WITHDRAWN

BURNS

928
B93m

A Biography of
Robert Burns
by
James Mackay

MAINSTREAM
PUBLISHING

Copyright © James Mackay, 1992
All rights reserved
The moral right of the author has been asserted

Reprinted 1993

First published in Great Britain in 1992 by
MAINSTREAM PUBLISHING COMPANY (EDINBURGH) LTD
7 Albany Street
Edinburgh EH1 3UG

ISBN 1 85158 462 5

No part of this book may be reproduced or transmitted in any form or by any
other means without the permission in writing from the publisher, except by a
reviewer who wishes to quote brief passages in connection with a review written
for insertion in a magazine, newspaper or broadcast.

A catalogue record for this book is available from the British Library

The publishers would like to acknowledge the financial assistance of the
The Scottish Arts Council in the production of this volume.

Typeset in 10½/12 Garamond by Blackpool Typesetting Services Ltd, Blackpool
Printed in Great Britain by Butler & Tanner Ltd, Frome, Somerset

For Lucie and Ross Roy

CAT Sep 13 '93

9-9-93 mls 31,58

ALLEGHENY COLLEGE LIBRARY

Robert Burns is a name entitled to the respect of posterity. Let us use it simply as 'Burns' – alone, and not maltreat it. He himself would have wished it so. The monosyllable needs neither prefix nor adjunct to define to whom it belongs. There is no other.

James Cameron Ewing, *Burns Chronicle*, 1933

Contents

Acknowledgments

M y thanks go, first and foremost, to Professor Donald Low of Stirling University who, some five years ago, suggested that all the research which had gone into editing *The Complete Works* and *The Complete Letters* ought to be distilled into a definitive biography of Burns. A suggestion along similar lines came from Ross Roy, now Emeritus Professor at the University of South Carolina. To both I am indebted in many ways that go far beyond the bounds of scholarship.

The research for this book was conducted in many libraries and archival institutions. I should like to thank the staff of the National Library of Scotland, and in particular the late Professor E. F. D. Roberts who took a keen personal interest in this project in the early stages. To Brenda Moon, Librarian of the University of Edinburgh, I am indebted for the opportunity to examine the Laing Collection. My thanks are due also to Roger Mortimer and his colleagues at the Cooper Library, University of South Carolina, Columbia, which now has the Ross Roy collection of Scottish literature including the rare works of many of Burns's contemporaries as well as the great rarities of Burns himself.

Nearer home, I have commuted between the Library of Glasgow University and the Mitchell Library. To the staffs of both institutions I am primarily indebted. In particular I should like to single out Joseph Fisher, lately keeper of the incomparable Burns Collection, and John Eaglesham, his successor. Hamish Whyte and Helen Miller were most helpful in the matter of rare books and manuscripts. The staff of the History and Topography section were unfailing in their courtesy in helping me track down obscure eighteenth-century farms and country houses from their excellent map collection. For the files of contemporary newspapers and directories my thanks are due to the staff of the Mitchell Library's Glasgow Room, as well as the staff of the Edinburgh City Library. I should also like to pay tribute to the late Jock Thomson and the present District Librarian of Kilmarnock and Loudoun District, William Anderson, and their staff at the Dick Institute, as well as Alistair Cowper, lately of the Ewart Library, Dumfries and his colleagues, and Lawrence Burness of the Coull-Anderson Genealogical Library, Arbroath.

A very special debt of gratitude is due to the Church of Jesus Christ of Latter Day Saints, and to Jeffrey F. Packe in particular. I should like to take this opportunity to pay tribute to the work of the members of the Mormon Church in rescuing old parish records, especially in England which has never been so well organised as Scotland in this respect. It is over a decade since I stumbled across the immense genealogical records in the Church Library at Salt Lake City, Utah. Since then over thirty branch genealogical libraries have been opened in Britain. The Mormon Church has helped me in two respects: firstly by microfilming every extant parish register, a task which has been going on since 1969, and secondly by computerizing these records which are now available as the International Genealogical Index, on microfiche. This has been the magnet that extracted countless needles from the haystack. Signposts may be a better metaphor, for the IGI has pointed the way to innumerable parish registers which I have studied in New Register House, Edinburgh, and at the Glasgow Room and the History and Topography section of the Mitchell Library, where the microfilms relevant to Glasgow and its environs are also available. To the staff of Old Register House, Edinburgh, I am indebted for the sight of Kirk Session minutes, registers of deeds and sasines. My thanks are due also to Dr Irene O'Brien of Strathclyde Regional Archives in Glasgow for help in resolving countless details.

I have also had a great deal of help from Marion Stewart, Archivist of Dumfries and Galloway, Miss M. J. Swarbrick, Chief Archivist at Victoria Library, and R. A. Bowden, Archivist at Marylebone Library, London, as well as the staff of the Greater London Records Office in tracing the movements of the sons of the poet. I have also to thank Graham Smith, lately Archivist of HM Customs and Excise, and his staff at King's Beam House, London, for additional information on Burns's Excise career. The staff of HM Customs and Excise, Greenock, Post Office Archives, London and the Public Record Office, Kew, have also helped in numerous ways. David Lockwood and his staff at Dumfries Burgh Museum have been extremely helpful at all times.

Many individuals have played a part in this project. It is a matter for regret that Clark Hunter of Houston, Renfrewshire, did not live to see this work completed, for he took a keen interest in its early stages and generously put his research into the origins of the Greenock Burns Club at my disposal. I am particularly indebted to James L. Hempstead of Dumbarton who has made detailed studies of many of the people associated with Burns, as well as researched the poet's connections with Dunbartonshire. To John Weir of North Logan, late Provincial Grand Master, I am indebted for much information on Burns's masonic connections. Samuel K. Gaw, past-President of the Burns Federation and now Secretary of Irvine Burns Club, was of particular help in unravelling Burns's Irvine interlude. Colonel Sir Bryce Knox deserves special thanks for helping to facilitate the loan of Highland Mary's Bibles for forensic examination. I am also indebted to Richard Henderson, Chairman, and Colin Kilpatrick, Secretary of the Trustees of Burns House and Monument at Alloway, and John Manson, Curator of the Museum. I should like to thank Tony Kerrigan of Ayr CID and the staff of Strathclyde Police forensic laboratory,

ACKNOWLEDGMENTS

especially Dr William Rodger and Campbell Stewart, for much help and advice. Dr William Murray of La Trobe University, Australia, was of considerable help regarding the political upheavals in the early stages of the French Revolution and their repercussions in Britain. I am grateful for the help given me by Dr A. W. O. Taylor of Saltoun, William Morrison, David Grey, Eric McCallum and James Russell in Galston and Newmilns, and to Ian McDowall and Frank Ryan in Dumfries who ferreted out vital information on the spot.

I am most grateful to Judy Diamond for her skilful editing of the manuscript, and to John Fleck who read the proofs and made a number of helpful suggestions.

To my wife Joyce, as always, I owe a far greater debt of gratitude than I can express in mere words, especially during a very intensive twelve-month period when millions of words in notes and reference material were being rendered down into more manageable proportions. Last, but by no means least, my very special thanks are due to John Inglis, past-President and former Secretary of the Burns Federation, who smoothed the way, effected introductions and helped in numberless ways. It is no exaggeration to say that, without his help and advice, this book would not be as thorough and as comprehensive as it is.

James A. Mackay
Glasgow
March 1992

Abbreviations

To save the tedium of overloading the text with numbers referring to the sources, I have used the system of referring to the poems and songs as CW, followed by their page numbers in *The Complete Works of Robert Burns* (1986), and the letters of the poet by CL, followed by their page numbers in *The Complete Letters of Robert Burns* (1987), published by the Burns Federation. This system is now widely used in books and periodicals. See also the note at the head of the Notes on Sources regarding abbreviations and shortened forms of titles used there.

Introduction

Professor Joel Egerer, compiler of *A Bibliography of Robert Burns* (Oliver and Boyd, Edinburgh, 1964), reckoned that his popularity in the nineteenth century may have been even greater than Shakespeare's. Certainly, if the wealth of literature is anything to go by, Burns has always enjoyed a far greater popular appeal. More than two thousand editions of his poems and songs have been published since 1786, and the number of extracts and anthologies is immeasurable. Over nine hundred volumes of biography, dealing either with the life of the poet as a whole or treating of some specific aspect of it, have poured from the world's presses since 1797, while the salient facts of Burns's life and career have appeared in the introductory sections of the editions of his poetry and letters.

Everyone knows about Robert Burns. He was a ploughman who wrote poetry, had seventy illegitimate children and drank himself into an early grave. A recent issue of *The Sunday Post* referred to Burns as 'an amorous rhymester', while an article in *Woman's Realm* in the series Intriguing People was headed 'The legendary poet and lover who died a pauper'. The fact is that, at the time of his death, Burns had net assets in excess of £200 (equivalent to over £40,000 in 1992). An Australian newspaper in 1991 claimed that following Burns's Edinburgh sojourn his face could be seen in virtually every pram in Princes Street. Some of the 'facts' are so grotesque as to defy rational understanding; perhaps they tell us more about the psychology of gossip and malicious rumour. The truth is that Burns had nine children by Jean Armour with whom he contracted an irregular, though perfectly legal, marriage in 1786. Out of wedlock he had daughters by Elizabeth Paton, Ann Park and possibly Helen Hyslop, and a son by Jenny Clow. It is easy to condemn someone from the standpoint of the present day, but birth control was non-existent in the eighteenth century. Burns's dubious record in bastardy was by no means out of the ordinary for the times he lived in.

Burns the alcoholic is a more difficult *canard* to dispel, but the man who ran a 170-acre farm, rode two hundred miles a week on Excise duties and kept four sets of Excise records, and still found time to compose such masterpieces as 'Tam o Shanter' besides conducting a voluminous correspondence and writing songs for two publishers simultaneously, was a workaholic, not an alcoholic. Burns's devotion to his family and his professional duties is well documented, and his letters to his music publisher, George Thomson, right down to within days of his death give the lie to the tales of dissipation and debauchery which circulated as soon as he was dead. He enjoyed a drink and, indeed, he did get drunk on occasion – as did everyone else, including his rather prissy friend Ainslie – but Robert Burns was not a hardened drinker, a habitual toper or an alcoholic as his detractors have so often claimed.

A great deal of nonsense was written, mostly in the nineteenth century, though lingering on fitfully till the 1930s, about 'Highland Mary', the one great, pure love of Burns's life which redeemed him from his worst excesses and saved him from himself. In the cult of Burns, which at times came very close to a religion, 'Highland Mary' assumed the role of the Blessed Virgin. This girl was so shadowy a figure that until now not even her date of birth, nor even her real name, has been known. 'Highland Mary' was almost entirely the invention of the nineteenth-century myth-makers.

When I embarked on this biography I wondered what I could possibly say that had not been said before; might this not, after all, be just yet another reprise of the old, old song? Despite the vast biographical outpourings, I soon discovered that ninety per cent of them merely repeated uncritically the 'facts', including a great many unsupported and unsupportable anecdotes, which had appeared originally in Currie (1800), Cromek (1808), Lockhart (1828) and Cunningham (1834). Currie, who was on the scene soon after the poet's death, could have got at the truth and given us the facts; but he was untrained and unskilled in editorship and biography and was hamstrung by so many of Burns's friends who retrieved their own letters and doctored the poet's correspondence to them. Cromek had more of the investigative journalist's instinct and succeeded in tracking down several of Burns's friends from whom he obtained anecdotal material; but he had such an unscholarly approach that the water has been muddied ever since, and it is impossible to sort the truth from the fiction in his *Reliques*. This established the pattern zealously adopted by Lockhart and raised to a fine art by Cunningham. 'Honest Allan' is now so suspect that any story originating in his biography and not corroborated from other sources must be discounted.

Robert Chambers, conducting investigations into the poet's life over a period from 1836 to 1851, brought a more sober, factual approach to bear, and this was continued by William Scott Douglas, writing between 1850 and 1879, and William Wallace who revised and virtually re-wrote Chambers' four-volume *Life and Works* for publication at the centenary of the poet's death in 1896. This was the best of the nineteenth-century biographies and later writers, such as Carswell (1930), Snyder (1932), Ferguson (1939), Lindsay (1954) and Fitzhugh (1970), relied very heavily on it. Of these, the most thorough and scholarly was written by Professor Franklyn Bliss Snyder, but it came just too soon to benefit fully from DeLancey Ferguson's two-volume edition of *The Letters of Robert Burns* (Oxford, 1931). Since then there has been the revised and expanded second edition by Ross Roy (1985) and James Kinsley's monumental three-volume edition of *The Poems and Songs of Robert Burns* (Oxford, 1968). In recent years there have been several thorough and excellent critical studies of Burns's verse, notably David Daiches' *Robert Burns* (1950), Christina Keith's *The Russet Coat* (1956), Thomas Crawford's *Burns: A Study of the Poems and Songs* (1960), *Critical Essays on Robert Burns* (1974), edited by Donald Low, and *The Art of Robert Burns* (1982), edited by Ronald Jack and Andrew Noble.

My approach has been to examine every so-called fact about the life of Robert Burns, and trace it right back to its source as far as possible in order to establish its provenance. More importantly, I have made use of primary sources – parish registers of baptisms, marriages and burials, Kirk Session books, masonic lodge minutes, Sheriff Clerk Office and Commissary records, and even the day-book of the surgeon who treated Burns in Irvine – as well as contemporary newspapers, periodicals and directories. The results have been nothing short of astonishing, for many of the discrepancies in the Burns story have now been resolved, the correct identities and subsequent history of several of the poet's heroines have now been revealed, and literally hundreds of other facts, great and small, have been ascertained for the first time. None of this materially alters the truth about Burns, but now it is possible, for the first time ever, to provide a definitive life of the poet.

Of one thing we may be certain: this will not be the last word on the subject. Perhaps some day a forensic examination of the remains re-interred at Greenock in 1920 may establish, for once and for all, the truth about 'Highland Mary'. The exact details of Jenny Clow's death and the early life of her son remain to be discovered. Hitherto unrecorded manuscripts of poems and letters of the poet may come to light, just as lost collections (notably the Law MSS including the poet's first commonplace book) may be retrieved.

This is a *life* of Burns and although it contains copious references to his poetry and letters, no attempt has been made to consider his writings from a critical viewpoint. For this, the reader is recommended to consult some of the works previously cited. It should also be noted that Professor Low's long-awaited *The Songs of Robert Burns*, in the press at the time of writing, will revise the general perception of Burns's later career; while Kirsten McCue's work on George Thomson, currently in progress, will no doubt give us a new perspective on Burns's meddling publisher.

ALLEGHENY COLLEGE LIBRARY

CHAPTER 1

Antecedents

In the cause of Right engaged,
   Wrongs injurious to redress,
Honour's war we strongly waged,
   But the heavens deny'd success.
Ruin's wheel has driven o'er us:
   Not a hope that dare attend,
The wide world is all before us,
   But a world without a friend.

Strathallan's Lament (CW 287)

The entire life of Robert Burns is riddled with half-truths, contradictions and myths. Even the origins of his family have been clouded by nonsense which persists to this day. In 1851 Robert Chambers, not the poet's first biographer by any means, but the first to bring a scholarly approach to bear on his subject, wrote:

> The first known ancestor of the Burnes family was one Walter Campbell, originally proprietor of a small domain in Argyleshire called Burnhouse. It is stated that, having offended his chief, the Duke of Argyle, by siding with the cause of the Stuarts at the Revolution he was, much about the time of the noted massacre of Glencoe, obliged to abandon his native country and wander to the Lowlands as a fugitive, accompanied by his only son Walter, then a boy. He dropped the name of Campbell, and was known by that of Burness, a corruption of Burnhouse, the place of his birth. He settled in the parish of Glenbervie, and there died.[1]

This account of the origins of the Burns family was derived immediately from a letter written in 1824 by John Burness (1771–1826), cousin of the poet and himself a poet of some merit, remembered nowadays as the author of *Thrummy Cap*. The letter was addressed to Provost James Burnes of Montrose, son of a cousin and one-time correspondent of Robert Burns.[2] John Burness gives as the source for this story the Revd. Alexander Greig, episcopal minister in Stonehaven, 'then a very old man, and well skilled in the records of the family, his mother being a Burness, and grand-daughter to the after-mentioned Walter'. This only takes the story back to about

1793 (the year of Greig's death), a century after the massacre of Glencoe; and although Dr Burnes got the tale from at least two other channels, he formed the opinion that 'it found its source in some obscure hint thrown out by Mr Greig, a devoted partisan of the Stuart Family'.[3]

Chambers was sceptical of this story and was quick to point out the discrepancies in the chronology.[4] It was inadmissible that the grandfather of a person known to have been born in 1656 (James Burnes of Brawlinmuir), could be liable after the Revolution of 1688-9 to change his residence on account of his political principles. Chambers, however, considered that the story, passed down from generation to generation, had become garbled and distorted, though he could not rule out the possibility of some social upheaval arising from the civil wars of an earlier period, particularly those of 1638-41. The fact that in some versions of the story the chief is given as the Earl of Argyll, rather than the Duke, tended to place it in the time of the eighth Earl, Archibald Campbell (1607-61), later first Marquis of Argyll, who broke with King Charles I and sided with the Covenanters in the defence of the national religion and liberties. To be sure, there was a place in Argyll known as Burnhouse, though it is known nowadays in a corrupted form of its Gaelic equivalent, *Tigh an uillt* - Taynuilt.

That this story was firmly believed by some members of the Burns family is borne out by the fact that Dr James Burnes (1801-62), son of Provost James Burnes, applied to the Lyon Court in 1837 to have his arms matriculated and incorporated in this the gyronny of eight or and sable (gold and black) emblem of Clan Campbell. At that time Dr Burnes maintained that the grandson of Walter Campbell of Burnhouse was Walter Burness, tenant in Bogjorgan, Kincardineshire, whose son was James Burness or Burnes, tenant in Brawlinmuir (noted above). Although Dr Burnes later discovered that this ancestry could not possibly fit the facts and applied to the Lyon Court in 1851 to have the Campbell element erased from his arms, '. . . from a recent investigation, a great doubt having arisen in regard to the origin of his name being from that of Campbell', the myth of the Campbell origin persists to this day.[5]

That a Walter Burness, farmer in Bogjorgan, was the common ancestor of the Burns, Burness or Burnes family of Bogjorgan and Brawlinmuir was first suggested by Dr James Burnes in 1851, later disputed by Scott Douglas[6] and amply demonstrated by Dr W. A. MacNaughton.[7] Walter Burnece, who died at Bogjorgan in November 1670, left a will (Commissariot of Brechin) in which his property totalled £91 sterling, a not inconsiderable sum for that time. The parochial records for this district date back no farther than 1721 (births) and 1748 (marriages), so this will is the earliest extant record of the Burness family. Both Bogjorgan and Brawlinmuir were farms on the estate of Inchbreck which was in the possession of the Stuart family at least as far back as 1547, and from this it has sometimes been stated that the Burness family's tenancy goes back just as far; but there is absolutely no proof to substantiate the claim that the ancestors of the poet were farmers in Kincardineshire from the time of Mary Queen of Scots.[8] Of course, Burns, Burnas, Burnes, Burness, Burnece, Burnase and other variants may be found in parish registers, wills and charters all over the north-east of Scotland, as well as Orkney and Shetland, back to the fourteenth century, derived from such common words as *bjorn* (Norse, bear), *beorn* (Anglo-Saxon, chief) or *burn* (a stream). The prevalence of various two-syllable versions, such as Burness and Burnase, lends credibility to the Burnhouse origin, but there were many burnside homesteads in the north-east of Scotland whose names alluded to the fact, so a Burnhouse origin could just as easily have come from this area as anywhere else. The Revd. J. C. Higgins, working on notes left by Dr Charles Rogers, introduced the fanciful notion of Norman descent for the poet on both sides, mentioning the fact that Sir John de Burnes was the envoy of King Edward I of England to Rome in 1290 and that the Browns of Ayrshire were descended from a Norman mercenary in the reign of King David I by the name of de Brun.[9]

All that can be said with any certainty is that Robert Burns could trace his ancestry back as far as his great-great-grandfather, Walter. While it is obvious that people called Burns lived in the Mearns for centuries, the legend of the Campbells of Burnhouse cannot be entirely dismissed. On three separate occasions Robert Burns made very definite assertions that his forefathers had suffered for their adherence to the Stuart cause in the Jacobite rebellion of 1715. Not a shred of evidence can be found for the truth of these assertions; on the contrary, all the information available is directly opposed to the idea that any of the Burnes family were openly identified with the Stuart cause. But, may it not have been that Burns's father carried the Campbell story from the Mearns to Ayrshire, and ultimately passed it on to his eldest son, with whose temperament it would so well accord and who naturally would receive it as authentic family history, albeit in a garbled and distorted form?[10]

Walter Burness was succeeded in the tenancy of Bogjorgan, 'sixty acres of Scots measure', by his second son William, the first of three of that name to occupy the farm. In turn, he was succeeded by his sons William II and James. William II was the grandfather of the poet John Burness previously mentioned. In 1705 James left his brother in Bogjorgan and went to occupy the farm of Inches two miles away. On this occasion an inventory was drawn up. This interesting document was first published by Chambers in 1851 but contained numerous errors and inaccuracies, which suggests that he saw only a carelessly transcribed copy and not the original. Unfortunately, subsequent biographers have merely copied Chambers and a correct version did not appear till 1931. The text is as follows:

Ane note off the biging of Bogjorgine belonging to William Stuart heritor theroff given up be William Burnesse present tenent off the sd Roum and James Burnesse late possessor off the halfe theroff upon the seventainth day off Jully 1705 yeare

Imp: ane ffyre house consisting off thrie couples four horsses tuo taill postes ane midle wall with ane post ffrom the ground with ane rooff tuo panes in the syd with ane door bandet locked and bared with ane windoue

off tuo lightes brodit bandet and snacked and with ane Loune all to be
sufficient

Item ane barne consisting off ffyve couples ffour horsses tuo till postes
ane Rooff thrie panes in the syd with ffor door locked and bandet and
back door bared and stepled all to be sufficient

Item ane Byre consisting off ffour couples tuo panes in the syd ane
Rooff with door and door cheikes bandet all to be sufficient

It is declared be both parties that iff ther be No other Inventur ffound
betwixt this and Whytsonday nixt Javii & six yeares that this shall be ane
true Inventur of the sd Biging and all that the sd William Stuart shall
requyre ffrom the sd William Burness at his Removall ffrom the sd Roum
In wittness yroff subt be both parties at BralinMuir day and year off God
fforsaid beffor thesse wittnesses Robert Midleton in Brombanck and
David Watson in polburn wryter heiroff

R Midletone Witnes   Will Stuart
D Watson Witness & Wryt   WB[11]

James Burnes (1656–1743), the eldest son of Walter and great-grandfather of the poet, occupied Brawlinmuir, the farm adjoining Bogjorgan.
Life was hard and farming one long grind of unremitting toil; but successive generations of Burneses managed, by careful husbanding of resources
and innate frugality, to save and add gradually to their hard-won capital.
On one occasion, when Highland caterans raided the Burnes home, they
failed to discover James's nest-egg, a poke of gold and silver coins concealed in an old box-wheel that lay across the mud puddle of his threshold
to form a stepping-stone. On his death he left 100 merks (about five
pounds sterling) to each of his sons to enable them to set up as tacksmen
in their own right. His eldest son Robert occupied the farm of Upper Kinmonth, from which he moved to the farm of Clochnahill in Dunnottar
parish. Clochnahill is usually referred to as the birthplace of William
Burnes, the poet's father, a statement which can be traced back to Dr
Rogers [12] who stated that the family bible of William Burnes contained the
entry: 'William Burnes, third son of Robert Burnes and Isabella Keith, was
born at Clochnahill on the 11th November 1721'. This is a good example
of the way in which Rogers, and other nineteenth-century biographers of
the poet, had a cavalier disregard for accuracy in both the minor and the
major details of the poet's life. The actual entry in the bible merely states:
'William Burnes was born 11 Novr. 1721'.[13]

The Kirk Session records of Glenbervie parish, however, show that
Robert Burness in Upper Kinmonth had two sittings in that church on
11 January 1723. The first reference to Robert as tenant in Clochnahill, in
the register of the neighbouring parish of Dunnottar, does not occur till
August 1725, so it seems reasonable to suppose that the parents of William
Burnes were living at Upper Kinmonth at the time of his birth, but moved
to Clochnahill while he was still a baby.

Just as the family's move to Clochnahill was misunderstood, so also its
removal has sometimes been erroneously stated. Early biographers of the

poet stated that Robert Burnes left Clochnahill in 1740, following a rather vague assumption by Rogers who gave it merely as 'probably at the close of 1740' that Robert retired, with his three unmarried daughters, to the cottage of Denside in Dunnottar parish. Dr James Currie, the poet's first major biographer, probably fixed this date from the statement by Gilbert Burns (brother of the poet) that his father left his home 'in his nineteenth year';[14] but in this Gilbert was mistaken. William Burnes did not leave the Mearns until 1748, as is proved by the certificate of character given to him by three Mearns landowners who testified that he was 'the son of an honest farmer in this neighbourhood . . . and a very well inclined lad himself'.[15] In fact it was not until Whitsunday 1745 that Robert Burnes removed from Clochnahill to Falside in the adjoining parish of Kinneff, of which farm he had a lease of seven years. In September 1747, however, owing to the culmination of financial troubles of long standing, he was forced to give up farming. What later became of Robert Burnes is not known for certain. In desperation Robert gave his landlord a bill at six months for the sum of £13 sterling; when the bill matured he could not cover it. Many biographers state, without any substantiation, that he was made bankrupt. Whether this legal process took place or not, however, the results were the same: after a lifetime on the land, Robert Burnes became a landless cottar. The statement by Rogers that he lived at Denside after 1747 with three unmarried daughters has been confirmed by an examination of the old parish registers of Kincardineshire. On 29 August 1752 Robert's eldest daughter, Elspit, married John Caird who lived in a cottage at Denside and it seems probable that old Robert spent his declining years with this couple.[16] Gilbert's Narrative mentions how William, his father, 'endeavoured to spare something for the support of an aged parent, and I recollect hearing him mention his having sent a bank-note for this purpose, when money of that kind was so scarce in Kincardineshire, that they hardly knew how to employ it when it arrived'. There is also the fanciful anecdote that William Burnes even approached his father's landlord privately and offered himself as an indentured labourer to work off Robert's debt, but this was refused.

Robert Burnes is a strangely shadowy figure and neither his birth nor death have been traced. He is believed to have been born some time before 1690 and he is known to have married Isabella, daughter of Alexander Keith, tenant farmer of Criggie in Dunnottar parish. He had a chequered career which strangely paralleled that of his son William. According to a statement made by Burns to John Ramsay of Ochtertyre, his grandfather had been a man of above average intellect and ability, sufficiently prosperous at one point to have silver cutlery on his dining table. In his heyday he had been employed by the Earl Marischal as his gardener at Inverugie Castle in Aberdeenshire; but Burns went on, rather obliquely, to say that he was 'plundered and driven out in the year 1715'.[17] In his famous Autobiographical Letter to Dr Moore (CL 249) Burns wrote, 'My Fathers rented land of the noble Keiths of Marshal, and had the honor to share their fate.' In a letter to Lady Winifred Maxwell Constable from Ellisland in December 1789 (CL 546) he drew attention to their shared misfortune of having ancestors who suffered for their adherence to the Jacobite cause: 'But with your Ladyship I have the honor to be connected by one of the strongest & most endearing ties in the whole Moral World – Common Sufferers in a cause where even to be unfortunate is glorious, the Cause of Heroic Loyalty.' He went on to say that though his Fathers had not illustrious honours and vast properties to hazard in the contest, they followed their leaders 'and shook hands with Ruin for what they esteemed the cause of their King and their Country'. Burns believed that his grandfather Robert had served under the Earl Marischal in the 1715 rebellion, although there is no evidence to support this, nor, indeed, to refute it. On the other hand, the estates of the Earl Marischal were forfeited after the rebellion and both employees and tenants would have suffered grievously as a consequence. By the time of the second Jacobite Rebellion in September 1745, Robert Burnes was the tenant of a farm at Falside of Kinneff. The agents of the Young Pretender must have been recruiting in the area, but Robert Burnes had other things to preoccupy him in that momentous autumn. Like many other farmers, he had suffered from the vagaries of the weather rather than the political climate; in particular, the very bad winter of 1740 destroyed standing crops and Robert Burnes, then tenant of Clochnahill, never got over this setback. By Whitsunday 1745 he was borrowing heavily from a former provost of Aberdeen to pay his arrears of rent and take on the lease of a more modest farm at Falside of Kinneff. His tenancy of that holding was very brief, however, as he was unable to pay the rent, for which he was sued shortly afterwards in Stonehaven Sheriff Court, by his landlord, George Kinloch of Keir.[18] This unfortunate trait of embarking on a disastrous course as a means of extricating himself from a farming failure was to be repeated in the next generation.

Robert Burnes had four sons. The youngest, named George, was born in April 1729 but apparently died very young. The eldest, James (1717–61), had the good sense to break with farming altogether, settling in the seaport of Montrose where he prospered in business and became a town councillor. This branch of the family made the switch from the peasantry to the bourgeoisie effortlessly. His son James (1750–1837) became a lawyer and notary public. First cousin of the poet, he and Burns carried on a lively correspondence which was terminated only by Robert's death and it was to cousin James that he turned for financial help as he lay dying. James III (1780–1852) followed in his father's footsteps and eventually became Provost of Montrose. His son James IV (1801–62) became Physician General of the Bombay Army and it was the receipt of his knighthood, in the Royal Guelphic Order of Hanover, which prompted him to matriculate his arms in 1837. His younger brothers, Sir Alexander Burnes and Charles Burnes, were murdered at Kabul on 2 November 1841, an atrocity which triggered off the Afghan War. Adam Burnes (1832–76), the eldest son of Dr Burnes, founded the first bank in Australia.[19]

While James Burnes gravitated to Montrose in 1748, his brothers Robert (1719–89) and William (1721–84) headed south to seek their fortune. One should not make too much of the fact that William Burnes felt the necessity to obtain a certificate from three Mearns landowners when he and his brother Robert left the district. Snyder[20] implies that the family must have been looked upon with some suspicion for such a 'clearance certificate' to have been necessary, and hints that the taint of Jacobitism was still strong, barely two years after Culloden; but it was normal practice when leaving one's native district to obtain a character certificate or reference from the local landowner or parish minister, so nothing sinister need be read into this action. It has often been used rather fancifully by Burns scholars, however, as further proof of the family's connection with the Jacobite movement.

William Burnes took up his father's former avocation and trained as a gardener, while his elder brother Robert appears to have been apprenticed to a stone-mason, although he, too, worked as a gardener in later life. Gilbert Burns, in his Narrative of 1797 described how his father and uncle left home:

> I have often heard my father describe the anguish of mind he felt when he parted with his elder brother Robert on the top of a hill, on the confines of their native place, each going off his several way in search of adventures, and scarcely knowing whither he went. My father undertook to act as gardener and shaped his course to Edinburgh, where he wrought hard when he could get work, passing through a variety of difficulties . . .[21]

Tradition puts this parting of the ways on the summit of Garvock Tap (813ft, 271m). Anguish would well describe the feelings of the brothers, from such a close-knit family, as they went their separate ways. Robert headed into England but in due course settled in Dreghorn, Ayrshire, and later Stewarton in the same county.

At Edinburgh William found no shortage of gardening work. Hope Park (now the Meadows, the great park south of the Royal Infirmary), was in the course of being laid out and for about two years Burnes worked there, landscaping the gardens.[22] According to Gilbert, William Burnes passed from Edinburgh into Ayrshire where he lived for two years as gardener to the laird of Fairlie in Dundonald parish, three and a half miles south-west of Kilmarnock. Alexander Fairlie of Fairlie was not untypical of his period, an improving landowner who was accustomed to spending the winter months in Edinburgh, returning to his country estate each spring. How William Burnes came in contact with Fairlie is not known, but possibly he was beginning to tire of the hustle and bustle of Auld Reekie and the opportunity to attach himself to one of the 'westering lairds' must have been very tempting. William found the work at Fairlie congenial. A rather shy man, who must have found the Ayrshire dialect well-nigh unintelligible, he kept himself to himself. He was a diligent employee and when he decided, about two years later, to move on, he got an excellent reference from Fairlie. More importantly, he received a certificate of good character signed by the parish minister and the session clerk of Dundonald. He moved to Carrick, the southerly part of Ayrshire, and found employment near Maybole. In 1754 he moved north again and engaged himself for two years as gardener to John Crawford at Doonside House near the hamlet of Alloway, two miles south of Ayr. Across the Doon, on the north bank of the river, William is said to have lodged at Doonside Mill for about three years, where he led a frugal, bachelor existence. During this period it seems likely that his father died, for William no longer had a need to send remittances to Denside for old Robert's maintenance. Now that he was able to save money on his own account, he began laying plans for the future.

He had ambitions to establish himself as a market gardener and, to this end, he feued seven and a half acres of land at Alloway from Dr Alexander Campbell of Ayr. The gently sloping site near the river lay to the west of the Ayr-Maybole highway, then little more than a track but nowadays the B7024 road. Today Alloway is a select suburb of Ayr but in the 1750s it was a tiny hamlet set in open countryside. While he continued to lodge at Doonside Mill, a few hundred yards east of the Auld Brig, William laid out his market garden and, in what time he had to spare, he began building, with his own hands, a cottage. At the same time, he hired himself as gardener to Provost William Fergusson, a London doctor who had amassed a fortune and recently retired to his native heath. Fergusson rebuilt the estate of Doonholm and considerably added to it, and in this project he relied heavily on his head gardener, Burnes.[23]

Doubtless there was some speculation locally regarding the cottage and William's plans, both business and matrimonial. Catherine Carswell paints a fanciful picture of William's tentative courtship of the miller's daughter, but states erroneously that she resided at the mill where William was a lodger.[24] In fact, Burnes was paying court to a girl at Alloway Mill, also on the north bank of the river but some way to the west and only 300 yards from the point at which the river entered the Firth of Clyde. The story goes that he painstakingly composed a letter proposing marriage to this girl, but then filed it away with his character references in his trunk to bide his time.

Then, one day in the summer of 1756, he met another girl at Maybole Fair and, as a result, he went home and promptly tore up the proposal of marriage. Physically, there was a great contrast between the tall, dark and taciturn nurseryman-gardener and the lively, red-head with the dancing brown eyes. At 24, Agnes Brown was comely rather than beautiful, but one can well imagine William Burnes being captivated by her vivacity. Agnes was the eldest of six children born to Gilbert Brown and Agnes Rainie and began life at Whitestone Cottage near Culzean.[25] When she was a few months old her parents moved to Craigenton Farm where Gilbert's father John was the tenant farmer. Agnes was only ten years old when her mother died in May 1742 of a pulmonary complaint. The story goes that as the poor woman lay dying her sister asked her, 'Are you not sorry to leave your husband and your children?' To which she replied, 'No – I leave my children to the care of God, and Gilbert will soon get another wife.'[26]

Such schooling as little Agnes had consisted of attendance at a dame school conducted in a weaver's cottage where, along with other girls, she learned the Psalms by heart and was taught, at length, to read after a fashion, sufficient to fit her for a life in domestic service. Writing, on the other hand, formed no part of this rudimentary education, and Agnes never learned how to write her name, far less anything more advanced. Gilbert Brown held that education was not for females. Like many men of his generation he felt that women should receive their perception of the world and religion through their menfolk, first a father and then a husband. In any case, Agnes was kept far too busy rearing her siblings to bother about book-learning. For two years she struggled to raise her brothers and sisters, her only help being Ann Gillespie who later married John Davidson, prototype of Souter Johnie.[27] True to Agnes Rainie's prophecy, Gilbert Brown decided to marry again and the little mother was then packed off to her maternal grandmother, Mrs William Rainie, in Maybole.

In fact, Gilbert Brown was married three times in all and fathered a further six children. On 26 June 1744 he married Margaret Blain, ten years his junior, and by her had Andrew (1745), Hugh (1747) and Jean (1750). Margaret died in June 1751 and Gilbert, at the age of fifty-seven and after almost fourteen years of widowerhood, married again on 16 April 1765. His third bride, Catherine Moat, was in her early twenties and bore four children: Margaret (1766), James (1768), Christian (1771) and Helen (1772).[28] Gilbert died on 31 October 1774 aged sixty-six. Agnes had no time for either of her stepmothers, particular Catherine who was several years younger than her, which probably explains why the poet had no contact with his maternal grandfather.

Whereas the Burnes family hailed from the north-east of Scotland, the Browns were firmly rooted in Ayrshire soil. Rogers[29] was probably responsible for the tale that the Browns were of good Covenanting stock, largely on the strength of having the same surname as John Brown, the 'Christian carrier' of Priesthill on the Muirkirk-Lesmahagow border, who was shot by Graham of Claverhouse in 1685, and the Browns of Cumnock who fought at Bothwell Brig in 1679 and were outlawed for their exploits; but it must be pointed out that Brown, next to Smith, is the commonest surname in the Lowlands of Scotland. Grandmother Rainie had herself known the persecution of the Killing Times.[30] Auld Granny was a hard taskmaster who set Agnes to spin indoors and plough outdoors. Her sole recreation seems to have been singing the old ballads to entertain Mrs Rainie and her bachelor son, a blind uncle of Agnes, who lodged with them. Love, of a sort, began to develop in the fields between Agnes and the gaudsman, Will Nelson, whose job was to hold the ploughshare to the furrows or help her at the flailing on the threshing-floor. By the time she was nineteen Agnes was betrothed and from her fiancé she picked up a great many of the auld sangs, but little else. Will earned the princely sum of £5 a year and so, until a better situation came along, there was no question of marriage. Unusually for the time and place, Agnes Brown was not the lass to yield to a lover's importuning before they were wed. Unfortunately for Agnes, Will Nelson was only human, and when, after seven years she discovered that he had been indulging in an affair on the side, she abruptly broke off their engagement. Agnes, raised in the dour Presbyterian idiom, could neither understand nor forgive Will's waywardness. She made a clean break, but her emotions were in a turmoil. In this vulnerable condition she met William Burnes, eleven years her senior. This shy, reserved man was in sharp contrast with the fickle gaudsman. He was the finest, the steadiest of men, and he loved her with a tenderness to which she was unaccustomed. Older in years, he was light years ahead of her in intellect. Agnes was spellbound – but she made him wait for twelve months nevertheless. On 15 December 1757 Agnes and William were wed and immediately he installed his bride as mistress of the new cottage at Alloway. Whatever memories of previous attachments on either side remained were soon forgotten. The couple lived in harmony and matrimonial felicity for twenty-six years. Thereafter Agnes was a widow for thirty-six years with no thought of remarrying.

Such, then, was the ancestry of Robert Burns. Scholars have long argued, debated and examined the antecedents of the poet in futile quest of any mark of genius. The Browns and the Burneses were of good, solid peasant stock – hardworking and hard–headed, thrifty and industrious, stolid and stoical in the face of innumerable hardships and disappointments, intensely loyal to the family and devoutly attached to their faith. The courage and integrity which distinguished the Montrose branch of the family, and brought *Iskander* Burnes a knighthood at the age of thirty-two, distinguished the younger surviving sons of the poet, both of whom rose to high rank in the service of the East India Company. From his mother, Robert Burns seems to have inherited his personal charm; from his father he undoubtedly derived his tenacity of purpose, amounting at times to stubbornness, and from the same source came his depressive, melancholic tendencies. Given the fact that the father's family was probably of Saxon and Norse origin, while the Browns were of Anglo-Norman descent, Burns himself, in physiognomy and temperament, betrayed a Celtic strain. There is no doubt that Celtic blood lingered on in southern Ayrshire, on the fringes of Galloway and overlooking Kintyre, long after it had disappeared from, say, Lanarkshire or the Lothians; although it is probably too fanciful to imagine that these Celtic traits were responsible for the lighter and more joyous elements in Burns's poetry as some biographers have asserted.[31]

CHAPTER 2

Alloway, 1759–66

Our monarch's hindmost year but ane
Was five-and-twenty days begun,
'Twas then a blast o Janwar win'
Blew hansel in on Robin.

Rantin, Rovin Robin (CW 268)

William ignored the old Scottish proverb 'He's a fule wha marries at Yule, for when the bairn's to bear, the corn's to shear'. As it turned out, his first-born did not come into the world till some thirteen months after the marriage took place. By that time the crops had long been safely gathered in, but that week was one of the stormiest on record. Nineteenth-century biographers – and a few of more recent vintage[1] – delighted in painting a lurid picture of the worried father fighting his way through the storm and riding through the swollen Slaphouse ford[2] to get the midwife, though none explains how this good woman would be expected to weather the journey back to Alloway. The inference is that Agnes was delivered of her first baby late at night, though this is nowhere recorded contemporaneously. Subsequent research into the Alloway of the mid-eighteenth century revealed that the village midwife was a next-door neighbour of the Burneses, Agnes McClure, wife of the blacksmith John Tennant and traditionally the same gossip who 'keekit in his loof' and foretold the poet's tempestuous future.[3] The following morning, the storm having abated slightly, William Burnes rode into Ayr to fetch the minister out to the cottage to baptise the infant. The Session clerk, David Tennant, laconically noted the details in his parish register:

> Robert Burns, lawful son to William Burns, in Alloway, and Agnes Brown, his spouse, was born January 25, 1759; bapd. 26, by Mr William Dalrymple. Witnesses: John Tennant and Jas. Young.[4]

The faded handwriting on the yellowing page is the most historic entry in the volume, though it differs in no respect from hundreds of others therein. Apart from the fact that this is the earliest record of Scotland's great national bard, it is of interest on several counts. First of all, it illustrates the custom of the time whereby babies were baptised as soon as possible after birth. The sacrament was carried out by the Revd. William Dalrymple, two years younger than William Burnes. Ordained in 1745, he became junior minister of Ayr the following year. Ten years later, in the year that William and Agnes began courting, he was elevated to the first charge. Dalrymple, son of the Sheriff-Clerk of Ayr, was one of the new breed of clerics who were beginning to give Presbyterianism a more liberal outlook. Dalrymple was no radical, however, and always took care not to break with the strict tenets of orthodoxy. William Burnes approved of the young minister whose religious views were very close to his own. In due course his services to the Church would be recognised by a doctorate of divinity, conferred by St Andrews University (1779), and two years later he attained the very pinnacle of the religious establishment when he became Moderator of the General Assembly. Dalrymple was above the middle rank of ministers of the period, being himself a minor landowner whose estate of Mount Charles actually lay not far to the west of Burns Cottage. Dalrymple was an uncle of Robert Aiken, the lawyer, benefactor and friend of the poet and the 'Orator Bob' of 'The Kirk's Alarm' (CW 359). Dalrymple himself was apostrophised by Burns in this satire as 'D'rymple mild! D'rymple mild! tho your heart's like a child! / An your life like the new-driven snaw'.

The identity of James Young is not known; but a long-hallowed tradition maintained that the other witness was John Tennant of Glenconner (1725–1810) – 'A worthy, intelligent farmer, my father's friend and my own' is how Burns was to describe him in a letter to Clarinda dated 2 March 1788 (CL 400). It was to Tennant that the poet turned when he sought impartial advice about the farm he was thinking of leasing. In the verse-epistle addressed to James Tennant (John's eldest son) Burns refers to the father affectionately as 'guid auld Glen, / The ace an wale of honest men' (CW 201). By that time Tennant had been for more than a decade factor to Elizabeth, Countess of Glencairn, and rented the farm of Glenconner (from which his descendants, raised to the peerage, were to derive their title), but at the time of the poet's birth he was the tenant of the farm of Laigh Corton. This is half a mile east of the present A77 Ayr–Maybole road, about a mile across country from Burns Cottage as the crow flies. Close friend he may have been, but it was unlikely that this John Tennant would be called in to witness the baptism. It was later ascertained that this farmer had a cousin of the same name who was the blacksmith in Alloway and whose wife was, in fact, the village midwife who attended the poet's birth. Smiddy Cottage, just along Alloway's main street from Burns Cottage, continued as a smithy until after the Second World War.[5]

It should also be noted that the Session clerk spelled the family surname as it was pronounced in Ayrshire, as a monosyllable, and dropped the second vowel. William Burnes continued to spell his name as he had been taught. Interestingly, the poet himself, to judge from his earliest letters, preferred the Ayrshire spelling – except when he began writing to his cousin James at Montrose in June 1783, when he used the old Mearns form of Burness. Several letters of the same period to other correspondents are similarly signed.[6]

About 4 February 1759 there was a storm of such severity that the roof and gable-end of the cottage were badly damaged and it was necessary to evacuate Agnes and baby Robert to a neighbouring farmhouse. Burns himself alluded to this stormy 'hansel' in his flippant celebration of his twenty-eighth birthday, 'Rantin, Rovin Robin' (CW 267–8), although the song conveys the impression that this incident took place immediately after his birth. The tradition that Burns cited it as prophetic of his tempestuous life seems to have arisen long after his death. Significantly, he makes no mention of it in his long autobiographical letter to Dr John Moore. The best account of it, in fact, was provided by Gilbert Burns for inclusion in Currie's revised edition of 1803:

> When my father built his 'clay biggin', he put in two stone–jambs, as they are called, and a lintel, carrying up the chimney in his clay-gable. The consequence was, that as the gable subsided, the jambs, remaining firm, threw it off its centre; and, one very stormy morning, when my brother was nine or ten days old, a little before daylight, a part of the gable fell out, and the rest appeared so shattered, that my mother, with the young poet, had to be carried through the storm to a neighbour's house, where they remained a week, till their own dwelling was adjusted.[7]

One can imagine poor William struggling through the stormy darkness to get his wife and baby safely lodged with a neighbour. By daylight, when the storm showed no sign of abating, he returned to the cottage to repair the ravages of the cruel west wind. Those neighbours who had watched the taciturn incomer building the cottage in the first place, doubtless smiled knowingly at his discomfiture while offering their sympathy. Undeterred by this setback, however, William set to with a will; and a testament to the care which he took is the fact that the 'auld clay biggin' has stood to this day. There is evidence to suggest that the main road originally ran along the back of the cottage, but the line of the road was altered by the road trustees in 1826. This explains the apparent discrepancies in early prints and paintings of the cottage, some of which show the front door level with the road, or with a winding footpath in front, or with seven steps leading down to the roadway.[8]

The cottage which William Burnes constructed was an unpretentious, single-storey building. It comprised two rooms, a living-room and a kitchen with a connecting door. From the kitchen another door led into the barn and byre or cowshed. The floors were paved with slabs of stone, but apart from the stone jambs mentioned in Gilbert's account, the cottage was entirely constructed of clay covered with lime and topped by a roof of thatch. The walls were very thick and sloped back slightly from their base to the roof. In the kitchen a wall recess contained a bed in the Scottish fashion, and it was here that Burns was born. A bed-stance, raised on planks above the stone floor, occupied a corner of the living-room and, in time, accommodated the growing brood. Both rooms had small windows to the back and front. Originally, only one of the front windows had glass in its upper part; the other windows were unglazed and light and ventilation were controlled by means of wooden shutters. Chimney places were positioned at either end of the house. Viewed from outside, the cottage presents a long, low appearance with chimneys protruding from the thatch on the extreme left and halfway along, but beyond the right-hand chimney lie the outbuildings. At first glance the cottage and its outbuildings appear to be in a straight line, but the structure is slightly curved to follow the line of the original roadway.

In due course three other children were born in this humble cottage. Gilbert was born on 28 September 1760, followed by Agnes and Annabella on 30 September 1762 and 14 November 1764 respectively.[9] It says much, both for the sturdy nature of the Burnes children and the careful nurture of their parents, that none of these boys and girls succumbed in infancy. At a time when infant mortality was high it is nothing short of remarkable that all seven children born to Agnes Burnes reached maturity and the family in this generation was not broken till October 1785 when the youngest son, John, died at the age of sixteen.

William's plans for a nursery garden never seem to have prospered. Before long he was taking refuge in the security of his job as head gardener at Doonholm. Provost Fergusson was steadily adding to his estate. To the original thirty acres which had formerly been the farms of Berriesdam and Warlockholm he added Fauldhead and Whinknowe as part of a deal with Crawford of Doonside. Subsequently he purchased the more extensive lands of South High Corton. The Doonholm estate eventually stretched all the way from Alloway's dilapidated and long-deserted church to Auchendrane. Around Fergusson's new mansion-house were laid out gardens, walks, shrubberies, an avenue of elms and copses and plantations of other trees. Laying out these grounds and maintaining them was a full-time occupation. Fergusson's offer was too tempting to turn down; and so Burnes tacitly abandoned his nursery scheme, disposing of a third of his land. In effect, the remaining five acres at the New Gardens (as this part of Alloway was then known) became a smallholding which was largely left in the capable hands of Agnes. It was she who cultivated this patch, kept as many as four cows at a time, produced milk and made cheeses, and tended her poultry. Agnes worked hard, and her bright-eyed, intelligent brood would be given little tasks as soon as they were old enough. Constant traffic along the Ayr–Maybole road that fronted the cottage would doubtless have provided the children with endless entertainment and wonderment, and for Robert and Gilbert at least, there were the expeditions into the nearby town on market days accompanying their father. The laddies would have found plenty of diversion, guddling for trout and paddling in the burns that led into the Doon itself, or exploring the ruined old church.

Kirk-Alloway, situated some 300 yards north of the Doon had had a rather mixed career. It was built about 1516 and served as a parish church until 1691 when Alloway was joined to the parish of Ayr. Over the course of half a century it was allowed to fall into disrepair, but in 1740 it was reroofed and for several years was used both for public worship and as a school. By the mid-1750s it was again vacant and when Robert was a boy the roof partially collapsed.[10] On the initiative of William Burnes himself, the villagers of Alloway made some attempt to repair the neglect to the kirkyard and tidy up the headstones, but the church itself remained ruinous and deserted. It is only too easy to imagine the spooky effect which this gaunt ruin would have on the receptive minds of young children, especially children brainwashed by the likes of old Betty Davidson.

This woman was the widow of a cousin of the poet's mother. Agnes gave her board and lodging and in return she helped about the house and the dairy. She also kept the children amused and spellbound with what Robert was later to describe as 'the largest collection in the country of tales and songs concerning devils, ghosts, fairies, brownies, witches, warlocks, spunkies, kelpies, elf-candles, dead-lights, wraiths, apparitions, cantraips, enchanted towers, giants, dragons, and other trumpery'.[11] Robert frankly admitted his indebtedness to this 'old Maid of my Mother's, remarkable for her ignorance, credulity and superstition'. Betty Davidson's repertoire

> cultivated the latent seeds of Poesy; but had so strong an effect on my imagination, that to this hour, in my nocturnal rambles, I sometimes keep a sharp look-out in suspicious places; and though nobody can be more sceptical in these matters than I, yet it often takes an effort of Philosophy to shake off these idle terrors.

One would not need to be unduly imaginative to associate the ruined church with the supernatural. On one occasion a Highland bullock strayed and eventually wandered into the old kirk where it got stuck and, being without food and water, went half-mad. A day or two later a local woman happened to be passing the kirk when she looked through the ruined window and saw a pair of horns, accompanied by loud bellowing. She fled in terror, convinced that the Devil had taken over the auld kirk. One of the Tennant boys was sent from Laigh Corton to investigate and found the poor beast. In extricating the maddened animal, however, one of its horns was knocked off. This was kept by the Tennant family as a trophy and in due course it was mounted with silver for use by the town crier of Ochiltree. It later reverted to the Tennant family and exists to this day.[12] The story of the bullock mistaken for the Deil spread rapidly through the district and would doubtless have reinforced Robert's opinion of Kirk-Alloway as 'a place so well known to be a favourite haunt of the devil and the devil's friends and emissaries'.[13]

As well as Betty Davidson, Agnes herself was a fund of old stories and songs. Following the habits of a lifetime, Agnes sang as she worked, and as she worked her eldest child would follow her around the steading listening and absorbing. Many of these songs were coarse in word and sentiment, reflecting the robust attitudes of the peasantry. His mother's favourite – and Robert's too – was an old ballad:

> Kissin is the key o love,
> An clappin is the lock,
> An makin o's the best thing
> That e'er a young thing got.

It seems strange, even in our enlightened times, to think that Agnes should entertain children of such tender years with a song whose subject was sexual intercourse. Given his consuming interest in songs from a very early age, it is ironic that young Robert never developed a talent for singing. Successive biographers have made increasing use of this supposed fact, culminating with Catherine Carswell:

> Robert himself could not sing. He tried – how the child tried! – with the violence of despair over his unaccountable, maddening failure. His mother did her best to teach him. But there it was. Though she could set the melody pulsing in him he could not release it. The rhythm was there. It was in his blood. But when he opened his mouth nothing came but unmeaning sounds. It was not that he could not distinguish each separate air. He could, even if they were hummed over without a word, But his baby sisters could sing a tune more correctly than he, and even Gilbert, who did not specially care for music, made a better showing.[14]

This view of the poet's lack of musicality derives solely from a brief comment by his schoolteacher John Murdoch in the account which he supplied to Dr Currie and which is given more fully, later in this chapter. I find Murdoch's statement very difficult to reconcile with the astonishing grasp of traditional Scottish music, with its notoriously difficult tones and rhythms. No one who wrestled with these old melodies and uncannily fitted words of the right metre and inflection to them could have been as tone-deaf and untunable as Murdoch made out. But then, Murdoch was speaking solely in the context of psalm-singing and I incline to the view that the thrawn wee laddie of six or seven lacked motivation, no matter how hard or how often Murdoch thrashed him.

Robert's attitude at this tender age is hinted at in his autobiographical letter to Moore:

> At these years I was by no means a favourite with anybody. I was a good deal noted for a retentive memory, a stubborn, sturdy something in my disposition, and an enthusiastic idiot piety. I say idiot-piety because I was then but a child.– Though I cost the schoolmaster some thrashings, I made an excellent English scholar . . .[15]

There was a family tradition that Robert Burnes, the poet's grandfather, had joined forces with other tenant farmers in his locality to provide a school for their children. The truth of this cannot now be ascertained; but this was what William Burnes did eventually. Himself educated rather above the average for the Scottish peasantry of the period, he clearly attached great importance to education, both for its own sake (hence the attention given to his daughters) and as a means of advancement in later life.

Although an Act of the Scottish Parliament had decreed in 1694 that there should be schools in every parish, practice often diverged widely from this ideal. Mention has already been made of the school at Kirk-Alloway which seems to have flourished between 1740 and 1752; but after that time it fell into abeyance. In default of a parish school nearer than the burgh school at Ayr (elevated to the rank of an academy in 1799), education was left to private enterprise. At the beginning of 1765 William Campbell opened a school at Alloway Mill near the mouth of the Doon and about a mile from the hamlet itself. William Burnes promptly enrolled his sons at this school and for a short time Robert and Gilbert were given the rudiments of reading and writing, although it is probable that Robert, at least, had already received some instruction from his own father. Running a one-teacher country school, with little or no aid from the heritors and relying on the pittance provided by the parents of the scholars, was a precarious existence and when, only a few weeks later, a job with prospects and certainly better remuneration turned up, William Campbell closed the school and went off to Ayr to become Master of the Workhouse.[16]

At this point William Burnes took the initiative in obtaining a tutor for his sons and those of four other families in the neighbourhood, including that of John Tennant of Laigh Corton. Tennant had a brother, David, who had been appointed English master at the burgh grammar school in Ayr in 1755 at the early age of twenty-one. With his scholastic duties he combined the offices of collector of the poor stent and Session clerk. Moreover, the Latin master at the grammar school, Alexander Paterson, was a native of Aberdeenshire with whom William and Agnes were on friendly terms. Paterson had been the Latin master at Tranent, East Lothian, before coming to Ayr in a similar capacity in 1751 – about the same time that Burnes himself had crossed country. He became rector (headmaster) in 1761, a position which he held until his death in 1768.[17] According to Gilbert Burns, on Sundays, after divine worship, the Burneses often paid a brief visit to the Patersons. The precentor at Ayr Auld Kirk was William Robinson, writing master at the grammar school, another friend of William Burnes. Through Tennant, Robinson and Paterson, therefore, William was singularly fortunate in securing the services of young John Murdoch. Born at Ayr on 25 March 1747, he was less than a dozen years older than Robert. He had been educated at Ayr Grammar School and had finished his studies in Edinburgh, before returning to his home town to look for a scholastic position. By this time, his father was the schoolmaster and Session clerk in Auchinleck.[18] Murdoch later furnished Currie (via the Irish antiquary, Joseph Cooper Walker) with an interesting account, shedding light not only on the early education of the future poet but also on his own character and teaching methods:

> In 1765, about the middle of March, Mr. W. Burnes came to Ayr, and sent to the school, where I was improving in writing, under my good friend Mr. Robinson, desiring that I would come and speak to him at a certain inn, and bring my writing-book with me. This was immediately complied with. Having examined my writing, he was pleased with it, – (you will readily allow he was not difficult), and told me that he had received very satisfactory information of Mr. Tennant, the master of the English school, concerning my improvement in English and in his method of teaching. In the month of May following, I was engaged by Mr.

Burnes, and four of his neighbours, to teach, and accordingly began to teach the little school at Alloway, which was situated a few yards from the argillaceous fabric above-mentioned. My five employers undertook to board me by turns, and to make up a certain salary, at the end of the year, provided my quarterly payments from the different pupils did not amount to that sum.

My pupil, Robert Burns, was then between six and seven years of age; his preceptor about eighteen. Robert, and his younger brother Gilbert, had been grounded a little in English before they were put under my care. They both made a rapid progress in reading, and a tolerable progress in writing. In reading, dividing words into syllables by rule, spelling without book, parsing sentences, &c, Robert and Gilbert were generally at the upper end of the class, even when ranged with boys by far their seniors. The books most commonly used in the school were, the *Spelling Book*, the *New Testament*, the *Bible, Mason's Collection of Prose and Verse*, and *Fisher's English Grammar*. They committed to memory the hymns, and other poems of that collection, with uncommon facility. This facility was partly owing to the method pursued by their father and me in instructing them, which was, to make them thoroughly acquainted with the meaning of every word in each sentence that was to be committed to memory. By the by, this may be easier done, and at an earlier period, than is generally thought. As soon as they were capable of it, I taught them to turn verse into its natural prose order; and sometimes to substitute synonimous expressions for poetical words, and to supply all the ellipses. These, you know, are the means of knowing that the pupil understands the author. These are excellent helps to the arrangement of words in sentences, as well as to a variety of expression.

Gilbert always appeared to me to possess a more lively imagination, and to be more of the wit, than Robert. I attempted to teach them a little church-music. Here they were left far behind by all the rest of the school. Robert's ear, in particular, was remarkably dull, and his voice untunable. It was long before I could get them to distinguish one tune from another. Robert's countenance was generally grave, and expressive of a serious, contemplative, and thoughtful mind. Gilbert's face said, *Mirth, with thee I mean to live*; and certainly, if any person who knew the two boys, had been asked which of them was most likely to court the muses, he would surely never have guessed that Robert had a propensity of that kind.[19]

The school was conducted by Murdoch in a tenement not far from Burns Cottage; it was still standing a century later, but was demolished in 1878. The fees paid by the pupils and their parents guaranteed the young schoolmaster sixpence a day, as well as free board and lodgings. One anecdote from this period was preserved by Joseph Train:

While a mere child, and at Mr Murdoch's school, some person called one day on the Teacher, who went out for a few minutes. As is quite customary in village schools a dreadful uproar commenced. Mr M at last returned – and in the meantime Robert whose seat was near the door, had slipped into a press [a shallow cupboard] quite contiguous to it. To quell the uproar Mr M struck the *tawz* loudly against the press-door. Rob was behind it and screamed out and began to cry so loudly that he was at last suffered to go home. His mother questioned what was the matter. Robert could not answer for some time – but by and by sobbed out 'The mas-master *payed* me!' '*Payed* you, Robbie. What for did the master pay ye? Where did he pay you on?' 'He pay-payed me on the press!' added poor Robert who created much amusement to his mother and [this] was long a standing joke at his expence.[20]

Murdoch has often been dismissed as a dreadful pedant, mainly for his affectation in referring to the auld clay biggin as an 'argillaceous fabric'. Elsewhere he alluded to it as a 'mud edifice' or 'tabernacle of clay', as if he had some aversion to calling it a cottage. But it is only fair to point out that he was writing, in relative old age, to a man of some rank in society and established literary reputation, so these 'pedantic absurdities' were perhaps pardonable and understandable. It is clear, however, that looking back on the days of his youth from a position of advanced years, Murdoch regarded his brief spell at Alloway with affection, and his lodging in the Burnes family with something approaching reverence. This was not merely hind-sight at the recollection of having played such a vital part in the formative education of Scotland's greatest poet, but an expression of genuine feeling for the poet's father. William Burnes, it is clear, had made an immense and lasting impression on Murdoch. Writing to Currie, Murdoch spoke of Burnes as 'the saint, the father, and the husband' and

a tender and affectionate father of whose manly qualities and rational and Christian virtues he would not pretend to give a description . . . In this mean cottage I really believe there dwelt a larger portion of content than in any palace in Europe.

Murdoch shared William's religious views, and this encouraged the older man to take the young dominie into his confidence. He had been working on a theological manual for the religious guidance of his children. He had commenced this about the time Robert was born, if not earlier, and had persevered with it ever since. This catechism took the form of a dialogue between father and son. In many respects William's *Manual of Religious Belief*, first published in 1875 almost a century after his death, was a remarkable document, reflecting the religious outlook of the second half of the eighteenth century and larded with the unreadable jargon in which ministers of the period took such delight. It was obviously the work of a man who had listened all too carefully to the long sermons preached by Dalrymple and his colleagues. But in presenting the manual in the form of a dialogue, in which the son was at liberty to question the father, it was ahead of its time. The only manuscript is not in William's handwriting and, to judge by extant specimens of his letters (in which he habitually spelled the first person pronoun as 'wee' and 'daughter' as 'douther'), definitely not in his spelling. Indeed, the full title of the published version reveals that although it was compiled by William Burnes it was

35

transcribed, with grammatical corrections, by John Murdoch, and it is in his beautiful copperplate hand that the manual was preserved. It seems probable that Murdoch transcribed this manuscript in 1765 during his residence at Alloway.

In his autobiographical letter to Dr Moore, Burns gave little more than a cursory glance at his early education, but he went on to record the effect which his early reading, under Murdoch's influence, had on him:

> The earliest thing of Composition that I recollect taking pleasure in was, The Vision of Mirza and a hymn of Addison's beginning – 'How are Thy servants blest, O Lord!' I particularly remember one half-stanza which was music to my boyish ear –
>
> > For though in dreadful whirls we hung,
> > High on the broken wave
>
> I met with these pieces in Masson's English Collection, one of my school-books.– The two first books I ever read in private, and which gave me more pleasure than any two books I ever read again, were, the life of Hannibal and the history of Sir William Wallace.– Hannibal gave my young ideas such a turn that I used to strut in raptures up and down after the recruiting drum and bagpipe, and wish myself tall enough to be a soldier; while the story of Wallace poured a Scotish prejudice in my veins which will boil along there till the flood-gates of life shut in eternal rest.[21]

Gilbert provided a more precise account of their early schooling:

> Under Mr. John Murdoch we learned to read English tolerably well, and to write a little. He taught us too the English grammar. I was too young to profit much from his lessons in grammar; but Robert made some proficiency in it, a circumstance of considerable weight in the unfolding of his genius and character; as he soon became remarkable for the fluency and correctness of his expression, and read the few books that came in his way with much pleasure and improvement; for even then he was a reader when he could get a book.[22]

From these accounts, therefore, we can see that, even at the tender age of six or seven, Robert was an avid reader. Not surprisingly, the textbooks used by Murdoch were of English, rather than Scottish origin. Inevitably the Bible, both Old and New Testaments, played a major role both as a manual of religious belief and as a medium for teaching reading. That Burns read his bible both as a boy and throughout his adult life is amply demonstrated by the number and range of the biblical quotations and allusions that peppered his poetry and letters. The grammar–book was compiled by a Mrs Slack of Newcastle, under the pseudonym of A. Fisher, and enjoyed widespread popularity. The eighth edition was published in London in 1763 and it seems likely that this was the edition used by Murdoch. The spelling book was probably Arthur Masson's *English Spelling Book* whose third edition appeared in Edinburgh in 1761. The preface contained an interesting statement:

> Some notice should be taken of several innovations which have been attempted, of late, in English Orthography; such as, in writing Honor, Favor, etc., for Honour, Favour . . . I approve of this method, and could wish Custom would authorise the throwing out as many silent letters in a word as possible.

It is possible that, under the influence of this work, Burns formed the habit of omitting the letter *u* in writing words of this class, and of using the contracted form *tho'* instead of though.[23]

Masson's *Collection of Prose and Verse* shows that Murdoch made a creditable attempt to introduce his youthful charges to the beauties of English literature, taking them far beyond what was required of the three Rs. It contained excerpts from the works of Shakespeare, Milton, Dryden, Addison, Thomson, Gray, Akenside and Shenstone (as well as a number of minor poets whose works are now unreadable and unread), together with a hodgepodge of moral, didactic and historical prose pieces, notably several of Elizabeth Rowe's *Moral Letters*.[24] A perusal of this rare work reveals to what extent Robert was influenced by it in later life. Many of the quotations which liberally sprinkled his correspondence come from poems memorised from this anthology, while the hand of the egregious Mrs Rowe can be discerned in Robert's earliest attempts at 'literary' prose. More importantly, he shaped his standards of value in conformity with those which he found exemplified in Masson.[25]

Though only six or seven years of age, Robert was Murdoch's star pupil. The precocity evinced by the small boy committing passages of Gray and Shenstone to memory, and the all-pervasive religiosity of the period, were also tinged with the insidious influence of the bawdy earthiness of the songs and stories of Agnes Burnes and Betty Davidson. These disparate strands were to come together, twenty years later, in the volume which included such works as 'The Cotter's Saturday Night' (CW 147-51) and 'Hallowe'en' (CW 151-7), or 'Despondency, an Ode' (CW 207-8) and 'Address to the Deil' (CW 161-4), or ' Prayer in the Prospect of Death' (CW 53-4) and the song 'The Rigs o Barley' (CW 49). The seeds sown in the boy's mind during his earliest schooldays had merely borne their natural fruit.[26]

CHAPTER 3

Mount Oliphant, 1766–77

My father was a farmer upon the Carrick border, O,
And carefully he bred me in decency and order, O.

My Father was a Farmer (CW 58)

Two things decided William Burnes to give up his smallholding at Alloway and take up the traditional occupation of his ancestors. Since the birth of Annabella in November 1764 the two-room cottage housing three adults and four children was getting cramped. More importantly, perhaps, William was aware that in a few months, a year at most, his elder son would be of an age at which he would normally be hired out as a day-labourer to some neighbouring farmer, or even sent off as a live-in gaudsboy at a farm farther away. William found such a course of action abhorrent. It upset all his carefully laid schemes to attain economic independence and it also interfered with his ambitions to do better for his sons. Farming seemed to offer an opportunity to keep the family together. William therefore decided to dispose of his few acres in Alloway and lease a farm. To this end he approached his employer, Provost Fergusson, who had only recently purchased the farm of Mount Oliphant, about two miles south-east of Alloway. This small farm of seventy acres Scots measure (about ninety English acres), on rising ground half a mile south of the Corton road and a similar distance east of the present A77, boasted a steading, but the land itself was in poor shape and was in urgent need of improvement. Fergusson was looking for a rent of £40 a year which, in view of the state of the farm, seems unduly optimistic and above the average of rents then prevailing in Ayrshire. Yet William Burnes was persuaded to agree these terms, for a period of six years, at the end of which the rent was to be raised to £45 per annum for a further six years. This twelve-year lease ran from Martinmas (11 November) 1765 till Martinmas 1777, but it contained a clause which gave the tenant the option of removing at the end of six years.[1]

William Burnes got no takers for the cottage and land at Alloway; he was therefore compelled to retain both the lease of the land and the proprietorship of the cottage and its outbuildings for fifteen years, letting the house to a succession of tenants. Eventually, in 1781, the land and house were put up for sale and were purchased by the Incorporation of Shoemakers in

39

Ayr for £160. The records of the Incorporation[2] reveal that the quondam Burnes house was occupied, at an annual rent of £10, by Matthew Dick, shoemaker in Ayr, from 1782 till 1801. It was Dick who, at some time after 1781, turned the cottage into an ale-house. John Maitland succeeded to the tenancy in 1801, paying £25 10s a year. He sublet the cottage in 1803 to John Goudie. From then until his death in 1842 'Miller' Goudie ran the cottage as a public house. John Keats visited the place in 1818 and described Goudie as 'a mahogany-faced old jackass who knew Burns; he drinks glasses, five for the quarter, and twelve for the hour'.[3] After Goudie's death, the business was carried on by his widow until her death in 1843. Thereafter her daughter and son-in-law (Mr and Mrs David Hastings) continued till Martinmas 1845, when the cottage was let to Davidson Ritchie. Two years later the Incorporation of Shoemakers erected a neat little hall alongside the cottage and this served as a Mecca for the increasing number of pilgrims who came from all over the country to visit the poet's birthplace. Here were gathered many Burns manuscripts and relics (some of which were actually genuine). The Ayr Burns Club held its annual suppers here and in 1859 the centenary of the poet's birth was enthusiastically celebrated. In 1881 the Incorporation sold its property for £4,000 to the Trustees of the Burns Monument (erected in 1823) 'to be preserved in the interests and for behoof of the public'. The cottage then lost its licence as an ale-house and was in due course restored to its condition and appearance at the time of the poet's birth.[4]

Under the terms of his lease, William Burnes had the use of the land at Mount Oliphant from Martinmas 1765, but could not take possession of the farmhouse and its outbuildings till after Whitsun 1766. At least this was a better time of year to be moving and setting up home anew and the Burnes family had an auspicious beginning, the weather in April and May 1766 being unusually mild, with the result that all growing things were, according to the newspapers, 'in great forwardness'. Even after the move to Mount Oliphant, Robert and Gilbert continued to trudge two miles each way to attend Murdoch's little school, downhill in the mornings and uphill in the evenings. School hours were longer than they are nowadays. In Scotland at that time schools were conducted six days a week and although the Sunday School movement in England did not begin until 1782, Sabbath schools were usually conducted in Scotland by the village dominies at the end of the afternoon church service. In Burns's case, not only was the actual time spent in school much longer than one might suppose, but the quality of tuition was remarkably good. Whatever his faults of pedantry, Murdoch was an excellent teacher whose methods, encouraging his pupils to think for themselves and work things out rather than accept everything by rote, were in advance of the time. In the case of pupils of the calibre of Robert and Gilbert, Murdoch's system of self–motivation was to pay handsome dividends. The boys continued to attend the Alloway school until early in 1768 when Murdoch obtained a teaching appointment at Dumfries.

This severed the family's last tenuous links with Alloway; but in other respects life at Mount Oliphant was very different from that at the New

Gardens. William Burnes was no longer head-gardener at Doonholm, in receipt of a modest but regular wage; he was now a tenant farmer starting off in the most disadvantageous circumstances. Unable to dispose of his holdings at Alloway, he could not release his capital; but in order to make a go of the new farm he needed a considerable sum of money for stock, seed and equipment. His late employer and new landlord, however, was quite ready to lend him £100 to get him started. It says a great deal for Fergusson's regard for his erstwhile employee that he not only accepted his offer for the tenancy but was so willing to advance a sum of money, equal to more than two years' rent, into the bargain. In retrospect, however, it was an enormous burden with which to saddle Burnes. Both Fergusson and Burnes proved unduly optimistic about the potential of the farm. Gilbert's laconic statement that Mount Oliphant had 'almost the very poorest soil I know of in a state of cultivation'[5] hints at the ruinous bargain this proved to be. Thirty years later, despite the revolution which had taken place in agriculture in the interim, the annual rental of Mount Oliphant was actually £5 less than Burnes had been paying.[6]

True to the old adage 'New house, new baby', Agnes gave birth to a third son on 30 July 1767, little more than a year after the family moved to Mount Oliphant. In the old Scottish tradition the Burnes boys had successively been named for the fathers of their parents; now the third son took the name of his father. There were two other children, who followed at two-yearly intervals: John was born on 10 July 1769 and Isobel on 27 July 1771.[7] Gilbert's narrative letter to Mrs Dunlop provides the most graphic description of this period:

> . . . there being no school near us, and our little services being useful on the farm, my Father undertook to teach us arithmetic in the winter evenings by candlelight, and in this way my two elder sisters got all the education they received.[8]

It is not known whether Murdoch found a successor at Alloway, though, on balance, this seems unlikely as, without the driving force of William Burnes, the little school could hardly have continued. In any case, Murdoch's departure provided a convenient pretext for taking Robert and Gilbert out of school and setting them to work on the farm. William could not afford to hire farm-hands and therefore performed all the heavy tasks himself.

The family must have felt the isolation of Mount Oliphant very keenly after living beside a busy highway. According to Gilbert:

> Nothing could be more retired than our general manner of living at Mount Oliphant; we rarely saw any body but the members of our own family. There were no boys of our own age, or near it, in the neighbourhood. Indeed the greater part of the land in the vicinity was at that time possessed by shopkeepers, and people of that stamp, who had retired from business, or who kept their farm in the country at the same time that they followed business in the town.[9]

Even today, there is an air of loneliness about this district, although the development of drainage ditches and the planting of hedgerows in the wake of the agrarian revolution towards the end of the eighteenth century belies the bleak desolation which must have so often been the outlook in the 1760s. Bleak and austere it might be, but the high ground of the aptly-named Mount afforded splendid views of the Firth of Clyde, with the dramatic bulk of Ailsa Craig on the left and the jagged grey-blue mass of Arran on the right. In none of his writings did Robert ever mention this stunning spectacle; indeed, Burns scholars have often commented on the fact that, for a nature poet in the sentimental era, he seems on the whole to have been oblivious to scenery. It has been postulated that Robert had a dread of the sea and that the inhuman expanse of the sea rather saddened and repelled him,[10] though some years later, during the period of his tours round Scotland, he did make two or three brief excursions by sailing vessels. Gilbert continues:

> My father was for some time almost the only companion we had. He conversed familiarly on all subjects with us as if we had been men, and was at great pains, while we accompanied him in the labours of the farm, to lead the conversation to such subjects as might tend to increase our knowledge, or confirm our virtuous habits.[11]

In these modern times when every town has a free public library and every village and hamlet is served by a mobile lending library, it is hard to comprehend how difficult it must have been to procure reading matter in the 1760s and 1770s. To be sure, the Ayr Library had been founded in 1762, but this was for the use of private subscribers only (William Burnes being one of them). It was housed in the burgh school and the English master was, *ex officio*, its librarian.[12] These duties fell to John Murdoch following his return to Ayr in 1772 and doubtless Robert benefited from accessibility to books. Gilbert recounts how Murdoch visited the farm shortly before he left the district in 1768:

> He brought us a present and memorial of him, a small compendium of English Grammar, and the tragedy of *Titus Andronicus*, and by way of passing the evening, he began to read the play aloud. We were all attention for some time, till presently the whole party was dissolved in tears. A female in the play (I have but a confused recollection of it) had her hands chopt off, her tongue cut out, and then was insultingly desired to call for water to wash her hands. At this, in an agony of distress, we with one voice desired he would read no more. My father observed that if we would not hear it out, it would be needless to leave the play with us. Robert replied that if it was left he would burn it. My father was going to chide him for this ungrateful return to his tutor's kindness; but Murdoch interposed, declaring that he liked to see so much sensibility; and he left the *School for Love* a comedy (translated I think from the French) in its place.[13]

Mention has already been made of the earliest books, other than the Bible and the Burnes *Manual*, which influenced the future poet. Gilbert corrected his brother's account of this, in his own narrative letter:

> Murdoch, whose library at that time had no great variety in it, lent him *The Life of Hannibal*, which was the first book he read (the school books excepted) and almost the only one he had an opportunity of reading while he was at school; for the *Life of Wallace* which he classes with it in one of his letters, he did not see for some years afterwards, when he borrowed it from the blacksmith who shod our horses.[14]

This blacksmith was Henry McCandlish of Purclewan, father of Robert's closest boyhood friend. On his own admission, Robert identified closely with the martial figure of Hannibal who came so close to overthrowing the Romans, a fantasy which did nothing to mitigate that 'stubborn sturdy something' in his character. A lasting legacy of this was the poet's oft-repeated hankering 'to go and be a sodger'. It has been observed shrewdly that as life had a way of appearing too difficult for Robert at frequent intervals this soldiering idea was a recurring source of comfort.[15]

William Burnes did his utmost to compensate for the lack of full-time education from 1768 onwards. To 'increase their knowledge, or confirm their virtuous habits', as Gilbert put it:

> He borrowed Salmon's *Geographical Grammar* for us, and endeavoured to make us acquainted with the situation and history of the different countries in the world; while, from a book-society in Ayr, he procured for us Durham's *Phisico and Astro-Theology*, and Ray's *Wisdom of God in Creation*, to give us some idea of astronomy and natural history. Robert read all these books with an avidity and industry scarcely to be equalled. My Father had been a subscriber to Stackhouse's *History of the Bible*, then lately published by John Meuros in Kilmarnock: from this Robert collected a pretty competent knowledge of ancient history: for no book was so voluminous as to slacken his industry, or so antiquated as to damp his researches. A brother of my mother who had lived with us some time, and had learned some arithmetic by our winter evening's candle, went into a bookseller's shop in Ayr, to purchase *The Ready Reckoner, or Tradesman's sure Guide* , and a book to teach him to write letters. Luckily, in place of *The Complete Letter-Writer*, he got by mistake a small collection of Letters by the most Eminent Writers, with a few sensible directions for attaining an easy epistolary style. This book was to Robert of the greatest consequence. It inspired him with a strong desire to excel in letter-writing, while it furnished him with models by some of the first writers in our language.

Stackhouse's *New History of the Holy Bible from the Beginnings of the World to the Establishment of Christianity* was originally published in two folio volumes in 1737. A second edition, revised and enlarged by the author, appeared in 1742. It seems probable that Burnes acquired the Edinburgh edition, which appeared in six volumes over a two-year period

(1765–7) at three shillings a volume (the total being equivalent to about two months' wages for a farm-worker at that time). Meuros was not the publisher in the modern sense, but rather the local distributor. Robert's autobiographical letter mentions that 'My knowledge of ancient story was gathered from Salmon's and Guthrie's geographical grammars' (CL 251). These works were *A New Geographical and Historical Grammar* by Thomas Salmon, and *A New Geographical, Historical and Commercial Grammar* by William Guthrie. The latter volume, in particular, published at London in 1770, is a fascinating compendium of 'the present state of the several kingdoms of the world' with well-written accounts of the 'population, inhabitants, customs, and manners' of each country, which would repay the student of Scotland, and the world at large, as they were in the poet's lifetime. Gilbert was slightly inaccurate in the name of one author and implied that a single volume was indicated. In fact, the Revd. William Derham, rector of Upminster, published his *Physico-Theology* in 1713 and the following year produced a sequel entitled *Astro-Theology, or, a Demonstration of the Being and Attributes of God.* Herein we find the accepted view of astronomy in the early eighteenth century, when theology rather than science was the author's chief interest. John Ray's *Wisdom of God Manifested in the Works of the Creation* first appeared in 1691 but was an extremely popular work that ran to many editions and was extensively translated. No creature was too humble or repulsive to stand witness to God's majesty. One wonders whether Burns recalled Ray's comment when he apostrophised that 'crowlin ferlie' (CW 181):

> Here, by the by, I can not but look upon the strange instinct of this noisome and troublesome creature the louse, of searching out foul and nasty clothes to harbour and breed in, as an effect of divine providence, designed to deter men and women from sluttishness and sordidness, and to provoke them to cleanliness and neatness.

Snyder was the first major biographer to draw attention to the fact that all of the books which came into the Burnes household, either as textbooks supplied by Murdoch, or borrowed or purchased by Burnes, were purely English.

> Indeed, it is obvious that all the early formal educational influence to which Burns was subjected, both secular and religious, tended to Anglicize him, so far as language and literary style were concerned. Had his native genius been less strong, it might easily have been warped entirely out of its destined orbit, and rendered as insipid as that of his contemporary Michael Bruce.[16]

After the light, sandy soil of Alloway, William Burnes had to wrestle with the mossy and moorish, the stony and inadequately drained land of this hill farm. The farmhouse at Mount Oliphant was a poor, rough little place. A fair idea of what it must have been like in Robert's day is provided by a sepia sketch by William Leitch, executed about 1827 as the basis of an engraving for one of the souvenir boxes manufactured by the Smith Brothers at Mauchline.[17] Little had changed in the half-century since William Burnes had given up his lease. Indeed, looking at the farm today and comparing it with Leitch's sketch, the resemblance is quite uncanny. The stone-built steading and its outbuildings were erected on three sides of a square with their back to the prevailing westerly winds. The farmhouse was little bigger than the cottage at Alloway, with a room and kitchen – the but and ben – on either side of the doorway and a single large window in each. This dwelling, however, had a slated roof, more steeply pitched than the Alloway thatch, and this provided the windowless attic accommodation for the four boys and any male visitors (such as John Murdoch who lodged here periodically in 1766-8).

When Cuthbert Hadden described Mount Oliphant towards the end of the nineteenth century he had to concede that, 'in spite of long cultivation, the farm is to this day but an indifferent one, the land being heavy, cold and stubborn'.[18] It is therefore easy to understand how, to the Burnes family, their eleven years' tenancy of Mount Oliphant were years of ceaseless, harassing struggle to keep the wolf from the door. Robert himself, in his autobiographical letter, has left a stark picture of this episode covering the most formative years of his life (CL 250):

> We lived very poorly. I was a dexterous ploughman for my age; and the next oldest to me was a brother who could drive the plough very well, and help me thrash the corn. A novel-writer might view these scenes with satisfaction; but so did not I.

William's ambitions to become financially independent and do well by his sons showed no signs of realisation. As Robert and Gilbert reached puberty they were too valuable as farm-hands to further their education. The above excerpt indicates how much the boys were exploited at a relatively tender age. Apparently it was a casual remark by John Murdoch, now back in Ayrshire after his spell in Dumfries and visiting the lonely hill farm in the summer of 1772, which gave further impetus to the boys' education. Gilbert narrates this episode:

> My brother was about thirteen or fourteen, when my father, regretting that we wrote so ill, sent us week about during a summer quarter, to the parish school of Dalrymple, which, though between two and three miles distant, was the nearest to us, that we might have an opportunity of remedying this defect.[19]

Dalrymple, south-east of Mount Oliphant on the B742 Coylton-Maybole road and some five miles north of the latter, is a pretty little village nestling on the banks of the Doon. The parish school of Robert's day was demolished many years ago and the White Horse Hotel now occupies the site. Those few intermittent weeks attending this school broadened Robert's horizons and gave him the opportunity to meet boys of his own age. One of those was James Candlish, or McCandlish, the blacksmith's son who later studied medicine at Glasgow and became a lecturer in the subject at Edinburgh. Two letters from Robert to Candlish have survived, and in one of them Burns addresses him as 'My ever dear old acquaintance' (CL 272). Robert also referred warmly to Candlish in a letter of 1791 to Peter Hill, the Edinburgh bookseller (CL 319) as 'the earliest friend except my only brother that I have on earth, & one of the worthiest fellows that ever any man called by the name of Friend'. Strangely enough, Robert himself makes no mention of his brief spell at Dalrymple school.

About this time, he was widening his literary experience. According to Gilbert:

A bookish acquaintance of my father's procured us a reading of Richardson's *Pamela*, which was the first novel we read, and the only part of Richardson's works my brother was acquainted with till towards the period of his commencing author. Till that time too he remained unacquainted with Fielding, with Smollett (two volumes of *Ferdinand Count Fathom*, and two volumes of *Peregrine Pickle* excepted), with Hume, with Robertson, and almost all our authors of eminence of the later times. I recollect indeed my father borrowed a volume of English history from Mr Hamilton of Bourtree-hill's gardener. It treated of the reign of James the First, and his unfortunate son, Charles, but I do not know who was the author; all that I remember of it is something of Charles's conversation with his children.[20]

Assuming that what Robert was reading, Gilbert read also, it says much for the precocity of the latter, a boy of eleven or twelve, that, defective though the scope of the literature available might be, he was reading works that would tax many an adult nowadays. Then John Murdoch returned to Ayr and his influence was felt directly once more. Gilbert continues:

About this time Murdoch . . . came to be the established teacher of the English language in Ayr, a circumstance of considerable consequence to us. The remembrance of my father's former friendship, and his attachment to my brother, made him do every thing in his power for our improvement. He sent us Pope's works, and some other poetry, the first that we had an opportunity of reading, excepting what is contained in *The English Collection*, and in the volumes of *The Edinburgh Magazine* for 1772; excepting also *those excellent new songs* that are hawked about the country in baskets, or exposed on stalls in the streets.

This is the first inkling that Robert read chapbooks and broadsides in which the popular ballads appeared in a *printed* form, although he himself claimed that his taste for vernacular literature was not developed till he was two or three years older. Then, in 1773, William Burnes sent his eldest son to Ayr:

to revise his English grammar, with his former teacher. He had been there only a week, when he was obliged to return, to assist at the harvest. When the harvest was over, he went back to school, where he remained two weeks; and this completes the account of his school education, excepting one summer quarter, some time afterwards, that he attended the parish school of Kirk-Oswald (where he lived with a brother of my mother's) to learn surveying.

During the two last weeks that he was with Murdoch, he himself was engaged in learning French, and he communicated the instructions he received to my brother, who, when he returned, brought home with him a French dictionary, and the *Adventures of Telemachus* in the original. In a little while, by the assistance of these books, he had acquired such a knowledge of the language, as to read and understand any French author in prose. This was considered as a sort of prodigy, and, through the medium of Murdoch, procured him the acquaintance of several lads in Ayr, who were at that time gabbling French, and the notice of some families, particularly that of Dr Malcolm, where a knowledge of French was a recommendation.

Observing the facility with which he had acquired the French language, Mr Robinson, the established writing-master in Ayr, and Mr Murdoch's particular friend, having himself acquired a considerable knowledge of the Latin language by his own industry, without ever having learnt it at school, advised Robert to make the same attempt, promising him every assistance in his power. Agreeably to this advice, he purchased *The Rudiments of the Latin Tongue*, but finding this study dry and uninteresting, it was quickly laid aside. He frequently returned to his *Rudiments* on any little chagrin or disappointment, particularly in his love afairs; but the Latin seldom predominated more than a day or two at a time, or a week at most. Observing himself the ridicule that would attach to this sort of conduct if it were known, he made two or three humorous stanzas on this subject, which I cannot now recollect, but they all ended, 'So I'll to my Latin again'. Thus you see Mr Murdoch was a principal means of my brother's improvement. Worthy Man![21]

Murdoch himself has left comments on this period:

Robert Burns came to board and lodge with me, for the purpose of revising English grammar, etc., that he might be better qualified to instruct his brothers and sisters at home. He was now with me day and night, in school, at all meals, and in all my walks. At the end of one week I told him, that, as he was now pretty much master of the parts of speech, etc., I should like to teach him something of French pronunciation, that when he should meet with the name of a French town, ship, officer, or the like, in the newspapers, he might be able to pronounce it something like a French word. Robert was glad to hear the proposal, and immediately we attacked the French with great courage.

Now there was little else to be heard but the declension of nouns, the conjugation of verbs, etc. When walking together, and even at meals, I was constantly telling him the names of the different objects, as they presented themselves, in French; so that he was hourly laying in a stock of words, and sometimes little phrases. In short, he took such pleasure in learning, and I in teaching, that it was difficult to say which of the two was most zealous in the business; and about the end of the second week of our study of the French, we began to read a little of the *Adventures of Telemachus*, in Fenelon's own words.

But now the plains of Mount Oliphant began to whiten, and Robert was summoned to relinquish the pleasing scenes that surrounded the grotto of Calypso, and, armed with a sickle, to seek glory by signalizing himself in the fields of Ceres – and so he did, for, although about fifteen, I was told that he performed the work of a man.

Thus was I deprived of my very apt pupil and, consequently, agreeable companion, at the end of three weeks, one of which was spent entirely in the study of English and the other two chiefly in that of French.[22]

Robert's proficiency in French has often been debated. To be sure, his letters were studded with French words and expressions and, more to the point, there are references to many French books which he was either reading, or was about to read, in his correspondence.[23] On the other hand, the occasional French phrases that occur in his poetry sometimes reveal, in either scansion or rhyme, that his pronunciation was idiosyncratic. Robert had one mild and innocuous affectation, a very prevalent one in polite society of the time, and that was his habit of peppering his conversation with French words and phrases. Significantly, it was Professor Dugald Stewart who alone commented somewhat adversely on this foible. There is a curious anecdote which may not be out of place at this juncture. Years later, when Robert was being lionised by Edinburgh society, Peggy Chalmers played a mean trick on the poet by introducing him to a real Frenchwoman and he, to his chagrin, found that she could not understand a word of his nor he a word of hers. Worse still, his maladroitness in the language landed him in some sort of foolish gaffe – so easy to do in French – and the lady, translated no doubt by Miss Chalmers, who must have been enjoying herself, rapped his knuckles for it smartly. One can imagine the fury that Robert, who was normally much too canny – or too lucky – to be involved in such contretemps, must have felt.[24] Hilton Brown quotes this tale without giving its source, and as Peggy Chalmers was the one correspondent to whom Robert persisted in writing in French, it does not ring true.[25]

The house in the Sandgate where Robert lodged with Murdoch in 1773 was still standing at the beginning of this century, but it was later demolished. A plaque was subsequently affixed to the wall of the building which took its place and this records that 'Here stood the house of John Murdoch, schoolmaster, in which Robert Burns lodged in his fourteenth year and received lessons in English and French'. One of Robert's fellow boarders with Murdoch was John Tennant, second son of 'guid auld Glen',[26] who later commented on Burns's familiarity with the Bible that he 'had the New Testament more at command than any other youth ever known'.[27] Regarding his brief sojourn at Ayr, Burns himself recalled to Dr Moore (CL 250):

My vicinity to Ayr was of great advantage to me. - My social disposition, when not checked by some modification of spited pride, like our catechism definition of Infinitude, was 'without bounds or limits.' I formed many connections with other Youngkers who possessed superiour advantages; the youngling Actors who were busy with the rehearsal of PARTS in which they were shortly to appear on that STAGE where, Alas! I was destined to druge (*sic*) behind the SCENES. - It is not commonly at these green years that the young Noblesse and Gentry have a just sense of the immense distance between them and their ragged Play-fellows. - It takes a few dashes into the world to give the young Great man that proper, decent, unnoticing disregard for the poor, insignificant, stupid devils, the mechanics and peasantry around him; who were perhaps born in the same village. - My young Superiours never insulted the clouterly appearance of my ploughboy carcase, the two extremes of which were often exposed to all the inclemencies of all the seasons. - They would give me stray volumes of books; among them, even then, I could pick up some observations; and ONE, whose heart I am sure not even the MUNNY BEGUM'S scenes[28] have tainted, helped me to a little French. - Parting with these, my young friends and benefactors, as they dropped off for the east or west Indies, was often to me a sore affliction.

In the previous chapter mention was made of Alexander Paterson, a fellow-countryman of William Burnes. Gilbert recounts how the intimacy established between Burnes and Paterson continued:

After his death, his widow, who is a very genteel woman, and of great worth, delighted in doing what she thought her husband would have wished to have done, and assiduously kept up her attentions to all his acquaintance . . . When she came to know my brother's passion for books, she kindly offered us the use of her husband's library, and from her we got the *Spectator, Pope's Translation of Homer*, and several other books that were of use to us.[29]

The few weeks spent under Murdoch's expert tuition in Ayr in the autumn of 1773 were like an oasis in a wilderness. For Robert, his life was all too often 'the chearless gloom of a hermit with the unceasing moil of a galley-slave'. This brought him to his sixteenth year, a little before which period he first 'committed the sin of RHYME'. In his letter to Dr Moore (CL 250-1) he recalled with fondness how his dour, humdrum life was enlivened by the advent of 'love and poesy':

You know our country custom of coupling a man and woman together as Partners in the labors of Harvest. - In my fifteenth autumn, my Partner was a bewitching creature who just counted an autumn less. - My scarcity of English denies me the power of doing her justice in that language; but you know the Scotch idiom, She was a bonie, sweet, sonsie lass. - In short, she altogether unwittingly to herself, initiated me into a certain delicious passion, which, in spite of acid disappointments, gin-horse prudence, and book-worm Philosophy, I hold to be the first of human joys, our chiefest pleasure here below. – How she caught the contagion I can't say; you medical folks talk much of infection by breathing the same air, the touch, &c. but I never expressly told her that I loved her. – Indeed I did not well know myself why I liked so much to loiter behind with her, when returning in the evenings from our labors; why the tones of her voice made my heartstrings thrill like an Eolian harp; and particularly, why my pulse beat such a furious ratann when I looked and fingered over her hand, to pick out the nettle-stings and thistles. – Among her other love-inspiring qualifications, she sung sweetly; and 'twas her favorite reel to which I attempted giving an embodied vehicle in rhyme . . . Thus with me began Love and Poesy; which at times have been my only, and till within this last twelvemonth have been my highest enjoyment.

Note how, in this passage, Robert makes a pose of underrating his command of English. Just why he should have struck such a pose so often is hard to fathom, although in this instance the pithy Scots expression was more apt than any English words.

Considering the importance of establishing exactly when Burns began writing songs, it is amazing that previous writers have so often been mistaken. Robert himself states unequivocally in this passage 'in my fifteenth autumn'. As he was born in January 1759 his first autumn would have been that of 1759, and therefore his fifteenth would have occurred in 1773. Several nineteenth-century editors, most notably Scott Douglas (1877), assigned the song to 1773 – though this was condemned by Iain MacDougall on the grounds that there was no authority for doing so.[30] Having just quoted the excerpt from the letter to Moore, however, MacDougall then wrote, 'I think, therefore, we can safely assume that the song was composed by Burns in his fifteenth year (1774) – certainly not earlier'. But 1774 was Robert's *sixteenth* year, having passed his fifteenth birthday that January. It is this failure to grasp simple arithmetic which has bedevilled the issue. Robert himself does not help matters, for he adds the comment to the copy of the song in the Stair MS that 'it was composed when he was a few months more than his sixteenth year'. What does this mean? Technically he entered that year on his fifteenth birthday, so presumably Robert meant a few months after that, in which case the song *was* composed in the summer or autumn of 1774. Perversely, MacDougall interprets this as meaning the autumn of 1775. I am inclined to think that Robert himself was guilty of a miscalculation when he wrote to Moore, and that the autumn of 1774 was intended. At any rate, that is the view generally accepted nowadays.

Not only do we have a problem over the precise date of composition, we also have a problem over the identity of the heroine. Notwithstanding the frequent references to it by the poet, he nowhere mentions the name of the 'bonie, sweet, sonsie lass' for whom the song was written, and she has come down to posterity as Handsome Nell, that being the title assigned to the song by Robert himself. Dr Currie did not identify the heroine in his editions. The first reference to her occurred in the 1819 edition produced by the Revd. Hamilton Paul of Ayr:

This nymph was afterwards married to a Carrick farmer, and became the mother of many sons and daughters, and who, when we saw her in 1811, still retained the characteristic of sonsieness, which so fascinated her helpmate in the work of the harvest as to betray him into the sin of rhyme. She sung delightfully, and he wrote a copy of verses to her favourite air or reel.[31]

The girl was first identified by the anonymous writer of a letter to *The Scotsman* in 1828, stating that she was Nelly Blair, a servant in the house of a friend of his, an extensive landed proprietor in Ayrshire. This unnamed friend stated that Burns had been a frequent visitor to his kitchen in his younger days and wrote many other songs about Nelly. The communication was based on the recollections of the lady herself. She said that she first knew Burns when 'a ploughman-lad', even at which period his peculiarities had made him an object of some notice, and of considerable attraction amongst both sexes of his own class. Burns was in great demand at rockings or spinning parties. The letter continues:

On these occasions my narrator remembers well the distinguished part Burns used to take in the business of the evening. Often has she met him at the head of a little troop, coming from a distance of three or four miles, with the spinning-wheel of his favourite, for the time being, mounted on his shoulders, and his approach announced by the bursts of merriment which his ready and rough jokes had excited amongst the group. It was always expected that some new effusion of his muse should be produced to promote the enjoyment of the party, and seldom were they disappointed, Rob Burns's last night's poem generally reaching the parlour in the course of the next day. At the kitchen of my friend's father Burns's visits were of such frequency and duration as to call down the animadversions of the lady of the house, the alertness of her damsels in the morning being at times impaired by his unreasonable gallantry. This was supposed to be occasioned by a penchant he had formed for a certain Nelly Blair, a pretty girl, a servant in the family, and whom he celebrated in more songs and odes than her name appears in – the only one likely to be applied to her now being one he himself transcribes . . . My friend describes him as being considered at that time as a clever fellow, but a 'wild scamp' . . .[32]

As a result, Nelly Blair was given as the heroine in the editions of Allan Cunningham (1834), Robert Chambers (1838) and John Wilson (1846). Not until the Chambers edition of 1851 was Nelly Kilpatrick substituted. This rested solely on the authority of Robert's sister, Isobel Burns (Mrs Begg), who, between 1847 and 1850 (when she was in her eightieth year) furnished Chambers with a number of incidents, circumstances and identifications. On the strength of Mrs Begg's recollections dating back to a period when she was a little girl, Chambers made a number of alterations which have been accepted by all subsequent writers without question. Isobel's statement was:

> The first touch of an emotion which afterwards gushed upon him was now experienced in his seventeenth autumn on the harvest-field, the cause being that 'bonie, sweet, sonsie lass', a year younger than himself, who had been assigned to him as the partner of his labours; Nelly Kilpatrick by name, and the daughter of the same blacksmith, it appears, who lent him his first book, the *Life of Wallace*.

In this instance, however, Mrs Begg's statement must be regarded with caution. She was only three years old in 1774, so her attribution could not have been based on personal observation. Her memory was clearest in respect to the Mossgiel years (1784–8), but regarding the earlier period her girlish recollections are not altogether accurate or reliable. In the above passage, for example, she directly contradicts the statements made by her famous brother, placing the composition at least a year after the later of his two versions. In other respects Isobel was manifestly wrong in her attributions (for example, she asserted that the heroine of 'My Nanie, O' was Peggy Thomson of Kirkoswald). Nevertheless, entirely on Isobel's statement, all editions from 1851 have obligingly replaced Nelly Blair with Nelly Kilpatrick. Dr Wallace, in his 1896 revision of the Chambers four-volume edition, added some details about Nelly Kilpatrick, 'the daughter of Allan Kilpatrick, miller at Parclewan, in Dalrymple Parish', with a footnote that Nelly married William Bone, coachman to the Laird of Newark, and died about the year 1820.[34]

The Dalrymple parish register, however, shows that Helen Kilpatrick was the daughter of John (not Allan) Kilpatrick in Parclewan and his spouse Jane Reid.[35] No other person of this name appears in the register of births. As she was baptised on 1 March 1759 (and presumably born a few days previously) she was only a few weeks younger than Robert, which does not square with his own description. A search through the birth registers of the Ayrshire parishes reveals no Helen Blair of the right period, which means either that the parish register has not survived, or more probably, that she was born elsewhere. On the other hand, a Helen Blair married John Smith at Dreghorn on 13 December 1788 and gave birth to a daughter Helen at Dailly on 18 February 1789. Several other children were recorded in subsequent years. Mrs Smith, née Blair, answers the description of a Carrick farmer's wife.[36]

About August 1783 Robert inscribed 'Handsome Nell' in his *First Commonplace Book*, followed by some rather exaggerated strictures which concluded:

> The expression is a little awkward, and the sentiment too serious . . . The seventh stanza has several minute faults, but I remember I composed it in a wild enthusiasm of passion, and to this hour I never recollect it but my heart melts, my blood sallies, at the remembrance.[37]

That Robert thought so well of his first poetic effusion is evident in his verse-epistle to the Guidwife of Wauchope House (CW 271), composed in

March 1787, in which he tells the story of its composition in the stanza beginning

> I mind it weel, in early date,
> When I was beardless, young and blate.

'Handsome Nell' is a simple, artless song which gives no hint of poetic genius; but it was composed to an existing tune with the title 'I am a man unmarried' and demonstrated at an early age Robert's knack of putting words to music. From the outset of his poetic career the ingredients of love, hard work and a snatch of music produced a song that is still regarded as one of his 'standards'. This basic formula permeated Robert's work from the earliest till the latest, although his muse often took him in other directions along the way.

Summer idylls such as this, however, were few and far between in the grim existence at Mount Oliphant. To the barrenness of the land must be added a run of sheer bad luck, starkly described by Gilbert:

> My father . . . soon came into difficulties, which were increased by the loss of several of his cattle by accidents and disease. To the buffettings of misfortune, we could only oppose hard labour and the most rigid economy. We lived very sparingly. For several years butcher's meat was a stranger in the house, while all the members of the family exerted themselves to the utmost of their strength, and rather beyond it, in the labours of the farm. My brother, at the age of thirteen, assisted in threshing the crop of corn, and at fifteen was the principal labourer on the farm, for we had no hired servant, male or female. The anguish of mind we felt at our tender years under these straits and difficulties was very great. To think of our father growing old (for he was now above fifty) broken-down with the long-continued fatigues of his life, with a wife and five other children, and in a declining state of circumstances, these reflections produced in my brother's mind and mine sensations of the deepest distress. I doubt not but the hard labour and sorrow of this period of his life, was in a great measure the cause of that depression of spirits with which Robert was so often afflicted through his whole life afterwards. At this time he was almost constantly afflicted in the evenings with a dull headache, which, at a future period of his life, was exchanged for a palpitation of the heart and threatening of fainting and suffocation in his bed, in the night-time.[38]

Gilbert, in referring to five other children, meant of course in addition to himself and Robert. That William Burnes could not afford the £4 or £6 a year which farm-labourers received is indicative of how near the poverty line the Burnes family was at this time. I feel that Burns himself was exaggerating his ragged appearance when he wrote of his Ayr schooldays; William and Agnes would have ensured that their children were well turned out for their Sunday excursions into the county town to attend religious services, and one imagines that while Robert lodged with John Murdoch he was as well attired as Agnes could manage. Nevertheless,

Robert must have been acutely aware of his 'clouterly', shabby appearance compared with his classmates. Seeing and experiencing the grinding poverty which beset his douce, hard-working, God-fearing father, and comparing this with the relative affluence of others, Robert could scarcely have been anything other than resentful. The fact that there is no mention in Robert's autobiographical letter, nor in Gilbert's Narrative, of social intercourse with neighbours in the Mount Oliphant period is highly significant. The weekenders and retirees who inhabited the scattered country houses of the neighbourhood would have considered themselves socially superior to the likes of small tenant farmers like William Burnes; and Burnes, for his part, would have felt contempt for such bourgeois pretensions and would have been unlikely to afford such neighbours the opportunity to air their petty superiority.

More significant is Gilbert's references to the headaches, palpitations and other afflictions which beset his brother even as a teenager. Robert, as a result of the hard physical effort required on the farm, developed a strong, thickset muscularity; but many contemporaries of his Edinburgh period commented on his round-shouldered appearance – his ploughman's stoop. The feelings of fainting and suffocation were put down by many biographers unthinkingly as the product of poor stamina, resulting from an inadequate diet, calmly ignoring the fact that neither Gilbert, nor any other member of the family who was reared on the same homely fare, suffered as Robert did. The diet of the Burnes family consisted mainly of oats in various forms such as porridge and bannocks, washed down by skimmed milk or buttermilk. Potatoes, turnips and other root crops did not come into widespread cultivation till some time later, but the Burnes family had a kailyard in which green vegetables, rich in iron and vitamins, were grown for domestic consumption. Some protein would have come from the cheeses which Agnes made (though these were mainly intended for sale rather than domestic consumption). On Gilbert's admission butcher's meat was never consumed, but barnyard fowls too old for egg-laying would have been consigned to the pot, as were those beasts which succumbed to disease and accident. The Scots were by no means averse to cooking braxy sheep (animals which had died of an unpleasant intestinal disease); indeed, braxy came to be synonymous with the salted flesh of diseased lambs and was widely relished by the canny peasantry. All things considered, one is left with the impression that the diet of the rural community in Ayrshire in the late eighteenth century was probably much healthier than that of more recent times.

CHAPTER 4

Kirkoswald, 1775

Now westlin winds and slaught'ring guns
Bring Autumn's pleasant weather;
The moorcock springs on whirring wings
Amang the blooming heather.

Now Westlin Winds (CW 44)

Gilbert casually mentions how his father had the right to get out of his
lease after six years and actually attempted to fix himself up in a
better farm in 1771, 'but failing in that attempt, he continued where he
was for six years more'[1] and with the added burden of a rent now raised
to £45 per annum. Burnes even tried to sub-let Mount Oliphant, but got
no takers; and without savings he was unable to lease a better farm. At
least Provost Fergusson was a kindly landlord, not unduly bothered if
William was a little late in paying his rent. So, in the end, William resigned
himself to carrying on at Mount Oliphant, hoping that somehow the situation would improve. In the meantime, however, he must see what he could
do to give his eldest son still further opportunity to get an education. In
the summer of 1775 William sent Robert away to continue his schooling.
Robert recalled this episode as one which 'made very considerable alterations in my mind and manners':

I spent my seventeenth summer on a smuggling coast a good distance from
home at a noted school, to learn Mensuration, Surveying, Dialling, &c. in
which I made a pretty good progress. – But I made greater progress in the
knowledge of mankind. – The contraband trade was at that time very successful; scenes of swaggering riot and roaring dissipation were as yet new
to me; and I was no enemy to social life.– Here, though I learned to look
unconcernedly on a large tavern-bill, and mix without fear in a drunken
squabble, yet I went on with a high hand in my Geometry; till the sun
entered Virgo, a month which is always a carnival in my bosom, a charming Fillette who lived next door to the school overset my Trigonometry
and set me off in a tangent from the sphere of my studies.– I struggled on
with my Sines and Co-sines for a few days more; but stepping out to the
garden one charming noon, to take the sun's altitude, I met with my
Angel,

> – Like Proserpine gathering flowers,
>   Herself a fairer flower –

It was vain to think of doing any more good at school. – The remaining week I staid, I did nothing but craze the faculties of my soul about her, or steal out to meet with her; and the two last nights of my stay in the country, had sleep been a mortal sin, I was innocent. –[2]

The lines quoted in this passage come from Milton's *Paradise Lost*, a work which was to become a firm favourite with Robert. One may imagine the pleasure he felt at being released from the drudgery of Mount Oliphant for a few weeks. There was also the excitement of new scenes and experiences, for Kirkoswald was a very different place from either Dalrymple or Ayr. The parish of Kirkoswald lay on the green, windswept slopes of Carrick high above the Firth of Clyde. The parish church, round which clustered the principal village, however, was just over a mile inland. Apart from the fishing village of Maidens, a small hamlet in Robert's time, nestling around an inlet, the coast is rugged and girt with cliffs and rocks.

It is not known how long Robert stayed at Kirkoswald, but it seems to have been about ten or eleven weeks. Many writers speak vaguely of Robert attending the parish school there for several months; others speak of an entire term, which would have run from the beginning of July till harvest-time in September, and this is confirmed by the reference to the sun entering Virgo (23 August). The choice of Kirkoswald was dictated by two factors. In the first place, the parish dominie, Hugh Rodger (1726–97), something of a self-taught genius by all accounts, enjoyed a wide reputation as a teacher of mathematics and was also in great demand locally as a land surveyor. He was in his fiftieth year and has been described as arid, supercilious and inclined to sarcasm – occupational characteristics of country dominies. Reading between the lines of Robert's account, we form the impression that mathematics was not his forte, but he was well aware of the effort and money which it had cost his poor father to send him to Rodger's school and he was determined to apply himself as diligently as possible. The weeks spent under Rodger's tutelage had little effect on Robert's intellectual development; on his own admission he 'made greater progress in the knowledge of mankind'. One sentence is very revealing, not for what it actually says but for what it implies. Can we really believe that Robert, then aged sixteen and a half, 'learned to look unconcernedly on a large tavern-bill, and mix without fear in a drunken squabble'? Apart from the fact that entering taverns ran counter to his upbringing, Robert could scarcely have had the cash to meet a large bill with equanimity. We may here detect him striking a pose. Casual remarks of this sort, which can be found elsewhere in his correspondence of later years, have been pounced on by biographers (mainly in the early nineteenth century) as evidence of the poet's drunkenness and debauchery but, as we shall see in due course, there was little substance in support of such a pose. In an age when an ability to hold one's liquor was a much-admired attribute of manliness, Burns could be forgiven for this harmless piece of self-dramatisation, but simple arithmetic alone ought to show how false this statement was. On the other hand, this may refer to an actual incident, which is noted later in this chapter.

There is no doubt that Kirkoswald was a pretty rough place in 1775. The parish boasted a deeply indented coastline extending some six miles along the Carrick shore, and its bays, inlets and coves provided convenient cover for those engaged in contraband. By 1790, when the blind minister, the Revd. Matthew Biggar, compiled his account of the parish for Sir John Sinclair, compiler of *The Statistical Account of Scotland* (21 vols., 1791–9), matters had improved. Smuggling had been an accepted aspect of his parishioners' way of life:

> Though the character and behaviour of those engaged in this business were, for the most part, in other respects good; yet, without doubt, it produced very bad effects on the industry of the people, and gave them a taste for luxury and finery that spoiled the simplicity of manners which formerly prevailed in this parish.[3]

It was a favourite destination for the smuggling vessels from the Isle of Man which brought French lace and silks, tea, tobacco, and above all brandy which was so plentiful that the entire population of the parish seems to have been soaked in it. When a lugger landed her illicit cargo it was not uncommon for whole families – men, women and children – to keep up a drunken orgy for three days and nights on end. Every cup and crock and can was needed to hold the neat spirit. On one farm, where not so much as a water-jug remained unfilled, the sodden servants would boil the breakfast porridge in proof brandy.[4] It was primarily to suppress this smuggling trade that the Duke of Atholl was forced to yield the sovereignty of the Isle of Man to the Crown, by the Revestment Act of 1765; but this measure seems to have had little effect, and Manx smugglers continued to be a major problem till the end of the century – as Burns the Exciseman was to discover for himself at a later date.

Matthew Biggar also spoke of 'others guilty of tuellying, as it is called, or fighting to the effusion of blood, in the church yard in the time of divine service'.[5] So frequent was the vice of drunkenness, even on the Sabbath, that we find the Session enacting that no inn-keeper should sell on that day more than two pints of ale to a company of three persons. Mr Biggar noted that the vice of adultery was also very prevalent. One incident alone will suffice to illustrate the magnitude of the problem caused by smuggling. The Kirkoswald Kirk Session, convened in October 1764, accused Samuel Brown (uncle of Robert Burns) of smuggling on the Lord's Day. From the record it appears that the Kirk elders were more concerned with the violation of the Sabbath than with the breaking of the law. Brown, on being interrogated by the Moderator of the Session, stoutly maintained that he had indeed attended church that day, before going down to the seashore to watch a Manx vessel. This proved to be a protracted affair for the Session was still dealing with the problem as late as 19 July 1765, when no fewer than forty-eight smugglers were hauled up before it for Sabbath-breaking on that occasion. The depositions in this case mention various men taking away ankers and casks of brandy from the Manxman. Among the four dozen smugglers admonished by the Session were Brown and several members of the Niven family, including Samuel's father-in-law. We are left with a rather comical picture of a troop of thievish, drouthy farmers and cottars, even involving their wives and children to carry away the spoils under the very nose of the commander of the King's wherry (revenue cutter) which tried to intercept the Manxman.[6]

While he studied at Kirkoswald, Robert lodged at Ballochneil, a farm about a mile to the south of the village. Here his maternal uncle, Samuel Brown (born in February 1739), had come as a farm-labourer to work for Robert Niven, the farmer and miller. Samuel fell in love with the farmer's daughter, Margaret, and as a result the young couple were haled before the Kirk Session on a charge of antenuptial fornication in April 1765. Their marriage was followed – around the time of the smuggling admonition – by the birth of their only child Jenny (later immortalised by Burns in his poem 'Hallowe'en'). Samuel and Margaret Brown lived with their daughter in a single apartment outside the mill, so it is unlikely that Robert, as some traditions maintain, actually slept under their roof. The alternative tradition – that he lodged with the miller in the farmhouse and shared an attic bed with his son John – seems more probable. Robert's 'cousin' (actually Uncle Samuel's brother-in-law) John was the only son of the miller by his wife Margaret Ross and was five years older than Burns. Some writers have mistakenly asserted that John Niven was a school-fellow of Burns, but he was already twenty-one years old when Robert lived at Ballochneil. The confusion has arisen because there *was* a classmate by the name of Niven – Willie Niven of Maybole, who was some months younger than Robert.[7] He, too, had been sent to Hugh Rodger's school for a good grounding in mathematics; his father David was a prosperous shopkeeper in Maybole and, in fact, was a younger brother of Robert Niven of Ballochneil. It seems strange that, instead of lodging with his relatives, he was boarded with Hugh Rodger himself; but David Niven could afford not to put his son to the inconvenience of lodging at such a distance from the school.[8]

The road that Robert took every morning from Ballochneil to Kirkoswald lay at that time on the other side of the Ballochneil burn from that on which the modern A77 Ayr-Girvan road runs, an ancient bridge on Minnybae Farm showing the place where it branched off. The parish school of Kirkoswald had originally been merely a lean-to attached to the parish church, just below the belfry, but at the beginning of 1775 this was removed and the heritors had rented (for a guinea a year) the ground floor of a two-storey house in the village for the use of the schoolmaster. This house is still standing and forms the second from the corner, right opposite the entrance to the churchyard. Next up the street stands the house which was once the home of the Thomson family. Rodger's school-room could accommodate up to sixty scholars, their playground being the street outside and the kirkyard itself. A strip of rising ground behind the houses, however, served for practical exercises in mensuration and surveying.

It was while engaged in taking an observation of the sun in this plot that Robert clapped eyes on thirteen year-old Peggy Thomson, the 'charming Fillette' referred to above.[9] Robert implies that this affair, though of short duration, was passionate on both sides, though in view of the girl's youth it was probably more emotional than physical that summer. From stray references in Robert's correspondence with Thomas Orr, however, it seems that the brief contact that summer of 1775 developed into an on-going, if intermittent relationship. Certainly Peggy made a lasting impression on Robert. A decade later she was singled out for receipt of a rare presentation copy of the Kilmarnock Poems which he inscribed on the fly-leaf:

> Once fondly lov'd, and still remember'd dear,
> Sweet early object of my youthful vows,

and six other lines in similar vein (CW 250). Robert thought well enough of the two stanzas, in spite of their affectedly doleful sentimentality, to transcribe them in the first volume of the Glenriddell MSS, and to add the following note by way of explanation:

> 'Twas the girl I mention in my letter to Dr Moore, where I speak of taking the sun's altitude.– Poor Peggy! Her husband is my old acquaintance, & a most worthy fellow.– When I was taking leave of my Carrick relations intending to go to the West Indies, when I took farewell of her, neither she nor I could speak a syllable. – Her husband escorted me three miles on my road, & we both parted with tears.

There has been some speculation regarding Robert's amour with young Peggy. Most writers tend to dismiss it as no more than a 'holiday romance' but the above quatrains and the comment in the Glenriddell MSS show it to have had a more lasting effect on the poet than might be imagined. I am inclined to think that, with Peggy, Robert attained that intimacy which ever afterwards he strove for at the first symptoms of passion.[10] One of the poet's friends from the Kirkoswald days was Thomas Orr whose father William and his wife Jean Robinson lived in a cottage on Laigh Park Farm, along with Jean's aged mother Julia, a reputed witch and certainly a notorious receiver of contraband goods. Thomas was likewise a pupil at Rodger's school and in subsequent years came as a harvest worker to help out at Lochlie. He later told Dr Currie that he had carried 'messages' (letters) between Robert and Peggy in the summers of 1782 and 1783. None of these amatory epistles has survived, but three letters from the poet to Orr are recorded. The last of these letters (CL 50), written from Mossgiel on 11 November 1784, was in answer to one from Thomas announcing the impending marriage of Peggy and William Neilson of Minnybae Farm. Thomas was probably rather diffident about breaking the bad news to her erstwhile suitor, but Robert assured him that the contents gave him no cause for concern. 'I am very glad that Peggy is off my hands as I am at present embarrassed enough without her' – an oblique reference to the trouble he had got into with Betty Paton. Peggy and William were, in fact, married on 23 November.

Several anecdotes have survived from the Kirkoswald period, which are worth recounting.[11] Most of them appear to have originated with Willie Niven who, somewhat younger than Burns, was much more sophisticated – one might even say 'street-wise' in the jargon of the present day. It was young Willie who told Robert that it was customary, on enrolling at the school, to take the dominie to a tavern for a liquid refreshment. In this strange manner Robert was initiated into the ways of ale-houses. Rodger's favourite howff was kept by two sisters, Jean and Anne Kennedy, and for this reason the pub was known locally as the Ladies' House. Jean Kennedy is said to have been the prototype of Kirkton Jean in 'Tam o Shanter'.

One hopes that the tavern-bill on this occasion was not too large! The statement in Robert's autobiographical letter, however, may have alluded to another incident, first published by Currie and doubtless originating with Niven. As the annual Kirkoswald Fair, early in July, approached, Robert proposed to Willie that they should organise a dance in one of the village pubs and invite their sweethearts to it. Willie knew little of dances or sweethearts, but he readily agreed, and some other boys were roped in. The dance took place, 'the requisite music being supplied by a hired band' (a solitary fiddler more likely) and about a dozen couples took part. Who Robert's partner was on that occasion is not recorded, but it could hardly have been young Peggy at this early stage in his Kirkoswald sojourn – unless, of course, the incident in the back green occurred much earlier than Robert conveyed to Dr Moore. At the end of the evening, the reckoning was called, and the tavern-bill was found to amount to 18s 4d. It was then discovered that almost everyone present had looked to his neighbour for the means of settling the bill. Robert, the originator of the scheme, 'was in the poetical condition of not being the master of a single penny'. The rest were equally penniless, apart from one youth who had a groat (fourpence) and young Willie who had half a crown (2s 6d). The story goes that Willie approached the landlord, made a candid admission, and induced him to take what they had and give credit for the rest. Very nobly, Willie took it upon himself to work off the 15s 6d debt. On a home visit he acquired a stock of pens and stationery at cost from his father and retailed them to his school-fellows at a profit. In no time at all he had raised enough, not only to pay off the debt but to treat the landlord to a bowl into the bargain. All of this was doubtless much to the credit of Willie Niven, but one would have liked to set alongside it the comments – or amendments – of Robert himself.[12]

Another of the Niven-inspired anecdotes illustrates Robert's ready repartee. The two daughters of the parish minister were about Robert's age and, despite his 'clouterly' appearance, there was something about him that intrigued and attracted them. One day the girls caught sight of him walking along the opposite side of the street, his shoulders hunched. He was muttering to himself and staring at the ground. The girls crossed the street and the bolder of the two accosted him with a giggle. 'Fancy looking at the ground and talking to yourself when we are here to be looked at and talked to!' Robert fixed the bold hussy with his lambent eye. 'Madam, it is a natural and right thing for man to contemplate the ground from whence he was taken, and for woman to look upon and observe man, from whom she was taken.' So much for Robert being bashful and awkward with the opposite sex in his younger days.

Tenuously related by marriage, Burns and Willie Niven became close friends and spent all their free time together that summer. On Saturday afternoons, when the week's schooling was over, they would tramp the four miles north-east to Maybole to spend the weekend at Willie's home above the village store. About the halfway point in their journey they would pass the magnificent ruins of Crossraguel Abbey, leading Robert, in a letter years later, to speculate as to why Presbyterian places of worship were 'such poor, pimping places'. Pacing together among the thyme-scented stones the two boys discussed theology, sought for a practical philosophy, dived into metaphysics, examined all they knew of life. What was there to be said for the Old Lights as compared with the New? Could one by right thinking or religion be consoled for the defeat of all one's natural ambitions? Might a man look for happiness with a woman above him in station or even gifts? Robert thought not.[13]

During the school day there was a two-hour midday break, between noon and two o'clock, which the boys liked to spend together. Instead of amusing themselves with a ball or any other sport like the rest of the scholars, they would take a stroll to the outskirts of the village and converse on all manner of subjects to improve their minds. In due course they hit upon a plan of holding disputations or arguments on speculative questions, one taking one side of the debate and the other the opposite, without much regard to their respective opinions on the point, the whole object being to sharpen their intellects. They asked several of their classmates to come along and take a side in these debates, but not one would do so; they only laughed at the young sophists. The matter at length came to the attention of Hugh Rodger. Like many dominies, before and since, Rodger had a limited grasp of matters outside his own narrow field of specialisation, and with that intolerance born of ignorance he determined to nip the ploy in the bud. One day, therefore, he went up to the desk where Burns and Niven were sitting opposite each other, and began to comment sarcastically on what he had heard of them. He had been led to believe that they had become great debaters and thought they were competent to settle affairs of importance which wiser heads usually let alone. He sincerely hoped that their disputations would not become quarrels, and that they would never think of coming from words to blows; and other sarcastic comments in like vein. The other pupils laughed heartily at the schoolmaster's mordant wit, but Niven was needled into making some suitable reply. He said he was sorry to find that he and Robert had given offence: it had not been intended; and indeed he had expected that the master would have been rather pleased to know of their endeavours to improve their minds. He assured Rodger that this was the sole object of the exercise. Rodger sneered at the idea of their improving their minds by nonsensical discussions, and contemptuously asked what were the subjects of their debates. Niven replied that generally there was a new subject every day; that he could not recollect all that had come under their attention; but the question of that day had been 'Whether is a great general or a respectable merchant the most valuable member of society?' Rodger laughed uproariously at what he called the silliness of this question, seeing there could be no doubt as to the correct answer. 'Well,' said Robert, 'if you think so, I will be glad if you take any side you please, and allow me to take the other, and let us discuss it before the school.' Rodger foolishly assented, and commenced the argument by a flourish in favour of the general. Robert answered with a pointed advocacy of the claim of the merchant, and soon had an evident superiority over his teacher. Rodger replied, but without success. 'His hand was observed to shake; then his voice trembled; and he dissolved the school in a state of vexation pitiable to behold.'[14]

There are many other anecdotes from the Kirkoswald interlude, cited by Currie, Cunningham, Lockhart and Chambers and repeated by more recent biographers down to Carswell and Lindsay. The chief interest of this district lies in the identification of various persons with the characters in Burns's great mock-epic 'Tam o Shanter' (CW 410–15). In the old kirkyard can be seen the graves of Douglas Graham and his wife Helen McTaggart of Shanter Farm, on the slope overlooking the shore about half a mile east of Turnberry Castle (Tam and Kate of the poem), John Davidson (Souter Johnie) and his wife Ann Gillespie who, as a girl, had worked at Craigenton Farm for Gilbert Brown, the poet's grandfather, and 'Kirkton Jean' Kennedy.[15] There is little, in actual fact, to link these good folk with the characters of the poem, other than the borrowing of the farm name. Douglas Graham, like his neighbours, dabbled in smuggling and enjoyed a dram; but his wife Helen had a reputation as a superstitious shrew – though this may have come from the benefit of hindsight, and few among the peasantry of the period were not superstitious to some degree. Helen died in 1798 at the age of fity-six and her husband followed her in 1811, aged seventy-three, so both were still alive when 'Tam o Shanter' was first published. No contemporary record exists, however, to say what they thought of the poem or whether they were aware of their connection with it. The poem put Kirkoswald on the map and to this day tourists come to Souter Johnie's cottage in the main street (now a National Trust property) to see the stone statues of Tam, the Souter, the landlord and the landlady, carved by James Thom in the early nineteenth century.

Willie Niven was the source of a highly dubious tale which would have us believe that Robert's great comic masterpiece was actually composed fifteen years earlier than generally stated! The first Thursday in July (the day of the Horse Fair at Ayr) was a school holiday in Kirkoswald, so Robert and Niven decided to go on a fishing trip. At Maidens they boarded the *Tam o Shanter*, a boat belonging to Douglas Graham.

When they had moved to some distance from the coast, they were assailed
by a strong gale from the east. Such a gale implied danger, but when
Niven proposed that they should steer shoreward, Burns objected, jocularly remarking that he would not abandon his purpose, though the breeze
should prove strong enough to blaw the horns off the kye.[16]

So much for Robert's terror of the sea! As the storm worsened, however,
they made for the shore and, thoroughly drenched, took shelter with Mrs
Graham at Shanter Farm. Her husband being late back from the Horse
Fair, the irascible Helen gave vent to her anger and 'energetically
expatiated on his convivial irregularities', assuring the boys that some day
he would fall into the Doon in an intoxicated stupor and be drowned. Mrs
Graham joined in her denunciation their neighbour Davidson, who had
accompanied her husband to Ayr to buy hides for shoe-leather. On the way
back to Ballochneil Robert remarked on the 'wanton censures' of the gude-
wife. 'Next day' – so the story goes – 'Burns seized a newspaper which lay
in the apartment, and on the margin inscribed some lines with a pencil: it
was his first draft of Tam o Shanter.' What, we must wonder, was Willie
Niven doing at Ballochneil (when he lodged with Hugh Rodger)? There is
some confusion here again with his cousin John. I doubt if any newspaper
of the period would have had margins broad enough to accommodate the
lines of such a poem. Needless to say, no manuscript answering this
description has ever come to light. Of course, Robert himself admitted that
all his poetry was the effect of easy composition, but of laborious correction, a point made by protagonists of this absurd story to support the view
that 'Tam' was drafted at Kirkoswald, even though it did not receive its
final polish till 1790.[17] Against Niven's veracity may be cited his claim to
have been the original recipient of Robert's 'Epistle to a Young Friend'
(CW 221), without any documentary evidence to support this assertion
and refute the universal belief that Andrew Hunter Aiken was the
addressee.

What is incontrovertible is that the verbal duels were subsequently commuted into an exchange of correspondence, Niven being the recipient of
the earliest letters of Burns still extant (CL 37–40). Robert himself refers
to this in his autobiographical letter:

I returned home very considerably improved. My reading was enlarged
with the very important addition of Thomson's and Shenstone's works. I
had seen mankind in a new phasis, and I engaged several of my school-
fellows to keep up a literary correspondence with me. This last helped me
on much in composition. I had met with a collection of letters, by the wits
of Queen Anne's reign, and I pored over them most devoutly. I kept
copies of any of my own letters that pleased me, and a comparison
between them and the composition of most of my correspondents, flattered my vanity. I carried this whim so far, that though I had not three
farthings worth of business in the world, yet every post brought me as
many letters as if I had been a broad plodding son of daybook and
ledger.[18]

Robert's pride in his letter-writing was self-evident. It is unfortunate that the earliest letter to have survived from the Niven correspondence is in very poor condition. Niven obviously treasured it immensely and seems to have carried it around in his wallet for years, to judge by its very worn condition and the fact that three-quarters of one page is missing, no doubt so creased at the fold that eventually it came adrift and was lost. The letter, even in its unintentionally mutilated form, is among the most extraordinary literary exercises Robert ever produced. Written from 'Lochlee' on 29 July 1780, it is a highly philosophical dissertation, quite unlike anything Robert wrote to anyone else, and thus confirming the metaphysical nature of their boyhood conversations. It is sad that no letters of an earlier vintage have survived, and certainly none of those 'messages' which Thomas Orr carried from Robert to Peggy Thomson. That young lady would prudently have destroyed such incriminating evidence prior to her marriage in 1784. Orr was another of the 'several school-fellows' with whom Robert engaged in correspondence. Orr even tried his hand at a verse-epistle, utterly banal in content and defective in metre and rhyme, but Robert, with characteristic generosity, responded by saying (17 November 1782) that 'I was extremely delighted with your letter'. Orr, who had been studying navigation under Hugh Rodger, went to sea in 1785 but was drowned on his first voyage.[19]

Burns the debater and belletrist was no ordinary farm-hand for whom eating, sleeping and purely animal pleasures were the only relief from the drudgery of the soil. That he seemed bound to a life of manual labour was never allowed to come between him and the intellectual pleasures of good conversation and correspondence. What he says about the amount of the latter, however, is palpably untrue. Of his early letters, the only survivals are two from 1780 (both to Willie Niven), seven from 1781 (including the amatory epistles to 'A' and 'E'), three from 1782 (including two to Tom Orr), three from 1783 and four from 1784 (including three to his cousin James Burness in Montrose)[20] – a mere nineteen letters in a period of five years. Of course, it can be argued that, before Robert achieved fame in 1786, few of his correspondents would have considered preserving his letters, and doubtless further letters to Niven, Orr and other friends of the Kirkoswald period were destroyed almost as soon as they had been read and answered. Currie's numerical list of letters addressed to Burns, with a précis of their contents,[21] does not include any letters prior to September 1786, so Robert was not in the habit of preserving the early letters of his friends either. Even so, had the volume of correspondence been as large as Robert asserted to Moore, we might have expected more examples from the poet in the period 1775–85. The plain fact of the matter is that the relatively expensive postage militated against this. Until the reforms of Rowland Hill in 1839–40, which introduced a system of uniform prepaid penny postage, it was customary for letter-writers to send their letters unpaid, leaving it to the addressee to pay the postage. In this period all but purely local letters would have cost at least twopence up to a distance of 80 miles, over which the charge rose to fourpence. By the Post Office Act of

1765 a cheaper rate of one penny for single-stage letters was introduced, but this would only have applied to letters within a mile or two of the post-town (in this case Ayr).[22]

When Robert returned home from Kirkoswald in September 1775 his schooldays had come to an end. To an elementary grounding in the three Rs at Alloway (1765–7) had been added a few weeks at Dalrymple improving his handwriting and grammar (1772), three weeks with Murdoch at Ayr improving his English and French and beginning with Latin (1773), and 'only a summer quarter not completed', studying the more advanced branches of mathematics at Kirkoswald (1775). Adding together the various periods, as some biographers have done, is a futile exercise. The equivalent of two years' full-time education belies the fact that, in Robert's case, a little formal schooling went a very long way. In teachers of the calibre of Murdoch (and Rodger, too, in his own way) Burns was singularly fortunate, not so much for what they actually taught, but for the manner in which they stimulated their eager pupil to carry on the process of self-education. Robert was a boy of extraordinary ability and soaring ambition, blessed with a truly phenomenal memory and powers of application (when sufficiently motivated). He may have lacked material things, but he came from a home where learning was highly regarded, and where books, as with Chaucer's poor clerk of Oxford, were more highly prized than furniture. The story that visitors to the Burnes home at meal-times invariably found the entire family (including the girls) seated at the table with a horn-spoon in one hand and a book in the other is apocryphal but probably not far short of the mark for all that. Certainly, among the poet's siblings, Gilbert and Isobel demonstrated an articulacy and a literary propensity far above the average. Too much has been made of formal education, ignoring the fact that for many individuals, both then and now, the process of education is an on-going one. Robert was a voracious reader, discriminating intelligently in what he devoured, and there is a wealth of evidence from his correspondence concerning the quantity and quality of his reading right down to the end of his life, demonstrating how the learning process never stopped. For someone who was largely self-taught, he had a remarkable grasp of theology, philosophy, history, heraldry, current affairs, politics and, of course, literature. As we shall see in due course, he also had to absorb a stupefying mass of Excise rules and regulations, while the multifarious duties of a gauger called for a high degree of competence in mathematics, so his time at Kirkoswald must have been well spent after all.

It is not known how, or by whom, Robert was introduced in the summer of 1775 to the poetry of William Shenstone (1714–63). Shenstone was very much a product of the English upper middle class, the son of a country squire and educated at Pembroke College, Oxford. On the death of his father in 1745 he withdrew to his country estate whose beautification was the chief work of his life. Shenstone lived up to the Horatian ideal, a country gentleman who corresponded with the leading literati of the day and who produced a mass of poetry which was published posthumously in three volumes. Quotations from Shenstone's elegies and his elegant essays pepper Robert's early correspondence (but only up to September 1788).[23] Today, Shenstone would be completely forgotten, but for the immortality conferred on him by Burns who was to quote him in the Preface to the Kilmarnock Poems: 'Humility has depressed many a genius to a hermit, but never raised one to fame'.

After his tragic death, Thomas Orr's personal effects came into the hands of Rodger's successor as Kirkoswald dominie. This included a bundle of papers containing the three extant letters of Burns to Orr, a letter of 1780 written by William Burnes and some scraps of paper with verses on them. These verses were not in Robert's handwriting, but they gave rise to some speculation that they might have been Orr's transcripts of poems by Burns. One of these contained a number of lugubrious verses in the Shenstonian idiom and one quatrain should suffice to give the flavour of them:

> While the sons of debauch to indulgence give way,
> And slumber the prime of their hours,
> Let us, my dear Stella, the garden survey
> And make our remarks on the flowers.

J. A. Westwood Oliver, son of the Kirkoswald schoolmaster who acquired these papers, advanced the theory that Robert was the author of this poem.[24] The 'sons of debauch' were clearly the villagers of Kirkoswald, while Stella was a poetic name for Peggy Thomson. The allusion to surveying the garden echoed Burns's reference to the peculiar circumstances in which he first met Peggy. William Wallace, however, stated that Burns, even under the influence of Shenstone, would have thrown a little of himself into any verses of his own composition, as he did in 'Handsome Nell'.[25] I am not so sure. The verses in question have never been traced to any other source. Despite their high-flown sentiment they are technically competent and accord with the mannered quality of Robert's prose of this period, as shown in the first of the Niven letters.[26]

CHAPTER 5

Lochlie: the Contented Years, 1777–81

Farewell, farewell, Eliza dear,
The maid that I adore!
A boding voice is in mine ear,
We part to meet no more!

Farewell to Eliza (CW 50)

In his autobiographical letter Robert passes with little further comment over the ensuing seven years of his life. What he does give, in his letter to Dr Moore (CL 250–1) is a very brief word-picture of the closing years at Mount Oliphant which shows that the situation, never rosy, went from bad to worse latterly:

My father's generous Master died; the farm proved a ruinous bargain; and, to clench the curse, we fell into the hands of a Factor who sat for the picture I have drawn of one in my Tale of two dogs.– My father was advanced in life when he married; I was the eldest of seven children; and he, worn out by early hardship, was unfit for labor.– My father's spirit was soon irritated, but not easily broken.– There was a freedom in his lease in two years more, and to weather these two years we retrenched expences . . . My father struggled on till he reached the freedom in his lease, when he entered on a larger farm about ten miles farther in the country.

Dr Fergusson died in 1776 and his estate was divided among his four daughters. The eldest, Mrs John Hunter, fell heir to Doonholm, where the youngest daughter, still unmarried, also resided. Provost Fergusson had dealt with his former gardener directly, but now the executry of the estate was handled by a 'factor' – probably one of the lawyers in the town of Ayr, although this individual is nowhere named. Doing the best for his clients, this factor wrote to Burnes concerning the arrears of rent. When Burnes either ignored these letters, or was evasive in his replies, the factor became more insistent and threatening. Legal jargon has a most chilling effect, especially on those who have never experienced it previously. More than their actual content, the effect which these missives had on the head of their household drove poor Agnes and her children to tears.

> Poor tenant bodies, scant o cash,
> How they maun thole a factor's snash:
> He'll stamp an threaten, curse an swear
> He'll apprehend them, poind their gear;
> While they maun stan, wi aspect humble,
> An hear it a', an fear an tremble![1]

Robert's 'Tragic Fragment' (CW 46–7), beginning with the poignant line 'All villain as I am – a damned wretch', is believed to have been written at this time, reflecting the misery of the Burnes family. Strangely enough, Gilbert Burns passes over this episode without mention. It seems likely that Robert's view of this wretched business was highly subjective, as the executors of the Fergusson estate settled the matter amicably by taking a mortgage on the Alloway smallholding which enabled Burnes to extricate himself from Mount Oliphant when the lease expired. Gilbert's narrative takes up the story, with his father's next essay in farming:

> He then took the farm of Lochlea, of 130 acres, at the rent of twenty shillings an acre, in the parish of Tarbolton, of Mr —, then a merchant in Ayr and now [1797] a merchant in Liverpool. He removed to this farm at Whitsunday 1777, and possessed it only seven years.[2]

Gilbert had to leave the landlord's name blank because he was still alive, and as the next passage dealt with the litigation which subsequently arose, he thought it more politic to preserve the landlord's anonymity. David McClure was the landlord in question. Despite William's not exactly brilliant track-record as a farmer, McClure reposed such confidence in his new tenant that he failed to draw up a written agreement making clear the terms of the lease. At the time, everything probably seemed clear enough; Burnes was due to pay £130 per annum. Gilbert says that a misunderstanding took place respecting the terms, but this is not borne out by the facts. It seems likely that McClure, like Fergusson before him, advanced a certain amount of money to his new tenant in order to get him started. Robert says as much in his letter to Dr Moore: 'The nature of the bargain was such as to throw a little ready money in [my father's] hand at the commencement; otherwise the affair would have been impracticable.' And McClure's depositions in the subsequent lawsuit bear this out.[3]

Lochlie[4] lies about two and a half miles north-east of the village of Tarbolton in the parish of the same name, and just over three miles northwest of the town of Mauchline. Because of the configuration of the roads, however, the farm may be regarded as equidistant between the two. It is today situated on the road between Largie Toll and Craigie, a mile and a half south of the A719 Ayr-Galston road. Much further inland than Mount Oliphant, the farm is about 400 feet (130m) above sea-level and, in the time of the Burnes family, was even more desolate than their previous abode, although nowadays a thick belt of woodland gives it shelter from the prevailing winds, and the ditches and hedgerows of later generations

have broken up what must have been a featureless landscape in the eighteenth century. More significantly, of all the farms which Burns inhabited,
Lochlie has probably altered the most so far as the farmhouse and outbuildings are concerned. The present house, a two-storey structure, was substantially rebuilt in the nineteenth century and the range of byres and barns is
much more extensive than it was in the 1770s. The farmhouse nestled in
a depression, near the marsh-ringed loch which gave the farm its name.
The farmland was, for the most part, higher than the farmhouse from
whose windows Robert would have looked out on the then sparsely
wooded ridge separating the valleys of the Ayr and the Irvine, though from
the crest of this ridge he would have had splendid views of the Firth of
Clyde. The loch was drained a century and a half ago and this brought to
light a prehistoric crannog or lake dwelling. In 1777, however, the loch was
very much in evidence, but did little to drain the soil which was very
boggy. William Burnes tried hard to improve the land, and part of the
dispute with McClure arose over the extent of these improvements.
According to the descendants of the tenant of the neighbouring farm of
Millburn, part of the agreement between Burnes and McClure dealt with
allowances to be made for making up the high lands of the farm (which
were very bare), by carting soil from the low-lying marshy ground. During
one winter of extreme, lengthened frost William Burnes carted more than
was equal to the half-yearly rent, and this was at the heart of the dispute.[5]

How much stock William Burnes owned when he took up the lease of
Lochlie has been a matter of some speculation. By the time of the sequestration in 1783 he allegedly owned four horses, two mares, thirteen cows,
two calves, one ewe, two lambs, four ploughs, five carts, two harrows and
a varied assortment of lint, tow, barley, corn and pease. McClure contested
this inventory, saying that thirteen black cattle seemed suspiciously inadequate for a farm of this size (it would have worked out at one cow for every
ten acres). 'Few as they are,' averred McClure, 'and notwithstanding your
Lordship's sequestration, the petitioner is well informed that since your
Lordship's warrant was execute the respondent has actually carried off and
sold part of that number at a public market.'[6] In his letter to Dr Moore
Robert told how:

> For four years we lived comfortably here but a lawsuit between him and
> his Landlord commencing, after three years tossing and whirling in the
> vortex of Litigation, my father was just saved from absorption in a jail by
> phthisical consumption, which after two years promises, kindly stept in
> and snatch'd him away – 'To where the wicked cease from troubling, and
> where the weary be at rest.'[7]

Three letters of William Burnes have survived from this period.[8] They
tell the reader little beyond the fact that William had a strong family affection, was meticulous in the details of his farming, and had a surprisingly
neat hand. There was also a jotting-book in which he carefully noted minor
transactions, such as work done by the blacksmith; interestingly, this

book, while mainly in William's hand, also contains entries by Robert. It eventually came into the hands of Isobel Burns (later Mrs Begg) who had the unfortunate habit of cutting bits out of it to present to souvenir hunters who applied to her for specimens of her famous brother's hand-writing.[9] Until the dispute with McClure arose, the Burnes family appear to have been reasonably happy and content at Lochlie. Robert touched lightly on it in his letter to Moore:

> I was, at the beginning of this period, perhaps the most ungainly, aukward being in the parish.– No Solitaire was less acquainted with the ways of the world.

He went on to list his reading matter during this period, showing an amazing catholicity in taste and interests. As well as the works of Salmon and Guthrie already cited, Robert mentioned that:

> my knowledge of modern manners, and of literature and criticism, I got from the Spectator.– These, with Pope's works, some plays of Shakespear, Tull and Dickson on Agriculture, The Pantheon, Locke's Essay on the human understanding, Stackhouse's history of the bible, Justice's British Gardiner's directory, Boyle's lectures, Allan Ramsay's works, Taylor's scripture doctrine of original sin, a select Collection of English songs, and Hervey's meditations had been the extent of my reading.[10] The Collection of Songs was my vade mecum.– I pored over them, driving my cart or walking to labor, song by song, verse by verse; carefully noting the true tender or sublime from affectation and fustian.– I am convinced I owe much to this for my critic-craft such as it is.

Gilbert's Narrative claims that the seven years in Tarbolton parish were not marked by much literary improvement, but he then hints darkly:

> during this time, the foundation was laid of certain habits in my brother's character, which afterwards became but too prominent, and which malice and envy have taken delight to enlarge on. Though when young he was bashful and awkward in his intercourse with women, yet when he approached manhood, his attachment to their society became very strong, and he was constantly the victim of some fair enslaver. The symptoms of his passion were often such as nearly to equal those of the celebrated Sappho. I never indeed knew that he *fainted, sunk and died away*: but the agitation of his mind and body exceeded anything of the kind I ever knew in real life. He had always a particular jealousy of people who were richer than himself, or who had more consequence in life. His love, therefore, rarely settled on persons of this description. When he selected any out of the sovereignty of his good pleasure to whom he should pay his particular attention, she was instantly invested with a sufficient stock of charms, out of the plentiful stores of his imagination; and there was often a great disparity between his fair captivator, and her attributes. One generally reigned paramount in his affections; but as Yorick's affections flowed out towards Madame de L— at the remise door, while the eternal vows to Eliza were upon him, so Robert was frequently encountering other attractions, which formed so many under-plots in the drama of his love.[11]

In many respects Gilbert's assessment of his brother in his late teens is perceptive. It is particularly interesting to note that Robert was considered bashful and awkward with girls, but subsequently became very much a 'lady's man'. Although Gilbert went on to qualify his remarks by saying that 'these connexions were governed by the strictest rules of virtue and modesty', it has to be said that, close as the brothers were, Gilbert was not with Robert at Kirkoswald. Something definitely happened to Robert in that brief interlude, and not just his initiation into the ways of taverns and tavern-bills. Nelly Kilpatrick and Peggy Thomson have been dismissed as juvenilia[12] but the fragmentary testimony of Thomas Orr, the poet's reference to her in his last letter, the dedication in her copy of the Kilmarnock Poems, and the songs she inspired[13] seem to place Peggy in a different category.

One of these songs was 'I Dream'd I Lay' (CW 45) which Robert, according to his annotation in the Glenriddell MSS, composed when he was seventeen. From its style and resemblance, in both ideas and expressions, it seems to have been closely modelled on Alicia Cockburn's exquisite song 'Flowers of the Forest', based on an old Border ballad and published in an anthology called *The Lark* in 1765. Certainly, in the two years which had elapsed between the composition of his first song and 'I Dream'd I Lay', the progress of the budding bard was striking. Despite its imitative quality, it is a much more mature work in every sense. Interestingly, compared with 'Handsome Nell', it contains only one Scottish word – drumlie, meaning gloomy (which, incidentally, also features in Mrs Cockburn's famous ballad).

New scenes, and especially new people, gave Robert fresh stimulus. The rivers Ayr and Irvine were fed by streams such as the Cessnock and the Faile, the Coyle, the Stinchar and the Lugar, which provided an abundant variety of well-wooded walks. In the Tarbolton years these were to be the inspiration of some of Robert's finest songs. The fair enslavers of Gilbert's narrative left more subtle marks on Robert's early works. In those few happy years at Lochlie he composed a number of fine pieces, which alluded to the new locale and some of the girls on whom he lavished his affections. 'My Nanie, O' (CW 45-6) is a case in point, but, even here, there is some confusion and mystery. In the original version (in all editions up to 1794) the opening line is 'Beyond yon hills where Stinchar flows', and in a letter to George Thomson on 26 October 1792 (CL 619) Robert confessed that the name of the river was 'horridly prosaic' and said that Girvan was the river that suited the idea of the stanza best, though Lugar was 'the most agreable modulation of syllables'. In both the first and second choice of river, it appears that Robert placed this poem in a south Ayrshire setting, which seems therefore to allude to the Kirkoswald period. Gilbert, answering an enquiry from George Thomson in 1819, cast his memory over the various Tarbolton females with the Christian name of Agnes, but could only hazard a guess that the Nanie of this poem was probably Agnes Fleming of Coldcothill or Doura Farms, a near-neighbour to the north-west of Lochlie. He added that 'Her charms were indeed mediocre, but what she had were sexual, which was the characteristic of the greater part of the poet's mistresses; for he was no Platonic lover, however he might otherwise pretend or suppose of himself'. Some doubt has been cast on Gilbert's identification.[14] Agnes, the daughter of John Fleming, was not born till 1765, so she would have been a girl of eleven or twelve when the Burnes family settled at Lochlie. The Revd. Hamilton Paul,[15] however, said that the song was inspired by Agnes Sherriff of Kilmarnock. It has been suggested that this was Miss Fleming's married name;[16] but there is no record of her having married, and for once Allan Cunningham may be right when he says that Nanie Fleming died unmarried at an advanced age. On the other hand, the same writer compromised himself by stating that Nanie dwelt on the banks of the Lugar, relying on the change which Burns made solely in the interests of euphony.[17]

Similarly it has been stated that the girl named in the fourth line of 'The Rigs o Barley' (CW 49) was Anne Rankine (1759–1843). She was the same age as Burns, and a close neighbour, being the daughter of John Rankine who farmed Adamhill near Lochlie. In this case the provenance is the lady herself; she claimed in later life that she had been surprised at finding herself mentioned in the song, and that Robert had then replied, 'Oh, aye! I was just wanting to give you a cast amang the lave.' Somehow, this does not have the ring of authenticity. In any case, Robert was reworking a well-known old ballad which existed, in various printed versions, as far back as 1681. This seems to be one of those instances in which a myth was fabricated around a girl's name which had been selected purely to fit the rhyme and metre of the verse. Annie could be anyone – or no one. Anne Rankine married John Merry, the inn-keeper at Cumnock, on 29 December 1782 and the story was handed down, like a family heirloom. In her own lifetime, however, the story that she had been the heroine grew, and in 1817 James Grierson of Dalgoner, an avid collector of anecdotal scraps concerning Burns, asked the old lady if she remembered nights with Rab among the rigs o' barley. She said 'No!' with considerable naïvety, but then added with a twinkle in her eye, 'I mind o' mony a happy night wi' him, though.'[18]

Just how unreliable this sort of identification can be, however, is shown by the fact that the heroine of 'Farewell to Eliza' (CW 50) has, until now, been variously given as Elizabeth Barbour or Elizabeth Miller, both of whom featured in the poet's life in 1785–6 but not earlier, whereas Robert told Dr Moore that he had composed this song before 1782.[19] It only goes to show the futility of trying to read too much between the lines, and putting flesh on what may have been names virtually chosen at random. If Gilbert is to be believed, there must have been a veritable army of fair enslavers, transient and ephemeral and leaving little, if any, mark on Robert's work. There is, in fact, one other lady who seems to fit the bill, but more of that later.

One other incident from the early years at Lochlie is puzzling. In his autobiographical letter to Dr Moore Robert wrote:

In my seventeenth year, to give my manners a brush, I went to a country dancing school.– My father had an unaccountable antipathy against these

meetings; and my going was, what to this hour I repent, in absolute defiance of his commands. – My father, as I said before, was the sport of
strong passions; from that instance of rebellion he took a kind of dislike
to me, which, I believe was one cause of that dissipation which marked
my future years.– I only say, Dissipation, comparative with the strictness
and sobriety of Presbyterean country life; for though the will-o'-wisp
meteors of thoughtless Whim were almost the sole lights of my path, yet
early ingrained Piety and Virtue never failed to point me out the line of
Innocence.

If Robert is to believed, this incident must have taken place in 1775 when
the Burnes family were still living at Mount Oliphant. Indeed, early
biographers, from Currie onwards, took this at face value and assigned the
episode to the Mount Oliphant period. The dancing class was said to have
been held in a barn at Dalrymple and some biographers even went so far
as to speculate that Nelly Kilpatrick was among the dancers who
attended.[20] Gilbert, however, tried to tone down this passage in his comments to Dr Currie:

I wonder how Robert could attribute to our father the lasting resentment
of his going to a dancing school against his will, of which he was incapable. I believe the truth was that he, about this time, began to see the dangerous impetuosity of my brother's passions, as well as his not being
amenable to counsel, which often irritated my father; and which he would
naturally think a dancing school was not likely to correct. But he was
proud of Robert's genius, which he bestowed more expence in cultivating
than on the rest of the family . . . He had indeed that dislike of dancing
schools which Robert mentions; but so far overcame it during Robert's
first month of attendance that he allowed all the rest of the family that
were fit for it to accompany him during the second month. Robert
excelled in dancing, and was for some time distractedly fond of it.[21]

Whatever else, Robert was invariably accurate in giving the age at which
various incidents and events took place, unlike Gilbert whose memory
either played him false, or who sometimes deliberately altered Robert's age
in order to make the chronology fit his own version. In this case it appears
that Gilbert confused the 1775 incident at Dalrymple with a similar incident several years later. It is more probable that neither Gilbert nor any
younger member of the family were aware of Robert's secret adventure and
the resultant defiance. A confrontation between William Burnes and his
children may have arisen again, in the winter of 1778–9. A letter from
James Candlish to Robert, dated 13 February 1779, says, 'You say you are
attending a dancing school this winter';[22] unfortunately, the letter which
Candlish thus answered has apparently not survived, otherwise Robert
himself might have shed more light on this business. It seems clear, therefore, that the dancing-school experience referred to by Gilbert belongs to
the Tarbolton period, when William Burnes was prostrated by his last
illness, and all the children had very much gone their own way.[23]

Tarbolton (pronounced Tarbowton), both the village and the parish, are vastly different today from the way they were in Robert's day. In 1777 the parish was going through a period of decline; the population had actually dropped since 1755, at a period when elsewhere the population was sharply increasing. It was a district which was beginning to improve in appearance; once 'rude and wild, bare and unsheltered, varied with inequalities of surface, marshy in the hollows, on the heights overgrown with heath', in the last decade of the century, 'the rude aspect of nature has here given place to the beauties and the wealth of industrious cultivation'.[24] The population in 1790 was about 1,200, of whom some 450 resided in the village. The parish had nineteen heritors (the landowning gentry), but there were several smaller properties around the village which were in the hands of 'portioners', and there were no fewer than 130 tenant-farmers. In the early nineteenth century the village became the centre of a flourishing coal-mining industry and mining towns, such as Annbank and Mossblown, mushroomed around it. Now the coal is worked out, the district has reverted to its rural character. In Robert's day peat and coal were the common fuel, the latter being obtained from no great distance; but the rich coal seams were not exploited till a generation later. The centre of the village, grouped around the intersection of the B730 Dundonald-Coylton road and the B744 Mauchline-Ayr road, has preserved sufficient of the buildings of two centuries ago for the visitor to form a fairly accurate picture of the place in the poet's Lochlie period. At first Tarbolton figured mainly as the place where William Burnes and his sons took their produce to market. From the sequestration inventory it appears that the main cash crops of Lochlie were oats and barley, but flax was also raised, and this was to loom large in Robert's career later on. As late as the 1790s the 'Friend of Statistical Inquiries' who compiled the account of the parish for Sir John Sinclair, in default of the parish minister, Mr Ritchie, observed that the cultivation of root crops was 'not yet fully established'. He noted that dairy-farming was now the main agricultural occupation, relying mainly on the Ayrshire breed whose reputation for an excellent milk yield was then being established. That Lochlie continued with the older breed of black cattle, raised for their beef rather than their milk, indicates the relative poverty of the Lochlie grazing. Agnes and the girls milked the cows and made some butter and a great deal of mild cheese, most of which was also destined for Tarbolton market.

On Sundays the entire family trekked into town to attend morning and afternoon services in the parish church and listen to the sermons of Dr Patrick Wodrow. The second of the three sons of the celebrated Robert Wodrow, chronicler of *The Sufferings of the Church of Scotland* during the Covenanting period, Patrick had been born in 1713. At the age of twenty-five he had been ordained at Tarbolton and spent the rest of his long life in that parish. He was sixty-five when the Burnes family began attending his church, and he continued to preach the Gospel till his death sixteen years later. He figures in Robert's first great religious satire, 'The Twa Herds' (CW 92) as:

Auld Wodrow lang has hatch'd mischief:
We thought ay death wad bring relief,
But he has gotten to our grief,
    Ane to succeed him,
A chield wha'll soundly buff our beef –
    I meikle dread him.

Taken out of context, this seems uncomplimentary to Auld Wodrow, but those whose beef was being buffed were the stern, unbending faction of Calvinists, so Wodrow (in Robert's eyes) must be regarded as inclining towards the liberal wing of Presbyterianism. The one who was marked out as his successor was the Revd. John McMath (1755–1825), the 'guid McMath' of the same poem, appointed as Wodrow's assistant in 1782. The 'Holy Tulzie' or brawl which was the subject of the poem was actually an unseemly dispute between two champions of Auld Licht principles, the Revd. Alexander Moodie of Riccarton and the Revd. John Russell of Kilmarnock, whose squabbles over the boundaries of their adjoining parishes led to much heated debate in the Presbytery of Irvine. Tarbolton parish was not directly involved, but doubtless the antics of the 'black-coats' of the county were highly entertaining to the likes of Robert and his friends, and he was not backward in expressing his views on the con-troversy in particular and the theological debate between the Auld and New Lichts in general. David Sillar, a 'brother poet', later wrote of Robert that 'I recollect hearing his neighbours observe, he had a great deal to say for himself, and that they suspected his principles'[25] which shows that, by his early twenties, Robert was gaining a reputation as a religious radical not afraid to speak his mind.

David Sillar (1760–1830) was the third of the four sons of Patrick Sillar, farmer in Spittalside near Lochlie. Though (like Robert) largely self-educated, he was appointed interim master of the parish school, but in 1781 the permanent post was awarded instead to John Wilson (1751–1839), the son of a Glasgow weaver. Wilson had had the benefit of a university education and taught for some time at Craigie (between Tar-bolton and Kilmarnock), so he was much better qualified academically and by experience for the job. Sillar subsequently established a private school at Commonside on the outskirts of the village but this venture was not a success and in 1783 he left the parish, to try his luck as a grocer in Irvine. Sillar was probably Robert's closest friend in the Lochlie period. They were much the same age, their educational and farming backgrounds were not dissimilar, and they shared an interest in versifying. Sillar was even to emulate Robert by getting John Wilson of Kilmarnock to publish his poems in 1789, but his verses were banal and inept and, not surprisingly, the pub-lishing venture was a failure. He would be all but forgotten nowadays were it not for the two great verse-epistles of Burns, composed in January 1785 and July 1786 (CW 86–9 and 213–14). He was also the recipient of three prose letters written in 1789–91 (CL 536–7) showing that Robert con-tinued to take a lively interest in his brother poet. Sillar, in his letter to

Robert Aiken[26] recorded the circumstances in which he came to meet the poet:

> Mr Robert Burns was some time in the parish of Tarbolton prior to my acquaintance with him. His social disposition easily procured him acquaintance; but a certain satirical seasoning, with which he and all poetical geniuses are in some degree influenced, while it set the rustic circle in a roar, was not unaccompanied by its kindred attendant – suspicious fear.

We are also indebted to Sillar for an excellent description of the poet's appearance in the early Lochlie period:

> He wore the only tied hair in the parish; and in the church, his plaid, which was of a particular colour, I think *fillemot*, he wrapped in a particular manner round his shoulders. These surmises, and his exterior, had such a magical influence on my curiosity, as made me particularly solicitous of his acquaintance. Whether my acquaintance with Gilbert was casual or premeditated, I am not now certain. By him I was introduced not only to his brother, but to the whole of that family, where, in a short time, I became a frequent, and, I believe, not unwelcome visitant. After the commencement of my acquaintance with the bard, we frequently met on Sundays at church, when, between sermons, instead of going with our friends or lassies to the inn, we often took a walk in the fields. In these walks I have frequently been struck by his facility in addressing the fair sex; and many times, when I have been bashfully anxious how to express myself, he would have entered into conversation with them with the greatest ease and freedom; and it was generally a death-blow to our conversation, however agreeable, to meet a female acquaintance.

The reference to Robert's hairstyle is interesting. At this period the menfolk of the peasantry cut their hair reasonably short, while the middle and upper classes of society either wore wigs or styled and powdered their hair as if they did. By wearing his hair long and gathered in a beribboned queue at the back, Robert was clearly showing that he regarded himself as a cut above his fellows. The unusual colour of his plaid (resembling the russet shades of fallen leaves in autumn), when everyone else was content with hodden grey, and the distinctive manner in which he wore it, were also designed to mark him out from the common herd.

David Sillar's reminiscences of this period continued:

> Some of the few opportunities of a noontide walk that a country-life allows her laborious sons, he spent on the banks of the river, or in the woods in the neighbourhood of Stair, a situation peculiarly adapted to the genius of a rural bard. Some book (especially one of those mentioned in his letter to Mr Murdoch) he always carried, and read when not otherwise employed. It was likewise his custom to read at the table. In one of my visits to Lochlea, in time of a sowen supper, he was so intent on reading, I think *Tristram Shandy*, that his spoon falling out of his hand, made him exclaim, in a tone scarcely imitable 'Alas, poor Yorick!' He had in his

youth paid considerable attention to the arguments for and against the doctrine of original sin, then making considerable noise in the neighbourhood of Ayr; and having perused Dr Taylor's book on that subject,[27] and also a book called *Letters concerning the Religion essential to Man*, his opinions, when he came to Tarbolton, were consequently favourable to what you Ayr people call the 'moderate side'. The religion of the people of Tarbolton at that time was purely that of their fathers, founded on the *Westminster Confession*, and taught by one generation to another, uncontaminated by reading, reflection, and conversation; and though divided into different sectaries, the *Shorter Catechism* was the line which bounded all their controversies. The slightest insinuation of Taylor's opinions made his neighbours suspect, and some even avoid him, as an heretical and dangerous companion. Such was Burns, and such were his associates when, in May 1781, I was admitted a member of the Bachelors' Club.

In his autobiographical letter to Moore Robert confessed, 'The great misfortune of my life was, never to have AN AIM'. In fact, as any psychologist would point out, he was hopelessly divided between two aims, equally powerful and mutually destructive. The one was hereditary: to be a successful farmer; while the other was intensely personal: to be a successful writer. Robert himself was acutely aware of the problem, as he confided to Dr Moore:

> I saw my father's situation entailed on me perpetual labor. – The only two doors by which I could enter the fields of fortune were, the most niggardly economy, or the little chicaning art of bargain-making: the first is so contracted an aperture, I never could squeeze myself into it; the last, I always hated the contamination of the threshold.

Robert did not see himself cut out to be a businessman, and judging by his subsequent dealings with Creech, Johnson and Thomson, he seems to have been too other-worldly or singularly unbusinesslike ever to have made a success in commerce.

Life on the farm was hard, but it was not a ceaseless round of unremitting toil. Robert had some leisure time in which to develop his immense appetite for sociability. He enjoyed the company of his peers of both sexes, though, as Sillar pointed out, girls always took priority over other friends. Robert himself commented at length on this:

> Thus, abandoned of aim or view in life; with a strong appetite for sociability, as well from native hilarity as from a pride of observation and remark; a constitutional hypochondriac taint which made me fly solitude; add to all these incentives to social life, my reputation for bookish knowledge, a certain wild, logical talent, and a strength of thought something like the rudiment of good sense, made me generally a welcome guest; so 'tis no great wonder that always 'where two or three were met together, there was I in the midst of them.'–[28] But far beyond all the other impulses of my heart was, un penchant à l'adorable moitiée de genre humain.– My heart was compleatly tinder, and was eternally lighted up by some

Goddess·or other; and like every warfare in this world, I was sometimes crowned with success, and sometimes mortified with defeat.- At the plough, scythe or reap-hook I feared no competitor, and set Want at defiance: and as I never cared farther for my labors than while I was in actual exercise, I spent the evening in the way after my own heart.- A country lad rarely carries on an amour without an assisting confidant.- I possessed a curiosity, zeal and intrepid dexterity in these matters which recommended me a proper Second in duels of that kind: and I dare say, I felt as much pleasure at being in the secret of half the amours in the parish, as ever did Premier at knowing the intrigues of half the courts of Europe.

Robert's role as a 'blackfoot', or go-between, in these parochial romances was reciprocated, if we are to believe the testimony of John Lees, a shoemaker in Tarbolton who claimed to have acted for Robert in a similar capacity. Lees said that once he had attracted a girl out of her home on the poet's behalf, Robert would say to him, 'Now, Jock, you can gang awa hame now.'[29] Somehow this does not seem to accord with the evidence of Gilbert Burns or David Sillar; it seems unlikely that Robert needed anyone's assistance in the conduct of his amatory warfare. As he wrote to Moore, it is obvious that he was able to take a detached, rather amused, view of these parish love affairs:

The very goosefeather in my hand seems instinctively to know the well-worn path of my imagination, the favorite theme of my song; and is with difficulty restrained from giving you a couple of paragraphs on the amours of my Compeers, the humble Inmates of the farm-house and cottage; but the grave sons of Science, Ambition or Avarice baptize these things by the name of Follies.- To the sons and daughters of labor and poverty they are matters of the most serious nature: to them, the ardent hope, the stolen interview, the tender farewell, are the greatest and most delicious part of their enjoyments.

One of the love affairs Robert is said to have helped along was that between David Sillar and Margaret Orr, a nurserymaid at Stair House. Following the local custom of being accompanied on his courting visits, Sillar chose Robert as his companion, to extol his good qualities and generally sustain his courage. At Stair, hospitality and entertainment were sensibly and pleasantly blended with matters of serious import, and the ballads that were sung so delighted Robert that he left a few of his own compositions. The story goes that these eventually fell into the hands of Mrs Stewart, the lady of the house, and so much was the lady captivated by the grace of their rhythm that, on her special request, the poet occasionally migrated from the servants' quarters to the drawing-room.[30] There is no documentary provenance for this story - Sillar never mentioned it in his letter to Aiken - but it may be confirmed by passages in the two extant letters to this lady. The first, written in September 1786 when Robert was planning to go abroad, accompanied a parcel of unpublished songs and poems which he had promised her. Perhaps he alludes to a much earlier period, the time of the Sillar courtship, when he says, 'One feature of your character I shall ever with grateful pleasure remember, the reception I got when I had the honor of waiting on you at Stair' (CL 125). And again, five years later, when he compiled the collection now known as the Afton Lodge MS, he added a dedication to 'The first person of her sex & rank that patronised his humble lays' (CL 126). In succeeding years, however, the tradition of Robert's early visits at Stair was reinforced by proud displays of those precious relics, the handleless china cups in which the poet is said to have tasted tea for the first time.

According to the custom of the period, the negotiations between Sillar and Miss Orr, superintended by Robert, eventually reached the stage of a compact, signalled by the exchange of a broken coin, hand-clasping and mutual vows. Despite the happy conclusion of this courting darg, however, Peggy Orr exercised the time-honoured prerogative of womankind and changed her mind; she finally married John Paton, an Edinburgh shoemaker, instead. The date of this courtship is not known, but an oblique reference to it in the first 'Epistle to Davie, a Brother-Poet, Lover, Ploughman and Fiddler' (CW 86) seems to place this in a much later period. On the other hand, the lines

> Ye hae your Meg, your dearest part,
> An I hae darling Jean

may be misleading. As Sillar left the neighbourhood by 1783, the courtship of Margaret Orr took place long before Robert had met Jean Armour – assuming, of course, that she was meant. On the other hand, as Robert did not send this verse-epistle till January 1785 (when Jean Armour's star was rising), it seems more probable that Meg was another Margaret altogether, a girlfriend of Sillar's in Irvine. It is sometimes suggested that Jean Gardner, an acquaintance of the poet's Irvine interlude, may have been meant; but this is discussed more appropriately in the next chapter.

By addressing Sillar as a 'brother fiddler' Robert implies that he had taken up the violin himself by this time. This is borne out by the reminiscences of Isobel Burns who said that, in emulation of his friend, Robert purchased an instrument for five shillings. When driven from the field by bad weather he would while away an idle hour with his fiddle. He never attained any proficiency on it, or the German flute which he subsequently attempted. That, at least, was Isobel's opinion, no doubt coloured by excruciating memories of her brother's gut-scraping attempts. Robert had quite a high regard for his musical ability, hence his reference to Sillar whom one assumes was a better fiddler than a poet. Nevertheless, Robert, as a result, could read music with reasonable fluency and even write musical notation, as examples may be found among his correspondence with George Thomson.

Though not the rowdy, anarchic place that Kirkoswald was in its smuggling heyday, Tarbolton was a much livelier place than Dalrymple. Unlike the neighbours at Mount Oliphant, the farms of Tarbolton parish were working farms, numerous, closely set and populous. Although coal-mining was beginning to make an impression on the neighbourhood, Tarbolton in the 1770s and 1780s was chiefly noted for its stockings and textiles; woollens, linen, cotton and even some silk were woven on the handlooms of its low-ceilinged cottages. After a hard day at the loom, the weaver lads would congregate on the street corners or crowd into Manson's Inn and the Cross Keys. The 'fair enslavers' of the first Lochlie period made little impact on Robert's poetry. Apart from the doubtful claim of Annie Rankine, already noted, one of the girls to become immortalised in song was Isabella 'Tibbie' Steven and then only after the poet suffered one of those defeats that mortified him so. 'O Tibbie, I hae seen the Day' (CW 47–8) dates from the very earliest days of the Lochlie tenancy when Robert was aged eighteen. Isobel Burns is the only source of the anecdote identifying the Tibbie of the song as Isabella Steven, daughter of the tenant in Littlehill, another farm near Lochlie; but as the poet's sister was only nine or ten at the time her information may not be reliable. This is countered (though not actually contradicted) by Tarbolton tradition which maintains that Tibbie Stein (an alternative form of Steven) lived in the village. Her house, no longer extant, stood on the west side of Burns Street, on the corner of Garden Street, and almost opposite Manson's Inn. The story goes that Isabella Steven came into a legacy of £75, on the strength of which she rejected Robert for a more prosperous suitor. Local legend maintains that one night Robert called at her home and the door was answered by a member of the household who said that Tibbie was entertaining another gentleman. The poet left the house and never returned. The song was composed shortly afterwards.[31] This legend supports (or may have been coloured by) the words of the song whose heroine has 'the name o clink' (money) and whose 'daddie's gear maks you sae nice'. In the end, however, the poet scorns the stuck-up heiress:

> There lives a lass beside yon park,
> I'd rather hae her in her sark
> Than you wi a' your thousand mark,
>   That gars you look sae high.

A thousand marks, in money of account, was by that time worth only £56 6s 8d sterling; a round sum, but near enough to the £75 of the legacy to have the ring of truth. The 'lass beside yon park' has often been identified as Elizabeth Paton (see Chapter 8) but without confirmation from the poet himself. There is also the shadowy figure of the young housekeeper at Coilsfield House, the residence of Colonel Hugh Montgomerie, later twelfth Earl of Eglinton. This locale became of greater relevance in the Mossgiel period. Robert took a traditional ballad entitled 'McMillan's Peggy' and wrote the song 'Montgomerie's Peggy' (CW 60). Robert was later to recall this episode in a lengthy reflective passage in his *First Commonplace Book* but suffice to say at this juncture that Isobel Burns many years later identified this young lady as someone whom her brother frequently met. 'They sat in the same church, and contracted an intimacy together; but she was engaged to another before ever they met.'[32]

If this is anything to go by, then it seems that the company of men, rather than women, stimulated Robert more in this period. In addition to David Sillar there was John Rankine, tenant in Adamhill not far from Lochlie. 'Rough, rude, ready-witted Rankine', as Burns apostrophized him in a verse-epistle and a mock-epitaph (CW 82–5), seems an odd choice of companion for a youth on the verge of manhood, for Rankine was old enough to be his father, and I am inclined to the view that the friendship, such as it was, belonged more to the second Lochlie period when Robert had more fully matured.

An acquaintance, rather than a friend, was the village tailor, Alexander Tait,[33] known locally as 'Sawney' or 'Saunders' Tait. Born at Innerleithen, Peeblesshire, on 14 August 1720, he was a relative newcomer to Tarbolton when the Burnes family themselves settled in the district. Tailoring in eighteenth-century rural Scotland was a nomadic business, closely allied to the sale of cloth, and Tait is believed to have roamed over the south of Scotland for many years before he came to rest in Tarbolton; but he soon established himself there as a respected figure. He is described as a well-formed man of middle stature with an inexhaustible supply of energy and a fund of funny stories. As a raconteur and wit he was much in demand at weddings, rockings and other merrymaking, but it was his prowess as a rhymester which brought him renown. In one of his autobiographical poems he recited his multifarious public duties:

> I'm Patron to the Burgher folks,
> I'm Cornal to the Farmers' Box,
> And Bailie to guid hearty cocks,
>   That are a' grand;
> Has heaps o houses built on rocks
>   Wi lime and sand.

The first line alludes to his success in managing the erection of the Secession or Burgher Church at Tarbolton in 1777, against the opposition of the parish minister and the heritors. The second line refers to his rank of 'Colonel' in the Universal Friendly Society of Tarbolton: a purely ceremonial one which entailed dressing up in a cocked hat and leading the Society's parade through the village to drum up support for this mutual-benefit organisation that did much to alleviate poverty and distress in the agricultural community.[34] The rest of the verse mentions his high civic office and the fact that he owned several properties around the village. At the age of seventy-five he enlisted in the West Lowland Fencibles and thus earned himself a lengthy footnote in Kay's *Edinburgh Portraits* in which we learn that 'Sawney' Tait could not write, although this did not prevent him publishing his poems.[35] Ungrammatical, defective in metre and deficient in rhyme, the works of the poetic tailor belong to the *genre* of William McGonagall. Most of his poems dealt with events and personalities of purely local interest. According to Kay, some of his songs obtained temporary popularity. One in particular, on Mrs Alexander of Ballochmyle, was much talked about, 'probably from the circumstance of the lady having condescended to patronise the village laureate by requesting his attendance at Ballochmyle, where he recited the piece, was rewarded, and afterwards continued to be a privileged frequenter of the hall'. This contrasted sharply with the way in which, to his chagrin, Robert himself was ignored by the Alexander family, and could hardly have endeared the doggerel-monger to him.

It appears that Robert 'made a song on him' and though the text is unknown we may suppose that Tait was the victim of Robert's barbed wit. Tait never forgot nor forgave him for this, but got his revenge some years later, in the aftermath of the wretched business of the sequestration. 'His posthumous reputation, such as it is, survives only because of the reflected genius of Burns. Had their paths never crossed, it is almost certain that Tait's coarse doggerel verses would have been consigned, long since, to discreet and everlasting oblivion.'[36]

Situated in the Sandgate was a substantial two-storey building which John Richard kept as an ale-house. The rooms on the upper floor were approached by an outside staircase at the rear of the building. In one of these top-floor rooms, on 11 November 1780, was founded the Bachelors' Club. It was the fulfilment of that ambition which Robert had shown at Hugh Rodger's school in Kirkoswald to promote the intellectual improvement of himself and his compeers. This club, probably the earliest rural debating society in Scotland and certainly the prototype of many Burns clubs the world over, was founded by Robert who became its first president. His fellow members were brother Gilbert, Hugh Reid, Alexander Brown, Thomas Wright, William McGavin and Walter Mitchell. David Sillar, however, did not become a member till May 1781. Later members included Matthew Paterson of Skioch (who shared Robert's interest in flax-growing), John Orr and James Paterson (a younger brother of Matthew), admitted in 1782. At the inaugural meeting the rules of the Club were drawn up. A copy exists to this day in Sillar's holograph, but without doubt Robert was the person chiefly responsible for drafting the rules, reproduced in full by Currie[37] and much-quoted in part by all subsequent biographers. The language of the rules is a curious mixture of sentimentalism, decorous formality and literary aspiration, of which the tenth and last rule gives a typical impression:

Every man proper for a member of this Society, must have a frank, honest, open heart; above anything dirty or mean; and must be a professed lover of one or more of the female sex. No haughty, self-conceited person, who looks upon himself as superior to the rest of the club, and especially no mean-spirited worldly mortal, whose only will is to heap up money, shall upon any pretence whatever be admitted. In short, the proper person for this society is a cheerful, honest-hearted lad, who, if he has a friend that is true, and a mistress that is kind, and as much wealth as genteelly to make both ends meet – is just as happy as this world can make him.

Although the manuscript copy of the rules, now on display in the Club, is not in Robert's handwriting, there can be little doubt that he was largely, if not wholly, responsible. The underlying note of class consciousness and the blend of defiance and sentimentalism were to be recurring themes of Robert's poetry in later years. The rules of the Bachelors' Club have his handiwork stamped all over them. As in the rules, so also in the subjects which were selected for debate. These included 'Whether do we derive more happiness from Love or Friendship?' and 'Whether is the savage man or the peasant of a civilized country in the most happy situation?' But the most telling topic was undoubtedly 'Suppose a young man, bred a farmer, but without any future, had it in his power to marry either of two women, the one a girl of large fortune, but neither handsome in person or agreeable in conversation but who can manage the household affairs of a farm well enough; the other of them a girl every way agreeable in person, conversation and behaviour, but without any fortune, which of them shall he choose?' It is on record that Robert took the side of the lass without the fortune.

A certain amount of social drinking accompanied these congenial debates, but no more, and probably a good deal less, than in similar circumstances in other venues at the same period. Tradition maintains that members were not permitted to spend more than threepence each on drink at any meeting, although this does not appear in the rules and regulations of the club. Quite apart from inclination, neither Robert nor Gilbert could afford it; and we have no reason to doubt the normally timid and mild-mannered Gilbert's assertion concerning his brother during the Lochlie period: 'I do not recollect, during those seven years . . . to have ever seen him intoxicated'.[38] Each meeting concluded with 'a general toast to the mistresses of the club'. The records of the club show that it continued for some years after the Burnes family left the district. Richard's ale-house languished in oblivion till 1937 when it was threatened with demolition by Ayr County Council. As a result, the Burns Federation joined forces with the National Trust for Scotland to obtain a postponement of the clearance order. The Trust later secured an option over the property but completion of the purchase was delayed by the Second World War and it was not until 1951 that this interesting old building was secured for the nation. It was subsequently restored and is now open to the public as a museum.

The Bachelors' Club had only been in existence a few weeks when Robert was allegedly enslaved by yet another fair young charmer. The heroine of this episode was identified by Dr Robert Chambers in his *Life and Works of Robert Burns*, published in 1851–2, as Alison Begbie, and all subsequent biographers and Burns scholars have accepted this unquestioningly. The sole source for this identification was Mrs Begg (Isobel Burns) to whom Chambers applied in 1847 when she was an old lady of seventy-six. As she was being asked to cast her mind back to a time when she was only nine or ten years old, the following statements must be regarded with extreme caution.

About two miles eastward from Lochlea, a shining stream, called Cess-nock Water, flows past in a northerly course through Galston parish into the River Irvine. A young woman, named Ellison Begbie, the daughter of a small farmer near Galston, was then in service with a family whose house was on Cessnock bank at the distance mentioned from the farm of William Burnes. The youthful poet had got acquainted with Ellison, and was so much charmed with her superior manners and agreeable person, that he courted her with all his ardour during several months, with a serious view to future marriage. It was on her that he composed the very poetic 'song of similes', called 'The Lass of Cessnock Banks'.[39]

John Muir, first editor of the *Burns Chronicle* (1892) latched on to this vague statement and embroidered it, identifying the house at which 'Ellison Begbie' was housekeeper as Carnell which, in Robert's day, was known as Cairnhill. According to one tradition 'which I have often heard repeated', says Muir, 'Burns took a fancy to her while passing her house with his cart for coals'. Robert and his father certainly went to Cairnhill kilns to obtain burnt lime to fertilize their sour fields. Muir went farther, however, and identified this girl as the daughter of a tenant-farmer in Old Place, a mile downstream. Old Place, which derived its name from the fact that it was originally the seat of the Campbells of Cessnock before they built a new residence in Galston parish, has long since been demolished and its land incorporated in the modern farm of Shawsmill.[40] Unfortunately Muir did not cite his sources, but his account was based inferentially on oral tradition, seldom the most reliable medium, especially so long after the event. In true nineteenth-century fashion, Muir could even cite one Campbell Wallace of Galston who possessed a pocket bible 'said to have been given by the poet to Ellison Begbie'. It was allegedly given by her father to the late John Gray, a Glasgow merchant, who gave it to Miss McWilliam of Glasgow, who gave it to Robert Wallace, the father of Campbell. Muir accepted this doubtful provenance without questioning, although he did observe that, unlike the celebrated two-volume bible given by Robert to 'Highland Mary', this volume bore no marks on the fly-leaf. Subsequent writers, while blindly accepting the myth of Alison Begbie, have merely commented on her shadowy figure. To strip away the accretions of legend and try to get at the truth is like peeling an onion; but the only solution is to rely on Robert's own statement to Dr Moore, his early letters and poetry, and the only primary source, the old parish registers.

Certainly in his autobiographical letter to Dr Moore, Robert says, somewhat out of context, that 'a belle-fille whom I adored and who had pledged her soul to meet me in the field of matrimony, jilted me with peculiar circumstances of mortification'.[41]

Gilbert may have had this incident in mind when he wrote, in the context of Robert's amours, 'As these connexions were governed by the strictest rules of virtue and modesty (from which he never deviated till his twenty-third year), he became anxious to be in a situation to marry.'[42] The writings of the poet provided no clue to the name or social position of the young woman he was thus so anxious to marry, and not till more than half a century after his death did any of his family or Tarbolton associates venture to throw some light on the matter. Four draft letters in Robert's handwriting, addressed to 'My dear E', were found among his papers at his death and were published in Currie's first edition (1800) as having been written 'about the year 1780'. These were withdrawn from the second and all subsequent editions, and were not even restored by Gilbert in his edition of 1820. Gilbert had been asked to inform George Thomson of what he knew concerning Mary Morrison, the subject of a song written in 1784-5 (CW 69), and he replied that if his brother had any particular person in his eye, certainly this was not the young woman's real name. This, however, did not deter A. N. Carmichael from erecting a tombstone in Mauchline kirkyard in 1825 in memory of his aunt – the poet's 'Bonnie Mary Morrison' – who died on 29 June 1791, aged twenty, following an amputation which led to septicaemia. It is ludicrous to suppose that Robert would have composed this song about a girl who was only nine or ten years old at the time. This only goes to show how pious frauds are perpetrated, and the headstone is there to this day, doubtless confusing and misleading tourists and Burns enthusiasts. Gilbert Burns, however, believed that 'Mary Morrison' must have been the same individual who formed the subject of the verses beginning 'And I'll kiss thee yet, yet, my bonie Peggy Alison' (CW 319); but who 'Peggy Alison' was, Gilbert did not explain. From time to time 'Highland Mary' Campbell has been tentatively suggested as the inspiration of this song, but the consensus of opinion is that the girl in question was the intended recipient of the E letters.

The only glimmer of light to be thrown on these early love letters came from Isobel Burns in 1847, twenty years after Gilbert's death. The foregoing information is the most tangible scrap of recollection we have to go on. Unfortunately Dr Chambers may have asked some leading questions, for it was Isobel who ventured the opinion that E may have stood for Ellison. Chambers seems to have prompted her, on the strength of the song extolling 'bonie Peggy Alison', and it was then that Mrs Begg came up with the name Alison or Ellison Begbie, Ellison being no doubt a broad-vowelled phonetic rendering of Alison. Many years later, when John Adam of Greenock, an avid Burns collector, turned up a fifth draft letter without any form of address, but containing the line 'I am a stranger in these matters A—' (CL 43), Scott Douglas naturally assumed that this letter pertained to the other four and, in fact, was the first of the series.[43] Mrs Begg then went on to state that Robert was so much charmed with Alison's superior manners and agreeable person that he courted her with all his ardour over a period of several months, with a serious view to future marriage.

Mrs Begg, once primed, could even recall how her brother went frequently of an evening to visit Ellison, and as he did not as a rule return till a late hour, his father at length became alarmed at the irregularity of his habits. The old man resolved one night to administer to his son the practical rebuke of sitting up to let him in, and also to give him a few words of advice. When Robert returned, William was lying in wait for him. On being asked what had detained him so long, the poet began a whimsical account of what he had met with and seen of natural and supernatural on his way home, concluding with the particulars afterwards wrought up in the well-known 'Address to the Deil' (CW 161). The old man was, in spite of himself, so much interested and amused by this recital that he forgot the intended scolding, and the affair ended in his sitting up for an hour or two by the kitchen fire enjoying the conversation of his gifted son.[44] It should be noted that Robert's 'Address to the Deil' was not actually composed till the winter of 1785–6; and one cannot but marvel at the power of recollection of Mrs Begg sixty-six years after the event.

Furthermore, it was in tribute to this young lady that Robert had composed 'The Lass of Cessnock Banks' (CW 51–2). This lengthy 'song of similes' runs to fourteen quatrains, in the course of which Robert worked himself into a white heat of indiscriminating passion. That such a paragon of matchless beauty could have escaped Gilbert's notice seems well-nigh incredible. Technically, it was also quite a *tour de force*. As each stanza ends with the line 'An she has twa sparkling rogueish een!' it entails fourteen lines ending with a syllable to match – and Robert succeeded without having to repeat himself. The similes themselves are often ingenious, although few women would like to be told that their teeth are 'like a flock of sheep, / With fleeces newly washen clean' (actually a borrowing of Burns from the Song of Solomon). This statement by Isobel Begg, taken in conjunction with Gilbert's hint regarding Peggy Alison, logically suggested that 'Peggy Alison' was a poetic alias devised by Robert because 'Begbie' was too prosaic and clumsy a name to be woven into verse. Unfortunately 'Peggy Alison' seems to have been something of a red herring which put scholars off the scent for almost a century and a half. The discrepancy between A and E in the draft letters was disingenuously explained away, due to the fact that Robert probably observed his correspondent signing her name 'Ellison Begbie' and not 'Alison Begbie', in accordance with the pronunciation of the Ayrshire peasantry. Indeed, John Muir was particularly pleased with himself, stating, 'This fact, trifling in itself, has not before been pointed out by any editor of the works of Burns.' I find it hard to believe, however, that any young lady – especially one as literate as the poet's correspondent obviously was – would have been so careless as to spell her name phonetically.

Ignoring this red herring, therefore, and assuming that Robert, even in drafting letters, would have got the right initials of his correspondents, it must now be supposed that these letters were addressed to not one but *two* young ladies. 'A', in fact, could refer to anyone by the name of Anne or Agnes. It has been remarked by some writers that Alison was a name unknown in Tarbolton parish; in fact, I have scoured the registers of *all* the neighbouring parishes without finding a single example of this girl's name before the early nineteenth century. Unless the actual letter, as sent, comes to light, it is unlikely that the identity of Miss A will ever be known. In any case, there is always the possibility that this letter was one which Robert drafted on behalf of one of his friends, one of the little services for which he was noted.[45]

Compared with the beauty and sheer genius of 'The Lass of Cessnock Banks', 'Mary Morrison' and 'Bonie Peggy Alison', the four letters addressed to 'My dear E' are unbelievably wooden, culminating in the stilted proposal of the third letter: 'If you will be so good and so generous as to admit me for your partner, your companion, your bosom friend through life, there is nothing on this side of eternity shall give me greater transport.' Small wonder, therefore, that the lady rejected the proposal. Indeed, it has been speculated whether such letters could ever have been sent; but the tenor of the final draft, a stiff upper lip acknowledgment of rejection, implies that this was part of a real correspondence. If the girl refused him 'with peculiar circumstances of mortification' as Robert says, one might have expected a much more impassioned tone in that final letter. If they *really* were intended for the lady Robert wished to wed, it shows how his honourable intentions could be scuppered by high-flown sentiment. We are not surprised, therefore, that the young lady refused to have anything to do with a man who told her that her company never gave him those giddy raptures so much talked of among lovers, and who announced that in his opinion married life was only friendship in a more exalted degree. If Isobel is to be believed, and Robert 'went frequently of an evening' to visit the girl, one has to question why he felt the need to put his feelings on paper when he was obviously far better at a verbal wooing.

The four letters in question are undated and bear no endorsement to suggest their would-be recipient. The first begins 'I verily believe, my dear E.', while the second and third are actually headed 'My dear E'. In the second letter 'my E.' or 'my dear E.' occurs thrice; in the third it occurs once in the text. Only in the last of the series, in which Robert copes with the finality of her rejection, is the initial omitted, but the letter tails off abruptly with 'I hope you will pardon it in, my dear Miss —, (pardon me the dear expression for once,) . . .'. It seems to me that the lady, whoever she was, must have had a name which began with E. On this assumption I made a search of the Galston parish register for the period coeval with Robert. I found no one of the name of Begbie (as suggested by Mrs Begg), but I found several families with the surname of Gebbie, all descended from a common ancestor at the beginning of that century. John Gebbie was the tenant in Millhill, while his brother Alexander was the miller at Cessnock Mill nearby. A third brother Thomas was tenant in Pearsland some distance away, but actually near to the village of Galston.[46] This answered the description of the poet's inamorata being the daughter of 'a small farmer near Galston'. The register shows that Alexander Gebbie had a daughter named Elizabeth, born on 21 November 1761, while Thomas had a daughter of the same name, born at Pearsland on 22 July 1762. Tracing their subsequent careers, we find that the older Elizabeth married Hugh Guthrie or Gutherey at Riccarton, south of Kilmarnock, on 30 April 1788. Guthrie was a wright or carpenter who soon after his marriage settled at Woodhead not far from his wife's birthplace. Here, their sons George and John were born on 28 February 1789 and 9 September 1790 respectively. This family continued to reside at Woodhead for many years.

Elizabeth's cousin and namesake, however, seems to have been the girl on whom the poet lavished his unrequited affections. In the last of the E letters Robert wrote in such a vein that we may form the impression that she had two beaux to her string and, having pondered their future prospects, she decided on someone other than Robert. Her letter breaking the bad news to Robert, to put it into his own words, was couched 'in the politest language of refusal' but its effect was devastating nonetheless. She was sorry she could not make him a return but she wished him all kind of happiness. She must have been quite a remarkable young lady, for few of her station in life at that time were able to read letters, let alone write them. After telling her that he expects 'to remove in a few days a little farther off' Robert continues, 'and you I suppose will perhaps soon leave this place, I wish to see you or hear from you soon'. It indicates that the girl herself had plans to leave the district as a result of the decision which included her refusal of Robert's proposal. This ties in with the fact that Elizabeth Gebbie married Hugh Brown at Newmilns in Loudoun parish on 23 November that year. Newmilns is, in fact, about a mile north-east of Pearsland. Hugh Brown was a man of more mature years, seven years older than Robert, and a stocking-maker to trade; to a girl who had not yet reached the age of twenty, he must have seemed a more dependable prospect than the son of Auld Lochlie.

The couple had two daughters, Helen born in November 1784 and Agnes born in June 1787. There are no further entries for Hugh Brown and Elizabeth Gebbie in Loudoun, Galston or, indeed, any of the other parishes in this part of Ayrshire. With a common name like Hugh Brown, it would seem that the needle could never be extracted from such a haystack. But now, enter Robert Hartley Cromek, whose *Reliques of Robert Burns* were published in 1808. Among the poet's early biographers, from Currie to Cunningham, Cromek has earned more opprobrium than most, being dismissed by Professor J. DeLancey Ferguson as the black sheep among the editors. 'He was indubitably a liar; he was almost certainly a cheat; there is some ground for thinking him a thief.'[47] He may have been all these things, but Cromek did what no previous editor had done, and which no editor since then could do: he took the trouble to track down as many of the friends and relatives of the late poet as he possibly could, and his *Reliques* contained the fruits of diligent research. Although he was not beyond faking material to suit his case, in one instance at least Cromek deserves credit: he was the first editor to publish 'The Lass of Cessnock Banks' (CW 51). 'This song was an early production. It was recovered by the Editor from the oral communication of a lady residing at Glasgow, whom the Bard in early life affectionately admired.'[48] The lady sang this 'song of similes' pretty much as Robert composed it but, due to a lapse of memory, omitted the eighth and ninth stanzas which were not published till Pickering's Aldine edition of 1839.[49] Pickering must have had access to a manuscript, but made a number of mistakes which were not corrected till 1927 when Davidson Cook collated the only known manuscript, then in the Law of Honresfield Collection.[50]

Cromek visited Scotland in 1807. The Glasgow Directory for that year contains the following entries:

Mrs Brown, bandbox-maker, 97 King Street
Mrs H. Brown, dyer, 297 High Street
Hugh Brown, stocking-manufacturer, 74 King Street
Mrs Brown, dealer in cotton and cotton yarn, 13 King Street
Mrs Brown, lets lodgings, Craig's Land, 47 Argyle Street[51]

It may be assumed that the stocking-manufacturer of King Street was the Hugh Brown who married Elizabeth Gebbie in 1781. A thorough search through the parish registers of Renfrewshire and Lanarkshire reveals that, at Glasgow, Elizabeth was born in June 1789 and Hugh in April 1791. Consulting the burial registers of the Glasgow parishes, however, I have been unable to trace Elizabeth Gebbie to the end of her life but she was dead by June 1823 when Hugh Brown, then a widower, made a will in favour of his children.[52] These registers were not so meticulously kept as the baptismal and marriage registers and there are many gaps. Even a search through the tombstones of Glasgow has so far proved fruitless. By 1825 Hugh Brown was listed as 'hosier and manufacturer' with a house at 22 North Frederick Street, renumbered 62 two years later. By 1829 Hugh Junior had taken over the business, now renamed Hugh Brown and Company with premises at 102 Virginia Street. Twenty years later Hugh Junior had expanded to premises on either side, at 100–104 Virginia Street and he resided in then fashionable Abercromby Place. In 1856 he purchased one of the splendid mansions in Park Terrace which was then being laid out. Clearly Elizabeth Gebbie had been a shrewd judge of character – or business sense at least – when she chose Hugh Brown and rejected Robert Burns.

From the foregoing, therefore, we can see that Robert courted Elizabeth Gebbie in the first half of 1781 and that she rejected him in favour of Hugh Brown with whom she eventually settled in Glasgow. She was probably known familiarly as Betty or Lizzie; but Robert was under the spell of *A Sentimental Journey* and *Tristram Shandy* at the time and we may assume that he bestowed on her the name of Sterne's heroine Eliza. Then 'Eliza Gebbie' could easily have become garbled to 'Ellison Begbie' in Mrs Begg's memory – after all, both surnames have the same letters, only the arrangement of the first syllable is different. Apart from a few letters, Eliza was obviously the recipient of 'Cessnock Banks' which she liked well enough to have memorised more or less correctly, in order to sing it for Cromek a quarter of a century later. It is strange that Robert never published this song himself, in the Kilmarnock or Edinburgh editions, or in the collections of Johnson and Thomson to which he contributed so generously. Perhaps the song triggered off such unhappy memories of his 'jilting' that he would rather turn his back on it.

Eliza Gebbie was undoubtedly the heroine of 'Farewell to Eliza' (CW 50) which previous editors associated with either Elizabeth Barbour or

Elizabeth Miller, without ever reconciling the discrepancy of the song having been composed before 1782 (on Burns's own admission to Moore), three years before either of these ladies swam into his ken, and ignoring Gilbert's comment that the song was one of Robert's early compositions. Certainly the two stanzas of this song would fit the mood of Burns at the time Miss Gebbie turned him down. The song closes with lines that inform Eliza that, no matter what, she will always be his heart-throb. The fact that, when it came to naming his daughters, Robert could never get beyond Elizabeth – so that all three who survived infancy were thus christened – may be a further clue to a love which he never got over till the end of his days.

Eliza obviously tried to let Robert down as gently as possible in her letter, but it certainly had a devastating effect on him. Afterwards he was to speak of her having jilted him – a difficult feat, when his own letters show that she had never actually accepted him in the first place. It seems probable that Eliza led him on, by the age-old method of tacit acceptance, while she was trying to make up her mind; and he may have taken her non-committal attitude as a sign of encouragement, so that her eventual rejection was all the harder to take. Robert had taken pride in both his skill in courtship and his elegance in correspondence; to find that a combination of these rare talents should fail so spectacularly dented his self-confidence.

Were it not for Isobel Burns identifying 'Ellison Begbie' and 'Montgomerie's Peggy' as two separate persons, one might suspect that they were one and the same. Both were housekeepers in country mansions, the one at Carnell House and the other at Coilsfield House; both had been bred 'in a style of life rather elegant', at least to the extent of being able to read joined-up writing (and some pretty high-flown sentiment at that); and both turned Robert down after being on the receiving end of his billets-doux. But Robert himself speaks of one of them as causing him mortification, whereas 'Peggy' (which may not have been her real name, but that borrowed from the old ballad) gently let him know that she was already engaged. Nevertheless, the admission that 'My Montgomerie's Peggy was my Deity for six, or eight months'[53] and the non-existence of any other 'billets-doux' which can be attributed to this girl inevitably leave one wondering.[54] And always at the back of one's mind is the speculation that 'Peggy Alison' may have been inspired by the Coilsfield housekeeper rather than the chateleine of Carnell. It is all very confusing. Of one thing we may be certain, however; not till the Clarinda episode of 1788 would Robert ever again place his trust in a postal wooing.

CHAPTER 6

Irvine, 1781–2

Tho fickle Fortune has deceived me,
  (She promis'd fair and perform'd but ill);
Of mistress, friends, and wealth bereav'd me,
  Yet I bear a heart shall support me still.

Fickle Fortune (CW 56)

About the time that Eliza Gebbie dashed his hopes of marriage, Robert decided on a change of career. Indeed, this decision may have been taken before that 'peremptory refusal' which caused him so much mortification, as he pondered his bleak prospects as the son of a poor tenant-farmer. 'My life flowed on much in the same tenor till my twenty third year,' he wrote to Moore. 'Vive l'amour et vive la bagatelle, were my sole principles of action.'[1] The year 1781 marked a turning point in Robert's poetic development, both stimulating his latent sentimentalism and helping to channel it into verse:

> The addition of two more Authors to my library gave me great pleasure; Sterne and Mckenzie.– Tristram Shandy and the Man of Feeling were my bosom favorites.– Poesy was still a darling walk for my mind, but 'twas only the humour of the hour.– I had usually half a dozen or more pieces on hand; I took up one or other as it suited the momentary tone of this mind, and dismissed it as it bordered on fatigue.– My Passions when once they were lighted up, raged like so many devils, till they got vent in rhyme; and then conning over my verses, like a spell, soothed all into quiet.– None of the rhymes of those days are in print, except, Winter, a dirge, the eldest of my printed pieces; The Death of Poor Mailie, John Barleycorn, And songs, first, second and third: song second was the ebullition of that passion which ended the forementioned school-business.–[2]

Lawrence Sterne published the first two volumes of *Tristram Shandy* in the very year that Burns was born. In 1768 Sterne further explored the feelings and failings of one character of that book, Parson Yorick,[3] in *A Sentimental Journey*, a seminal work which, if it did not actually invent the word, certainly made 'sentimental' fashionable in the original sense of resulting from feeling rather than reason. Critics, however, soon gave the word its pejorative meaning of having an excess of superficial sentiment, and this is the sense in which it is largely used to this day. Yorick, of course, derived his name from the greatest theatrical prop of all time, the jester's skull in *Hamlet*; this symbolises the sentimental process whose heroes look around, select an object, fasten their attention on it and dramatise the feelings that arise from this contemplation.[4] Henry Mackenzie (1745–1831) was closer to Robert's own age and place and, as we shall see, played no small part in the poet's later career. The son of an Edinburgh physician, he had studied law in Edinburgh and London before returning to his native city to practise in the Scottish Court of Exchequer in 1768. His novel *The Man of Feeling* appeared anonymously in 1771 and achieved instant acclaim. A sequel, *The Man of the World*, was published two years later under his own name. Other works followed, and Mackenzie also edited *The Mirror* and subsequently *The Lounger*. By the 1780s Henry Mackenzie was one of the pillars of the Scottish literary establishment. Robert had an exaggeratedly high opinion of Mackenzie, long before the latter deigned to notice him. In a letter of 15 January 1783 to John Murdoch, Robert said that *The Man of Feeling* was 'a book I prize next to the Bible'. In the same sentence he also enumerates 'Man of the World, Sterne, especially his Sentimental journey' (CL 55). Robert carried an octavo copy of *The Man of Feeling* everywhere with him and the original volume became so tattered as a result that he had to purchase a replacement.

Eliza Gebbie's rejection was a short, sharp shock. In an instant Robert saw the lack of aim or purpose in his life. He resolved to do something about it:

> My twenty third year was to me an important era.– Partly thro' whim, and partly that I wished to set about doing something in life, I joined with a flax-dresser in a neighbouring town, to learn his trade and carry on the business of manufacturing and retailing flax.–[5]

The neighbouring town was Irvine, about ten miles away to the northwest. One of the oldest royal burghs in Scotland, it had received its charter from King Alexander II (1214–49). It was here that the Capitulation of Irvine was signed in 1297 which brought the first struggle against English domination to a humiliating conclusion; but the burgh had its powers and privileges confirmed and extended by a grateful Robert Bruce for its support during a crucial early stage of the Wars of Independence in the early fourteenth century. Towards the end of the seventeenth century it was regarded as Scotland's third seaport in terms of importance and volume of trade. The gradual silting up of its harbour led to the decline of this trade, much of which was transferred to Greenock and Port Glasgow. Even the appearance of the town was considerably altered by the vagaries of shifting sands. The Seagate Castle, which in ancient times stood guard over the harbour, is now quite a long way from the mouth of the River Irvine which winds and loops between the town and the Firth of Clyde.

Irvine was the birthplace of the 'Christian Poet', James Montgomery (1771-1854) but the town's most famous son was John Galt. The son of a ship-owner trading with the West Indies, Galt was born two years before Robert's sojourn, and though he moved with his family to Greenock when he was only ten, he has left us a vivid picture of life in Irvine as it was in the closing years of the eighteenth century, in his great novel *The Provost* published in 1822. His *Annals of the Parish* (1821), based on the nearby village of Dreghorn, was described by the historian G. M. Trevelyan as 'the most intimate and human picture of Scotland during her period of change in the reign of George III'.

It has been suggested by some writers[6] that Robert was sent to Irvine by his father; but this is not borne out by the facts. Apart from Robert's own statement, quoted above, we have the testimony of brother Gilbert, who said that Robert's matrimonial prospects were poor so long as he remained at Lochlie:

> He began, therefore, to think of trying some other line of life. He and I had for several years taken land of my father for the purpose of raising flax on our own account. In the course of selling it, Robert began to think of turning flax-dresser, both as being suitable to his grand view of settling in life, and as subservient to the flax raising. He accordingly wrought at the business of a flax-dresser in Irvine for six months, but abandoned it at that period, as neither agreeing with his health nor inclination.[7]

Robert himself mentioned in his first letter to Willie Niven, as early as July 1780 (CL 38), 'I have three acres of pretty good flax this season'. It is not known whether the Irvine experiment was the end of Robert's interest in flax, the wonder crop of the 1780s. In January 1783 the Commissioners and Trustees for Fisheries, Manufactures and Improvements in Scotland, a quasi-governmental body which had been established in the aftermath of the Act of Union in 1707, belatedly awarded a premium of three pounds 'Being for lintseed saved for sowing' to 'Robert Burns, Lochlee, Tarbolton'.[8] The Trustees evidently wished to encourage flax and awarded sums totalling £369 18s to 154 farmers in respect of the 1781 crop. Two-thirds of the awards went in the first class for raising flax, 'being twenty shillings per acre; no premiums being allowed to any one person for more than six acres', whereas the second class was for linseed, no limit being placed on the amount that could be paid. The bulk of the prizes went to farmers in Dunbartonshire (fifty-five) and Lanarkshire (sixty-two), while only fifteen awards went to Ayrshire. Robert's name was the second last on the list, immediately followed by that of Matthew Paterson in Skioch (a close neighbour) who got £3 14s. Only six of the farmers in the first class qualified for the maximum of six pounds, but several in the second class did quite well. James Currie of Lanark Crofts got £6 5s and Thomas Nuckell of Stewarthall, St Ninians, in Stirlingshire got £8 6s, but the biggest pay-out (£14 5s) went to Robert Williamson of Calder (Cadder) in Lanarkshire. On the other hand many of the awards were as low as one pound, and Robert was certainly above the average. If these sums seem small it should be remembered that three pounds was equivalent to half a year's wages for the average farm-worker of the period. Robert and Gilbert sub-leased small parcels of land from their father, which implies that this was a sideline in which William had no direct interest.

Flax is a generic term for a number of different plants of the *Linaceae* family, but the type grown in the British Isles is *Linum usitatissimum* or Common Flax. It is an annual plant with erect, slender stems standing about half a metre (18 inches) high. Its narrow, lanceolate leaves are arranged alternately and at some distance from each other. The flowers are large and purplish-blue in colour. It is a fairly demanding crop requiring quite heavy soils and plenty of water. Fortunately, the clay soils of Lochlie and the moisture-laden westerlies which give this part of Ayrshire a higher than average rainfall were ideally suited to the cultivation of flax. When ready, the entire plant was pulled by hand. Flax-growing in Scotland was only a commercially viable crop in the eighteenth century when labour was very cheap. In the nineteenth century the cost of labour rose sharply, an incentive to the mechanisation of farming wherever possible. Unfortunately, the harvesting of flax could not be done mechanically without losing a substantial part of the yield, so that it became commercially feasible only in countries where land was very cheap and the growers could afford to lose part of the crop in mechanised cutting. For this reason flax-growing tended to be concentrated in the United States and the Baltic regions of Russia, though by the twentieth century production in these areas had declined sharply in face of competition from South America and Australia. Flax-growing survived in the British Isles longest in Ulster, but even that was forced into oblivion by the influx of much cheaper imports from Riga and St Petersburg.

The seeds were separated from the main plant at an initial stage, and from the crushed seed were obtained linseed oil and oil-cake, a high-protein cattle feed. Later strains of the flax plant were developed either for seed or fibre, but in Robert's day both were products of the same plant and had to be carefully separated by hand. Dressing flax entailed removing the seeds and then separating the bark and stem of the plant from the fibres (retting). Once the woody core had rotted down, the fibres were removed, dried, broken and scutched by beating the flax with a crescent-shaped hammer. The bundles of scutched fibres were full of impurities known as shives (splinters of woody material) and these had to be removed, and the fibres separated, by the process known as heckling. This was achieved by pairs of specially designed hand-combs, pre-heated in a comb-pot. A bundle of fibres (about 250g) was worked into one comb, then the heckler sat and worked the combs, one across the other, until a long, flat tress was combed out. This produces long, fairly straight strands known as line, and the shorter, tangled and often damaged strands known as tow. These were prepared for spinning by the final process of carding which parts the fibres, breaking any snags and locks and producing a light, fluffy mass. The wastage in flax-processing was very high, as much as half the fibres ending up as tow, too short for spinning and fit only for use as wadding or packing material. Dressed flax was now returned to the farms so that the womenfolk could spin it into yarn, using treadle-operated wheels. The resulting yarn was stronger than cotton, but brittle and not amenable to the powered loom until 1824 when Maberley of Aberdeen succeeded in modifying one to suit.

If the premiums paid by the Trustees are any guide, Ayrshire was not such an important area of Scottish flax-growing in the late eighteenth century as has been suggested[10] nor is it true to say that Irvine developed as a centre of the lint-processing industry. The account of the parish compiled by the Revd. James Richmond,[11] while going into minute detail concerning the various jobs and professions in Irvine – the town boasted one physician, two druggists, three surgeons, four tinkers, five writers (lawyers), six butchers, six barbers, twenty-four smiths, fifty-six shoe-makers, 116 weavers and 150 coal-hewers – is silent on the subject of flax-dressers. There is no reason to suppose that this trade was not still being carried on by 1790 when this report was written, but it suggests that it was a minor occupation.

According to Dr John Cumming of Milgarholm, a former provost of Irvine, he and Charles Hamilton, the aged and ailing incumbent of that office (who attended his last council meeting in April 1781), had a joint venture in textile manufacturing and bleachfields, and took the credit for encouraging Burns to come to the town to learn the trade of flax-dressing. In support of his claim, Dr Cumming prized a pair of heckling combs which he asserted had belonged to the poet. Certainly Provost Hamilton's son John, then a medical student, became a close friend of Robert during this period. But there is nothing in the writings of the poet, nor any explicit reference in the memoirs of Gilbert Burns or Mrs Begg, to throw some light on Robert's contacts in Irvine. Even the date on which he left Lochlie and came to the town is unknown. On 12 June 1781, however, Robert wrote a letter to his old friend Willie Niven (CL 39). Dated from 'Lochlee', this letter states, 'I know you will hardly believe me when I tell you, that by a strange conjuncture of circumstances, I am intirely got rid of all connections with the tender sex. I mean in the way of courtship; it is, however absolutely certain that I am so; though how long I shall continue so, Heaven only knows; but be that as it may, I shall never be involved as I was again.' This pinpoints the Gebbie rejection, and as the last letter in the courtship correspondence (CL 47–8) stated that the writer expected 'to remove in a few days a little farther off', it may be deduced that Robert departed for Irvine shortly afterwards. He was still in Tarbolton for the seventh meeting of the Bachelors' Club on 25 June, and attended his first masonic meeting there on 4 July.[12] He probably left for Irvine a day or two later. Local tradition – and it is not unlikely – maintains that Gilbert convoyed Robert for several miles along the road (now the B730) which ran in a north-westerly direction through Bogend and Dundonald.

When he wrote to Dr Moore, Robert was maddeningly vague about the Irvine interlude, which 'turned out a sadly unlucky affair'. The bald facts as stated by Robert were:

> My Partner was a scoundrel of the first water who made money by the
> mystery of thieving; and to finish the whole, while we were given (*sic*) a
> welcoming carousel to the New year, our shop, by the drunken careless-
> ness of my Partner's wife, took fire and was burnt to ashes; and left me
> like a true Poet, not worth sixpence.

From the foregoing it seems likely that Robert invested a sum of money in
the venture, hence the reference to a partner. Even the identity of this
individual is not known for certain, although an Irvine tradition which
dates back no farther than the 1820s gives some details which may, or may
not, be true. It is unfortunate that it was not until the formation of the
Irvine Burns Club in 1826 (which included two close friends of the poet,
David Sillar and Dr John Mackenzie, as founder-members) that a serious
interest was taken, by Maxwell Dick and others, in retracing the poet's
history in the burgh.[13] Much of the recollection of old age, however, is
confusing and contradictory.

The work of dressing flax was carried on in heckling-sheds where the
smell and the choking dust from shorts and shives must have been unbear-
able. Two heckling-shops compete for the doubtful honour of being the
one that left Burns sixpenceless. Robert's reference to his partner as a
scoundrel and the allegation that he was a thief may have been coloured by
a sense of grievance and indignation at having put some money into the
business in return for instruction in the techniques of flax-dressing, only to
be cheated. Robert's first partner was a man called Peacock, but there is
some confusion over his first name.[14] Early accounts add that he was a
kinsman – even a half-brother – of Agnes Brown, the poet's mother,[15] and
nearer relations than that have cheated one another. Inevitably, someone
as straight as Robert would find 'a scoundrel of the first water' hard to
tolerate, so a split was not surprising, but when did it take place? Before
or after Hogmanay 1781? If Burns and Peacock had parted company
before that date, who then was the partner with 'the drunken careless
wife'? John Strawhorn recounts the tradition that Robert had broken with
'Alexander and Sarah Peacock' before the fire.

Alexander Peacock had a house in the Glasgow Vennel opposite Bog Ha'
(Temple Dean, which belonged to a maltster named Joseph Francis). In the
yard of Peacock's house stood the heckling-shop. One room was the
heckling-shed as such, while the other was a stable and store, in the loft of
which Robert made his bed. After a time, however, he obtained better
lodgings, renting a small room in a tenement farther down the Vennel for
a shilling a week. The Glasgow Vennel was restored by Cunninghame District Council and the heckling-shop now forms part of a museum devoted
to Burns and the flax industry. Peacock's house was demolished before
1826 and the site redeveloped; this building now forms the front portion
of the museum. House number four in the Vennel was traditionally
regarded as the place where Robert lodged. This was a two-storey building
with a stair on either side of the lobby. The right-hand stair led to an attic
at the back of the house, reputedly the room in which Robert resided. This

house was partly damaged by fire on 13 September 1925 but the walls and mantelpiece, being made of stone, survived the blaze. Miraculously, so also did the wooden lintel of the mantelpiece on which someone had crudely carved the inscription 'R.B. 1782'. The house was later rebuilt, but the mantelpiece and its inscription were preserved.[16] After the quarrel with Peacock, Robert continued to live in the Glasgow Vennel but entered into partnership with someone else in Montgomery Boyd's Close and was there burned out. For many years the location of this second building rested on the testimony of various old inhabitants such as Robin Cummell and John Boyd, a retired weaver of Eglinton Street who recalled, as a young man, throwing snowballs into the fire. This anecdote was confirmed by Adam Fairie, a nonagenarian native of Irvine who made the journey from Montreal to attend the Burns Centenary Dinner at Irvine in 1859. He was about ten or eleven at the time of the fire and averred that the heckling-shop was in a close a few doors up the High Street from the King's Arms Hotel where the dinner was being held. The heckling-shop later became a bakehouse and one nineteenth-century tenant could recall an old door on which ROBERT BURNS had been crudely cut with a penknife. It is only fair to point out that many spurious relics of the poet were embellished with his name or initials, so the presence of such features tends to rouse our suspicions. The notion of two heckling-shops and two partners, however, is at variance with the admittedly scanty facts given by the poet. Proof that Robert *did* work in Montgomery Boyd's Close, however, was provided by the burgh cess books which record that 'Robert Burns, flaxdresser' paid seven shillings cess for the term (i.e. the period ending 31 March 1782).[17] This entry is also of interest in helping to pinpoint the actual time Robert spent at Irvine, although he may well have departed before the term was up.

Nor is the persistent local tradition that Robert himself started the fire, by accidentally knocking over a candle, in keeping with the reference to the drunken carelessness of the partner's wife. It is worth mentioning, perhaps, that dressed flax fibre is extremely flammable. Huge quantities of very dry dust are released and float around the workshop, so that the slightest spark could easily ignite it. Early flax mills were notorious fire hazards and, as a result, became pioneers in fireproof construction, using stone and iron instead of wood wherever possible. It should also be noted that Dean Castle in Kilmarnock was gutted by fire in 1735 when a serving-maid accidentally ignited a quantity of lint which she was spinning.

Robert's autobiography covering this period is tantalisingly vague, lacking hard detail and tending to dart around, so that the chronology is difficult to follow. The impression one is left with is that, on account of the uncongenial nature of the work and the chicanery of his partner or partners, this was an episode which he had done his best to forget:

> I was obliged to give up the business; the clouds of misfortune were gathering thick round my father's head, the darkest of which was, he was visibly far gone in a consumption; and to crown all, a belle-fille whom I adored and who had pledged her soul to meet me in the field of

matrimony, jilted me with peculiar circumstances of mortification. – The finishing evil that brought up the rear of this infernal file was my hypochondriac complaint being irritated to such a degree, that for three months I was in diseased state of body and mind, scarcely to be envied by the hopeless wretches who have just got their mittimus, 'Depart from me, ye Cursed.'[18]

Two of the reasons cited in this paragraph for Robert giving up the flax-dressing business are a trifle specious. The rejection by Eliza Gebbie, as we have already seen, took place before Robert went to Irvine, while the wretched affair of the dispute with the landlord McClure did not blow up until 17 May 1783. On the other hand, Eliza's rejection would have continued to prey on Robert's mind and one can imagine only too well the poor fellow dwelling on those 'peculiar circumstances of mortification', whatever they may have been. Similarly, although David McClure did not commence legal action till May 1783, this was only initiated after repeated attempts to get Burnes to pay his rent arrears which, by that date, amounted to no less than £500. At the rate of £130 per annum, it appears that William had paid little, if any, rent since 1779 or 1780 (if, as we assume, a capital loan at the commencement of the lease were also involved). But the illness which gravely affected Robert for three months should not be under-estimated. It is important to distinguish between the present-day meaning of hypochondria (a morbid preoccupation with one's health) and the sense in which Robert used the word – a physical ailment brought about by his depressed mental state. Here again, people nowadays use the term 'depression' when they really mean low spirits; but in Robert's case the depression was very real, in the full clinical sense. There was a smallpox epidemic in Irvine in 1781, and though the number of victims who succumbed is not listed, this was a year in which deaths (137) exceeded live births (112).[19] This gave rise to speculation that Burns's hypochondria was a mental state brought on by a physical condition,[20] although it was actually the other way round. Robert, in other words, suffered for much of the time in Irvine from what is now termed a psychosomatic ailment. That this was brought on by acute depression did not in any way lessen the severity of the physical aspects of the illness which were compounded by the ravages of overwork and an unhealthy atmosphere. Robert, in fact, suffered a nervous breakdown at Irvine, the first but, unhappily, by no means the last which periodically cast a deep shadow on his life.

This period of 'violent anguish' beset Robert in the last three months of 1781. He was well enough on 1 October, the evening on which, momentarily back at Tarbolton, he was passed and raised at a meeting of his masonic lodge.[21] But his health deteriorated so sharply at the end of that month or early in November that William Burnes himself was impelled to make a trip to Irvine to visit his sick son. In 1955 the day-book of Dr Charles Fleeming was discovered in the attic of his former house at 49 Kirkgate and this is now in the care of the Irvine Burns Club. It covers the period from 1757 to 1798, and under November 1781 it contains a number of very interesting entries concerning 'Robert Burns, lint-dresser'.[22] In the first place, for Robert to have called in a doctor at all is evidence of the seriousness of his illness. Fleeming visited his patient five times in the space of eight days. On the first occasion (14 November) he prescribed ipecacuanha (the powdered root of a South American plant which was then widely used as an emetic) and 'sacred elixir', a powerful laxative composed of powdered rhubarb and aloes. Robert was given this elixir in powdered form which he would then have had to dissolve in fortified wine, such as port or madeira. Thus Fleeming's answer to severe depression was a good vomiting and purging. Having in this way rather crudely cleansed the patient of the black bile (the literal meaning of melancholy) Fleeming visited Burns again on 19 November. On this occasion he prescribed 'an anodyne', probably some form of opium which was employed as a painkiller or astringent. He returned on 20, 21 and 22 November, to prescribe massive doses of powdered cinchona (the dried bark of a South American tree which contained quinine in its raw form). This was the standard treatment for a high fever, such as occurred in smallpox.

Two people, Marion Hunter and Gilbert Baird, asserted years later that Burns was pock-marked, but such scarring may have been merely acneous.[23] Had Robert contracted smallpox he would surely have mentioned this in his autobiographical letter to Moore. It should be noted also that smallpox was very much a townsman's disease which bred in the fetid atmosphere of the overcrowded slums. Country-people, on the other hand, rarely caught the disease in its virulent form, partly because they were not living in confined spaces, but mainly because most folk caught the cowpox instead. This was a very mild form of the disease which did not disfigure the victim and actually provided immunity to smallpox. Although Edward Jenner gets the credit for discovering the principles of vaccination – coincidentally, he was working on the rationale of this practice in 1781 – he did not put his theories to the test until 1796. Long before that date, however, the belief that cowpox and smallpox were mutually antagonistic was widely held in rural districts, and Robert himself was an enthusiastic advocate of some primitive form of inoculation.[24] It seems reasonably safe to conclude that, whatever caused Robert's high fever, it was not smallpox.

Similarly malaria, a disease often associated with seaports in that period, may be ruled out because of its recurrent character – and Robert never mentioned such attacks in later life. The other disease which was more or less endemic in seaports at that time was typhoid. To be sure, the symptoms of this are lassitude, headaches and discomfort, together with sleeplessness and feverishness, particularly at night. The peculiar course of the temperature is one of the most important diagnostic evidences of this fever, attaining its peak about the eighth day – which certainly does not tie in with Fleeming's visits from 20 to 23 November. In a favourable case, a gradual return to normal begins to take place during the fourth week from onset, but convalescence progresses slowly. As Fleeming did not visit his patient after 23 November it must be assumed that Robert showed a marked improvement by the time of the last consultation – well before the usual signs of recovery in even mild typhoid cases. Of course, this is only speculation, and it is unfortunate that Fleeming nowhere specifies the actual illness he is treating, but from the details of the other patients whom he treated in the same period, an outbreak of what Burns himself later, in another context, was to describe as 'a malignant fever', typhoid in one of its milder forms can be ruled out entirely. Nevertheless, whatever Robert suffered from, severe morbid depression was undoubtedly a major constituent.

Robert was still getting over the attack on 27 December when he wrote to his father the only extant letter that ever passed between them (CL 41–2). Addressing him as 'Honored Sir', he began:

> I have purposely delayed writing in the hope that I would have the pleasure of seeing you on Newyearday but work comes so hard upon us that I do not chuse to come as well for that, as also for some other little reasons which I shall tell you at meeting.– My health is much about what it was when you were here only my sleep is rather sounder and on the whole I am rather better than otherwise tho it is but by very slow degrees.– The weakness of my nerves has so debilitated my mind that I dare not, either review past events, or look forward into futurity; for the least anxiety, or perturbation in my breast, produces most unhappy effects on my whole frame.

Despite his illness, Robert was struggling manfully to continue with the flax-dressing which, by this time, he must have come to loathe heartily. One wonders what were those 'other little reasons' which he did not wish to commit to paper; the suspicion that his partner was cheating him, perhaps? The last few lines of this paragraph, however, succinctly convey Robert's nervous state at this time. It has been conjectured[27] that William Burnes made a detour to Irvine in mid-November, on his way to or from Ayr where he had been settling the sale of the Alloway cottage which was purchased by the Incorporation of Shoemakers at Martinmas that year for £160. In view of William's growing financial problems at that time, it seems natural that he should make a point of giving Robert this piece of good news in person.

The rest of Robert's letter to his father shows him in a very morbid state, calmly – fatalistically almost – contemplating death. This was a time when his Calvinistic upbringing came to the fore; religion was now his only comfort:

> . . . my principal, and indeed my only pleasurable employment is looking backwards & forwards in a moral & religious way – I am quite transported at the thought that ere long, perhaps very soon, I shall bid an eternal adieu to all the pains, & uneasiness & desquietudes of this weary life; for I assure you I am heartily tired of it, and, if I do not very much deceive myself I could contentedly & gladly resign it.

He then goes on to quote lines from Pope's *Essay on Man*: 'The Soul uneasy & confin'd from home, / Rests & expatiates in a life to come', and dwells on the last three verses in the seventh chapter of *Revelation* (a promise of a much better life in the hereafter): 'I am more pleased with [these] verses than any ten times as many verses in the whole Bible, & would not exchange the noble enthusiasm with which they inspire me, for all that this world has to offer.' There is more in a similar vein, but even after making allowances for the fact that Robert was writing to a deeply religious father, it is obvious that the sentiments were real enough. Robert spoiled the spiritual effect, however, with a materialist postscript: 'my meal is nearly out but I am going to borrow till I get more'!

Bearing in mind that this depressing letter was penned only days before the calamitous fire that left Robert penniless, it is a wonder that he did not pack his bags and head for home immediately. Yet, according to Isobel Burns, he did not return to Lochlie till the beginning of the following March. In his cheerless garret and languishing under the darkest melancholy, Robert turned to his muse for consolation. The acknowledged output of the Irvine period, in poetry as well as prose, is very meagre. The exact date of composition of the few Irvine pieces is unknown, but it is clear that they belong to the period when Robert was at his nadir. One of these was 'Winter, a Dirge' (CW 50-1) which he annotated in the Glenriddell MSS as having been composed 'just after a tract of misfortunes'. This mournful song of resignation to the will of the Supreme Power aptly fits the poet's mood at this time. Though it appeared on page 166 of the Kilmarnock volume it was 'the eldest of my printed pieces' as he told Moore. To this period also belong the verses 'To Ruin' (CW 53) which reflect Robert's sombre mood in every syllable. 'A Prayer in the Prospect of Death' (CW 53-4) and 'Stanzas, on the Same Occasion' (CW 54-5) were followed by the very poignant 'Prayer under the Pressure of Violent Anguish' (CW 55) which Robert annotated in his first *Commonplace Book* (March 1784):

> There was a certain period of my life that my spirit was broke by repeated losses and disasters, which threatened, and indeed effected the utter ruin of my fortune. My body too was attacked by that most dreadful distemper, a Hypochondria, or confirmed Melancholy: in this wretched state, the recollection of which makes me yet shudder, I hung my harp on the Willow tree, except in some lucid intervals, in which I composed the following.

'Fickle Fortune' (CW 56) – 'An extempore under the pressure of a heavy train of Misfortunes' – and 'Raging Fortune' (CW 56) also belong to the winter of 1781-2, followed by the 'pick yourself up, dust yourself down, start all over again' defiance of 'I'll Go and be a Sodger' (CW 56-7). One imagines Robert penning these defiant lines around the time of his twenty-third birthday:

O, why the deuce should I repine,
  And be an ill foreboder?
I'm twenty-three, and five feet nine,
  I'll go and be a sodger!

I gat some gear wi meikle care,
  I held it weel thegither;
But now it's gane – and something mair:
  I'll go and be a sodger!

More in keeping with his sombre mood of religiosity, however, are the two paraphrases, of the first and ninetieth psalms (CW 57–8). He felt that in the lines of these psalms there was much that was relevant to his condition, and he derived immense comfort from them. These exercises in versification were for him the natural outcome. Another composition which dates from the early months of 1782 shows Robert more his old self. The song with autobiographical undertones, 'My Father was a Farmer' (CW 58–9), written to the tune of 'The Weaver and his Shuttle, O', shows how Robert 'courted Fortune's favour' but 'Some cause unseen still stept between, to frustrate each endeavour'. 'Then sore harass'd, and tir'd at last, with Fortune's vain delusion' he dropped his schemes, 'like idle dreams' and came to the conclusion that 'the past was bad, and the future hid, its good or ill untried', so henceforth he would live for the moment, taking each day as it came. The rest of this rollicking song is in similar philosophic vein, and Robert concluded that he would prefer to be 'a cheerful honest-hearted clown' than powerful and wealthy.

It must not be supposed that the months in Irvine were without their lighter, happier moments. Not far along the High Street from his lodgings, and hard by the Old Tolbooth, stood the bookshop of William Templeton. This narrow four-storey building was still standing in the early years of this century, when it was an ice-cream salon, but it was swept away in the inner-city redevelopment of more recent times and its site is now occupied by the Co-operative supermarket on the east side of the street, south of the Cross. Part of Templeton's stock in trade consisted of popular ballads, which appeared in the form of long strips, rather like newspaper columns. Templeton had several vivid memories of Robert, a frequent visitor to the shop in quest of the latest ballads. If there was anything new in that line he would seat himself on the counter, read them over and, coming on something that satisfied his taste, would read it aloud.[26] Templeton later subscribed to the Kilmarnock Poems and also served as the poet's local agent, collecting all the subscriptions due in Irvine and forwarding them to Robert.

There is a local tradition that Robert, in the first flush of his enthusiasm for freemasonry, would have frequently attended meetings of Lodge St Andrew, which were held in the Wheat Sheaf Inn in the High Street, but there is no actual record of this in the lodge's minutes. It is more likely that Robert's attendances at masonic meetings were confined to Kilwinning Lodge Navigation Irvine (sometimes known as the Harbour lodge), which later transferred to Troon.[27]

Similarly there is some doubt concerning Robert's church attendance, but this is due to lack of records for the relevant period. The Revd. James Richmond, then parish minister, believed that Robert took the sacrament of Communion at Irvine for the first time, but there is a gap in the Communicants' Roll covering the years 1781-2, and his name does not figure anywhere in the records of the Kirk Session. It may be supposed, however, that what Richmond claimed was true enough, and certainly Robert would have attended the parish church fairly regularly. The church in which he 'sat under' Richmond was relatively new, having been built in 1774. Beautifully situated on rising ground to the south of the town, it is now very much a focal point of the old town, and its magnificent steeple is one of the principal landmarks.

Irvine's ancient festival of Marymas took place that year in the week beginning Monday, 20 August. Robert would undoubtedly have witnessed these festivities and participated in them; yet he has left us no record of them and the droll goings-on never inspired one of his shrewd poetic observations of human behaviour.

With a population of 4,391 in 1781, Irvine was the largest town in Ayrshire at that period. Richmond commented that 'Perhaps in no sea-port town of the same extent are the inhabitants more sober and industrious than in this. They are social and chearful, but seldom riotous . . . The people, in general, are in easy circumstances; many of them are wealthy, and all of them remarkably hospitable. They are happy in each other's society, and entertain frequently and well.'[28] One can well imagine the impact of this lively, jolly, kindly place on the young farmer. Irvine was a go-ahead town where the latest ideas, in fashion and religion, found a ready acceptance. Ayrshire was still a bastion of the old-style Calvinism, with its dour beliefs in predestination and God's elect; but new ideas were in the air and the heresies of Arminianism and Socinianism were rife. Robert, by upbringing and inclination, was a liberal in religious matters but we have seen how he was always ready to adopt any side in a debate, purely for the sake of argument, and at Irvine it is recorded that one elderly person (in the 1820s) could remember that, during the latter part of the poet's stay in Irvine, he and his companion were in the habit of spending Sunday evenings together. 'Religion was often the subject of their conversation, in the discussion of which the poet commonly ranged himself on the side of Calvin; but from this station his companion took the credit of withdrawing him, saying with some complacency that Burns was indebted to him for a more liberal way of thinking.'[29] I suspect that Robert was merely adopting a stance in order to make the debate more lively; and therefore the notion of a conversion to New Licht principles at Irvine can be discounted.

More importantly, as Robert confessed to Moore:

From this adventure I learned something of a town-life. – But the principal thing which gave my mind a turn was, I formed a bosom-friendship with a young fellow, the first created being I had ever seen but a hapless son of misfortune.– He was the son of a plain mechanic; but a great Man in the neighbourhood taking him under his patronage gave him a genteel education with a view to bettering his situation in life.– The Patron dieing just as he was ready to launch forth into the world, the poor fellow in despair went to sea; where after a variety of good and bad fortune, a little before I was acquainted with him, he had been set ashore by an American Privateer on the wild coast of Connaught, stript of every thing.– I cannot quit this poor fellow's story without adding that he is at this moment Captain of a large westindian man belonging to the Thames.

Captain Richard Brown was six years older than Robert. The son of William Brown and Jean Whamie, he was born on 2 June 1753.[30] If young Willie Niven, the Maybole shopkeeper's son, had seemed worldly wise at Kirkoswald, Richard Brown the seafarer must have been the very epitome of sophistication. The circumstances in which Burns and Brown met are not recorded and there seems to be no truth in the speculation that Brown may have been a distant relative (through the poet's Brown connections on his mother's side). Robert often alluded, in letters to Brown, to the fact that they had been companions in misfortune. Brown's career was at a low ebb, thanks to the attack by a privateer in the closing stages of the American War of Independence, and from the circumstances of Robert's being similarly unfortunate I would hazard a guess that they met in January 1782. What is certainly true, however, is that Richard Brown exerted a greater and more profound influence on Robert than any man, other than his father of course, and possibly John Murdoch. As Robert related to Moore:

> This gentleman's mind was fraught with courage, independance, Magnanimity, and every noble, manly virtue.– I loved him, I admired him, to a degree of enthusiasm; and I strove to imitate him.– In some measure I succeeded: I had the pride before, but he taught it to flow in proper channels.– His knowledge of the world was vastly superiour to mine, and I was all attention to learn.– He was the only man I ever saw who was a greater fool than myself when WOMAN was the presiding star; but he spoke of a certain fashionable failing with levity, which hitherto I had regarded with horror.– Here his friendship did me a mischief . . .

The too fastidious Dr Currie replaced the words 'a certain fashionable failing' with 'illicit love'.[31] What, one wonders, lay behind this intriguing piece of editorial licence? This question was never posed until recently; until the more liberated atmosphere of the 1960s, perhaps, it would have been unthinkable. Robert's sexuality was never in any doubt, surely? A man who was so irresistibly drawn to the opposite sex (even when their charms were not so obvious), who had had so many affairs, and fathered at least thirteen children, must have been wholeheartedly heterosexual. And yet some doubt has been raised by at least one writer whose penetrating analysis of so many aspects of Robert's life is matched only by the formidable array of his expertise in many different scientific disciplines. Richard

Fowler feels that 'the first part of Burns's assertion implied that Brown was somewhat *gauche* in his approach to heterosexual intercourse'[32] and taking this in conjunction with the rest of that sentence quoted above he infers 'a familiar approach to the alternative activity'. He points out that sodomy was still a capital offence in the late eighteenth century, hence Currie's justification in eliminating it.

If the admission of sodomy by a man who was now dead could have so upset Dr Currie what, we must ask ourselves, would have been the effect of the self-same admission to Dr Moore, or Mrs Dunlop who was privileged to have a preview of the autobiographical letter? Looking at the sentence again, my interpretation of 'a greater fool than myself when WOMAN was the presiding star' is that Richard Brown was even more 'girl-daft' than Burns himself. Robert candidly admitted that he suffered from 'amorous madness', falling in and out of love very readily. Brown was an even greater Lothario, according to Robert. In that context the second part of the sentence, about 'a certain fashionable failing', probably referred to whoring which was commonplace, then as now, though Robert had arguably never encountered the ladies of the street before he came to Irvine. On the other hand, Brown the sailor would no doubt have been familiar with brothels in every port he visited and one assumes that he recounted some of his experiences in the stews and bordellos in a light-hearted manner. One can easily imagine the horror with which Robert reacted to Richard's stories. Ever afterwards he felt instant revulsion whenever the subject was raised. In May 1789, for example, he wrote to his younger brother William who was then trying to get work in Newcastle (CL 516). His closing words of advice were, 'I need not caution you against guilty amours – they are bad and ruinous everywhere, but in England they are the very devil'. To William in London, Robert wrote in February 1790 (CL 518):

> Another caution; I give you great credit for your sobriety with respect to that universal vice, Bad Women.– It is an impulse the hardest to be restrained, but if once a man accustoms himself to gratifications of that impulse, it is then nearly or altogether impossible to restrain it.– Whoring is a most ruinous expensive species of dissipation; is spending a poor fellow's money with what he ought clothe & support himself nothing? Whoring has ninety nine chances in a hundred to bring on a man the most nauseous & excruciating diseases to which Human nature is liable; are disease & an impaired constitution trifling considerations? All this is independant of the, criminality of it.

To my way of thinking 'illicit love' was only Currie's way of beating about the same bush. It is unfortunate that neither Burns to Moore, nor Currie when contemplating publication, could call a spade a spade and thus leave posterity in no doubt.

Another writer, Alan Dent, devotes an entire chapter to Robert's supposed homosexual leanings, fleshing out the innuendo of those Sunday afternoon walks together in Eglinton Woods:

We shall probably never know by exactly how much Brown broadened Burns's outlook on that unforgotten day long ago in Eglinton Woods. Or whether the two young men compared notes, or gathered conkers, or brambles, or bluebells, according to the season of the year. Or just read Burns's verses aloud to one another till the sun went down. One might call it, without speculating too far, an afternoon of two fauns instead of one, and leave it at that.[33]

Dent backs up this ludicrous picture of two Wildean aesthetes in the woods by quoting from letters of Robert to Brown, especially the last letter of 4 November 1789 (CL 422), 'When you & I first met, we were at a green period of human life when the twig would easily take a bent – but would as easily return to its former state' and ends with a cheap jibe at the naïvety of local Burnsians who erected a plaque in Eglinton Woods, inscribed 'Favourite Walk, 1781–82, of Robert Burns and his sailor friend, Richard Brown'. As if this were not enough he hints at a homosexual relationship between Burns and John Richmond when they slept together at Mrs Carfrae's in Edinburgh. This insinuation is discussed in a later chapter. That Robert was a warm-hearted, passionate man cannot be gainsaid, and his friendships with other men were on the same ardent level as his amours with the ladies. Friendship of such intensity, unfortunately, seldom lasts the course; but we cannot read anything into these relationships.

Richard Brown married Eleonora Blair at Irvine on 30 May 1785[34] and early in January 1788 moved to Port Glasgow which remained his home until his death in 1833. Seven letters from Burns to Brown are extant (CL 418–23) covering the period from 30 December 1787 till 4 November 1789. Ironically, the very last of these letters contains the pathetic passage: 'You are the earliest Friend I now have on earth, my brother excepted, & is not that an endearing circumstance?' In view of the professions of friendship which earlier passed between them, the silence of the last seven years of the poet's life is deafening. Richard Brown was one of the very few recipients of a presentation copy of the Kilmarnock Poems, but years later the volume was discovered quite by accident, stuffed down the back of a drawer in a sideboard, when this piece of furniture was purchased at a sale of the late captain's effects. Brown attained eminence and respectability in his adopted town and in later life played down his connection with the poet. The story goes that he became estranged from Burns when he discovered that the poet had been telling people that Brown had initiated him into the arts of seduction. 'Richard Brown never quite forgave Burns for representing him in the Moore letter as a person of loose morals,' wrote Charles Brodie,[35] blithely ignoring the fact that the letter was not made public till 1800 – four years after Burns's death. This also makes a nonsense of the 'traditional' claim that the breach between Burns and Brown arose out of the same subject. 'To one of his own ship captains Richard Brown related the circumstances of the final quarrel. This captain in turn related the story to a friend of the writer's,' wrote Brodie. 'It would be

profitless to repeat it, but Brown and Burns never saw each other again.'
Brown was certainly incensed when Currie's version of the revealing comments in the autobiographical letter were published in 1800, although
there was nothing to link Brown specifically with them; but at that time,
less than twenty years after the event, there would have been plenty of
people in Irvine who would readily recognise Richard Brown as the person
mentioned. He was asked for his view on this reference which implied that
he had introduced Burns to illicit love. 'Illicit love! Levity of a sailor!
When I first knew Burns he had nothing to learn in that respect,' he is
reported to have said.[36] One is therefore left wondering whether the
friendship withered for some other reason; but what, it would be impossible to guess.

Brown deserves to be remembered rather as the person who first gave
Robert the idea of getting his poetry published. Writing to Brown at Irvine
from Edinburgh on 30 December 1787 Robert acknowledged his indebtedness to his friend:

> for steeling my mind against evils of which I have had a pretty decent
> share.- My will o' wisp fate, you know: do you recollect a Sunday we
> spent in Eglinton woods? you told me, on my repeating some verses to
> you that you wondered I could resist the temptation of sending verses of
> such merit to a magazine: 'twas actually this that gave me an idea of my
> own pieces which encouraged me to endeavour at the character of a Poet.

Attractive as this notion was, however, Robert never actually did anything
to implement it until economic necessity forced publication upon him four
years later. It is strange, nevertheless, that Robert never submitted any of
his poems to the newspapers and literary periodicals of the time. It was on
the anniversary of the poet's birth and its own centenary, in 1927, that
Irvine Burns Club erected the aforementioned memorial at St Bryde's Well
(the Drukken Steps) in Eglinton Woods to commemorate the occasion
which led indirectly to the publication of Robert's poems four and a half
years later.

David Sillar did not move to Irvine till 1783, over a year after Robert
had left. Joseph Train argued that, in the 'First Epistle to Davie' (CW 88),
'my darling Jean' referred not to Jean Armour (who came later) but Jean
Gardner, the daughter of James Gardner, a butcher in Irvine.[37] Robert's
hint at 'a certain fashionable failing' probably implied that Brown had
encouraged him to succumb to temptation – as if Robert needed any
encouragement or guidance in such matters. Jean Gardner is the only
woman whose name was linked to the poet in this period, but this belongs
in the realm of oral tradition, and there is nothing in Robert's letters or
poems to connect him with this girl. It seems exceedingly doubtful that
Robert was romantically involved with this woman, if for no other reason
than that she was thirteen years his senior.[38] The Gardner family had
a lodger, the Revd. Hugh Whyte or White, the minister of the Relief
Congregation (which had seceded from the established church). A few

months after Robert left Irvine, Whyte preached a sermon at Glasgow which so attracted one of the congregation that she followed him back to Irvine. This was Elspat Buchan (1738–91) who 'began spreading some fanatical notions of religion' (as Robert himself put it in a letter to his cousin James Burness a few years later). Whyte supported 'Luckie' Buchan (who claimed to confer immortality on her flock merely by breathing upon them), and was suspended by the Relief Presbytery as a result. The Buchanites now seceded from the Relief Church, but a mob rose up and drove them out of Irvine in May 1784. According to Andrew Innes, a fellow Buchanite, Robert discovered that his quondam 'darling Jean' had gone with the followers of Mother Buchan and he went post-haste to the barn at New Cample (facetiously known to the local inhabitants as Buchan Ha') in Dumfriesshire to try to talk her out of it, but without success.[39] This, however, is an embroidering of the testimony of Innes given to Joseph Train:

> When I was sent back from Thornhill for Mr Hunter, Jean Gardner came back with me from Irvine to Closeburn, and when we were in the neighbourhood of Tarbolton she seemed to be in fear, and rather in a discomposed condition. When I enquired the cause, it was lest Burns the Poet should see her, for if he did he would be sure to interrupt her, for they had long been on terms of intimacy. But we proceeded on our journey without meeting with any obstruction.[40]

'Terms of intimacy', in its eighteenth-century context, meant no more than that Burns and Jean Gardner had known each other well, and Andrew Innes, interviewed by Train half a century after these events, was hardly likely to be the most objective or reliable of witnesses. Innes by that time was living the life of a recluse at Auchengibbert, guarding the remains of the prophetess which were laid out on the bed in the next room. Every night, through a hole in the wall, Andrew religiously spread a blanket over the remains to keep the saintly bones warm.

Of other friends and acquaintances of the Irvine period, little is recorded. Robin Cummell (Robert Campbell) was coeval with Burns and later claimed a close acquaintance.[41] He alleged that he frequently met with the poet in the Wheat Sheaf Inn, their companions being 'Richie Brown, the sailor, Keelivine the writer; and Tammie Struggles frae the Briggate'. No one of the name of Struggles appears in any of the Irvine parish records, so it must be assumed that this was a nickname, as, indeed, was Keelivine (lead pencil in Lallans) – an apt sobriquet for a lawyer's clerk. When the Irvine Burns Club was founded thirty years after the poet's death, five of the original members claimed personal friendship with Burns. The first names on the list were Dr John Mackenzie (of whom more later) and David Sillar;[42] the other three who had known Robert personally were James Orr, John Peebles (adjutant to Hugh Montgomerie) and Dr John Fletcher.[43]

CHAPTER 7

Lochlie: the Litigious Years, 1782–4

I once was by Fortune carest,
I once could relieve the distrest,
Now life's poor support, hardly earn'd,
    My fate will scarce bestow:
And it's O, fickle Fortune, O!

The Ruined Farmer (CW 68)

By the time the winter snows had thawed sufficiently for Robert to retrace his steps from Irvine to Lochlie at the end of February or beginning of March 1782 'the clouds of misfortune' were indeed gathering thick and fast round his father's head. There is no doubt that the soil at Lochlie was acidic, probably more than most at that time, for a programme of liming to counteract this was clearly a major part of the verbal agreement with David McClure. It is arguable how much improvement could have been wrought, given the basic geological and pedological conditions,[1] but from the outset McClure did not keep his side of the bargain. The documentary evidence was not made public till very long after the event, so that for well over a century this wretched business contained many elements that were perplexing and confusing and tended to show William Burnes in an uncharacteristically bad light. Neither Robert in his autobiographical letter to Moore, nor Gilbert in his narrative supplied to Currie via Mrs Dunlop, gave any details of this episode. Robert dismissed the events leading up to the sequestration in half a sentence in which he fancifully speaks of 'three years tossing and whirling in the vortex of Litigation', while Gilbert merely spoke of 'my father's affairs grew near a crisis'. The earliest account of this sorry affair was given by Dr John Mackenzie of Mauchline who said that he had attended William Burnes at Lochlie towards the end of his life and from him received 'a detail of the various causes that had gradually led to the embarrassment of his affairs; these he detailed in such earnest language, and in so simple, candid, and pathetic a manner as to excite both my astonishment and sympathy'.[2]

Mention has already been made of Alexander 'Saunders' Tait, the Tarbolton doggerel-monger. There is no denying that Tait's poetry was very poor stuff, but no better nor worse than the products of other parish and village rhymers of the period. His reputation has suffered, however, solely because he vented his spite against the Burnes family; but he deserves to be charitably remembered for the light he sheds (rightly or wrongly) on the dispute between Burnes and his landlord. Though originally an incomer himself, he had become sufficiently well established in the parish by 1777 to join in on one side of the 'us and them' assessment of the latest arrivals. It would have been well known that Burnes had had troubles with the factor of Dr Fergusson's estate and therefore the newcomers would be treated with caution. The country parish has always a large measure of caution in its reception of the stranger. The process of ticketing, docketing, weighing up the incomer is an endless pursuit and woe betide the stranger who does not wait for this assessment and launches forthwith into local affairs. One can almost imagine the attitudes of many parishioners: on the one hand, a family whose presence only arose from their financial difficulties elsewhere; on the other, here is an argumentative youth rapidly gaining a reputation for his quick wit and ready satire. Instead of keeping a low profile, he flouts convention in dress and hairstyle. He is hardly here five minutes before he is organising a young men's debating society. A country parish will inevitably look askance at this, and herein lies the key to Tait's scurrilous verses.[3]

No doubt Tait's nose was put out of joint by the appearance in the parish of another rhymer to challenge his position as the village bard. At some stage he was a victim of Robert's mordant wit and took his revenge in a poem entitled 'B–rns in his Infancy' which was published in his *Poems and Songs* at Paisley in 1790. The clue to Tait's animus is provided in the opening stanza which begins 'Now I maun trace his pedigree / Because he made a sang on me'. This was followed by a poem entitled 'B–rns in Lochly' which, in seven stanzas of Standard Habbie, provides a pithy commentary on the dispute between the Burnes family and their landlord. A few lines from this will suffice to give both the quality of the verse and the salient facts as Tait saw them:

> Man! I'm no speakin' out o' spite,
> Else Patie wad upo' me flyte,
> M'L–re ye scarcely left a mite
>   To fill his horn,
> You and the Lawyers gi'ed him a skyte,
>   Sold a' his corn.
>
> M'L–re he put you in a farm,
> And coft you coals your arse to warm,
> And meal and maut – Ye did get barm,
>   And then it wrought,
> For his destruction and his harm,
>   It is my thought.
>
> He likewise did the mailing stock,
> And built you barns, the doors did lock,
> His ain gun ye did at him cock,

> And never spar'd,
> Wi't owre his head came a clean knock,
> Maist kill'd the Laird.

> The horse, corn, pets, kail, kye and lures,
> Cheese, pease, beans, rye, wool, house and flours,
> Pots, pans, crans, tongs, brace-spits and skeurs,
> The milk and barm,
> Each thing they had was a' M'Lure's,
> He stock'd the farm.

'Patie' in the first stanza was the Revd. Patrick Wodrow. Elsewhere occurs the line 'Five hundred pounds they were behind', an obvious reference to the arrears accumulated by William Burnes. The silence of Robert on the matter in his otherwise frank and candid letter to Moore was taken as proof that the Burnes family were in the wrong. This was the view expressed by W. E. Henley[4] and others, and although it has since been refuted the notion lingers to this day that McClure was hard done by. The Henley-Henderson edition of 1896 was already in the press when the Centenary Exhibition was held in Glasgow. Among the exhibits on display were several documents bearing on the Lochlie sequestration, lent by a descendant of Gilbert Burns. These were first published (though inaccurately) in 1904 by David Lowe[5] and reprinted in the *Burns Chronicle* six years later.[6]

The first document consisted of the service copy of the Petition by David McClure, merchant in Ayr, against William Burns in Lochill (*sic*), part of the barony of Halfmark in the parish of Tarbolton, at the rent of £130 Sterling yearly by Set from the Petitioner, alleging that William Burns owed him upwards of £500, besides the current year's rent, wherefore warrant of sequestration was asked for and interim warrant granted on 17 May 1783, the date of the service. To this were appended Replies for David McClure to the Answers of William Burns. From McClure's petition it is known that the dispute between landlord and tenant regarding the rent due for Lochlie had been 'submitted to arbiters and then laid before Mr Hamilton of Sundrum as Oversman'; but Hamilton's award was not included in the bundle, so that only McClure's side of the dispute was available. By inference, however, it was clear that William Burnes denied that he was owing over £500 as McClure alleged.

In the meantime William Burnes had to suffer the trauma of having his goods and chattels pried over by the Sheriff's officer and his men, and the intense humiliation of hearing the Tarbolton town-crier going through the parish at tuck of drum warning everyone against buying any of the sequestrated property. Saunders Tait put it pithily in his poem, already quoted:

> He sent the drum Tarbolton through
> That no man was to buy frae you;
> At the Kirk door he cry'd it too;
> I heard the yell;
> The vera thing I write 'tis true,
> Ye'll ken yersel.

Hamilton's Decreet Arbitral, which all along had lain undisturbed in the Sheriff Court books of Ayrshire under date 18 August 1783, was not turned up by researchers until 1934 and was subsequently transcribed in full.[7] From the various documents it is therefore possible to piece together an accurate account of the dispute. David McClure of Shawwood came of a line of minor landowners and merchants who, earlier in the century, had prospered; but he was among those who had lost heavily in the crash of the ill-fated Douglas, Heron and Company Bank in 1772. Although he managed for some time to extricate himself from that débâcle, unlike many others who were bankrupted and ruined immediately, McClure was in no position to adopt an indulgent attitude towards his tenants, as the late Dr Fergusson of Doonholm had done. McClure's petition alleged that William 'having upon frivolous Pretences refused payment of the rent, his claims of Retention came at last to be submitted to arbiters and then laid before Mr Hamilton of Sundrum as oversman', but as there was no written 'Tacks or minute of bargain' between them William Burnes was preparing to quit the farm and sell his stock and crops 'to disappoint the petitioner of his fund of payment'.

To pre-empt Burnes, therefore, McClure had applied for the warrant of sequestration, and this was duly served on 17 May by the Sheriff's officer, James Gordon, who promptly made an inventory of the farm in the presence of Robert Doak (McClure's servant) and John Lees, a Tarbolton shoemaker. The pathetic list of William's worldly goods was summarised in Chapter 5. In the Replies to the Answers submitted by William Burnes, McClure denied that there was any missive of agreement as Burnes apparently was alleging. He went on to state, however, that Burnes had some time previously made out an account in his own handwriting, 'which he called an account of Charge and Discharge betwixt him and the petitioner'. McClure conceded that Burnes had ploughed and sown part of the land, 'but whither so much as ought to have been done he cannot say'. He queried William's account regarding the number of cattle he was raising, and accused him of surreptitiously selling off part of his stock. In particular, McClure contested William's claim to have paid up all arrears of rent to Martinmas last (i.e. November 1782), as 'a mere allegation without the smallest foundation'.

From this we glean that McClure claimed £500 of back rent, whereas Burnes denied the charge and asked that the warrant of sequestration be recalled. It was speculated that Robert held the pen for his ailing father in framing his Replies, 'perhaps with the help of his legal friends in Ayr'.[8]

The Decreet Arbitral gives the oversman's award first, followed by the text of the Submission and the minutes of the arbiters. In the interests of clarity, the following summary of the affair deals with the Submission first. The arbiters were named as James Grieve in Boghead and Charles Norval, gardener at Coilsfield, 'mutually elected and chosen by the said parties' to the dispute. Grieve was a friend of McClure, while Burnes was probably drawn to Norval by virtue of shared interests in gardening. The text of this legal document was written by William Chalmer, a lawyer in Ayr, and dated there on 24 September 1782. It was signed by McClure and Burnes in the presence of Chalmer and John Simson.

The minutes of the arbiters were written by William Humphrey at Tarbolton on various dates from 7 October 1782 onwards (the clerk being brother of James Humphrey, of whom more anon). The first meeting was brief, and was adjourned because it was 'the throng of Hervist' (the busiest part of harvest-time). When they met again on 19 November they decided that proof would be required of statements made by both parties, and promptly adjourned till 4 December when the depositions of sundry witnesses were considered. A date of 18 December was fixed for both parties to lodge their claims. In due course this was followed by a meeting on 26 December at which petitioner and respondent were to give in their answers to each other's claims. The matter dragged on until 9 April 1783 when the arbiters concluded that they were unable to agree, and therefore referred the matter to the umpire or oversman, John Hamilton.

Over the ensuing months Hamilton studied the dispute and gave his decree on 18 August in the presence of William Wallace (the county sheriff) and James Neill and Robert Miller, solicitors in Ayr, who appeared for McClure and Burnes. Hamilton found that, sometime in 1776, bargains involving a thirty-eight-year lease had been struck on two separate occasions 'in the presence of Dr John Campbell of Air (sic)'. Under the first agreement Burnes was to take possession at Martinmas 1777 and the rental was to be fifteen shillings an acre for the first eight years and twenty shillings for the remaining thirty years. Under a second agreement, however, Burnes was to enter at Martinmas 1776 and pay twenty shillings per acre from the outset. The farm was to be enclosed, sub-divided and limed by McClure at the rate of 100 bolls of lime per acre, 'and also the said William Burnes was to be allowed 12 tons of limestone at Cairnhill lime quarry for each acre of said farm as a second dressing, and one shilling per ton for coals to burn the same'. Such precise terms reveal Burnes as a canny negotiator, but the fact that he never had anything in writing tells against him. Moreover, the actual rental of £130 was almost three times what had been expected at Mount Oliphant, and Burnes must have been exceedingly rash (or recklessly desperate) to take on such a commitment. Fowler speculates that McClure evaded a written lease 'because he felt, or knew, that his title to the land was far from clear',[9] and, indeed, there is circumstantial evidence in support of this interesting theory, discussed later.

Hamilton's decree mentions a verbal agreement between Burnes and McClure whereby William undertook to pay rent on 'the miln damb' – presumably the lochan which gave the farm its name – as and when McClure got around to draining this portion of the land. Furthermore, for agreeing to the higher rental set out in the second bargain, William was 'to receive a compensation' although what precisely this meant was not specified. David Scott, accountant to the banking-house of Hunter and Company, (which was in the course of salvaging the wreckage from the Douglas, Heron fiasco), determined that the amount which Burnes was entitled to hold back in respect of 'the advance rent' was £210 1s 6d. In addition to this sum, Hamilton found that, because McClure had not kept his end of the agreement regarding the liming of the ground, Burnes was entitled to an allowance for the work which he had himself undertaken in this regard. 'I allow the said William Burns to retain out of the rents of said farm the sum of £86 13s 4d Sterl. as the value of 2600 bolls of lime at eight pence per boll for liming said 26 acres' but as William had limed these acres out of 726 tons of limestone delivered to him, and coals at a shilling a ton, 'being part of what has been furnished by the said David McClure for the second dressing', Hamilton decreed that William would have to lay on a further 2,600 bolls of lime at his own expense by Lammas 1784 and produce vouchers to support this. William was also entitled to £18 10s in respect of some dykes which he had made. House-building and grass-sowing of ten acres undertaken by Burnes entitled him to a further rebate of £80 18s 6d. No rent was chargeable for the mill dam, as it had not yet been drained. As a result, the colossal sum of £775 (five and a half years' back rent) which McClure had been claiming was reduced by the amount actually paid out by Burnes on improvements, together with the aforementioned sums. The net result, therefore, was that Burnes was deemed to be owing no more than £231 2s 8d, which William was ordered to pay 'together with the interest thereof from the said term of Whitsunday 1782 and in time coming untill payment'. An account of the sum awarded to McClure, less the credit allowed to Burnes, was appended to the decree showing how the due amount was reached.

The sum of £231 was a vast improvement over the £775 originally claimed and William was anxious to settle the matter. But now another action was raised, over which Burnes had no control but in which he was implicated. It transpired that David McClure was in financial difficulties and had mortgaged his estates to John McAdam of Craigengillan.[10] The rents due on these estates amounted to £8,000 and in pursuing this sum McAdam brought legal action against all the debtor tenants, including William Burnes. Within nine days of Hamilton's decree, Burnes took the case to the Court of Session and applied for a suspension of the charge, but his appeal was rejected on a technicality. From the text of William's petition for suspension it appears that he continued to nurse a grievance against his landlord who had acted 'under the pain of poinding &c. most wrongously and unjustly'.[11] Because of McAdam's intervention, however, Burnes felt that he could not pay the sum he still owed, without McAdam's consent, 'And therefore the foresaid Charge ought to be Simpliciter Suspended'. John Swinton, clerk of the court, added that the Lord Ordinary had considered this petition but it was refused because 'In respect the complainer has not specially stated before what Court he is sued at Craigengillan's instance nor has produced any evidence of such action, nor has raised any multiplepoinding'.

McAdam was not McClure's only creditor who tried to get hold of the sum awarded in Hamilton's decreet, and once more William Burnes was obliged to take the matter to the Court of Session. On this occasion an action of Multiplepoinding (a suit brought by the holder of money, goods and chattels claimed by different parties) was raised at the instance of William Burns, Tenant in Lochlie, against John McCulloch, Merchant in Ayr, David Ewen, Merchant there, Jas. Hume, Writer there, Douglas, Heron & Co., late Bankers there, and George Home of Branxton, their factor and manager, John Campbell of Wellwood, David McClure of Shawwood, and George McCree of Pitcon, mentioning that where the pursuer is daily charged, troubled, molested and pursued by the persons before named, defenders, for payment making to them of the rents due by the pursuer for the said farm of Lochlie belonging in joint property to the said John Campbell, David McClure and George McCree, most wrongously, considering that the pursuer can only be liable in once and single payment of the rents of the said farm and that to the person or persons who shall be found by the Lords of Council and Session to have best right thereto, and therefore the said John McCulloch, David Ewen and Jas. Hume, Douglas, Heron & Co. and their said factor and manager, John Campbell, David McClure and George McCree, ought and should exhibit and produce before the said Lords the several rights and grounds of debt by which they claim right to the foresaid rents and should discuss the same before the said Lords, to the end that the party having the best right thereto may be preferred to the said rents after deduction and allowance to the pursuer of the expense of this process, and the remanent persons should be by Decreet foresaid discharged from further molesting and pursuing the said pursuer thereafter in time coming.[12]

All the defenders were cited personally or at their dwelling places with the exception of George McCree who was cited 'by affixing and leaving for him the like just copy of citation at and upon each of the Mercat Cross of Edinburgh and the Pier and Shore of Leith, as being furth of Scotland at the time'. William Burnes was represented by the advocate Robert Blair who appeared also for Douglas, Heron and their factor. The other defenders failed to appear. On behalf of the failed bank a number of documents was produced to the court. The first of these was an Extract Heritable Bond and Disposition of 2 August 1773 (registered in the Books of Council and Session on 17 June 1779), by John Campbell, David McClure and George McCree, whereby they disposed to trustees for the bank 'the five merk land of Easter and Wester Douries and others', in security of the principal sum of £8,600, and £1,720 of penalty and interest. This was supported by an Extract Instrument of Sasine, recorded in the General Register of Sasines at Edinburgh on 17 September 1773. An Extract Bond and Assignation of 18 October 1774 (registered 7 March 1777) by Campbell, McClure and McCree corroborated the sums of £8,600 and £1,720. The last productions in this bundle were the Instrument of Intimation of the writs before narrated by George Hume to William Burnes, dated 18 September 1783, and a copy of the Decreet Arbitral by Hamilton of Sundrum showing the balance due to McClure as £231 2s 8d.

The case ultimately came before Lord Braxfield, the Lord Ordinary, who found 'that the sums in the hands of the raiser of the Multiplepoinding amounted at Whitsunday 1782 to the foresaid sum of £231 2s 8d, besides the sum of £130, both sterling, as another year's rent fallen due since, and therefore preferred the said Messrs. Douglas, Heron & Co. to the foresaid two sums, for payment to them *pro tanto* of the sums contained in their interest produced'. The Lord Ordinary was that Robert Macqueen of Braxfield in Lanarkshire (1722–99) who is nowadays remembered for the savage sentences pronounced on the Friends of the People in the notorious treason trials of 1793–4. William Burnes won his case, but at what a cost. McClure's sequestration order was quashed but William's legal costs exceeded the cash he could raise, while even the elements seemed to conspire against him. The summer of 1782 had been the worst in recorded memory, but the season of 1783 was almost as bad. All over Scotland crops failed and the harvest was disastrous. As Robert said ruefully to Moore of his father's experience, 'his all went among the rapacious hell-hounds that growl in the kennel of justice'. To crown all, the successful litigant was now in the last throes of tuberculosis. Braxfield's decision was no sooner handed down than William Burnes died on 13 February 1784.

Summarising this unfortunate episode, it can be seen that the traditional views expressed by nineteenth and early twentieth-century biographers, that the Burnes family tried to swindle their landlord, and that William only escaped the horrors of jail by his untimely death, are utterly unfounded.[13] On the contrary, the foregoing documents show that McClure claimed more than twice the rent to which he was entitled, and also reneged on his original agreement in regard to the draining and liming of the ground. More importantly, the documents now preserved in Register House, Edinburgh, show beyond any shadow of doubt that William Burnes was not only able to pay the balance actually due, but was perfectly willing to do so once the dispute was fairly settled. In light of this, McClure's action in pursuing an action for sequestration was invalid and uncalled for. It should also be pointed out that McClure overstepped the mark when he attempted to seize grain in respect of bygone rent for years of which it was not the crop. This action was contrary to Scots law which laid down that the produce of a farm could only be hypothecated for the rent of the year in which it had been harvested. This point was not overlooked by Sheriff Wallace who granted interim warrant to sequestrate only for payment of the current year's rent and also the 'crop in the barn and barnyard for payment of the year's rent whereof it is the growth'.

When he raised the action for multiplepoinding, William Burnes paid the £231 2s 8d into the court, apparently without difficulty and without needing to dispose of his stock. That he was able to do so gave the lie to McClure's allegation that sequestration was necessary because of the respondent's inability to pay his arrears. In his Replies McClure insinuated that he had not received any payments on account, when he must have known this to be untrue. Three cash payments, of £60, £11 8s and £40 respectively, had been made by Burnes, and receipts for those amounts were produced accordingly to the oversman who consequently gave William credit for them. In mitigation, it has to be said that McClure's precipitate action was due entirely to the fact that he was in dire financial straits. He himself was sequestrated on 23 November 1783, his debts by that time amounting to the staggering sum of £45,382 19s 6d.[14]

It has been suggested that McClure's evasiveness about giving Burnes a written agreement in the first instance was due to there being some doubt regarding his title to Lochlie. This is, in fact, borne out by the legal position in 1776-7 when the bargain was being struck. The farm of Lochlie, along with other lands, was vested in John Campbell of Wellwood, David McClure of Shawwood and George McCree of Pitcon, by a sasine recorded on 16 March 1771, proceeding on a disposition to them by Thomas Rigg of Morton on 17 December 1770. To judge from the manner in which they juggled with the title, none of the three appears to have been above suspicion, and one of them, McCree, seems to have absconded.[15]

When Douglas, Heron failed, the position of George Home of Branxton, their factor and general manager, must have been anything but enviable; but the hundreds of actions to be found in the Minute Book of the Court of Session are eloquent testimony to his assiduity in chasing up the debts due to the bank. One of these actions was a 'Process of Ranking of the Creditors and Sale of the estates of John Campbell, David McClure and George McCree, all merchants in Ayr, raised at the instance of Douglas, Heron & Co., late Bankers in Ayr'. On 26 July 1786 these estates, in various parcels, were exposed to public judicial sale. The first lot, comprising the lands of Halfmark (including Lochlie), was knocked down to David Erskine, Clerk of the Signet, who made the purchase on behalf of Miss Henrietta Scott of Scotstarvet.[16]

If the Court were satisfied that Lochlie was the joint property of Messrs Campbell, McClure and McCree (which none of them ever denied), then Campbell and McCree ought to have concurred both in the granting of the lease and in the petition for sequestration. In the oversman's decree Hamilton mentioned Dr John Campbell of Ayr as a witness to the bargain; was he the same person as John Campbell of Wellwood? But neither Campbell nor McCree was party to the sequestration of William Burnes, and thus McClure's petition was invalid. It is small wonder, therefore, that Robert formed a bad opinion of factors, landlords and lawyers as a result of this episode.[17]

If the winter of 1781-2 had been a terrible period for Robert, the winter of 1783-4 must have been infinitely worse for the whole family. Until Braxfield's judgment on 27 January 1784, the fear of ruin and the cruel 'absorption in a jail' stared William in the face. The stress probably accelerated the final stage of that 'phthisical consumption, which after two years promises, kindly stept in and snatch'd him away' as Robert later expressed it to Moore. If, as Robert states, this tubercular illness had been going on for two years, William's physical condition towards the conclusion of the litigation must have been pretty poor indeed. In the light of this, we cannot but admire the indomitable spirit he showed in resisting the bitter and unwarranted claims of a devious and unscrupulous landlord. Until these legal documents were discovered barely half a century ago, William Burnes was always characterised only as the upright, high-principled 'saint, father and husband' immortalised in the verses of 'The Cotter's Saturday Night' (CW 147–51). In pursuing this litigation all the way to the Court of Session, however, Burnes exhibited a dour, unrelenting streak; though it cost him life itself, he refused to be beaten. To his previous attributes there now fell to be added, as John McVie put it, 'that of a keen, hard-headed businessman, who did not suffer fools gladly and was prepared to fight for his rights to the last ditch'.[18]

Saunders Tait had a side-swipe at Burns in another of his poems entitled 'A Compliment', the recipient being the James Grieve in Boghead who had been McClure's arbiter in the dispute. Grieve was unofficial provost of Tarbolton, and tenant of a small farm not far from Lochlie. Tait apostrophises Grieve:

> Sir, for M'Lure he fought so fair
> 'Gainst Burns and Lawyers in Air,
> He trimm'd their jacket to a hair
>   So wantonlie,
> No toil nor travel he did spare
>   To win the plea.

Robert singled out James Grieve as the butt of one of his Tarbolton epitaphs (CW 67), written in April 1784, two months after William's death:

> Here lies Boghead amang the dead
>   In hopes to get salvation;
> But if such as he in Heav'n may be,
>   Then welcome – hail damnation.

This unhappy business overshadowed the family's last years at Lochlie. Gilbert's Narrative provides a sketchy picture of this period, amplified by the letters and poetry of Robert himself, and a few memoirs of his contemporaries. First Gilbert:

> During this period also he became a freemason, which was his first introduction to the life of a boon companion. Yet, notwithstanding these circumstances, and the praise he has bestowed on Scotch drink (which seems to have misled historians), I do not recollect, during these seven years, nor till towards the end of his commencing author, (when his growing celebrity occasioned his being often in company) to have ever seen him intoxicated; nor was he at all given to drinking. A stronger proof of the general sobriety of his conduct need not be required, than what I am about to give. During the whole of the time we lived in the farm of Lochlea with my father, he allowed my brother and me such wages for our labour as he gave to other labourers, as a part of which, every article of our clothing manufactured in the family was regularly accounted for.[19]

Local tradition (unsupported by documentary evidence) states that Robert was introduced to freemasonry by Alexander Wood, a Tarbolton tailor. This ancient and honourable institution probably dates back to medieval times in Scotland, although the Scottish Code of 1599 named lodges of Edinburgh as 'the first and principall' and Kilwinning 'the secund'. The latter came to be called the Mother Lodge, because of the numerous offshoots that sprang from it in the eighteenth century when freemasonry was organised on the lines followed to this day. The Grand Lodge of England was founded in 1717, soon emulated by similar bodies in Ireland (1725) and Scotland (1736). Ayrshire in general and Kilwinning in particular have played a notable part in the development of the craft throughout Scotland and the rest of the world. Daughter lodges of Kilwinning combined that name with their own; and the Tarbolton Kilwinning Lodge was warranted in 1771 for the sum of one merk Scots. Sadly, freemasonry was soon rent by differences of opinion in much the same way as religion was divided. In Tarbolton this led to a group breaking away from the parent lodge in 1773. Twenty brethren, led by Sir Thomas Wallace, Bart., petitioned the Grand Lodge of Scotland for a charter, and this was granted on 26 February 1773 as Lodge St David, No. 174 on the Grand Lodge roll. The remaining members of the original lodge soon affiliated with the Grand Lodge and became St James Tarbolton Kilwinning, No. 178 on 27 May 1774. In 1781 the two Tarbolton lodges came together and effected a 'junchen', in the quaint phonetic language of the minute-book kept by Lodge St David. This union came into effect on 25 June 1781, the combined lodge retaining the name of the older lodge, according to Grand Lodge charter, but ignoring the fact that Lodge St James Kilwinning was actually by far the older lodge. From the outset, therefore, grounds for further dissension were laid.

Nine days after the 'junchen', Robert Burns was entered as a member of the combined Lodge St David. The lodge minute for 4 July 1781 merely states that 'Robt. Burns in Lochly was entered an Apprentice'.[20] His entry fee of 12s 6d was paid on the same date. It has often been stated that Lodge St David met in Manson's Inn (used by Lodge St James), but the meetings were held in a room of the public house kept by John Richard, who was for some time steward of the lodge. As previously stated, the room in which Robert was initiated was that used by the Bachelors' Club. No further meeting of the lodge took place until 1 October when Robert made the twelve-mile journey from Irvine for this express purpose. This was a very important meeting for him, as the minute-book reveals: 'Robert Burns in Lochly was passed and raised, Henry Cowan being Master, James Humphrey Senr. Warden and Alexr. Smith Junr. Do., Robt. Wodrow Secy. and James Manson Treasurer, and John Tannock Taylor and others of the Brethren being present.' Two of these brother masons were later the subject of mock epitaphs. Manson inspired the couplet 'On an Innkeeper in Tarbolton' (CW 67):

Here lies 'mang ither useless matters,
A Manson wi his endless clatters.

119

while James Humphrey, the senior warden roused Robert to a quatrain. The title 'Epitaph on a Noisy Polemic' (CW 70) alluded to Humphrey's smattering of book-learning which induced him to engage in endless arguments with the poet:

> Below thir stanes lie Jamie's banes;
>   O Death, it's my opinion,
> Thou ne'er took such a bleth'rin bitch
>   Into thy dark dominion.

Manson was also referred to in the lines addressed to Dr Mackenzie (CW 237): 'An taste a swatch o Manson's barrels'. Robert Wodrow, son of the parish minister and secretary of the lodge, played a prominent role in the break-up of the combined lodge. Manson and Wodrow, as leading members of the older lodge, had never been happy at the suppression of its name and its supersession by St David. Along with Captain James Montgomerie, Wodrow called one evening upon John Richard, who kept the charter chest of the lodge (with the minute-books, archives and other belongings). After ordering a couple of gills of punch, they sent Richard to Manson's Inn on some trumped-up errand and, removing the effects of Lodge St James from the chest during Richard's absence, carried them off. Proceedings at Ayr Sheriff Court ensued and eventually the matter was referred to the Grand Lodge in Edinburgh. The Grand Committee ordered the recalcitrant Wodrow to return the property, but Wodrow would not budge. In the end Sheriff Wallace decided that, as the union had been a voluntary one, there was nothing to prevent a voluntary separation. The St James minute-book contains the entry, 'Tarbolton, June 17, 1782. St James Lodge met upon the same footing as it was before the junction. James Montgomerie, Gr. Mr. for the night'.[21]

Robert went with the seceders, but his name does not feature in the lodge minutes until 27 July 1784, when he was elected Depute Master of St James, at Manson's Inn to where it had moved only the previous month. The Master of the lodge was Sir John Whitefoord (1734–1803), third baronet of Blairquhan and a noted agricultural improver. He was served heir of the Ballochmyle estate but, in the collapse of Douglas, Heron he was forced to sell to Claud Alexander (1753–1809) who had made his fortune as paymaster-general of the Bengal Army. John Kay, in his *Edinburgh Portraits*, described Sir John as 'a remarkably smart, active little man'. His brother Caleb was a celebrated wit and amateur versifier whom Oliver Goldsmith described in 'The Retaliation' as 'the best-natured man with the worst-natured muse'. Sir John Whitefoord was the first member of the landed gentry that Robert was to know personally and his connections were later to stand the poet in good stead. In his masonic capacity Sir John was the recipient of a letter in Robert's handwriting, probably sent in November 1782 (CL 51). The letter, as sent, has not apparently survived, and it is known only in the form of an unsigned and undated draft (on the back of the sheet bearing the letter to 'A'); but a conjectural date can be assigned on the basis of its contents. The letter was drafted on behalf of the warden of the lodge and although Robert had no official standing at the time it is clear that his fluency with words marked him out for the delicate task of broaching the subject of the recent secession. After a preamble reviewing the philanthropic and charitable character of freemasonry, he goes on:

> We are sorry to observe that our lodge's affairs with respect to its finances have for a good while been in a wretched situation.– We have considerable sums in bills which lye by without being paid or put in execution; & many of our members never mind their yearly dues or anything else belonging to the lodge.– And since the separation from St David's, we are not sure even of our existence as a Lodge.– Their (*sic*) has been a dispute before the Grand Lodge but how decided, or if decided at all we know not.– For these & other reasons we humbly beg the favor of you as soon as convenient to call a meeting & let us consider on some means to retrieve our wretched affairs.

The minute-book contains three minutes in Robert's handwriting, beginning with the meeting of 1 September 1784. Twenty-nine minutes were signed by Robert in his capacity as Depute Master, and they are of particular interest as pinpointing the date at which he changed the spelling of his surname. Prior to 1 March 1786 they are signed 'Robt. Burness', but on that date brother Gilbert got his second and third degrees in the lodge, and both he and the Depute Master signed their names 'Burns'. The longer version of the surname is intriguing, as William invariably spelled it 'Burnes'. The earliest letters of the poet, from 1781 onwards, were signed 'Burns', but Robert went through a brief phase in which he used the variant 'Burness'.

This affectation began, logically enough, on 21 June 1783 with a long letter which Robert penned to his cousin James Burness at Montrose (CL 57–8). In adopting the East Coast spelling Robert was consciously emphasising his kinship with the older man who was now a lawyer and a prosperous burgess. In all, some nine letters were written by Robert to his cousin (the last written virtually on his deathbed) and the first four (up to 5 July 1786) were signed 'Burness'. After Robert made his name illustrious, however, he dropped the pretence and invariably signed the later letters 'Burns'. James's father James was William's elder brother. That their families inevitably drifted apart is shown by a letter from William Burnes to his nephew James in April 1781 giving an account of himself and his family since his marriage to Agnes Brown in 1757. James Burness thereafter kept up a desultory correspondence with his Burnes relatives and it was in response to one dated 10 June 1783 that Robert took up the pen on his father's behalf. William was 'in his own opinion, & indeed in almost ev'ry body's else, in a dying condition'. Apart from the melancholy circumstances – 'he has only, with great difficulty, wrote a few farewel lines to each of his brothers-in-law' – Robert's letter is of more than passing importance for its commentary on 'the present wretched state of this country' (i.e. Ayrshire). He paints a sombre picture of short supplies and high prices, with famine imminent, after the bad harvest of 1782. Manufactures were depressed and farming was at a very low ebb. 'Our Landholders, full of ideas of farming gathered from the English, and the Lothians and other rich soils in Scotland; make no allowances for the odds of the quality of land, and consequently stretch us much beyond what, in the event, we will be found able to pay.' There are perceptive comments on the failure of 'a miserable job of a Douglas, Heron & Co.'s Bank, which no doubt you have heard of', on smuggling on the coast and the moral decline of those individuals who engaged in the contraband trade: 'but Fortune, as is usual with her when she is uncommonly lavish of her favours, is generally even with them at the last; & happy were it for numbers of them if she would leave them no worse than when she found them'.

A second letter from Lochlie (CL 59) was written to James Burness only four days after William Burnes died. Robert was replying to a letter of 13 December 1783, which he would have answered sooner

> had it not been that I waited to give you an account of that melancholy event which for some time past we have from day to day expected.– On the 13th Current, I lost the best of fathers. Though to be sure we have had long warning of the impending stroke still the feelings of Nature claim their part and I cannot recollect the tender endearments and paren-tal lessons of the best of friends and the ablest of instructors without feeling, what perhaps, the calmer dictates of reason would partly condemn.–

The only other letters written by Robert in the later Lochlie period com-prise two to Thomas Orr in the autumn of 1782 and a long epistle to his old schoolmaster John Murdoch. The letters to Orr, dated 7 September and 17 November (CL 49–50), are in that philosophic vein he had previ-ously reserved for William Niven, but we do not have to read too much between the lines to see Robert's state of mind at this time, with the McClure dispute gathering momentum. In the first letter he wrote:

> To be rich & to be great are the grand concerns of this world's men, & to be sure if moderately pursued it is laudable; but where is it moderately pursued? the greater part of men grasp at riches as eagerly as if Poverty were but another word for Damnation & misery whereas I affirm that the man whose only wish is to become great & rich; whatever he may appear to be, or whatever he may pretend to be; at the bottom he is but a miserable wretch.– Avoid this sordid turn of mind if you would be happy.

And in the second, his mood may have reflected the unfriendly attitudes of his neighbours, as he acknowledged his friend's verse-epistle:

> I was extremely delighted with your letter. I love to see a man who has a mind superior to the world & the world's men – a man who, conscious of his own integrity, & at peace with himself, despises the censure & opinions of the unthinking rabble of mankind.

The long letter to Murdoch (CL 54–5), written on 15 January 1783, when the McClure dispute was coming to a head, dwelt on the same theme. After assuring his former mentor that he has 'indeed, kept pretty clear of vicious habits' and that his conduct would not disgrace the education he has gotten, he confesses that, as a man of the world, he is 'most miserably deficient'. He hints at his Irvine experiences: 'I seem to be one sent into the world, to see, to observe; and I very easily compound with the knave who tricks me of my money . . .' He carries on philosophically before getting to the heart of the matter:

> I scorn to fear the face of any man living: above every thing, I abhor as hell, the idea of sneaking in a corner to avoid a dun – possibly some pitiful, sordid wretch, who in my heart I despise and detest. 'Tis this, and this alone, that endears eo-conomy to me.

Elsewhere in this letter he mentions casually, 'Though indolent, yet so far as an extremely delicate constitution permits, I am not lazy' – the matter-of-fact way in which he thus touches upon his health is an indication that the illness of the Irvine period had left such a lasting mark that he had come to accept physical impairment as the norm. He concludes this sentence significantly: 'and in many things, especially in tavern matters, I am a strict eoconomist; not, indeed, for the sake of the money; but one of the principal parts in my composition is a kind of pride of stomach'.

This letter is also of interest as showing the escapist nature of Robert's reading matter in this troubled period. He admits that his favourite authors are of the sentimental kind, such as Shenstone, Mackenzie and Sterne. He also mentions *Ossian* by James Macpherson (1736–96). When this epic was first published in 1761 it had created a minor sensation. Within twenty years Macpherson had obtained a lucrative sinecure (London agent of Mohammed Ali, Nabob of Arcot), entered Parliament and become a country gentleman. His reputation went into eclipse when, shortly after his death, the authenticity of his 'translations' of ancient Gaelic songs was questioned, and subsequently the doubtful morality of his transactions obscured the fact that he was a great writer; but in the latter part of the eighteenth century Macpherson's works were still highly regarded. 'These are the glorious models after which I endeavour to form my conduct,' wrote Robert with enthusiasm.

During Robert's tenure as Depute Master two gentlemen were admitted to the Lodge as honorary members. The first was Professor Dugald Stewart of Catrine, who later played a part in the development of the poet's career, and Claud Alexander, brother of the lady whom Robert was to immortalise as the 'Bonie Lass o Ballochmyle' (CW 199–200).

The sequestration of May 1783 had a cataclysmic effect on the already ailing William Burnes and he was forced to take to his bed. Concerned at his father's rapid deterioration, Robert summoned the nearest doctor. There being no medical man in Tarbolton at that time, Robert applied to Dr John Mackenzie who had recently, at the instigation of Sir John

Whitefoord, set up in practice as 'Doctor and Midwife' in premises at Mauchline Cross.[22] Mackenzie was born at Ayr and studied medicine in Edinburgh before returning to his native county. In 1810 Mackenzie furnished Josiah Walker with an illuminating description of his first visit to Lochlie, of particular interest on account of the poor first impression which William's eldest son made on him:

> When I first saw William Burns he was in very ill health, and his mind suffering from the embarassed state of his affairs. His appearance certainly made me think him inferior, both in manner and intelligence, to the generality of those in his situation; but before leaving him, I found that I had been led to form a very false conclusion of his mental powers . . . His wife spoke little but struck me as being a very sagacious woman, without any appearance of forwardness, or any of the awkwardness in her manner which many of these people show in the presence of a stranger. Upon further acquaintance with Mrs Burns I had my first opinion of her character fully confirmed. Gilbert and Robert Burns were certainly very different in their appearance and manner, though they both possessed great abilities, and uncommon information. Gilbert partook more of the manner and appearance of the father, and Robert of the mother. Gilbert, in the first interview I had with him at Lochlea, was frank, modest, well informed and communicative. The poet seemed distant, suspicious, and without any wish to interest or please. He kept himself very silent in a dark corner of the room; and before he took part in the conversation, I frequently detected him scrutinising me during my conversation with his father and brother. But afterwards, when the conversation, which was on a medical subject, had taken the turn he wished, he began to engage in it, displaying a dexterity of reasoning, and ingenuity of reflection, and a familiarity with topics apparently beyond his reach, by which, his visitor was no less gratified than astonished.[23]

Mackenzie paints a very vivid picture of the sickroom, with Gilbert, even poor old William, taking part in the discussion, but – rather disconcertingly – the saturnine figure sits well back in the shadows, observing rather than observed, his penetrating gaze sizing up the earnest young doctor, getting the measure of the man before deigning to join the conversation. Later, however, Mackenzie got to know Robert well and was ever afterwards under his spell:

> From the period of which I speak, I took a lively interest in Robert Burns; and, before I was acquainted with his poetical powers, I perceived that he possessed very great mental abilities, an uncommonly fertile and lively imagination, a thorough acquaintance with many of our Scottish poets, and an enthusiastic admiration of Ramsay and Fergusson. Even then, on subjects with which he was acquainted, his conversation was rich in well chosen figures, animated, and energetic. Indeed, I have always thought that no person could have a just idea of the extent of Burns's talents, who had not an opportunity to hear him converse. His discrimination of character was great beyond that of any person I ever knew; and I have

often observed to him, that it seemed to be intuitive. I seldom ever knew him to make a false estimate of character, when he formed the opinion from his own observation, and not from the representation of persons to whom he was partial.

Later Mackenzie was to get to know Robert even more intimately, after the poet and his family moved to Mossgiel, barely a mile north of Mauchline.

Between the rejection of William's first petition to the Court of Session on 25 August 1783 and the presentation of his plea of multiplepoinding on 26 November, the Burnes family were in a turmoil of perplexity and despondency. What transpired in the interim can only be inferred from a letter which Robert wrote on 18 October to Gavin Hamilton, a Mauchline lawyer (CL 65). The letter, written from 'Machline', deals with the 'offer of a private bargain of your cows you intend for sale' and in a brief post-script adds 'Whatever of your dairy utensils you intend to dispose of we will probably purchase'. There is nothing in this brief letter to suggest that Robert and Gilbert were negotiating with Hamilton for anything more than cows and dairy utensils; yet, underlying this, was the clandestine agreement struck between the lawyer and the Burns boys who, foreseeing disaster if the Court of Session decided against their father, took steps to secure the lease of another farm. This agreement, kept secret for the time being, was finalised in November 1783, three months before William's death. It has been simplistically dismissed by one biographer as 'a piece of rather sharp practice'[24] but more accurately assessed by another as 'no more than a pragmatic stratagem'.[25] I incline to the latter view. It was a bold stroke, probably conceived by Robert and Gilbert without reference to their dying father; and in their desperate predicament a drastic solution was needed to combat the wily McClure. From the fact that a bargain was suggested by Gavin Hamilton – it could scarcely have been suggested by Robert or Gilbert – it seems probable that Hamilton was one of the poet's friends who gave legal advice on how best to defend the case involving McClure, and later to conduct the actions in the Court of Session. It may also have been on his advice that William Burnes agreed upon the sum of £7 each as annual wages for Robert and Gilbert, with smaller wages for the other members of the family, in order to give them the status of preferred creditors should the worst come to pass. This intriguing episode is described by Gilbert:

When my father's affair grew near a crisis, Robert and I took the farm of Mossgiel, consisting of 118 acres, at the rent of £90 per annum (the farm on which I live at present), from Mr. Gavin Hamilton, as an asylum for the family in case of the worst. It was stocked by the property and indi-vidual savings of the whole family, and was a joint concern among us. Every member of the family was allowed ordinary wages for the labour he performed on the farm. My brother's allowance and mine was £7 per annum each.[26] And during the whole time this family concern lasted, which was four years, as well as during the preceding period at Lochlea, his expenses never in any one year exceeded his slender income. As I was intrusted with the keeping of the family accounts, it is not possible that there can be any fallacy in this statement in my brother's favour. His temperance and frugality were everything that could be wished.[27]

It must have been very obvious to Robert and Gilbert by that time that their father had not long to live. His death would have cancelled the Lochlie lease, though not the debt.

Gavin Hamilton (1751–1805) was the fifth son of John Hamilton of Kype by his first wife, Jacobina Young, and he followed in his father's footsteps as an attorney and clerk of the regality of Mauchline, before branching out in a legal practice of his own. At one point he purchased the twelfth-century tower known locally as Mauchline Castle and built a modern villa alongside it. Later he sold both to the Earl of Loudoun but leased them back. The Ayrshire parishes, according to the reports given by their ministers in Sir John Sinclair's *Statistical Account*, frequently speak of the rising menace of beggars, due to the influx of Irish vagrants in the second half of the century. This reached such a pitch that there was a very real fear that the 'deserving poor' (those actually born or resident in the parish) would be denied their just deserts. To counter the activities of 'travelling professional beggars', therefore, each parish established a stent, or tax for the relief of the parochial paupers. In the case of Mauchline, this action took place in 1771, the stent being set at a penny in the pound of rental value. Young Gavin Hamilton was appointed collector of the stent in 1775. The story of Hamilton's implication in a dispute with the Mauchline Kirk Session over Sabbath-breaking is well known and belongs to the next chapter. What was not apparent, however, until relatively recently was that Hamilton was involved in disputes with the Kirk Session on three separate occasions between 1777 and 1787.[28]

Henley and Henderson (1896) cited Cromek (1808) as authority for the statement that the Revd. William Auld had quarrelled with Gavin's father, and this allegation was repeated by Hecht[29] who grafted on an unsupported contention of Lockhart (1826) that the Hamilton family had Episcopal tendencies and had persecuted the Presbyterians during the religious upheavals of the seventeenth century. These allegations, however, have no foundation in any recorded facts pertaining to the well-documented history of the Covenanting period. On the other hand, no biographer of Burns has hitherto taken the trouble to consult the minute-books of the Mauchline Kirk Session now preserved in Register House, Edinburgh. In 1771 the heritors of Mauchline parish had agreed to raise the sum of £19 10s 2d per annum, according to their rental value, for the relief of the poor. Gavin Hamilton, whose tombstone describes him, in the words of Burns, as 'the poor man's friend in need'[30] has, until lately, enjoyed a reputation as a champion of the poor and one who was not afraid to stand up to the Auld Lichts of the parish. Dr Andrew Edgar touched briefly on the first dispute but gave as the reason for Hamilton's intransigence the view that he considered himself accountable to the heritors and not the Session.[31] The Kirk Session minutes, however, show a rather different story.

The minutes of 5 February, 6 March, 3 April, 5 June and 12 June 1777 show that the Session was experiencing great difficulty in getting their hands on the poor stent, and appointed a committee (James Lamie, John Sillar, William Fisher and the Session Clerk, Andrew Noble) to grapple with the problem. The matter continued to drag on until 3 December 1778 when the committee was empowered by the Session 'to represent to Mr Hamilton, late collector of the poors stint, the hardship the poor are in for want of monthly supply, and to insist that some part at least of the said money due at Whit. last shall be paid to the Session before their next monthly meeting in January next'. A minute of 4 March 1779 reads: 'This day the Session were obliged to stop any further disbursements until Mr Hamilton, collector of the stint, shall pay up the arrears in his hand. The former Committee are appointed anew to apply to him immediately for the above purpose.'

On 7 May 1779 it was minuted that 'John Sillar reports that Mr Hamilton told him that he would give papers and money in a little time'. The committee was appointed to receive Hamilton's accounts in time for the next meeting of the Session, but nothing happened. By 24 February 1780 James Lamie was being ordered to speak to Mr Hamilton and to get accounts settled for stent 1776, 1777 and 1778. Lamie and William Fisher (the 'Holy Willie' of Robert's satire) were appointed on 12 June 1781 to pursue the matter again. Further committees and deputations from the Session were appointed for the same fruitless purpose on 18 October and 27 December 1781, the latter in the forlorn hope of getting Hamilton to settle his accounts by the end of January 1782.

Finally, the matter came to a head on 19 June 1783. On that date Lamie and Sillar reported that they had spoken to Gavin Hamilton about the arrears of the poor stent for the years in which he had been collector (1776-8), only to be told blandly that he had none of this money in his hand. The Session Clerk was instructed to write to Hamilton with extracts of the minutes and 'signifying their desire to have an account from him of the said stint outstanding . . . and beg his answer in the space of two weeks as they wish much to end the matter amicably but if that is not done their duty as administrators for the poor will oblige them to apply to Law for justice'. Even after this very reasonable but firm approach the Session were reluctant to make good their threat. By 20 July 1784 the minutes recorded that Mr Hamilton continued to refuse to settle his accounts for 1776-8. The sum involved was about £7 and after several further verbal approaches the Session had been forced to take out a summons against him, which resulted in his appearance before the Justices at Kilmarnock. Incredibly, this long dispute was still running at the time the Burns family left Tarbolton and settled in the neighbouring parish of Mauchline.

In addition to several extant letters, Robert's prose work from the latter part of the Lochlie period includes his *First Commonplace Book* which he commenced in April 1783.[32] The keeping of such a book (as distinct from a journal or diary) was a pastime of the upper classes possessed of the necessary education and refinement as well as the abundance of leisure in which to contemplate the world around them and make philosophical comments in their notebooks. Such volumes became the repository of ephemeral matters, *bon mots*, fragments of poetry, quotations from books read, and thoughts, moral, religious and contemplative. Robert's motive for keeping such a book was stated some ten years later when he began preparing the manuscript volume known as the *Abridgement of the First Commonplace Book* for Robert Riddell of Glenriddell (CL 483–4):

> On rummaging over some old papers, I lighted on a M.S.S. of my early years, in which I had determined to write myself out; as I was placed by Fortune among a class of men to whom my ideas would have been nonsense – I had meant that the book would have lain by me, in the fond hope that, some time or other, even after I was no more, my thoughts would fall into the hands of somebody capable of appreciating their value . . .

Nowadays a commonplace has become synonymous with some trite or obvious observation, but in the Age of Enlightenment it had a more elevated meaning, as Robert himself implied in the rather self-conscious title which he inscribed on the opening page: 'Observations, Hints, Songs, Scraps of Poetry, etc., by Robt. Burness'. As he confessed to Riddell, from the outset Robert wrote with at least one eye on posterity:

> As [the author] was but little indebted to scholastic education, and bred at a plough-tail, his performances must be strongly tinctured with his unpolished, rustic way of life; but as I believe, they are really his own, it may be some entertainment to a curious observer of human-nature to see how a Ploughman thinks, and feels, under the pressure of Love, Ambition, Anxiety, Grief, with the like cares and passions, which, however diversified by the Modes, and Manners of life, operate pretty much alike I believe, in all the Species.

Note how Burns the tenant-farmer sees himself here as a simple ploughman, a pose that was consonant with his sentimental notions. There follows a strange compendium of poetry and songs, some original and others borrowings from his favourite authors which Robert copied out for his own edification. There are numerous essays and trial-pieces, from early versions of now-familiar songs to experiments in blank verse. There is a great deal of amateurish philosophising, the outpourings of his hopes and ambitions for the future, as well as opinions and reflections, many of them as remarkable as anything he ever wrote, and all pertaining to a period when he was completely unknown. There are numerous examples of that 'critic-craft' on which Robert set such great store. From the outset he realised the importance of being able to take a long, hard look at his own work and, as a result, the criticisms which follow many of the poems and songs are invaluable for showing Robert's thought processes and his views on his own compositions. These criticisms were often detailed and precise, analysing songs line by line. Many entries are dated, though by no means all, so that it is possible to trace the poet's development as well as link his writings to the appropriate incidents in the family history. Under March 1784, for example, a few weeks after William Burnes died, we find 'A Penitential Thought, in the Hour of Remorse, Intended for a Tragedy' followed by twenty lines of blank verse which served as the basis for 'Tragic Fragment' (CW 46-7).[33] This was immediately followed by a paragraph which is clearly the genesis of the 'Address to the Unco Guid' (CW 74-6):

> I have often observed, in the course of my experience of human life, that every man, even the worst, have (*sic*) something good about them; though very often nothing else than a happy temperament of constitution inclining him to this or that virtue; on this likewise depend a great many, no man can say how many of our vices; for this reason, no man can say in what degree any other person, besides himself, can be, with strict justice, called wicked. Let any of the strictest character for regularity of conduct among us, examine impartially how many of his virtues are owing to constitution & education; how many vices he has never been guilty of, not from any care or vigilance, but from want of opportunity, or some accidental circumstance intervening; how many of the weakness's of mankind he has escaped because he was out of the line of such temptation; and, what often, if not always, weighs more than all the rest; how much he is indebted to the world's good opinion because the world does not know all: I say any man who can thus think, will scan the failings, nay the faults & crimes, of mankind around him, with a brother's eye.

Clearly both the great poem illustrating the notion of natural sympathy as the root of moral consciousness, and this prose jotting of the poet's thoughts on the subject, gain considerably in significance when read in the context of the turbulent period which triggered them off.

Isobel Burns supplied Robert Chambers and James Grierson with various anecdotes which relate to the latter part of the Lochlie period. On one occasion their mother had been visiting a neighbour's child who was on the point of death. On her return she said to Rab, 'You should have been there – you never heard such a prayer as James Lee gave beside the poor child.' Robert replied, 'Oh, mother! Can you or Jamie Lee be so daft as to think that his prayer can be of any service to the dying bairn, or keep the devil at a distance? Would God send a child into the world to damn it?' On this, his mother lifted the fire tongs to strike him, but he dodged out of the way.[34]

Mrs Begg's most vivid recollections, however, pertained to her father, especially in his last years. Broken down as he was in constitution, he sustained his natural and habitual cheerfulness. He was always trying to make his children happy; and the impression Isobel conveyed was of a man who could crack a joke, who was always affable and approachable. She could only recollect him angry on two occasions. The first time, his anger was directed at a young lad for wasting some hay, when he had just returned to the farm weary and irritated from an interview over his unfortunate lawsuit. The second time arose when some old man, to whom he had shown much kindness, told lies about him. On that occasion an altercation took place in the kitchen and Mrs Burnes gave her husband a reproachful look. Sternly he replied, 'There must be no gloomy looks here.' To the modern reader this seems inconsequential, perhaps; but it was held up as a solitary example of severity towards his wife which, in retrospect, gave much pain to all concerned. Agnes herself recalled that William never beat any of their children, apart from one occasion when he took a strap to his eldest daughter Agnes for showing obstinacy while he was teaching her to read, 'and it had had a good effect upon the child's temper'. Isobel's memories of her father were happier. When she was eleven or twelve her main occupation was tending the cattle in the fields. William would often visit her and sit beside her, telling her the names of the various flowers and plants. Isobel had a terror of thunder and lightning, and whenever a storm was brewing William would come out to the fields to bring her back to the farmhouse.

Various stories have been told concerning William's death-bed scene, but probably the most factually accurate was that communicated by Isobel to Dr Chambers. She remembered being at William's bedside that morning along with Robert. Seeing her cry bitterly at the thought of parting, her father tried to speak but could only murmur a few words of comfort, enjoining her 'to walk in virtue's paths and shun every vice'. After a pause, he said there was one of his family for whose future conduct he feared. He repeated the expression, and then Robert came up to the bed and asked, 'Oh, father, is it me you mean?' The old man said it was. Robert turned to the window, with the tears streaming down his cheeks.[35]

Two dozen poems, songs and surviving fragments are reckoned to have been composed during the Lochlie years (including the Irvine interlude), and doubtless others (such as the song satirising Saunders Tait) were regarded by Robert as too ephemeral to preserve. The unrelenting moil and toil of farm-work and the stress of the dispute with McClure were hardly conducive to literary inspiration; but the score and more pieces from this period show the passion and the fire that were the hallmarks of Robert's best work in later years. In addition to those compositions of the earlier years already mentioned, the later Lochlie period was notable for the reworking of the old ballad 'John Barleycorn' which Robert inserted in his *Commonplace Book* a year later. 'I once heard the old song, that goes by this name, sung, and being very fond of it, and remembering only two or three verses of it, viz. the 1st, 2nd and 3rd, with some scraps which I have interwoven here and there in the following piece.' Previously Robert had composed entirely new words to old melodies, but here we see the germ of that facility for mending and reworking traditional ballads which was to dominate the latter part of his poetic career.

Under June 1785 Robert inserted 'The death and dyin' words o' poor Mailie – my ain pet ewe – an unco mournfu' tale' (CW 62–4) but it belongs more properly to the closing part of the Lochlie period. Gilbert later told Dr Currie that Robert had partly by way of frolic, bought a ewe and two lambs from a neighbour, and she was tethered in a field adjoining the house at Lochlie . . . He and I were going out with our teams, and our two younger brothers to drive for us, at mid-day, when Hugh Wilson, a curious-looking, awkward boy, clad in plaiding, came to us with much anxiety in his face, with the information that the ewe had entangled herself in the tether, and was lying in the ditch. Robert was much tickled with Hughoc's appearance and posture on the occasion. Poor Mailie was set to rights, and when we returned from the plough in the evening, he repeated to me her *Death and Dying Words* pretty much in the way they now stand.[36]

It will be remembered that James Gordon's inventory of the stock at Lochlie in May 1783 included 'one ewe, two lambs'. The sequel, entitled 'Poor Mailie's Elegy' (CW 64-5), was not composed till the following year.

The early pages of the *First Commonplace Book* include several mock epitaphs. In addition to the lines on James Grieve already mentioned, there were the verses in more serious, sincere vein on 'my own friend and my father's friend, Wm. Muir in Tarbolton Mill' (CW 70) and the quatrain on William Hood, Senior, later published as 'Epitaph on a Celebrated Ruling Elder' (CW 70). The epitaph on 'Wee Johnie' (CW 71), one of the concluding pieces in the Kilmarnock edition, was at one time believed to lampoon John Wilson, Burns's printer – a singularly tactless act were that the case, given the uncomplimentary nature of the punch-line – but later another John Wilson (a resident of Tarbolton discussed in the next chapter) was generally regarded as the butt of this poem. This *canard* was exposed in 1910 when a copy of the first Edinburgh Edition (1787) was discovered in Dumfries with annotations in the poet's handwriting. In particular, Robert had identified all the persons alluded to in his poems, and opposite Wee Johnie was the comment that the person meant was the Revd. John Kennedy, assistant to the Revd. George Reid at Ochiltree until 1781 when he was translated to Terregles parish. The circumstances in which Robert might have known Kennedy at this early stage are not known.

The other epitaph belonging to this period, however, was written reverentially, from the heart. In the *First Commonplace Book* it was entitled 'Epitaph on my Ever Honoured Father', but this was toned down, in the Kilmarnock Edition, to 'For the Author's Father' (CW 71). Neither Robert nor Gilbert explained why the body of their father was taken all the way back to Alloway for burial in the yard of the old ruined kirk, rather than be interred at Tarbolton; but one can easily imagine that the family had no desire to leave their patriarch in a place which held only unhappy memories. By contrast, Alloway had been the scene of William's early hopes and achievements, when he married, began raising a family, built his cottage and planned his nursery garden. He had taken a keen interest in the kirkyard and had personally tidied the ancient headstones. It therefore seemed the most appropriate place for William's remains. The coffin was slung from two poles inserted in the stirrups between two horses in tandem.[37] Tradition states that John Tennant of Glenconner supplied one of the horses and Gilbert led the other beast. The friends and relatives of the deceased followed behind, as they traversed the eight miles along rough country roads. Robert lost no time in getting an impressive headstone erected, bearing the eight lines which end with

> The friend of man – to vice alone a foe;
> For 'ev'n his failings lean'd to virtue's side'.[38]

The present headstone is the third to have been erected, the first two having been mutilated by souvenir hunters. It was to here in December 1858 that the poet's youngest sister Isobel was brought for burial and her daughters, Isabella and Agnes Begg, were also buried there in due course.

CHAPTER 8

Mossgiel, 1784–6

O, leave novéls, ye Mauchline belles –
Ye're safer at your spinning-wheel!
Such witching books are baited hooks
For rakish rooks like Rab Mossgiel.

O, Leave Novels (CW 79)

ecause the papers relating to the conclusion of the dispute between
B Burnes and McClure were not published till 1935 all of the major
biographers of Burns[1] take the view that death alone saved William from
a debtors' gaol and that the family were forced out of Lochlie by
bankruptcy.[2] There was also much waffle about William being only narrowly saved from the ignominy of a pauper's grave. The critic Catherine
Carswell even provides a vivid account which had Robert advertising the
sale of the Lochlie corn on a notice tacked to the door of Tarbolton kirk,
with David McClure standing outside the kirk on the Sabbath day warning
worshippers against buying from Burns. This nonsense, based on the scurrilous rhymes of Saunders Tait, obviously confuses the leaving of Lochlie
in March 1784 with the sequestration of May 1783.[3]

The truth was probably more prosaic. By the time of William's death
McClure must have been out of the picture anyway, overtaken by his own
financial problems; and after Braxfield's judgment in January 1784 the
money paid into court would have gone to McClure's preferred creditors.
There was nothing to prevent the Burnes family from moving out of
Lochlie whenever they chose. In any event, had he not died, William's
verbal lease would have expired in the normal course at Whitsun 1784,
when he would assuredly have exercised his option to terminate after seven
years. He was no sooner laid to rest than Robert and Gilbert put the finishing touches to their best-laid scheme hatched the previous autumn and
made the move to their new farm, some two miles to the south-east; but as
it was in the neighbouring parish of Mauchline Robert had to obtain the
obligatory certificate of character from Tarbolton Kirk Session to show to
his new minister that he was a communicant in good standing.

The Mauchline parochial account, written seven years later for Sir John
Sinclair, was compiled by the Revd. Dr William Auld, known to posterity

as Daddy Auld and, in his own way, immortalised by the Burns connection. Auld was writing at a time when the spelling of the parish name was not quite stabilised. Robert himself used Machline as well as Mauchline in his correspondence, but Auld noted Machlin, Machlein and Machlene as earlier variants, and derived the name from Gaelic *mo achadh léine* – 'my field of flax'; but lest it be assumed that flax-raising was an ancient form of agriculture in the area it should be noted that the word translates more accurately as bog-cotton, a hardy plant which thrives only in the poorest, most acidic and boggiest of soil. Auld noted that the parish was generally flat, except for Mauchline Hill, north-east of the town, running in an east-west ridge that terminated at Shioch-hill in Tarbolton parish (that same Skioch where Robert's neighbour, Matthew Paterson, also grew flax). The town of Mauchline was situated on the southern side of this slope, declining towards the River Ayr.

About 1710 Mauchline had possessed a charter, but Auld said it had been lost. 'This is much to be regretted, as that privilege, if properly exercised, might contribute much to the public good, by checking riots and disorder, which are at present too frequent, and promoting the good order, peace and happiness of the community.'[4] In 1755 the parish had a population of 1,169 but by 1791 this had risen to 1,800 – an increase of fifty per cent. About 1,000 lived in the town itself, and the rest in the surrounding countryside. Auld gave a detailed breakdown of the trades and professions of the parish, which included one clergyman (himself), two lawyers (including Gavin Hamilton), one surgeon (Dr John Mackenzie) and one university student, compared with ten merchants, ten tailors, twelve shoemakers, twelve wrights or carpenters, twenty weavers and twenty stone-masons. The landward area of the parish supported seventy-three farmers whose stock comprised some 240 horses and 1,080 black cattle. The Mauchline Friendly Society had been founded in 1781 and paid out two shillings a week to unemployed members and three shillings a week in sickness benefit. Members paid a guinea (£1.05) on entry.

Auld passed judgment on the character of his parishioners:

In such a number there must be some exceptions; but, in general, they are a sober, industrious people, charitably disposed; Careful and even punctual in attending the church on Sunday and on sacramental occasions . . . 50 years ago, and for some time thereafter, there were only two or three farms in the parish who made use of tea daily; now it is done by, at least, half of the parish and almost the whole use it occasionally. At that period, good two-penny, strong-ale, and home spirits were in vogue; but now even people in the middling and lower stations of life deal much in foreign spirits, rum-punch and wine . . . As to dress, about 50 years ago there were few females who wore scarlet or silks. But now, nothing is more common, than silk caps and silk cloaks; and women, in a middling station, are as fine as ladies of quality were formerly. The like change may be observed in the dress of the male sex, though, perhaps, not in the same degree.

The minister observed that the Scottish dialect was the language spoken, 'but is gradually improving nearer to English'. In one respect at least Mauchline was worse off than Tarbolton: the parish schoolmaster had a salary of only £10 per annum, compared with the £50 paid at Tarbolton.

Both Robert and Gilbert are silent on the actual move from Lochlie to Mossgiel. Robert described this to Moore, colourfully but imprecisely:

> . . . we made a shift to scrape a little money in the family amongst us, with which, to keep us together, my brother and I took a neighbouring farm. – My brother wanted my harebrained imagination as well as my social and amorous madness, but in good sense and ever sober qualification he was far my superiour.– I entered on this farm with a full resolution, 'Come, go to, I will be wise!'–[5] I read farming books; I calculated crops; I attended markets; and in short, in spite of 'The devil, the world and the flesh', I believe I would have been a wise man; but the first year from unfortunately buying in bad seed, the second from a late harvest, we lost half of both our crops: this overset all my wisdom, and I returned 'Like the dog to his vomit, and the sow that was washed to her wallowing in the mire –'.[6]

Gilbert, needless to say, provided a more factual account of the farm where he continued to live until 1798:

> The farm of Mossgiel lies very high, and mostly on a cold wet bottom. The first two years that we were on the farm were very frosty, and the spring was very late. Our crops in consequence were very unprofitable, and notwithstanding our utmost diligence and economy, we found ourselves obliged to give up our bargain, with the loss of a considerable part of our original stock.[7]

Fowler's detailed soil analysis[8] indicates that Mossgiel was no better than Lochlie in many respects, though part of it was composed of lanfine soil in the higher elevations and this would have been the most easily cultivated soil that Robert and Gilbert had encountered up to that time. It was less stony, that much is certain, but the drainage was just as bad. Indeed, until the advent of tile-drainage in the 1830s, there could have been little room for real improvement. The candid admission by Robert that he had bought bad seed has, more than anything else, earned him the scorn of previous biographers, the consensus of whose opinion was that Burns was an indifferent farmer. Only a more scientific examination of prevailing conditions by Fowler has at long last set the record straight.[9] The 1780s are now known to have been one of those clusters of severe weather towards the tail-end of the 'Little Ice Age' (1550–1850) and Gilbert does not exaggerate when he speaks of the two very frosty years (1784–5). They were preceded by three years of exceptionally long and hard frosts (1781–3) resulting in poor harvests and crop failures all over Scotland. In particular, 1783 was a year of atrocious weather, with snow lying till April and piercing cold wind in May followed by continuous heavy rain in late May and

June. Ten days of hot weather in early July were followed by torrential rain and cold storms that lasted for six weeks, so that August was as cold as February. A hurricane struck central Scotland on 24 August and devastated the standing wheat. Two weeks of fine weather in September, when the crops were still green, gave way to boisterous winds, followed by hard frosts early in October. Cereal crops, such as they were, could not be harvested till well into November, but severe frosts and deep snow were so intense that the mill-lades froze.[10]

As a result, almost all of the seed available for the 1784 sowing would have been of a very poor quality, giving yields in a ratio of four to one or even lower. The continuing bad weather in 1785 would only have exacerbated an already desperate situation. Although the description of the 1783 weather pertained to southern Perthshire it would have not been very different from that which Robert and Gilbert had to contend with, as their new farm lay in the upland part of the parish, at an average height of just over 600 feet (197m) above sea-level, exposed to westerly gales and having an average rainfall of forty-five inches per annum.

Even the name of the farm ought to have sounded a note of warning. It appears on maps and in documents variously as Mossgavill, Mossgaville, Mossgill and Mossgiel. Boyle[11] rightly says that it is doubtful if any man in literature ever made a name so famous by so brief an association, and Angellier[12] waxed lyrical with 'Mossgiel, Mossgiel, how that name sings itself into every Scottish heart'. The derivation of the second syllable is obscure but there can be no doubt about the prefix 'moss' which, in the language of Scotland, meant boggy ground or moorland.[13] The light soil, eroded by poor husbandry and the relentless effects of the weather, lay above thick clay which prevented surface water from running off. Gilbert, commenting on the circumstances in which Robert composed 'Death and Dr Hornbook' (CW 96–100), casually mentioned that Robert recited the verses to him 'as I was holding the plough and he was letting the water off the field beside me'.[14] This conjures up a picture of waterlogged fields which must have made the task of ploughing doubly difficult.

The ultimate responsibility for improving the land lay with James Mure-Campbell, fifth Earl of Loudoun. His cousin, the fourth Earl, had been a noted improver who planted over a million trees (especially willows), built roads, and began an ambitious programme of land drainage; but at Earl John's death in 1782 he was succeeded by a professional soldier who had little if any previous experience as a landowner, and even if he had the expertise and inclination to carry on the good work, he was beset by domestic and financial problems. His wife, Flora McLeod, died in 1780 giving birth to their only daughter, and a natural tendency to melancholy was aggravated by farming failures and financial problems which culminated in April 1786 when he shot himself.[15]

Before proceeding with the story of the Burns family at Mossgiel it is necessary to deal with an episode which was, in some respects, a legacy of the Lochlie period, especially as it is erroneously believed to this day to have taken place about the time the family were preparing to leave their old farm and start life anew at Mossgiel. Elizabeth Paton, a female servant employed briefly at Lochlie in the winter of 1783-4, did not follow the Burns family to Mossgiel. Instead, she returned to her own home in the hamlet of Largieside, about a mile south-west of Lochlie, where she was a near neighbour of the Rankines of Adamhill. The circumstances in which Robert seduced this girl, twenty months his junior, are unknown and the only details we have about this shadowy figure have come to us indirectly, from Isabella Begg, daughter of Isobel Burns and thus the poet's niece. In the 1840s she communicated with Robert Chambers about Elizabeth Paton:

> She was an exceedingly handsome figure, but very plain looking; so active, honest and independent a creature, that she had become a great favourite with her mistress, who, when her situation became known, was most anxious that Burns should have married her, but both my aunts [Agnes and Annabella Burns] and uncle Gilbert opposed it. The girl herself acknowledged he had broken no promise to her. They thought the faults of her character would soon have disgusted him. She was rude and uncultivated to a great degree; a strong masculine understanding, with a thorough (tho' unwomanly) contempt for every sort of refinement . . . My mother says she does not believe that ever woman loved man with a more heartfelt devotion than that poor creature did him.[16]

This passage is significant in showing how important decisions affecting Robert's life were taken by other people. His mother was all for him marrying Betsey Paton, but Gilbert and his sisters opposed it, and their wishes were obeyed. There is no mention in this account of how Robert felt when he found himself in his predicament. Isabella Begg goes on to state that Robert's affection for Betsey had been very different from hers for him, 'but he never treated her unkindly'. Most biographers speak vaguely of an affair having briefly arisen following the death of William Burnes, and the inference is that the seduction took place some time between mid-February and March, when the family moved to Mossgiel; but as Betsey did not give birth to 'Dear-bought Bess' until 22 May 1785, conception must have occurred in August 1784.[17] Of course, the affair could have started in February that year, or even earlier, but the weather would have been too cold for intimacy out of doors, and practical problems must have made it well-nigh impossible for Robert to have engaged in sexual intercourse with Betsey in the crowded conditions of Lochlie. By high summer, however, Robert would have had ample time and opportunity to pursue the erstwhile farm-servant.

At this period he had formed a close frienship with John Rankine, the tenant in Adamhill. John, the 'rough, rude, ready-witted Rankine' of the verse-epistle (CW 82-4), was twice Robert's age, but the budding poet shared the farmer's Rabelaisian sense of humour and boisterous pranks. Allan Cunningham (1834) gave a sample of Rankine's coarse wit, while Chambers (1851) quoted daughter Annie as saying that Robert was amused by a trick which her father had played on a 'sanctimonious professor' whom he had invited to a jorum of toddy in his farmhouse. 'The hot-water kettle had, by pre-arrangement, been primed with proof-whisky, so that the more water Rankine's guest added to his toddy for the purpose of diluting it, the more potent the liquor became.'[18] A somewhat similar story was told against the Revd. John McMath, Wodrow's assistant in Tarbolton parish, who was also the victim of Rankine's misguided wit. At any rate it would appear that the affair had progressed as far as it could go by August.

John Lambie, a Stevenston thatcher whom Grierson interviewed in August 1817, had, many years earlier, been employed by Robert as a ploughboy, allegedly at Lochlie, though the events he recounted actually took place at Mossgiel. This error alone tends to make us wary of Lambie's evidence, although it was an easy mistake to make, so many years after the event. According to Lambie, Robert actually boasted to him of his exploits on the very night he 'brought the pairtrick to the grun' (an allusion to the celebrated poaching metaphor in the epistle to John Rankine), after Lambie had trailed Robert 'to a neighbour's farm where Bess Paton was then working'.[19]

Those eleven lines of bawdry, 'My Girl She's Airy' composed by Robert to the tune of the coarse old ballad 'Black Joke' (CW 82), are believed to extol the physical charms of Elizabeth Paton. Whether the farm at which Betsey was then working was Adamhill or not, John Rankine was certainly one of the first to learn of the girl's pregnancy, as a note to that effect provoked the poetic response entitled 'Reply to an Announcement by John Rankine' (CW 85). The two stanzas beginning 'I am a keeper of the law' are not without interest. The last lines of the first verse, 'The breaking of ae point, tho sma', Breaks a' thegither', are a paraphrase of James 2: 10, 'For whosoever shall keep the whole law, and yet offend in one point, is guilty of all'. But the second stanza begins, 'I hae been in for't ance or twice, / And winna say o'er far for thrice', implying that the affair with Paton was not his first essay in fornication, though the first time that pregnancy had resulted. The punch-line, 'A whaup's i' the nest!' is a more apt and colourful way of putting it than the modern vulgarism, 'a bun in the oven'. The metaphor was subse-quently expanded in the verse-epistle itself (especially the seventh to eleventh stanzas) in which Robert likens himself to a poacher taking a partridge. The news of Betsey's pregnancy must have reached Robert in late September or early October, and he alludes to his embarrassment in the letter to Thomas Orr already quoted in Chapter 4, written on 11 November 1784.

The penultimate stanza of the verse-epistle to Rankine suggests that Robert had to pay a guinea by way of a fine to the Tarbolton Kirk Session, and also do penance for fornication. Robert outrageously dismisses this fine as 'the buttock-hire' in 'The Fornicator' (CW 113–14) which also graphically describes the penitential performance, during which he is incor-rigibly exposed to further temptation:

Before the Congregation wide
    I pass'd the muster fairly,
My handsome Betsey by my side,
    We gat our ditty rarely;
But my downcast eye by chance did spy
    What made my lips to water,
Those limbs so clean where I, between,
    Commenc'd a Fornicator.

If the last line is taken literally, Robert would have us believe that he lost his virginity to Betsey Paton; but it is more probable that, so far as Robert was concerned, fornication did not count unless you were found out. Until 1909 it was believed that Elizabeth Paton's baby was born in November 1784 (hence Chambers's belief that she had either given birth, or was just about to, when the Orr letter was written). This tied in with the tradition that Betsey had become pregnant in February or March of that year. The truth did not emerge until Duncan McNaught was shown a document dated 1 December 1786 and drawn up by Gavin Hamilton at Robert's request, which clearly stated the birth of the baby as 22 May 1785.[20] Mrs Carswell gives a highly coloured account of Robert and Elizabeth Paton doing penance in Mauchline Kirk[21] when, in fact there is no indication in the Session books of that parish that either of the two came under official censure at that time. Snyder, commenting on the apparent discrepancy between this omission and Robert's candid admission in verse[22] overlooked the fact that such censure would have taken place in Tarbolton Kirk and, regrettably, its records for the period have not survived.

Isabella Begg, on the information supplied by her mother, said that some time afterwards, when the poet was about to marry Jean Armour, he offered to take the little girl:

> When Burns went to Ellisland, the child Elizabeth Burns came to Mossgiel to my grandmother [Agnes Brown], and attended school at Mauchline till the poet's death. Her mother took her home, where she lived till she was married to John Bishop, who acted as land-steward to Baillie of Polkemmet. She was a good, upright creature, and when she died, the minister of the parish wrote a beautiful character of her to my grandfather.[23]

Bess, in fact, died at the age of thirty-two in 1817. Elizabeth Paton herself survived the scandal, married John Andrew, a farm-hand and a widower, on 9 February 1788. By him she had four children (1789–93) and died some time later, for Andrew took, as his third wife, Jean Lees on 8 March 1799.[24]

When Robert received news that Betsey Paton had given birth to a girl, his immediate reaction was one of elation. Strangely, he made no reference to this incident in his autobiographical letter, and Gilbert, too, was silent on the matter. To be sure, Robert was exposed as a fornicator, but that was no uncommon occurrence in rural Ayrshire, as Andrew Noble noted casually in the Mauchline minutes ('only 24 fornicators in the parish since last sacrament'); but this was the first instance 'that entitled him to the venerable appellation of father'. This was the subtitle to one of the several versions Robert wrote of the poem which, in the published form, is known as 'A Poet's Welcome to his Love-Begotten Daughter' (CW 112–13), but which Robert, more pithily and in private, referred to as the 'Welcome to his Bastart Wean'. Compared with the sexual boastfulness of his epistle to Rankine, however, this poem expresses only warm tenderness. The only defiant note appears in the second stanza:

> What tho they ca' me fornicator,
> An tease my name in kintra clatter,
> The mair they talk, I'm kend the better,
>   E'en let them clash!
> An auld wife's tongue's a feckless matter
>   To gie ane fash.

Robert later transcribed this poem in the Glenriddell MS but it was not published in his lifetime.

At one time there were three farms in the area north-west of Mauchline, distinguished as Near (East), Far (West) and Nether (South) Mossgiel. The last named disappeared early in the nineteenth century and is marked today by little more than a scatter of overgrown stones in a copse about fifty yards from the Mauchline-Tarbolton road, opposite the road-end of West Mossgiel. West Mossgiel is a working farm to this day, as is East Mossgiel, where the Burns family lived. Tile-drainage and regular top-dressing have completely transformed the farm, and it is prosperous and productive. The farmhouse was substantially rebuilt between 1858 and 1870, when a second storey and a new roof were added. When the farmhouse was partially demolished in 1858, crowds of souvenir hunters converged on the place and bore away pieces of the decaying roof timbers, many of which ended up as snuff-boxes and other products of the Smith Boxworks in neighbouring Mauchline. Today, only the foundations and the lower courses of masonry on the outer walls date from the eighteenth century. The range of outbuildings bears no relation to the stable, barn and byre of Robert's day, while the fields have been enclosed. A hedge, traditionally planted by Robert but probably installed by Gavin Hamilton, was only knee-high when Gilbert left Mossgiel in 1798; today it is over twelve feet (four metres) tall and obscures the house from the road. Robert might not recognise Mossgiel itself, but the outlook from the farm, spreading out to the south and west, remains the same. William Wordsworth, who visited Mossgiel in 1802, was entranced by the view and was inspired to write one of his finer poems

> Far and wide
> A plain below stretched seaward, while, descried
> Above sea-clouds, the peaks of Arran rose;
> And, by that simple notice, the repose
> Of earth, sky, sea, and air was vivified.[25]

Significantly, neither the stunning view nor the farm itself ever moved Robert in the same manner.

Gavin Hamilton himself transformed the original 'but and ben' and built the small farmhouse which he had intended to use as a summer home. For a prosperous burgess with aspirations to gentility, Hamilton built on an exceedingly modest scale, but if it was never intended as anything more than a weekend retreat from his town residence only a mile south, then it would have served its purpose. As the home of the widow Burnes, her four sons and three daughters, Mossgiel can have been no improvement over their previous abode. The farmhouse had the customary two rooms on the ground floor, with a floored loft above used, like Lochlie, as the sleeping accommodation of the menfolk. This area, approached by means of movable wooden steps, sloped down to the eaves and was divided into three tiny rooms. One, at the far end, served as little more than a storage closet and was separately reached from the kitchen; the middle apartment accommodated the bed where Robert and Gilbert slept, while the remaining chamber, at the other end, was occupied by John and William. This end bedroom had a tiny four-pane window in the gable. The middle room had a much larger window, also of four panes, set in the rear roof like a skylight. Below this window stood a small table with a single large drawer underneath where Robert kept his writing materials.

Downstairs, old Agnes and her youngest daughter slept in the usual recess bed in the kitchen, while Agnes and Annabella had fixed beds along the back wall in the larger adjoining room. Some of the early biographies stated incorrectly that Robert shared his bed with John Blane, one of the farm-servants who was responsible for some personal reminiscences of the poet which may or may not be accurate, particularly bearing on his method of treating those palpitations that often assailed him in the night. In fact, from the outset, the male servants, two ploughmen and a gaudsboy, slept in the loft over the stable.

One of Robert's longer poems of the early Mossgiel period, 'The Vision' (CW 114–21), was set in this farmhouse. The best room, 'ben the house', is referred to in the second stanza: 'Ben i the spence, right pensivelie, I gaed to rest'. The 'ingle–cheek' was the hearth where the poet 'sat an ey'd the spewing reek'. The reference to 'The auld clay biggin' in the third stanza, and 'the restless rattons' squeaking 'about the riggin' seemed to refer to the more homely architecture of Lochlie, placing composition in 1783 or earlier; but Kinsley argued for a date in 1785, and Robert added several verses in 1786–7. The eighth stanza begins 'When click! the string the snick did draw'; and William Patrick, who had been herd-boy at Mossgiel in 1784–8, later recalled that the front door was opened by means of a string through a hole which lifted the sneck or latch.[26]

Willie Patrick was only eight years old when he came to work at Mossgiel. At various times Robert also gave employment to Robert Allan, a relative of his mother, as ploughman. Agnes Brown and Jean Allan were step-sisters, and Robert was Jean's son. James Hamilton, as a very young boy, was briefly employed about the farm and ran errands. His sole recollection of this period was taking a sealed letter to Mauchline one day in 1785 with strict instructions to deliver it into the hands of Jean Armour personally. John Blane, the gaudsman whose main task was to drive the plough team of four horses, later became driver of the Lord Nelson coach which plied between Kilmarnock and Cumnock. Davie Hutcheson, known at the time as 'Girning Davie', was immortalised by Robert in 'The Inventory' (CW 195), the poetic answer to a mandate from Robert Aiken (in his capacity as Surveyor of Taxes), as 'wee Davoc'. Although at least seven labourers are known to have lived at Mossgiel, there were never more than three at any one time, the 'three mischievous boys, / Run-deils for fechtin an for noise'. The reason that 'A gaudsman ane, a thrasher t'other' had to be enumerated was that, among the fiscal measures introduced to restore the country's fortunes after the American War, William Pitt had levied a tax on male servants, with a higher rate for bachelors than for married men. In this poetic tax return Robert admits, 'I've nane in female servan' station' and adds parenthetically, 'Lord keep me ay frae a' temptation' – a rueful reference to the trouble he had got into with Betsey Paton.

According to James Grierson's notes, John Blane sat beside Robert in church on the day when the incident of the louse crawling across the hair of the young lady in the pew in front was observed. Blane 'was surprized when Burns awakened him, the middle of the same night, & repeated to him all the stanzas, requesting his opinion of them, – this was the most surprizing Proofs of the facility with which Burns composed, that Came within J. B.'s Knowledge'. Unfortunately Blane's claim to have shared a room, if not a bed, with the poet was later shown to be untrue, so this statement has to be taken with a pinch of salt. He may have been on firmer ground in his other observations:

> In the laborious employment of husbandry, the Peculiarities of Burns's mind were easily discernable – While engaged in Thrashing, it was evident that his mind was particularly occupied, from the varied alternations from slow to quick which rendered it dangerous & even impossible for another to Keep time with him but in an hour or two he was quite exhausted & gave in altogether . . . A simple occurrence commented on by Burns in his own commanding way, has never since failed to Impress this persons mind, in regard to Cruelty to animals. When walking together, J. B. having a whip in his hand, gave a slight touch of it at a sparrow, & deprived it of some of its feathers – Upon this occasion Burns made so solemn an appeal to his Conscience, upon the unnecessary & wanton barbarity of the action that he has Ever since been Influenced by his admonition to resist similar Temtations – Burns uniformly digested & arranged his Compositions mentally, before he committed them to paper –[27]

Equally suspect was the testimony of John Lambie, who claimed to have worked as a labourer at Lochlie, but furnished Grierson with details of incidents which, from other evidence, were actually associated with Mossgiel. Lambie claimed to have been with Robert at the plough on the day that they turned up the mouse, and had been rebuked by the poet for chasing the poor creature 'wi murdering pattle'. Lambie recalled that the mouse:

> had an uncommonly large nest. Next day, while [Burns] was composing the Poem on the Mouse he was driving and unloading two carts, earth and lime, which his brother and another man filled from a heap at a distance – so absorbed was he Burns that one time he forgot to unload one of the Carts and returned it with its Load to the heap, not much to the pleasure of his Brother. Influence of the Poetic fever, not steady – then he was silent with his lips frequently in motion. So good natured that his boys directed him rather than he the boys.[28]

An apocryphal version, still part of oral tradition in Mauchline, claims that Robert subsequently showed Lambie the draft of the poem 'To a Mouse' with the words, 'Well, what do you think of your mouse now?'

Willie Patrick was eighty-four years of age when William Jolly interviewed him in the centenary year of Robert's birth, but he was mentally alert and had good recall of the years he had spent at Mossgiel.[29] He worked there from the age of eight till twelve and was originally employed to feed the poultry, do little tasks around the farmyard, muck out the byre, peel potatoes, help the womenfolk in the kitchen and run errands. He could remember going down into the town a mile away for Robert's newspapers. 'He had a lairge leebrary and he read ony books that cam in his way; in fac' he was ay readin'. Willie, however, never heard Robert read or recite any of his own works, though it was well known even then (1784) that he had composed a great deal. The boy also carried Robert's letters into Mauchline to post, remarking that they were much more numerous than was then common. Patrick tripped himself up, however, when he claimed to have led Robert's horse named Jenny Geddes when, in fact, this 'yauld, poutherie Girran' was purchased by Robert in Edinburgh some years later. Similarly, one tends to look critically at Willie's comment that Robert 'soon made up the lasses . . . he could ay speak up to them in a fresh, open, cheerful manner with smart daffin [flirtation] and banter'. Burns was 'smart, manly and good-looking, liked by all, except the stricter sort who feared his reputed wildness'. Patrick never once saw the poet the worse for liquor. He was 'a guid kind maister', being liked for his gentle nature and kindly helpfulness by all his servants. Gilbert was a 'douce, sensible man' but otherwise seems to have made no impression.

Willie's favourite in the Burns family was Isobel, whom he habitually referred to as Bell. According to him, Bell used to creep up the garret steps to have a fly peep at Robert's poems. If Robert was aware of his young sister's curiosity, it may explain why an entry in the *Commonplace Book* under September 1785, containing an unpublished version of the first stanza of 'Now Westlin Winds' (CW 44) had the last line altered from 'To muse upon my charmer' to 'To muse on ***** *****'. My asterisks were represented in the manuscript by squiggles, a secret cypher which Robert had devised to keep his innermost secrets from little prying eyes; but it does not take a skilled cryptologist to crack this simple code and reveal the name as Jeany Armour.

William Tannahill, a joiner in Ardrossan by 1817 when Grierson interviewed him, recalled that as a youth he was employed as errand-boy by Robert Bowie, a merchant in Kilmarnock. From time to time these errands took him to Mossgiel where he was usually met by Bell Burns. He was a shy lad who would never give his name, but merely said that he hailed from Stewarton. On one occasion he called at the farmhouse and Agnes Brown answered the door. Seeing him she cried ben the house, 'Bell, here's the Stewarton boy wanting you again – his breeches wouldn't be mittens to a ploughman'. The lady of the house had been a woman of some humour. Bowie courted Bell for some time, and Tannahill remembered that she had a talent for extempore verse when his employer was with her. The wooing failed and Bowie never married, whereas Bell eventually married a Mauchline quarrier named John Begg.

Both family and farm-hands ate together and shared the same simple repast; but Patrick said that after the evening meal the servants retired to their stable loft early and were never present for evening prayers which was a strictly family affair. This contradicts the statement of another quondam gaudsman (at Lochlie) named William Ronald who maintained that Robert's conduct of the family worship after his father's death was unequalled. Otherwise his memoir of Burns is not without interest. Though he was the kindest of masters, 'he was then sometimes an ill guide of himself'. He was much more kindly than Gilbert who, as farm manager, took a tougher line with the servants. Robert was 'always anxious to solace and cheer and assist the younger labourers and was ready with a helping hand and a look of encouragement', as an unidentified farm-hand informed Dr Carruthers of the *Inverness Courier*.[30]

The move to Mossgiel widened Robert's social horizons but did not lessen his Tarbolton connections. This was mainly due to his enthusiasm for freemasonry, a movement which embodied so many of his ideals. To his enthusiasm must be added his natural wit and intelligence which marked him out for rapid advancement, so that he was elected Depute-Master on 27 July 1784. Sir John Whitefoord was Master, but this was largely an honorific position, and the day-to-day running of the lodge was in the hands of the Depute-Master. According to some of his masonic friends he was 'so keen a mason that he would hold lodges for the admission of new members in his own house'.[31] The song 'No Churchman am I' (CW 66), which belongs to early 1784, alludes to the convivial nature of these meetings. Earlier editors assigned it to 1781, and associated it with the Bachelors' Club, but a suppressed stanza (in the Huntington MS) contains the lines, 'Sir Pit at his Finance may set him to work, / And Hastings be libell'd a robber by Burke', which date it to the parliamentary commission of enquiry into Warren Hastings (1783–4) and the appointment of William Pitt the Younger as Chancellor of the Exchequer in December 1783. To this song Robert added a stanza which makes the masonic context perfectly clear:

Then fill up a bumper and make it o'erflow,
And honours Masonic prepare for to throw:
May ev'ry true Brother of the Compass and Square
Have a big-belly'd bottle, when harass'd with care!

This bacchanal has been used by some of the poet's detractors as evidence of over-indulgence in alcohol at a relatively early stage in his life; but in fact, it is nothing of the sort. 'The bacchanalianism of his verse did not come from the heart, as his amatory frenzy usually did,' wrote Chambers. 'It was merely the literary expression of a recognised common sentiment'[32] and, indeed, it merely echoed many of the Anacreontics which were exceedingly popular in the eighteenth century.

Dr John Mackenzie himself became a freemason in 1784, being inducted as a member of St James Lodge, Tarbolton, in default of a lodge in Mauchline itself. It is not known whether Robert was the means of persuading the good doctor to join, though this is not unlikely, given Robert's zeal for the movement at this time. Certainly, the friendship which had begun at Lochlie in 1783 ripened over the course of the ensuing years. It was cemented, both socially and professionally, in the late summer of 1784 when Robert's health suffered a relapse. No letters are extant between 17 February (when Robert wrote from Lochlie to cousin James in Montrose announcing his father's death) and 3 August (when he again wrote to his cousin). The latter epistle (CL 59–60) stated 'we are all in health at prest' but this does not rule out the possibility that Robert may have been suffering from a general recurrence of those psychosomatic ailments which had so beset him at Irvine. The next extant letter, dated 13 September 1784 (CW 72–3), was addressed to his old school friend, John Tennant, Junior, now living at Glenconner in the parish of Ochiltree, whither his father had gone as factor to the Countess of Glencairn. This letter, dealing with local, domestic and business matters, began ominously:

My unlucky illness of Friday last did not do me a greater disservice than in disappointing me of the pleasure I had promised myself in spending an hour with you. – I got so much better on Saturday as to be able to ride home, but I am still in a kind of slow fever, as I trouble you with this small letter rather to relieve a little the langor of my spirits than any thing particular I have to tell you.

It is not known where Robert was that unhappy weekend, but we may assume that he was in the vicinity of Ochiltree. Contemporary eye-witness accounts quoted by Chambers[33] state that Robert's health gave way 'to a somewhat serious extent' that summer, implying that the bout in early September was a recurrence of the same problem. 'The movements of his heart were affected, and he became liable to fainting fits, particularly in the night-time.' John Blane was the source of the tale that Robert, by way of remedy, had recourse to cold baths. 'A barrel of water was placed near his bedside, and into this he was obliged to plunge when threatened by his ailment.' No doubt Robert's friend Dr Mackenzie kept an eye on him, though the doctor has left no actual record of attendance or medicines and treatment prescribed as we have from the Irvine period. It is thus unsafe to assert, as Maurice Lindsay has done, that Mackenzie instructed his patient to plunge into cold baths and to get rid of the melancholy by still harder farm work when clearly Robert should have been ordered complete rest.[34] There is absolutely no evidence to support these assertions. Mackenzie's own memoir makes no mention of attending Burns during this illness. As for the cold tub treatment, Robert probably got this from *Domestic Medicine* by Dr William Buchan (1729–1805), first published in 1769 and going through twenty-two editions by 1826 (not counting numerous pirated editions). If not every household, certainly every farmhouse would have had a copy of this indispensable manual. That Robert was familiar with it, and knew that his readers would also be familiar with it, is demonstrated by the casual reference in 'Death and Dr Hornbook' (CW 98): 'He's grown sae weel acquaint wi *Buchan*'. Buchan was an ardent believer in the efficacy of hard labour to snap people out of depression and, reflecting the relative ignorance of cardiovascular disorders at the time, vigorously propounded cold bathing, especially in sea water, for the relief of rheumatism, 'nervous fevers' and the violent palpitations accompanying nervous disorders. This point is particularly significant not only in absolving Mackenzie but also perhaps in mitigating the harsh verdict which posterity has cast on Robert's last physician, Dr William Maxwell of Dumfries.

From December 1781 onwards references to illness, injuries and ailments permeate the prose writings of Burns no fewer than seventy-seven times.[35] Crichton-Browne (1925)[36] and Anderson (1928)[37] both came to the conclusion that Robert had suffered rheumatic fever which, being a disease contracted in childhood, led them into the unsupportable morass of claiming such an attack in the Alloway or Mount Oliphant years, although neither Robert nor Gilbert mentioned anything of the sort. Biographers latched on to Robert's casual references to 'a rheumatic fever' in a letter to Robert Cleghorn (CL 279) and 'a most severe Rheumatic fever' in a letter to Mrs Dunlop (CL 215) – both written in January 1796 near the end of his life – as proof that he had suffered chronic rheumatic fever since early boyhood. Fowler [38] quite rightly rejects this and points out that the use of the indefinite article makes a world of difference. The label of rheumatic fever for a specific disease was not commonly used by the medical profession till 1812. When Robert used the term he was describing a fever with cramps and pains in his bones and muscles. Taking the available evidence of the dull night-time headaches mentioned by Gilbert from Robert's adolescence onwards, together with Robert's own graphic descriptions of his illnesses at Irvine and later on, everything points to recurring clinical depression, accompanied by severe anxiety attacks and psychosomatic disorders – Robert's 'hypochondria'. The recurrence of this illness in the summer of 1784 resulted in an entry in the *First Commonplace Book* about August, under the heading 'A prayer, when fainting fits, & other alarming symptoms of a Pleurisy or some other dangerous disorder, which, indeed still threatens me, first put Nature on the alarm'. Below this appears 'A Prayer in Prospect of Death' (CW 53-4) which most scholars now believe to have been written during the Irvine period. Its insertion in the *Commonplace Book* at this time, however, seems to tie in with the recurrence of illness. Those who argue for a later composition, at the time it appeared in the *Commonplace Book*, point to the pervasive feelings of remorse in this poem – 'a remorse which there is no good ground for believing he had any reason to feel when he was in Irvine'.[39] This fitted the erroneous belief of biographers until early this century that Elizabeth Paton would have been heavily pregnant by August 1784, and that Robert therefore had much to be remorseful about.

Robert was certainly well enough on 27 July 1784, the evening on which he was elected Depute Master of St James Lodge. The entries in the lodge minutes show that he was a regular attender from that time onwards, but meetings were intermittent and therefore provide few clues to Robert's state of health during this period. The next meeting did not take place until 1 September 1784 and, though the minute is unsigned, it is unmistakably in Robert's handwriting. From his letter to Tennant, we know that he was ill about ten days later. The *Commonplace Book* is no help either, except in a negative sense. After the stanzas beginning 'Why am I loth to leave this earthly scene?' (CW 54-5), the only entry under September 1784 is the song 'O Tibbie, I Hae Seen the Day' (CW 47-8). There is no further entry until April 1785.

Hitherto Robert's poetic progress had been rambling and desultory, without any clearly defined aim. Gilbert spoke of the Tarbolton years as being a period marked by little intellectual improvement, though the Bachelors' Club gave Robert an opportunity to sharpen his debating skills. After the move to Mossgiel, however, we see the rapid development of Robert's literary power. To this period belongs the 'Ballad on the American War' (CW 72-4), Robert's most ambitious occasional poem to date. As a commentary on political events in the aftermath of the War of Independence, it exhibits a technical deftness matched by familiarity with the incidents and personalities of the period. The pawky references to the political heavyweights, such as 'Chatham's boy' (William Pitt) and 'slee Dundas' (Henry Dundas, later Viscount Melville) were pretty daring but too politically sensitive for inclusion in the earliest editions of Burns's works. Likewise the 'Address to the Unco Guid or the Rigidly Righteous' (CW 74-6), with its vernacular paraphrase from Ecclesiastes, was early evidence of Robert's courage in speaking out against Calvinist hypocrisy.

Several pieces which date from 1784, however, had a more local interest. 'The Ronalds of the Bennals' (CW 76-8) dealt with a family whose 200-acre farm, to the east of Mossblown about a mile north of the A758 Ayr-Mauchline road, is in existence to this day. It was the home of William Ronald and Jean Boyd and, unlike the Burnes family, Ronald owned his farm. This put the Ronalds in a rather superior class, though not quite the 'laird' which Burns speaks of in the second stanza. The Ronalds had one son, Hugh, and four daughters, one of whom (Jean) was allegedly courted by Gilbert Burns, without success – she married John Reid of Langlands Farm near Tarbolton. Jean Ronald was ages with Robert and eighteen months older than Gilbert. A hoary old tradition (inspired, no doubt, by the relevant verses of the song itself) claims that Robert was keen to pay court to Anne Ronald but was afraid of being rebuffed on account of the family's wealth and social position.[40] Perhaps it was she who was the recipient, or intended recipient, of the undated A letter (CL 43) mentioned in Chapter 5. Certainly it was couched in terms that suggested that the declaration of love would come like a bolt from the blue. Perhaps Robert could not bring himself to speak to the girl in person and decided that the written word would serve his purpose best. This is idle speculation, of course, but it might explain the tradition of an intention which was never realised and also why Robert consoled himself by poking mild poetic fun at this prosperous family's expense. Incidentally, Anne Ronald married Robert's friend and neighbour of the Lochlie period, Matthew Paterson of Skioch, whose prowess as a flax-grower has already been noted. Neither of the other daughters – Isabella (born in 1756) and Mary (born in 1769) – is mentioned in the poem, probably because Isabella was already married to Alexander Bruce of Shaw by that time and Mary was scarcely in her teens. Regarding his supposed passion for Anne Ronald, the poet declared himself in the ninth stanza:

> I lo'e her mysel, but darena weel tell,
> My poverty keeps me in awe, man;
> For making o rhymes, and working at times,
> Does little or naething at a', man

Ronald is a common surname, unfortunately; for most Burns scholars from the earliest until very recently[41] have fallen into the trap of assuming that William Ronald of the Bennals was the person referred to by Robert in a letter to his brother William dated 10 November 1789 (CL 517–18), telling him that 'Mr Ronald is bankrupt. – You will easily guess that from his insolent vanity in his sunshine of life, he will now feel a little retaliation from those who thought themselves eclipsed by him . . .' This furnishes a prime example of the manner in which biographers of Burns have been all too ready to jump to conclusions. Fortunately Heather Ronald, wife of William's great-great-great-grandson, herself a writer of considerable scholarship and integrity, has succeeded in removing the unwarranted stigma. Puzzled by the fact that the Bennals remained in the Ronald family until 1885 – hardly consonant with a bankruptcy in 1789 – Mrs Ronald discovered documents pertaining to the sequestration of William Ronald, merchant and tobacconist in Mauchline, on the petition of John Muir of Glasgow.[42] This William Ronald, incidentally, was the recipient of a parcel from Burns in April 1787 containing a letter (CL 220) and two copies of the first Edinburgh Edition intended for George Reid of Barquharrie near Ochiltree.[43]

Another poem of the same vintage is 'The Tarbolton Lasses' (CW 78-9), six verses of light-hearted fun at the expense of the local belles. No attempt was ever made to identify Peggy ('She kens her father is a laird, / And she forsooth's a leddy'), Sophy ('Wha canna win her in a night, / Has little art in courtin'), Mysie ('She's dour and din, a deil within, / But aiblins she may please ye), her sister Jenny ('If ye'll dispense wi want o sense / She kens herself she's bonie') and Bessy, the pride of them all:

> There's few sae bonie, nane sae guid
> In a' King George' dominion;
> If ye should doubt the truth o this,
> It's Bessy's ain opinion!

From the same period, during the first year at Mossgiel, probably dates the song 'O, Leave Novels' (CW 79-80):

> O, leave novéls, ye Mauchline belles –
> Ye're safer at your spinning-wheel!
> Such witching books are baited hooks
> For rakish rooks like Rob Mossgiel.

The sexual boastfulness of this song and the frank warning of Robert's predatory outlook show a tremendous self-confidence. Robert's reputation as the parish poet was becoming established. When it came to paying a compliment to those 'Belles of Mauchline' (CW 79), however, Robert was not slow to identify them. The reference to 'Their carriage and dress, a stranger would guess, in Lon'on or Paris, they'd gotten a'' accords with William Auld's comment on the fashions of his female parishioners:

> Miss Miller is fine, Miss Markland's divine,
>   Miss Smith she has wit, and Miss Betty is braw,
> There's beauty and fortune to get wi Miss Morton;
>   But Armour's the jewel for me o them a'.

Helen Miller (born in September 1762) was the elder daughter of John Miller of the Sun Inn, Mauchline, and on 29 August 1791 she married Dr Mackenzie. Their son, John Whitefoord Mackenzie (1794-1884) was a noted antiquarian and literary figure. Helen's sister Betty (born February 1768) married William Templeton, a Mauchline merchant, but died in 1795 giving birth to their only child. The tradition that Robert was sweet on her was entirely based on the supposition that she was the heroine of 'From Thee, Eliza, I must go' (CW 50), composed at least three years before he met her. Jean Markland (1765-1851), daughter of a Mauchline shopkeeper named George Markland, had the curious distinction in 1779 of being charged, along with her parents, of making a false accusation of witchcraft against the wife of a rival shopkeeper. Tradition avers that she was the Jenny who, sitting in church one day in her fine balloon-bonnet, played hostess to the 'ugly, creepin, blastit wunner' which inspired

Robert's ode 'To a Louse' (CW 181–2). Eventually she married James Findlay, the Tarbolton exciseman who subsequently gave Robert his practical instruction in gauging and excise book-keeping. Robert is believed to have introduced the couple. The witty Jean Smith (1768–1854) was the sister of James Smith, one of Robert's closest cronies of the Mauchline years, and she married another of Robert's friends, James Candlish, by whom she was the mother of the Revd. Dr James Candlish, the theologian and Free Church leader. Christina (or Christian as her baptismal entry shows) Morton was born in August 1760 and married Robert Paterson, a draper and general merchant of Mauchline, in December 1788. She bore him four sons and two daughters.[44]

The place of honour in the punch-line was reserved for Jean Armour who, traditionally, was also the subject of the little song entitled 'The Mauchline Lady' (CW 80). A further dozen poems or songs were to extol the merits of Robert's 'bonie Jean', the last being the exquisite song, 'Their Groves o Sweet Myrtle' (CW 550), sent to George Thomson in April 1795. Songs like 'Tho Cruel Fate' (CW 251), the last of the valedictory pieces composed before he intended taking ship for Jamaica in 1786, and 'Of a' the Airts' (CW 329), a song of longing and separation, when he was at Ellisland and she was still in Mauchline, are among some of the tenderest and most passionately sincere that Robert ever wrote. So far as Robert ever really loved any woman, he loved Jean and she continued to inspire him, from time to time, almost until his death.

Remarkably little is known about Jean and even her date of birth is variously given, in those works which even mention it at all.[45] This confusion may have arisen because Robert Burns-Begg (a great-grandson of Isobel Burns) published a memoir of Jean Armour and gave her birth date as February 1767, from the entry in a Burns family bible (27 February 1767). Yet the Mauchline parish register unequivocally gives her baptismal date as 25 February 1765, while the Armour family bible, containing entries made by James Armour himself, gives her birth date as 16 February 1765.[46] The entry in the Burns family bible, it should be noted, was made by Robert about 1791 so the error is, perhaps, understandable. Jean was the second in a family of eleven and the eldest daughter, born to James Armour and Mary Smith who were married on 7 December 1761. Several of the Armour children died in infancy, which explains why three of the sons were christened Robert and two daughters were named Mary (after their mother).[47] The Armours appear to have been stone-masons for several generations, as were the Smiths. This tradition was carried on in the next generation when the poet's cousin William Burnes was apprenticed to James Armour. James himself was a master-mason and 'contractor' and was responsible for a number of bridges in Ayrshire, still standing, as well as working on Dumfries House at Cumnock and Skeldon House, Dalrymple. The Burnes family were living at Mount Oliphant when James Armour and his father-in-law Adam Smith were engaged by the Earl of Cassillis in building Greenan Bridge over the River Doon only two miles away. Both masons are named on the plaque which was removed when the bridge was demolished in 1861 and replaced by the present road bridge, the plaque being then built into the wall of the cottage and shop on the west side of the road.[48] Armour was never the 'pretty considerable architect in Ayrshire' which Robert liked to make out when trying to impress his cousin James Burness (CL 63) but he was a tradesman of solid worth, who could afford to rent one of the most expensive pews in the body of the kirk, at a cost of 10s 8d per annum.[49] James Armour was numbered among the unco guid of the parish. 'He appears to have been exemplary in his life but, like many worthy men, he was somewhat rigid and austere in his disposition and belonged to the stricter sect of religionists called the Auld Lichts,' wrote Robert Burns-Begg.[50] This writer also credited Jean's mother with having 'partaken somewhat of the gay and frivolous', though on what grounds this was based I have been unable to determine; and this vague character sketch is at variance with Robert's admittedly subjective view of his prospective mother-in-law, as we shall see later.

Similarly, nothing is known about Jean's childhood, upbringing or education. Indeed, so little was known concerning the last named that many Burns scholars supposed her to be virtually illiterate. It was long supposed that her education was not above that typical of country girls of the period, and that she would have been taught to read the printed word (i.e. the Bible and devotional works), but would not have been taught to read or write cursive script beyond making her signature. But Jean was the eldest daughter and her father's favourite, and appears to have received a more liberal education than was the norm. Jean's signature, in a bold round hand, appears in the Session books of Mauchline and also in some receipts granted to Gilbert Burns.[51] What gave the lie to the *canard* that Jean was no scholar was the fact that Robert himself wrote to her at least four letters (CL 477-9) and the first of these, written from Ellisland in September 1788, actually begins, 'My dear Love, I received your kind letter with a pleasure which no letter but one from you could have given me'. No letters from Jean to Robert have survived, but several personal letters from Jean to the Marchioness of Hastings, James Glencairn Burns (her son) and Betty Burns (her step-daughter) spanning the years 1816-33 are known to exist.[52] These show that Jean was not only literate but had a good command of spelling and grammar; in other words, she wrote a good letter. The suggestion that they were actually written by an amanuensis does not stand up, as the handwriting is very similar over a period of seventeen years, and also bears the characteristics found in those specimens of Jean's signature from a much earlier period. In view of the evidence of Jean's high standard of literacy, the notion (prevailing to this day) that Robert was unable to treat with his wife on an intellectual level may need to be revised.

Robert himself confided to Peggy Chalmers in September 1788 (CL 238) that 'Mrs Burns . . . although she scarcely ever in her life, except the Scriptures of the Old and New Testament, and the Psalms of David in metre, spent five minutes together on either prose or verse.– I must except from this last, a certain late publication of Scots poems, which she has perused very devoutly'.

Jean, named after her maternal grandmother, was born and raised in Mauchline and lived all her life until the age of twenty-one in her parents' substantial stone house on the west side of the Cowgate, a few yards south of Loudoun Street. The Whitefoord Arms stood on the west side of the junction of these streets and the Armour house was immediately behind the public house, and separated from it by a very narrow lane. Just up the Cowgate on the opposite side from the Whitefoord Arms stood another inn, Poosie Nancie's, on the corner with Main Street. Opposite Loudoun and Main Streets stands the parish church and the kirkyard, on the far side of which is the Castle, with Gavin Hamilton's house on the western side and Morton's ballroom on the eastern side. Mauchline owes its importance as a market town to its location at the intersection of the A758 Edinburgh-Ayr and A76 Kilmarnock-Dumfries roads. Although today it has a population in excess of 2,000 and has expanded considerably in comparatively recent years, the old village around the kirk and the cross has not changed much since the late eighteenth century. It had a population of about a thousand in 1791 and a century later this had risen to 1,454.[53] Long noted for its horse and cattle fairs, it preserves the air of a small country town to this day. The church in which the Armour and Burns families worshipped was dismantled in 1827 and the present building erected in its place; but the kirkyard has not changed much since it was the location of Robert's 'Holy Fair' (CW 133–9) and the visitor can consult the chart on the outside wall of the church indicating the burial places of the poet's family and associates, and inspect the well-tended graves of Gavin Hamilton and the Alexanders of Ballochmyle, of 'Holy Willie' Fisher and Nance Tannock, of Daddy Auld and Racer Jess, and that poignant lair containing the bones of Jean Armour's four daughters.[54]

From the twelfth-century pile, known locally as the Castle (but actually a daughter house of Melrose Abbey), the High Street runs eastwards. Opposite the junction with the Back Causeway (Castle Street) was Nance Tannock's inn, built in 1712 (and still standing, though no longer a licensed hostelry). Across the street is Bauldy Muckle's house where Robert and Jean first set up home (now a museum), the house of Dr Mackenzie, and the homes of Robert's boon companions, James Smith and John Richmond. The Back Causeway runs north-west to join the Knowe, while the lane curving southwards at this juncture is the Backholm which meanders in a southerly direction to link up with Loudoun Street. At the bend where the Back Causeway and Backholm meet stood a pub known as the Elbow tavern, kept by a retired sailor known, appropriately, as 'The Old Tar'. This ale-house has long gone, as has the much more respectable Whitefoord Arms which gave succour and sustenance to many a weary cattle-drover and horse-dealer.

On the other hand Poosie Nancie's (Agnes Gibson's), a disreputable dive in Robert's day, has been beautifully preserved and even boasts a number of relics associated directly or indirectly with the poet. In the 1770s and 1780s it was classed as a lodging-house, which was thoroughly misleading as it was little more than a dosshouse for vagrants. It seems ironic that, since Robert would never have considered frequenting such a place, it owes its present undeniable attraction to the works of the poet. It is, first and foremost, associated with 'The Jolly Beggars' (CW 182–91), that glorious cantata of love and liberty which was Robert's only attempt at a dramatic work. Agnes Ronald, better known to posterity by her nickname of Poosie (pussy) Nancie, was the wife of George Gibson – the black-bearded Geordie of 'Adam Armour's Prayer' (CW 198–9) – and the mother of Jock and poor half-witted Hav'rel Jean in the same poem. Jean Gibson, otherwise known as Racer Jess from her fleetness of foot as she ran errands around the village, also figures in 'The Holy Fair' – 'There Racer Jess and twa-three whores, / Are blinkin at the entry'.

The Kirk Session was responsible for the maintenance of law and order, both spiritual and temporal, and its minute-books make fascinating reading. Here are preserved the foibles and peccadilloes of the parish, the allegations of witchcraft, the petty-thieving, the drunkenness and, above all, the fornication both ante-nuptial and extra-marital. Among the entries for 1773, for example, we find the Session recording that Agnes Ronald is 'habitually drunk, troublesome to her neighbours, and frequently disturbs the sober passengers' of the stage-coaches. Being hailed before the Session she told the assembled minister and elders that 'she was resolved to continue in her disorderly way'. Thereupon it was minuted, on the motion of Mr Auld, that 'the Session, considering the aforesaid foolish resolution and expression, do immediately exclude her from the privileges of the church until she shall profess her repentance'. Later the same year we find the Session declaring that 'George Gibson keeps a very irregular house, and that his wife and daughter are guilty of resetting stolen goods, knowing the same to be stolen'. More will be said later of the Gibsons in connection with a fracas in 1786 which inspired some of Robert's Rabelaisian verses.

The precise date of Robert's first meeting with Jean Armour – even the year – is a matter of debate. Many early writers, confused by some of the undated or disjointed entries in the *First Commonplace Book*, placed this in April 1784 during the week of the annual horse races.[55] It cannot be ruled out that, in a small place like Mauchline, Robert may have known of Jean Armour by that time, but at that date he was becoming heavily involved with Betsey Paton. After Betsey became pregnant that autumn, however, Robert turned his attentions elsewhere, as he related in a letter to Mrs Dunlop on 21 August 1788 (CL 154–5):

> You would know an Ayr-shire lad, Sandy Bell, who made a Jamaica fortune, & died some time ago. – A William Miller, formerly a Mason, now a Merchant in this place, married a sister german of Bell's for the sake of 500£ her brother had left her. – A Sister of Miller's who was then Tenant of my heart for the time being, huffed my Bardship in the pride of her new Connection; & I, in the heat of my resentment resolved to burlesque the whole business, & began as follows –

He then quoted the hilarious poem entitled 'The Mauchline Wedding' (CW 157–8) about the marriage of William Miller and the heiress Agnes

Bell which took place in July 1785. The poem satirises the pomp and circumstance, but especially the groom's sisters who got up three and a half hours early to dress for the occasion. Robert took immense delight in describing this lengthy operation, but in deference to his matronly correspondent he cut out two obscene lines which, regrettably, have never been recovered. The Nell and Bess of this risqué production were Helen and Elizabeth Miller, two of the Mauchline belles previously mentioned. It was the latter whose head was turned from Burns by 'Jamaica siller', though she did not actually wed William Templeton till 8 September 1794. The tentative identification of Elizabeth Miller with the Eliza of Robert's farewell song has already been examined and discarded.

The importance of this, however, is in helping to fix the beginning of the affair with Jean Armour. Bess Miller's rejection would have come some time before July 1785, and may have been due rather to the scandal involving Betsey Paton which would have erupted with the birth of the baby (22 May), if not prior to that. The first meeting with Jean Armour is traditionally associated with Race Week in April, and there is no reason to doubt that. But surely Robert would have been too busy with the move into Mossgiel to have attended the races of 1784. It seems more probable, therefore, that Jean and Robert met in April 1785, rather than twelve months earlier.

Even the exact circumstances of their first encounters are open to doubt. Near the Castle in Mauchline stood the building known as Morton's ballroom, but which was in fact little more than a barn in which dances were held to the accompaniment of a fiddler who played for a penny a reel. The generally accepted story goes like this. At the end of Race Week a dance was held in this hall and Robert and Jean were both present, but dancing with other partners, when some confusion and merriment were excited by Robert's collie literally dogging his footsteps through the room. Robert playfully remarked to his dancing partner that 'he wished he could get any of the lasses to like him as well as his dog did'.[56] Some writers, projecting from this wistful statement, claim that Robert was a bit of a wallflower!

Not long afterwards he happened to be walking through the washing-green, a patch of ground between the Backholm and the Mauchline Burn north of the Castle, where Jean was busy bleaching linen in the time-honoured manner by spreading it out on the grass to expose it to the bright sunshine. Robert was accompanied by his collie, still little more than a puppy, which frisked and frolicked in the manner of puppies and intruded itself among the cloth that Jean was trying to lay out. She called to Robert to bring his dog to heel. He instantly complied and then apologised for the collie's behaviour, and in the course of the ensuing conversation Jean is said to have remarked, 'Have you found any lassie yet to love you as well as your dog?' accompanied by a fascinating archness of expression which must have gone straight to Robert's highly impressionable heart. 'With two such natures an acquaintanceship thus begun on a key-note so suggestive, could lead to only one result – an immediate attraction to each other, by the tenderest and most overpowering predilection which sways the human heart' is how their grand-nephew Robert Burns-Begg describes it, though Chambers states more laconically at the end of the bleaching-green incident, 'That was the beginning of their intimacy'.

This version, which has acquired the power of Holy Writ, implies that Jean made the first move, a matter which she herself hotly denied when questioned on the subject in 1827:

> The first time I ever saw Burns was in Mauchline. His family then lived in Mossgiel, about a mile from the village. I was then spreading clothes in a bleach-green along with some other girls, when the poet passed in his way to call on Mr Hamilton. He had a little dog which ran on the clothes, and I scolded, and threw something at the animal. Burns said, 'Lassie, if ye thought ought o' me, ye wadna hurt my dog!' – I thought to mysel – 'I wadna think much o' you at ony rate!' I saw him afterwards at a dancing-room, and we fell acquainted.[57]

Jean was just turned twenty at this time, in the prime of life and, as one of the Mauchline belles, probably quite good-looking. It is unfortunate that the only authentic portraits were not painted until she was well into her fifties and a grandmother, and these contradict each other. Samuel Mackenzie's portrait (with her favourite grandchild Sarah) shows a strong, careworn face with heavily chiselled, almost gypsy, features; whereas the Gilfillan portrait, seven years earlier, depicts a chubbier person, with dark brown curls peeping out from under her bonnet. The small mouth is pursed (Jean is on record as not being happy at having to pose for her portrait), but there is a sagacious look in those penetrating dark eyes. The Gilfillan portrait certainly accords more closely with one's perception of Jean as the comfortable, uncomplaining – not to say long-suffering – housewife and helpmeet. There are no descriptions of 'bonie Jean' after the 1780s so later writers have been left to exercise their imaginations. Catherine Carswell makes her 'a girl of nineteen or twenty, in short-gown and kilted petticoat' – so far, so good – 'She had a pleasant, square face, small square hands and frank, widely-opened, desirous eyes. Not his type, perhaps – the eyes were too dark, but there were lights in the straight brown hair which a poet might easily describe as golden. Her bare legs were strong and shapely, her feet remarkably small. She was as shy and as bold as a blackbird.'[58] Yvonne Stevenson, herself a great-great-grandniece of Jean Armour, plumped for 'a bewitching and gracious brunette', possessing a charming soprano voice, 'light as thistledown on her feet and the most popular dancing partner in the Penny Reels'. Later on, 'her cheek flamed scarlet and her jet black eyes sparkled dangerously'.[59] Poor Jean – to be reduced to the level of a Mills and Boon heroine!

Quite rightly, Snyder points out that it is purely a matter of conjecture as to how fast the friendship between Robert and Jean developed. The affair with Betsey Paton had ended before the baby was born. Apart from taking the infant off Betsey's hands as soon as she was weaned, so that she could be brought up in the Mossgiel household, Robert had nothing further to do with Miss Paton, apart from making some legal arrangement through Gavin Hamilton in the summer of 1786. In the spring and early summer of 1785 he had his eye on Bess Miller, but that was over by July, although there is strong evidence that it revived some twelve months later in the emotionally tangled summer of 1786. Whether other 'fair enslavers' flitted across the scene thereafter is unknown; but by the autumn of 1785 Robert and Jean were courting. Again local tradition maintains that James Armour did not approve of his eldest daughter walking out with young Mossgiel, but 'love will find a way'. A window at the rear of the Whitefoord Arms looked on to the window of Jean's bedroom, with only a very narrow lane intervening; and it is supposed that, like Pyramus and Thisbe, a verbal courtship was carried on across this barrier. At any rate, the affair progressed in a logical manner, so that, ere the year was out, Jean found herself 'As women wish to be who love their lords'.[60] The repercussions are discussed later.

By the summer of 1785, when he recovered from his depressive illness, Robert seems to have entered a more euphoric period which was significantly productive of both poetry and prose. The entries in the *Commonplace Book* now begin to reveal his ambitions and the awakening realisation that he might become more than just another parochial rhymer. In the early Lochlie years he had studied the works of Allan Ramsay (1686–1758); towards the end of the Irvine period he had begun reading the poems of Robert Fergusson (1750–74). In August 1785 Robert wrote:

> However I am pleased with the works of our Scotch Poets, particularly the excellent Ramsay, and the still more excellent Ferguson (*sic*), yet I am hurt to see other places of Scotland, their towns, rivers, woods, haughs, &c. immortalized in such celebrated performances, whilst my dear native country, the ancient Bailieries of Carrick, Kyle, & Cunningham, famous both in ancient & modern times for gallant, and warlike race of inhabitants; a country where civil, & particularly religious Liberty have ever found their first support, & their last asylum; a country the birthplace of many famous Philosophers, Soldiers, & Statesmen, and the scene of many important events recorded in Scottish History, particularly a great many of the actions of the GLORIOUS WALLACE, the SAVIOUR of his country; yet, we have never had one Scotch Poet of any eminence, to make the fertile banks of Irvine, the romantic woodlands & sequestered scenes of Aire, and the heathy, mountainous source, & winding sweep of Doon emulate Tay, Forth, Ettrick, Tweed, &c. This is a complaint I would gladly remedy, but Alas! I am far unequal to the task, both in native genius & education.
>
> Obscure I am, & obscure I must be, though no young Poet, nor Young Soldier's heart ever beat more fondly for fame than mine.

Later the same month Robert inserted a long passage which reveals an astonishingly deep perception of the traditional ballads of Scotland even at this early stage, giving the lie to the popular fallacy, still widely held, that

he did not turn to song to any large extent till he took up with James
Johnson and George Thomson some years later. This extremely detailed
analysis begins:

> There is a certain irregularity in the old Scotch Songs, a redundancy of
> syllables with respect to that exactness of Accent & measure that the
> English Poetry requires, but which glides in, most melodiously with the
> respective tunes to which they are set.

He then goes on to illustrate his points, using the old ballad 'The Mill, Mill
O' as an example. This passage also shows that Robert was familiar with
Bremner's collection of Scottish songs, for he compares the old ballad with
'To Fanny fair' in that volume:

> how flat & spiritless will the last appear, how trite, and lamely methodi-
> cal, compared with the wild-warbling cadence, the heart-moving melody
> of the first.– This particularly is the case with all those airs which end
> with a hypermetrical syllable.– There is a degree of wild irregularity in
> many of the compositions & Fragments which are daily sung to them by
> my compeers, the common people – a certain happy arrangement of old
> Scotch syllables, & yet, very frequently, nothing, not even *like* rhyme, or
> sameness of jingle at the ends of the lines. This has made me sometimes
> imagine that perhaps, it might be possible for a Scotch Poet, with a nice,
> judicious ear, to set compositions to many of our most favorite airs, par-
> ticularly that class of them mentioned above, independent of rhyme
> altogether.
> There is a noble Sublimity, a heart-melting tenderness in some of these
> ancient fragments, which show them to be the work of a masterly hand;
> and it has often given me many a heartake to reflect that such glorious old
> Bards – Bards, who, very probably, owed all their talents to native genius,
> yet have described the exploits of Heroes, the pangs of Disappointment,
> and the meltings of Love with such fine strokes of Nature, and, O mor-
> tifying to a Bard's vanity their very names are 'buried 'mongst the wreck
> of things which were'.

The final paragraph of this long passage shows clearly that Robert identified himself very closely with these nameless bards of old. He wrote
deprecatingly of himself as one who 'though far inferiour to your flights,
yet eyes your path, and with trembling wing would sometimes soar after
you'. In particular, Robert empathised with the ancient bards whose poetic
genius compensated them for more than their fair share of life's knocks and
setbacks:

> Some of you tell us, with all the charms of Verse, that you have been
> unfortunate in the world – unfortunate in love; he too has felt all the
> unfitness of a poetic heart for the struggle of a busy, bad World; he has
> felt the loss of his little fortune, the loss of friends, and worse than all, the
> loss of the Woman he adored! Like you, all his consolation was his Muse
> – She taught him in rustic measures to complain – Happy, could he have
> done it with your strength of imagination, and flow of Verse!

This very revealing passage, in which Robert discusses himself dispassionately and objectively in the third person, shows that he was still smarting from Eliza's rejection four years earlier – this at a time when he had dallied with Annie Rankine, had had an affair with Betsey Paton, had also tentatively set his sights on the housekeeper at Coilsfield and Elizabeth Miller, and was now embarked on an affair with Jean Armour.

The Coilsfield housekeeper is the least substantial of all Robert's heroines. An undated entry in the *Commonplace Book*, but belonging, from its position, to August or September 1785, deals with this episode, by way of providing the background to the song 'Montgomerie's Peggy' (CW 60). This was closely modelled on a traditional ballad entitled 'McMillan's Peggy', sung to the tune of 'Galla Water'.

> My Montgomerie's Peggy was my Deity for six, or eight months. She had been bred, tho' as the world says, without any just pretence for it, in a style of life rather elegant.– But as Vanbrugh says in one of his comedies, my 'damn'd Star Found me out'[61] there too, for though I began the affair, merely in a *gaieté de coeur*, or to tell the truth, what would scarcely be believed, a vanity of showing my parts in Courtship, particularly my abilities at a Billet doux, which I always piqu'd myself upon, made me lay siege to her; and when, as I always do in my foolish gallantries, I had battered myself into a very warm affection for her, she told me, one day in a flag of truce, that her fortress had been for some time before the rightful property of another; but with the greatest friendship and politenes, she offered me every alliance, except actual possession.– I found out afterwards, that what she told me of a preengagement was really true; but it cost me some heart Achs to get rid of the affair.

This courtship, such as it was, is only of interest in revealing the way Robert regarded a wooing as a military operation; the references to the siege, the fortress and the flag of truce – and similar metaphors elsewhere in his writings – show a subconscious view of woman as a target or a quarry, if not actually an enemy, to be stormed and captured. It also indicates Robert's propensity, in 'these foolish gallantries', to work himself up into such a state that he *felt* a warm affection for whichever fair charmer he had in his sights at the time; and in that passionate frame of mind he could write such tender love songs.

Further comments on fragments of songs which he was gathering then follow: 'By the way, these old Scottish airs are so nobly sentimental that when one would compose to them; to *south* the tune, as our Scotch phrase is, over & over, is the readiest way to catch the inspiration and raise the Bard into that glorious enthusiasm so strongly characteristic of our old Scotch Poetry.' The song 'Fickle Fortune' and the poem 'Raging Fortune' (CW 56), composed in the winter of 1781–2, were inserted in the book at this point, followed by a lengthy commentary confirming the date of composition. Robert adopted a fairly philosophical attitude that, even in the depths of misery, his muse 'all rustic, akward (*sic*) and unpolished as she is' would not desert him. She had 'more charms for me than any other of the pleasures of life beside'. Robert might claim, as he did in one of his earliest verse-epistles (CW 170), 'I rhyme for fun'; but poetry, from adolescence onwards, was much more than that. Snyder sums it up very neatly as 'sheer creative instinct', but I would go further. Even at this early period Robert was aware that his was no ordinary talent; already he could see that his verses were far superior to anything produced by the village poets like Saunders Tait. In lavishing praise on the productions of Thomas Orr, David Sillar and John Lapraik, Robert was unconsciously elevating his own genius. But allied to a self-confidence that could be overweening at times was a curious diffidence and indecisiveness; he had not yet reached the point at which he was ready to expose his poetic ambitions before a wider public. Richard Brown (1781-2) and brother Gilbert (1784) urged Robert to try for publication, but on both occasions he shied off.

Robert says of 'Raging Fortune' that it was at this time (1781-2) that he 'set about composing an air in the old Scotch style' (ignoring his earlier, juvenile efforts, right back to 'Handsome Nell'), but he modestly added, 'I am not Musical Scholar enough to prick down my tune properly, so it can never see the light, and perhaps 'tis no great matter'. Below the words of this song appears an entry made in October 1785:

> If ever any young man, on the vestibule of the world, chance to throw his eye over these pages, let him pay a warm attention to the following obser-vations; as I assure him they are the fruit of a poor devil's dear bought Experience.– I have, literally like that great Poet and great Gallant, and by consequence, that great Fool, Solomon, – 'turned my eyes to behold Madness and Folly'[62] – Nay I have, with all the ardor of a lively, fanciful and whimsical imagination, accompanied with a warm, feeling, Poetic heart – shaken hands with their intoxicating friendship.
>
> In the first place, let my Pupil, as he tenders his own peace, keep up a regular, warm intercourse with the Deity . . .

Here, in mid-sentence, the *First Commonplace Book* comes to an abrupt end.

In a letter to Dr Currie, written on 2 April 1798, Gilbert shed some light on what has since come to be regarded as Robert's *annus mirabilis*, when his poetry suddenly came into full flower:

> Among the earliest of his poems was the *Epistle to Davie*. Robert often composed without any regular plan. When any thing made a strong impression on his mind, so as to rouse it to poetic exertion, he would give way to the impulse, and embody the thought in rhyme. If he hit on two or three stanzas to please him, he would then think of proper introduc-tory, connecting, and concluding stanzas; hence the middle of a poem was often first produced. It was, I think, in summer, 1784, when in the inter-val of harder labour, he and I were working in the garden (kail-yard), that he repeated to me the principal part of this epistle. I believe the first idea of Robert's becoming an author was started on this occasion. I was much pleased with the epistle, and said to him I was of opinion it would bear

being printed, and that it would be well received by people of taste . . .
Robert seemed very well pleased with my criticism, and we talked of
sending it to some magazine, but as this plan afforded no opportunity of
knowing how it would take, the idea was dropped.[63]

In the end, it was to be sheer necessity, arising out of the desperate
predicament in which he found himself, that forced Robert to think of
himself as a poet rather than as a farmer, and to take practical steps to see
his poetry in 'guid black prent'.

Shortly after the last abrupt entry in the *Commonplace Book* tragedy
struck the Burns family for the second time. On 28 October 1785, perhaps
even as Robert was penning those last words, his youngest brother John
died at the age of sixteen. The cause of death is unknown, and the parish
register of burials merely records the fact: 'Died, John Burns, Mossgiel,
buried Nov. 1st 1785'. The final column of the account-book entry notes
that a second quality mort-cloth was used for the funeral, perhaps an indication of the family's relative poverty.[64]

Robert's output of letters in 1784-5, despite the recollections of his
errand-boys, was small. The letters to James Burness, John Tennant Junior
and Thomas Orr written in 1784 have already been mentioned briefly. The
letter to Tennant (CL 72-3) is of passing interest for some cynical comments concerning a mutual acquaintance, Robert Paterson, a Mauchline
draper who, a few years later, married Christina Morton, one of the
Mauchline belles. Whether Christina was the 'Miss C' referred to in this
letter is not known – any more than that 'Miss R' can definitely be identified as Anne Ronald – but Robert confessed that he had so often admired
her 'sweet, sonsie face' and her 'engaging frank, honest-hearted manner'.
The lady had financial prospects worth £300 a year:

> We talk of air & manner, of beauty & wit, and lord knows what unmean-
> ing nonsense; but – there – is solid charms for you – Who would not be
> in raptures with a woman that will make him 300£ richer? – And then to
> have a woman to lye with when one pleases, without running any risk of
> the cursed expence of bastards and all the other concomitants of that
> species of Smuggling. These are solid views of matrimony –

With the exception of an undated letter to Margaret Kennedy of
Daljarrock (to which she replied on 15 October) all the extant letters from
Robert to his friends in 1785 were in verse. The response to John
Rankine's twitting him about the impending birth of Betsey Paton's
bastard was sent off some time between December 1784 and the following
March, the epistle to David Sillar in January. Seven other verse-epistles
were composed in the ensuing months, culminating in the poetic letter to
James Smith the following winter.[65]

This dramatic burst of epistolary poetry, however, was presaged by
several long poems. The first of these can be dated to a time immediately
after a judgment given by the Presbytery of Ayr in January 1785. Robert's

own note on 'Holy Willie's Prayer' (CW 93-5) which he wrote for the Glenriddell MS explains:

> Holy Willie was a rather oldish bachelor elder in the parish of Mauchline, and much and justly famed for that polemical chattering which ends in tippling orthodoxy, and for that spiritualized bawdry which refines to liquorish devotion. In a sessional process with a gentleman in Mauchline – a Mr Gavin Hamilton – Holy Willie and his priest Father Auld, after full hearing in the presbytery of Ayr, came off but second best; owing partly to the oratorical powers of Mr Robert Aiken, Mr Hamilton's counsel, but chiefly to Mr Hamilton's being one of the most irreproachable and truly respectable characters in the country. On losing his process, the Muse overhead him at his devotions.

There is a minor distortion of the facts here, as William Fisher (1737–1809) was only forty-eight at the time and married to Jean Hewatson. Fisher was the tenant-farmer in Montgarswood and undeniably one of Mr Auld's chief lieutenants; but a careful examination of the Mauchline Session books does not reveal that persecution of Gavin Hamilton which Robert's poem hints at. Fisher's name crops up regularly in the long-drawn-out disputes with Gavin Hamilton, to be sure, but so do others, notably that of James Lamie (James Smith's overbearing step-father), and Fisher was no more than a member of the sub-committee or delegation appointed to deal with the recalcitrant attorney. In a stanza of 'The Kirk's Alarm' (CW 361), written in the autumn of 1789, Burns makes a definite allegation against Fisher: 'Holy Will, Holy Will, There was wit i' your skull, / When ye pilfered the alms o the poor'. This libel was not printed in Robert's lifetime but, as manuscript copies circulated widely, it was published in the legal sense. That Fisher never took action against his poetic detractor has been taken as clear proof of guilt, and 'Honest Allan' Cunningham (1834) latched upon it to fabricate a definite charge of robbing the poor box at the kirk-door. Later biographers gleefully followed suit without bothering to verify the allegation.

A careful examination of the Session minutes shows no reference to any such allegation and lest it be thought that Daddy Auld had suppressed the peccadilloes of his stalwart, it should be noted that even Holy Willie was not immune from rebuke when occasion demanded. A minute of 14 October 1790 recorded that William Fisher was solemnly rebuked by Mr Auld for drunkenness and thus warned, 'Be on your guard in all time coming against this bewitching sin, shun bad company, avoid taverns as much as possible, and abhor the character of a tippler'.[66] This lapse was not sufficient to demote him from his position as elder and he continued in that position till 1799 when he moved to occupy the farm of Tongue-in-Auchterless in the parish of Sorn. Indeed, so highly regarded was he that, at a special meeting of the Session in 1798 for the admission of young communicants, he was called up by the new minister of Mauchline to 'engage with them in the exercise of prayer'.

Cromek was responsible for the *canard* that William Fisher had perished in a ditch, into which he had fallen when coming home from a debauch, and this story received widespread currency in many later editions; but the circumstances of Fisher's death seem to have been rather different. On 13 February 1809 Fisher, then aged seventy-two, had come into Mauchline for a meeting with his landlord. That evening he set off to walk back to his farm about four miles east of the town, and appears to have got halfway when a snow-storm came up suddenly and enveloped him. In the blizzard the poor man stumbled into a ditch where his frozen corpse was discovered the following morning. He may have been drinking, of course, but the fact that he managed to walk two miles points to him being 'nae that fou, but just a drappie in his e'e'.

In the previous chapter we have seen how Gavin Hamilton and the Mauchline Kirk Session had been at loggerheads for several years. Matters came to the boil on 13 November 1784 when the Session received a letter from Gavin Hamilton, who wrote, 'You must be conscious to yourselves that the manner in which you have recorded my characters in your minutes of the 22 July and 3 August did not proceed from any good cause or foundation but from some private pique and ill nature.' These last words, 'highly calumnious and injurious to their character', stung the Kirk Session who then resolved to 'verify his lybell or to acknowledge the injury, reserving the right to bring their complaint against him before the Revd. Presbytery and Commissary of Glasgow'.[66]

The Session itself seems not to have been unanimous in its battle with the Mauchline lawyer. On 3 December none other than the Session clerk himself was censured for having divulged the minutes of 3 August to Gavin Hamilton. These minutes contained some confidential matters relating to persons who were to be admonished for non-attendance at church. The Session now decided to ask Gavin Hamilton to choose one gentleman and they another 'to be final determinators and amicable compositors in all questions and differences' between them. On 23 December Hamilton rejected this. In the meantime, however, he had appealed to the Presbytery (24 November) and tabled a lengthy complaint consisting of more than twenty folio pages. The Session (20 January 1785) were understandably aggrieved because they had not been represented at that meeting. Gavin's complaint centred on the minute of 3 August about private admonitions to be administered to certain persons prior to giving them tokens to attend the annual Communion service. The Session defended themselves, saying that the admonition had been given without protest or appeal from those admonished, and that the matter had ended there. In turn, they now complained that 'one of the persons had stole a march on them' and entered a complaint in their absence. The Session now counter-attacked and accused Hamilton on the grounds that 'he has been absent from Church 2 Sabbath days in Dec. and 3 Sabbath days in January together; that on the third Sabbath of January he set out on his journey to Carrick tho' advised and admonished against it by the Minister'; and that he 'habitually if not totally neglects the worship of God in his family'. Hamilton was cited to appear before the Session on

30 January 1785 to answer three charges on these grounds, as well as a fourth charge arising out of the 'offensive and injurious letter of Nov. 13'.

On 30 January Gavin Hamilton appeared before the Session and admitted the charges. He did not consider them to be sufficiently serious, however, as to warrant a summons from the Session, but asked them to get on with it in his presence. The Session wanted to adjourn the proceedings till the following Thursday, but he insisted that they go ahead, as he would be away that day. The Session suggested some other day after that; but Hamilton then produced the decision of the Presbytery (a victory for his defence counsel, 'Orator Bob' Aiken) which ordered the Session to strike out the minutes of 22 July and 3 August from their records. The Session asserted that they were not bound by that decision and decided to appeal.

On 3 February the Session appealed to the Synod of Glasgow and Ayr. The reasons for their appeal occupied eleven pages of the minute-book and speak of 'the despotic procedure' and 'the cruel piece of injustice' of the Presbytery's decision which 'opened a door to all sorts of illegal and litigious complaints from disaffected parishioners'. While the Synod were digesting this appeal, Gavin Hamilton wrote to the Session on 3 March asking them for their judgment and sentence, with the words, 'I am determined to have an end and a check put to the disgraceful manner you have for some time past treated me'.

The same day the Session met and passed judgment, an extract from their minutes being sent to Hamilton. He was to be rebuked and admonished for his frequent and habitual neglect of public ordinances, for setting out on a journey on the Lord's day, and for his total neglect of family worship. With regard to the abusive letter, unless some satisfactory acknowledgment were made, the Session reserved the right to complain and seek proper redress afterwards.

Gavin Hamilton attended the meeting on 13 March at which the sentence was pronounced. He now asked the members of the Session if they had been present at the meeting ten days earlier, and if they adhered to this sentence. Mr Auld told him that he had no right to dictate to the Session like this or put such questions. Lamie and Sillar, however, adhered to the sentence, but Aird and Guthrie had been absent. Hamilton then asked the Session to 'eraze the charges so wantonly and groundlessly brought against him and to show him that such are erazed and at an end'. The Session refused point-blank, whereupon Hamilton protested, reading out a lengthy prepared script denouncing them. The meeting was adjourned till 23 March when the Session managed to get hold of this document. They decided not to enter it in the minutes, but appointed the minister, with William Fisher and James Lamie, to prepare replies to it.

This dispute dragged on and on, until 17 July when the Session admitted defeat and granted Gavin a certificate that he was 'at present free from public scandal or ground of church censure'. Even so, they could not resist appending a note, 'The poor have already suffered in your retaining 5 shillings for 2 private baptisms of your children formerly; due both by act and practise. It is therefore hoped that you will pay 7/6 along with the other dues.'

The reason for this capitulation is not given, though it may be inferred that the Presbytery had intervened to force the issue to a conclusion. As Gavin Hamilton continued to defy the Session by neglecting public and family worship, they decided to have another go at him. On 27 October it was minuted that Hamilton was continuing to give more and more offence, 'and that in disobedience to the recommendation and advice of the Presbytery'.

This was the last entry in respect to the second dispute; but the earlier dispute was not forgotten. On 29 December the Session minuted that Hamilton was owing them the sum of £6 8s 3¾d and decided to lay the matter before the heritors 'hoping they will order payment with interest'. The manner in which the Session tenaciously plugged away at these two long and bitter quarrels justified Robert Burns in describing the Kirk elders as 'the holy beagles'.

The third dispute was entirely ignored by Snyder (1932) and only hinted at by Hecht (1936), who dismisses it with 'The peace thus unwillingly established was not of long duration, but the resumption of the conflict is of no great importance to us'.[67] Henley and Henderson (1896), however, state that Hamilton 'was again prosecuted by the Session for causing his servants to dig new potatoes in his garden on the last Lord's day of July, 1787'. This dispute lasted for more than five months and illustrates the extreme Sabbatarianism of Mr Auld and his Session. On 2 August 1787 Robert Bryan was summoned 'for digging potatoes in Mr Hamilton's garden upon the last Lord's day by order of Mr Gavin Hamilton'. Three days later Bryan appeared and acknowledged that 'according to the desire of his master he did digg two rows and a half of potatoes in Mr Hamilton's garden last Lord's day and that the young girl Mr Hamilton's daughter gathered them. The said Robert Bryan answered that it was not a sin but necessary to please the children'. Again, this piffling matter dragged on and on, and ultimately Gavin Hamilton wrote at considerable length to the Session on 11 September giving his side of the incident, a perfectly innocent business arising out of his children asking for some new potatoes for their dinner that day. Gavin obviously hoped that this reasonable explanation would settle the matter; but perhaps he had not reckoned with Daddy Auld and his Session, who duly minuted that Hamilton 'makes no acknowledgment of anything sinful or wrong in so doing'. Furthermore, they doubted Gavin's claim that there were no new potatoes in the house at the time, and summoned a number of witnesses including Jean Jamieson (Bryan's wife), Ann Shankland and Agnes Aird, servants of the defendant. They deponed that the heinous crime of tattie-howking had taken place in the forenoon, during the hours of divine worship 'when the Defender ought to have been in some neighbouring church, seeing he has quite forsaken his parish church'. In comparing his action to other servile labours in gardens on the Sabbath, Hamilton compounded his felony. Consequently the Session now ordered Hamilton to appear before the Presbytery of Ayr on 19 September to answer a charge of contumacy.

The Presbytery seems to have had a better perspective on the matter, for they dismissed the contumacy charge on a technicality (that the reason for the charge was not given). Nothing daunted, the Mauchline Session now ordered Hamilton to appear before them on 30 September to answer for the sin of profaning the Lord's day. Gavin must have been wearying of this silly business, but he duly appeared and reminded them of his side of the story as set out in his letter, and that the Presbytery had dismissed the charge. When he tried to dictate answers to the accusation, however, he was cut short and his answers ignored. The Session were now side-tracked into a debate as to whether Hamilton could be allowed to submit written declarations or give his evidence *viva voce*. In the end they decided to adjourn, but Gavin demanded an immediate decision, 'so they argued re time but he refused delay'.

Again the ding-dong dispute continued. By 22 November the Session was recording that Hamilton had 'obstinately refused to attend upon the Session'. Instead of appearing personally he had bombarded them with further letters. Even worse, Gavin was now ignoring the Session as a court, and writing to individual elders to canvass their support. In the end it came to the decision that Hamilton had been guilty of profaning the Sabbath by causing his servant Robert Bryan to 'digg two and one half rows of potatoes with a spade on the Lord's day mentioned . . .' and also of 'an habitual or total neglect and desertion of God's public ordinances'. Hamilton was then sentenced to appear before the Session to profess his repentance 'and promise amendment and good behaviour in both respects for the future, after which he shall submit to a rebuke from the Chair, and shall then be absolved from the foresaid scandal'. But still the wrangle went on. On 2 December the Session Clerk reported that Hamilton had summoned him to the house of John Dove (publican of the Whitefoord Arms, and the 'Paisley John' of Burns's verse-epistle to Hamilton of 3 May 1786) where he had protested against the sentence and appealed to the Presbytery at Ayr on 28 December. On this occasion the dispute went all the way to the Synod of Glasgow before it was thrown out in March 1788. In the end, having failed to net the big fish, the Mauchline Session had to be content with publicly humiliating the servant. On 6 January 1788 Robert Bryan appeared before the Session and submitted to public rebuke, in the presence of the congregation, on 13 January, after which he received absolution.

There is a curious tailpiece to this story. The Mauchline parish register of births contains an entry: 'Robert Bryan, labourer in Mauchline, & Jean Jamieson his spouse, their son born 11 and Baptd. 18 Jan. 1784 & named Gavin Hamilton'. This child was probably the first in the parish ever to have two baptismal names; but these particular names must have stuck in Daddy Auld's throat as he performed the sacrament of baptism. It is in light of this that one can understand why Auld singled out the hapless Bryan for punishment four years later.

To this day Burns scholars debate the rights and wrongs of this sordid business, the consensus of opinion being that Daddy Auld was finding it inconvenient to his Auld Licht conscience to have a New Licht official functioning for him, hence the framing of Gavin Hamilton on the original charge of withholding the poor's stent. When Hamilton ignored this (arguing that he had never collected the money in the first place because those from whom it was being levied could not afford to pay) Auld stopped the parochial distribution of money to the poor on the grounds that the necessary money had been fraudulently retained by Hamilton. When this ploy failed, Auld tried to get at Hamilton for Sabbath-breaking and neglect of God's ordinances. I have set out the facts, as shown in the various records, and while it must be conceded that most of these occur in the Session minutes (and might therefore be biased against Hamilton), the picture that emerges is not as clear-cut as was formerly believed.

Whether Gavin Hamilton collected the stent or not has never been made clear. What is in no doubt is that this series of petty disputes escalated over a period of ten years, and provided the religious liberals with abundant ammunition against the Auld Lichts. Robert was not a man to remain a disinterested onlooker. He nailed his colours to the mast in his dedicatory poem in the Kilmarnock Edition (CW 216–19). The lines:

> O ye wha leave the springs o Calvin,
> For gumlie dubs of your ain delvin!   [muddy holes]

have an oddly prophetic ring, anticipating the Great Potato Dispute which erupted a year after they were published; but there are plenty of sly digs at the hypocrisy and pharisaical attitudes of Auld and his faction.

Long before this *cause célèbre* was resolved, however, Robert was finding plenty of material in the antics of the Auld Lichts for his satirical poetry. In his autobiographical letter to Dr Moore he wrote:

> I now began to be known in the neighbourhood as a maker of rhymes. – The first of my poetic offspring that saw the light was a burlesque lamentation of a quarrel between two reverend Calvinists, both of them dramatis personae in my Holy Fair.– I had an idea myself that the piece had some merit; but to prevent the worst, I gave a copy of it to a friend who was very fond of these things, and told him I could not guess who was the Author of it, but that I thought it pretty clever.– With a certain side of both clergy and laity it met with a roar of applause.

This was 'The Twa Herds: or, the Holy Tulzie' (CW 90–2), 'an unco mournfu tale' concerning the unseemly dispute which arose between two parish ministers, here cast in the role of 'herds' (shepherds, to give pastors their literal meaning). A 'tulzie' may be defined as a brawl occasioning actual bodily harm. The protagonists in this dispute were the Revd. John Russell of the Chapel of Ease (now the High Church) in Kilmarnock and the Revd. Alexander Moodie of Riccarton (now a suburb of Kilmarnock, but then a separate parish on the south bank of the River Irvine). 'Black Jock' Russell was invested by Burns with unforgettable distinction; no other cleric gets so much attention.[66] He is mentioned in 'The Holy Fair' (CW 138), 'The Ordination' (CW 192) and 'The Kirk's Alarm' (CW 360) as well as the present poem. Robert apostrophises him as 'Black Russell', 'Windy Russell' and 'Rumble John', a man noted for his powerful, stentorian voice which could quite literally be heard a mile off when the wind was in the right direction. He was born in 1740 in Morayshire and was the schoolmaster in Cromarty, attracting the better-class scholars of three counties. He entered the ministry in 1768 and was licensed by the Presbytery of Chanonry before being translated to Kilmarnock in 1774. He has been described as 'an uncompromising disciplinarian, a strict Sabbatarian, and a preacher of great power'.[68] Russell found much room for his zeal at Kilmarnock after a decade of New Licht doctrines under the liberal William Lindsay.

Across the river was another redoubtable zealot of the old school who had come there from Culross in 1761. At first Moodie and Russell made common cause, but there was a falling-out which arose in a ridiculous manner. The story goes that as they were riding home one evening from Ayr, Moodie amused himself by tickling his colleague's horse. The maddened animal careered off down the road, much to the amusement of bystanders but greatly to the discomfiture of the rider who never forgave Moodie. Some time later, a question of parish boundaries arose between them, escalating as these parochial matters tended to do, until the squabble came before the Presbytery. There in open forum before a vast throng (including, according to Lockhart, Burns himself)[69] the reverend gentlemen lost their tempers and abused each other roundly, 'with a fiery virulence of personal invective such as has long been banished from all popular assemblies, wherein the laws of courtesy are enforced by those of a certain unwritten code'.[70]

About the same time, possibly slightly earlier, Robert composed a long poem entitled 'Death and Dr Hornbook' (CW 96–100).[71] The eponymous hero derived his epithet from the hornbooks or primers used by children to learn the alphabet, and was, in fact, John Wilson (1751–1839), the schoolmaster and Session clerk of Tarbolton. In April 1785 Robert attended a meeting of St James Lodge at which Wilson was present. Gilbert supplied Dr Currie with some background information on this episode:

> To eke out a living Wilson had set up a shop of grocery goods. Having accidentally fallen in with some medical books, and become almost hobby-horsically attached to the study of medicine, he had added the sale of a few medicines to his little trade. He had got a shop-bill printed, at the bottom of which, overlooking his own incapacity, he had advertised that 'Advice would be given in common disorders at the shop gratis'.[72]

It is said that Wilson and Burns got into a medical argument at the masonic meeting when the dominie paraded his therapeutics too offensively. Be that as it may, going home that night Robert conceived and partly composed the poem. 'These circumstances,' added Gilbert, 'he related when he repeated the verses to me next afternoon . . .'

Lockhart[73] was the source of the *canard* that Wilson was not merely compelled to shut up shop as an apothecary by the satire which bore his name, but so irresistible was the tide of ridicule that his pupils deserted him and he was forced to give up the school. Unfortunately, the Session minutebooks of Tarbolton for the late eighteenth century have disappeared so there is no way of pinpointing the exact date of Wilson's departure from the parish, but as he was the secretary of St James Lodge from 1782 till 1787 and continued as parish schoolmaster till 1793, Lockhart's tale has no foundation whatsoever. Nevertheless, this nonsense persists in many quarters to this day.

Nor is there any truth in the story that Wilson and Burns fell out as a result of this mild satire. Wilson admitted to Gilbert Burns many years later that he had been quite flattered to have been singled out by the poet; and there is the concrete evidence of a kind and thoughtful letter from Robert to Wilson, written from Ellisland on 11 September 1790 (CL 566). At that time Wilson was unhappy with his situation and decided that a career move would be a good idea. He wrote to Robert for help and advice, with a view to gaining employment as a clerk or copyist in an Edinburgh office, possibly in the Excise. Robert replied (keeping up the medical metaphor of the poem):

> I fear that the remedy you propose, is worse than the disease.– The life of an Edinburgh Quill-driver at twopence a page, is a life I know so well – that I should be very sorry any friend of mine should ever try it.

Robert pointed out that Wilson was too old and had too many children to gain entry to the Excise – 'No man above thirty, or who has more than two children, is admissible'. Robert was anxious to help his old friend as much as possible and enclosed a card introducing Wilson to John Somerville, an Edinburgh lawyer of his acquaintance. Burns closed the letter with the advice, 'let me beg of you for Mrs Wilson's sake & your sweet little flock, not to quit the Present, poor as it is, untill you be pretty sure of your hold on the Future'. Wilson took Robert's advice and held on till 1793 when he went to Glasgow. There he taught at a school in the High Street before obtaining the lucrative position of Session clerk to Gorbals parish, an appointment which he held for thirty years.

In August 1785 Robert sent a verse-epistle to John Goldie of Kilmarnock (1717–1811), one of the most remarkable men of his time and place.[74] This miller turned mechanic, cabinetmaker, wine-merchant, scientist, astronomer, projector of mines, canals and railroads, popular theologian and prolific author, attained national importance in 1780 with the publication of his three-volume work, *Essays on various important Subjects, Moral and Divine, being an attempt to distinguish True from False Religion*. Not surprisingly, this immensely popular work soon came to be known more simply as 'Goudie's Bible'. When a second and greatly expanded six-volume edition appeared in 1785, Burns sent an enthusiastic greeting to the redoubtable author, beginning with the memorable lines 'O Goudie, terror o the whigs, Dread o Blackcoats and reverend wigs!' (CW 121). In the second stanza, Robert's favourite target at the time, the Revd. John Russell, was satirised as 'Black Jock' – a dig at the minister's swarthy appearance. Robert hailed Goldie for his part in vanquishing those enemies – 'sour Bigotry, poor gapin, glowrin Superstition, Enthusiasm' (in the original meaning of fanaticism) and auld Orthodoxy, linking Goldie with Dr John Taylor of Norwich whose *Scripture Doctrine of Original Sin* was generally regarded as the manual of New Licht rationalism. Goldie subsequently called in at Mossgiel on his way home from a business trip to Mauchline, and thus began a personal friendship which was to have important repercussions nine months later.

Robert's religious satires and the many jibes at the expense of the Auld Lichts to be found in the verse-epistles of 1785 have left an impression that he was irreligious and atheistic. In fact, the exact opposite was the case. Robert deserves to be better remembered as a religious reformer who helped to overturn the totalitarianism of the extremely puritanical Auld Lichts, just as much as John Knox is remembered for overturning the corrupt autocracy of the unreformed Church over two centuries earlier. Robert's religious views, deeply thought-out and forcefully expressed in his poetry and letters, were a positive inspiration to many people during and after his lifetime. A glance at any Burns bibliography, or the footnotes at the end of this volume, will show a high proportion of reverend authors; and from Hamilton Paul in 1801 to John Weir Cook in the 1990s there has been no shortage of ministers ready to propose the toast of the Immortal Memory at countless Burns suppers. 'The Twa Herds' circulated widely in manuscript copies in the summer of 1785 and, as Robert put it to Moore, 'With a certain side of both clergy and laity it met with a roar of applause'. The Revd. Hamilton Paul (1773–1854) published an edition of *The Poems and Songs of Robert Burns, with a Life of the Author* in 1819 and defended the religious satires with an enthusiasm which, itself, verges on zealotry. Paul was positively lyrical in his praise of 'Holy Willie's Prayer' (CW 93–5) which lambasted William Fisher, reflecting the admiration and favourable sentiments among the Ayrshire divines of the New Licht persuasion. 'That performances so blasphemous should have been, not only pardoned, but applauded by ministers of religion, is a singular circumstance', commented Lockhart (1828) half a century after the event. Burns himself spoke of the countryside being 'half-mad' with religious ferment. The squabbles and disputes seem petty nowadays, but often resulted in riots and civil disturbances, such as the ugly scenes provoked by the induction of the Revd. James Mackinlay at Kilmarnock's Laigh Kirk in August 1785, which inspired Robert's satirical poem 'The Ordination' (CW 192–4). Robert threw himself into the thick of battle with a recklessness which was no doubt intoxicating at the time, but which soon rebounded on his head.

Gilbert has left us further reminiscences of this momentous period:

> It was, I think, in the winter following, as we were going together with carts for coal to the family (and I could yet point out the particular spot),

that the author first repeated to me the 'Address to the Deil' (CW 161–4). The curious idea of such an address was suggested to him, by running over in his mind the many ludicrous accounts and representations we have, from various quarters, of this august personage.[75]

Snyder ranked this poem among Burns's half-dozen masterpieces and Hecht perceptively suggested that Burns 'lets a gentle ray of hope of redemption fall upon the Prince of Hell himself, thus echoing, unconsciously perhaps, ideas already expressed by Origenes'.[76]

Gilbert also shed some light on the poetic correspondence that passed between Robert and John Lapraik that summer:

The 'Epistle to John Lapraik' (CW 101–4) was produced exactly on the occasion described by the author. He says in that poem, 'On Fasten-e'en we had a rockin' . . . It was at one of these *rockings* at our house, when we had twelve or fifteen young people with their *rocks* [distaffs for spinning], that Lapraik's song beginning 'When I upon thy bosom lean', was sung, and we were informed who was the author.

John Lapraik (1727–1807) was not much younger than Robert's own father and bordering on sixty when they first became acquainted. Robert described him as 'a worthy, facetious old fellow, late of Dalfram near Muirkirk, which little property he was obliged to sell in consequence of some connection as security for some persons concerned in that villainous bubble, the Ayr Bank'. As a result of the collapse of Douglas, Heron and Company, Lapraik was made bankrupt and thrown into the gaol at Ayr where he whiled away the time by composing rhymes. Ironically, what inspired Burns to write his first verse-epistle to Lapraik was the song which, half a century later, was found to have been strongly based on an anonymous ballad in *Ruddiman's Weekly Magazine* of 14 October 1773. Lapraik's version was pretty rough, despite Robert's fulsome praise of it, and when Burns published it in *The Scots Musical Museum*, he appears to have wrought a number of improvements. Lockhart (1828) comments, 'Burns was never a fastidious critic; but it is not very easy to understand his admiration of Lapraik's poetry'.[77] Robert, however, could afford to be generous in praising the work of rival rhymers, secure in the knowledge that his own poetry was far superior. The first epistle to Lapraik is chiefly memorable for Robert's avowal of his own poetic philosophy, in the ninth and tenth stanzas, beginning with 'I am nae poet, in a sense; / But just a rhymer like by chance'. This epistle was sent off about 1 April 1785 and provoked a prompt response from the old farmer-bard which he gave to his son to deliver by hand. The younger Lapraik later reminisced how he found the goodman of Mossgiel in a field engaged in sowing. 'I'm no sure if I ken the hand,' said Robert as he took the letter; but no sooner had he glanced at its contents, than, unconsciously letting go the sheet containing the grain, it was not till he had finished reading that he discovered the loss he had sustained.[78]

Though complaining of fatigue – 'Forjeskit sair, with weary legs' – Robert replied on 21 April with a further letter running to eighteen stanzas in the Standard Habbie measure which he was now making his *métier* (CW 104–7), dwelling on the misfortune which both poets had suffered and culminating in a glorious declaration of the value of humility and contentment. A third epistle (CW 127–8) of half the previous length followed on 13 September. Lapraik himself included this poem in the slim volume published at Kilmarnock in 1788, emulating Robert's own efforts. *Poems on Several Occasions*, printed by John Wilson, had little literary merit and failed to attract much attention. The farmer-poet suffered, as so many of his contemporaries did, from poor harvests and bad luck; and about 1796 he gave up farming altogether, in favour of running the inn and post office in the village of Muirkirk.

Four days after the third epistle to Lapraik was on its way, Robert penned a long letter in similar vein to the Revd. John McMath, then acting as assistant to old Patrick Wodrow in Tarbolton parish. Four years older than the poet, McMath was licensed to preach in 1779 but not ordained at Tarbolton till a decade later when Wodrow retired. He was an excellent preacher and, like Wodrow, a moderate. He enjoyed the friendship of the Montgomeries of Coilsfield and Robert found him to be a kindred spirit in more ways than one, for the young minister was a champion of Gavin Hamilton. Robert may also have felt another bond with him, for McMath also suffered bouts of severe depression. Later, however, he turned to drink and in 1791 was forced to resign his charge; thereafter he enlisted as a private soldier. Nothing else is known about him except that he eventually retired to the Ross of Mull where he died in 1825. McMath got to hear of 'Holy Willie's Prayer' and asked Robert for a copy, which the poet duly sent along with the verse-epistle which refers to their mutual friend, 'There's Gau'n, misca'd waur than a beast' (CW 129–31).

But undoubtedly Robert's most ambitious production of this prolific period was 'The Holy Fair' (CW 133–9). The annual sacrament of communion was held in Mauchline on the second Sunday in August and attracted a vast multitude from the town and the surrounding district. William Auld came from a rather higher class in society than the majority of his parishioners, being the younger son of the Laird of Ellanton in the parish of Symington. Born in 1709, he took his master's degree at Edinburgh and studied theology at Glasgow and Leyden. For some time he was tutor to the family of the Campbells of Shawfield but was licensed by the Presbytery of Hamilton in 1739 and ordained at Mauchline three years later. The Session books show him to have been a fair man, though a stickler for church discipline. His parishioners, the Hamilton disputes notwithstanding, remembered him as a kindly, courteous man, though this is oddly at variance with the unseemly quarrel he picked with his neighbour, the normally peaceable Patrick Wodrow, pursuing the matter all the way to the General Assembly in Edinburgh. This disreputable incident showed an opinionative, self-willed streak. Like Gavin Hamilton, he had a reputation as a zealous friend of the poor, though probably with greater justification, if the Session records are any guide. He has been accused of Calvinistic rigidity, largely as a result of Burns's polemics, but in fairness it must be pointed out that he stamped on a number of abuses. He succeeded in abolishing cock-fighting, got the heritors to fence the kirkyard so that it was no longer the scene of dissipation of former days, and he put an end to the use of the church door as a public noticeboard. For all his faults, Auld was a popular pastor during whose long ministry the number of communicants on the roll rose from 578 in 1750 to 1,400 in 1768.[79] As this number considerably exceeded the adult population of the parish it means that Auld must have poached a goodly number of communicants from adjoining parishes.

The annual communion, attracting people from all over the outlying areas of the parish and even sermon-tasters from other parts of the county, was arguably the single largest social event in the year. Inevitably, it attracted a great many less desirable aspects, degenerating into a curious mixture of solemnity and carnival, hence the title of the poem. In many respects it symbolised the bizarre double standards of the Church at that time. Central to the Calvinist faith was the doctrine of predestination 'that sends ane to Heaven an ten to Hell'. This bred a certain fatalism in people who, if not numbered among the Elect, felt that they might as well do as they pleased, for they were damned anyway; while those who had been chosen took the view that as there was more rejoicing in heaven over a reformed bawd than a blameless virgin, the more they sinned in this life the greater would be their redemption in the next. That was no doubt Holy Willie's view, but it was not untypical of the sanctimonious humbug and hypocrisy that was the other side of the puritanical coin.

It is important to note that Robert's satire was focused on the people in the kirkyard. The sacrament itself and the building in which it was held form no part of the picture. That Robert's description is not exaggerated is borne out by a pamphlet which attacked the manner in which the annual communion had degenerated:

In Scotland they run from kirk to kirk, and flock to see a sacrament, and make the same use of it that the papists do of their pilgrimages and processions – that is, indulge themselves in drunkenness, folly, and idleness. Most of the servants, when they agree to serve their masters in the western parts of the kingdom, make a special provision that they shall have liberty to go to a certain number of fairs, or to an equal number of sacraments; and as they consider a sacrament, or an occasion (as they call the administration of the Lord's Supper), in a neighbouring parish in the same light in which they do at a fair, so they behave at it much in the same manner. I defy Italy, in spite of all its superstition, to produce a scene better fitted to raise pity and regret in a religious, humane, and understanding heart, or to afford an ampler field for ridicule to the careless and profane, than what they call a field-preaching upon one of those occasions. At the time of the administration of the Lord's Supper, upon the Thursday, Saturday and Monday we have preaching in the fields near the church. At first, you find a great number of men and women lying together upon the grass; here they are sleeping and snoring, some with their faces towards heaven, others with their faces turned downward, or covered with their bonnets; there you find a knot of young fellows and girls making assignations to go home together in the evening, or to meet in some ale-house; in another place you see a pious circle sitting round an ale-barrel, many of which stand ready upon carts for the refreshment of the saints. The heat of the summer season, the fatigue of travelling, and the greatness of the crowd, naturally dispose them to drink; which inclines some of them to sleep, works up the enthusiasm of others, and contributes not a little to produce those miraculous conversions that sometimes happen at these occasions; in a word, in this sacred assembly there is an odd mixture of religion, sleep, drinking, courtship, and a confusion of sexes, ages, and characters. When you get a little nearer the speaker, so as to be within the reach of the sound, though not of the sense of the words, for that can only reach a small circle, you will find some weeping and others laughing, some pressing to get nearer the tent or tub in which the parson is sweating, bawling, jumping, and beating the desk; others fainting with the stifling heat, or wrestling to extricate themselves from the crowd; one seems very devout and serious, and the next moment is scolding and cursing his neighbour for squeezing or treading on him; in an instant after, his countenance is composed to the religious gloom, and he is groaning, sighing, and weeping for his sins; in a word, there is such an absurd mixture of the serious and comic, that were we convened for any other purpose than that of worshipping the God and Governor of Nature, the scene would exceed all *power of farce.*[80]

In the poem the narrator falls in with a trio of girls on their way to Mauchline for the Holy Fair, allegories of Fun, Hypocrisy and Superstition whose dress and expressions symbolise the ambivalent character of the occasion. Successive stanzas describe the people gathered for the event, both the preachers and their congregation, ranging from the general to the highly particular. Auld himself is not named, but five ministers from neighbouring parishes, there to assist in the day-long services, are satirised: the Revd. Alexander Moodie of Riccarton who 'speels the holy door / Wi tidings o damnation'; the New Light moderate, George Smith of Galston, opening out 'his cauld harangues, / On practice and on morals'; William Peebles 'frae the water-fit' (Newton-on-Ayr), 'up he's got the word o God, / An meek an mim has view'd it'; wee Alexander Miller of Kilmaurs 'An Orthodoxy raibles'; and last but not least, 'Black Russell' himself, 'the Lord's ain trumpet'. The hellfire and damnation of the preachers is nicely contrasted with the earthly pleasures of the communicants so neatly summed up in the final stanza:

> There's some are fou o love divine;
> There's some are fou o brandy;
> An monie jobs that day begin,
> May end in houghmagandie
> Some ither day.

Once the meagre harvest of 1785 was gathered in, Robert and Gilbert must have realised that, once more, a farm had turned out a ruinous bargain. Gilbert probably felt that, bred a farmer, he would have to struggle on somehow; but Robert, now producing the brilliant poetry on which his fame was largely to rest, had yearnings for a literary career. Those closing entries in the *Commonplace Book* made about this time clearly reveal his ambitions. But he lacked the purposefulness to turn his dreams into reality. Why he never submitted any of his poems to one or other of the newspapers and periodicals, which regularly published verse at the time, is a mystery. Perhaps Robert, while happy to bask in a reputation that now extended over several Ayrshire parishes, baulked at exposing his writings to the colder glare of national scrutiny. Gilbert later recalled how, in the course of a Sunday stroll, Robert recited to him 'The Cotter's Saturday Night' and how 'the fifth, sixth and eighteenth stanzas thrilled with ecstasy through my soul'.

Much of Burns's reputation in his own lifetime, and throughout the nineteenth century, rested on this poem. In lavishing high praise upon it, however, the critics were not blind to its defects. Lockhart (1828) summed up the view of his time when he said, 'In spite of many feeble lines and some heavy stanzas, it appears to me that even Burns's genius would suffer more in estimation by being contemplated in the absence of this poem, than of any other single poem left us.' 'November's chill' in the second stanza indicates the period of the year when Robert began composing this poem, and it was completed by 17 February 1786 when he mentioned the fact in a letter to John Richmond (CL 76). It was heavily inspired by Thomas Gray's famous 'Elegy written in a Country Churchyard' (1750) and closely modelled on Robert Fergusson's 'The Farmer's Ingle' (1774).[81] Modern critics, such as Snyder (1932), Edwin Muir (1936), David Daiches (1971), Maurice Lindsay (1981) and Alan Bold (1991)[82] have taken a harsher line and agreed that the two poems furnished excellent examples of the genuine and the false use of language, Fergusson's being a far finer work. It may be added that this judgment was not very different from Robert's own view, and was reflected in his very high regard for the poet who was 'By far my elder brother in the Muse' (CW 269). But these were the views of professionals judging another practitioner; in the heart of the general public, the sentimentalism of this poem struck a very responsive chord. The homely picture of the cotter, obviously based on William Burnes, conducting family worship, was a powerfully emotive image in the 1780s. According to Gilbert, Robert thought there was something peculiarly venerable in the phrase, 'Let us worship God', used by a decent, sober head of a family introducing domestic worship. Many lines and phrases from this poem have a noble ring, ensuring their inevitable debasement as clichés which remain current to this day. Despite its many faults, it was a most impressive effort for the twenty-six-year-old poet, and did more than anything else in the Kilmarnock Edition to ensure the rapturous acclaim of the contemporary literati.

It can hardly be doubted that Robert, seeing the effect his poetry had on his brother (whom he regarded as an intellectual equal), must often have wondered whether he would ever be known as Robert Burns the poet, and not just as Rob Mossgiel, tenant-farmer. Further, might not his poetry somehow be the means of extricating them from their financial embarrassment. Although actual steps towards publication were not taken till several months later, it seems probable that Robert began entertaining the notion more seriously in the autumn of 1785. The *Commonplace Book* was neglected from October onwards because Robert was now engaged in revising manuscripts and composing fresh works with an eye to publication.

While the sobersided Gilbert was Robert's closest friend, confidant and intellectual sounding-board, his boon companions of this period were two lads who lived in the town. James Smith and John Richmond were both six years younger than Robert, young scamps who idolised Burns much as he had looked up to Richard Brown. Smith (brother of one of the Mauchline belles) lost his father when he was only ten. His mother remarried, and in James Lamie – second only to William Fisher among God's Elect – he had a step-father whose ideas on parental discipline were harsh and restrictive. Not surprisingly, young James rebelled against this domestic tyrant. By 1785 he was beyond Lamie's control and had set up in business on his own account, with a draper's shop almost opposite Nance Tannock's inn. Richmond was employed as clerk in the law office of Gavin Hamilton, and it was probably there that he first met Burns whom he later introduced to his boon companion, Smith. The three soon formed a close friendship; 'a happy triumvirate in village revelry' is Snyder's apt phrase. Interestingly, Richmond was the younger son of Holy Willie's landlord, Richmond Senior being the Laird of Montgarswood. Robert Chambers, who visited Mauchline in 1833 to gather material for his forthcoming edition, interviewed a number of local residents who could still remember the poet and his companions of fifty years previously. On the word of Richmond himself Chambers was the source of the myth, much embroidered by later writers, that Burns, Smith and Richmond were habitués of Poosie Nancie's – as if a tenant-farmer, a solicitor's clerk and a draper would have frequented such a place. But what Chambers actually wrote was that, *on a solitary occasion* the trio:

> dropped accidentally, at a late hour, into the humble hostlery of Poosie Nansie . . . After witnessing much jollity amongst a company who by day appeared abroad as miserable beggars, the three young men came away, Burns professing to have been greatly amused by the scene, but particularly with the gleesome behaviour of an old maimed soldier. In the course of a few days he recited a part of the poem to Richmond, who informed me that, to the best of his recollection, it contained, in its original form, songs by a sweep and a sailor, which did not afterwards appear.[83]

Robert himself left no record of the circumstances surrounding the composition of 'The Jolly Beggars' (CW 182–91). Prudently he did not include it in the Kilmarnock Edition and was easily dissuaded from printing it in the Edinburgh Edition by Hugh Blair who condemned it and another poem, a religious satire entitled 'The Prophet and God's Complaint'. The latter is not known in any form, and it is every Burns scholar's ambition that some day the long-lost manuscript may turn up. As for Robert's great dramatic work of love and liberty, he was remarkably offhand about it when (early in September 1793) George Thomson raised the subject. In reply (CL 644) he wrote:

> I have forgot the Cantata you allude to, as I kept no copy, & indeed did not know that it was in existence; however, I remember that none of the songs pleased myself, except the last – something about
>
> > Courts for cowards were erected,
> > Churches built to please the priest.

How could Robert have forgotten such a splendid work! In 1787 he did not trust his own judgment and deferred to the views of the Edinburgh literati; but in the context of September 1793, when a paranoid government was hell-bent on suppressing freedom of expression, Robert must have been thanking his lucky stars for taking Blair's advice; the last thing the up-and-coming Excise officer wished to be reminded of was such a gloriously anarchic production.

Burns actually quoted Blair in the heading of one of the verse-epistles which appeared in the Kilmarnock Edition. The 'Epistle to James Smith' (CW 169–73) develops Robert's rip-roaring denunciation of the censorious, hypocritical religious bigots of the time, but is chiefly memorable for the seventh stanza which declared his intention 'To try my fate in guid, black prent'. The manuscript of this epistle in the Dick Institute, Kilmarnock, does not bear a superscription, so it is not known exactly when it was written, or whether Smith was still in Mauchline at the time. But after 'an affair cognizable by the Kirk Session'[84] – he had made pregnant his mother's servant Christian Wilson (a woman fifteen years his senior) – he left Mauchline at the end of 1785 and started a calico-printing business at Linlithgow, so the epistle may have been directed to him there.

Richmond himself had an affair with Jenny Surgeoner, as a result of which he was publicly rebuked before the congregation and compelled to do penance in January 1785. Although Jenny subsequently bore a daughter, Richmond repudiated the girl he had seduced and later took himself off to Edinburgh. Interestingly, Robert upbraided his friend about his despicable behaviour in a letter of 1 September 1786 (CL 78–9), 'You are acting very wrong My friend; her happiness or misery is bound up in your affection or unkindness . . .' – sentiments which later governed his own decision to settle down with Jean Armour, although in the self-same letter, in the very preceding paragraph, he said he would never marry her (as clear a case of 'don't do as I do, do as I say' as ever was). Richmond returned to Mauchline in 1787[85] and married the long-suffering Jenny four years later.

These three young bloods, with a shoemaker William Hunter, formed a sort of bachelors' club which met informally in the Whitefoord Arms and was known jocularly as the Court of Equity, parodying the Tarbolton

Bachelors' Club and the Mauchline Kirk Session. Robert was chairman of course, Smith the fiscal (public prosecutor), Richmond the clerk of the court and Hunter the messenger at arms. This mock court proceeded to examine some of the scandals of Mauchline and bring to book the offenders against the moral code who had so far managed by various ploys to evade the penalty of their transgressions. The result was 'Libel Summons' (CW 227-30), a long poem rich in humanity and tenderness, but which was considered too coarse for publication. When Catherine Carswell published it as an appendix (1930) she was savagely condemned for her action.[86]

The other interesting development in the closing months of 1785 was that 'striking and picturesque description of local customs and scenery'[87] which Burns entitled simply 'Hallowe'en' (CW 151-7). This, the fourth in the group of ambitious essays in 'manners-painting', dealt with ancient customs surrounding Hallowe'en, allegedly obsolete even by Robert's time. The old customs associated with All Hallows' Eve had virtually died out when Robert rescued them from oblivion and popularised them to such an extent that many are observed to this day. This poetic record derived much of its material from the fund of stories and superstitions told to Robert by his mother and old Betty Davidson. Here we see Burns, the budding folklorist. At times, indeed, the poem is overwhelmed by the mass of antiquarian data which Robert felt constrained to supply, by way of footnotes. Robert was inordinately pleased with this production, as the concluding part of his headnote shows:

> The passion of prying into Futurity makes a striking part of the history of Human-nature, in its rude state, in all ages and nations; and it may be some entertainment to a philosophical mind, if any such should honour the Author with a perusal, to see the remains of it, among the more enlightened in our own.

The letter to Richmond in February 1786 also mentioned that 'I have likewise compleated my Poem on the dogs, but have not shown it to the world' (CL 76). From this James Kinsley inferred that the poem had been 'begun earlier than the other poems and that it was planned, and probably in part written, before Richmond left Ayrshire in November 1785'.[88] According to Gilbert the poem was 'composed after the resolution of publishing was nearly taken'. He went on to explain that Luath, the 'gash an faithfu tyke', was based on Robert's own dog:

> which had been killed by the wanton cruelty of some person, the night before my father's death. Robert said to me that he should like to confer such immortality as he could bestow upon his old friend Luath, and that he had a great mind to introduce something into the book under the title of Stanzas to the Memory of a Quadruped Friend; but this plan was given up for the poem as it now stands. Caesar was merely the creature of the poet's imagination, created for the purpose of holding chat with his favourite Luath.[89]

Here again, Robert was indebted to Fergusson for his model, the dialogue in octosyllabic couplets entitled 'Mutual Complaint of Plainstanes and Causey' which later inspired 'The Brigs of Ayr' (CW 244-9) as well. Robert's feelings for his late dog come across clearly in the affectionate description and the sensitive dialogue. When the time came to publish, he ranked this as his finest performance and gave it pride of place at the beginning of the volume.

CHAPTER 9

Two Loves

She has my heart, she has my hand,
By secret troth and honor's band!
'Till the mortal stroke shall lay me low,
I'm thine, my Highland lassie, O!

My Highland Lassie, O (CW 224)

As the winter of 1785–6 drew to a close Robert Burns and Jean Armour had reached that stage in their relationship where intimacy, in an era before birth control, had led inevitably to pregnancy. Assuming that the twins were born at full term, Jean must have conceived round about Christmas 1785. She may not have realised her predicament until the end of January or the beginning of February 1786.

At that time there was a second connection between the Armour family and Mossgiel. An entry in the Kirk Session minutes of 6 March 1786 refers to Agnes Wilson, servant to George Gibson, as being 'of lewd and immoral practices and the ocasion of the late disturbance'. This is believed to relate to an incident which Robert made the subject of 'Adam Armour's Prayer'. Jean's brother (born in 1771) was only fifteen and small for his age, hence the references in the poem to him being 'little' and 'scarce as lang's a guid kail-whittle'. By way of a prank which got out of hand, he and a gang of Mauchline laddies set upon George Gibson's 'jurr' (journeywoman). Agnes Wilson, described as a vagrant and considered the model for the 'tozie drab' of 'The Jolly Beggars', had come to Mauchline with a bad reputation for harlotry and had been plying her trade at Poosie Nancie's for about six months when the incident occurred. Adam Armour and his pals decided to teach 'Geordie's jurr' a lesson, so they 'stang'd her through the place, / An hurt her spleuchan'. In other words, they punished the woman by riding her out of town on a rough wooden rail formed out of the trunk of a pine-tree, which (in an era when women wore no drawers) would have severely bruised and lacerated her genitalia. The jurr's employers resented this outrage and threatened its perpetrators with criminal proceedings, in consequence of which Adam ran off to Mossgiel to lie low till the affair had died down. The poem, which has mock undertones of that longer and more savagely satirical prayer of Holy Willie, expresses the mock remorse of young Adam and his gang, now hunted as outlaws for disturbing the peace; but it ends on a triumphant note of self-justification:

> As for the jurr – puir worthless body! –
> She's got mischief enough already;
> Wi stanget hips and buttocks bluidy
>   She suffer'd sair
> But may she wintle in a woody,
>   If she whore mair!

The village audience for this piece would doubtless have relished the coarse brutality of it, but there is an unattractive blend of sadism and hypocrisy about it – to 'wintle in a woody' is to dangle in a noose – which shows the age-old double standards at work. Robert (and many of his friends) had a fundamentally amoral attitude towards the fair sex; but though farm-girls and serving-maids were considered fair game, Robert had a marked aversion to prostitution. His antipathy seems to have been directed against the trade itself, rather than individual practitioners, though a measure of ambivalence may be detected in his ballad of Muirland or Monkery Meg (CW 602). On the other hand, he seems to have had a down on Jean Glover from whom he obtained the song 'O'er the Moor amang the Heather' for *The Scots Musical Museum*, though this may be due to the fact that she was a thief as well as a prostitute.

Later Robert was to defend an Edinburgh prostitute and namesake, and exhibit far more common sense and compassion. In his letter of 2 February 1790 to Peter Hill (CW 315–6) he lashed out at 'those flinty-bosomed, puritanic Prosecutors of Female Frailty & Persecutors of Female Charms', the Edinburgh magistrates who had banished Margaret Burns for keeping a brothel. And he composed the quatrain 'Cease ye prudes, your envious railing' (CW 375) at the time of the banishment, followed by a mock epitaph in 1791 (CW 418), which turned out sadly prophetic as the 'frail sister' died about a year later.

It is impossible to tell from Robert's poems and correspondence exactly when he was apprised of Jean Armour's condition. He was certainly well aware of this by 17 February 1786 when he wrote to John Richmond. This letter is more preoccupied with a resumé of Robert's prolific poetic output over the past winter, but after mentioning that his chief patron now was Robert Aiken in Ayr he went on to say:

> I have no news to acquaint you with about Machlin, they are just going on in the old way. – I have some very important news with respect to myself, not the most agreeable, news that I am sure you cannot guess, but I shall give you the particulars another time.– I am extremely happy with Smith; he is all the friend I have NOW in Machlin.

It seems that Jean's pregnancy was, if not common knowledge, certainly the stuff of gossip, and the reference to James Smith being the only friend he had left, emphasising the present time, may imply that 'the rakish rook Rob Mossgiel' had scandalised the town as a result. Jean was her father's favourite daughter. William Jolly, interviewing William Patrick in 1859, and suggesting that James Armour must have been a person of some consequence, elicited the offhand response that 'he was only a bit mason body, wha used to snuff a guid deal and gae afen tak a bit dram!' Chambers asked him why Armour objected to Burns so strongly and Patrick replied, 'The thing was, he hated him, and would raither hae seen the Deil himsel comin to the hoose to coort his dochter than him! He cu'dna bear the sicht o'm, and that was the way he did it!'[1]

Nineteenth-century biographers, taking their cue from Currie, spoke of a lengthy courtship between Robert and Jean which, only after more than a year's duration, reached the point at which intimacy took place with the inevitable results. I suspect that the affair only became serious late in 1785. The next problem which biographers had to contend with was Robert's reaction on discovering that Jean was pregnant. That Burns was inclined to repudiate the girl he had seduced was a view expressed by Lockhart (1828) and subsequent writers, on the strength of a fragment of an undated letter (CL 117) addressed to James Smith: 'Against two things I am fixed as fate – staying at home, and owning her conjugally. The first, by Heaven, I will not do! – the last, by hell, I will never do.' The full text was not published till 1931, after Professor Ferguson examined the original manuscript in the Gribbel Collection. The letter being undated, Ferguson assigned it to about the beginning of August 1786, although it may have been written about six weeks earlier. Certainly it was well after February-March and therefore cannot be regarded as expressing Robert's initial reaction to the trouble he now found himself in for the second time in less than a year.

Arising from the assumption that this letter proved Robert's first reaction, biographers tried to create some other mitigating circumstances. The farm was doing badly and Robert was therefore in no condition to marry Jean. The only solution was to make a clean break, go abroad, make his fortune, and then return to make her his wife. To this end, so the argument ran, Robert gave Jean a document constituting some sort of long-term promise. Followers of this school of thought went to elaborate lengths to minimise the importance and legal validity of this 'acknowledgment'. Protagonists of this view were led by the Revd. Dr Edgar of Mauchline who stated that 'It is certain that Burns, in the spring of 1786, gave Jean some writing regarding their marriage; but it seems to me not quite so certain what was the precise tenor of that writing.'[2]

It was therefore held that, even supposing that the 'unlucky paper' as Robert termed it contained a declaration by him that Jean was his wife, it was questionable if the law would on that account have held them to be married persons. This was the view of, among others, Chambers and Wallace who cited some of the leading legal authorities in support of their contention. Lord Fraser, one of the nineteenth-century law lords, said that, although some writers on law had, before 1786, affirmed that *sponsalia de presenti* constituted marriage, their opinion was not supported by any judicial authority. Lord Braxfield (1796) declared from the bench that consent *de presenti* did not constitute marriage 'without the priest's blessing or something equivalent'; and Sir Ilay Campbell – mentioned in 'The Author's Earnest Cry and Prayer' (CW 176) – said, 'I deny in principle that consent makes marriage without ceremony or coitus'. Church courts, for most of the eighteenth century, scarcely knew what to recognise as marriages, as the frequency with which this vexed matter came before Kirk Sessions shows. Chambers averred that had Robert's alleged marriage by the unlucky paper come before the civil courts in 1786, and the fact of consent *de presenti* been clearly established, it was at least doubtful if the marriage could have been affirmed, adding, 'There is reason to think that all the length the Court would have gone, would have been to grant an order to compel solemnisation.'[3]

On the other hand, John Erskine took the view that marriage might be without doubt perfected by the consent of parties declaring in writing, 'provided the writing be so conceived as necessarily to impart their present consent'. The proof of marriage was not confined to the testimonies of the clergymen and witnesses at the ceremony. 'The subsequent acknowledgment of it by the parties is sufficient to support the marriage, if it appear to have been made not in a jocular manner, but seriously, and with deliberation.'[4]

All the wrangling and disputation over this moot point might have been resolved had the unlucky paper survived. With all the facility with words at his command, Robert would surely have made the position abundantly clear. But if Robert made a written declaration of marriage, as one might reasonably suppose, the obvious question is why go to that trouble when the couple could have been married in church at the earliest opportunity? That they did not do so leaves one with the inescapable conclusion that the 'acknowledgment' stopped short of that. It may be that Jean, worried for her future, wrung the document from Robert and he obligingly wrote out something in his best epistolary style, in order to reassure her. Speculation that James Smith may have witnessed this document[5] is no more than that, unsupported by any reference to it in the Burns-Smith correspondence. To have had any practical validity the paper had to be either a promise of marriage or an acknowledgment that the couple already regarded themselves as married. The eminently practical Scots law, which even nowadays makes provision for 'marriage by habit and repute', would have paid scant regard to the document as such, and concentrated instead on the fact and admission of agreement without requiring further proof.

At any rate Jean, armed with some sort of compromise, felt that she could break the news to her parents, hoping that Robert's document would soften the blow. But far from it. James Armour would, of course, already have known about young Mossgiel's love-begotten daughter, and probably – more to the point – the parlous state of his finances. It is said that Armour fainted at the news, and had to be revived with a cordial administered by the only marginally less distraught Mary Armour. The next part of the story is rather confused. Some writers speak of the document being in Ayr in the safe custody of Robert Aiken, Burns's lawyer friend, the inference being that Aiken was Robert's lawyer and had had a hand in drawing it up. To be sure, Aiken had been a friend of Robert's since about 1783, but their relationship had been entirely literary. Aiken was the dedicatee of 'The Cotter' and Burns subsequently addressed his 'Epistle to a Young Friend' (CW 221–3) to his son Andrew. 'Orator Bob' was renowned for the power and beauty of his voice and Burns later confessed that he had never fully appreciated his own work until he heard Aiken reading it aloud. 'My first poetic patron' is how Robert described Aiken in November 1786 (CL 99). The late-nineteenth and twentieth-century references to Aiken as the 'custodier of the declaration of marriage'[6] use this interpretation needlessly to bolster the validity of the marriage necessary to legitimise the children born after the event. If Robert felt it necessary to consult a lawyer regarding the document he would surely have gone to Gavin Hamilton. Certainly Gavin knew of the document's existence, as Robert referred to it as 'that unlucky paper' in a letter to his lawyer on 15 April, quoted more fully below.

The earliest accounts, however, speak of the paper as being in Jean's possession from the time Robert gave it to her. No doubt she brandished this before her parents when she broke her news. It may be that Jean was pathetically naïve in the faith she placed in this scrap of paper; perhaps not. But equally her father, simple, honest stonemason that he was, seems to have been naïve in thinking that the validity of the document could be annulled by the simple expedient of taking it to a lawyer and getting him to cut out the portions bearing the names of the contracting parties. This is where Robert Aiken came into the story. My view is that Armour had to consult a lawyer in Ayr for the simple reason that he would distrust (and heartily detest) a New Licht reprobate like Gavin Hamilton. As the only other lawyer in Mauchline was Gavin's brother and partner, Armour had no alternative but to seek legal assistance elsewhere. We can imagine the stormy scene as the angry Armour confronted Aiken (a little man of very rotund proportions) and demanded that he excise the names. Aiken was too competent a lawyer to suggest that such an act would invalidate the document; but menaced by the angry mason he probably went through the motions merely to humour him. For the plain fact of the matter was that Aiken could no more nullify the marriage – if such it were – by mutilating the paper, than a murderer could erase the foul deed by destroying the incriminating evidence.

It is said that when a rumour of this business reached Burns there was a coolness between him and Aiken. Indeed, some biographers who ought to have known better have even cast doubt on Aiken's part in the affair.[7] A glance at the extant correspondence, however, easily resolves this matter. As late as 3 April Burns was writing to Robert Aiken in answer to 'your kind letter' which informed him of the 'flattering instance of Mrs C—'s notice' (the lady has never been satisfactorily identified). Robert asked Aiken to thank the lady and ended by saying, 'My Proposals for publishing I am just going to send to the Press. – I expect to hear from you first opportunity' (CL 91). So far so good; there is no mention of the Armour affair here. Exactly when Jean broke the news to her parents is not known, although most writers have opted for March, applying simple arithmetic and common sense. The chances are, however, that the poor young lady delayed telling her mother and father as long as she dared, and only dropped her bombshell when things began to show. The date on which Armour rushed off to Robert Aiken is beyond doubt and is certainly proven by a letter from Burns to Gavin Hamilton (CL 65–6). By that time Robert was in the course of distributing his 'proposals' (subscription lists) among his friends. To Gavin he now wrote (CL 65–6):

> I must consult you, first opportunity, on the propriety of sending my *quondam* friend, Mr Aiken, a copy. – If he is now reconciled to my character as an honest man, I would do it with all my soul; but I would not be beholden to the noblest being ever God created, if he imagined me to be a rascal.– Apropos, old Mr Armour prevailed with him to mutilate that unlucky paper, yesterday. – Would you believe it? tho' I had not a hope, nor even a wish, to make her mine after her [damnable *deleted*] conduct; yet when he told me, the names were all cut out of the paper, my heart died within me, and he cut my very veins with the news.– Perdition seize her falsehood, and perjurious perfidy! but God bless her and forgive my poor, once-dear, misguided girl.– She is ill-advised.– do not despise me, Sir: I am indeed a fool, but a *knave* is an infinitely worse character than any body, I hope, will dare to give the unfortunate Robt Burns.

This letter is undated, but it can be assigned to 15 April because we know, from other sources, that Robert took delivery of the proposal sheets from Wilson of Kilmarnock on 14 April. From this, too, we can date the mutilation of the document to the very same day. This letter is important for two other reasons as well. In the first place it shows that if there were any coolness between Burns and Aiken it was not on Robert's side; he was only concerned lest Aiken should think badly of him. No other letters to Aiken are known prior to late September 1786 but the opening line of the next extant letter (CL 92) – 'I never end a letter to you of late but I think of Mr Ballantine' – implies that other letters, now lost, passed between them in the intervening period.[8] Secondly, however, it is important in showing (despite the confused, almost hysterical state he was in when he wrote this) that Robert's reaction had been to do the decent thing by Jean. This is the man who wrote the bawdy song, 'Wha'll Mowe Me Now?' (CW 605–6), whose concluding stanza expressed his views:

> But deevil damn the lousy loun,
> Denies the bairn he got!
> Or lea's the merry arse he lo'ed
> To wear a ragged coat!

Admittedly, he did not always live up to this ideal; but he would have married Betsey Paton if his family had not talked him out of it, and at least he assumed responsibility for raising her little girl. And in Jean Armour's case the white-hot passion he felt comes over clearly enough in the letter quoted above. Robert's 'honourable intentions' were also manifest in the opening sentences of a long letter to John Arnot of Dalquhatswood. The original itself has not apparently survived, but Robert kept a copy of it and later transcribed this for the Glenriddell MS with an introductory note which shows how his memory could play him false. In the note he thought that the letter was written 'about the latter end of 1785, as I was meditating to publish my Poems', but as the letter was sent with a subscription proposal it must have been written about the middle of April 1786. In the note prepared for Robert Riddell (who, one presumes, was well acquainted with Mrs Burns) Robert wrote coyly:

> The story of the letter was this.– I had got deeply in love with a young Fair-One, of which proofs were every day *arising* more & more to view.– I would gladly have covered my Inamorato (*sic*) from the darts of Calumny with the conjugal Shield, nay, had actually made up some sort of Wedlock; but I was at that time deep in the guilt of being unfortunate, for which good & lawful objection, the Lady's friends broke all our measures, & drove me au desespoir.

The letter itself describes in amusing but bawdy terms, full of sexual braggadocio, how Robert had successfully besieged and captured Jean, but was subsequently outflanked by James Armour. Here we see the military metaphors most fully developed. Little is known about the recipient of this very long letter and from the opening preamble, 'I have long wished for some kind of claim to the honor of your acquaintance', it appears that he was virtually a total stranger. Yet, a couple of paragraphs on, Robert is confiding in Arnot, in the most intimate terms:

> Sad & grievous, of late, Sir, has been my tribulation, & many & piercing, my sorrows . . . I have lost, Sir, that dearest earthly treasure, that greatest pleasure here below, that last, best gift which compleated Adam's happiness in the garden of bliss, I have lost – I have lost – my trembling hand refuses its office, the frightened ink recoils up the quill – Tell it not in Gath – I have lost – a – a – A WIFE!
>
> > Fairest of God's creation, last & best!
> > *How art thou lost –*[9]
>
> You have doubtless, Sir, heard my story, heard it all with all its exaggerations; but as my actions, & my motives for action, are peculiarly like myself, & that is peculiarly like nobody else, I shall just beg a leisure-moment & a spare-tear of you, untill I tell my own story my own way –

In this extraordinary letter Robert then embarked on one of those remarkably candid passages of self-revelation:

> I have been all my life, Sir, one of the rueful-looking, long-visaged sons of Disappointment.– A damned Star has always kept my zenith, & shed its

baleful influence, in that emphatic curse of the Prophet – 'And behold, whatsoever he doth, it shall not prosper!'[10] – I rarely hit where I aim; & if I want any thing, I am almost sure never to find it where I seek it.– For instance, if my pen-knife is needed, I pull out twenty things – a plough-wedge, a horse-nail, an old letter or a tattered rhyme, in short, every thing but my pen-knife; & that at last, after a painful fruitless search, will be found in the unsuspected corner of an unsuspected pocket, as if on purpose thrust out of the way.– Still, Sir, I had long had a wishing eye to that estimable blessing, a wife.– My mouth watered deliciously, to see a young fellow, after a few idle, common-place stories from a gentleman in black, strip & go to bed with a young girl & no one durst say black was his eye; while I, for just doing the same thing, only wanting that ceremony, am made a Sunday's laughing stock, & abused like a pick-pocket.

After much more in similar vein, Robert switched to the military phraseology which he sustained in a virtuoso performance to describe the seduction of Jean Armour:

whilst I was vigorously pressing on the siege; had carried the counter-scarp, & made a practicable breach behind the curtin in the gorge of the very principal bastion; nay, had found means to slip a choice detachment into the very citadel: while I had nothing less in view than displaying my victorious banners on the top of the walls – 'Heaven & Earth, must I remember'! my damned Star wheeled about to the zenith by whose baleful rays Fortune took the alarm, & pouring in her forces on all quarters, front, flank & rear, I was utterly routed, my baggage lost, my military chest in the hands of the enemy; & your poor devil of a humble servant, commander in chief forsooth, was obliged to scamper away, without either arms or honors of war, except his bare bayonet & cartridge-pouch; nor in all probability had he escaped even with them, had he not made a shift to hide them under the lap of his military cloak . . .

After a further couple of pages, in which he confessed that this defeat left him 'nine parts & nine tenths, out of ten, stark staring mad', followed by the entire gamut of emotions, Robert brought his tale of woe up to date, switching to hunting metaphors:

But this is not all.– Already the holy beagles, the houghmagandie pack, begin to snuff the scent; & I expect every moment to see them cast off, & hear them after me in full cry; but as I am an old fox, I shall give them dodging & doubling for it; & by & bye, I intend to earth among the mountains of Jamaica.

Indeed, the holy beagles were already in hot pursuit, as these entries in the Session book graphically indicate:

April 2, 1786. The Session being informed that Jean Armour, an unmarried woman, is said to be with child, and that she has gone off from the place of late, to reside elsewhere, the Session think it their duty to enquire . . . But appoint James Lamie and William Fisher to speak to the parents. April 9, 1786. James Lamie reports that he spoke to Mary Smith, mother to Jean Armour, who told him that she did not suspect her daughter to be with child, that she was gone to Paisley to see her friends, and would return soon.[11]

This helps to clarify the sequence of events. Jean probably informed her parents towards the end of March. Once James Armour recovered from the shock his anger intensified. Uppermost in his mind were two things: (a) the scandal affecting his good name, and (b) his pathological hatred of the young blackguard who had violated his daughter. Scandal might be averted by swift action, so Jean was promptly packed off to relatives in Paisley. As for Burns, Armour seems to have considered unwed motherhood and bastardy as infinitely more acceptable than Rob Mossgiel as a son-in-law. This decision was not taken lightly and without due consideration, hence the delay in Armour seeking the help of Robert Aiken. Doubtless James became increasingly desperate once the 'houghmagandie pack' got on the scent. The fact that Fisher and Lamie spoke with Mrs Armour implies that James had taken good care to absent (or conceal) himself when they came calling on their sacred inquisition. The circumstances leading up to Jean's flight to Paisley are unknown, so whether she went of her own volition to escape a righteous father's wrath, or whether Mary Armour had packed her off to avoid gossip in the village, or whether James himself insisted on this ploy, are matters of fruitless speculation which do not materially affect the situation.

From late March till early June, about nine weeks in all, Jean lived in the Sneddon with her mother's sister Elizabeth and her husband Andrew Purdie. He was a wright or carpenter and probably of an argumentative nature, for there survives a record of an action which he raised against the Society of Wrights before Paisley magistrates (he won his case). While she resided in Paisley Jean was visited on several occasions by Robert Wilson, a prosperous weaver from Mauchline, four years her senior, from whom she is said to have borrowed money. Inevitably, wind of this got back to Burns and fanned the flames of his indignation at Jean's 'desertion'. Two poems have been alleged to refer to this incident, but 'To the weaver's gin ye go' (CW 306–7) was Robert's reworking of a traditional chorus to which he added new words for *The Scots Musical Museum* some years later, and it appears to be stretching credulity to believe that the 'bonie, westlin weaver lad' of the song was intended to allude to Robert Wilson. Similarly, 'The Gallant Weaver' (CW 464), tied more specifically to Paisley by its opening line 'Where Cart rins rowin to the sea', is a reworking of an ancient ballad which bears no resemblance in content to the supposed wooing of Jean by Robert Wilson.

The repudiation of his unlucky paper by the Armours, followed by Jean's flight to Paisley, hit Robert very hard. In his highly emotional state his feelings about Jean were confused, to put it mildly. In April and May, while Jean took refuge with the Purdies, Robert found other distractions. The one was the publication of his poems, discussed separately in the next chapter, and the other was Margaret Campbell. When Jean fled to Paisley Robert may only have sighed with relief; an intractable problem was, for the time being, shelved. But assuming that Robert and Jean met, if only briefly, before she ran off to her aunt and uncle, Robert must have been left in no doubt as to her parents' feelings. Until 14 April, however, Robert probably considered himself married to Jean, despite parental hostility. Only when Bob Aiken told him about the mutilation of the document did Robert think that the irregular marriage had been annulled. This raises a fine point; how did Aiken break the news and what did he actually tell him? One would have thought that the lawyer was bound to point out that the charade of cutting out the names in no way altered the legal position. But Robert and Jean appear to have taken this act at face value and considered themselves legally severed. Certainly, from that date forward, Robert acted in the sincere belief that he was a single man.

Six letters of Burns written in April 1786 have survived, addressed to Robert Aiken (3 April), Gavin Hamilton (15), the Ayr merchant and banker John Ballantine (exact date unknown), the Ayr lawyer David McWhinnie (17), John Kennedy of Dumfries House, Cumnock, a cousin of Gavin's wife (20), and that prolix letter to John Arnot quoted above. Apart from the quotations already discussed, these letters dealt with poetic matters in general and the subscription lists in particular. May produced only one extant prose letter, a very brief note to John Kennedy enclosing a copy of the 'Epistle to John Rankine' (16), but in this month Robert wrote two verse-epistles to Gavin Hamilton and the long 'Epistle to a Young Friend' (CW 221–3) which he sent to Orator Bob's son Andrew Hunter Aiken on 15 May. It was a sadder and wiser man who imparted advice to his youthful friend. The fifth stanza is particularly interesting:

> Ay free, aff han', your story tell,
>   When wi a bosom cronie;
> But still keep something to yoursel
>   Ye scarcely tell to onie:
> Conceal yoursel as well's ye can
>   Frae critical dissection:
> But keek thro ev'ry other man,
>   Wi sharpen'd, sly inspection.

At first sight this seems odd coming from a man who could unbosom himself to virtual strangers like John Arnot; but Robert had by now learned a valuable lesson. On the rebound from Jean, he now embarked on an affair with Margaret Campbell which he not only managed to conceal at the time, but seemed very coy about mentioning in later life. This is hardly surprising, for the affair with 'Highland Mary' must have taken place between the middle of April (when he admitted to Arnot that he was looking for 'another wife') and the second Sunday in May – four weeks at the most. This affair, which is discussed in proper detail later, seems to have been pretty intense, if we are to believe Robert's assertion that 'My Highland lassie was a warm-hearted, charming young creature as ever blessed a man with generous love'.[12] Margaret Campbell then vanishes from the scene, and three weeks later Jean was back in Mauchline. Again we are indebted to a long, confused and hysterical letter by Burns to a hitherto unknown correspondent, David Brice, written from Mossgiel on 12 June (CL 111–12). Brice was a native of Mauchline who had gone to work in Glasgow as a shoemaker,[13] but it is clear from the letter that he and Robert were on terms of close friendship:

> I have no news to tell you that will give me any pleasure to mention, or you, to hear.– Poor, ill-advised, ungrateful Armour came home on friday last. – You have heard all the particulars of that affair; and a black affair it is. – What she thinks of her conduct now, I don't know; one thing I know, she has made me compleatly miserable.– Never man lov'd, or rather ador'd, a woman more than I did her; and, to confess a truth between you and me, I do still love her to distraction after all, tho' I won't tell her so, tho I see her, which I don't want to do.– My poor, dear, unfortunate Jean! how happy have I been in her arms!– It is not the losing her that makes me so unhappy; but for *her* sake I feel most severely.– I foresee she is on the road to, I am afraid, *eternal* ruin; and those who made so much noise, and showed so much grief, at the thought of her being *my wife*, may, some day, see her connected in such a manner as may give them more real cause for vexation.– I am sure I do no wish it: may Almighty God forgive her ingratitude and perjury to me, as I from my very soul forgive her! and may His grace be with her, to bless her in all her future life!– I can have no nearer idea of the place of eternal punishment than what I have felt in my own breast on her account.– I have tryed often to forget her: I have run into all kinds of dissipation and riot, Mason-meetings, drinking matches, and other mischief, to drive her out of my head, but all in vain; and now for a grand cure, the Ship is on her way home that is to take me out to Jamaica, and then, farewel dear old Scotland, and farewel dear, ungrateful Jean, for never, never will I see you more!

Here we can sense Robert's emotional turmoil, his mood oscillating frequently – one minute howling about Jean's treatment of *him*, the next invoking God's forgiveness for her ingratitude and perjury – and, running like a golden thread throughout, the searing intensity of a love that had reduced him to such abject misery.

From this letter we learn that Jean had returned to Mauchline on Friday, 9 June. On Sunday 18 (according to the Session book) she was 'called, compeared not' which means that Mr Auld cried out for her to come forward from the body of the kirk and be solemnly rebuked. Jean, sensible girl, however, had chosen to absent herself from divine worship that morning. Instead, she had already written a letter to the minister (on 13 June). This was duly recorded in the minute-book:

> I am heartily sorry that I have given and must give your Session trouble
> on my account. I acknowledge that I am with child, and Robert Burns in
> Mossgiel is the father. I am, with great respect, your most humble
> servant, Jean Armour.

Regrettably, the letter itself has not survived, but its grovelling import is
clear enough. Jean could not have apologised more profusely, and now she
was waiting meekly to accept whatever humiliation the Kirk Session might
mete out by way of penance. We do not know how she felt on her return
from Paisley, or, indeed, why she decided to come back when she did.
Why, for example, did she not remain with the Purdies until her confinement ten weeks later? She returned to find that Robert was planning to
leave Scotland; worse, that he had not been slow in replacing her in his
affections. In her letter to the Session Jean could have mentioned her marriage, irregular though it might be. That she chose not to is an indication
that she, like Robert, considered herself to be single. She implied no claim
upon him at all.

  Robert himself was hailed before the Session on 25 June and
acknowledged his responsibility in the affair. The Session, far from taking
their revenge on the uppity young poet as they are alleged to have done by
insisting on three penitential appearances, actually let him off quite lightly.
Three acts of public penance was the usual punishment, but instead of
mounting the stool of penitence – the creepy chair, as Burns called it –
Robert was allowed to stand in his own place at fortnightly intervals, thereafter. On the evening before the first of these rituals, Robert took up his
quill to write to John Richmond, who had endured a similar experience the
previous year in regard to his 'antenuptial incontinence' with Jenny
Surgeoner:

> I have waited on Armour since her return home; not by [God] from any
> the least view of reconciliation, but merely to ask for her health; and – to
> you I will confess it, from a foolish hankering fondness – very ill-plac'd
> indeed.– The Mother forbade me the house; nor did Jean shew that peni-
> tence that might have been expected.– However, the Priest, I am
> inform'd will give me a Certificate as a single man, if I comply with the
> rules of the Church, which for that very reason I intend to do.–

The rest of the letter was written on 'Sunday morn':

> I am just going to put on Sackloth (*sic*) & ashes this day.– I am indulged
> so far as to appear in my own seat.– Peccavi Pater, misere (*sic*) mei – My
> book will be ready in a fortnight – If you have any Subscribers, return me
> them by Connell.–
>   The L[ord] stand wi' the Righteous –

James Connell, referred to in this and other letters, was the Mauchline
carrier. Incidentally, Burns – and Connell – were breaking the Postmaster-
General's monopoly (a criminal offence), as the transmission of a letter

other than by the proper postal service was only permitted if it accompanied a parcel. In fairness to Burns and Connell, however, it must be pointed out that this infringement of the postal regulations was common in an age when postage was expensive.

The penance was more fully described in a second letter to Brice, written on 17 July (CL 112):

> I have already appeared publicly in Church, and was indulged in the liberty of standing in my own seat.– I do this to get a certificate as a bachelor, which Mr. Auld has promised me.– I am now fixed to go for the West Indies in October.– Jean and her friends insisted much that she should stand along with me in the kirk, but the minister would not allow it, which bred a great trouble, I assure you, and I am blamed as the cause of it, tho' I am sure I am innocent; but I am very well pleased, for all that, not to have had her company.[14]

Further penitential appearances took place on 23 July and 6 August. On the last occasion Robert, Jean and three other fornicators were formally rebuked by Daddy Auld and were 'absolved from scandal' in the sonorous formula of the Established Church:

> You appear there to be rebuked, and at the same time making profession of repentence for the sin of fornication.
>
> The frequency of this sin is just matter for lamentation among Christians, and affords just ground of deep humiliation to the guilty persons themselves.
>
> We call you to reflect seriously in contrition of heart on all the instances of your sin and guilt, in their numbers, high aggravation, and unhappy consequences, and say, having done foolishly, we'll do so no more.
>
> Beware of returning to your sin as some of you have done, like the dog to his vomit, or like the sow that is washed to her wallowing in the mire.[15]

This was not to be the last appearance of Robert and Jean before the Kirk Session; but for the moment the Kirk had done with them both. Robert got his bachelor's certificate and Jean had to look forward to life as an unmarried mother. James Armour, knowing that Robert planned to go abroad and was about to publish his poems, now showed a vengeful and calculating streak; but young Mossgiel, for once, anticipated his next move and acted first. On the day before the second penitential appearance Robert drew up a Deed of Assignment (CL 115–16), effectively making over to Gilbert all his property, including his share of the tack of Mossgiel, 'all and Sundry Goods, Gear, Corns, Cattle, Horses, Nolt, Sheep, Household furniture, and all other moveable effects of whatever kind'. Robert particularised the profits that might arise from the publication of his poems, and also entrusted Gilbert with the copyright of the poems for behoof of his natural daughter Elizabeth, so that Gilbert could carry out his part of the contract to 'aliment, clothe and educate' Robert's natural child 'in a suitable manner as if she was his own'. This document, on which stamp duty was paid in the prescribed manner, was subsequently lodged with the Sheriff-Clerk in Ayr, in whose office it is preserved to this day. It is to Robert's credit that he remembered where his priorities lay. A second document, dated 1 December 1786 and drafted by Gavin Hamilton, was an undertaking by Burns to Elizabeth Paton that he would continue to maintain 'dear-bought Bess'.[16]

Having executed the Deed of Assignment at Mossgiel on 22 July and made his penitential appearance the following day, Robert fled from the parish. By now Armour had obtained a writ *in meditatione fugae* (literally 'in contemplation of flight') in order to recover substantial damages on his daughter's behalf, and Robert was being hounded. Having suffered the trauma of Jean's rejection and desertion and the public humiliation of ecclesiastical rebuke, he was now threatened with imprisonment. Small wonder, therefore, that his mood now alternated between impotent anger and sheer wretchedness. He took refuge with the Allans at Old Rome Foord (Rumford) on the River Irvine near Gatehead, west of Kilmarnock. Jean Allan was Agnes Brown's half-sister, so she and her husband James were Robert's aunt and uncle. Their son Robert was employed at Mossgiel as a ploughman. From this refuge Burns wrote a despairing letter to Richmond on 30 July (CL 77–8):

> My hour is now come. – You and I will never meet in Britain more.– I have orders within three weeks at farthest to repair aboard the Nancy, Captain Smith, from Clyde, to Jamaica, and to call at Antigua.– This, except, to our friend Smith, whom God long preserve, is a secret about Mauchlin.– Would you believe it? Armour has got a warrant to throw me in jail till I find security for an enormous sum.– This they keep an entire secret, but I got it by a channel they little dream of; and I am wandering from one friend's house to another, and like a true son of the Gospel, 'have no where to lay my head'.–[17] I know you will pour an execration on her head, but spare the poor, ill-advised Girl for my sake; tho', may all the Furies that rend the injured, enraged Lover's bosom, await the old Harridan, her Mother, untill her latest hour! May Hell string the arm of Death to throw the fatal dart, and all the winds of warring elements rouse the infernal flames to welcome her approach! For Heaven's sake burn this letter, and never show it to a living creature.– I write it in a moment of rage, reflecting on my miserable situation, – exil'd, abandon'd, forlorn –
>
> I can write no more – let me hear from you by the return of Connel.– I will write you ere I go.

The 'channel they little dream of' seems to have been Jean herself who, in defiance of her father's wishes, must have continued seeing Robert and tipped him off about the petition for the writ which she had signed under duress. Old Rome Foord would have been very convenient for Robert, slipping into Kilmarnock to check the proofs of his book at Wilson's printing shop in the Star Close. From the reference to wandering from one friend's house to another, it seems probable that Robert stayed with one or more of his Kilmarnock friends, the better to supervise his book through the press. The book itself was ready on Monday, 31 July. In the early weeks of August Robert continued to live in and around Kilmarnock, whence he wrote letters to various friends dealing with book sales. Jean Armour had now receded for the time being. Instead, his mind was full of the imminent departure. There were frequent references to this, in letters to John Kennedy (CL 84), John Logan (CL 123) and James Smith (CL 118). The last-named, to his closest confidant, was the most explicit concerning his plans:

> I went to Dr Douglas yesterday fully resolved to take the opprtty of Capt Smith; but I found the Doctor with a Mr and Mrs White, both Jamaicans, and they have derang'd my plans altogether.– They assure him that to send me from Savannah la Mar to Port Antonio will cost my Master, Charles Douglas, upwards of fifty pounds; besides running the risk of throwing myself into a pleuratic fever in consequence of hard travelling in the sun.– On these accounts, he refuses sending me with Smith for pas[sage]; but a vessel sails from Greenock the first of Sept:, right for the place of my destination; the Captn of her is an intimate of Mr Gavin Hamilton's, and as good a fellow as heart could wish: with him I am destined to go.– Where I shall shelter, I know not, but I hope to weather the storm.– Perish the drop of blood of mine that fears them. I know their worst, and am prepared to meet it –
>
> > I'll laugh, an' sing, an' shake my leg,
> > As lang's I dow.[18]
>
> Thursday morning, if you can muster as much self denial as be out of bed about seven o' clock, I shall see you as I ride thro' to Cumnock.–
> I could not write to Richmond by Connel, but I will write by the Kilmck Carrier.– After all, Heaven bless the Sex. I feel there is still happiness for me among them.–
>
> > O woman, lovely woman sure Heaven design'd you,
> > To temper Man, we had been brutes without you:[19]

From this letter it is possible to reconstruct Robert's movements. He was in Kilmarnock on 10 August, but the following weekend (12–13) he was in Ayr discussing his plans with Dr Patrick Douglas. Very early on the morning of Thursday, 17 August, Robert would have ridden through Mauchline, under the very noses of the Armour family. A letter written from 'Mr J. Merry's Saturday morn' to Thomas Campbell (CL 124) shows that Robert reached New Cumnock on 18 August and put up for the night at the inn where his old sweetheart Annie Rankine had been the innkeeper's wife since December 1782. From there he rode westwards, through Dalmellington to Maybole, arriving there about Friday, 25 August. There he stayed with his old school chum Willie Niven, visiting subscribers in the district and collecting money for copies of his book. At Maybole he was royally received and introduced by Willie to his friends. Judging by a bread and butter letter written soon afterwards (CL 40) Willie laid on a party at which Robert had more to drink than he ought: 'I am afraid the conduct you forced me on may make them see me in a light I would fondly think I do not deserve.' His fame now spread like wildfire, and the acclaim which his poems received emboldened him to return to Mossgiel and brazen things out. He was home again by 30 August, on which date he wrote to Niven.

Two days later Robert wrote to Richmond (CL 78):

> I am still here in statu quo, tho I well expected to have been on my way over the Atlantic by this time.– The Nancy, in which I was to have gone, did not give me warning enough.– Two days notice was too little for me to wind up my affairs and go for Greenock. I now am to be a passenger aboard the Bell, Capt Cathcart, who sails the end of this month.– I am under little apprehension now about Armour.– The warrant is still in existence, but some of the first Gentlemen in the country have offered to befriend me; and besides, Jean will not take any step against me, without letting me know, as nothing but the most violent menaces could have forced her to sign the Petition.– I have called on her once and again, of late, as she, at this moment, is threatened with the pangs of approaching travail; and I assure you, my dear Friend, I cannot help being anxious, very anxious, for her situation.– She would gladly now embrace that offer she once rejected, but it shall never more be in her power.

The excuse for not catching the boat which sailed from Greenock on 1 September is pretty lame, in view of the fact that Robert had been told the date of sailing seventeen days previously. The inescapable conclusion is that, as the time drew nearer, Robert's enthusiasm for Jamaica waned. His feelings regarding Jean were as confused as ever.

Ironically, this is the self-same letter in which Burns proceeded to deliver a lecture to his friend on his cavalier behaviour towards poor Jenny Surgeoner:

> I saw Jenny Surgeoner of late, and she complains bitterly against you.– You are acting very wrong, My friend; her happiness or misery is bound up in your affection or unkindness.– Poor girl! she told me with tears in her eyes that she had been at great pains since she went to Paisley, learning to write better; just on purpose to be able to correspond with you; and had promised herself great pleasure in your letters. Richmond, I know you to be a man of honour, but this conduct of yours to a poor girl who distractedly loves you, and whom you have ruined – forgive me, my friend, when I say it is highly inconsistent with that manly INTEGRITY that I know your bosom glows with.– Your little, sweet Innocent too – but I beg your pardon; 'tis taking an improper liberty.

Two days later Jean gave birth to twins, a boy and a girl. Adam Armour was sent up to Mossgiel to break the news to the father and found Burns at the plough. Robert continued with his ploughing, but that evening he came down to the town 'with a guinea and some Tea and Sugar, which was thought very handsome'.[20] This anecdote, relayed to Train, is charming but defective surely, for 3 September was a Sunday and Robert would not have compounded his previous felonies by daring to plough on the Sabbath. That day, however, he penned a brief note to Richmond (CL 79): 'Wish me luck, dear Richmond! Armour has just now brought me a fine boy and girl at one throw. God bless them poor little dears!' To this he appended four lines of the old ballad 'Green grow the rashes, O' which he was then reworking. The stanza ends with the memorable lines: 'A feather bed is no sae saft, / As the bosoms o' the lasses, O'. Burns was clearly back on form.

Incidentally, it is a wonder that the Kirk Session did not show their disapproval of this twin birth on a Sunday. The notion was still prevalent at that time that a birth on the Sabbath reflected conception on the Lord's day and this, even within the sanctity of marriage, was regarded as a profanity. On this occasion, however, the Session clerk was content to record:

> Burns, Robert, Tenant in Mossgiel, and Jean Armour had Twin Children Born 3rd and Baptized 5th Septr called Robert and Jean.[21]

This seemingly innocuous entry revealed the illegitimate nature of the births. The convention of naming first-born children for the father's father (William) and mother's mother (Mary) did not apply in such cases; the names of the guilty parties were used instead. The key-words 'spouse' and 'lawful' which invariably appeared in the record of legitimate births were conspicuous by their absence.[22]

To the wine-merchant Robert Muir, one of the coterie of Kilmarnock businessmen who had played a noble part in guaranteeing the publication of the poems, Robert wrote the following Friday morning, addressing him warmly as 'My Friend My Brother' (CL 86–7):

> You will have heard that poor Armour has repaid my amorous mortgages double.– A very fine boy and girl have awakened a thousand feelings that thrill, some with tender pleasure and some with foreboding anguish thro' my soul –

He closed this letter with a fleeting reference to his plans: 'I believe all hopes of staying at home will be abortive, but more of this when, in the latter end of next week, you shall be troubled with a visit.' As Armour's anger abated and Robert's fortunes seemed, at long last, to prosper, the attraction of Jamaica receded. It might have been supposed that the rift with the Armour family would have disappeared and the paternal feelings aroused in Robert by the sight of Jean's twins would have brought the erstwhile lovers together again; but although Robert's attitude towards the girl he had seduced visibly softened, on one point he remained adamant: he had no intention of marrying her. There is no further mention of Jean in his correspondence of 1786; instead, he was completely engrossed in his plans, first to emigrate, and then to promote his literary career. But, deep down, something continued to gnaw at him. About 8 October he wrote a

long letter to Robert Aiken (CL 93). After commenting on 'the consequence of my follies', he went on:

> besides I have for some time been pining under secret wretchedness, from
> causes which you pretty well know – the pang of disappointment, the
> sting of pride, with some wandering stabs of remorse, which never fail to
> settle on my vitals like vultures, when attention is not called away by the
> calls of society or the vagaries of the muse. Even in the hour of social
> mirth, my gaiety is the madness of an intoxicated criminal under the
> hands of the executioner. All these reasons urge me to go abroad; and to
> all these reasons I have only one answer – the feelings of a father. This,
> in the present mood I am in, overbalances everything that can be laid in
> the scale against it.

The uneasiness that pervades this letter seems oddly at variance with the
up-beat mood of others written in the preceding weeks. It was as if Robert,
after a brief period of euphoria, had been brought back to earth with a
bump. Snyder says that the reason for this perturbation was that he was
harassed not only by the results of his intimacy with Jean, but also by the
fact that he had at this very time promised to marry another girl.[23] This
seems too pat a solution, and does not accord with 'pining under secret
wretchedness, from causes which you pretty well know' which surely is an
allusion to the affair with Jean Armour. Obviously Robert was still deeply
in love with her and seeing her with her babies – as he was bound to do in
such a small community – would inevitably provoke those 'stabs of
remorse'.

We shall see later that, for Robert, love was no abstract concept, and he
invariably found it difficult to entertain the deepest feelings for a fair
charmer in her absence, especially when he had the physical presence of a
counter attraction to contend with. To be sure, his feelings for Jean, one
way or the other, seemed to be in suspension at this time; but nowhere in
his correspondence or (more significantly) in his poetry do we find any
reference to Margaret Campbell during the period, from May to October,
when he was allegedly betrothed to her.

More has been written about 'Highland Mary' (and arguably less known)
than any of Burns's other heroines. Certainly she has always far outranked
Jean Armour, the woman who actually set up house with him and bore
most of his children. Statues of Highland Mary are to be found as far afield
as Dunoon, Liverpool and New York, but Jean has never had that honour.
At this remove in time it is difficult to understand the immense emotional
appeal of this very shadowy figure; but therein lies the key to her attraction. It was her very shadowiness, her ethereal quality which first intrigued
and then captured the imagination of Burns worshippers. Around her
countless myths were woven, until the cult of Highland Mary reached its
zenith in the late nineteenth century. Only as the centenary of Robert's
death approached did responsible biographers begin to raise doubts. This
culminated in the centenary year itself when William Ernest Henley

attacked the Mary cult head-on, dismissing it merely as 'an episode'. This sparked off a dispute between the Episodists and the Mariolaters which had all the zealous vehemence and belligerent fanaticism of the struggle between the Auld and New Lichts a century earlier, or the sectarianism of the Covenanting wars a century before that. The argument flared up again in 1930 following the publication of *The Life of Robert Burns* by Catherine Carswell, which was greeted with an unprecedented campaign of vituperation equalled in modern times only by the reception of Salman Rushdie's *Satanic Verses*.

Prior to 1850 the so-called Highland Mary episode in Burns's life had neither beginning nor ending. After that date, Scott Douglas fixed Sunday, 14 May 1786 as the end of the affair. The facts, such as they are, were contained in a passage of the *Reliques* which Cromek allegedly transcribed from the interleaved copy of *The Scots Musical Museum* which Burns prepared for Robert Riddell of Glenriddell. Referring to the *Reliques* we find the day and the month pointedly indicated – 'the second Sunday in May' – but not the year. The year 1786 was adopted by Scott Douglas on the *prima facie* assumption that the poet's songs in honour of 'Mary' were composed during the period of his proposed emigration. When James Dick rediscovered the Glenriddell volume in 1903, after a period of closest seclusion extending for almost a century, it was found that the page which bore the text of 'The Highland Lassie, O' and Burns's annotation thereon had been removed (along with some sixteen others), and to this day it has never come to light. For many years, therefore, Cromek was suspected of having fabricated the whole thing, and as his editorial conscientiousness and reliability in other matters had been found sadly wanting, the consensus of opinion was that Cromek had deliberately concocted numerous spurious notes. The discovery of a Burns manuscript of twelve folio pages in the Laing Collection at Edinburgh University Library in 1921 (showing that many of Cromek's notes which J. C. Dick had rejected as spurious, were, in fact genuine, though taken from a source other than Cromek had claimed) went a long way to restoring Cromek's tarnished reputation. Nevertheless, the missing page from the volume prepared by Burns for Robert Riddell of Glenriddell means that we still have no alternative but to fall back on Cromek's transcript:

> *The Highland Lassie, O.* This was a composition of mine in very early life, before I was known at all in the world. My Highland lassie was a warm-hearted, charming young creature as ever blessed a man with generous love. After a pretty long tract of the most ardent reciprocal attachment, we met by appointment, on the second Sunday of May, in a sequestered spot by the banks of Ayr, where we spent the day in taking farewel, before she should embark for the West Highlands to arrange matters among her friends for our projected change of life. At the close of Autumn following she crossed the sea to meet me at Greenock, where she had scarce landed when she was seized with a malignant fever, which hurried my dear girl to the grave in a few days, before I could even hear of her illness.[24]

It is unfortunate that Cromek should have been discredited from 1903 till 1921 (indeed, he has never been fully rehabilitated and continues to languish under a cloud along with Currie and Cunningham), for in that period the pendulum swung too far in the opposite direction. The year 1786 was no longer accepted unquestioningly and scholars began looking to a much earlier period, between 1782 and 1784. The parameters were set by the date of the two-volume bible which Burns gave to the young lady (which clearly appeared in the printer's colophon) and the beginning of the Mossgiel period. This therefore placed the Mary episode well clear of the entanglements with either Betsey Paton or Jean Armour; the idea that Robert had two affairs running simultaneously was unthinkable.

Burns must have been chuckling in his mausoleum at this manipulation of the chronology; for it appears that he did his best to obscure the issue himself. As far back as 1893 Eric Robertson[25] drew attention to the deliberate obscuring of the girl's memory, not only by Burns and his friends, but, more surprisingly, by her own family. Instead of receiving a clear account of her who inspired 'Thou Lingering Star' (CW 372-3) he found that all concerned in the story had exhibited the most manifest anxiety to conceal the facts, and prevent posterity from gaining any certain knowledge of them. Robert himself went out of his way to avoid mention of the girl, and Robertson thought it strange that, at the time when Burns fell out with the Armours, the line 'And such a leg! my bonie Jean' in 'The Vision' (CW 116) should be replaced by 'my Bess, I ween' if, indeed, he were having an affair with his Highland lassie by that time. On the other hand, I feel that the Mauchline belle Bess Miller, rather than Bess Paton, could have been intended here. Much has also been made of the fact that Robert's otherwise very candid autobiographical letter to Moore is completely silent on the Mary episode, although this account took the narrative down to August 1787.

The controversial annotation quoted by Cromek (assuming it to have been authentic) was not made by Burns until August 1792, but even here we find Robert being uncharacteristically economical with the truth by referring to it 'in very early life'. Snyder disingenuously shrugs this off as a phrase used to indicate the time before the Kilmarnock volume had brought him fame.[26] Burns repeatedly referred to the Mary songs as products of his earliest years. In a letter of November 1792 to George Thomson (CL 621) he wrote of 'Highland Mary' (CW 470), 'The Subject of the Song is one of the most interesting passages of my youthful days'. Consequently Currie, Cromek, Lockhart, Motherwell and Hogg, Cunningham, Wilson and (originally) Chambers all swallowed the line that the Mary affair belonged to Burns's earliest days, hence the general idea that she had died in 1782. It was not until January 1850 that Scott Douglas showed how all these biographers had been duped.[27] He not only correctly dated the bible which Robert gave to the young lady – he could hardly have done otherwise, as the date in roman numerals formed part of the printer's colophon – but even deciphered the partially obliterated word 'Mossgavill' on the fly-leaf of one volume. As Burns did not take up residence there till

April 1784 the Mary affair must have taken place some time after that. Incidentally, it is a sad commentary on mid-nineteenth-century scholarship that no one had thought to examine the two-volume bible itself before Scott Douglas late in 1849, although the precious relic had been enshrined in the Burns Monument at Alloway since December 1840.

Scott Douglas also, for the first time, linked the episode and the song 'My Highland Lassie, O' with Robert's plan to emigrate, a design which 'we hear at no earlier period of his life than the spring of 1786'. This was also borne out by a passage in another letter to Thomson, written on 26 October 1792 (CL 619) in which Robert commented, in connection with the song 'Will Ye Go to the Indies, my Mary' (CW 468):

> In my very early years, when I was thinking of going to the West Indies, I took the following farewell of a dear girl.– It is quite trifling . . . You must know, that all my earlier love-songs were the breathings of ardent Passion

implying yet again that the song, like the plan to emigrate, belonged to a much earlier period. Gilbert Burns was even more reticent, claiming, for example, that 'Sweet Afton' (CW 351) had been written in compliment to Mrs Stewart of Stair, though her Christian name was Catherine, and did not accord with the 'Mary' referred to in the song. In the early editions by Currie the song appears without comment, but in the fourth edition (1803) the story concerning Mrs Stewart of Stair appeared for the first time. Scott Douglas was convinced that the story was a little ruse got up by Gilbert, 'to divest Currie's readers of the natural conjecture that Highland Mary was here again the theme of his lays'.[28] If, however, we accept Gilbert's word, then the name Mary rather than Catherine was used purely because it suited the metre better. In any case, as the song was not composed till 1789, Burns may not have had any specific girl in mind.

Robert Chambers took up the scent from Scott Douglas and pressed Isobel Burns on the date of Mary's death. At first Isobel was non-committal, but when Chambers insisted that it must have been in 1786 Mrs Begg confessed, 'You are quite right; the facts have all along been known to the family. I, like Gilbert, wished to say as little as possible.'

Like so many other aspects of Robert's life, the circumstances in which he considered emigrating to Jamaica are not precisely known. In the 1780s many a young Scotsman went east or west, to India and the Far East or America and the Caribbean, and although the mortality rate in both areas was very high, the fortunes that could be made were immense. The Indies, East or West, were the traditional resort of young men in trouble of a financial or amatory nature, giving them the chance to redeem themselves and make good. It is worth noting that James Smith, having failed in his calico business at Linlithgow, went off to St Lucia where he died at the beginning of the nineteenth century. When he was in trouble over Betsey Paton Robert hinted in his 'Epistle to John Rankine' that the alternatives were to enlist – 'I'd better gaen an sair't the King' – or go to the plantations – 'Tho I should herd the buckskin kye [American cattle] / For't, in Virginia'. At this period there was, indeed, many a close connection between Ayrshire and both Virginia and Jamaica, though since the end of the American War in 1783 the former, for the time being, seemed to offer fewer opportunities.

Patrick Douglas of Garallan in Cumnock parish had trained as a surgeon, but in 1776 he succeeded to the family estates which included property in Jamaica which his brother Charles personally supervised. Either Burns applied to Dr Douglas personally, or more probably had one of his Ayr friends (either Robert Aiken or John Ballantine) intercede on his behalf. An unfounded tradition, current in the nineteenth century, stated that Dr Douglas even arranged for Robert to take ship direct from Ayr, but that he baulked at this at the last moment. What is certain, however, is that Dr Douglas wrote to his brother who responded by offering Burns the position of book-keeper on his plantation in the neighbourhood of Port Antonio on the north-east coast of the island, at a salary of £30 per annum for three years. The salary was meagre, but Robert had no alternative but to accept it. Without the money for his passage and other necessary expenses Robert would have been obliged to indenture himself to his new master. He would, in effect, have ended up little better than the negro slaves he was overseeing, and less able than they to withstand the rigours of the tropical climate. His original plan, to land at Savannah la Mar on the south-west coast, would have entailed a journey of more than two hundred miles overland costing more than a year's pay. Once the plans were altered and delayed, however, Robert's enthusiasm began to wane. Thus we find him writing again to John Richmond on 27 September (CL 79–80):

> I received yours of Connel's last return, and I have just a moment at present to tell you that I am in the land of the living, and in the place of hope.– I am going perhaps to try a second edition of my book – if I do, it will detain me a litle longer in the country; if not, I shall be gone as soon as harvest is over.–
> Bettsey Miller waits me –

As the *Bell* set sail from Greenock on 20 September, it is obvious that the prospect of a second edition now overturned plans to emigrate. If the promise of a second edition did not materialise then Robert would be off to the Indies as soon as the crops were safely gathered in. But even when John Wilson of Kilmarnock dashed his hopes early in October Robert no longer regarded emigration as an alternative. In a long letter to Aiken written about 8 October (CL 92–4) Robert discussed his hopes for publication but made no mention at all of the emigration scheme. This seems to have been tacitly dropped by that time; instead, we find the earliest reference to another plan which was then beginning to form in his mind: 'I have been feeling all the rotations and movements within, respecting the excise', followed by a careful consideration of all the factors for and against such a move.

Nowhere in Robert's correspondence of this period do we find any reference to his Highland lassie. The last four words of the letter to Richmond, however, indicate that Elizabeth Miller may have been, however temporarily, in the ascendant. It is on this basis that many previous biographers have attributed the song 'Farewell to Eliza' (CW 50) to her, ignoring Burns's own statement that it was composed several years earlier. Gilfillan (1872) confused the issue by promoting the claim of Elizabeth Black, who married an innkeeper of Alloa and maintained that she was the heroine of the song.[29] The only significance in the reference to Bettsey Miller is that she may have briefly supplanted Jean Armour in Robert's affections. This view was taken by Chambers who says, 'She appears to have been an amiable girl, and it is not improbable that she had sympathised with Burns during his various distresses. Gratitude may have inspired a kind of affection, which, as usual, he expressed in the language of adoring love.' Chambers uses this statement to introduce a footnote:

> Another 'Betty' figures in the list of the loves that Ayrshire legend has assigned to Burns. It is still believed in the parish of Stair that he courted and was accepted by Betty Campbell, a servant in Stair House, that he gave her 'lines', and that these were destroyed by the girl after a quarrel with the poet.[30]

Betty Campbell does not appear anywhere else, and Chambers does not cite his source. This tale has the hallmarks of a half-truth half-remembered and distorted by the passage of time. I have been unable to trace any girl of this name in Stair parish in this period. But Coilsfield, less than a mile away on the other side of the River Ayr, did have a girl named Campbell among its employees, and she was the Highland lassie to whom Robert referred in his note on the song. Snyder apologised for retelling the story which was so clearly set out in the Chambers-Wallace edition of 1896, but he sounded a note of caution: 'even in the chronicle of these conservative and dependable scholars there is much unverifiable gossip and tradition interwoven with a small amount of ascertainable fact'. The result was an account 'of such a nature as to leave the reader constantly bewildered, and uncertain, when he comes to the end of the tale, as to whether any element of it can be unquestioningly believed'.[31] Unhappily even sources which Snyder believed to be reliable have since proved to be tainted, while primary sources which ought to have been checked have never been examined until now.

Snyder concluded that 'the most trustworthy anchor to windward' on which the student of Burns and Highland Mary could rely was the fact that, early in the nineteenth century, long before the mythmakers had begun their work with Burns, Greenock tradition unhesitatingly identified a grave in which a girl named Mary Campbell had been buried, and, furthermore, knew her to have been the Highland Mary of Burns's lyrics. For proof, Snyder adduced a minute of the Greenock Burns Club:

23d Feb. 1803. It was unanimously decided to request permission from
Mr. M'Pherson to allow the Club to add a tablet to the memory of Mary
Campbell on his lairs.[32]

Snyder quoted from the Chambers-Wallace edition of 1896 rather than
from the original, for the very good reason that the minute-book had long
since vanished. Neither he nor William Wallace would have had any reason
to doubt the authenticity of this document; but there are now good
grounds for considering it to have been a mid-nineteenth-century fabrication. Before examining the Highland Mary legend it is necessary to check
the antecedents of the Greenock Burns Club which claims to have been
founded in 1801, within five years of the poet's death. There existed, as
recently as 1902, a small volume bound in thick brown calf board, purporting to have been an Excise notebook found in Robert's home at the time
of his death and subsequently presented to the Greenock Burns Club by
Adam Pearson of the Excise in 1801. An inscription to this effect appeared
on the fly-leaf of the volume. The book itself mysteriously disappeared
some time after 1902 but a detailed description of the book, together with
'an old oaken, brass-bound chest' in which it was kept, was given in an
article in the *Greenock Telegraph* of 24 January 1902. Clark Hunter
brought this to the attention of the Librarian of HM Customs and Excise
who immediately expressed surprise at the description. Excise books of the
period were, in fact, invariably bound in red leather with the Excise
emblem stamped in gold on the cover.[33] For some unfathomable reason the
book subsequently disappeared, and only the two pages (fly-leaf and title)
reproduced in the centenary booklet of 1902 are now preserved in the
Watt Library, Greenock. Why they should have been detached from the
rest of the book in the first place, and why they alone have survived, is
open to conjecture. One is left inescapably and reluctantly with the conclusion that, at some time after 1902, the so-called minute-book of 1801 was
exposed as yet another spurious relic. Brief transcripts from this book, purporting to be from 1802-4, were printed in the Centenary brochure, but
these reveal a number of inconsistencies and discrepancies.

Hunter also found a reference to a strong oak chest of the kind formerly
furnished to Excise officers for keeping their offical papers. This had been
in the Thornhill office while Burns was a gauger in that area (1789-91) and
had been used by him. This was lent to the Greenock Burns Club by
R. W. Train of HM Inland Revenue, by whose father Joseph Train, the
eminent antiquary, it had been purchased at a sale of the poet's effects. It
seems, therefore, that the chest had come to the Greenock club between
the death of Joseph Train (1852) and the Burns Centenary celebrations
(1859) at which it was proudly exhibited. Whether the mysterious book
now missing was acquired at this time, or at a much earlier date, of course
cannot be verified. The only documentary evidence that there was a
Greenock Burns Club in 1803 is a press cutting advertising a visit of the
Burns Club of Greenock and Ayrshire Society to Alloway and purporting
to be from the *Greenock Advertiser* of 20 January 1803. Clark Hunter

consulted the files of this newspaper, only to discover that there was no issue of the paper on that date; and a search of other issues from November 1802 to March 1803 failed to turn up the mysterious advertisement. A search of the contemporary Glasgow newspapers likewise drew a blank. To date, *no* newspaper of 1803 has been found with the curious announcement contained therein. The Greenock Burns Club's earliest extant minutes date from 1825 only, but references to its annual Burns supper may be found in the *Greenock Advertiser* from 1811 onwards. Hunter's deductions were that, while the Greenock Burns Club was indeed one of the oldest in existence, and may even have held informal meetings before 1811, there was no concrete evidence known at present to sustain the tradition that the Club dated from 1801.

This matter is of importance in the wrangle between the Greenock and Paisley Burns Clubs for the premier title, the latter having been established in 1805 and possessing incontrovertible proof of the fact. This rivalry between the two Renfrewshire clubs need not concern us; but, in the words of Clark Hunter, 'a tradition which, until now, has not been critically examined' has important bearing on the so-called Highland Mary story. It should be noted that, despite the alleged minute of February 1803, no actual move to erect a monument over the girl's grave was made until 1841 (following the repatriation of the two-volume bible from Canada) when local Burnsians raised about £100 to defray the costs of the memorial unveiled on 25 January 1842.

Snyder has therefore based his assumptions on what now appears to be a false premise. By 1803 only Currie's and Heron's lives of Burns had been published. Heron did not mention the Highland Mary incident at all, while Currie treated it briefly and cryptically, without naming the young lady. The earliest reference to the girl as Mary Campbell is to be found in Cromek's *Reliques* (1808), wherein is given the description of their fond farewell on 14 May 1786:

> This adieu was performed with all those simple and striking ceremonials, which rustic sentiment has devised to prolong tender emotions, and to inspire awe. The lovers stood on each side of a small purling brook – they laved their hands in the limpid stream – and, holding a Bible between them, pronounced their vows to be faithful to each other. They parted – never to meet again.[34]

Just where Cromek got this twaddle from is anyone's guess; it does not accord with any known betrothal custom and as no witnesses were present and both participants were dead by 1808 it must be assumed that the story was one of Cromek's own invention. It was repeated verbatim by Lockhart (1828) and 'Honest Allan' Cunningham, needless to say, seized upon it and embroidered it even further in his own edition of 1834. Lockhart added:

> It is proper to add, that Mr Cromek's story, which even Allan Cunningham was disposed to receive with suspicion, has been confirmed

very strongly by the accidental discovery of a Bible, presented by Burns to 'Mary Campbell', which was found in the possession of her sister at Ardrossan.[35]

He then went on to describe the small, two-volume bible, describing the inscriptions, in pen and ink, on the inside front covers of both volumes. Typically, Cromek was careless both with the transcriptions from the Old and New Testaments and with the inscriptions on the fly-leaves. In particular, he stated that the names of both the donor and the recipient were given, averring that the girl's name had been virtually erased by someone rubbing the inscription with a wet finger so that only the first letters 'Ma' remained.

A slightly more accurate description was given by James Grierson of Dalgoner:

Met with Campbell spouse to James Anderson mason in Ardrossan 1817 and sister to Highland Mary Burns friend. She says Mary was tall, fair haird with blue eyes – they were daughters of Arch. Campbell mariner who resided at Dunoon Parish & Agnes Campbell his spouse, he died in Grenock 1815 & is buried in a lair of the new burying ground he bought from Widow McPherson & his widow lives there in Scots land long vennal. Their sons are Robert & Archd Carpenters there – Mrs Andersons sons possess the Bibel Burns gave her in exchange – it is printed by Alexander Kincaids assignies at Edin 1782. The booksellers mark 5/6 2 vol small 12° on each volume is his mason mark >-X-I>. this son a mason works presently in Paisley . . . Mrs showed the Bible to J.G. which she sent to Paisley to her son for, on purpose – on the first vol is in Burns hand writing 'And ye shall not swear by my name falsely' – 'I am the LORD' 'Levit 19 Chap 12 verse' his name had been there but carefully rubed out except some letters On the second vol there is also wrote in his hand 'Thou shalt not forswear thyself but shalt perform unto the Lord thine Oath' 'Matth: 35 Ch 33 verse On this vol had also been the mason mark & his name with date 1786. but papers had been pasted on & torn off so the writing is much defaced.

Leaves are folded in at or near various places as Isaiah 30 & 21. 34 & 10. 43 & 17. 55 & 16 [or 17 or 19] Jerem: x 27 [or x & 7, or Jerem 7; or Jerem 1 & 7]. 31 & 5. Ezek 18. 36 & 33. Hosea 4th 11 & 8. Zach. 13 Luke 17 & 14 John 13 & 14. 20 & 7. Rev 4 & It seems evident that those two texts wrote at length in his hand, each *only* part of a verse & inscribed one in each vol. given to mary were intende strongly to alude to some secret known to them alone & it is more than probable this was some promise or Oaths he has not Oaths as in the original but *Oath* & he was not one of these men who had no meaning for what they did.– probably it was her who erased the name, conscious too of the meaning and not chusing to have the books in her possession on which were the texts connected with the name.[36]

Whatever the imperfections of Grierson's near-illiterate scrawl, he at least had noted the date 1782 in the colophon, a matter which Lockhart or

Train overlooked (or chose to overlook). Significantly, Grierson makes no mention of any name other than Robert's on the fly-leaves of the two volumes. He implies, however, that though Robert's masonic mark appeared on both volumes, his name and date 1786 appeared only on the second one. Scott Douglas, who examined the bibles very carefully in 1849, gave his own version of the inscription on the left-hand page of the first volume as: 'And ye shall not swear by my name falsely, I am the Lord. – Levit. chap. xix. v. 12'. On the second volume the inscription was given as, 'Thou shalt not forswear thyself, but shalt perform unto the Lord thine oaths. – St. Matth. chap. v. 33'. According to Scott Douglas, however, both volumes had, on the right-hand fly-leaf, 'Robert Burns, Mossgavill' with his masonic mark, but there was no mention of the year 1786.

Although the Biblical quotations are intact, someone, at some time or another, has attempted to rub out the inscriptions in the upper areas of the right-hand pages, by wetting a finger and disturbing the surface of the paper. When Cromek examined the volumes in 1807 he noted that paper had been pasted over these inscriptions, but that it was possible to read them by holding the pages up to the light. Some time within the ensuing decade the strips of paper had been removed and the inscriptions partially erased by rubbing the surface with a wet finger. As a result all that can be read of the name on one volume is 'Robert —ns', though 'Mossgavill' can be deciphered. On the other volume the obliteration of the name was more thorough and only the initial 'M' and part of the adjoining letter, together with 'll' at the end, are visible to the naked eye. This was interpreted as 'Mary Campbell', the name of the recipient. In January 1992 I examined these volumes with a view to clearing up the discrepancy concerning the girl's name, which, from the Dunoon parish register, I had found was Margaret, not Mary. The inscription below 'Robert Burns', however, had been so badly defaced that little was now visible to the naked eye.

Permission was subsequently obtained from the Trustees of Burns Monument and Birthplace Museum to have the volumes examined in a forensic laboratory. Under ultra-violet light nothing was visible and very little could be seen with infra-red light; but under blue-green light the faded and mutilated inscriptions came up clearly. In fact, the inscriptions on the right-hand fly-leaves of both volumes are 'Robert Burns' in one line and 'Mossgavill' below. What had been taken to be the name of Mary (or Margaret) Campbell now turns out to have been Robert's address in both books. Neither the date, nor the girl's name, nor any presentational inscription, appear on the right-hand pages.

In the course of examination, however, it was discovered that three blank pages at the end of one volume were covered with inscriptions in pencil. At some point these pencil marks had been rubbed out. This had been done so efficiently that neither Cromek (1807) nor Grierson (1817), far less any later investigator, had even noticed them; although sufficient traces remain that anyone examining the bibles in good light would notice that some writing had been there. Under infra-red light the remnants of the graphite marks show up clearly but unfortunately where the graphite was removed nothing can be seen. More advanced techniques for examining documents, such as laser-microscopy and ESDA (used by the Metropolitan Police forensic laboratory with such dramatic effect to prove tampering with the notes of interrogations in certain well-publicised cases) are not yet available in Scotland, so the text of the three pages cannot at this stage be fully ascertained. What is beyond doubt, however, is that the handwriting was that of Robert Burns himself. The second and third pages are headed with roman numerals 'ii' and 'iii' implying some connected text; but the first page has arabic numerals '2' and '3' as central heading to two short passages, so the pencil marks may represent little more than the poet's random jottings. Here and there full words can be deciphered – 'His wonder then . . .' near the top of the first page, 'god of . . .' and 'is the gt work of the Lord' further down – which seem to suggest either Biblical quotations or religious musings. The second page is virtually indecipherable apart from the word 'Day' near the centre. On the third page the tantalising snatches are 'is everybody . . . delight . . . friend . . . poesy was a . . . that means . . . stolen . . . Sis . . .' with what appears to be a signature near the foot.

What now becomes clear is that the two-volume bible, for which Robert paid five shillings and sixpence, was his own personal bible. This seems to be borne out by the inscriptions on the fly-leaves and the extensive notes or jottings on the end papers. That Robert gave the books to his Highland lass is not in doubt; what now has to be reassessed is the significance of the gift. Contrary to popular belief, the girl's name does not appear on the fly-leaf, far less any formula indicating the gift. The bibles were given to the girl as a memento of friendship; whether they could be regarded as a pledge is open to doubt. Indeed, Robert may have intended ambiguity in the matter. Despite the quotations from Leviticus and Matthew there was certainly nothing *specific* which could be regarded as a declaration or promise of marriage. Robert may have meant the bibles as a parting gift, nothing more; at the same time, however, he may have conveyed to the trusting girl that they were a token of betrothal. The biblical quotations – the words from the Good Book – would have been regarded as sacred. Significantly no attempt was ever made to erase the quotations, despite the mutilation of the inscriptions opposite.

The surname of the girl is not in doubt. Cromek had his shortcomings as an editor, but he was indefatigable in searching out a great deal of background information concerning Burns and his associates. The Christian name was naturally assumed from the writings of the poet himself. Now let us examine the poems, songs and letters which add to the meagre store of knowledge.

The note to 'My Highland Lassie, O' was Robert's only admission concerning the affair, giving the day and month but not the year, but implying a very early date. This may have been done deliberately to throw Robert Riddell off the scent. After all, Robert was by that time married to Jean Armour and would not be minded to reveal too much about an affair which had been in existence after he had seduced Jean. Riddell would have understood 'blessed a man with generous love' to mean sexual intercourse, and while it was unlikely that Jean would ever get to see her husband's notes in Glenriddell's interleaved volume, Robert would doubtless prefer to draw a discreet veil over his behaviour of not so many years before. Reduced to their lowest terms, therefore, the song and the annotation told of Robert's love for a Highland lassie, of their intention to marry, of their parting on the second Sunday of May in the year he was planning to emigrate to the West Indies, and of her death the following autumn.

No name was given to the girl in either the song or the note which accompanied it. But Robert sent a song, 'Will ye go to the Indies, my Mary' (CW 468), to George Thomson in a long letter of 26 October 1792 (CL 618–19). Robert had taken a traditional ballad entitled 'Will ye go to the Ewe-Bughts, Marion', replaced the prosaic sheep-folds of the original with the Indies, and, in order to compensate in the metre, replaced Marion by Mary. The relevant passage of the letter reveals a little of this song's origins:

> In my very early years, when I was thinking of going to the West Indies,
> I took the following farewell of a dear girl. – It is quite trifling, & has
> nothing of the merit of 'Ewebughts'; but it will fill up this page.

The only new element here is the proper name, Mary. All the rest was either stated or implied in 'My Highland Lassie, O'. As we shall see later, the girl's name was actually Margaret. Robert may have inserted Mary in the song in yet another attempt to distance himself from the reality of the episode which, six years after the event, still caused him considerable pain, hence the tenderness implicit in the reference to the dear girl – just as he tried to mislead everyone regarding the exact period of the affair.

The letter to John Arnot, previously quoted, was written in the middle of April 1786 and mentioned that Robert was seeking 'another wife', which would tie in with the brief courtship of the Highland girl. The letter to Brice dated 12 June 1786 speaks of the 'dissipation and riot . . . and other mischief' by which Robert tried to erase the memory of Jean; Snyder suggests that the 'other mischief' referred to the brief affair with this other girl. Finally, the letter to Robert Aiken about 8 October is full of remorse – 'the consequence of my follies, which may perhaps make it impracticable for me to stay at home'. What was the 'secret wretchedness from causes which you pretty well know'? After all, the trouble with the Armours had now blown over, Robert had achieved a measure of fame with the publication of his poems, and he even had his certificate of bachelorhood from Daddy Auld. He was free, unencumbered by debt or a forced marriage with Jean, his life lay before him with the prospects of a dazzling literary career. Snyder dwells on the futurity of the word *may*. What was Robert dreading that might conceivably drive him from Scotland, as the Armour affair had done?

Snyder also cites a letter to Mrs Dunlop of 7 July 1789 (CL 175). This letter began 'Yours . . . has given me more pain than any letter, one excepted, that I ever received'. He argues that this may allude to an incident, reported by Isobel Burns to Chambers in 1850 (although it may well have alluded to the letter of rejection from Eliza Gebbie in 1781). Isobel recounted how, one afternoon in the autumn of 1786, when the family was gathered in the Mossgiel farmhouse after the harvest, 'a letter was handed in. [Robert] went to the window to open it and read it, and she was struck by the look of agony which was the consequence. He went out without uttering a word.'[36] The inference is that this letter told of the girl's death. Who wrote this letter will probably never be known. Maurice Lindsay speculates that one of the girl's brothers must have written it, but Robert Campbell was seventeen and Archibald only eight at the time. Fourteen-year-old Annie is highly unlikely, while it is doubtful whether old Agnes would be capable of writing a letter though she may have been able to read printed words. This leaves only Captain Campbell himself, and by all accounts he had no time for Robert Burns. It may be supposed therefore that, if the letter came from him, he would not have minced his words. Ever afterwards Burns would be more than usually 'Novemberish' at the beginning of that month each year, as he was sharply reminded of Margaret's death.

On 8 November 1789 Burns wrote to his mother confessor, Mrs Dunlop, 'I shall send you a Song I made the other day, of which your opinion, (sic) as I am too much interested in the subject of it, to be a Critic in the composition'. The song was 'Thou lingering star, with lessening ray' (CW 372). This melancholy song seems to have been composed around the third anniversary of the girl's death. It contained those memorable lines 'My Mary from my soul was torn' and 'O Mary dear departed shade!' (the latter occurring twice, in the first and fourth stanzas). Like 'Ewe-Bughts', the proper name in this song may have been dictated by the title of the tune to which it was set – 'Mary weep no more for me' – rather than as a reflection of the actual name of the dear departed, or it may have suited Robert once again to conceal the true identity of the unfortunate heroine. This song, however, was the clearest indication that Robert had loved a Mary from whom he parted in a 'hallow'd grove . . . by the winding Ayr'; that she had died; that he could not forget her; and that he asked her ghost, 'See'st thou thy lover lowly laid? Hear'st thou the groans that rend his breast?' Reading these anguished lines in conjunction with Robert's guarded comment to Mrs Dunlop, the verses seem to warrant Scott Douglas's remark, 'When we find Burns, after eighteen months' experience of loving wedlock with his own Jean, suddenly appealing to the shade of Mary . . . we feel constrained to say, If this is not the language of remorse, what is it?'[37] And Snyder adds what occasion had Burns to feel *remorse* at all?

Burns was still in a state of conscience-stricken anguish when he wrote to Mrs Dunlop on 13 December 1789 (CL 181–2). He had at that time been ill for almost three weeks, 'groaning under the miseries of a diseased nervous System' and suffering a nervous headache which was so severe that he had been unable to attend to his Excise books, far less ride over the ten parishes of his survey district. This letter contains long, gloomy passages with morbid musings on the hereafter. One is forcibly reminded of the letter which Robert penned to his father from Irvine when he was suffering acute depression. This strange letter continues:

> If there is another life, it must be only for the just, the benevolent, the amiable, & the humane; what a flattering idea, then, is a World to come! Would to God I as firmly believed it, as I ardently wish it! There I shall meet an aged Parent, now at rest from the many buffetings of an evil world against which he so long & bravely struggled. There should I meet the friend, the disinterested friend of my early life; the man who rejoiced to see me, because he loved me & could serve me – Muir, thy weaknesses were the aberrations of human nature, but thy heart glowed with every thing generous, manly & noble; and if ever emanation from the All-Good Being animated a human form, it was thine! – There should I, with speechless agony of rapture, again recognise my lost, my ever dear MARY! whose bosom was fraught with Truth, Honor, Constancy & Love.

After quoting the closing four lines of 'Thou Lingering Star', he gives vent to further bursts of morbid religiosity concluding, 'Your goodness will excuse this distracted scrawl which the Writer dare scarcely read, and which he would throw into the fire, were he able to write any thing better, or indeed any thing at all.'

This is the clearest reference to 'Highland Mary', both in verse and prose, that Robert ever wrote, even to the extent of printing her name in capitals. For three years since her death he had assiduously kept all direct allusions to her out of his correspondence. Snyder wrote, 'Then, in a sudden outburst, he let the name appear, accompanied by such expressions as only love and remorse could well provoke.' For whatever reason, the death of this girl weighed very heavily on Robert. It preyed on his mind and he could not exorcise her spirit. He wanted to get it off his chest, but remorse prevented him from making a clean breast of the sorry business. In the end he compromised by blurting out the salient details but concealed the girl's identity in a pseudonym. Having already conjured up a Mary, for the purpose of a couple of songs, he began to think of his dear girl by this name. In this manner the legend of Burns's Highland Mary was born.

Barely a fortnight after venturing to submit 'Will ye go to the Indies, my Mary', Robert wrote again to Thomson (CL 620-1) on 14 November 1792 sending 'Highland Mary' (CW 470) to the tune 'Katherine Ogie':

> I agree with you that the song, K. Ogie, is very poor stuff, & unworthy, altogether unworthy, of so beautiful an air.– I tried to mend it; but the awkward sound, 'Ogie', recurring so often in the rhyme, spoils every attempt at introducing *Sentiment* into the Piece. The foregoing Song pleases myself; I think it is in my happiest manner; you will see at first glance that it suits the air.– The Subject of the Song is one of the most interesting passages of my youthful days; & I own that I would be much flattered to see the verses set to an Air which would insure celebrity.–

> Perhaps, after all, 'tis the still glowing prejudice of my heart, that throws
> a borrowed lustre over the merits of the Composition.

This song was obviously composed in November 1792 and no earlier. Coming hard on the heels of the previous song which gave the dead girl a name and linked her with the emigration period, it shows Robert becoming more daring in facing the spectre of his lost love, although 'youthful days' hardly accords with the man who was twenty-seven years old at the time of the affair and was only thirty-three when he recalled it. He could not bear to reveal her true name, but by substituting Mary for Margaret he could at least look on the episode more objectively. Perhaps he could exorcise her ghost by writing a song in her honour. 'Highland Mary' was just that. The opening lines even set the scene – 'Ye banks and braes and streams around / The castle o Montgomery' refer clearly to Coilsfield, the residence of Colonel Hugh Montgomerie, later twelfth Earl of Eglinton, where the girl had been employed as a dairymaid or byre-woman. 'How rich the hawthorn's blossom' in the second stanza placed the time of parting in mid-May. Half a century after the event Burns's Thorn or Mary's Tryst, a hawthorn bush on the Coilsfield estate, became an object of pilgrimage, until it was literally whittled away by souvenir hunters. When nothing remained above ground, the gardener obligingly dug up the roots and broke them up to satisfy the demands of pilgrims. The third stanza tells of the tender parting and the girl's death so soon afterwards, while the fourth dwells on the lips, the sparkling glance and the heart 'that lo'ed me dearly', all 'mouldering now in silent dust'. The last line of each stanza ends with the words 'Highland Mary' and the poignancy of the final stanza was heightened by the closing lines 'But still within my bosom's core / Shall live my Highland Mary'. This song, more than anything else, established the very special place of Mary in the Burns cult which was likened by the Episodists to the veneration of the Virgin Mary in Roman Catholicism. The song was – and still is – undeniably popular, and the combination of a haunting melody and plaintive lines helped to stoke the fires of intrigue concerning the poet's lost mistress.

George Thomson, responding to this letter, wrote to the poet a day or two later at great length, and concluded with a postscript:

> Your verses upon 'Highland Mary' are just come to hand: they breathe
> the genuine spirit of poetry and, like the music, will last for ever. Such
> verses, united to such an air, with the delicate harmony of Pleyel super-
> added, might form a treat worthy of being presented to Apollo himself. I
> have heard the sad story of your Mary; you always seem inspired when
> you write of her.[38]

So far as can be ascertained, Burns and Thomson never met. There is no doubt that they were never intimate personal friends; yet Thomson had heard the story of 'Highland Mary', obviously from the lips of some mutual acquaintance. Robert undoubtedly determined, at the outset, to keep the story of his intercourse with the girl a complete secret, and the world might never have heard her name, but for the circumstances of the production of his verses, 'Thou Lingering Star'. Despite some rather obvious attempts to obscure the facts about this unfortunate girl, even to the extent of deliberately distorting the chronology and giving the lassie an alias, Robert could not get her out of his mind. That, however, was as far as he was prepared to go, and after his death both his family and the remaining family of the girl herself conspired to keep her identity concealed from inquisitive individuals. Robert himself never referred to the affair again.

So we have a shadowy figure who, in Robert's lifetime, was known as his Highland Mary and who, by 1808, was named by Cromek as Mary Campbell. The first independent corroboration of this occurred under the heading of Bills of Mortality in the *Gentleman's Magazine* for October 1827:

> Scotland, Sept. 27, at Greenock, aged 85, the mother of Burns's 'Highland Mary'. Among the little stores of the deceased, there was nothing to be found as mementoes of the gifted bard, but the Bible which he gave his beloved Mary on that day when they met by the banks of Ayr . . . It has written on the first leaf in Burns's handwriting . . . 'Thou shalt not forswear thyself, but perform unto the Lord thine oaths'. It is to be regretted that two letters which he wrote after her death to the afflicted mother have been destroyed; the old woman said she could never read them without tears.[39]

So who was Robert's Highland lassie? Scott Douglas suggested that the earliest biographers were reticent to mention this painful episode so long as Jean Burns was alive. As fragments of the tale began to emerge, Cromek, Motherwell, Lockhart, Cunningham, Chambers and Professor Wilson named the girl as Mary Campbell and placed the affair at various times between 1781 and 1784, before Robert met Jean. They could be excused on the grounds of delicacy for the feelings of Robert's widow, but by the time of Jean's death, in 1834, the fable had become so well entrenched that no one dared disturb it. In 1849, however, Wood's *Songs of Scotland* was published and contained a note from Thomas Thorburn of Ryedale dated 9 February 1849 stating that he had received some particulars of Highland Mary. 'She was born in the parish of Dunoon in 1761 or 1762 and died of an epidemic at Greenock on or about 17 September 1784.' Scott Douglas, who for some years previously had been attempting to construct a chronological list of Burns's poems and songs, and had long entertained doubts about the Highland Mary episode, immediately contacted Thorburn to elicit the source of this statement. From Thorburn he learned that the facts had been supplied by John Munro, Session Clerk of Greenock. Munro, however, subsequently admitted that he had made a mistake regarding the girl's death. Armed with this admission, and his own deductions, Scott Douglas published his paper of January 1850 which launched him on his illustrious career as one of the more original and independent-minded

Burns scholars of the nineteenth century. It was his startling findings which forced Robert Chambers to rethink his version of the story (published in 1838), and led to his definitive edition of 1851, to which all subsequent biographies have been heavily indebted.

John Munro's son Archibald himself developed a consuming interest in the story and this culminated in the publication of *The Story of Burns and Highland Mary* (Paisley, 1896). This volume of 180 pages is certainly the fullest account of the episode, but it was very short on hard facts, and many of those were incorrect or inaccurate. The fifteen other works on Highland Mary cited in the Mitchell Library's *Catalogue of the Robert Burns Collection* more or less follow the same pattern, ranging from the Mariolatry of Allan Bayne (1906) and the Revd. Lauchlan M. Watt (1933) to the frankly sceptical approach of Henley and Henderson[40] and Robert M. Lockhart.[41]

From these we learn that Mary was the eldest child of Archibald Campbell in Dalling who married Agnes Campbell in Auchamore, parish of Dunoon and Kilmun, 'who gave in their names to be proclaimed in marriage' on 19 June 1762. Archibald and Agnes had eight children (Chambers), five children (Carswell) or four children – Mary, Robert, Annie and Archibald (all other biographers). Mary was the eldest (most writers, except Munro who says that Robert was the eldest). Mary was born in Dunoon (all writers except Cunningham, who says she was born in Ardrossan, and William Gunnyon who gives Ardentinny as her birthplace). She was born in 1763 (Hilton Brown, Maurice Lindsay and later writers), 1764 (some nineteenth-century writers), 1768 (Chambers, though with some reservations; Munro without doubts), while the ever-cautious Snyder gives her dates as (? - 1786) and other biographers, such as Gilfillan do not hazard a guess at all. Archibald Campbell had been a seaman aboard a Revenue cutter and had lost an eye in a skirmish with smugglers. Later he went into partnership with two others and bought a coal sloop of which he was the captain. He plied between Ardrossan, Troon and Campbeltown, carrying coal from Ayrshire to Kintyre. Some authors give the move to Campbeltown as taking place in 1776, but Munro says specifically that the family moved from Auchamore to Campbeltown at Whitsun 1773 and that they lived in a cottage in Broombrae, Dalintober, at the head of Saddell Street (demolished in the 1880s), next door to Elizabeth McNeill (*née* Campbell), a cousin of Agnes. Munro had a deposition from Archibald Mains before a justice of the peace in 1886 when he was ninety-six years old, saying that he had known Janet Clark, a relative and schoolmate of Mary's in Dunoon, who remembered her as good at her schoolwork and a very gentle girl.

It seems strange that, whereas Chambers or his informants had taken the trouble to consult the Dunoon parish registers for the marriage of Archibald and Agnes Campbell, none of the nineteenth-century biographers had examined the register of births. Or did they? The doubt expressed by Chambers regarding the 1768 birth-date implies that perhaps a search was made and nothing was found which tied a Mary Campbell to

Archibald and Agnes. To be sure, there *was* a Mary Campbell born in Dunoon in that year, on 23 October 1768 to be precise, but her parents were Archibald Campbell and Janet Brown. Still, the father's name was right enough; therefore, this must be 'Highland Mary' – hence the 1768 date which was so positively accepted by Archibald Munro.

I examined the Dunoon register of births, now preserved in New Register House, Edinburgh, and was puzzled to find that only three Mary Campbells were born in the parish in the course of a decade – two in 1759 (probably too old) and the other in 1768; but the parents in none of these cases accorded with Archibald and Agnes. A search from 1762 onwards, when the couple got married, however, revealed an entry of a baptism dated 18 March 1766 of one Margaret Campbell, lawful daughter of Archibald Campbell and his spouse *Anne* Campbell. Doubtless this entry was overlooked, or ignored, as the baby's name was wrong and the mother's name did not accord with the Agnes of the marriage entry. But the fact that both parents had the same surname ought to have been a clue, even in Argyll, the Campbell clan country. No entries appeared in the burials register, so one must suppose that this Margaret Campbell survived infancy. No other entries for Archibald and Anne or Agnes Campbell appear in the Dunoon registers.

The birth register of Campbeltown parish, however, reveals that Robert was baptised on 3 February 1769, the parents being named as Archibald Campbell and Agnes Campbell. Two other entries in the Campbeltown register were Ann, daughter of Archibald and Ann Campbell, baptised on 23 February 1772, and Archibald, whose parents were similarly named, baptised on 2 November 1778. From this we see that Agnes Campbell was probably known familiarly as Annie, hence the confusion over these baptismal entries. Her second daughter was habitually known as Annie and was clearly meant to be named after her. There can be no doubt, therefore, that the eldest of the four children was called Margaret and not Mary as has hitherto been supposed. From the baptismal entries it appears as though the move to Campbeltown took place in 1768 – certainly some time before Robert's birth the following February. In view of this, it is ludicrous to suggest that Margaret attended school in Dunoon. No doubt Janet Clark remembered a Mary Campbell – probably the one whose mother was Janet Brown – who, born in 1768, would have been the same age; but that child certainly could not have been Burns's heroine.

Everything else that Archibald Munro dredged up about the girl must therefore be treated with reservation. According to Munro the Campbell children were educated at a little school in Watson's Row near their Broombrae home. Here brother Robert learned to read and write English thus 'enabling him to read Robert Burns's letters to Mary before he recklessly committed them to the flames'. What this alluded to can only be conjectured; presumably it was intended to refer to the period between May and September 1786 when the girl was back home in Campbeltown after parting from Burns on the banks of Ayr. But why letters from the poet should have been consigned to the flames at this time is a puzzle. This tale smacks of recollections in hindsight, confused with the widespread tradition that the Campbell family were later to execrate the very name of Burns.

According to Munro the elder Campbell daughter entered domestic service as a day labourer with a family in Kirk Street, Campbeltown, in 1778 (when she was twelve, and not ten as he thought). This job did not last long because her employers made her work longer hours than had been stipulated. Margaret moved by the end of that year to Lochranza in Arran where she was employed as a housemaid in the manse of the Revd. David Campbell, allegedly a kinsman of the girl's mother. From there she moved to the mainland 'about 1780' but where exactly Munro did not say. There is a tradition that 'Highland Mary' was working in Irvine in 1781–2 and that Burns first became acquainted with her then – but this preposterous story was invented by those who tried to cling to the notion that the affair of Burns and his Mary belonged to a period long before he met his bonie Jean. Here again, there were at least three Mary Campbells living in the parish of Irvine at that time, all actually born there.

In the 1880s an antiquary, making research into some parish records, stumbled across a Mary Campbell in the Dundonald Kirk Session book who, in April 1784, in the neighbouring parish of Mauchline, had given birth to a child by John Hay in Paulstone, Dundonald. Hay at first denied the charge, but in February 1786 was compelled to pay £4 a year for the maintenance of the child who was, by that time living with the mother in Stair parish. The Session of Stair was accordingly informed in order that they might 'take the said Mary Campbell under discipline for her guilt of fornication'. The matter ended in December 1787 when John Hay confessed that he had fathered children on three other women, as well as admitting fornication with a further two girls who fortunately did not become pregnant. George Aitken used this damning evidence to trounce the Mariolaters in the third Aldine edition, published in 1893.[42] His 'strong presumption' that this Mary Campbell was Burns's heroine gave the defenders of the girl's reputation as Robert's maiden pure divine a great deal of hard work,[43] which they might have been spared had they taken the trouble to ascertain who she really was. Of all the red herrings in the Burns story 'Highland Mary' was by far the biggest of them all.

According to Munro, Miss Campbell obtained her position as a dairymaid with the Montgomerie family through the mediation of a Miss Arbuckle of Campbeltown who later married into the family of the Earl of Eglinton. Chambers, however, states that she was induced by another relative of her mother, a Mrs Isabella Campbell, who was housekeeper to a family in Ayrshire, to come to that county and take a situation as a servant. Isobel Burns, the fount of so much knowledge of the Mauchline years, was the source of the statement (made to Chambers in 1850) that her brother 'became acquainted with Mary Campbell, who was acting as nursemaid in the family of Gavin Hamilton, which situation she left to become dairymaid at Coilsfield. I said he just then became acquainted with her, but he must have known her previous to that, though his love-fit had only begun then.' Mrs Begg, who would only have been fourteen at the time, admitted that she had no definite recollection of the girl at Mossgiel, except from the poet himself, when he told John Blane one day that 'Mary had refused to meet him in the old castle' – the dismantled tower of the priory near Hamilton's house.[44]

No records of servants' service have survived, except one which, in a negative sense, is of some help in pinpointing Margaret Campbell's movements in the neighbourhood. Mention has already been made of Gavin Hamilton's long-running battle with the Mauchline Kirk Session. A minute of 20 January 1785 lists Gavin's servants as Hugh Sterling, Helen Herris and Jean Rennie, while James Wylie of Sorn, Agnes Cameron of New Street and Mary Vallance of Cumnock, Flora Weir of Woodend and Janet Caldwell of Maybole were named as having previously been in his employ. From this it appears that Gavin employed a groom and two maids on a half-yearly basis and consequently these people would have been employed between Martinmas 1783 and Whitsunday 1785.[45] Margaret Campbell could not have been working in Mauchline during this period; by the same token, she could have been at Coilsfield up to the latter date. John Blane, gaudsman at Mossgiel in 1785, always asserted that he was in the service of Gavin Hamilton along with 'Highland Mary', which statement, if reliable, fixes the date of her engagement there possibly at Whitsunday 1785, but certainly before Martinmas of that year. Gavin's daughter Wilhelmina (Mrs Todd) stated that the Highland girl came to their house as a nursemaid to her brother Alexander who was born on 13 July 1785. She was probably there only until the following November when, at the half-yearly feeing of Martinmas, she returned to Coilsfield and reverted to her position as byre-woman. She would have worked six months there, then left at Whitsunday 1786, which ties in with the second Sunday in May mentioned by Burns. Robert's 'pretty long tract of reciprocal attachment' is about as long as a piece of string, so it is impossible to say whether he had an affair with Margaret during her first period of service at Coilsfield, as many writers maintain, or whether it began during the four months spent at Gavin Hamilton's house, or whether it did not commence until he had been 'deserted' by Jean Armour in April 1786. Mrs Begg's statement is contradictory, for Margaret could not have still been working for the Hamiltons in April 1786. Mrs Todd, on the other hand, stated that the girl left the Hamiltons 'and entered the service of General Montgomerie, then living at Coilsfield'.[46]

McNaught[47] took the view that the girl must have been emotionally linked to Burns during the latter half of 1785, while she was working in Mauchline. He conceded, therefore, that Burns was probably involved with the Campbell girl and Jean Armour simultaneously, but dropped the former when the latter became pregnant, and only reverted to the Highland lassie when the Armours rejected him. This scenario fitted the anecdote about Robert complaining to Blane that the girl had refused to meet him in the old castle adjoining her employer's house, after he had for months neglected her, and his preference for Jean had become the talk of the village. McNaught subscribed to Andrew Smith's view that when Robert took up with Margaret Campbell in April 1786 it was but the renewal of an old courtship.

According to another old tradition, Robert first saw Margaret in Tarbolton church which she attended with the Coilsfield family and retainers, 'although her acquaintance with the English language was somewhat imperfect; her pronunciation of it, indeed, was so tainted with the Gaelic accent that she soon obtained the more familiar name of Highland Mary'.[48] In Gaelic Margaret is rendered as Mairghread, pronounced 'Myrat', whereas Mary is spelled Màiri and pronounced 'Marri'. The similarity of the Gaelic forms for Agnes (Una) and Ann (Anna, pronounced in a very nasal fashion so that it sounds like 'A-oona') may explain why the mother's name was confused; it may also explain the confusion over Margaret and Mary in Miss Campbell's case. Strangely enough, a similar confusion arose a few years later in the case of another Highland lassie with whom Burns had an affair – Margaret Cameron, known variously as May, Meg or Peggy.

Munro[49] is the source of the story that Burns clapped eyes on Margaret in church. Though Mossgiel is much nearer Mauchline than Tarbolton, Robert frequently attended services at the latter even after he left that parish. The poet was charmed with the appearance of the young stranger and the propriety of her conduct. One of Margaret's noticeable habits during the church service was a close attention to her bible while the minister was reading from it, or referring to passages illustrative of his text. It has been surmised that her assiduous attention to the Good Book gave Burns the idea of exchanging bibles with her when they plighted their troth. More probably, however, Robert may have seen this as a way of alleviating the anxiety of a girl who, as a result of 'the most ardent reciprocal attachment', now found herself pregnant. The Biblical quotations, in Robert's handwriting, may have been wrung from him by the girl to whom, after the Armour fiasco, he was not minded to give anything so binding as a document acknowledging their irregular marriage. If Margaret gave Robert a bible at the same time (a single-volume edition has been mentioned) it has not survived. We must suppose that Robert prudently divested himself of such an incriminating piece of evidence at the first opportunity. Whether an exchange of pointedly inscribed bibles would have been deemed in any Scottish law-court of the 1780s as tantamount to acknowledgment of an irregular marriage is debatable. Some writers have, however, argued that it was and that, technically, Robert became a bigamist by this act. If he was a bigamist, he was an unwitting one; for he was absolutely convinced (as his letters at this time clearly show) that his marriage to Jean had been repudiated and annulled. More seriously, if Robert regarded the exchange of bibles with Margaret Campbell as a contract, he concealed it from friends and family; if Daddy Auld had got wind of this Robert would never have got his bachelor's certificate so readily. Robert's subsequent actions were not those of a man who now considered himself married to Margaret Campbell. Nor, it must be admitted, were the girl's actions consonant with someone who had just got married, however irregularly and informally.

Many nineteenth-century writers held firmly to the view that Burns treated Jean Armour and Margaret Campbell on two different planes. The consensus of opinion was that he entertained one set of sentiments towards Jean who was liberal with her charms, and another towards the Highlander 'who seems to have discouraged, if ever he offered, advances of irregular love'. This notion was particularly dear to those who repudiated the Episode theory and considered that 'Mary' was the truly great spiritual love of Robert's life. Some even went so far as to suggest that she spurned Robert's too amorous advances (the Mauchline Castle incident) and as a result he switched his attentions to the more pliant Jean. Such a view of things was necessary in order to maintain the image of 'Highland Mary' as the maiden, pure and unsullied. For the same reason, therefore, it was necessary to dismiss the Grierson Papers in Edinburgh University Library as Joseph Train's *Histoires Scandaleuses* and to pour scorn on his chief informants James Grierson of Dalgoner and John Richmond. Some of the facts gathered by Train were undoubtedly little more than rumours and scraps of gossip, but it was not until 1943 that serious research by Professor Fitzhugh showed that many of the anecdotes rejected by earlier scholars had, in fact, a sound basis.[50]

For this reason it is no longer tenable to reject out of hand the story which most of all raised the hackles of the Mariolaters. According to the Train manuscript:

Her character was loose in the extreme. She was *kept* for some time by a brother of Lord Eglinton's, and even during the period of Burns' attachment it was well known that her meetings with Montgomery were open and frequent. The friends of Burns represented to him the impropriety of his devotedness to her, but without producing any change in his sentiments. Richmond told Mr Grierson that Montgomery and Highland Mary frequently met in a small ale-house called the Elbow, and upon one occasion he and some of Burns's friends – knowing they were actually together in the Elbow and having often in vain tried to convince Robert of her infidelity – upon this occasion they promised to give ocular proof of their assertions. The party retired to the Elbow. Richmond (Mr Grierson's informant) was one, and they took their seats in the kitchin (*sic*) from which two rooms branched off to the right and left – being all the accommodation the house contained . . . After waiting long, and when Burns was beginning to ridicule their suspicions, Mary Campbell appeared from one of the rooms, was jeered by the party, in a general way – blushed and retired. Another long interval elapsed and Burns began to rally his spirits, which were much sunk. Montgomery walked out of the same room. Burns coloured deeply – compressed his lip – and muttered '*damn* it'. After enduring considerable bantering from his friends, he soon gave way to the general hilarity of the evening, and his friends thought he had seen enough of Highland Mary, but in a few days after, he returned 'like the dog to its vomit'.[51]

Writers who rejected this as absurd and preposterous pointed out that (a) Lord Eglinton had no brother, (b) there was no pub in Mauchline called the Elbow, (c) Richmond left Mauchline in November 1785 and (d) that Gavin Hamilton would surely never have retained in his service as nurse-maid a girl who was so openly somebody's mistress. On the first point it was certainly true that the person who held the title Earl of Eglinton in 1785-6 had no surviving brother. But Richmond was interviewed by Grierson on 17 December 1817 by which time the holder of the title had a brother who did have close connectons with Mauchline in the 1780s. Archibald Montgomerie, the eleventh earl, had succeeded his brother Alexander in 1769; a career soldier who rose to the rank of lieutenant-general, he died childless in 1796 and was succeeded as twelfth earl by his cousin Hugh Montgomerie of Coilsfield, the 'sodger Hugh' of the fifteenth stanza in 'The Author's Earnest Cry and Prayer' (CW 174-9). Hugh's younger brother was James Montgomerie, captain in the 93rd Regiment, one-time Master of Tarbolton St James lodge, and ultimately Lieutenant-General Montgomerie of Wrighthill and MP for Ayrshire in 1818-29. If Margaret Campbell had been James's mistress it is possible that 'Montgomerie's Peggy' (CW 60) referred to her. Robert's annotation of this song seems to combine a reference to Coilsfield with the circumstances of his epistolary courtship of Eliza Gebbie. If this is the case, then Robert's statement that 'Peggy was my Deity for six, or eight months' lends weight to the belief that his on-off affair with Margaret Campbell did, indeed, begin in 1785. It seems like just one more example of the way in which Burns playfully concealed the truth of his amorous exploits with misleading statements.

As for the statement that there was no ale-house called the Elbow, we have already seen that there was just such a place, kept by a superannuated seaman known as the Old Tar. To be sure, this pub had long since vanished by the 1880s when the Laing MSS came to light. It is a measure of the subjective nature of scholarship at that time that the pundits who rubbished the Train collection did not even take the trouble to find out who was his informant, the indefatigable Grierson, and for many years thereafter suspicion fell on William Grierson of Baitford (1773-1852), secretary of the Burns Mausoleum committee in Dumfries and a close friend of John Syme. In the same way poor John Richmond had opprobrium heaped upon him for sullying the hallowed memory of Burns's Highland lassie with his vile story. Far from proving that the tale was false because Richmond had left the district by November 1785, it merely reinforces the view that Burns was sweet on the girl anterior to that date. Too much reliance has been placed on Gavin Hamilton's sensibilities regarding giving employment to a 'lightskirts' (that expression of Henley's has a delightfully Victorian ring). Although Richmond's account of the incident at the Elbow gave grave offence to the late-Victorians, there is nothing in it which actually brands Margaret Campbell as a harlot. The behaviour of James Montgomerie and his serving wench has to be seen in the context of the eighteenth century when public morals, at all levels of society, were at a low ebb. Besides,

Margaret Campbell had probably already left Hamilton's employment before embarking on an affair with the gallant captain.

Just as Campbeltown in the Mull of Kintyre can hardly be regarded as the West Highlands, as stated in the note on 'My Highland Lassie, O', so Robert's vague statement about the girl arranging 'matters among her friends for our projected change of life' is open to question. For 'friends' read 'family' (Robert used the same word when referring to Jean's family in respect of the penitential appearances); but 'our projected change of life' may mean simply settling down to married life together, or it may have meant that Robert intended to take the girl with him to the West Indies. Certainly he showed no intention of the latter course; as soon as the subscription money from his book began to come in he booked a single passage to Jamaica for himself alone, at a cost of £9.

Munro further confuses the narrative regarding the date of Margaret's departure from Ayrshire. According to Margaret's nephew Archibald Campbell, one John Blair recalled a day early in August 1786 meeting the girl on the road between Kilmacolm in Renfrewshire and Greenock. She said that she had come by gig from Kilmarnock as far as Kilmacolm, and that her lover had driven her there. As a parting gift he had pressed upon her a copy of the Kilmarnock Poems, just off the press.[52] This story, needless to say, has been ignored by everyone as it does not fit any of the generally accepted facts, far less the statements of Burns himself. Moreover, it seems a very roundabout way of getting to Campbeltown, at a time when the girl's own father was plying regularly between his home port and Troon, a mere ten miles from Coilsfield which a strapping country girl could easily have walked in a few hours. A Mr Andrews of Tarbolton is said to have been sweet on Margaret Campbell, but lost out to Burns. This disappointed suitor is alleged to have convoyed her and her trunk to the carrier when she left Coilsfield to go back to Argyll. According to him, she was plain in appearance but virtuous and amiable.[53]

Munro was also the source of the story that, far from preparing for her forthcoming marriage, Miss Campbell's sojourn in Campbeltown was 'no different from that of any other servant girl who spends with her parents a brief period between her resignation of one situation and her entrance to another'. Margaret appears therefore to have spent the summer at her parents' home without any thought of marriage, although during this period she allegedly received letters from Burns.[54] Through the ever-helpful Mrs Isabella Campbell, who seems to have been running some kind of employment agency, Margaret eventually obtained a post with a Colonel McIvor in Glasgow and was due to take up this appointment at Martinmas (11 November) 1786. It was to this end that, late in September or early October, she crossed the sea from Campbeltown to Greenock. According to Munro's informants, the girl's departure from Campbeltown was delayed because her father's sloop was not ready earlier. Captain Campbell intended taking his daughter up the Clyde to Greenock in mid-September and then planned a second trip in October with his son Robert who was due to begin his apprenticeship as a carpenter in Scott's shipyard. In the end, however, the first voyage was cancelled and Margaret and Robert travelled together early in October. Margaret was met on the quay by the well-known shipowner Andrew Munro (1744–1834). Andrew thought that Margaret looked poorly; she had a slight cough, due to the inclement weather. He escorted the brother and sister to the tenement house at 31 Charles Street, occupied by Peter McPherson whose wife, Mary Campbell, was a cousin of Agnes Campbell.

The commonly accepted story is that there was a brothering-feast at which the seventeen-year-old Robert was admitted to his craft and his sister helped wait upon the company. Next morning, Robert was so indisposed as to be unable to go to work. When McPherson came home to breakfast he asked what had detained the lad. Margaret playfully suggested that he had probably had too much to drink the night before. McPherson, keeping up the badinage, replied, 'It's just as well I've agreed to purchase that lair in the kirkyard.' The Register of Lairs in Greenock shows that this portion of the burial ground had been assigned on 14 January 1760 to Duncan Robinson, a carpenter, but on 12 October 1786 he transferred it to 'Peter McPherson, ship-carpenter in Greenock'.[55] With the grave went a headstone whose upper panel bore carved emblems of the carpenter's trade. Below this McPherson inserted the inscription 'This Burying-place belongs to Peter Mcpherson, ship-carpenter in Greenock, and Mary Campbell his spose (*sic*), and their children, 1787'.

Young Robert's illness proved more serious than was at first supposed and his sister attended him with great tenderness and assiduity. In a few days he began to recover, but at the same time Margaret sickened and was confined to her bed. The story goes that her friends believed that she suffered from the cast of an evil eye, and recommended the father to go to a cross burn, a place where two streams met, and select seven smooth pebbles from the channel, boil them in fresh milk, and then give her the liquor to drink. Highland superstition, however, failed to save the poor girl from 'the malignant fever'. Fowler[56] points out that there is quite a high survival rate for *uncomplicated* typhus in young people, but typhus supervening in advanced pregnancy would have meant almost certain death in 1786. The 'two planes' theory of Robert's attitude towards women of his own class can be discounted. To brother William he was later to give the famous advice to 'try for intimacy as soon as you feel the first symptoms of the passion' (CL 516) and his candid admission to Robert Riddell is not in the least ambiguous. There seems little doubt that Robert had carnal knowledge of the young lady, and he had a distressing propensity for impregnating women, but these facts alone would not be sufficient proof that Margaret Campbell was actually pregnant when she and Burns parted company. Nevertheless the promises implicit in the bible ceremony and the terrible remorse that haunted the poet for years after the girl's death both point in that direction.

It is a matter for regret that the burial registers of Greenock West parish, apart from the period 1722 to 1747, have not survived. We have therefore no concrete evidence either of the date of Margaret's death, or whether an unbaptised child was interred with her. If Peter McPherson purchased the lair on 12 October specifically for the purpose of having a plot of ground in which to bury his unfortunate young kinswoman, then we may assume that she died on or about that date. The composition of 'Thou Lingering Star' sent to Mrs Dunlop on 8 November 1789, traditionally some little time after the third anniversary of Margaret's death, would seem to place the event towards the end of October rather than the beginning. The date 20 October is given by some writers, but without either proof or justification for this. The letter referred to by Mrs Begg arrived at Mossgiel 'at the end of harvest-time', which would tie in with a death in late October.

What that letter contained, or who wrote it, we can only speculate. It has been assumed that the writer was Captain Campbell who stood in relation to his eldest child and her lover in much the same position as James Armour with regard to Jean and Robert. Had Margaret died of typhus, pure and simple, an announcement of her death would have been a big enough blow, especially if Robert really did intend to emigrate with her. But there is absolutely no evidence to suggest that Robert went to Greenock to meet Margaret (as he suggested to Riddell). Robert's laconic phrase 'she crossed the sea to meet me at Greenock, where she had scarce landed . . .' implies that they were to meet there prior to taking ship for the West Indies; but as we have already seen Robert's enthusiasm for emigration had cooled by that time. Besides, there is nothing in this statement to suggest that that was what Burns had in mind. The contents of the letter, and the tone in which it was written, will never be known; but Snyder, having concluded that the girl must have died in childbirth, was in no doubt of the devastating effect which the notification of her death must have had upon him. 'For the only time in his career, so far as we know, Burns's lawless love of a woman had cost her her life, and the life of her child.'[57]

This would explain the remorse, the veiled references to 'follies' and 'other mischief', the evasiveness concerning the date of the affair and even the identity of the young woman. It appears to be clinched by the attitude of the Campbell family towards Burns from this time forward. Margaret's parents and other close relatives who later settled in Greenock shrank from all acknowledgment of Burns as her lover. Captain Campbell, rather than brother Robert, is believed to have burned the poet's letters written in the summer of 1786. Annie Campbell, the younger daughter, recalled that these letters contained poems and songs which her sister recited to her. In turn, Annie used to sing these pieces to her children. Her granddaughter, Mary Kilgour of Chicago, told Chambers of this tradition, but could not recall any of the songs which may therefore be completely lost. William Anderson, son of Annie Campbell, gave some of the songs he had heard his mother singing to William Motherwell who died before they could be published. Captain Campbell is said also to have forbidden all mention of Burns's name, and although this is only an oral tradition it seems to be confirmed by the deliberate mutilation of the names in the two-volume bible.

In 1823 Mrs Campbell, through an intermediary, J. Archibald of Largs, approached Sir Walter Scott with a view to his purchasing the bible. Sir Walter's offer of £5 was rejected as far too small. On the old lady's death this relic passed to Annie, her sole surviving child, who gave a volume to each of her daughters, but their brother William purchased the books from them when he emigrated to Canada in 1834. Six years later, in straitened circumstances, he sold them for $100 (then worth £25) to a group of Scottish-Canadian businessmen who arranged for the bible to be sent to Ayr for deposit in the Burns Monument at Alloway. The survival of the bible was fortuitous, for it was the only positive proof of the strange affair between Robert Burns and Margaret Campbell more than half a century earlier.

Agnes Campbell was not so unforgiving as her husband, and even learned to sing 'My Highland Lassie, O' to her grandchildren. She was probably the source of the story that, after Margaret's death, Robert wrote to the parents begging some memento of their daughter; but his letter was destroyed unanswered. Her grand-nephew, J. C. Douglas of Greenock, is said to have asked her if she thought Burns might have married her daughter. She replied that she could not tell what might have happened had Margaret survived, but 'she did not think her sweet lassie could have ever been happy with so wild and profane a genius as Burns – yet she would immediately add that he was a real warm-hearted chield, for such was the impression he had made upon her when he had subsequently paid her a visit'.[58]

What may strike the reader as strange is the fact that, nowhere in the posthumous accounts of the girl who was allegedly to Burns what Beatrice was to Dante or Laura was to Petrarch, did anyone apparently demur at the name 'Mary'. We find no mention of those earnest seekers of the truth, from Cromek onwards, being corrected in this assumption. Captain Campbell died in 1815, his sons Archibald and Robert died in 1817 and 1821 respectively, and Annie apparently soon after her mother in 1828. By the time enquiries were being made about the poet's mysterious 'Highland Mary' the members of the immediate family were all dead and their reluctant recollections of the dead girl and her famous lover were, at best, transmitted at second hand to the next generation. By that time 'Highland Mary' the legend was so well established, that there would not have seemed any point in pointing out the truth; 'Highland Margaret' does not have quite the same poetic ring. Besides, the real name did not accord with the romantic legend and the songs which it inspired.

The story has a curious epilogue. During the First World War the shipyard of Caird and Company applied for an extension which would entail the demolition of the Old West parish church and its kirkyard. The matter was hotly debated and the passage of the necessary Act was blocked in Parliament, due to pressure brought to bear by the Burns Federation. When members of the Federation visited the grave of 'Highland Mary' after the war they were shocked to find it in a squalid and dilapidated condition. To leave it in that state would have been a greater offence than to remove the remains and reinter them elsewhere. As a result it was decided to accede to the wishes of Greenock Corporation and Messrs Harland and Wolff (successors to Caird) and have the remains removed to a more suitable location. On 13 November 1920, in the presence of a large number of Burnsians and local dignitaries, a coffin containing the remains was reverently placed in Greenock Cemetery. Earlier in the week, the remains had been exhumed and placed in an oak coffin. Archibald Macphail, a member of Greenock Burns Club, described the entire proceedings for the local newspaper.[59]

Fourteen men were present at the exhumation on 8 November, including the Superintendent of Cemetery and Parks, the Chief Constable, the Convener of the Parks Committee, ex-Bailie Hillhouse Carmichael, Ninian McWhannell (President of the Burns Federation), four members of the Greenock Burns Club and staff of the cemetery. The first earth had been removed before the Burns contingent arrived and already several small bones had been unearthed. The grave turned out to be only four feet deep, 'stopping at gravel and clay'. The excavation took two hours, four men relieving each other by turns. Four large boxes had been provided to hold the soil and a smaller box for bones and other remains. Three skulls were unearthed, as well as a thigh and smaller bones and part of a jawbone 'with four teeth in good state of preservation'. There were also some human remains which were black and quite hard. 'One got a better idea of the number of interments from the considerable quantity of wood unearthed . . . At the foot of the grave the bottom of an infant's coffin was found. This while sodden was quite sound.' Bailie Carmichael later described the bottom of the grave as 'at the bottom of the North lair, in the north-west corner'.

Snyder implied that only the girl whom we now know to have been Margaret Campbell was interred in the lair and therefore jumped at the apparently damning evidence of the infant's coffin board as a strong presumption that 'the coffin brought to light was that of a child whose mother was buried in the same grave; and since Highland Mary was buried in this grave she may well have been the mother, and Burns, who at the time of her death was her betrothed lover, was the father'.[60] But *three* skulls, a jawbone and a surprising quantity of wood indicate that there had been other occupants of the lair. What of Peter McPherson and the *real* Mary Campbell, his 'spose'? Presumably they, too, were interred in this grave, even if their children were not. It is singularly unfortunate that no forensic examination of the remains was carried out at the time to determine the ages and sexes of the bodies. Hilton Brown has suggested that an intelligent working carpenter from the nearby shipyard, far less a timber expert, might have been able to determine the age of the infant's coffin board, to within half a century.

Oddly enough, the infant's coffin board excited no comment at the time. The fact was reported in Macphail's article, but without speculation. Not till the publication of Catherine Carswell's biography of Burns in 1930 did the matter come to the fore. Hilton Brown hints darkly at a conspiracy of silence in the Burns Federation after 1920, noting that Highland Mary vanished 'almost entirely' from the pages of the *Burns Chronicle*. Well, 'almost entirely' was hardly tantamount to a conspiracy of silence; and following Mrs Carswell's revelation – 'She gave birth to a premature infant' are the exact words, without any explanation or supporting evidence – the Mariolaters had a field day.[61] The *Burns Chronicle* never reviewed Mrs Carswell's book, but the 1932 volume contained a long and savage side-swipe by the Revd. Dr Lauchlan MacLean Watt of Glasgow Cathedral, aimed at 'a kind of school which seems to love to unveil the sad stains upon the soul of the great'.[62] Later the reverend doctor returned to the fray[63] to take issue with Snyder over the inferences drawn from the infant's coffin board. Watt's criticisms were based largely on his experience as a parish minister over thirty-five years. Both in rural and urban areas he had found it a universal custom that, when a mother died in childbirth, the mother and the child were buried in the *same* coffin, the dead infant normally being laid on the mother's breast. There was, in all his vast experience, *never* a separate coffin, and he cited the largest undertaker in Glasgow to prove this point.

The flaw in this argument was to suggest that the mother and child died simultaneously; but if there were a gap of several days or weeks between the deaths, then separate coffins would have been necessary. The presence of the infant's coffin board in the same lair as the remains of at least two adults proved nothing in regard to Margaret Campbell. Despite the circumstantial evidence and all the theorising, there is absolutely no proof whatsoever that Margaret was pregnant, far less that she died in childbirth. Margaret was intending to take service with Colonel McIvor at Martinmas (11 November), but this does not help us one way or the other; for had she been pregnant by Burns she would have had her child at least some weeks earlier and it could then have been adopted out. In support of this theory, of course, there is the awkward question of what Margaret was doing all summer, between leaving Ayrshire and coming to Greenock. It is assumed that she took no work during this period; but, here again, this is an assumption and nothing more. She may have come to Greenock for the express purpose of bearing a child away from the prying eyes and gossip in Campbeltown. It would not have been the first time that accommodating relatives in another town had helped a poor girl in such an embarrassing situation. 'The child may have been born and lived there for some weeks and died of the same fever as its mother,' suggests Hilton Brown,[64] but adds the rider, 'I am not saying that there is evidence for this; only that, on general principles, the one thing is about as likely as the other.' When Burns parted from Margaret in May 1786 she may have been a month gone with child, or two, or four – or, of course, not 'gone' at all. There are simply no *facts*; and Dr Watt's argument was no stronger than any other inference proceeding from general expectation.

Nevertheless his letter to the *Times Literary Supplement* yielded unexpected results. Duncan M. Hendry of Greenock (a friend of Archibald Macphail and W. Hillhouse Carmichael) responded with the claim that an ancestor, Captain Duncan Hendry, had brought his wife from Campbel-town (now there was a coincidence!) to Greenock at the end of 1826 for her confinement. A girl, Agnes Hendry, was born on 4 January 1827 but died on 27 February. By another odd coincidence, Captain Hendry's neighbour was allegedly none other than Peter McPherson and he gave per-mission for the infant to be interred in his family lair, alongside Highland Mary. To support this extraordinary claim, a Miss J. Hendry testified that she had often heard her father speak of this incident, and that it was a tra-dition in the Hendry family that they had an aunt buried with Highland Mary. Why, the details were even recorded in a family tree in her posses-sion! So certain of this was Duncan M. Hendry that when Highland Mary's grave was opened he confidently anticipated that a baby's coffin would be found in it, and when one duly appeared he knew whose it was. Dr Watt set forth all of this in a second letter to the *Times Literary Supple-ment*. He then weakened his case with some rather irrelevant argument, but backed it up with a corroborative letter from ex-Bailie Carmichael who, it will be remembered, had been a witness at the exhumation:

> On the bottom of the North lair, in the north-west corner, was found the bottom board of an infant's coffin. It was perfect in shape, but sodden with water. I told my friend Mr Hendry of this, when he told me that in all probability the bottom board belonged to the coffin which had con-tained the body of Captain Duncan Hendry's child, buried in 1827.

Carmichael's letter was not as useful as Watt supposed. Apart from fur-nishing the precise location of the bottom board, it merely repeated what Hendry said. Indeed, the fact that Carmichael should happen to tell a friend about the find – and that that friend should just happen to have an infant relative buried in that very grave – sounds like another of those astonishing coincidences. The burial records of the Old West parish for the relevant period have not been preserved, but once more we are left lament-ing that no expert examined that bottom board even from the viewpoint of establishing an approximate date. There are more than forty years between 1786 and 1827; surely any man ordinarily used to handling wood could have said which of these dates was the more probable for it. But it was not done, and cannot be done now.

Hilton Brown, who examined this curious business thoroughly in 1949, concluded that the Hendry evidence did not clear up the matter beyond any shadow of doubt. There were obvious defects in Hendry's story, though Brown was at pains to avoid casting aspersions: 'The argument that it appeared extraordinarily pat to Dr Watt's *Times Literary Supplement* letter may be ruled out – Dr Watt would never have put his name to it if he had not been certain of its antecedents, and the suggestion would be a wholly unwarrantable slur on Mr Hendry himself.' Nevertheless, he could not help pointing out that, in view of the publicity given to the exhumation and the subsequent tumult in Burns circles by the publication of Mrs Carswell's book as far back as 1930, it was a little surprising that neither

Hendry nor Carmichael had come forward earlier with this crucial piece of information.

The entire episode consisted of hearsay and uncorroborated oral tradition; and while family traditions and family trees have their value they are not in the nature of scientific proof. The coincidences, and the involvement of the extraordinarily accommodating Peter McPherson in two burials forty years apart, lead one to suspect a confusion and overlapping of stories. The Hendry story is fatally flawed in two respects. Peter McPherson was dead at least a decade before the Hendry family came on the scene and burials in the old cemetery had ceased some time earlier than that.

Robert Fitzhugh (1970) concluded that the infant was not Mary Campbell's,[65] relying on the dates of birth and death of Agnes Hendry (4 January and 27 February 1827) which were 'taken from the Hendry family register of her brother Daniel S. Hendry, and were certified in a document . . . by Duncan M. Hendry on October 23, 1933, sent by W. Hillhouse Carmichael'. Even this record does not stand up to corroborative examination, however, for the only baptism in the Greenock West parish register which approximates roughly with this story was that of Agnes Stewart Hendry, daughter of Daniel Hendry, on 13 January 1828. Assuming this baby to have been the one at issue, both the year of birth and the father's name do not accord with the Hendry family tradition. Agnes Stewart Hendry and Agnes Hendry appear to have been one and the same and she did, indeed, have a brother called Daniel Stewart Hendry, the presumed compiler of the family register; but it only goes to show how unreliable these unofficial family registers and lists in family bibles can be.

Hilton Brown summed it up neatly:

> All one can say is that if the coffin-board does not prove the Carswell-Snyder theory, the Hendry-Carmichael story does not disprove it; that the Highland Mary mystery is on the whole darkened by the exhumation results rather than clarified; and that the *Greenock Telegraph* article and Dr Watt's Mr Hendry have between them pretty well ruined the infant's coffin-board as a Material Object of any final significance.[66]

How, then, does Margaret Campbell stand? Was she a 'maiden, pure, divine' or a 'lightskirts'? Who were right: the Episodists or the Mariolaters, Auguste Angellier or William Ernest Henley? Was she the white rose amid Burns's passion-flowers, or just another country girl who fell for a farmer with the gift of the gab and a strange light in his eyes? One can only fall back upon that commonsense old Scottish verdict, and say that the case is 'not proven' either way. The nineteenth century notion of the unsullied virgin who inspired Burns to some of his finest work is no longer tenable; the clutch of 'Mary' songs hardly rise above the second-rate at best, and are pretty banal at worst. Did Margaret and Robert, in the usual way of a ploughman with a dairymaid, come together in that late spring of 1786 and (given Robert's previous track-record) inevitably produce a baby whose remains are now among the 'rickle o banes' in that oaken casket in the Greenock Cemetery? Again, 'not proven'. No jury on earth would convict on the existing evidence; but few juries would be left without a strong suspicion of guilt. I do not think one can say more – or less – than that at this moment in time.

As it happens, forensic science now has a method of proving the matter. Microscopic amounts of undegraded nucleic material are used to produce a DNA profile. Not only can this be produced from actual materials such as mucous, saliva, semen and blood, it can be produced from hair, bones, or even inanimate objects which have come in contact with a person, such as the sweatband lining a hat, a pair of gloves or undergarments. Plenty of such relics, including locks of hair, of Robert Burns have survived for a DNA profile to be obtained without disturbing his remains; but in order to compare this with a DNA profile from the infant remains in the Greenock Cemetery it would be necessary to exhume the coffin put there in 1920. Much would also depend on such factors as temperature, humidity and bacteria in determining whether undegraded nucleic material would be available to make such a genetic comparison.[66] Perhaps some day a desire to satisfy universal curiosity will overcome a natural reticence about disturbing the dead, and settle the controversy for once and for all.

CHAPTER 10

Kilmarnock, 1786

Go, Fame, an canter like a filly
Thro a' the streets an neuks o Killie;

Tam Samson's Elegy (CW 241)

Kilmarnock vies with Alloway and Dumfries, the places where he was born and died, as a Mecca for devotees of Robert Burns. Although he never resided within the burgh or parish, the poet had numerous connections with the district and both his poetry and his correspondence are peppered with allusions to Kilmarnock and its inhabitants. About 1750 William Burnes had worked as a gardener at Fairlie House two miles south-west of the town. In April 1775 Jean Brown, the twenty-five-year-old half-sister of Agnes Brown and thus the poet's aunt, married James Allan, a carpenter on the Fairlie estate. Robert lodged with this couple at Old Rome Foord, on the east side of the Kilmarnock-Troon road, while he was on the run from a vengeful James Armour in the summer of 1786. When William Burnes moved his family from Mount Oliphant to Lochlie in 1777, the centre of their world shifted from Ayr to Mauchline, but Kilmarnock, only a few miles to the north, was now their nearest town. The same was true when Robert and Gilbert took the lease of Mossgiel and moved there after their father's death in 1784. While Mauchline provided the poet with social intercourse and was the nearest market, he would also have been familiar with Kilmarnock during this period. There is yet another of those hoary traditions that Burns was accustomed to visit the area to purchase coal from Norris Bank, a mine located south of the Cessnock Water but now long since vanished from the map. An old inhabitant who had been a contemporary of Burns recalled seeing him on his way to Norris Bank, reading a book as he strolled along.[1] When Robert went to Irvine in 1781 he would almost certainly have passed through Kilmarnock. After the move to Mossgiel in 1784 he became an increasingly frequent visitor to the town.

Even then, his reputation as a forceful and witty personality ensured entry to Kilmarnock's social scene, and Robert became an habitué of the Bowling Green House, an inn on the east side of Portland Street opposite the north side of West George Street. The inn took its name from the bowling green nearby which, between 1780 and 1790, was located in open ground to the west of Bank Street. Before the end of the century the ground was redeveloped and the inn demolished. In the 1780s it was kept by Sandy Patrick whose house was a rendezvous for the merchants and shop-keepers and the few professional men of the town; they would meet for a social glass or two after a game of bowls. It was here that Robert is said to have met the seedsman Thomas 'Tam' Samson (who was Patrick's father-in-law), his brother John and his nephew Charles, the vintner Robert Muir, the poet Gavin Turnbull, the physician William Mure, the brothers William and Hugh Parker, the businessman and Town Clerk William Paterson, the brewer Bailie Thomas Greenshield and the merchant William Brown, among many others. Sandy Patrick brewed his own caup ale, a superior beverage which drew the more discerning tipplers of the burgh to his pub.

Several of these gentlemen were later immortalised in Robert's poetry, most notably Tam Samson, the subject of the famous 'Elegy' (CW 240–1). The opening lines of this comic ballad also mention the Revd. James Mackinlay and the Revd. John Robertson, both of whom, in death, lie alongside Tam Samson in the Laigh Kirkyard. The third stanza refers to 'The Brethren o the mystic level' – the members of St John's Lodge Kilwinning No. 24 (now number 22), to which Tam and many other worthy citizens then belonged. Major William Parker was the Right Wor-shipful Master of the lodge and his brother Hugh, a prominent banker in Kilmarnock, was another of the poet's friends. Hugh was the recipient of a verse-epistle (CW 322–3) written in mid-June 1788.

Robert Muir, only a few months older than Burns, was probably the closest of the poet's Kilmarnock friends. Gilbert furnished an interesting account of the young wine-merchant who died in 1788, soon after the pub-lication of Robert's first Edinburgh Edition. That the death of Muir in his thirtieth year affected Burns very greatly may be determined from the curious 'conscience' letter to Mrs Dunlop (CL 181–2), referred to in the previous chapter. Robert also composed the lines for his friend's epitaph (CW 322).

The popular tradition is that, after the composition of 'The Twa Herds' and the circulation of manuscript copies of this satire, John Goldie of Kilmarnock called at Mossgiel one day during the harvest of 1785 and that Robert drew his visitor aside, sat down behind a stook, and recited several of his poems. 'Goldie, delighted with what he heard, suggested that the poems ought to be published, and invited their author to visit him in Kilmarnock. There, at Goldie's table, it is said, Burns met a group of the leading men of the town.'[2] Here again, this popular tradition is unsup-ported by actual documentary evidence. The truth was probably much less dramatic, with Robert gradually widening his circle of friends. If such a meeting was arranged by 'the terror o the whigs' it did not result in any immediate plans for publication.

In June 1785 the Revd. John Mutrie died and Kilmarnock's second charge became vacant. There was considerable excitement and tension in the town. Would the Earl of Glencairn, who was patron of the living, select a moderate from the New Lichts, or a zealot of the Auld Licht per-suasion? When it was learned that the Earl had chosen the Revd. James

Mackinlay, the Auld Lichts were overjoyed. They remembered with horror and distaste how moderate or 'common-sense' theology had been preached by Mutrie's predecessor, Lindsay, and they lamented the effects of so long a reign of terror. Now Mutrie's place had been taken by a zealot who could be relied upon to repair the damage. The New Lichts were chagrined at the appointment, and in anticipation of the induction ceremony Robert composed 'The Ordination' (CW 192). The ceremony itself did not take place till 6 April 1786, but long before that, clandestine copies of the satirical verses under the *noms de plume* of 'Rob Rhymer' or 'Ruisseaux' (the French word for brooks or rivulets, i.e. burns in Scots) were in circulation.

The poem shows that Robert was very familiar with Kilmarnock. The town was then a lively place of about 4,000 inhabitants most of whom were engaged in the weaving of coarse woollen goods, carpet manufacture, leather-dressing and shoemaking. These trades were alluded to in the opening lines of the poem. The Laigh Kirk was the Low Church, the original parish church of Kilmarnock. 'Then aff to Begbie's in a raw' referred to the Angel tavern in Market Lane on the other bank of the Kilmarnock Water from the church. To get from one to the other, thirsty parishioners between Sunday services had to cross a narrow footbridge in single file.

Robert's poetic output during the winter of 1785–6 was prodigious. Richard Brown, brother Gilbert and now John Goldie had urged him to publish his works. The success of 'The Ordination', which brought him fame as far afield as Kilmarnock, spurred him on even more. On 20 March 1786 he wrote to Robert Muir, one of the leading wine-merchants and spirit-dealers of the town, and appropriately enclosed a copy of his poem 'Scotch Drink' (CW 165–8):

> I hope, sometimes before we hear the Gowk, to have the pleasure of seeing you, at Kilmarnock, when, I intend we shall have a gill between us, in a Mutchkin-stoup; which will be a great comfort and consolation

From the reference to the cuckoo it appears that Robert planned to visit Kilmarnock early the following month. At the time this brief letter was written he was beginning to suffer the first pangs of anxiety over Jean and her family's reaction to the news of her pregnancy. It may be that he was already contemplating publication in the forlorn hope of raising some money. At this juncture he may have turned to his old friend and landlord Gavin Hamilton for advice, for the latter is said to have urged him to publish his poems by subscription, believing that his fame had already secured him a sufficient number of friends to make the sale of a small volume certain, and to a moderate extent profitable.[3] Robert's movements at this crucial period are not known in detail, but it is worth noting that on 27 March he was in Loudoun parish, and was introduced at a meeting of the Newmilns masonic lodge that evening by Gavin Hamilton. This lodge, incidentally, was closely associated with the Arnots of Dalquhatswood. James Arnot had been Master in the 1750s, but two of his sons held that office on a number of occasions. William Arnot was Master in 1768, 1769, 1772 and 1777 while Robert's correspondent, John Arnot, was Master in 1770, 1771, 1773, 1781 and 1783. Among the members of this lodge was John Rankine of Adamhill, Robert's rabelaisian friend from the Lochlie days, and Rankine himself was Master in 1794–5.[4]

There is an unsubstantiated story that Robert sought a publisher in Glasgow, the firm of Dunlop & Wilson being mentioned. But there is no record of the poet visiting the metropolis of western Scotland until late November 1787, and it would have been logical for Robert to try a printer closer to hand first. At that time Kilmarnock boasted the only printing-house in Ayrshire. The first wooden printing-press was imported into Kilmarnock in the mid-eighteenth century by a Mr McArthur. About 1780 he was succeeded by John Wilson, born in Kilmarnock in 1759. He had a bookshop in one of the buildings which stood where Portland Street opened into the Cross. The printing-works occupied the attics of the tenement on the left of the Star Inn Close as entered from Waterloo Street. Wilson removed to Ayr in 1803 where he launched the *Ayr Advertiser*, the first newspaper in the county, and it was not till 1831 that printing was revived at Kilmarnock. Most of the printing done on the wooden press was simple jobbing work, such as bills, tradesmen's cards and letterheads; but in 1785 Wilson brought out an edition of Milton's *Paradise Lost*. The landlord of the Star Inn Close was James Robertson whose sister, Mrs Bunten, used to recount how, when living in the close, she frequently saw Burns visiting the premises while his work was going through the press.

Though much of what Robert was composing in 1785–6 was not intended for general consumption (to judge from the significant omissions from the Kilmarnock Edition) it is out of the question that he would have composed such an amazing quantity of poetry without at least giving some thought to the most logical means of attaining that fame which he craved. Despite Robert Fergusson, 'my elder brother in misfortune, / By far my elder brother in the muse', there was at that time no fashion for vernacular poetry, and to embark on such a course was quite daring and original. It is worth noting that Gavin Turnbull, an exact contemporary of Burns, confined his effusions to pure English in the style of the English lyric poet, William Shenstone. By late 1785 Robert had already tested the market, so to speak, by circulating many of his pieces among friends and acquaintances. An undated verse-epistle addressed to James Smith of Mauchline around this time (CW 169–73) contains the earliest hint of his ambition to see his work published:

> This while my notion's taen a sklent
> To try my fate in guid, black prent;

From this it may be inferred that the idea was in his mind some time before this epistle was composed. The most prolific period of Robert's entire life was the nine months from July 1785 till the end of March 1786, and it was broken only by the crisis over Jean Armour. Soon afterwards he contemplated leaving the country but needed money for his ticket to Jamaica. It was then that the notion of publishing, so often considered in the past, surfaced again. In his long autobiographical letter to Dr Moore Robert gave a somewhat fanciful account of the circumstances leading up to his decision to publish:

> Before leaving my native country for ever, I resolved to publish my Poems.– I weighed my productions as impartially as in my power; I thought they had merit; and 'twas a delicious idea that I would be called a clever fellow, even though it should never reach my ears a poor Negro-driver, or perhaps a victim to that inhospitable clime gone to the world of Spirits.– I can truly say that pauvre Inconnu as I then was, I had pretty nearly as high an idea of myself and my works as I have at this moment.– It is ever my opinion that the great, unhappy mistakes and blunders, both in a rational and religious point of view, of which we see thousands daily guilty, are owing to their ignorance, or mistaken notions of themselves.– To know myself had been all along my constant study.– I weighed myself alone, I balanced myself with others; I watched every means of information how much ground I occupied both as Man and as a Poet; I studied assiduously Nature's DESIGN where she seem'd to have intended the various LIGHTS and SHADES in my character.– I was pretty sure my Poems would meet with some applause; but at the worst, the roar of the Atlantic would deafen the voice of Censure, and the novelty of west-Indian scenes make me forget Neglect.

Unfortunately, he gave no clue to the precise steps which he then took to realise his ambition, but, given his circle of friends in Kilmarnock, it seems obvious that he should approach the one printer in the county. Whether Burns was acquainted with John Wilson prior to this time is not known, but it seems probable that he was, as they moved in the same circles. Robert would undoubtedly have seen Wilson's edition of Milton and noted that it was a creditable performance. That Wilson approached the venture with caution may be seen in the need for Robert to obtain sureties against financial loss. But as Robert saw this project as a means of making money, he clearly had the confidence that Wilson lacked.

Successive letters were written in March 1786 to John Kennedy (Gavin Hamilton's brother-in-law) enclosing 'The Cotter's Saturday Night' and to Robert Muir, already noted. Then, on 3 April, he wrote to Robert Aiken (CL 91) enclosing the lines which he had inscribed in a work by Hannah More when presenting this book to a young lady. Almost as an after-thought, however, he added the bald statement, 'My Proposals for publishing I am just going to send to the Press.' Clearly something of the sort must have been discussed with Aiken, and probably other friends, previously. The subscription blanks, which were printed by Wilson over the ensuing days, were delivered to Robert on the evening of 14 April; one of the first people to receive a copy was Gavin Hamilton, to whom Robert wrote the following day (CL 65): 'I know you would wish to have it in your power to do me a service as *early* as any body, so I inclose you a sheet of them.' The document which announced Robert's intentions to the world was brief and to the point:

PROPOSALS
FOR PUBLISHING BY SUBSCRIPTION
SCOTCH POEMS,
BY ROBERT BURNS

The Work to be elegantly Printed, in One Volume, octavo. Price Stitched *Three shillings.*

As the Author has not the most distant *Mercenary* view in Publishing, as soon as so many Subscribers appear as will defray the *necessary* Expence, the Work will be sent to the Press.

There then followed a six-line quotation from Allan Ramsay beginning 'Set out the brunt side o your shin', and the printed portion of the sheet concluded with a heading 'We, under Subscribers, engage to take the above mentioned Work on the Conditions Specified'. This left about half the quarto sheet for the names of the subscribers to be entered. Robert had ninety-six copies of this notice printed, 'a great deal more than I shall ever need', as he told David McWhinnie on 17 April (CL 106). Only one example of this document has apparently survived and is now preserved in the Burns Museum at Alloway. This advertisement is doubly interesting. It shows that Robert originally intended to confine his book to poems in the vernacular. Characteristically, it also shows the poet's repugnance at being seen to make money from his poems. In view of the fact that he had finally been spurred into publication to raise the fare to Jamaica, his strident disclaimer has a rather hollow ring.

The sole surviving prospectus bears the signatures of sixteen subscribers, but four were subsequently crossed out, and opposite the name of a fifth, William Lorimer, the words 'sent per Charles Crichton' were crossed out and the entry endorsed 'The Blockhead refused it'. These subscriptions were collected by William Johnston who personally took three copies of the book. His initials appear in the margin opposite each name as the subscribers paid up. Finally, there is a note on the right-hand side in the handwriting of Gilbert Burns: 'W. Johnston paid me for 11 Copies'. This sheds an interesting light on the manner in which the production of the book was funded. McWhinnie, to whom Robert sent four subscription sheets, secured twenty orders. John Kennedy of Dumfries House near Cumnock got as many more, as did John Logan of Laight. Gavin Hamilton (forty), James Smith (forty-one), Gilbert Burns (seventy), Robert Muir (seventy-two) and Robert Aiken (a hundred and forty-five) were the principal subscribers, but David Sillar secured fourteen, Willie Niven seven, Walter Morton of Cumnock six, and even William Neilson, Peggy Thomson's husband, got five. There were also several individual subscriptions.

References to the subscriptions occurred in letters to Gavin Hamilton (CL 65–6) on 15 April, the day after they came to hand, to John Ballantine (CL 97), to David McWhinnie on 17 April (CL), John Kennedy on 20 April

(CL 106) and to John Arnot (CL 107), undated but probably written in April as well. Another letter to Kennedy on 16 May (CL 84) mentioned that 'In about three or four weeks I shall probably set the Press agoing'. No other letters are extant until 12 June when Robert wrote to David Brice (CL 111–2) and concluded:

> You will have heard that I am going to commence Poet in print; and tomorrow, my works go to the press.– I expect it will be a Volume about two hundred pages.– It is just the last action I intend to do; and then turn a wise man as fast as possible.

To his cousin, James Burness, Robert wrote on 5 July (CL 60–1): 'I intend to send you a letter accompanied with a singular curiosity, in about five or six weeks hence'. A second letter to Brice, written on 17 July (CL 112) mentions having 'been so throng [busy] printing my Poems', implying that Robert, as tradition avers, spent a great deal of time in Kilmarnock checking his proofs as the sheets went through the press. Strangely enough, none of Robert's surviving letters mentions the actual publication of *Poems Chiefly in the Scottish Dialect* which took place on 31 July.

The book was a remarkable performance by any standards. The Preface, which ran to three and a half pages, created the myth of the 'Heaven-taught ploughman' as Henry Mackenzie so succinctly expressed it later:

> The following trifles are not the production of the Poet, who, with all the advantages of learned art, and perhaps amid the elegancies and idlenesses of upper life, looks down for a rural theme, with an eye to Theocrites or Virgil . . . Unacquainted with the necessary requisites for commencing Poet by rule, he sings the sentiments and manners, he felt and saw in himself and his rustic compeers around him, in his and their native language.

Robert spoke of 'the little creations of his own fancy, amid the toil and fatigues of a laborious life' and he ended by begging his readers 'particularly the Learned and the Polite, who may honor him with a perusal, that they will make every allowance for Education and Circumstances of Life'. The Learned and the Polite responded on cue, and thus the myth of the noble peasant, the Heaven-taught ploughman, was born.

The Kilmarnock Edition contained forty-four poems, but ten of them consisted of epigrams and epitaphs, inserted towards the end of the volume to fill it up. The thirty-four poems forming the body of the book established Robert's reputation and, to a large extent, his reputation rests on them to this day. The book began with 'The Twa Dogs' (CW 140–6) which Robert obviously regarded as his masterpiece. This was followed, strangely enough, by 'Scotch Drink' (CW 165–8) and 'The Author's Earnest Cry and Prayer' (CW 174–9), then come 'The Holy Fair' (CW 133–9) and 'Address to the Deil' (CW 161–4), 'The Death and dying words of poor Mailie' (CW 62–4) and 'Poor Mailie's Elegy' (CW 64–5). 'A Dream' (CW 233–6), 'The

Vision' (CW 114–21), 'Halloween' (CW 151–7), 'The Auld Farmer's new-year morning Salutation' (CW 158–61), 'The Cotter's Saturday Night' (CW 147–51) and the nature poems, 'To a Mouse' (CW 131–2), 'To a Mountain-Daisy' (CW 203–4) and 'To a Louse' (CW 181–2) represented the cream of Robert's great poems written by that time. Seven verse-epistles showed Robert's mastery of this poetic form and four songs gave a hint of greater things to come. Half a dozen dirges, including 'Despondency, an Ode' (CW 207–8), are an interesting reflection of Robert's depressive bouts, as well as betraying the influence of English poets, notably Edward Young whose *Night Thoughts on Life, Death and Immortality* and similar works had a profound effect on the budding poet. Conversely, Robert thought it prudent to omit 'The Jolly Beggars' (CW 182–91) and six of his great satires, for obvious reasons. Less understandable was the omission of eight verse-epistles and the lyrics of three dozen songs, including his first-ever production, 'Handsome Nell' (CW 43), which, though a juvenile performance, was one that Robert was particularly pleased with. Many of these, however, found a place in the first Edinburgh Edition.

Less than a month after the volume was ready, 599 copies had been disposed of, and only thirteen remained on hand. Robert himself received his first copy on 3 August and took a couple more on 4 and 5 August respectively; but he presented all three personal copies to friends – Richard Brown, Peggy Thomson and James Burness – and the Mossgiel household ended up with none. The breakdown of the subscription list was itemised in Wilson's account, rendered to the poet on 28 August.[5] Each sheet bore sixteen pages of text, making 240 in all. Printing fifteen sheets at 19s cost £15 5s; nineteen reams thirteen quires at 17s a ream cost £16 14s; carriage cost 8s 9d, and stitching 612 copies in blue paper covers at a penny three-farthings cost £4 9s 3d, bringing the total outlay to £35 17s. As the number of advance subscriptions amounted to 428, this yielded an income of £64 4s – more than enough to defray the costs of the paper, ink and press-work. In addition, Wilson took seventy copies for his bookshop and credited Robert with ten guineas. The rest of the bill was paid in cash – £6 3s on 19 August, £14 13s on 28 August and a final tranche of £3 4s on 6 October. Later, Robert was to claim that he cleared only £20 from the sale of his poems, but as all 612 copies were soon sold out Robert's profit must have been in excess of £54. Even making allowances for some incidental if unspecified expenses, it is impossible to reconcile the facts with his statement in the autobiographical letter to Moore:

> I threw off six hundred copies, of which I had got subscriptions for about three hundred and fifty.– My vanity was highly gratified by the reception I met with from the Publick; besides pocketing, all expences deducted, near twenty pounds.– This last came very seasonable, as I was about to indent myself for want of money to pay my freight. So soon as I was master of nine guineas, the price of wafting me to the torrid zone, I bespoke a passage in the very first ship that was to sail.

One can understand the rounding down of the number of copies printed, but 350 subscriptions was very wide of the mark – which is strange, for authors are not in the habit of understating their sales. Nor, in an age before the invention of income tax, was there any need for creative accoùnting on Robert's part to minimise his profit. Moreover, such a wide divergence between £20 and £54 cannot be explained by a lapse of memory, for the letter to Moore was written less than a year after the events here described. Robert paid his nine guineas to James Allen, a ship-ping agent in Irvine, rather than to the insurance-broker James Brown in Glasgow or Captain Andrew Smith at Greenock.[6] The ticket appears to have been transferable, for Robert later changed to the *Bell* and finally, in late October, to the *Roselle* which was due to sail from Leith and not the Clyde. One wonders whether he obtained a refund when his plans to emi-grate were finally abandoned.

Throughout August Robert was preoccupied with the distribution of his Poems and gathering in the money from subscribers. The business involved in publication and marketing the volume must have died down in Septem-ber when, one hopes, Robert found some time to help on the farm with the harvest. He was also busy with his preparations to leave the country, and several letters and poems of this period allude to farewells taken of family and friends. The 'Farewell to the Brethren of St James's Lodge, Tarbolton' (CW 237–8) was written during this period. Robert signed the lodge minutes as Depute Master on 18 August, 5 October and 10 November and tradition maintains that the poem was recited on the last occasion, although the minutes make no reference to it. John Lees, however, used to say that 'Burns came in a pair of buckskins, out of which he would always pull the other shilling for the other bowl, till it was five in the morning. An awful night *that*!'[7]

On 6 October Robert was in Kilmarnock settling up with John Wilson. A letter to Aiken two days later (CL 92–4) recounted that Robert:

> made him the offer of a second edition, on the hazard of being paid out of *the first and readiest*, which he declines. By his account, the paper of a thousand copies would cost about twenty seven pounds, and the printing about fifteen or sixteen; he offers to agree to this for the printing, if I will advance for the paper; but this, you know, is out of my power; so farewell hopes of a second edition till I grow richer! an epocha which, I think, will arrive at the payment of the British national debt.

It will be observed that the estimated cost of printing a new edition of a thousand copies was very reasonable and compared favourably with the printing cost for the first edition. It might have been supposed that Wilson still had the type standing, so that fresh press-work would have been con-fined to additional material, but few printers of the period had such a large stock of type that they could afford to immobilise it in this manner and it is more probable that the formes had already been broken up and the type distributed, so that any new edition would have to start from scratch.

Robert, despite his busy schedule, had continued to write new poems and songs at an astonishing rate, 'The Brigs of Ayr' (CW 244–9) being the major production of this period. Indeed, as he confessed to Aiken, one of his regrets in not securing a second edition was that this fine poem, dedicated to John Ballantine, would not appear in print:

> There is scarcely any thing hurts me so much in being disappointed of my second edition, as not having it in my power to shew my gratitude to Mr Ballantine . . . I would detest myself as a wretch, if I thought I were capable, in a very long life, of forgetting the honest, warm and tender delicacy with which he enters into my interests.

But John Wilson probably took the view that Robert's friends had exhausted the local market and he was therefore not inclined to risk publishing without some payment in advance. It is a sad commentary on Robert's husbanding of his new-found fortune that the fifty-odd pounds profit appears to have gone so rapidly that he could not afford to lay out the sum required to purchase the paper. It also explains why, in writing to Moore a year later, Robert reduced the net amount received to 'near twenty pounds'. Where the money went is a complete mystery. It may seem a trifle in modern parlance, but £50 was a year's salary by the time Robert entered the Excise. Few parish schoolmasters earned as much, and it was seven times the wages which Robert and Gilbert allocated themselves on the farm. Previous biographers have been content to take Robert's statement at face value without checking the arithmetic. During August, September and October Robert travelled extensively all over the county, so one assumes that a large part of the money must have been frittered away in travelling expenses. Those large tavern bills, which, at Kirkoswald, he had learned to look upon without concern, must have been fairly frequent during this hectic period. Besides, Robert needed some money to fit himself out for the Jamaican trip. The remaining £20 would have to be carefully husbanded. Snyder sums it up beautifully: 'This being the case, and neither author nor publisher having much faith in the marketability of a second printing, the two men brought their relations to a close, each having done more to make the other known to the world than he could well have dreamed.'[8]

The response to the Kilmarnock Poems was instant and highly gratifying. Robert Heron, whose *Memoir of the Life of the Late Robert Burns*, was published in 1797, commented on the public reaction to this volume:

> Old and young, high and low, grave and gay, learned or ignorant, all were alike delighted, agitated, transported. I was at that time resident in Galloway, contiguous to Ayrshire; and I can well remember how that even plough-boys and maid-servants would have gladly bestowed the wages which they earned the most hardly, and which they wanted to purchase necessary clothing, if they might but procure the works of Burns . . . On a Saturday evening I opened the volume, by accident, while I was undressing to go to bed. I closed it not, till a late hour on the rising Sunday morn, after I had read over every syllable it contained.[9]

The adulation Robert received was not all from people of his own class, or his own circle of acquaintances. For the first time he was approached by complete strangers. Perhaps some of his unspecified expenses went on postage as well-wishers wrote unexpectedly to congratulate him. This attention from professional men and the landed gentry had an intoxicating effect, and Robert responded accordingly. John McAdam of Craigengillan, the landowner who had been suing David McClure when he was in dispute with William Burnes, was one of the first to write 'a card' (in effect, a brief note) which provoked a seven-stanza verse-epistle in return (CW 274). Incidentally, because McAdam and his family appeared only in the addenda and not the main subscription list of the first Edinburgh Edition, it has been suggested that the note was not sent till the spring of 1787, but the subtitle refers to 'the commencement of my poetic career' which would place composition in the autumn of 1786. Sir William Cunninghame of Robertland and Mrs Alexander Stewart of Stair (to whom Robert twice sent manuscript packets of songs) both seem to have praised the Poems and to have admitted the author to their circle. Gavin Hamilton and Major Logan of Park were recipients of further verse-epistles at this time which reflect the euphoric effect which the praises of the 'great folk' had on Burns.

More important in the long term, however, was the notice taken of the poet by the Revd. George Lawrie, minister of Loudoun parish not far to the north-east of Mossgiel. He was a prime example of the moderate or New Licht clergy; Chambers described him as 'sensible, upright, kind-hearted, and with no despicable taste in literature'. He was the personal friend of several of the leading literary figures of the day, including those reverend doctors Hugh Blair and Thomas Blacklock. Lawrie had read the Kilmarnock Poems and sent a copy to Blacklock at Edinburgh, asking his opinion of it and hoping that he would, in turn, show the volume to Blair. On 4 September 1786 Blacklock wrote back to Lawrie. Blacklock was a truly remarkable man. Born at Annan in the same year as William Burnes, he had lost his sight to smallpox while still an infant. Despite this handicap he became an accomplished musician, a poet and a man of considerable classical and scientific education. In 1762 he was ordained minister of Kirkcudbright, but his parishioners rejected him on account of his blindness. He retired on a small annuity to Edinburgh where his wife kept a boarding-house for university students. He eked out his pension by giving tuition, and the roll-call of young men who passed through his hands was both long and distinguished. As one of Edinburgh's literati, Blacklock had even played host to Samuel Johnson on his visit to Edinburgh in 1773.

The blind littérateur got his friend, Professor Dugald Stewart, to read some of Robert's poems to him. To Lawrie he admitted, 'I have little intercourse with Dr Blair, but will take care to have the poems communicated to him by the intervention of some mutual friend.' He then continued:

> It has been told me by a gentleman, to whom I shewed the performances, and who sought a copy with diligence and ardour, that the whole impression is already exhausted. It were therefore much to be wished, for the

sake of the young man, that a second edition, more numerous than the former, could immediately be printed; as it appears certain that its intrinsic merit, and the exertion of the author's friends, might give it a more universal circulation than any thing of the kind which has been published within my memory.

Lawrie communicated this letter to Gavin Hamilton, although after an unaccountable delay of about two weeks, and Gavin in due course showed it to Robert. His account of this period, in the letter to Moore, is interesting for the interpretation he placed on the events of that hectic period:

I had for some time been skulking from covert to covert under all the terror of a Jail; as some ill-advised, ungrateful people had uncoupled the merciless legal Pack at my heels.– I had taken the last farewel of my few friends, my chest was on the road to Greenock; I had composed my last song I should ever measure in Caledonia. 'The gloomy night is gathering fast',[10] when a letter from Dr Blacklock to a friend of mine overthrew all my schemes by rousing my poetic ambition.– The Doctor belonged to a set of Critics for whose applause I had not even dared to hope.– His idea that I would meet with every encouragement for a second edition fired me so much that away I posted to Edinburgh without a single acquaintance in town, or a single letter of introduction in my pocket.

The exaggeration of the hounding by James Armour is pardonable; but the latter part of this paragraph was incorrect in several respects. Blacklock's letter merely suggested that a second, larger impression ought to be produced, but said nothing about Edinburgh. The immediate effect of this letter, which Robert must have read about the last week of September, was to encourage him to approach John Wilson; but when the printer dampened Robert's hopes with his calculations of paper and printing costs, the poet became resigned to the fact that his poems would never see a second edition. Robert, in fact, allowed two months to elapse before he set out for Edinburgh. His head was still filled with thoughts of emigration. Indeed, were it not for the fact that the brigantine *Nancy* was delayed till 5 September[11] Robert might have been on his way across the Atlantic long before any temptation arose to induce him to visit Edinburgh. To be sure, the birth of Jean's twins on 3 September must also have influenced his future course of action to some degree, not to mention Margaret Campbell, whose own trip to Greenock from Campbeltown had been delayed about this time.

At the 'end of autumn' Robert paid a visit to St Margaret's Hill, the pleasantly situated manse of Loudoun parish on the outskirts of Newmilns, above the River Irvine. The date of this visit has not been ascertained but it probably took place at the end of September or the beginning of October. Here Robert was cordially received by Dr Lawrie and his charming family. Lawrie's son Archibald was then a youth of eighteen and a divinity student at Edinburgh University. He was later to marry Anne Adair, sister of Robert's friend Dr James McKitterick Adair who, in turn, married Charlotte Hamilton, Gavin's half-sister. On 13 November Robert lent young Archibald a two-volume set of Macpherson's *Ossian* and a volume of songs, which he sent in a parcel with a covering letter (CL 127):

> My most respectful compliments to Mr. and Mrs. Lowrie (*sic*); and a poet's warmest wishes for their happiness to the young ladies; particularly the fair Musician, whom I think much better qualified than ever David was, or could be, to charm an evil spirit out of a Saul.[12]

The 'fair Musician' was Louisa Lawrie, youngest of the minister's four daughters and then aged seventeen. Gilbert later recalled that the first time Robert heard a spinet was at St Margaret's Hill and he is believed to have told the keyboard-player that she knew the magic way to a poet's heart. The Lawries were a musical family and at least one of the older girls, Christina, was also an accomplished performer whom Burns later heard playing the piano in Edinburgh. In addition, however, Dr Lawrie was a keen dancer, believing that this pastime was conducive both to health and cheerfulness. After dinner on the evening of Robert's visit, a dance was improvised in which the poet and other guests joined. Robert, though somewhat heavy-limbed, was a good dancer, the Tarbolton lessons now paying off. One of the daughters of the manse afterwards commented that he kept time admirably. Robert retired for the night, deeply touched by the simple refinement, good nature and mutual affection of the family, as well as by the kindness shown to himself. In the morning Archibald was sent up to rouse the poet who appeared to have slept in, but met Robert on the stair. Archibald asked him how he had slept, and Burns replied, 'Not well. The fact is, I have been praying half the night. If you go up to my room, you will find my prayers on the table.'[13] The lad did so, and found the lines, afterwards published by Burns, with the title 'Lying at a Reverend Friend's House one Night, the Author left the following Verses in the Room where he slept', but now generally better known as 'Prayer – O Thou Dread Power' (CW 261). Robert also repaid the family's hospitality with the song 'The Night was Still' (CW 262), intended to be sung to the old tune 'Irvine's Bairns are bonnie a'' which also formed the punchline at the end of the second verse. In this case Irvine signified the river rather than the town, and was a charming compliment to Dr Lawrie's brood. Still preserved at the new manse next door is an old six-pane window from the poet's bedroom. On one of the panes was scratched in Robert's angular handwriting 'Mrs Lawrie. She's all charms'.

Dr Lawrie was more than ever convinced that it would be a tragic loss to Scotland should Burns carry on with his plan to emigrate, but he was in no position to suggest a better alternative. On the way back to Mossgiel from Newmilns Robert had to traverse a bleak stretch of moorland. As he trudged along the lonely road through Sornhill and Middleyard his mind was strongly affected by parting for ever with a scene where he had experienced so much elegance and social pleasure, and depressed by the contrasting gloom of his surroundings which seemed to symbolise his uncertain prospects in the West Indies. The aspect of nature harmonised with his feelings. It was a lowering and heavy evening at the end of autumn. The wind was up, and whistled through the rushes and long spear-grass which bent before it. The clouds were driving across the sky and cold pelting showers at intervals added discomfort of body to cheerlessness of mind.[14] It was under these circumstances, and in a very sombre mood, that Robert composed what he considered as 'the last song he should ever measure in Caledonia'. 'The Gloomy Night is Gath'ring Fast' (CW 250) was later annotated by Robert:

> I composed this song as I conveyed my chest so far on my road to Greenock, where I was to embark in a few days for Jamaica. I meant it as my farewell dirge to my native land.

This does not accord with the version given to Walker, in conversation a few months later, and there appears to be some poetic licence in this head-note. This is Robert's only recorded reference to definite intentions and actual preparations for the voyage, but whether he ever got around to packing his chest, far less conveying it in the direction of Greenock, is open to doubt. The continuing and positive reaction to his Poems must have exerted a very strong pull on him to stay where he was. Dugald Stewart, whose introduction to the poems of Burns came at Dr Blacklock's home, had a country house at Catrine Bank on the River Ayr, a little south of Mauchline. He was six years older than Robert and a close friend of Dr John Mackenzie who was the means of introducing the poet and the profes-sor. Dugald Stewart invited Mackenzie and Burns to dinner on Monday afternoon, 23 October. Among the other guests on that occasion was Basil William Hamilton Douglas, Viscount Daer, second son of the fourth Earl of Selkirk. Born in the same year as Burns, he succeeded to the courtesy title on the death of his elder brother, Sholto. He had attended classes at Edinburgh University where he boarded with Professor Stewart. He took a keen interest in socio-political questions and contributed a number of papers on the subject to the Speculative Society of Edinburgh. When Robert met him, Lord Daer had just returned from France where he had met some of the men who afterwards took a prominent part in the early phases of the Revolution (notably Condorcet) and had contracted their sentiments. As a result, he became a staunch advocate of parliamentary reform. Well above average height, he had a striking appearance matched by an unassuming nature. Robert, who had never met any of the nobility on equal terms before, was bowled over by the young aristocrat and dashed off the extempore verses, 'On Dining with Lord Daer' (CW 254–5), which he sent to Mackenzie with a covering letter (CL 113) on the Wednesday morning. It is clear that Robert's prejudices against the Great took a bit of a knock. 'I sidling shelter'd in a nook, / An at his Lordship steal't a look / Like some portentous omen', wrote Robert, uncannily echoing Macken-zie's description of his first impression of the poet when William Burnes was dying.

Professor Stewart left a very perceptive account of his own first meeting with the poet:

> His manners were then, as they continued ever afterwards, simple, manly, and independent; strongly expressive of conscious genius and worth, but without anything that indicated forwardness, arrogance, or vanity. He took his share in conversation, but not more than belonged to him; and listened with apparent attention and deference on subjects where his want of education deprived him of the means of information. If there had been a little more of gentleness and accommodation in his temper, he would, I think, have been still more interesting; but he had been accustomed to give law in the circle of his ordinary acquaintance, and his dread of anything approaching to meanness or servility rendered his manner somewhat decided and hard. Nothing, perhaps, was more remarkable among his various attainments than the fluency, and precision, and originality of his language, when he spoke in company; more particularly as he aimed at purity in his turn of expression, and avoided, more successfully than most Scotchmen, the peculiarities of Scottish phraseology.[15]

Robert himself left his first impression of Stewart, in his letter to John Mackenzie:

> I never spent an afternoon among great folks with half that pleasure as when, in company with you, I had the honor of paying my devoirs to that plain, honest, worthy man, the Professor. I would be delighted to see him perform acts of kindness and friendship, though I were not the object; he does it with such a grace.

On Thursday that week Robert was in Kilmarnock, being inducted as an honorary member of Lodge St John, whose Master was his old friend Major William Parker of Assloss. The lodge met in the old Commercial Inn in Croft Street, demolished in the 1880s. On this occasion Burns responded with the 'Masonic Song' (CW 255–6) addressed to 'Ye sons of old Killie, assembled by Willie'. Four days later, on 30 October, he was addressing another Willie – William Logan, a half-pay army officer who lived with his sister Susan at Park Villa near Ayr. This verse-epistle (CW 256–8) greeted him as 'thairm-inspirin, rattlin Willie!' – a reference to Logan's skill with the fiddle. This poem is chiefly important for the antepenultimate stanza containing the line 'Ance to the Indies I were wonted' (meaning 'once I had reached the Indies'), which shows that Robert was still thinking of going to Jamaica. The unsettled condition of Robert's mind at this time and the uncertain character of his prospects are evident in the fact that on the very evening when he wrote the rollicking verses to Logan, there was held in the nearby town the inaugural meeting of the Mauchline Conversation Society. Currie vaguely mentioned the fact that 'after the family of our bard had removed from Tarbolton to the neighbourhood of Mauchline, he and his brother were requested to assist in forming a similar institution there . . . Though the records of the Society at Tarbolton are lost, and those of the Society at Mauchline have not been transmitted, yet we may safely affirm that our poet was a distinguished member of both these Associations, which were well calculated to excite and develop the powers of his mind.'[16]

The minute book of the Mauchline Conversation Society, however, was discovered in 1892.[17] It reveals that Robert and Gilbert had been living at Mossgiel for more than two years before the society was formed, and that Robert never attended any of its meetings. The minute-book runs from 30 October 1786 till 20 November 1797 and shows that Gilbert played a prominent part throughout that period. The subjects of the debates, however, have the stamp of Robert, if at second-hand through his no less articulate brother.

There was no further reference to Jamaica or the Indies in any of Robert's letters of this period. By Saturday 18 November this project had definitely been abandoned and Robert was now intent on going to Edinburgh to seek a second edition of his poems. A brief note to Robert Muir on that date (CL 87), enclosing 'Tam Samson's Elegy' (CW 239–41), made it clear that 'I am thinking for my Edinburgh expedition on Monday or Tuesday, come se'ennight, for pos', with a promise to visit Muir on Tuesday first (21 November).

A few days earlier, on 15 November, Robert received a letter from another member of the Ayrshire gentry. Frances Anna Wallace, Mrs Dunlop of Dunlop, was twenty-nine years the poet's senior and a widowed grandmother. At the age of eighteen she had made a love-match with John Dunlop of Dunlop (twenty-three years older than her) and bore him seven sons and six daughters. In 1761, on the death of her mother, Frances fell heiress to the estate of Lochryan in Galloway. When her father, Sir Thomas Wallace of Craigie, died in 1774 the estate, which had been in the family's possession since the Middle Ages, passed to her eldest surviving son, Thomas Wallace. Mrs Dunlop liked to think of herself as a descendant of the illustrious Guardian of Scotland, but her ancestor was actually the younger brother of Sir William Wallace of Ellerslie. No matter, hers was a proud and ancient lineage which brought out the patriotic fervour in Burns. The Dunlop family, however, never recovered from their involvement in the collapse of the ill-fated Ayr Bank and in 1783 the ancestral lands of Craigie had to be sold to pay off debts, a blow which caused Mrs Dunlop considerable personal distress. She was just getting over this disaster when her elderly husband died, on 5 June 1785. This was more than she could bear; she suffered 'a long and severe illness, which reduced her mind to the most distressing state of depression'. Then Miss Betty McAdam, a daughter of the laird of Craigengillan, gave her 'The Cotter's Saturday Night' to read. The sentimental lines (including the reference to 'Wallace's undaunted heart') triggered an emotional release and Mrs Dunlop immediately got in touch with the poet. Gilbert later recorded:

Mrs Dunlop sent off a person express to Mossgiel, distant fifteen or sixteen miles, with a very obliging letter to my brother, desiring him to send her half-a-dozen copies of his *Poems*, if he had them to spare, and begging he would do her the pleasure of calling at Dunlop House as soon as convenient. This was the beginning of a correspondence which ended only with the poet's life (nearly); the last use he made of his pen was writing a short letter to this lady a few days before his death.[18]

Robert was away from home when Mrs Dunlop's letter arrived, but he replied the following day (CL 130-1). He was flattered by her comments, and the reference to her 'illustrious Ancestor' was the cue for Robert to embark on a long reminiscence on his boyhood, when he made his pilgrimage to Leglen Wood. The letter closed on a business note:

I have only been able to send you five Copies: they are all I can command.- I am thinking to go to Edinburgh in a week or two at farthest, to throw off a second Impression of my book: but on my return, I shall certainly do myself the honor to wait on you, and thank you in person for the obliding notice you have been pleased to take . . .

Mrs Dunlop wrote back on receipt of the books, suggesting that Robert should appoint her as his literary critic:

I have been told that Voltaire read all his manuscripts to an old woman and printed nothing but what she would have approved. I wish you would name me to her office.

Robert ignored this, but, no matter, Frances Dunlop took this role upon herself. She wrote long letters in a close, cramped hand, often badly spelled and invariably lacking in punctuation. She gossiped incessantly, she scolded Robert as if he were a wayward son, particularly when his politics or robust attitude towards sexual matters were aired, and she criticised his poems and songs. She could be as huffy as a schoolgirl, and was very quick to accuse Robert of ignoring or failing to read her letters. But she meant well and exerted herself on several occasions on his behalf, although her plans, to secure him the newly created professorship of agriculture at Edinburgh University or an army commission, perhaps mercifully, came to naught. Nevertheless, Robert's correspondence with Mrs Dunlop was larger and longer than that with any other person.

Gilbert stated that, when it came to John Ballantine's knowledge that shortage of cash was preventing a second Kilmarnock edition, 'he generously offered to accomodate Robert with what money he might need for that purpose, but advised him to go to Edinburgh, as the fittest place for publishing.'[19]

Just when Robert thought that his poetic genius had enabled him to crash through the class barrier, he received what, to him, was a crushing setback. He was out for an autumn stroll one evening along the banks of the River Ayr when he trespassed on the Ballochmyle estate. Here he clapped eyes on Miss Wilhelmina Alexander, sister of the new laird, Claud Alexander. On his return home he composed the song 'The Bonnie Lass of

Ballochmyle' (CW 199–200) which he sent, along with a high-flown letter (CL 216–17) on 18 November. The purpose of the letter was to seek permission to publish the song in his forthcoming second edition (though as Miss Alexander was not actually named in the song, this was not actually necessary). Wilhelmina had probably been startled by the figure in the shadows as she took her afternoon constitutional, especially as he was on private property. Her initial reaction to the song and the letter was one of puzzled scepticism. She was already in her thirties and not, by any stretch of the imagination, 'a bonnie lass'. She thought that the writer was trying to take a rise out of her; so, before replying, she made some enquiries about him. The reports of Robert's character were so unfavourable that her suspicions were confirmed. 'Feeling it to be necessary to decline yielding to his request, she thought that her decision would be intimated most delicately to him by allowing his letter to remain unanswered.'[20] Miss Alexander never married, but long before she died in 1843 at the age of eighty-seven, the song and the letter had become her most cherished possessions. Belatedly appreciating the immortality conferred on her by the genius of Burns, her nephew commemorated the brief encounter of the poet and his aunt by erecting on the very spot the Fog House, a rustic summer-house, and in this was hung a facsimile of the manuscript. The summer-house and its contents, however, were destroyed by vandals in 1944.

Robert, on the other hand, never forgot the tacit rebuff and years later he still smarted at the memory. When he transcribed the song and the letter for the Glenriddell MS (CL 217) he added this note:

> Well, Mr Burns, and *did* the lady give you the desired permission? No! She was too fine a Lady *to notice* so plain a compliment. As to her great brothers, whom I have since met in life on more equal terms of respectability – why should I quarrel their want of attention to me? When Fate swore their purses should be full, Nature was equally positive that their heads should be empty. 'Men of their fashion were surely incapable of being impolite?' Ye canna mak a silk-purse o' a sow's lug.

Burns never forgot nor forgave those 'great folks' who ignored him – or rather his poetry. On a subsequent occasion Robert composed elegiac verses to the memory of Lord President Robert Dundas of Arniston, and sent the poem with a letter to the Solicitor General, Robert Dundas Junior. Dundas never acknowledged either letter or elegy, thereby provoking in Burns feelings of anger and anguish thereafter every time he saw a mention of the Dundas family in any newspaper.[21]

Two days after writing to Wilhelmina Alexander, Robert sent a joint-letter to William Chalmers, an Ayr lawyer, and John McAdam, in the form of a public writ. With this he enclosed a 'certain ***, nefarious, abominable, and wicked SONG or BALLAD'. Presumably the bawdy ballad was still with the 'writ' when Currie recorded the latter for his edition of 1800, but the song itself has not been identified. The same day he wrote to Ballantine enclosing a copy of 'A Winter Night' (CW 258), intimating that he would be happy to have his opinion on Friday 24 November when he intended to be in Ayr:

> I hear of no returns from Edinburgh to Mr Aiken respecting my second edition business, so I am thinking to set out beginning of next week for the City myself. If my first poetic patron, Mr Aiken, is in town, I want to get his advice, both in my procedure and some little criticism affairs, much; if business will permit you to honour me with a few minutes when I come down on Friday.

This shows that the projected trip to Edinburgh was far more carefully planned than Burns later implied, and that Robert Aiken had been busy in his young friend's interest. Meanwhile Dr Blacklock, too, was continuing to interest himself in the young poet. On 27 November he wrote to his friend George Lawrie saying that he had heard a rumour the previous week that 'a second edition of the Poems was projected, consisting, according to some, of twelve, or, according to others, of five thousand copies, at the expense of the gentlemen of Ayrshire, for the author's benefit'.[22] Blacklock wished to remonstrate against the size of this edition 'as it might too long postpone another with additions'. Lawrie, it will be remembered, wished the Poems to be brought to the attention of Hugh Blair, then regarded as the chief among the Edinburgh critics; but Blacklock now replied: 'I will venture to assure you that most, if not all, of the Scots poems will fail of gaining his approbation. His taste is too highly polished, and his genius too regular in its emotions to make allowances for the sallies of a more impetuous ardour.'

It was with high hopes and a sense of adventure that Robert finalised his preparations to take the capital by storm.

CHAPTER 11

Edinburgh: the First Winter, 1786–7

Edina! Scotia's darling seat!

Address to Edinburgh (CW 262)

Three things finally impelled Robert to take the plunge and make the long-projected but forever-delayed trip to Edinburgh. Uppermost in his mind now was the hope of a second edition of his poems; but there was also the prospect of Jamaica and he still had a sailing ticket which would secure him a passage to the West Indies aboard the *Roselle*, due to set sail from Leith at the end of December. If he were disappointed regarding the poems he could always fall back on his original plan. There was, however, a third reason which was now beginning to form in Robert's mind. In his letter to Aiken about 8 October he mentioned his feelings concerning 'all the various rotations and movements within, respecting the excise'[1] and on 4 December Sir John Whitefoord wrote to Burns, in reply to a letter from the poet three days earlier, making a passing reference to 'your wish to be made a gauger'. That the motivation to become an Exciseman came from Robert himself, and not from external forces or other individuals, is important in light of the insinuation that Burns was hijacked into the Excise as a means of muzzling him.[2] At this juncture Robert had not entirely given up his plans to emigrate, but he was also beginning to feel that perhaps he ought to settle down with Jean Armour, and the Excise seemed to offer a measure of security which farming quite patently did not. Detested as the Excise generally was, it was the only branch of government service which extended into every district and parish. By contrast, for example, Mauchline's post office was not established till early in 1788, and the salary of the postmaster amounted to a little over £10 a year. Excise officers at this time earned £35 a year, but various perquisites could augment that figure very considerably. Although some half-baked notion of getting a secure position in the Excise lurked at the back of Robert's mind, it seems to have been fairly low down in his list of priorities, and the idea remained dormant during his first winter in the capital, if the absence of any mention of it in his correspondence is anything to go by.

Early on the morning of Monday, 27 November, Robert mounted a pony borrowed from George Reid of Barquharie and rode eastwards, through Sorn and Muirkirk and Douglas along the route of the present A70 Ayr-Edinburgh road. At Hyndford Brig-end he made a detour southwards to Covington Mains farm, a mile north of Thankerton. The reason for the detour was that George Reid had not only provided the 'pownie' but had made arrangements for the poet to break his journey and spend the night with Archibald Prentice. The farmhouse was situated in the middle of the combined parish of Covington and Thankerton, in a natural amphitheatre formed by Wellbrae Hill to the west, Tinto and Culter Fell to the south and the striking cone of Quothquan Law to the east. All the farmers of the district had by now read the Kilmarnock Poems and were eager to meet their author. They were all asked to meet at Covington for a late dinner, and the signal of Burns's arrival was to be a white sheet attached to a pitch-fork, put on the top of a cornstack in the centre of the barnyard. The farmer's son, Archibald Junior, has left a vivid account of the poet's reception.

> My father's stackyard, lying in the centre, was seen from every house in the parish. At length Burns arrived . . . Instantly was the white flag hoisted, and as instantly were the farmers seen issuing from their houses, and converging to the point of meeting. A glorious evening, or rather night, which borrowed something from the morning, followed, and the conversation of the poet confirmed and increased the admiration created by his writings. On the following morning, he breakfasted with a large party at the next farmhouse, tenanted by James Stodart, brother to the Stodarts, the pianoforte-makers of London; took lunch also with a large party at the Bank, in the parish of Carnwath, with John Stodart, my mother's father, and rode into Edinburgh that evening.[3]

The Stodarts farmed at Alleyhead. James Stodart's son James later recalled how, as a boy on his way to Covington school that morning, he had passed the Mains and noted the pony tethered at the gate, waiting for the poet to be on his way. The stalwart 'Bauldy' Prentice had come out of the farm-house and ordered him and other schoolboys to stop and hold the stirrup for the man that was to mount, adding, 'You'll boast of it to your dying day.' The boys said, 'We'll be late, and we're feart o' the maister.' 'Stop and haud the stirrup,' said Bauldy, 'I'll settle wi the maister.' The boys took courage as Prentice stood six foot three, and the dominie was but an ordinary mortal. James Junior, recounting this anecdote when he was in his eighties, said, 'I think I'm prouder of that forenoon frae the schule than a' the days I was at it.'[4] In 1986 a plaque, set in a cairn, was unveiled at Covington Mains, to celebrate the bicentenary of the poet's visit.

Burns himself referred to his eventful journey in a letter to George Reid, written on 29 November (CL 220). Originally he was supposed to entrust the pony to James Connell, the Mauchline–Edinburgh carrier, but John Samson (brother of the immortal Tam) begged the loan of it for his own return journey to Ayrshire. Robert took the opportunity to give Samson a letter of thanks and apology to Reid. In this letter he mentioned 'a most agreeable little party in the evening'. Robert was clearly touched by his reception. 'For Mr Prentice no words can do him justice', he wrote. 'Sound sterling sense and plain warm hospitality are truly his.'

At Carnwath Robert rejoined the line of the present A70 and continued north-east along the northern flanks of the Pentland Hills and the Water of Leith, through the paper-mill towns of Balerno, Currie and Colinton, into the capital. He arrived on the evening of 28 November, a historic day marked by the arrival of the first of John Palmer's mailcoaches from London, thereby accelerating the mails between the capital cities to a mere sixty hours.

The remaining money from the Kilmarnock Poems had to be carefully husbanded, so Robert could not afford sumptuous lodgings. He appears to have arranged beforehand to lodge with his old friend John Richmond. Gavin Hamilton's former clerk was now articled to an Edinburgh lawyer, and rented a room in Baxter's Close, Lawnmarket, for which he paid two shillings and sixpence a week. His landlady, a Mrs Carfrae, put the rent up to three shillings (fifteen pence) when she found that Richmond had sub-let a portion of his bed to his friend Burns.[5] The friends shared the rent, and for eighteenpence a week Robert had the part-use of 'a deal table, a sanded floor and a chaff bed'. He was fatigued and jaded after his sixty-mile ride, and perhaps more than a little hungover from the bucolic hospi-tality he had enjoyed *en route*, and immediately took to his bed where he remained all of the next day.

The tenement in Edinburgh's Old Town where Burns lodged was demolished many years ago and incorporated into Lady Stair's Close, over the entrance to which a bronze tablet, erected by the Edinburgh Pen and Pencil Club, records that 'in a house on the East side of this close, Robert Burns lived during his first visit to Edinburgh, 1786'. Lady Stair's House itself now serves as a museum containing many manuscripts and relics of Burns and Sir Walter Scott. At the head of the close was the shop of James Johnson, with whom Robert was to be associated in the compilation of *The Scots Musical Museum*. In medieval times the walled city of Edinburgh perched on the ridge that ran from the Castle Rock down to Holyrood-house, the famous Royal Mile. Each burgess had a house and enclosure separated from his neighbours by a narrow lane, closed at night. In the course of time, however, the expanding populace, unable to spread out-wards, had to double the density of building by erecting tenements in the enclosures. These structures eventually reached as high as seven storeys. Until the draining of the Nor' Loch and the development of the New Town in the 1760s, Edinburgh must have been one of the most densely packed cities anywhere in the world. By the time of Robert's first visit the New Town had been laid out from its east end as far as Hanover Street, reliev-ing the congestion in the Old Town to some extent; but the Royal Mile was still largely the bustling, crowded human ant-heap which it had been for centuries. Its coffee-houses and taverns were still the favourite resort of professional and businessmen, and for a country boy like Burns, whose only experience of urban living had been confined to Irvine and Kilmar-nock, Edinburgh must have been a traumatic experience.

The Royal Mile was roughly divided into three sections. The uppermost portion, nearest the Castle, was the Lawnmarket, which had taken its name from the shops where lawn (fine linen) had been sold. The name survives to this day, although the shops and booths have long since given way to trendy boutiques and antique shops. The central section was the High Street, frequented by clergymen from St Giles, doctors from the medical school, professors from the colleges and lawyers from the courts around the old Parliament House. Further south, beyond the Netherbow, lay the Canongate where the artisans had their homes. Up and down this narrow cobbled canyon, hemmed in by the overhanging grey stone 'lands', thronged a continual mass of humanity. Above the tenements lay the perpetual pall of smoke from a thousand chimneys, giving Edinburgh its well-deserved nickname of Auld Reekie. In the evenings the city acquired a more pungent odour as countless windows were raised and chamber-pots and slop pails were emptied on to the street below, to the warning cries of 'Gardyloo!' (a corruption of the French *gardez l'eau* – watch out for the water). Woe betide the pedestrian who did not duck for cover in the nearest close-mouth while this deadly torrent of raw sewage rained forth.

By the middle of the twentieth century the Royal Mile had degenerated into a sprawling slum, an eyesore in the Athens of the North; but in more recent times it has been expertly and lovingly restored, so that it is not difficult, as one trudges up the Lawnmarket, to imagine Burns there two centuries ago. But, despite the preservation of the façade, the Lawnmarket of today is a vastly different place from what it was in Burns's day. It was even quite different from the town which William Burnes had known barely thirty years earlier. For a graphic comparison of Edinburgh in 1763 and 1783 we must consult the writings of William Creech, the man who was to play the most crucial part in Robert's Edinburgh interludes:

In 1763 it was fashionable to go to church, and people were interested about religion. Sunday was strictly observed by all ranks as a day of devotion; and it was disgraceful to be seen on the streets during the time of public worship. Families attended church, with their children and servants; and family worship was frequent . . .

In 1783 attendance on church was greatly neglected, and particularly by the men. Sunday was by many made a day of relaxation; and young people were allowed to stroll about at all hours. Families thought it ungenteel to take their domestics to church with them. The streets were far from being void of people in the time of public worship; and, in the evenings, were frequently loose and riotous; particularly to bands of apprentice boys and young lads . . .

In no respect were the manners of 1763 and 1783 more remarkable than in the decency, dignity, and delicacy of the one period, compared with the looseness, dissipation, and licentiousness of the other. Many people ceased to blush at what would formerly have been reckoned a crime . . .

In 1763 the fines collected by the kirk treasurer for bastard children amounted to £154; and, upon an average of ten succeeding years, they were £190.

> In 1783 the fines for bastard children amounted to £600, and have since greatly increased . . .
> In 1763 there were five or six brothels, or houses of bad fame, and a very few of the lowest and most ignorant order of females sculked about the streets at night. A person might have gone from the Castle to Holyrood House (the then length of the city), at any hour in the night, without being accosted by a single street-walker. Street-robbery and pocket-picking were unknown.
> In 1783 the number of brothels had increased twenty-fold, and the women of the town more than a hundred-fold. Every quarter of the city and suburbs was infested with multitudes of females abandoned to vice . . . Street robbers, pick-pockets, and thieves, had much increased.[6]

The skyscrapers themselves symbolised the stratification of Edinburgh society, with the different levels of society occupying the same tenement, but on different floors: the poorer classes occupied the lower storeys, closer to the noise and the smells of the street, while the merchant classes lived in the upper storeys, with the nobility in the flats at the top of the building. But the common closemouth and the narrow stair-well were the great levellers of society, for all, both high and low, had to use them to come and go, and the elegant ladies with their cork rumps and hooped skirts had to squeeze past the coarsely garbed artisans and tradesmen on the stairs. Robert himself was tickled by the incongruous juxtaposition of the different sorts and classes. In a long letter to John Ballantine, dated 14 January 1787 (CL 100–1) he described his landlady, Mrs Carfrae, and the problems she was having with some of her other tenants:

> I have just had a visit from my Landlady who, is a staid, sober, piously-disposed, sculdudery-abhorring Widow, coming on her grand climacter-ick.– She is at present in sore tribulation respecting some 'Daughters of Belial' who are on the floor immediately above.– My Landlady who as I said is a flesh-disciplining, godly Matron, firmly believes her husband is in Heaven; and having been very happy with him on earth, she vigorously and perseveringly practices some of the most distinguishing Christian virtues, such as attending Church, railing against vice, &c. that she may be qualified to meet her dear quondam Bedfellow in that happy place where the Unclean & the ungodly shall never enter.– This, no doubt, requires some strong exertions of Self-denial, in a hale, well-kept Widow of forty-five; and as our floors are low and ill-plaistered, we can easily distinguish our laughter-loving, night-rejoicing neighbours – when they are eating, when they are drinking, when they are singing, when they are &c., my worthy Landlady tosses sleepless & unquiet, 'looking for rest but finding none,'[7] the whole night.– Just now she told me, though by the by she is sometimes dubious that I am, in her own phrase, 'but a rough an' roun' Christian' that 'We should not be uneasy and envious because the Wicked enjoy the good things of this life; for those base jades who, in her own words, lie up gandygoing with their filthy fellows, drinking the best of wines, and singing abominable songs, they shall one day lie in hell, weeping and wailing and gnashing their teeth over a cup of God's wrath!'

It was on the encouragement of Dr John Mackenzie that Robert screwed up the courage to write to Sir John Whitefoord on 1 December. Whitefoord, formerly Master of the Tarbolton masonic lodge, had been living in Edinburgh since selling Ballochmyle to Claud Alexander. He and his family resided in a flat in the Anchor Close, at the foot of which one William Smellie had his printing office. Mackenzie had told Burns that Sir John would be pleased to do what he could for him, so Robert took the bull by the horns. This letter ended on a curious note: 'I was surprised to hear that any one, who pretended in the least to the *manners of the gentleman*, should be so foolish, or worse, as to stoop to traduce the morals of such a one as I am, and so inhumanly cruel, too, as to meddle with that late most unfortunate, unhappy part of my story.' This was a clear reference to the affair with Jean Armour, and it appears that Robert had many enemies who were only too ready to spread malicious gossip about him in Edinburgh, just as they had traduced his character in Ayrshire. From Mackenzie, Robert learned that Sir John Whitefoord had stoutly defended him. 'With a tear of gratitude, I thank you, Sir, for the warmth with which you inter-sposed in behalf of my conduct. I am, I acknowledge, too frequently the sport of whim, caprice, and passion – but reverence to GOD, and integrity to my fellow-creatures, I hope I shall ever preserve.'

Sir John, in replying a few days later, confessed that he had not much interest (i.e. influence), 'but what I have I shall be ready to exert in procur-ing the attainment of any object you have in view'. He was inclined to dismiss the Excise idea and suggested what appeared to be a more practical alternative. 'I submit it to your consideration, whether it would not be more desirable, if a sum could be raised by subscription for a second edition of your poems, to lay it out in the stocking of a small farm. I am persuaded it would be a line of life much more agreeable to your feelings, and in the end more satisfactory.'[8]

Towards the end of 1785 work had begun on the erection of the new bridge at Ayr. The foundation stone had been laid with full masonic honours by James Dalrymple, an Ayr businessman and nephew of the Revd. Dr William Dalrymple who had baptised Burns. James Dalrymple, some seven years older than the poet, was an ardent freemason and an amateur versifier of note. Burns and Dalrymple appear to have been intro-duced through the medium of John Ballantine. In 1785 James succeeded his father to the estate of Orangefield in Monkton parish (now the site of Prestwick Airport). Dalrymple was in Edinburgh when Robert arrived and seconded the idea that John Samson should take Reid's pony back to Ayr-shire. Dalrymple, in fact, was the key that opened the door to Edinburgh society for the young poet. His background and connections illustrate the extraordinary mobility of Scottish society in the eighteenth century.

About 1677 there was born at Ayr a boy named James Macrae. His father died when he was a baby and his mother eked out a precarious existence as a washerwoman. Young James herded cattle and ran errands, but he was befriended by a poor Irish 'violer' (fiddler) named Hew McQuyre who was like a father to the boy and saw to it that he got at least a rudimentary education. At the age of fifteen James went to sea, and nothing more was heard of him for almost forty years. By 1720, however, he had risen to the rank of captain in the service of the East India Company and was entrusted with a delicate mission to Sumatra. As a result, he rose rapidly in the company's hierarchy and was appointed Governor of Madras in 1725. When he resigned five years later he had amassed a personal fortune of more than £100,000 in gold and diamonds. In 1731 he set sail for his native land and began searching for his relatives. He himself had never married, but he found that his only sister had married the violer's son, Hugh McGuire. He promptly wrote to her at Ayr, enclosing a large sum of money to provide for herself and her family. McGuire earned a living as a carpenter and part-time fiddler, but he had never seen so much money before, and he and his wife went on a spree which illustrates both their idea of happiness and the state of poverty in which they had been living. They procured a loaf of sugar and a bottle of brandy, and scooping out a hole in the sugar they poured in the brandy, and supped up the sweetened spirit with spoons 'until the excess of their felicity compelled them to close their eyes in peaceful slumber'.[9]

The wealthy nabob settled in Ayrshire and purchased a number of estates. He became a burgess of Ayr in 1733 and two years later presented the bronze statue of William III to the city of Glasgow. He died on 21 July 1744 and was buried in Monkton kirkyard where his imposing monument may be seen to this day. Having no family of his own, he bequeathed his fortune to the family of Hugh McGuire. Hugh himself got the estate of Drumdow and became a landed gentleman, but his son James inherited the barony of Houston, Renfrewshire, on condition that he adopted the surname of Macrae. To the eldest daughter Elizabeth, born in 1725, he left a large dowry and the barony of Ochiltree which enabled her, after a whirlwind courtship, to marry William Cunningham, thirteenth Earl of Glencairn, only a month later. Lizzie McGuire in early life had been a farm-servant to John Tennant of Laigh Corton and, in turn, she repaid his kindness to her by appointing his eldest son John (of Glenconner) as factor of the Glencairn estates, a position which he held for eleven years. Lizzie's sister Margaret received the estate of Alva and married James Erskine who was later elevated to the bench under the title of Lord Alva, while Macrae, the youngest sister who inherited the Governor's residence and lands at Orangefield, married Charles Dalrymple of Ayr in 1750.[10]

Thus it was that the fourteenth Earl of Glencairn, James Dalrymple of Orangefield and Captain James Macrae of Houston and Holmains, all distinguished members of Edinburgh society, were first cousins through common descent from Hugh McGuire. The thirteenth Earl had died in 1775, and since then the dowager countess had resided at Coates House on the outskirts of the city, with her unmarried daughter, Lady Betty Cunningham. The fourteenth Earl, James Cunningham (1749-91), was her second son, but his elder brother having predeceased him, James had inherited the title and estates. As principal heritor of Kilmarnock parish and patron of the living, Earl James had been responsible for the selection of the Revd. James Mackinlay which inspired 'The Ordination'.

The Cunninghams were also connected by blood and marriage to another powerful Edinburgh family. In 1785 the Revd. John Cunningham, younger brother of Lord Glencairn, married Lady Isabella Erskine, sister of the Earl of Buchan and the Hon. Henry Erskine, Dean of the Faculty of Advocates. Through James Dalrymple, Burns was introduced to both families and they, in turn, secured his introduction to many others ranked among the great and the good. In a letter of 6 December to John Mackenzie (CL 114) Robert revealed that his circle of acquaintances had been widened, on different levels:

> I have now been a week in Edinburgh and have been introduced to a great many of the Noblesse.– I have met very warm friends in the Literati, Professors Stewart, Blair, Greenfield, & your namesake, the Author of The man of feeling. I am likewise kindly & generously Patronised by the Duchess of Gordon; Countess of Glencairn, with my lord & Lady Betty; Sir John Whitefoord, the Dean of the Faculty, the honorable Mr H. Erskine, with several others.– Our worthy friend Mr Stewart, with that goodness truly like himself, got me in the periodical paper, The Lounger; a copy of which I here inclose you.–

Dugald Stewart, on leaving Catrine at the beginning of November for the start of the winter term at Edinburgh University, had taken with him a copy of the Kilmarnock Poems which he showed to his friend Henry Mackenzie (1745–1831). The son of an Edinburgh physician, Mackenzie was then at the zenith of his literary powers. A lawyer and a freemason, he had published his first novel, *The Man of Feeling*, anonymously in 1771. This curiously sentimental work attained enormous popularity and established its author as the foremost literary figure in Edinburgh. Robert himself held an exaggeratedly high opinion of Mackenzie and his novel, 'a book I prize next to the Bible';[11] he carried a copy with him at all times and he eventually had to replace it because the covers became so worn. In 1786 Mackenzie was conducting a literary periodical, *The Lounger*, which was published by William Creech. Creech, incidentally, had been at school with Lord Glencairn and later accompanied him on the customary Grand Tour before entering the publishing business. Mackenzie read and admired the poems, and published a generous, if rather patronising, review in the issue of 9 December. After philosophising on the contemplation of genius and the discovery of 'talents generally unknown', Mackenzie went on:

> . I know not if I shall be accused of such enthusiasm and partiality, when I introduce to the notice of my readers a poet of our own country, with whose writings I have lately become acquainted; but if I am not greatly deceived, I think I may safely pronounce him a genius of no ordinary rank. The person to whom I allude, is *Robert Burns*, an Ayrshire Ploughman, whose poems were some time ago published in a country town in the west of Scotland, with no other ambition, it would seem, than to circulate among the inhabitants of the county where he was born, to obtain a little fame from those who had heard of his talents. I hope I shall not be

thought to assume too much, if I endeavour to place him in a higher point of view, to call for a verdict of his country on the merit of his works, and to claim for him those honours which their excellence appears to deserve.

After quoting from 'The Vision' and 'To a Mountain Daisy' and commenting on them at great length, Mackenzie continued:

Though I am very far from meaning to compare our rustic bard to Shakespeare, yet whoever will read his lighter and more humorous poems, his 'Dialogue of the Dogs', his 'Dedication to G- H-, Esq.'; his 'Epistles to a young Friend', and 'to W. S-n', will perceive with what uncommon penetration and sagacity this Heaven-taught ploughman, from his humble and unlettered station, has looked upon men and manners.

And he concluded:

Burns possesses the spirit as well as the fancy of a poet. That honest pride and independence of soul which are sometimes the muse's only dower, break forth on every occasion in his works. It may be, then, I shall wrong his feelings, while I indulge my own, in calling the attention of the public to his situation and circumstances. That condition, humble as it was, in which he found content, and wooed the muse, might not have been deemed uncomfortable; but grief and misfortunes have reached him there; and one or two of his poems hint, what I have learnt from some of his countrymen, that he has been obliged to form the resolution of leaving his native land, to seek under a West Indian clime that shelter and support which Scotland has denied him. But I trust means may be found to prevent this resolution from taking place; and that I do my country no more than justice, when I suppose her ready to stretch out her hand to cherish and retain this native poet, whose 'wood-notes wild' possess so much excellence. To repair the wrongs of suffering or neglected merit; to call forth genius from the obscurity in which it had pined indignant, and place it where it may profit or delight the world; these are exertions which give to wealth an enviable superiority, to greatness and to patronage a laudable pride.

Henry Mackenzie's review, long and laudatory though it was, was not the first notice to be shown of Burns. The *Edinburgh Magazine, or Literary Miscellany* of November and December 1786 reprinted poems by Burns. Robert Anderson (1750-1830), who assisted James Sibbald (1745-1803) in the production of this periodical, brought the poems to the attention of his employer.[12] It was probably Sibbald himself who penned the anonymous review which appeared in the October issue, the earliest notice of Burns's work in print. Sibbald, too, was influenced to some extent by Robert's peasant background, rather than assessing his poetry purely on its own merits:

The author is indeed a striking example of native genius bursting through the obscurity of poverty and the obstructions of laborious life. He is said to be a common ploughman; and when we consider him in this light, we cannot help regretting that wayward fate had not placed him in a more favoured situation. Those who view him with the severity of lettered criticism, and judge him by the fastidious rules of art, will discover that he has not the doric simplicity of Ramsay, nor the brilliant imagination of Ferguson (*sic*); but to those who admire the exertions of untutored fancy, and are blind to many faults for the sake of numberless beauties, his poems will afford singular gratification. His observations on human characters are acute and sagacious, and his descriptions are lively and just. Of rustic pleasantry he has a rich fund; and some of his softer scenes are touched with inimitable delicacy. He seems to be a boon companion, and often startles us with a dash of libertinism, which will keep some readers at a distance . . .

Burns himself may have been gratified by the letter which appeared in the *Edinburgh Evening Courant* on 13 November 1786, under the pseudonym of Allan Ramsay. After quoting the old adage about a prophet having no honour in his own country, the writer castigated the 'Peers, Nabobs and wealthy Commoners' of Ayrshire, none of whom had stepped forth as a patron to the author of a collection of poems in the Scottish dialect, 'the production of a common farmer in Ayrshire of the name of Burns. His language is nervous, and his sentiments would do honour to a much more enlightened scholar. In short, he appears to be not only a keen satirist, but a man of great feeling and sensibility.' The letter-writer, who hailed from Dunbartonshire, concluded with a plea:

To this self-taught poet I am an entire stranger, but his productions have afforded me so much pleasure that if this hint should raise an emulation in that county to rescue from penury a genius which, if unprotected, will probably sink into obscurity, I will most cheerfully contribute towards it, and I know many others who will follow the example. Should my efforts to serve this man with the laity be ineffectual, I propose as a *dernier resort* to address the clergy of that county, many of whom he hath taken particular notice of in his poems.

The newspaper printed a short letter two days later, written from Glasgow on 14 November and taking Allan Ramsay of Dunbartonshire to task. The writer begged that Ramsay be informed that the greatest part of the edition of six hundred copies were subscribed for, or bought up by, the gentlemen of Ayrshire, many of whom had taken particular notice of the author. 'Allan Ramsay's reflection upon the county does therefore little credit either to his information or to the politeness of his stile.' The letter was merely initialled 'G. H.', but there can be little doubt that Gavin Hamilton, dedicatee of the Kilmarnock Poems, was its author.[13]

To Gavin Hamilton himself Robert wrote on 7 December (CL 66–7). It is clear that Hamilton was anxious to know how the auction of the Loudoun estates had gone. The Earl had committed suicide the previous April, beset with financial worries, and the executors of his will, acting on behalf of his little daughter Flora, had put up certain of the estates for sale at the Exchange Coffeehouse on 5 December. Robert had been asked to provide the results of the sale at the earliest opportunity. After furnishing brief details regarding the successful bidders for each lot, Robert turned to his own affairs:

> I am in a fair way to becoming as eminent as Thomas a Kempis or John Bunyan; and you may expect henceforth to see my birthday inserted among the wonderful events, in the Poor Robin's and Aberdeen Almanacks, along with the black Monday, & the battle of Bothwell bridge.– My Lord Glencairn & the Dean of Faculty, Mr H. Erskine, have taken me under their wing; and by all probability I shall soon be the tenth Worthy, and the eighth Wise Man of the world. Through my lord's influence it is inserted in the records of the Caledonian Hunt, that they universally, one & all, subscribe for the 2d Edition. – My subscription bills come out tomorrow, and you shall get some of them next Post.

Robert evidently had no illusions about his sudden fame. His sardonic reference to his inclusion in the two popular almanacs of the period was intended as a joke; little did he realise then, or later, how accurate his prophecy was. More to the point, however, was the patronage of the Earl of Glencairn who had secured a publisher for the much-desired second edition, and a practical guarantee of its success by persuading the noblemen and gentlemen of the Caledonian Hunt to subscribe *en bloc*.

Burns wrote to Ballantine on 13 December (CL 99–100), shedding a little light on his doings during his first two weeks in the capital. Oddly enough, he misstated the time of his arrival by saying that he had only been a week in Edinburgh when, in fact, he had been there two weeks. More seriously, however, he admitted that he had 'suffered ever since I came to town with a miserable headache and stomach complaint', though he was now a good deal better. Contrary to the imaginary account provided by Allan Cunningham, that he had spent his first days aimlessly wandering around the city, viewing the sights of Arthur's Seat, the Palace and the Castle, and visiting the grave of Fergusson and the house of Allan Ramsay, we have Richmond's own testimony[14] that he was in such a depressed state much of the time that he took to his bed where his friend would read to him until sleep overtook him.

In his letter to Ballantine Robert stated that Dalrymple of Orangefield had introduced him to Lord Glencairn, 'a man whose worthy and brotherly kindness to me I shall remember when time will be no more'. In this letter he elaborated on the promise by the Hunt: 'They are all to take each a Copy of the second Edition, for which they are to pay one guinea'. In this, however, he had been sadly misinformed, for the Hunt got their one hundred copies at the normal subscription price of five shillings. Nevertheless, it was a major boost to the success of the edition, a matter which Robert duly repaid in his fulsome dedication. After reciting the names of the nobility and literati who had taken him under their wing, he continued:

An unknown hand left ten guineas for the Ayrshire Bard in Mr Sibbald's hand, which I got. I since have discovered my generous unknown friend to be Patrick Miller Esq. brother to the Justice Clerk; and drank a glass of claret with him by invitation at his own house yesternight.– I am nearly agreed with Creech to print my book; and, I suppose, I will begin on monday.– I will send a subscription bill or two next post; when I intend writing my first, kind Patron Mr Aiken. I saw his Son [Andrew Hunter Aiken] today, and he is very well.

Significantly this letter ended with a postscript: 'If any of my friends write me, my direction is Care of Mr Creech Bookseller.' Two days later Robert wrote to Robert Muir (CL 87–8). As usual, he reeled off the names of the celebrities who had patronised him before continuing:

I believe I shall begin at Mr Creech's as my publisher. I am still undetermined as to the future; and, as usual, never think of it. I have now neither house nor home that I can call my own, and live on the world at large. I am just a poor wayfaring Pilgrim on the road to Parnassus; thoughtless wanderer and sojourner in a strange land.

The uncertainty and indecisiveness mingled with self-pity strike us as strange. In point of fact, Robert had by this time concluded a deal with William Creech who, on the day before this letter was written, advertised the second edition as 'in the press, to be published by subscription for the sole benefit of the Author'.

The exact circumstances in which Robert and Creech came to an agreement to publish the Edinburgh Edition are not known, although they can be fairly deduced from the poet's correspondence, and the recollection of his contemporaries. John Moir, who later became one of Edinburgh's leading printers, recounted how he was serving his apprenticeship in 1786 with a well-known typographer in the High Street.

One day a plain-looking man, of rustic appearance, who afterwards proved to be Robert Burns, came to inquire about the printing of a volume of poems. Unluckily the master took his visitor for some poor crack-brained versifier, who might give him a good deal of trouble, but was not likely to yield much solid return in the way of business. He therefore received the application with marked coldness; spoke of being a good deal engaged at present, and of his habit of requiring effective guarantees of payment from any strangers for whom he worked. The visitor, manifestly offended, went away, but not till he had taken occasion to pull out and show a quantity of money sufficient to convince the printer that, if more favourably received, he might have proved a good customer. This was not an end of the typographer's mortifications; for, being vexed at missing so good a job as the printing of Burns's poems, he resolved to lose no second customer of that sort who might come in his way, and accordingly took the risk, soon after, of printing the productions of a poet from Aberdeenshire, which proved a complete failure, so that he lost fully as much by the one concern as he might have gained by the other.[15]

Instead, Robert was introduced to William Creech, probably by Lord Glencairn, his quondam travelling companion. Creech was, at that time, the leading publisher in Edinburgh, enjoying a close connection with the London firm of Cadell and Davies. He was the publisher of Beattie, Campbell and Mackenzie and an intimate friend of Hugh Blair and Dugald Stewart. Elected to the Town Council six years previously, Creech was to become a magistrate in 1788 and eventually Lord Provost in 1811. He was also Secretary of the Edinburgh Chamber of Commerce. Socially and politically he was the very model of conformity and propriety. Robert left a most perceptive word sketch of Creech in his *Second Commonplace Book* which he started in Edinburgh. Unlike the first volume, this was never intended for publication, and therefore contained very candid descriptions of the people he met, and his assessment of their character:

> My worthy bookseller, Mr Creech, is a strange, multiform character. His ruling passions of the left hand are an extreme vanity and something of the more harmless modifications of selfishness. The one, mixed as it often is with great goodness of heart, makes him rush into all public matters and take every instance of unprotected merit by the hand, provided it is in his power to hand it into public notice; the other quality makes him, amid all the embarassment in which his vanity entangles him, now and then to cast half a squint at his own interest.

An Edinburgh bookseller of the mid-nineteenth century, who had been in Creech's employment in his early years, provided Robert Chambers with a memoir of his habits and curious method of conducting business:

> Being so much occupied with literary people, he seldom handled his own money. His clerk balanced the cash every night, and carried on *that* to next day. He had a *levée* in his house till twelve every day, attended by literary men and printers. Between twelve and one he came to the shop, where the same flow of company lasted till four, and then he left us, and we saw no more of him till next day. He was a very good-natured man, and was never known to prosecute any one for a debt.[16]

He might have added that Creech had the same lackadaisical attitude towards his own debts, as Burns was soon to discover. Among his contemporaries Creech was renowned for his meanness, and the frugal quality of the refreshments provided at his levées was proverbial. It is ludicrous to suppose that Creech had any sinister motive in delaying the payment of money owed to Burns, as has been suggested;[17] he treated everyone like that.

Robert seems to have been equally unbusinesslike in his dealings with his parsimonious publisher. According to Maurice Lindsay, Lord Glencairn asked Creech whether he would undertake a second edition of the poems, but Creech recommended a subscription edition, for which he undertook to subscribe five hundred copies,[18] but I can discover no evidence either for Glencairn's intercession or the discussion of alternative methods of publication. We have nothing more than the vague hints conveyed by Robert himself in various letters to his friends. The exact nature of the relationship between Burns and Creech was revealed in Robert's letter to Aiken on 16 December (CL 94) in which he refers to Creech as 'my agent forsooth'. Creech undertook to get the subscription bills printed and distributed, and when the book was produced he would offer his own subscription copies for retail sale, but that was as far as he was prepared to go. Both Smellie the printer and William Scott the bookbinder dealt directly with Burns in all matters, including payment for their work on the project. In this way Creech covered himself from any loss that might arise, should sales fail to reach expectations, while at the same time gaining the credit for adding another 'notable' to his list of authors. One ought not to emphasise Creech's canniness in adopting this procedure; it was pretty well the standard method of the period. In any case, Robert would have been hard-pressed to find an agent better qualified than the 'little, upright, pert, tart, tripping wight' whom he described in an unpublished fragment.[19]

In his letter to Aiken on 16 December, Robert mentioned that Lord Glencairn had sent a parcel of subscription bills to the Marquis of Graham 'with downright orders to get them filled up with all the first Scottish names about Court'. He had also written to the Duke of Montague and was about to write to the Duke of Portland 'for their Graces' interest in behalf of the Scotch Bard's Subscription', though neither of their names appeared in the published subscription list. Robert promised to send Aiken one or two more bills when he had an opportunity of a carrier. No example of the subscription bill appears to have survived, but we may suppose that it followed the pattern of the Kilmarnock bill. Subscribers were to get their copies for five shillings, but the general public, who bought the poems from a bookseller afterwards, had to pay six shillings. Thus Creech stood to make a shilling on every copy he sold, a clear profit of £25.

Robert Muir, one of Robert's closest friends in Kilmarnock, had subscribed for seventy-two copies of the Kilmarnock Edition. Now he proposed to take sixty of the Edinburgh Edition. Burns, knowing that his friend was in straitened circumstances owing to his efforts in clearing his estate at Loanfoot from the debts with which it had been encumbered at his father's death, tactfully reduced it to forty. On 20 December (CL 88) he wrote, 'Your affair of sixty copies is also like you; but it would not be like me to comply.'

Meanwhile Robert was playing up to the image of the Heaven-taught ploughman which Sibbald and Mackenzie had created. To Dr Moore he wrote exultingly:

> The baneful Star that had so long shed its blasting influence in my Zenith, for once made a revolution to the Nadir; and the providential care of a good God placed me under the patronage of one of his noblest creatures, the Earl of Glencairn: 'Oublie moi, Grand Dieu, si jamais je l'oublie!'

I need relate no farther.– At Edinburgh I was in a new world: I mingled among many classes of men, but all of them new to me; and I was all attention 'to catch the manners living as they rise.'–[20]

John Logan (1748–88), formerly a parish minister in Scotland who had moved to London in 1785 to edit the *English Review*, was the first critic to see through the pose. In an unsigned review, published in February 1787, he pointed out that:

> Robert Burns, though he has been represented as an ordinary ploughman, was a farmer, or what they call a tenant in Scotland, and rented land which he cultivated with his own hands. He is better acquainted with the English poets than most English authors that have come under review.

Logan's questioning of the Burns legend provoked a response from none other than Henry Mackenzie, who was mainly responsible for creating the myth in the first place. Logan wrote a letter to Mackenzie on 28 February, defending his position. He had read Burns's works under considerable disadvantage:

> I received three letters from Edinburgh full of irrational and unbounded panegyric, representing him as a poetical phenomenon that owed nothing but to Nature and his own Genius. When I opened the book I found that he was as well acquainted with the English poets as I was, and I could point you out a hundred imitations . . . I have given Burns' poems to several English gentlemen who cannot discern their beauties. When that rage and Mania which seizes Edinburgh at least once a year has subsided, I am confident that your own opinion will coincide with Mine . . . An enthusiastic lover always discovers new and concealed beauties in his Mistress.[21]

Not since Dr Johnson had come to Edinburgh thirteen years before had Edinburgh lionised a literary figure so enthusiastically as it did Burns. After he was taken up by Glencairn and Henry Erskine, every door in polite society was open to him. Robert, ever afterwards, was fulsome in his gratitude to Glencairn, 'my titular Protector' (CL 497). To Mrs Dunlop he wrote on 22 March 1787 (CL 134), 'The noble Earl of Glencairn, to whom I owe more than any man on earth, does me the honor of giving me his strictures; his hints, with respect to impropriety or indelicacy, I follow implicitly'. In his *Second Commonplace Book*, however, Robert philosophised ruefully:

> There are few of the sore evils under the sun give me more uneasiness and chagrin than the comparison how a man of genius –, nay, avowed worth – is everywhere received with the reception which a mere ordinary character, decorated with the trappings and futile distinctions of Fortune meets.

He deeply and bitterly resented the fact that some men, because of inherited titles and wealth, were deferred to just as much as, if not more than, he was. Because they were born into a superior station in life, so he reasoned, why should they be treated with more respect than he, who had made his way in the world by his own efforts and talents? This bitter mood was triggered off by a particular incident:

> The noble Glencairn has wounded me to the soul here, because I dearly esteem, respect, and love him. He showed so much attention – engrossing attention one day to the only blockhead, as there was none but his lordship, the dunderpate, and myself, that I was within half a point of throwing down my gage of contemptuous defiance; but he shook my hand and looked so benevolently good at parting – God bless him! though I should never see him more, I shall love him until my dying day! I am pleased to think I am so capable of the throes of gratitude, as I am miserably deficient in some other virtues.

For all his egalitarian sentiments, so often and so stridently expressed, Robert was both flattered and overawed by the attention he received from the aristocracy. In the case of James Glencairn (after whom he was to name his fourth son) Robert's feelings were highly emotional, to put it mildly. The fourteenth earl was nine years older than the poet, but his charm was matched by his boyish good looks. He had wealth and position (for several years he was one of the Representative Scots Peers in the House of Lords) and he was one of the most eligible bachelors of the time; but he never married, and I have not been able to trace any hint of a romantic attachment with women. With Burns he appears to have been extremely generous, if the silver snuffbox that is now the most prized possession of the Dumfries Burns Club is anything to go by. Robert never mentioned this gift, allegedly a birthday present in January 1787, in any of his writings, but there is no reason to doubt the authenticity of the fulsome inscription engraved upon it. Although made of silver it is of immense value, as the silver crown mounted on the lid was one struck at Oxford during the Civil War and fewer than a dozen examples are believed to exist. How Glencairn came by such a rare coin is not known, but its great value was appreciated even in the 1780s. Glencairn also gave Robert a jewelled signet ring, the loss of which some years later caused the poet indescribable anguish.

There is absolutely no suggestion of a homosexual relationship between Glencairn and Burns; not even Alan Dent, who made much of Robert's relationships with Richard Brown, John Richmond and Robert Ainslie, felt able to suggest that there was any impropriety between the nobleman and the poet. But there can be no doubt that Robert regarded Glencairn with adulation bordering on hero-worship and was completely captivated by him. Thus, when the earl quite innocently behaved in a polite way towards a third party who perhaps lacked Robert's intellectual capacity, the latter was furious. Such a startling passage in the *Commonplace Book* (which was intended as a confidential record, not for publication) tells us more about Burns than Glencairn. The relationship between the earl and the poet, however, was extremely beneficial to the latter. Glencairn seems to have had the happy knack of extending the benefits of his superior upbringing and patronage without upsetting the poet's sensibilities. That Robert was an apt pupil is obvious in the various pen-portraits of him which eye-witnesses of his first winter in Edinburgh society have left. The best of these was that written by Dugald Stewart:

> He came to Edinburgh early in the winter following, and remained there for several months. By whose advice he took this step, I am unable to say. Perhaps it was suggested only by his own curiosity to see a little more of the world; but I confess I dreaded the consequences from the first . . . The attentions he received during his stay in town from all ranks and descrip-tions of persons, were such as would have turned any head but his own. I cannot say that I could perceive any unfavourable effect which they left on his mind. He retained the same simplicity of manners and appearance which had struck me so forcibly when I first saw him in the country; nor did he seem to feel any additional self-importance to the number and rank of his new acquaintances. His dress was perfectly suited to his station, plain and unpretending, with a sufficient attention to neatness. If I recol-lect right, he always wore boots; and, when on more than usual ceremony, buck-skin breeches.
>
> The variety of his engagements, while in Edinburgh, prevented me from seeing him so often as I could have wished. In the course of the spring he called on me once or twice, at my request, early in the morning, and walked with me to Braid Hills in the neighbourhood of the town, where he charmed me still more by his private conversation than he had ever done in company. He was passionately fond of the beauties of nature; and I recollect once he told me, when I was admiring a distant prospect in one of our morning walks, that the sight of so many smoking cottages gave a pleasure to his mind, which none could understand who had not witnessed, like himself, the happiness and the worth which they contained . . .
>
> I should have mentioned before, that notwithstanding various reports I have heard . . . of Burns's predilection for convivial and not very select society, I should have concluded in favour of his habits of sobriety, from all of him that ever fell under my own observation . . .
>
> In the course of [the summer of 1787] I was led by curiosity to attend for an hour or two a Mason-Lodge in Mauchline, where Burns presided. He had occasion to make some short unpremeditated compliments to different individuals from whom he had no reason to expect a visit, and everything he said was happily conceived, and forcibly as well as fluently expressed . . . His manner of speaking in public had evidently the marks of some practice in extempore elocution.[22]

Alexander Dalziel, Professor of Greek, also provided a description of Burns in a letter to his friend, Sir Robert Liston, 25 January 1787:

> We have got a poet in town just now, whom everybody is taking notice of – a ploughman from Ayrshire – a man of unquestionable genius, who has produced admirable verse, mostly in the Scottish dialect, though some

of them are nearly in English. He is a fellow of strong common sense, and by his own industry has read a good deal of English, both prose and verse. The first edition of his poems was published at Kilmarnock, and sold in that part of the country very soon, insomuch that they are now not to be got. I, among others, have seen them, and admire some of them exceedingly. A new edition is now in the press, and he is encouraged by a most numerous subscription. It is thought he will get some hundred pounds by it, which will enable him to take a small farm. He runs the risk, however, of being spoiled by the excessive attention paid him just now by persons of all ranks. Those who know him best, say he has too much good sense to allow himself to be spoiled. Everybody is fond of showing him everything here that the place furnishes. I saw him at an assembly t'other night. The Duchess of Gordon and other ladies of rank took notice of him there. He behaves wonderfully well; very independent in his sentiments, and has none of the *mauvaise honte* about him, though he is not forward.[23]

Such was the favourable impression which the 'ploughman poet' made on some of the most sophisticated people of the period. Incidentally, Dugald Stewart's comment is also authoritative rebuttal of the posthumous charges of dissipation levelled against Burns.

Stewart's predecessor in the chair of Moral Philosophy was Adam Ferguson (1723–1816). Although he had retired in 1785 he continued to take a leading role in the cultural life of Edinburgh and, in his house at Sciennes Hill, he often entertained the literati. Here one afternoon early in 1787 Walter Scott, then a boy of sixteen but recently entered as a clerk in his father's law office, encountered Burns:

I saw him one day at the late venerable Professor Ferguson's, where there were several gentlemen of literary reputation, among whom I remember the celebrated Dr Dugald Stewart. Of course we youngsters sate silent, looked, and listened. The only thing I remember which was remarkable in Burns' manner was the effect produced upon him by a print of Bunbury's, representing a soldier lying dead on the snow, his dog sitting in misery on the one side, on the other his widow, with a child in her arms . . .

Burns seemed much affected by the print, or rather, the ideas which it suggested to his mind. He actually shed tears. He asked whose the lines were [written below], and it chanced that nobody but myself remembered that they occur in a half-forgotten poem of Langhorne's, called by the unpromising title of 'The Justice of the Peace'. I whispered my information to a young friend present, who mentioned it to Burns, who rewarded me with a look and a word, which, though of mere civility, I then received, and still recollect, with very great pleasure.

His person was strong and robust; his manners rustic, not clownish; a sort of dignified plainness and simplicity, which received part of its effect perhaps from one's knowledge of his extraordinary talents . . . I would have taken the poet, had I not known what he was, for a very sagacious country farmer of the old Scottish school; that is, none of your modern agriculturists, who keep labourers for their drudgery, but the *douce guidman* who held his own plough. There was a strong expression of sense and shrewdness in all his lineaments; the eye alone, I think, indicated the poetical character and temperament. It was large, and of a dark cast, and glowed (I say literally *glowed*) when he spoke with feeling or interest. I never saw such another eye in a human head, though I have seen the most distinguished men in my time.

His conversation expressed perfect self-confidence, without the slightest presumption. Among the men who were the most learned of their time and country, he expressed himself with perfect firmness, but without the least intrusive forwardness; and when he differed in opinion, he did not hesitate to express it firmly, yet at the same time with modesty . . . I have only to add, that his dress corresponded with his manner. He was like a farmer dressed in his best to dine with the laird. I do not speak *in malam partem*, when I say I never saw a man in company with his superiors in station and information, more perfectly free from either the reality or the affectation of embarrassment. I was told, but did not observe it, that his address to females was extremely deferential, and always with a turn either to the pathetic or humorous, which engaged their attention particularly. I have heard the Duchess of Gordon remark this.[24]

Ferguson's house, jocularly known in Burns's time as Kamchatka because of its isolation on the bleak, windswept Siberian wastes to the south of the city, is today in the midst of a heavily built-up district, a tenement whose original front now faces a drying-green, enclosed on three sides by tenements and on the fourth by a factory wall. A bronze tablet was erected on the wall on 12 March 1927 by the Edinburgh and District Association of Burns Clubs, in conjunction with the Edinburgh Sir Walter Scott Club, to mark the historic meeting of Scotland's greatest literary figures. Sir Adam Ferguson (1771-1854), a school-friend of Scott and the eldest son of Professor Ferguson, had secured his chum's invitation to the weekly conversazione where Burns was present, and he, too, has left a record of the occasion:

Professor Stewart on this occasion offered to bring Burns, and Dr Ferguson readily assented. The poet found himself in the most brilliant literary society which Edinburgh then contained. Black, Hutton, and John Home were amongst those present . . . Burns seemed at first little inclined to mingle easily in the company; he went round the room, looking at the pictures on the walls. The print described by Scott arrested his attention; he read aloud the lines underneath, but before he reached the end his voice faltered, and his eye filled with tears. A little after, he turned with much interest to the company, pointed to the picture, and with some eagerness asked if any one could tell him who had written these affecting lines. The philosophers were silent; no one knew; but, after a decent interval, the pale lame boy near by said in a negligent manner: 'They're written by one Langhorne'. An explanation of the place where they occur followed, and Burns fixed a look of half-serious interest on the youth, while he said: 'You'll be a man yet, sir'. Scott may be said to have derived literary ordination from Burns.[25]

Another of the academic figures who patronised Burns was Professor Hugh Blair (1718-1800). He was the only child of John Blair, an Edinburgh merchant who speculated heavily in the Darien Scheme and lost everything as a result. The poet Robert Blair, best remembered nowadays for 'The Grave', was a close relative. Hugh was educated at the High School before going on to the University and graduating in 1739. Two years later he was licensed to preach and soon afterwards became tutor in the family of Simon Fraser, Master of Lovat. After a succession of parish appointments he became minister of St Giles, the High Church of Edinburgh, in the year of the poet's birth. In the same year he also began lecturing at the University with such success that the Chair of Rhetoric and Belles Lettres was created specially for him in 1762. His lectures on taste won widespread approval and from then onwards Blair was recognised as the arbiter of taste, a kind of Scottish Seneca. Posterity has dealt harshly with him, however; Gosse derided his sermons as 'a bucket of warm water' and Leslie Stephen wrote of Blair 'mouthing sham rhetoric'. Snyder dismissed him as 'pompous and vain, rather too scrupulous concerning his dress, obviously self-satisfied, and somewhat lacking in a sense of humor'.[26] The sexual metaphors in Burns's 'Epistle to John Rankine' (CW 82–4) escaped him altogether.

Blair, in fact, was very much a product of his time, when the Scots were hell-bent on turning their backs on their indigenous culture and anglicising themselves with a dour determination. His canons of taste had been formed by a study of the classics and the Augustan writers of England. Remember that Dr Blacklock considered Blair's taste 'too highly polished and his genius too regular in its emotions to make allowances for the sallies of a more impetuous ardour'.[27] Burns, in his *Second Commonplace Book*, has left a shrewd impression of the learned divine:

> I never respect him with humble veneration; but when he kindly interests himself in my welfare, or, still more, when he descends from his pinnacle and meets me on equal ground, my heart overflows with what is called *liking*: when he neglects me for the mere carcase of greatness, or when his eye measures the difference of our points of elevation, I say to myself with scarcely an emotion, what do I care for him or his pomp either? . . .
> In my opinion Dr Blair is merely an astonishing proof of what industry and application can do. Natural parts like his are frequently to be met with; his vanity is proverbially known among his acquaintances; but he is justly at the head of what may be called fine writing . . . He has a heart, not of the finest water, but far from being an ordinary one. In short, he is truly a worthy and most remarkable character.

Despite the great disparity in their ages – Blair was more than forty years Robert's senior – the professor took more than a passing interest in the young poet. Josiah Walker (introduced to Burns by Blacklock) later recalled an unfortunate incident:

> The day after my first introduction to Burns, I supped in company with him at Dr Blair's. The other guests were very few, and as each had been invited chiefly to have an opportunity of meeting with the poet, the doctor endeavoured to draw him out, and to make him the central figure of the group.

Though he therefore furnished the greatest proportion of the conversation, he did no more than what he saw evidently was expected. Men of genius have often been taxed with a proneness to commit blunders in company, from that ignorance or negligence of the laws of conversation which must be imputed to the absorption of their thoughts in a favourite subject, or to the want of that daily practice in attending to the petty modes of behaviour which is incompatible with a studious life. From singularities of this sort Burns was unusually free; yet on the present occasion he made a more awkward slip than any that are reported of the poets or mathematicians most noted for absence. Being asked from which of the public places he had received the greatest gratification, he named the High Church, but gave the preference as a preacher to the colleague of our worthy entertainer, whose celebrity rested on his pulpit eloquence, in a tone so pointed and decisive, as to throw the whole company into the most foolish embarassment. The doctor, indeed, with becoming self-command, endeavoured to relieve the rest by cordially seconding the encomium so injudiciously introduced; but this did not prevent the conversation from labouring under that compulsory effort which was unavoidable, while the thoughts of all were full of the only subject on which it was improper to speak. Of this blunder he shewed the return of good sense by making no attempt to repair it. His secret mortification was indeed so great, that he never mentioned the circumstance until many years after, when he told me that his silence had proceeded from the pain which he felt in recalling it to his memory.[28]

Blair's colleague, for whom Burns had so tactlessly expressed a preference, was the Revd. William Greenfield, a man of immense abilities but whose character was fatally flawed. The son of Captain John Greenfield of Dalkeith and Grizel Cockburn, he had been educated at the High School and the University, from which he graduated MA in 1778. He was ordained in 1781 and appointed minister of Wemyss, Fife. He had been translated from Wemyss to St Andrew's Church in Edinburgh in November 1784, and in February 1787 he became Blair's colleague at the High Church. In the same year he also succeeded Blair to the Chair of Rhetoric and Belles Lettres.[29] In the *Second Commonplace Book* Robert described him:

Mr Greenfield is of a superior order. The bleedings of humanity, the generous resolve, a manly disregard of the paltry subjects of vanity, virgin modesty, the truest taste, and a very sound judgment, characterise him. His being the first [i.e. best] Speaker I ever heard is perhaps half owing to industry. He certainly possesses no small share of poetic abilities; he is a steady, most disinterested friend, without the least affectation, of seeming so; and, as a companion, his good sense, his joyous hilarity, his sweetness of manners and modesty, are most engagingly charming.

Both Blair and Greenfield were recipients of at least one letter apiece from the poet. To Greenfield, Robert wrote in December 1786 (CL 221) enclosing two songs, 'the composition of two Ayrshire mechanics' (though more probably his own work which a natural diffidence concealed by this harmless artifice). This curious lack of confidence, in a lofty academic setting, was explained in the letter:

> I am willing to believe that my abilities deserved a better fate than the veriest shades of life; but to be dragged forth, with all my imperfections on my head, to the full glare of learned and polite observation, is what, I am afraid, I shall have bitter reason to repent.

And he concluded this letter on a prophetic note, showing that he had no illusions about the evanescence of his new-found fame:

> I mention this to you, once for all, merely, in the Confessor style, to disburthen my conscience, and that – 'When proud Fortune's ebbing tide recedes'[30] – you may bear me witness, when my bubble of fame was at the highest, I stood, unintoxicated, with the inebriating cup in my hand, looking forward, with rueful resolve, to the hastening time when the stroke of envious Calumny, with all the eagerness of vengeful triumph, should dash it to the ground.–

Ironically, Greenfield attained the very pinnacles of his career – Almoner to King George III (1789), Doctor of Divinity (1796) and Moderator of the General Assembly (1796–8) – before 'envious Calumny' dashed *him* to the ground. In December 1798 he suddenly resigned the moderatorship, demitted his charge and fled the country. The Presbytery of Edinburgh, meeting later that month, deposed and excommunicated him on account of 'certain flagrant reports concerning his conduct, which his desertion seemed to preclude the Presbytery from considering as groundless'. The University stripped him of his degrees and he lived in the north of England under the alias of Rutherford, until his death in 1827. For the last three decades of his life he supported himself by teaching and writing. In 1809 Walter Scott introduced him to the London Scot, John Murray, who published his work in the *Quarterly Review* under the pen name of Richardson. What his flagrant conduct was can only be guessed at, though DeLancey Ferguson suggested (not unreasonably) some sexual scandal and referred to him as 'the eloquent but incontinent Greenfield'.[31]

As for Blair himself, he overlooked Robert's dreadful gaffe and continued to take an interest in his work. Blair never forgot that he had been responsible for giving James Macpherson the encouragement to persevere with *Ossian*, a fact to which he referred in a letter to Burns on 4 May 1787,[32] and he took upon himself the role of censor in the matter of Robert's latest productions. This was in reply to a letter (CL 288), written when Robert was on the point of leaving Edinburgh and thanking Blair for his kindness, patronage and friendship. During the early months of 1787 Robert had consulted Blair on a number of matters, and submitted to him copies of his latest works for criticism. Blair was reponsible (in part at least) for the exclusion of 'The Jolly Beggars' from the Edinburgh Edition.

Indeed, his criticism of this work seems to have been so trenchant that, in September 1793, when asked by George Thomson about this major work, Robert confessed, 'I have forgot the Cantata you allude to, as I kept no copy, & indeed did not know that it was in existence' (CL 644). The loss of a work of such importance would have been calamitous; as it was, another work submitted to Blair with the intriguing title of 'The Prophet and God's Complaint' has never been recovered. It was on the advice of Blair, however, that Robert altered the phrase 'tidings of salvation' to 'damnation' in 'The Holy Fair', revealing a pawky humour under the layers of pomposity.

Incidentally, although the cantata related to a supposed incident at Mauchline in 1785 and was largely written around that period, it seems probable that Robert reworked or refined portions of it a year later, in the early part of his first Edinburgh sojourn. In the second stanza of the cairds' song occur the lines:

> An by that stowp! my faith an houpe!
> And by that dear Kilbaigie!

Why this obscure Clackmannanshire distillery should have been singled out for mention has long been a mystery; but it may have been a sly reference to the trial of its proprietor James Stein, at the High Court on 4 December 1786, on a charge of attempting to bribe John Bonar, the Solicitor of the Excise no less. On 2 September Stein had taken breakfast with Bonar and complained bitterly of the hardship of the Scotch Distillery Act, recently passed. It was this iniquitous Act which inspired Robert to compose 'The Author's Earnest Cry and Prayer' (CW 174-9). After wailing about being harassed by the 'expectants' (junior Excise officers), Stein got up to leave, but as he did so he slipped a packet into Bonar's pocket, saying that it was a pair of gloves. Bonar, however, patted the packet and said that if it was what he thought it was, then Stein would be hearing more about the matter. Afterwards, Bonar opened the envelope and found £500 in banknotes, wrapped in a paper inscribed 'This is to be repeated once every year'. As a result, Stein was arraigned on a charge of bribery. He had the good fortune, however, to secure Henry Erskine as defending counsel. Harry exerted all his wit and eloquence to demonstrate how the new Act was unjust. Consequently, although the jury found that Stein had, in fact, given Bonar the money, the charge of bribery was 'not proven' and the defendant was discharged.[33]

Burns also risked giving offence to another learned divine. About 12 December 1786 Dr Blacklock wrote to his friend Lawrie saying that he had heard that 'Mr Burns is, and has been some time, in Edinburgh. This news I am sorry to have had at second hand; they would have come much more welcome from the bard's own mouth.' Presumably a few days later Dr Lawrie wrote to Robert to reproach him for being so remiss, and it appears that the poet made a point of visiting Blacklock shortly afterwards; but it was not until 5 February 1787 that he got around to writing back

(CL 263–4), by which time he could say with hand on heart that he had now seen Blacklock several times. 'In Dr Blacklock, whom I see very often, I have found what I would have expected in our friend, a clear head and an excellent heart.' Burns and Blacklock were to exchange verse-epistles in October 1789 (CW 370–2) but the only extant prose letter from Robert was written from Mauchline in November 1788 when he was on the point of leaving for Ellisland (CL 490–1). It seems likely, however, that other letters passed between them. In the verse-epistle Robert castigates Robert Heron (1764–1807), Hugh Blair's assistant, to whom he had apparently entrusted a letter for Blacklock which was never delivered, and in the letter of 1789 he mentions a previous letter of June 1789, 'but either it had not found you at all; or, what I dread more, it found you or Mrs Blacklock in too precarious a state of health & spirits, to take notice of an idle Packet.'

New friends of a completely different kind were the Duke and Duchess of Gordon. George Alexander, fourth Duke of Gordon (1745–1827) had, in 1767, taken as his wife Jane, the second daughter of Sir William Maxwell of Monreith. Jane was born in February 1746 to Sir William and his vivacious wife Magdalen Blair of Blair, in Hyndford's Close, Edinburgh, where Lady Maxwell had a second-floor apartment. Jane's elder sister Betty married Sir Thomas Wallace of Craigie, the eldest son of Mrs Dunlop of Dunlop. As teenagers, the Maxwell girls were high-spirited tomboys who often scandalised genteel Edinburgh society by their boisterous antics. On one memorable occasion Betty and Jane rode down the High Street on the backs of pigs, turned loose from a neighbouring enclosure. By the Duke of Gordon Jane had two sons and five daughters (who all made good marriages, three of them marrying the Dukes of Richmond, Manchester and Bedford, though Jane's plans to marry another daughter off to the prime minister, William Pitt, was foiled by her arch enemy, Henry Dundas). She was a celebrated beauty, as testified by the portrait painted by Reynolds. She was also noted for her business acumen, her ready wit and good nature as well as 'singular coarseness of speech'. In Edinburgh she was the leader of polite society and arbiter of fashion, but because of her unconventional, forthright manner she made many enemies who circulated malicious gossip and outrageous stories about her.[34] One of the milder and more publishable accounts of the duchess was contained in a letter written in February 1786 by James Drummond, a member of the Scottish Bar, to a friend in India:

> The good town is uncommonly crowded and splendid at present. The example of dissipation set by her Grace the Duchess of Gordon is far from showing vice her own image. It is really astonishing to think what effect a single person will have on public manners, when supported by high rank and great address. She is never absent from a public place, and the later the hour, so much the better. It is often four o'clock in the morning before she goes to bed, and she never requires more than five hours' sleep, Dancing, cards, and company occupy her whole time.[35]

272

Rumours of indiscretions, which ranged from the snide comment that at least one of her children was not the duke's bairn to the apparently unfounded (though still widely believed) tale that she rewarded each recruit to the newly raised Gordon Highlanders (1794) with a kiss, and the fact that she once confessed to Sir Walter Scott that Burns was the only man whose conversation carried her off her feet, have given rise to the *canard* that she had an affair 'of agricultural severity' with Burns in the winter of 1786-7;[36] but Jane was the same age as Jean Gardner – thirteen years older than Robert – and in the eighteenth century that was too large a gap to make a liaison at all likely.[37] One may be sure that, had Robert seduced – or been seduced by – the duchess he would have been unable to contain himself; but neither in letters to his closest confidants nor in his verses do we find the slightest hint of impropriety. Furthermore, I can trace no gossip that linked the names of Burns and the duchess in anything but the most innocuous of terms. Robert was introduced to her by Henry Erskine, to whom she was related. On 10 January 1787 Alicia Cockburn wrote:

> The town is at present agog with the ploughman poet, who receives adulation with native dignity, and is the very figure of his profession, strong and coarse, but has a most enthusiastic heart of love. He has seen Duchess Gordon and all the gay world: his favourite for looks and manners is Bess Burnet – no bad judge, indeed . . . The man will be spoiled, if he can spoil; but he keeps his simple manners, and is quite sober. No doubt he will be at the Hunters' Ball tomorrow, which has made all women and milliners mad. Not a gauze-cap under two guineas – many ten, twelve.[38]

If Glencairn provided an *entrée* to polite society, it was the Duchess of Gordon who ensured Robert's social success.

Henry Erskine, Dean of the Faculty of Advocates, was the same age as Jane. Connected with the Gordons by blood and the Cunninghams by marriage, Burns was introduced to him on 7 December 1786 by Dalrymple of Orangefield, at a meeting of the Canongate Kilwinning Lodge No. 2 where Erskine was Past Master. Among the other members of this lodge were William Maule of Panmure, Patrick Miller of Dalswinton, the High School's classics master William Nicol and the attorney Alexander Cunningham. All of them played some part in Burns's later career and even beyond, for Maule was to obtain an annuity of £50 for the poet's widow, while Miller was Robert's landlord at Ellisland; and Cunningham, the staunchest friend of all, took a leading role in the campaign to raise funds for the poet's family, and helped to secure the services of Dr Currie as biographer. No meeting of the lodge took place in January 1787, but the minutes of the meeting on 1 February record that Burns was entered as an apprentice:

> The R.W. Master having observed that Brother Burns was at present in the Lodge, who is well known as a great poetic writer, and for a late

publication of his works, which had been universally commended, submitted that he should be assumed a member of this Lodge, which was unanimously agreed to, and he was assumed accordingly.[39]

It is a popular myth in masonic circles that Robert was at the meeting of 1 March formally inaugurated as poet laureate of the lodge. In fact, the minute of that date does not mention him at all. The notion that he had, somehow, been appointed laureate of the lodge did not apparently materialise until 24 June 1802 on which date the lodge approved the purchase of four prints, one of which was an engraving by Paton Thomson of the Skirving head bearing the inscription 'Robert Burns, the Scottish Bard, Poet Laureat Lodge No. 2 Canongate Kilwinning'. There is no evidence, however, that the lodge claimed Burns as its laureate until 8 June 1815 when a subscription was started for the mausoleum of 'Robert Burns, who had been Poet Laureat to the Lodge'. The resolution to this effect was signed by Charles More who, as Depute Master, had signed the minute of the meeting of 1 February 1787 at which Burns had been affiliated. As More had an unbroken record of service from that time till 1815, he must have been in possession of the true facts. Moreover, in 1815 there were about a hundred gentlemen who had been members of the lodge since 1787, if not earlier. It might have been expected that some at least of them would have been present on the evening when Burns's laureateship was formally asserted, yet nobody appears to have dissented. Again, some of these men were still alive as late as 1835 when James Hogg was elected to succeed Burns as poet laureate, on which occasion Hogg expressly acknowledged the compliment, and the lodge toasted Burns as 'the last Poet Laureate of the Lodge'.

It seems as if, the later the recollection, the more convinced people were that some kind of laureate ceremony had taken place. Thus in 1845 William Petrie was able to state with conviction that he had been present on 1 March 1787 when Burns was inaugurated, and supplied details to Stewart Watson who painted the picture entitled 'The Inauguration of Robert Burns as Poet-Laureate of Lodge Canongate Kilwinning, 1 March 1787' which hangs on the wall of the Grand Lodge, Edinburgh. Watson, born in 1800, was entered in Canongate Kilwinning in 1828 and must have known many other members who could recall the events of 1787.

The principal grounds on which the tradition has been assailed are the absence of any record in the minutes, and the absence of any mention of the fact by Burns. The defence is that the minutes were very carelessly kept at the time, and that the secretary took more pains to record formalities than exceptional occurrences; and that, as Burns did not mention even his affiliation to the lodge, it is not surprising that there is no allusion to the laureateship in any of his extant letters. On the other hand, such a singular honour touching on his poetical skills would, I am sure, have occasioned some epistolary comment from Robert had it taken place.[40]

It is also possible that the notion of the laureateship had grown out of another, unrelated incident. Two days after Robert arrived in Edinburgh there had taken place a Grand Visitation to mark St Andrew's Day. All the masonic lodges in Edinburgh, with representatives from every part of the country, assembled in the New Church at midday to witness the election of Francis Charteris of Amisfield as Grand Master, and other office-bearers in the Grand Lodge of Scotland.[41] There is no record of Burns having been present on that occasion, but a little over a month later, on Friday, 12 January 1787, Robert attended a meeting at St Andrew's lodge, visited by Grand Master Charteris and all the Grand Lodge of Scotland, accompanied by Alexander Fergusson of Craigdarroch, Provincial Grand Master of the Southern District (and subsequently a close friend of the poet in his Dumfriesshire period). A full account of this auspicious meeting was in due course relayed by Robert to Ballantine on 14 January (CL 100-1):

> The meeting was most numerous and elegant; all the different Lodges about town were present in all their pomp. The Grand Master who presided with great solemnity, and honor to himself as a Gentleman and a Mason, among other general toasts gave 'Caledonia and Caledonia's Bard, brother B—' which rung through the whole Assembly with multi-plied honors and repeated acclamations. As I had no idea such a thing would happen, I was downright thunder struck, and trembling in every nerve made the best return in my power. Just as I finished, some of the Grand Officers said so loud as I could hear, with a most comforting accent, 'Very well indeed,' which set me something to rights again.

On 8 March 1787 Robert wrote to Gavin Hamilton (CL 67-8) and men-tioned that his songs 'The Lass o Ballochmyle' (CW 199) and 'Young Peggy' (CW 125), honourng Wilhelmina Alexander and Peggy Kennedy respectively, had been:

> tried by a jury of the Literati, and found defamatory libels against the fastidious Powers of Poesy and Taste; and the Author forbid to print them under pain of forfeitures of character.– I cannot help almost shed-ding a tear to the memory of two Songs that cost me some pains, and that I valued a good deal, but I must submit.

Some time previously, probably at the end of December, Robert had written to Henry Erskine (CL 224) enclosing his ballad on the American War, 'When Guilford good' (CW 72-4). Though composed in 1784 shortly after the war ended, Robert had not included it in the Kilmarnock Edition as he was unsure of it, suspecting that his political tenets 'such as they are, may be rather heretical in the opinion of my best friends'. Glen-cairn, whom Robert first consulted, seemed to think that the piece was fit to print, but thought that, as a precaution, a copy should be submitted to Erskine for his comments. Erskine's response is not recorded, but as the ballad was included in the first Edinburgh Edition it clearly passed muster.

While Burns sought such legal advice, and was also prepared to submit his work to literati such as Hugh Blair and his patroness and mother-confessor Mrs Dunlop (even if he was selective in the advice which he accepted), he also had to endure the well-meaning if patronising and ignorant advice thrust upon him by his social superiors. In this category the prime example was provided by David Erskine, eleventh Earl of Buchan. The elder brother of the Dean of the Faculty was a man of mediocre abilities, vain, eccentric and parsimonious, yet keen to be regarded as a patron of literature. On 1 February he wrote to Robert with unsolicited advice which he thought his rank entitled him to offer to a mere 'ploughing poet':

> I have redd (*sic*) with great pleasure several of your poems, and have subscribed in Lady Glencairn's list for six copies of your book for myself, and two for Lady Buchan.
>
> These little doric pieces of yours in our provincial dialect are very beautiful, but you will soon be able to diversify your language, your Rhyme and your subject, and then you will have it in your power to show the extent of your genius and to attempt works of greater magnitude, variety and importance. Take care, however, that you do not suffer the wings of your Pegasus to be sullied or curtailed by the grosser or more polished invaders of your genuine Invention, but let him fly with the rein, but not the curb. Keep your Eye upon Parnassus and drink deep of the fountains of Helicon, but beware of the Joys that is dedicated to the Jolly God of wine.

There was more in the same highfalutin vein, ending 'May the Apollo of my Nypa who sits on the fork of Eildon enable you to produce the genuine offspring of Genius, sentiment, and skill – never to die'.[42] Robert replied on 7 February (CL 266–7) in similar style. We may assume that he had his tongue in his cheek as he guyed Lord Buchan's inane pomposities in the form of a rhetorical sermon delivered against himself by 'a long-visaged, dry, moral-looking Phantom'. He drew this screed to a close with:

> This, my Lord, is an unanswerable harangue. I must return to my rustic station, and in my wonted way woo my rustic Muse at the Ploughtail. Still, my Lord, while the drops of life, while the sound of Caledonia, warm my heart; gratitude to that dear-priz'd country in which I boast my birth, and gratitude to those her distinguished Names who have honored me so much with their Approbation and Patronage, shall, while stealing through my humble Shades, ever distend my bosom, and at times, as now, draw forth the swelling tear.

Lord Buchan, however, was responsible for touching 'the darling chord of my heart when you advise me to fire my Muse at Scottish story and Scottish scenes'. With the toast to 'Brother Burns, Caledonia's Bard' still ringing in his ears, Robert needed little encouragement of this sort. From this time probably dates his hankering to embark on a tour of Scotland. For the moment, however, he was too preoccupied with work on his Edinburgh Edition and enjoying the continuing adulation of polite society. No one made a greater impression upon him at this time than the beautiful and graceful Elizabeth Burnet, youngest daughter of Lord Monboddo

(1766-90). When she succumbed to tuberculosis at Braid Farm near Edinburgh some three years after Robert first met her, he was moved to compose his 'Elegy on the Late Miss Burnet of Monboddo' (CW 416). Earlier, she was singled out for mention in 'Address to Edinburgh' (CW 262-4), an uncomfortable ode, composed in the stiff Augustan English favoured by poets of the late eighteenth century.[43]

This was one of the rather forced pieces which Robert produced in response to the advice of the literati. Perhaps there was some substance to the laureateship, for this long poem has all the hallmarks of those odes commissioned for specific public occasions, although it was composed soon after arriving in Edinburgh, as a copy of it was sent to William Chalmers of Ayr on 27 December (CL 218-19):

> Fair B— is the heavenly Miss Burnet, daughter of lord Monbodo (*sic*), at whose house I have had the honor to be more than once.- There has not been any thing nearly like her, in all the combinations of Beauty, Grace and Goodness the great Creator has formed, since Milton's Eve on the first day of her existence.

Less generous witnesses recount that she had exceedingly bad teeth, but concealed this unsightly blemish by opening her mouth as little as possible.

In extolling the various wonders of the metropolis, Burns strove self-consciously to 'fire his muse at Scottish scenes' as Buchan later exhorted; but even Robert had to admit that the result was second-rate. Similarly, he tried to repay the kindness of Lord Glencairn as only he could, in poetry; but the high-flown verses which he felt suitable to a person of Glencairn's exalted rank were not only fulsome but probably embarrassing to their recipient. On 13 January 1787 Robert wrote to Glencairn (CL 226-7) enclosing the verses, saying that:

> I intended to have written [them] below a Picture or Profile of your Lord-ship, could I have been so happy as to procure one with any thing of a likeness.- As I will soon return to my shades, I wanted to have something like a material object for my gratitude: I wanted to have it in my power to say to a Friend, there is my noble Patron, my generous Benefactor!

He then asked for permission to publish the verses, concluding,

> Almost every Poet has celebrated his Patrons, particularly when they were Names dear to Fame, and illustrious in their Country; permit me then, my Lord, if you think the lines have intrinsic merit, to tell the World how much I have the honor to be Your Lordship's highly indebted, and ever grateful, humble servant.

There is no record of Glencairn's reaction; but as the verses remained unpublished until the Chambers edition of 1851 we may suppose that the earl tactfully drew Robert aside and gently dissuaded him. At any rate, Glencairn's refusal did not provoke the same bitter response from the poet which Wilhelmina Alexander's silence roused. During his six months in Edinburgh, in fact, Robert produced very little new poetry, and even less that he considered worthy of immediate publication. Three stanzas to Susan Logan, sister of William Logan of Park, were inscribed in a copy of *The Minstrel* by James Beattie which Robert sent her as a New Year's gift on 1 January 1787 (CW 267). A mock elegy on the death of Robert Ruisseaux (CW 268), a French translation of his own surname, also belongs to this period and reflected his ambivalent attitude towards his temporary fame. There were the lines to Miss Isabella McLeod of Raasay (CW 273), to whose family Robert may have been introduced by Gavin Hamilton; and there were the extempore epigrams (CW 273) which were dashed off during a visit to the Court of Session to hear the case of Campbell v. Montgomerie, when Robert produced lightning sketches in verse describing the Lord Advocate, Sir Ilay Campbell, and his adversary, Harry Erskine, both of whom were friends and patrons of the poet. Robert's interest in this case arose from the fact that his friend, Captain James Montgomerie, had run off with a Mrs Campbell who bore him a child in 1784. Maxwell Campbell, the plaintiff, sued for damages without divorcing his wife (whose estates and property he would thereby have lost). When the case went against him the gallant captain fled to the West Indies, that last refuge of so many Scottish scoundrels and reprobates of the period. Robert must have viewed the proceedings with mixed feelings. In his letter to Gavin Hamilton (CL 67–8) on 8 March, the day after the case was tried, Robert commented:

> Poor Captain Montgomerie is cast.– Yesterday it was tried whether the husband could proceed against the unfortunate Lover without first divorcing his wife, and their Gravities on the bench were unanimously of opinion that Maxwell may prosecute for damages directly, and need not divorce his wife at all if he pleases . . . O all ye Powers of love unfortunate and friendless woe, pour the balm of sympathising pity on the grief-torn, tender heart of the hapless Fair One!

Two verse epistles belong to this period. At this time Robert received a great deal of what would now be called fan mail, and a costly exercise this must have been in an age when letters were usually sent unpaid, leaving the recipient to pay the postage. Robert was inundated with letters couched in indifferent verse and he must often have regretted the craze for poetic epistles which he had unwittingly triggered off. But amid this welter of doggerel the lines from Mrs Elizabeth Scott of Wauchope near Jedburgh stood out, and Robert was inspired to reply in similar vein. Mrs Scott was a niece of Alicia Cockburn, herself a famous poetess, and she was impelled to write to Burns after borrowing a copy of the Kilmarnock Poems in December 1786. Her epistle from 'The Guidwife of Waukhope-House to Robert Burns, the Ayrshire Bard'[44] provoked his response the following month (CW 271–2). A brief note from John McAdam of Craigengillan is now believed to have been written in March 1787, rather than late 1786, as McAdam and his family appear only in the addenda to the subscription list published in the Edinburgh Edition. Robert himself annotated his rhyming reply (CW 274) to 1786, when he inserted a copy in the Glenriddell MS, but this may have been due to faulty memory.

A new departure for Robert, however, was the Prologue (CW 275-6) which he wrote for the actor William Woods (1751-1802) on 16 April 1787, his benefit night at the Theatre Royal. The Scottish Roscius, Woods was the leading actor of the Edinburgh stage for the last three decades of his life, and very much at the height of his fame and popularity in the period of Robert's first visit. Woods had begun his dramatic career in Southampton but moved to Edinburgh in 1772 and remained there ever since. He was a close friend and champion of Robert Fergusson, and it was this that drew Burns to him. In the Prologue, Robert was astute enough to include flattering references to Harley, hero of Henry Mackenzie's *Man of Feeling*, and to John Home's epic tragedy *Douglas* which had roused considerable patriotic pride at the time of its début in 1756, memorable for the cry from the audience 'Whaur's your Wullie Shakespeare noo?' The play on the occasion of the actor's benefit night was, in fact, Shakespeare's *Merry Wives of Windsor*. The line 'It needs no Siddons' power in Southern's song' alluded to the famous actress Sarah Siddons who had made her Edinburgh début in 1784 and had returned the following year, on both occasions taking the city by storm. When she next appeared on the Edinburgh stage, in 1788, she took the role of Lady Randolph in *Douglas*, a perennial favourite with Scottish audiences.

William Woods is said to have taken Robert Fergusson regularly to the theatre and given him a free seat. Whether Burns was similarly honoured is not recorded, but it would be true to say that he was introduced to the pleasures of theatrical performances at this time, a taste which he later developed enthusiastically at Dumfries where he took a leading role in the foundation of the Theatre Royal in that town. Whether an interest in the drama was purely passive at this period, or whether Robert now felt his first hankering to write for the theatre, is debatable. To be sure, 'The Jolly Beggars', with its theatrical possibilities, showed what Robert could do; but Dr Blair had effectively nipped that in the bud.

Robert's profound admiration for the works of Robert Fergusson (1750-74) was matched only by the burning sense of indignation which he felt at the way the wretched poet had been treated. Allan Cunningham, exercising his imagination to the full, recounted how Burns, soon after his arrival in Edinburgh, had made a pilgrimage to the Canongate kirkyard and had prostrated himself on the grave of Fergusson and kissed the sod. The truth, however, appears to have been more prosaic. Not until some time in February 1787 did Robert make enquiries regarding the grave of 'my elder brother in misfortune, / By far my elder brother in the muse', only to discover that Fergusson was buried in an unmarked grave. His poems had been published in 1773, only a year before his death in the Edinburgh madhouse. Eight years later, during his sojourn in Irvine, Burns had stumbled upon this slim volume, at a time when he, too, was almost engulfed by despair. Fergusson's mastery of the vernacular inspired Burns to even greater heights, but both in the structure and the subject matter of his poems Robert was considerably influenced by his predecessor. He was not slow to acknowledge his debt to Fergusson, notably in the 'Epistle to William Simpson' (CW 107) and the 'Apostrophe to Fergusson' (CW 269) which he inscribed in a copy of Fergusson's poems which he presented to the poetess Rebekah Carmichael on 19 March 1787; but his gratitude took a more practical form when he wrote to the bailies of the Canongate on 6 February (CL 265), seeking permission to erect a headstone over Fergusson's grave. The bailies forwarded his request to the managers of the Canongate Kirk and this was duly noted in their minutes of 22 February:

> Thereafter the said managers, in consideration of the laudable and disinterested motion of Mr Burns, and the propriety of his request, did, and hereby do, unanimously, grant power and liberty to the said Robert Burns, to erect a headstone at the grave of the said Robert Fergusson, and to keep up and preserve the same to his memory in all time coming.[45]

About April 1789 Robert wrote to Peter Stuart, the founder and editor of the *Star*, London's first evening newspaper. Peter's elder brother Charles had been a school-fellow of Fergusson and he himself was an ardent devotee of his poetry. After launching the *Star* in May 1788 he offered him payment for any contributions he cared to make. He showed Burns 'repeated instances of kindness' which Robert belatedly acknowledged in his letter (CL 520) which enclosed the lines which he composed for Fergusson's tombstone. Chambers-Wallace[46] assigned this undated letter to February 1787 on the strength of its contents, but as it included the text of the actual stone, it clearly belongs to a much later date. In fact, exactly five years elapsed before Robert settled his account with his near namesake, the Edinburgh architect Robert Burn, who designed the stone and superintended its erection. In a letter to Peter Hill on 5 February 1792 (CL 321) Robert gave instructions for Burn's bill to be paid, adding:

> He was two years in erecting it, after I commissioned him for it; & I have been two years paying him, after he sent me his account; so he & I are quits. – He had the hardiesse to ask me interest on the sum; but considering that the money was due by one Poet, for putting a tomb-stone over another, he may, with grateful surprise, thank Heaven that ever he saw a farthing of it.

Two stanzas in addition to the lines actually inscribed on the stone were subsequently inserted in the *Second Commonplace Book*. A further two quatrains on Fergusson (CW 270) were written by Robert in a copy of *The World*, a periodical to which he subscribed for five years (1785–90), but it was not actually published (in the *Scots Magazine*) until November 1803. Robert threw off some epigrams, one on James Elphinstone's translation of Martial and another addressed to an unnamed painter who was working on a picture of Jacob's dream (CW 270). All of these poems were written in standard English and nowadays rank among the least consequential of his *oeuvre*.

On the other hand, the Edinburgh period was notable for three works in the vernacular. John Richmond[47] was the source of the story that 'Address to a Haggis' (CW 264) allegedly originated at a dinner held at the home of the Kilmarnock solicitor, David Shaw, in Craigie Kirkdyke at the end of the 1785 harvest. Burns sat down in the company of five lawyers at what was then constituted the Haggis Club. Matthew Dickie of Edinburgh was preses (chairman) and asked Robert to say a grace, but instead he addressed the haggis which was the main dish of the evening. Another tradition maintains that the closing stanza was declaimed extempore at a dinner at the home of John Morrison, a Mauchline cabinet-maker, shortly before Robert left Ayrshire, but the rest of the poem was written soon after he arrived in Edinburgh, for the complete text appeared in the *Caledonian Mercury* of 20 December 1786 – the first time that any poem of Burns was first published in a newspaper. Haggis, contrary to the modern view which regards it as 'traditional' fare, was then something of a novelty (as Richmond pointed out) and its recipe first appeared earlier that year in *Cookery and Pastry* by Susanna MacIver.

Finally, two songs belong to this period. Hitherto Robert had composed few lyrics, although those include several which are sung to this day and hinted at the power and range to come. In 'And Maun I Still on Menie Doat' (CW 266-7) Robert took an ancient chorus and added seven verses; but although the chorus contains several vernacular words, the song itself was only lightly sprinkled with Scotticisms – not enough to mar its Augustan elegance, but sufficient to endear it to English singers for whom Scots songs were then very fashionable on account of their slightly exotic flavour. By contrast, 'Rantin, Rovin Robin' (CW 267-8) was liberally peppered with Scots words and phrases. It is thought that this autobiographical song was composed in a light-hearted celebration of Robert's twenty-eighth birthday on 25 January 1787, but not jotted down in the *Second Commonplace Book* until about 9 April. Interestingly, the original version was merely titled 'A Fragment' to the tune 'Daintie Davie', and it was 'Davie' rather than 'Robin' who was named in each punch line. Otherwise the text of this draft followed closely on that of the song as it was finally published.[48]

The closing stanza of this song had the gossip prophesying Robert's easy way with women – 'I doubt you gar / The bonie lasses lie aspar [legs apart]'. Remarkably little is known of his amorous adventures in this period. It was not until 1 December 1786 that Elizabeth Paton finally accepted his settlement of her claim, and the memory of Margaret Campbell and her tragic death must still have been seared into his mind. In the circumstances one might have expected Robert to concentrate on cultivating his new-found contacts with a view to furthering his Excise career and getting his poems before a wider audience. He had visited the home of Lord Monboddo 'more than once' and his captivation with Elizabeth Burnet was widely known (presumably also to Monboddo himself), but although by the standards of the time Bess was unconventional – she rode every-where with her father and thought nothing of commuting in the saddle between Edinburgh and their country estate in Kincardineshire – she occupied a position in society so exalted that Robert could never have dared to woo her. Answering an invitation to dine, he wrote to Lord Mon-boddo on Saturday, 30 December, enclosing the manuscripts of three (unnamed) songs 'by way of a peace-offering' for having neglected to send Miss Eliza a song which she had wished to have. Although couched in tones of easy familiarity, there was nothing in this note to hint at anything serious between the poet and the society beauty.

The earliest letter of the Edinburgh period to hint at his emotional state was written on 7 January 1787 to Gavin Hamilton (CL 67). The letter itself has long since vanished. When Robert Chambers published it in 1838 it had been reduced to a fragment which looks as if only the bottom half of a sheet had survived. Probably the upper half had come adrift through frequent folding and unfolding, rather than as a result of any deliberate concealment. Tantalisingly, the first recorded portion of this letter began at a point where Robert was obviously confiding to Gavin that, deep down, he still yearned for Jean Armour:

> . . . To tell the truth among friends, I feel a miserable blank in my heart, with want of her, and I don't think I shall ever meet with so delicious an armful again. She has her faults; and so have you and I; and so has every body.
>
> > Their tricks and craft hae put me daft;
> >   They've ta'en me in and a' that;
> > But clear your decks, and here's the Sex,
> >   I like the jads for a' that.
> > For a' that and a' that,
> > And twice as muckle's a' that . . .[49]

It seems probable that this quotation from his unpublished cantata had been continued overleaf, but the verso of this half sheet concluded:

> I have met with a very pretty girl, a Lothian farmer's daughter, whom I have almost persuaded to accompany me to the west country, should I ever return to settle there. By the bye, a Lothian farmer is about an Ayr-shire squire of the lower kind; and I had a most delicious ride from Leith to her house yesternight in a hackney-coach, with her brother and two sisters, and brother's wife. We had dined all together at a common friend's house in Leith, and danced, drank, and sang till late enough. The night was dark, the claret had been good, and I thirsty . . .

Chambers was unable to identify the young lady, though Snyder was 'vir-tually certain' that the woman in mind was Margaret Chalmers.[50] How such a deduction was arrived at is impossible to say; but Margaret's antecedents do not answer the description given in Robert's letter. Quite apart from the fact that Margaret had been born at Fingland,

Kirkcudbrightshire, and that latterly her father had tenanted a farm near Mauchline – hardly the Lothians – there is also the inescapable fact that the woman Robert described to Gavin was someone unknown to the latter, whereas Margaret Chalmers and Gavin Hamilton were actually related, her mother and Gavin's stepmother being sisters. To this day, therefore, the identity of the Lothian farmer's daughter remains a complete mystery. On the strength of this tentative identification, however, DeLancey Ferguson proposed Margaret Chalmers as the recipient of the letter (known only from an undated draft) addressed 'My Dr Countrywoman' (CL 230). In this letter Robert wrote:

> I know you will laugh at it, when I tell you that your Piano and you together have play'd the deuce somehow, about my heart.– I was once a zealous Devotee to your Sex, but you know the black story at home. My breast has been widowed these many months, and I thought myself proof against the fascinating witchcraft; but I am afraid you will 'feelingly convince me what I am.'– I say, I am afraid, because I am not sure what is the matter with me.– I have one miserable bad symptom: when you whisper, or look kindly to another, it gives me a draught of damnation.– I have a kind of wayward wish to be with you ten minutes by yourself; though, what I would say, Heaven above knows, for I am sure, I know not.– I have no formed design in all this; but just in the nakedness of my heart write you down a meer matter-of-fact story.– You may perhaps give yourself airs of distance on this, and that will completely cure me; but I wish you would not; just let us meet if you wish in the old, beaten way of friendship.

Many years later, Margaret Chalmers confided to the poet Thomas Campbell that Burns had once proposed marriage to her; but she had gently pointed out that she was already engaged to Lewis Hay, whom she eventually married in December 1788. Certainly this letter (if, indeed, it was intended for her) shows that Robert was madly in love with her; but their relationship subsequently matured into a close friendship in which Burns treated her as a confidante and intellectual equal. It only terminated on her marriage to the banker Lewis Hay; Robert had no wish to share his confidences with a woman who might then tell all to her husband.

Even this attribution is not definite, for the musical allusion seems to apply just as well to Christina Lawrie. On 5 February 1787 Robert wrote to the Revd. George Lawrie (CL 263), 'By far the most agreable hours I spend in Edinburgh must be placed to the account of Miss Lowrie (*sic*) and her Piano forte'. This seems to be borne out by brief notes which Robert wrote to Archibald Lawrie, Christina's brother. One which belongs to this period is quite revealing:

> As tonight the Grand Master and Lodge of Masons appear at the Theatre in form, I am determined to go to the play.– I am afraid it will be impossible to form a Partie with our female friends for this night, but I shall call on you a few minutes before the Theatre opens, when if Miss Lawrie can I shall be very happy; if not, I suppose you will have no objection to take a seat in the Pit with toujours le votre R. Burns.

This implies that Robert was then courting Christina. Archibald, then a divinity student at the University, was only eighteen at this time so it is not known whether his 'female friend' was Anne Adair, whom he married in 1794; but Anne was the sister of Dr James McKittrick Adair who accompanied Robert on his Stirlingshire tour and who wooed and won Charlotte Hamilton, Gavin's step-sister and the closest confidante of Margaret Chalmers. At any rate, it illustrates the closely-woven web of Robert's intimate friends of approximately his own age, if rather above his rank in life.

A letter to James Dalrymple of Orangefield in February (CL 269–70), in reply to a rhyming epistle, contains an intriguing paragraph:

> For the blind, mischief-making little urchin of a Deity, you mention, he and I have been sadly at odds ever since some dog tricks he play'd me not half a century ago.– I have compromised matters with his godship of late by uncoupling my heart and fancy, for a slight chase, after a certain Edinburgh Belle.– My devotions proceed no farther than a forenoon's walk, a sentimental conversation, now and then a squeeze of the hand or interchanging an oeillade, and when peculiar good humor and sequestered propriety allow –
>
> – 'Brethren, salute one another with a holy kiss,' –
>
> Paul

Whether the Edinburgh Belle and the Lothian farmer's daughter were one and the same is not known. Piecing together the chronology of Robert's movements and activities in Edinburgh, I am left with the conclusion that his love life was, in fact, at an uncharacteristically low ebb. When he was smitten momentarily by Isabella Lindsay during his Border tour, he noted in his journal, 'My heart is thawed into melting pleasure after being so long frozen up in the Greenland bay of indifference, amid the noise and nonsense of Edinburgh'.

On 11 January 1787 Robert wrote to John Mackenzie (CL 114). In passing he mentioned Sir John Whitefoord's son John who had just become engaged to Miss McAdam of Craigengillan. 'Between friends, John is desperately in for it there; and I am afraid will be desperate indeed.' Robert breakfasted with Lord Maitland and his brother, sons of the Earl of Lauderdale: 'They are exceedingly easy, accessible agreable fellows; and seemingly pretty clever'.

Early in January Robert initiated a correspondence with Dr John Moore which was to have immense significance for future students and biographers of the poet. Born at Stirling in 1729, John was the son of the Revd. Charles Moore. He was educated at Glasgow Grammar School and the University where he studied medicine. In 1747 he became surgeon's mate in the 54th (Duke of Argyll's) regiment and served in the Low Countries till peace was secured in 1748. He then went to Paris where he continued his medical studies. In 1770 he graduated MD at Glasgow and from 1772 till 1778 was tutor and travelling companion to two successive young Dukes of Hamilton. In 1778 he settled in London where he continued to practise medicine till his death in 1802.

In 1779 he published his two-volume *View of Society and Manners in France, Switzerland and Germany*, followed two years later by a further two volumes devoted to Italy. Among his other publications were *Medical Sketches* (1786) and a novel entitled *Zeluco*, a bestseller which Burns hailed enthusiastically as 'a glorious story'. In the autumn of 1786 his long-time friend Mrs Dunlop sent him one of the copies of the Kilmarnock Edition which she had recently obtained from the author. Moore was intrigued and interested, but rather than write to the poet direct he replied to Mrs Dunlop, asking her to tell Burns to get in touch. Robert delayed writing to the great man, telling Mrs Dunlop on 15 January 1787 (CL 132):

> I wished to have written to Dr Moore before I wrote to you; but though, every day since I received yours of Dec. 30, the idea, the wish to write to him, has constantly pressed on my thoughts, yet I could not for my soul set about it. I know his fame and his character, and I am one of 'the sons of little men.' To write him a mere matter-of-fact letter, like a merchant's order, would be disgracing the little character I have; and to write the author of *The View of Society and Manners*, a letter of sentiment – I declare every artery runs cold at the thought. I shall try, however, to write to him tomorrow or next day.

Robert was as good as his word, and despatched a letter to Moore a day or two later (CL 246–7), thanking him for his criticisms, relayed by Mrs Dunlop, but regretting that they had arrived too late for incorporation in the forthcoming Edinburgh Edition. Robert had an incredibly inflated notion of Moore's literary standing, but fortunately chose in the end to ignore the good doctor's advice, well-meaning but utterly mistaken as it was. Moore replied on 23 January, urging Burns to give up writing in the Scottish dialect and concentrate on standard English, producing something like Thomson's *Seasons*, only livelier. Helen Maria Williams, three years Robert's junior, was employed by Moore as his amanuensis, but she was an aspiring poetess. On reading Burns's poem 'To a Mountain Daisy' (CW 203), she was inspired to compose a sonnet addressed to the poet, containing the memorable lines which give a flavour of its high-flown sentiment:

> Scotia! from rude afflictions shield thy Bard,
> His Heav'n taught numbers Fame herself will guard.

The doctor forwarded the poem and Robert responded courteously in a letter to Moore on 23 April (CL 247–8), expressing the hope that he would probably endeavour to return her poetic compliment in kind, though he never did.

The one good and lasting thing to come out of this epistolary association (for they never met) was the long Autobiographical Letter, written late in

July 1787 and despatched from Mauchline on 2 August. Why Moore should have been singled out for this detailed and, at times, extremely candid, self-assessment is a mystery, for the correspondence was still in its infancy. Indeed, although Burns and Moore continued to exchange letters from time to time over the ensuing four years, and Moore subsequently presented copies of *View of Society and Manners* and *Zeluco* to the poet, there were only four other letters from Robert in all. His diffidence, after unburdening himself in the Autobiographical Letter, seems to have been summed up in the very next letter of the series, written from Ellisland on 4 January 1789:

> As often as I think of writing to you, which has been three or four times every week these six months, it gives me something like the idea of an ordinary sized Statue offering at a conversation with the Rhodian Colossus that my mind misgives me; and the affair always miscarries somewhere between Purpose and Resolve . . .

Although the correspondence fizzled out in February 1791, contact was maintained indirectly through Mrs Dunlop. It was through Moore, incidentally, that Dr James Currie, Burns's first editor and full-length biographer, was introduced to the poet's works, and Captain Graham Moore, RN, the doctor's son, was the dedicatee of Currie's 1800 edition.

It was also in January 1787 that Burns made the acquaintance of Robert Ainslie (1766–1838), then completing his articled clerkship in the law office of Samuel Mitchelson in Carrubber's Close on the north side of the High Street. In later life Ainslie became a Writer to the Signet and an elder of the Kirk whose chief pastime was writing theological treatises; but in 1787 he was just turned twenty-one and 'as thoughtless and light-hearted as a writer's apprentice could well be'.[51] He was to become Robert's most trusted confidant, and the recipient of letters which usually showed the poet in a playful mood. Unfortunately, some of them also reveal Robert in a singularly unattractive light. For allowing these letters to be published Ainslie has earned the opprobrium of Burns devotees, who chose to overlook the fact that perhaps the letters ought never to have been written in the first place. It was Ainslie who accompanied Robert on the first part of his Border tour in May 1787. When Ainslie had to return to his studies in Edinburgh Burns missed him sorely. 'I have not had one hearty mouthful of laughter since that merry-melancholy moment we parted,' Burns wrote to him later (CL 327). The nature of their relationship was put succinctly in another letter, written from Mauchline on 23 July 1787 (CL 328):

> There is one thing for which I set great store by you as a friend, and it is this – that I have not a friend upon earth, besides yourself, to whom I can talk nonsense without forfeiting some degree of his esteem. Now, to one like me, who never cares for speaking anything else but nonsense, such a friend as you is an invaluable treasure. I was never a rogue, but have been

a fool all my life; and, in spite of all my endeavours, I see now plainly that I never shall be wise. Now it rejoices my heart to have met with such a fellow as you, who, though you are not just such a hopeless fool as I, yet I trust you will never listen so much to the temptations of the devil, as to grow so very wise that you will in the least disrespect an honest fellow because he is a fool. In short, I have set you down as the staff of my old age, when the whole list of my friends will, after a decent share of pity, have forgot me.

Meanwhile work on the proposed volume of poems went ahead at a cracking pace. In a letter to Ballantine on 14 January (CL 101) Robert said, 'I have this day corrected my 152d page', but it was not until 22 March that he was able to announce to Mrs Dunlop, in a lengthy postscript (CL 135):

> I have today corrected the last proof sheet of my poems and have now only the Glossary and subscribers names to print. Printing this last is much against my will, but some of my friends whom I do not chuse to thwart will have it so.– I have both a second and a third Edition as the second was begun with too small a number of copies.– The whole I have printed is three thousand.– Would the profits of that afford it, with rapture I would take your hint of a military life, as the most congenial to my feelings and situation of any other, but 'what is wanting cannot be numbered'.

Previously Mrs Dunlop had suggested an army career, if he could raise the money to purchase a commission. The military life was a recurring fantasy of Robert's, but earlier in the same letter he said, 'I guess that I shall clear between two and three hundred pounds by my Authorship; with that sum I intend, so far as I may be said to have any intention, to return to my old acquaintance, the plough, and, if I can meet with a lease by which I can live, to commence Farmer.' But the truth was that Robert could not make up his mind what to do, and for the moment he was content to drift along, enjoying the sights, sounds and sensations of the capital, and concentrating on seeing his poems through the press. In answer to Mrs Dunlop, he wrote, 'You kindly interest yourself in my future views and prospects; there I can give you no light'. The passage which ensued voiced Robert's innermost ambitions, but his innate hard-headedness shone through:

> The appellation of, a Scotch Bard, is by far my highest pride; to continue to deserve it is my most exalted ambition. – Scottish scenes, and Scottish story are the themes I could wish to sing.– I have no greater, no dearer aim than to have it in my power, unplagued with the routine of business, for which Heaven knows I am unfit enough, to make leisurely pilgrimages through Caledonia; to sit on the fields of her battles; to wander on the romantic banks of her rivers; and to muse by the stately towers or venerable ruins, once the honored abodes of her heroes.–
> But these are all Utopian ideas: I have dallied long enough with life; 'tis time to be in earnest.– I have a fond, aged Mother to care for; and some other bosom-ties, perhaps equally tender.– Where the Individual only

287

suffers by the consequences of his own thoughtlessness, indolence or folly, he may be excusable; nay shining abilities, and some of the nobler virtues may half sanctify the character; but where God and Nature have entrusted the welfare of others to his care, those whose weal or woe must depend upon his, where the trust is sacred and the ties are dear, that man must be far gone in unfeeling selfishness, or strangely lost to reflection and thought, whom those connections will not rouse to active attention and serious resolve.

Incredibly, the postscript quoted earlier was not published till 1898,[52] but it solves the mystery of the numerous discrepancies in the Edinburgh Edition, of which the most glaring occurred in 'Address to a Haggis', with the correct form 'skinking' and the much less common error 'stinking'. The correct version appeared in the first state, produced in an edition variously estimated at 1,500 or 2,000. Smellie had only a finite quantity of type, and as one part was set and printed, the type was broken up and distributed for the setting of the next part. The printer had got as far as the end of signature Mm before it was realised that the number printed was not sufficient to cope with all the subscriptions, so Smellie was compelled to reset the first half of the text (A-Ii and Ll–Mm). Because of the haste with which the second impression of 1,000 or 1,500 was set and rushed through the press a number of errors escaped the eye of the proof-reader, probably Robert himself. No mention of these production problems leaked out, and so far as the public were concerned there was only one Edinburgh Edition, released on 17 April.

Part of the problem was Robert's own relative inexperience. The printer's son Alexander vividly remembered the poet's visits to the composing room:

> Burns would walk up and down the room three or four times, cracking a whip which he carried, to the no small surprise of the men. He paid no attention to any of his own *copy* that might be in hand, but looked at any other which he saw lying in the cases. One day he asked a man how many languages he was acquainted with. 'Indeed, sir,' replied the man, 'I've enough ado wi' my *ain*.' Burns remarked that behind there was one of his companions setting up a Gaelic Bible, and another composing from a Hebrew Grammar. 'These two,' said the compositor, 'are the greatest dolts in the house.' Burns seemed amused by the remark, and said he would make a note of it.
>
> There was a particular stool in the office which Burns uniformly occupied while correcting his proof-sheets; as he would not sit on any other, it always bore the name of Burns's Stool . . . At this time Sir John Dalrymple was printing in Mr Smellie's office an *Essay on the Properties of Coal Tar*. One day it happened that Sir John occupied the stool when Burns came into the correcting-room looking for his favourite seat. It was known that what Burns wanted was the stool; but before saying anything to Sir John on the subject, Burns was requested to walk into the composing-room. The opportunity was taken in his absence to request Sir John to indulge the bard with his favourite seat, but without mentioning

his name. Sir John said: 'I will not give up my seat to yon impudent staring fellow,' Upon which it was replied: 'Do you not know that that staring fellow, as you call him, is Burns the poet?' Sir John instantly left the stool, exclaiming: 'Good gracious! Give him all the seats in your house!' Burns was then called in, took possession of his stool, and commenced the reading of his proofs.[53]

Smellie's laid-back attitude towards the production of the Edinburgh Edition was reflected in his easy-going, convivial nature. It was he who introduced Robert to yet another aspect of Edinburgh, the world of the gentlemen's clubs, each of which was founded on some whim or conceit which gave a distinctive character to its proceedings. Smellie himself had founded the Crochallan Fencibles, taking the first part of its name from the Gaelic song 'Cro Chalein' (Colin's cattle) which was a great favourite with Daniel 'Dawney' Douglas, landlord of the tavern in Anchor Close where the club met, and the second part of the name from the regiments raised for the defence of the country during the late American War. It was a rule of the club to subject candidates for admission to a rigorous initiation test by way of proving their temper; and Burns declared that, on his installation, he was 'thrashed' in a style beyond all his experience, though what particular form this hazing took is not known. At this club Robert met several of the men whom he had already encountered at the Canongate Kilwinning lodge, among them William Dunbar, by day a Writer to the Signet and ultimately Inspector General of Stamp Duties for Scotland, but by night Colonel of the Crochallan Fencibles and the 'Rattlin, Roarin Willie' immortalised in Robert's poem (CW 320).

The printer himself was immortalised in Robert's humorous sketch (CW 433) which conveyed his unkempt appearance in contrast to the sharpness of his intellect. The son of a Duddingston stonemason, he was an antiquary, natural historian and prolific essayist, best remembered as the first editor of the *Encyclopaedia Britannica* founded at Edinburgh in 1768, and the founder of the *Edinburgh Magazine* in 1773. Smellie's biographer, however, stated that 'many letters from Burns to Smellie . . . being totally unfit for publication . . . have been burnt'.[54] Only one letter from Robert survived the holocaust, and this, written from Dumfries in 1792, served to introduce Maria Riddell with a view to getting her Caribbean memoirs published (CL 597). Some at least of the bawdy ballads which eventually saw the light of day in *The Merry Muses of Caledonia*, clandestinely published three years after Robert's death, were originally composed for the delectation of the Crochallan Fencibles.

It is unfortunate that Henry Raeburn, then Scotland's foremost portrait painter, was in Italy at the time of Robert's visit, and thus never produced an authentic portrait of the poet, although he may have touched up one of the several paintings produced by Alexander Nasmyth at the behest of George Thomson.[55] If legend is true, then pride of place must go to the naïve hatted portrait, in oils on a wooden panel, which was executed by Peter Taylor, a coach-painter and signwriter. The story goes that, in

December 1786, Burns and Taylor met at a dinner party which extended into the early hours, and the poet agreed on the spur of the moment to sit for his portrait the very next morning. There were three sittings in all before the work was completed, the last (according to Taylor's widow) taking place in May 1787 shortly before Robert left Edinburgh. Taylor died in 1788 and the existence of the portrait was concealed by his widow until 1812 when she showed it to James Hogg. This curious little work is now in the National Portrait Gallery, Edinburgh.

Although the Taylor portrait predates the Nasmyth portraits, the latter are the best known. The first was commissioned by Creech to serve as the basis of an engraving for the frontispiece. Nasmyth was a landscapist rather than a portraitist and was rather diffident about his abilities; but Creech invited him to breakfast one morning to meet the poet. Only a few months older than Burns, Nasmyth established an instant rapport and agreed to tackle the project. Robert gave several sittings to the artist at his lodgings in Wardrop's Court. The first bust-portrait was never completed, Nasmyth reaching a point at which he was scared to go farther lest he spoil the result. The canvas was then handed over to John Beugo to produce a copperplate engraving. Beugo took infinite pains with the work, and had several sittings from the poet for the purpose of retouching the plate. In a brief note to Ballantine on 24 February (CL 102), Robert wrote, 'I am getting my Phiz done by an eminent Engraver; and if it can be ready in time, I will appear in my book looking, like other fools, to my title page'. Gilbert Burns later confessed to George Thomson that he thought Beugo's engraving showed more character and expression than the painting itself.[56] Incidentally, the painting cost Creech nothing because Nasmyth refused to take any payment, and eventually presented it to Robert's wife as a mark of esteem.

Both the painter and the engraver subsequently became close friends of the poet. Nasmyth and Burns frequently went for long walks and expeditions into the surrounding countryside together. James Nasmyth, son of the artist, was the source of a number of anecdotes, some of which must be treated with caution. There is, however, no reason to doubt the story that, on one occasion, after a convivial meeting in a High Street tavern which lasted till an early hour in the morning, they agreed not to go home at all, but to start on an excursion to the Pentland Hills:

> At that time of the year [13 June] the night is very short, and morning comes early. Burns, on reaching the street, looked up to the sky. It was perfectly clear, and the rising sun was beginning to brighten the mural crown of St Giles' Cathedral. Burns was so much struck with the beauty of the morning, that he put his hand on my father's arm and said, 'It'll never do to go to bed on such a lovely morning as this! Let's awa' to Roslin Castle.' No sooner said than done. The poet and painter set out. Nature lay bright and lovely before them in that delicious summer morning. After an eight-miles' walk they reached the castle at Roslin. Burns went down under the great Norman arch, where he stood rapt in speechless admiration of the scene. The thought of the eternal renewal of

youth and freshness of nature, contrasted with the crumbling decay of man's efforts to perpetuate his work, even when founded upon a rock, as Roslin Castle is, seemed greatly to affect him. My father was so much impressed with the scene that, while Burns was standing under the arch, he took out his pencil and paper, and made a hasty sketch of the subject. This sketch was highly treasured by my father, in remembrance of what must have been one of the most memorable days in his life.[57]

There were, in fact, *two* sketches, one of which is now in Irvine Burns Club while the other is in the National Galleries of Scotland. The former later served as the basis for a small oil painting of a full-length portrait which Robert Chambers commissioned in 1827 and engraved the following year for Lockhart's *Life of Burns*.

Stray references to all-night sessions in the taverns off the High Street doubtless helped to create the *canard* of Burns's hard drinking, perpetuated by Heron, Currie and other early biographers. We have already seen, however, how Dugald Stewart firmly refuted such malicious gossip at the time, and numerous other references to Burns in contemporary letters and memoirs are united in making the point that fame did not corrupt him. 'It does not appear that Burns's character was either spoiled by the aristocracy and gentry, or debauched by the tradesmen and clerks.'[58] On the contrary, the tone of his burgeoning correspondence throughout the early months of 1787 is remarkable for sobriety in every sense of the word. When Dugald Stewart spoke of Robert keeping 'not very select society' he meant people like William Dunbar, William Smellie, William Nicol and Alexander Cunningham, gentlemen who were not of the same rarefied stratum as himself and the literati, but who nonetheless were eminently respectable in their own right. It is obvious that, if Robert could keep his end up in the most refined society of the aristocracy or among the keenest intellects of the day, he could relax more in the company of the Crochallan Fencibles, or with young men like Richmond and Ainslie, where he found kindliness and conviviality, rollicking joviality and good humour, not a little wit and cleverness, and a hearty appreciation of his own talents. And Dugald Stewart made the telling point that Robert had told him that 'the weakness of his stomach was such as to deprive him entirely of any merit in his temperance'. The plain fact was that, neither then nor later, did Robert have the ability to drink large quantities of alcohol in any form. A little made him intoxicated, but too much made him sick.

His faults were cerebral rather than physical. Josiah Walker, who chronicled Robert's gaffe in praising Greenfield over Hugh Blair, also criticised his tendency to be opinionated, a failing which he shared with Thomas Carlyle. Cromek, however, dredged up the greatest breach of decorum, often cited by later biographers with as much justice as one might ascribe bad temper to a man who once gave way to passion:

At a private breakfast-party, in a literary circle in Edinburgh, the conversation turned on the poetical merit and pathos of Gray's 'Elegy', a poem of which he was enthusiastically fond. A clergyman present, remarkable for his love of paradox and for his eccentric notions upon every subject, distinguished himself by an injudicious and ill-timed attack on this exquisite poem, which Burns, with generous warmth for the reputation of Gray, manfully defended. As the gentleman's remarks were rather general than specific, Burns urged him to bring forward the passages which he thought exceptionable. He made several attempts to quote the poem, but always in a blundering, inaccurate manner. Burns bore all this for a good while with his usual good-natured forbearance, till at length, goaded by the fastidious criticisms and wretched quibblings of his opponent, he roused himself, and with an eye flashing contempt and indignation, and with great vehemence of gesticulation, he thus addressed the cold critic: 'Sir, I now perceive a man may be an excellent judge of poetry by square and rule, and after all be a d— blockhead!'[59]

Commenting on this story, William Wallace put the matter in perspective. The incident had occurred at the home of Alexander Christison (1753–1820), one of the masters at the High School, and the unfortunate cleric was the Revd. William Robb (1738–97), minister of Tongland parish, Kirkcudbrightshire. Wallace pointed out that a man of warm and sensitive nature might on occasion be goaded into an outburst of this kind, but that was a totally different thing from a habit of outraging propriety in conversation. Besides, Cromek had omitted to tell the whole of the story that was so often quoted to Burns's discredit. Christison's wife Margaret, beside whom Robert was sitting, had an infant on her lap. Immediately after crushing the clergyman, Robert turned to the child and said softly, 'I beg your pardon, my little dear.'[60]

There are also several versions of a story concerning a rather pushy society lady who, without a proper introduction, insisted that Robert attend one of her soirées. He riposted that he would come along on condition that she also invited the Learned Pig. This sagacious animal was the sensation of Edinburgh in the spring of 1787 and its proprietor, a Mr Nichols, made a small fortune by charging a shilling admission to the offices of the *Edinburgh Intelligencer* where the Pig was put through its paces. By the middle of April Nichols was advertising that this was positively the last opportunity to see the animal as it was setting out for Glasgow the following week. The Edinburgh papers, however, carried advertisements a week later saying that the Pig's stay in the capital had been extended a further week, the price of admission being now reduced to sixpence. Even the Theatre Royal cashed in on the porcine celebrity with a farce entitled *The Learned Pig's Levée*, billed as ' a rhiming, chiming, snorting, squeaking, grunting rhapsody'.[61]

It is clear that Robert attempted to be detached and objective in his observation of men and their manners, hence the *Second Commonplace Book*. This was a belated notion, for it was not until 9 April 1787, near the end of his first visit to Edinburgh, that he began keeping a record of his impressions and descriptions of the people he met. The volume itself was a post-folio manuscript book of 240 foolscap pages bound in half-calf and costing 4s 3d (the price appears in the upper left-hand corner of the cover). Under the price Robert wrote, rather self-consciously, 'R. Burns was born 25th Jan. 1759'. On the opening pages was a lengthy preamble setting out his motives:

> As I have seen a good deal of human life in Edinr., a great many characters which are new to one bred up in the shades of life as I have been, I am determined to take down my remarks on the spot. Gray observes in a letter of his to Mr Palgrave, that 'Half a word fixed upon or near the spot, is worth a cart-load of recollection.'[62] I don't know how it is with the world in general, but with me, making remarks is by no means a solitary pleasure. I want some one to laugh with me, some one to be grave with me; some one to please me and help my discrimination with his or her own remark, and at times, no doubt, to admire my acuteness and penetration. The World are so busied with selfish pursuits, ambition, vanity, interest or pleasure, that very few think it worth their while to make any observation on what passes around them; except where that observation is a sucker or branch of the darling plant they are rearing in their fancy . . .
>
> For these reasons, I am determined to make these pages my Confidante. I will sketch every character that anyway strikes me, to the best of my observation, with unshrinking justice; I will insert anecdotes, and take down remarks, in the old law phrase, without feud or favor; where I hit on any thing clever, my own applause will, in some measure, feast my vanity; and (begging Patroclus' and Achates' pardon) I think a lock and key a security at least equal to the bosom of any friend whatsoever.
>
> My own private story likewise, my amours, my rambles, the smiles and frowns of Fortune on my Bardship, my Poems and fragments that must never see the light, shall be occasionally inserted: in short, never did four shillings purchase so much friendship since Confidence went first to market, or Honesty was set to Sale.[63]

Sadly, Robert did not stick to his intentions. The character sketches were confined to brief portraits of Lord Glencairn, Hugh Blair, William Greenfield, Dugald Stewart and William Creech, all of which have been quoted earlier in this chapter. As for his own private story, this part of the promise was never honoured at all. Robert lacked the brutally self-revealing candour of a Boswell, with the result that we know virtually nothing of his amatory adventures in either Edinburgh period. What little we know has come from either his correspondence or external sources, but on the subject of amours the *Commonplace Book* is deafeningly silent. Similarly anecdotes and remarks, the very stuff of most commonplace books of the period, were completely absent. In effect, the volume very soon assumed the character of its predecessor, as a repository of Robert's poetic compositions, but without any of the analyses and criticisms that distinguished the first volume. The only other prose passage, in fact, was written on 14 June 1788, a rather pathetic and introspective piece which reflected his loneliness and homesickness at Ellisland when he first moved there, followed incongruously a couple of days later by copies of the letters he wrote to the Earls of Buchan and Eglinton two years previously.

The other point worth noting about the preamble was the injection of some classical allusions, showing a half-hearted attempt to follow the precepts of the literati to broaden his scope. Robert also judiciously sprinkled his correspondence in this manner, but only when he was making a self-conscious effort to show his professorial or clerical correspondents that he was just as well-read as they.

On 17 April 1787 the first Edinburgh Edition was published. The prefatory dedication, to the Noblemen and Gentlemen of the Caledonian Hunt, was written some two weeks previously and played up the image of the Heaven-taught ploughman for all it was worth:

> The Poetic Genius of my Country found me as the prophetic bard Elijah did Elisha – at the *plough*; and threw her inspiring mantle over me. She bade me sing the loves, the joys, the rural scenes and rural pleasures of my natal Soil, in my native tongue; I tuned my wild, artless notes, as she inspired. She whispered me to come to this ancient metropolis of Caledonia, and lay my Songs under your honoured protection: I now obey her dictates.

Though much indebted to their goodness, however, Robert felt impelled to assert his independence. 'I do not approach you, my Lords and Gentlemen, in the usual style of dedication, to thank you for past favours; that path is so hackneyed by prostituted Learning, that honest Rusticity is ashamed of it.'

On the very day that the copies were ready for distribution Robert made an agreement with Creech. A memorandum of agreement was drawn up by their mutual friend, Henry Mackenzie:

> By advice of friends, Mr. Burns having resolved to dispose of the property of his *Poems*, and having consulted with Mr. Henry M'Kenzie upon the subject, Mr. Creech met with Mr. Burns at Mr M'Kenzie's house upon Tuesday, the 17th April 1787, in the evening, and they three having retired and conversed upon the subject, Mr. Burns and Mr. Creech referred the sum to be named by Mr. M'Kenzie, as being well acquainted with matters of this kind, when Mr. M'Kenzie said he thought Mr. Burns should have a hundred guineas for the property of his *Poems*.
>
> Mr. Creech said that he agreed to the proposal, but as Scotland was now amply supplied with the very numerous edition now printed, he could write to Mr. Caddell of London, to know if he would take a share of the Book, but at any rate Mr. Burns should have the money named by Mr. M'Kenzie, which Mr. Burns most cordially agreed to, and to make over the property upon these terms, whenever Mr. Creech required him,
>
> Upon Monday, the 23rd of April 1787, Mr. Creech informed Mr. Burns that he had remained in Town, expecting Mr. Caddell's answer, for three days, as to his taking a share of the property of the *Poems*; but that he had received no answer; yet he would, as formerly proposed and agreed to, take the whole matter upon himself, that Mr. Burns might be at no uncertainty in the matter.
>
> Upon this both parties considered the transaction as finished.

To the original document were appended two notes. The first, dated at Edinburgh, 23 October 1787, was 'On demand I promise to pay Mr. Robert Burns, or Order, One Hundred Guineas, value received' and signed by Creech. The other laconically recorded 'Received the contents – May 30, 1788. Robert Burns'.[64]

In this transaction, however, Robert forgot to mention that he had already assigned his rights to the Kilmarnock Poems (which comprised two-thirds of the contents of the Edinburgh Edition) to his brother Gilbert as part of the legal manoeuvre to prevent Jean Armour or her father making any claim against him. One can only assume that Robert (who, on his own admission, was no businessman) was unaware of the full implications of his Deed of Assignment to Gilbert, or had forgotten it. The latter excuse is often cited by biographers,[65] although it seems highly improbable that Robert could have forgotten a document which he had signed barely nine months previously. Those who have considered that Robert was hard done by in the arrangement with Creech would do well to remember that he was selling something which he had already disposed of elsewhere. Nor does the view that Robert had virtually given his copyright away stand up to serious examination. A hundred guineas (£105) would later represent two years' salary as an Excise officer and, translated into modern currency, would be the equivalent of £30,000. No wonder Mr Burns most cordially agreed to the arrangement. By the same token, the notion that Henry Mackenzie had some sinister motive in conspiring with Creech to cheat the Ayrshire bard is not worth a second glance.

Rather more serious is the charge that Creech deliberately withheld payment. As the document shows, Creech made no immediate move to honour the agreement by making payment. Indeed, it was not until 23 October, some six months later, that Creech was brought to the point at which he put his promise in writing, and not until 30 May 1788, more than a year after the agreement was negotiated, before he actually paid up. As we shall see, only the most persistent pressure from Robert finally induced Creech to part with all the money which he was owing.

Apart from the purchase of the copyright, Creech had a substantial stake in the Edinburgh Edition. Other subscribers might be expected to put their money up front, but Creech, who was the largest subscriber of them all, owed Robert £125 in respect of the five hundred copies which he sold on to the general public. From Creech's advertisement in the Edinburgh newspapers, it is clear that he also acted as the distribution centre for the copies subscribed by private individuals. In this capacity he would have taken in a large part of the subscription money and no doubt Robert allowed him a commission on the proceeds, although no details of such an arrangement are known. To be sure, Creech must have turned over to Robert considerable sums of subscription money as the business proceeded, but it was not until late in March 1789 – almost two years after publication – that the account was finally squared. Robert's later dealings with his niggardly publisher belong more properly to a subsequent chapter.

According to the poet's earliest biographer, the whole sum paid by Creech to Burns for his copyright and the subscriptions amounted to almost £1,100. From this sum, the expenses of printing had to be deducted.[66] According to the subscribers' lists published in the Edinburgh Edition almost 1,500 people subscribed for 2,876 copies, but even these statistics have to be qualified. To take one example only: the Earl of Eglinton gave Robert ten guineas (£10 10s), as a result of which he was entered in the lists as a subscriber for forty-two copies. Dr Moore, writing to Burns on 23 May, put him wise:

> You seem to think it incumbent on you to send to each subscriber a number of copies proportionate to his subscription money, but you may depend upon it, few subscribers expect more than one copy, whatever they subscribed; I must inform you, however, that I took twelve copies for those subscribers, for whose money you were so accurate as to send me a receipt, and Lord Eglintoun told me he had sent for six copies for himself, as he wished to give five of them as presents.[67]

Robert was not always as meticulous about recording subscriptions and supplying receipts, as he confessed to Ballantine on 18 April, the day following publication, when he sent him five parcels containing a hundred copies (CL 102): 'Several of the Subscription bills have been mislaid, so all who say they have subscribed must be served at subscription price; otherwise those who have not subscribed must pay six shillings.' This lamentable state of affairs was also admitted in a tailpiece to the subscribers' lists in the book, 'Some subscriptions have not yet come to hand, and perhaps some have been mislaid'. This was hardly a businesslike approach, but in mitigation it must be remembered that Robert was not at all keen to pander to the vanity of his supporters by publishing their names, and only gave way reluctantly. His reluctance was understandable, as the lists occupied thirty-eight pages and must have added not inconsiderably to the production costs. For this reason one must not attach too much weight to which names appeared in the main list and which (like the McAdam family) were relegated to the supplementary list. It would be unwise, as some biographers have done, to suppose from this that these people only subscribed at the last moment and therefore only got to know the poet latterly.

Presumably the thirty-six copies which the Earl of Eglinton had theoretically paid for but did not require, along with all the other copies oversubscribed by similarly generous patrons, were at Robert's disposal and could either be sold to late subscribers or those whose subscriptions had been mislaid, or, better still, sold to non-subscribers at six shillings. Either way, Robert was in the happy position of having an unknown but quite substantial quantity of books which could be effectively sold twice over. This factor makes a nonsense of any attempt to calculate with accuracy the profits of the venture. Snyder failed to take this into account when he considered Creech's figure of £1,100 rather too large for acceptance.[68] Snyder did his sums on the basis of an edition of 3,000 copies. Had all been sold at the subscription rate of five shillings, Robert would have netted £750; had a couple of hundred been sold at the full price the gross figure, together with the copyright money, would not have exceeded £950. But in view of Dr Moore's comments, and a closer look at some of the theoretically large numbers for which some individuals subscribed, I am inclined to the view that Creech was probably correct after all.

To Dr Moore Robert wrote on 4 January 1789 (CL 257-8) regarding his financial transactions with Creech:

> I believe I shall in whole, £100 Copy-right included, clear about £400, some little odds; and even part of this depends upon what the gentleman has yet to settle with me. I give you this information because you did me the honor to interest yourself much in my welfare; but I give it to yourself only, for the world would accuse me of ingratitude, and I am still much in the gentleman's mercy. Perhaps I injure the man in the idea I am sometimes tempted to have of him: God forbid I should.

And to Mrs Dunlop Robert confided on 25 March the same year (CL 170):

> By Mr. Creech, who has at last settled amicably & fully as fairly as could have been expected, with me, I clear about 440 or 450£.

But too much reliance must not be placed on Robert's arithmetic, bearing in mind how inaccurate were the figures of the profit he claimed from the Kilmarnock Edition. It seems probable, therefore, that the profit from the Edinburgh Edition, after deducting the production costs, was considerably higher than he thought. In fairness to Robert, however, he was writing two years after publication and in the intervening period money would have come in by fits and starts. He did not keep an accurate record and therefore had only a hazy notion of the profit which accrued from the venture. Doubtless much of the difference between the true profit and the imagined profit merely disappeared in the interim, as money tends to do, like snow off a dyke.

Admittedly the costs of paper, printing and binding would have been much greater than had been the case with the Kilmarnock Edition. In place of a volume of 240 pages in blue paper covers there was now a book of 408 pages more permanently bound in French grey paper boards. In place of 612 copies, the Edinburgh Edition ran to five times as many, and these were produced in what were virtually two editions. The costs of production must therefore have been at least £200 and probably closer to £250. In addition Robert discovered that he had to offer booksellers a discount – 'the unconscionable, Jewish tax of 25 pr Cent'. mentioned in his letter to John Ballantine. Such a discount would have made considerable inroads into the gross figure quoted by Creech.

Apart from the thirty-eight pages of subscribers' names, itself a useful commentary on cultivated Scottish society,[69] the new volume differed from its predecessor in several important respects. The glossary of Scottish words and phrases was expanded from five to twenty-four pages – a valuable and, until relatively recently, underrated linguistic tool.[70] This, more than anything else, demonstrated that Burns was now reaching a much wider readership than before. Previously he had been aiming at an audience in the south-west of Scotland, most of whom would have been familiar with a high proportion of the Scots words. Now, however, he acted on the advice of Mrs Dunlop and Dr Moore[71] and considerably enlarged the glossary, even to the extent of including fairly obvious variants of English, such as *aff* (off) and *aits* (oats), in order to make his works acceptable to English readers. For the same reason Robert tinkered with the text of his poems, changing the old Scottish gerund or gerundive forms ending in *an* or *in* to the more modern forms in *ing*.

The Edinburgh Edition added just over a hundred pages of hitherto unpublished poetry. Three relatively insignificant pieces which appeared in the Kilmarnock Edition merely to fill the space – 'Epitaph on a Henpecked Country Squire' (CW 209), 'Epigram on said Occasion' (CW 209) and 'One Queen Artemisa' (CW 210) – were now discarded. On the other hand, major new works included this time were 'When Guilford good our pilot stood' (CW 72–4), 'Address to the Unco Guid' (CW 74–6), 'Death and Dr Hornbook' (CW 96–100), 'The Ordination' (CW 192–4), 'The Brigs of Ayr' (CW 244–9), 'Tam Samson's Elegy' (CW 239–41) and 'The Calf' (CW 252). The first four had been composed before the Kilmarnock Edition went to press but were prudently omitted on grounds of taste. Several new stanzas were added to 'The Vision' (CW 114–21), and five previously unpublished religious poems and a similar number of songs were included. By contrast, the 'Address to Edinburgh' (CW 262–4) and the 'Address to a Haggis' (CW 264–5) were the only products of the Edinburgh sojourn which Robert considered worthy of inclusion. In fact, most of the uncollected poetry which appeared for the first time in this volume dated back before the spring of 1786. In the nine months which elapsed between the decision to publish the Kilmarnock Poems and late December when the Edinburgh Edition went to press, Robert had had precious little time for poetic composition. When we remember that in those crowded months Robert had been supervising the production of the Kilmarnock Poems, dodging the wrath of the Armour family, courting Margaret Campbell (and possibly Betsey Miller as well), scurrying about Ayrshire attending to the publication of his poems, preparing to emigrate, coping with the devastating tragedy of Margaret Campbell's death, planning the trip to the capital and being lionised by Edinburgh society, it is a wonder that he found any time for literary pursuits at all.

Superficially the Edinburgh Edition marked a big advance over its predecessor; in truth there was little, if any, real progress in Robert's poetic talent. His reputation was made by the Kilmarnock Edition and merely confirmed and widened by the Edinburgh Edition. On the one hand, the pretentious 'Address to Edinburgh' provided a warning of what could happen if Robert were to heed too slavishly the well-meaning advice of the literati. On the other, there was the hint of things to come in 'Green Grow the Rashes O' (CW 81), a brilliant reworking of an old ballad.

Only three months after the first review of Burns's poems had appeared in the *English Review* critiques of the Edinburgh Edition were beginning to appear not only in the Edinburgh and Glasgow periodicals but farther afield. The *Universal Magazine* for May 1787 was fulsome, if not entirely accurate, in its praise. 'These Poems, the author of which is in the humble station of a ploughman, in the Highlands of Scotland, possess uncommon excellence, whether we consider them as adorned with beautiful sentiments, picturesque imagery, or harmonious versification.' In August the *New Town and Country Magazine*, while giving some idea of the wide range of Burns's poetic skills, lamented that, 'These poems being chiefly in the Scottish dialect, it must necessarily confine their beauties to a small circle of readers; however, the author has given good specimens of his skill in English. The following stanza is not only very elegant, but highly poetical', and the ninth stanza of 'The Cotter's Saturday Night' (CW 148) was printed below. A suspiciously similar review (either from the same anonymous pen or blatantly copied from it) appeared in the *General Magazine*. James Anderson, who had taken notice of the Kilmarnock Poems in the December 1786 issue of the *Monthly Review*, returned to this theme twelve months later:

> We are glad to find, by the numerous and respectable list of subscribers prefixed to the volume before us, that this Bard of Nature has no reason to complain that 'a poet is not honoured in his own country'. It appears that he has been very liberally patronized by an indulgent Public; and we rejoice to see that he may now have it in his power to tune his oaten reed at his ease. Whether this change in his circumstances will prove beneficial to the cause of literature, or productive of greater happiness to the individual, time alone can discover; but we sincerely wish it may prove favourable to both.[72]

Although most reviews were favourable, there was the occasional sour note. None was as overtly condemnatory as James Maxwell, 'Poet in Paisley' who, with rather more skill and elegance than Saunders Tait, launched a violent diatribe in rhyming couplets:

> Of all British poets that yet have appear'd,
> None e'er at things sacred so daringly sneer'd,
> As he in the west, who but lately is sprung
> From behind the plough-tails, and from raking of dung.

And much, much more in similar vein.[73] An anonymous writer, under the pen name of 'A Friend to Virtue', rushed into print with a lampoon of 'To a Mountain Daisy' (CW 203), prefaced by the following statement:

> On reading Burns's poems, and some other productions in his defence, my feelings have been shocked, so that I should think it criminal not to

contribute with the virtuous few who have already appeared on the side of injur'd truth. – It is certainly a very agreeable article of licentious faith, that although led astray by fierce passions and wild pleasures, 'Yet the light that led us astray is light from heaven.' – Burns's vision, page 140. – Such articles, together with the contaminating spirit that runs through this work, are calculated to do more injury to religion, and virtue, than all the atheistical, deistical, and heretical books that have been written this last century.[74]

These attacks, however, were mere pinpricks which did not diminish the ever-widening popularity of Burns's poems. Originally promised 'within days' of the Edinburgh Edition, the first London Edition, by A. Strahan and Thomas Cadell, appeared on 5 July (Creech having negotiated a deal as he had hoped); but before the year was out, editions had also been published by William Gilbert in Dublin and James Magee in Belfast. The first American edition appeared at Philadelphia on 7 July 1788 (published by Peter Stewart and George Hyde), and six months later J. and A. McLean of New York brought out their edition. The Irish and American editions were pirated, so neither Burns nor Creech profited from their appearance. The Ayrshire farmer-poet who had ridden into Edinburgh on a borrowed pony was unknown outside a few parishes; within eighteen months he was well on the way to becoming a celebrity of international importance.

As soon as the Edinburgh Edition was out, Robert dutifully despatched presentation copies, often accompanied by letters. Appropriately, the first of these went to George Reid, whose pony Robert had borrowed, and his daughter Jenny (CL 220). To William Dunbar, who had previously given him the works of Edmund Spenser, Robert wrote on 30 April (CL 282):

> The tatter'd Rhymes I herewith present you, and the handsome volumes of Spencer for which I am indebted to your goodness, may perhaps seem as out of proportion to one another as to their late owners but be that as it may, my gift, though far less valuable, is as sincere a mark of esteem as yours.

The only other presentation copy recorded raises an intriguing question. At the Centenary Exhibition in Glasgow, 1896, there was displayed a copy of the 1787 Poems bearing a holograph inscription on the fly-leaf:

> To Miss Farquhar as a mark of the most respectful PERSONAL esteem, and sincere gratitude for many kindnesses he owes to her nearest Relations and dearest Friends, from, THE AUTHOR.

The present whereabouts of this volume is unknown. Was Miss Farquhar the Edinburgh Belle, referred to so coyly in Robert's letter to Dalrymple of Orangefield? She may have been Isobella, the daughter of James Farquhar of 11 Princes Street (who has been identified as one of the subscribers) and his wife Jean Menzies. In August 1787 Robert dined with Farquhar and his family and afterwards wrote to Archibald Lawrie about it (CL 128), adding:

I ate some Newhaven broth, in other words, boiled mussles with Mr
Farquhar's family t'other day – Now I see you prick up your ears – They
are all well and Madamoiselle is particularly well.– She begs her respects
to you all.

This implies that Lawrie, rather than Burns, was sweet on Miss Farquhar;
and Archibald, who was at this time back home in Newmilns, would doubtless appreciate the compliment. On the other hand, were she and
Archibald courting, she would not have needed to pay her respects via
Robert or any other third party. Either way, it does not rule out the possibility that Miss Farquhar and the Edinburgh Belle whose hand he squeezed
and at whom he stole the occasional glance were one and the same person.

Robert now prepared to leave Edinburgh on the first of his projected
tours of Scotland; but before he went he ordered three dozen prints of
Beugo's engraving on India paper from James Kirkwood, at a cost of a shilling apiece, and distributed them, with 'bread and butter' letters, to those
who had shown him so much kindness during his stay in the capital. These
engravings, usually accompanied by letters, were sent to Hugh Blair (CL
288), Henry Mackenzie (CL 289–90), William Tytler (CL 291), the Earl of
Glencairn (CL 227), a Mr McCartney and Dr Charles Fyfe of Leith Walk
(CL 304) on 4 May. Characteristically, Mackenzie endorsed Robert's letter
'Robt. Burns May 1787 Remarkable Anecdote to shew the good Effects of
Moral Reading' before he filed it away in his precise lawyer's manner.

The same day, however, Robert, while packing his bags to leave
Edinburgh on tour, possibly for ever, dashed off a note to James Johnson,
an engraver who had his workshop in Bell's Wynd on the south side of the
High Street but who later moved to Lady Stair's Close off the
Lawnmarket. Johnson (1742–1811)[75] had invented a process for reproduc-
ing sheet music on pewter plates and some time before Robert came to
Edinburgh he conceived the idea of collecting the words and music of all
the old Scots ballads. When he first met Burns, the first volume of *The
Scots Musical Museum*, containing a hundred songs, was already in the
press. Robert needed little encouragement to become involved in the
project, and as he was on the point of leaving the city he sent a brief letter
(CL 292) accompanying a song by an anonymous author, to an air by
McGibbon. 'Keep the original of this Song till we meet again, whenever
that may be.'

CHAPTER 12

The Tours, 1787

Admiring Nature in her wildest grace,
These northern scenes with weary feet I trace;
O'er many a winding dale and painful steep,
Th' abodes of covey'd grouse and timid sheep,
My savage journey, curious I pursue,
Till fam'd Breadalbane opens to my view.

Verses Written with a Pencil (CW 287)

B etween late spring and the end of autumn 1787 Robert made four extended journeys through different parts of Scotland and even included a couple of forays into England. Snyder describes them as vacation tours,[1] implying that Robert was on holiday, but it would be truer to describe them as business, rather than pleasure, trips. The best analogy would be to liken these tours to the gigs of today's pop groups who have to go on the road to maintain faith with the fans who buy their records. The warm reception he had received at Covington had not been lost on Robert. Indeed, shortly before embarking on his tour of the Borders, he paid a flying visit to Covington on 1 May. Archibald Prentice, like many farmers of the time, kept a journal which was mainly a record of the weather and work done on the farm. Under 1 May appears the laconic entry, 'Cold land. Making bear (*sic*). Mr Burns here'. John Prentice, the farmer's grandson, who preserved this journal, had no doubt that Burns had been at Covington that day; Chambers felt that:

> if such an excursion took place, it was probably connected with some circumstances about which Burns desired to observe silence. He says of one of his songs, in which a Clydesdale heroine is celebrated . . . that it 'alludes to a part of my private history, which it is of no consequence to the world to know'. The present might be a similar case, if not the same.[2]

The song to which Chambers refers was 'Yon Wild Mossy Mountains' (CW 284-5). As John's father, Archibald Junior, was not even born at the time of this visit, his remarks must be regarded at best as no more than a family tradition. It is hard to imagine that Robert would have had the time for amorous dalliance during his brief, crowded visit to Covington in

November 1786. Perhaps his visit the following May had a more prosaic explanation. A few days before embarking on his Border tour, Robert purchased for £4 a mare which he named Jenny Geddes, after the woman who hurled her footstool at Bishop Lindsay in St Giles Cathedral on 23 August 1637 when he was trying to introduce the *Book of Common Prayer*, execrating as she did so the poor cleric who dared 'say Mass at my lug'.

The Border tour was no sudden whim. Indeed, although the itinerary appears quite aimless, the trip must have required a certain amount of planning. In the first place Robert was to be accompanied on the first part of it by young Ainslie, who arranged to get two weeks' leave from Samuel Mitchelson; and as the two men received a certain amount of hospitality during their peregrinations there must have been some correspondence (probably by Ainslie) to set this up. Robert himself took his leave of many of his Edinburgh friends, and sufficient letters have survived to show the motives for the tour.

Robert always had a hankering for travel, and those brief interludes at Kirkoswald and Irvine had shown him aspects of life other than those he experienced at home. But, as a farm-worker, he had been very much tied to the soil, and at Mount Oliphant, Lochlie and Mossgiel there had been precious little opportunity to get away, other than fleeting visits to Ayr and Kilmarnock. Although the Irvine period is often dismissed as the dreariest episode in his life, Robert's friendship with Richard Brown must have stimulated his interest in seeing something of the wider world. Robert was, perforce, an armchair traveller; among his voracious reading were many books of a geographical or historical nature, including such French exotica as Jean-François Marmontel's *Les Incas, ou la destruction de l'empire du Perou* and Rochette de la Morlière's *Angola, histoire indienne*. It was inevitable that, when Robert finally had a large amount of money at his disposal, he should expend some of it on travel. It might have been supposed that he would take the opportunity to visit London, but he seems to have had an aversion to going there. Later, when Peter Stuart tried to woo him away from the Excise with the promise of a lucrative journalistic appointment, Robert shrank at the prospect, and in his letters to his brother William, when the latter was about to set off for the metropolis, Robert gave him stern advice which reflected his own prejudices.

If he had little or no interest in seeing what England had to offer, Robert was keen to explore his own country. Even if the Earl of Buchan and Mrs Dunlop had not planted the idea in his head, Robert would have been enthusiastic about visiting other parts of Scotland whose bard he now considered himself. There are frequent references in his letters in April 1787 to returning to his shades, as he termed his reversion to obscurity, but before he was resigned to the farming life he was determined to see a little more of the world and its people. The same consciousness of the significance of what he was doing that impelled him to make copies of important letters and embark on the *First Commonplace Book* induced him to keep journals of his tours. Like the *Second Commonplace Book*, however, Robert's good intentions soon fell by the wayside. The best and fullest of the journals was that covering the Border tour. By contrast, the journal of the Highland tour was little more than a series of disjointed jottings and headings which Robert may have regarded merely as an *aide-mémoire* for a fuller account, to be written at his leisure but which never materialised. In addition to these main tours were shorter forays into the West Highlands and to Stirlingshire. Both of these were made for emotional reasons and it is significant that Robert made no attempt to keep a journal of either.

Burns and Bob Ainslie left Edinburgh on the morning of Saturday, 5 May, riding east, through Haddington and Gifford, before heading south across the Lammermuirs to Longformacus and Duns. The first entry in the new journal was terse:

> Left Edinburgh – Lammermuir Hills miserably dreary, but at times very picturesque. Lanton-edge, a glorious view of the Merse – reach Berrywell . . .

By contrast, Robert's description of the Ainslie family was six times as long, and although the portraits he penned of Bob's parents, brother Douglas and sister Rachel were brief, he managed to convey in a few deft phrases acute assessments of their characters as well as their physical appearance. For Robert, landscapes were secondary to the men and women, especially the women, who peopled them. The following day Robert joined the Ainslies at worship in Duns parish church and afterwards recorded that the minister, Dr Bowmaker (1731–97) was 'a man of strong lungs and pretty judicious remark; but ill-skilled in propriety, and altogether unconscious of his want of it'. Though Robert left it at that, Ainslie later recalled that the poet made a neat impromptu, conveying a graceful compliment to his sister. Bowmaker chose a text containing a severe denunciation of obstinate sinners, and during the sermon Robert observed Miss Rachel, seated next to him, diligently searching through her bible for the text, in a state of great agitation at Bowmaker's hell-fire preaching. Robert was moved to inscribe these extempore lines on the fly-leaf of her bible:

> Fair maid, you need not take the hint,
>   Nor idle texts pursue;
> 'Twas guilty sinners that he meant,
>   Not angels such as you.

On Monday the two travellers set off due south. The Journal noted, 'Coldstream – went over to England – Cornhill – glorious river Tweed – clear and majestic – fine bridge'. These staccato phrases, worthy of a Mr Jingle, were filled out by Ainslie, forty-five years after the event:

> The weather was charming, the travellers youthful and in good spirits, and the poet delighted with the fine scenery and the poetical associations connected with it. When they arrived at Coldstream, where the dividing

line between England and Scotland is the Tweed, Mr Ainslie suggested
going across to the other side of the river by the Coldstream Bridge, that
Burns might be enabled to say he had been in England. They did so, and
were pacing slowly along on English ground, enjoying their walk, when
Mr Ainslie was surprised to see the poet throw away his hat, and, thus
uncovered, kneel down with uplifted hands, and apparently rapt in a fit
of enthusiasm. Mr Ainslie kept silence, uncertain what was next to be
done, when Burns, with extreme emotion, and an expression of countenance which his companion could never forget, prayed for and blessed
Scotland most solemnly, by pronouncing aloud, in tones of the deepest
devotion, the two concluding stanzas of the 'Cotter's Saturday Night'.[3]

Snyder dismissed Ainslie's picture of Burns on his knees in an ecstasy of
patriotic fervour as probably apocryphal, but such an act, half-serious, half-
joking, would not have been out of the character of Caledonia's Bard, and
obviously the local Burnsians thought so too, for in 1926 they erected a
bronze plaque at the mid-point of the bridge to commemorate the incident.
At Coldstream Burns and Ainslie dined with Robert Foreman, a young
man of about his own age whom Burns beat in a dispute over Voltaire.[4]
They went on to tea with the celebrated traveller and author Patrick
Brydone (1741–1818) at Lennel House where Robert was gratified by an
'extremely flattering' reception. They slept at Coldstream and the following day went to Kelso where they breakfasted before visiting the ruins of
Roxburgh Castle. Here again, the people he encountered provoked greater
comment than the scenery and landmarks. Robert was introduced to
Robert Scott of the Royal Bank – 'an excellent modest fellow' – and later
dined with David McDowal at Caverton Mill who provided much useful
information on sheep husbandry, all of which Robert the farmer dutifully
recorded. Towards nightfall the travellers came up the Teviot and the Jed
'to Jedburgh to lie, and so wish myself a good night'. They lodged at
27 Canongate, adjoining Dean's Close (where yet another plaque was
erected, in 1913).

Burns and Ainslie spent three days here, making excursions into the surrounding countryside. This was one of the most interesting periods of the
tour, to judge by the fulness of the entries. His host for much of this period
was the lawyer James Fair (died 1796) whose sight had been greatly
impaired by the misplaced attentions of a quack doctor. Robert had by now
got into his stride as the detached observer of the human condition around
him, and there are amusing passages in the journal concerning, for
example, 'a squabble between Mrs F[air], a crazed, talkative slattern, and
a sister of hers, an old maid, respecting a Relief minister', a widower whom
the sister, a Miss Lookup, had been trying to trap into matrimony. They
dined at Mossburnford with Captain John Rutherford (1746–1830) who
had soldiered in America and been a prisoner of the Chippewah Indians.
His lady was 'exactly a proper matrimonial second part for him' but Robert
considered his daughter to be 'a beautiful girl, but too far gone woman to
expose so much of a fine swelling bosom – her face very fine'. After
accompanying some ladies to a couple of local beauty spots, Robert was

introduced to Mr Potts, 'writer, a very clever fellow', and the Revd. Dr Thomas Somerville (1741–1830), 'the clergyman of the place, a man, and a gentlemen, but sadly addicted to punning'. After this passage was published by Currie in 1800 Dr Somerville is said to have absolutely abandoned punning.

The sisters, Mrs Fair and Miss Lookup, who squabbled over the clerical widower, did not improve on a second acquaintance. 'These two appear still more comfortably ugly and stupid, and bore me most shockingly. Two Miss Fairs, tolerably agreable, but too much of the Mother's half-ell mouth and hag-like features.' The other young ladies in the party, however, proved to be much more agreeable. Miss Hope of Cowdenknowes was 'a tolerably pretty girl, fond of laughing and fun', but her companion, Isabella Lindsay (1764–1800), made an even greater impression:

> Miss Lindsay, a good-humoured, amiable girl; rather short *et embonpoint*, but handsome, and extemely graceful – beautiful hazel eyes, full of spirit, and sparkling with delicious moisture – an engaging face *un tout ensemble* that speaks her of the first order of female minds – her sister, a bonnie, strappan, rosy, sonsie lass. Shake myself loose, after several unsuccessful efforts, of Mrs F and Miss L, and somehow or other get hold of Miss Lindsay's arm . . . Miss seems very well pleased with my bardship's distinguishing her; and after some slight qualms, which I could easily mark, she sets the titter round at defiance, and kindly allows me to keep my hold; and when parted by the ceremony of my introduction to Mr Somerville, she met me half, to resume my situation. *Nota Bene* – The poet within a point and a half of being d–mnably in love – I am afraid my bosom is still nearly as much tinder as ever.
>
> The old, cross-grained, whiggish, ugly, slanderous Miss L, with all the poisonous spleen of a disappointed, ancient maid, stops me very unseasonably to ease her bursting breast, by falling abusively foul on the Miss Lindsays, particularly on my Dulcinea; – I hardly refrain from cursing her to her face for daring to mouth her calumnious slander on one of the finest pieces of the workmanship of Almighty Excellence! Sup at Mr F–'s; vexed that the Miss Lindsays are not of the supper-party, as they only are wanting. Mrs F– and Miss L– still improve infernally on my hands.

Early on Thursday morning Burns and Ainslie set off for Wauchope, breakfasting at Rule *en route* with Dr Gilbert Elliot, a retired army surgeon and a cousin of Lord Heathfield, defender of Gibraltar. The good doctor then convoyed them by Bonchester and Wolflee Hill, almost as far as Wauchope itself. Here Robert met Mrs Elizabeth Scott, who had 'all the sense, taste, intrepidity of face, and bold, critical decision, which usually distinguish female authors'. Back at Jedburgh later Robert discovered from Dr Somerville that Miss Lookup, the malicious old maid aforementioned, had been the means of keeping the Misses Lindsay from the supper-party; so he prevailed on the minister to invite the entire family to breakfast the following day. In the event, only Isabella kept the appointment. 'I find

Miss Lindsay would soon play the devil with me,' noted Robert, 'I met with some little flattering attentions from her.' Later Isabella accompanied the party which went off to visit Esther Easton, a gardener's wife who had a prodigious memory for poetry and could recite the whole of Pope's 'Homer'. 'She is very much flattered that I send for her, and that she sees a poet who has *put out a book*, as she says,' Robert recorded with self-satisfaction. Mrs Easton, though now soberly married, had allegedly been a prostitute in her younger days – 'suspected for some of the tricks of the Cytherean Déesse' as Robert delicately put it. Robert and Isabella took a stroll in Esther's beautiful flower garden,

> and after some little chit-chat of the tender kind, I presented her with a proofprint of my *Nob*, which she accepted with something more tender than gratitude. She told me many little stories which Miss L– had retailed concerning her and me, with prolonging pleasure – God bless her! Was waited on by the Magistrates, and presented with the freedom of the burgh.

Robert was presented with his burgess ticket, partly printed and partly handwritten on parchment, but did not sign the burgess roll. The ticket itself surfaced in 1911, came up for sale in 1939, and was presented to Jedburgh thirty years later. The story goes that there was some confusion over who should meet the cost of the riddle of claret customarily consumed on such occasions and the new burgess offered to pay; but in the end the provost and bailies stumped up. Considering that this was the first time that Burns was made an honorary burgess, it is significant that it was dismissed in the journal almost as an afterthought, the burgeoning romance with the fair Isabella being uppermost in the poet's mind. Incidentally, it is interesting to note the use to which Robert put the prints of Beugo's engraving – much as pop stars now bestow signed photographs on their fans. It was with a heavy heart that Robert reluctantly pulled himself away from Jedburgh. He himself described it as 'some melancholy, disagreeable sensations' and went on to apostrophise:

> Jed, pure be thy crystal streams, and hallowed thy sylvan banks! Sweet Isabella Lindsay, may peace dwell in thy bosom, uninterrupted, except by the tumultuous throbbings of rapturous love! That love-kindling eye must beam on another, not on me: that graceful form must bless another's arms; not mine!

Isabella married Adam Armstrong only twenty-four days later. Her 'easy manners' with the poet, despite her impending marriage, caused tongues to wag locally. Armstrong later obtained a post with the Russian government. Isabella died young, leaving four children, but her youngest son became a general and director of the Imperial Mint at St Petersburg.

At Kelso on 11 May Robert dined with the Farmers' Club and spent the night at the home of Gilbert Kerr of Stodrig who offered to accompany

Robert into England when Bob Ainslie's holiday was up and he had to return to Edinburgh. They dined with Sir Alexander Don, 'a pretty clever fellow, but far from being a match for his divine lady' (Harriet Cunningham, sister of the Earl of Glencairn). After spending two nights at Stodrig Burns and Ainslie set out on Sunday morning for Melrose. The day was wet and cold and the weather did not improve when they visited the ruins of Dryburgh Abbey. They pressed on, dined at Melrose, visited the ruined abbey, and rode along the Ettrick to Selkirk. Dr Clarkson and a couple of friends were sitting in Veitch's Forest Inn over a glass when the rain-sodden travellers arrived, 'like twa droukit craws'. Through the window, the doctor and his companions watched the riders dismounting and formed a poor impression of them from their dishevelled appearance. When the travellers sent the innkeeper to Clarkson to ask if they might join his company, the doctor objected and asked Veitch what they were like. Veitch could not really say. One spoke *rather* like a gentleman, but the other was a drover-looking chap; so they refused to admit them, sending them word that they were sorry they were engaged elsewhere, and obliged to go away. Clarkson saw them ride off the following day, and it was only a couple of days later that he discovered that he had spurned the celebrated poet. 'That refusal hangs about the doctor's heart like a deadweight to this day, and will do till the day of his death, for the bard had not a more enthusiastic admirer,' wrote James Hogg.[5]

Robert was disappointed with his visit to the Vale of Yarrow, noting 'the whole country hereabout, both on Tweed and Ettrick, remarkably stony'. That day it rained incessantly and the travellers were confined to the inn. Robert whiled away the tedium by composing the lament, in twelve stanzas of Standard Habbie, entitled 'Willie's Awa' (CW 277–9), which he despatched with a covering letter (CL 305) to William Creech who was then in London making arrangements with Strahan and Cadell for the first English edition. The letter reflects Robert's low spirits that day:

> The inclosed I have just wrote, nearly extempore, in a solitary Inn in Selkirk, after a miserable wet day's riding.– I have been over most of East Lothian, Berwick, Roxburgh, & Selkirk Shires; and next week I begin a tour through the north of England.– Yesterday, I dined with Lady Hariot, sister to my noble patron, – Quem Deus conservet! – I would write till I would tire you as much with dull Prose as I dare say by this time you are with wretched Verse; but I am jaded to death.

On Monday, 14 May, Burns and Ainslie made a twenty-mile detour up the Tweed to Innerleithen, solely for the purpose of seeing the locations of places celebrated in the traditional ballads, 'The Bush aboon Traquair' and 'Elibanks and Elibraes'. After taking tea with Alexander Horsburgh of Pirn,[6] the travellers lodged at the inn in Piccadilly (now the High Street). The old thatched inn was demolished in the 1860s, but a granite tablet, erected in 1913, commemorates Robert's brief sojourn there. The following day he and Ainslie doubled back to Caddonfoot, then went across country, presumably to Galashiels, though this was not mentioned, and thence to Earlston where they dined. This inn later became the venue for the Ercildoune Burns Club, one of the oldest in existence. The travellers viewed the ruins of the castle where Thomas the Rhymer had lived, and passed the scene immortalised in the ballad 'Cowdenknowes' before riding on, through Gordon and Greenlaw, to Berrywell. That evening Robert dined with the local Farmers' Club and met another punning cleric, the Revd. Andrew Smith (1741–89), and the celebrated mechanic, Andrew Meikle (1719–1811) of Houston Mill who had invented the threshing-machine.

At Duns parish church, after morning worship on 6 May, Robert was introduced to Symon Gray, a retired London businessman and amateur versifier who made many charitable bequests and is commemorated in the local literary society. He pestered Robert with a specimen of his work on which he wanted his views. Robert gave it a hasty perusal and returned it with the endorsement, 'Symon Gray, You're dull to-day'. Gray, unabashed, immediately sent a fresh packet which Robert just as promptly returned with another couplet on the outside:

> Dulness, with redoubled sway,
> Has seized the wits of Symon Gray

Two rebuffs were insufficient to take the edge off Gray's vanity, and he sent a third packet containing several of his most elaborate performances. It came too late for Robert to pay it immediate attention, as he was about to depart on his excursion to Kelso, Jedburgh and Selkirk, but it was waiting for him when he returned to Berrywell on 15 May. Robert now responded with a brief verse-epistle (CW 279–80) which ended with the crushing quatrain:

> Such damn'd bombast no time that's past
>   Will show, or time to come,
> So, Cimon dear, your song I'll tear,
>   And with it wipe my —.

Gray's reaction to this *coup de grâce* is not recorded; but he never had the temerity to foist any more of his effusions on the long-suffering poet.

After breakfast at Berrywell on Thursday 17 May Burns and Ainslie visited a farmer named James Thomson who had recently married Patty Grieve, an old flame of Ainslie's.[7] Even on tour Robert was unable to get away entirely from mundane business matters, for he wrote a letter on 17 May to Alexander Pattison of Paisley whom he facetiously addressed as 'Bookseller' because he had been so successful in disposing of a considerable number of copies of the Edinburgh Edition (CL 308). Robert had arranged for his mail to be forwarded to him at Berrywell and he must have been gratified to receive Pattison's letter of 11 May enclosing a bank draft for £22 7s in respect of ninety books. Pattison had heard a rumour that

Burns was going to London, but Robert now soundly refuted this. Most of the letter was taken up with business matters and problems arising out of the non-supply of books to James Cowan of Paisley. The same day, therefore, Robert wrote to Creech's assistant, Peter Hill (CL 308), asking him to supply Pattison, Cowan and anyone else to whom copies had been sent on credit 'what number they demand when they require it; provided always that those who are non-subscriber shall pay one shilling more than subscribers'. Robert concluded this business letter in a curious manner: 'This I write to you when I am miserably fou, consequently it must be the sentiments of my heart'. This letter, now preserved in the City Museum, Edinburgh, gives the lie to Robert's confession of drunkenness, for the handwriting is as vigorous and well formed as usual, and the letter is free of mistakes, which would not have been the case had he been as 'miserably fou' as he claimed. This masquerade of drunkenness is a curious feature in several letters of later years and may have genuinely misled his earliest biographers; though, judging from the quality and contents of these epistles, we may judge that Robert, as usual, had his tongue in his cheek.

On 18 May he rode with Ainslie to Berwick, 'An idle town, rudely picturesque', and while they were wandering round the city walls they encountered the Earl of Errol. Robert duly recorded 'His Lordship's flattering notice of me'. Robert had an invitation from John Renton of Lamerton to visit him at his residence, Mordington House. He responded to the invitation with six lines of verse (CW 280), but there was no indication in the journal that the meeting took place. Instead, he dined with John Clunie who had been mayor in 1783–4 and was a partner in the timber and iron company of Clunie and Home ('nothing particular in company or conversation'), then went on to Eyemouth to sup and sleep at the home of William Grieve. The following day Grieve, a keen freemason, introduced Burns and Ainslie at the St Ebbe's lodge whose records show that:

> At a general encampment held this day the following Brethren were made Royal Arch Masons – namely, Robert Burns, from the Lodge of St James's, Tarbolton, Ayrshire, and Robert Ainslie, from the Lodge of St Luke's, Edinburgh . . . Robert Ainslie paid one guinea admission dues; but on account of R. Burns's remarkable poetical genius, the encampment unanimously agreed to admit him gratis, and considered themselves honoured by having a man of such shining abilities for one of their companions.[8]

Afterwards William's brother and partner, Robert Grieve, took the visitors for a sail to view the fishing boats in the harbour. Here (though he made no mention of it) Robert parted company with Ainslie whose leave was up and who had to head back to Edinburgh.

Having dismissed Sunday 20 May with 'A Mr Robinson, brewer at Ednam, sets out with us to Dunbar', Robert returned to the subject of his host at Eyemouth: 'Mr William Grieve's attachment to the family circle so fond, that when he is out, which by the bye is often the case, he cannot go to bed till he sees if all his sisters are sleeping well'. Of these sisters he also noted, 'The Miss Grieves very good girls. – My bardship's heart got a brush from Miss Betsey'. Patty Grieve, Ainslie's old flame, was her sister. On Sunday the travellers passed Coldingham Abbey and Pease-bridge and dined with George Sherriff, scion of a well-known Longformacus family ('talkative and conceited'). Later Robert was to regale his late companion Ainslie with an account of that evening (CL 327). Sherriff was a crashing bore, but fortunately his landlord called and detained him on business till almost eleven o'clock, leaving Robert with a free hand to chat up his sister 'till I was, in the language of the royal Voluptuary, Solomon, "Sick of Love!".' In the journal Robert noted that he 'talked of love to Nancy the whole evening, while her brother escorts home some companions like himself'. George Sherriff was a tenant of Sir James Hall of Dunglass (1761–1832) who called at breakfast the following day to take Robert off to show him round his estate. Robert was invited to dine at Dunglass but 'he would not stay dinner', and returned to Sherriff's for his mare in order to ride on to Dunbar. By now the poet was done with Nancy Sherriff, with whom he had such a nauseating dose of love-talk on the previous evening, but was consternated to find that she had taken him seriously. What followed was briefly described in the journal, and more fully in the letter to Ainslie. The incident shows Robert in a rather ungallant light. In his diary he wrote of the young lady who

> will accompany me to Dunbar, by way of making a parade of me as a sweet-heart of hers, among her relations. She mounts an old cart-horse, as huge and as lean as a house; a rusty old side-saddle without girth or stirrup, but fastened on with an old pillion-girth – herself as fine as hands could make her, in cream-coloured riding-clothes, hat and feather, &c.– I, ashamed of my situation, ride like the devil and almost shake her to pieces on old Jolly – get rid of her by refusing to call at her uncle's with her.

The farmer in Burns cast an experienced eye over the countryside, noting 'the most glorious corn country I ever saw, till I reached Dunbar, a neat little town'. Half a page was devoted to an account of his doings in Dunbar, of dining with Provost Robert Fall ('an eminent merchant, and most respectable character, but undescribable, as he exhibits no marked traits') and calling on a Miss Clarke ('a maiden, in the Scotch phrase, *Guid enough, but no brent new*') with his travelling companion Mr Robinson, who was the subject of a lengthy description; but of the historic town itself, and its connections with Oliver Cromwell, there was no mention. There was, in fact, no evidence anywhere in the journal that Robert had the slightest interest in the larger historical associations of the places he visited or passed by (such as Pinkie and Flodden), although he often went out of his way to visit places celebrated in Scottish song.

By 22 May Robert was at Skateraw where the farmer, a Mr Lee, persuaded him to stay the night. At dinner that evening Robert met up with the Revd. Dr Bowmaker again ('a reverend, rattling old fellow'). The following morning he left Skateraw for Duns with 'a lad of slender abilities, and bashfully diffident to an extreme'. He was back in Duns before dinner, and went out to his friend's home where he found

> Miss Ainslie, the amiable, the sensible, the good-humoured, the sweet Miss Ainslie, all alone at Berrywell.– Heavenly powers, who know the weakness of human hearts, support mine! What happiness must I see only to remind me that I cannot enjoy it! . . . How well-bred, how frank, how good she is! Charming Rachel! may thy bosom never be wrung by the evils of this life of sorrows, or by the villainy of this world's sons!

Rachel, who was just nineteen at this time, lived to a ripe old age but never married.

At Berrywell Robert dealt with his business mail before setting off, on Thursday 24 May, with Gilbert Kerr to visit the north of England. They had not got very far, however, when they paused to dine at the home of Thomas Hood. We may sense the alarm with which Robert recorded:

> I am taken extremely ill with strong feverish symptoms, and take a servant of Mr Hood's to watch me all night – embittering remorse scares my fancy at the gloomy forebodings of death.– I am determined to live for the future in such a manner as not to be scared at the approach of death – I am sure I could meet him with indifference, but for 'The something beyond the grave'.

Thomas Hood agreed to accompany Robert and Kerr on their jaunt into England, provided they could wait till Sunday. In the interim Robert accompanied his host on Friday to see the roup of an unfortunate farmer's stock – 'rigid economy, and decent industry, do you preserve me from being the principal *dramatis persona* in such a scene of horror!' That day Robert met Ainslie's father who called on Hood to take farewell of the poet. 'This day I feel myself warm with sentiments of gratitude to the Great Preserver of men, who has kindly restored me to health and strength once more.'

On Sunday the party crossed the Tweed and traversed wild moorland until they came to Alnwick. Thomas Wilkin (1737–98), steward to the Duke of Northumberland, showed them over the castle and its policies. The following day they travelled along country byways to Warkworth and spent the night at Morpeth and went on to Newcastle on 29 May. Newcastle itself was not described, though Robert mentioned 'a very agreeable, sensible fellow, a Mr Chattox' who dined with them. Tuesday 29 May was a total blank so far as the journal went; instead, on that day, Robert penned a long, rollicking letter to Ainslie (CL 327–8), although, reading between the lines, we can sense his loneliness:

> Here am I, a woeful wight on the banks of Tyne.– Old Mr. Thos. Hood has been persuaded to join our Partie, and Mr. Kerr & he do very well, but alas! I dare not talk nonsense lest I lose all the little dignity I have among the sober sons of wisdom & discretion.

It is interesting, however, to compare Robert's journal entry concerning Nancy Sherriff who insisted on escorting him to Dunbar, and his Rabelaisian description in the letter to his bosom companion. After treating Ainslie to a very full and unflattering description of the pertinacious lady's physical attributes and accoutrements, he continued:

> In the words of the Highlandman when he saw the Devil on Shanter-hill in the shape of five swine – 'My hair stood and my p– stood, and I swat & trembled.'– Nothing could prevail with her, no distant insinuation, no broad hint would make her give over her purpose; at last vexed, disgusted, enraged, to a high degree, I pretended a fire-haste and rode so hard that she was almost shaken to pieces on old Jolly, and, to my great joy found it convenient to stop at an uncle's house by the way: I refused to call with her, and so we quarreled & parted.

By Wednesday 30 May Robert and his companions were on the move again. They breakfasted at Hexham and got as far as the celebrated spa of Wardrew that night. The following day they dined at Longtown and there parted company. Robert rode on alone towards Carlisle where he met

> a strange enough romantic adventure by the way, in falling in with a girl and her married sister – the girl, after some overtures of gallantry on my side, sees me a little cut with the bottle, and offers to take me in for a Gretna Green affair. I, not being quite such a gull as she imagines, make an appointment with her, by way of *vive la bagatelle*, to hold a conference on it when we reach town. I meet her in town and give her a brush of caressing and a bottle of cyder; but finding herself *un peu trompée* in her man, she sheers off.

There is no record in the journal of an incident at Carlisle when Robert let his mare stray on to the municipal park known as the Bitts. As a result, the horse was impounded and Robert was promptly brought before a magistrate, but on learning the identity of the horse's owner the mayor ordered that the case be dropped lest Burns make a poem about the incident. Burns, however, was alleged to have produced a quatrain:

> Was e'er puir poet sae befitted,
> The maister drunk – the horse committed;
> Puir harmless beast! tak thee nae care,
> Thou'll be a horse when he's nae mair [mayor].

This verse, ignored by early editors, first appeared in Wilmot's edition of 1863, and as no holograph manuscript has ever come to light it is now regarded as spurious. Scott Douglas (1877) doubted the authenticity of this epigram, on the grounds that the journal was very detailed regarding the visit to Carlisle, but Robert made no mention of such an incident therein, nor in his letter to William Nicol. On 1 June Robert met 'my very good friend, Mr Mitchell', senior partner in the calico printery of Mitchell,

Ellwood and Company, who took him on a walk round the town and its environs and a tour of inspection through the printworks where four or five hundred people were employed. After dining with Mitchell, Robert rode off, crossed the Sark into Scotland and took the coast road to Annan. 'Overtaken on the way by a curious old fish of a shoemaker, and miner from Cumberland mines,' wrote Robert; and at this point the manuscript ended abruptly.

It is ironic that Robert's only known letter in the vernacular should have been written when he was in England (CL 342–3). Headed 'Carlisle 1st June 1787 – or I believe the 39th o' May rather' and addressed to 'Kind, honest-hearted Willie', it was an extraordinary production showing Robert's mastery of Scots prose. It is to be regretted that, apart from the occasional word or phrase, he never repeated the exercise. His description of the two girls who captured his fancy will suffice to give a flavour of the letter:

> I met wi' twa dink quines in particular, ane o' them a sonsie, fine, fodgel lass, baith braw and bonie; the tither was a clean-shankit, straught, tight, weel-far'd winch, as blithe's a lintwhite on a flowerie thorn, and as sweet and modest's a new-blawn plumrose in a hazle shaw. They were baith bred to mainers by the beuk, and onie ane o' them had as muckle smeddum and rumblgumption as the half o' some presbytries that you and I baith ken. They play'd me sic a deevil o' a shavie that I daur say if my harigals were turn'd out, ye wad see twa nicks i' the heart o' me like the mark o' a kail-whittle in a castock.

At Dumfries Robert got a good reception and on 4 June the freedom of the burgh was conferred on him. There is no truth in the widely held tradition that Burns was invited to Dumfries by the magistrates for the express purpose of honouring him. Dumfries lay on his route from Carlisle to Dalswinton, where he was to meet Patrick Miller. Robert reached the county town on the evening of 1 June and stayed there three days; and it was only on the last day that the magistrates, taking note of the distinguished visitor to the town, belatedly honoured him. Chambers commented on the fact that no record had survived of any public ceremony having taken place on the occasion,[9] but many years previously the Burgh Council had enacted that no 'gratis' burgess tickets were to be entered in the Council books, so as not to confuse them with those who paid burgess composition with the intention of exercising the rights and privileges thus obtained.[10] In fact, there *was* a record of the event, entered in a small quarto volume headed 'List of Honorary Burgess Tickets furnished by Archd. Malcolm and John Aitken, Town Clerks of Dumfries, by order of the Magistrates to the persons following'. This book contained entries from 9 December 1777 till 9 July 1795. Under the date of 4 June 1787 we find that 'Mr. Robert Burns, Ayrshire' and 'The Revd. Mr. George Gordon, Preacher of the Gospel' were granted their tickets by the provost (William Clark) and Bailies Lawson and Wilson.[11] At that period would-be burgesses had usually to pay ten merks (if the sons of burgesses) or £80 Scots (£6 13s 4d sterling) for the privilege, but the Council seem to have been remarkably liberal with honorary burgess tickets, as no fewer than thirty-eight were granted in 1787 alone, and in some other years the number was twice as large. Most of the honorary burgesses were gentlemen who frequented the town in October for the annual race meetings, balls and assemblies, and following the outbreak of the French war in 1793 it became customary to grant the freedom of the burgh to the officers of the regiments billeted there. The custom was sadly abused, and the Council minutes frequently implored the magistrates to confer the tickets 'as cautiously as possible, so as the burgh be not hurt'; but to no avail, as even the servants of visiting gentlemen were often honoured just as indiscriminately. The worst case occurred on 24 April 1784 when William Mitchel, steward to the Duke of Queensberry, was honoured – along with seven other servants from Drumlanrig, including two footmen and the Duke's groom! It is interesting to note, among other honorary burgesses, the names of Harry Erskine, the Revd. John Kemp and the Duke of Gordon (1779), Robert Dundas of Arniston (1780), Professor Dugald Stewart (1782), Patrick Miller of Dalswinton and his son of the same name (1783), the Earl of Eglinton (1784), Fergusson of Craigdarroch and Collector John Mitchell (1788), and William Smellie, printer of the Edinburgh Edition (1792) – all gentlemen connected directly or indirectly with Burns. The honorary burgesses paid a fee to the Town Clerk for their tickets – two shillings gilt or one shilling plain. Robert's ticket was one of the more modest variety. What later became of it is not known for certain – it was probably scooped up with everything else sent to Currie – but it turned up in 1859 in time for exhibition at the Centenary Music-hall Banquet in Edinburgh, and was sold at Sotheby's in 1904 for £55, the purchaser being John Thomson, proprietor of the Hole i' the Wa' public-house in Dumfries where it was displayed until its transfer to the Dumfries Burgh Museum about 1975. The Revd. George Gordon, honoured along with Burns, was licensed as a preacher at Edinburgh in 1779 and ordained minister of Sorn parish in 1789. He was twice married, his second wife being Ann Lawrie, daughter of the poet's friend the Revd. Dr George Lawrie of Newmilns.[12]

According to Chambers[13] Robert also at this time received the bad news that he had got an Edinburgh domestic servant into serious trouble. Some doubt as to the *year* exists, however, because Robert's letter to Ainslie dealing with the matter is known only by the undated draft now preserved in the Birthplace Museum. DeLancey Ferguson (1931), and subsequent editors of the poet's correspondence, however, assigned it to 1788, because of a confession, in a letter to Ainslie of 30 June 1788 (CL 334), that 'I am vexed at that affair of the girl' which was thought to allude to this affair. On the other hand, DeLancey Ferguson[14] contradicted himself eight years after the publication of his edition of the Letters when he placed this incident in 1787 and noted that in another letter to Ainslie, dated 29 July that year (CL 329), Robert cast some light on this hitherto perplexing incident. This letter was in reply to one from young Bob confessing that he, too, had got a girl in trouble. Robert characteristically made light of another man's predicament with 'Welcome, Sir, to the society, the venerable Society, of FATHERS!!!' After quoting the metrical version of Psalm 127: 3–5 about Love's children being God's heritage, he mentioned Jean Armour (of which more later) and then, as an afterthought, 'and Peggy will bring me a gallant half-Highlander – and I shall get a farm, and keep them all about my hand'. Professor Ferguson might have added, but apparently over-looked, that the affair was also alluded to in the fragmentary letter from Robert to Ainslie from Arrochar on 25 June 1787 (CL 328). Currie and all subsequent editors till Ferguson (1931) omitted the tantalising snatch '. . . the Devil's Day-book only April 14 or fifteen so cannot yet have increased her growth much. I begin, from that, and some other circumstances to suspect foul play; and to tell the truth I w . . .' From this we infer that Robert had intercourse with Margaret Cameron for the first time about 14 or 15 April. By 26 May she might have realised that she was pregnant, but it would not have begun to show. If Margaret asserted that her pregnant *appearance* had led to her dismissal, Robert would have been quite right to suspect that he was now taking the blame for someone else.

That 'Peggy' and the girl whose disagreeable news reached Robert as soon as he reached Dumfries were one and the same is borne out by the writ *in meditatione fugae* taken out against him in July 1787.[15] This unequivocally places the episode with Miss Cameron in the spring and summer of that year, and not 1788. Thus the undated draft must be of a letter to Ainslie written at Dumfries about 1 June 1787:

> My first welcome to this place was the inclosed letter.– I am very sorry for it, but what is done is done.– I pay you no compliment when I say that except my old friend Smith there is not any person in the world I would trust so far.– Please call at the James Hog mentioned, and send for the wench and give her ten or twelve shillings, but don't for Heaven's sake meddle with her as a *Piece*.– I insist on this, on your honor; and advise her out to some country friends.– You may perhaps not like the business, but I just tax your friendship thus far. – Call for God's sake, lest the poor soul be starving. Ask her for a letter I wrote her just now, by way of token. It is unsigned. – Write me after the meeting –

Further confirmation that this incident occurred in 1787 is provided by some disjointed notes which Robert scribbled in the notebook containing the journal of the Border tour. On the page following the last diary entry there appear several names and addresses, among them 'James Hog, Shoe-maker, Buchanan's Land, head of Canongate'. Curiously enough, some confusion has arisen over the name of Robert's second Highland lassie. The earliest biographies omit all mention of this episode[16] while the Revd. George Gilfillan (1872) either overlooked the news Robert received at Dumfries or confused it with the later affair with Jenny Clow.[17] Wallace (1896), however, stated that at Dumfries Robert received a pitiful letter, dated 26 May, from a domestic servant in Edinburgh, named May Cameron, asking help, as she was 'in trouble'. The poor girl, who had to get a friend to write for her, did not reproach Burns, nor did she say directly that he was the cause of her 'trouble'. She decribed herself as his 'sincere well-wisher', and apologised for writing: but 'out of quarters, without friends, my situation at present is really deplorable. I beg, for God sake, you will write and let me know how I am to do. You can write to any person you can trust to get me a place to stay in till such time as you come to town yourself.'[18]

It has been surmised that the person who wrote the letter on the girl's behalf was the wife of the James Hog mentioned in Robert's letter to Ainslie. Tantalisingly, Wallace gave no details of the source of his quotation, but presumably he had access to the girl's letter, or a transcript of it. Robert himself never referred to the matter again. Some writers,[19] taking the poet too literally, thought that the girl was the same as 'a Highland wench in the Cowgate [who] bore me three bastards at a birth' to whom Robert alluded in a letter to George Thomson of September 1793 (CL 644), blithely ignoring the fact that Burns meant it merely as a colourful metaphor for his surprise at Thomson's opinion of the song 'Dainty Davie'. Others have even speculated that 'May' Cameron and Jenny Clow were one and the same.[20] No Burns scholar, it seems, has ever attempted to identify these girls or the children they bore. Doubtless Chambers was relying on oral tradition when he named the girl as May Cameron. DeLancey Ferguson, by identifying the girl with the Peggy of the letter to Ainslie quoted earlier, referred to her eight times as Meg Cameron.[21] Although this is a common name, the only person called Margaret Cameron recorded in the parish registers of Edinburgh at the right time was a girl in the Tolbooth parish who married a cattle-drover named Mungo Forbes of New Greyfriars parish on 5 September 1788. Subsequent research has revealed that she was born at Fortingall, the daughter of Hugh Cameron and Catherine Kennedy, on 19 August 1766. Her husband was a first-cousin and hailed from the neighbouring parish of Dull and was born on 18 January 1766 to Neil Forbes and Christian Kennedy. It looks as if Margaret met up with her childhood sweetheart when they were both working in Edinburgh. The eldest child of this marriage was Katherine Campbell Forbes, born at Edinburgh on 4 April 1790. This child must have died young, for a second daughter, born on 20 June 1804, was christened Catherine. The only other child was David Forbes, born on 9 May 1795.[22] If this were the Margaret Cameron who was seduced by Burns she would have been twenty-one at the time. No record of a birth to Margaret Cameron in 1787 is to be found in the Edinburgh parish registers, which points to the possibilities that the infant was prematurely stillborn – not an unusual occurrence for that time – or that Margaret miscarried. That the problem resolved itself in some way seems to have been confirmed by a document of 15 August 1787 which freed Burns from the restraints of the writ previously taken out against him. Robert preserved this document, on the back of which he scribbled 'with a pencil in his own hand, a couple of verses of an old and broadly humorous song, which he had probably heard sung somewhere, and wished to preserve'.[23] Thereafter Margaret Cameron disappears from the Burns story. When Sir James Shaw, the Kilmarnock-born Lord Mayor of London (and a nephew of Gilbert Burns through his marriage to Jean Breckenridge), made enquiries regarding the illegitimate children of the poet in 1804–5, he could find no trace of any offspring of Burns by this girl.

On 18 June 1787 Robert wrote to William Nicol (CL 344):

> I have been with Mr Miller at Dalswinton, and am to meet him again in August. – From my view of the lands and his reception of my Bardship, my hopes in that business are rather mended; but still they are but slender.

Robert first made the acquaintance of Patrick Miller of Dalswinton soon after his arrival in the capital, when the latter had left ten guineas for him at Sibbald's bookshop. Subsequently Robert learned of his benefactor's identity and they had met at Miller's Edinburgh residence on 12 December. A month later Robert wrote to Ballantine (CL 100):

> My generous friend, Mr Peter Miller (sic), brother to the Justice Clerk, has been talking with me about a lease of some farm or other in an estate called Dasswinton (sic) which he has lately bought near Dumfries. – Some life-rented, embittering Recollections whisper me that I will be happier any where than in my old neighbourhood, but Mr Miller is no Judge of land; and though I dare say he means to favour me, yet he may give me, in his opinion, an advantageous bargain that may ruin me.– I am to take a tour by Dumfries as I return and have promised to meet Mr Miller on his lands some time in May.

In view of the fact that he later settled in Dumfries, it is interesting to note Robert's favourable impression, in a letter to Nicol dated 18 June (CL 344):

> I am quite charmed with Dumfries folks.– Mr Burnside the Clergyman, in particular, is a man I shall ever gratefully remember; and his wife, Gude forgie me, I had almost broke the tenth commandment on her account.– Simplicity, elegance, good sense, sweetness of disposition, good humour, kind hospitality, are the constituents of her manner and heart; in short – but if I say one word more about her, I shall be directly in love with her.

Dr Burnside (1751–1838), then minister of the New Church (now Greyfriars), was translated to St Michael's parish church in 1794. His wife Anne was a few months younger than the poet and quite a beauty; it is hardly surprising that Robert was dazzled by her.

Some time after 4 June, therefore, Robert rode the six miles out from Dumfries and conferred with Patrick Miller. Apart from a brief reference to this in the letter to Nicol, however, Robert did not mention his visit, so it is not known whether he made a tour of inspection of the farms on the Dalswinton estate at this time. It seems probable that the meeting was not as brief and inconsequential as many writers have supposed. Although it might have been thought that Robert was anxious to get back home to Mossgiel, he dallied on the way from Dumfries and did not reach Mauchline until the evening of Friday 8 June. Curiously enough, he was in no hurry to be off out to the farm, for he put up at John Dow's tavern for the night. The reason for this seeming dilatoriness was conveyed in a letter to James Smith, written at Mauchline on 11 June (CL 118–19):

> I cannot settle to my mind – Farming the only thing of which I know any thing, and Heaven above knows, but little do I understand even of that, I cannot, I dare not risk on farms as they are. If I do not fix, I will go for Jamaica. Should I stay, in an unsettled state, at home, I would only dissipate my little fortune, and ruin what I intend shall compensate my little ones, for the stigma I have brought on their names.

This letter shows Robert at his most indecisive. The last sentence, however, reveals that he was beginning to feel some sense of responsibility for his three illegitimate children. Apparently it had been agreed with the Armour family that as soon as baby Robert was weaned he should go to Mossgiel to be raised by the poet's mother along with 'dear-bought Bess' while baby Jean remained with her mother. Soon after arriving at Mauchline, probably the following morning, Robert called at the Armour residence, ostensibly to see his infant daughter. 'If any thing had been wanting to disgust me compleatly at Armour's family, their mean servile compliance would have done it,' he wrote scornfully to Smith. By contrast to the manner in which the Armours had hounded him the previous summer, they now seem to have gone out of their way to extend a warm welcome to the local boy made good. Far from being relieved that James Armour's anger had abated, Robert was merely revolted. I cannot help thinking that subconsciously he was repelled by women who took an active rather than a passive role – just as Nancy Sherriff had done on the ride to Dunbar. No doubt poor, long-suffering Jean was overjoyed to see her erstwhile lover again; and equally her parents were bowled over by his fame and reputed fortune.

Margaret Cameron's unwelcome news was doubtless still ringing in his ears as he was trying to disentangle himself from Jean's cloying embrace. In trying to steel his heart, Robert turned to Milton's *Paradise Lost* and besought a spirit like his favourite hero, Satan:

> Hail, horrors! hail,
> Infernal world! and thou, profoundest Hell,
> Receive thy new possessor! one who brings
> A mind not to be chang'd by *place* or *time*![24]

In a letter to Mrs Dunlop on 30 April (CL 136) Robert had announced that he had resolved to study 'the sentiments of a very respectable personage, Milton's Satan'; now, in the letter to Nicol, Robert revealed that he was beginning to identify himself with Milton's fallen angel:

> I have bought a pocket Milton which I carry perpetually about with me, in order to study the sentiments – the dauntless magnanimity; the intrepid, unyielding independance; the desperate daring, and noble defiance of hardship, in that great Personage, Satan.

And later in the same letter he returned to a favourite introspective theme, the 'thoughtless follies and hare-brained whims' which, like some will o' the wisp, 'sparkle in the idly-gazing eyes of the poor heedless Bard, till, pop, he falls like Lucifer, never to hope again' – a quotation this time from Shakespeare's *Henry VIII*. Nicol was now in the ascendant as Robert's principal male confidant.

Mrs Dunlop, of course, continued in her role as mother confessor. Later Robert was to write to her (CL 149) 'On my éclatant return to Mauchline, I was made very welcome to visit my girl.– The usual consequences began to betray her'. Robert had left Mauchline penniless and unknown, and had returned a national celebrity. In Edinburgh and on the Border tour he had rubbed shoulders with the high and the mighty, the great and the good of the land. He had been fêted by the nobility and lionised by the literati. He had lost his heart in rapid succession to a whole series of attractive young ladies (although his only actual conquest had been an illiterate Highland serving wench); yet on his return home he found Jean just as 'delicious an armful' as ever, and her parents now positively threw her at him. Despite his protestations of disgust, Robert soon found himself as hopelessly in love with Jean as before. Lying in her warm embrace once more gave him an acute perspective on life in general and his future course of conduct. The adulation of his friends and acquaintances unsettled him: 'the servility of my plebeian brethren, who perhaps formerly eyed me askance, since I returned home, have nearly put me out of conceit altogether with my species', he wrote to Nicol. Mauchline must have seemed small and claustrophobic after his sojourn in the metropolis.

Significantly, Robert made no mention in his correspondence of the reception he got at Mossgiel on his return. He seems never to have bothered writing to Gilbert during his six months' absence. What later developed into the long autobiographical letter to Dr Moore, completed at Mauchline on 2 August 1787 (CL 248), began:

> For some months past I have been rambling over the country, partly on account of some little business I have to settle in various places; but of late I have been confined with some lingering complaints originating as I take it in the stomach.– To divert my spirits a little in this miserable fog of Ennui, I have taken a whim to give you a history of MYSELF.

Restless, aimless, bored, unhappy and doubtless finding life at Mossgiel a terrible come-down, Robert tarried less than two weeks before he was off on his travels again. He saddled his mare and rode off in search of new sights and more congenial company. Currie (1800) stated that he remained at Mauchline only a few days before proceeding again to Edinburgh, 'and immediately set out on a journey to the Highlands'. There is no evidence to support this assertion. Robert was still at Mauchline on 18 June when he wrote to Nicol, with a postscript 'I shall be in Edinr about the latter end of July'. The next letter, written six days later, was a brief note to Creech from Glasgow (CL 305) asking him to send fifty copies of the book to John Smith, one of that city's leading booksellers. According to Isobel Burns, she had the impression that her brother had gone direct to Glasgow where he purchased bolts of *mode* silk which he despatched home to his mother and sisters, 'sufficient to make a bonnet and cloak to each, and a gown to his mother and youngest sister, the whole being a recognition of their title to a share of his good-fortune'. Mrs Begg remembered going for rather more than a week to Ayr, to assist in the making up of these dresses; and when she came back on a Saturday (30 June) Robert had returned, and she recollected being requested by him to put on her dress, that he might see how smart she looked in it.[25]

The so-called West Highland tour may have been, as Robert hinted to Moore, in the nature of a business trip like the Border tour, but the facts that he made the journey unaccompanied and did not attempt to keep a journal seem to imply some hidden, deeper motive. Snyder felt that the West Highland trip was motivated by a desire to visit the family of Margaret Campbell. 'If he actually went to Glasgow, a trip down the Clyde to Greenock, where lay the body of the woman he had promised to marry, would have seemed inevitable.'[26] From this developed the implausible theory that he took a ship across the Firth of Clyde and visited old Agnes Campbell at Campbeltown, but this would have entailed a voyage of several days with poor Jenny Geddes in the cattle-hold, and there just was not the time to do it. Of course, the date on the letter to Creech could be wrong, and Robert might already have left Glasgow some days before 24 June. More probably, however, the date of the very next recorded letter, to Ainslie from Arrochar on 25 June (CL 328), was wrong and, indeed, Currie assigned 28 June to it when he first published it in 1800. By that time Robert could report that his last stage had been Inveraray and that his next stop would be at Dumbarton.

It is not impossible that Robert rode from Glasgow to Greenock, made a quick pilgrimage to the girl's grave, then took the ferry to Dunoon, a short sea-crossing. From there he could have ridden north through Sandbank, past Margaret's birthplace and up the side of Lock Eck to Strachur, then round the head of Loch Fyne to Inveraray. This is pure conjecture, of course, unsupported by any documentary evidence, but it would explain how he was able to reach Inveraray within two days of leaving Glasgow.

On the other hand, if the letter to Creech was erroneously dated but actually written on 22 June, Robert could have travelled overland to Inveraray. The letter to Smith is incomplete and Currie, when first publishing it in 1803, mentioned that it was part of a letter communicated to him since the publication of the previous edition. It is extremely regrettable that the whole of this letter has not survived for it might have solved the mystery of Robert's motives and movements. But the words 'On our return' with which the extract begins imply two things – that Robert did not travel alone, as has often been supposed, and that when he travelled from Inveraray to Glasgow he was merely retracing his steps. This would rule out the visit to Greenock and the sea-crossing with Jenny Geddes.

That Robert was actually accompanied on the journey would conform to the pattern of his other tours. He was not only a gregarious being who revelled in the company of like-minded individuals, but a rather timid traveller who would scarcely have ventured 'through a country where savage streams tumble over savage mountains, thinly overspread with savage flocks, which starvingly support as savage inhabitants'[27] without the comfort of seasoned travelling companions. It seems likely that, in Glasgow, Robert called on Dr George Grierson who, having ordered thirty-six copies, was by far the largest subscriber to the Edinburgh Edition in that city. It may be that Grierson agreed to accompany Robert on his projected foray into the West Highlands; and it may be that George Gairdner of Ladykirk completed the party, for reasons given later. A fellow mason, Grierson was made an honorary member of Tarbolton St James's lodge on 25 July that year. The minute recording this occasion was made by Robert himself, in his capacity as Depute Master.[28] An extensive correspondence between Burns and Grierson is said to have been in the possession of John Reid of Kingston, Glasgow, who also had Grierson's manuscript of the West Highland tour, but the Reid Collection was destroyed in 1831 when the Clyde burst its banks and inundated the Kingston district.

Why Robert should have been so keen to get to Inveraray, apparently the furthest point of his journey into Argyll,[29] is a complete mystery, but the fact that the Duke and Duchess of Argyll headed the subscribers' list seems to offer a clue. Perhaps Robert had a long-standing invitation to visit the duke; but, as it turns out, he could not have chosen a worse moment. It was singularly unfortunate that John Campbell, fifth Duke of Argyll (1723–1806), was in the course of hosting a large gathering of the British Fishery Society of which he was President, prior to departing the following day for the Hebrides to select a site for a new fishing port in the island of Mull (Tobermory, established two years later). The castle was full and the members and officials of the Society had spilled over to the local inn; as a result, the innkeeper, John Frazer, was too preoccupied with the duke's guests to serve the travel-weary poet.[30] Robert had recently acquired a diamond-pointed stylus, such as was used by glass-engravers, and now gave vent to a peculiar form of graffiti. On one of the window-panes at the inn he allegedly scratched the lines:

Whoe'er he be that sojourns here,
  I pity much his case.
Unless he come to wait upon
  The lord *their* god, 'His Grace'.

There's naething here but Highland pride,
  And Highland scab and hunger;
If Providence has sent me here,
  'Twas surely in an anger.

No trace of the window now exists, although two different versions of the epigram were in print by the beginning of the nineteenth century.[31] A third version was given by Hately Waddell in his revised edition of 1870, annotated 'The above lines were written at the inn at Inveraray, by R. Burns in presence of George Grierson'. Waddell, in fact, was quoting from the manuscript compiled some years after the event by Grierson who stated that the lines were written on a pane of glass in his presence. What puzzles me about the Grierson manuscript[32] is that it begins at Inveraray, thereby undermining the theory that Grierson travelled all the way from Glasgow to Inveraray and back with Burns. But it must be borne in mind that all we have to go on regarding the manuscript is that portion of it which Hately Waddell chose to reproduce. Presumably, if the original were destroyed in 1831 as he claimed, Waddell was working from a copy; what, one wonders, has become of that?

From Inveraray Robert rode back by Clachan and Cairndow, then through the pass aptly named Rest and be Thankful and down Glen Croe to Crocharibas on the heights overlooking Loch Long, where he wrote to Ainslie; and then a couple of miles round the head of the loch to Arrochar. According to Grierson, they stayed the night of 27 June at Tarbert Inn (which Waddell and some subsequent writers confused with the place of that name on Loch Fyne, but which ought to have been rendered by Grierson as Tarbet). Here Robert wrote a poem addressed to Mary McLachlan, the innkeeper's daughter, but this has not survived, apart from the final couplet:

To fair Maria add McLachlan,
Quod Burns, a rhymer lad frae Mauchlin.

The following day Robert and his travelling companions 'fell in with a merry party, at a Highland gentleman's hospitable mansion, and danced 'till the ladies left us, at three in the morning'. This comes from a long undated letter without the superscription of the addressee (Allan Cunningham gave James Smith at Linlithgow as the recipient) which was written on or shortly after 30 June (CL 119–21) and describes in graphic detail this hectic social event:

When the dear lasses left us, we ranged round the bowl till the good-fellow hour of six; except a few minutes that we went out to pay our

devotions to the glorious lamp of day peering over the towering top of
Benlomond. We all kneeled; our worthy landlord's son held the bowl;
each man a full glass in his hand; and I, as priest, repeated some rhyming
nonsense, like Thomas a Rhymer's prophecies I suppose.- After a small
refreshment of the gifts of Somnus, we proceeded to spend the day on
Lochlomond, and reached Dumbarton in the evening. We dined at
another good fellow's house, and consequently push'd the bottle; when
we went out to mount our horses, we found ourselves 'No vera fou but
gaylie yet'.[33] My two friends and I rode soberly down the Loch side, till
by came a Highlandman at the gallop, on a tolerably good horse, but
which had never known the ornaments of iron or leather. We scorned to
be out-galloped by a Highlandman, so off we started, whip and spur. My
companions, though seemingly gayly mounted, fell sadly astern; but my
old mare, Jenny Geddes, one of the Rosinante family, she strained past
the Highlandman in spite of all his efforts, with the hair-halter: just as I
was passing him, Donald wheeled his horse, as if to cross before me to mar
my progress, when down came his horse, and threw his rider's breekless
a-e in a clipt hedge; and down came Jenny Geddes over all, and my bardship between her and the Highlandman's horse. Jenny Geddes trode over
me with such cautious reverence, that matters were not so bad as might
well have been expected; so I came off with a few cuts and bruises, and
a thorough resolution to be a pattern of sobriety for the future.

Dr Grierson's account amplifies this. According to his notes, he accompanied Robert back to Glasgow from Inveraray and stayed with the poet
at Bannachra, near the southern side of Luss parish where the Fruin Water
debouches into Loch Lomond. Duncan McLachlan, son of Archibald
McLachlan of Bannachra, was the young man who was commanded by
Burns to bring out the largest punch-bowl in the house. Robert composed
an invocation to the Sun which he chanted extempore as dawn broke
while the assembled company knelt down. As well as Grierson and the
McLachlan family there were present a Mr McFarlan from Jamaica, a
Glasgow merchant John Shedden with his unmarried sister, a Mr Gardner
(sic) of Ladykirk and the two Misses Butters from Edinburgh. John
Shedden appears in Jones's Directory of Glasgow for 1787 as a merchant
residing on the west side of Dunlop Street. Mr Gardner of Ladykirk was,
in fact, George Gairdner who inherited the Ladykirk estate from his father
in 1780. William Gairdner had previously been a lawyer in Ayr but moved
to the Borders about 1774. Gairdner was about a year older than the
poet.[34] The 'Misses Butters' were Elizabeth (born 1767) and Margaret
(born 1775), daughters of Henry Butter of Pitlochry whose town-house
was in the newly fashionable George Street.[35] The other members of the
party have not been traced.[36]

The following afternoon Robert, accompanied by Grierson and Gairdner, left Bannachra and rode down the lochside to Dumbarton. 'Burns
pursued the Highlandman, till he was thrown from his horse into a thorn
tree and cut his face,' reported Grierson, confirming Robert's tale of
his reckless race. In 1787 the tacksman of Bannachra was Archibald

McLachlan, while a Peter McLauchline of Bannochray (probably a relative) was listed as a subscriber to the Edinburgh Edition. The 'good fellow' at whose house Robert dined and 'pushed the bottle' was long the matter of speculation; but according to Grierson's account, he, Burns and Gairdner dined at Arden, about two and a half miles north of Balloch on the loch-side. We can therefore assume that their host was George Buchanan, a Glasgow tobacco lord, whose country mansion was Arden House. Buchanan himself was a subscriber to the Edinburgh Edition and McLachlan of Bannachra was one of his tenants.

The letter to Smith makes no reference to events at Dumbarton, but Grierson supplied some details:

> They came that night safe to Dumbarton – when the magistrates did them all the honour of conferring the freedom of their city; and Oliphant preached next day, being the Fast-day, against the parties foresaid, and found great fault [with] the magistrates for conferring honours on the author of *vile*, *detestable*, and *immoral* publications.

For well over a century it was believed in Dumbarton that Burns had been made an honorary burgess in 1787; but no record of this existed and the Revd. James Oliphant was blamed for this omission. Oliphant (1734–1818) was an Auld Licht who had previously been minister of Kilmarnock's High Church (1764–73) and, as such, had been lampooned by Burns in 'The Ordination' in 1786. He was on good terms with his successor at Kilmarnock, 'Black Jock' Russell, and no doubt had heard from him about the young anti-clerical poet. The absence of any record of the burgess ceremony, however, has a more prosaic explanation. Like Dumfries, previously noted, honorary burgess tickets were then dispensed with unseeming profligacy and the honour had become so debased that it no longer seemed worth the trouble of entering the details in the burgh records. 'In Dumbarton between 1767 and 1787 many hundred honorary burgesses were made for no other reason than to give the Town Clerk a fee of 3s 6d for each burgess ticket out of the revenue of the Burgh.'[37] Robert's burgess ticket, bearing the date 29 June 1787, came to light in 1911, thereby ending any lingering doubts as to whether the poet had been honoured or not.

Dumbarton was assuredly one of those places in which Robert had 'some little business', as quite a number of subscribers to the Edinburgh Edition resided in that locality. John Kennedy (1757–1812), kinsman of Gavin Hamilton's wife, had moved from Dumfries House near Cumnock to Dumbarton where he was factor to the Breadalbane estates and it was probably he who introduced Robert to John McAulay, the Town Clerk, who helped to secure a number of subscriptions. An analysis of the subscribers' list shows that most of those in the Dumbarton and Renton area were freemasons, lending weight to the belief that Robert used his masonic connections to good purpose.[38] According to local tradition, Burns and his companions were hospitably entertained at Levengrove House, the residence of John McAulay, on the night of 28 June. As well as receiving the freedom of the burgh, Robert is said to have visited the Freemasons' Lodge whose Master, Robert Lindsay, was a subscriber to the Edinburgh Edition; although there is no reference to this in the lodge minutes it would have been not unlikely.

Robert's movements thereafter are not known for certain. According to one account, he was seen in Paisley around noon on the same day as he was receiving his burgess ticket at Dumbarton. This would not have been impossible, for there was, even then, a continual ferry service between Yoker and Renfrew across the Clyde. It is more probable, however, that the writer was mistaken in the date, as there is no mention of the injuries sustained in the riding accident, and Robert is believed to have been in Paisley at the beginning of August – at least that was his intention, expressed in a letter to Mrs Dunlop, noted later.

It must have been on Friday the 29th of June, about noon, that Dr John Taylor of Paisley, who had been charmed with the poems of the Ayrshire Ploughman, readily recognised him from his portrait, as he stood in the street with his friend Mr Alexander Pattison. Having induced both Burns and Pattison to go to his house, notwithstanding some hesitation on the part of the poet, who expressed himself as eager to proceed on his journey, Dr Taylor entered into conversation on what was with himself a favourite subject – poetry. Burns made the observation that perhaps people were ready to attach more merit to poetry than was its due, for that, after all, it was only natural ideas expressed in melodious words; to which his host assented, and, in illustration, remarked that nothing was more common than for children in a winter's night to say: 'What will become of the puir birdies the nicht?' But what says the poet?

> Ilk happing bird, wee, helpless thing,
> That, in the merry months o' spring,
> Delighted me to hear thee sing,
>   What comes o' thee?
> Whare wilt thou cower thy chittering wing,
>   An' close thy e'e?[39]

The compliment pleased: Burns started on his feet, and bowing, expressed his thanks for the obliging quotation. After this, Burns seemed to forget the haste which he had before alleged; the conversation became animated, and, as it appeared, interesting to both. Burns spoke of his reception at Edinburgh, and dwelt much on the kindness which he had experienced from the Earl of Glencairn, showing a ring that he wore, a gift from that nobleman. However fond Burns was of the produce of his Muse, the other was probably no less so of his young family, who were all summoned. One of the children, a fat chubby boy, the poet took on his knee, and said 'he would make an excellent subject for a poem'; an idea which the father assured him he should be highly gratified to see carried into effect. An elder one was sent for, and desired to go in; but from the great talk he had heard about poets, and particularly about Poet Burns, this one did not feel well assured that it was safe for him to trust his person within the poet's clutches. He therefore watched his opportunity, and ventured merely to pass from one door to another through the room, taking the best look he could of the poet, as he stood up with a small black profile of Mrs Taylor's in his hand, which he was then examining. The small black profiles, called silhouettes, were then coming into fashion. From that time, although the observer was then hardly more than a child, the remembrance of the poet's figure, face, and general appearance, has never been lost; the recollection of him is distinct, and is that of a big, stout, athletic man, of a brown, ruddy complexion, broad-chested, erect, and standing firmly on his legs, which perhaps were rather clumsy, though hid in yellow topped-boots. His dress was a blue coat and buckskin breeches, and his *caste* seemed what we should now style that of a gentleman-farmer. The impression made by the poet on his host was highly favourable, but the lady was struck with a certain gloominess that seemed to have possession of his countenance and general bearing.[40]

Writing to his old friend Smith soon after his return to Mossgiel from the West Highlands (CL 120), Robert had confessed:

I have yet fixed on nothing with respect to the serious business of life. I am, just as usual, a rhyming, mason-making, rattling, aimless, idle fellow. However, I shall somewhere have a farm soon. I was going to say a wife too; but that must never be my blessed lot. I am but a younger son of Parnassus, and, like other younger sons of great families, I may intrigue, if I choose to run all risks, but must not marry.

I am afraid I have almost ruined one source, the principal one, indeed, of my former happiness – that eternal propensity I always had to fall in love. My heart no more glows with feverish raptures – I have no paradisaical evening interviews, stolen from the restless cares and prying inhabitants of this weary world.

Thus Robert declared emphatically that he had no intention of marrying Jean Armour with whom he was about to resume their affair. Indeed, if calculations concerning Jean's second pregnancy are correct, and she carried her second twins to full term, intimacy must have begun again by 14 June – fully two weeks before Robert wrote to Smith (30 June)!

The next part of the letter poses yet another of those interminable mysteries. The name of the lady, represented by asterisks in Currie's 1802 edition and all subsequent transcriptions, had either been obliterated by Currie's correspondent, or deleted by him. No manuscript of this letter has been traced:

I have only ****. This last is one of your distant acquaintances, has a fine figure, and elegant manners; and in the train of some great folks whom you know, has seen the politest quarters in Europe. I do like her a good deal; but what piques me is her conduct at the commencement of our acquaintance. I frequently visited her when I was in —, and after passing regularly the intermediate degrees between the distant formal bow and the familar grasp round the waist, I ventured in my careless way to talk of friendship in rather ambiguous terms; and after her return to — I

wrote to her in the same style. Miss, construing my words farther I
suppose than ever I intended, flew off in a tangent of female dignity and
reserve, like a mounting lark in an April morning; and wrote me an answer
which measured me out very completely what an immense way I had to
travel before I could reach the climate of her favour. But I am an old
hawk at the sport; and wrote her such a cool, deliberate, prudent reply as
brought my bird from her aerial towerings, pop, down at my foot like
corporal Trims hat.

Just who was the young lady, described here in such predatory terms, is not
known for certain, though Chambers hazarded a guess that Margaret
Chalmers was meant.[41]

Back at Mossgiel after his West Highland jaunt, Robert spent July
exactly as he described to Smith, in an aimless and idle manner. It is clear,
however, that the fall which he took on Loch Lomondside was giving him
a great deal of pain and discomfort. In a letter to Richmond on 7 July (CL
80) he described the 'drunken race' and admitted, 'so I have got such a
skinful of bruises and wounds, that I shall at least be four weeks before I
dare venture on my journey to Edinburgh'. While he recuperated,
however, he conducted his business by post, writing to Peter Hill with
instructions to pay Scott the bookbinder. He was sufficiently recovered
to preside over the meeting of St James's lodge on 25 July at which his
new friend George Grierson was admitted an honorary member. This
was the meeting of which Dugald Stewart (himself similarly honoured)
wrote so flatteringly regarding Robert's extempore speech-making. Claud
Alexander, brother of the Wilhelmina who had ignored him, was also
granted honorary membership on this august occasion.

His muse did not desert Robert entirely during this period, though the
results did not represent the poet at his best. Sir James Hunter Blair, the
Ayrshire-born Lord Provost of Edinburgh, died on 1 July. On reading of
his death in a newspaper, Robert felt constrained to compose an elegy in
his most elegant Augustan manner (CW 281–2). Robert sent copies of this
elegy to Robert Aiken (14 July) and Susan Ferrier who had requested one
of his poems. To the latter Robert addressed some twenty lines (CW 283)
in a more relaxed, characteristically jovial mood. Then, on 20 July 1787,
John McLeod of Raasay died and Robert, who had met his sister Isabella
in Edinburgh the previous winter, immediately dashed off an elegy in his
memory (CW 283–4), though he contrived to mention Isabella herself four
times in two dozen lines. Transcribing this poem later for the Glenriddell
MS, Robert added the comment, 'This poetic compliment, what few poetic
compliments are, was from the heart'.

In the course of July Robert also wrote at length to Nicol and Ainslie
(twice) as well as Mrs Dunlop. The last named, anxious at not having heard
from her poet friend for some time, sent a servant twenty miles to enquire
after his health. He bore a packet containing a letter and some verses
which Robert assured her 'Without any Poetic licence . . . upon the honor
of plain, unfettered, truth-delivering Prose, are excellent'. In his undated

reply, dated by Ferguson and Roy about 30 or 31 July but more likely 2 August (CL 137), Robert told her that he had a long letter to Dr Moore just ready to put into the post: 'It is on a subject you have done me the honor to interest yourelf in, so if you dare face twenty pages of an epistle, a reading of it is at your service.' He had no copy of this letter, but sent it back to Dunlop House with the servant so that she could read it before it was posted. 'If you can contrive no better way, I shall call for it myself tomorrow, as I am going for Edinr by way of Paisley & Glasgow, tomorrow morning.' The letter to Dr Moore, dated 2 August (CL 248–57), was retrieved by Robert a day or two later when he called at Dunlop House, but in the hustle and bustle of Glasgow he forgot to post it, and did not discover it among other papers until he unpacked his bags at Edinburgh on 23 September at the end of his Highland tour. He must then have made a copy of it, before posting it, as he later favoured Mrs McLehose with a sight of it.

Robert's movements in the first half of August are not known. After the long letter to Moore there is none actually dated until 14 August, when he wrote to Archibald Lawrie at Newmilns, but from its reference to dining with the Farquhars 't'other day' it is inferred that Robert had been back in Edinburgh for several days. It is generally accepted that he returned to the city on 7 August, from the fact that he later stated to Moore that Creech had kept him waiting for his money from 7 August 1787 till 13 April 1788. At first Robert went to lodge with John Richmond in the Lawnmarket as before, and from here he wrote a short undated note to William Tytler (CL 291). Sent on 'Monday noon', it was probably written on 13 August, and is of particular interest for the light it sheds on Robert's passion for old ballads:

> Inclosed I have sent you a sample of the old pieces that are still to be found among our Peasantry in the West. I once had a great many of these fragments and some of these here entire; but as I had no idea then that any body cared for them, I have forgot them.– I invariably hold it sacriledge to add any thing of my own to help out with the shatter'd wrecks of these venerable old compositions.

According to tradition, Robert quarrelled with Richmond soon after his return and moved out of the flat in Baxter's Close. There is no evidence to support this, and from the fact that at least two letters couched in friendly terms are recorded from Robert, in October 1787 and February 1788, the story of a quarrel appears to be unfounded. Richmond, who supplied James Grierson of Dalgoner with a number of anecdotes in 1817, strenuously refuted the story of the quarrel but would not elaborate on the circumstances in which Robert moved out of his old lodgings. The plain fact, however, was that Robert could afford something more comfortable than a half-share of a chaff bed, and Richmond soon took in a new lodger. As Robert was now planning to tour the Highlands with William Nicol it was perfectly logical that he should move into the schoolmaster's house above the Buccleuch Pend near St Patrick Square. The Pend was demolished many years ago and the exact location is unknown. Nicol and his family occupied the attic storey, as Robert described in his letter to Archibald Lawrie. In his cheerless garret Robert counted the strokes of the clock outside, bored senseless. To Lawrie he confessed that he was alone with

> a friend whose kindness I shall largely experience at the close of this line – there – thank you – A Friend, my dear Mr Lowrie, whose kindness often makes me blush; A Friend who has more of the milk of human kindness than all the human race put together, and what is highly to his honor, peculiarly a friend to the friendless as often as they come in his way; in short, Sir, he is, without the least alloy, a universal Philanthropist; and his much beloved name is, A BOTTLE OF GOOD OLD PORT!

Previously Robert's drinking had been confined to social occasions, when he would take a glass in the company of fellow masons and boon companions. This confession of solitary drinking, however, was much more serious and, taken in conjunction with the feelings of morose self-pity, boredom and loneliness that permeate this letter, it would appear that Robert had turned to the bottle for consolation. Perhaps there had been a quarrel with his old friend Richmond, perhaps he was beginning to regret the move to the Nicol residence; Robert's hopes of an early settlement with his wily agent Creech had already been dashed, he still had the worry of Margaret Cameron's writ hanging over him (though that wretched matter was settled the very next day), and after the euphoria over the publication of the Edinburgh Edition in April had died down Robert's importance as a literary lion had correspondingly diminished, as he suspected it would. Add to all this continuing anxieties about his future, coupled with an inability to take any steps to resolve them, and probably also pangs of longing for the Mauchline mason's daughter whose wholehearted devotion he had sampled yet again, and the curious manner with which Robert had begun his letter to Lawrie becomes crystal clear:

> Here am I – that is all I can tell you of that unaccountable BEING – Myself.– What I am doing, no mortal can tell; what I am thinking, I myself cannot tell; what I am usually saying, is not worth telling.

On 23 August Robert wrote two very different letters. To the members of his lodge at Tarbolton he wrote apologising for his absence from their quarterly meeting and dealing in a commensense manner with the problem of those whose membership dues were now in arrears (CL 352). To Ainslie, now back home at Berrywell, he wrote in ebullient mood. Apparently Ainslie had written from Innerleithen informing his friend that the girl he had seduced had now borne him a son. In a postscript Robert suggested a biblical name – so long as 'Burns' was the boy's middle name. Zimri Burns Ainslie had a fine ring to it, or Achithophel etc, etc: 'look your bible for these two heroes'. Robert tried to write this letter while Nicol was correcting homework. The schoolmaster and his wife were 'gabbling latin so loud that I cannot hear what my own soul is saying in my own scull,' complained Robert:

> Tomorrow I leave Edinr in a chaise: Nicol thinks it more comfortable than horseback, to which I say, Amen; so Jenny Geddes goes home to Ayr-shire, to use a phrase of my Mother's, 'wi' her finger in her mouth'.

On a more practical note he asked Ainslie to write to him, if before 1st September, at the post office in Inverness, the next week at Aberdeen and the next at Edinburgh.

At first glance, the choice of travelling companion on this tour seems rather odd. William Nicol was fifteen years older than Robert. Although his origins were quite humble – his father was a tailor at Dumbretton in the parish of Annan who died when William was quite young – Nicol had got the rudiments of an education from John Orr, a travelling teacher, and then set up a school in his mother's house while still a boy. Later he attended classes at Annan Academy and the University of Edinburgh where he studied for the ministry, then switched to a medical course, before opting for the classics. In 1774, at the age of thirty, he won appointment as classics master at the High School in open competition, and he remained in that post until 1795 when, as a result of a violent quarrel with the Rector, Dr Adam, he resigned and opened a school of his own, which he ran successfully till his death two years later. A man of undoubted talents, Nicol was vain, touchy and irascible. Lord Cockburn, who had been a pupil under Nicol, has left a savage description of a classroom tyrant with an ungovernable temper. 'Unacquainted with the nature of youth, ignorant even of the characters of his own boys, and with not a conception of the art or of the duty of alluring them, he had nothing for it but to drive them: and this he did by constant and indiscriminate harshness.'[42]

The cantankerous Latin pedant, however, had some redeeming features in Robert's eyes. 'Kind, honest hearted Willie' probably summed it up pretty neatly. Where or when they first met is not known. Nicol did not move in the more elevated circles of Edinburgh society, nor did he unbend sufficiently to be a welcome addition to the Crochallan Fencibles. But he liked a dram and convivial relaxation, and perhaps Robert met him in one of the pubs of Edinburgh. In deference to his age (Willie was in his mid-forties) Robert agreed to hire a post-chaise, which was a relatively expensive mode of transport. It was to be Robert's last extravagance before he settled down. Nicol was certainly in no position to pay his share; his salary was not sufficient to take care of his family and he had to eke out his scholastic income by translating into Latin the theses of the university graduates, for which he was ill-paid. Alexander Young of Harburn, Writer to the Signet, was responsible for putting a lot of this work in Nicol's direction, and considered him to be one of the greatest Latin scholars of the age. Nicol was not only poorly remunerated for his translations, he was also often kept waiting for his money. Young was employed by him to recover many of these debts, mainly from English students. On one occasion Young told Nicol that the Liverpool lawyer William Roscoe (acting for the students) felt that his claims were doubtful. Nicol 'fell into an extravagant rage, swore the most unseemly of oaths & uttered the grossest blasphemies . . . In consequence of these and similar exhibitions, I thought it prudent to detach myself from such companions [Burns and Nicol]; but I never had any quarrel with them,' wrote Young primly.[43] It is worth noting that Roscoe was James Currie's closest friend and may have been the source of the tales of dissipation which Currie had firmly planted in his head when he heard of Burns's death.

Charles Hope, later Lord Granton and Lord Adocate in the Addington administration (1801–4), expressed himself much more forcibly:

> I met Burns several times at dinner in different Houses, when he first came to Edinr but I was not at all intimate with him. That visit of his to Edinr was a great misfortune to him, & led to all his after follies & misconduct, & ultimately to his ruin & premature death – to all of which his intimacy with Nicol mainly contributed – Nicol . . . was a good scholar; but I did not consider him as a *better* scholar than Adam[44] or Fraser[45] – His passions were quite ungovernable, & he was altogether a most ungovernable savage – He persecuted poor Adam by every means in his power; & at least was guilty of a brutal assault on him.[46]

This was a grossly partisan viewpoint, written retrospectively and hardly the comment of an unbiased observer. Nevertheless, it was probably not untypical of a view of Robert in which the polite society of the capital – or an important section of it – later took refuge. Robert was never forgiven for those lines in the epistle to William Simpson (CW 107) cursing 'your whunstane hearts, Ye E'nbrugh gentry' for their scandalous neglect of poor Robert Fergusson.

Robert kept a diary of his Highland tour, along the same lines as the journal of the Border tour. On this occasion, however, he was able to make notes as they went along, rather than writing up his journal at the end of each day. For this reason the Highland journal has a greater sense of immediacy; but, written as they jolted along the rutted Highland roads, it was also much more disjointed and fragmentary.[47] Unfortunately, a rather different impression was created by successive biographers, from Lockhart (1828) and Cunningham (1834) to Chambers-Wallace (1896). The extent of their tinkering with the text only became apparent when James C. Ewing published his facsimile edition in 1927.[48]

One need look no further than the opening entry to see a prime example of the handiwork of the nineteenth-century meddlers. Robert began 'I set out for the north in company with my good friend Mr N', but the emendors have not only given his name in full but added the clause 'whose originality of humour promises me much entertainment'. Robert then wrote, 'from Corstorphine by Kirkliston and Winsburg, fine, improven, fertile country; near Linlithgow the land's worse; light and sandy'. Lockhart, however, could not leave it at that, but inserted a long philosophical passage:

> The more elegant and luxury among the farmers, I always observe, in equal proportion the rudeness and stupidity of the peasantry. This remark I have made all over the Lothians, Merse, Roxburgh, &c. For this, among other reasons, I think that a man of romantic taste, a 'Man of Feeling', will be better pleased with the poverty, but intelligent minds, of the peasantry in Ayrshire (peasantry they are, all below the Justice of Peace) than the opulence of a club of Merse farmers, when at the same time he considers the vandalism of their plough-folks, &c. I carry this idea so far that an uninclosed, half-proven country is to me actually more agreeable, and gives me more pleasure as a prospect, than a country cultivated like a garden.

This is literary vandalism of the very worst kind. A similar purple passage occurs under 26 August where Lockhart interpolated what he imagined Burns must have felt about the battlefield of Bannockburn. Fortunately, these are the worst cases. Robert obviously started out with the admirable intention of keeping a fairly detailed diary, and the earlier entries (despite Lockhart and Cunningham) were quite discursive. His description of Linlithgow, which they visited on the first day, illustrates this intention at its best:

> What a poor, pimping business is a Presbyterian place of worship, dirty, narrow and squalid, stuck in a corner of old Popish grandeur such as Linlithgow and, much more, Melrose! Ceremony and show, if judiciously thrown in, absolutely necessary for the bulk of mankind, both in religious and civil manners.

By the following day, however, Robert had slipped back into his old way of making disjointed headings. Thus what he actually wrote about the scene of Scotland's greatest victory was: 'Come on to Bannockburn – shown the old house where James 3d was murdered – the field of Bannockburn – the hole where glorious Bruce set his standard – Come to Stirling'. Unlike the Border journal, even the descriptions of the people he met were treated in the same perfunctory manner. In most cases names alone were jotted down with little or no attempt at even the swiftest and most impressionistic of pen-portraits. Exceptions include the trio Robert met at Stirling: Doig, 'a queerish fellow and something of a pedant', Bell, 'a joyous, vacant fellow, who sings a good song' and Captain Forrester of the Castle, 'a merry, swearing kind of man, with a dash of the Sodger'.

As usual, historic landmarks received short shrift. An exception was the Druids' temple in Glenlyon which received a comparatively meticulous description concluding characteristically 'say prayers in it'. Otherwise, the journal is virtually a list of places passed through and people met. At Dunkeld, however, the travellers met the celebrated fiddler Niel Gow (1727–1807), 'a short, stout-built, honest highland figure, with his grayish hair shed on his honest social brow – an interesting face, marking strong sense, kind open-heartedness mixed with unmistrusting simplicity'.

From Linlithgow Burns and Nicol travelled to Falkirk where they stayed at the Cross Keys Inn in the High Street; a bust of the poet now marks the spot, though no trace remains of the lines 'Sound be his sleep and blithe his morn / That never did a lassie wrang', which he allegedly inscribed on a window pane with his diamond stylus.[49] The following morning they made a slight detour to Carron where they hoped to inspect the famous iron-works, soon to become even more celebrated for the light cannon, known as carronades, used so extensively during the French Revolutionary and Napoleonic Wars. It being Sunday, however, the works was closed and the caretaker refused to admit them. In high dudgeon Robert crossed the road to the inn and gave vent to his disappointment in the epigrammatical squib (CW 286) which he scratched on a window-pane.

At Stirling Robert wrote to Robert Muir (CL 88–9), catching up on correspondence he had meant to deal with before leaving Edinburgh. Whatever the shortcomings of the journal, Robert now compensated in his highly emotional description of his feelings at the tomb of Sir John Graham and at the borestone on the field of Bannockburn. The following morning Robert left his companion at Stirling while he made a foray to the Devon valley to visit Gavin Hamilton's relations at Harvieston. He received a warm welcome, but was disappointed to find that Margaret Chalmers was temporarily absent in Edinburgh, and he returned to Stirling that night. The laconic entry in the journal, merely recording the names of the people and places, was amplified by a long letter to Gavin Hamilton, written at Stirling the following day (CL 68–9) telling him all about his step-brother and sisters whom Gavin had not seen for several years. Robert upbraided his landlord for not keeping up a correspondence with his father's second family: 'Such relations, the first Peer in the realm might own with pride; then why but you keep up more correspondence with these so amiable young folks?' That evening Burns and Nicol dined with Doig, Bell and Forrester whose descriptions have already been noted.

Another bond between Burns and Nicol was their Jacobite sentiment. In Robert's case, at least, this was little more than a romantic notion, spring-ing out of the erroneous supposition that his ancestors had suffered for the cause in the rebellion of 1715. Nicol's reasons for adherence to a dead cause are not known, but he held his Jacobite views, as he did everything else, with angry vehemence. The ruinous state of the ancient hall of Stirling Castle, in which parliaments had occasionally been held, outraged them both, and moved Robert to vandalise the window of his room at the inn with the ten lines beginning 'Here Stewarts once in glory reigned' (CW 286) and ending with an injudicious attack on the House of Hanover, 'An idiot race, to honour lost; / Who know them best despise them most'. Robert's earliest biographers and editors prudently omitted this incident and the lines, but almost half a century later Allan Cunningham gave the story, adding some details of his own which may or may not be accurate, stating that Robert aggravated his offence by adding a mock reproof beginning 'Rash mortal, and slanderous poet, thy name'.[50] The 'old Mansfield' was the Earl of Mansfield, Lord Chief Justice in 1756–88. Subsequently, however, Robert inserted a note in the Glenriddell MS, under the title of 'The Poet's Reply to the Threat of a Censorious Critic': 'My imprudent lines were answered, very petulantly, by *somebody*, I believe a Revd. Mr Hamilton'. In a manuscript, where he came across the verses by the Revd. George Hamilton of Gladsmuir parish taking him to task for prostituting his genius by basely attacking his monarch, Robert added the impromptu endorsement:

> With Aesop's lion, Burns says, sore I feel
> Each other blow, but d–n that ass's heel.

He was unrepentant, and resented the impertinence of anyone who took him to task for his immoderate views. On his next visit to Stirling, however, about 4 October, Robert smashed the pane bearing the offending lines; but the damage had been done by that time. The verses on the window pane had not passed unnoticed; and copies were eagerly made and circulated, not always by the poet's well-wishers.

After breakfasting with Captain Forrester on Tuesday morning, 28 August, Burns and Nicol left Stirling. They dined at Crieff and went to Aberuchill where Robert noted tersely 'cold reception at Arbruchill'. The next day they left Crieff and went by Glen Almond to Ossian's grave. 'Taymouth – described in rhyme' alludes to lines which Robert wrote with his pencil over the chimney-piece in the parlour of the inn at Kenmore, beginning 'Admiring Nature in her wildest grace' (CW 287–8). These verses were published in the *Edinburgh Evening Courant* of 6 September 1787, allegedly communicated by 'O. B. of Kenmore who, a few days ago, being on a visit to Taymouth, . . . found the following verses (by the celebrated Ayrshire bard) written on the walls of the Hermitage there'. It is more likely that Robert himself contributed the poem to the newspaper.

On Thursday 30 August the travellers came down the Tay to Dunkeld and supped with Dr Stewart at Inver that night. On the way they had passed through Aberfeldy and, standing under the Falls of Moness nearby, Robert composed 'The Birks of Aberfeldie' (CW 288–9). The following day Robert met Niel Gow and as a compliment to him composed the song 'Amang the Trees' (CW 289). By now his muse was in her stride, and Robert produced a number of other works directly connected with the places he visited. On Friday he and Nicol travelled up the Tummel to Blair Atholl where they stopped at the inn. In Edinburgh, at the home of Dr Blacklock, Robert had made the acquaintance of Josiah Walker, tutor to the family of the Duke of Atholl; now, with a letter of introduction from Hugh Blair to the duke, Robert sent word of his arrival. Walker left a record of this meeting:

> I hastened to meet him at the inn. The Duke, to whom he had brought
> a letter of introduction, was from home; but the Duchess, being informed

of his arrival, gave him an invitation to sup and sleep at Athole-house [Blair Castle]. He accepted the invitation, but as the hour of supper was at some distance, begged I would in the interval be his guide through the grounds. It was already growing dark; yet the softened, though faint and uncertain, view of their beauties, which the moonlight afforded us, seemed exactly suited to the state of his feelings at the time. I had often, like others, experienced the pleasures which arise from the sublime or elegant landscape, but I never saw those feelings so intense as in Burns. When we reached a rustic hut on the river Tilt, where it is overhung by a woody precipice, from which there is a noble waterfall, he threw himself on the heathy seat, and gave himself up to a tender, abstracted, and voluptuous enthusiasm of imagination. I cannot help thinking it might have been here that he conceived the idea of the following lines, which he afterwards introduced into his poem on Bruar Water, when only fancying such a combination of objects as were now present to his eye . . . It was with much difficulty I prevailed on him to quit this spot, and to be introduced in proper time to supper.

My curiosity was great to see how he would conduct himself in company so different from what he had been accustomed to. His manner was unembarrassed, plain and firm. He appeared to have complete reliance on his own native good sense for directing his behaviour. He seemed at once to perceive and to appreciate what was due to the company and to himself, and never to forget a proper respect for the separate species of dignity belonging to each. He did not arrogate conversation, but when led into it, he spoke with ease, propriety, and manliness. He tried to exert his abilities, because he knew it was ability alone gave him a title to be there. The Duke's fine young family attracted much of his admiration; he drank their healths as *honest men and bonie lasses*, an idea which was much applauded, and with which he has very felicitously closed his poem.

Next day I took a ride with him through some of the most romantic parts of that neighbourhood, and was highly gratified by his conversation. As a specimen of his happiness of conception and strength of expression, I will mention a remark which he made on his fellow-traveller, who was walking, at the time, a few paces before us. He was a man of robust but clumsy person; and while Burns was expressing to me the value he entertained of him, on account of his vigorous talents, although they were clouded at times by coarseness of manners; 'in short,' he added, 'his mind is like his body, he has a confounded strong in-knee'd sort of a soul'.

Much attention was paid to Burns both before and after the Duke's return, of which he was perfectly sensible, without being vain; and at his departure I recommended to him, as the most appropriate return he could make, to write some descriptive verses on any one of the scenes with which he had been so much delighted. After leaving Blair, he, by the Duke's advice, visited the Falls of Bruar, and in a few days I received a letter from Inverness with the verses enclosed.[51]

The verses were 'The Humble Petition of Bruar Water' (CW 290–2). According to the accompanying letter which Robert wrote to Walker (CL 354):

it was, at least most part of it, the effusion of the half hour that I spent at Bruar.– I don't mean it was extempore, for I have endeavoured to brush it up as well as Mr Nicol's chat and the jogging of the chaise would allow.– It eases my heart a good deal, as Rhyme is the coin with which a Poet pays his debts of honor or gratitude: what I owe to the noble Family of Athole of the first kind, I shall ever proudly boast; what I owe of the last, so help me God in my hour of need! I shall never forget!

The journal, as usual, merely recited a list of the persons Robert met at Blair Atholl:

> Mrs Graham, *belle et aimable* – Miss Cathcart – Mrs Murray, a painter – Mrs King – Duchess and fine family, the Marquis, Lords James, Edward and Robert – Ladies, Charlotte, Emelia and Elizabeth – children dance – sup – Duke – Mr Graham of Fintray – Mr Mlaggan, Mr and Mrs Stewart.

In this list we find the name of Robert Graham of Fintry. The Mrs Graham mentioned was not Fintry's wife but the wife of Thomas Graham who, in middle age, volunteered for the army, became a general and was later to distinguish himself in the Peninsular campaign, for which he was raised to the peerage as Lord Lynedoch. Robert Graham's 'charms of conversation' were singled out for mention by Burns in his letter from Inverness to Josiah Walker, but otherwise the impressions made by Graham on Burns and vice versa were not recorded. Yet this was the man who played an important part in the change of direction which was to give Robert, if not the main purpose in life, certainly the security of steady employment. Graham, ten years older than Burns, was a descendant of the Grahams of Strathcarron and numbered the notorious persecutor of the Covenanters, John Graham of Claverhouse, among his kinsmen. Claverhouse, later Viscount Dundee, won the battle but lost his life at Killiecrankie in 1689, thus sealing the fate of the older Stuart line. Burns, who had come through the pass of Killiecrankie on his way to Blair, was probably drawn to Graham on account of shared Jacobite sentiment. Graham, however, also shared Robert's apparently paradoxical politics, being a Whig rather than a Tory. This did not bar his appointment, earlier that year, as one of the Commissioners of the Scottish Board of Excise, thus giving the lie to the view that Prime Minister William Pitt, through his trusted lieutenant Henry Dundas, had all of the public appointments in Scotland tightly sewn up in the Tory interest. Interestingly, in view of his half-conscious desire to secure an Excise appointment (first expressed almost a year previously), Robert does not appear to have seized the opportunity to broach the subject with Graham; and Graham certainly did not make any suggestions of this sort to Robert. This is borne out by Robert's first letter to Graham on 7 January 1788 (CL 424) which began 'When I had the honor of being introduced to you at Atholehouse, I did not think of putting that acquaintance so soon to the test'.

Robert spent two days at Blair (Friday 31 August and Saturday 1 September) and afterwards looked back on them as among the happiest days of his life. The duke's family were as captivated by the poet as he was with them. They entreated him to stay, and he would have complied, but for the eagerness of Nicol to get away. There is no mention of the invitation to stay at the castle being extended to Nicol and it is presumed that he had to kick his heels at the inn, along with Mr Carnegie, the chaise-driver, while Robert was fêted up at the big house. If this were the case, then Nicol's mounting resentment was perfectly understandable. To Josiah Walker fell the task of keeping Nicol in a reasonably good mood. Fortunately, he discovered that the schoolmaster was a keen angler, so he furnished him with rod and tackle and showed him the best beats on the Tilt and the Garry. 'This quite absorbed his attention and allayed his jealousy, while the poet was made a pet of in the mansion,' wrote Walker implying that Nicol was not himself a house guest there. He also related to Currie that:

> the ladies, in their anxiety to have a little more of Burns's company, sent a servant to the inn, to bribe his driver to loosen or pull off a horse's shoe. But the ambush failed. *Proh mirum!* The driver was *incorruptible.*

It was the more to be regretted that Robert did not tarry a little longer at Blair Atholl, as Henry Dundas himself was daily expected as a guest and, in fact, arrived the very next day. Dundas (1742–1811), then Treasurer of the Navy, was the most powerful man in Scotland. As the election agent of the Tory party in Scotland, he manipulated the election of virtually all the Scottish members of parliament and exercised a tight control over all those government appointments which were subject to patronage. Oddly enough, one of the few areas of public service where this patronage did not extend was the Excise. Contrary to a belief held in some quarters, the Excise required a very high degree of professionalism in its officers, so that admission and promotion were on merit alone, and any suggestion of canvassing would have automatically debarred a candidate. Of the five Commissioners of Excise in 1787, at least two were Whigs – clear proof that the arch-Tory Dundas could not always get things his own way. Dundas, while often portrayed as something of a philistine, was not indifferent to contemporary literature and was himself no mean versifier; Lockhart thought that Dundas would have helped Burns because Dundas 'was a warm lover of his country and, in general, of whatever redounded to her honour'. The name of Henry Dundas, however, was conspicuously absent from the list of subscribers to the Edinburgh Edition; and Lockhart's encomium has to be viewed in light of the fact that he was Sir Walter Scott's biographer and son-in-law and shared Scott's high-Tory politics. In 1802 Dundas was raised to the peerage as Viscount Melville, but later the same year a parliamentary commission into financial mismanagement led to his impeachment in 1806. When Melville was acquitted, Scott took a leading part in the celebratory dinner. Like his political master Pitt, Dundas had a formidable reputation for hard drinking which made him, in Lockhart's malicious words, 'very especially qualified to appreciate Burns as a companion'.[52] Had Burns and Dundas met socially at Blair, the latter might have been induced to do something for the poet. It would have been a very easy matter for him to confer a well-paid sinecure on Robert, just as, a generation later, Wordsworth was cushioned against the harsh reality of life by the £300 per annum which the sinecure of Distributor of Stamps for Westmorland brought him. His future secured, Robert might have had the leisure to develop his talents and, freed from the worry and the debilitating effects of trying to combine farming with the riding-work of an Exciseman, he might have lived a great deal longer. But this is one of the great 'might-have-beens' of Scottish history. Burns and Dundas never met, and if their paths ever crossed they did so but indirectly. Henry IX, uncrowned King of Scotland, had previously featured in two of Robert's poems. In 'Ballad on the American War' (CW 74) a reference was made to Henry's political management in Scotland:

> While slee Dundas arous'd the class
> Be-north the Roman wa', man:

and in 'The Author's Earnest Cry and Prayer' (CW 176) he appeared as 'a chap that's damned auld-farran' [sagacious] – 'Dundas his name'. Later, however, this all-powerful mandarin figured in Robert's 'Ode on the Departed Regency Bill' (CW 353), penned in March 1789, where he appears less flatteringly in the lines:

> Paint Ruin, in the shape of high Dundas
> Gaping with giddy terror o'er the brow:

but by that time something had happened to make Robert execrate the name of Dundas. This matter, in its proper perspective, belongs to the next chapter.

On Sunday Nicol could not smite the waters with his rod and, deprived of his sport, he was impatient to be off. Robert could not trust his friend's temper and so wriggled out of the invitation up to the castle that day by saying that he had a headache. As soon as they had breakfasted, therefore, Burns and Nicol rode off up the Garry, pausing at the Falls of Bruar before going on to Dalwhinnie where they dined amid snows seventeen feet deep. The warmth of the reception at Dalwhinnie thawed the frozen travellers and prompted Robert to pen the quatrain entitled 'A Highland Welcome' (CW 292). Later they crossed the Spey and came down Glen Truim to 'Pitnim' (Pitmain, as Kingussie was then called, after a neighbouring mansion). Pausing only to note the ruined barracks at Ruthven ('wild and magnificent') they drove on to Aviemore. The following day they entered Strathspey and dined with Sir James Grant of Grant, half-brother of Henry Mackenzie, and 'came through mist and darkness to Dulsie to lie'. On Tuesday they came down by the Findhorn to Cawdor ('saw the bed in which King Duncan was stabbed') and dined at Kilravock with Mrs Elizabeth Rose, a cousin of Henry Mackenzie who had given Robert a letter of introduction to her. Writing to her from Edinburgh on 17 February 1788 (CL 441–2), Robert commented:

> There was something in my reception at Kilravock so different from the cold, obsequious, dancing-school bow of politeness, that it almost got into my head that friendship had occupied her ground without the intermediate march of acquaintance.

At Kilravock Robert heard her niece, Miss Rose of Kildrummie, sing two Highland ballads which he subsequently sent to James Johnson for inclusion in the second volume of *The Scots Musical Museum*.

After passing Fort George, Burns and Nicol arrived at Inverness on the evening of Tuesday 4 September. Robert had with him a letter of introduction from William Dunbar to William Inglis, then a bailie and one of the town's leading merchants who became provost in 1797. From Ettles Hotel Robert penned a brief note to Inglis enclosing Dunbar's letter (CL 353). He apologised for not waiting on the bailie personally with Dunbar's letter but he was 'jaded with the fatigue of to-day's journey'. As he planned remaining at Inverness till the Thursday morning, however, Robert had ample time to see the Highland capital and its environs. From here he made a brief excursion south-west along the east side of Loch Ness as far as the Falls of Foyers and the hut occupied by General Wade while constructing the military road in 1727. Here he pencilled the fragment, an uncompleted poem of twelve lines (CW 292), beginning 'Among the heathy hills and ragged woods'. Back in Inverness that evening he and Nicol dined with the Inglis family at Kingsmills House (now a hotel). According to an unnamed eye-witness, however, Robert was thoughtful and silent during the evening.[53]

On Thursday the travellers retraced their steps, via Culloden ('reflections on the field of battle'), to Kilravock where they breakfasted with the Rose family. They dined at Nairn with Dr Alexander Stewart 'who had been long abroad with his father' John Stewart of Bonskeid, a noted Jacobite, and Hugh Falconer, a kinsman of the Roses of Kilravock, 'a spare, irascible, warm-hearted Norland, and a non-juror'. They spent the night at Brodie as guests of the clan chief ('truly polite, but not just the Highland cordiality'), James Brodie of Brodie (1744–1824), who was still grieving the loss of his wife, a daughter of the Earl of Fife, accidentally burned to death in Brodie House the previous year. On Friday Burns and Nicol crossed the Findhorn to Forres and breakfasted at Elgin with an unnamed friend of Dunbar's. They inspected the venerable ruins of Elgin Cathedral ('A grander effect at first glance than Melrose, but nothing near so beautiful') and crossed the Spey to Fochabers – 'fine palace, worthy of the generous proprietor'.

This was Gordon Castle, the palatial residence of the Duke and Duchess of Gordon. Robert noted in his journal, 'The Duke makes me happier than ever great man did – noble, princely; yet mild, condescending and affable, gay, and kind. The Duchess charming, witty, and sensible – God bless them!' As well as the Duke's family, a number of local worthies was assembled to meet the celebrated poet, and one of these, Dr Robert Coupar, subsequently furnished Currie with an account of the occasion:

> In the course of the preceding winter Burns had been introduced to the Duchess of Gordon at Edinburgh; and, presuming on this acquaintance, he proceeded to Gordon Castle, leaving Mr Nicol at the inn of the village. At the castle, our poet was received with the utmost hospitality and kindness; and the family being about to sit down to dinner, he was invited to take his place at table as a matter of course. This invitation he accepted, and after drinking a few glasses of wine, he rose up, and proposed to withdraw. On being pressed to stay, he mentioned, for the first time, his engagement with his fellow-traveller; and his noble host offering to send a servant to conduct Mr Nicol to the castle, Burns insisted on undertaking that office himself. He was, however, accompanied by a gentleman, a particular acquaintance of the Duke, by whom the invitation was delivered in all the forms of politeness. The invitation came too late; the pride of Nicol was inflamed into a high degree of passion by the neglect to which he thought he was being subjected. He had ordered the horses to be put to the carriage, being determined to proceed on his journey alone; and they found him parading the streets of Fochabers, before the door of the inn, venting his anger on the postillion for the slowness with which he obeyed his commands. As no explanation nor entreaty could change the purpose of his fellow-traveller, our poet was reduced to the necessity of separating from him entirely, or of instantly proceeding with him on their journey. He chose the latter of these alternatives; and seating himself beside Nicol in the post-chaise, with mortification and regret he turned his back on Gordon Castle, where he had promised himself some happy days.[54]

Robert made no mention of this incident in his journal; but on 20 October (CL 361–2) he wrote to James Hoy, the Duke's librarian who had probably been the messenger accompanying Robert on that unfortunate occasion, and enclosed 'Castle Gordon' (CW 293), blaming Nicol for

> that unlucky predicament which hurried me, tore me away from Castle Gordon.– May that obstinate Son of Latin Prose be curst to Scotch-mile periods, and damn'd to seven-league paragraphs; while Declension & Conjugation, Gender, Number and Time, under the ragged banners of Dissonance and Disarrangement eternally rank against him in hostile array!!!!!!

This unfortunate incident illustrated only too well the problems faced by Robert in moving across the debatable land between two different ranks in society. 'To play the lion under such circumstances, must be difficult at best; but a delicate business indeed, when the jackals are presumptuous,' Lockhart neatly summed it up.[55] We can imagine the strained silence between the travellers as they rode on to Cullen that night. Robert must have been remarkably forbearing in spite of his friend's prickly sensitivities. When Robert wrote to William Cruikshank on 3 March 1788 (CL 360) he confessed, 'I would send my compliments to Mr Nicol, but he would be hurt if he knew that I wrote to any body and not to him'. Josiah Walker regarded the abrupt curtailment of the visit to Gordon Castle as just as calamitous as the similar incident at Blair. It was 'not only a mortifying disappointment, but in all probability a serious misfortune; as a longer stay among persons of such influence might have begot a permanent intimacy, and on their parts, an active concern for his future advancement'.[56]

Allan Cunningham is the source of the intriguing story that the Duchess of Gordon, knowing that Henry Addington (later Lord Sidmouth) was a warm admirer of Burns, planned a meeting between them, with Dr Beattie, at Gordon Castle. 'The future premier was unable to accept the invitation; but wrote and forwarded, it is said, these memorable lines – memorable as the first indication of that deep love which England now entertains for the genius of Burns,' wrote Honest Allan, following this with the sonnet beginning 'Yes! pride of Scotia's favoured plains, 'tis thine'. But Addington (1757–1844) had only been MP for Devizes for four years and his potential for patronage must have been limited at this time. To be sure, he owed his position to William Pitt, who secured his elevation to Speaker of the House in 1789, and he might have been able to put a good word for the poet in the right ear; but his name does not appear in the subscribers' list in the Edinburgh Edition, and his interest in Burns in the summer of 1787 is debatable. As for the sonnet, however, this may well have been genuine enough; Addington, while an undergraduate at Oxford, had shown a taste for writing English verses in which he occasionally indulged in later life, though with no great success,[57] and Cunningham in 1834 (when he published this) would surely never have risked being exposed as a forger by Lord Sidmouth who, though seventy-seven at that time, was still mentally alert and in full command of his faculties. It seems to me, however, that the hypothetical question of a meeting between Burns and Dundas at Blair or Addington at Gordon Castle is immaterial. The Dukes of Atholl and Gordon were powerful enough in their own right to have taken steps to ensure that Robert's future was secure, and they were by no means the only influential people who could have helped him if they so chose.

Robert's practised eye took in the changes in the countryside as they journeyed along the Moray Firth. He noted the wastes of sand and was depressed by the bleak landscape:

> The country is sadly poor & unimproven, the houses, crops, horses, cattle, etc., all in unison – cart-wheels with low, coarse, unshod, clumsy work: an axle-tree which had been made with other design than to be a resting shaft between the wheels.

There is a tradition that Burns visited Thornybank, a mile south of Buckie, whose farmhouse had been built in the year of the poet's birth.[58] But, late at night, as Burns and Nicol rode on in angry silence from Fochabers to

Cullen, sightseeing would have been the last thing on their minds. The song 'Lady Onlie, Honest Lucky' (CW 295), which mentions 'A' the lads o Thorniebank', was probably collected by Burns at Cullen the following morning. It was to be one of the fruits harvested on this tour and subsequently mended or reworked for Johnson's *Scots Musical Museum*.

Matters improved after breakfasting at Banff with Dr George Chapman, (headmaster of the Academy and a former colleague of Nicol's at Dumfries).[59] Chapman's star pupil and later dux of the Academy, George Imlach (1775–1863), who had been asked to join the party, later recalled how Burns made some quips at Nicol's expense 'about some misunderstanding which took place between them at Fochabers . . . and the good old doctor seemed much amused with the way the poet chose to smoothe down the yet lurking ire of the dominie'.[60] After breakfast, Dr Chapman despatched his pupil to the bookshop for a copy of Cordiner's *Antiquities and Scenery of the North of Scotland* which he presented to Nicol. Later the boy accompanied Burns and Nicol in the chaise to guide them to Duff House, the residence of the Earl of Fife, with a note to the steward of the mansion that the travellers might be allowed to see the interior, with its valuable library and pictures. During the coach ride out to Duff House Nicol asked the lad if he knew Burns's poems. When he replied in the affirmative Nicol asked him which ones he liked best. The boy cited 'The Twa Dogs' and 'Death and Dr Hornbook' but added that he liked 'The Cotter's Saturday Night' best, confessing, 'It made me greet when my father had me to read it to my mother.' At that Burns gave a start, looked intently in the boy's face and patting him on the shoulder, said, 'Well, my callant, I don't wonder at your greeting at reading the poem; it made me greet more than once when I was writing it at *my* father's fireside.' At Duff House, while Nicol loitered in the library looking at the fine collection of old classics there, Burns took the boy with him as a guide through the public rooms. Robert was particularly interested in the portraits of the Stuart dynasty in the great drawing-room. The boy could not remember the poet's remarks, 'but the face and look of Robert Burns were such as, either boy or man, he never could forget'.

Although the journal mentioned Duff House Robert made no comment on his visit there. Instead he noted the 'pleasant ride along the shore – country almost wild again between Banff and Newbyth – quite wild as we come thro' Buchan to Old Dear, but near the village both lands and crops rich'.

On Sunday 9 September Burns and Nicol left Old Deer and headed across the north-east corner of Buchan for Peterhead, rejoining the coast near the famous Bullers of Buchan. They dined at Ellon and passed by the seat of George Gordon, third Earl of Aberdeen (1722–1801), on whom Robert commented cryptically, 'entrance denied to everybody, owing to the jealousy of three-score over a kept country-wench'. This alluded to the amorous activities of the earl. In 1782 he formed an attachment with Penelope Dering of Petting Grove, Kent, whom he met through her friendship with one of his four daughters. By Miss Dering the elderly nobleman had a daughter, also named Penelope (1782), and a son Alexander (1783). The following year he began the rebuilding of Ellon House as a love-nest, hence Robert's rather bitchy reference in his journal. It is worth noting that 'Geordie Gordon the bad Earl' also maintained mistresses and their offspring at Cairnbulg Castle, Tilney Street, London and Wiscombe Park, Devon, as well as his countess and legitimate brood at Haddo House.[61]

That night Burns and Nicol reached Aberdeen where they lodged at the New Inn in Castle Street. Subsequently their visit was briefly noted by the *Aberdeen Journal* whose editor, James Chalmers (1742-1810), 'a facetious fellow', entertained Burns on Monday 10 September. At the newspaper office Robert was introduced to Andrew Shirrefs (1762-1807), an aspiring poet whose own volume entitled *Poems Chiefly in the Scottish Dialect* (1790) was a poor imitation of Robert's work. 'Mr Ross, a fine fellow, like Professor Tytler' was John Ross, professor of Hebrew at King's College, while 'Professor Gordon, a good-natured, jolly-looking professor' was Thomas Gordon (c.1714-97), professor of philosophy. The identity of 'Mr Marshall, one of the *poetae minores*' has never been satisfactorily settled. Chambers opted for William Marshall (1748-1833), factor to the Duke of Gordon and author of *A Collection of Reels* (1781), but Marshall's biographer considered it doubtful whether Burns ever met the composer.[62] Another suggestion was William Marshall (1745-1818), the experimental agriculturalist whose *Rural Economy of England* Burns claimed to have read.[63] Neither of these, however, seems as likely as John Marshall, a noted Aberdonian poet of the period.[64]

No such doubts surround the other gentleman whom Burns met on this occasion: 'Bishop Skinner, a non-juror, son of the author of Tullochgorum; a man whose mild, venerable manner is the most marked of any in so young a man.' Born in 1744, John Skinner was the son of the Episcopal deacon of Longside where he ministered for sixty-four years. In 1753 father and son were imprisoned for six months for evading the Toleration Act. Both were men of considerable abilities. John Senior published *An Ecclesiastical History of Scotland* (1780) in two volumes, but is best remembered nowadays for his *Poems*, published in 1809, two years after his death. These included such gems as 'Tullochgorum', which Robert declared to be 'the best Scotch Song ever Scotland saw'. When Robert discovered, in conversation with Bishop Skinner, that his father was still alive and, in fact, dwelling at Linshart near Lonmay, he expressed great regret that he had not learned the fact before leaving Banff, as he would gladly have gone twenty miles out of his way to have seen the author of 'Tullochgorum'.

Bishop Skinner later sent his father a lively account of his meeting with the poet; and subsequently old John sent Burns a verse-epistle which provoked, by way of response, two letters dated 25 October 1787 and 14 February 1788 (CL 363-4). In his letter to his father, the bishop wrote:

> Our time was short, as he was just setting off for the south and his companion hurrying him; but we had fifty 'auld sangs' through hand, and spent an hour or so most agreeably.- 'Did not your father write the

Ewie wi' the crooked horn?' – 'Yes.' – 'O, an I had the lown that did it!' said he, in a rapture of praise; 'but tell him how I love, and esteem, and venerate his truly Scottish muse.' On my mentioning *his Ewie*, and how you were delighted with it, he said it was all owing to yours, which had started the thought. He had been at Gordon Castle, and come by Peterhead. 'Then', said I, 'you were within four Scottish miles of *Tullochgorum's* dwelling.' Had you seen the look he gave, and how expressive of vexation; – had he been your own son you could not have wished a better proof of affection. 'Well', said he at parting, and shaking me by the hand as if he had been really my brother, 'I am happy in having seen you, and thereby convey my long-harboured sentiments of regard to your worthy sire; assure him of it in the heartiest manner, and that never did a devotee of the Virgin Mary go to Loretto with more fervour than I would have approached his dwelling and worshipped at his shrine.' He was collecting on his tour the 'auld Scots sangs' he had not before heard of, and likewise the tunes that he might get them set to music. 'Perhaps', said he, 'your father might assist me in making this collection; or, if not, I should be happy in any way to rank him among my correspondents.' 'Then give me your direction, and it is probable you may hear from him sometime or other.' On this he wrote his direction on a slip of paper, which I have enclosed that you may see it under his own hand. As to his personal appearance, it is very much in his favour. He is a genteel looking young man of good address, and talks with as much propriety as if he had received an academical education. He has indeed a flow of language, and seems never at a loss to express himself in the strongest and most nervous manner. On my quoting with surprise some sentiments of the Ayrshire *Plowman*, 'Well', said he, 'and a plowman I was from youth, and till within these two years had my shoes studded with a hundred *tackets*. But even then I was a reader, and had very early made all the English poets familiar to me, not forgetting the old bards of the best of all poetical books – the Old Testament.'[65]

From Aberdeen Burns proceeded southwards into Kincardineshire, the land of his forebears and still the home of many of his paternal kith and kin. From Inverness on 4 September (CL 61) Robert wrote to his cousin James Burness:

I shall be in Stonhive sometime on monday the 10th instant, and I beg the favor of you to meet me there. – I understand there is but one Inn at Stonhive so you cannot miss me. – As I am in the country, I certainly shall see any of my father's relations that are any way near my road; but I do not even know their names, or where one of them lives, so I hope you will meet me and be my guide.

Right on schedule, Robert reached Stonehaven where another cousin, Robert Burnes, a lawyer in that town, met him. Burns described his cousin and namesake as 'one of those who love fun, a gill, a punning joke, and have not a bad heart – his wife a sweet, hospitable body, without any affectation of what is called town-breeding'. Although he does not say so in his journal, Robert met James Burness at Stonehaven as planned, and it was

James who then introduced him to Robert Burnes and other relatives in the area. After breakfast with cousin James the following morning, the poet travelled to Laurencekirk; a plaque on the wall of the Gardenstone Arms Hotel commemorates the visit. Here Robert met 'a jolly, frank, sensible, love-inspiring widow' – one of the very few ladies on this trip to rouse something of the old passion in him, though he did not record her name. The details of the brief sojourn in the land of his ancestors were conveyed in a letter to brother Gilbert on 17 September (CL 357–8), soon after his return to Edinburgh. This was doubtless not the first time that Robert wrote to Gilbert, but it is the first letter that has survived:

> I spent two days among our relations, and found our aunts, Jean and Isbal still alive and hale old women, John Caird, though born the same year with our father, walks as vigorously as I can; they have had several letters from his son in New York. – William Brand is likewise a stout old fellow; but farther particulars I delay till I see you, which will be in two or three weeks.

John Caird had farmed at Denside in Dunnottar parish and retired to Stonehaven, while William Brand was a dyer in Auchenblae. They were the respective husbands of Robert's aunts Elspeth and Isabel Burnes.

At Montrose Robert visited the home of his cousin James. James's son, also James, later recalled being dandled on the poet's lap. Robert would have tarried longer at Montrose but, as he explained in a letter to his cousin written from the Townfield inn at six o'clock on the morning of 13 September (CL 61):

> Mr Nicol and Mr Carnegie have taken some freak in their head and have wakened me just now with the rattling of the chaise to carry me to meet them at Craigie to go on our journey some other road and breakfast by the way.– I must go, which makes me very sorry.

In fact, they breakfasted at Auchmithie on the coast about four miles north of Arbroath. At this little fishing village they boarded a smack and sailed along the rugged coast to see the famous caverns of which the Geary or Gaylet Pot ('Garriepot' in the journal) is the most spectacular. They landed at Arbroath, dined there, and inspected the ruined abbey before driving on to Dundee ('a low-lying but pleasant town'). Robert visited the ruins of Broughty Castle and then breakfasted the following morning at the manse of Auchterhouse with the daughters of the Revd. David Scott. One of them, Bess, reminded Robert of William Greenfield's wife and he added laconically 'my bardship almost in love with her', though she was nine years older than him.[66]

Later Burns and Nicol came 'thro' the rich harvests and fine hedgerows of the carse of Gowrie' to Perth where they lodged in the High Street. On Saturday 15 September they drove out to Scone Palace and viewed the pictures of the Young Chevalier and his sister. They later visited Castle

Gowrie, site of the notorious conspiracy against King James VI, before going to Strathalmond to see the location of the tragic heroines Bessie Bell and Mary Gray, subjects of an old ballad. The day ended with the entry 'Come to Kinross to lie – reflections in a fit of colic'. This may have been induced by a convivial evening with Ebenezer Michie, the schoolmaster of Cleish nearby. Michie fell into an alcoholic stupor, provoking Robert to dash off an extempore epitaph (CW 286).

The tour ended the following day, dismissed with a few words: 'Pass through a cold, barren country to Queensferry – dine – cross the ferry, and on to Edinburgh.' To his brother Robert wrote the following day giving him a digest of the tour which had lasted twenty-two days and covered almost six hundred miles 'windings included'. Two days later he wrote again to James Burness (CL 62) enclosing nine copies of the Edinburgh Edition 'which you will transmit as marked on the blank leaves'. These were presumably presentation copies to Kincardineshire relatives, although one, marked for Lord Gardenstone, was to be despatched as soon as possible.

Interestingly, Robert asked his cousin to address his correspondence to him care of Andrew Bruce, a merchant in Bridge Street. Robert had previously used this address when he first arrived in Edinburgh and may, in fact, have actually lodged briefly with him and his wife Matty, to whom he referred in a letter to Robert Muir in December 1786 (CL 88). Andrew was a partner in the firm of John Bruce and Company and had family connections with Kilmarnock. The previous letter to Burness had asked him to send mail care of Creech, showing that Robert had already decided (before the tour had ended) to move out of the Nicol residence but was undecided where to go.

Back in Edinburgh Robert tried to get to grips with Creech but he was too other-worldly in his approach to business matters to be able to pin down that wily operator. He tried, with similar lack of success, to secure for his younger brother William, then a youth of twenty, a position as a saddler. William was, by all accounts, an amiable young man, but lacking in drive and direction. Perhaps Robert saw something of himself in his brother to whom (at Longtown and London) he later sent affectionate advice. Certainly Robert himself was once more at one of those crossroads in his life. Discouraged by Creech's behaviour, he realised that he had to find some career that would provide security. The only thing he knew anything about was farming – but his past experience in this field made him wary about returning to the land. He allowed twelve days to pass after his return to Edinburgh before he got around to writing to Patrick Miller at Dalswinton (CL 241–2), broaching the subject of a farming tenancy. He began by apologising for not waiting on Miller at Dalswinton about the latter end of August as he had promised. There was actually no good reason why he could not have kept this appointment, and we must suppose that he put off the evil of having to take a decision, by going off on his Highland tour instead. Robert had learned that Miller was due to return to Edinburgh about the end of October; that was good enough reason for delaying a decision still further. So, reasoned Robert, 'within that time I shall certainly wait on you, as by that time I suppose you will have settled your scheme with respect to your farms'. What was intended to be the final paragraph of the letter gave Miller the verdict on the Highland tour:

> My journey through the Highlands was perfectly inspiring; and I hope I have laid in a good stock of new poetical ideas from it.– I shall make no apology for sending you the inclosed: it is a small but grateful tribute to the memory of our common Countryman.

The letter has survived without its contents, but it seems probable that the poem referred to was the 'Elegy on the Death of Sir James Hunter Blair' (CW 281–2), a fellow Ayrshireman. The first half of the letter was undated but it seems likely that several days elapsed before Robert completed it with a postscript which was just as long. With this he enclosed the lines on the death of John McLeod of Raasay (CW 283–4). Significantly, in this postscript Robert stated, 'I am determined not to leave Edinburgh till I wind up my matters with Mr. Creech, which I am afraid will be a tedious business.' Just how tedious, he could not have foreseen.

The following day Robert wrote a long letter to Josiah Walker (CL 355–6), recalling the happy times at Blair and hoping that Walker would consider entering into a regular correspondence, or as regular as Robert was capable of:

> I have no idea of corresponding as a clock strikes; I only write when the spirit moves me.– Direct to me at Mauchline, as it is now a post-town.– On Thursday I shall be at Auchtertyre, where I shall remain for five or six days, and then a day or two at Edinburgh sends me for the West Country.

Robert was unduly optimistic in thinking that a few days would resolve his problems with Creech. In the meantime, however, he intended making another tour. Unlike his previous excursions that year, the trip to Stirlingshire was purely for pleasure. At the back of his mind were thoughts of the Excise as a safe career, but he continued to swither over a return to farming. It would be so much easier to make up his mind if he were married; and not just married, but having made a good match. By now Robert must have been aware that Jean Armour was pregnant again, but his actions demonstrate that, at this juncture, he had no notion of marrying her. He had his sights set on richer game. He was infatuated with Margaret Chalmers, and it was with a view to pressing his suit that he set off on 4 October to visit Harvieston where the charming Peggy was now in residence.

Like the West Highland foray, no journal was kept on this occasion, but it is possible to piece together a fair idea of the itinerary from Robert's letters, and the account which was supplied to Dr Currie in 1798 by Robert's travelling companion. Unfortunately, previous editors of the poet's letters have wrongly dated several letters, thereby upsetting the chronology considerably. Two letters, written from 'Auchtertyre' on a Monday, were incorrectly assigned by DeLancey Ferguson and all subsequent editors to 8 October. Chambers-Wallace, however, gave 15 October in both cases, and this must be correct.

As his companion on this important expedition Robert selected Dr James McKittrick Adair (1765–1802). Although there can be little doubt that the real reason for the trip was to visit Harvieston where Robert was a-wooing, the immediate pretext for the journey was to visit Sir William Murray of Ochtertyre in Strathearn near Crieff, who had extended an invitation to the poet when they met at Blair Atholl. That, at any rate, was what he told Josiah Walker, to whom he wrote on 29 September. Somewhat confusingly, Robert also had a long-standing invitation to visit John Ramsay of Ochtertyre, on the River Teith four miles north-west of Stirling. From the surviving correspondence, written between 15 and 20 October, the impression was given that the excursion to Strathearn in Perthshire was the principal reason for the tour. By contrast, the visit to Harvieston was passed off casually as a mere jaunt; but by the time Robert wrote to Nicol, Cruikshank and Miller of Dalswinton, the real reason for the trip was best forgotten.

In fact, Burns and Adair left Edinburgh on or about 4 October, called at Ochtertyre near Stirling on the way, and then spent eight days at Harvieston (5 to 12 October inclusive). Adair says 'about ten days', while Burns later recalled his sojourn there as 'eight days'. He had not intended to stop so long, but was 'storm-steaded two days at the foot of the Ochel hills with Mr Tait at Herveystoun & Mr Johnston at Alva', as he recalled to William Cruikshank (CL 359). As central Scotland was hit by a severe storm and heavy floods on 10 October it appears that Robert did not proceed to Ochtertyre near Crieff until Friday 12 October at the earliest. This places the letters written from there on a Monday as dating from 15 October, and not 8 as Ferguson, Roy and I have hitherto supposed. To both Nicol and Cruikshank Robert wrote that he intended leaving the Crieff Ochtertyre on Wednesday (17 October) and as he proposed spending a couple of days with the Ramsay family at Ochtertyre near Stirling on the way back, we can assume that he was there from 17 to 19 October, returning to Edinburgh on 20 October. Chambers-Wallace and Snyder both fell into the trap of supposing that Robert spent most of the time at Harvieston, with mere day-trips to the two Ochtertyres, although his letters suggest otherwise.

Young Dr Adair was the son of an Ayr physician and a relative of Mrs Dunlop; Robert had been introduced to him by the Revd. Dr Lawrie of Loudoun parish. Like many others who were asked to provide their recollections some years after the event, Adair got his dates confused, and told Currie that the tour had taken place in August; but taken in conjunction with Robert's letters and known movements, the tour must be assigned to the early part of October. A letter to Miller of Dalswinton, dated 20 October (CL 242), confirms this, for Robert did not return to Edinburgh till that day. A pardonable lapse concerning the precise dates, however, in no way invalidates the facts of the tour given by Adair:

At Stirling we met with a company of travellers from Edinburgh, among whom was a character in many respects congenial with that of Burns. This was Nicol, one of the teachers of the High Grammar-School at Edinburgh – the same wit and power of conversation; the same fondness for convivial society, and thoughtlessness of to-morrow, characterised them both; Jacobitical principles in politics were common to both of them; and these have been suspected, since the revolution in France, to have given place in each to opinions apparently opposite. I regret that I have preserved no *memorabilia* of their conversation, either on this or other occasions, when I happened to meet them together. Many songs were sung; which I mention for the sake of observing, that then when Burns was called on in his turn, he was accustomed, instead of singing, to recite one or other of his own shorter poems, with a tone and emphasis, which though not correct or harmonious, were impressive and pathetic. This he did on the present occasion.

From Stirling we went next morning through the romantic and fertile vale of Devon to Harvieston, in Clackmannanshire, then inhabited by Mrs Hamilton, with the younger part of whose family Burns had been previously acquainted. He introduced me to the family, and then was formed my first acquaintance with Mrs Hamilton's eldest daughter to whom I have been married for nine years.[67] Thus was I indebted to Burns for a connexion from which I have derived, and expect further to derive, much happiness.

During a residence of about ten days at Harvieston, we made excursions to various parts of the surrounding scenery, inferior to none in Scotland in beauty, sublimity, and romantic interest; particularly Castle Campbell, the ancient seat of the family of Argyll; and the famous cataract of the Devon called the Caldron-linn; and the Rumbling Bridge, a single broad arch, thrown by the devil, if tradition is to be believed, across the river, at the height of about one hundred feet above its bed.

A visit to Mrs Bruce of Clackmannan, a lady above ninety, the lineal descendant of that race which gave the Scottish throne its brightest ornament, interested his feelings powerfully. This venerable dame, with characteristic dignity informed me on my observing that I believed she was descended from the family of Robert Bruce, that Robert Bruce was sprung from her family. Though almost deprived of speech by a paralytic affection, she preserved her hospitality and urbanity. She was in possession of the hero's helmet and two-handed sword, with which she conferred on Burns and myself the honour of knighthood, remarking that she had a better right to confer that title than *some people*. You will of course conclude that the old lady's political tenets were as Jacobitical as the poet's, a conformity which contributed not a little to the cordiality of our reception and entertainment. She gave us her first toast after dinner, 'Awa Uncos', or Away the Strangers! Who these strangers were, you will readily understand.

At Dunfermline we visited the ruined abbey, and the abbey church, now consecrated to Presbyterian worship. Here I mounted the cutty stool, or stool of repentance, assuming the character of a penitent for fornication; while Burns from the pulpit addressed to me a ludicrous reproof and exhortation, parodied from that which had been delivered to himself in Ayrshire, where he had, as he assured me, once been one of the seven who mounted the *seat of shame* together.[68]

In the church, two broad flag-stones marked the grave of Robert Bruce for whose memory Burns had more than common veneration. He knelt and kissed with sacred fervour, and heartily (*suus ut mos erat*) execrated the worse than Gothic neglect of the first of Scottish heroes.

At Harvieston Robert spent eight of the happiest days of his life. Some time during this period he summoned up the courage to propose marriage; but Peggy turned him down with such gentleness and tact that she remained one of his closest friends, right up until she married Lewis Hay in December 1788. Almost a year after his visit to Harvieston, Robert wrote from Ellisland a very long – and, as it happened, his last – letter to Peggy (CL 237–9). In the course of pouring out all the pent-up feelings exacerbated by intense loneliness (for Jean, though now married to him, was then still at Mauchline), Robert wrote:

> when I think I have met with you, and have lived more of real life with you in eight days than I can do with almost anybody I meet with in eight years – when I think on the improbability of meeting you in this world again – I could sit down and cry like a child!

At Ochtertyre in Strathearn, after the disappointment of Peggy's rejection, Robert relaxed in congenial surroundings. In his letter to Nicol, he confessed, 'I find myself very comfortable here, neither oppressed by ceremony nor mortified by neglect'. Sir William Murray was an amiable and intelligent man who seems to have understood the sensitive nature of his guest. His wife, Lady Augusta Mackenzie, was interesting to Robert from associations with her parentage, for she was the youngest daughter of the Jacobite Earl of Cromartie who so narrowly escaped accompanying the Earl of Kilmarnock and Lord Balmerino to the scaffold on Tower Hill in 1746. Lady Augusta was, in fact, born in the Tower of London where her mother had taken up temporary residence while pleading for her husband's life.

Robert could not have spent more than five days with the Murrays at Ochtertyre, yet little more than three years later he exaggerated the length of his stay when annotating the lines 'On Scaring some Water-fowl in Loch Turit' (CW 296–7) in the Glenriddell MS: 'This was the production of a solitary forenoon's walk from Oughtertyre-house. I lived there, Sir William's guest, for two or three weeks.' By April 1791, therefore, it appears that Robert had erased the Harvieston visit from his memory. At Ochtertyre Robert met Sir William's young cousin, Euphemia, daughter of Mungo Murray of Lintrose. She was then a beautiful girl of eighteen, known locally as the 'Flower of Strathmore'. Robert made her the subject of a pastoral song, 'Blythe was She' (CW 295–6) to the melody of the old ballad 'Andro and his Cutty Gun'. Seven years later Euphemia married

David Smythe of Methven, afterwards a judge of the Court of Session. A letter from one of her relatives later recalled that

> Mrs Smythe always manifested a disinclination to speak on the subject of her meeting with Burns. But she once told me that she remembered his reciting the poem 'On Scaring the Wild-fowl' one evening after supper, and that he gave the concluding lines with the greatest possible vigour.[69]

Robert was given a letter of introduction from Dr Blacklock to John Ramsay of Ochtertyre (1736–1814), on whom he called with Adair on the way to Harvieston on 5 October. Two weeks later, in response to an invitation, he stopped at the Menteith Ochtertyre on the way back to Edinburgh. Ramsay had trained as a lawyer but never practised as he had inherited the family estate, and thereafter was content to live the life of a country gentleman in the Horatian ideal. A keen classical scholar, he placed a Latin inscription over his door, expressing his wish 'to live in peace and die in joyful hope in the small but pleasant inheritance of his fathers'. In a copse of willows which he planted on the estate he placed an eighteen-line Latin inscription expressing similar sentiments at greater length. Robert admired these lines and asked for copies of them. Later Ramsay supplied Currie with some interesting details of the poet's brief sojourn:

> I have been in the company of many men of genius, some of them poets, but never witnessed such flashes of intellectual brightness as from him, the impulse of the moment, sparks of celestial fire! I never was more delighted, therefore, than with his company for two days *tête-à-tête*. In a mixed company I should have made little of him, for, in the gamester's phrase, he did not always know when to play off and when to play on . . . I not only proposed to him the writing of a play similar to the 'Gentle Shepherd,' *qualem decet esse sororem*, but Scottish Georgics, a subject which Thomson has by no means exhausted in his *Seasons*. What beautiful landscapes of rural life and manners might not have been expected from a pencil so faithful and forcible as his, which could have exhibited scenes as familiar and interesting as those in the 'Gentle Shepherd,' which every one who knows our swains in their unadulterated state instantly recognises as true to nature! But to have executed either of these plans, steadiness and abstraction from company were wanting, not talents.[70]

Ramsay clearly felt that Robert had it in him to become a playwright and even furnished him with a suitable subject which the poet found attractive. This was the story of Omeron Cameron, the Highlander who sheltered an Earl of Mar when he had to hide from his enemies, and himself suffered exile as a consequence, only to be rewarded eventually by the Earl with a grant of land.

During one of their conversations, Ramsay asked Robert whether the Edinburgh literati had mended his poems by their criticisms. 'Sir,' said the poet, 'these gentlemen remind me of some spinsters in my country, who spin their thread so fine, that it is neither fit for weft nor woof.' Robert told Ramsay that he had not changed anything except one word, to please Dr Blair.[71] On 22 October 1787, a few days after the poet's visit, Ramsay wrote to him with further advice which reflected some of their dicussions:

> I approve of your plan of retiring from din and dissipation to a farm of very moderate size, sufficient to find exercise for mind and body, but not so great as to absorb better things. And if some intellectual pursuit be well chosen and steadily pursued, it will be more lucrative than most farms in this age of rapid improvement . . . Let those bright talents which the Almighty has bestowed on you, be henceforth employed to the noble purpose of supporting the cause of truth and virtue. An imagination so varied and forcible as yours may do this in many different modes; nor is it necessary to be always serious, which you have been to good purpose; good morals may be recommended in a comedy, or even in a song.

It soon becomes apparent to anyone reading Robert's journals and the letters written during or about his tours, that he differed quite radically from most of the other travellers of the period. 'In an age given to lengthy, sentimental, and pseudo-scientific chronicling of voyages and tours, Burns was laconic to the point of taciturnity', is how Snyder summed it up.[72] To be sure, Robert was as acute and penetrating as ever in his observations of the people he encountered along the way; but it is significant that when he repaid his hosts and hostesses 'in the coin with which a Poet pays his debts' the results were strained and lacking in spirit. Dr Adair commented on this curious shortcoming:

> I am surprised that none of these scenes should have called forth an exertion of Burns's Muse. But I doubt if he had much taste for the picturesque. I well remember that the ladies at Harvieston, who accompanied us on this jaunt, expressed their disappointment at his not expressing in more glowing and fervid language his impressions of the Caldron Linn scene, certainly highly sublime, and somewhat horrible.[73]

That Robert fully intended to ply his poetic trade while on these tours is borne out by the fact that he borrowed a copy of the Edinburgh Edition belonging to the Revd. Dr John Geddes, a Roman Catholic bishop whom he had met in Edinburgh.[74] This volume had had additional blank leaves bound in at both ends. It was obviously Robert's intention to fill the blank pages with fresh compositions as he went along, but wisely he refrained from so doing. Of the twelve poems which he subsequently inserted in these end-pages, only four were composed on tour.[75] The others included the elegies on John McLeod, Sir James Hunter Blair and Lord President Dundas, and three poems composed after his move to Ellisland.[76]

If the tours failed to rouse Robert's extempore powers, he was still confident that they would provide fresh inspiration. To Patrick Miller of Dalswinton he had written on 28 September, 'My journey through the Highlands was perfectly inspiring; and I hope I have laid in a good stock of new poetical ideas from it'. But to his old friend John Richmond, then back at Mauchline, Robert was nearer the truth when he wrote (CL 81):

> I have been rambling over the world ever since I saw you, through the heart of the Highlands as far as Inverness and back by the north coast the whole rout to Dundee.– I have done nothing else but visited cascades, prospects, ruins and Druidical temple, learned Highland tunes and pickt up Scotch songs, Jacobite anecdotes, &c. these two months.

Robert's best writing was inspired by human nature in all its aspects. Moreover, although he often tried to tune his lyre to the charms of some young lady encountered along the way, it must be admitted that he was only really at home writing about those whom he knew most intimately and for whom he cared deeply. His best poetry came from the heart, and it succeeded so well because it reached out to the hearts of his readers.

The four tours of May-October 1787, however, were by no means a waste of time. Robert saw a great deal of Scotland and sampled a little of England and thereby broadened his outlook immeasurably. These months had given him ample opportunity to measure himself against other men and to take stock of his position and, more importantly, ponder at length on his future course of action. It is clear that he lacked no amount of well-meant advice on the latter score, the consensus of opinion being that he ought to return to farming. This seemed sound advice, for was it not as a ploughman that he had found his muse in the first place? Thus the society which had briefly lionised him neatly categorised him. But, throughout his peregrinations and often haphazard wanderings that summer, Robert rapidly developed his hitherto latent interest in traditional ballads. Many of the men he met in his travels subsequently became good friends who supported what was to become the main achievement in the last years of his short life. All that had gone before, even the Kilmarnock and Edinburgh Editions, seemed to Robert as little more than the apprenticeship for his main aim in life,

> That I for poor auld Scotland's sake
> Some usefu plan or book could make,
>   Or sing a sang at least.[77]

CHAPTER 13

Edinburgh: the Second Winter, 1787–88

When dear Clarinda, matchless fair,
  First struck Sylvander's raptur'd view,
He gaz'd, he listened to despair–
  Alas! 'twas all he dared to do.

Sylvander to Clarinda (CW 301)

When Robert returned to Edinburgh on 20 October 1787 he had three matters on his mind: to wind up his affairs with Creech, to settle the business of leasing a small farm and to obtain a position in the Excise. His immediate priority, however, was to find new lodgings. Fortunately, another of his schoolmaster friends came to the rescue and Robert was given a room by William Cruikshank, a colleague of Nicol's at the High School. Cruikshank hailed from Duns, where he had received his education under his uncle and namesake. After graduating from Edinburgh University he was appointed rector of the Canongate High School and two years later became one of the classics masters in the High School of Edinburgh. By contrast with Nicol, Cruikshank was fondly remembered by his pupils, Lord Brougham describing him as 'a very able and successful teacher, as well as a worthy man'. Robert had met Cruikshank earlier that year and they had become close friends. The Cruikshank family occupied the two upper floors of a lofty building in an airy situation in the New Town, at 2 (later renumbered 30) St James's Square, now incorporated in Register House. The building was comparatively new in 1787 and this was undoubtedly the most commodious and comfortable of the poet's lodgings. Robert had two attic rooms. His bedroom was a large room at the back of the house with a window facing St Andrew Square and the green at the rear of Register House. From this a door led into a smaller front room, with a sloping ceiling and a small skylight window looking on to St James's Square.[1]

Cruikshank's twelve-year-old daughter Jean became a firm favourite of the poet. Josiah Walker later recalled how

About the end of October, I called for him at the house of a friend, whose daughter, though not more than twelve, was a considerable proficient in music. I found him seated by the harpsichord of this young lady, listening with the keenest interest to his own verse, which she sung and accompanied, and adjusting them to the music by repeated trials of the effect. In this occupation he was so totally absorbed, that it was difficult to draw his attention from it for a moment.[2]

This vividly illustrates the trouble Robert went to in marrying his words to music. For young Jean he composed one of his most beautiful and enduring songs, 'A Rose-bud by my Early Walk' (CW 318), to the tune 'The Shepherd's Wife'. In February 1788, as he was leaving Edinburgh, Robert presented Jean with a book on whose fly-leaf he inscribed the lines beginning 'Beautous rose-bud, young and gay' (CW 367–8) which he later published under the title 'To Miss Cruikshank, a Very Young Lady'. The 'rose-bud' married the Jedburgh lawyer James Henderson in 1804 and died in 1835.

When Robert came back to Edinburgh on 20 October he was in the grip of a heavy cold which compelled him to retire to his bed for several days. Ill or not, Robert put his enforced leisure to good account by catching up on his correspondence – which gives a good indication of his priorities at the time. To Patrick Miller he wrote that day (CL 242):

> I was still more unlucky in catching a miserable cold for which the medical gentlemen have ordered me into close confinement, 'under pain of Death!' the severest of penalties.– In two or three days, if I get better, and if I hear at your lodgings that you are still at Dalswinton, I will take a ride to Dumfries directly.

On the same day, however, Robert also wrote to James Hoy, the librarian of the Duke of Gordon (CL 361–2), to describe a project which had recently caught his interest and which was to become the chief pursuit in the few remaining years of his life:

> An Engraver, James Johnson, in Edinburgh has, not from mercenary views but from an honest Scotch enthusiasm, set about collecting all our native Songs and setting them to music; particularly those that have never been set before.– Clarke, the well known Musician, presides over the musical arrangement; and Drs Beattie & Blacklock, Mr Tytler, Woodhouslee, and your humble servant to the utmost of his small power, assist in collecting the old poetry, or sometimes for a fine air to make a stanza, when it has no words.– The inclosed is one which, like some other misbegotten brats, 'too tedious to mention,'[3] claims a parental pang from my Bardship.– I suppose it will appear in Johnson's second Number; the first was published before my acquaintance with him.– My request is; 'Cauld kail in Aberdeen' is one intended for this number; and I beg a copy of his Grace of Gordon's words to it, which you were so kind as repeat to me.– You may be sure we won't prefix the Author's name, except you like; tho' I look on it as no small merit to this work that the names of many of the Authors of our old Scotch Songs, names almost forgotten, will be inserted.

Johnson was born in Ettrickdale in April 1742, the son of Robert Johnson and Elizabeth Dickson. He came to Edinburgh and served his apprenticeship as a music engraver under James Read before setting up in business on his own account. Although he was poorly educated and betrayed the fact by his atrocious spelling, Johnson was a man of an inventive turn of mind, whose chief claim to fame up to 1787 had been to devise a cheap method of printing sheet music using etched pewter plates. By failing to patent his invention, however, he made little money out of it; and after 1795 it was rapidly eclipsed by the miracle of lithography. When he died in 1811, he was virtually penniless and his destitute widow was forced into the Edinburgh Charity Workhouse where she died eight years later. Poor as he himself was, however, Johnson contributed £4 to the fund for the poet's widow and orphans.

When Robert first came to Edinburgh Johnson had his premises in Bell's Wynd on the south side of the High Street, and it was from here that the first volume of his *Scots Musical Museum* was issued on 22 May 1787. Shortly thereafter, however, he moved to larger premises at the head of Lady Stair's Close on the opposite side and further up the thoroughfare, off the Lawnmarket. Robert was not speaking the truth when he said that the first volume was published before his acquaintance with Johnson. To be sure, the first volume had probably been in gestation for some time before Robert was introduced to Johnson by fellow Crochallan Fencibles, William Dunbar and William Smellie, but it is unlikely that it had gone to press. Johnson was eager to meet the young poet, as he wished to secure his co-operation. As a result, the first volume contained two songs acknowledged to 'Mr Burns' – 'Green grow the Rashes' (CW 81) and 'Young Peggy blooms our bonniest lass' (CW 125-6). Robert also contributed the last four lines to 'Here awa', there awa' (CW 480) and a reliable version of the old ballad 'Bonie Dundee' (CW 280) which he had taken down early in February and to which he added new stanzas.[4]

It will be remembered that one of Robert's last acts before leaving the capital on 5 May had been to write to Johnson, enclosing a song for his collection (CL 292). Now that he had settled back in Edinburgh, Robert lost no time in contacting Johnson again. An undated fragment of a letter (CL 292-3) written about this time furnished Johnson with addenda and corrigenda to his first volume. Before long, however, Johnson had tacitly delegated the editorship to his enthusiastic young collaborator. From then until his death less than nine years later, Robert was the editor of the *Museum* in all but name, contributing at least 160 songs of his own, as well as emending and revising many others; his system of identifying authors by a complex letter code only served to disguise the true extent of his own contribution. Three further volumes appeared in Robert's lifetime and the fifth volume was ready for the press at the time of his death. By contrast, it took Johnson a further seven years to get out the sixth and final volume. The musical editorship was held by Stephen Clarke (1744-97), organist of the Episcopal Chapel in the Cowgate; after his death, the music for the sixth volume was arranged by his son William. The chief driving force behind the *Museum* was undoubtedly Robert. Clarke was indolent and careless – on one occasion he lost a packet of songs, not all of which Robert was able to reconstitute from memory. The poet's correspondence with Clarke is confined to a single surviving letter (CL 615) which jocularly upbraided the musician for being so remiss in not answering letters:

> Mr B– is deeply impressed with, & awefully conscious of, the high impor-
> tance of Mr C–'s time, whether in the winged moments of symphonious
> exhibition at the keys of Harmony, while listening Seraphs ease their own
> less delightful strains; – or in the drowsy, hours of slumbrous repose, in
> the arms of his dearly beloved elbow-chair, where the frowsy but potent
> Power of Indolence, circumfuses her vapours round, & sheds her dews on,
> the beard of her Darling son – but half a line conveying half a meaning
> from Mr C– would make Mr B– the very happiest of mortals.

This mock-formal epistle apparently did the trick.

If Johnson had hoped to make his fortune from the *Museum* he was soon sadly disabused; and it was often quite a struggle to keep going with the project. When Johnson lost heart, it was Robert who encouraged him to continue. In a letter of 15 November 1788 (CL 295) Robert wrote:

> Perhaps you may not find your account, *lucratively*, in this business; but
> you are a Patriot for the Music of your Country; and I am certain,
> Posterity will look on themselves as highly indebted to your Publick
> spirit. – Be not in a hurry; let us go on correctly; and your name shall be
> immortal.

And on 19 June 1789 (CL 296) Robert felt constrained to write:

> What are you doing, and what is the reason that you have sent me no
> proof sheet to correct? Though I have been rather remiss in writing you,
> as I have been hurried, puzzled, plagued & confounded with some dis-
> agreable matters, yet believe me, it is not owing to the smallest neglect or
> forget of you, my good Sir, or your patriotic work.– Mr Clarke & I have
> frequent meetings & consultations on your work.

Even as he was dying, Robert was exhorting his friend (CL 303) to finish what they had so well begun:

> Your Work is a great one; & though, now that it is near finished, I see if
> we were to begin again, two or three things that might be mended, yet I
> will venture to prophesy, that to future ages your Publication will be the
> text book & standard of Scotish Song & Music.

When Robert wrote to James Hoy he estimated that the *Museum* might eventually run to three volumes, 'each number a handsome pocket volume, to consist of a hundred Scotch songs, with basses for the harpsichord, &c'. Hoy replied on 31 October, thanking Robert for his letter which had enclosed the lines on 'Castle Gordon' (CW 293):

> Your song I shewed without producing the author; and it was judged by the Duchess to be the production of Dr Beattie . . . When the Duchess was informed that you were the author, she wished you had written the verses in Scotch.

Apparently Hoy had conveyed to Robert that the Duke, while agreeable to having his song published in the *Museum*, declined to have it attributed to him. This impelled Robert to write:

> I wish my Lord Duke would pay a proper attention to the Christian admonition – 'Hide not your candle under a bushel,' but 'let your light shine before men.' I could name half-a-dozen dukes that I guess are a devilish deal worse employed; nay, I question if there are half-a-dozen better: perhaps there are not half that scanty number whom Heaven has favoured with the tuneful, happy, and I will say glorious, gift.

The Duke, 'a plain, unpretentious laird',[5] however, remained obdurate, and his song (number 162 in the second volume) appeared anonymously.

Robert's enthusiasm for Scottish songs permeated the long letter which he wrote to Margaret Chalmers a day or two after returning to Edinburgh (CL 231), enclosing the first volume of the *Museum* for her cousin Charlotte. 'I am determined to pay Charlotte a poetic compliment, if I could hit on some glorious old Scotch air, in number second,' he wrote, enclosing a rough draft of 'The Banks of the Devon' (CW 298-9). This was set to an old Gaelic air which Robert had recovered during his visit to Inverness. Charlotte was not mentioned by name, but the lines

> But the bonniest flow'r on the banks of the Devon
> Was once a sweet bud on the braes of the Ayr

would have clearly identified her. Robert composed two songs in compliment to Peggy Chalmers herself, 'My Peggy's Charms' (CW 297) and 'Where, Braving Angry Winter's Storms' (CW 298), which he sent sometime in November, with the intimation that he planned to publish them in the next volume of the *Museum*. Peggy was embarrassed, and wrote promptly to dissuade him. Robert responded (CL 232-3) with a spirited defence of his actions:

> The poetic compliments I pay cannot be misunderstood. They are neither of them so particular as to point *you* out to the world at large; and the circle of your acquaintances will allow all I have said. Besides, I have complimented you chiefly, almost solely, on your mental charms. Shall I be plain with you? I will; so look to it. Personal attractions, madam, you have much above par; wit, understanding, and worth, you possess in the first class. This is a cursed flat way of telling you these truths, but let me hear no more of your sheepish timidity.

About the same time he was writing to Johnson (CL 293) urging him to publish 'My Peggy's Charms', adding that if the words did not suit the tune he would have to find some other air 'as I have a very strong private reason for wishing them in the 2nd Volume'. Robert seems to have been determined to let the world know of his love for Peggy; perhaps he hoped that his recklessness would make her change her mind. In the end, however, he was forced to compromise. While 'Where, Braving Angry Winter's Storms' did appear in the second volume (number 195), 'My Peggy's Charms' had to wait almost fifteen years before it first saw the light of day, in George Thomson's *Select Collection of Scotish Airs* – and then divorced from the beautiful Gaelic melody which Burns had selected. It also appeared in the sixth volume of the *Museum* in 1803. Peggy's reticence was understandable. She was still secretly engaged to Lewis Hay who might not have taken very kindly to his fiancée being paraded before the world as the mistress of the notorious poet Burns. Although Robert more or less successfully managed to put his relationship with Peggy on a platonic level, Mrs McLehose saw through this. When Robert wrote to her as Clarinda on 10 January 1788 that 'the name I register in my heart's core is *Peggy Chalmers*', Mrs McLehose replied a few weeks later with the question, 'Why did not such a woman secure your heart? O the caprice of human nature, to fix on impossibilities.'[6]

Robert's interest in Johnson's *Museum* was the one bright spot in his life during late October and November 1787. A truer idea of how he felt at this time appears in a letter to Ainslie on 25 October. That evening he and Bob were to have visited the latter's second-cousin and namesake, the bookseller Robert Ainslie who resided at 2 North St David's Street, but Burns was not up to it.

> On looking over my engagements, constitution, present state of my health, some little vexatious soul concerns, &c., I find I can't sup abroad tonight. I shall be in to-day till one o'clock, if you have a leisure hour.
>
> You will think it romantic when I tell you, that I find the idea of your friendship almost necessary to my existence. You assume a proper length of face in my bitter hours of blue-devilism, and you laugh fully up to my highest wishes at my good things. I don't know, upon the whole, if you are one of the first fellows in God's world, but you are so to me. I tell you this just now, in the conviction that some inequalities in my temper and manner may perhaps sometimes make you suspect that I am not so warmly as I ought to be your friend.

Blue devils was an expression of Robert Fergusson's. Interestingly, the phrase also appeared in a lengthy 'Epistle to Robert Burns, the Ayrshire Poet', published by the *Edinburgh Evening Courant* on 12 December 1786, by an anonymous writer who had just seen the Kilmarnock Poems. By way of explanation he added a footnote that Fergusson used these words 'for the depression of the spirits generally consequent to a debauch and which he suffered in a most dreadful extreme'. Incidentally, this was the first poetic tribute to Burns to appear in print.[7]

Young Ainslie had recently moved to a flat on the north side of St James's Square so that he and Burns were close neighbours. Other residents of the square at this time included Alexander Nasmyth the portrait painter, John Beugo the engraver of Robert's portrait, and George Thomson (1757–1851) with whom the poet later collaborated in the production of the *Select Collection*. Captain Matthew Henderson, who lived next door to the Cruikshank family, was the subject of one of Robert's best elegies (CW 337–40). The scion of a once-wealthy family with estates in Ayrshire and Lanarkshire, and connected by marriage to James Boswell, Henderson had dissipated his fortune in high living, and when Robert knew him he was living in straitened circumstances, but maintaining an air of indigent gentility to the last. When he died in November 1788 Robert penned the elegy dedicated to 'a gentleman who held the patent for his honours immediately from almighty God!'

At number six resided another law student, Alexander Cunningham (1763–1812), to whom Robert addressed the lines beginning 'My godlike Friend – nay, do not stare' (CW 328). At this time Cunningham was courting Anne Stewart, the Anna referred to in this poem. Sadly, Anne Stewart rejected Cunningham in favour of a surgeon named Forrest Dewar. In January 1789, when Robert read of Miss Stewart's marriage in an Edinburgh newspaper, he wrote a long letter of commiseration to his friend (CL 456):

> As you are the single only instance that ever came within the sphere of my observation of her human nature, of a young fellow, dissipated but not debauched, a circumstance that has ever given me the highest idea of the native qualities of your heart, I am certain that a disappointment in the tender passion must, to you, be a very serious matter . . . I myself can affirm, both from bachelor and wedlock experience, that Love is the Alpha and the Omega of human enjoyment.– All the pleasures, all the happiness of my humble Compeers, flow immediately and directly from this delicious source.– It is that spark of celestial fire which lights up the wintry hut of Poverty, and makes the chearless mansion warm, comfortable and gay.– It is the emanation of Divinity that preserves the Sons and Daughters of rustic labour from degenerating into the brutes with which they daily hold converse.– Without it, life to the poor inmates of the Cottage would be a damning gift.
>
> I intended to go on with some kind of consolatory epistle, when, unawares I flew off in this rhapsodical tangent.

Despite the fact that Robert's attempt to console his friend must rather have rubbed salt in the poor fellow's wounds, Cunningham and the poet remained on the best of terms. Indeed, he was one of the few men who remained loyal to Robert till the end of his life, and even beyond; for he played one of the principal roles in promoting the fund on behalf of the poet's widow and orphans.

Ainslie and Cunningham formed with Burns a trio which must have reminded the poet of the Court of Equity of his Mauchline days. Cunningham eventually got over his unfortunate love affair and in 1792 married Agnes Moir who brought as her dowry the wealth of an estate in

South Carolina. But in the winter of 1787–88 Cunningham and Ainslie, and especially the latter, were Robert's closest male companions. Ainslie, though not yet fully qualified as a lawyer, was a young man of independent means which he proclaimed by maintaining a wine-cellar. In fact, this was nothing more than the recess under a bunker-seat in one of the windows of his apartment. His stock of wine consisted of five bottles of port, all that remained of a dozen of good quality which had been presented to him by a friend, a wine-merchant. On Burns calling on him one day, Ainslie proposed that they should spend the afternoon over a bottle; but Burns said, 'No, my friend, we'll have no wine today. To sit dozing in the house on such a fine afternoon as this would be insufferable. Besides, you know that you and I don't require wine to sharpen our wit, nor its adventitious aid to make us happy. No; we'll take a ramble over Arthur's Seat to admire the beauties of nature, and come in to a late tea.' They did so; and Ainslie used to declare that he had never known the poet's conversation so amusing, so instructive, and altogether so delightful, as during the cheerful stroll they had over the hill, and during the sober tea-drinking which followed.[8]

Old friends were by no means forgotten. On 25 October Robert wrote to John Richmond, now back in Mauchline again during the long summer recess (CL 81). Robert estimated that he would be in Edinburgh at least another fortnight, so that if Richmond were back in town for the winter session of the law courts he hoped that they would meet 'once more in Auld Reekie'. It will be remembered that Richmond had seduced Jenny Surgeoner who bore him a daughter out of wedlock. In 1791 he married Jenny, but in 1787 he enjoyed the same sort of *ad hoc* relationship with his mistress that Robert had with Jean Armour:

> I long much to hear from you, how you are, what are your views, and how your little girl comes on.– By the way, I hear I am a girl out of pocket and by careless, murdering mischance too, which has provoked me and vexed me a good deal.– I beg you will write me by post immediately on receipt of this, and let me know the news of Armour's family, if the world begins to talk of Jean's appearance any way.

The casual reference to the death of baby Jean is sometimes taken out of context by Burns's detractors to show him in a callous light, but the full quotation shows that, far from making light of the little girl's death, Robert was sorely vexed by the news. Little Jean had remained with her mother in Mauchline while her twin brother had gone to Mossgiel. The circumstances of the baby's death, on 20 October, are not known but 'murdering mischance' hints at gross negligence. Robert's anxiety about the child's mother was understandable but perhaps premature. If she was four months' pregnant by this time, the chances are that her condition would not be so obvious. Had she been tall and slim, the swelling in her abdomen would have been more noticeable; but Jean was naturally on the plump side and it seems more likely that, for the moment, she was managing to conceal the truth from her parents and the ever-watchful eyes of the 'holy beagles'.

Some time afterwards, Robert paid a flying visit to Dalswinton, looked briefly at the unimproved farms which Patrick Miller had to offer, and returned to Edinburgh again without making a detour to Mauchline either going or coming. For all his concern about Jean, Robert could not stomach another confrontation with her formidable parents. Who broke the bad news about baby Jean is not known; probably this unpleasant task would have fallen to Gilbert. The date of the visit to Dumfries is not known for certain. In a letter of 21 October (CL 231) to Margaret Chalmers Robert said, 'I go on Thursday or Friday to Dumfries to wait on Mr Miller about his farms'. As two long letters were written from Edinburgh on 25 October it seems unlikely that Robert would have gone to Dumfries that day. Even the following day seems doubtful. The problem is compounded by attempts by scholars to date three letters to Peggy. If modern editors are correct, the first of these, headed 'Edinburgh, December 1787', belongs to 6 November (although there is nothing in the text to support DeLancey Ferguson's decision to ignore the date which Burns put on it). This supposition may have been based on a remark near the close of the letter. 'This day will decide my affairs with Creech', however, could apply to virtually any time up to the following February. One letter alone bears a clear date (CL 233) – 21 November 1787 – but this contains no reference to persons or events which would help to clarify the details of the trip to Dumfries. The third letter, tentatively ascribed by Ferguson and Roy to about 1 December, however, begins 'I have been at Dumfries'. Either the visit to Dalswinton took place much later than generally supposed, or the date suggested for this letter is wrong. The problems concerning the poet's correspondence with Margaret Chalmers stem from the fact that, according to Cromek, Robert's letters were burned by her cousin 'Mrs Adair of Scarborough' (Charlotte Hamilton), but he omits to mention whether his text was taken from the charred fragments rescued from the fire, or from partial transcripts made before the originals were destroyed. Allan Cunningham stated that 'nothing was saved except such fragments as were found among the Bard's memoranda', but this seems doubtful. Several of the fragmentary letters are dated, whereas Robert very seldom dated his drafts.

It would seem that, were Robert contemplating a fairly arduous journey on horseback, he would do so earlier rather than later, so on balance I think that the Dumfries visit must have taken place on or about 26 October. Unfortunately, few of the surviving letters of this period are clearly dated. Robert was certainly back in Edinburgh on 6 November when he wrote his second letter to James Hoy (CL 362), and he was in the capital eight days later when he wrote to Robert Patterson of Alnwick (CL 365). On 16 November he was in Linlithgow where he was made an honorary burgess. Dr Wallace had a sight of this interesting document for he gave a transcript of it,[9] and it seems probable that it was then in the possession of Neilson Mitchell, a Glasgow tobacco merchant, who lent it to Alexander Thomas, a native of the town, who produced it for the inspection of the Town Council on 4 January 1859 when the birth centenary celebrations were imminent.[10] Neilson Mitchell (1801–89) was the grandson of Stephen

Mitchell V (1732–1800), one of the bailies present on the occasion of the burgess ceremony. It might have been supposed that Neilson Mitchell would have donated this interesting relic to his birthplace, but apparently this was not the case. It is perhaps worth noting that Neilson's eldest brother Stephen VII (1789–1874) was the Glasgow tobacco magnate who bequeathed his fortune to found the great library that bears his name, but there is no record of the Linlithgow burgess ticket ever having formed part of the incomparable Burns collection in the Mitchell Library.[11] Burns himself never referred to this civic honour in any of his letters or poems.

Again Robert was unduly sanguine in his hopes of leaving Edinburgh. On 24 November, after a gap of four months, he wrote to Mrs Dunlop (CL 137–8) and concluded by saying, 'I expect to leave Edinburgh in eight or ten days, and shall certainly do myself the honour of calling at Dunlop house as I return to Ayrshire'. To what extent he had been able to pin down the slippery Creech is starkly evident in the codicil to the Memorandum of Agreement made the previous April. It was not until 23 October that Robert actually got as far as wringing a written promise from Creech to pay him the hundred guineas for his copyright. The final line 'Received the contents' was not dated till 30 May 1788 – fully seven months later.

The notion that Creech was involved in a conspiracy to keep the poet short of cash and thereby make it easier for Dundas and his henchmen to inveigle Burns into joining the Excise[12] does not stand up to serious examination. Creech's tight grasp on money was proverbial in his own lifetime. While it is true to say that Creech never settled an account till it became impossible to put off his creditor any longer – and Robert was by no means the only person who received this frustrating treatment – it is only fair to point out that the practice in the book trade at that time was for a publisher to render royalty accounts to an author annually, either on 30 June or 31 December but always at least six months after publication. The money due on these accounts was not paid until six months later. In this case, therefore, money due to Robert in respect of sales from 17 April till the end of June 1787 would not require to be accounted for until 31 December, and would not become payable until the end of June 1788. On the other hand, by merely acting as the author's *agent*, Creech was not risking his own money. The sums which passed through his hands were subscription money and not author's royalties in the true sense. Furthermore, there was no valid reason for delaying payment on the copyright, within a month or two at latest, after the Memorandum of Agreement was signed by the contracting parties. No doubt Creech regarded himself as the publisher and the money as royalties and behaved accordingly; but Robert had good grounds for his mounting irritation with Creech. From the various references to the matter in the poet's correspondence, it seems obvious that Creech kept promising an early settlement, but then fobbed him off. Robert, unsophisticated and unskilled in the ways of publishers, was baffled and increasingly angered; but if Creech gave the matter a second thought it was probably to feel hurt at the poet's hardening attitude. Wily William would not have considered his conduct to be out of the ordinary.

In the meantime, while Robert busied himself with his new-found interest in Johnson's *Museum*, he had other ways of passing the time. Having been embarrassed by a Frenchwoman at one of the fashionable assemblies, when she could not understand his French nor he hers, Robert had decided to improve his fluency in speaking the language. To this end he and his engraver friend John Beugo enrolled for tuition under Louis Cauvin. Though born in Scotland, Cauvin was the son of a native Frenchman. Both father and son gave individual tuition in French and Louis later stated that Burns learned more in three months than most of his pupils in three years. A brief, undated note from Robert to Beugo is preserved in the National Library of Scotland (CL 368):

> a certain sour faced old acquaintance called Glauber's salts hinders me from my lesson tonight. Tomorrow night I will not fail.

We can only speculate why Robert needed to dose himself with this powerful laxative; 'old acquaintance' implies habitual use at that. It was commonly believed at the time that a good purging was the best cure for depression, and Robert certainly had much to be depressed about. In his letter to Margaret Chalmers following the visit to Dumfries to view Miller's farms, Robert admitted:

> I am rather hopeless in it; but as my brother is an excellent farmer, and is, besides an exceedingly prudent, sober man, (qualities which are only a younger brother's fortune in our family), I am determined, if my Dumfries business fail me, to return into partnership with him, and at our leisure take another farm in the neighbourhood.

About this time Robert also wrote to Gavin Hamilton (CL 70). It appears that Gavin had been very ill when Robert was briefly in Mauchline during the summer, but he was now fully recovered. This provided Robert with the pretext for a homily in ironical terms, at the expense of both Daddy Auld and Hamilton himself. Having preached to his friend 'never at one time to drink more than a pint of wine (I mean an English pint) & that you will never be witness to more than one bowl of punch at a time', Robert continued sardonically:

> as I understand you are now in habits of intimacy with that Boanerges of gospel powers, Father Auld, be earnest with him that he will wrestle in prayer for you, that you may see the vanity of vanities in trusting to, or even practising the carnal moral works of Charity, Humanity, Generosity & Forgiveness; things which you practised so flagrantly that it was evident you delighted in them; neglecting or perhaps prophanely despising the wholsome doctrine of 'Faith without Works, the only anchor of salvation'.

Ross Roy surmises that this joke misfired and may, in fact, have contributed to the coolness which developed between Burns and Hamilton.[13]

Having brought Creech to the point of actually putting his promise to pay a hundred guineas into writing, Robert felt that he had got as far as he could for the time being with his niggardly publisher and had decided to return to Mossgiel about 4 December. This much seems evident in a curious letter dated 'Saturday noon'. As he mentions his plan to leave Edinburgh 'in three or four days' it has been dated to 1 December. The recipient of this letter was Isabella Mabane, of whom nothing has been previously recorded beyond the tantalising scraps furnished by Chambers (1851): 'Died in Edinburgh many years ago' and Scott Douglas (1877): 'She became Mrs Col. Wright, but there is no tradition of any connecting link between her and Burns except this short letter'.[14] All that I can add is that she was the natural daughter of Thomas Mabane and Margaret Tait and was born at Melrose on 20 April 1735. Robert had evidently visited Miss Mabane and promised to try and get some small object of vertu, possibly a patch-box, repaired.

Robert's alternative plan of securing an Excise appointment, which he had aired a number of times between October and December 1786, had been in limbo for twelve months while he oscillated between returning to farming and making some sort of literary career for himself; but it was always at the back of his mind. During his first winter in Edinburgh Robert made the acquaintance of Miss Erskine Nimmo, to whom he was probably introduced by Margaret Chalmers. This seems clear from the reference to the lady in Robert's letter of 21 October 1787 (CL 231): 'Miss N. is very well, and begs to be remembered in the old way to you'. Robert, in fact, had tried to persuade this lady to accompany him on his trip to Harvieston, but 'all in vain. My rhetoric seems quite to have lost its effect on the lovely half of mankind', showing that he and Miss Nimmo had been on close terms for some time. Erskine Ebenezer Nimmo was not much younger than Mrs Dunlop, having been born in Edinburgh in October 1731, the youngest of eight children born to James Nimmo and Mary Erskine. She lived in a first-floor apartment in Alison Square where she kept house for her nephew, William, who was six years Robert's senior. At this time William Nimmo was a Supervisor in the Excise, and it has been suggested that Robert cultivated this friendship with a view to gaining entry to the service;[15] but Nimmo was actually based at Lanark, and a Supervisor was only one rank higher than an Exciseman.[16] There is no evidence to suggest that Robert had any ulterior motive in visiting Miss Nimmo in the autumn and winter of 1787 and it is significant that although the lady herself is mentioned a dozen times in letters between October 1787 and October 1790, there is not a single mention of her nephew. So much, therefore, for the importance of William Nimmo.

Whether Robert was serious about returning to Mossgiel around 4 December cannot be ascertained; but that afternoon he attended a tea party hosted by Miss Nimmo which, if it did not change his life, certainly precipitated one of the most curious episodes in it. Present on that auspicious occasion was Mrs Agnes Craig McLehose – Nancy to her friends – an intimate friend of the hostess, and then residing with her children in the first floor of a house at the back of General's Entry, Potterrow. Until now it has always been believed that Agnes Craig was three months younger than Burns, the statement that she was born in April 1759 having originated with her grandson and biographer, William Craig McLehose.[17] No doubt he got this detail from the lady herself before she died at an advanced age in 1841. In the circumstances, the lie was quite understandable; indeed, the lady may have misled Burns himself. Nancy was not only nine months older than Robert, she was a good deal older than any other woman with whom he ever became emotionally involved. She was also married and, although his journals reveal that Robert was occasionally attracted fleetingly to comely young matrons, this factor alone would in ordinary circumstances have rendered a closer association taboo; but Nancy had separated from her husband.

Born on 26 April 1758 and baptised on 8 May, Nancy was the daughter of a prominent Glasgow surgeon, Andrew Craig. Nancy's biographer claimed that she was the youngest of five children, three of whom had died before she was born. In fact, she was the third of four daughters, her sisters being Margaret (born 27 June 1752), Lilias (born 25 July 1754) and Mary (born 11 May 1764). According to the McLehose biography, Nancy herself was a sickly child but her health gradually improved from the age of five and she developed into an exceptionally pretty girl. Her mother, Christian McLaurin, died in 1767 and both Lilias and Mary died in infancy; thereafter Nancy had only her sister Margaret, six years her senior, for companionship. On 30 April 1771 Margaret married Captain James Kennedy of Kailzie, but died in childbirth a year later. At the age of fifteen, 'pretty Miss Nancy' was the toast of Glasgow's Hodge Podge Club. She had a somewhat erratic education, but at the age of fifteen she was sent to a boarding-school in Edinburgh to improve her handwriting and grammar and give her the polish required to launch her into society. The pretty little blonde with the pert figure and dancing eyes, however, attracted the attention of James McLehose, a young Glasgow lawyer who was determined to get to know her much better. He was either discouraged by Nancy's father or failed to get a proper introduction to her, but he discovered that she was about to leave Glasgow by stage-coach. Having ascertained the time of her departure he engaged all the seats in the interior of the coach, except the one booked by Miss Craig. On the appointed day the coach left Glasgow at eight in the morning and arrived at Edinburgh ten hours later. 'Mr McLehose, who possessed a handsome person and a most insinuating address, improved the opportunity which he had purchased.' Nancy was bowled over by the dashing young lawyer and on her return from Edinburgh six months later she consented to marry him, despite all the entreaties of her family. On 1 July 1776 the regular marriage of 'James M'Elhose, writer in Glasgow, and Agnes Craig, residing there' was duly entered in the register of Glasgow parish.

Having entered matrimony not long after her eighteenth birthday, Nancy was the mother of four children by the time she was twenty-three. The marriage, however, was an unhappy one. According to Nancy's own statement, 'Our disagreement rose to such a height, and my husband's treatment was so harsh, that it was thought advisable by my friends a separation should take place, which accordingly followed in December 1780.' The eldest child, William (born in May 1777) had died in infancy; Andrew Craig (June 1778) and a second William (April 1780) followed. Shortly before the last child was born Nancy moved out of the matrimonial home and returned to her father's residence in the Saltmarket. There, on 21 April 1781, her son James was born. James McLehose, having already got custody of the two elder children, subsequently took possession of the youngest boy as soon as he was weaned. To make matters worse, Nancy's father died on 13 May 1782, though fortunately he made sure that his property could not be touched by his rascally son-in-law. As he died after a long illness, however, Andrew Craig had dissipated his savings; his property was sufficient to provide Nancy with an annuity of £8, augmented by £8 per annum from the Faculty of Physicians and Surgeons and later £10 a year from the Glasgow Faculty of Procurators, in respect of James McLehose's profession. Meanwhile, James had parked his three children on his widowed mother and other relations and made no provision for the upkeep of his wife or family. Nancy soon recovered her children and in August 1782 moved to Edinburgh, where she was to spend the rest of her long life. Her slender income of ten shillings a week was augmented from time to time by 'some worthy, benevolent friends, whose kindness no time can erase from my grateful heart'.[18]

McLehose himself went to London. After two and a half years of dissipation he was thrown into a debtors' gaol from which he was rescued by his long-suffering relatives, on condition that he leave the country. In November 1784, shortly before he sailed for Jamaica, James tried to effect a reconciliation with his young wife, to whom he wrote: 'For my part, I am willing to forget what is past, neither do I require an apology from you'. Not surprisingly, Nancy was outraged at his condescension and hypocrisy and never bothered to reply. By that time her youngest son James had died, while the second William was a sickly child, prone to boils and abscesses.

When Nancy settled in Edinburgh her youth, beauty and sad story excited the sympathy of many. She was lucky in one respect; she was not without influential connections. Her late father's brother was the Revd. William Craig whose son, William (1745–1813), was then one of the country's rising lawyers. In 1787 Nancy's cousin was appointed Sheriff-depute of Ayrshire. Most biographies of Burns refer to him as Lord Craig, although he did not acquire this judicial title until 1792 when he was raised to the bench on the death of Lord Hailes. William Craig, however, was also a prominent member of Edinburgh's literati. He took a leading role in the foundation of *The Mirror* published by Creech and, after Henry Mackenzie, was that magazine's most prolific contributor. To Craig also belongs the credit for having first brought the young poet Michael Bruce to the attention of the public. He was himself a talented versifier, strongly influenced by *The Man of Feeling*. He showed his cousin great kindness, paying many of her bills and generally providing material and emotional support when she needed it. When reports of James McLehose's success in Jamaica reached Scotland the Surgeons and the Procurators terminated their annuities to his wife, in the belief that the wayward James would now support her. No help being forthcoming, however, William Craig took it upon himself to make good the deficit. When he died in 1813, Lord Craig left a substantial sum, as well as his library, to Nancy's sole surviving son, Andrew.

By contrast John McLaurin (1734–96), Nancy's second cousin, was a petty, vindictive, morose hypocrite. In 1788 he became a Senator of the College of Justice with the title of Lord Dreghorn. He, too, had literary pretensions, and published a number of tracts on such diverse topics as the law, religion and poetry. An early ambivalence towards prostitutes turned into an obsessive hatred, and he was largely responsible for cleaning up the city in 1789 by closing Edinburgh's brothels and banishing their inmates. This provoked Burns to write to Peter Hill (CL 315) execrating Dreghorn and his colleagues:

> May Woman curse them! May Woman blast them! May Woman damn them! May her lovely hand inexorably shut the Portal of Rapture to their most earnest Prayers & fondest essays for entrance! And when many years, and much port and great business have delivered them over to Vulture Gouts and Aspen Palsies, *then* may the dear, bewitching Charmer in derision throw open the blissful Gate to tantalize their impotent desires which like ghosts haunt their bosoms when all their powers to give or receive enjoyment, are for ever asleep in the sepulchre of their fathers!!!

Lord Dreghorn suspected that his pretty cousin, living on her own, was on the brink of depravity and refused steadfastly to acknowledge her, far less help her. 'He used me in a manner unfeelingly harsh beyond description, at one of the darkest periods of my chequered life,' Nancy later recorded.[19]

Nancy settled into a precariously genteel routine in Edinburgh and steadily widened her circle of friends and acquaintances. Conscious of the shortcomings in her formal education, she read voraciously, polished her conversational skills and wrote elegant verses. When Burns was the lion of the 1786–7 season Nancy read his poems and determined to meet him, but cousin William despised 'that ploughman with pretensions to poetry' and refused to invite Robert to his soirées. It was not until 4 December 1787 that Nancy's wish was granted. One contemporary described her at this period as 'short in stature, her form graceful, her hands and feet small and delicate. Her features were regular and pleasing, her eyes lustrous, her complexion fair, her cheeks ruddy, and a well-formed mouth displayed teeth beautifully white', while another said of her that she was 'of a some-what voluptuous style of beauty, of lively and easy manners, of a poetical cast of mind, with some wit, and not too high a degree of refinement or delicacy'.[20] She was, in fact, just the kind of woman to whom Robert would be instinctively drawn. 'Golden locks were a sign of amourousness',

Robert noted in the margin of his copy of Sterne's *Koran*, perhaps mindful of Margaret Campbell.

Nancy went home that night and dashed off a note inviting Robert to her flat for tea on Thursday, 6 December. Robert fully intended to keep this appointment, but on that day he was unavoidably detained. He immediately sent a letter (CL 371–2), saying, 'I had set no small store by my tea-drinking tonight, and have not often been so disappointed. Saturday evening I shall embrace the opportunity with the greatest pleasure.' He went on to add that he planned to leave Edinburgh on 13 December.

> Our worthy common friend Miss Nimmo, in her usual pleasant way, rallied me a good deal on my new acquaintance, and in the humor of her ideas I wrote some lines which I inclose you, as I think they have a good deal of poetic merit; and Miss N– tells me, you are not only a Critic but a Poetess.

And he concluded by saying of Miss Nimmo and his new acquaintance, that 'there are scarcely two people on earth by whom it would mortify me more to be forgotten, tho, at the distance of nine-score miles'. Strong stuff, indeed, to a lady whom he had just met. It is not known what verses were enclosed with this letter.

Both Robert and Nancy appear to have been looking forward to their *tête-à-tête* on the Saturday evening; but fate intervened. Robert had been wining and dining on Friday night and had taken a hackney cab back to his lodgings in the early hours of Saturday morning. In a letter to Margaret Chalmers (CL 234) on 12 December he stated that 'a drunken coachman' was the cause of the accident in which he sustained 'a bruised limb' which he had to keep extended on a cushion. This implies that the coach had a collision, or overturned, as a result of the driver's drunken carelessness; but in a letter of apology to Nancy herself, written on Saturday evening (CL 372), Robert was more specific, saying that 'an unlucky fall from a coach has so bruised one of my knees that I can't stir my leg off the cushion'. Ten weeks after the accident, however, he wrote to John Tennant (CL 222) and explained, 'I fell and dislocated the cap of my knee, which laid me up a cripple'. Robert's surgeon friend Alexander 'Sandy' Wood found that no bones were broken, and managed to reset the knee-cap. He ordered the poet to immobilise his injured leg and keep it extended on a cushion for a few days till the swelling abated. This put paid, not only to Robert's date with Nancy, but to his plans to leave Edinburgh.

The physical injury was the lesser of Robert's ailments, however, as he confided to Peggy Chalmers: 'misfortune, bodily constitution, hell and myself, have formed a Quadruple Alliance to guarantee the other [evil]'. Enforced idleness did not come easy to such an active man, and Robert turned to his bible for consolation; within a few days he had 'got through the five books of Moses, and half way in Joshua. It is really a glorious book'. Disappointment at not seeing the charming young grass-widow probably contributed in no small measure to his depression. In his note of

8 December he added that he was 'intoxicated with the idea' of seeing her. 'I shall not rest in my grave for chagrin', he promised if he did not see her again. One can imagine how Nancy's heart fluttered when she read the closing lines:

> I cannot bear the idea of leaving Edinburgh without seeing you.– I know not how to account for it – I am strangely taken with some people; nor am I often mistaken. You are a stranger to me; but I am an odd being: some yet unnamed feelings; things not principles, but better than whims, carry me farther than boasted reason ever did a Philosopher.

Nancy replied immediately with a long letter sent the same evening. For six weeks Burns was virtually confined to his room. Had his injury not immobilised him Robert would undoubtedly have spent a great deal of his time in Nancy's delectable company; whether this would have led to physical intimacy is a matter of speculation, but it would not have resulted in such a voluminous correspondence. The series of letters which subsequently developed, fast, furious and frequent, relied heavily on the excellent service of the Edinburgh Penny Post, a private enterprise which had been operated by 'Indian' Peter Williamson since 1773.[21] One of Williamson's receiving offices was located in the Register Office next to Robert's lodgings, and another, run by a Mrs Anderson, was in Chapel Street on the corner of Potterrow where Nancy resided. Letters and small parcels were 'delivered every hour throughout the day, from nine o'clock in the morning till nine at night, for one penny each letter or bundle, within an English mile of the cross of Edinburgh'.[22] Between December and mid-March at least eighty letters (forty-two from Robert) passed between them; at the height of this epistolary romance, as many as two letters in each direction passed between them on some days.

Nancy, who had experienced so many crushing disappointments in her young life, admitted that, inured as she was to life's cruel knocks, 'I never felt more, nay, nor half so severely, for one of the same nature!' After hoping that Robert would soon recover from his injury she confessed, 'I am much flattered at being a favourite of yours. Miss Nimmo can tell you how earnestly I had long pressed her to make us acquainted. I had a presentiment that we should derive pleasure from the society of each other.' There was much, much more in similar vein. She latched on to Robert's 'unnamed feelings':

> These 'nameless feelings' I perfectly comprehend, tho' the pen of a Locke could not define them. Perhaps *instinct* comes nearer their description than either 'Principles or Whims'. Think ye they have any connection with that 'heavenly light which leads astray'? One thing I know, that they have a powerful effect on me, and are delightful when under the check of *reason* and *religion* . . . Pardon any little freedoms I take with you . . . If I was your *sister*, I would call and see you; but 'tis a censorious world this; and in this sense 'you and I are not of this world'. Adieu. Keep up your heart, you will soon get well, and we shall *meet[t]*. *Farewell. God bless you.*[23]

The poem which Nancy sent has not survived. In her letter she had indulged in a bout of self-deprecation: 'Be sincere, and own that, whatever merit it has, it has not a line resembling poetry'. This provoked the desired response. When Robert replied on 12 December (CL 372) he claimed gallantly: 'Your lines, I maintain it, are Poetry; and good Poetry,' but, rather carelessly, he did not preserve them. The lines obviously spoke of friendship, for Robert reacted fulsomely, 'Your friendship, Madam! By heavens, I was never proud before . . . I swear solemnly, (in all the tenor of my former oath,) to remember you in all the pride and warmth of friendship until – I cease to be!'

It appears that Miss Nimmo was at the party on that fateful Friday night and afterwards felt herself partly responsible for Robert's injury, implying that Robert may have drunk too much and thus been at least a contributor to the accident. This may be inferred from Nancy's next letter, dated 'Sunday, Noon' (16 December), in which she went on to give Robert sound advice on following Dr Wood's instructions. But Nancy was also uneasy that Robert had gone too far in his professions of friendship, 'a friendship which, had I been so blest as to have met with you *in time*, might have led me – God of love only knows where'. Tremulously, but coquettishly, she responded:

> When I meet you, I must chide you for writing in your romantic style. Do you remember that she whom you address is a married woman? or, Jacob-like, would you wait seven years, and even then, perhaps, be disappointed, as he was? No; I know you better: you have too much of that impetuosity which generally accompanies noble minds.[24]

Robert had come a long way since those stilted letters to Elizabeth Gebbie. First of all, he was in no hurry to reply and although his next letter was undated it appears to have been sent after a decent interval of four days (CL 373). He adopted a mixture of friendly banter and affection, making her eat her own words:

> 'Pay my addresses to a married woman!' I started, as if I had seen the ghost of him I had injur'd: I recollected my expressions; some of them indeed were, in the law phrase, 'habit and repute,' which is being half guilty.– I cannot positively say, Madam, whether my heart might not have gone astray a little; but I can declare upon the honor of a Poet that the vagrant has wandered unknown to me.

Having protested his innocence and declaring that his intentions were perfectly honourable, he proceeded to subject her to an intense bout of verbal love-making, ending:

> I have just now looked over what I have written, and it is such a chaos of nonsense that I daresay you will throw it into the fire, and call me an idle, stupid fellow; but whatever you think of my brains, believe me to be, with the most sacred respect, and heart-felt esteem, My Dear Madam, your humble servant.

Several letters must have passed between these pen-friends in the ensuing week but none has survived. It is clear that, in the course of that week, Robert and Nancy moved from the formality of Sir and Madam to the Arcadian conceit of Sylvander and Clarinda. If these *noms de plume* were adopted on grounds of prudence – Williamson's Penny Post was not bound by the same constraints as His Majesty's mails and Edinburgh was little more than a village where gossip was concerned – then it seems likely that the one who had most to lose by being compromised if the letters fell into the wrong hands was Nancy. In the next extant letter, written on Friday 28 December (CL 374), Robert says, 'You cannot imagine, Clarinda, (I like the idea of Arcadian names in a commerce of this kind)' which implies that Nancy had taken the initiative. The use of such classical pseudonyms in love letters was a not uncommon practice in the eighteenth century and it is the sort of notion which Nancy might have picked up at her Edinburgh boarding-school. Sylvander ('man of the woods') was the hero of a romance published at Edinburgh in 1768, while Clarinda had been a popular name with romantic poets since the days of Edmund Spenser. Damon and Celia would have done just as well, but the three-syllable names were that little bit more distinctive. One would have thought that, less than ten years later, Nancy would have had no difficulty remembering the name she had used. When, soon after Robert's death, his friends Alexander Cunningham and John Syme launched a public appeal for the loan of the poet's letters for publication in 'a posthumous volume of the poetical remains', Cunningham received a letter from Mrs McLehose seeking the return of her 'Letters wrote the Bard under the Signature of Clitander' – a Freudian slip, surely! Hard on the heels of this strange request, Cunningham had a visit from Robert Ainslie, Writer to the Signet (and Nancy's man of business), demanding her letters. That the trustees did not accede to that demand until some months later – and then only on one condition – is shown by a letter of 9 January 1797 from the lady to Syme, 'I am happy you have consented to return my letters at last, and that my pledge has pleased you'.[25] What that pledge was may be guessed: Nancy was only prepared to release Robert's letters provided hers were returned to her unpublished. In fact, Dr James Currie (1800) treated Robert's second winter in Edinburgh very cursorily and made no reference to the Clarinda episode at all. It was not until two years later that some of Robert's letters to Clarinda appeared as an appendix in Thomas Stewart's compilation of Burns's poems 'including a number of original pieces never before published', and not until 1843 that both sides of the correspondence were published by Clarinda's grandson.[26] About 1854, however, an undated volume entitled *The poetical and prose works of Robert Burns . . . from the collection of Sir Egerton Brydges* was published with an appendix containing sixteen letters of Clarinda. Fifteen of these corresponded roughly to letters in the McLehose edition of 1843, but had been heavily doctored or completely rewritten to put the authoress in a better light, thereby replacing the simplicity, spontaneity and vigour of the originals with something that was dull, laboured and artificial. A sixteenth letter, however, was based on one which did not appear in the McLehose edition. This piece, dated 20 December 1787, confirms that the initiative for the Arcadian names came from the lady herself:

> I have proposed to myself a more pastoral name for you, although it be not much in keeping with the shrillness of the *Ettrick Pipe*. What say you to *Sylvander?* I feel somewhat less restraint when I subscribe myself CLARINDA.[27]

On Christmas eve Nancy, now signing herself Clarinda, sent Robert a verse-epistle in six stanzas. In his previous letter Robert had said that he had written this scrawl because he had nothing else to do. Now she took this as the theme of her poem, the punch line in each stanza ending 'you'd nothing else to do'. Robert later transcribed three of the stanzas in the Glenriddell MS, but the rest of this witty poem has not survived. Robert produced the extempore rejoinder 'Sylvander to Clarinda' (CW 301–2), ten stanzas in the same metre. As each stanza ended with the word 'do', Robert showed his skill and ingenuity in finding appropriate rhymes for the second line in each verse.

Before the year was out, Robert had pressed forward to the point at which he was writing in a strange mixture of restraint and recklessness. In the letter of 28 December, in which he addressed her as Clarinda and signed himself 'Sylvander' for the first time, he was professing:

> I do love you if possible still better for having so fine a taste and turn for Poesy.– I have again gone wrong in my usual unguarded way, but you may erase the word, and put esteem, respect, or any other tame Dutch expression you please in its place.– I believe there is no holding converse or carrying on correspondence, with an amiable woman, much less a *gloriously amiable, fine woman*, without some mixture of that delicious Passion, whose most devoted Slave I have more than once had the honor of being

and much, much more in the same vein. Nancy probably had a fit of the vapours on receipt of this torrid epistle. Now she sought shelter in religion, her standby during all her past tribulations which she now summarised for him before continuing:

> Religion, the only refuge of the unfortunate, has been my balm in every woe. O! could I make her appear to you as she has done to me! Instead of ridiculing her tenets, you would fall down and worship her very semblance wherever you found it!
>   . . . Good night; for Clarinda's 'heavenly eyes' need the earthly air of sleep. Adieu. CLARINDA
>   *P.S.* – I entreat you not to mention our corresponding to one on earth. Though I've conscious innocence, my situation is a delicate one.

Without waiting for an answer Clarinda wrote to Sylvander on 1 January 1788, 'Many happy returns of this day, my dear, pleasant friend!' and followed with a letter of almost 1,300 words, ranging over philosophy and religion and poetry, in an attempt to put their burgeoning relationship on a purely platonic level. The skilful mixture is best exemplified in the much-quoted passage:

> My heart was formed for love, and I desire to devote it to Him who is the source of love! Yes: we shall surely meet in an 'unknown state of being', where there will be full scope for every kind, heartfelt affection – love without alloy, and without end. Your paragraph upon this made the tears flow down my face!

She had spent the weekend with 'a dear female friend, who has long been an admirer of yours, and was once on the brink of meeting with you in the house of a Mrs Bruce'. The friend was Mary Peacock and it appears that Robert narrowly missed meeting her at Clackmannan Tower, when he and Dr Adair paid their respects to Mrs Catherine Bruce during the so-called Stirlingshire tour that autumn. Nancy seems to have had some idea of diverting this dangerous poet to her young friend:

> She would have been a much better *Clarinda*. She is comely, without being beautiful, – and has a large share of sense, taste and sensibility; added to all, a violent penchant for poetry. If I ever have an opportunity, I shall make you and her acquainted.

Robert did meet Mary Peacock subsequently and even corresponded with her in a desultory way, though he confessed to Nancy in March 1793 (CL 410):

> There is a fatality attends Miss Peacock's correspondence and mine. Two of my letters, it seems, she never received; and her last, which came when I was in Ayrshire, was unfortunately mislaid, and only found about ten days or a fortnight ago, on removing a desk of drawers.

If Nancy was in a turmoil, Robert's senses were reeling. He was head over heels in love again, and experiencing all those bitter-sweet pangs so familiar to him. On 30 December 1787 he wrote his first letter to his old friend from his Irvine days, Captain Richard Brown (CL 418–19):

> Almighty Love still 'reigns and revels' in my bosom; and I am at this moment ready to hang myself for a young Edinr widow, who has wit and beauty more murderously fatal than the assassinating stiletto of the Sicilian Banditti, or the poisoned arrow of the savage African.

Never before had Robert worked himself up into such a passion – and all over a fluffy, frothy matron whom he had met for only a few minutes at an elderly spinster's tea-party.

On Monday 24 December Robert wrote a brief letter (CL 414) to Charles Hay (1747–1811), one of the coterie of lawyers who belonged to the Crochallan Fencibles. Hay, in fact, rejoiced in the facetious rank of Muster-Master-General, responsible for drilling the new recruits in conviviality. Lord Cockburn said that Hay was noted for 'law, punch, whist, claret and worth', while Forbes Gray added that 'his bibulous performances were really remarkable at a time when drinking records were not easily established'.[28] He was alleged to have no taste for literature, so it is usually assumed that his friendship with Burns was purely convivial, although Robert's comments in this letter suggest otherwise. From this it appears that Hay (who was to be raised to the bench with the judicial title of Lord Newton in 1806) had suggested to Robert that he ought to compose an elegy on the death of the Lord President of the Court of Session. This was Robert Dundas, Lord Arniston, who had died on 13 December 1787. Burns confessed that

> the inclosed Poem was in consequence of your suggestion, last time I had the pleasure of seeing you.– It cost me an hour or two of next morning's sleep, but did not please me; so it lay by, an ill-digested effort, till the other day I gave it a Critic brush.– These kind of subjects are much hackneyed; and besides, the wailings of the rhyming tribe over the ashes of the Great, are damnably suspicious, and out of all character for sincerity.– These ideas damp'd my Muse's fire; however, I have done the best I could.

Writing to Alexander Cunningham more than three years later (CL 461–2) Robert recalled this occasion with some bitterness:

> My very worthy & most respected Friend, Mr Alexander Wood, Surgeon, urged me to pay a compliment in the way of my trade to his Lordship's memory.– Well, to work I went, & produced a copy of Elegaic verses, some of them I own rather common place, & others rather hide-bound, but on the whole though they were far from being in my best manner, they were tolerable; & had they been the production of a Lord or a Baronet, they would have been thought very clever.– I wrote a letter, which however was in my very best manner, & inclosing my Poem, Mr Wood carried altogether to Mr Solicitor Dundas that then was, & not finding him at home, left the parcel for him.– His Solicitorship never took the smallest notice of the Letter, the Poem, or the Poet. From that time, highly as I respect the talents of their Family, I never see the name, Dundas, in the column of a newspaper, but my heart seems straitened for room in my bosom; & if I am obliged to read aloud a paragraph relating to one of them, I feel my forehead flush, & my nether lip quivers.

Lord Arniston was the father of Henry Dundas, previously noted, and Robert Dundas (1758–1819) the Solicitor General to whom Burns addressed his letter and elegy. The poet had his revenge in January 1796 when Dundas of Arniston defeated Robert's friend Harry Erskine in the election for Dean of the Faculty of Advocates. In the ballad composed soon after the election (CW 562–3) Robert satirised the new Dean as 'pious

Bob' or 'simple Bob' and lampooned his 'purblind mental vision'. Young Arniston's failure to acknowledge 'the Letter, the Poem or the Poet' was probably an innocent oversight; but, like the imagined snub by Wilhelmina Alexander, Robert neither forgot nor forgave. The last day of the Old Year was the sixty-seventh birthday of Prince Charles Edward Stuart, the Young Pretender, and Robert was invited by some fellow Jacobites to attend a celebratory dinner. Dr Currie, writing in 1800, was mindful of the fact that Jacobitism could still be regarded by the Hanoverian régime as a subversive activity, and was at pains to point out that those present did not seriously entertain 'any hope of . . . the restoration of the house of Stewart; but over their sparkling wine, they indulged the generous feelings which the recollection of fallen greatness is calculated to inspire . . . Burns took upon himself the office of poet-laureate'. The Jacobitism of Robert and his friends did not extend beyond a mild attachment of a purely sentimental nature. It is worth noting that none other than 'the witless youth', the Prince of Wales (later King George IV), shared these sentiments but took practical steps to ensure that his distant kinsman and rival for the throne should end his days in comfort by settling a pension on him. Sadly, Bonnie Prince Charlie, after a lifetime of debauchery, died only a month later. Robert's 'Birthday Ode' (CW 303–4) is arguably his most bathetic work, although the lines on the same theme, from his 'Address to Wm. Tytler' (CW 276), which he inscribed in answer to James Steuart's invitation (CL 416) come very close, beginning: 'Tho' something like moisture conglobes in my eye'. Earlier that month, the news that Prince Charles had belatedly recognised his illegitimate daughter Charlotte, born in 1753 to his mistress Clementina Walkinshaw, and had sought her ennoblement at Paris under the title of the Duchess of Albany, inspired Robert to compose the poignant song 'The Bonie Lass of Albanie' (CW 302–3). Poor Charlotte, however, outlived her father by little more than a year.

Some doubt has been expressed as to whether Robert was well enough to attend the Jacobite dinner.[29] This is based, however, on the tentative assumption of every previous editor that a brief, undated letter to Clarinda was written on Thursday 3 January (CL 375). In this Robert wrote,

> My limb is vastly better, but I have not any use of it without my crutches.
> – Monday, for the first time, I dine at a neighbour's next door: as soon
> as I can go so far, *even in a coach*, my first visit shall be to you.– Write
> me when you leave town and immediately when you return, and I
> earnestly pray your stay may be short.

The reference to Nancy leaving town, however, must place this letter a week earlier than hitherto supposed. If it were written on Thursday 27 December, then it fits the description of the 'fragment scrawl I sent you yesterday' for which Robert apologised in a long letter dated 28 December. Nancy answered both letters on Friday evening, saying that she was going to the country early the following morning, but would be home by Tuesday 1 January. If the short letter were written on 27 December, then the dinner to which Robert referred must, indeed, have been the Jacobite celebration. The dinner was held by James Steuart, a lawyer whose house was in Cleland's Gardens adjoining the north-east corner of St James's Square. It would therefore have been a relatively easy matter for Robert to hobble round the corner to attend this dinner. Robert's reply to the invitation (CL 416) was written on 'Weden even' (i.e. 26 December) and shows that he was deeply honoured to be invited. Among the guests assembled on that poignant occasion was Lawrence Oliphant of Gask, father of the song-writer, Lady Nairne.

The confusion over Robert's letter of 27 December, and the erroneous assumption that it was penned a week later, arose from the reference in it to some verses of Clarinda's. As it is known that she sent him the stanzas beginning 'Talk not of Love! it gives me pain' on 3 January, it was always assumed that these were the 'last verses' referred to by Robert in his short letter; but beyond the fact that he said, 'I have copied them in among some of my own most valued pieces', there is nothing to identify the particular poem. The only other verses which Robert transcribed were those, previously mentioned, in which Clarinda had twitted him on having nothing else to do; and as these were sent on Christmas eve it seems highly probable that these were the lines Robert acknowledged on 27 December. Although Robert's poetic rejoinder was allegedly written extempore on receipt of Clarinda's poem she may not have received them till her return from the country. Her prolix letter with New Year's greetings may actually have been written a day earlier, while briefly out of town. Thus her letter of Thursday 3 January beginning 'I got your lines: they are in *kind*!' undoubtedly acknowledged 'Sylvander to Clarinda' and not some poem now lost, as Chambers imagined.[30] Referring to this exchange of poems, Nancy wrote:

> I can't but laugh at my presumption in pretending to send my poor ones
> to *you*! but it was to amuse myself. At this season, when others are joyous,
> I am the reverse. I have no *near* relations; and while others are with theirs,
> I sit alone . . .

Turning from her own loneliness at the festive season, Nancy enquired whether Robert was well enough to pay her a visit. 'Do you think you could venture this length in a coach, without hurting yourself?' She was going out of town again the following Monday for a few days. 'I wish you could come to-morrow or Saturday. I long for a converation with you, and lameness of body won't hinder that. 'Tis really curious – so much *fun* passing between two persons who saw one another only *once*!' On this occasion Nancy merely signed herself 'A. M.'

Sylvander, however, addressed his 'dear Clarinda' later the same day. This letter, hitherto assigned to 4 January, must now be re-dated 3 January (CL 376–7); in it Robert speaks of visiting her 'tomorrow evening' (i.e. Friday 4 January). As this was followed by a letter headed 'Saturday noon' (5 January) referring to their meeting 'yesternight', the visit must have taken place on the Friday evening. Nancy's allegation of irreligiosity stung Robert and he was quick to refute it: 'If you have, on some suspicious evidence, from some lying oracle, learned that I despise or ridicule so sacredly-important a matter as real religion, you have, my dear Clarinda, much misconstrued your friend'. He went on to compliment her on the verses 'Talk not of Love', adding that he had found an excellent old Scots air that suited the measure, and that he intended to publish the resultant song in Johnson's *Museum*. 'The latter half of the first stanza would have been worthy of Sappho. I am in raptures with it.' He was not too bedazzled, however, to point out defects and alternative words which would improve the meaning and the rhyme. In his long letter of 3 January, on a more practical note, Robert mentioned that he planned to take a sedan-chair the following evening, in order to visit a much-valued old friend at Park Place, possibly William Nicol. 'If I could be sure of finding you at home . . . I would spend from five to six o'clock with you, as I go past. I cannot do more at this time as I have something on my hand that hurries me much.' He would call on Clarinda first, his old friend second, and Miss Nimmo as he returned home. 'Do not break any engagement for me, as I will spend another evening with you at any rate before I leave town.'

The 'something on my hand' was undoubtedly his application to the Excise, about which he wrote to Robert Graham of Fintry on 7 January (CL 424). In this letter he reminded Graham of their meeting at Blair Atholl and came straight to the point. After quoting *King Lear* he wrote:

> I now solicit your Patronage.– You know, I dare say, of an application I lately made to your Board, to be admitted an Officer of Excise.– I have, according to form, been examined by a Supervisor, and today I give in his Certificate with a request for an Order for instructions.

Whether the Supervisor who examined him was Miss Nimmo's brother, William, is not known. The certificate (which has not been preserved) had to be attested by the parish minister and certified that the candidate was over twenty-one and under thirty. If married, he had to have no more than two children. At this time Robert was just short of his twenty-ninth birthday. Although he had two children living – Bess (born 1784) and Bobbie (born 1786) – neither was relevant as Robert was technically a bachelor. Perhaps this document was the 'certificate of bachelorhood' which he had been so anxious to obtain from Daddy Auld after doing penance for fornication in 1786. The supposition that Robert lied about his age, his marital status or the number of his children in his application to the Excise – central to the views held by one writer[31] – is groundless.

Robert's arrangement to fit her in between calls on Nicol and Miss Nimmo was sufficiently casual as to guarantee that Nancy would be on tenterhooks. The meeting took place as planned. Despite the fact that Nancy, no doubt under the intense strain of anticipation, was suffering a headache, the meeting was evidently a huge success:

Some days, some nights, nay, some *hours*, like the 'ten righteous persons in Sodom,' save the rest of the vapid, tiresome, miserable months and years of life. One of these *hours* my dear Clarinda blest me with yesternight.

Robert recalled those precious moments in his noonday letter of 5 January (CL 378) and we can infer that much of the time was taken up with a recital of his life story. Contrary to what he had previously told Mrs Dunlop, Robert *did* have a copy of his long autobiographical letter to Dr Moore and this was mentioned during the visit. Now he sent it to Nancy for her perusal: 'I am afraid you will hardly be able to make sense of so torn a piece'. The surviving fragments of this document, which appears to have been Robert's original draft, were used by Currie in 1800 and are now in the National Library of Scotland, whereas the copy actually sent to Moore is in the British Library. Robert even told Clarinda about his unfortunate affair with Jean Armour and spoke of his infant son. From the fact that his letter appears to be answering some questions, it is inferred that Nancy herself had followed up the meeting with a letter (now lost). 'My little fellow is all my namesake,' explained Robert, adding, 'I am truly happy your headache is better. Oh, how can pain or evil be so daring, unfeelingly, cruelly savage, as to wound so noble a mind, so lovely a form!' Nancy, of course, may have feigned a headache as the time-honoured female method of holding too impetuous a suitor at bay.

On Monday night, 7 January, Clarinda wrote to Sylvander another of her very long letters. Over the weekend she had read his autobiographical letter twice and had been reduced to tears as a consequence. The account of Robert's first love-scene delighted her and she promised to take him into her confidence regarding her own earliest experiences of love – 'only mine did not go so far'.

> Ah, my friend! our earliest love emotions are surely the most exquisite. In riper years we may acquire more knowledge, sentiment, &c.; but none of these can yield such rapture as the dear delusions of heart-throbbing youth! Like yours, mine was a rural scene, too, which adds much to the tender meeting. But no more of these recollections.

Despite his protestations of religiosity, Nancy was hurt to discover that Robert was an enemy of Calvinism and she set out to convert him to her own doctrinally narrow brand of Presbyterianism. An interesting point which permeates so many of her letters, is the way that Nancy switches from the first to the third person, letting her Clarinda persona take over, especially when delivering a homily or expressing regret at something in Robert's views with which she disagreed. Towards the end of the letter she turned the tables on her correspondent:

> You told me you never had met with a woman who could love as ardently as yourself. I believe it; and would advise you never to tie yourself, till

you meet with such a one . . . I think you had almost best resolve against wedlock: for unless a woman were qualified for the companion, the friend, and the mistress, she would not do for you.

Of course, as Nancy could not have him herself, she had no desire to see anyone else marry him. Tantalisingly, she touched on 'infidelity in a husband' which had made Robert stare at her. 'This, and other things, shall be matter for another letter, if you are not wishing this to be the last'. The letter ends with a curiously hard-headed postscript:

> Don't detain the porter. Write when convenient.
>   I am probably to be in your Square this afternoon, near two o'clock. If your room be to the street, I shall have the pleasure of giving you a nod. I have paid the porter, and you may do so when you write. I'm sure they sometimes have made us pay double. Adieu!

Users of Williamson's service had the options of prepaying the postage, contrary to the usual custom then prevalent in letters of the General Post; but it should have been obvious from the postmarks whether the letters were prepaid or sent unpaid. Williamson made use of porters, or 'caddies', in his service, but perhaps Robert and Nancy sometimes sent letters by unofficial messengers.

Thereafter the love affair escalated in intensity. During the remainder of January Sylvander met his Clarinda at her home on at least six occasions and interspersed these meetings with letters exchanged on virtually a daily basis. Robert stoutly defended his religious tenets and in so doing provided useful insights into what he sincerely believed:

> My creed is pretty nearly expressed in the last clause of Jamie Dean's grace, an honest weaver in Ayrshire:– 'Lord, grant that we may lead a gude life! for a gude life maks a gude end: at least it helps weel!'

Similarly he would not yield when Clarinda was outraged at the way he regarded Milton's Satan as his heroic ideal. Nancy's fervour was marred, to some extent, by concern for her children. A second child had died some time previously, leaving only William and Andrew. Now, she was troubled by the 'crazy state of health' of little William which kept her awake for several nights. Nancy, in her voracious reading, had become an avid devotee of Fielding, and doubtless the other sentimental novelists so popular in the eighteenth century. She saw herself as another Amelia, and Robert was quick to play up to this notion (CL 380): 'Your sentiments on that subject, as they are on every subject, are just and noble' and he quoted back her own words (from a letter of 9 January), 'To be feelingly alive to kindness – and to unkindness'.

Nancy, given Robert's version of his affair with Jean Armour, commented in her letter of 9 January, 'I can't understand that bonny lassie: her refusal, after such proofs of love, proves her to be either an angel or a dolt'.

She admitted, however, that she did not know all the circumstances, then added rather callously, 'I love you for your continued fondness, even after enjoyment: few of your sex have souls in such cases'; Jean Armour was very much on Nancy's mind when she fervently wished 'a certain affair happily over'. In a postscript written the following morning she hinted, 'Keep a good heart, Sylvander; the eternity of your love-sufferings will be ended before six weeks'. But Nancy's actions belied her words. Several times she took a stroll down to the New Town to promenade before his windows, in the hope that, even though she could not see him, he might behold her. On Thursday 10 January Sylvander wrote,

> I am certain I saw you, Clarinda; but you don't look to the proper story for a poet's lodging . . . I could almost have thrown myself over, for very vexation. Why didn't you look higher? It has spoilt my peace for this day.

On 12 January, though they were due to meet that evening, two letters went from Robert and at least one from Nancy. The second letter (CL 382) was couched in anguish at the tone and content of Clarinda's (which has not survived). Hers was obviously a rather tearful missive, for it provoked a similar response in Robert,[32] as well as agitating him 'into a violent headache'. He was expecting a friend to tea, else he would have come sooner; but he promised to take a chair and be with her about eight o'clock.

That Saturday evening, Robert and Nancy had their third meeting. By the time they met, both had violent headaches. What transpired on that emotionally charged encounter need not be guessed at; for Clarinda's long letter the following evening was, in effect, a post mortem:

> I will not deny it, Sylvander, last night was one of the most exquisite I ever experienced. Few such fall to the lot of mortals! Few, extremely few, are formed to relish such refined enjoyment. That it should be so, vindicates the wisdom of Heaven.

Well, did they, or didn't they? After such a rapturous opening it might be supposed that the love, which had been fanned into a white heat largely by means of the written word, would at last have been consummated. But, no. We read on and find that 'our enjoyment did not lead beyond the limits of virtue'. What is more, the lady's Sabbath conscience was now troubling her:

> to-day's reflections have not been altogether unmixed with regret. The idea of the pain it would have given, were it known to a friend to whom I am bound by the sacred ties of gratitude,[33] no more, the opinion Sylvander may have formed from my unreservedness; and, above all, some secret misgivings that Heaven may not approve, situated as I am – these procured me a sleepless night; and, though at church, I am not at all well.

This was a prelude to a long, tedious bout of sermonising, mercifully terminated eventually. 'If my head did not ache, I would continue the subject', though it did not prevent her from adding a page-long postscript the following day. By now, Robert should have begun to realise, if he had not earlier, that, much as she might lead him on, Mrs McLehose was not going to yield 'the portal of love' to him. For his part, Robert waited apprehensively on the Monday for what he feared would be the inevitable reaction after their bout of relative intimacy on Saturday. By eleven o'clock that night, when he had not heard from her, he consoled himself by writing a long letter (CL 382-3) peppered with lengthy quotations, but then gave the game away:

> I like to have quotations for every occasion. They give one's ideas so pat, and save one the trouble of finding expression adequate to one's feelings.

Robert was truly smitten. He had looked for a letter from Clarinda all that day, and when one was handed in at nine o'clock that evening his heart had soared – only to sink to his boots when he found that it was nothing more than yet another verse-epistle from one of the doggerel-mongers who continued to plague him. When Clarinda's long letter of Sunday, with a prolix postscript added at mid-day on Tuesday, reached him he was more vexed and perplexed than ever. But by this time he had decided to return to Ayrshire. There is a hint of resignation in his letter of 15 January in which he reminded her of this intention:

> Oh, my angel! how soon must we part! – and when can we meet again? I look forward on the horrid interval wih tearful eyes. What have not I lost by not knowing you sooner! I fear, I fear, my acquaintance with you is too short to make that lasting impression on your heart I could wish.

Nancy replied on Wednesday morning, suggesting a further meeting either the next day or Friday. 'Come to tea if you please; but eight will be an hour less liable to intrusions.' The boys would be sound asleep by that hour. Although Robert was still crippled by his wounded knee, Nancy advised him to come on foot. 'A chair is so uncommon a thing in our neighbourhood, it is apt to raise speculation.' Going home was not such a problem: the neighbours 'are all asleep by ten'. In this letter Nancy revealed a catty side to her nature. In a previous letter (10 January) she had complained to Robert about the sister of Lord Napier who had 'cut' her at the house of a mutual friend on Sunday between sermons. 'By her ill-breeding I should have taken her for the daughter of some upstart tradesman!' Robert apparently tried to defend Miss Napier, or point to some mitigating circumstances (presumably in a letter no longer extant), and this provoked Nancy to respond tartly,

> 'You carry your warmth too far as to Miss Napier . . . She is comely, but a thick bad figure, waddles in her pace, and has rosy cheeks.

Wha is that clumsy damsel there?
'Whisht! it's the daughter of a Peer,
  Right Honorably Great!'

The daughter of a Peer, I cried,
  It doth not *yet* appear
What we *shall* be (in t'other world),
  God keep us frae this here!
That she has *Blude*, I'se no dispute,
  I see it in her face;
Her honor's in her *name*, I fear,
  And in nae other place.

In John Taylor's reminiscences of his meeting with Burns in Paisley in the summer of 1787 he mentioned the fact that the poet was intrigued by a small black profile of his mother. These silhouettes, or shades as they were then popularly known, were just coming into fashion. In 1786 a Leeds profilist named John Miers came to Edinburgh and opened a studio where he produced silhouette profiles on card (sixpence), plaster (half a guinea) or ivory (four guineas). Miers used a powerful candlelight to project the sitter's shadow on to a sheet of oiled paper on which he traced the outline. This served as the master for reduced outlines, filled in in black ink. After the invention of the pantograph it was possible to make accurate reductions in any size desired and Miers claimed in his advertising labels 'Perfect likenesses in miniature profile – with the most exact symmetry and animated expression of the features'. Some time, probably in November 1787, Robert paid a visit to Miers and sat for his profile. Several examples of court-card sized silhouettes of the poet exist and Robert presented them to close friends. Miers was a rapid and skilful worker – 'when I sat to Mr Miers, I am sure he did not exceed two minutes,' he wrote to Ainslie in June 1788 (CL 334). Soon after his accident in December 1787 Robert sent a tiny version of his silhouette to Francis Howden, a jeweller in Parliament Square, to have it set 'just as you did the others you did for me, in the neatest and cheapest manner; both to answer as a breast-pin, and with a ring to answer as a locket'. This particular silhouette was intended as a wedding present, but neither of the parties was named, though the groom was 'a very particular acquaintance of mine'. From this undated letter to Howden (CL 417) it appears that Robert had miniature plaster silhouettes set as jewellery for presentation to other close friends.

Some time in January 1788 he urged Clarinda, suitably chaperoned of course, to visit Miers and have her profile done. In her letter of 16 January, she wrote, 'I'll certainly go to Miers to please you, either with Mary or Miss Nimmo'.

In due course the lovers met on Friday evening 18th January, provoking a very long letter from Robert, begun on Saturday morning and completed at 'Night, Half after Ten'. The first half was a virtuoso performance of religiosity, quoting appropriate lines from Hervey's *Meditations* and Young's *Night Thoughts*; but the second half began impetuously, 'What luxury of bliss I was enjoying this time yesternight!' Again, lest it be assumed that, at long last, towering passion had reached its logical conclusion, Robert continued:

> My ever dearest Clarinda, you have stolen away my soul: but you have refined, you have exalted it; you have given it a stronger sense of virtue, and a stronger relish for piety.

And he concluded:

> Clarinda, when a poet and poetess of Nature's making – two of Nature's noblest productions! – when they drink together of the same cup of Love and Bliss, attempt not, ye coarser stuff of human nature! profanely to measure enjoyment ye can never know.

This smacks of the disappointed lover making the best of a bad job, still hoping by all his seductive verbal skills to overcome the lady's qualms. The flowery language and high-flown sentiment, however, barely concealed his bafflement. For a more realistic assessment of how the affair was progressing, we have Clarinda's version of Friday night. Late the following evening, Nancy took up her quill and began plaintively, 'I am wishing, Sylvander, for the power of looking into your heart'. But what, we wonder, produced the admission,

> Last night must have shown you Clarinda not 'divine' – but as she really is. I can't recollect some things I said without a degree of pain . . .
> For many years, have I sought for a male friend, endowed with sentiments like you; one who could love me with tenderness, yet unmixed with selfishness; who could be my friend, companion, protector, and who would die sooner than injure me.

Before she sent this already long letter, Nancy wrote as much again the following evening, after listening to a sermon delivered at the Tolbooth church by the Revd. John Kemp (1745–1805), Nancy's minister and father-confessor. Kemp was, quite literally, a ladies' man, (his second and third wives were Lady Mary Carnegie and Lady Elizabeth Hope, both daughters of earls) and only escaped being cited by Sir James Colquhoun of Luss as co-respondent in a rather messy divorce case by dying before the matter came to court. John Ramsay of Ochtertyre commented on this curious affair, 'An intrigue with a Lady that has been near 30 years married was never I suppose heard of in the commissary court'.[34] Referring to the fact that Kemp's son David (a weaver by trade) had married Colquhoun's daughter, Ramsay concluded: 'Lady Colquhoun might have made religion her darling luxury, without trusting too much to a protestant father confessor, whose son, under that guise, stole the heart of her fair, amiable daughter! The popish ones had no sons bred wabsters to spread their nets.' The Revd. George Drummond neatly summed up this strange affair in a couplet:

> Doom to a weaver's arms the well-born miss,
> Then greet the mother with a holy kiss.[35]

Pious, devout, comely young matrons like Nancy McLehose were fair game to sanctimonious lechers like John Kemp. The better part of a thousand words were expended in giving poor Sylvander a replay of Kemp's sermon on the text 'Let me live the life of the righteous'. The uplifting effect of this homily was spoiled for Nancy by the recollection of a rather disagreeable encounter that very morning. As she crossed Parliament Square she met the judges, among whom was her kinsman Lord Dreghorn in his new robes of purple:

> I looked steadfastly in his sour face; his eye met mine. I was a female, and therefore he stared; but, when he knew who it was, he averted his eyes suddenly. Instantaneously these lines darted into my mind:
>
> > Would you the purple should your limbs adorn,
> > Go wash the conscious blemish with a tear.
>
> The man who enjoys more pleasure in the mercenary embrace of a courtezan than in relieving the unfortunate, is a detestable character, whatever his bright talents may be. I pity him! Sylvander, all his fortune could not purchase half the luxury of Friday night!

This extraordinary epistle concluded with the mild reproof: 'Want of passions is not merit: strong ones, under the control of reason and religion – let these be our glory'. With this letter Clarinda sent Robert verses entitled 'To a Blackbird Singing on a Tree'. Nancy had composed this poem at Morningside some four years previously; Robert revised it and added four lines (CW 319) which he sent back to her two days later. Under the title 'To a Blackbird, by a Lady', it appeared as number 190 in the second volume of *The Scots Musical Museum*.

Robert had a recurrence of his depression on 20 January and with the greatest difficulty penned a few lines to Clarinda (CL 386) that night: 'The impertinence of fools has joined with a return of an old indisposition, to make me good for nothing today . . . I can no more, Clarinda; I can scarce hold up my head: but I am happy you don't know it, you would be so uneasy'. The reason for Robert's depressive state may have been the receipt of a letter from brother Gilbert containing nothing but bad news. Jean, now more than six months' pregnant, had been turned out of doors by her harsh, unforgiving father into the uncertainties of a Scottish winter. Things were not going too well at Mossgiel either and Gilbert appealed to his relatively affluent brother for financial assistance. That Robert had sent money to Gilbert on previous occasions might seem to be denied by the absence of any letters from Robert to Mossgiel; but all that this proves is that Gilbert took good care to suppress his brother's letters. Currie, in fact, got remarkably little out of Gilbert while compiling his biography.

But the truth was fleetingly revealed amid the random jottings at the back of Robert's journal of his Border tour, for there we find the numbers, dates and details of two five pound notes which he sent to his brother at that time; and there can be no doubt that Gilbert was in receipt of similar sums at regular intervals.

Now Robert was impelled by Gilbert's latest communication to write to one of those friends who had helped to sell his book. Neither the date of the letter nor the name of the addressee appear, but from references to Robert Aiken it is most likely that John Ballantine was the recipient. The letter to Ballantine (CL 102-3) was sent under cover of another which was written to Gilbert. Naturally, the covering letter has not survived, but Robert refers in Ballantine's letter to 'My brother, the bearer of this' to whom he wished the money accruing from sales of his book to be given. 'Should he want half a dozen pounds or more, dare I ask you to accommodate him?' As to the date of this letter, the reference to Robert's health – 'I am got a good deal better, but can walk little yet without my crutches' – places it on or after 21 January. On that day Robert wrote a dated letter to Mrs Dunlop (CL 139):

> After six weeks' confinement, I am beginning to walk across the room. They have been six horrible weeks, anguish and low spirits made me unfit to read, write, or think.

The following morning, however, Robert felt much better but still had 'a horrid languor on my spirits'. By the next day he was asking Clarinda querulously, 'Why are your sex called the tender sex, when I never have met with one who can repay me in passion? They are either not so rich in love as I am, or they are niggards where I am lavish.'

On Wednesday 23 January Robert and Nancy met again, at her house. We can only assume that Robert became rather physical and Nancy had the utmost difficulty in keeping control. As soon as she awoke the following morning she 'received a summons from Conscience to appear at the Bar of Reason'. Two dozen lines conveyed her turbulent emotions couched in high-flown allegory before she let the mask of Clarinda slip:

> to drop my metaphor, I am neither well nor happy to-day; my heart reproaches me for last night. If you wish Clarinda to regain her peace, determine against everything but what the strictest delicacy warrants. I do not blame you, but myself. I must not see you on Saturday, unless I find I can depend on myself acting otherwise.

Nancy held off posting this letter all that day; but by nightfall, when she had not heard from Robert, she added a lengthy passage to the letter, beginning, 'Why have I not heard from you, Sylvander? Everything in nature seems tinged with gloom today. Ah! Sylvander' and she quoted back to him his lines, 'The heart's ay the part ay / That makes us right or wrang'. By now Nancy was hinting of the relief which Robert's return to Ayrshire would bring:

Absence will mellow and restrain those violent heart-agitations which, if continued much longer, would unhinge my very soul and render me unfit for the duties of life. You and I are capable of that ardency of love, for which the wide creation cannot afford an adequate object. Let us seek to repose it in the bosom of our God.

Ironically, when she finally brought this tortured epistle to a close on Friday morning (which was Robert's twenty-ninth birthday) Nancy concluded:

My servant (who is a good soul) will deliver you this. She is going down to Leith, and will return about two or three o'clock. I have ordered her to call then, in case you have ought to say to Clarinda to-day.

Nancy's maidservant was a twenty-year-old girl from Newburgh in Fife, the youngest of a family of eight born to Alexander Clow and his wife Margaret Inglis.[36] Jenny Clow obediently delivered her mistress's letter on her way from the Old Town to the port of Leith, and just as obediently called in at the house on St James's Square that afternoon to pick up the reply. In the interim, Robert had had plenty of time to read and re-read a letter which, he later claimed, 'wounded my soul'. He was mortified to think that his actions had caused such misery; but he was hurt to the core that Nancy should now refuse to see him the following night and wished that the hour of parting had come. 'But why, My Love, talk to me in such strong terms; every word of which cuts me to the very soul?' he upbraided her and himself. 'Now, my Love, do not wound our next meeting with any averted looks or restrained caresses.' He was stunned by the peremptory harshness of her command to 'Take care'. Suddenly he panicked at the thought that his beloved would not allow him to see her again. 'O, did you love like me, you would not, you could not, deny or put off a meeting with the Man who adores you; who would die a thousand deaths before he would injure you; and who must soon bid you a long farewell!' As his goose-quill feverishly covered the pages, Robert was in a turmoil. Having grovelled and pleaded and brought the letter to a close with the hysterical line, 'O Clarinda, the tie that binds me to thee is entwisted, incorporated, with my dearest threads of life!' reaction would have set in. By the time wee Jenny had called at his lodgings to collect his answer, Robert was probably in a pugnacious mood. If he could not have Nancy McLehose he would have to work off his pent-up emotions somewhere else. Young Jenny, a waif-like innocent, might serve his immediate needs.

Throughout this strange, overheated correspondence, Nancy wrestled with her conscience and fought for Robert's eternal soul. Mr Kemp was quoted continually, and at one point Nancy even exhorted Robert to accompany her to the Tolbooth kirk ('You'll easily get a seat'). But running like a golden thread through this strange mish-mash of religiosity was the deep-seated passion for the man to whom propriety and her strict Calvinistic faith had decreed she could never surrender her body. It is a matter for speculation to what degree Robert reciprocated her feelings. He had never had love letters from any woman before (and never would again); it has to be said that Nancy's, for all their religiosity, have a fresher, more appealing and more sincere ring to them. In Robert's case we are left with the suspicion that, much of the time, he treated the correspondence as an interesting exercise to pass the time and the tedium of his injury. But this is not to doubt the sincerity of his feelings; during the three months when this courtship by correspondence was at its height Robert truly believed that he loved Nancy, and no other.

A new dimension was added to the relationship on 26 January. On that day Robert wrote (CL 390) to say that he proposed calling for tea around seven o'clock with his dearest friend, Bob Ainslie:

> We only propose staying half an hour,– 'for ought we ken.'– I could suffer the lash of Misery eleven months in the year, were the twelfth to be composed of hours like yesternight.– You are the soul of my enjoyment: all else is of the stuff of stocks & stones.

Mary Peacock was present on this occasion, so they made a pretty foursome. Thus was Nancy introduced to the man who was to become her lawyer and who, in due course, would take young Andrew McLehose as his pupil. After Robert left Edinburgh, Ainslie to a large extent took his place as that 'male friend, companion and protector' whom Nancy so earnestly sought. Just how far Ainslie went beyond the bounds of professionalism may be guessed from an undated letter to Nancy in which he speaks of the 'end of the week which you appointed as the Termination of my Banishment'.[37]

Graham of Fintry's response to Robert's letter soliciting his patronage is not known, but matters concerning the Excise had progressed, by 27 January, as far as Robert being subjected to some form of preliminary vetting by a Mrs Stewart, a friend of Miss Nimmo. Nothing is known of this lady but she was obviously a person of considerable standing and Robert resented the way in which she probed him. 'I have been question'd like a child about my matters, and blamed and schooled for my Inscription on Stirling window.' If Robert's politics were at all suspect at this time, it was his sentimental attachment to the Jacobite cause. Bonnie Prince Charlie, however, was now a spent force (he died only three days later), and there must have been few people who believed in the nominal claim of his brother Prince Henry, Duke of York and Bishop of Frascati – least of all the Bishop himself who was content to live in the Vatican. Robert was in despair again: 'I have almost given up the excise idea,' he wrote, still smarting from Mrs Stewart's inquisition, 'Why will Great people not only deafen us with the din of their equipage, and dazzle us with their fastidious pomp, but they must also be so very dictatorially wise?' By that evening, however, his equanimity had been restored, following a visit to Miss Nimmo. The previous Thursday he had dined with Johann Georg Schetky (1740–1824), the Darmstadt cellist and composer, who had settled in

Edinburgh in 1773. Robert gave his new friend and drinking companion the lines 'Clarinda, Mistress of My Soul' (CW 320) to set to music. Now, Schetky had sent Robert the song and it, too, duly appeared in the *Museum* as number 198. 'I have carried it about in my pocket, and thumbed it over all day,' he wrote to Clarinda.

Robert followed this coolly with, 'I trust you have spent a pleasant day: and that no idea or recollection of me gives you pain'. By Tuesday morning, 29 January, however, he was in a remorseful mood. This followed another meeting, on Monday night, in the course of which Robert had said something hurtful and they had parted in an unhappy frame of mind. He resorted to some of those quotations which he had 'pat for all occasions' to atone for his behaviour and ended, 'I send you a poem to read till I call on you this night, which will be about nine'. How that meeting went is not known; there were no further letters till Thursday when Clarinda wrote to tell Robert that Mary Peacock was a happy woman, because the celebrated poetess Alicia Cockburn had read Mary's poem 'Henry' and liked it. Then, coquettishly, she let him know that 'I only tremble at the ardent manner Mary talks of Sylvander! She knows where his affections lie, and is quite unconscious of the eagerness of her expressions'. Robert, meanwhile, had favoured Nancy with a perusal of the letters he had received from Peggy Chalmers, provoking her to comment 'Why did not such a woman secure your heart?' It seems as if Nancy was now intent on deflecting Robert away from herself.

Robert, however, saw through this ploy. His letter, written at seven o'clock the following morning, began, 'Your fears for Mary are truly laughable. I suppose, my love, you and I showed her a scene which, perhaps, made her wish that she had a swain, and one who could love like me.' He then confessed that he had been out dining the previous evening with a baronet 'and sat pretty late over the bottle'. A quotation from Proverbs ('who hath woe, who hath sorrow? they that tarry long at the wine') provided the pretext to comment on King Solomon, 'my favourite author', and how human nature had not changed since biblical times. The loves in the 'Song of Songs' were all in the spirit of Lady Mary Wortley Montagu and Ninon de l'Enclos – 'modern voluptuaries'. Perhaps Robert had in mind the rather stilted love letters of Alexander Pope to Lady Mary, seeing a parallel between Pope and himself.

What was more significant in this latest exchange was the fact that the clandestine affair was now out in the open. Mary Peacock and Bob Ainslie knew what was going on, and we may be sure that these two did not keep the matter to themselves. Before the middle of February the curious affair was common knowledge and gossip had even reached the ears of Nancy's cousin, William Craig. The Revd. John Kemp may even have had an inkling of the affair from Nancy herself, during one of those heart-to-heart little chats in the Tolbooth vestry. On 8 February Nancy had gone to Miers's studio. Very daringly, she was unchaperoned; Mary was out of town, and Nancy did not care to ask Miss Nimmo along for fear that she would realise why her young friend was having her silhouette done. Robert appreciated the risks she was taking and told her to urge Miers to have the plaster silhouette completed by the middle of the following week at the latest. 'I want it for a breast-pin, to wear next my heart.' He proposed to keep sacred set times, when he would wander in the woods and wilds and meditate upon her. 'Then, and only then, your lovely image shall be produced to the day, with a reverence akin to devotion.' Nancy's side of the correspondence has not survived, but it is clear that her conduct had come to the attention of Messrs Craig and Kemp. One or the other, it is not known which, but probably the latter, wrote her a letter of reproof which she subsequently sent to Robert on Wednesday evening, 13 February, with a covering note.

Robert was on the point of leaving for a dinner party when this shocking news arrived and rivetted him to the spot. Nancy told him that he must cease to love her; but he would not agree. 'I must love, pine, mourn, and adore in secret; this you must not deny me.' Then he turned to the enclosed letter:

> I have not patience to read the Puritanic scrawl. Damned sophistry. Ye heavens, thou God of nature, thou Redeemer of mankind! ye look down with approving eyes on a passion inspired by the purest flame, and guarded by truth, delicacy, and honour; but the half-inch soul of an unfeeling, cold-blooded, pitiful Presbyterian bigot cannot forgive anything above his dungeon-bosom and foggy head.

A much longer letter followed at midnight, when Robert returned from his dinner party. Now he attacked 'your friend's haughty dictatorial letter' at considerable length. The following day – St Valentine's Day – a further two letters went from Sylvander to Clarinda. 'How shall I comfort you,' he asked rhetorically, 'who am the cause of the injury? Can I wish that I had never seen you? That we had never met? No; I never will!' Here, perhaps, we have the genesis of 'Ae Fond Kiss' (CW 434), composed four years later.

The second letter, written at two o'clock that afternoon, was much calmer, more resigned in tone. Robert had just 'now received your first letter of yesterday, by the careless negligence of the penny post'. After a poetic resumé of their friendship, he continued:

> I esteem you, I love you, as a friend; I admire you, I love you, as a woman, beyond any one in all the circles of creation. I know I shall continue to esteem you, to love you, to pray for you, nay, to pray for myself for your sake.

They met that evening at eight o'clock, as usual. The following day Robert wrote, 'I am yours, Clarinda, for life'. He urged her to take a more philosophic view of matters. If Kemp and Craig had withdrawn their worldly support, what did that matter? Soon she would get over it.

A decent means of livelihood in the world, an approving God, a peaceful conscience, and one firm trusty friend – can anybody that has these be said to be unhappy. These are yours.

He promised to be with her on Saturday evening about eight, 'probably for the last time till I return to Edinburgh'. It appears that, although Craig and Kemp had been told that Nancy was keeping company with a man, they did not as yet know the rascal's identity. Robert exhorted Nancy not to divulge this: 'I do not think they are entitled to any information. As to their jealousy and spying, I despise them.'

Although letters and visits to Nancy McLehose took up a great deal of Robert's time in the first half of February he did not let Clarinda obstruct his other aims. On the first of the month he wrote to Lord Glencairn (CL 227–8): 'I wish to get into the Excise; I am told that your Lordship's interest will easily procure me the grant from the Commissioners'. Significantly, Robert was diffident in making this approach, sensing that Glencairn would disapprove of his intentions. This letter also shed a little more light on the state of affairs at Mossgiel:

My brother's lease is but a wretched one, though I think he will probably weather out the remaining seven years of it.– After what I have given and will give him as a small farming capital to keep the family together, I guess my remaining all will be about two hundred pounds.– Instead of beggaring myself with a small dear farm, I will lodge my little stock, a sacred deposite, in a banking-house.– Extraordinary distress, or helpless old age have often harrowed my soul with fears; and I have one or two claims on me in the name of father: I will stoop to any thing that honesty warrants to have it in my power to leave them some better remembrance of me than the odium of illegitimacy.

With this letter Robert enclosed a copy of 'Holy Willie's Prayer' (CW 93–5) and, in a postscript, promised to call on his lordship at the beginning of the following week 'as against then I hope to have settled my business with Mr Creech'.

Robert was now thoroughly disenchanted with Edinburgh. Writing to Richmond at Mauchline on 7 February (CL 81–2):

As I hope to see you soon, I shall not trouble you with a long letter of Edinr news.– Indeed there is nothing worth mentioning to you; every thing going on as usual – houses building, bucks strutting, ladies flaring, blackguards sculking, whores leering, &c. in the old way.– I have not got, nor will not for some time, get the better of my bruised knee; but I have laid aside my crutches.– A lame Poet is unlucky; lame verses is an every day circumstance.– I saw Smith lately; hale and hearty as formerly.– I have heard melancholly enough accounts of Jean; 'tis an unlucky affair.

On the same day, and on a more positive note, Robert wrote to an old family friend, John Tennant of Glenconner (CL 222). 'Old Glen' had been a close neighbour when the Burnes family were at Mount Oliphant; later he had been factor for the Dowager Countess of Glencairn. Curiously enough, while his cousin and namesake, the blacksmith at Alloway, had been a witness at Robert's baptism, Tennant of Glenconner was himself a witness at the baptism of Robert Junior. Now that he was thinking seriously of taking up Patrick Miller's offer of a farm he sought Tennant's practical experience in helping him come to a decision – 'if you will do me the favour to accompany me, your judgement shall determine me'. Robert asked after George Reid, whose pony he had borrowed on his first visit to Edinburgh. Reid was Tennant's son-in-law, having married Agnes, the old man's eldest daughter by his second wife. The letter closed on a sombre note: 'I am at present crazed with thought and anxiety, but particulars I refer till meeting'. Now that he was preparing to return to Ayrshire, Robert found thoughts of poor Jean crowding his mind.

Meanwhile, work on the second volume of the *Museum* was going on apace. Of the hundred songs in this volume almost forty were either wholly written by Burns or revised and expanded by him.[38] Although the Preface was unsigned (and therefore, by implication, the work of the editor, Johnson) it was assuredly from Robert's pen. The concluding paragraph has his genius all over it:

> Ignorance and Prejudice may perhaps affect to sneer at the simplicity of the poetry or music of some of these pieces; but their having been for ages the favorites of Nature's Judges – the Common People, was to the Editor a sufficient test of their merit. Materials for the third Volume are in great forwardness.

This volume was published on 14 February, as a letter of that date to the Revd. John Skinner (CL 364) testifies, although it was advertised in the *Edinburgh Courant* of 20 February as 'published this day' while the Preface was actually dated 'March 1, 1788'. Skinner, however, had to wait till the appearance of the third volume two years later to see his own contributions in print. Conversely, 'Cauld Kail in Aberdeen', though anonymously presented on page 170, appeared in the Index as being by 'The D- of G-'. Songs by Smollett, Ramsay, Fergusson, Hamilton of Gilbertfield, Struan Robertson and 'Ossian' (James Macpherson) were included, along with works by Dr Blacklock and two 'By a Lady' – Nancy McLehose. As the only female contributor, Nancy, though not named, was recklessly conspicuous. Authors of airs were not generally given, but an exception was the melody to Robert's 'Thickest night, surround my dwelling', which was credited to Allan Masterton, writing master at a private school in Stevenlaw's Close, to whom Robert was introduced by William Nicol. Burns, Nicol and Masterton later collaborated in the jollification of October 1789 which produced that splendid bacchanal, 'Willie Brew'd a Peck o Maut' (CW 364).

During the torrid correspondence with Clarinda, Robert let his other letter-writing slide. As he prepared to leave Edinburgh, however, he snatched a few moments to write to some old friends. Mrs Dunlop, having expected a visit from the poet on his way home late in January, had written immediately; but Robert did not get around to answering this letter till 12 February. He had intended to compose a fine verse-epistle by way of reply, or at least 'such a Post-sheet as would be a pennyworth at sixpence', but he failed in both respects. 'Some important business respecting my future days, and the miserable dunning and plaguing of Creech, has busied me till I am good for nothing'. Mrs Dunlop did not think much of Robert's elegy on the late Lord President. Robert agreed. 'I am sick of writing where my bosom is not strongly interested.– Tell me what you think of the following? there, the *bosom* was perhaps a little *interested*' and he enclosed 'Clarinda, Mistress of my soul'. He was leaving Edinburgh on Saturday morning, presumably by coach, as he added that 'If my horse meet me at Glasgow, I will probably do myself the honor of calling at Dunlop-house'. He also mentioned having been at a party in George Street in the New Town, at the home of Dowager Lady Wallace, Mrs Dunlop's stepmother, and had met Miss Keith Dunlop ('I was delighted to find Miss Dunlop a daughter of the Mother'). Robert may also have met Anthony Dunlop (1775–1828) at this time, as he was then residing with his grandmother; an undated letter to Anthony enclosing 'Holy Willie's Prayer' (CW 93–6) wished the boy well as he was about to start his career in the merchant navy (CL 433).

There were also letters to Mrs Elizabeth Rose of Kilravock (CL 441–2) and Margaret Chalmers (CL 236), both written on 17 February. A previous, but undated, letter to Peggy, tentatively assigned to 22 January (CL 235) is of interest for the light it sheds on Robert's state of mind:

God have mercy on me! a poor damned, incautious, duped, unfortunate fool! The sport, the miserable victim, of rebellious pride; hypochondriac imagination, agonizing sensibility, and bedlam passions!

But he took comfort from Peggy's friendship and ended stoically, 'life at present presents me with but a melancholy path: but – my limb will soon be sound, and I shall struggle on'. The beginning of this letter has not survived, but the fragment starts with news of the latest round in the on-going saga with Creech:

I have broke measures with — and last week I wrote him a frosty, keen letter. He replied in terms of chastisement, and promised me upon his honor that I should have the account on Monday; but this is Tuesday, and yet I have not heard a word from him.

Robert's fury with Creech eventually boiled over. To mid-February may belong the incident later recorded by James Grierson:

A person met Burns coming up Leith walk brandishing a sapling & with much violence in his face & manner, said, Burns what is the matter? I am going to smash that S[hite] Creech.[39]

But the letter to Peggy on 17 February was much more ebullient. Robert intended leaving Edinburgh the following day. By now he had abandoned his farming plans – 'A farm that I could live in, I could not find' – and was now seriously contemplating the alternative:

> You will condemn me for the next step I have taken. I have entered into the excise. I stay in the west about three weeks, and then return to Edinburgh for six weeks instructions; afterwards, for I get employ instantly, I go *où il plait a Dieu, – et mon Roi*. I have chosen this, my dear friend, after mature deliberation. The question is not at what door of fortune's palace shall we enter in; but what doors does she open to us?

Captain Richard Brown had answered Robert's original letter of 30 December, and now Robert wrote again on 15 February (CL 419) saying that he would arrive in Glasgow on Monday evening. He proposed putting up for the night at George Durie's Black Bull Inn in Argyle Street (a plaque on the wall of Marks and Spencer's department store, which now stands on the site, records this occasion) where the Edinburgh coaches terminated, but would keep all day Tuesday free. He hoped that Richard would manage up to town: 'I am hurried as if haunted by fifty devils, else I would come to Greenock'. If that date were unsuitable he urged Brown to write to him at Glasgow or Mossgiel to suggest an alternative within the next fortnight. As it happened, Richard Brown did not wait for Tuesday but came to Glasgow on Monday afternoon to meet Robert off the coach. As a bonus, Robert had the company of his younger brother William who had also come to meet him, no doubt bringing Jenny Geddes. The three men had a jolly evening: 'guess my pleasure; to meet you could alone have given me more', Robert wrote enthusiastically to Nancy at nine o'clock that night (CL 398).

Having promised to write to Nancy every day, Robert found that a crowded itinerary made this impossible. It was not until the following Friday, 22 February, that he found the time to write again, from Kilmarnock (CL 398-9). He had gone to Paisley on the Tuesday but did not get a chance to write. 'My worthy, wise, friend Mr Pattison, did not allow me a moment's respite.' Robert was in Paisley for ten hours, 'during which time I was introduced to nine men worth six thousands; five men worth ten thousand; his brother, richly worth twenty thousands; and a young Weaver who will have thirty thousands good'. It seems more probable that the meeting recorded by John Taylor as having taken place the previous August actually belonged to this date. From Paisley Robert had ridden to Stewarton where he had spent the past two days at Dunlop House. He had paused at Kilmarnock on the way home. Nancy had made two shirts for Jean's son Bobbie and Robert mentioned this: 'in about two hours I shall present your twa wee sarkies to the little fellow'. Nancy was still uppermost in his mind:

> My dearest Clarinda, you are ever present with me; and these hours that drawl by among the fools and rascals of this world, are only supportable

in the idea that they are the forerunners of that happy hour that ushers me to 'The Mistress of my soul.'– Next week I shall visit Dumfries, and next again, return to Edinr.– My letters, in these hurrying dissipated hours, will be heavy trash – but you know the Writer.

Robert appears to have changed his mind, and instead of making straight for Mossgiel he rode to Tarbolton where he called in at Willie's Mill. Acording to Jean Armour herself[40] her father had become angry when he discovered that she and Burns were still communicating. Her mother warned her of her father's anger and advised her to leave home until he calmed down. It was then that she visited the Muirs of Tarbolton Mill. This implies that Jean took the initiative in pre-empting her father and that she made her own arrangements to live at Tarbolton. William Muir (1745–93) is a very shadowy figure; beyond the fact that he is said to have been a long-standing friend of the Burnes family, nothing is known of him. But Gilbert once let slip that Robert kept his assignations with Mont-gomerie's Peggy (who may, in fact, have been Margaret Campbell) at 'Tarboth Mill' which was another name for the same place. There can be no doubt that Muir was a very intimate friend of both Robert and his father; he was the subject of a mock epitaph (CW 70) composed in April 1784 with the clumsy title 'Epitaph on my own friend and my father's friend, Wm. Muir in Tarbolton Mill', and the third and fourth lines convey something of the relationship:

> The friend of man, the friend of truth,
> The friend of age, and guide of youth:

It seems probable that Robert spent the night of 22 February with Jean under the hospitable roof of the Muirs. Now that he was back in the dis-trict Jean assumed chief priority. Anxiety – and a measure of longing for 'that delicious armful' – combined to send Robert to Tarbolton before going across to Mauchline.

There, on the morning of 23 February, Robert found an exceedingly long letter from Clarinda which she had begun on the night of Tuesday 19, taken up at eleven o'clock the following morning, and completed that afternoon. Nancy had had a visit from her stern, unbending, hypocritical minister. 'He did not name you; but spoke in terms that showed plainly he knew.' Kemp knew Nancy's weak spots and sadistically told her that he was withdrawing his friendship, reducing the poor woman to tears. She had sought some comfort from Miss Nimmo who soothed her with praises of Robert as a man of worth, honour and genius. 'Oh, how I could have listened to her for ever!' The following morning the ever-faithful Mary Peacock was at her bedside by eight o'clock. 'She tells me her defence of you was so warm, in a large company where you were blamed for some trivial affair, that she left them impressed with the idea of her being in love. She laughs and says 'tis pity to have the skaith and nothing for her pains.' Nancy had other worries on her mind: 'I am a little anxious about

Willie; his leg is to be lanced this day, and I shall be fluttered till the operation is fairly over. Mr Wood thinks he will soon get well, when the matter
lodged in it is discussed.' But by the afternoon, when Nancy finished the
letter, Sandy Wood had not turned up, and her misery and anguish were
greater than ever. She would have delayed sending the letter, but was
anxious that it should be waiting for Robert at Mauchline when he got
there on Thursday.

Robert hastened to reply the same day (CL 399–400). 'I have just now,
My ever dearest Madam, delivered your kind present to my sweet, little
Bobbie; who I find a very fine fellow.' The next paragraph, however, dealt
with the far less agreeable subject of Kemp's visit, a matter which Robert
confessed 'opens a wound, ill-closed, in my breast'. Then, switching tack,
he continued:

> Now for a little news that will please you.– I, this morning as I came
> home, called for a certain woman.– I am disgusted with her; I cannot
> endure her! I, while my heart smote me for the prophanity, tried to
> compare her with my Clarinda: 'twas setting the expiring glimmer of a
> farthing taper beside the cloudless glory of the meridian sun.– Here was
> tasteless insipidity, vulgarity of soul, and mercenary fawning; there,
> polished good sense, heaven-born genius, and the most generous, the
> most delicate, the most tender Passion.– I have done with her, and she
> with me.

This smacks of the morning after the night before; note how Robert is at
pains to place his reunion with Jean 'this morning as I came home'. The
posturing and artificiality which characterise so much of Robert's correspondence with Nancy reached a new low in this letter. It takes little
imagination to visualise the scene at Willie's Mill when poor Jean, now
eight months pregnant, greeted the return of her lover. After all the
brutal, callous treatment she had received from her own family, Jean would
have reacted to Robert's timely reappearance with abject devotion mingled
with immense relief. Despite the nearness of her time, Robert no doubt
succumbed all too easily, relieved the pent-up emotions of the previous
months – and then suffered a fit of remorse and revulsion afterwards.

To Richard Brown, Robert wrote on 24 February (CL 419–20), 'I
arrived here, at my brother's, only yesterday; after fighting my way thro'
Paisley and Kilmarnock against those old powerful foes of mine, the Devil,
the World, and the Flesh; so terrible in the fields of Dissipation'. A letter
to Mrs Dunlop, despatched with a parcel of books (Spenser for Mrs
Dunlop, Marmontel's *Bélisaire* for Miss Fanny and Gray's poems for Miss
Keith), was dated 29 February but actually written several days earlier.
Robert post-dated the letter to go with the parcel by carrier; for by the end
of the month he was in Dumfriesshire. According to his letter to Clarinda,
Robert intended to set off for Dumfriesshire the following day, but he was
still at Mossgiel when he wrote to Richard Brown and he may not actually
have departed till a day or two later.

Robert's movements between 24 and 27 February are not known, but during this period he arranged for Jean to move back to Mauchline. She did not return to her parents' home but was accommodated in an apartment in the house of his old friend Dr John Mackenzie. The house, opposite Nanse Tannock's hostelry, has been preserved as a Burns Museum, and the upstairs room and kitchen which Robert is said to have rented have been restored, although it is more likely that Robert only rented the kitchen. This ensured that, when her time came, Jean would have the best medical attention ready to hand. It would appear (from a letter to Ainslie quoted below) that Robert affected a reconciliation between Jean and her mother at this time, and arranged for Mrs Armour to attend her daughter during her confinement.[41]

Robert's next letter was written from the inn at Cumnock (where his old girlfriend Annie Rankine was landlady) on 2 March (CL 400). He apologised to Clarinda for the week-long silence: 'I have been tosst about thro' the Country ever since I wrote you'. He was now on his way back to Mossgiel from Dumfriesshire where, accompanied by John Tennant, he had inspected Patrick Miller's farms:

> I am thinking my farming scheme will yet hold.– A worthy, intelligent farmer, my father's friend and my own, has been with me on the spot: he thinks the bargain practicable.– I am myself, on a more serious review of the lands, much better pleased with them.– I won't mention this in writing to any body but you and Mr Ainslie.– Don't accuse me of being fickle: I have the two plans of life before me, and I wish to adopt the one most likely to procure me independance.

Before parting, Sylvander and Clarinda had made a pact. Every Sunday evening at eight o'clock they would meditate upon each other. 'Tonight, at the sacred hour of eight, I expect to meet you – at the Throne of Grace'. More to the point, he hoped that he would find a letter from her waiting for him at Johnnie Dow's which, since the previous summer, had served as Mauchline's post office. 'If I settle on the farm I propose, I am just a day and a half's ride from Edinr – we will meet'.

The following day, back at Mossgiel, Robert wrote to William Cruikshank (CL 359–60). In Glasgow Robert had tracked down some cocoa, to which Cruikshank was partial, and had sent it off by carrier; now he hoped that it had arrived safely. He apologised for not having written sooner:

> Apòlogies for not writing are frequently like apologies for not singing – the apology better than the — song.– I have fought my way severely through the savage hospitality of this Country – to send every guest drunk to bed if they can.

Robert told his erstwhile landlord of his visit to Dumfriesshire: 'I am just returned from visiting Mr Miller's farm'. This implies that Robert, having previously examined farms on both banks of the Nith, had provisionally settled on Ellisland, on the west bank and detached from the rest of the Dalswinton estate by the river, and had only required Tennant's judgment to confirm his choice. Robert had his doubts about the wisdom of choosing Ellisland whose unimproved, stony soil was poor compensation for the splendid views it offered. But Tennant 'was highly pleased with the farm; and as he is without exception the most intelligent farmer in the Country, he has staggered me a good deal'. It was this apparently curious judgment which lent weight to the notion that Tennant was part of the Byzantine conspiracy to trap Burns into the Excise.[42] But Robert had the last word:

> I have the two plans of life before me; I shall balance them to the best of my judgement; and fix on the most eligible.– I have written to Mr Miller, and shall wait on him when I come to town which will be the beginning or middle of next week: I would be in sooner, but my unlucky knee is rather worse, and I fear for some time will scarcely stand the fatigue of my Excise instructions.

In this and in other letters of this period Robert promised to be a more regular correspondent once he was settled in the routine of life, either as an Excise officer or as a farmer. Little did he realise then that for three years he would attempt to combine both of these very exacting occupations.

Robert wrote to Patrick Miller the same day (CL 242-3), enclosing John Tennant's report on Ellisland. Robert's letter was one of the most businesslike he ever wrote. The farm was in such a run-down condition that it would be impracticable for him to take up the lease at Whitsun. 'I'll pay for the grass & houses whatever they deserve for the summer, and if you please, make my entry to my lease at Martinmas.' The lease was to be for seventy-six years, in four nineteen-year periods, with an annual rent of £50 for the first three years and £70 thereafter. Miller allowed Robert £300 for the erection of a new farmhouse and for much-needed repairs, drainage and fencing.

The reference to his 'unlucky knee' in the letter to Cruikshank is significant, for it has given Robert's apologists a way out of an unpleasant dilemma. A third letter, which may have been written on 3 March, was addressed to Bob Ainslie (CL 331-2). The opening paragraph is more or less the same as that in the letter to Cruikshank, but it then switches to sexual bombast:

> I have been through sore tribulation and under much buffeting of the Wicked One since I came to this country. Jean I found banished, like a martyr – forlorn destitute and friendless: All for the good old cause. I have reconciled her to her fate, and I have reconciled her to her mother. I have taken her a room. I have taken her to my arms. I have given her a mahogany bed. I have given her a guinea, and I have f—d till she rejoiced with joy unspeakable and full of glory. But, as I always am on ever occasion, I have been prudent and cautious to an astonishing degree. I swore her privately and solemnly never to attempt any claim on me as

a husband, even though anybody should persuade her she had such a claim (which she had not), neither during my life nor after my death. She did all this like a good girl, and I took the opportunity of some dry horse litter, and gave her such a thundering scalade that electrified the very marrow of her bones. Oh, what a peacemaker is a guid weel-willy pintle! It is the mediator, the guarantee, the umpire, the bond of union, the solemn leage and covenant, the plenipotentiary, the Aaron's rod, the Jacob's staff, the prophet Elisha's pot of oil, the Ahasuerus' Sceptre, the sword of mercy, the philosopher's stone, the Horn of Plenty, and Tree of Life between Man and Woman.

The opening paragraph, together with a closing paragraph about Robert's plans to return to Edinburgh, were published by Allan Cunningham in 1834. The complete text, however, appeared in *The Merry Muses* with the spurious publication date of 1827 (but actually 1872). Ross Roy[43] mentions a nineteenth-century transcript, but the original manuscript has never been traced. It may well have been the very letter which the antiquarian book-seller James Stillie and some like-minded friends purchased for £4 and put in the fire. 'This Ainslie was one of Burns' worst enemies, and an odious character,' reminisced Stillie many years later.[44] This passage, showing Robert at his most caddish, is indefensible. In mitigation, it smacks of the kind of immature bragging to which some men are prone, feeling some compulsion to give their intimate friends a blow-by-blow account of their sexual exploits. This kind of behaviour is usually aural and Robert probably indulged in that as well; but he made the cardinal error of committing this braggadocio to paper, and just as big an error in placing his trust in Ainslie. Soon after the poet's death, Ainslie got the return of his letters to Burns, which he apparently destroyed.[45] We can only conjecture that whatever Burns wrote to Ainslie, he was repaid in kind.

Burns's biographers have interpreted the notorious 'horse-litter' letter in various ways. The novelist James Barke[46] dismissed it as a *jeu d'esprit* intended purely for Ainslie's titillation. Alastair Campsie,[47] however, saw this as a piece of deliberate misinformation to throw the inquisitors of the Excise off the scent (on the assumption that Ainslie was some sort of spy or informer). This was necessary to support the theory that Robert lied to the Excise about the number of children he had. Far from admitting to the existence of the second set of twins born to Jean a few days later, Robert allegedly concocted this tale of sexual prowess to conceal the fact that Jean was even pregnant. This theory, of course, was based on a false premise, as Burns was technically a bachelor when he applied for his Excise certificate, so the number of children, out of wedlock, was irrelevant. Campsie was on firmer ground when he pointed to the immense difficulty, if not well-nigh impossibility, of Robert having sexual intercourse with his injured knee, and this alone ought to have alerted everyone to the 'thundering scalade' as a figment of Robert's imagination. On the other hand, Robert was unlikely to let a little matter like a sore knee – any more than Jean's advanced pregnant state – get in the way of his pleasure.

Those biographers who have taken this boast at face value have had the added problem of the putative injury which penetrative sex might have done to the unborn foetuses.[48] If Jean's statement, recorded by McDiarmid, is correct the twins, both girls, were born on 3 March; but there are good grounds for thinking that the birth occurred up to six days later. If Robert had sexual intercourse on 22 February, only ten or fifteen days before the babies were born, was he guilty of contributing to their deaths? To be sure, obstetricians advise against penetrative sex during the last few weeks of pregnancy, but there is no absolute case for blaming Robert for the sad outcome.[49] If Jean's date of 3 March is correct, Robert's behaviour at this period shows him in a rather callous light, which is quite out of character. On the assumption of 3 March as the birth date, Robert has been castigated by some writers; he was too busy writing his indecent letter to Ainslie that day to ride down to the village and visit Jean and the new-born infants. On 6 March Sylvander wrote to Clarinda (CL 401), mentioning that:

> yesterday I dined at a friend's at some distance; the savage hospitality of this Country spent me the most part of the night over the nauseous potion in the bowl; this day – sick – head-ache – low-spirits – miserable – fasting, except for a draught of water or small-beer now eight o'clock at night – only able to crawl ten minutes' walk into Mauchline, to wait the Post in the pleasurable hope of hearing from the Mistress of my soul.

Of course, the omission of any mention of Jean and her twins does not imply that Robert was unaware of them, or had not been to visit them; he was hardly likely to admit this in a letter to Clarinda. But the wining and dining on 5 March seem to indicate that the birth had not yet taken place. This is reinforced by a letter of 7 March to Richard Brown (CL 420) in which he indulged in some appropriate nautical metaphors:

> I found Jean – with cargo very well laid in; but unfortunately moor'd, almost at the mercy of wind and tide: I have towed her into convenient harbour where she may lie snug till she unload; and have taken the command myself – not ostensibly, but for a time, in secret. – I am gratified by your kind enquiries after her;

Richard Fowler, taking the alleged birth date of 3 March as correct, waxes indignant at Robert's cavalier behaviour:

> The anticipated 'unloading' mentioned to Brown had already taken place – four days before the letter was written, and one of the newborn twin girls, with only three more days to live, must have been visibly failing. Poor Jean. When the bardolaters make their move to have Robert of Mossgiel canonized, the events of a few weeks early in 1788 will make the task of the *advocatus diaboli* a very brief one.[50]

But the recording of the date of birth goes back no further than Jean's reminiscences to McDiarmid recorded in 1825, almost forty years after the event, and Robert's letters must surely cast doubt on 3 March as the date. It seems inconceivable that Robert would have been ignorant of the birth, had it taken place on 3 March; nor was there any way that he could have remained in ignorance of such an event, especially one which was daily expected, and to suggest that he was so indifferent to Jean is an unwarranted calumny. The letter to Brown implies that the event was still imminent, and there would have been no reason for Robert to lie to his old friend. It must be assumed, therefore, that the twins were not born until some time after 7 March.

It is most likely that they were born on 9 March, or even as late as the following day. Robert wrote to William Nicol on 8 March (CL 345–6) and made no mention of Jean and her predicament. No further letters were written till 12 March. Chambers stated that 'The birth of these infants is not recorded in the parish registers of Mauchline – probably because they did not live to be baptized'.[51] This has been accepted without question until now, but, following the assertion by Campsie that the twins lived and moved with Robert and Jean to Ellisland, I checked the matter with the records preserved in Register House, Edinburgh. I found that, contrary to accepted belief, the burial register of Mauchline has been preserved. Page 304, headed 'Burials 1788', has two identical entries of 'Jean Armour's Child, unbaptized', one on 10 March and the other on 22 March. The last column in the page indicated the charge for burial, but in both instances a line was drawn through, showing that no charge was made in either case. This was apparently normal in the case of still-births and the death of unbaptised infants. Putting this matter in perspective, it should be noted that this page records nineteen burials between 11 February and 11 May, and of these no fewer than seven were of unbaptised new-born infants.[52] It is possible that one girl died at or shortly after birth, while the other was so weak that she died less than two weeks later. It is strange, nevertheless, that the second girl should not have been baptised, given the fact that baptisms normally took place within a matter of days of birth at that time. Whatever the circumstances of their life and death, these baby girls never featured in any of Robert's letters; but the entire episode must have been extremely painful to him and it is hardly surprising that he should wish to erase it from his memory.

In Chapter 8 I quoted a passage from Gilbert's Narrative which referred to giving up 'our bargain'. The latter part of the closing sentence is something of a puzzle which has either been totally overlooked by previous writers, or merely shrugged off as probably referring to Gilbert's giving up the farm in 1797 when he exercised his option to break the lease. But Robert had been out of the Mossgiel picture from November 1786 and died more than a year before Gilbert left Mossgiel; so the generally accepted view does not square with the reference to 'we found ourselves'. If Gilbert was referring to his family in general this might be acceptable; but if he meant his elder brother and himself as joint-tenants of the farm, then we ought to consider some drastic step taken much earlier, possibly even as early as 1788 when

Robert effectively abandoned Mossgiel to his brother. Surely this is what Gilbert implies, by bracketing the surrender of the original bargain with the unprofitability of the farm, despite 'utmost diligence and economy' – a 'cause and effect' situation. The reference to the loss of 'a considerable part of our original stock' also seems to give the lie to the notion of the abandonment of the lease in 1797 – fully ten years later. Unfortunately, the legal papers of Gavin Hamilton appear to have disappeared (or been destroyed long ago), so unless they subsequently come to light we may never find the answer to this intriguing mystery. A clue, however, lies in the correspondence of Burns with Gavin Hamilton. This consists of six letters in all, written between 18 October 1783 (previously quoted) and 7 March 1788. The second to fifth letters are written from one close friend to another, discussing poetry and mutual friends; but the last, like the first, is a business letter (CL 70–1). Written from Mossgiel, it was known only in a draft which has since vanished, so the actual addressee was not named; but from the contents only Gavin Hamilton could have been meant. Clearly Hamilton wanted Robert to stand surety for Gilbert in a very substantial sum, but Robert was unable, or unwilling, to go further, having, by this time, lent his brother at least £180, a substantial part of the profits from his Edinburgh Edition:

> The language of refusal is to me the most difficult language on earth, and you are the man of the world, excepting One of Rt Honble designation, to whom it gives me the greatest pain to hold such language.– My brother has already got money, and shall want nothing in my power to enable him to fulfil his engagement with you; but to be security on so large a scale even for a brother, is what I dare not do, except I were in such circumstances of life as that the worst that might happen could not greatly injure me.– I never wrote a letter which gave me so much pain in my life, as I know the unhappy consequences; I shall incur the displeasure of a Gentleman for whom I have the highest respect, and to whom I am deeply obliged.

The friendship between Burns and the Mauchline lawyer seems to have terminated abruptly at this point, probably soured on both sides by the way that yet another 'ruinous bargain' had turned out. We are left with the impression that this wretched business did not reflect to the credit of Gavin Hamilton. Many previous writers have taken the contrary view, maintaining that the friendship survived, if not quite sustaining its earlier ardour, and support this contention by citing a letter which Robert wrote to an unnamed correspondent as late as 16 July 1793. Hately Waddell, who first published it in 1871, considered that Robert Aiken was the recipient; but Scott Douglas (1877) and all subsequent writers till 1985 thought Gavin Hamilton was the addressee. Ross Roy[53] then re-examined the text objectively and came to the conclusion that Waddell's original verdict was more likely, and with this I concur. There is therefore no documentary evidence to suggest that there was anything but a total break in the relationship between Burns and Hamilton from March 1788 onwards.

Although Sylvander wrote to his Clarinda from Glasgow, Kilmarnock, Mossgiel and Cumnock by 2 March, she had only written to him once in that period, and then when next she wrote on 5 March, had the temerity to upbraid him for not writing more often: 'believe me, it will be some time ere I can cordially forgive you the pain your silence has caused me! . . . I accept of your apologies; but am hurt that any should have been necessary betwixt us on such a tender occasion'. She had just received his letter from Cumnock and 'to show you my good nature' had sat down to reply immediately. She was happy that the farming scheme promised so well. 'There's no fickleness, my dear Sir, in changing for the better. I never liked the Excise for you; and feel a sensible pleasure in the hope of your becoming a sober, industrious farmer.'

If she could not have Sylvander in the flesh, Clarinda had had the consolation of frequent visits from Mr Ainslie, to whom she had 'been under unspeakable obligations'. While she was writing this letter, in fact, Nancy had a visit from their mutual friend who told her that he had heard from Robert, although we presume he did not divulge the contents of the 'horse-litter' letter. Nancy had also made her peace with her minister. 'I supped at Mr Kemp's on Friday. Had you been an invisible spectator [and seen] with what perfect ease I acquitted myself, you would have been pleased, highly pleased, with me.'

Nancy was interrupted by a visit from a Miss R— (not identified). She was obviously a mutual friend who was aware of the relationship between Robert and Nancy, as she enquired kindly after him. Then Nancy resumed her letter: 'I hope you have not forgotten to kiss the little cherub for me. Give him fifty, and think Clarinda blessing him all the while. I pity his mother sincerely, and wish a certain affair happily over.' Though usually interpreted as a reference to Robert's affair with Jean, this may have had the more specific meaning of referring to Jean's confinement. This seems to be borne out by the very next sentence which discussed the health of her own son: 'My Willie is in good health, except his leg, which confines him close since it was opened; and Mr Wood says it will be a very tedious affair. He has prescribed sea-bathing as soon as the season admits.'

An indication of the efficiency of the eighteenth-century postal service is the fact that Robert received this letter the very next day and replied immediately. Another letter, written on 7 March, appears to have answered one of Clarinda's of the previous day, accusing him of unkindness. Robert protested his innocence of 'a sin so unlike me, a sin I detest more than a breach of the whole Decalogue' and was hurt that she should suppose 'that a short fortnight could abate my passion'. By now he must have begun to find Nancy's possessiveness rather tiresome. Although he apologised at great length, he posed the question: 'Could you not, my ever dearest Madam, make a little allowance for a man, after long absence, paying a short visit to a country full of friends, relations, and early intimates?' Nancy replied on 8 March 'agreeably surprised' to receive an answer to hers of Wednesday that morning. 'I thought it always took two days, a letter from this to Mauchline, and did not expect yours sooner than

Monday.' Although she admitted that this was the fifth from Robert and now her fourth to him, it did not prevent her from reproaching him for not writing from Dumfries as he had promised. She expended the better part of a page to lecturing him on the matter, and then made matters worse by attacking his Paisley friend Pattison: 'In the name of wonder how could you spend ten hours with such a —? What a despicable character!' And off she went again with another sermon. Towards the end of this long tirade, Nancy changed the subject: 'Love and cherish your friend Mr Ainslie. He is your friend indeed'. One suspects that, by this time, Ainslie was insinuating himself in the lady's affections. He was, after all, a more genteel, refined person; and doubtless better able to adapt his views to her religious moods.

What is indisputable is that Robert left Mossgiel about the time that Jean was giving birth to his twins. To Robert Muir he wrote on 7 March saying that he planned to leave on Monday morning (10 March), as he had to collect some sums of money in Galston and Newmilns owing to him on the Edinburgh Edition 'and I shall set off so early as to dispatch my business and reach Glasgow by night'. This reinforces my belief that the birth of the twins did not take place until some time that day. If one infant were still-born, it would be buried the same day.

In Glasgow Robert had to pick up a parcel of books for Nancy from Dunlop and Wilson in the Trongate. He would have stayed there, probably at the Black Bull as before, and caught the Edinburgh coach the following morning.

The letter to Muir (CL 89-90) is of interest for its expression of Robert's philosophy at this time. Muir, only a few months older than Robert, had been seriously ill – Robert hoped that 'the Spring will renew your shattered frame' – but he was now dying, and they never met again. Perhaps Robert had some inkling or premonition of this, for he consoled his friend:

> an honest man has nothing to fear.- If we lie down in the grave, the whole man a piece of broke machinery, to moulder with the clods of the valley, – be it so; at least there is an end of pain, care, woes and wants: if that part of us called Mind, does survive the apparent destruction of the man – away with old-wife prejudices and tales! Every age and every nation has had a different set of stories; and as the many are always weak, of consequence they have often, perhaps always been deceived: a man, conscious of having acted an honest part among his fellow creatures; even granting that he may have been the sport, at times, of passions and instincts; he goes to a great unknown Being who could have no other end in giving him existence but to make him happy; who gave him those passions and instincts, and well knows their force.

Robert Muir died barely a month later. It is to be hoped that he derived some comfort from this letter, containing Burns's frankest declaration of his religious beliefs.

By 13 March Robert was back in Edinburgh. A letter to Margaret Chalmers on 14 March (CL 236) mentioned that 'Yesternight I compleated a bargain with Mr Miller, of Dalswinton, for the farm of Ellisland'. DeLancey Ferguson and Roy have dated a batch of undated letters from Sylvander to Clarinda to this week. These letters are merely headed 'Wednesday Morning' and 'Friday, Nine o'clock Night', but they have been assigned to 12 and 14 March respectively. The first letter (CL 403–4) says 'that arch-rascal Creech, has not done my business yesternight, which has put off my leaving town till Monday morning. Tomorrow at eleven, I meet with him for the last time'.

We look in vain in any of Robert's letters of the ensuing month for any direct reference to the tragic affair of Jean and her twins. The nearest we come to this is in a letter to Richard Brown of 20 March in which he says 'these eight days I have been positively crazed', but by what he did not elaborate.

By now Robert was much too busy dealing with Creech, negotiating his lease with Miller and settling his Excise preliminaries to worry overmuch about matters at Mauchline. On Sunday 16 March Robert sent the missives concerning Ellisland to Patrick Miller and signed the lease two days later at John Gordon's law office.[54] On Monday morning he concluded his Excise affair, writing at noon to tell Clarinda:

> I have got my order for instructions: so far so good. Wednesday night I am engaged to sup among some of the principals of the Excise: so can only make a call for you that evening; but next day, I stay to dine with one of the Commissioners, so cannot go till Friday morning.

Never before had a raw recruit been inducted into the Excise with so much pomp and circumstance. Who the principals were, whom Robert mentioned in this letter, are not known, but we may suppose them to have been some of the senior 'practical officers' of the department. The Commissioner, however, was probably Robert Graham of Fintry, the 'Great Man' referred to in a letter to Clarinda dated Tuesday morning (18 March).

The matter with Creech was also resolved at this time. The letter to Richard Brown from Glasgow on 20 March (CL 421) points to this having preoccupied Robert the previous day:

> I have been getting my tack extended, as I have taken a farm; and I have been racking shop accounts with Mr Creech; which, both together, with watching, fatigue, and a load of Care almost too heavy for my shoulders, have in some degree actually fever'd me.– I really forgot the directory yesterday, which vexes me: but I was convuls'd with rage a good part of the day.

Perhaps the 'load of Care' was an allusion to Jean, whose second twin daughter was now dying. No doubt Gilbert was keeping him informed of the grim situation at Mauchline. But the reference to being 'convuls'd with rage' can only apply to Robert's dealings with Creech. As late as the following January, memories of this business still rankled bitterly, as Robert confessed to Dr Moore (CL 258):

I cannot boast of Mr Creech's ingenuous fair-dealing to me.- He kept me hanging on about Edinburgh from the 7th August 1787 until the 13th April 1788, before he would condescend to give me a Statement of affairs; nor had I got it even then, but for an angry letter I wrote him which irritated his pride.

The angry letter may well have been the same as the 'frosty, keen letter' which Robert mentioned to Margaret Chalmers in January 1788, but is more likely to have been a second letter, written on 12 March. None of Robert's letters to Creech have survived and unfortunately he did not keep copies of them; but this was mentioned in the letter to Clarinda of that date, 'I have just now written to Creech such a letter, that the very goose-feather in my hand shrunk back from the line . . . I am forming ideal schemes of vengeance. O for a little of my will on him!' But it is clear that, even by 19 March, Robert had still not managed to get Creech to settle the accounts. There may have been more than a simple withholding of money to upset Robert. A rumour was going around Edinburgh at the time that Creech had smuggled an edition into the market unknown to Burns. Creech is alleged to have asked John Beugo for the copper plate on which Burns's portrait was engraved. Beugo was suspicious of Creech's intentions, so he put a secret mark on the engraving. 'Report addeth that numberless copies of the Poems afterwards appeared with this private mark upon the portrait.'[55] If, indeed, Robert suspected his agent of literary piracy, his convulsion with rage would have been understandable. Robert had promised to procure a directory for Brown, but with everything on his mind he forgot about it 'yesterday'. From this, previous editors have suggested that Jones's *Directory of Glasgow*, first published in 1787, was meant; but Richard Brown could have purchased a copy of this for himself quite easily. Perhaps Williamson's *Post Office Directory of Edinburgh* was meant instead; if so, it would lend weight to the notion that Robert was still in Edinburgh as late as 19 March.

Sylvander's last letters to Clarinda were written on 'Monday, Noon' (17 March) and 'Tuesday morn' (18 March).[56] In the first he promised to meet her the following evening by appointment but, in fact, must have met her the very same night. On that occasion Robert made Nancy a farewell present of a pair of small drinking-glasses, along with the verses 'To Clarinda' (CW 321). Now that the affair was virtually over, there was no need for secrecy any longer. The pen-friends had gone for an evening stroll together. As Robert recalled the following morning, 'The walk – delightful; the evening – rapture.– Do not be uneasy today, Clarinda; forgive me.' The brief letter of 18 March ended on a characteristic note: 'The Father of Mercies be with you, Clarinda! and every good thing attend you!'

CHAPTER 14

Ellisland, 1788–91

O, were I on Parnassus hill,
Or had o Helicon my fill,
That I might catch poetic skill
  To sing how dear I love thee!
But Nith maun be my Muse's well,
My Muse maun be thy bonie sel,
On Corsincon I'll glowr and spell,
  And write how dear I love thee.

O, Were I on Parnassus Hill (CW 329)

The farm of Ellisland extends to some 170 acres and lies on the west bank of the River Nith, some five and three-quarter miles north of Dumfries.[1] The farm buildings are approached by a farm road running about a quarter of a mile east of the A76 Dumfries-Kilmarnock road. In the eighteenth century the main Dumfries-Glasgow post-road lay some way to the east, on the other side of the river through the hamlet of Dalswinton. At Auldgirth the post-road crossed the river by means of a fine stone bridge erected in 1782. The fathers of Allan Cunningham and Thomas Carlyle were two of the stonemasons employed in its construction. The present main road south of Auldgirth, which runs close to Ellisland, was in Burns's day an unmetalled secondary road running south to Brigend. The cluster of cottages standing at the western end of Devorgilla's bridge, origi-nally accommodating the workers at the grain-drying kilns, had, in the course of the nineteenth century, grown into a town of 2,000 inhabitants, beyond the control of the burgh of Dumfries on the east bank and prover-bial for its lawlessness. Sir John Fielding, a prominent London magistrate, summed it up neatly when he said that Metropolitan detectives could trace a thief over the entire kingdom if he did not get to the Gorbals of Glasgow or Brigend of Dumfries. This appalling state of affairs was not rectified till 1810 when Brigend was erected into a burgh of barony under the name of Maxwelltown. Burns would go there from time to time, as work on his new farm permitted, to cross the ancient stone bridge and collect his mail from the post office. North of Ellisland it was but a short ride to Auldgirth and thence along the post-road, through Sanquhar and Cumnock, to Mauchline, some forty-five miles to the north-west.

Ellisland lies in the parish of Dunscore in Nithsdale and in legal documents is described as 'the forty shilling or three merk lands of old extent', being part of the ancient barony of Closeburn. Dunscore parish is shaped like an hour-glass, tapering to little more than a few yards at its narrowest point. Although otherwise undistinguished, Dunscore was home to two of the greatest literary figures in Scottish history. It has, at its most westerly extremity, the moorland farm of Craigenputtock where, early in the nineteenth century, Thomas Carlyle established his formidable reputation with such works as *Sartor Resartus*. Ellisland, at the most easterly end of the parish, is forever associated with some of Burns's finest work, particularly 'Tam o Shanter'. This area originally formed part of the lands of the Comyns seized by King Robert Bruce early in the fourteenth century, and from him passed to the Kirkpatrick family.

The estate of Dalswinton, on the opposite bank of the Nith, lay in the parish of Kirkmahoe and passed successively into the hands of the Stewarts and latterly the Maxwells. Dalswinton estate was purchased for £25,000 in 1785 by Patrick Miller (1731–1815), who separately purchased the farm of Ellisland for £1,300 the following year from James Veitch of Elliock, one of the Senators of the College of Justice. Miller, a director and later Deputy-Governor of the Bank of Scotland, a director of the Carron Ironworks and a prominent businessman with interests in many diverse spheres, is best remembered for inventing the carronade and for his experiments with paddleboats. A twin-hulled boat propelled by manually operated paddles was sailed to Sweden under his direction in 1787. The King of Sweden presented Miller with a sumptuous gold box containing a packet of turnip seeds. In this curious manner swedes became one of the staples of Scottish agriculture in the late eighteenth century. The following year Miller commissioned James Taylor and William Symington to build a twin-hulled boat whose paddles were powered by steam. This vessel, the prototype for steam navigation, made its maiden voyage on Dalswinton Loch on 14 October 1788. Thomas Carlyle said of Miller that 'he spent his life and his estate in that adventure, and is not now to be heard of in these parts, having had to sell Dalswinton and die quasi-bankrupt, and I should think, brokenhearted'.[2] This was quite untrue; Miller actually died at Dalswinton House on 9 December 1815 and, far from being near bankrupt, he left a considerable property which was the subject of a long-running dispute among his heirs.[3] When his executors disposed of Dalswinton in 1822 they received £120,000 for it, representing a very handsome return on Miller's original investment. Five years after he purchased Ellisland he had the good sense to rationalise his holdings by selling the farm to John Morrin of Laggan for £1,900.

Both the Dalswinton estate in general, and Ellisland farm in particular, were in a run-down state when Miller purchased them. In 1812 he wrote an account which casts light on this episode:

> When I purchased this estate about five and twenty years ago, I had not seen it. It was in the most miserable state of exhaustion and all the tenants in poverty. When I went to view my purchase, I was so much disgusted for eight or ten days that I never meant to return to this county.[4]

Patrick Miller, however, was an agricultural reformer, among his many other talents, and determined to effect far-reaching improvements. He conducted agricultural experiments, introduced the Swedish turnip, invented a drill plough and an improved threshing machine, and introduced the feeding of cattle on steamed potatoes. The purchase of Ellisland was a quixotic act, defying sound judgment and common sense. Although it marched with his estate it was on the wrong side of the river, entailing a three-mile detour to Auldgirth Bridge before it could be reached by road. A man on horseback, however, could ford the Nith with little difficulty. Gilbert Burns was inaccurate on several counts in the details of the lease which he furnished to Dr Currie. 'I never understood that Mr Miller gave my brother the choice of any farm but Ellisland, on which Mr Miller fixed the rent himself, but allowed my brother fifty-seven years of a lease, and to point out what restrictions he should be under in the management.'[5] In fact, as we have seen, the lease was for seventy-six years and Robert was certainly given a choice of farms. According to Allan Cunningham, whose father acted as Miller's steward at this period, Burns was offered three in all: Foregirth, a fine piece of the haugh on the east bank of the Nith on rich, level ground bearing heavy crops of wheat; Bankhead nearby, marginally less fruitful; and Ellisland. Robert should have chosen Foregirth which, even in the famine year of 1800, yielded £40 an acre, and whose eventual tenant gave up his lease £3,000 the richer.

Ellisland was the poet's choice; there is no evidence to suggest that either Miller or Tennant or both dissuaded him from selecting one or other of the low-lying farms on the Dalswinton side of the river, or that they swayed him by unduly singing the praises of Ellisland, as some writers have insinuated. Robert may have had his doubts about a return to farming in general and farming in Dumfriesshire, an area with which he was unfamiliar, in particular; but once he had decided on this course of action Ellisland appealed to him far more than the richer but less inspiring farms across the river. The farm lies in a rolling landscape above the steep banks of the river and affords a commanding view of the Dalswinton estate and fine vistas up and down the river. But the ground was just as stony as Mount Oliphant. The soil was poor, the land undrained, unfertilised and unimproved. It had potential, as John Morrin shrewdly perceived; but a great deal of hard work and the expenditure of considerable sums of money were required to bring it up to a level at which it would be profitable. This Robert soon found to his cost, but for the moment he was trying to fit in arrangements for his farm along with practical instruction in the Excise.

On 21 March he wrote to an unnamed correspondent, tentatively identified as William Stewart of Brownhill near Closeburn (CL 444). Stewart (1749-1812) was the factor of the Closeburn estate and the son of the landlord of the inn at Brownhill. Burns and Stewart were later to become firm friends, sharing an interest in bawdy poetry. Stewart's daughter Mary (1775-1847) was the heroine of the song 'Lovely Polly Stewart' (CW 523). Polly had a turbulent love-life, forming an irregular marriage with a farmer named George Welsh (grand-uncle of Jane Welsh Carlyle) before eloping with a Swiss soldier of fortune named Fleitz. Stewart was to be a good friend not only to Robert but also to Gilbert, and it was through Stewart's good offices that Gilbert secured the lease of Dinning farm in 1798.

Robert informed his correspondent that he had signed his tack with Miller and intended to commence operations on Whitsunday (25 May):

> I am an entire Stranger in your Country; and Heaven knows shall need advice enough: will you be so very good as take a poor devil of a sojourning Rhymster under your care?

Robert planned to spend Thursday night, 27 March, at Brownhill and asked for a meeting the following day:

> I want two men servants for the summer; if you know of any, please bespeak me them, or direct me to them.– I could like one of them a married man, as I can give him a house, and perhaps for this summer, a cow's grass; but I won't make a custom of that any more than this season.

From this it may be inferred that there was a farmhouse of sorts available. This may have been the building at the southern extremity of the farm which was later inhabited by David and Agnes Cullie, but whether they were the married couple alluded to in this letter cannot be ascertained.

Meanwhile, Robert was preoccupied with his Excise plans. On 25 March he wrote to Robert Graham of Fintry (CL 425) saying that he had arranged with James Findlay, the Tarbolton Exciseman, to undergo his six weeks' instruction under him. This deviated from the original arrangements which had stipulated that Robert was to be instructed by Alexander Dickson, an Excise officer in Edinburgh of some twelve years' standing. Dickson was very well thought of at headquarters and was, in fact, promoted to Supervisor soon afterwards. Edinburgh was much less convenient to Robert, now that he was set on taking Ellisland, and on his own initiative he approached Findlay whom he knew personally. Indeed, it was Robert who introduced Findlay to his future wife, Jean Markland, one of the Mauchline belles. But Findlay was bound by the red tape of the Excise service and had to regularise the position with George Johnston, his Supervisor at Ayr; and the latter, according to Robert, was 'superstitiously strict' and insisted that he reapply to the Secretary of the Excise, Adam Pearson, for a new order for instruction. To expedite matters, therefore, Robert now approached Graham of Fintry. Robert spoke highly of Findlay, 'an Excise Officer here who is exceedingly clever, and who enters with the warmth of a friend in my ideas of being instructed'.

Graham acted immediately, for a new order for instruction was signed by Adam Pearson on 31 March and directed to Burns a day or two later. The order to Findlay for instruction showed:

> That you instruct the bearer, Robert Burns, in the art of gauging and practical dry gauging casks and utensils; and that you fit him for surveying

victuallers, rectifiers, chandlers, tanners, tawers, maltsters, etc; and when he has kept books regularly for six weeks at least, and drawn true vouchers and abstracts therefrom (which books, vouchers and abstracts must be signed by your supervisor and yourself, as well as the said Robert Burns) and sent to the Commissioners at his expense; and when he is furnished with proper instruments, and well instructed and qualified for an officer, then (and not before, at your perils) you and your supervisor are to certify the same to the Board, expressing particularly therein the date of this letter; and that the above Robert Burns hath cleared his quarters, both for lodging and diet; that he has actually paid each of you for his instruction and examination and that he has sufficient at the time to purchase a horse for his business.[6]

Robert paid his visit to Brownhill on Friday or Saturday, 27 or 28 March, and rode back to Mauchline on Sunday. A letter written from Mauchline the following day (CL 274) to fellow-Crochallan Fencible Robert Cleghorn of Saughton Mills mentioned that he had ridden 'thro' a parcel of melancholy, joyless muirs, between Galloway and Ayrshire', and it being Sunday, Burns's mind turned to 'Psalms, hymns and spiritual Songs'. Cleghorn shared Robert's propensity for bawdry, and no doubt what the poet actually had in mind were those bawdy parodies known as the Cumnock Psalms. In his head was the tune 'Captain Okean' and as he rode along Robert composed the song 'The small birds rejoice in the green leave returning' (CW 322) which he sent to Cleghorn. But he had little time or inclination for composition:

> I am so harassed with Care and Anxiety about this farming project of mine, that my Muse has degenerated into the veriest prose-wench that ever picked cinders, or followed a Tinker.

Something of that care and anxiety was due to the fact that Robert, having to expend quite a sum on his Excise training, was running short of cash. On the same day he wrote to William Creech (CL 306) asking for the payment of the hundred guineas due in respect of his copyright. He had instructed his friend John Somerville to call on Creech for the money. But Robert showed a woeful lack of business sense, for he virtually countermanded the request by adding 'but as I do not need the sum, at least I can make a shift without it till then, any time between now and the first of May, as it may suit your convenience to pay it, will do for me'. This was as good as telling Creech to forget the matter for at least another month. In fact, it was not until 30 May that Creech finally paid up.

Robert began his course of Excise instruction at Tarbolton during April. The exact date of this is not known, but it was probably about Monday, 7 April. He had been invited to spend a day or two at The Mount, the residence of Mrs Dunlop's son Major Andrew Dunlop who managed the Dunlop estate, but had to turn this down (CL 143) as quite impracticable. To Alexander Blair at Catrine House he wrote on 3 April (CL 447) turning down a similar invitation 'as I am much harassed with the care and anxiety of farming business'. And to Margaret Chalmers he wrote on 7 April (CL 236–7):

> I am going on a good deal progressive in *mon grand bùt*, the sober science of life. I have lately made some sacrifices for which, were I *viva voce* with you to paint the situation and recount the circumstances, you would applaud me.

This is taken to refer to Robert, at long last, doing the decent thing by Jean. The only sacrifices which Peggy could have applauded would have been that he had given up his independence and bachelorhood and finally acknowledged Jean as his wife – 'by habit and repute', if not in the eyes of the Kirk. It seems that Robert was now living quite openly with Jean in the upstairs apartment of Dr Mackenzie's house in the Back Causeway. Joseph Train, whose father was steward on the Gilminscroft estate near Mauchline about this time, may have received from this source the detail that 'Robert Burns and Jean Armour were privately married in Gavin Hamilton's office by John Farquhar of Gilminscroft, a local magistrate'.[7] This seems to be a more plausible account than the local traditions which averred that the civil marriage took place in Hugh Morton's dance-hall and was conducted by Farquhar Gray (*sic*),[8] or that Robert and Jean were married in Loudoun Street in the hostelry of John Ronald, a Mauchline carrier and publican.[9] In fact, the magistrate's name was John Farquhar-Gray and his estate lay in the neighbouring parish of Sorn. No documentary evidence of this civil marriage has ever been found.

Robert also wrote to William Dunbar on 7 April (CL 283), revealing something of the hectic life he was then leading and hinting at the radical change in his domestic situation:

> I have been roving over the Country, as my farm I have taken is forty miles from this place, hiring servants and preparing matters: but most of all, I am earnestly busy to bring about a revolution in my own mind.

He confessed that 'my late scenes of idleness and dissipation have enervated my mind to an alarming degree', but now he had dropped 'all conversation and all reading (prose reading) but what tends in some way or other to my serious aim' and he concluded:

> I have scarcely made a single Distic since I saw you.– When I meet with an old Scots Air that has any facetious idea in its Name, I have a peculiar pleasure in following out that idea for a verse or two.

Three weeks then passed before Robert again took up pen and paper to write to any of his friends. James Smith, still working at the Avon Printfield, Linlithgow, was the recipient of a long letter of 28 April (CL 121–2) which revealed that Robert had, in fact, taken the plunge:

there is, you must know, a certain clean-limb'd, handsome bewitching young Hussy of your acquaintance to whom I have been lately and privately given a matrimonial title to my Corpus. –

'Bode a robe, and wear it;
'Bode a pock, and bear it,'

says the wise old Scots Adage! I hate to presage ill-luck; and as my girl in some late random trials has been *doubly* kinder to me than even the best of women usually are to their Partners of our Sex, in similar circumstances; I reckon on twelve times a brace of children against I celebrate my twelfth wedding-day . . .

After some whimsical musings about such a large family, Robert got down to brass tacks:

I intend to present Mrs Burns with a printed shawl, an article of which I dare say you have variety, 'tis my first present to her since I have *irrevocably* called her mine, and I have a kind of whimsical wish to get her the said first present from an old and much valued friend of hers & mine . . . The quality, let it be of the best: the Pattern I leave to your taste.– The money I'll pay to your sister, or transmit to any Correspondent of yours in Edinburgh or Glasgow . . . Mrs Burns ('tis only her private designation) begs her best Compliments to you.

This letter contains the earliest mention of Jean as Mrs Burns. The reference to this as a private matter, however, implies that, whatever form the marriage in Gavin Hamilton's office took, it was clandestine and irregular. But a simple declaration before two witnesses, such as Gavin Hamilton and John Farquhar-Gray, would have constituted a perfectly valid marriage at that time, and it seems odd that, having taken that step, Robert should have been at some pains to keep the matter private. Jacobina Hamilton, the lawyer's eldest daughter, later stated that the first she knew of the marriage was at her father's breakfast table one morning when Burns and Robert Aiken were present. Her mother apologised to Aiken for not being able to give him his usual boiled egg, whereupon the poet interjected that if she cared to send over the way to Mrs Burns she might have some.[10]

It is perhaps worth noting that, in the same year that Burns broke off his connection with Clarinda and married Jean Armour, Johann Wolfgang von Goethe, his senior by ten years and his 'elder brother, not certainly in misfortune, but in the muses' and erotic passion, broke off his long-running affair with the Countess von Stein and took Christiane Vulpius to live with him as his wife, although he did not go through any wedding ceremony till 1806.

On 28 April Robert also wrote to Mrs Dunlop (CL 143-4). The old lady had previously written, upbraiding him for being such a tardy correspondent – a recurring theme. Robert now hastened to defend his seeming remissness:

As I commence Farmer at Whitsunday, you will easily guess I must be pretty throng; but that is not all. As I got the offer of the Excise business without solicitation; and as it costs me only six weeks attendance for instructions to entitle me to a Commission: which Commission lies by me, and at any future period on my simple petition can be resumed; I thought five & thirty pounds a year was no bad dernier resort for a poor Poet, if Fortune in her jade tricks should kick him down from the little eminence to which she has lately helped him up.– For this reason, I am at present attending these instructions to have them completed before Whitsunday.

Robert's account of his Excise activities was inaccurate on two points. The cost of the training period was certainly much greater than he implied; and whatever document he received at the end of his training, it certainly was not his commission. It is probable that what he referred to was the certificate of fitness but even that would not have been issued by Supervisor Johnston until the training period had been completed. Burns's Excise commission was not issued till 14 July. This lengthy document, setting out in immense detail the vast range of disparate duties and responsibilities of the Excise officer, bore the signatures of the Chief Commissioner Thomas Wharton and two other Commissioners, George Brown and James Stoddard, but not, curiously enough, that of Robert Graham.

Robert had apparently intended to come to The Mount on Sunday 6 April, despite his misgivings about being able to keep the appointment; but in the end his health had let him down. On the Saturday he had been back at Mossgiel, meaning to set out early the following morning, but

for some nights preceding I had slept in an apartment where the force of the winds and rains was only mitigated by being sifted thro' numberless apertures in the windows, walls, &c. In consequence I was on Sunday, Monday & part of Tuesday unable to stir out of bed with all the miserable effects of a violent cold.

Whatever the temporary quarters at Ellisland, whether lodging with the Cullies or in some other hovel at the farm, one may imagine the rigours of the still-wintry weather in late March. Nevertheless, Robert's movements do not square with the privations described to Mrs Dunlop, and it may be that the violent cold was of the diplomatic variety and other matters of a domestic nature detained him instead. He ended by stating that he would be going and coming frequently to Ayrshire through the summer. If he did not manage to visit Dunlop, he hoped to be in Edinburgh some time before midsummer and would then pay her a visit at Morham West Mains near Haddington, the farm of Mrs Dunlop's son John where she was accustomed to spend part of the summer. Mrs Dunlop had lent Robert some volumes of the classics, notably Dryden's translation of Virgil. Further letters to Mrs Dunlop passed on 4 May (CL 145) and 27–29 May (CL 145–7) but it was not until 13 June (CL 147–8) that Robert got around to telling his mother-confessor what she had already learned elsewhere – that he was married. On her interrogation, he revealed a little more of his changed circumstances in a letter of 17 July (CL 148–50). Why he should have been so diffident about letting her know is a mystery, though Robert seems to have thought that Mrs Dunlop would not approve.

Two days after he sent off the long letter of 27–29 May, Robert had some second thoughts, and tackled the problem of breaking the news of his marriage in a characteristically roundabout manner. This time he wrote to Major Andrew Dunlop (CL 452). Perhaps he felt that Andrew, a confirmed bachelor, might understand matters better. After commenting philosophically on the decline of his brief fame, he changed direction abruptly:

> Your Mother never hinted at the report of my late change in life, and I did not know how to tell her.– I am afraid that perhaps she will not entirely enter into the motives of my conduct, so I have kept aloof from the affair altogether.– I saw, Sir, that I had a once, & still much-lov'd fellow-creature's happiness or misery among my hands; and I could not dally with such a matter.

It may be significant that Robert only blurted out the fact by dribs and drabs, as occasion demanded. Thus a letter from 'Masgiel' (*sic*) on 4 May gave the news to Robert's uncle, Samuel Brown at Kirkoswald (CL 451), purely because he was 'impatient to hear if the Ailsa fowling be commenced for this Season' as he wished to obtain three or four stones (56lbs, 25kg) of feathers, presumably for pillows or a mattress. Remembering that Uncle Samuel had been involved in smuggling, Robert resorted to appropriate metaphor to explain his new domestic situation:

> I engaged in the smuggling trade and God knows if ever any poor man experienced better returns – two for one.– But as freight and Delivery has turned out so D–md Dear I am thinking about taking out a Licence and beginning in a Fair trade.– I have taken a Farm on the Banks of Nith and in imitation of the old Patriarchs get Men servants and Maid Servants – Flocks and herds and beget sons and Daughters.

Just as he could not come straight out with the facts when writing to James Smith, Robert had to break the news to his uncle in a jokey manner. Again, why he should have befogged the issue by implying that marriage was imminent, rather than an accomplished fact, is mystifying.

To James Johnson, Robert wrote from Mauchline on 25 May (CL 293–4). The immediate cause for writing was mounting anxiety at Creech's inability to settle his account. Robert hoped that Johnson would be able to grapple with Creech on his behalf:

> A hundred guineas can be but a trifling affair to him, and 'tis a matter of most serious importance to me. Tomorrow I begin my operations as a farmer, and God speed the Plough!

Robert took this opportunity to give Johnson a rather flippant account of his changed status:

I am so enamoured with a certain girl's prolific twin-bearing merit, that I have given her a *legal* title to the best blood in my body; and so farewell Rakery!

He followed this, on a more serious note, with a paragraph about 'a long and much loved fellow-creature's happiness or misery' which was virtually identical to that in the letter to Major Dunlop.

Although Robert entered into his lease on 25 May, he did not actually commence work on his farm till 11 June. Some time during the previous week, about 4 or 5 June, he was in Glasgow,[11] and called on Andrew Dunlop on his way back to Ayrshire. From Andrew he doubtless was apprised of the fact that he had given the matrimonial news to his mother. Mrs Dunlop herself wrote from Haddington one of her longer letters on 4 June, expressing her feelings of hurt:

I am told in a letter that you have been a month married. I am unwilling to believe so important an era in your life has past, and you have considered me as so very little concerned in what concerned you most as never to give me the most distant hint of your wishing such a change or of its accomplishment, while I have had the favour of hearing two or three times of you during that interim. Allow me, however, married or unmarried, to wish you joy.

A week later Robert was in Dumfriesshire which would henceforward be his home. The first letter he wrote from 'Ellesland' (*sic*) was to Mrs Dunlop and dated 13 June (CL 147–8):

This is the second day, my honored Friend, that I have been on my farm. A solitary Inmate of an old smoky SPENCE: far from every Object I love or by whom I am belov'd . . .

Doubtless Robert was overwhelmed with homesickness, compounded by depression as the truth of his ruinous bargain rapidly sank in. The following day he wrote to Ainslie (CL 333) in similar vein:

This is now the third day, My dearest Sir, that I have sojourned in these regions; and during these three days you have occupied more of my thoughts than in three weeks preceeding . . . My Farm gives me a good many uncouth Cares & Anxieties, but I hate the language of Complaint.– Job, or some one of his friends, says well – 'Why should a living man complain?'[12]

On the same day Robert resumed entries in his *Second Commonplace Book* with a passage which began:

This is now the third day I have been in this country. Lord, –what is man! what a bustling little bundle of passions, appetites, ideas, and fancies! and what a capricious kind of existence he has here! If legendary stories be true, there is, indeed, an *elsewhere* . . . I am such a coward in life, so tired of the service, that I would almost at any time, with Milton's Adam,

> '. . . gladly lay me in my Mother's lap,
> And be at peace;'

but a wife and children – in poetics, 'the fair partner of my soul, and the little dear pledges of our mutual love' – these bind me to struggle with the stream, till some chopping squall overset the silly vessel, or, in the listless return of years, its own craziness drive it a wreck. Farewell now to those giddy follies, those varnished vices, which though half sanctified by the bewitching levity of Wit and Humour, are at best but thriftless idling with the precious current of existence . . .

Wedlock, the circumstance that buckles me hardest to care, if virtue and religion were to be anything with me but mere names – was what in a few seasons I must have resolved on; in the present case it was unavoidably necessary. Humanity, generosity, honest vanity of character, justice to my own happiness for after life, so far as it could depend (which it surely will a great deal) on internal peace – all these joined their warmest suffrages, their most powerful solicitations, with a rooted attachment, to urge the step I have taken. Nor have I any reason to rue it. I can fancy *how*, but have never seen *where*, I could have made it better. Come then, let me return to my favourite motto, that glorious passage in Young –

> 'On Reason build Resolve –
> That column of true majesty in man.'

The last sentences imply that the Robert who wore his heart on his sleeve still hankered after Nancy McLehose, but the hard-headed Robert realised that such a relationship had been beyond his grasp and he must settle for what was possible. Although the *Commonplace Book* was used subsequently for drafts of poems, Robert never again committed his innermost thoughts in prose to paper in this manner.

In his letter of 13 June, Robert confirmed to Mrs Dunlop that:

> I am indeed A HUSBAND. This information I from my inmost soul wished to give you but till you yourself should mention it, I did not know how to do it.

But he provided no explanation for his motives in withholding the information. This was followed by a variation on the theme of the 'once much loved and still much lov'd Female' which he had previously employed in writing to James Johnson and Andrew Dunlop. 'There is no sporting with a fellow-creature's happiness or misery', he added as a prelude to a description of his wife:

> The most placid good-nature & sweetness of disposition; a warm heart, gratefully devoted with all its powers to love one; vigorous health and sprightly chearfulness, set off to the best advantage by a more than common handsome figure; these, I think, in a woman, may make a tolerable good wife, though she should never have read a page but The

Scriptures of the Old & New Testament, nor have 'danced in a brighter Assembly than a Penny-pay Wedding.–'

Ainslie had previously been the recipient of a rather guarded letter of 26 May (CL 332) in which Robert had broken the good news of his marriage:

> I have the pleasure to tell you that I have been extremely fortunate in all my buyings and bargainings hitherto; Mrs Burns not excepted, which title I now avow to the World.– I am truly pleased with this last affair: it has indeed added to my anxieties for Futurity but it has given a stability to my mind & resolutions, unknown before; and the poor girl has the most sacred enthusiasm of attachment to me, and has not a wish but to gratify my every idea of her deportment.

This was a bold step, and Robert must have realised as he wrote this letter that Bob Ainslie would lose no time in passing on the glad tidings to Nancy McLehose with whom he was now on intimate terms. For nine months Nancy kept silent, but in March 1789 she wrote to Robert. Eight years later, when she managed to retrieve her letters from the poet's trustees, this was one which she took good care to destroy. We may guess something of its angry, bitter contents from Robert's dignified reply, written on 9 March 1789 (CL 405–6):

> The letter you wrote me to Heron's carried its own answer in its bosom: you forbade me to write to you, unless I was willing to plead Guilty, to a certain Indictment that you were pleased to bring against me.– As I am convinced of my own innocence, and though conscious of high imprudence & egregious folly, can lay my hand on my breast and attest the rectitude of my heart; you will pardon me, Madam, if I do not carry my complaisance so far, as humbly to acquiesce in the name of, Villain, merely out of compliment even to YOUR opinion; much as I esteem your judgement, and warmly as I regard your worth.– I have already told you, and I again aver it, that at the Period of time alluded to, I was not under the smallest moral tie to Mrs B–; nor did I, nor could I then know, all the powerful circumstances that omnipotent Necessity was busy laying in wait for me.– When you call over the scenes that have passed between us, you will survey the conduct of an honest man, struggling successfully with temptations the most powerful that ever beset humanity, and preserving untainted honor in situations where the austerest Virtue would have forgiven a fall – Situations that I will dare to say, not a single individual of all his kind, even with half his sensibility and passion, could have encountered without ruin; and I leave you to guess, Madam, how such a man is likely to digest an accusation of perfidious treachery!
>
> Was I to blame, Madam, in being the distracted victim of Charms which, I affirm it, no man ever approached with impunity? – Had I seen the least glimmering of hope that these Charms could ever have been mine – or even had not iron Necessity – but these are unavailing words.–
>
> I would have called on you when I was in town, indeed I could not have resisted it, but that Mr A– told me that you were determined to avoid

your windows while I was in town, lest even a glance of me should occur in the Street.–

When I have regained your good opinion, perhaps I may venture to solicit your friendship: but be that as it may, the first of her Sex I ever knew, shall always be the object of my warmest good wishes.–

But back in June 1788 Ainslie was Robert's chief confidant, to judge by the number of letters – four in the space of two weeks alone – which went from Ellisland to Edinburgh. The last of these, however, did not mull over old friendships so much as deal with a vexatious matter which Ainslie had just raised. It will be remembered that Ainslie had been the bearer of bad news concerning Margaret Cameron in June 1787; now he had to inform Robert that Jenny Clow – Nancy's maid-servant no less – was pregnant. Ainslie had problems of his own, not the least being the sudden death of Samuel Mitchelson to whom he was apprenticed. Mitchelson's death, however, did not prove disadvantageous as Ainslie was appointed a Writer to the Signet a few months later, at the astonishingly early age of twenty-two.

Robert began his reply to Ainslie's brief epistle in a flippant manner, paying out his laziness by taking a long sheet of writing paper '& begun at the top of the page, intending to scribble on to the very last corner'. But then he turned serious, to the matter in hand:

I am vexed at that affair of the girl, but dare not enlarge on the subject until you send me your direction, as I suppose that will be altered on your late Master and Friend's death.

And he went off at a tangent to philosophise about man being at the mercy of 'such a whoreson, hungry, growling, multiplying Pack of Necessities, Appetites, Passions & Desires'. Then he changed the subject completely, dealing with a petty matter of a silhouette by Miers of young Hamilton of Bangour which Robert was duped into paying for. This matter, entailing a few paltry shillings, annoyed and irritated him far more than poor Jenny's predicament. He concluded this very long letter with a postscript about the map of Scotland then being published by Bob's kinsman, the land-surveyor John Ainslie: 'If you are in the shop, please ask after the progress; and when published, secure me one of the earliest Impressions of the Plate'.

We look in vain for further references to Jenny Clow in Robert's correspondence with Ainslie. Of course, there may have been a letter, or letters, no longer extant which might have shed some light on the subject. But it appears that Jenny, having relieved the poet's unassuaged passion for Clarinda the previous February, was now in an unfortunate condition. By the end of June, when Ainslie had written, Jenny would have been about eighteen weeks pregnant. What precisely was meant by 'the affair of the girl' is not known, for Ainslie, like Clarinda, took good care to retrieve his letters years later; unlike Clarinda, Bob promptly destroyed *all* of his. We can only speculate that, even if her condition were not yet readily apparent, Jenny would have confided her predicament to Nancy and she, in turn, would have communicated the problem – and doubtless her own sense of outrage – to Ainslie. For aught we know, good Mr Ainslie may even have acted for the girl in the matter of the writ *in meditatione fugae* which she took out against Robert later that year. In November Jenny gave birth to a son who, according to the custom of the time, automatically took his father's names. On 6 January 1789 Robert wrote to Ainslie (CL 336-7) congratulating him on becoming a Writer to the Signet and enclosing the words of 'Robin, Shure in Hairst' (CW 348), a sly dig at Ainslie's own sexual peccadilloes. Robert followed this with a paragraph dealing with matters then hanging over his head:

> I shall be in town in about four or five weeks, & I must again trouble you to find & secure for me a direction where to find Jenny Clow, for a main part of my business in Edinburgh is to settle that matter with her, & free her hand of the process.

Sadly, this matter had no happy ending. Nearly three years later, in November 1791, Mrs McLehose wrote to Robert at Dumfries informing him that Jenny

> to all appearances is at this moment dying. Obliged, from all the symptoms of a rapid decay, to quit her service, she is gone to a room almost without common necessaries, untended and unmourned. In circumstances so distressing, to whom can she so naturally look for aid as to the father of her child, the man for whose sake she suffered many a sad and anxious night, shut from the world, with no other companions than guilt and solitude? You have now an opportunity to evince you indeed possess these fine feelings you have delineated, so as to claim that just admiration of your country. I am convinced I need add nothing further to persuade you to act as every consideration of humanity, as well as gratitude, must dictate. I am, Sir, your sincere well-wisher,
>
> A. M.

One can just imagine the relish with which Nancy reminded Robert of what he had done. Robert replied immediately (CL 407-8). Even at a time like this, he could not prevent himself flirting with her:

> It is extremely difficult, my dear Madam, for me to deny a lady anything; but to a lady whom I regard with all the endearing epithets of respectful esteem and old friendship, how shall I find the language of refusal? I have, indeed, a shade of the lady, which I keep, and shall ever keep, in the *sanctum sanctorum* of my most anxious care. That lady, through an unfortunate and irresistible conjuncture of circumstances has lost me her esteem, yet she shall be ever to me 'Dear as the ruddy drops that warm my heart.'[13]

In the ensuing paragraphs he took up Nancy's curiously formal habit of writing in the third person, giving as good as he got. It is almost as if he were addressing Nancy as two separate personalities, mixing the second and third person pronouns:

> By the way, I have this moment a letter from her, with a paragraph or two conceived in so stately a style, that I would not pardon it in any created being except herself; but, as the subject interests me much, I shall answer it to you, as I do not know her present address. I am sure she must have told you of a girl, a Jenny Clow, who had the misfortune to make me a father, with contrition I own it, contrary to the laws of our most excellent constitution, in our holy Presbyterian hierarchy.
>
> Mrs M- tells me a tale of the poor girl's distress that makes my very heart weep blood. I will trust that your goodness will apologise to your delicacy for me, when I beg you, for Heaven's sake, to send a porter to the poor woman - Mrs M., it seems, knows where she is to be found - with five shillings in my name; and, as I shall be in Edinburgh on Tuesday first, for certain, make the poor wench leave a line for me, before Tuesday, at Mr Mackay's White Hart Inn, Grassmarket, where I shall put up; and before I am two hours in town, I shall see the poor girl, and try what is to be done for her relief. I would have taken my boy from her long ago, but she would never consent.

Jenny Clow, by now far gone in tuberculosis, died in January 1792.[14] Why Robert made no attempt at that time to reclaim his son, now aged three, is not known; and the subject never again occurred in his correspondence.

All previous biographies are silent on the subject, but Jenny's little son Robert Burns survived, became a prosperous merchant and married well.[15] It seems strange that he should never have made any attempt to capitalise on his connection with Scotland's national poet, but no doubt bitter memories of poverty and deprivation in his childhood were contributory factors. Later, however, his views seem to have mellowed, for he named his own elder son Robert and told him who his grandfather was.[16] Robert Burns III, born in 1820, was educated at Gerrit van de Linde's boarding-school in Islington[17] and about 1840 went out to the East Indies. He discovered extensive deposits of antimony and coal in North Borneo and wrote an account of his travels there. He inherited his grandfather's detestation of tyranny and injustice and returned to Britain in 1849 to present evidence of atrocities by Sir James Brooke, the white rajah of Sarawak, to Joseph Hume and other MPs who raised the matter in Parliament.[18] As a result, a Royal Commission was established at Singapore to enquire into the matter. Although the verdict was 'not proven' Brooke was deprived of his post as governor of the crown colony of Labuan. Burns resided at Darvel Bay on the north-east coast of Borneo where he had married the daughter of a Kayan chief. On 12 September 1851 his schooner *Dolphin* was captured off Maludu Bay by pirates and Burns, his partner Robertson and five of their crew were murdered. The pirates, however, were themselves apprehended at Labuk a short time afterwards and paid the supreme penalty on the orders of Sherif Yassin. The following January vessels of the Royal Navy and the East India Company took part in a punitive expedition against the pirates of Illanun and destroyed the village of Raja Muda by way of reprisal.[19] Descendants of the poet, through Robert Burns III, are believed to live in Sabah to this day.

Back in the summer of 1788, however, Robert continued to commute between Ellisland and Mauchline, spending a week or ten days in each place. From Mauchline on 26 June Robert confided to James Smith (CL 122):

> I have waited on Mr Auld about my Marriage affair, & stated that I was legally fined for an irregular marriage by a Justice of the Peace.– He says, if I bring an attestation of this by the two witnesses, there shall be no more litigation about it.– As soon as this comes to hand, please write me in the way of familiar Epistle that, 'Such things are.'–

The first two sentences, on their own, would seem to lend weight to the belief that Robert and Jean had been married by John Farquhar-Gray in the presence of Gavin Hamilton and at least one other; but the furtive manner in which Robert gradually let the fact of his marriage leak out belies this. Snyder[20] was sceptical of such a marriage having actually taken place and took the view that in his interview with Daddy Auld, Robert had invented a 'pious fiction'. When Mr Auld demanded proof of the irregular marriage – a receipt for the money paid by way of a fine, for example – Robert was nonplussed, hence the appeal to an old friend, now living far from Mauchline, to back him up. Whether Smith perjured himself to order is not known, and there seems to have been no further correspondence between him and the poet. Subsequent events seem to demonstrate that Auld did not believe Robert's story, but found a pragmatic solution. The annual communion was due to be held on 10 August that year, but five days earlier the Kirk Session met to consider the matter. Andrew Noble, the Session clerk recorded:

> Compeared Robert Burns with Jean Armour his alledged Spouse. They both acknowledged their irregular marriage, and their Sorrow for that irregularity, and desiring that the Session will take such steps as may seem to them proper, in order to the solemn confirmation of said marriage.
> The Session, taking this affair under their consideration, agree that they both be rebuked for their acknowledged irregularity, and that they be taken solemnly engaged to adhere faithfully to one another as husband and wife all the days of their life.
> In regard the Session have a tittle (sic) in Law to some fine for behoof of the Poor, they agree to refer to Mr. Burns his own generosity.
> The above sentence was accordingly executed, and the Session absolved the said parties from any scandal on this acct.
> William Auld, modr. Robt. Burns Jean Armour
> Mr. Burns gave a guinea note for behoof of the poor.[21]

Not content with recording the rebuke in the Session minutes, the Session clerk also inserted an entry in the parish register of marriages:

Burns, Robert, in Mossgiel and Jean Armour in Machlin came before the Session upon 5 Augt. and Acknowledged that they were irregularly married some Years ago. The Session rebuked both parties for their irregularity and took them solemnly bound to adhere to one another as Husband & Wife all the days of their life.[22]

That evening Burns wrote to Robert McIndoe, a Glasgow silk-merchant in Horn's Land off Virginia Street (CL 476). Robert had previously purchased from him the silk for the gowns and petticoats made for his mother and sisters. Now he ordered fifteen yards of the finest black lutestring silk for Jean. Robert had been celebrating his ecclesiastical marriage, or rather the Holy Fair of which it had formed a minor part, and confessed that he was unable to write in a straight line. On receipt of the silk, however, he promised the money 'and a more coherent letter', adding, 'I shall choose, some sober morning before breakfast, and write you a sober answer, with the sober sum which will then be due from, dear Sir, fu' or fasting, yours sincerely, Robt. Burns'. A memorandum on this letter stated that the price of the silk was 5s 6d or 5s 9d a yard, which means that Robert expended £4 2s 6d or £4 6s 3d – more than six months' wages of a farm-worker – on this 'wedding present'.

Local tradition maintains that Jean continued to reside in Mackenzie's house in the Back Causeway for several months, but that she went out to Mossgiel each day to learn the duties of a farmer's wife and the skills of looking after the dairy side of the business. This tradition, however, has no verifiable facts. One would have thought that Jean would either have been reconciled with her parents, once the cause of their anger and anguish was removed, or have moved into Mossgiel where her sole surviving child, Robert Junior, had been living for more than eighteen months. In support of the Back Causeway story, however, there remains only the testimony of Jacobina Hamilton and the story of Robert Aiken's boiled egg. On the other hand, one can imagine that Jean and Robert liked the privacy of their own apartment, away from both the Armours and the extended family at Mossgiel. Nevertheless, with Robert away much of the time, Jean must have found the little apartment lonely. One would have expected that she would have resumed the care of her son Bobbie by this time but he appears to have remained with his half-sister Bess and his aunts and uncles at Mossgiel. Indeed, when Jean eventually moved south to Ellisland, little Bobbie was left behind at Mossgiel for some time.

From Ellisland Robert wrote to his new friend William Stewart one Wednesday evening in July enclosing a number of ribald songs. These eventually appeared in *The Merry Muses*, published clandestinely by an unknown hand little more than three years after Robert's death. In this instance, however, the songs were not of Burns's composition, as he explained in the letter (CL 444-5). 'The Plenipotentiary' was the work of a Captain Morris who published his *Songs Drinking, Political and Facetious* in 1790, while 'The Bower of Bliss' was composed by a Reverend Doctor of the Church of Scotland – Would to Heaven a few more of them would turn their fiery Zeal *that way*. There they might *spend* their Holy fury, and shew the *tree* by its *fruits*!!!²³ There, the *in-bearing workings* might give hopeful presages of a *New-birth*!!!!

Robert concluded, 'I have no copies left of either, so must have the precious pieces again'. This appears to be the earliest reference to his specific interest in bawdy ballads, which he was collecting as a separate group from the fragments of traditional songs which he was mending for James Johnson.

A letter erroneously dated 10 August but bearing the Bishop postmark of 17 July (applied in transit through Edinburgh to Haddington) informed Mrs Dunlop (CL 148–50):

> Yours of the 24th June is before me.– I found it, as well as another valued friend – MY WIFE – waiting to welcome me to Ayrshire. I met both with the sincerest pleasure.

Robert, having previously admitted to being married, now fully unbosomed himself. 'Mrs Burns,' he confessed, 'is the identical woman who was the mother of twice twins to me in seventeen months . . .' He then gave her a detailed account – from his viewpoint, of course – of the circumstances which preceded his recognition of Jean as his wife:

> When she first found herself – 'As women wish to be who love their lords,'²⁴ as I lov'd her near to distraction, I took some previous steps to a private marriage.– Her Parents got the hint; and in detestation of my guilt of being a poor devil, not only forbade me her company & their house, but on my rumoured West Indian voyage, got a warrant to incarcerate me in jail till I should find security in my about-to-be Paternal relation.– You know my lucky reverse of fortune.– On my eclatant return to Mauchline, I was made very welcome to visit my girl.– The usual consequences began to betray her; and as I was at that time laid up a cripple in Edinr, she was turned, literally out of doors, and I wrote to a friend to shelter her, till my return.– I was not under the least verbal obligation to her, but her happiness or misery were in my hands, and who could trifle with such a deposite? – To the least temptation to Jealousy or Infidelity, I am an equal stranger.– My preservative from the first, is the most thorough consciousness of her sentiments of honour, and her attachment to me; my antidote against the last, is my long & deep-rooted affection for her.

He went on to weigh up the pros and cons of marriage compared with continuing bachelorhood. Jean was an excellent housewife and a quick learner and he was pleased to point out that 'during my absence in Nithsdale, she is regularly & constantly apprentice to my Mother & Sisters in their dairy & other rural business'.

> In short, I can easily *fancy* a more agreable companion for my journey of Life, but, upon my honor, I have never *seen* the individual Instance!– You

are right that a Bachelor state would have ensured me more friends; but from a cause you will easily guess, conscious Peace in the enjoyment of my own mind, and unmistrusting Confidence in approaching my God, would seldom have been of the number.

Robert need not have worried at Mrs Dunlop's reaction. When she answered this letter on 22 July she sent him a 'luckpenny . . . as a pledge of future good-will to the contracted pair' in the form of a bank-draft for five pounds. Robert, very sensitive about the slightest suspicion of being patronised by the gentry, wrote back on 2 August (CL 150) rather ungraciously, 'I am indeed seriously angry with you at the Quantum of your Luckpenny'. To the end of his life, acts of kindness and generosity brought out the stiff awkwardness in him. A very generous man himself, with his time, his talents and even his money when he had some, Robert was never happy when he himself was on the receiving end. It offended that sense of manly independence in which he took such an inordinate pride.

One other letter from this period is of interest for the light it sheds on Robert's strange and sometimes tragic domestic situation during this turbulent time of his life. On 27 July he wrote to Alexander Cunningham from Ellisland (CL 455). Again he announced his marriage in terms of 'a much-lov'd Female's positive happiness, or absolute Misery among my hands' – obviously this was a turn of phrase with which he was particularly happy – but he then went on to make the only reference, albeit an indirect, negative one, to the twins who had died in March:

> When I tell you that Mrs Burns was once, *my Jean*, you will know the rest.– Of four children she bore me, in seventeen months, my eldest boy is only living.– By the bye, I intend breeding him up for the Church; and from an innate dexterity in secret Mischief which he posses (*sic*), & a certain hypocritical gravity as he looks on the consequences, I have no small hopes of him in the sacerdotal line.

In this letter he mentioned 'Mrs Burns does not come from Ayr-shire, till my said new house be ready'. At this period Robert lodged with David and Agnes Cullie. Their cottage, at the southern extremity of the farm where it was virtually in the shadow of the Isle Tower, was a poor hovel, run-down and sadly in need of repair, like the farm in general. The Isle Tower took its name from the piece of land looped by the Nith almost to form an island. The tower, an ancient stronghold of the Fergussons, was erected in 1587 but was in a ruinous state by 1788. It adjoined a farmhouse (the site of the present mansion which was erected in 1882) which was then used as a summer residence by David Newall, a Dumfries lawyer and property developer who also acted as factor to the Isle and Steelston estates.

Robert's temporary host, David Cullie, was an ardent member of the Anti-Burgher Congregation of Loreburn Church in Dumfries, and it was in this humble cottage that Burns first met the Revd. William Inglis for whom he had such a high regard. Inglis was accustomed to visit Cullie's house to hold the pre-Communion catechism, and this was followed by a dinner at which Robert, and later Jean Armour, were frequently among the guests. Jean's *Memoir* contains some interesting details of this period:

> Before this time Burns had written the 'Holy Fair' and an impression had gone abroad that he was rather a scoffer or a freethinker. David Cullie and his wife were aware of this; and although they treated him civilly as the incoming tenant, during the five months he resided under their roof, still they felt for him as for one who was by no means on the right path. On one occasion Nance and the bard were sitting in the spence, when the former turned the conversation on her favourite topic, religion. Mr Burns, from whatever motive, sympathised with the matron, and quoted so much Scripture that she was fairly astonished. When she went ben she said to her husband, 'Oh! David Cullie, how they have wranged that man; for I think he has mair o the Bible off his tongue than Mr Inglis himsel'. The bard enjoyed the compliment . . .[25]

Part of the agreement regarding Robert's tenancy was that he was to pay David Cullie for the crops harvested at the end of the first season. A receipt in Robert's handwriting, dated at Ellisland on 19 November 1788 and signed by David Cullie, reads:

> Received from Robert Burns in Ellisland the sum of thirty-six pounds, one shilling and sixpence sterling, being the first half of the sum he owes me for the crop he bought of me in Ellisland farm of this year's growth in terms of bargain.[26]

All the time that Robert was commuting between Mauchline and Ellisland, he continued to work on the songs for the third volume of Johnson's *Museum*. On 28 July he wrote from Ellisland (CL 294) enclosing 'another cargo of Songs'. Robert's editorial work was discussed: 'I have still a good number of Dr Blacklock's Songs among my hands but they take sad hacking & hewing'. Robert also mentioned another consignment of songs which he had sent some weeks previously but which Johnson had not acknowledged. 'I am in hopes that I shall pick some fine tune from among the Collection of Highland airs which I got from you at Edinburgh', he continued, adding that he had had 'an able fiddler' already working two days on it. 'I have got one most beautiful air out of it, that sings to the measure of Lochaber.– I shall try to give it my very best words.' A letter written from Mauchline at the end of August was entirely devoted to matters arising out of various songs and melodies, showing Robert at his most brisk and workmanlike, and in another, from Mauchline on 15 November (CL 295) Robert exhorted Johnson to carry on with the good work. By now the third volume was well advanced and Robert promised that he was preparing 'a flaming Preface' for it. He assured Johnson that the quality of his work would endure:

I see every day, new Musical Publications, advertised; but what are they? Gaudy, hunted butterflies of a day, & then vanish for ever; but your Work will outlive the momentary neglects of idle Fashion, & defy the teeth of Time.

Though meant for Johnson, Robert probably addressed those same last words to himself often enough.

Although Robert claimed to have little time for fresh poetic composition, he made incredibly good use of the time spent in the saddle. As he jogged along the rough country road that wound through the Cumnock Hills between Ayrshire and Dumfriesshire he would hum over a Scottish melody and fit words to it. Many a song was composed in this manner; with the rough draft firmly in his head, Robert would then refine and polish it later, working far into the night to produce yet another timeless gem of Scottish song. While the bulk of his output in this period – and, indeed, right on to the end of his short life – consisted of songs, he did not entirely neglect works which were meant to be read or recited. Within days of entering his farm Robert penned a long verse-epistle to Hugh Parker (CW 322-3), complaining of the uncouth clime and the peat-smoke in the hut where he lodged:

> The red peat gleams, a fiery kernel
> Enhusked by a fog infernal.

During August 1788, when he was still trying to get settled on his farm, Robert had to cope with two matters which must have given him a certain amount of heartache. The first concerned his younger brother William, now aged twenty-one. Intelligent and personable but gentle and diffident, William had more than his fair share of the aimlessness that Robert had detected in himself. Although he had served his apprenticeship as a saddler, he had the greatest difficulty in getting work and Robert was acutely disappointed in his attempts at this time to find a situation for him in Edinburgh. Eventually William moved in with his brother and sister-in-law and lodged at Ellisland for several months until he obtained saddlery work at Longtown near Carlisle, before moving to Newcastle-upon-Tyne where he worked for Messrs Walker and Robson. On completing his apprenticeship he became a journeyman saddler with William Barber in the Strand, London. Poor William had only been in the metropolis a few months when he succumbed to 'a putrid fever' and died on 24 July 1790. The ten letters extant from the poet to his younger brother, written between 2 March 1789 and 16 July 1790 (CL 514-19), reveal an endearing side of his nature. Although only eight years older than William, Robert was something of a father-figure to him. The letters are full of good advice, although he only imparted the more elaborately sententious aspects when William specifically sought them. Robert's advice to William concerning falling in love (CL 516), however, was ruefully self-revealing.

431

Ainslie, whom Robert hoped would be able to fix up the young man with a job, was involved in the other matter which caused a great deal of upset in the late summer of 1788. Robert's friendship with William Nicol had been a source of irritation to Nancy. She had no time for the irascible dominie at all and was very quick to pass on malicious gossip about him to Robert. Only half believing these stories, and suspecting that their source was Dr Alexander Adam, rector of the High School, Robert had repeated one of these tales to Cruikshank, referring to his informant only as a lady of his acquaintance. Cruikshank had repeated the slander back to Nicol and the matter might have rested there (Cruikshank having no more liking for the rector than Nicol), had not a fresh quarrel erupted between Adam and Nicol which led to litigation. Nicol demanded to know the identity of Burns's informant, but he refused to divulge this. Robert recounted the sorry business to Ainslie in a letter of 23 August (CL 335–6):

> last post Mr N– acquaints me, but in very good natured terms, that if I persist in my refusal, I am to be served with a summonds (*sic*) to compear & declare the fact.

Robert wrote to Nicol saying that he 'would not give up his female friend till farther consideration' but had instructed Ainslie to call on him and discuss the matter, with or without disclosure of Nancy's name as he and she should decide. Neither the letter to Nicol, nor one to Nancy formally putting her in the picture, has survived. As Robert heard no more about this vexatious matter it is assumed that Ainslie exercised his diplomatic skills with Nancy and Nicol and persuaded the latter to back down.

It might have been supposed that all the rushing back and forwards between Ayrshire and Dumfriesshire, the hard work on the farm and the building of the farmhouse, not to mention preoccupation about his brother and disagreement among his friends, would have left Robert with no time for socialising; but he was at heart a very social being. Within two weeks he had met, or been introduced to, Robert Riddell of Glenriddell, who owned Friars' Carse, the adjoining estate to the north. It has been suggested that Robert was introduced to Riddell by Patrick Miller himself, but there is no actual record of this. Riddell, four years the poet's senior, was not untypical of the country gentlemen of the period. Born in the locality, he had been educated at Dumfries (where James Currie, the future biographer of Burns, was a classmate) and the universities of St Andrews and Edinburgh. Commissioned into the Scots Greys, he became a captain in the Eighty-third Regiment and retired on half pay at the end of the American War. Friars' Carse, as its name suggests, was originally a monastic foundation, under Melrose Abbey, secularised at the Reformation and later forming part of the estate of Glenriddell. Walter Riddell of Newhouse, grandfather of Robert, had married his cousin Anne, the heiress of Glenriddell, and thus acquired the estate. Captain Riddell inherited the estate on the death of his father in 1788. He sold the bulk of it but retained the territorial title, and continued to live at Friars' Carse, a pleasant red sandstone mansion on an eminence overlooking a bend in the river.

An enthusiastic amateur musician and composer of some talent, Robert Riddell was just the man who would be immediately drawn to Burns through a shared interest in Scottish song. About three years earlier, Riddell had compiled a volume of music *for the Piano Forte or Harpsichord composed by a Gentleman Consisting of a Collection of Reels, Minuets, Hornpipes, Marches and two Songs in the Old Scotch Taste, with Variations to Five Favourite Tunes*. The publisher was none other than James Johnson, and it may be that he, rather than Patrick Miller, was the means of bringing Burns and Riddell together. Robert used several of Riddell's airs for the songs he wrote for the *Museum*. Whatever the circumstances of their first meeting, Riddell made Burns very welcome. He was also a keen antiquary whose enthusiasm occasionally outran his scientific approach to the subject, inducing him to create a fake Druids' circle and a hermitage, after the manner of the cell of a medieval anchorite. This folly, situated among the woods at the southern end of his estate, was close to the boundary of Ellisland farm. Riddell gave the poet a key to this little summer-house so that he could meditate therein whenever the mood took him. By 28 June 1788 this had yielded its first fruits, 'Verses in Friars' Carse Hermitage' (CW 324). A substantially longer version (CW 325-6) was composed several months later. These poems were but the first of several inspired by the friendship between Burns and Riddell.

Robert returned to the genre of longer poems with a strong local flavour in 'The Fête Champêtre' (CW 326-7), ostensibly about the supper and ball given by William Cunninghame to celebrate inheriting the family estate of Annbank and Enterkin. The dissolution of Parliament was imminent and it was suspected that young Cunninghame was using this celebration to canvass votes. In the event, however, he stood down. Nevertheless, the occasion provided Robert with his first opportunity to compose an electioneering ballad. A copy of this long poem was sent to John Ballantine with a relatively short letter (CL 103). Interestingly, Robert apologised: 'A bruised finger hindered me from transcribing my Poem myself; so I am oblidged to send you the inclosed, rather incorrect one'. Normally Robert transcribed his poems himself, a task which he delighted in, and over which he usually took infinite pains. Biographers who point to the amount of poetry which Robert composed right down to the end of his life, and the volume and complexity of the letters he wrote, tend to overlook the fact that these letters were often accompanied by handwritten copies of the latest poetic compositions. When one considers the sheer scale of this labour of love alone – in some cases as many as seven or eight transcripts in the poet's holograph are known of particular poems – one wonders where Burns could ever have found the time for the drinking and dissipation at which his early biographers hinted.

By early autumn Robert was busy superintending his first harvest at Ellisland, as he confessed to John Beugo in a letter of 9 September (CL 368-9), but for all that most pleasurable part of Life called, Social Communication, I am here at the very elbow of Existence.- The only things that are to be found in this country, in any degree of perfection, are Stupidity & Canting.- Prose, they only know in Grace, Prayers, &c. and the value of these they estimate as they do their plaiding webs – by the Ell; as for the Muses, they have as much idea of a Rhinoceros as of a Poet.

Burns the poet had been briefly the sensation of the 1786–7 Edinburgh season; here in Nithsdale Robert was judged solely on his merits as a farmer. His remarks about his country neighbours were hardly accurate or fair, for Robert Riddell must have become a congenial companion by that time, and it is more likely that he had the extremely Whiggish parish minister, Joseph Kirkpatrick, in his mind as he wrote this. It was perhaps more true that Robert had not yet settled in his new surroundings, and the rhyming mania was only really upon him when he was back in Ayrshire with his 'darling Jean'

then I, at *lucid intervals*, throw my horny fist across my be-cobwebbed Lyre, much in the same manner as an old wife throws her hand across the spokes of her Spinning wheel.

With all the zeal of the recently converted, Robert extolled the merits of the wedded state:

Depend upon it, if you do not make some damned foolish choice it will be a very great improvement on the Dish of Life. – I can speak from Experience; tho' God knows, my choice was as random as Blind-man's-buff.- I like the idea of an honest country Rake of my acquaintance, who, like myself, married lately.- Speaking to me of his late Step: 'L–d, man,' says he, 'a body's baith cheaper and better sair't!'

By the time the meagre harvest was in, Robert took stock of his situation. It was beginning to dawn on him that Ellisland would require a great deal of hard work before it became profitable, if even then. Now he swung back to his alternative of the Excise. On 10 September he wrote to Robert Graham of Fintry (CL 425–6). The system was that once a candidate had received his commission he went on the Expectants' List to await an appointment whenever a position fell vacant. This process was strictly in order of seniority and could take months if not years. Now Burns sought not only to speed up the process but to wangle an appointment in his own district; both steps were highly irregular and Robert exerted all his skills in prose and poetry to pull strings. What he proposed was quite outrageous. The present encumbent, Leonard Smith, was to be ousted to make way for Robert, so that he would have the convenience of combining the Excise job with his farm. He reasoned that:

as the gentleman, owing to some legacies, is quite opulent, a removal could do him no manner of injury; and on a month's warning, to give me a little time to look again over my Instructions, I would not be afraid to enter on business . . . It would suit me to enter on it, beginning of next Summer; but I shall be in Edinr to wait upon you about the affair, sometime in the ensuing winter.

The *hardiesse* of this rather unscrupulous letter was mitigated by the inclusion of the verse-epistle beginning 'When Nature her great masterpiece designed' (CW 330–3), an absurd piece of poetic flattery, given the fact that Burns and Graham were, as yet, but slightly acquainted, with the incongruous threat of an independent posture thrown in for good measure. In particular, I find these lines unpalatable:

> Why shrinks my soul, half-blushing, half-afraid,
> Backward abash'd to ask thy friendly aid?
> I know my need, I know thy giving hand,
> I tax thy friendship at thy kind command.

That both the letter and the verse-epistle cost Robert a considerable amount of thought and effort is borne out in a reference he made to having written 'my long-thought-on letter to Mr Graham', in one of the few letters he ever wrote to Jean Armour (CL 478). He obviously considered the verse-epistle a fine piece of work and sent a draft of it to Mrs Dunlop as early as 2 August (CL 151), despatching the final version to her on 5 September – five days before he sent it to Graham himself. He later sent copies to William Dunbar, Dr Moore, Dugald Stewart, Lady Elizabeth Cunningham and Henry Erskine.[27]

Graham replied on 14 September in terms of kindness mingled with politeness. Because of the harvest, compounded by an attack of influenza, Robert did not get to Dumfries to collect his mail till 22 September and wrote to Graham the following day (CL 427–8). After thanking his new benefactor most effusively for his 'friendly assurances of patronage and protection' he got to the heart of the matter. Regarding his wish for an Excise division the following summer, he wondered whether,

> as I am only a little more than five miles from Dumfries, I might perhaps officiate there, if any of these Officers could be removed with more propriety than Mr Smith; but besides the monstrous inconvenience of it to me, I could not bear to injure a poor fellow by ousting him to make way for myself: to a wealthy Son of good-fortune like Smith, the injury is imaginery, where the propriety of your rules admit.

Ironically, more than a year was to elapse before Robert's wishes were fulfilled. Any notion that Burns was somehow dragooned into the Excise ought to be dispelled by this time factor alone, but well-meaning friends, from Miller of Dalswinton to Mrs Dunlop herself, urged Robert to stick to farming. This view was very generally held, as a paragraph in the *Edinburgh Advertiser* of 28 November 1788 bears out:

Burns, the *Ayrshire Bard*, is now enjoying the sweets of retirement at his farm. Burns, in thus retiring, has acted wisely. Stephen Duck, the *Poetical Thresher*, by his ill-advised patrons, was made a parson. The poor man, hurried out of his proper element, found himself quite unhappy; became insane; and with his own hands, it is said, ended his life. Burns, with propriety, has resumed his *flail* – but we hope he has not thrown away the *quill*.

Increasingly, however, Robert regarded the Excise commission in his pocket as a guarantee of security and peace of mind, as the ruinous bargain of his farming venture became more and more apparent. There are numerous references to this in his letters in the ensuing months.[28] To Dr Moore, on 4 January 1789 (CL 258), he confided his ambitions:

If I were very sanguine, I might hope that some of my Great Patrons might procure me a Treasury warrant for Supervisor, Surveyor-General, &c. If farming will not do, a simple petition will get me into employ in the Excise somewhere; & poor as the salary comparatively is, it is luxury to what either my wife or I were in early life taught to expect.– Thus, secure of a livelihood, 'to thee sweet Poetry, delightful maid,' I consecrate my future days.

To the latter part of 1788 belong two of the four extant letters from Robert to his wife. Addressed to 'My dear Love' or 'My dearest Love', they were written in tender but simple terms from Ellisland at a time when Robert was expecting to come up to Mauchline to bring her back to the farm. The first one, dated 12 September (CL 477–8) began:

I received your kind letter with a pleasure which no letter but one from you could have given me.– I dreamed of you the whole night last; but alas! I fear it will be three weeks yet, ere I can hope for the happiness of seeing you.– My harvest is going on.– I have some to cut down still, but I put in two stacks today, so I am as tired as a dog.

Agnes Cullie was obliquely referred to in this letter. 'I have just consulted my old Landlady about table-linen and she thinks I may have the best for two shillings per yard'. Jean was now making preparations for the imminent move to Ellisland.

A month passed, however, before Robert was ready to receive his wife. On Tuesday 14 October (CL 478) he wrote telling Jean not to come the following Sunday to meet him on the road, as he was engaged to dine that day with John Logan of Laight, a close friend of Gavin Hamilton who introduced him to the poet. From this we may assume that Jean had been in the habit of walking south along the road to Catrine and Auchinleck to meet her husband on his return from Dumfriesshire. Then Robert would help her up to ride pillion behind him back to Mauchline. Although work on their farmhouse had been delayed, Robert had some good news:

You must get ready for Nithsdale as fast as possible, for I have the offer of a house in the very neibourhood with some furniture in it, all of which I shall have the use of for nothing till my own house be got ready; and I am determined to remove you from Ayrshire immediately, as I am a sufferer by not being on the farm myself.– We will need a Maid servant, of consequence: if you can hear of any to hire, ask after them.– The apples are all sold & gone.– I am extremely happy at the idea of your coming to Nithsdale, as it will save us from these cruel separations.– The house is one in which a Mr Newal lived during the summer, who is gone to Dumfries in Winter.– It is a large house, but we will only occupy a room or two of it.

How this happy arrangement came about is not known; but Burns and David Newall were close friends during the poet's years in Dumfries and Robert was a frequent guest at the lawyer's town house, Bushybank, where his daughter Catherine would play old Scottish airs on the piano for Robert's delectation. They may have been introduced by Robert Riddell or Patrick Miller; at any rate, David Newall became an intimate friend of the poet very early in his Dumfriesshire period. Interestingly, the letter quoted above was written on the very day on which the poet's landlord was making his historic contribution to the Steam Age. A popular belief is that Burns himself was a passenger on the maiden voyage of Miller's steamboat, but the various eye-witness accounts merely state that Robert, accompanied by Sandy Crombie, the stonemason who was building Ellisland farmhouse at the time, downed tools, crossed the Nith and went to watch the fun from the banks of Dalswinton Loch.[29] Had Robert actually been on the deck of this, the world's first steam-propelled boat, he would certainly have mentioned it in his correspondence, and might even have composed an ode suitable to the occasion. Sadly, he did neither, and lost the opportunity to herald the era of steam navigation in elegiac form.

From this letter it is obvious that Robert planned to go up to Mauchline on Sunday 19 October to collect Jean, but her move to Ellisland was unaccountably delayed for several more weeks. Robert made two further trips to Ayrshire, probably ferrying Jean's goods and chattels, including a splendid four-poster bed, the gift of Mrs Dunlop. From Sanquhar, on his way back from Ayrshire, Robert wrote to his benefactress on 23 October, adding a postscript at Ellisland three days later. From the fact that this letter (CL 157) refers to 'my officious landlady', it appears that Robert was still lodging with Nance and David Cullie, and the letter concluded: 'I believe I shall move, bag & baggage, to Nithsdale at Martinmas. I am getting the loan of a neighbouring house till my own be ready.' Martinmas was 11 November and, indeed, Robert was in Mauchline at that time, for he wrote from there to Mrs Dunlop on 13 November (CL 159). Two days later he wrote to Dr Blacklock (CL 490), 'In a fortnight, I move, bag & baggage to Nithsdale . . .' He continued to commute between Ellisland and Mauchline, as his correspondence testifies. From Sanquhar he wrote to John McMurdo, chamberlain to the Duke of Queensberry at Drumlanrig, on 26 November (CL 492), 'I am just baiting on my way to Ayr-shire'. By

7 December, however, Robert and Jean were definitely settled at the Isle, for on that day Robert wrote to Mrs Dunlop (CL 160–3) one of the longest and bulkiest packets, enclosing a number of songs, poems, epigrams and fragments.

Little Bobbie continued to live with his grandmother at Mossgiel that winter, and was not brought to Ellisland till the following summer. A letter from Gilbert to Robert, written at Mossgiel on 1 January 1789, ended with seasonal greetings from 'Your mother and sisters, with Robert the second'.[30] In fact, the little boy was not reunited with his parents till the middle of August – and then in circumstances which must have been rather traumatic for him.

According to tradition, the week before Jean moved to Ellisland, 'two servant-lads and a servant-girl had come from Mauchline'. If this is true, it implies that Robert had laid off the farm-workers he had employed till Martinmas, as there would have been no need of additional labour at that time of year. There is no doubt that a female servant accompanied Jean. According to Chambers,[31] this girl stated that Jean was anxious, on going to a district where she would be a stranger, to have the services of a girl whom she already knew. She was accordingly engaged; but her father, in his anxiety for her moral welfare, exacted a formal promise from Robert that he would keep a strict watch over her conduct and, in particular, would 'exercise her duly in the Catechism', a promise which she said he had faithfully kept. The girl was seventeen-year-old Elizabeth Smith, a cousin of Jean's (her father Hugh Smith and Jean's mother were brother and sister), and many years later she furnished an account of the ceremony attending the move to the new farmhouse:

> Burns made her take the Family Bible and a bowl of salt, and placing the one upon the other, carry them to the new house, and walk into it before anyone else. This was the old *freit* appropriate to the taking possession of a new house, the object being to secure good-luck for all who should tenant it. He himself, with his wife on his arm, followed the bearer of the Bible and salt, and so entered upon the possession of his home.[32]

Elizabeth was uncertain about the date but it could not have been earlier than mid-April 1789 and was perhaps some weeks later.

Even after Jean moved to Ellisland, Robert occasionally rode up to Mauchline to collect various bits and pieces for his new household. It was on one of these jaunts, early in January 1789, that he put up at Bailie Edward Whigham's, the only tolerable inn in Sanquhar. As he told Moore in a letter of 23 March (CL 259):

> The frost was keen, and the grim evening and howling wind were ushering in a night of snow and drift.– My horse & I were both much fatigued with the labors of the day, and just as my friend the Bailie and I were bidding defiance to the storm over a smoking bowl, in wheels the funeral pageantry of the late great Mrs. Oswald, and poor I, am forced to brave all the horrors of the tempestuous night, and jade my horse, my young favourite

horse whom I had just christened Pegasus, twelve miles farther on, through the wildest moors & hills of Ayrshire, to New Cumnock, the next Inn.

Robert vented his spleen by composing his bitter 'Ode, Sacred to the Memory of Mrs Oswald of Auchencruive' (CW 342-3), a copy of which he despatched to Mrs Dunlop from Mossgiel the following Wednesday (CL 165). Mrs Dunlop tried to put the matter in perpective by responding with the comment, 'Are you not a sad wicked creature to send a poor old wife straight to the Devil, because she gave you a ride in a cold night?'

Earlier in the letter to Moore Robert said of Mrs Oswald that 'I spent my early years in her neighbourhood, and among her servants and tenants I know that she was detested with the most heartfelt cordiality'. Sending the ode to Peter Stuart of the London *Star* that April, Robert commented on the old lady as 'a purse-proud Priestess of Mammon' (CL 522).

During the winter of 1788-9 Robert and Jean lived in the ground-floor rooms in David Newall's house at the Isle while work on the building of the Ellisland farmhouse continued fitfully. According to Allan Cunningham, Robert worked energetically, 'digging foundations, collecting stones, seeking sand, carting lime and even laying on the stones of the house',[33] but it is more likely that he left this work to the contractor's men and concentrated on the farm itself. The design and construction of the farmhouse were superintended by Thomas Boyd (1753-1822), a stonemason, building contractor and architect of Dumfries who is also remembered for erecting the New Bridge over the Nith (1791-4) and the Theatre Royal (1792). The actual building was carried out by Alexander Crombie, stonemason of Dalswinton, who also erected cottages in Dalswinton village and worked on Miller's mansion. Cunningham's story goes that Burns, as an ardent freemason, performed the laying of the foundation stone of the farmhouse according to the proper masonic rites, removing his hat with a flourish and invoking the blessing of Almighty God on his future home.

The farmhouse is described as a single-storey building, but there was access to the loft space which was converted into attics where the domestic and farm-servants were accommodated. In Robert's time the roof was thatched, but in the nineteenth century this was replaced by slates. The ground floor contained five apartments arranged in the form of a letter T. The farmhouse had a parlour on the east, looking down upon the Nith, a west room known as the spence, where distinguished guests would dine with the poet, a kitchen and a bedroom lying between, and a garret. The well from which Jean drew the water lay below the bank beyond the house and close to the river. The kitchen garden was enclosed by a stone wall, at the far corner of which was the privy, still extant. A granary, stackyard, byre (cowshed) and stable were behind the dwelling-house.

It is commonly, though erroneously, believed that the present farmhouse is the identical cottage built in 1788-9, but this is not the case. In the first place, the present building is much more commodious than could have been provided for the £300 allowed by Patrick Miller. Secondly, there is

439

the testimony of James Grierson of Dalgoner (who lived less than five miles from Ellisland and knew Burns intimately) that Burns's residence was demolished in 1812 and the house subsequently rebuilt.[34] A detailed study of the structure itself, however, reveals that that portion of the building containing the kitchen and the parlour appears to be original. The kitchen ceiling still has the meat-hooks on which Jean Armour smoked her hams, and the Carron range which Burns installed for his young bride – the latest in culinary technology two centuries ago – is doing good service even yet. The light and airy parlour, with windows on two sides, was used by Burns as an office and study, and it was here that he would laboriously write up his Excise reports and accounts, as well as transcribe his poetic compositions. How much of this room is original and how much dates after 1812 is a matter for conjecture. The original stonework can still be discerned in the south-eastern corner, but the pane of glass allegedly engraved with inscriptions by Burns is quite patently not in his hand at all and bears little resemblance to other examples of his handiwork with the diamond stylus; so the window is not contemporary with the poet's residence. Nevertheless, as one stands in the present-day parlour, now serving as a museum of Burns memorabilia, it is easy to imagine Robert there two centuries ago. The parlour occupies the south-eastern end of the building and from the gable window one catches beautiful glimpses of the Nith beyond the tree-shaded path where Robert regularly exercised.

We tend to think that the over-optimism of builder and contractors in regard to the erection of houses is a modern phenomenon, but Burns suffered endless delays at the hands of Boyd and Crombie as his correspondence shows. On 22 January 1789 Robert wrote to Peter Morison, the Mauchline carpenter and cabinetmaker who was making furniture for Ellisland (CL 501):

> Necessity oblidges me to go into my new house, even before it be plaistered.– I will inhabit the one end untill the other be finished.– About three weeks more, I think, will at farthest be my time beyond which I cannot stay in this present house.– If ever you wished to deserve the blessing of him that was ready to perish; if ever you were in a situation that a little kindness would have rescued you from many evils; if ever you hope to find rest in future states of untryed being; get these matters of mine ready.– My servant will be out in the beginning of next week for the Clock.

It would appear that Newall's loan of the Isle had been due to expire about the middle of February; but it was later extended. Three brief letters to Thomas Boyd and a bill connected with the building of Ellisland have survived (CL 513). The first letter, written from 'Isle, Sunday morn' (undated but assigned to 8 February 1789 from internal evidence), reads:

> I see at last, dear Sir, some signs of your executing my house within the current year. I am obliged to set out for Edinburgh tomorrow se'ennight so I beg you will set as many hands to work as possible during this week.

I am distressed with the want of my house in a most provoking manner. It loses me two hours work of my servants every day, besides other inconveniences. For God's sake let me but within the shell of it!

The second letter, also undated from the Isle but assigned to 1 March 1789, is terse, but not without a peculiar touch of humour:

I arrived from Edinburgh yesternight and was a good deal surprised at finding my house still lying like Babylon in the prophecies of Isiah (*sic*). I beg, dear Sir, for humanity's sake, that you will send me out your hands tomorrow, and oblidge.

Isaiah 13: 19-20 reads: 'And Babylon, the glory of kingdoms, the beauty of the Chaldees' excellency, shall be as when God overthrew Sodom and Gomorrah. It shall never be inhabited, neither shall it be dwelt in from generation to generation.' It shows that both Burns and Boyd were thoroughly familiar with the Old Testament. Work on the house, however, proceeded in a leisurely fashion and a further six weeks at least elapsed before it was sufficiently completed for the Burns family to move in. As late as 15 April 1789 (CL 515) Robert was still dating his letters from the Isle, more than ten months after he had begun work on his farm.

The third letter shows that Robert got his revenge on the dilatoriness of his architect by delaying the settlement of his account. Dated 16 June 1791 from Ellisland, it reads:

As it is high time that the account between you and me were settled, if you will take a bill of Mr Alexr Crombie's to me for twenty pounds in part, I will settle with you immediately; at least against Wednesday se'ennight, as I am to be out of the country for a week. Mr Crombie cannot take it amiss that I endeavour to get myself clear of his bill in this manner, as you owe him and I owe you.

Robert had rashly agreed to discount a bill of Crombie's for £20 and was thereby saddled with a debt which he could ill afford. By this ploy, however, he managed to cancel the debt. The bill, dated 6 April 1791, was directed to Alexander Crombie, mason in Dalswinton, and read: 'Sir Three months after date pay to me or my order at the Coffee house in Dumfries the sum of twenty pounds sterling for value received from Robt. Burns'. The bill bears the signatures of Burns, William Lorimer (father of 'Chloris') and Crombie himself.

Robert had to start from scratch with unimproved ground, which he set about liming and clearing of stones. It is thought that he reorganised the old rigs or ploughing ridges into straight fifteen-foot rigs to facilitate drainage through surface run-off. William Clark, who was hired as a ploughman, later furnished Robert Chambers with an interesting account of the half year which he spent in the farmer-poet's service, from Martinmas 1789 till Whitsunday 1790:

Burns kept two men and two women servants; but he invariably, when at home, took his meals with his wife and family in the little parlour. Clark thought he was as good a manager of land as the generality of the farmers of the neighbourhood. The farm of Ellisland was said to be moderately rented, and was susceptible of much improvement, had improvement been in repute. Burns sometimes visited the neighbouring farmers, and they returned the compliment; but that way of spending time and exchanging civilities was not so common then as now, and, besides, the most of the people thereabouts had no expectation that Burns's conduct and writings would be so much noticed afterwards. Burns kept nine or ten milch cows, some young cattle, four horses, and several pet sheep; of the latter he was very fond. During the winter and spring time, when he was not engaged with the Excise business, he occasionally held the plough for an hour or so, and was a fair workman, though the mode of ploughing now-a-days is much superior in many respects. During seed-time, Burns might be frequently seen, at an early hour, in the fields with his sowing-sheet; but as business often required his attention from home, he did not sow the whole of the grain. He was a kind and indulgent master, and spoke familiarly to his servants, both in the house and out of it, though, if anything put him out of humour, he was gey guldersome for a wee while: the storm was soon over, and there was never a word of upcast afterwards. Clark never saw him really angry but once, and it was occasioned by the carelessness of one of the woman-servants who had not cut potatoes small enough, which brought one of the cows into danger of being choked. His looks, gestures, and voice on that occasion were terrible: W.C. was glad to be out of his sight, and when they met again Burns was perfectly calm. If any extra work was to be done, the men sometimes got a dram; but Clark had lived with masters who were more flush in that way to their servants. Clark, during the six months he spent at Ellisland, never once saw his master intoxicated or incapable of managing his own business . . . Burns, when at home, usually wore a broad blue bonnet, a blue or drab long-tailed coat, corduroy breeches, dark-blue stockings and cootikens, and in cold weather a black-and-white-checked plaid wrapped round his shoulders. Mrs Burns was a good and prudent housewife, kept everything in neat and tidy order, was well liked by the servants, for whom she provided abundance of wholesome food. At parting, Burns gave Clark a certificate of character, and, besides paying his wages in full, gave him a shilling for a fairing.[35]

Robert later switched from arable farming to dairying, leaving Jean and the farm servants to cope with the milking and making butter and cheeses while he concentrated on his Excise duties. Robert usually kept about ten cows as well as heifers and calves. For one cow and her calf he got £18 – a record price at a time when the average price was £2 10s. To Robert is given the credit for introducing Ayrshire cattle to Nithsdale, and this experiment was carried on with all the enthusiasm and single-mindedness that were the hallmarks of every endeavour he put his mind to. The description of Dunscore parish, contributed by the Revd. Joseph Kirkpatrick to Sinclair's *Statistical Account*, contained a paragraph under the heading 'Cattle and Sheep':

The black cattle, in general, are of the Galloway breed; but Mr. Robert Burns, a gentleman well known by his poetical productions, who rents a farm in this parish, is of opinion that the west-country cows give a larger quantity of milk.[36]

This gives the lie to the fallacy, sometimes expressed by nineteenth-century writers, that Robert was an indifferent farmer. It should also be noted that Colonel Fullarton of Fullarton near Irvine, who visited Ellisland in 1791, later wrote:

In order to prevent the danger arising from horned cattle in studs and strawyards, the best mode is to cut out the budding knob, or root of the horn, while the calf is very young. – This was suggested to me by Mr Robert Burns, whose general talents are no less conspicuous, than the poetic powers, which had done so much honour to the county where he was born.[37]

Clark mentioned four servants, two of each sex, during his time at Ellisland in 1789-90, but in the earlier period the number of farm-hands varied. In the autumn of 1788, during the first harvest, Robert employed three men. The first letter to Robert Riddell (CL 480), written on 16 September, thanked his neighbour for the loan of a lad that day and asked if he could use him the following day:

I would not ask even that one, did not staring Necessity compel me. I have not a person I can command but three; your servant makes a fourth, which is all my forces.

Clark's testimony, and the letters quoted above, show that Robert was no gentleman farmer in the Horatian ideal, dabbling in pastoral pursuits while giving himself up to the study of literature and the composition of poetry. He was, first and foremost, a working farmer, intelligent, energetic and resourceful, determined to make a success of his farm against all the odds. Farming was the life to which he had been bred, and he asked for nothing more than to make a go of Ellisland. But poetry was in his breath and blood, and even while asking Riddell a favour he was busy composing 'The Day Returns' (CW 333) which he was setting to Riddell's air 'The Seventh of November' in honour of his neighbour's wedding anniversary.

At one point Robert had as many as five horses, but Clark mentioned that there were only four on the farm while he worked there. One of these was called Pegasus, after the winged horse of Greek mythology, and it featured in the verse-epistle which Robert addressed to John Taylor of Wanlockhead (CW 344) when he was trying to get the horse's shoes frosted, the better to grip the icy roads. A second horse was William Nicol's ancient bay mare Peg Nicholson. Just as Robert had named his mare Jenny Geddes after the woman who provoked a riot in St Giles Cathedral, so Nicol, perhaps on the same analogy, chose for his mare the name of the deranged Margaret Nicholson who tried to assassinate King

George III in 1776. To name a horse after a mad assassin was the sort of dangerously anarchic thing which endeared Nicol to Burns. Peg Nicholson was the subject of the 'Elegy on Willie Nicol's Mare' (CW 380), which Robert sent to her erstwhile owner on 9 February 1790 with a covering letter (CL 346): 'That damned mare of yours is dead. I would freely have given her price to have saved her: she has vexed me beyond description.' In this letter Robert mentioned that he 'drew her in the plough, one of three, for one poor week'. It seems that Nicol had purchased a spavined jade, 'quite strained in the fillets beyond cure before you had bought her'.

The inordinate delay in getting into the farmhouse was the last straw. By the time Robert moved his wife from the Isle and brought his son down from Mauchline Jean was far advanced in her third pregnancy and, in fact, a second son, named Francis Wallace in honour of Mrs Dunlop, was born on 18 August. From a letter which Robert wrote to his brother William four days previously (CL 516–17) it appears that the confinement was attended on this occasion by Robert's mother and sisters who had brought Bobbie, now almost four years old, with them. The little boy was reunited with his mother as she was about to go into labour. The day after the birth Robert wrote to Mrs Dunlop (CL 177):

> More luck still! About two hours ago I welcomed home your little Godson.– He is a fine squalling fellow with a pipe that makes the room ring.– His Mother as usual.– Zelucco I have not thoroughly read so as to give a critique on it . . .

The casual and laconic reference to Jean, sandwiched between the announcement of the birth and a discussion of Dr Moore's novel, leaves us with the uneasy feeling that Jean was, by now, of little account. The dozen songs associated with her were compositions of the courtship and honeymoon period; and after the spate of 'much-loved fellow creature' confessions to correspondents in 1788 Jean virtually disappeared from Robert's letters, beyond the occasional perfunctory reference to 'my Rib' or 'my Goodwife' or 'Mrs B' in the closing salutation. She was an infinitely better wife than he ever appreciated or deserved; but beyond the strictly domestic duties of a wife, mother and dairywoman, Jean played no part in Robert's life, intellectually or socially.

By the end of July 1789 Burns was confessing to Graham of Fintry (CL 425), 'I am deliberating whether I had not better give up farming altogether'. By 11 January 1790 he had had enough. 'This Farm has undone my enjoyment of myself,' he complained to Gilbert (CL 358), 'It is a ruinous affair on all hands. But let it go to hell! I'll fight it out and be off with it.' By now his career in the Excise promised to be more lucrative and less of a gamble, even although it was involving him in up to 200 miles riding across ten parishes of Upper Nithsdale every week. The die was cast on 27 January 1790 when Robert was placed on the list of officers eligible for promotion to Examiner or Supervisor. The following July he was transferred to the Dumfries Third Division.

Thereafter he was keen to divest himself of what had proved to be a bad bargain. Fortunately, he was allowed to get out of the lease because the farmer of the adjacent property, Laggan, offered Miller £1,900 for Ellisland. Patrick Miller himself was anxious to dispose of the farm, detached from the rest of his property by the river. In the autumn of 1791 Robert wrote to Peter Hill (CL 320), 'I have sold to my Landlord the lease of my farm, & as I roup off every thing then, I have a mind to take a week's excursion to see old acquaintances'. After discussing his excellent prospects in the Excise, he went on, 'I have not been so lucky in my farming. Mr Miller's kindness has been just another as Creech's was . . .' It has been said that relations between tenant and landlord were pretty strained by that time, but Patrick Miller treated Burns fairly and even made him some unspecified payment in respect of the remainder of the lease. At any rate they both put the matter behind them.

On 25 August 1791 Robert's crops were auctioned. Over thirty people engaged in a drunken riot for three hours after the roup. 'Such a scene of drunkenness was hardly ever seen in this country,' he wrote to Thomas Sloan (CL 104):

Nor was the scene much better in the house. No fighting, indeed, but folks lieing drunk on the floor, & decanting, until both my dogs got so drunk by attending them, that they could not stand. You will easily guess how I enjoyed the scene as I was no farther over than you used to see me.

This last, incidentally, gives the lie to the myth of Burns as a hard drinker; his disgust at the drunken behaviour of those attending the auction comes across very clearly in this letter.

The Ellisland lease was formally renounced on 10 September 1791, but the Burns family continued to occupy the house until Martinmas (11 November) when they moved to Dumfries. An interesting document pertaining to this business was the award for repairs on the farm, dated 19 January 1792:

We, Joseph Henning, in Merkland, and Patrick Barr, in McCubbinstown, Barleymen, at the desire of Mr John Morrin of Laggan, we went this day and viewed the Houses upon Ellisland lately possessed by Mr Robert Burns, and find that the byre and stable will take ten shillings for thatch and workmanship, the Barn thirteen shillings for thatch and workmanship, the dwellinghouse for Glass six shillings, for sclate and workmanship five shillings. This we give as our opinion to put the House in a tenantable condition.

The total sum due for dilapidations was £1 14s, a relatively trifling sum, due, no doubt, to the fact that the extensive buildings were still fairly new at the time the inspection was carried out. One aspect, however, deserves comment and that is the sum due in respect of glass needed to replace broken windows. Robert's old habit of inscribing verses on glass with his diamond stylus continued unabated at Ellisland and many of the window-panes were liberally decorated in this curious fashion. On the day of the removal Burns and John Morrin had a violent quarrel. Morrin disagreed with the poet's valuation of a heap of manure which he left behind, and also insisted that the fences and outbuildings should be left in good order. Robert felt that he was being harshly treated, in view of the work he had been put to in clearing what was virtually waste-ground. On the day of the flitting several things happened to try Burns's temper. To get his own back on Morrin, Robert sent his young brother-in-law, Adam Armour (who was then working as a stonemason at Dalswinton and lodging at Ellisland) back to the farm under cover of darkness to smash every pane of glass that bore the poet's handwriting. According to Armour this piece of deliberate vandalism was punctiliously carried out, Robert paying Adam six shillings for his services.[38] John Morrin was later the butt of one of the poet's savage epigrams (CW 495):

> When Morine, deceas'd, to the Devil went down,
> 'Twas nothing would serve him but Satan's own crown.
> 'Thy fool's head,' quoth Satan, 'that crown shall wear never:
> I grant thou'rt as wicked, but not quite so clever.'

The episode of the broken window-panes was recounted by Adam Armour to a Dumfriesshire man in 1813. Young Armour's signature appeared on the southern window of the parlour, along with that of Fanny Burns, the poet's cousin. By the late nineteenth century this window-pane was liberally covered in graffiti, little, if any, being the work of Burns himself. One line, a favourite of Robert's, was a quotation from Alexander Pope: 'An honest man's the noblest work of God'. This was in handwriting which *might* have been the poet's, but all the rest was dismissed as spurious. Even this line was not left untouched. An irreverent hand subsequently scored through the word 'man' and substituted 'lass' and, as if that were not enough, a further improvement was sought in writing it afresh, so as to read, 'A charming woman's the noblest work of God', a line which neither Burns nor Pope could have scanned. The names of 'Jean Lorimer, Kemys Hall' and 'John Gillespie', who was one of Robert's Excise colleagues, appeared more than once, and had been scored through several times, like all the rest of the writing. As we shall see in a subsequent chapter, Robert helped Gillespie in his courtship of 'Chloris' whose home was almost in sight on the other side of the Nith; but that episode occurred after Burns had left Ellisland and settled in Dumfries, so the appearance of these names on the window in Robert's handwriting would have been an anachronism.

Among the relics on display at Ellisland is a fishing-rod, alleged to have been the poet's. There is some controversy concerning whether Robert, who had such a horror of injuring living creatures, would have indulged in the sport of angling; but taking trout or salmon from the river for the dining-table may have been a very different matter (as Robert's letters indicate). Dr Currie, in his biography of Burns,[39] repeated the ludicrous testimony of two English visitors who allegedly came upon the poet in the summer of 1791, wearing 'a cap made of a fox's skin on his head, a loose great-coat fixed around him by a belt from which depended an enormous Highland broad-sword' and fishing in the Nith. The truth of this story was denied later by Jean Burns, who stoutly maintained that her husband was not an angler.

Sir Samuel Egerton Brydges visited Ellisland in company with Ramsay of Ochtertyre and later published a more accurate reminiscence of his meeting with Burns:

> I had always been a great admirer of his genius and of the many traits in his character; and I was aware that he was a person moody and somewhat difficult to deal with. I was resolved to keep in full consideration the irritability of his position in society. About a mile from his residence, on a bench, under the tree, I passed a figure, which from the engraved por-traits of him, I did not doubt was the poet; but I did not venture to address him. On arriving at his humble cottage, Mrs Burns opened the door; she was the plain sort of humble woman she has been described: she ushered me into a neat apartment, and said that she would send for Burns, who was gone for a walk. In about half an hour he came, and my conjecture proved right: he was the person I had seen on the bench by the roadside. At first I was not entirely pleased with his countenance. I thought it had a sort of capricious jealousy, as if he was half inclined to treat me as an intruder. I resolved to bear it, and try if I could humour him . . .

One can imagine Robert's feelings at the intrusion of such a patronising buffoon. Brydges continued:

> While we were talking, Mrs Burns, as if accustomed to entertain visitors in this way, brought in a bottle of Scotch Whisky, and set the table. I accepted this hospitality. I could not help observing the curious glance with which he watched me at the entrance of this signal of homely enter-tainment. He was satisfied; he filled our glasses: 'Here's a health to auld Caledonia!' The fire sparkled in his eye, and mine sympathetically met his.[40]

As hopes of making a success of the farm faded, Robert turned more and more to the Excise as a solution to his mounting problems. He visited Edinburgh from 16 to 27 February 1789, settling accounts with Creech and resolving the embarrassing matter of the paternity suit brought by Jenny Clow. He also took the opportunity of pressing his future career in the Excise, but he was not as successful as he had wished. To Mrs Dunlop (CL 169–71) he confessed that his hope of an Excise division in his own locality had been thwarted by the regulations of the Excise Board, 'not-withstanding Mr. Graham's warmest exertions'. Mrs Dunlop had offered to write to Graham herself on the poet's behalf and sent Robert a draft of the proposed letter. He approved of her petition, but warned her that 'I must not seem to know any thing of the matter'. People might solicit patronage quite shamelessly, but there were still some limits.

Unfortunately, the Excise archives are silent on the matter, but we may assume that Mrs Dunlop wrote to Robert Graham at the beginning of April 1789 on the poet's behalf. Graham pulled strings and early the following month was able to write to Burns enclosing a letter to John Mitchell, Collector of Excise at Dumfries. Although Mitchell was very busy on the day Burns called on him, he received the poet with the utmost politeness and made Robert promise to call on him again soon. Robert wrote to Graham on 13 May (CL 428), reporting progress. He noted that Graham and his cousin, Sir William Murray of Ochtertyre (whom Robert had met during his tour in 1797), were proposing to visit Dumfries during the summer, and he extended an invitation to them to visit his 'humble domicile' and partake of a Farmer's dinner of 'good old beef, a chicken, or perhaps a Nith salmon fresh from the ware'. It is not known, however, whether the visit ever took place.

Graham wrote on 19 July and Burns replied at the end of the month (CL 429–50). He reported that Mitchell had not waited for him to call, 'but sent me a kind letter giving me a hint of the business, and on my waiting on him yesterday, he entered with the most friendly ardour into my views and interests'. Mitchell apparently agreed with Robert that Leonard Smith could be removed from his post without disadvantage to the Revenue or detriment to him. Robert's ruthlessness in this matter has often been criticised by his biographers and, taken out of context, it does place him in a bad light. But it is obvious that Robert must have discussed the matter with Mitchell and Findlater and they may have suggested the idea first. Leonard Smith had been in the service nine years, the last three of them in Dumfriesshire. He was very comfortably off, having come into a fortune through the estate of his mother-in-law, and he occupied a farm near Ellisland. More importantly, however, he was not highly regarded by his superiors. His official character read 'Pretty good, drinks', which was actually pretty damning by Excise standards. It should also be noted that, by the rules of the service, Excisemen could expect to be uprooted every three or four years; for it was official policy not to keep officers too long in one place in order to prevent over-familiarity with the merchants and traders. Smith and his wife had no family, so the upheaval of 'removes' as they were called would have been minimal. Apart from his drinking, however, Smith was unsatisfactory in many respects, and showed a lack of urgency and interest in his Excise business. In 1790 he was actually suspended from duty for a time, but subsequently reinstated, only to be suspended again in 1796. He was never re-employed, although he twice petitioned for a post.[41]

Robert's actions should also be viewed against the customs of his time, when patronage was all-important in virtually every walk of life; and although the Excise was the least susceptible of all government employment to this, it was not entirely free of the occasional string-pulling. Robert posed two alternatives. Should the Board accede to his importuning and appoint him to a division in which he lived, he would be 'at the top of my wishes'. Alternatively, 'should it be judged improper to place me in this Division, I am deliberating whether I had not better give up farming altogether, and go into the Excise wherever I can find employment'. Even so important a man as Commissioner Graham, however, was powerless to manipulate appointments; only the Collector of the district had the power to move men within his collection or recommend to the Board that an officer should be moved out of his collection. It was for this reason, then, that Graham did the next best thing by giving Robert a letter of introduction to John Mitchell.

The prospect of an Excise appointment was now made more attractive because the salary had been raised to £50 a year. This seems paltry, but it is necessary to multiply this by 150 to 200 to get a rough approximation of its worth, relative to the depreciated currency of the present day. Meanwhile, the friendship between Burns and Graham, though largely on paper, was growing steadily. They shared interests in poetry and the theatre. Robert was to play a leading role in the foundation of the Theatre Royal in Dumfries (1792) and had ambitions to become a playwright; Graham, on the other hand, was an enthusiastic devotee of amateur theatricals. It was Graham's copy of Adam Smith's *Wealth of Nations* which Robert read in the summer of 1789. It is evident from Robert's letters that Graham lent him several books, including Marshall's *Yorkshire*, Morliere's *Angola*, Fontaine's *Contes* and two other French works, including one whose title was *Chansons Joyeuses*. By the end of July Robert was set on an Excise career. He told Graham that:

> I do not think that I must trouble you for another cargo of books, at least for some time, as I am going to apply to Leadbetter and Symons on Gaging, and to study my Sliding rule, Branan's rule &c., with all possible attention.[42]

Eventually the Excise Board acceded to Robert's wishes and, exceptionally, he was given an appointment in the district where he resided. Because of the traditional opprobrium attached to the work, it was Board policy never to employ officers in their home districts, so the rules were quite significantly bent on this occasion. About 7 August 1789 Robert heard unofficially from Graham that he was to be appointed riding-officer of the First Dumfriesshire Itinerary, with the responsibility of surveying the ten parishes of Upper Nithsdale. Robert responded immediately with the sonnet beginning 'I call no Goddess to inspire my strains' (CW 362) which he sent to his patron on 10 August. On 19 August he wrote to Mrs Dunlop (CL 177), 'I suppose I shall begin doing duty at the commencement of next month'. The appointment dated from 7 September 1789 and from then until the following July he was riding 'five days a week, up to 40 miles a day, ere I return, besides four different kinds of book-keeping' as he told Mrs Dunlop on 2 October (CL 179-80). Robert's name appeared on the official list of Excise officers on 10 October, with a note to the effect that he was now on active service. This was formally ratified by the justices of the peace at Dumfries Quarter Sessions on 27 October. On that date Alexander Findlater, Supervisor of Excise, was sworn in as an extraordinary officer of the Customs, and Robert Burns was sworn in as an Officer of Excise 'by taking and swearing the oath of alleageance (*sic*)'.[43]

To Ainslie on 1 November (CL 338–9) Robert admitted his good luck in having cut corners and gained an appointment as a fully-fledged Exciseman without having had to serve as an expectant or probationer. The comment 'Never Tryed' opposite his name in the official list alluded to the fact that he had not served the customary probationary period. The rigours of the business were spelled out to Richard Brown on 4 November (CL 422). Moreover, he had no prospect of snatching a day off to meet his old friend on his home ground. 'I cannot meet you anywhere; no less than an order from the Board of Excise at Edinr is necessary before I can have so much time as meet you in Ayr-Shire. – But, do you come and see me!' When brother Gilbert married Jean Breckenridge at Kilmarnock on 21 June 1791, however, Robert merely wrote a brief note to Collector Mitchell (CL 563) saying that he required three days' leave 'for which I shall take your permission as granted, except I be countermanded before Sunday, the day I set out'.

Among the few Excise records still extant which have a bearing on Robert's service is a statistical survey of officers dated 10 October 1789 which shows that the Burns family had swollen to six. This does not mean that Robert and Jean now had four children, as one writer has deduced.[44] In fact, the family now consisted of Robert Junior and Francis Wallace, together with the poet's young cousins John and Fanny – a fact mentioned by Robert in a letter to James Burness dated 9 February 1789 (CL 62–3):

We have lost poor uncle Robert[45] this winter.– He has long been weak and with very little alteration in him, he expired January 3rd.– His son William, has been with me this winter, & goes in May to bind himself to be a Mason with my fatherinlaw who is a pretty considerable architect in Ayrshire. – His other Son, the eldest, John, comes to me, I expect in summer.– They are both remarkable stout young fellows, & promise to do well.– His only daughter Fanny has been with me ever since her father's death and I purpose keeping her in my family till she be quite woman grown, & be fit for better service.– She is one of the cleverest girls, and has one of the most amiable dispositions that I have ever seen.

In fact, Fanny eventually married Jean's brother Adam at Mauchline on 5 June 1792. Incidentally, it is interesting to note Robert's pardonable exaggeration of James Armour's importance when writing to his cousin.

A few anecdotes concerning the early part of Robert's Excise service have survived. Profesor Gillespie of St Andrew's recalled how, as a boy of twelve, he had seen Robert Burns at a Thornhill fair in August 1790. In Old Street lived a poor woman, Kate Watson, who on these gala days kept a shebeen:

I saw the poet enter her door, and anticipated nothing short of an immediate seizure of a certain greybeard and barrel, which to my certain knowledge contained the contraband commodities our bard was in search of. A
nod, accompanied by a significant movement of the forefinger, brought
Kate to the doorway, and I was near enough to hear the following words
distinctly uttered: 'Kate, are ye mad? Dinna you know that the supervisor
and I will be in upon you in the course of forty minutes? Good-bye t'ye
at present.' I had access to know that the friendly hint was not neglected.
It saved a poor widow from a fine of several pounds for committing a
quarterly offence by which the revenue was probably subject to an annual
loss of five shillings.[46]

Kirkpatrick Durham was the location of a story recovered by Joseph Train,
concerning Jean Dunn, 'a suspected trader' who saw Burns and Robertson,
a fellow Exciseman, approaching her house on the morning of a fair. She
slipped out of the back door to evade scrutiny, leaving in her house only
her little daughter and a girl who was looking after her. 'Has there been
any brewing for the fair here today?' enquired Robert as he entered the
cottage. 'Oh no, Sir,' replied the servant, 'we hae nae licence for that.'
'That's no' true!' cried the child, 'the muckle black kist is fu o the bottles
o yill that my mither sat up a' night brewin for the fair.' 'Does that bird
speak?' asked Robertson, pointing to one in a hanging cage. 'There is no
use for another speaking-bird in this house,' commented Burns, 'while that
lassie is to the fore. We are in a hurry just now; but as we return from the
fair we'll examine the muckle black kist.' Thus warned, Jean Dunn
managed to get her stock of beer out of the house before the Excisemen
returned.

These stories have often been quoted to show Robert's distaste for the
petty bureaucracy which his profession forced upon him and as illustrations of his essential humanity, compassion and good sense. In the late
nineteenth century, however, a different interpretation was placed on such
incidents and in the centenary year of the poet's death letters appeared in
the national press condemning Burns for his action in these cases, saying
that he was only too ready to let off a defaulter because she was a woman,
and that he was false to the interests of the revenue he had sworn to uphold
when he accepted the King's commission. This was a view of Burns from
the standpoint of the rigidly-righteous late-Victorian era. Fortunately,
other writers put the matter in perspective. From the 1660s anyone could
brew beer without a licence, for sale at fairs in Scotland, provided the
proper duty had been paid in advance. Such persons whose brewing was
confined to fairs were known as bye-brewers (as distinguished from
common brewers who made a full-time living from this occupation). By a
general order of 25 October 1740, bye-brewers were required to give
notice of their intention to sell beer at a fair. The officers were instructed
to insist on their paying the duty before selling any part of the beer. If they
sold more than they had paid duty for they were liable to prosecution. It
should also be noted that, prior to 1880, anyone could brew beer for purely
domestic consumption without a licence or the need to pay duty. In light

of this, therefore, Robert's treatment of Kate Watson and Jean Dunn (probably well known as old offenders) was fair. He had no proof of sale, and in the case of such poor persons his instructions were to prevent evasion of the law, hence the friendly warnings. As a conscientious, energetic officer, he did his duty effectively and, at the same time, mercifully, by these domiciliary visits on the morning of the fair.[47]

When it came to dealing with real smugglers and other offenders, however, Robert was as zealous as any other Exciseman, and more efficient than most. To Graham of Fintry (CL 433) Robert explained his methods:

> I recorded every Defaulter; but at the Court, I myself begged off every poor body that was unable to pay, which seeming candour gave me so much implicit credit with the Hon. Bench that with high Compliments they gave me such ample vengeance on the rest that my Decreet is double the amount of any Division in the District.

As the detecting officer was entitled not only to half of all fines imposed in the courts, but also to half the produce of seizures, it may be imagined that Burns was able to add substantially to his basic salary. The fines accruing to Robert on this particular occasion, following the apprehension of a band of smugglers, amounted to about £60 – more than a whole year's salary. The prospect of doubling one's wages by arresting smugglers must have been a real incentive to vigilance.

All too often, however, Robert found that people, great and small, had an ambivalent attitude towards the Excise. In an age when the Excise duties were manifold and all-pervasive, there was a widespread belief that to evade such petty imposts was not only understandable but actually desirable. Something of the frustration which Robert felt when his zeal in tracking down malefactors was set at naught by their powerful friends comes across in a letter which he wrote to John Mitchell (CL 563). Robert had reported a farmer, Thomas Johnston of Mirecleugh, for illicit maltings. As a result, Johnston had been tried and convicted and fined £5, but he appealed against the fine. Fergusson of Craigdarroch and Riddell of Glenriddell, in their capacity as magistrates, ordered Collector Mitchell to suspend proceedings till Johnston's appeal could be investigated. Robert, who had been exceedingly busy at the time, was clearly annoyed at the intervention of Fergusson and Riddell on Johnston's behalf, and there was more than a hint of exasperation in the final sentence of this letter:

> In short, Sir, I have broke my horse's wind, & almost broke my own neck, besides some injuries in a part that shall be nameless, owing to a hard-hearted stone of a saddle, & I find that every Offender has so many Great Men to espouse his cause, that I shall not be surprised if I am committed to the strong Hold of the Law tomorrow for insolence to the dear friends of the Gentlemen of the Country.

On the other hand, Robert could appeal to the self-same magistrates when he felt that the occasion warranted some compassionate gesture. From the

Globe Inn one Wednesday in October 1789 he wrote to Fergusson of Craigdarroch (CL 538):

> I have sought you all over the town, good Sir, to learn what you have done, or what can be done, for poor Robie Gordon. The hour is at hand when I must assume the execrable office of whipper-in to the bloodhounds of justice, and must, must let loose the ravenous rage of the carrion sons of bitches on poor Robie. I think you can do something to save the unfortunate man, and I am sure, if you can, you will.

The work was arduous but not unpleasant, and as he rode around the countryside Robert had the opportunity to add to his store of old ballads and pass the time in the saddle with composing new verses. With the onset of winter, however, the hardships of riding work began to tell. On 10 November 1789, for example, Robert wrote to his brother William, then working as a saddler in Newcastle (CL 517-18). He complained, 'I am so hurried and fatigued with my Excise-business, that I can scarcely pluck up resolution to go through the effort of a letter to any body'. His robust physique was now undermined by a psychosomatic ailment which he explained to Mrs Dunlop on 13 December (CL 181-2):

> I am groaning under the miseries of a diseased nervous System; a System of all others the most essential to our happiness – or the most productive of our Misery. For now near three weeks I have been so ill with a nervous head-ach, that I have been obliged to give up for a time my Excise books, being scarce able to lift my head, much less to ride once a week over ten muir Parishes . . .

This rather pathetic letter is oddly at variance with the lengthy epistle to Robert Graham two days earlier, accompanying a veritable parcel of his latest effusions (CL 431-3):

> I have found the Excise business go on a great deal smoother with me than I apprehended; owing a good deal to the generous friendship of Mr Mitchell my Collector, and the kind assistance and instruction of Mr Findlater my Supervisor.

Having bent the rules by obtaining a position in his own locality, Robert next engineered a transfer to the much more lucrative Dumfries Third (Port) Division. Graham was apparently in Dumfries in December 1789, for Robert entrusted to him a letter addressed to Provost Robert Maxwell of Lochmaben (CL 548). It is tempting to speculate that during Graham's visit Robert may have propositioned the Commissioner about this transfer. He confided to Mrs Dunlop as early as 6 March 1790 (CL 184-5),

> I can have in the Excise-line what they call a foot-walk whenever I chuse; that is an appointment to a Division where I am under no necesity of keeping a horse. There is in every Sea-port town, one or two Officers,

called Port Officers, whose income is at least seventy pounds per annum. I will petition Mr Graham & stretch all my interest to get one of these; and if possible on the Clyde. Greenock & Port Glasgow are both lucrative places in that way & to them my views are bent.

This letter also graphically illustrates the alacrity with which Robert was ready to use whatever connections Mrs Dunlop possessed, in this instance the friendship of a Mrs Corbet whose husband just happened to be William Corbet, one of the two Supervisors-General of Excise:

Were he to interest himself properly for me, he could easily by Martinmass 1791 transport me to Port Glasgow port Division, which would be the ultimatum of my present Excise hopes.

Robert was prudent enough to remind Mrs Dunlop that this was for her most private ear. 'It would be of considerable prejudice to me to have it known at present.'

On 15 October 1790 Ainslie paid a visit to Ellisland and later reported back to Nancy McLehose. Burns was just getting over a severe quinsy and prolonged fever which, however, did not depress his spirits, it being the kirn-nicht or harvest home, a party held to celebrate the gathering in of the crops. Ainslie found that the household had swollen to include sisters of both Robert and Jean, one female and two male cousins (Uncle Robert's children), as well as a few homely neighbours. Ainslie was astonished at the change in his friend's appearance. The elegant blue coat with its buff and blue facings had now given way to the coarse homespuns and the clumsy gaiters of the country farmer. Robert, by now well into his Excise duties, might boast of being 'a mighty tax-gatherer before the Lord', but in the relaxed atmosphere of the harvest home Ainslie noted with pursed-lip disapproval that his old friend was very free and easy with both Jean and the servants. Ainslie's impression of 'Bonie Jean' was of a somewhat slatternly woman who laughed coarsely and had let her figure go – she was actually pregnant at the time and, in due course, would give birth to William Nicol Burns. Ainslie did not think much of the company Robert was now keeping. To Nancy he wrote from Dumfries two days later:

We spent the evening in the way common on such occasions – of dancing, and kissing the lasses at the end of every dance . . . Our friend is as ingenious as ever, and seems happy with the situation I have described. His mind, however, seems to me to be a great mixture of the poet and exciseman. One day he sits down and writes a beautiful poem – and the next seize a cargo of tobacco from some unfortunate smuggler, or roups out some poor wretch for selling liquors without a licence. From his conversation, he seems to be pretty frequently among the great . . . Having found that his farm does not answer, he is about to give it up, and depend wholly on the Excise.[48]

Robert himself has left rather an unflattering impression of Jean at this time, in a letter to Mrs Dunlop of 11 April 1791 (CL 194–5), two days after the baby was born:

Mrs Burns is getting stout again, & laid as lustily about her today at
breakfast as a Reaper from the cornridge.- That is the peculiar priviledge
& blessing of our hale, sprightly damsels, that are bred among the hay &
heather.- We cannot hope for that highly polished mind, that charming
delicacy of soul, which is found among the Female world in the more
elevated stations of life

and he ended philosophically with a recital of the homely virtues which
were 'the charms of lovely woman in my humble walk of life'.

In the autumn of 1790 James Cunningham, fourteenth Earl of Glencairn, went to Portugal for the sake of his health, but by now his consumption was too far gone. He set sail for England but died shortly before his
ship reached Falmouth on 30 January 1791. Robert was grief-stricken
when he heard the news, and wrote immediately to Alexander Dalziel (CL
506) to enquire when the Earl's remains would be interred in the family
burial ground, 'that I may cross the country & steal among the croud, to
pay a tear to the last sight of my ever revered Benefactor'. But the Earl was
interred at Falmouth, and Robert, who went to the expense of a grey tail-
coat and black gloves, was not even invited to the requiem service in Ayrshire. Nor did his beautiful and poignant 'Lament' (CW 423-5) evoke a
response when he sent it to the late Earl's sister, Lady Betty Cunningham,
(CL 499-500), and his request for permission to publish it was ignored.
Nothing daunted, Robert wrote out another copy of the long poem and
sent it with a covering letter to Betty's sister, Lady Harriet Don (CL 280),
but it, too, was ignored. Such were Robert's sincere feelings for the late
Earl that he overlooked the snub on this occasion and in 1793 sent Lady
Betty a presentation copy of the second Edinburgh Edition.

The wheels of the Excise ground exceeding slow and nine months passed
before Corbet again wrote to Burns, on 17 January 1791, informing him
that 'he may soon expect to hear of his promotion'. Ten days later, Robert
was placed on a list of officers eligible for promotion to the rank of
Examiner or Supervisor. This was not a promotion as such, merely the
prospect of advancement in due course. In fact, had he lived, Robert would
have attained the rank of Examiner late in 1796 and was scheduled to
become Supervisor at Dunblane the following year.[49] But in 1791 Robert
was optimistic that his promotion would circumvent the normal rules of
seniority. To Peter Hill he wrote (CL 320):

I do not know if I ever informed you that I am now got ranked on the list
as a Supervisor; & I have pretty good reason to believe that I shall soon
be called out to employ.- The appointment is worth from one to two
hundred a year, according to the place in the country in which one is
settled.

This was a palpable untruth, the facts distorted by wishful thinking.
Perhaps something of the same sort had led William Nicol, a year earlier,
into believing that Robert had, even at that early date, been promoted to

Examiner – months before his name was even put on the list for eventual promotion. In a letter of 13 August 1790 addressed to Ainslie, Nicol wrote:

> As to Burns, poor folks like you and I must resign all thoughts of future correspondence with him. To the pride of applauded genius is now super-added the pride of office. He was lately raised to the dignity of an Examiner of Excise, which is a step preparative to attaining that of a Supervisor.[50]

For the moment, Robert would have to be content with a transfer to the Dumfries Third Division in July 1790. It was promotion of a sort, as it was a much more lucrative position attracting perquisites which boosted the salary to £70 a year. More importantly, it was a foot-walk, confined to the town itself, so that the Exciseman was not put to the additional expense of maintaining a horse although, so long as his home was six miles out of town, Robert could not dispense with Pegasus. Robert's transfer to this division, in fact, made a move from Ellisland inevitable. For about a year and a half, therefore, Robert commuted between Dumfries and his farm. As a rule, he would ride home at the end of each day but sometimes, if the weather was inclement, or he was detained in town rather late, he would put up at the Globe Inn for the night.

This hostelry in the High Street of Dumfries had been in existence since 1610. A century and a half later it was purchased by William Hyslop of Lochend who combined the farming of his small estate with the trade of vintner in Dumfries. The Globe was Robert's 'howff' till the end of his life and, as such, was to feature largely in his Dumfries years. In the latter part of the Ellisland period, however, it was mainly a convenient lodging as occasion demanded. William Hyslop's father John had married, in 1733, a lady named Ann Park.[51] Her great-niece was a girl of the same name who came to work at the Globe as barmaid about 1789, so she was, in fact, second-cousin to William Hyslop, and not the niece of his wife Jean (one of the Maxwells of Terraughty), as has been stated in every work on Burns till now; but as Ann Park was ages with William's son John (born in 1770) it is probable that she regarded the landlord and landlady of the tavern as aunt and uncle, hence the popular misconception. Ann was the daughter of Joseph Park, an Edinburgh coachmaker and his wife Elizabeth Dick; she was barely nineteen when she and Robert began an affair which had the inevitable consequences. Chambers was probably correct when he said that 'Tradition – more probably mischievous slander – in Dumfries affirms that Anne Park was quite as much the sinner as the sinned against in the affair'.[52] 'Honest Allan' Cunningham started the *canard* that blackened the girl's reputation in order to mitigate the temptation to which Robert succumbed: 'She had other pretty ways to render herself agreeable to the customers at the inn than the serving of wine';[53] and he further claimed that George Thomson refused to publish the love song 'Yestreen I had a Pint o Wine' (CW 407–8) because he knew the 'free character' of the heroine.

It is true that the ever-fastidious Thomson rejected the song when Robert offered it to him two years later, but he never gave his reasons and it may be supposed that it was rejected purely because it did not accord with Thomson's notions of a love song fit for the drawing-room.

Chambers felt that it was significant that Mrs Hyslop did not forbid Burns the inn 'in spite of her niece's misfortune' and Hilton Brown, much nearer the present day, commented that corroboration of the view that the girl was 'common property' was suggested by the easy manner in which all concerned took her 'disgrace'.[54] There is not a single shred of evidence to support the notion that Ann was a 'lightfoot', to use the quaint expression beloved of Robert's early biographers. Cunningham might logically have followed his innuendo with doubts as to Robert's paternity of the baby resulting from this liaison but he did not, and it is clear that Robert himself accepted full responsibility. Nevertheless, the biographers of the nineteenth and early twentieth centuries found it very difficult to come to terms with Robert's 'solitary lapse' from marital fidelity after he had avowed Jean as his wife. There are good grounds, however, for thinking that the affair with Ann Park was not an isolated occurrence, as will become clearer in a subsequent chapter. But if they could not avoid the issue, the poet's biographers felt obliged to condemn it in the strongest terms possible. 'Burns's intrigue with her was a lamentable and absolutely indefensible lapse from that ideal of conjugal fidelity which he had placed before himself when he married Jean Armour', intoned Chambers,[55] while Duncan McNaught regarded it as 'the most grievous error of Burns's life'.[56]

Chambers tried to whitewash Burns by recording that Jean was 'imprudently' away on long visits to Mauchline in the summer of 1790: 'It was natural for Jean to wish to spend a little time with her own relatives, and to show them her children. But it was an injudicious step for the wife of so passionate and impressionable a man: it tended to break the good domestic habits which he had unquestionably set himself to form'[57] and backed this with the testimony of Robert's unmarried sister Agnes, who was at Ellisland superintending the dairy, and who averred that 'she never knew him fail to keep good hours at night till the first unlucky absence of her sister-in-law in Ayrshire'. So the blame for this peccadillo was placed fairly and squarely on poor Jean's shoulders. But this excuse just will not do at all. Jean can be traced more or less continuously at Ellisland from December 1788 right through 1790, and she must certainly have been accessible within ten days of that crucial intercourse with Ann which resulted in the girl's pregnancy. For the plain fact of the matter is that Robert impregnated both his wife and his girlfriend within a matter of days of each other.

Burns's song extolling the 'gowden locks of Anna' was, by his own admission to George Thomson in April 1793 (CL 628), 'the best love-song I ever composed in my life; but in its *original* state is not quite a lady's song'. For this reason he sent Thomson two versions – the unexpurgated one to be passed on to Harry Erskine and the 'altered' version for publication. Even in its toned-down form Thomson found it a little too broad to his taste. Robert's exultant verses frankly praised the girl's physical charms, and he never made any pretence of deep affection for her; but to him she was 'my Anna' and no one else's.[58] There was no question of contesting paternity, as in the case of Margaret Cameron. Ann Park, in fact, was just another simple country girl who fell for the poet's charms.

Ann Park returned to her parents in the latter stage of her pregnancy and gave birth to a daughter, whom she named Elizabeth, at Leith on 31 March 1791. Nine days later Jean herself gave birth, to William Nicol Burns. The rest of the story has so far been shrouded in mystery and contradiction. According to Chambers the baby girl was sent for a period to Mossgiel, which presupposes that she was weaned by that time. This statement, however, has been overlooked by some later writers who assumed that, within days or weeks of the birth, the baby was sent to Ellisland where Jean, lactating for her own baby, generously took on the additional task of breast-feeding little Elizabeth. Snyder alone of twentieth-century biographers took note of Chambers-Wallace and stated that the girl was reared at first by Robert's mother (who already had the upbringing of 'Dear-bought Bess'). 'It is a curious fact,' noted Snyder, 'that no one knows what became of Anne (sic) Park after the birth of her daughter. She vanishes from the record as completely as if she had never existed.' Some modern biographers, such as Duncan McNaught, Robert Fitzhugh and Hugh Douglas, follow the line that Ann Park died giving birth to Elizabeth; Hilton Brown repeated the story, adding sceptically, 'but this is by no means proved'. Fowler alone, trying to be a little more original, came up with the theory that Ann must have died from puerperal infection, or milk fever as it was once called, some days or weeks after Elizabeth was born.[59] Others, notably William Wallace and Maurice Lindsay, quoted two alternatives. Either Ann died giving birth to Elizabeth, or she subsequently married a soldier and died giving birth to his child.

A detailed study of the parish registers of Edinburgh and Leith, however, reveals that Ann Park did not die in March 1791 as had been suspected. She appears to have weaned the infant and then persuaded the father to shoulder responsibility. This explains the apparent mystery – or error – whereby both Robert's illegitimate daughters were christened Elizabeth; in this case Ann Park had named the child after her own mother, proving that at that early stage there was little thought of handing the baby over to Burns. Having unloaded her burden, Ann obtained a domestic situation in Edinburgh, where she married a carpenter named John Greenshields on 11 November 1794. I have not been able to trace Ann's date of death, but Greenshields married again, taking Jane Boyd as his wife on 27 September 1799. There were no children of either marriage.[60]

At any rate, the little girl eventually came to be reared by Jean Armour whose equanimity in the matter is nothing short of astounding. She is said to have shrugged it off with a laugh and the words, 'Our Rab should have had twa wives'.

By the summer of 1791 Robert had had enough of farming. Thereafter, it was only a matter of extricating himself from his lease (which he apparently did with some pecuniary advantage, as Miller was now anxious to sell the farm) and, at long last, Robert would be free of farming forever.

Despite the relative obscurity to which Robert returned when he resumed farming, there were times when visitors beat a path to his door, or otherwise sought him out. Helen Maria Williams (1762-1827) was Dr Moore's secretary in the 1780s and on reading 'To a Mountain Daisy' had composed a sonnet in Robert's honour which Moore forwarded to him on 25 June 1787. On hearing of Robert's approval, she replied that 'a much less portion of applause' from him would have been gratifying.[61] In 1788 when the controversy over the repeal of the slave trade was reaching fever pitch, Miss Williams wrote a very long poem on the subject which was submitted to Burns for his criticism. On this occasion Robert went to great lengths, sending her a long letter in late July or early August 1789 with a detailed critique (CL 532-5).[62]

There were the congenial visits of like-minded individuals. In October 1789 Willie Nicol and Allan Masterton visited Dumfriesshire and Robert rode over from Ellisland to meet them at Willie's Mill near Craigieburn on the outskirts of Moffat. This inn has long since disappeared but it is forever immortalised as the site of Robert's glorious bacchanal, 'Willie Brew'd a Peck o Maut' (CW 364). Nicol's wife, one of the Cairns of Torr, inherited some money about this time and Willie decided to invest this windfall in a small country estate. He eventually settled on Lagganpark in Glencairn parish on the southern flank of the Keir Hills, and asked Robert to take a look at it on his behalf. The poet was too ill at the time to carry out a personal inspection but sent two friends instead. On 13 December 1789 he wrote to Nicol giving him a full report and recommending purchase (CL 346). On 26 March 1790 Nicol completed the purchase of the 340-acre farm from William Riddell of Camieston, a cousin of Glenriddell. Two months later Robert got around to inspecting the property himself and reported to Nicol on the rich deposits of limestone which he found there. The letter of 28 May (CL 348) is quite technical and reveals a sound grasp of geology. Robert concluded that the farm itself was a most beautiful one, and 'an exceeding cheap purchase' (Nicol had paid £1,700). Nicol regarded it as a long-term investment, probably with some notion of settling there when he retired, but as his health began to fail and he realised the impossibility of this ambition he put it up for sale. The roup of Lagganpark took place in April 1797, only a few days before Nicol died.[63]

In August 1791 Robert received an invitation from the Earl of Buchan to attend a pompous ceremony on 22 September, at Ednam, Roxburghshire, birthplace of James Thomson (1700-48). Thomson was a prolific poet and dramatist, whose epic work *The Seasons* attained a measure of popularity in the eighteenth century. He also wrote the lyrics for Mallet's long-running musical about Alfred the Great – now long-forgotten, but for its hit number 'Rule Britannia'. Although Burns regarded Ramsay and Fergusson as his mentors in vernacular poetry, Thomson more than any other poet guided Robert's daily life. In particular, two lines from *Alfred* were virtually Robert's motto, quoted in several letters and the commonplace books, and praised to Ainslie (CL 336) 'tho' I have repeated them ten thousand times, still they rouse my manhood & steel my resolution like Inspiration'. The lines that buoyed Robert up against countless setbacks and disappointments were:

> What proves the hero truly great,
> Is never, never to despair!

Lord Buchan, in asking Robert to attend the ceremony, at which a bust of Thomson was to be crowned with a laurel wreath, hoped that he would compose an ode suitable to the occasion. The bust was a plaster cast of the sculpture in Poets' Corner in Westminster Abbey which had been generously sent to Buchan by Thomas Coutts (1735–1822), the Edinburgh-born London banker. Robert could not spare the time from Excise duties and the exigencies of the harvest to undertake the arduous eighty-mile cross-country journey, but he dutifully wrote his 'Address to the Shade of Thomson' (CW 421). Having cast his eye over the ode to Thomson by Collins, Robert felt unequal to the occasion as he confessed to Buchan (CL 267–8). In fact, the 'Address' was influenced very heavily by Collins' 'Ode to Evening'. In the event, the ceremony was a fiasco, the bust having got broken in a midnight frolic on 16 September during Race Week, and Lord Buchan had to substitute a copy of Thomson's *Seasons* which were apostrophised, not in the words of Burns after all, but in lines composed by the dead poet's kinsman, the Revd. William Thomson of Queen's College, Oxford.[64]

Although Robert probably had little regrets in leaving Ellisland in November 1791, the place was not without its memories, some happy, others poignant. It might be 'the very riddlings of Creation', but its outlook was infinitely more inspiring than that of any other farm on which Robert had laboured. He was twenty-nine years old, full of high hopes and firm resolution, when he entered his lease. For a time his work prospered and his life was happy. Here, too, some of his best poetry was written. Some 230 of the 700 extant letters of the poet were written during the Ellisland period, though not all, of course, were actually written from here. Some editors have ascribed the song 'I hae a Wife o my ain' (CW 450) to the period when Robert set up home for Bonie Jean at Ellisland, but James Kinsley, on internal evidence, dated it more accurately to 1792.

Nevertheless, the Ellisland period was to see over 130 poems and songs – about a quarter of Burns's total output – beginning in June 1788 with the 'Epistle to Hugh Parker' (CW 322), 'Verses in Friars' Carse Hermitage' (CW 324) and the verse-epistle to Alexander Cunningham on 27 July (CW 328). The beautiful love songs 'Of A' the Airts' and 'O, Were I on Parnassus Hill' (CW 329) were both composed 'out of compliment to Mrs Burns' in the summer of 1788 when the poet would gaze longingly to the Cumnock Hills beyond which dwelled his young wife. Many old ballads were reworked and fragments mended and rewritten, including 'Auld Lang Syne' (CW 341), arguably the most widely sung ballad in the history of world music. There were experiments in occasional odes, such as that on the departed Regency Bill (CW 352), as well as the political ballads for the parliamentary elections of 1789 and 1790. The old satirical anti-clericalism was not dead, as 'The Kirk's Alarm' (CW 359-61) testifies. This long poem, ridiculing some of the leading Auld Licht divines of Ayrshire, was provoked by the controversy surrounding the charges of heterodoxy brought against the Revd. William McGill (1732-1807) on account of his treatise *The Death of Jesus Christ* published in 1786. The General Assembly established a commission of enquiry into the affair ('Holy Willie' Fisher being one of its number), but the case collapsed in July 1789 when McGill hastily recanted and made a grovelling apology to the Presbytery. Robert also had ambitions to write epic poems and from this resulted the lengthy fragment entitled 'The Poet's Progress', intended as part of a much longer autobiographical work. He never got further with this project, however, and eventually incorporated it into his 'Epistle to Robert Graham' (CW 330-2).

There was also that very moving song, 'Thou Lingering Star' (CW 372-3), allegedly composed about the third anniversary of Margaret Campbell's death. Lockhart, quoting John McDiarmid who allegedly got the facts from Jean, was the source of the highly embellished (and equally improbable) story:

> Burns spent that day, though labouring under cold, in the usual work of his harvest, and apparently in excellent spirits. But as the twilight deepened, he appeared to grow 'very sad about something, and at length wandered out into the barn-yard, to which his wife, in her anxiety for his health, followed him, entreating him in vain to observe that frost had set in, and to return to the fireside. On being again and again requested to do so, he always promised compliance – but still remained where he was, striding up and down slowly, and contemplating the sky, which was singularly clear and starry. At last Mrs Burns found him stretched on a mass of straw, with his eyes fixed on a beautiful planet, 'that shone like another moon;' and prevailed on him to come in. He immediately on entering the house, called for his desk, and wrote exactly as they now stand, with all the ease of one copying from memory, the sublime and pathetic verses, 'Thou lingering star'.[65]

This story was accepted without question by most biographers, though Hately Waddell's version of McDiarmid's account omits it entirely. Snyder, robustly sceptical as ever, put it succinctly:

> If Burns wrote a poem to the morning star while lying on a mass of straw in his barnyard during the early evening, he was making himself unnecessarily and inappropriately ridiculous.[66]

Robert's anguish was assuaged by the stanzas composed to the melancholy air 'Mary weep no more for me' which, incidentally, helped to conceal the dead girl's true identity behind the fictional Mary.

On the morning of 19 April 1789, as he was out at an early hour, sowing in the fields, Robert heard a shot and presently saw a poor little wounded doe hare, which 'set my humanity in tears and my indignation in arms', as he subsequently wrote to Mrs Dunlop (CL 171). The 'Ode on the Wounded Hare' (CW 354) was the result. James Thomson, the son of a neighbouring farmer, stated that having shot and wounded a hare he saw it run past Burns. 'He cursed me and said that he would not mind throwing me in the water and I'll warrant he could hae done it, though I was but young and strong.'[67] Interestingly, Robert's indignation was not at the wounding of the hare so much as 'at the inhuman fellow who could shoot a hare at this season when they all of them have young ones; & it gave me no little gloomy satisfaction to see the poor injured creature escape him', as he confided to Alexander Cunningham a few days later (CL 457). Subsequently Robert sent a copy of the poem to Dr James Gregory for his comments, but the good doctor was unduly severe and prolix in his criticism when he replied on 2 June, taking exception to the coarseness of many words. Gregory's pomposity makes us chuckle now, but Robert was mortified. He should have known what to expect; indeed, in a letter to Dugald Stewart the previous January (CL 449), Robert had commented wryly on 'the justness (Iron justice, for he has no bowels of compassion for a poor poetic sinner) of Dr Gregory's remarks'.

Indubitably the greatest product of Robert's muse in this period was 'Tam o Shanter' (CW 410-15). On 17 July 1789 Robert wrote to Mrs Dunlop (CL 176-7):

> Captain Grose, the well-known Author of the Antiquities of England & Wales, has been through Annandale, Nithsdale & Galloway, in the view of commencing another Publication, The Antiquities of Scotland.– As he has made his headquarters with Captain Riddel (sic), my nearest neighbour, for these two months, I am intimately acquainted with him . . . His delight is to steal thro' the country almost unknown, both as favorable to his humor & his business . . . if you discover a cheerful-looking grig of an old, fat fellow, the precise figure of Slop, wheeling about your avenue in his own carriage with a pencil & paper in his hand, you may conclude 'Thou art the man!'[68]

Robert took to Grose immediately and their friendship inspired the witty poem 'On the Late Captain Grose's Peregrinations through Scotland' (CW 373-4) as well as the lines 'On Captain Grose' and 'Epigram on Francis Grose the Antiquary' (CW 415). Robert suggested that Grose include Kirk Alloway in his projected volume. Grose agreed, provided that Robert supplied him with a tale of witchcraft to accompany the engraving of the ruined church. In June 1790 Robert sent him three prose tales associated with the church (CL 557-9); the second of these recounted the story of the drunken farmer who had interrupted the witches' dance with his cry 'Well luppen Maggy wi' the short sark!' and whose horse had lost her tail as he fled across the bridge of Doon. Robert concluded this anecdote with the unsightly, tailless condition of the vigorous steed was to the last hour of the noble creature's life, an awful warning to the Carrick farmers, not to stay too late in Ayr markets.

On 1 December 1790 Robert wrote again to Captain Grose (CL 559-60), 'Inclosed is one of the Aloway-kirk Stories, done in Scots verse. Should you think it worthy a place in your Scots Antiquities, it will lengthen not a little the altitude of my Muse's pride'. Grose, not surprisingly, preferred the poetic version which duly appeared in the second volume of *The Antiquities of Scotland*, published in April 1791. The poem, however, first appeared in the March issue of the *Edinburgh Magazine*. A local tradition, which goes back no further than Lockhart in 1828 but which persists to this day in face of all the evidence to the contrary, and is now enshrined in one of the several plaques which festoon Ellisland, maintains that Robert's great masterpiece was the work of a single day. William McDowall, omitting some of Lockhart's more purple passages, expressed this tradition in typically fanciful prose:

For one day at least all prosaic business must be set aside, that the poet may, by doing full justice to his theme, gratify his friend. He is seen in the forenoon pacing to and fro along his favourite walk southward of the house, beside the river. Some hours afterwards Mrs Burns, with her two children, Robert and Francis Wallace, join him; but perceiving that he is deeply absorbed 'busy crooning to himself' she, guided by true womanly tact, retires with her little prattlers, and from behind some 'lang yellow broom' growing upon the bank, she keeps a loving lookout, unperceived by the poet. He becomes increasingly excited; his manner is that of a pythoness, so strange and wild are his gesticulations, and, though now at the remote end of the promenade, she can perceive that he is '*agonized with an ungovernable access of joy*'. It is his masterpiece of Tam o' Shanter with which he is busy. He is so far advanced with it that heroic Tam has been brought in full sight of the fantastic dancers, and then the poet bursts out with the apostrophe so loud that his listening wife hears every line –

> Now, Tam! o Tam! had thae been queans,
> A' plump and strapping in their teens

The fine frenzy of Burns continued till the poem was completed, and, lest the glow of his first fresh conceptions should in any degree cool down, he, with a sod-dyke for desk, committed the poem to paper. Then, returning to the house, he read it in triumph to Bonnie Jean. Even as the farmyard of Ellisland witnessed the agonizing throes in which the poet's most pathetic effusion was produced, so this walk of his, trodden by hosts of admiring visitors, was the scene of his most joyful ecstasy and of his proudest achievement.[69]

'Tam o' Shanter,' says Alexander Smith, with pardonable exaggeration, 'was written in a day – since Bruce fought at Bannockburn, the best single day's work done in Scotland.'[70] That Lockhart was wrong in stating that this long poem was the work of a single day is amply shown by Robert's letters of the period. The notion that the poem was originally written at Kirkoswald, and was a product of the poet's early career, only polished up some years later, can be dismissed. More plausible is the reminiscence of Ainslie who, during his flying visit on 15 October that year, heard Robert reciting his mock-epic on that occasion. Ainslie could even remember a couplet after the line 'The landlord's laugh was ready chorus':

> The crickets joined the chirping cry,
> The kittlin chased her tail for joy.

which is not known in any manuscript, far less any printed version.[71] In April 1788 Mrs Dunlop had been travelling from Edinburgh to Hadding-ton and fell in with a personable youth on the road who lightened her journey with his sparkling wit and interesting conversation. What struck her particularly, was that the young man expressed an unbounded admira-tion for Burns and claimed to know him intimately. The young fellow was, in fact, Bob Ainslie, then on his way to Berrywell. On his way north from Ellisland in October 1790 Ainslie had called at Dunlop House and shown Mrs Dunlop either a fragment or a rough draft of 'Tam o Shanter'. Later, presumably in response to her entreaty, Ainslie sent her a copy of the text. A very long letter from Mrs Dunlop to Burns, simply headed 'Novr 1790' but belonging to the early part of that month (as the next letter was dated 16 November), was continued the following morning:

> I waked this morning to read a piece which no hand but [one] could have produced. Let me rejoice with you, my friend, that the torch of Hymen has not extinguished the little stars of imagination which shine in all the sparkling brightness of a clear frosty evening in the tale now before me

and she quoted two passages, totalling sixteen lines, back to him. This letter implies that the poem had come to her from someone other than Burns himself. There was certainly no mention of it in Robert's previous letter to her, dated 6 October.

Robert's next letter to Mrs Dunlop, lacking a date but ascribed to November 1790 (CL 192), states, 'I am much flattered by your approba-tion of my Tam o' Shanter'. It would appear that composition of this long poem had been in progress, off and on, for a month or more. A copy of the complete work was sent to Mrs Dunlop on 6 December (CL 192–3) and to Captain Grose five days earlier (CL 559–60). Finally, Robert mentioned to Mrs Dunlop the following April (CL 194) that the poem had 'a finishing polish that I despair of ever excelling'.

Though Francis Grose is forever associated with 'Tam o Shanter', the poem is also an enduring monument to the close friendship of Burns and Robert Riddell without whose antiquarian interests and connections it may never have been written. Riddell's reputation as an antiquary and man of letters suffered a knock in the late nineteenth century and reached its nadir in the 1930s when Snyder could pour scorn on his scholarship and reduce him to no more than one of 'the large group of persons who are remembered because of their association with Burns'[72] and DeLancey Ferguson, going one better, dismissed him as 'A loud blustering squire, a hollow and unsubstantial mind'.[73] It is unfortunate that Riddell the antiquary 'skill'd in rusty coins' is today not so well remembered as Riddell the participant in the contest for the whistle, immortalised in Robert's rollicking ballad (CW 368-70), which took place at Friars' Carse on 16 October 1789. The prize was a little ebony whistle brought to Scotland by a Dane in the service of Prince George of Denmark who married Princess (later Queen) Anne in 1683. He lost it in a drinking contest to Sir Robert Laurie, first baronet of Maxwelton, one of whose daughters married Walter Riddell of Glenriddell. The whistle thus passed into the Riddell family. Sir Robert Laurie, third baronet, attempted to emulate his grandfather in this drinking contest with his cousins Robert Riddell and Alexander Fergusson of Craigdarroch. The latter consumed upwards of eight bottles of claret before blowing the victory blast. John McMurdo of Drumlanrig was the judge of the contest and Burns was a witness and recorder of the event. The occasion was well documented, in Burns's notes on the song, in a letter to Riddell on the actual day, referring in jocular fashion to the forthcoming event (CL 481-2) and Robert's poetic answer to an invitation from Riddell to be present (CW 370). The letter, however, does not make any reference to Burns having a prior invitation and it seems that only after Riddell had received the letter was an invitation hastily extended to the poet, hence his poetic acceptance. This is borne out by the text of the actual bet itself, in the form of a memorandum of agreement between the contestants whose signatures appeared at the foot. In the lower left-hand corner, however, headed 'Cowhill, 10 October 1789', appeared the names of John McMurdo as judge, George Johnston as witness and Patrick Miller '*witness*, to be pre. if possible'.[74] It is not known whether Miller was able to attend the contest.

In the nineteenth century there was some controversy over whether Burns was actually present at the contest; but Robert Chambers assiduously investigated the matter in 1851 and obtained statements from surviving eye-witnesses. William Hunter of Cockrune was a servant at Friars' Carse at the time:

> Burns was present the whole evening. He was invited to attend the party, to see that the gentlemen drank fair, and to commemorate the day by writing a song. I recollect well that when the dinner was over, Burns quitted the table, and went to a table in the same room that was placed in a window that looked south-east: and there he sat down for the night. I placed before him a bottle of rum and another of brandy, which he did not finish, but left a good deal of each when he rose from the table after the gentlemen had gone to bed . . . When the gentlemen were put to bed, Burns walked home without assistance, not being the worse for drink. When Burns was sitting at the table in the window, he had pen, ink, and

paper, which I brought to him at his own request. He now and then wrote on the paper, and while the gentlemen were sober, he turned round often and chatted with them, but drank none of the claret which they were drinking.[75]

Doubts were cast on the accuracy of this statement made more than sixty years after the event, but solely on the claim that Robert composed the ballad during the contest. No doubt what he produced was a rough draft subsequently reworked and polished before it was rendered in its final form. But as a commentary on the poet's sobriety relative to the standards of the day it is invaluable. McDiarmid likewise got Jean Armour's reminiscence of the occasion. Jean remembered that 'the Bard, tho' present at the contest, came home in ordinary trim'.[76] Isobel Burns and her mother were still staying at Ellisland at the time, helping Jean while she recuperated after the birth of Francis Wallace, and Isabella Begg likewise told Chambers that she had heard from her mother that Uncle Robert had returned quite sober from the contest.

The assessments of Snyder and DeLancey Ferguson regarding Riddell were grossly unfair, as Robert Thornton amply proved.[77] It is clear that Riddell's contemporaries had a very high regard for his diligence as a scholar, bibliophile, numismatist, folklorist and all-round antiquary. Richard Gough looked upon Riddell as 'the first Antiquary of his Country'. Lord Hailes, the Earl of Buchan, Lord Oxford and George Paton (founder of the Advocates' Library) all wrote very highly of Riddell, whose services were recognised by the award of a doctorate by the University of Edinburgh.

Nineteenth and early twentieth-century biographers of Burns minimised Riddell's achievements in order to highlight the poet's. In so doing, they were less than fair to both men. This found expression most obviously in the matter of the Monkland Friendly Society. The facts of the matter may be briefly summarised. Riddell was very disappointed with the account of Dunscore parish compiled by the Revd. Joseph Kirkpatrick, so he prevailed on Robert to send a supplementary report (CL 586–7) to Sir John Sinclair, giving details of the Monkland Friendly Society. Whose idea this literary organisation was in the first place is not clear, but from the fact that it was intended 'to store the minds of the lower classes with useful knowledge' and give them 'a turn for reading and reflection' the idea probably originated with Burns who put it to Riddell.

> Impressed with this idea, a gentleman of this parish, ROBERT RIDDELL, Esq.; of Glenriddel, set on foot a species of circulating library, on a plan so simple, as to be practicable in any corner of the country; and so useful, as to deserve the notice of every country gentleman, who thinks the improvement of that part of his own species, whom chance has thrown into the humble walks of the peasant and the artisan, a matter worthy of his attention.

Robert's account described how Riddell got a number of his own tenants and farming neighbours to form themselves into a society for the purpose of having a library among themselves. The members were bound by a legal agreement for three years, at the end of which the books were auctioned off among the members.

> At the breaking up of this little society, which was formed under Mr. Riddell's patronage, what with benefactions of books from him, and what with their own purchases, they had collected together upwards of 150 volumes . . . A peasant who can read, and enjoy such books, is certainly a much superior being to his neighbour, who, perhaps, stalks beside his team, very little removed, except in shape, from the brutes he drives.

It is clear from this that Riddell was the instigator of the library, but in his covering letter to Sir John Sinclair he wrote:

> Mr Burns was so good as to take the whole charge of this small concern. He was treasurer, librarian, and censor to this little society, who will long have a grateful sense of his public spirit and exertions for their improvement and information.

The impression from this account is that the society was of brief duration, but in fact the library continued until 2 February 1931 and many of its books are preserved to this day at Ellisland. The library, founded by Burns and Riddell in March 1789, took its name from Monkland Cottage in the village of Cottack (now Dunscore) where it was originally located.

Many of the books were purchased from Peter Hill, Creech's former assistant who had now branched out as a bookseller on his own account, and Robert's letters to him make copious references to orders for the library. Sometimes Robert was reduced to devious ploys in order to influence the choice of reading matter. Thus, in a letter of 2 March 1790 (CL 317), when he was forced by the vote of the majority of subscribers to order an additional copy of Watson's *Body of Divinity*, he neatly sidestepped this:

> This last heavy Performance is so much admired by many of our Members, that they will not be content with one Copy, so Captain Riddel our President & Patron agreed with me to give you private instructions not to send Watson, but to say that you could not procure a Copy of the book so cheap as the one you sent formerly & therefore you had to wait farther Orders.

According to Robert's account, the members paid five shillings on entry and sixpence at each meeting, held on the last Saturday of the month, thus providing the funds to purchase books.

Of infinitely greater and more lasting importance, however, were two products of the friendship between Burns and Riddell. The third volume of *The Scots Musical Museum* was published in February 1790 and a fourth volume, containing some sixty songs by Burns, appeared in August 1792. Robert Riddell had the four volumes of the *Museum* rebound with interleaving throughout and then prevailed on his friend, by now in Dumfries, to insert explanatory notes on the blank leaves opposite each song. Mention of this invaluable manuscript has already been made in the context of the 'Highland Mary' legend. The interleaved *Museum* served as the basis for Cromek's *Reliques* (1808), but the surviving notes were not published in an accurate transcript until a century later when James Dick published his *Notes on Scottish Song by Robert Burns*.[78] It should be observed that Robert Riddell added quite a number of notes of his own. Anyone who cares to examine these notes in their proper context will find that Riddell stimulated Burns into a scholarly examination of the old fragments, as distinct from his original inclinations merely to recover, mend and add to these fragments.

Early in their friendship, however, Robert seems to have promised to make a manuscript collection of his favourite pieces for Riddell. He had already, about September 1786, supplied 'a parcel of songs' to Mrs Catherine Stewart of Stair (now known as the Stair MS) and five years later compiled a collection of thirteen then unpublished poems, including 'Tam o Shanter', which he presented to the same lady (the Afton Lodge MS). Twelve songs and poems had been inscribed on the end pages of the Edinburgh Edition belonging to Bishop Geddes. Robert seems to have been only too delighted to perform this labour for those whose friendship he esteemed most highly. In the case of Robert Riddell, however, Burns was prepared to go a great deal further.

It seems as if the idea arose informally in conversation. Probably Robert promised to make up a collection of manuscripts for his friend, and Riddell went one better by procuring two handsome calf-bound quarto volumes with his armorial crest embossed on the bindings. These he handed over to Robert with the intention that the first volume should contain poetry and the second a selection of the poet's letters. Work on the first volume began about May 1789,[79] when Robert sent his friend an undated letter (CL 481):

> I wish from my inmost soul it were in my power to give you a more substantial gratification & return for all your goodness to the Poet, than transcribing a few of his idle rhymes . . . If my Poems which I have transcribed & mean still to transcribe into your Book were equal to the grateful respect & high esteem I bear for the Gentleman to whom I present them, they would be the finest Poems in any language.

At the end of the first volume Robert wrote, 'Let these be regarded as the genuine sentiments of a man who seldom flattered any, and never those he loved'. The transcription was completed on 27 April 1791, the date applied by Robert to the preface (CL 482) which ended:

> As, from the situation in which it is now placed, the M.S.S. may be preserved, & this Preface read, when the hand that now writes & the

heart that now dictates it may be mouldering in the dust; let these be regarded as the genuine sentiments of a man who seldom flattered any, & never those he loved.

This volume contained fifty-seven unpublished poems, together with the autobiographical letter to Dr Moore. It appears to have been handed over to Riddell soon after the preface was written. Work on the second volume, which eventually contained twenty-seven of the letters which Robert considered his most important, continued at a leisurely pace and was still in progress at Christmas 1793 when Robert wrote to Mrs Dunlop (CL 208-9):

I have lately collected, for a Friend's perusal, all my letters; I mean, those which I first sketched in a rough draught, & afterwards wrote out fair.– On looking over some old musty papers, which, from time to time, I had parcelled by, as trash that were scarce worth preserving & which yet at the same time, I did not care to destroy I discovered many of these rude sketches, & have written & am writing them out, in a bound M.S.S., for my Friend's Library.– As I wrote always to you, the rhapsody of the moment, I cannot find a single scroll to you, except one, about the commencement of our acquaintance.– If there were any possible conveyance, I would send you a perusal of it.

The prose volume, however, was abruptly terminated soon after this letter was written. A day or two later occurred an incident (related in more detail in Chapter 16) which caused an irreparable breach between the two friends. Sadly, Robert Riddell died on 20 April 1794 before the quarrel could be patched up. It is worth noting that, although Burns continued to be estranged from the Riddell family till the end of 1794, his personal feelings for his erstwhile friend were unchanged, as can be seen by the obvious sincerity of his 'Sonnet on the Death of Robert Riddell' (CW 513).

After Riddell's death Burns managed to retrieve the first volume from his widow and both volumes were in Robert's possession until his own death two years later. Subsequently they were sent with all other manuscript material to Dr Currie at Liverpool. Currie had a very cavalier attitude to the poet's manuscripts entrusted to his care and omitted to return them to Jean Burns after the publication of his four-volume work in 1800. When Dr Currie died in 1805 the two quarto volumes came into the hands of his son William Wallace Currie, and when he died in 1853 his widow presented the volumes to the Liverpool Athenaeum. The Athenaeum did nothing with them for twenty years when they were put on exhibition. On 3 June 1913, however, the Athenaeum sold them by private treaty, through Messrs Sotheby, Wilkinson and Hodge, to a London bookseller J. Hornstein for £5,000. Contrary to many press reports of the time, Hornstein was not acting as the agent of the American millionaire, J. Pierpoint Morgan, although he did have a potential customer in mind and lost no time in sending the volumes across the Atlantic. Meanwhile, vociferous protests from all over the British Isles gathered momentum, especially when the Athenaeum tactlessly announced that the proceeds would form a Currie Memorial Fund. The Burns Federation took the lead in questioning the legality, let alone the ethics, of the Athenaeum transaction, and as the opening round of what promised to be a lengthy legal battle, Miss Annie Burns of Cheltenham obtained a decree in Dumfries Sheriff Court as executrix of her grandfather. But this was locking the stable door after the horse had bolted; by that time the manuscripts were not only in America but had found a new owner, John Gribbel of Philadelphia. At a meeting of the St Andrew's Society of Philadelphia on St Andrew's Day 1913, Gribbel broke the news that he strongly disapproved of the manner in which these precious relics had been hawked around the world. His generosity in purchasing the volumes was matched only by his public spirit in making a gift of them to the Scottish nation. Gribbel's deed of gift stipulated that a trust, consisting of Lord Rosebery and the Lord Provosts of Edinburgh and Glasgow *ex officio*, should look after the manuscripts until such time as a National Library of Scotland was established. The story ended, on 1 June 1926, on a happy note when Sir William Sleigh, Lord Provost of Edinburgh, handed over the volumes to Sir Herbert Maxwell, Chairman of the Board of Trustees of the National Library, in whose keeping they have been preserved ever since.[80]

Apart from Robert Riddell, Burns had few friends in the Ellisland period. His official position as an Exciseman to some extent kept him apart from the society of his peers, but there were some notable exceptions. John McMurdo (1743–1803), the judge at the whistle contest, succeeded his father in 1780 as chamberlain to the Duke of Queensberry at Drumlanrig and lived with his large family in the elegant mansion itself. Robert first met McMurdo in the summer of 1788 when he was just settling in at Ellisland. Between November of that year and 1793 McMurdo was the recipient of at least eight letters from the poet (CL 492–5). Robert transcribed many of his unpublished poems for McMurdo and also lent him his collection of bawdy ballads (CL 493–4):

> I think I once mentioned something to you of a Collection of Scots Songs I have for some years been making. I send you a perusal of what I have gathered.– I could not conveniently spare them above five or six days, & five or six glances at them will probably more than suffice you . . . There is not another copy of the Collection in the world, & I should be sorry that any unfortunate negligence should deprive me of what has cost me a good deal of pains.

This letter, the poet's first specific reference to his collection of bawdry, prompted Dr Currie to add the words, after Songs, 'a few of them are my own' in order to minimise the extent of Robert's authorship of the collection. This deceived all subsequent biographers and scholars until 1931 when DeLancey Ferguson gave the correct, unemended text of this letter.[81] Robert went on adding to this collection and his letters to certain correspondents, such as Cleghorn, included examples of his own composition in this genre. Robert never intended these 'cloaciniads' (literally 'songs of the sewer') as he called them, to see the light of day, far less be attributed to himself. What became of this collection after Robert's death is not known; the probability is that it was destroyed, but not before it fell into unknown hands which ensured that it should appear, about 1800, under the title of *The Merry Muses of Caledonia*. Only two copies of the first edition are extant, and both have had the printer's colophon defaced.[82] Burns's name did not appear as author on this edition, but Robert's connection with the collection was common knowledge and in the later nineteenth-century editions, believed to date from 1872 but masquerading under a transposed date of 1827, had his name writ large on the title page, under the subtitle of 'a choice collection of favourite songs gathered from many sources'. For good measure, the '1827' editions also included 'two of his letters and a poem – hitherto suppressed – and never before printed' – the notorious 'horse litter' letter to Ainslie (CL 331-2) and the letter to Johnson containing the passage 'I am so enamoured with a certain girl's prolific twin-bearing merit . . .' (CL 293). Why the latter should have been singled out is a complete mystery, as the letter had appeared in Chambers (1856) and all subsequent editions and is in no sense indecent. The poem referred to was 'Libel Summons' (CW 227-8) composed for Robert's facetious Court of Equity in 1785. It was not till the 1960s that scholars like James Kinsley and Gershon Legman[83] were able to sort the wheat from the chaff and identify those productions which were definitely written or reworked by Burns.[84]

McMurdo married Jane Blair, daughter of a provost of Dumfries. Both were mentioned in the 'Election Ballad' of 1790 (CW 404) as 'McMurdo and his lovely spouse'. Mrs McMurdo herself received a letter from Burns on 2 May 1789 (CL 529), thanking her for her hospitality and enclosing a poem, probably 'To John McMurdo, Esq., of Drumlanrig' (CW 356). Robert composed 'To the Woodlark' (CW 550) at her request. Her sister Rebecca married Colonel Arent Schuyler De Peyster, a friend of Burns in the Dumfries years. The lines beginning 'Blest be McMurdo to his latest day!' (CW 356) were inscribed by Robert on a window-pane in the chamberlain's quarters at Drumlanrig. The McMurdos had seven sons and seven daughters. The eldest daughter Jean (1777-1839) and her sister Philadelphia (1779-1825) were taught to play the piano by Robert's friend and collaborator, Stephen Clarke, whom he persuaded to come down from Edinburgh. Jean Armour sang an old song which Clarke transcribed and taught to the McMurdo girls, and as a compliment to the eldest Miss McMurdo Robert composed the lyrics of 'Bonie Jean' (CW 493). The exact circumstances of the composition of this song were given to the lady herself in July 1793 (CL 693-4) in unequivocal terms which make it perfectly clear that Jean McMurdo and not Jean Armour was the eponymous heroine. Philadelphia, more familiarly known as Phillis, was a noted beauty and inspired several of Robert's songs: 'Phillis the Fair' (CW 495), 'Philly and Willy' (CW 529) and 'Adown Winding Nith' (CW 497).

After the Burns family moved to Dumfries in 1791 the friendship between the poet and the chamberlain was maintained. In 1793 McMurdo bought the estate of Hardriggs near Annan as an investment, but had a town house in Dumfries. He took a keen interest in municipal politics and became provost in 1794. The McMurdos were an ancient yeoman family, well connected by marriage with many county families, to which Burns consequently had entrée. These included the Charteris of Amisfield, the Sharpes of Hoddam and the Duncans of Torthorwald and Lochrutton, and through the last named the McMurdos were related to Dr James Currie, Burns's biographer.

Robert's relationship with his landlord was ambivalent. Patrick Miller had shown him kindness and an offer of friendship from his earliest Edinburgh days, and the offer of a farm was no doubt well meant. It also tickled Miller's fancy to have the celebrated poet as one of his tenants, and this underlay a certain patronising attitude which Robert very soon came to resent. Early biographers hinted that there was resentment on both sides, with the assertion that Burns 'found that Mr Miller's relation to him was that of the patron, who expected deference, and passively, if not actively, resented Burns's independence'.[85] Robert confided to Peter Hill about October 1791 (CL 320) when he was on the point of leaving Ellisland, and quoted a couple of lines apostrophising his landlord:

> His meddling vanity, a busy fiend,
> Still making work his selfish craft must mend.

Robert had been on his farm a couple of months before he was invited up to the big house for dinner on 15 August 1788, an event which he described fully to Mrs Dunlop the following day (CL 152-3):

> I was yesterday at Mr Miller's to dinner; the first time since I have been his Tenant.– My reception was quite to my mind: from the lady of the house, quite flattering.– I believe in my conscience that she respects me more on account of marrying a woman in circumstances something similar to her own; when she commenced Mrs Millar.–[86] See what it is to be rich! I was going to add, & to be great; but to be rich is to be great.– She sometimes hits on a Couplet or two, impromptu.– She repeated one or two, to the admiration of all present.– My suffrage as a professional man, was expected: I for once went, agonizing over the belly of my conscience – Pardon me, ye, my adored Household gods, Independance of Spirit; & Integrity of Soul! In the course of conversation, Johnson's musical Museum, A Collection of Scots Song with the music, was talked of.– We got a song on the Harpsichord, beginning 'Raving winds around her blowing' – The Air was much admired: the lady of the house ask'd me whose were the words. 'Mine, Madam' – they are my very best verses! sacre Dieu! she took not the smallest notice of them! The old Scots Proverb says well – 'King's caff is better than ither folks' corn.'– I was going to make a New Testament quotation about 'casting Pearls,' but that would be too virulent.

The only other reference to Miller in the poet's letters to Mrs Dunlop occurs in a letter of 25 March 1789 (CL 170):

My master, Mr Miller, out of real tho' mistaken benevolence, sought me industriously out, to set me this farm, as he said to give me a lease that would make me comfortable & easy . . . I am sorry to tell you this Madam, but it is a damning truth; though I beg, as the world think that I have got a pennyworth of a farm, you will not undeceive them.

Robert's pride would not let him admit (to anyone other than his mother-confessor) that he had made a mistake. Despite the poor first impression which Mrs Miller made on Burns they seem to have been on quite cordial terms eventually, if the criterion of letters and poems is anything to go by. Mrs Miller was the recipient of a letter on 2 November 1789 (CL 245) enclosing his verses on Captain Grose (CW 373) and a political ballad (CW 367) about Sir James Johnstone, but really attacking the Duke of Queensberry. Sir James was the Tory candidate in the parliamentary election of 1790 who lost his seat to Patrick Miller Junior (1773-1845). At the tender age of sixteen, Miller retired from the army with the rank of captain (which had been purchased for him the previous year) and entered politics. With the aid of the Duke of Queensberry (who had temporarily changed sides), he was elected as member for the Dumfriesshire Burghs when he was not yet seventeen. The corrupt electoral system of the time debarred children under sixteen from electing and being elected (along with women, paupers, lunatics, convicted criminals, Nonconformists, Catholics, Quakers, Jews and agnostics). William Pitt the Younger, by contrast, was a relatively old man of twenty-one when he entered parliament at his second attempt, becoming Chancellor of the Exchequer a year later and Prime Minister at the age of twenty-four. The Dumfriesshire Burghs – Dumfries, Annan, Lochmaben, Kirkcudbright and Sanquhar – were the Five Carlins of Robert's poem (CW 364) in which young Miller was described as 'a sodger boy, wha spak wi modest grace'. In the 'Election Ballad' composed at the close of that election and addressed to Robert Graham of Fintry (CW 402-6), the winning candidate was referred to in the lines:

> Miller brought up th'artillery ranks,
> The many-pounders of the Banks,

a punning reference to Captain Miller's brief military career and his father's connections with the Bank of Scotland. Burns, in a letter of 9 December 1789 (CL 431-2), described 'Captain Miller, my landlord's son' as 'a youth by no means above mediocrity in his abilities; and is said to have a huckster-lust for shillings, pence & farthings'. We get some idea of the corrupt electioneering of the eighteenth century in this letter, as well as a graphic account sent to Mrs Dunlop on 9 July 1790 (CL 188-90):

I have just got a summons to attend with my men-servants armed as well as we can, on Monday at one o'clock in the *morning* to escort Captain Miller from Dalswinton to Dumfries to be a Candidate for our Boroughs which chuse their Member that day.– The Duke of Queensberry & the

Nithsdale Gentlemen who are almost all friends to the Duke's Candidate, the said Captain, are to raise all Nithsdale on the same errand. The Duke of Buccleugh's, Earl of Hopeton's people, in short, the Johnstons, Jardines, and all the Clans of Annandale, are to attend Sir James Johnston who is the other Candidate, on the same account.– This is no exaggeration.– On Thursday last, at chusing the Delegate for the boro' of Lochmaben, the Duke & Captain Miller's friends led a strong party, among others, upwards of two hundred Colliers from Sanquhar Coal-works & Miners from Wanlock-head; but when they appeared over a hill-top within half a mile of Lochmaben, they found such a superiour host of Annandale warriors drawn out to dispute the Day, that without striking a stroke, they turned their backs & fled with all the precipitation the horrors of blood & murther could inspire.– I shall go to please my Landlord, and to see the Combustion; but instead of trusting to the strength of Man, I shall trust to the heels of my horse, which are among the best in Nithsdale.

A great deal of confusion has existed over another of Robert's acquaintances of the Ellisland period. In the autumn of 1790 William Lorimer took from Robert Riddell a lease of Kemys Hall or Kemmishall, a farm about two miles south of Ellisland on the other side of the Nith. Lorimer appeared in Burns's subscription list of 1 November that year for Dr James Anderson's forthcoming literary periodical *The Bee* (CL 571). Lorimer had previously farmed at Craigieburn near Moffat and it was there that his daughter Jean was born in 1775. Burns got to know the family well and, as we shall see later, formed an attachment to Miss Lorimer who was to become the Chloris and the 'lass with the lintwhite locks' of several love songs. Robert's familiarity with the Lorimers has been criticised on the grounds that William Lorimer was a smuggler and illicit trader in spirits. This assumption rested entirely on a letter of Burns to his supervisor, Alexander Findlater (CL 540). Robert got into hot water over his failure to check the Lorimer stock properly, but in mitigation he pointed out that he had been unable to carry out his task because Lorimer had gone to Edinburgh:

> The surveys I have made during his absence might as well have been marked '*key absent*' as I never found any body but the lady, who I know is not mistress of keys, &c. to know any thing of it, and one of the times it would have rejoiced all Hell to have seen her so drunk . . . I know, Sir, & regret deeply, that this business glances with a malign aspect on my character as an Officer; but as I am really innocent in the affair, & as the gentleman is known to be an illicit Dealer . . . I shall be peculiarly unfortunate if my character shall fall a sacrifice to the dark manouevres of a Smuggler.

For an Exciseman to be on friendly terms with a known smuggler with a drunken wife was one of the cardinal sins, and this has often been used by Robert's detractors to illustrate an ambiguous attitude towards the service that employed him. But Lorimer is a common surname in Dumfriesshire and Ayrshire, and the father of Chloris was no more an illicit dealer than he was the 'blockhead' who refused the Kilmarnock Poems. Kirkmahoe parish, in which Kemys Hall lay, was not one of those in Robert's survey and that alone ought to have alerted previous writers to the false premise on which their criticism of the poet-Exciseman were made. In fact, the William Lorimer referred to in this letter was the tenant of Cairnmill on the Scaur Water, about half a mile south of Penpont and very much within Robert's jurisdiction.[87]

Burns the farmer, Exciseman, poet and song-writer also had ambitions to become a playwright and polemicist. Ramsay of Ochtertyre, who accompanied Sir Samuel Egerton Brydges on his visit to Ellisland in the autumn of 1790, left a vivid account of his meeting with the poet, which sheds some light on one of Robert's unrealised ambitions:

> We fell into conversation directly and soon got into the *mare magnum* of poetry. He told me that he had now gotten a story for a drama, which he was to call *Rob Macquechan's Elshon*, from a popular story of Robert Bruce being defeated on the Water of Cairn, when the heel of his boot having loosened in flight he applied to Robert Macquechan to fit it, who, to make sure, ran his awl nine inches up the King's heel.[88]

That Robert had ambitions to become a playwright was also revealed in a letter to Lady Elizabeth Cunningham on 23 December 1789 (CL 498-9):

> I have some thoughts of the Drama. Considering the favorite things of the day . . . does not your Ladyship think that a Scottish Audience would be better pleased with the Affectation, Whim & Folly of their own native growth, than with manners which to by far the greatest of them can be only second hand?– No man knows what Nature has fitted him for untill he try; and if after a preparatory course of some years' study of Men and Books, I should find myself unequal to the task, there is no great harm done – Virtue and Study are their own reward.– I have got Shakespeare, and begun with him; and I shall stretch a point & make myself master of all the Dramatic Authors of any repute, in both English and French, the only languages which I know.

Regrettably Robert's ambitions to follow in the footsteps of Shakespeare were never realised, and his cantata 'The Jolly Beggars' remains his only dramatic work.

As a polemicist, however, Robert had more success, although it did not increase his income. From 19 December 1786 when 'Address to a Haggis' appeared in the *Caledonian Mercury*, till October 1797 when 'Address to the Toothache' (CW 553) appeared in the *Scots Magazine*, some thirty poetic works first appeared in newspapers and magazines; in some cases, the same poem appeared in two or three different periodicals before its incorporation in the latest edition of Burns's works.[89]

Robert's first prose contribution to a newspaper was published in the *Edinburgh Evening Courant* on 22 November 1788 (CL 487-8) under the pen name of 'A Briton'. It was inspired by the celebrations that marked the centenary of the Glorious Revolution which led to the flight of James VII and II and the accession of William and Mary. Robert, a Jacobite by sentiment, was revolted by the 'harsh political prejudice' in the diatribe by the Revd. Joseph Kirkpatrick from the pulpit of Dunscore church at the local centenary celebration on 5 November, and in this essay he called for moderation and a proper perspective on the House of Stewart, concluding by drawing a parallel between the rebels of 1688 and the Americans of 1776. In this courageous and well-expressed essay Robert showed a new maturity and breadth. He concluded prophetically:

> I dare say, the American Congress, in 1776, will be allowed to have been as able and enlightened, and a whole Empire will say, as honest, as the English Convention in 1688; and that the fourth of July will be as sacred to their posterity as the fifth of November is to us.

The fourth of July, as it has turned out, is celebrated just as fervently today, whereas the fifth of November is nowadays remembered only in the context of an earlier *coup d'état*, the attempt by Guy Fawkes to blow up the Houses of Parliament in 1605.

On 9 February 1789 the same newspaper published an open letter to William Pitt, the Prime Minister, protesting at the government's unfair treatment of the Scottish distillers (CL 509–11). This time Robert used 'John Barleycorn' as his *nom de plume*.

On 2 April 1789 Robert wrote to Peter Hill (CL 313–14) in extravagantly ebullient mood. Near the close, however, he became more serious and wrote:

> Write me first post and send me the address of Stuart, Publisher of *The Star* newspaper: this I beg particularly, but do not speak of it . . . By Stuart I mean the famous Stuart who differed with the rest of the proprietors and set up by himself.

In the 1770s the brothers Charles and Peter Stuart had left Edinburgh and established themselves in London as printers. In 1778 they were joined by a younger brother, Daniel. Charles, the eldest, had been a schoolmate and close friend of Robert Fergusson. He left the family business to become a successful playwright. Peter and Daniel obtained in 1788 the contract to print the *Morning Post* and seven years later became proprietors of both this newspaper and the equally popular *Oracle*. Peter, however, left the *Morning Post* in 1788 to start *The Star*, the first evening paper in Britain to appear every day, and appointed fellow-Scot Andrew Macdonald as editor. *The Star* made its debut on 3 May 1788 and continued till 1831. Peter Stuart fell out with his partners over the Regency controversy – he championed the Prince of Wales against the Prime Minister – and on 13 February 1789 he and his brother Charles, with James Mackintosh (brother of his fiancée), founded a rival *Star*, later renamed *Stuart's Star and Evening*

Advertiser, and later still the *Morning Star*, which ceased publication in mid-June 1789. Stuart subsequently returned to the *Oracle* and had a glittering career. He had an uncanny eye for new talent and at the turn of the century employed a galaxy of writers including Coleridge, Lamb, Southey and Wordsworth. In April 1789 he wrote to Burns offering him 'for communications to the paper, a small salary quite as large as his Excise office emoluments',[90] but Robert did not wish to tie himself to one particular paper, and he declined the offer, although he agreed to submit items from time to time, for which Stuart put him on the complimentary list. Robert thanked him for this courtesy (CL 520) and included the text of the verse and inscription which he had arranged to be placed on Fergusson's tombstone (CW 269).

Robert and Stuart, however, got off to a bad start within a matter of days, when the newspaper printed four lines, purporting to be by Burns, on the Duchess of Gordon's reel-dancing. A paragraph attributing these lines to 'Mr Burns, the ploughing poet', appeared on Friday 27 March and prompted an anonymous correspondent to submit a further three stanzas (CW 358), hinting that this was but a sample, and he was prepared to produce the entire poem if desired. This addendum was published on 31 March. Four days later, *The Star* published an even longer piece giving further background details regarding the poem and Burns's hand in the matter. The mysterious correspondent who furnished this material gave his name as Dr Theodore Theobald Theophilus Tripe, who claimed that Burns had given him the manuscript at Mauchline the previous summer. To add further insult to injury Dr Tripe now left two more stanzas concluding:

> But frae thy mow, O Gordon fair!
>   Could I but get ae kiss sae frisky
> For a' the sharney queans in Ayr   [shitty maidens]
>   I wadna gi' a glass of whisky!

Thus the mysterious author managed to cast a slur on the personal hygiene of the girls in Ayr *and* make an insinuation about Burns's love of whisky. By this time Peter Stuart had a shrewd suspicion that Burns was not the author of these scurrilous verses and appealed to him to clarify the matter.

Robert got to hear of this on 12 April and immediately wrote to Stuart to complain. In the meantime, however, he had been told by a friend that *The London Gazetteer and New Daily Advertiser* had printed the original four lines in its issue of 28 March, and on 10 April wrote to the editor of that paper (CL525):

> had you only forged dullness on me, I should not have thought it worth while to reply; but to add ingratitude too, is what I cannot in silence bear.

The *Gazetteer* in due course published Robert's disclaimer, adding a footnote:

> Mr Burns will do right in directing his petulance to the proper delinquent, the Printer of *The Star*, from which Paper the Stanza was literally copied into the Gazetteer. We can assure him, however, for his comfort, that the Duchess of Gordon acquits him both of the ingratitude and the dullness. She has, with much difficulty, discovered that the *Jeu d'Esprit* was written by the right honourable the Treasurer of the Navy, on her Grace's dancing at a ball given by the Earl of Findlater; this has been found out by the industry and penetration of Lord Fife. The lines are certainly not so dull as Mr Burns insinuates, and we fear he is jealous of the poetical talents of his rival, Mr Dundas.

To be accused of libelling a lady for whom Robert had only the highest respect was bad enough; to discover that the jape at his expense had been perpetrated by none other than Henry Dundas must have been galling in the extreme, given Robert's Pavlovian reaction whenever he saw the hated name in print. Peter Stuart endeavoured to make amends by printing Robert's letter to him in full, together with an explanatory headnote and a flattering footnote which went a long way to soothing the poet's agitated breast. On 4 May Robert wrote at length to Alexander Cunningham (CL 457) in reply to a letter of his:

> Thank you, my dearest Sir, for your concern for me in my contest with the London News-men.– Depend upon it that I will never deign to reply to *their* Petulence.– The Publisher of the Star has been polite.– He may find his account in it; though I would scorn to put my name to a News-paper Poem.

Robert went on to mention that he had made an exception in the case of the verses which he had previously sent to his friend (CW 328); as Anne Stewart had 'prostituted her character' Robert no longer felt bound to set any store by the poem, which he had sent to Stuart 'as a bribe, in my earnestness to be cleared from the foul aspersion respecting the Duchess of Gordon'. The extraordinary lengths to which Robert went to refute his authorship of the poems were explained by some biographers as due to the poet's anxiety lest the matter damage the chance of patronage at a crucial moment in his Excise plans, but the plain fact is that Robert was genuinely grateful to the Duke and Duchess of Gordon who had shown him great kindness both in Edinburgh and at Castle Gordon and he was always very sensitive to anything that might cast aspersions on his character. Criticism of his poetry he had learned to live with, but anything that was calculated to show him as ungrateful or base cut him to the quick. Chambers, however, probably exaggerated the malevolence of Henry Dundas towards Burns. By representing Burns as the ploughing poet, fond of women and whisky and capable of ridiculing a patroness in verse, Dundas showed himself as no warm friend or admirer of the poet, and Burns, for his part, would realise that Dundas would not facilitate his rapid promotion.[91] But that is to read far too much into the affair. Dundas was, first and foremost, out to make fun of the Duchess, and Burns was a secondary victim of the jest. In any event Dundas seems not to have interested himself in Burns's Excise career, one way or the other; and Robert enjoyed as much preferment and advancement as the strict regulations of the service permitted.

After this minor *contretemps*, however, Robert settled down to an amicable relationship with Peter Stuart to whom he sent occasional poems and letters. The latter, usually dealing with major topics of political importance, were published under pseudonyms such as 'Tim Nettle'. Stuart's offer of a regular salary was reiterated the following year but again declined, though Robert continued to send him amusing, satirical and often politically inspired pieces, of which the 'Ode on the Departed Regency Bill' (CW 352-4) and the splendid burlesque, 'A New Psalm for the Chapel of Kilmarnock' (CW 354-5), were the best. Robert responded to the complimentary copies which Stuart sent him by composing the lines 'To a Gentlemen who had sent a newspaper, and offered to continue it free of expense' (CW 379-80) which formed a brilliant poetic summary of the world's current affairs. When Stuart's newspaper became rather erratic, Robert sent him a gentle reminder in verse beginning 'Dear Peter, Dear Peter' (CW 358).

It was during the Ellisland period that Robert's health, never of the best, began to give him grave concern. Although the long-held view that Robert's health had been permanently impaired by rheumatic fever as a teenager has recently been critically re-examined,[92] there is ample testimony from the poet's correspondence, and the eye-witness evidence of his contemporaries, that his health, for one reason or another, deteriorated in this period. The arduous tasks of running an unrewarding farm, as well as hard riding across the upland parishes of Nithsdale in all weathers, would have taken their toll of a constitution more robust than Robert's. From his letters we know that Robert suffered 'this fashionable influenza' in September 1788. By December of the same year, however, Robert was confessing to Cruikshank (CL 360) that 'My knee, I believe, never will be entirely well; and an unlucky fall this winter has made it still worse'. To Mrs Dunlop on 8 November 1789 (CL 180) he complained, 'I have somehow got a most violent cold; and in the stupid, disagreable predicament of a stuffed, aching head and an unsound, sickly crasis . . .' By 13 December (CL 181) he was 'groaning under the miseries of a diseased nervous System; a System of all others the most essential to our happiness – or the most productive of our Misery.– For now near three weeks I have been so ill with a nervous head-ach' which, to some extent had been brought on by anguish and remorse at the memory of Margaret Campbell who had died three years earlier. To Gilbert he confessed on 11 January 1790 (CL 358), 'My nerves are in a damnable State.– I feel that horrid hypochondria pervading every atom of both body and soul'.

Matters gradually improved; by the end of the month, Robert could inform Mrs Dunlop that his health was 'greatly better'. Though he never mentioned it himself, Robert suffered an attack of quinsy in late September, early October 1790, as reported by Ainslie to Mrs McLehose on 18 October. Three months later, however, there was a fall, 'not from my horse but with my horse', which interrupted his correspondence with Mrs Dunlop for several weeks. On 7 February 1791 (CL 193) he wrote, 'I have been a cripple some time, & this is the first day my arm & hand have been able to serve me in writing'. A few weeks later Janet Little, the poetic milk-maid and a protégée of Mrs Dunlop's, paid a visit to Ellisland on her way to Ecclefechan where her family resided. Robert was not at home when she called, but was expected shortly. When he did appear, however, he was in a dishevelled state, having fallen off his horse and broken his arm. Janet related in verse her embarrassment at greeting the illustrious poet in such circumstances and her intense feelings for Jean who was reduced to tears by the spectacle.[93] It was not until 11 April that Robert could resume his correspondence with Mrs Dunlop (CL 194) 'with my own hand', thanking her for 'your kind anxiety in this last disaster that my evil genius had in store for me' and he closed lugubriously, 'This is the greatest effort my broken arm has yet made.'

More than six months elapsed before he took up his pen to write to Mrs Dunlop again, on 26 October (CL 195) when he was on the point of removing to Dumfries. In the same month he moaned to Peter Hill (CL 320):

> I was never more unfit for writing.– A poor devil nailed to an elbow chair, writhing in anguish with a bruised leg, laid on a stool before him, is in a fine situation truly for saying bright things.

It is perhaps worth stating that most of Robert's ailments in the Ellisland period were due to physical injuries and riding accidents and, on the whole, there is little evidence of the depressive illness which he himself described as 'hypochondria'. His mental state, throughout this period, was excellent. To be sure, his farm had proved a disappointment, but it never provoked the hysterical anguish evident in the closing year at Mount Oliphant. By 1790 Robert had largely delegated the dairy farm to Jean and the servants; the Excise work, though arduous and daunting, was a challenge to which he rose nobly; and there was the constant intellectual stimulus of friends like Riddell and correspondents like Mrs Dunlop, not to mention the on-going work on the *Museum* and plans for future diversification of his talents. His zest for life was in no way diminished.

CHAPTER 15

Dumfries: the Wee Vennel, 1791–3

Ye men of wit and wealth, why all this sneering
'Gainst poor Excisemen? Give the cause a hearing.
What are your Landlord's rent-rolls? Taxing ledgers!
What Premiers? What ev'n Monarchs? Mighty Gaugers!
Nay, what are Priests (those seeming godly wise-men)?
What are they, pray, but Spiritual Excisemen!

Kirk and State Excisemen (CW 363)

William Ernest Henley, in his brilliant but flawed and distorted essay on Burns, drew his narrative to a close with the dismissive words, 'I propose to deal with the Dumfries period with all possible brevity'.[1] The biographical sketch of Burns which appeared in all editions of the *Encyclopaedia Britannica* till 1973, but which was actually written by Professor John Nicol for the ninth edition in 1876, sums up the popular view of Robert's declining years which has persisted to this day:

Unfortunately the 'Rock of Independence' to which he had proudly retired was but a castle of air, over which the meteors of French political enthusiasm cast a lurid gleam. In the last years of his life, exiled from polite sociey on account of his revolutionary opinions, he became sourer in temper and plunged more deeply into the dissipations of the lower ranks, among whom he found his only companionship and sole, though shallow, sympathy.[2]

These widely accepted views of the Dumfries period had their origins in malicious gossip which grew around the poet in the last decade of his life. Even before his brief fame in 1786–7 Robert was acutely aware that malice, envy, resentment and jealousy conspired to blacken his character. As a young man, he had often acted recklessly and little heeded the consequences of his savage wit and biting satire. While many New Lichts applauded his attacks on religious orthodoxy, an even larger group was offended and outraged by his attacks on their devoutly held beliefs. When they counter-attacked, they denounced Burns as a blasphemer and an atheist. Neither charge stood up to serious examination, of course, but the mud stuck. Even after he 'settled down' with a wife and family and a steady job in government service, that ready wit of his could still be his undoing, even though he did his best to curb it. His epigrammatic brilliance sometimes ran ahead of innate caution and consequently alienated many who might have befriended him. Robert could be rude, tactless and thoughtless and for a man who was ultra-sensitive to imagined slights and snubs on the part of others he could be remarkably obtuse in giving offence. Eventually he even alienated his closest correspondent, Mrs Dunlop, and he never realised why she stopped writing to him. Sentimental Jacobitism was one thing; a radical political outlook, especially in the 1790s, was something else. We have already seen how his lines at Stirling almost jeopardised his attempt to get into the Excise; in the paranoia which enveloped the country with the downfall of the French monarchy the liberal views expounded by Burns were regarded as seditious. Robert, as a humble placeman, sailed very close to the wind at times. In Dumfries he was soon targeted by the Tory faction as a dangerous dissident. Far from learning to trim his sails and curb his tongue, Robert often lashed out with epigrammatic squibs which only exacerbated the situation. Consequently, even the obituary notices in the newspapers, both local and national, implied that he had spent his last years in abject poverty and a close approximation to disgrace. Robert Heron (1797) and James Currie (1800) were strongly influenced by these malicious reports when compiling the earliest memoirs of Burns, and once the die was cast later biographers fell over each other in painting an even blacker picture. Thus what had merely been innuendo in Heron, or a discreet drawing of the veil by Currie, became the signposts to other writers. Lockhart (1828) and Cunningham (1834) laid on with a will, embroidering the sorry tale with many fantasies of their own fabrication. Subjectivity was the keynote of the biographies of the nineteenth and early twentieth centuries. Burns the drunken debauchee, redeemed only by the brilliance of his poetry, was a powerful image. Incidentally, it fitted the views of the Victorian biographers to paint a vivid picture of Burns redeemed from his moral turpitude by the pure, undefiled love of 'Highland Mary', which explains why this ethereal, and ephemeral, young lady was given such prominence and why statues of her exist to this day, whereas 'Bonie Jean', the real love of Robert's life, was totally neglected.

Chambers-Wallace (1896) began the trend towards a more objective view, but it was not until Snyder (1932) that a positive reassessment was fully accomplished. DeLancey Ferguson (1939), Daiches (1952), Lindsay (1954) and Fitzhugh (1970) continued the process. With Thornton (1963) and Fowler (1988), however, the pendulum has swung back against Burns. Thornton,[3] in seeking to rehabilitate the poet's first major biographer Dr Currie, has had to defend him against the charge of maligning Burns and this, perforce, has tended to put the poet in a bad light; and Fowler,[4] pursuing his own theories regarding Burns's last illness, has come up with lead poisoning from the litharge used as a preservative in wine, and thus revived the hoary chestnut of the poet's heavy drinking.

Carswell (1930) began her Dumfries chapter brilliantly with the aphorism, 'A man's failure is doubled when he fails under the eyes of his wife'[5] and maintained that Jean was not backward in blaming her husband for the Ellisland fiasco. But we have no shred of evidence concerning how Jean felt or reacted, any more than we can conclude that the Ellisland episode was a fiasco. There is no doubt that, in November 1791, Robert was congratulating himself on having extricated himself from his seventy-six year lease so well, even receiving a small consideration from Patrick Miller in order to relinquish the tenancy. The sales of crops, stock and equipment had gone remarkably well, and Robert, once more, had a sizeable amount of ready cash in his hands.

The move to Dumfries was eminently sensible, for that, after all, was where his work was centred. As for Jean, it is debatable whether she regretted the move from the isolated and uncomfortable farmhouse into the town. To be sure, she must have found their new quarters very cramped after the relative spaciousness of Ellisland, but she was a town girl herself, born and bred in an urban environment. If she had any regrets, Jean was probably sad that her 'nice wee cow', which she had insisted on bringing with her to Dumfries to provide fresh milk for her young family, could not be pastured in the tiny garden at the rear of their tenement in the Wee Vennel and reluctantly this had to be let go. Otherwise, life in Dumfries could not have been so very different from life in Mauchline, and if the upstairs flat was cramped and inconvenient, it was more than made up for by the convenience of shops and the company of women of her own age.

Dumfries in 1791 was a compact and prosperous county town on the east bank of the Nith at that point where it was still navigable and just fordable. There had been a settlement here for countless centuries, but Dumfries, (from Gaelic *Dùn phreas*, the fort on the wooded ridge or hill-fort among shrubs) rose to importance when Scotland emerged as a nation. It was made a royal burgh by King William the Lion in 1186 and became a major bulwark in the defence of the western Borders. The town's motto 'a Loreburn' was used as a war-cry to rally the townspeople to the Lore Burn, the stream which formed a natural obstacle to English invaders.

It had also been a place of some ecclesiastical importance and a stronghold of the Balliol family in medieval times. Devorgilla, mother of King John Balliol, was a prominent benefactress, remembered for having erected a bridge across the Nith, and the forerunner of the fifteenth-century bridge that stands to this day. In the chapel of the Minorites or Grey Friars (at the head of present-day Friars' Vennel) Bruce had stabbed the Red Comyn and made his bid for the Scottish crown in 1306, thereby triggering off the Wars of Independence. In the centuries of struggle with England, Dumfries was of immense strategic importance. The town played its turbulent part in the feuds of the Maxwells and the Johnstones, favoured the Lords of the Congregation against Mary Queen of Scots, and suffered in the struggles of the Covenanters and the 'Killing Time'. Memorials on the Whitesands and in the town's cemeteries testify to those martyred for their faith. The grandfather of Robert Riddell of Glenriddell, and the Whig provost Andrew Crosbie of Holm, were taken hostage by the Jacobite army of Prince Charles Edward Stuart in 1745, and the following year, on his retreat north, the Young Pretender himself established his headquarters in the Blue Bell Inn (later the County Hotel and now part of a department store). The large chamber in which he held court was preserved as Prince Charlie's Room, until the hotel was demolished in the 1980s. It also had a Burns Room, used by the Dumfries Burns Club, thus linking two of Scotland's most colourful and romantic figures. In June 1787 Robert had been made a freeman of the burgh at the conclusion of his Border tour; little did he realise then that, barely four years later, he would be setting up house there.

In 1791 Dumfries had a population of 5,600, densely packed within a small area along the ridge at the bend of the river. Well over a thousand of these residents were actively engaged in trade or business. A further 1,400 people lived in the landward portion of the parish. The High Street ran along the ridge, parallel to the river, and from it extended about a dozen vennels, or lanes, at right angles, running down to the Whitesands, a stretch of level ground along the river. When the river was in spate and burst its banks the Whitesands regularly flooded (a distressing problem which continues to this day). The Burns family took up their abode on the middle floor of a tenement on the north side of the Wee Vennel about a hundred yards from the riverbank. This was the same river that had provided such tempting vistas from the spence at Ellisland, but Robert and Jean would have had to crane their necks to get a glimpse of the Nith from their new lodgings. The Wee Vennel, otherwise known as Cavart's Vennel, was also less flatteringly (though probably more accurately) known as the Stinking Vennel from the rubbish and raw sewage which coursed down its gutters and discharged straight into the river. Today it is an altogether more salubrious thoroughfare rejoicing in the name of Bank Street, an allusion to the fact that many of the town's banks have their premises there.

Dumfries, as the county town, had a substantial middle-class population. Chambers noted that it was 'cursed rather than blessed by the partial or entire idleness of large classes of its inhabitants'.[6] A high proportion of its population consisted of retired gentlemen, well-to-do professional men and tradesmen whose shop-duties did not occupy much of their time. For this reason the tavern was an important focal point of society, as it was in Edinburgh for that matter. In 1793 Dumfries boasted three large inns, the George, the Bell and the King's Arms, all situated at the southern end of the High Street, several taverns, of which the Globe, the Jerusalem and the Hole i' the Wa' in the High Street and the Coach and Horses on the Whitesands near the corner of the Wee Vennel, were certainly frequented by the poet, a coffee-house and no fewer than seventy-five smaller premises licensed for the sale of spirituous liquors – one for every ninety souls in the parish. In addition, about twenty people were prosecuted annually for running illegal drinking-dens.

On the other hand, Dumfries provided a focus for polite society. It was the largest town between Carlisle and Ayr and provided a genteel mode of living. The Revd. Dr Burnside, minister of the Second or New Church (now Greyfriars), wrote of his parishioners:

In their private manners they are social and polite; and the town, together with the neighbourhood a few miles around it, furnishes a society amongst whom a person with a moderate income may spend his days with as much enjoyment, perhaps, as in any part of the kingdom whatever.[7]

Dumfries joined with the four other Dumfriesshire burghs in returning a member to Parliament and, as such, was 'Maggie by the banks o Nith, / A dame wi pride eneugh' in 'The Five Carlins' (CW 364-6). Burns's 'Mimmou'd Meg o Nith' was more sedately known as the Queen of the South and 'the cynosure of the Southern Counties', symbolising its attractiveness which continues to this day. In 1990 a nationwide socio-economic survey found that Dumfries came second only to Nottingham as the most desirable town in the United Kingdom. The town has always been an important communications centre, since Devorgilla erected the first bridge in the thirteenth century. A bridge suitable for carriages was erected between 1790 and 1795 higher up the river, its architect being the Thomas Boyd who designed the farmhouse at Ellisland. With the opening of the New Bridge in 1794 Buccleuch and Castle Streets were rapidly developed, shifting the emphasis of the town away from the High Street. In Burns's time the river was navigable as far as the Caul, and there were docking facilities south of the Whitesands where Dock Park now stands. Almost two hundred ships entered the Nith and cleared each year, doing a bustling coastal trade in coal, potatoes, tobacco and wine which made the Dumfries Port Division of Excise one of the more lucrative appointments in the south-west of Scotland.

Then as now, Dumfries enjoyed cultural and social amenities out of proportion to the size of its population. It was the centre of a large and comparatively rich district and many of the county families had their winter residences in the town. It boasted an excellent grammar school, two public libraries, a prestigious infirmary providing a high level of medical services, two established churches and a range of alternatives, from the Anti-Burgher Seceders and Relief congregation to Episcopal, Methodist and Roman Catholic chapels. Long before the Theatre Royal was established, Dumfries had provided facilities for travelling players and a keenly appreciative audience for their productions. The Assembly Rooms in George Street gave the well-to-do residents a social round which was as rich and diverse as any to be found in Edinburgh itself. In the late eighteenth century, especially after the outbreak of the French Revolutionary War, Dumfries was an important garrison town and the officers of the fencible infantry and cavalry regiments stationed there added immeasurably to the glittering social life. During the sessions of the Circuit courts, during the cattle and horse fairs, and at the autumn season when the Dumfries and Galloway Hunt joined with the Caledonian Hunt to hold races on nearby Tinwald Downs, Dumfries was *the* place for routs, assemblies, balls and all manner of social events.

Intellectually and socially stimulating, however, Dumfries was not the healthiest place to be. Even today, approaching the town from Annan,

Moffat or Lochmaben, its presence can often be detected from a distance by the pall of cloud hanging low over it. In Burns's day, long before the advent of anti-pollution measures, smog must have been a major problem. The town lay in a hollow along a winding river with extensive tracts of undrained marsh on all sides. It was humid and oppressive in summer and dank and chilly in winter. 'Consumptions and rheumatisms are frequent here,' noted Dr Burnside; and certainly Robert's health was not improved by his transfer to the town.

Dumfries is broadly stamped with his name, and his term of residence in the burgh (1791–6) flashed on the popular mind so vividly as to have been at once and till the present day regarded as an epoch – 'the time of Burns'. The places in Dumfries associated with the poet far outnumber those in Ayr, Irvine, Kilmarnock, Mauchline, Tarbolton and Edinburgh, and Dumfries probably has as many statues, memorials, plaques and tablets honouring Burns as the rest of Scotland put together. In St Michael's kirk-yard are the tombstones of many people associated with the poet in his last years, dominated by the neo-classical mausoleum. Within the church itself a brass plaque marks the spot where he and his family regularly wor-shipped. Nearby stands Burns House in Burns Street, where he died in 1796 (now preserved as a museum), while, across the river, stands the splendid Burns Centre, a recent conversion from the ancient town mill. Burns's white marble statue is one of the town's most prominent land-marks, in the centre of the roundabout linking Buccleuch, Castle and High Streets. A bas-relief of Burns adorns the wall of the Theatre Royal, which the poet played a part in founding in 1792, and which is now the oldest provincial theatre in Scotland. Further plaques, busts and memorials to Burns may be found on the former Loreburn Church, in the burgh museum, in the Globe Inn and the Hole i' the Wa' public house, and on the wall of the original Burns house in Bank Street (which has also inspired the Burns Café and the Burns hairdressing salon nearby), while a park has been laid out with flowers and shrubs associated with the poet. It would be no exaggeration to say that the tourism of Dumfries and district depends very heavily on Burns and associations with the poet.

On 11 November 1791 Robert and Jean moved into their Vennel apart-ment with their three sons, Robert, Francis Wallace and William Nicol. Bess, raised by the poet's mother, was now almost seven years old and con-tinued to live at Mossgiel with Gilbert and his young bride. By that time baby Elizabeth was probably also at Mossgiel where, according to Cham-bers, 'the bulk of the evidence that can now be ascertained points to November 1792 as the date of her removal from Mossgiel',[8] though tan-talisingly no evidence was adduced. The apartment on the middle floor of what is now 11 Bank Street consisted of three small rooms with a kitchen overlooking the back green. Robert Chambers provided a graphic descrip-tion of the poet's first home in Dumfries:

> He had three little rooms on the first floor, all overlooking the street, and a small kitchen behind. The central room, about the size of a bed-closet,

was the only place in which he could seclude himself for study. On the ground floor, John Syme of Ryedale, who became an intimate friend, had his office for the distribution of stamps. On the floor above lived a black-smith called George Haugh. On the opposite side of the street was the house of his landlord, Captain Hamilton, a connection of the Craiks of Arbigland.[9]

John Hamilton of Allershaw (1734-1813), scion of an ancient Douglasdale family, owned several properties in Dumfries and was also the poet's land-lord when he moved to more spacious accommodation in the Mill Hole Brae in May 1793. It is more probable that Robert was introduced to Captain Hamilton through Helen Craik of Arbigland, to whom he had been introduced early in 1790 by Robert Riddell. The Craik family have earned their small niche in history, partly through their connection with the poet and partly from the fact that their gardener was the father of John Paul, later Paul Jones, the co-founder of the American Navy, who was born in a cottage on the Arbigland estate.

The house occupied by the Burns family was next door to the Coach and Horses tavern, not one of the pubs that Robert was likely to frequent over-much. This hostelry of doubtful repute extended from the lower end of the Vennel along the Whitesands and was the haunt of the waterfront low-life and the cattle-drovers who flocked to Dumfries during the great Whitsun and Martinmas fairs. In the upstairs rooms a brothel was conducted by Margaret Hog (died 1811), alias Monkery Meg and immortalised by Burns as 'Muirland Meg' (CW 602). Access to the Burns apartment was through a long, open pend or doorway, then up a spiral stairway. At the rear of the building was a tiny, part-concealed courtyard just large enough to have stabled the poet's pony. George Haugh, who died in January 1828 at the age of eighty, was the source of several anecdotes concerning Burns. The rental of this apartment was very modest, a mere six or seven pounds a year.

In her reminiscences to John McDiarmid Jean Burns left an account of her husband in this period:

> Burns was not an early riser, except when he had anything particular to do in the way of his profession. Even though he had dined out, he never lay after nine o' clock. The family breakfasted at nine. If he lay long in bed awake he was always reading. At all his meals he had a book beside him on the table. He did his work in the forenoon, and was seldom engaged professionally in the evening. He dined at two o' clock when he dined at home; was fond of plain things, and hated tarts, pies, and pud-dings. When at home in the evening he employed his time in writing and reading, with the children playing about him. Their prattle never dis-turbed him in the least.[10]

The period spent in the Wee Vennel was not the happiest in Robert's life. The earliest letter written from here, and which can be definitely dated, was addressed to Nancy McLehose on 23 November 1791 (CL 407) and dealt with the distressing matter of the dying Jenny Clow. Robert had no sooner settled in Dumfries than he had to go to Edinburgh to sort out this embarrassing matter and also take his last, poignant farewell of Mrs McLehose. A letter from the poet to Ainslie (CL 339), undated but attributed by all previous editors to November 1791, was written in a fit of depression:

> *Misérable perdu* that I am! I have tried every thing that used to amuse me: here must I sit, a monument of the vengeance laid up in store for the wicked, slowly counting every chick of the clock as it slowly – slowly, numbers over these lazy scoundrels of hours, who, d–n them, are ranked up before me, every one at his neighbour's backside, and every one with a burden of anguish on his back, to pour on my devoted head – and there is none to pity me. My wife scolds me! my business torments me, and my sins come staring me in the face, every one telling a more bitter tale than his fellow. When I tell you even [bawdry?] has lost its power to please, you will guess something of my hell within, and all around me.

Further on, he cautions Ainslie not to address letters to him as 'Supervisor' for that was an honour he could not pretend to, no matter what Ainslie or Nicol had previously been led to believe:

> I am on the list, as we call it, for a Supervisorship, and will be called out by and bye to act as one; but at present I am a simple gauger, tho' t'other day I got an appointment to an excise division of £25 *per annum* better than the rest. My present income, down money, is £70 *per annum*.

Unless this was a piece of wishful thinking, however, the letter must date from the following February, for that was when Robert's transfer to the lucrative Dumfries Port Division was ratified.

As a result of Nancy's letter regarding Jenny Clow, Robert obtained a week's leave and went off to Edinburgh on 29 November. He lodged at Mackay's White Hart Inn in the Grassmarket and before he was two hours in the capital he had sought out the consumptive Jenny and given her an undisclosed sum of money from the rapidly dwindling proceeds of the Ellisland roup. Why he made no attempt to take charge of their son, now three years old, or failed to obtain custody of the boy, is not known. From what he told Nancy it can be assumed, however, that Robert would have quite cheerfully taken the lad into his own household.

On 6 December, the last day of his sojourn, Robert visited Mrs McLehose. Something of the old magic briefly sparked between them. They kissed, exchanged locks of hair and parted. Three weeks later Robert sent her three songs which she had inspired: 'Ance mair I hail thee, thou gloomy December' (CW 433), 'Behold the hour, the boat arrive!' (CW 503) and, of course, 'Ae Fond Kiss' (CW 434). The sense of heartbreak conveyed by this song makes it one of the most poignant of all Burns's productions. After the visit, the correspondence was briefly rekindled. Robert had not even waited till his return home before writing a letter to

Nancy. From Leadhills at noon on Thursday 8 December he wrote enclosing his 'Lament of Mary Queen of Scots' (CW 400) with a note (CL 408):

> Misfortune seems to take a peculiar pleasure in darting her arrows against 'Honest Men and bony Lasses.'– Of this You are too, too just a proof; but may your future fate be a bright exception to the remark.– In the words of Hamlet – 'Adieu, adieu, adieu! Remember me!'

A crisis was, indeed, approaching in Nancy's life. After years of silence from her ne'er-do-well husband James, she had received a draft for £50 and a letter inviting her to come to Jamaica so that they could be reconciled. James also wished that their sole surviving son Andrew (William had died in August) should be enrolled at a good boarding-school and taught French and fencing. Having got the boy installed at school Nancy began preparing for the long and arduous voyage to the West Indies. By a curious coincidence, she was booked on Captain Liddell's ship *Roselle*, the very ship which was to have borne Burns from Leith to Jamaica four years previously. From mid-December till the following February when she set sail, Robert bombarded Nancy with letters, often enclosing his latest effusions. On 15 December (CL 409) he told her that he had sent a lock of her hair to Bruce the jeweller in Princes Street, Edinburgh to be made up into a ring for himself. He had revised his song 'Sensibility how charming, Dearest Nancy, thou canst tell' (CW 402) and sent it to Johnson for the fourth volume of the *Museum*, and he concluded 'from a man who is literally drunk, accept & forgive!!!'

Nancy wrote on Robert's thirty-third birthday. She had apparently written a letter on 21 January, but had forgotten to post it and now could not be sure whether she had sent it after all. She was 'agitated, hurried to death' as she had been ordered aboard in three days' time to weigh anchor on 29 January:

> And now, my dearest Sir, I have a few things to say to you, as the last advice of her who could have lived or died with you! I am happy to know of your applying so steadily to the business you have engaged in; but, oh remember, this life is a short, passing scene! Seek God's favour, – keep His commandments, – be solicitous to prepare for the happy eternity! There, I trust, we will meet, in perfect and never-ending bliss.

Nancy and her poet never met again. She duly arrived at Kingston where she suffered the humiliation of being left unmet on the quay. Later she discovered that her husband had, in her absence, acquired a negro mistress, Ann Chalon Rivvere, who had borne him a bonny octoroon daughter, Ann Lavinia McLehose. In 1829 Nancy told Grierson of Dalgoner that she had found the heat and the mosquitoes very trying, and for climatic reasons she had returned to Scotland by the first available vessel. She made no attempt to resume her correspondence with Burns who did not learn of her whereabouts till March 1793. During her absence Robert composed the beautiful pastoral 'My Nanie's Awa' (CW 532). It seems possible that his reworking of the old ballad 'Wandering Willie' (CW 480) was intended as a poetic conception of the feelings of Nancy as she strove for a reconciliation with her husband. That appears to be implied in the final stanza beginning 'But if he's forgotten his faithfullest Nanie'. The earliest version of this song was sent with an undated letter to John McMurdo some time early in 1793 (CL 494), a revised version being despatched to George Thomson on 27 March that year (CL 624).

Having been expressly warned by Nancy 'as you value my peace, do not write to me to Jamaica, until I let you know you may with safety', Robert had kept his own counsel. Instead, Nancy had exhorted him to write to her friend Mary Peacock who would act as a go-between; but Robert's letters to Miss Peacock seem to have been accident-prone. Two of them apparently went astray, and he would probably never have written a third time but for the fact that, on 6 December 1792, he suddenly realised that that day was the anniversary of his meeting with Nancy. He penned a brief note (CL 684):

> I have written so often to you and have got no answer, that I had resolved never to lift up a pen to you again, but this eventful day, *the sixth of December*, recalls to my memory such a scene! Heaven and earth! when I remember a far distant person!

Mary answered immediately, telling him that Nancy had returned to Scotland, but that she had been ill as a result of her trip to Jamaica. This letter arrived while Robert was absent in Ayrshire. Jean probably laid it aside for him but it was unfortunately mislaid, and only found some months later where it had fallen down the back of a chest of drawers. When Robert belatedly discovered that Nancy was back in Edinburgh he wrote to her (CL 410):

> I suppose, my dear Madam, that by your neglecting to inform me of your arrival in Europe, a circumstance which could not be indifferent to me, as indeed no occurrence relating to you can – you meant to leave me to guess & gather that a correspondence I once had the honor & *felicity* to enjoy, is to be no more.

With this letter Robert sent Nancy a copy of the two-volume edition of his poems which Creech had just published. He promised to let her have a copy of the fourth volume of the *Museum* which had been published the previous August. This long letter closed with a passage that shows how Robert, the married man, could still work himself into a lather over his quondam Clarinda:

> Shall I hear from you? – But first, hear me! – No cold language – no prudential documents – I despise Advice, & scorn Controul – If you are not to write such language, such sentiments, as you know I shall wish, shall delight to receive; I conjure you, By wounded Pride! By ruined

Peace! By frantic disappointed Passion! By all the many ills that constitute that sum of human woes – A BROKEN HEART! – To me be silent
for ever!!! – If you insult me with the unfeeling apothegms of cold-
blooded Caution, May all the – but hold – a Fiend could not breathe a
malevolent wish on the head of *MY* Angel! – Mind my request! – If you
send me a page baptised in the font of sanctimonious Prudence – By
Heaven, Earth & Hell, I will tear it into atoms!

Not long afterwards Robert copied this letter into the volume he was
preparing for Robert Riddell, omitting the date and deliberately obscuring
the period to which it belonged with the annotation, 'I need scarcely
remark that the foregoing was the fustian rant of enthusiastic youth'.

If Nancy was seldom far from his thoughts during his first year in
Dumfries, Robert now had more time for old correspondents as well as the
opportunity to make new friends. His first letter to Mrs Dunlop was not
sent till 14 January 1792 (CL 196-7). What with the move to Dumfries,
'getting deeply engaged in a line of our business to which I was an entire
Stranger; not to mention hunting of Smugglers once or twice every week',
and the jaunt to Edinburgh, he had had no time for private correspondence. But things were now settling down and he hoped that he would
have more time to devote to composition as well as letter-writing. By now
he had recovered his equilibrium and could look back on his changed circumstances philosophically:

Indeed, CHANGE, was, to me, become a matter of necessity. – Ruin
awaited me as a Farmer; though by that peculiar Good Luck that for some
years past has attended all my motions, I have got rid of my farm with
little, if any loss.

And he devoted the greater part of the letter to commiserating with Mrs
Dunlop on the recent loss of her stepmother, Lady Wallace, to whom she
had been very attached, and enquiring after Susan Dunlop. Susan, Mrs
Dunlop's second daughter, had married a Frenchman named James Henri
from Bernaldean in 1788. He is invariably, but inaccurately, described as
an *émigré* though he had left France a year before the French Revolution
had erupted, and long before it acquired those ominous overtones which
impelled the aristocracy and many of the middle classes to flee their
country. The Henris rented Loudoun Castle from the girl-countess Flora
and thus became the employers of Janet Little, the rhyming milkmaid and
emulator of Burns. On 22 June 1789, however, James Henri had died,
leaving his young wife four months pregnant. A son was born in due
course, inspiring Robert's moving lines 'On the Birth of a Posthumous
Child' (CW 406). Robert seems to have had a premonition of Susan
Henri's doom, likening her to the tragic Lady Randolph in Home's *Douglas*
in a letter of 6 December 1790 (CL 193). In his first Dumfries letter
Robert was pleased to get good news of Susan and her baby son – 'the little
Floweret & the Mother-plant'. Rather rashly Mrs Henri had taken her son

to France, probably with a view to establishing his claim to the family estate at Muges, Aiguillon, near Bordeaux. Since the birth of her child, however, Susan had been in poor health, and Robert's concern was evident in his comment, 'Her worth & her misfortunes would interest the most hardened Bandit in her fate.' When Mrs Dunlop wrote in October 1792 to tell Robert that Susan had died at Muges, he replied immediately (CL 201) with a very tender letter of condolence. The sad news affected him deeply and triggered off a bout of depression which was reflected in the letter:

> What shall I say to comfort you, my much-valued friend? I can but grieve with you; consolation I have none to offer, except that which religion holds out to the children of affliction . . . Alas, Madam! who would wish for many years? What is it but to drag existence out until our joys gradually expire, and leave us in a night of misery; like the gloom which blots out the stars one by one from the face of night, and leaves us without a ray of comfort, in the howling waste!

It may have been through William Stewart that Robert became acquainted with James Clarke, the schoolmaster at Moffat. About two years younger than the poet, Clarke had been born at Closeburn and educated at Wallacehall Academy before taking up his appointment at Moffat in 1786. In 1790 he married Jane Simpson from Cumbria. The following year he fell foul of some parents who complained to the Earl of Hopetoun, as principal heritor of the parish, that he was guilty of undue severity in the corporal punishment meted out to his pupils. There was a move to dismiss Clarke from his post. Burns was outraged when he got wind of this piece of petty injustice and he went to quite extraordinary lengths to campaign on Clarke's behalf. On 11 June 1791 he wrote a long letter to his Edinburgh lawyer friend Alexander Cunningham (CL 462–3) and gave it to Clarke to deliver in person. For a man who never lifted a finger against his own children, and firmly believed in teaching them by stimulating their interests, Robert dismissed the charges in an uncharacteristically robust manner:

> God help the Teacher, a man of genius & sensibility, for such is my friend Clarke, when the blockhead Father presents him his booby son, & insists on having the rays of science lighted up in a fellow's head whose scull is impervious & inaccessible by any other way than a positive fracture with a cudgel!

Robert argued his case with such vehemence and passion that Cunningham cannot fail to have been moved. The patrons of Moffat School were the ministers, magistrates and Town Council of Edinburgh, with whom Robert hoped Cunningham would argue the case. Robert also drafted a letter for Clarke to present to the Lord Provost of Edinburgh to seek a fair hearing. In a subsequent letter to Cunningham, dated 5 February 1792 from Dumfries (CL 464), Robert mentioned that he had enlisted the help of John McMurdo of Drumlanrig, Fergusson of Craigdarroch and Robert

Riddell. In February 1792 Clarke went to Edinburgh to seek redress. Robert wrote to him before he went (CL 595):

> Courage, mon ami! The day may, after all, be yours; but at any rate, there is other air to breathe than that of Moffat, pestiferously tainted with the breath of that Arch Scoundrel, Johnston.

Robert took advantage of Clarke's impending trip to the capital to give him a letter for Peter Hill (CL 321) enclosing six pounds and a shilling. Most of this money was to be used to settle the stonemason Robert Burn's bill for erecting Fergusson's tombstone – a matter which had been outstanding for some time:

> He was two years in erecting it, after I commissioned him for it; & I have been two years paying him, after he sent me the account; so he & I are quits.– He had the hardiesse to ask me interest on the sum; but considering that the money was due by one Poet, for putting a tomb-stone over another, he may, with grateful surprise, thank Heaven that ever he saw a farthing of it.

When Burn had rendered his account on 23 June 1789 he had facetiously added, 'I shall be happy to receive orders of a like nature for as many more of your friends that have gone hence as you please'.[11]

By mid-February 1792, as the Moffat School dispute was coming to a head, matters looked black for Clarke. Robert not only tried to brace his friend for the shock of dismissal, as this letter implies, but took practical steps to secure him alternative employment. A second letter, dated 17 February, indicates that he had interceded with Riddell who had hopes of getting a clerical position for the poor schoolmaster in Manchester where his wife Elizabeth had family and business connections. But even as he wrote this letter (CL 595–6), Robert received the good news that Clarke had been vindicated. 'Apropos, I just now hear that you have beat your foes, *every tail hollow*. Huzza! Io triomphe!' Clarke, in fact, remained at Moffat till 1794 when he was promoted to Forfar. Though hard-pressed himself, Robert lent his friend a considerable sum of money which Clarke was still paying off at the time of the poet's death. Burns's last letter, less than a month before he died (CL 596), acknowledged one of these repayments, and appealed for another by return of post.

At the beginning of 1792 Robert Riddell's brother Walter (1764–1802) purchased the estate of Holm of Dalscairth, four miles south-west of Dumfries. By a strange coincidence, this had been the estate of Andrew Crosbie who, with Walter's father and namesake, had been taken hostage by the Jacobites in 1745. Provost Crosbie had subsequently sold it to Colonel Goldie who renamed it Goldielea in compliment to his wife whose maiden name was Leigh. Walter Riddell had married Ann Doig, the daughter of an Antigua sugar magnate and plantation owner, but she died a year later. While in Antigua sorting out the inheritance from his late wife's estate, Walter had met the daughter of the island's governor, William Woodley, and after a whirlwind courtship they were married at Nichola Town, St Kitts, on 16 September 1790. Walter's second wife was not quite eighteen years of age.

Maria Banks Woodley was born on 4 November 1772, the second-youngest of a family of seven born to Woodley and his vivacious wife Frances Payne. Frances was the daughter of Sir Ralph Payne, a Whig MP who later found it more expedient to become a Tory, and Frances Lambertina de Koebel whose father was a baron of the Holy Roman Empire and a general in the Imperial service. She had come to England as a lady-in-waiting to Princess Charlotte of Mecklenburg-Strelitz, the future wife of King George III. Thus Maria Riddell was English, with an exotic dash of the Continental aristocracy in her blood. Nothing is known of her early life or upbringing, but she had a precocious taste for literature, and some witty verses written by her at the age of fifteen, in answer to a mock proposal from the celebrated wit Joseph Jekyll, have been preserved.[12] The metre may be faulty, but the lines show an astonishingly intimate knowledge of the contemporary political scene.

Later the same year, 1788, the Woodleys went out to the West Indies taking young Maria with them. She whiled away the voyage with her diary and sketch-book and out of this obtained the material which was subsequently distilled into a book with the title of *Voyages to the Madeira and Leeward Caribbee Islands; with Sketches of the Natural History of these Islands*. It was during this trip that Maria met her future husband. The young couple settled on Doig's Estate but Maria was homesick and they must have returned to England soon afterwards, for it was in London, at her father's house in South Audley Street on 31 August 1791, that Maria gave birth to her daughter Anna Maria Riddell. A few months later Walter took his young wife and baby daughter north and settled in his native county. Walter's first act was to change the name of his new estate from Goldielea to Woodley Park, emulating Colonel Goldie in paying a delicate compliment to his wife. Details of the purchase of this property are obscure, but it seems that Walter never paid over the balance due to the previous owner, although he did lay out about £2,000 in improving the mansion-house and landscaping its grounds.

While this work was in progress Walter and Maria lived at Friars' Carse and it was probably there that Maria was introduced to her brother-in-law's friend, the poet Burns. Robert was thirty-three and Maria just turned nineteen when they first met. Robert was captivated by her, though not so enamoured that he was blind to her faults. When she discovered that he had good literary contacts in Edinburgh Maria begged Robert to introduce her to William Smellie. As well as printing Robert's Edinburgh Edition, Smellie was a man of wide-ranging interests in science and literature and a prolific contributor to the *Encyclopaedia Britannica*. The Walter Riddells were planning to visit Edinburgh and stay with Walter's cousin, Alexander Fergusson of Craigdarroch. This would give Maria the opportunity to find a publisher for the account of her West Indian tour, and by way of introduction Robert wrote to Smellie on 22 January 1792 (CL 597). In view of Maria's role in the closing years of the poet's life, this letter is not without considerable interest:

> Mrs Riddel who takes this letter to town with her, is a Character that even in your own way, as a Naturalist & a Philosopher, would be an acquisition to your acquaintance.– The Lady too, is a votary of the Muses; and as I think I am something of a judge in my own trade, I assure you that her verses, always correct, & often elegant, are very much beyond the common run of the Lady Poetesses of the day . . . lest you should think of a lively West-Indian girl of eighteen, as girls of eighteen too often deserve to be thought of, I should take care to remove that prejudice – To be impartial, however, the Lady has one unlucky failing; a failing which you will easily discover, as she seems rather pleased with indulging it; & a failing which you will as easily pardon, as it is a sin that very much besets yourself; – where she dislikes, or despises, she is apt to make no more a secret of it – than where she esteems & probably respects.

Two days after writing this letter, Robert joined a party at Friars' Carse. A week later Maria wrote a vivid description of the expedition in a letter to her mother. The Walter Riddells were setting out for Edinburgh, but first Maria insisted on a detour to inspect the lead mines at Wanlockhead. Elizabeth and Robert Riddell had agreed to accompany them on this jaunt and Burns was prevailed to join what turned out to be a very strenuous and hazardous outing. They set out two hours before sunrise on a cold wintry morning and after breakfast at Sanquhar took a post-chaise to Wanlockhead, the highest village in Scotland. Maria wrote, 'The beauties of the majestic scenery, joined to the interesting remarks and fascinating conversation of our friend Burns, not only beguiled the tediousness of the road, but likewise made us forget its danger'. They entered the mine, 'a dark and narrow cavern carved out of the solid rock' lit only by the tapers which each of them carried. Almost doubled up, they clambered along the low tunnel, wading up to mid-leg in muddy water and drenched by the continual drip of water from the roof. Maria found the beams so wet and slimy that she soon cut her gloves to pieces by clinging to the points of the rocks.

> After we had proceeded about a mile in the cavern, the damp and confined air affected our fellow adventurer Burns so much, that we resolved to turn back, after I had satisfied my curiosity by going down one of the shafts. This you will say was a crazy scheme – assailing the Gnomes in their subterranean abodes! Indeed there has never been before but *one* instance of a *female* hazarding herself thither.[13]

This was an incredible expedition to make in the depths of winter, a journey of about twenty miles in each direction, on horseback, by carriage and on foot. The rest of the party, considerably older than Maria, must have been remarkably forbearing, but they must have found her high spirits and selfishness rather trying. What Robert thought of the jaunt has never been recorded.

The Riddells took a whole week to reach Edinburgh, partly due to bad weather and partly due to the headstrong Maria's desire to make lengthy detours and excursions. On Sunday 29 January, however, they arrived at Craigdarroch's town house in St Andrew Square and that evening Maria called on Smellie. The high-spirited girl and the crusty old printer-publisher were instantly drawn to each other. A lively correspondence ensued and on 7 March Maria wrote from Woodley Park enclosing the manuscript of her book. In passing, Maria mentioned the poet:

> Robie Burns dined with us the other day. He is in good health and spirits; but I fear his muse will not be so frequent in her inspirations, now that he has forsaken his rural occupations.[14]

Smellie was agreeably surprised when he read Maria's manuscript and replied on 27 March:

> When I considered your youth and still more, your sex, the perusal of your ingenious and judicious work, if I had not previously had the pleasure of your conversation, the devil himself could not have frightened me into the belief that a female human creature could, in the bloom of youth, beauty and, consequently, of giddiness, have produced a performance so much out of the line of your ladies' works. Smart little poems, flippant romances, are not uncommon. But science, minute observation, accurate description and excellent composition are qualities seldom to be met with in the female world.

Maria had modestly hoped for a privately printed volume, a piece of vanity publishing, but Smellie felt that the book was commercially viable and in due course it was advertised in the November 1792 issue of the *Scots Magazine*. Smellie printed it, but it was actually published by Burns's friend Peter Hill at Edinburgh and by Thomas Cadell in London. One of the recipients of a presentation copy was Robert Burns, who acknowledged the compliment in a brief note (CL 601).

Robert's own correspondence with Maria Riddell began shortly after her return from Edinburgh. Obviously all this gallivanting round the countryside in the depths of winter had taken its toll, for Maria was confined to her bed for some time. Robert's first letter (CL 601) is undated but belongs to February 1792. Addressing her as 'My Dearest Friend', he counselled her:

> God grant that now when your health is re-established, you may take a little, little more care of a life so truly valuable to Society and so truly invaluable to your friends! As to your very excellent epistle from a certain Capital of a certain Empire, I shall answer it in its own way sometime next week: as also settle all matters as to little Miss. Your kindness there is just like your kindness in everything else.

Unfortunately, the letter which Maria wrote to Robert from Edinburgh has not survived so what he meant by this passage is not known; but it is a matter for conjecture whether Maria had been deputed by Robert to undertake some delicate commission regarding Ann Park's baby daughter Elizabeth.

During September 1792 Smellie himself made a trip to Dumfries and spent some time with Maria and Burns. Maria even persuaded the eccentric Smellie to present his extraordinary figure at one of the assemblies then being held in the town, and there is an unsubstantiated tradition that he and Burns received some kind of civic reception.

In February 1790 Mrs Dunlop had written to Robert and, in passing, enquired whether her friendship with a Mrs Corbet, whose husband was one of the senior officials of the Excise, might be of help in advancing Robert's career. William Corbet (1755–1811) had been Acting Supervisor General at Edinburgh since 1789 and in 1791 this appointment was made permanent. In the interim, Mrs Dunlop had used her connection with the Corbets judiciously, though she could do no more than bring her protégé's name before the Supervisor General for there was little, in practice, that Corbet or anyone else could have done to manipulate the very strict Excise code of practice. Two years later, however, Mrs Dunlop enquired whether Corbet had been able to help. Robert replied (CL 197–8) saying that he hoped to see the Supervisor General when he visited Dumfries later that year. Robert had no illusions about getting a supervisorship, but he had his eye on the next best thing:

> there is what is called a Port Division, here, &, entre nous, the present incumbent is so obnoxious, that Mr C–'s presence will in all probability send him adrift into some other Division, & with equal probability will fix me in his stead.– A Port Division is twenty pounds a year more than any other Division, beside as much rum & brandy as will easily supply an ordinary family; which last consideration brings me to my second head of discourse, namely your unfortunate hunting of Smugglers for a little brandy; an article I believe indeed very scarce in your country.– I have however hunted these Gentry to better purpose than you, & as a servant of my brother's goes from here to Mauchline tomorrow morning, I beg leave to send you by him a very small jar, sealed full of as genuine Nantz as ever I tasted.

This letter has been quoted by the poet's detractors on two counts: to show his unscrupulous string-pulling to oust a brother officer and to demonstrate that, in handling contraband goods, Burns was little different than the smugglers he was chasing. Part of the problem concerning the string-pulling has been the assumption by most writers that the transfer involved promotion. In fact, it was nothing of the sort, and the exchange of divisions which Robert proposed, and which was eventually acceded, was common practice within the service. The 'obnoxious incumbent' was an elderly man named George Grey who had risen to the lucrative Dumfries First Foot-walk by dint of seniority. By 1792, however, he was no longer capable of managing the most difficult and complex job in the entire Dumfries district with the high degree of competence and precision which it demanded, so a transfer to a less exacting position would have been inevitable anyway. A survey of the other officers in the Dumfries collection reveals that there was really only one Exciseman of the right calibre for the job. Burns would undoubtedly have been transferred to this post, whether he had used what little influence he had or not.

The only two letters extant from Robert to Corbet deal with this matter. The first, undated but clearly belonging to February 1792 (CL 598), puts the matter in context. Robert was extremely diffident about taking up his pen in 'the language of supplication', but the letter shows that he was not taking the initiative in this matter:

> Mr Findlater tells me that you wish to know from myself, what are my views in desiring to change my Excise Division.- With the wish natural to man, of bettering his present situation, I have turned my thoughts towards the practicality of getting into a Port Division.- As I know that the General Supervisors are omnipotent in these matters, my honored friend, Mrs Dunlop of Dunlop, offered me to interest you in my behalf.- She told me that she was well acquainted with Mrs Corbet's goodness, & that on the score of former intimacy she thought she could promise some influence with her: and added, with her usual sagacity & knowledge of human nature, that the surest road to the good offices of a man was through the mediation of the woman he loved.- On this footing, Sir, I venture my application; else, not even the known generosity of your character would have emboldened me to address you thus.

Corbet had previously written to Findlater seeking an assessment of Robert's character and ability, and Findlater had replied on 23 December 1791, saying that he was 'an active, faithful and zealous officer . . . capable of achieving a more arduous task than any difficulty that the theory or practice of our business can exhibit'. As a result Robert was notifed within two months that the Excise Board had approved the exchange. He was formally appointed on 26 April, the exchange to come into effect on 5 May. Robert was later to write to Corbet (CL 598-9) expressing his gratitude, although he felt that 'a simple letter of thanks will be a very poor return for so much kindness'. This letter acknowledged his debt to Mrs Corbet and Mrs Dunlop. In due course Mrs Corbet was to be one of those privileged to receive a presentation set of the 1793 volumes of his Poems.

The allegation that, in handling a jar of illicit Nantes brandy, Robert was no better than a common smuggler himself, can easily be dismissed. One of the perquisites of the Exciseman was a share in the contraband goods confiscated, or a share in the cash proceeds from the sale thereof. The same remark applies to the contraband charge raised in respect of a pair of French gloves which Robert obtained for Maria Riddell in April 1793. In fact, the poet's critics objected not to his handling of the gloves (which had been confiscated from a haberdasher in Dumfries) but from his flippant attitude expressed in a letter to Maria (CL 602-3); but the jocular, half-flirtatious, half-bantering tone is pretty much what one might have expected from Robert in the circumstances:

You must know that FRENCH GLOVES are contraband goods, &
expressly prohibited by the laws of this wise-governed Realm of ours.– A
Satirist would say, that this is one reason why the ladies are so fond of
them; but I, who have not one grain of GALL in my composition, shall
alledge, that it is the PATRIOTISM of the dear Goddesses of man's idolatry, that makes them so fond of dress from the LAND OF LIBERTY &
EQUALITY.

The gloves, in fact, were part of the stock impounded by the revenue
officers from three different Dumfries merchants who were subsequently
prosecuted. By that time Britain was at war with France and imports from
the enemy country were strictly forbidden. This letter could have proved
far more embarrassing to Robert on account of the whiff of sedition it contained; remarks which might be written in jest would have been taken all too
seriously by the authorities had this letter fallen into the wrong hands.[15]

Shortly before his third and final transfer, there occurred the most dramatic incident in Robert's entire Excise career. During the eighteenth
century the Solway coast was the favourite haunt of smugglers, mainly
operating out of the Isle of Man. Under the Revestment Act of 1765 the
Duke of Atholl (then Lord of Man) had sold his rights to the Crown. This
abolished the exemption of the island from British Customs and had the
desired effect of curbing the smuggling trade with the Solway coast, but
did not entirely eliminate it. The Revenue officers belonging to the
Customs and Excise (then quite separate services), assisted by detachments
of troops, patrolled the coast on a constant lookout for smugglers and their
vessels. The smugglers would land their illicit cargoes of tobacco and
brandy at Sarkfoot, where the River Sark debouches into the firth. A
nearby house called Alisonbank has a series of deep cellars to this day,
believed to have been used by the smugglers. From Alisonbank the contraband was taken by pack-mule up a lane, known even now as Whisky
Loaning, up to Gretna and Springfield for onward distribution.

Sarkfoot was at the eastern extremity of the Dumfries Port Division,
and thus came within the area covered by Burns prior to his transfer to the
Dumfries First Foot-walk. He was therefore involved, with fellow Excisemen John Lewars and Walter Crawford, in the seizure of the brig
Rosamond on 29 February. Various accounts of this incident appeared in
the Glasgow and Edinburgh newspapers the following week, but the fullest
version was that printed in the *Edinburgh Evening Courant* of 8 March. A
highly coloured and inaccurate account of the seizure was given by
Lockhart (1828) which gave Robert undue prominence in the affair at the
expense of his colleagues, and also included a wholly imaginary account of
the composing of 'The Deil's awa wi th' Exciseman' (CW 467). To
Lockhart also we owe the story that Robert subsequently purchased four
carronades from the ship which he sent to the French Convention with a
letter requesting that body to accept them as a mark of his admiration and
respect. The present, and its accompaniment, were intercepted at the
Customs House of Dover.

Allan Cunningham (1834) cast doubt on the tale of the carronades, and subsequent biographers were sceptical of the whole incident. Lockhart, son-in-law of Sir Walter Scott, had used manuscripts which had been given to Sir Walter by Joseph Train, Supervisor of Excise at Castle Douglas. These documents consisted of (a) the journal of Walter Crawford, riding-officer of Excise, (b) an account of the seizure in the handwriting of Burns himself, and (c) a statement written by John Lewars, detailing the circumstances of Robert purchasing the carronades. Train acquired these documents from the widow of Lewars. Sir Walter, unable to find any reference to the carronades in *Le Moniteur*, the French official newspaper of the time, applied to the Customs House authorities in London. They, after considerable search, found that the guns had been seized at the port of Dover, as stated by Lewars in his memorandum.

For many years these documents were apparently mislaid at Abbotsford, and this merely added to the scepticism. As recently as 1932 Snyder dismissed the *Rosamond* affair as a complete myth: 'No more picturesque legend was ever invented by the ingenious brain of a romantic biographer . . . The whole thing would do full justice to Gilbert and Sullivan'.[16] Following the publication of his biography, however, a concerted effort was made to locate the missing papers and the very next year a mass of miscellaneous papers at Abbotsford was sorted and catalogued by the National Library of Scotland, and two of the documents came to light. Unfortunately, the Lewars memorandum has not been found, although a fourth document, in Lewars' handwriting, was discovered and consists of an inventory of the ship and her equipment. The record of the seizure at Dover was apparently destroyed at some time after 1828 when Scott made his enquiries.[17]

Walter Crawford had been appointed only the previous month, having mustered out of the South Fencibles at Edinburgh and entered the Excise with the specific duty of patrolling the coast between Dumfries and Gretna. From his journal it appears that a landing of smugglers had been expected some time that week. On 27 February news reached Crawford that a landing was in progress. He set out from Dumfries late that night with John Lewars, leaving Burns, William Penn and an officer named Rankine to follow as quickly as possible. Crawford and Lewars reached Annan at 5 a.m. and immediately set out with a party of dragoons. They searched Mr McDowall's, 'a notorious smuggler', and other premises associated with smuggling, and about noon rode down to the shore.

The ship was waiting the tide to make sail. Crawford and his soldiers tried to board her, but were stopped by the crew which threatened to fire on them. As the Excisemen and soldiers were only armed with pistols, Crawford alone went on board. He found twenty-four men on board, with fifteen rounds of shot each. He went ashore and consulted his men. Clearly a larger force was required. Lewars was despatched to Dumfries to bring up another twenty-four dragoons, while Crawford went to Ecclefechan for reinforcements, with which he patrolled the shore till Lewars returned with the Dumfries force.

About 9 a.m. on 29 February Crawford mustered his forces. He had twenty-three dragoons from Dumfries, thirteen from Annan and eight from Ecclefechan – forty-four men mounted and fully armed. Meanwhile the *Rosamond* slipped down the firth about a mile from where she had been the previous day. The depth of the water and the swiftness of the current made it impossible for the troops to get out to the ship on foot or horseback, so Crawford and his men searched the shore for suitable boats.

> But the Country People guessing our design got the start of us and staved every Boat on the Coast before we Could reach them, the vessel in the mean time keeping up a fire of grape shott and musquetry, we resolved as last resource to attempt the passage on foott as the quick sands made the ridding on horseback dangerous or rather impossible.

The troops were divided into three groups – fore, aft and broadside:

> The first party being Commanded by Quarter Master Manly, the Second by myself and the third led by Mr Burns. Our orders to the Millitary were to reserve their fire till within eight yards of the vessel, then to pour a volley and board her with sword & Pistol. The vessel keept on firing thou without any damage to us, as from the situation of the fire they could not bring their great guns to bear on us, we in the mean time wading breast high, and in Justice to the party under my Command I must say with great alacrity; by the time we were within one hundred yards of the vessel the Crew gave up the cause, gott over side towards England which shore was for a long long way dry sand. As I still supposed that there were only Country people they were putting ashore and that the Crew were keeping under Cover to make a more vigourous immediate resistance, we marched up as first concerted, but found the vessel compleatly evacuated both of the Crew and every movable on board except as per inventory, the Smugglers as their last instance of vengeance having poured a six-pounder Carronade through her Broadside. She proved to be the Roseomond of Plymouth, Alexander Patty Master, and about one hundred tons burthen, schooner rigged.

The second document consisted of two pages on the backs of blank Excise receipt forms, in Robert's handwriting, with the exception of corrections and the prices which were written by Crawford. This consisted of a list of the expenses incurred in watching the captured vessel and subsequently repairing it at Kelton on the Nith estuary. The expenses included £1 2s for advertising the sale of the ship in the Edinburgh, Dumfries and Whitehaven newspapers. The third surviving document was the ship's inventory, written by John Lewars in the form of a draft advertisement.

Among the fifty-three items listed were 'Four four Pounders Carronade Guns mounted on carriages with takle and furniture compleat Round Carr double headed & Grape Shot &c. &c. &c.' The guns weighed 33cwt (1,680kg) and were sold at half a crown per hundredweight, making a total of £4 2s 6d. Robert Chambers (1851) stated that Train had a copy of the

sale catalogue annotated in Robert's handwriting, showing that he had purchased the four guns for £3. The apparent discrepancy between the two
sums may be explained by the fact that Robert was entitled to a fourth part
of the net proceeds of the sale. The journal of John Lewars, which allegedly
detailed Robert's purchase of the carronades and their despatch to France,
has not yet come to light, but the existence of the other documents in the
Abbotsford Collection affords strong presumptive proof that it was also
handed by Train to Scott.

The story, as presented by Lockhart, by romanticising Robert's role in
the affair – he was represented as leading the assault, sword in hand, and
being the first to board the ship – led to the tale of the carronades being
dismissed as pure fantasy. It was pointed out that there was no such body
as the French Convention in February or March 1792, and that it did not
come into being till the following September. This was a slip on Lockhart's
part which, however, did not necessarily invalidate the possibility of
some quixotic gesture by Burns towards the Legislative Assembly, the
democratic body which at that moment was supporting the Constitutional
party around King Louis XVI. At that time the French Revolution was still
in its infancy; the old order had been overthrown but the moderates were
in the ascendancy and France did not pose any threat to her neighbours.

Just why Burns should have spent money he could ill afford to send a
bulky package of cannon to the infant French democracy has been treated
as a mystery, thereby lending weight to the sceptics who denounced this
story as preposterous. But by the end of 1791 the Austrian Emperor
(brother of Marie Antoinette) was gathering around him the forces of reaction and repression. Many French aristocrats had fled to the territory of
the Holy Roman Empire and were planning a counter-coup. In the latter
part of January 1792 a fund was opened at Glasgow 'to aid the French in
carrying on the war against the emigrant princes or any foreign power by
whom they may be attacked . . . It is said that £1200 have already been
subscribed'.[18] Robert's action, therefore, was a somewhat eccentric and
audaciously generous one, but was in no sense an 'absurd and presumptuous breach of decorum', far less construed as a treasonable act. There was
certainly no question of his actions being called to account by his Excise
superiors. As to the logistical problem of despatching thirty-three hundredweight of guns from Dumfries to France, this would have cost a pound or
two but was certainly not impossible. There was, even at that time, a
highly sophisticated network of carrier services operating both overland
and by coastal vessels, which made the conveyance of very bulky and heavy
goods perfectly feasible and straightforward.

About this time Charles Maurice de Talleyrand-Périgord, erstwhile
Bishop of Autun and latterly member of the Assembly, visited England as
an envoy of the French government and was cordially received by Pitt and
Grenville. Talleyrand, incidentally, used his time in London to take lessons
in conversational English from none other than John Murdoch, Burns's
former school-teacher. Talleyrand proposed a treaty of friendship, convinced that Britain would not intervene against France unless the latter

launched a pre-emptive strike on the Netherlands. Talleyrand's tact and diplomacy equally convinced the British government of France's friendly intentions, leading Pitt to declare in his budget speech, 'Unquestionably there never was a time in the history of this country when from the situation in Europe we might more reasonably expect fifteen years of peace than at the present moment'.[19] Talleyrand returned to Paris on 10 March 1792 and persuaded Dumouriez, then Foreign Minister, to establish an embassy in London. The former Marquis Chauvelin was appointed ambassador, with Talleyrand as his adviser. But the situation deteriorated rapidly after France declared war on Austria, and the provocative attitude of Chauvelin undid all Talleyrand's good work. Meanwhile the Revolution was moving ever further to the left; the monarchy was overthrown on 10 August and the September massacres alienated the British. The new Convention adopted a bellicose stance and by setting aside the rights of the Dutch over the Scheldt estuary brought France and Britain to the brink of war. The execution of Louis XVI on 21 January 1793 was the last straw, and Britain joined in the war between France and her European neighbours. Dumouriez, having defeated the Austrians at Jemappes in November 1792, was beaten at Neerwinden the following March and, faced with arrest by the emissaries of the Convention, arrested them instead. When his army failed to back him he fled to the Austrians taking with him two aristocrats who had originally backed the Revolution, the Duc de Chartres (later King Louis-Philippe) and his brother, the Duc de Montpensier. Robert's composition of a street ballad going the rounds that winter, entitled 'The black-headed eagle' and dealing with Dumouriez's victory at Jemappes,[20] has been disputed; but there is no doubt that, in the early stages of the Revolution Robert sympathised with the French and his satirical song, 'You're welcome to Despots, Dumourier' (CW 484), composed soon after the general's defection, clearly shows that even after Britain was at war Robert was recklessly espousing the republican cause.

But back in the spring of 1792 peace seemed assured, and the liberal movement in France was generally well received in Britain. The only other matter concerning the *Rosamond* that requires clarification is the composition of 'The Deil's awa wi th' Exciseman. The earliest account of this song was given by Cromek (1808) who said that, at a meeting of Excisemen in Dumfries, Robert was asked for a song and wrote the verses on the back of a letter and handed them to the chairman. That the song was composed more or less extempore at one of the periodic Excise dinners in the King's Arms seems more probable than Lockhart's tale of composition at Sarkfoot while waiting to board the smuggling vessel. A third version, however, circulated in Annan and is widely believed to this day; as it does not rule out the King's Arms story, it may well be correct.

In connection with his duties in the Port Division, Robert occasionally had to stay overnight at Annan where he habitually lodged at a house in the High Street (now the Café Royal). This house belonged to a local merchant named Thomas Williamson (1752–1840), provost of the burgh in

1831–3. Miss Harkness, the provost's great-granddaughter, claimed that Burns had inscribed verses on window-panes of his bedroom. According to Williamson, Burns one evening left a large company assembled in the house, remarking that he would come back shortly and recite something new. He walked to Annan Bridge, evidently working out his ideas, and on his return wrote down the song which he recited to great applause. Williamson often described in later years the sensation caused by the poet's recital. A stone tablet in the wall looking towards the Town Hall records the occasion. It therefore seems probable that Robert composed the song at Annan, but first sang it at the Excise dinner a month later.

One of the *canards* still widely held is that Burns was shunned by Edinburgh society after he settled in Dumfries, if not while he was on his farm at Ellisland. Catherine Carswell (1930) makes the point that Walter Scott never once visited Burns during the eight-year period (1789–96) when his professional duties took him frequently to Dumfriesshire.[21] Nevertheless, it was on 10 April 1792 that Robert received a singular honour, his diploma as a member of the Royal Archers of Scotland, the sovereign's ceremonial bodyguard. He fully intended sending his thanks appropriately in rhyme, but he never seemed to be in the right mood, and consequently never got around to acknowledging the honour. Five months passed before he wrote to Alexander Cunningham (CL 465–7) who seems to have nominated him for the award:

> Amid all my hurry of business, grinding the faces of the Publican & the Sinner on the merciless wheels of the Excise; making ballads, & then drinking, & singing them; & over & above all, the correcting the Press-work of two different Publications.

This was Robert at his best, in a very long letter, written near 'witching time of night' and a nipperkin of toddy at his elbow. By turns whimsical and philosophical, and at all times extravagant in his use of language and metaphor, he touched on a wide range of topics. Cunningham had recently married Agnes Moir, having eventually got over being jilted by Anne Stewart, and this prompted Robert to enquire:

> Apropos, how do you like, I mean *really* like, the Married Life? – Ah, my Friend! Matrimony is quite a different thing from what your love-sick youths & sighing girls take it to be! – But Marriage, we are told, is appointed by God & I shall never quarrel with any of HIS institutions.– I am a Husband of older standing than you, & I shall give you *my* ideas of the Conjugal State.– (En passant , you know I am no Latin, is not 'Conjugal' derived from 'Jugum' a yoke?) Well then, the scale of Good-wife ship I divide into ten parts.– Good Nature, four; Good-Sense, two; Wit, one; Personal Charms, viz. a sweet face, eloquent eyes, fine limbs, graceful carriage, (I would add a fine waist too, but that is so soon spoilt you know) all these, one: as for the other qualities belonging to, or attending on, a Wife, such as, fortune, connections education, (I mean, education extraordinary) family-blood, &c. divide the two remaining degrees among

them as you please; only remember that all these minor properties must be expressed by *fractions*; for there is not any one of them, in the aforesaid scale, entitled to the dignity of an *integer*.

He rhapsodised about Miss Lesley Baillie, 'the most beautiful, elegant woman in the world', and told his friend how he had lately convoyed the girl and her family fifteen miles on their journey, 'out of pure devotion to admire the loveliness of the works of God' which inspired the songs 'Bonie Lesley' (CW 435) and 'Blythe hae I been on yon hill' (CW 490).

He described this incident in greater detail to Mrs Dunlop, in a letter from Annan Waterfoot on 22 August 1792 (CL 198-9) and confessed that he was *almost* head over heels in love. A dithyrambic passage describing his feelings concluded 'so delighting, & so pure, were the emotions of my soul on meeting the other day with Miss Lesley Bailie, your neighbour at Mayfield' – Mayville House on the outskirts of Stevenston.

In his letter to Cunningham, Robert mentioned that he was involved in two separate publications. Ironically, it was thanks to Cunningham that he was soon to become involved in a third. During the spring and summer of 1792 Robert was, indeed, very preoccupied with the fourth volume of the *Museum*. In addition to correspondence with James Johnson on this matter there is a solitary letter from Robert to his musical collaborator Stephen Clarke. It will be remembered that Robert promised the McMurdo family that he would get his friend Clarke down to Drumlanrig to give the girls piano and singing lessons. Clarke appears to have ignored Robert's original request, but a mock-formal letter of 16 July (CL 615) did the trick:

Mr B– is deeply impressed with, & awefully conscious of, the high importance of Mr C–'s time, whether in the winged moments of symphonious exhibition at the keys of Harmony, while listening Seraphs cease their own less delightful strains; – or in the drowsy, hours of slumbrous repose, in the arms of his dearly beloved elbow-chair, where the frowsy but potent Power of Indolence, circumfuses her vapours round, & sheds her dews on, the beard of her Darling Son – but half a line conveying half a meaning from Mr C– would make Mr B the very happiest of mortals.

The fourth volume of the *Museum* was published in August 1792; this time two-thirds of the songs were by Burns who also wrote the Preface:

When the Editor Published the third Volume of this work, he had reason to conclude that one volume more would finish the Publication.– Still however, he has a considerable number of Scots Airs and Songs more than his plan allowed him to include in this fourth volume.– These, though in all probability they will not amount to what he has hitherto published as one volume, he shall yet give to the world; that the Scots Musical Museum may be a Collection of every Scots Song extant.– Tho those who object that his Publication contains pieces of inferior, or little value, the Editor answers, by referring to his plan.– All our Songs cannot have equal merit. Besides, as the world have not yet agreed on any unerring balance, any undisputed standard, in matters of Taste, what to one person yields no manner of pleasure, may to another be a high enjoyment.

In April 1792, however, Robert received a letter, out of the blue, from none other than William Creech, who proposed a new edition of the poems in two volumes and coolly asked how much new material Robert was prepared to furnish. Robert replied on 16 April (CL 306–7), estimating that he could add about fifty pages.

> I would also correct and retrench a good deal. These said fifty pages you know are as much mine as the thumb-stall I have just now drawn on my finger which I unfortunately gashed in mending my pen. A few books which I very much want are all the recompence I crave, together with as many copies of this new edition of my own works as Friendship or Gratitude shall prompt me to present. There are three men whom you know and whose friendly patronage I think I can trouble so far – Messrs McKenzie, D. Stewart, and F. Tytler: to any of these I shall submit my MSS for their strictures.

The same gentlemen, Robert proposed, would be arbiters of what his labour on the new edition should be worth in terms of books to be supplied. As 'the Man of Feeling' and Professor Stewart were busy with works of their own, Robert supposed that Alexander Fraser Tytler would be the best man to refer his manuscripts to. A letter of 6 December that year (CL 579) implies that Robert did consult Tytler. No other letter of this year has survived, but the December letter implies an on-going correspondence by stating: 'I again trouble you with another, & my last, parcel of Manuscript.– I am not interested in any of these; blot them at your pleasure.' It was as a result of Tytler's strictures that Robert agreed to delete the four lines from 'Tam o Shanter' dealing with lawyers' tongues and priests' hearts.

The letter to Creech concluded with a desire to correct the proof-sheets which could be sent to Dumfries by the thrice-weekly fly; 'I would earnestly wish to correct them myself,' he added. The absence of further correspondence between poet and publisher created the impression that Robert dragged his heels in the project, repaying the business of the delayed settlement by himself delaying the correcting of the copy of the 1787 edition which Creech sent to him for that purpose. This was confirmed by Robert himself, who wrote to Peter Hill (CL 320):

> By the way, I have taken a damned vengeance of Creech.– He wrote me a fine, fair letter, telling me that he was going to print a third Edition; & as he had a brother's care of my fame, he wished to add every new thing I have written since, & I should be amply rewarded with – a copy or two to present to my friends! – He has sent me a copy of the last Edn to correct, &c.– but I have as yet taken no notice of it; & I hear he has published without me.– You know & all my friends know, that I do not value money; but I owed the gentleman a debt, which I am happy to have it in my power to repay.[22]

That Robert took no interest in revising material which had hitherto been published is borne out by the text of the previously published poems in the 1793 edition which remained virtually unaltered. On the other hand, Robert kept his promise and sent a substantial amount of manuscript material for the new edition, confirmed by the re-emergence of a letter to Creech discussing these very matters. This letter did not appear in any biography of Burns or any edition of his letters, and its existence was overlooked by both DeLancey Ferguson (1931) and Ross Roy (1985). It lacks a date but clearly belongs to the autumn of 1792 (CL 307):

> I have been from home, and very throng for some time, else I would have sent you the remaining MSS. I suppose that there will be fifteen or eighteen pages yet, at least. Please send me, by first carrier, Darwin's Botanic Garden, and his Loves of the Plants, as also Professor D. Stewart's Elements of the Philosophy of the Human Mind. If I exceed in this commission I will pay the balance. Adieu! They gallop fast whom the Devil drives, and I am just going to mount on an excise ride.

Robert ended by quoting four lines from 'The Deil's awa wi th'Exciseman' and closed with the greeting 'Ça ira!' – the slogan of the French revolutionaries. Creech, however, was very offhand about keeping his author informed of impending publication. One may detect just a hint of exasperation in Robert's last-known letter to his publisher, dated 28 February 1793 (CL 307):

> I understand that my Book is published.– I beg that you will, *as soon as possible*, send me twenty copies of it.– As I mean to present them among a few Great Folks whom I respect, & a few Little Folks whom I love, these twenty will not interfere with your sale.– If you have not twenty copies ready, send me any number you can.– It will confer a particular obligation to let me have them by first Carrier.

Creech replied on 2 March and dutifully sent the parcel of books. Over the ensuing month Robert sent presentation copies of his latest edition to Thomas Sloan (CL 577), Nancy McLehose (CL 410), Patrick Miller of Dalswinton (CL 245), Mrs Graham of Fintry (CL 556), Robert Riddell (CL 484), John McMurdo (CL 494), Maria Riddell (CL 602), David Blair of Birmingham (CL 503), Thomas White (CL 687) and John Francis Erskine (691). Despite the offhand treatment he had received at the hands of the Glencairn family after the death of the fourteenth Earl the previous year, Robert swallowed his pride and sent presentation copies to John, fifteenth Earl (brother of the deceased) and his sister Lady Elizabeth Cunningham (CL 500). The copy which went to Earl John was accompanied by a comparatively long letter (CL 686) which revealed the depth of Robert's feelings for the late Earl. Rather touchingly, a presentation copy also went to Mossgiel for 'Dear-bought Bess', now twelve years of age. The fly-leaf was simply inscribed 'her father's gift – THE AUTHOR'.

There was a rather artless quality about *The Scots Musical Museum*, from Clarke's simple harmonies to Robert's somewhat idiosyncratic punctuation. In a letter to Mrs Dunlop, when she was contemplating getting her own poems published, he once said airily (CL 192) that 'you have only to spell it right, & place the capital letters properly: as to punctuation, the Printers do that themselves'. In this case, however, Johnson was a man of very limited education and, knowing his own limitations, he relied entirely on Robert. For this reason, Robert's own wayward way with commas and dashes, a hallmark of his correspondence, can clearly be seen in the prefaces and notes in the *Museum*.

Robert's preface in the fourth volume struck a rather defensive note. Perhaps there was a feeling that, in attempting to be all-embracing, he was not so discriminating in his choice of material. We may be sure that certain genteel souls in the polite society of Edinburgh thought so. At any rate one of them at least was prepared to do something about it, although he had the good sense to realise that, without the active collaboration of Robert Burns, the project would be severely handicapped, if not doomed to failure. George Thomson (1757–1851) was the son of the schoolmaster at Limekilns near Dunfermline and on top of a good basic education he had trained as a lawyer's clerk. He might have become a lawyer and ended his days as a Writer to the Signet, but in 1780 his career changed direction slightly. On the recommendation of the playwright John Home, young Thomson exchanged his desk in a law office for a desk in the office of the Board of Trustees for the Encouragement of Art and Manufacture in Scotland. He spent the rest of his very long and uneventful career in this office, eventually becoming chief clerk. This quasi-governmental organisation had been established under the terms of the Act of Union in 1707 to promote trade and industry in Scotland with money disbursed by Parliament partly as compensation for the Darien disaster and partly in recognition of Scotland's assumption of a portion of the National Debt. Part of Thomson's duties, soon after taking up his appointment, would have been to work out the exact amounts of the premiums payable to the farmers, including Robert Burns in Lochlie, for raising flax.

Thomson's otherwise humdrum existence was enlivened by a passion for music. A keen amateur musician, he played in the orchestra for the St Cecilia concerts. Some idea of the refinement of his taste may be gained from his partiality to the Italianate rendition of Scottish songs by Tenducci and other castrati who gave concerts in Edinburgh from time to time. In 1792 Pietro Urbani (1749–1816), a Milanese singer who had settled in Edinburgh seven years earlier, launched his *Selection of Scots Songs*. Although Thomson admired Urbani's singing, he was disconcerted by the appearance of the first volume of Urbani's *Selection* which he dismissed as 'a water-gruel collection'. This spurred him on to realise his own long-felt ambition of producing a select volume of the best Scottish airs, with words to match and the sort of florid musical arrangements that would raise them to the level of concert performance. The fussiness and pomposity of Thomson's taste were better suited to the mid-Victorian era than the simpler Augustan elegance of the late eighteenth century. Fortunately, Thomson lived long enough to see his views become the norm, and he died in the year of the Great Exhibition which was designed, among other things, to restore sanity to taste and fashion. Whereas simple, unlettered, unpretentious James Johnson was content with the services of Stephen Clarke, Thomson preferred Continental composers, such as Beethoven and Haydn. Haydn's star pupil, Joseph Ignaz Pleyel (1757–1831), became his chief musical collaborator.

By the summer of 1792 Thomson's plans for his *Select Collection of Scotish Airs* were well matured and he had secured the support of Captain Andrew Erskine, youngest son of the fifth Earl of Kellie, a man who had enjoyed the close friendship of James Boswell and who was well known in Edinburgh literary circles. All that remained was to enlist the aid of Burns. To this end Thomson got Alexander Cunningham to write to Robert a letter of introduction. With this was enclosed a longer missive from Thomson setting out his ideas for the projected work. Thomson's letter was despatched in mid-September:

> For some years past I have, with a friend or two, employed many leisure hours in collating and collecting the most favourite of our national melodies, for publication. We have engaged Pleyel, the most agreeable composer living, to put accompaniments to these and also to compose an instrumental prelude and conclusion to each air, the better to fit them for concerts both public and private. To render this work perfect, we are desirous to have the poetry improved wherever it seems unworthy of the music; and that it is so, in many instances, is allowed by every one conversant with our musical collections. The editors of these seem in general to have depended on the music proving an excuse for the verses; and hence some charming melodies are united to mere nonsense and doggerel, while others are accommodated with rhymes so loose and indelicate as cannot be sung in decent company. To remove this reproach would be an easy task to the author of 'The Cotter's Saturday Night'; and, for the honour of Caledonia, I would fain hope he may be induced to take up the pen.

Thomson hastened to add that 'Profit is quite a secondary consideration' although he was willing to pay 'any reasonable price' for Robert's co-operation.

> Tell me frankly, then, whether you will devote your leisure to writing twenty or twenty-five songs, suitable to the particular melodies which I am prepared to send you. A few Songs exceptionable only in some of their verses, I will likewise submit to your consideration; leaving it to you, either to mend these or make new Songs in their stead. It is superfluous to assure you that I have no intention to displace any of the sterling old · Songs: those only will be removed which appear quite silly or absolutely indecent. Even these shall be examined by Mr Burns, and if *he* is of opinion that any of them are deserving of the music, in such cases no divorce shall take place.

Robert replied immediately on receipt of this letter with characteristic
enthusiasm (CL 617–18). Thomson had struck a responsive chord in referring to the honour of Caledonia:

> As the request you make will positively add to my enjoyments in comply-
> ing with, I shall enter into your undertaking with all the small portion of
> abilities I have, strained to their utmost exertion by the impulse of
> enthusiasm. Only, don't hurry me: 'Deil tak the hindmost' is by no means
> the *Crie de guerre* of my muse.

He asked Thomson for a list of the airs, and their first lines. Straight away
he warned Thomson that if he was looking for English verses 'there is on
my part an end of the matter'. While conceding that there were English
verses by Scotsmen which had merit and would be eligible for inclusion –
here he cited a number of works including his own compositions – he railed
against

> such insipid stuff as 'To Fanny fair could I impart' &c., usually set to 'The
> Mill, Mill O', 'tis a disgrace to the collections in which it has already
> appeared and would doubly disgrace a collection that will have the very
> superior merit of yours.

Robert promised that he would not alter except where he himself thought
that he should amend. Then followed the crucial paragraph which showed
Robert at his most impetuous and unbusinesslike. After his experiences
with Creech, he ought to have been more cautious in dealing with a gentleman who was, at this juncture, a total stranger.

> As to remuneration, you may think my songs either *above* or *below* price;
> for they shall absolutely be the one or the other. In the honest enthusiasm
> with which I embark in your undertaking, to talk of money, wages, fee,
> hire, &c., would be downright Sodomy of Soul!

And he added a postscript, 'I have some particular reasons for wishing my
interference to be known as little as possible'. Presumably he did not want
to hurt Johnson's feelings.

When this letter was published by Currie in 1800 the editor showed a
nice sense of moral distinction by replacing 'Sodomy' by 'Prostitution'.

Thomson's proposal was a shot in the arm to Robert. As winter
approached with its attendant blue devilism, he had an exciting and
challenging new project to absorb his interests. Now that the *Museum* was
losing momentum – although work on a fifth volume had begun it was not
to see the light of day till some months after Robert's death – Robert
needed some new sense of purpose to relieve the *ennui* which always came
over him in the closing months of the year. Besides, Thomson's project
promised to be an altogether superior production. Before the year was out
Robert had sent Thomson eight songs and others followed in quick succession. When Thomson published the first volume of *Select Scotish Airs* the

following June it contained the original twenty-five songs which Robert
had promised.

Thomson has tended to be lumped with Creech as one who treated
Burns shabbily; but it must be remembered that Burns himself made it
very clear at the outset that he had no desire to sully his part of the undertaking with any mercenary considerations. Thomson had to cope with a
man whose pride could sometimes rise to ridiculous heights and who was
perennially and unduly sensitive to any suspicion of being patronised. If
ever an arrangement had called for a proper contract between the parties,
this was it. It has been argued that had Thomson known better how to
cope with Burns's pride, or had someone like Henry Mackenzie draw up
a proper settlement, the ticklish problem of payment need never have
arisen.[22]

When the volume was published Thomson sent Robert a copy and
enclosed a five-pound note, with the explanation:

> I cannot express to you how much I am obliged to you for the exquisite
> new songs you are sending me; but thanks, my friend, are a poor return
> for what you have done. As I shall benefit by the publication, you must
> suffer me to enclose a small mark of my gratitude, and to repeat it after-
> wards when I find it convenient. Do not return it, for, by Heaven! if you
> do, our correspondence is at an end.

Robert's immediate reaction would have been to return the money but, to
make matters worse, by that time he was in no position to make such a
gesture. Since the outbreak of war between Britain and France four
months earlier, the drastic interruption in trade had severely reduced his
Excise perquisites. About April 1793 he had written to Peter Hill (CL 321)
hoping that 'this unlucky blast which has overturned so many, & many
worthy characters who four months ago little dreaded any such thing'
would spare him, and to Thomson himself he lamented (CL 630) the fact
that a friend of his had 'fallen a sacrifice to these accursed times' adding
that his own loss, 'as to pecuniary matters, is trifling'. But his financial
problems were swept aside when he responded to Thomson's gesture
(CL 631):

> I assure you, my dear Sir, that you truly hurt me with your pecuniary
> parcel.– It degrades me in my own eyes.– However, to return it would
> savour of bombast affectation; But as to any more traffic of that Debtor
> & Creditor kind, I swear by that HONOUR which crowns the upright
> Statue of ROBt BURNS'S INTEGRITY! – On the least motion of it, I
> will indignantly spurn the bypast transactions, & from that moment com-
> mence entire Stranger to you! – BURNS'S will, I trust, long outlive any
> of his wants which the cold, unfeeling, dirty Ore can supply: at least, I
> shall take care that such a Character he shall deserve.

Despite his protests at receiving this money, Robert was more than
a little relieved at this unexpected windfall. Significantly, for one who

protested about Sodomy of Soul, Robert had a rather cavalier way with settling minor debts. The bill for ten shillings, owing to Jackson of the *Dumfries Journal* for advertising the sale of his stock at Ellisland, was still unpaid, some twenty months after the event, and Robert did not settle this account till 12 July that year, doubtless using some of the money sent by Thomson.

Wisely Thomson made no attempt to repeat the gesture. More tactfully he arranged for payment in kind. Only when he lay dying, with the imagined threat of bankruptcy over him, did Robert swallow his pride and appeal to Thomson for a further five pounds which the latter despatched immediately. Pleyel, by contrast, received £131 5s in 1793 as his payment for the musical arrangements. It is only fair to add that, having made his impassioned declaration, Robert went on to congratulate Thomson on the 'elegance and correctness' of the volume:

> Your Preface, too, is admirably written; only your partiality to me has made you say too much: however, it will bind me down to double every effort in the future progress of the Work.

Thomson took Robert at his word and soon expanded the project to exploit the eagerness and enthusiasm of the poet to fullest advantage. Sadly, although *Select Scotish Airs* was to get the bulk of Robert's poetic attention right down to the day he died, and he continued to send songs to Thomson till 12 July 1796, no subsequent volume appeared in his lifetime. The first volume was reissued in 1798 and the following year the second appeared. Four other volumes of Scottish songs were published fitfully up to 1841, together with companion volumes containing the songs of Wales (1809–14) and Ireland (1814–16). Robert contributed about a hundred and fourteen songs to this project, although it is fair to add that the true number that ought to be credited to him was probably much larger, as several songs belonging to other authors were polished and subtly transformed by him.

Apart from selling himself short, Robert made the cardinal mistake of treating Thomson as he regarded Johnson. They were the editors of their respective works, and he was happy to abide by their decisions. Johnson had the good sense and humility to know his own limitations and had always been happy to take Robert's verdict as final. Thomson, however, was vain, pompous and pretentious and was imbued with a sense of his own superiority in matters of taste and elegance. Consequently he was forever altering and meddling in matters where he was not competent. Thomson was not slow in making alternative suggestions, or criticising Robert's contributions. As early as 26 October 1792 (CL 618) Robert felt constrained to comment, 'Let me tell you, that you are too fastidious in your ideas of Songs & ballads' but he undermined his own argument by politely conceding 'I own that your criticisms are just'. As the project developed, however, and Thomson meddled more and more, Robert was increasingly compelled to defend and justify his actions. As a result, the fifty-seven letters which Robert wrote between 1792 and 1796 have furnished us with an invaluable insight into the mechanics of composition and a far better analysis of the mending and reworking of old ballads than can be gleaned from the poet's annotations in Riddell's interleaved *Museum*.

When Robert argued a point and gave his reasons for a particular line of action Thomson seldom countered with a fresh argument; he knew exactly how far he could go in trying the patience and reasonableness of his principal collaborator. But he 'ganged his ain gait' anyway, and discreetly altered a line here, a stanza there, without telling the poet; and after his death he blithely ignored Robert's wishes regarding the melodies to which his words had been composed, often substituting inferior or unsuitable airs of his own choosing. Robert treated Thomson's antics with remarkable tolerance, not to say good humour. The key lay in Robert's attitude that the project was potentially the most worthwhile one he had ever been involved in. On 7 April 1793 he wrote to Thomson (CL 626):

> You cannot imagine how much this business of composing for your publication has added to my enjoyments.– What with my early attachment to ballads, Johnson's Museum, your book; &c. Ballad-making is now so compleatly my hobby-horse, as ever Fortification was Uncle Toby's, so I'll e'en canter it away till I come to the limit of my race.

To ballad-making was added another interest which, in Robert's last years, provided him with considerable intellectual stimulus. When he settled in Dumfries theatrical entertainments were given by itinerant companies in the old Assembly Rooms in George Street. One such company, which performed at Dumfries in 1789-90, was managed by George Stephens Sutherland, to whom Robert sent a New Year Prologue (CW 376). A few days later Robert had sent a copy of this to Gilbert with a letter reporting that Sutherland had 'spouted to his Audience with great applause' (CL 358). The following March Robert had written a Scots Prologue for Mrs Sutherland (CW 399) which she delivered on her benefit night. Sutherland was sufficiently encouraged by the response of his audiences to make approaches to certain influential gentlemen of the district, with a view to securing a permanent theatre. Robert himself, an avid patron of dramatic performances, discussed this matter with William Nicol to whom he wrote on 2 February 1790 (CL 346-8):

> Our theatrical company, of which you must have heard, leave us in a week. Their merit and character are indeed very great, both on the stage and in private life; not a worthless creature among them; and their encouragement has been accordingly. Their usual run is from eighteen to twenty five pounds a night; seldom less than the one, and the house will hold no more than the other. There have been repeated instances of sending away, six, and eight, and ten pounds in a night for want of room. A new theatre is to be built by subscription; the first stone is to be laid on Friday first to come. Three hundred guineas have been raised by thirty subscribers, and thirty more might have been got if wanted. The manager, Mr Sutherland, was introduced to me by a friend from Ayr; and a

worthier or clever fellow I have rarely met with. Some of our clergy have slipt in by stealth now and then.

A meeting of the subscribers took place on 18 February 1790, at which Sutherland announced that he had feued a portion of the gardens at East Barnraws (now Queen Street) as a site. A design, based on that of the Theatre Royal in Bristol, was submitted to Thomas Boyd who drew up the plans. The Founding Deed for the theatre was drafted in the name of Robert Riddell of Glenriddell, to whom was granted by Thomas and William Bushby land 'on the South East side of the street called the Barn-raws, or Shakespeare Street'. Riddell was to pay £5 a year to Thomas Bushby who was also entitled to two 'Brass Tickets' which gave him free admission to all performances (except benefit nights). Each of the original subscribers of ten guineas or more was similarly granted free admission, receiving as a token of this a silver medal which had a vignette of the theatre on the obverse and the subscriber's name engraved on the reverse.

Robert was unduly optimistic about the funds raised, for the original capital was exhausted before the work was completed. A further £500 had to be raised before the theatre was ready. John Brown Williamson, actor-manager formerly with the Theatre Royal in the Haymarket, London, was appointed to manage the theatre, with Sutherland as his assistant. The opening ceremony, on Saturday, 29 September 1792, was a gala occasion:

> The united elegance and accommodation of the house reflected equal honour on the liberality and taste of the proprietors and design and execu-tion of the artists, and conspired with the abilities of the performers in giving universal satisfaction to a crowded and polite audience. In a word, it is allowed by persons of first taste and opportunities that this is the handsomest provincial theatre in Scotland.[23]

This report added that Thomas Boyd was the architect and that Alexander Nasmyth had designed the scenery and interior decor, for which he received a fee of one hundred guineas. At that time, Nasmyth was down on his luck. His open advocacy of parliamentary reform and a reckless espousal of the French Revolution had alienated his wealthy Edinburgh clientele, and it seems highly probable that he secured the commission to work on the new theatre as a result of the intervention of his most famous sitter. A sketch is preserved in the National Gallery of Scotland entitled 'Design for a scene for the Dumfries Theatre, done at the desire of Robert Burns, by Alexander Nasmyth'.

The theatre was designed in the classical fashion then prevailing, with a pillared portico. The interior consisted of a pit, a dress circle of boxes arranged in a horseshoe and, above and behind that, the gallery. Seats in these areas cost two, three and one shillings respectively. Behind the boxes ran a semi-circular passage, off which opened the doors to the boxes. Each box was divided into compartments containing several seats. The baize-covered door to each box had an oval glass panel in the centre, and was tastefully festooned by crimson curtains. The theatre was capable of accommodating up to six hundred people. It was enlarged in 1830 and rebuilt in 1876; in 1911 it was converted into a cinema and in 1954 became a casualty of the television age. It remained closed till 1 October 1960 when it reopened as a theatre again, under the auspices of the Guild of Players, and has flourished ever since.

Though not one of the subscribers, Robert was on the free list of patrons, thanks to his friend Riddell, and was a regular attender at new performances. Robert certainly repaid Riddell's generosity in the appropriate coin, continuing to write prologues and occasional addresses. At this time Robert was captivated by the company's leading lady, the beautiful and petite Louisa Fontenelle, who charmed everyone with her role of Little Pickle in *The Spoiled Child*. For her benefit night on 26 November 1792 she took the lead in Wycherley's *Country Girl*. The performance was followed by a re-enactment of Drake's victory over the Spanish Armada 'with Fire Ships &c., &c.', but the high-point of the evening came when Miss Fontenelle came on stage and declaimed 'The Rights of Woman' (CW 471-2). These lines, mirrored on fellow-Exciseman Tom Paine's *Rights of Man*, placed Burns in the very forefront of the feminist movement, although, in view of the subsequent furore over his political leanings, Robert may have regretted the closing lines:

> Let Majesty your first attention summon,
> Ah! ça ira! THE MAJESTY OF WOMAN!

Louisa Fontenelle (1773–99) married Williamson three years later and emigrated with him to the United States where she died of yellow fever at Charleston, South Carolina, on 30 October 1799. She was a woman of immense charm and beauty and it was inevitable that Robert should be attracted to her. He sent a copy of 'The Rights of Woman' to her with a highly complimentary letter (CL 682) beginning fulsomely, 'To you, Madam, on our humble Dumfries boards, I have been more indebted for entertainment, than ever I was in prouder Theatres'. A shorter letter, written soon afterwards, sought her permission before sending the poem for publication. For Miss Fontenelle he also composed, the following year, the prologue beginning 'Still anxious to secure your partial favor' (CW 508) and enclosed a copy with a letter written about 1 December 1793 (CL 683). The stanzas beginning 'Sweet naivete of feature' (CW 509) were probably sent to her at the same time.

Events on the other side of the Channel were rapidly spinning out of control. The refugee aristocrats had roused the anger and anxiety of Prussia and Austria which were now at war with revolutionary France. The royal family had been imprisoned and the king deposed. Thousands of loyalists were massacred in Paris in September and the National Convention, which had replaced the National Assembly, was increasingly authoritarian. The bellicose republic, in the first flush of revolutionary fervour, threatened to topple monarchy everywhere. The revolutionary ideas which had seemed innocuous in February had, by October, acquired an ominous overtone. Paine's *Rights of Man*, published on 31 March 1791, had an enormous circulation before the government took fright and endeavoured to suppress it. Paine was indicted for treason in May 1792 but before he came to trial he left the country and was elected by the *département* of Calais to the National Convention. Poor Paine, who understood neither French nor the dreadful difficulties of the revolution, rapidly made himself unpopular with the Jacobins. Robespierre had him thrown into prison and he only escaped the guillotine by the merest accident. Paine, the revolutionary, was overtaken by the Revolution itself. His legacy in Britain was the mushroom growth of reform societies under the general name of Friends of the People. Their aims were laudable, 'to stem the torrent of corruption and bring about a redress of real grievances'. To this end they sought a 'full, free, and equal representation of the people' and a shortening of the duration of parliaments (which then lasted a maximum of seven years). They disavowed all extreme and dangerous courses and sought reform by constitutional means. Forty years later, the first of their moderate aims was achieved by the Reform Act of 1832, though a further half-century elapsed before the principle of 'one man, one vote' was secured.

The principles which the Friends of the People advocated, including adult suffrage and a secret ballot, have long since become regarded as the very fundamentals of democracy; but in the atmosphere of 1792–3, a paranoid government took fright and began a campaign of reaction and repression. As the international situation deteriorated and war with France seemed imminent, the authorities took extraordinary steps to secure the loyalty of its officials and cow the populace into submission. The Whigs, who stood for liberalism and reasonableness, were no match for the Tory ascendancy and the ruthless party machine operated by Henry Dundas. Harry Erskine became the fearless leader of the reform movement in Edinburgh, while Dugald Stewart propounded the doctrines of reform to his students in philosophical and rhetorical terms. Enlightened gentry, such as Patrick Miller and Robert Riddell, sympathised with the reformers but could do little in the face of the severe measures taken by the government. It became an act of sedition for more than three or four people to meet together for any purpose other than divine worship. When guests assembled for dinners in honour of the birthday of Charles James Fox, the leader of the parliamentary opposition, their numbers were restricted to a dozen, and their names reported to the authorities by the sheriff officers. Strict Tory tests were laid down for all would-be advocates before their admission to the Bar.

In various parts of Scotland effigies of Henry Dundas were ceremonially burned. Henry IX was now the most unpopular figure in the country; but everywhere his network of spies and informers helped to hold a rebellious people in check. That, at least, was the perception of Scotland prevalent in Whitehall. The wave of paranoia and repression that swept the country was to culminate in the notorious treason trials of 1793–4, but even in the late autumn and winter of 1792 the atmosphere was tense. In view of this,

Robert seems to have been singularly naïve, not to say extremely fool-hardy, in not curbing his enthusiasm for the Revolution and Reform, or at least behaving in a more discreet manner.

A retired army officer with radical political views, Captain William Johnston, founded a left-wing newspaper, the *Edinburgh Gazetteer*, in November 1792. Robert obtained a prospectus for this paper and wrote to its proprietor on 13 November (CL 681):

> If you go on in your Paper with the same spirit, it will, beyond all compar-ison, be the first Composition of the kind in Europe.– I beg leave to insert my name as a Subscriber; & if you have already published any papers, please send me them from the beginning . . . Go on, Sir! Lay bare, with undaunted heart & steady hand, that horrid mass of corruption called Politics & State-Craft! Dare to draw in their native colors these 'Calm, thinking VILLAINS whom no faith can fix'–[24] whatever be the shibboleth of their pretended Party.

Two weeks later he wrote again to Johnston asking that Robert Riddell be added to the subscription list, and enclosed an essay by Glenriddell on the extension of the franchise, under the *nom de plume* of Cato. Robert himself did not resort to polemics, but his lines 'On Some Commemorations of Thomson' (CW 421) and 'The Rights of Woman' (CW 508) were subse-quently published in the *Gazetteer*. A sympathy with this seditious news-paper was one of the charges laid against Burns shortly afterwards by an unnamed informer. But as 1792 drew to a close, Robert was ignorant of the trouble which was brewing. To this period belongs his song 'Here's a health to them that's awa' (CW 473). Based on an old Jacobite ballad, Robert updated its political flavour and alluded to the leading radicals of the time. 'Tammie, the Norlan' laddie' was Thomas Erskine (1750–1823), Tom Paine's defence lawyer and younger brother of the redoubtable Harry. James Maitland, eighth Earl of Lauderdale (1759–1839), John Henry Petty Fitzmaurice, Earl of Wycombe (1765–1809) and Colonel Norman MacLeod of MacLeod (1754–1801) were singled out for mention, along with Charles James Fox himself. Maitland was one of the sixteen representative Scottish peers and one of the founders of the Friends of the People, while Wycombe was an ardent supporter of parliamentary reform. MacLeod was then MP for Inverness-shire and was the principal speaker at an assembly of delegates from the various reform societies held in James's Court, Edinburgh, on 22 November. At this meeting Captain Johnston was unanimously asked to take the chair but declined. He was arrested and imprisoned early in 1793, and the same fate befell his successor. Even his printer, an honest Jacobite by the name of Moir, found that his concern in the newspaper stopped his credit at the banks and made him a marked man. Business only recovered when he enlisted in one of the loyal volun-teer regiments then being formed.[25]

Robert had other matters on his mind at this time. On 21 November Jean gave birth yet again. To Mrs Dunlop on 24 September (CL 200)

Robert had written with some misgivings about the impending birth. He hoped it would not be a daughter: 'I am not equal to the task of rearing girls.– Besides, I am too poor: a girl should always have a fortune'. His worst fears were realised, however, and the child was named Elizabeth Riddell Burns, in compliment to the wife of Robert's friend Glenriddell. Despite Robert's misgivings, the little girl turned out to be her father's favourite and he was often to be seen dandling the infant in his lap and crooning to her. Although the Burns family nominally worshipped in St Michael's parish church, the poet was allegedly not on the best of terms with the aged Dr Mutter and preferred to make use of the minister of the neighbouring parish of Caerlaverock, the Revd. William McMorine. Meeting this gentleman in Dumfries one market-day, Robert asked him to call the following morning in order to baptise baby Elizabeth. McMorine called, but at an earlier hour than was perhaps expected. On being shown into one of the rooms in the flat he was amazed to find the poet and two companions, apparently prolonging a drinking-session commenced the night before, the two visitors being very much the worse for drink. 'The poet seemed taken by surprise, but quickly recovered his self-possession and soon put things in order for the ceremony,' McMorine afterwards related. 'I was shocked by the idea of so prolonged a debauch, and thought meanly of the appearance of the two guests.'[26] This embarrassing incident was touched on obliquely by Robert in a letter to Mrs Dunlop of 5 January 1793 (CL 204):

> Your cup, my dear Madam, arrived safe.– I had two worthy fellows dining with me the other day, when I, with great formality, produced my whig-maleerie cup, & told them that it had been a family-piece among the descendants of Sir William Wallace.– This roused such enthusiasm that they insisted on bumpering the punch round in it; & by & by, never did your great Ancestor lay a *Suthron* more compleately to rest, than for a time did your cup my two friends.

The 'whigmaleerie cup' was, in fact, a polished coconut, with a silver rim and ornamental pedestal which later passed into the hands of Archibald Hastie, the celebrated collector of Burns manuscripts who also acquired the poet's polished stone punch-bowl that had been a wedding present from James Armour.

Robert was due some leave and on 6 December he wrote at great length to Mrs Dunlop (CL 201–2) whom he hoped to visit. Near the end of this letter he casually mentioned the political ferment in Dumfries:

> We, in this country, here have many alarms of the Reform, or rather the Republican spirit, of your part of the kingdom.– Indeed, we are a good deal in commotion ourselves, & in our Theatre here 'God save the king' has met with some groans & hisses, while Ça ira has been repeatedly called for.– For me, I am a *Placeman*, you know, a very humble one indeed, Heaven knows, but still so much as to gag me from joining in the cry.– What my private sentiments are, you will find out without an

Interpreter.– In the mean time, I have taken up the subject in another view, and the other day, for a pretty Actress's benefit-night, I wrote an Address, which I will give on the other page, called *The Rights of Woman*.

This letter refers to an incident at the Dumfries Theatre on the evening of Thursday 28 October when Robert was, indeed, present. He was alleged to have remained seated with his hat on his head during the playing of the national anthem, and to have joined in the clamour for 'Ça ira', the French republican song. The only eye-witness account of this incident was written forty years later by one Charles Sharpe who was only eleven years old at the time:

> I know that he was most woefully indiscreet on that point, and I remember one proof. We were at the play in Dumfries in October 1792 – the Caledonian Hunt being then in town. The play was 'As you like it', Miss Fontenelle, *Rosalind*, when 'God save the King' was called for and sung; we all stood up uncovered, but Burns sat still in the middle of the pit with his hat on his head. There was a great tumult, with shouts of 'Turn him out! – Shame, Burns!' which continued a good while. At last he was either expelled or forced to take his hat off – I forget which; nor can my mother remember. This silly conduct all sensible persons condemned.[27]

Such a rumpus in the theatre pit would have been upsetting for a boy of eleven, but recollecting the event so long after it happened, some allowance for misinterpretation must be made. The Sharpe family disliked Burns and always spoke or wrote disparagingly of him in any case. Taken out of context, Robert's conduct seems pretty damning, as witnessed by an excited eleven-year-old, but it actually fits with the poet's own description to Robert Graham, written on 5 January 1793 (CL 436), in which the matter is put in its proper perspective:

> I was in the playhouse one night, when Ça ira was called for.– I was in the middle of the pit, & from the Pit the clamour arose.– One or two individuals with whom I occasionally associate were of the party, but I neither knew of the Plot, nor joined in the Plot; nor ever opened my lips to hiss, or huzza, that, or any other Political tune whatever.– I looked on myself as far too obscure a man to have any weight in quelling a Riot; at the same time, as a character of higher respectability, than to yell in the howlings of a rabble.– This was the conduct of all the first Characters in this place & these Characters know, & will avow, that such was my conduct.

When young Sharpe says that 'God save the King was called for', he unwittingly implied that, far from being the customary expression of loyalty played at the end of the evening, it was, in this context, being indecorously used by the Loyal Natives, a right-wing faction, to shout down the clamour of the left-wing rabble who had called for *their* anthem. By sitting tight and trying to ignore the clash and counter-clash of the hotheads, Robert was clearly disassociating himself from both factions. Robert had made no secret of his political views and such a kenspeckle figure would have been a natural target for the Tory diehards. Admittedly, to have remained seated with his hat on his head was, in itself, a provocative action which Robert probably regretted immediately the heat of the moment had passed. That right-wingers made a habit of calling for the national anthem during theatrical performances as a provocative gesture is borne out by accounts of disturbances at the theatre in Edinburgh at this period. A voice would call out for 'God Save the King' followed by a shout of 'Off hats!' as the signal for an attack on those who refused to comply. These disturbances culminated in a showdown on 12 October 1792. A report of the incident implied that both parties had come prepared with bludgeons, and while the affray lasted both sides fought with ferocity:

> Many dreadful blows were given, which brought several individuals to the ground; and the wounded were in danger of being trampled to death in the general confusion. The party, however, who insisted on keeping on their hats, being at length overcome, left the house, and the wounded were carried out. The pit was the principal scene of action.[28]

There was certainly a concerted movement by right-wing elements in Dumfries which culminated, in 18 January 1793, with the foundation of a club known as the Loyal Natives. Similar clubs sprang up all over the country as war fever mounted, and held the simplistic view that 'Gallicism' (the espousal of the French Revolution) and any form of opposition to the Tory government was synonymous. In Dumfries, the activities of the Loyal Natives seem to have consisted mainly of noisy dinners in the King's Arms when provocative toasts would be called for. The highlight of the social year was the king's birthday on 4 June, and this, naturally, became the occasion for raucous demonstrations of fanatical loyalty when the Loyal Natives paraded through the streets wearing patriotic sashes embroidered by their wives and daring those who held other views to block their way. Not surprisingly, these confrontations frequently led to fisticuffs and breaches of the peace.

It is only fair to point out that a minute examination of the contemporary newspapers, both local and national, has failed to reveal the slightest notice of any tumult at the Dumfries Theatre in October 1792. On the contrary, the local paper, published two days after the incident, was content to report:

> The entertainments of the hunting races, balls, and assemblies, by the Caledonian and the Dumfries and Galloway Hunts being now over, we embrace the earliest opportunity of informing the public that they have been conducted with the utmost propriety, and, we believe, have given general satisfaction ... The performances of the stage in the evening gave high entertainment to crowds of genteel people collected at the theatre. Lady Hopetoun's box on Thursday evening, being the play asked by the Caledonian Hunt, exhibited an assemblage of nobility rarely to be seen in one box in the theatres of the metropolis.[29]

Nevertheless, whatever the exact circumstances that fateful night, some anonymous informer communicated this to the Board of Excise who began gathering other shreds of evidence pointing to the poet-Exciseman's 'disaffection'. The case against him was compiled while he was absent on leave in Ayrshire. He spent four idyllically happy days at Dunlop House and returned to Dumfries towards the end of the month, to be told on 31 December by Collector Mitchell that he had received an order from the Board to enquire into Burns's political conduct.

Robert was aghast at this and immediately wrote a hysterical letter (CL 435-6) to Robert Graham of Fintry who, as a member of the Board, must have been well aware of the circumstances. Robert was 'surprised, confounded & distracted' and appealed to Graham:

> Sir, you are a Husband – & a father – you know what you would feel, to see the much-loved wife of your bosom, & your helpless, prattling little ones, turned adrift into the world, degraded & disgraced from a situation in which they had been respectable and respected & left without the necessary support of a miserable existence.

And much, much more in similar vein. Robert hotly denied the charge of disaffection. 'To the British Constitution, on Revolution principles, next after my God, I am most devoutly attached,' he declared, alluding to the revolution of 1688-9 which had resulted in the establishment of the constitutional monarchy. Then he changed tack and embarked on a long, grovelling passage reminding Graham of their close friendship:

> Fortune, Sir, has made you powerful & me impotent, has given you patronage, & me dependance.– I would not for my *single Self* call on your Humanity; were such my insular, unconnected situation, I would despise the tear that now swells in my eye.

He ended, 'Pardon this confused scrawl.– Indeed I know not well what I have written'. Unfortunately, no documents are extant to shed any light on the precise nature of the charges laid against Burns, nor the manner in which the Excise Board dealt with the matter. The impression conveyed by early biographers was that the affair was very grave indeed, and cited as proof a letter which Robert wrote in April 1793 in which he admitted that, but for the intervention of Graham, he would have been dismissed 'without so much as a hearing'. But such evidence as has survived, both direct and indirect and mainly negative, seems to suggest that the matter was a storm in a teacup which Robert, with his propensity for self-dramatisation, had greatly magnified and distorted out of all proportion.

It was a prudent matter for the Excise Board to take the precaution of making some judicious enquiries about the suspected political leanings of its staff. After all, it was not so very long ago that Tom Paine had been an Excise officer at Lewes in Sussex. But there is a world of difference between suspecting and actually *blaming* someone; Robert immediately jumped to the wrong conclusion and panicked accordingly. Alexander Findlater, who was Supervisor of Excise at Dumfries and therefore Robert's immediate superior, felt that whatever hint of disapprobation or warning was given to Burns must have been very slight and insignificant, for the simple reason that all disciplinary matters, great and small, came through him, and no such censure had passed through his hands. Diligent examinations of the Excise records at various times from 1827 to 1896 and even since then have failed to yield the slightest indication of any reprimand on this occasion. Considering that the Excise records were so detailed that they could even reveal that, in all his service, Robert had had only two 'admonishments', this gives the lie to anything more serious on this particular occasion.

The volumes still extant in Excise archives show that Robert was admonished on two occasions, in 1792 and 1795. On 10 May 1792 he entered a grocer's stock of green tea as 160 lbs instead of 16 lbs, causing an apparent increase of 144 lbs. He rectified the error on his next visit. On 25 May 1795 he neglected to visit a tanner and the omission was detected the very next day by Findlater. That these were very minor errors is indicated by the fact that, until 1804, admonitions were recorded only at a local level and not reported to Edinburgh. At that time a table of discipline contained the following entry:

> 6 admonishments = 1 reprimand
> 3 reprimands = 1 suspension
> 2 suspensions = dismissal

In a general order of 1815 the rules for the promotion of officers put this into perspective by stating that selection was to be made from the most senior officers, and the officer with the fewest censures was to be appointed. 'An admonishment shall not be deemed a censure.'[30] Findlater himself published a letter which set out the scale of disciplinary measures which rose from a verbal caution (no record being kept), via admonishment, sharp admonishment and reprimand, to severe reprimand and warning prior to suspension.[31]

Incidentally, in the same year the regulations were modified to permit the promotion of officers to the rank of Examiner or Supervisor after seven years' service, instead of nine as formerly. As Robert completed only seven years' service at the time of his death, one cannot put any adverse interpretation on the fact that he had not been promoted. On the contrary, he was selected for accelerated promotion and was to serve as Acting Supervisor in place of Findlater between 22 December 1794 and late April 1795. In the Character Book previously mentioned Robert's name also appears in a list of officers recommended for the post of Examiner, showing that he would have attained this rank late in 1796 or early in 1797.

How Robert was regarded by his superiors can be gauged by the tantalisingly few documentary scraps which have survived, as well as the poet's record of service. There exists a list of Excise officers in the Dumfries

Collection, drawn up some time after 26 April 1792.[32] Twelve names appear on this list and above their names Findlater had added cryptic comments. The letter (a) appears above the names of Burns, William Penn, John Lewars and Walter Crawford, denoting that these officers were regarded as above average ability. James McQuaker and Alexander Easton were marked 'weak', James Hosack was marked 'In' (indifferent), John McCulloch was 'doubtfull' and Peter Warwick 'does his best'. The Character Book of the Scottish Excise Board contains an alphabetical list of all officers. Many of the names have no annotation, but others were singled out as 'a good officer', 'a carefull officer' or, occasionally, even 'a carefull good officer'. Robert alone was annotated, 'The Poet, does pretty well'.

Robert had been in the middle of writing a letter to Mrs Dunlop when Findlater broke the news about the Board's enquiry, and as a result the letter to his patroness was not completed till 5 January 1793 (CL 203-5). Ironically, this was in response to Mrs Dunlop's offer to use her influence with Supervisor General Corbet's wife to get him promoted to Supervisor. After pointing out that he would not be eligible for promotion for several years, Robert continued:

> Besides, some envious, malicious devil has raised a little demur on my political principles, & I wish to let that matter settle before I offer myself too much in the eye of my Superiors.

Before he despatched this letter, however, Robert received a courteous and kindly letter from Graham of Fintry on 5 January. This outlined the charges which had been made against him. Robert replied immediately (CL 436-8), rebutting the charges in more reasoned, measured language than his initial outburst. His refutation of the incident in the theatre has already been dealt with. More seriously, however, he was questioned about his association with a seditious publisher named Johnston in Edinburgh. Robert admitted that he had subscribed to the *Gazetteer* but stoutly denied that he had ever written a line of prose for it. He conceded that he had sent poetry to that paper, and enclosed copies of 'The Rights of Woman' and extempore stanzas on the Commemorations of Thomson to show that they were entirely innocent and apolitical. And he added:

> As to France, I was her enthusiastic votary in the beginning of the business. When she came to shew her old avidity for conquest, in annexing Savoy, &c., to her dominions, & invading the rights of Holland, I altered my sentiments.

Robert even had the temerity to suggest that, assuming his explanation put all to rights again, he might stand in as Supervisor for Mr McFarlane of the Galloway District 'who is & has been for some time very ill'. Robert followed this up two days later with a separate letter (CL 438) stating that Collector Mitchell had that very day formally applied to the Board for someone to officiate in the Galloway District till McFarlane recovered.

The response of Graham or the Board to this is not known, but Robert did not get the job. It is clear that, despite his hysterical fear of instant dismissal when first told of the enquiry, he was unaware of the gravity of the matter and seemed to think that a letter to Graham would immediately blow the trouble away, otherwise his hint of taking over from McFarlane would never have been made. Perhaps he was lulled into a sense of false security by Mitchell who may have told him that he had nothing to worry about as *he* was satisfied with Robert's conduct.

It is also obvious that rumours flew round Edinburgh at this time. On 10 February 1793 Robert received a letter from William Nicol addressing him as 'Dear Christless Bobbie'. Nicol took his old friend gently to task for his reported indiscretions.

> What concerns it thee whether the lousy Dumfriesian fiddlers play 'Ça ira' or 'God save the King'? Suppose you *had* an aversion to the King, you could not, as a gentleman, wish God to use him worse than He has done. The infliction of idiocy is no sign of Friendship or Love; and I am sure damnation is a matter far beyond our wishes or ideas.

He went on to remind Robert of the Vicar of Bray who trimmed his political and religious sails so finely that he managed to survive through eight reigns in perfect security. Robert replied to this letter ten days later (CL 349–50) with a facetious screed of mock contrition:

> How infinitely is thy puddle-headed, rattle-headed, wrong-headed, round-headed slave indebted to thy super-eminent goodness, that from the luminous path of thy own right-lined rectitude thou lookest benignly down on an erring wretch, of whom the zig-zag wanderings defy all the powers of calculation, from the simple computation of units up to the hidden mysteries of fluxions!

On the same day, however, he also wrote to Alexander Cunningham (CL 467–8) giving pungent expression to the sentiments on politics which had been to some extent the outcome of his own experience. This took the form of a political catechism:

> Quere, What is Politics?
> Answer, Politics is a science wherewith, by men of nefarious cunning, & hypocritical pretence, we govern civil Polities for the emolument of ourselves & our adherents. –
> Quere, What is a Minister?
> Answer, A Minister is an unprincipled fellow, who by the influence of hereditary, or acquired wealth; by superiour abilities; or by a lucky conjuncture of circumstances, obtains a principal place in the administration of the affairs of government. –
> Q. What is a Patriot?
> A. An individual exactly of the same description as a Minister, only, out of place.

The Excise records are silent on how the matter of the poet's alleged disaffection was eventually resolved, but we can glean the facts from a letter which Robert wrote to John Francis Erskine, later twenty-seventh Earl of Mar, on 13 April 1793 (CL 689–91). He was the grandson of the last Earl of Mar, attainted for his part in the Jacobite rebellion of 1715, and it was not until 1824 that Erskine had his lands and titles restored to him. The scion of an ancient Jacobite family, Erskine, like his namesakes Henry and Thomas, was a liberal in politics and an advocate of parliamentary reform. He and Burns never met, but when he heard the rumour that the poet had been dismissed from the Excise he wrote to Robert Riddell offering to head a subscription on Burns's behalf. Burns was very touched by this and wrote to thank his new-found patron. The details of Erskine's generous act were set out in the headnote to the copy of this letter in the Glenriddell MS. By the time Robert made this copy for Riddell the matter had long since blown over, so he could afford to adopt a fairly jocular attitude towards the whole business:

> In the year 1792/93, when Royalist & Jacobin had set all Britain by the ears, because I unguardedly, rather under the temptation of being witty than disaffected, had declared my sentiments in favor of Parliamentary Reform, in the manner of that time, I was accused to the Board of Excise of being a Republican; and was very near turned adrift on that account.

By the time he wrote to Erskine Robert's customary 'manly independence' as he liked to call it, was beginning to reassert itself. Now that the crisis had passed, he was smarting under the recollection of his panic, and the grovelling way in which he had immediately responded to the threat. Referring to the threat of dismissal, he wrote:

> Had I had any other resource, probably I might have saved them the trouble of a dismissal, but the little money I gained by my Publication, is almost every guinea embarked, to save from ruin an only brother; who, though one of the worthiest, is by no means one of the most fortunate of men.

Robert conveyed to Erskine the gist of his defence against the charges, namely that, whatever its imperfections, the British constitution was better than any 'untried, visionary theory'. As a government employee he had forborne taking any active part 'either personally, or as an author', in the present Reform debate, but that 'where I must declare my sentiments, I would say that there existed a system of corruption between the Executive Power & the Representative part of the Legislature, which boded no good to our glorious Constitution'.

> Some such Sentiments as these I stated in a letter to my generous Patron, Mr Graham, which he laid before the Board at large, where it seems my last remark gave great offence; & one of our Supervisors general, a Mr Corbet, was instructed to enquire, on the spot, into my conduct, & to

document me – 'that *my* business was to *act*, not to think; & that whatever might be Men or Measures, it was my business to be silent & obedient' – Mr Corbet was likewise my steady friend; so, between Mr Graham & him, I have been partly forgiven; only, I understand that all hopes of my getting officially forward are blasted.

There is no actual record of the Supervisor General's visit to Dumfries, though it appears to have taken place in the second week of January. Robert was suitably cowed by his interview with Corbet. What passed between them was not tantamount to an 'admonishment' in Excise parlance, but there is no doubt that Robert was given a verbal caution to behave in future. On 26 January (CL 622–3) Robert replied to a letter from Thomson suggesting a collection of Jacobite songs, and his new-found caution was well to the fore:

> I do not doubt but you might make a very valuable Collection of Jacobite songs, but would it give no offence? In the mean time, do n't you think but some of them, particularly 'The Sow's tail to Geordie', as an *Air*, with other words, might be well worth its place in your Collection of lively Songs?

Thereafter Robert tried to keep a low profile. He got on with his Excise duties, redoubling his efforts to prove how efficient he was; and he had the consolation of his work on Thomson's forthcoming *Select Collection* which increasingly absorbed what little leisure time he possessed. Even before he moved to Dumfries, Robert had made the acquaintance of David Staig (1740–1824) who served as agent of the Bank of Scotland in the town for upwards of forty years. Staig took a leading part in civic affairs and between 1783 and 1817 held the office of provost no fewer than nine times, covering a total of twenty years in office. During his administration Dumfries was efficiently modernised, following a reform of civic revenues in 1788. The new academy, the bridge over the Nith, the shipping quay and the mail-coach service were all due to his initiative and drive. Staig was also an enthusiastic theatre-goer, and it was this that prompted letters from Robert in March 1790 and January 1793 (CL 551–2).

About the end of the latter month, however, Robert wrote to Staig on official business, making recommendations for a substantial increase in the burgh's revenue by applying the twopenny tax on ale brewed in the Bridgend (Maxwelltown), Annan and even across the border, which was consumed in the town. It was no part of Robert's official duties to record Ale Certificates, showing that municipal tax had been paid on such beer, but he could not help noting that while the Dumfries brewers paid this tax their competitors were getting off scot-free. The Collector (John Mitchell) was entitled to a small percentage of the tax levied on imported beer, but as it was no great object to him he never bothered with it. Robert suggested, therefore, that Provost Staig should approach Supervisor Findlater:

He is an abler and keener man; &, what is all-important in the business, such is his official influence over, & power among, his Officers, that were he to signify that such was his wish, not a 'pennie' would be left uncollected.– It is by no means the case with the Collector.– The Officers are not so immediately among his hands, & they would not pay the same attention to his mandates . . . These crude hints, Sir, are entirely for your private use.– I have by no means any wish to take a sixpence from Mr Mitchel's income: nor do I wish to serve Mr Findlater: I wish to shew any attempt I can, to do any thing that might declare with what sincerity I have the honor to be your obliged humble servant.

A postscript added that 'a variety of other methods might be pointed out, & will easily occur to your reflection on the subject'.

About this time Robert composed the song 'Young Jessie' (CW 486) which he sent to Thomson in April. It was intended as a compliment to Staig's daughter (1775-1801) who subsequently married Major William Miller of Dalswinton, eldest son of Robert's erstwhile landlord. By now Robert Junior was six years of age and showing great promise. He had his father's alert, lively mind, combined with a certain docility and gravity, and Burns had high hopes that the boy might go far, if he were given the right education. At this time Robert remembered that Dumfries had made him an honorary burgess in June 1787 so he decided to apply for the privileges that went with that rank. A much lower scale of school fees applied to the sons of burgesses than to those of non-burgesses, and Robert, feeling the pinch from the reduction in imports arising from the war, took the bull by the horns. In March he wrote formally to 'the Honble the Lord Provost, Bailies, & Town Council' of Dumfries (CL 553-4). After praising their 'literary taste and liberal spirit' in improving the school, he said that he wished to give his children a good education, but the high-school fees payable by a 'stranger' would bear hard on him:

> Some years ago your good Town did me the honor of making me an Honorary Burgess.– Will your Honors allow me to request that this mark of distinction may extend so far, as to put me on the footing of a real Freeman of the Town, in the Schools?

He reminded them that, by bringing the twopennies on foreign ale within their limits, he had already yielded a revenue, in a matter of a few weeks, amounting to nearly £10, and pointed out that he was the only Exciseman – 'except Mr Mitchell, whom *you pay* for his trouble' – who had taken an interest in this matter. The Town Council considered the matter and promptly granted this concession.

Robert, who already had free entry to the theatre, was the same month admitted a member of the Dumfries Library free of the customary half-guinea entry fee and quarterly payments. This library, operating on a subscription basis, had been founded in September 1792. Although not a subscriber, Robert presented a copy of the first Edinburgh Edition of his poems only a few days after the library was founded. A minute of the library committee of 3 March 1793 stated that by a great majority, resolved to offer him a share of the library free from the usual admission money out of respect and esteem for his merits as a literary man; and they directed the secretary to make this known to Mr Burns as soon as possible, that the application which they understood he was about to make in the ordinary way might be anticipated.[33]

Robert later presented four books to the library at the end of September. These were Smollett's *Humphrey Clinker*, Mackenzie's *Julia de Roubigné*, Knox's *History of the Reformation* and De Lolme's *British Constitution*. The last named was inscribed by the poet on the back of the frontispiece: 'Mr Burns presents this book to the Library, & begs they will take it as a Creed of British Liberty – untill they find a better. R.B.' Nowadays no one would take these sentiments amiss, but in the autumn of 1793, when a paranoid government found sedition in any voice of dissent, such an expression was open to misinterpretation and could easily have landed the poet in the gravest trouble, leading to his dismissal from the Excise. Robert thought better of his rashness and, hurrying very early the following morning to the home of William Thomson with whom the books had been deposited, he asked for the De Lolme, saying that he was afraid that he had written something in it 'which might bring him into trouble'.[34] On the volume being produced, he glued the back of the frontispiece to the adjoining fly-leaf in order to seal up his seditious secret. This volume, like many others in the original library, passed into the hands of the Dumfries and Maxwelltown Mechanics' Institution and is now on display in the Robert Burns Centre. The offending page has been unstuck and is on prominent display, the glue marks round the edge of the page being a mute reminder that the freedom of speech which we take for granted did not always exist.

At Friars' Carse in 1790 Robert had been introduced to members of the Craik family whose estate at Arbigland has already been mentioned. Helen Craik (1750–1825) was the recipient of two letters from the poet. The first, from Ellisland on 9 August 1790 (CL 561), mentioned an imminent second visit to Arbigland, implying that Robert had visited her home some time previously. A second letter, written from Dumfries on 12 January 1792 (CL 562), stated: 'Now that I have, by my removal to town, got time & opportunity, I shall often intrude on you'.

It was on just such a visit to Arbigland that Robert met Anna Dorothea Benson (1773–1856), the daughter of a York wine-merchant and, in later life, a close confidante of Jane Welsh and Thomas Carlyle. Afterwards Miss Benson recounted her impression of the poet:

> I dined with Burns at Arbigland; he was witty, drank as others drank, and was long in coming to the tea-table. It was then the fashion for young ladies to be busy about something – I was working a flower. The poet sat down beside me, talked of the beauty of what I was imitating, and put his hand so near the work that I said: 'Well, take it and do a bit yourself'. 'O ho!' said he, 'you think my hand is unsteady with wine. I cannot work a flower, madam; but' – he pulled the thread out of the needle and re-threaded it in a moment, 'Can a tipsy man do that?' He talked to me of

his children, more particularly of his eldest son, and called him a promising boy. 'And yet, madam', he said, with a sarcastic glance of his eye, 'I hope he will turn out a glorious blockhead, and so make his fortune'.[35]

When Cunningham's book was published Miss Benson wrote to him on 25 February 1834 to correct the impression that Burns 'drank as [other men] drank'. Burns, she averred, was incapable of rudeness or vulgarity . . . well bred and gentlemanly in all the courtesies of life. Even during the meetings of the Caledonian Hunt, she 'never saw Burns once intoxicated, though the worthy Member for Dumfries and the good Laird of Arbigland and twenty more . . . were brought home in a state of glorious insensibility'.[36]

That Robert enjoyed a convivial dram there can be no doubt. In addition to social occasions in the houses of the gentry where excessive drinking was the norm, and the ocasional all-night carouse at home such as the Revd. William McMorine witnessed, there were evenings at the Globe with like-minded friends which sometimes went on till the early hours. One such late-night session took place on Friday 17 May 1792 – perhaps a celebration of Robert's transfer to the more lucrative Dumfries Port Division earlier that month – and terminated early the following morning when Burns and his Excise colleague, John Lewars, staggered off down to the Whitesands to clear their heads with a brisk walk by the Nith. They walked along the footpath known as Waterside (now Waterloo Street) where the foot of the gardens of the town houses of the well-to-do in Irish Street terminated in a long wall, in which were set the doors used by tradesmen and domestic servants to gain access to the backs of the houses.

Later, Jean Murdoch, servant to Wellwood Maxwell of Barncleugh, was to depone that, about five o'clock that morning, she and Janet Anderson were washing clothes in Mr Maxwell's wash-house at the foot of the garden when John Lewars and 'another person whom the declarant does not know' were walking past on the road. Lewars saw the girls on the garden steps and hammered noisily on the door which was locked. When the girls refused to unlock the door, Lewars put his shoulder to the door, broke the lock and entered the wash-house. When the girls asked him to leave, Lewars became abusive, 'cursed & swore and used such obscene indecent language, as she or no modest woman can mention'.[37] Jean raised a porringer full of boiling water to ward him off, whereupon Lewars threw a half-gallon pig (crockery vessel) of soap-suds at the girl. It struck her before shattering on the floor, but before she could retaliate Lewars attacked her, laying his hands on her so roughly that her neck, breast and left arm were bruised and scratched. When Jean cried to Janet to go and fetch their master, Lewars gripped her also and knocked her head against the wall, threatening to duck both of them in the copper cauldron of boiling water.

Burns – the other man – was standing out in the lane when this altercation began, but he rushed to the wash-house and asked the girls who their master was. When they told him he remonstrated with Lewars and managed to get him back into the lane, begging the girls to say nothing of what had happened. Jean Murdoch declared that it might be 'about three quarters of an hour from the forcing of the lock until the time that the other man got Lewars out of the Garden'. This was probably a subjective impression; the actual time-span of the disturbance may have been no more than a few minutes.

It is interesting to note that, so far from being a great celebrity, Burns was unknown to the servant-girls, though Jean knew John Lewars. As a result of his drunken and disorderly behaviour, occasioning actual bodily assault of one of the girls, Lewars was charged with 'crimes of a heinous nature'. Remarkably, Robert was kept out of the affair, although Lewars named him in his own statement to the Procurator Fiscal, though he could recall nothing on account of his inebriety. Fortunately for Lewars, the Procurator Fiscal – none other than David Newall (a friend of the poet) – with the consent of the magistrates, 'deserted this process pro loco et tempore' after a plea of mitigation was entered on 29 May, 'on account of several favourable circumstances to the def. which have come to his knowledge since raising this summons'. John's defending lawyer in the case was Francis Shortt, one of the town's diehard Tories. Which magistrates tried the case are not named, but as they included Fergusson of Craigdarroch, David Staig and Robert Riddell, the leniency shown in this unfortunate matter affecting Burns can be understood.[38] Robert Thornton, who discovered this bundle of documents, makes much of the case to bolster his view of drunkenness and dissipation in the Dumfries years, but Jean Murdoch's statement makes it quite clear that the defendant's unnamed companion had done his best to calm the situation and did not, himself, contribute to the fracas. That Robert was drunk is quite probable, but he was not so intoxicated that he lost all sense of propriety. While Thornton makes much of this case – 'What makes this binge unique is not its hilarious high jinks, but the extent of its documentation' – it is perhaps worth noting that this bundle is only one of many hundreds dealing with similar offences, none of which had the slightest connection with Burns or, for that matter Lewars, who thereafter led a respectable and blameless life and eventually attained the rank of Supervisor in the Excise.

CHAPTER 16

Dumfries: Mill Hole Brae, 1793–4

Contented wi little, and cantie wi mair,
Whene'er I foregather wi Sorrow and Care,
I gie them a skelp, as they're creepin alang,
Wi a cog o guid swats and an auld Scottish sang.

Contented wi Little (CW 531)

The birth of Elizabeth Riddell Burns and the arrival of Ann Park's daughter Betty late in 1792 made a more commodious house imperative, but it was not until the following May that the Burns family were able to move from the Vennel. Captain John Hamilton of Allershaw, Robert's landlord, came to the rescue by offering the poet one of his larger properties in the town, a substantial two-storey dwelling-house several hundred yards to the south-east. One fine day in late spring, therefore, Robert and Jean and their children followed the cart that bore their furniture up the Vennel, first right into Irish Street, past the Assembly Rooms into St Michael Street, then first left into the turning and twisting, up-hill and down-dale lane known then as the Mill Hole Brae, but later Millbrae Vennel or Mill Street and now more appropriately as Burns Street. The house at number 24 was to be the poet's last abode. Long after his death, his widow Jean was to reside here for thirty-eight years – longer, in fact, than Robert's entire life – until her own death in March 1834.

The move to a larger house became possible with Robert's transfer to the Dumfries Port Division, with no actual increase in salary but the prospects of £15–£20 more in perquisites from seizures. Unfortunately, however, the move came just as the war with France was beginning to bite. Previously in an average month there might be as many as ten bankruptcies in Scotland; by July 1793 this had quadrupled. Foreign imports were brought virtually to a halt and Robert's Excise emoluments suffered accordingly. What with the expenses of moving house and laying out cash on fittings, such as the new fire-grate which he purchased from Crombie for £1 8s, Robert soon got into arrears with his rent. Four letters from the poet to Hamilton of Allershaw are extant (CL 703–4) and deal almost exclusively with this matter. The first letter, dated 24 March 1794, gives a statement of Robert's payment of £5 in cash, together with allowances totalling £2 3s in respect of a 'quey calf' and some furniture.

One can imagine the anguish of Burns, a man who fiercely prided himself on his independence, when he wrote to Hamilton about July 1794, 'I assure you, Sir, it is with infinite pain that I have transgressed on your goodness', going on to allude to an unfortunate business with Alexander Crombie whose bill for £20 he had so rashly discounted: 'I had a sum to pay which my very limited income & large family could ill afford'. This matter, however, had arisen in April 1791 and got Robert into trouble with the banker, James Gracie, at that time (CL 582); but in the end he had extricated himself from this embarrassing situation by using Crombie's bill in partial settlement of his debt to Thomas Boyd who, in turn, owed money to Crombie. It seems rather odd that Robert should be trotting this out as an excuse for his precarious financial position three years later. On 29 January 1795 he managed to pay off three guineas of his arrears to Hamilton and promised to settle all soon: 'I shall not mention your goodness to me: it is beyond my power to describe . . . the feelings of my wounded soul at not being able to pay you as I ought.' Hamilton hastily replied, asking if he had in any way offended the poet. Robert replied by return on 31 January and we may read between the lines the bitter memories of the humiliation which debt had brought upon his father:

> It is not possible, most worthy Sir, that you can do any thing to offend any body; my backwardness proceeds alone from the abashing consciousness of my obscure situation in the ranks of life.– Many an evening have I sighed to call in & spend it at your social fireside; but a shyness of appearing obtrusive amid the fashionable visitants occasionally there kept me at a distance.

The poet's eldest son, Robert Junior, furnished an interesting account of life in the Mill Street house, indicating that the self-contained detached house, whose rental was £8 a year, was of the kind then occupied by the better class of burgesses:

> My father and mother always had a maid-servant, and sat in their parlour. That apartment, together with two bedrooms, was well furnished and carpeted; and when good company assembled, which was often the case, the hospitable board which they surrounded was of a patrician mahogany. There was much rough comfort in the house, not to have been found in those of ordinary citizens; for, besides the spoils of smugglers, the poet received many presents of game and country produce from the rural gentlefolk, besides occasional barrels of oysters from Hill, Cunningham, and other friends in town; so that he possibly was as much envied by some of his neighbours, as he has since been pitied by the general body of his countrymen.

It would appear that Hamilton could have extracted a much higher rent if he had wished. According to Dr Burnside's manuscript report for the *Statistical Account*, a house of that size (three rooms and a kitchen) yielded an average annual rental of £10 or £12 at that time, and attracted a police tax of ninepence in the pound for paving and cleaning the streets. John Hamilton, however, felt amply recompensed to have such a distinguished tenant.

Robert had not long settled in his new house when he had a visit from an old friend, Archibald Lawrie of Newmilns. Lawrie put up at the King's Arms on 19 June and sent a message to the poet. Robert arrived shortly afterwards. Lawrie's diary furnished a graphic description of their meeting:

> He came into the room where I was supping with a number of strangers, and there he sat from 11 at night till 3 next morning. I left them about 12, and had a most confounded and extravagant Bill to pay next morning, which I grudged exceedingly, as I had very little of Burns's company; he was half drunk when he came, and completely drunk before he went away in the morning.
>
> Thursday, 20th. After breakfast called on Mr B., found him at home, took a plate of broth with him, and afterwards he took a walk with me thro the town of Dumfries, and along the banks of the Nith, which was extremely pleasant. After having walked some time with Mr B., I returned again with him to his house, where I stayed and dined and spent the day; after dinner we had some charming music from a Mr Fraser, master of a band of soldiers raised by and belonging to Lord Breadalbane; having drunk tea, we went to a wood upon the banks of the river Nith, when Mr Fraser took out his hautboy and played a few tunes most delightfully, which had a very pleasing effect in the wood. We then left this rural retirement, walked back to the town, where I parted with Mr B., and continued my walk with a Mr Lewis, a friend of Burns, who dined in company with me. The night coming on, I went with Mr Lewis and supped with him on cold mutton and eggs, at 12 o'clock left his house; went to the Inn, King's Arms, and ordered the chambermaid to show me to bed; having rested my mare one day more, which she had not the slightest occasion for, but the temptation of Burns company I could not withstand.[1]

Thomas Fraser was ages with Burns and a recent arrival in Dumfries. An accomplished oboist and composer, he was bandmaster of the Breadalbane Fencibles and soon made the poet's acquaintance. A few days after Lawrie's visit, Robert wrote to George Thomson (CL 630), 'You know Fraser, the Hautboy player in Edinburgh' and went on to say that he was now in Dumfries. Robert admired many of Fraser's compositions, particularly 'The Quaker's Wife', a slow arrangement of the traditional reel 'Liggeram Cosh', to which Robert set the song 'Blythe hae I been on yon hill' (CW 490). Another of Fraser's favourites was the ancient air 'Hey tutti taitie', which Robert subsequently confessed (CL 638) 'with Fraser's Hautboy, has often filled my eyes with tears'. In this letter, written about the end of August 1793, Robert went on to say that there was a tradition, which he had encountered in many parts of the country, that this had been Robert Bruce's march at the Battle of Bannockburn:

This thought, in my yesternight's evening walk, warmed me to a pitch of enthusiasm on the theme of Liberty & Independance, which I threw into a kind of Scots Ode, fitted to the Air, that one might suppose to be the gallant ROYAL SCOT'S address to his heroic followers on that eventful morning.

To this was subjoined the text of 'Scots wha hae' (CW 500). The circumstances in which Robert's great patriotic song, for long regarded as Scotland's national anthem, had been composed were elaborated in a postscript to the same letter:

I showed the air to Urbani, who was highly pleased with it, & begged me to make soft verses for it, but I had no idea of giving myself any trouble on the Subject, till the accidental recollection of that glorious struggle for Freedom, associated with the glowing ideas of some other struggles of the same nature, *not quite so ancient*, roused my rhyming Mania.

These details, however, were contradicted by John Syme. In the summer of 1793 Robert made the first of two tours through Galloway with his friend. Syme (1755–1831) had trained as a lawyer, became a Writer to the Signet, served as an ensign in the 72nd regiment and then retired to manage his father's country estate at Barncailzie in Kirkcudbrightshire; but Syme Senior was hard hit by the failure of the Ayr Bank and the estate had to be sold. John Syme obtained the sinecure of Distributor of Stamps for Dumfries and Galloway and moved to Dumfries shortly before the poet, in 1791. He had a modest villa at Ryedale on the west bank of the Nith and his Stamp Office on the ground floor of the Vennel tenement where the Burns family first resided. 'Stamp Office Johnie' soon became a firm friend of the poet, the bosom companion of his last years and a staunch friend of the family after Robert's death. Close proximity has deprived posterity of letters from Burns to Syme, apart from one written about May 1795 (CL 708–9) and an impromptu quatrain accompanying a dozen bottles of porter (CW 560), sent from the Jerusalem Tavern in May 1794.

Syme gave Dr Currie an account of their travels. Robert had given up the luxury of a horse when he was transferred to the Dumfries Port Division, but Syme procured him a grey Highland shelty for the journey. They set out on 27 July 1793 and dined that afternoon with the Glendenwyne (Glendinning) family at Parton and made an evening excursion to Airds, the one-time home of the minor poet John Lowe who was best remembered for 'Mary, weep no more for me'. They pressed on to Kenmure Castle that night and supped with John Gordon (1750–1840) and his wife. Gordon was the grandson of the sixth Viscount Kenmure who had taken part in the rebellion of 1715 and paid the supreme penalty as a consequence. John Gordon was restored to the title in 1824, more than a century after the event. Robert was drawn to the Gordons by virtue of shared Jacobite sentiment, and spent three happy days at Kenmure in their company. When Mrs Gordon's lap-dog Echo died she prevailed on Robert to compose a suitable epitaph. Robert rose dutifully to the occasion, though his reluctance is evident in the high-flown sentiment of the lines beginning 'In wood and wild, ye warbling throng' (CW 495).

On leaving Kenmure the travellers went to Gatehouse. It was a not untypical day at the end of July, with thunder and lightning, a leaden sky and a cold wind. 'The poet enjoyed the awful scene – he spoke not a word, but seemed rapt in meditation,' commented Syme as they rode along the moorland track through some of the most desolate and savage scenery in Galloway. Presently it began raining and kept up a torrential downpour for three hours. By the time they reached the Murray Arms they were thoroughly soaked and 'to revenge ourselves, Burns insisted on our getting utterly drunk'.

According to Syme, Robert's splendid new top-boots, which had cost him £1 2s, were completely ruined by being soaked and then dried in such a manner that it was impossible to get them on again. The implication is that the boots were soaked on the ride from Kenmure to Gatehouse, but a Mr Carson, who, with the parish minister John Gillespie, was one of the party at Kenmure Castle, has left a fuller account which sheds a different light on the incident:

> On the evening preceding their departure, the bard having expressed his intention of climbing to the top of 'the highest hill that rises o'er the source of Dee,' there to see the arbour of Lowe, the author of the celebrated song 'Mary's Dream,' Mr Gordon proposed that they should all sail down the loch in his barge *Glenkens*, to the Airds Hill below Lowe's seat. Seeing that this proposal was intended in compliment by the worthy host both to the bard and to Mr Gillespie, who had been the patron of Lowe, the gentlemen all concurred; and the weather proving propitious next morning, the vessel soon dropt down to the foot of Loch Ken with all the party on board. Meanwhile, Mr Gordon's groom led the travellers' horses round to the Boat-o'-Rhone, saddled and bridled, that each rider might mount on descending from the poet's seat; but the barge unfortunately grounded before reaching the proposed landing-place – an obstruction not anticipated by any of the party. Mr Gordon, with the assistance of an oar, vaulted from the prow of the little vessel to the beach, and was soon followed in like manner by Mr Syme and myself; thus leaving only the venerable pastor of Kells and the bard on board. The former, being too feeble to jump, as we had done, to land, expressed a desire to remain in the vessel till Mr Gordon and I returned; upon hearing which, the generous bard instantly slipt into the water, which was, however, so deep as to wet him to the knees. After a short entreaty, he succeeded in getting the clergyman on his shoulders; on observing which, Mr Syme raised his hands, laughed immoderately and exclaimed: 'Well, Burns, of all the men on earth, you are the last that I could have expected to see *priest-ridden*!' We laughed also, but Burns did not seem to enjoy the joke. He made no reply, but carried his load silently through the reeds to land.[2]

When Syme's account of the Galloway tour was published by Currie in 1800 the Glenkens people were surprised that it omitted the boating incident. Syme, however, better than most, would have been aware of Robert's ill humour at ruining a pair of boots that had cost him a week's wages, compounded with the ill-timed quip about being priest-ridden. Matters did not improve when, the following day at Gatehouse, Robert tore his shrunken boots in a rage while trying to get into them. This put him into a foul mood, compounded by the hangover from the previous night's hard drinking. Syme described the poet's temper:

> We were going to St Mary's Isle, the seat of the Earl of Selkirk, and the forlorn Burns was discomfited at the thought of his ruined boots. A sick stomach and a headache lent their aid, and the man of verse was quite *accablé*. I attempted to reason with him. Mercy on us, how he did fume and rage! Nothing could reinstate him in temper. I tried various expedients, and at last hit on one that succeeded. I showed him the house of Garlieston, across the Bay of Wigton. Against the Earl of Galloway, with whom he was offended, he expectorated his spleen and regained a most agreeable temper. He was in a most epigrammatic humour indeed!

Just why Robert should have taken such a dislike to John Stewart, seventh Earl of Galloway, is not known for certain, although the Earl's high Tory politics probably accounted for the poet's animosity. The bitter epigram (CW 494) which Robert produced on the spur of the moment was:

> What dost thou in that mansion fair?
> Flit, Galloway, and find
> Some narrow, dirty, dungeon cave,
> The picture of thy mind!

The Earl, when informed of Burns's ill-natured epigram against him, replied with dignity that 'it would not become him, when his good old master the King despised and disregarded the paltry attacks of a Peter Pindar, to feel himself hurt by those of a licentious, rhyming ploughman'. When the Earl's comment was conveyed to him, Robert riposted:

> Spare me thy vengeance, Galloway!
> In quiet let me live:
> I ask no kindness at thy hand,
> For thou hast none to give.

Apart from politics there was certainly no reason for the poet's hostility, and Robert's jaundiced view of the earl was oddly at variance with all published references to a man who was noted for his piety and his generosity to his servants.

Syme's account continued:

> Well, I am to bring you to Kirkcudbright along with our poet without boots. I carried the torn ruins across my saddle in spite of his fulminations and in contempt of appearances; and what is more, Lord Selkirk carried them in his coach to Dumfries. He insisted they were worth mending.

We reached Kirkcudbright about one o'clock. I had promised that we should dine with one of the first men in our country, John Dalzell. But Burns was in a wild and obstreperous humour, and swore he would not dine where he should be under the smallest restraint. We prevailed, therefore, on Mr Dalzell to dine with us in the Inn, and had a very agreeable party. In the evening we set out for St Mary's Isle. Robert had not absolutely regained the milkiness of good temper and it occurred once or twice to him, as he rode along, that St Mary's Isle was the seat of a Lord; yet that lord was not an aristocrat, at least in his sense of the word. We arrived about eight o'clock, as the family were at tea and coffee . . . we found all the ladies of the family (all beautiful) at home, and some strangers, and among others who but Urbani.

John Dalzell of Barncroch was a man who enjoyed convivial company and he and Burns were already well acquainted. According to Mrs Dalzell, the poet often called at their house, even for breakfast.[3] One must presume that Robert's waywardness on this occasion was due to his continuing ill humour over the wretched business of the ruined boots. Unlike the Earl of Galloway, Dunbar Douglas, fourth Earl of Selkirk (1722–99) was a radical with a long record of resisting Tory manipulation of the Scottish representative peers in the House of Lords. His second son was that liberal-minded Lord Daer whom Burns had met at the home of Dugald Stewart in October 1786, thus forcing the poet to revise his prejudices against the nobility.

The Heid Inn in Kirkcudbright's High Street, now the Selkirk Arms, where Burns and Syme lodged on this tour, claims that it was here that 'Burns wrote the Selkirk Grace in 1794', as a plaque on the exterior wall affirms. In fact, the so-called Selkirk Grace was not actually written down by Burns, and it was given extempore at St Mary's Isle in 1793.[4] Syme's account of the evening spent at St Mary's Isle makes no mention of Burns saying grace, and this omission gave rise to the view that the story was suspect. It was not referred to in any of the nineteenth-century biographies, from Currie to Chambers, with one notable exception. In its vernacular form, however, the grace made its début in Cunningham (1834)[5] with the headnote:

On a visit to St Mary's Isle, Burns was requested by the noble owner to say grace to dinner; he obeyed in these lines, now known in Galloway by the name of 'The Selkirk Grace'.

Interestingly, it was omitted from later editions of Cunningham's compilation, and it is intriguing to speculate on the reasons for this. For half a century the grace was in limbo until 1896 when Scott Douglas included it in the revised edition of his work, adding a cautious headnote:

Allan Cunningham records that this very characteristic Grace before Meat was uttered by Burns at the table of the Earl of Selkirk while on his tour of Galloway with Syme in 1793. If so, it is strange that Syme who,

in his account of that journey, gives sundry epigrams produced by Burns
in the course of it, has omitted this.

The edition of Chambers revised by William Wallace and published later
the same year, likewise restored the grace to the canon but without
comment.[6] Since 1896 the Selkirk Grace has appeared in about thirty per
cent of the new editions of Burns, despite the fact that it was frequently
pointed out that the vernacular version existed long before 1793 and was
known either as the Galloway Grace or the Covenanters' Grace. James
Grierson of Dalgoner, however, though not present at St Mary's Isle on
the historic occasion, acquired a transcript of what Burns actually said. He
had been asked for a grace towards the end of the meal, when the other
guests had reached the tea, coffee and dessert. What Burns actually recited
was an *English* version of the traditional grace, only the final line 'Sae the
Lord be thankit' retaining the vernacular. The Grierson transcript dated
from about 1805 and is therefore much older than the oldest publication of
the vernacular version given by Cunningham.[7] In the English form, it was
added to the canon by Kinsley in 1968 and has appeared in standard editions of Burns since then (CW 408).

Instead, Syme described the very agreeable atmosphere at Lord Selkirk's
country home, where the Italian singer and composer Pietro Urbani was a
house-guest. Burns was asked to recite 'Lord Gregory' (CW 482) which he
did so effectively that a dead silence ensued.

> 'Twas such a silence as a mind of feeling must necessarily preserve when
> it is touched, as I think sometimes and will happen, with that sacred
> enthusiasm which banishes every other thought than the contemplation
> and indulgence of the sympathy produced. We enjoyed a very happy
> evening – we had really a treat of mental and sensual delights – the latter
> consisting in abundance and variety of delicious fruits etc. – the former
> you may conceive from our society – a company of 15 or 16 very agreeable
> young people.

That Burns and Syme arrived at the earl's home just as dinner was concluding, seems, on the face of it, to rule out St Mary's as the venue of the
grace. On the other hand, according to the upper-class custom of the
period, the meal did not end with the serving of coffee, but was followed
by dessert. If, as we suppose, Burns and Syme were invited to draw up
their chairs to the table and partake of the 'variety of delicious fruits etc.',
it is not impossible that the poet would be asked to say a grace. He was
apparently as famous for his poetic graces as for his epigrams – both being
uttered extempore. There is certainly a down-to-earth informality about
the Selkirk Grace which would have been in keeping with this.

Syme concluded his account of the evening at St Mary's Isle:

> We enjoyed a most happy evening at Lord Selkirk's. We had in every
> sense of the word a feast, in which our minds and our senses were equally
> gratified. The poet was delighted with his company, and acquitted

himself to admiration. The lion that had raged so violently in the morning was now as mild and gentle as a lamb. Next day we returned to Dumfries and so ends our peregrination.

I told you that in the midst of the storm on the wilds of Kenmure, Burns was rapt in meditation. What do you think he was about? He was charging the English army, along with Bruce, at Bannockburn. He was engaged in the same manner on our ride from St Mary's Isle, and I did not disturb him. Next day he produced me the following address of Bruce to his troops, and gave me a copy for Dalzell:

> Scots, wha hae wi' Wallace bled, &c.

If Syme is to be believed, this stirring patriotic song was composed on 1 August 1793, *before* Burns visited St Mary's Isle. Yet Robert's own account, to Thomson, suggests that it was at Urbani's instigation that he composed the 'soft verses'. The probability is that the idea of 'Scots wha hae' occurred to him during the ride from Kenmure, and it was very much in his mind when he discussed the tune with Urbani. No doubt the song was substantially drafted on that day or the following morning but revised and polished in the course of the ensuing month, before the finished article was sent to Thomson. Robert, it will be remembered, had visited the field of Bannockburn on 26 August 1787 during his Stirlingshire tour and had been visibly affected by the sight of the borestone where Bruce had planted his standard. This emotive incident had been locked away in Robert's memory since then, but it was brought to mind in August 1793 by 'the glowing ideas of some other struggles, *not quite so ancient*'. In fact the increasingly repressive situation in which Robert found himself lay at the back of the mercurial moods and irritability which Syme noted during their tour. The government was, in his view, embarked on a course which would ruin the country, but he was powerless to raise his voice in protest. A hint of exasperation along these lines, but couched in very general terms, occurred in the opening passage of a letter to George Thomson (CL 629) on 25 June 1793:

> Have you ever, my dear Sir, felt your bosom ready to burst with indigna-tion, on reading of, or seeing, how these mighty villains who divide kingdom against kingdom, desolate provinces & lay Nations to waste out of wantonness of Ambition, or often from still more ignoble passions?

It was not so much the wretched matter of the ripped boots, nor the sight of Galloway House, that roused the poet's ire, but the feelings of frustration mingled with fear and foreboding at events then dramatically unfolding. Burns and Syme were at Gatehouse on the very day that Thomas Muir passed through the village on his way to stand trial for sedi-tion at Edinburgh. Thomas Muir of Huntershill was six years Robert's junior and from a very different background. His father was a wealthy Glasgow merchant and proprietor of the Huntershill estate in the parish of Cadder. Muir studied at Glasgow University and was called to the bar where he achieved a notable success as a defending counsel. In many respects the careers of Muir and Harry Erskine were very similar. Both were men of a radical liberal outlook. When the movement for parliamentary reform got under way, Muir joined the Friends of the People and threw himself into the campaign with all the enthusiastic zeal of youth. Towards the end of 1792, when the country was in a ferment between the diehard 'Loyal Natives' and the reformers, James Tytler was arrested for publishing a seditious handbill, in fact an advertisement for a meeting of the Friends of the People.

Tytler (1747–1805) was a friend of Burns who had led a chequered career. A son of the manse, he had studied medicine but failed as a doctor before turning to literature. He edited the second and third editions of the *Encyclopaedia Britannica* and wrote popular ballads, several of which were published by Johnson in the *Musical Museum*. Tytler deserves to be better known as the father of British aviation, having made the first balloon flights in the United Kingdom (1784), as a result of which he was ever afterwards known as 'Balloon' Tytler. Burns described this kenspeckle figure in his *Second Commonplace Book* as 'an obscure, tippling, but extraordinary body . . . a mortal who . . . drudges about Edinburgh as a common printer'. It was in this capacity that he fell foul of the law.

On 2 January 1793 Thomas Muir was on his way from Glasgow to Edinburgh to attend Tytler's trial when he himself was apprehended at Holytown by Williamson, the King's Messenger, in whose custody he completed the journey. Muir was charged with sedition, but released on bail to appear before the court the following month. He immediately set off for London and thence to Paris with the intention of interceding on behalf of King Louis XVI who was executed on 21 January. War between Britain and France broke out a few days later and Muir was trapped and unable to return to Edinburgh to stand trial. As a result he was formally declared an outlaw on 25 February. His enemies maintained that he had fled from justice knowing that he was guilty; but eventually Muir succeeded in boarding a ship ostensibly bound for America but which called at Ireland. After a short period in Dublin, where he became a member of the Society of United Irishmen and was warmly received by the reformers of that city, he sailed for Scotland in July with the avowed intention of standing trial. On landing at Stranraer he was promptly arrested by a Customs official and after a spell in the local gaol he was conducted by Williamson, via Dumfries, to Edinburgh where he was brought to trial on 30 August. The case was heard before the Lord Justice Clerk, Lord Braxfield, and four Lords Commissioners of Justiciary, Lords Henderland, Swinton, Dunsinnan and Abercromby. The fifteen members of the jury consisted of nine landed gentlemen (including Gilbert Innes of Stow, the richest man in Scotland). Those not of the gentry comprised three merchants, two bankers and the bookseller James Dickson.[8] In the indictment Muir was charged with creating disaffection by means of seditious speeches and harangues. He was found guilty and sentenced to transportation to Botany Bay for fourteen years.

During the trial much was made of the fact that Muir had possessed Paine's *Rights of Man* which he had lent to like-minded friends. Burns, in a panic, promptly passed his copies of Paine's books for safe-keeping to his friend, the Dumfries tinsmith George Haugh, who resided on the top floor of the Vennel tenement.

A month later, the Revd. Thomas Fyshe Palmer, Unitarian minister of Dundee, was similarly tried and sentenced to seven years' transportation. Early in 1794 William Skirving, Maurice Margarot and Joseph Gerrald were likewise brought before Lord Braxfield and drew sentences of four-teen years apiece. At Gerrald's trial on 13 and 14 March two of the fifteen jurors were William Creech and Peter Hill. During the trial preliminaries Gerrald actually challenged the impartiality of Bailie Creech on the grounds that the latter had made no secret of his intention of condemning any member of the British Convention, should he be called upon to pass upon their assize. Gerrald asserted, 'I wish to refer it to his own con-science, and his oath, whether he has not pre-judged the principles upon which I am to be tried'.[9] Lord Braxfield disallowed the objection on the grounds that Creech had only been speaking in a loose way. Richard Fowler, claiming this as a new discovery, averred that Burns must have been unaware that two of his friends had served as jurors in this sedition trial,[10] otherwise he would not have remained on cordial terms with them; but, in fact, Robert could hardly have been ignorant of this fact as the names and occupations of the jury were customarily published in all the leading newspapers of the period. It should be noted that Creech also served on the jury that convicted the notorious Deacon Brodie in October 1788. Interestingly, in the very newspapers which gave the names of the jurors in the Gerrald trial, publicity was given to the debate in which Robert Adam had drawn attention to the fact that Creech had published an account of the trial of Thomas Muir 'written by a person not at all in the interests of the Defence'.[11] Yet, less than two months after Gerrald's conviction, Robert wrote to Peter Hill (CL 322–3) with neither reproach nor reference to the case. There is no evidence, however, that Robert remained 'on cordial terms' with Creech. On the other hand, Ross Roy has proved that Burns, having taken nothing to do with the 1793 Edition, superintended the 1794 Edition published by Creech.[12] In fairness to Hill, there was nothing he could have done in the circumstances. In this trial none of the jurors were landed gentry unless we except the banker, Sir William Forbes of Pitsligo. The other fourteen comprised three book-sellers, two jewellers, a seal-engraver, a watch-case-maker, a smith, a manu-facturer, a brewer, a tailor and three general merchants, the very epitome of solid bourgeoisie.

In fact, the poet's correspondence from mid-1793 onwards was remark-ably apolitical. We examine Robert's letters in vain for the kind of political indiscretions which peppered his correspondence a year earlier. Apart from the oblique reference in the letter that accompanied 'Scots wha hae', the sole side-swipe at the contemporary situation was so mild that it has escaped most commentators altogether. In an undated note, assigned to

August 1793 because Stephen Clarke, who also signed it, was in Dumfries-shire at the time, Robert wrote to Thomson (CL 633):

> I hold the pen for our Friend Clarke, who at present is studying the Music
> of the Spheres at my elbow.– The Georgium Sidus he thinks is rather out
> of tune; so, untill he rectify that matter, he cannot stoop to terrestrial
> affairs.

The Georgium Sidus (literally the 'George star') was the name given by Sir William Herschell to the planet Uranus when he discovered it in 1781, out of compliment to King George III.

The spectacle of Thomas Muir in shackles being taken from Stranraer to Edinburgh served as a salutary warning, reinforcing the caution adminis-tered at the turn of the year. Thereafter Robert got on with his Excise duties and sought an outlet for his nervous energies in his 'hobby-horse', ballad-making. Between the end of June and the following November the vast majority of his letters were addressed to George Thomson. The second half of 1793 witnessed, in fact, a resurgence of that astonishing creativity, almost manic in its intensity. No fewer than eighteen letters were sent to Thomson in the space of four months, several of these running to many pages. By contrast, only one letter was written to his mother-confessor, Mrs Dunlop, and that, in August (CL 206), was mainly in a bid to secure her interest in furthering the career of John Drummond, a promising young bank-clerk; apart from a passing reference to 'these accursed times', Robert kept well clear of political matters. Twenty-two songs (including two versions of 'Scots wha hae') were sent to Thomson in this period, but the letters were mainly taken up with discussing moot points in songs which had previously been submitted. This extraordinary correspondence peaked early in September when Robert despatched a letter discussing one by one and often at great length the list of one hundred songs which Thomson had sent at the poet's request (CL 641–6). Two letters earlier (CL 639) Robert had apologised:

> I dare say, my dear Sir, that you will begin to think my correspondence
> is persecution.– No matter – I can't help it – a Ballad is my hobby-horse;
> which, though otherwise a simple sort of harmless, idiotical beast enough,
> has yet this blessed headstrong property, that when once it has fairly
> made off with a hapless wight, it gets so enamoured with the tinkle-gingle,
> tinkle-gingle of its own bells, that it is sure to run poor Pilgarlick, the
> bedlam Jockey, quite beyond any useful point or post in the common race
> of MAN.

By contrast, while Robert was so wholeheartedly committed to Thomson, his collaboration with James Johnson seemed to have tailed off. Between October 1792 (shortly after agreeing to work with Thomson) and early 1794, only one letter passed from Robert to Johnson. To be sure, this letter, written about October 1793 (CL 298) mentioned that he and Stephen Clarke had been busy sorting out material for the fifth volume of the *Museum*. When next he wrote, about February 1794, Robert sent Johnson a packet containing forty-one songs, which shows that he had not neglected his old friend. It has often struck critics and commentators as strange that Robert should have endeavoured to serve two masters simultaneously. His innate sense of loyalty to Johnson ensured that he continued to collaborate with him in his rather homespun project; but the attraction of working with an altogether superior collection, with music arranged by a composer of international standing, was too strong to resist. Although Robert appreciated Johnson's sterling worth he was not blind to the physical shortcomings of the *Museum*. Thomson's *Select Collection*, on the other hand, promised to be a much more prestigious project, and Robert was spurred on by professional pride. He was suitably gratified when the first set appeared in May 1793, and when the end-product was so superlative he could afford to put up with the editor's pettifogging niggles. It was his innate sense of achievement that kept Robert so wholeheartedly committed to Thomson, despite the latter's irksome meddling. Robert viewed his work on Scottish songs in an almost mystical light. He had no qualms about taking payment for his poems: 'The profits of the labours of a Man of genius are, I hope, at least as honorable as any other profits whatever,' he had written to the Revd. Patrick Carfrae in April 1789 (CL 527) when the latter was soliciting his interest in the poems of the late James Mylne. But the songs were an entirely different matter, hence that outburst about Sodomy of Soul in his first letter to Thomson, when he made it absolutely clear that his songs were *above* or *below* price. Robert regarded the songs of Scotland as a sacred trust and saw himself as some sort of high priest charged with their protection and preservation. It is in this light also that one must regard the pain and anguish which he suffered whenever anyone abused that trust, and this goes some way towards explaining the circumstances in which he appeared to surrender his copyright.

At some point Robert drew up a deed assigning the copyright of the songs composed for the *Select Collection* to George Thomson. On the face of it, this seems a very rash thing to do, but it was not quite as sweeping as it might be supposed. It certified that all the songs of Burns's composition, published and yet to be published by Thomson, were so published by the poet's authority and consent. 'In particular,' it went on, 'I never authorised any other person to publish *any* of those songs which were written by me for his work.' This was Robert's response to the pirates who published songsheets hawked the length and breadth of Scotland and, in default of a rigorous law on copyright, stole many an author's work.

Furthermore, Robert added a rider to the deed, reserving to himself the power of publishing these songs, 'at any future period, & in any manner I may think proper'. Thomson was empowered to prosecute 'in terms of law any person or persons pirating, publishing, or vending the said Songs, or any of them, without his consent; & that at his own expence & for his own behoof'. Previous scholars have tentatively assigned this document to August 1793, although it is undated. If this is so, it may seem rather strange that Thomson did not use this document when he published his second number, dated 1 January 1794. On the other hand, given the eventual use he made of it, he had good reasons for holding back till Burns was dead before utilising the deed of assignment to serve his own ends. In the second set of the first volume, probably as early as 1798 but certainly by 1799, Thomson published a warning:

> I do hereby certify, that all the Songs of my writing, published, and to be published, by Mr GEORGE THOMSON of Edinburgh, are so published by my Authority. And moreover, that I never empowered any other person to publish any of the Songs written by me for his Work. And I authorise him to prosecute any person or persons who shall publish or vend ANY of those Songs without his consent. In testimony whereof, &c. ROBERT BURNS.

This is an important point, for by tampering with the text of the original, Thomson tried to use this document to secure the copyright of Robert's songs in the *Select Collection*, specifically to block James Johnson, whose *Museum* also contained some of these songs. Robert, however, had made it clear to Thomson on 7 April 1793 (CL 626):

> Though I give Johnson one edition of my songs, that does not give away the copy-right; so you may take 'Thou lingering star, with lessening ray', to the tune of Hughie Graham, or other songs, of mine.

Robert had a rather casual attitude towards his property, but it is obvious that he did not intend that either Johnson or Thomson should have exclusive rights over his work. Indeed, he wrote to Thomson about 18 May 1796 (only two months before his death) enclosing 'a Certificate' which may, in fact have been the deed of assignment hitherto ascribed to 1793. It is clear that Thomson had been anxious to secure the copyright of material used in his *Select Collection* and had got a lawyer named McKnight to draw up a deed, which was then sent to Robert for his approval. In replying, however, Robert, altered the document which he said, 'though a little different from Mr McKnight's model, I suppose will amply answer the purpose; & I beg you will prosecute the miscreants without mercy' (CL 679). He then went on:

> When your Publication is finished, I intend publishing a Collection, on a cheap plan, of all the songs of which I wish to be called the Author.– I do not propose this so much in the way of emolument, as to do justice to my Muse, lest I should be blamed for trash I never saw, or be defrauded by other claimants of what is justly my own.

Significantly, Robert was just as vexed at the hucksters who tried to pass off their own worthless ballads as his, as he was at those who pirated his work. In November 1794 he wrote to Thomson (CL 664):

> I myself, have lately seen a couple of Ballads sung through the streets of Dumfries, with my name at the head of them as the Author, though it was the first time ever I had seen them.

It is one of the great tragedies of literature that Robert never lived to fulfil his intention. No fewer than 160 songs in the *Museum* and about 114 in the *Select Collection* were his work, but there were others where the extent of Robert's reworking is debatable. Such a definitive collection of his own songs would not only have cleared up these lingering doubts but would have established much earlier Burns's reputation as one of the foremost song-writers of any age. At the same time, it would have magnificently refuted that nineteenth-century *canard* of the poet's final years as a period of dissipation and decadence.

Thomson had originally secured the services of John Wolcott, a minor English poet who wrote under the pen name of Peter Pindar (mentioned previously in connection with his scurrilous squibs aimed at the king). Wolcott was to have done for English airs what Burns was doing for the Scottish; but by August 1793 he had grown weary of the project. Thomson now turned to Robert for help. The latter had previously made it clear that he would have nothing to do with English words, saying the previous April, 'I have not the command of the language that I have of my native tongue. In fact, I think my ideas are more barren in English than in Scottish'. But in response to Thomson's plea he wrote about 25 August (CL 636):

> You may readily trust, my dear Sir, that any exertion in my power, is heartily at your service.– But one thing I must hint to you, the very name of Peter Pindar is of great Service to your Publication; so, get a verse from him now & then, though I have no objection, as well as I can, to bear the burden of the business.

The letters of George Thomson to Burns reveal the fussiness of the former, constantly coming up with a battery of criticisms whenever Robert sent him a packet of new songs. Robert showed incredible tolerance and, indeed, good humour in dealing with Thomson's niggles and wrong-headedness. In the long letter commenting on Thomson's list Robert disagreed vehemently with Thomson over the way in which 'Dainty Davie' should be sung, adding pithily, 'nothing, since a highland wench in the Cowgate once bore me three bastards at a birth, has surprised me so much, as your opinion on this Subject' – an unfortunate metaphor, as some biographers have taken Robert literally![13] When Thomson, in September 1793, had the temerity to criticise 'Scots wha hae', adding that he had shown it to 'three friends of excellent taste' who agreed with him in objecting to the line 'Welcome to your gory bed', Robert was impelled to reply (CL 646-7):

> 'Who shall decide, when Doctors disagree?'[15] – My Ode pleases me so much that I cannot alter it.– Your proposed alterations would, in my

opinion, make it tame.– I am exceedingly obliged to you for putting me on reconsidering it; as I think I have much improved it . . . I have scrutinized it over & over; & to the world some way or other, it shall go as it is. – At the same time, it will not in the least hurt me, tho' you leave the song out altogether . . .

After all, there was always Johnson's *Museum* to fall back on, and James Johnson would never dream of opposing the poet's wishes. It soon became apparent that Burns and Thomson were poles apart in their tastes. Robert summed it up neatly (CL 649) when he commented, 'What pleases me, as simple & naive, disgusts you as ludicrous & low'. At times Thomson's genteel refinement must have seemed quite baffling. In fairness to Thomson, however, he was not untypical of his time and place. At a time when Scotland was being regarded increasingly as North Britain, the rising middle classes were hell-bent on anglicising their speech and manners. Whereas Robert regarded the vernacular traditions in poetry and song as matters to be preserved at all costs, many of his fellow countrymen were ashamed of their native language. One of the few things which could be said in Lord Braxfield's favour was that he was the last High Court judge to conduct his business in broad Scots.

Even more heinous than his distaste for the vernacular was Thomson's constant meddling with the airs to which Robert set his words. This was a matter with which he took infinite pains. Not only was he fully conversant with all the published songs of Scotland, but he had an intimate knowlege of their melodies, and when composing his own songs he would hum the tunes to ensure that the rhythm and cadence of the words fitted exactly. It must have been extremely irritating when Thomson, time and again, had his own views on what melodies should be used. This was bad enough in ordinary circumstances, but when Thomson's choice meant that the poet's words no longer fitted, Robert's patience must have been strained to the utmost.

This interference was at its worst in the matter of 'Scots wha Hae'. On 5 September 1793 Thomson wrote to Burns, replacing 'Hey Tutti Taitie' with 'Lewie Gordon'. Unfortunately, the last bars of this melody would have entailed inserting two more syllables in the final line of each verse. Not content with altering the melody, Thomson intruded his own alterations of the last lines. In four verses, where he could think of nothing fresh, he lamely proposed to repeat words or phrases to make up the deficiency. Thus some verses would have ended (Thomson's additions are italicised):

> *Chains* – chains and slavery
> Let him, *let him* turn and flee
> But *they shall*, they shall be free
> Let us, *let us* do – or die.

'Lewie Gordon', quite apart from the different length of the last line, was totally unsuited to Robert's heroic words. Incredibly, Thomson won this battle, against the poet's better judgment; surprisingly, Robert yielded and supplied a revised text, weaker in every stanza than the original. When the second volume appeared in 1799, this song was included in its emasculated form. But posterity has rectified this injustice and 'Hey Tutti Taitie' has long since been restored with Robert's original words. Even Thomson perceived the error of his ways and reverted to Robert's original version when the song was reprinted in the third volume.

In retrospect it seems strange that Robert should have given in to Thomson so readily, rather than trust his own instincts; but in his relations with Thomson (whom he never met) he seems always to have regarded him as a superior judge in these matters. By the same token he sometimes showed a tendency to belittle his own work. The most striking example of this occurred in January 1795 (CL 669) when he sent Thomson his great hymn to the brotherhood of man, 'A Man's a Man for a' that' (CW 535) with the understatement of all time:

> A great critic, Aikin on songs, says that love & wine are the exclusive themes for song-writing.– The following is on neither subject, & consequently is no Song; but will be allowed, I think, to be two or three pretty good *prose* thoughts, inverted into rhyme . . . I do not give you the foregoing song for your book, but merely by way of vive la bagatelle; for the piece is not really Poetry.

I am inclined to think that, by quoting John Aikin whose *Essays on Song-Writing* (1772) he had borrowed from Dugald Stewart,[15] Robert was writing with his tongue in his cheek. Aikin never made such a preposterous claim as Robert inferred, and it was patently ludicrous to suggest that 'A Man's a Man' was no song. More significantly, however, Robert, by emphasising the *prose* thoughts which he had inverted into rhyme, was giving a signal regarding the source of the sentiments expressed in the song. It has been suggested that Robert had been reading Paine's *Rights of Man* and had borrowed both ideas and phraseology from it; and there are, indeed, several strong verbal similarities between this song and certain passages in Paine.[16] That being so, Robert's putting-down of his own work is understandable, given the political climate of the period. In any case, this song ranks among the top ten of Burns's lyrics; technically flawless, brilliant in phrasing and burning with passionate intensity, it has assured the poet's international reputation beyond anything else he ever wrote. It encapsulates Robert's socio-political philosophy, matured in the last years of his life. The old rebellion against the status quo was undiminished; the contempt for 'yon birkie ca'd a lord' echoes the bitterness of a passage in his autobiographical letter to Dr Moore (CL 250). The opening stanzas speak of the 'honest poverty' of the common man whose solid innate worth rises above his material condition and surroundings:

> The rank is but the guinea's stamp,
> The man's the gowd for a' that.[17]

In the third and fourth stanzas the scope is widened to point to the artificiality of the stratified social system with its ranks and titles. Finally, the poem reaches its magnificent crescendo with the horizon broadened to encompass the whole of humankind. In these eight lines alone Robert earned his title as the Bard of all Humanity; it is this stirring verse which, more than anything else, has endeared him to the whole world. Whether 'Scots wha hae' should be regarded as Scotland's national anthem may be debatable; but 'A Man's a Man' is unassailable as a universal anthem. Of the 263 words that compose this song, 240 are monosyllables. If anyone ever doubted that the simplest words had the greatest impact, this lyric should dispel these doubts. Its power is enhanced by its very simplicity. It has been translated into over forty languages and, miraculously, retains its sense, spirit and cadence in them all. In 1919 Karl Liebknecht, the Spartakist leader, died before a firing squad with these words (in the translation of Ferdinand Freiligrath) on his lips:

> For a' that, an a' that,
>   It's comin yet for a' that,
> That man to man, the world o'er
>   Shall brithers be for a' that.

The relationship of Burns and Thomson has never enjoyed the prominence which it richly deserves. Indeed, it has been the custom for many biographers to regret that Robert wasted so much of his time in his last years in song-writing, totally missing the point that this was arguably his greatest and most enduring contribution to Scottish literature. For almost four years Robert devoted a great deal of his time and creative energy to work on a project which, to a large extent, he never lived to see fulfilled. Through the medium of the lengthy correspondence we can see Robert giving Thomson his immediate and undivided attention; going to inordinate lengths to explain or defend his views; bending over backwards to accommodate Thomson, even to the extent of working on English and Irish airs which went far beyond his original undertaking; always meticulous and painstaking, a true master of his lyrical craft. Even when he was burdened with the manifold additional duties of acting Supervisor of the Excise, and cut off by snowdrifts at Ecclefechan in February 1795, his commitment to Thomson was paramount (CL 671). Even when he was racked by pain and fever in April 1796 he gave Thomson's business priority (CL 677–8). Only nine days before his death (CL 679–80), when he had been forced by fear of bankruptcy to ask Thomson for £5, he promised 'to furnish you with five pounds' worth of the neatest song genius you have seen' and that very morning composed 'Fairest maid on Devon's banks' (CW 568) to go with the air 'Rothiemurchie' which Thomson wished to use:

> The measure is so difficult that it is impossible to infuse much genius into the lines – they are on the other side.– Forgive, forgive me!

No poet ever served his editor so well; it is a matter for supreme regret that Robert's unflagging devotion to the project was not repaid with greater integrity and generosity of spirit.

After Robert's death, George Thomson made available to Dr Currie the fifty-seven letters from the poet. It was bad enough that Currie interfered with the text from time to time, with the well-meaning if misplaced intention of improving style or grammar, but this was as nothing compared with the emendations contributed by George Thomson. None of the biographers or editors of Burns prior to 1929 mentioned the fact that many passages in the Thomson letters had been cancelled, and the matter was only raised by DeLancey Ferguson when compiling his edition of the poet's correspondence.[18] Of the fifty-five letters in the Morgan Library, New York, twelve contained cancelled passages, ranging from a single word to several lines, and totalling a little more than three hundred words. Ferguson carefully distinguished between Robert's own vigorous deletions, invariably a single stroke of the pen through the deleted word, Currie's tampering (bracketing the words or phrases he wished to omit from the printed text) and those other passages which were heavily blotted out by spiral sweeps of a broad-nibbed pen. Fortunately, with the passage of time, the ink used by Thomson in his obliterations has faded more rapidly than the original writing, so that with the aid of a good magnifying glass DeLancey Ferguson was able to decipher most of Robert's text.

At first glance the substance of these cancelled passages seemed so trivial that Ferguson wondered why Thomson should have been at such pains, and even after investigation one or two remain bewildering. But, examining these cancellations in their proper context, it soon became apparent that Thomson had three distinct motives, all of them selfish.

The first was vanity. About half the cancelled passages are outspoken criticisms of Thomson's taste or judgment, or flat refusals to comply with Thomson's recommendations. Of course, Thomson let many other differences of opinion stand, but these were mainly concerning matters where either might have been right. When it came to a confrontation with the poet, where the latter accused him of 'whim & caprice of taste', that could not be allowed to remain. In one letter Thomson deleted a reference to the bawdy song 'Oonagh's Waterfall', lest the reader suppose that he was familiar with such a 'blackguard ditty'.

The second motive was more serious. Having shown such a wilful and blatant disregard for the poet's wishes regarding the airs for which his words were written, Thomson attempted to conceal his wrong-doing. Apart from 'Scots wha hae' there are numerous instances in which Thomson flagrantly ignored the poet's wishes, and the fact that Robert died before the next volume of the *Select Collection* was published enabled the unscrupulous editor to get away with it. When they crossed swords in correspondence, as when Thomson refused to use Lady Elizabeth Heron's 'Banks of Cree' for the song 'Here is the glen' (CW 513) and insisted on using 'Jockey was the blithest lad' instead, Robert replied that if he were not prepared to accede to his wishes the song would have to be omitted.

Thomson blotted this out and subsequently published the song to the tune 'The Flowers of Edinburgh'.

The originals of Thomson's letters to Burns have not survived. Instead, Thomson made available to Currie his own carefully re-edited version of the scroll copies which Currie naïvely published as having 'little addition or variation' from the originals. This enabled Thomson to put himself in a better light and fit in with the mutilated letters of the poet. The most blatant example of this was a letter which Thomson claimed to have written to Burns on 5 February 1796:

> I have still about a dozen Scotch and Irish airs that I wish 'married to immortal verse.' We have several true-born Irishmen on the Scottish list; but they are naturalised, and reckoned our own good subjects. Indeed, we have none better.

In a letter from Robert written early in February 1796 (CL 676–7) there occurs this passage. The italicised portions represent Thomson's deletions:

> The *twenty-five* Irish airs, *in one number, is a business that you will find your account in more than anything.*– I shall chearfully undertake the task of finding verses for *them*.

This implies that what Thomson actually wrote was an acceptance of Robert's notion of a supplementary number, so long as he would provide words for these Irish airs. Later in the same letter (CL 677) Robert wrote:

> I have already, you know, equipt three Irish airs with words and the other day I strung up a kind of rhapsody to another Hibernian melody which I admire much.

And he gave the words of 'Hey for a lass wi a tocher' (CW 563) to the tune 'Balinamona and ora'. Then he continued:

> If this will do, you have now four of my Irish engagement. – Humours of glen, Captain Okean, Oonagh's Waterfall, & Ballinamona.

Sadly, Robert died a few months later with his Irish project unrealised and after the poet's death Thomson not only abandoned the scheme and incorporated some Irish airs among the Scottish (contrary to Robert's wishes), but even went so far as to set Robert's 'Come let me take thee to my breast' (CW 498), which had been composed for 'Cauld Kail in Aberdeen', to the Irish air 'Ally Croker'. This was particularly indefensible, as it was the poet's dying wish, expressed in his penultimate letter of 4 July 1796 (CL 679), that the song should be suppressed entirely. Thomson not only disregarded Robert's specific request, but he set the condemned words to a 'rank Irish' air, and then attempted clumsily to cover up his behaviour by mutilating the letter.

In the very long letter of September 1793 one passage was so badly mutilated (CL 645) that even today several words remain illegible. Significantly, this passage dealt with Urbani and Johnson, publishers of rival collections. Sufficient can be deciphered, however, to show that Robert was suggesting that Thomson should co-operate with them. In light of Thomson's attempt to secure the rights of Robert's songs for his exclusive use, this particular doctoring of a letter puts the editor in an unflattering light.

DeLancey Ferguson summed up this discreditable performance pungently:

> In one sense, these restored passages cannot damage Thomson's reputation, because as a man of taste in literature and in music he has little reputation to lose. The judgment of posterity has long since damned to eternal ridicule the meddling amateur who did not hesitate to suggest 'improvements', and to make unauthorized alterations, in the poetry of Burns and the music of Beethoven. But, with the light which his treatment of these letters sheds on his character and motives, it is no longer possible to regard him merely as a well-meaning but silly meddler. He stands convicted, not only of childish vanity, but of petty meanness and of a deliberate disregard of the dying wish of the poet who had devoted time and energy, without material recompense, in furthering his schemes.[19]

Although Thomson was absorbing most of Robert's spare time from the middle of 1793 onward, he did not entirely neglect his friends. Between October and the end of the year some seven letters passed from Robert to Maria Riddell (CL 604-6). Most of them were fairly brief, apologies for appointments which had to be broken on account of the exigencies of the Excise business, or promises to meet, either at Woodley Park or at the theatre where the Riddells had a box. They were, for the most part, undated, but Maria docketed them with serial numbers so that they were preserved in chronological order. One note, about November, is worth quoting:

> I meant to have called on you yesternight, but as I edged up to your Box-door, the first object which greeted my view was one of these lobster-coated PUPPIES, sitting, like another dragon, guarding the Hesperian fruit.

Since the outbreak of war Dumfries had become an important garrison town and two regiments, of fencible infantry and cavalry, were stationed there. Local trade depended increasingly on the soldiery, and the officers were a valuable addition to Dumfries society; but Robert instinctively resented their presence, partly on account of the idiotic war which they represented and partly because they belonged to a superior class. There does not appear to be any substance to Allan Cunningham's claim that Robert imputed his betrayal to the Excise Board to the officers of a regiment then stationed at Dumfries, some of whom, he believed, reported his rash language.[20]

Dorothea Benson was visiting Helen Craik at Arbigland in 1793 and attended a ball of the Caledonian Hunt. She was on the dance-floor with a young officer when the whisper of 'There's Burns!' ran through the assembly:

> I looked round and there he was – his bright dark eyes full upon me. I shall never forget that look; it was one that gave me no pleasure. He soon left the meeting. I saw him next day. He would have passed me; but I spoke. I took his arm and said: 'Come, you must see me home.' 'Gladly, madam,' said he; 'but I'll not go down the plainstones, lest I have to share your company with some of those *epauletted puppies* with whom the street is full.'[21]

The young army officers looked splendid in their scarlet tunics and gold braid, but 'their tinsel show' meant nothing to Robert; the empty-headed ensigns and lieutenants who swarmed round the county belles such as Maria Riddell earned only his contempt. Just as the Loyal Natives tried to provoke incidents at the theatre there were loud-mouths only too ready to goad known radicals such as Burns into indiscretions. And all too often he fell into their trap. Local tradition, backed by eye-witness accounts and even the poet's own correspondence, testified to some of Robert's fool-hardy toasts. On one occasion when a toast to William Pitt the Prime Minister was called for, Robert responded with a toast to 'a better man, George Washington'. On another occasion, when called upon to propose a toast, he called for 'the last verse, of the last chapter, of the Book of Kings'. At some social event in the King's Arms, one Saturday evening in January 1794, he was cornered into proposing a toast, and when he responded with the ambivalent words 'May our success in the present war be equal to the justice of our cause', he roused the ire of Captain James Dodd (or Dods) of Chapel in Dunscore parish. The following morning Robert wrote to Samuel Clark who had been present:

> I was, I know, drunk last night, but I am sober this morning.– From the expressions Captain Dods made use of to me, had I had nobody's welfare to care for but my own, we should certainly have come, according to the manners of the world, to the necessity of murdering one another about the business.– The words were such as generally, I believe, end in a brace of pistols; but I am still pleased to think that I did not ruin the peace and welfare of a wife & a family of children in a drunken squabble.– Farther, you know that the report of certain Political opinions being mine, has already once before brought me to the brink of destruction.– I dread lest last night's business may be misrepresented in the same way – YOU, I beg, will take care to prevent it.– I tax your wish for Mr Burns's welfare with the task of waiting as soon as possible, on every gentleman who was present, & state this to him, & as you please shew him this letter.– What after all was the obnoxious toast?– 'May our success in the present war be equal to the justice of our cause' – a toast that the most outrageous frenzy of loyalty cannot object to.– I request & beg that this morning you will wait on the parties present at the foolish dispute.– The least delay may be

of unlucky consequence to me.- I shall only add, that I am truly sorry that a man who stood so high in my estimation as Mr Dods, should use me in the manner in which I conceive he has done.

Clark, ten years younger than Robert, was, like his father before him, a lawyer in Dumfries, and later became Conjunct Commissary Clerk and Clerk of the Peace for the County. Apart from this plea of intercession with the irascible Dodd, only one other letter to Clark from the poet has survived. It, too, is undated, but is believed to belong to the same period (CL 702):

> I recollect something of a drunken promise yesternight to breakfast with you this morning.- I am very sorry that it is impossible.- I remember too, your very oblidgingly mentioning something of your intimacy with Mr Corbet our Supervisor-General.- Some of our folks about the Excise Office, Edinburgh, had & perhaps still have conceived a prejudice against me as being a drunken dissipated character.- I might be all this, you know, & yet be an honest fellow, but you know that I am an honest fellow and am nothing of this.

These letters are of particular interest as showing how concerned Robert was that there should be no recurrence of the bad reports which had gone to the Excise Board the previous winter. Although he made a conscious effort to be more circumspect, his ready tongue sometimes got the better of him, especially over a bowl of punch or a bottle of wine. It is also interesting to note that a reputation for drunkenness existed in Robert's own lifetime and that he strenuously rebutted it. How much worse, therefore, was the blackening of his character when he was no longer around to defend himself from such calumnies.

The letters to Maria Riddell, however, usually touched on more pleasant and congenial matters. The lady was something of a poetess herself and Robert flattered her by suggesting that one of her compositions would be ideally suited to the fine pathetic air 'My lodging on the cold ground' for inclusion in Thomson's *Select Collection*. Even more flattering was his alteration of his song 'The last time I came o'er the moor' (CW 486) to include a reference to Maria. He even flirted with her over this, saying 'I am afraid that my song will turn out a very cold performance, as I never can do any good with a love theme, except when I am really & devoutely in love' and returning to this theme at the end of the letter, 'It will be absolutely necessary for me to get in love, else, I shall never be able to make a line worth reading on the subject'. Later (CL 605) he altered the opening lines of the song again and submitted it to her for her approval, adding, 'Tell me, thou first & fairest of Critics, is it mended?'

Late in November he wrote to her, enclosing two very different poems. 'Passion's Cry' (CW 501-2) had been commenced in 1788 during the courtship of Clarinda. It was revised a year later but not completed till late 1793. It represented Robert's persistence in trying to write elegant

Augustan verses, but demonstrated just as well that this was not really his métier. By contrast, this poem was accompanied by 'another piece of Poetry of mine, that is also from the heart' – 'Scots wha hae' which he concluded with the comment, 'So much for my two favourite topics, Love & Liberty'.

The last Sunday of November coincided with the termination of an Excise accounting period '& may probably keep me employed with my pen until Noon.– Fine employment for a Poet's pen!' he wrote to Maria (CL 606) in a despondent 'Novemberish' mood,

> a damn'd melange of Fretfulness & melancholy; not enough of the one to rouse me to passion; nor of the other to repose me in torpor; my soul flouncing & fluttering round her tenement, like a wild Finch caught amid the horrors of winter & newly thrust into a cage.

An undated letter assigned to December 1793 reminded Maria that she had 'a spice of Caprice' in her composition, which she often disavowed even when her opinions were irrefragably proving it. Robert continued mysteriously:

> Could *any thing* estrange me from a Friend such as you?– No!– Tomorrow, I shall have the honor of waiting on you. Farewell, thou first of Friends, & most accomplished of Women; even with all thy little caprices!!!

On 15 December Robert began a long letter to Mrs Dunlop (CL 207–9), to whom he had not written for several months:

> As I am in a compleat Decemberish humour, gloomy, sullen, stupid, as even the deity of Dullness herself could wish, I will not drawl out a heavy letter with a number of heavier apologies for my late silence.– Only one I shall mention, because I know you will sympathise in it: these four months, a sweet little girl, my youngest child, has been so ill, that every day, a week or less threatened to terminate her existence.

Robert's little girl, Elizabeth Riddell, seems to have been a very sickly child, and although she eventually recovered from this unspecified illness, she was to die twenty months later. The toddler's illness was an unwelcome reminder of his own mortality and this set Robert on a morbid train of thought:

> I cannot describe to you, the anxious, sleepless hours these ties frequently give me. I see a train of helpless little folks; me, & my exertions, all their stay; nipt off, at the command of Fate; even in all the vigor of manhood as I am, such things happen every day.– Gracious God! what would become of my little flock!

The letter was continued on 20 December and finished on Christmas Day on a more cheerful note. Robert exchanged his copy of Moore's *Zeluco* with Mrs Dunlop's copy, so that she could have the benefit of his marginal comments:

> Tell me, how you like my marks & notes through the Book. I would not give a farthing for a book, unless I were at liberty to blot it with my criticisms.

This volume is now preserved in the Cooper Library at the University of South Carolina, and Robert's pencilled marginalia reveal how closely he had read and studied the good doctor's novel. In this letter Robert also mentioned the manuscript volume of letters which he was then compiling for Robert Riddell. 'If there were any possible conveyance, I would send you a perusal of it.'

Within days of this letter, however, there occurred an unfortunate incident which caused a rift between Robert and the Riddells. The exact circumstances – even the precise location – are not known and have been disputed. Indeed, the name by which this incident is now generally known, the Rape of the Sabine Women, actually dates back no further than 1915. In all the biographies up to the end of the nineteenth century it was assumed that the incident had taken place at Woodley Park. Chambers noted that Walter Riddell was notorious for the drunkenness and debauchery of his dinner-parties, one at least almost leading to a duel,[22] but Walter Riddell was, in fact, in the West Indies at this time.[23] An undated letter from Robert to 'Mrs R****' (CL 697–8), apologising for his unseemly behaviour, was long regarded as having been addressed to Maria. When it was published by Currie in 1800 Maria Riddell wrote to him:

> I am puzzled to guess how you came by it. I had somehow mislaid it, and it was certainly not among those I delivered for your perusal. Some other person must have pirated a copy. It is a pity you inserted it, at any rate; the stile is not fanciful enough for the intention of the composition, and it is not altogether a creditable one to Burns.[24]

Whatever actually took place that fateful night at the end of December 1793, it was not the first of Robert's drunken indiscretions. Ironically, his New Year resolution at the beginning of that year, expressed in a letter to Mrs Dunlop (CL 203), had been:

> ocasional hard drinking is the devil to me.– Against this I have again & again bent my resolution, & have greatly succeeded.– Taverns, I have totally abandoned: it is the private parties in the family way, among the hard drinking gentlemen of this country, that does me the mischief – but even this, I have more than half given over.

A month or two later, however, this resolution was broken, and he had occasion to write to John McMurdo (CL 494):

I believe last night my old enemy, the Devil, taking the advantage of my being in drink (he well knows he has no chance with me in my sober hours) tempted me to be a little turbulent.– You have too much humanity to heed the maniac ravings of a poor wretch whom the power of Hell, & the potency of Port, beset at the same time.

On that occasion a judicious apology, accompanied by a new song, 'Lang here awa' (CW 480), sufficed and the recalcitrant poet was soon forgiven. Other apologies the morning after are on record, not only to Samuel Clark (previously quoted) but also to William Robertson of Lude on 3 December the same year (CL 695). The lines beginning 'The friend whom, wild from Wisdom's way, / The fumes of wine infuriate send' (CW 568) were also intended as a remorseful apology which some early editors assumed were addressed to Maria Riddell but which are now thought to have been intended for Simon McKenzie. But Robert's behaviour in the company of the Riddells in December 1793 went far beyond the bounds of what could be forgiven so readily.

It is not known how Currie came by the letter addressed to Mrs Riddell, but he consulted Glenriddell's sister-in-law, Miss Rachel Kennedy (Elizabeth's elder sister), on the matter and she had replied on 20 January 1798:

I think that the letter ought not to appear as it refers to some circumstances of improper Conduct of Burns to Mrs Walter Riddell, which she represented to Mr Riddell and which he thought (in his brother's absence) he ought to resent and therefore declin'd taking any further notice of Burns'.[25]

This implies that Maria Riddell was the recipient of Robert's apology (CL 697–8), but if this were the case it makes a nonsense of Robert expressly stating that it was the husband of the offended lady who had made him drink too much. DeLancey Ferguson originally held the view that the incident had taken place at Friars' Carse, but later came to the conclusion that some other lady of Nithsdale fitted the description 'Mrs R'.[26] Rachel Kennedy implies that Robert Riddell was not present when the unfortunate incident took place; but, writing four years after an event at which she herself was not present, she may have been mistaken. The likeliest explanation is that the incident did take place at Friars' Carse and that Maria was, in fact, Robert's victim; but that the letter of apology was addressed to Elizabeth Riddell, the hostess of the dinner-party.

What actually happened on that fateful evening at Friars' Carse? The consensus of opinion is that, after the ladies retired to the drawing-room, the men sat at the dining-table pushing the port around, and none other than Robert Riddell himself had seen to it that Burns drank more than he would have chosen. Somehow the tipsy conversation brought up the subject of the Roman myth known as the rape of the Sabine women, and someone suggested that it would be rather a lark to re-enact the scene.

Local tradition (for it is no more than that) maintains that the instigators of the jape were army officers, determined to take the uppity poet down a peg. To each 'Roman' a Sabine maiden was allocated, it being decided that to the poet should be awarded the younger Mrs Riddell. Robert, long accustomed to the peasant frolics of kirn-nights and his prudence eliminated by a surfeit of fortified wine, apparently led the attack as the men charged towards the drawing-room. He carried out his part of the assault with enthusiasm and, throwing caution to the winds, grabbed hold of Maria – only to discover, to his horror, that he was alone. His fellow-conspirators held back at the doorway, leaving him to charge ahead on his own. Robert's discomfiture was compounded by the ladies' sense of outrage and the simulated shock of the gentlemen. Before the assembled company, the gauger-poet was humiliated. Two of the ladies, a Miss I. and a Mrs G., saw through the ploy and tried to intercede on Robert's behalf; but the gentry closed ranks and the offender was bundled out of the house in disgrace.

One can imagine the feelings of Robert, shame mingled with rage – at himself and the 'gentlemen' who had set him up – as he rode back to Dumfries that winter's night, and the agonising anguish that doubtless deprived him of sleep. In the cold grey light of the following morning he sat at his desk and penned one of the most difficult letters of his entire life (CL 697-8):

> Madam,
>   I daresay this is the first epistle you ever received from the nether world. I write you from the regions of Hell, amid the horrors of the damned. The time and manner of my leaving your earth I do not exactly know, as I took my departure in the heat of a fever of intoxication, contracted at your too hospitable mansion; but, on my arrival here, I was fairly tried, and sentenced to endure the purgatorial tortures of this infernal confine for the space of ninety-nine years, eleven months, and twenty-nine days, and all on account of the impropriety of my conduct yesternight under your roof. Here am I, laid on a bed of pityles furze, with my aching head reclined on a pillow of ever-piercing thorn, while an infernal tormentor, wrinkled and old, and cruel, his name I think is *Recollection*, with a whip of scorpions, forbids peace or rest to approach me, and keeps anguish eternally awake. Still, Madam, if I could in any measure be reinstated in the good opinion of the fair circle whom my conduct last night so much injured, I think it would be an alleviation to my torments. For this reason I trouble you with this letter.

The extravagant language of this apology has been interpreted as an attempt by Robert to inject some humour into the situation and thus defuse what was, in all honesty, a very grave breach of etiquette. Writing 'from the regions of Hell, amid the horrors of the damned' was definitely not the correct approach; and Elizabeth Riddell, who was not noted for her sense of humour, would have been offended rather than mollified. The grotesque posture of penitence and the serio-comic description of the torments he was enduring – no hangover was ever better described – suggest that the letter was written in a mood diametrically opposed to that it was supposed to represent. It was, in effect, the tongue-in-cheek apology of a man who was pretty confident of ready forgiveness. Not for the first time, however, Robert had grossly underestimated the degree of offence he had given and was blissfully deluding himself that he would get away with it. But Elizabeth Riddell was one of those rather prim and proper ladies, and her sense of propriety had been outraged. She probably also resented the next part of the letter which sought to put the matter in perspective, particularly by apportioning some of the blame to her husband and the other gentlemen present:

> To the men of the company I will make no apology.– Your husband, who insisted on my drinking more than I chose, has no right to blame me; and the other gentlemen were partakers of my guilt. But to you, Madam, I have much to apologize. Your good opinion I valued as one of the greatest acquisitions I had made on earth, and I was truly a beast to forfeit it.

It was this last reference which misled previous scholars into supposing that Maria Riddell had been the recipient of the letter; but the sentiment does not preclude Elizabeth Riddell, as the wife of one of Robert's closest friends over the past five years. The fact that Robert named his daughter after Glenriddell's wife shows the very high regard in which he held her. Robert singled out the two ladies who had tried to speak up on his behalf, hoping that he had not outraged them beyond all forgiveness, and then continued:

> To all the other ladies please present my humblest contrition for my conduct, and my petition for their gracious pardon. O, all ye powers of decency and decorum! whisper to them that my errors, though great, were involuntary – that an intoxicated man is the vilest of beasts – that it was not in my nature to be brutal to any one – that to be rude to a woman, when in my senses, was impossible with me – but –

Currie placed a line of asterisks across the page at this point, indicating a passage which he considered unfit for publication. As the actual letter itself, or the scroll copy which Robert presumably made of this literary exercise (and from which Currie probably got the text), has not survived we have no way of knowing what, or how much, was deleted. The letter ends in a characteristically dramatic and exaggerated fashion:

> Regret! Remorse! Shame![27] ye three hell-hounds that ever dog my steps and bay at my heels, spare me! spare me! Forgive the offences, and pity the perdition of, Madam,
>
> Your humble
slave

That Elizabeth Riddell was the recipient of this extraordinary letter is confirmed by Robert's letters to Maria. Number fourteen (CL 606–7), written very early in January 1794, within days of the Sabine incident, was in reply to a letter from Maria which (like all her other letters) has not survived. Robert's letter dealt with literary matters; he lent Maria his copy of Goethe's *Werther* 'truly happy to have any, the smallest, opportunity of obliging her'. Then he went on:

> 'Tis true, Madam, I saw you once since I was at Woodley park; & that once froze the very life-blood of my heart. Your reception of me was such, that a wretch, meeting the eye of his judge, about to pronounce sentence of death on him, could only have envied my feelings & situation.– But I hate the theme, & never more shall write or speak of it.

This proves beyond any shadow of doubt that the drunken incident had taken place somewhere other than Woodley Park. More importantly, this letter does not read like a sequel to the 'letter from Hell', showing that some other 'Mrs R.' than Maria had been its addressee. A day or two later Robert sent Maria a brief note with his epigram on Lord Buchan's assertion that 'Women ought to be flattered grossly, or not spoken to at all'. The lines beginning 'Praise woman still!' (CW 501) were directed to Maria in no uncertain terms:

> Maria, all my thought and dream,
> Inspires my vocal shell:
> The more I praise my lovely Theme
> The more the truth I tell.

What Maria's reaction was to these overtures of reconciliation is not known, but it seems that, just as Elizabeth Riddell ignored the 'letter from Hell', so Maria ignored these letters. Robert made one last attempt to heal the breach, writing on 12 January (CL 607–8):

> I return your Common Place Book.– I have perused it with much pleasure, & would have continued my criticisms, but as it seems the Critic has forfeited your esteem, his strictures must lose their value.–
> If it is true, that 'Offences come only from the heart;'–[28] before you I am guiltless:– To admire, esteem, prize and adore you, as the most accomplished of Women & the first of Friends – if these are crimes, I am the most offending thing alive.–
> In a face where I used to meet the kind complacency of friendly confidence, *now* to find cold neglect & contemptuous scorn – is a wrench that my heart can ill bear.

Angus Macnaghten[29] has interpreted this one-sided correspondence as suggesting that Robert visited Woodley Park *after* the Sabine incident, and that the encounter in which Maria 'froze' Robert must have been in the streets of Dumfries. It seems to me more likely, however, that the visit to

Woodley Park could refer to some previous visit *before* the Sabine incident, and that the 'freezing' referred to Maria's reaction when the drunken poet seized her and clumsily tried to smother her with kisses. At any rate, Robert tried to restore the situation as best he knew how, by means of the written word. The dignity with which he concluded his letter of 12 January echoes the dignified restraint which he showed when Clarinda reproached him in March 1789. Indeed, there are echoes of the former occasion (CL 406) in his conclusion to Maria:

> With the profoundest respect for your exalted abilities; the most sincere esteem & ardent regard & for your gentle heart & amiable manners; & the most fervent wish & prayer for your welfare, peace & bliss – I have the honor to be, MADAM, your most devoted humble servt.

Maria ignored this last-ditch attempt at healing the breach. The tacit snub was more effective than any retort. Robert hated being ignored above everything else, as witness his violent reaction to the silence that greeted his overtures to Wilhelmina Alexander and Robert Dundas. The intense emotional feelings Robert had for Maria turned almost overnight into a violent hatred which was to manifest itself in a prostitution of his talents. Robert who once confessed that he 'rhymed for fun' and who often, throughout his turbulent life, used verse as a kind of safety valve for his feelings, now gave free rein to his acidulous muse. The first fruits of this was 'Monody on a lady famed for her caprice' (CW 511–12) to which he tacked one of the satirical epitaphs for which he was noted:

> Here lies, now a prey to insulting neglect,
>   What once was a butterfly, gay in life's beam;
> Want only of wisdom denied her respect,
>   Want only of goodness denied her esteem.

Ironically, this was sent to Mrs McLehose the following June, accompanied by a long, rambling letter (CL 411–12) which ended:

> The subject of the foregoing is a woman of fashion in this country, with whom, at one period, I was well acquainted.– By some scandalous conduct to me, & two or three other gentlemen here as well as me, she steered so far to the north of my good opinion, that I have made her the theme of several illnatured things. The following Epigram struck me the other day, as I passed her carriage.

Note how, in his sullen mood, Robert twisted matters round, excusing his attitude on account of Maria's 'scandalous conduct' to him. This was followed by the scurrilous lines beginning 'If you rattle along like your Mistress's tongue' (CW 514). What Clarinda thought of these verses is not known, for she never answered this letter and thus, on this jarring note, the correspondence of Burns and Agnes McLehose came to an end. Robert thought the 'Extempore, Pinned to a Lady's coach' uncommonly clever, for he submitted it to Captain Patrick Miller for possible inclusion in Perry's *Morning Chronicle* (CL 700). Whether Miller forwarded the lines is not known, but the newspaper never published them. Robert's crowning insult was to insert these lines in the Glenriddell Manuscript when the poetic volume was returned to him.

This was followed by a mock epitaph for Walter Riddell, an innocent figure in the dispute as he was out of the country till the middle of 1794. The quatrain beginning 'So vile was poor Wat, such a miscreant slave' (CW 516) shows that Robert, who never had a high opinion of Walter's abilities, was only too ready to vent his spleen on anyone connected with the detested Maria. The longest piece inspired by his animosity was entitled 'From Esopus to Maria' (CW 539-41). Taking the advice of the Edinburgh literati that he should look to classical themes for inspiration, Robert used Esopus, the leading actor in Rome at the time of Cicero, to conceal the identity of James Williamson, the manager of a theatrical company which had occasionally played in Dumfries before the foundation of the theatre. When they were playing at Whitehaven the Earl of Lonsdale imprisoned Williamson's troupe as vagrants.[30] Robert used this incident to hit back at both Maria and Lord Lonsdale whom he disliked as the worst kind of arrogant nobleman. Williamson, like Burns, had been admitted into the Riddells' social circle. This long poem of eighty-one lines was written in Augustan English. As a satire on Maria it is pretty tame, apart from some slighting references to her pretensions to poesy; but as a commentary on contemporary events it is not without interest for it contained jibes against Maitland Bushby and the noted lothario, Colonel McDougal of Logan, as well as a passage which was pretty daring for its time:

> The shrinking Bard adown the alley skulks,
> And dreads a meeting worse than Woolwich hulks,
> Though there, his heresies in Church and State
> Might well award him Muir and Palmer's fate:

Scholars and biographers have often speculated over the virulence of Robert's attacks on Maria Riddell, especially as neither Robert Riddell nor his wife attracted such hostility. Hugh Gladstone, however, got right to the heart of the matter:

> It is possible that Burns felt the estrangement from Maria more severely than from the other members of the family, because a greater, a more sentimental, intimacy had existed between them. That she should alienate herself in a similar manner to her relations may have stung him to the exceptional vituperation in which he indulged.[31]

What, one wonders, was Robert Riddell's reaction? Burns's drunken behaviour, given the circumstances, was understandable. If Riddell had, indeed, been the instigator, his own conduct was quite inexcusable; if Burns were guilty of abusing Glenriddell's hospitality, Glenriddell was guilty of the greater sin of conspiring in such a dastardly trick on a man who was a guest in his house. In this case one could have understood it had Burns shown bitterness towards his old friend. But the poet was virtually silent on the matter. The reason is not far to seek. Robert Riddell, the hardened drinker who could put away seven bottles of claret before passing out, died on 21 April 1794 at the age of thirty-eight. Charitably Macnaghten suggests that some hereditary taint, perhaps due to inbreeding, may have contributed to his early death, rather than riotous living and excessive drinking. Interestingly, his brothers also died young: Walter died in his thirty-eighth year, in 1802, and Alexander John died aged thirty, two years later; so there may well have been some truth in the hereditary factor. At any rate, Robert Riddell died before he and the poet could be reconciled. Robert's reaction, when he heard of Glenriddell's death, was one of intense distress. At noon on that very day Robert wrote to a mutual friend, John Clark of Locharwoods (CL 706):

> This morning's loss I have severely felt.– Inclosed is a small heart-felt tribute to the memory of the *man I loved*. I shall send it to some Newspaper with my name.

With this note was the sonnet 'On the Death of Robert Riddell' (CW 513) which was published in the *Dumfries Weekly Journal* the following day. Maria herself acquired a copy of the sonnet, 'taken *verbatim* from one in Burns' own hand a few days after the death of my much-loved and respectable brother', as she wrote to Currie in 1800. Whether Robert gave or sent this copy to her personally is not known.

Some time after Riddell's death, Robert paid a surreptitious visit to Friars' Carse. He strolled through the wooded policies and visited the little hermitage one last time, in order to scratch impromptu lines on the window (CW 513):

> To Riddell, much lamented man,
>   This ivied cot was dear:
> Wand'rer, dost value matchless worth?
>   This ivied cot revere.

There is no record of Robert offering his condolences to the widow; but a few weeks later he wrote to a close member of Glenriddell's family (CL 707). The identity of the lady has never been satisfactorily ascertained. Currie, who was in a position to know the truth, merely printed the letter without attaching a name other than 'Miss –'. Wallace (1896) suggested Miss Woodley, but that was impossible as both of Maria Riddell's sisters were married. DeLancey Ferguson (1931) suggested that the recipient may have been 'a Miss Kennedy', sister of Elizabeth Riddell – Rachel Kennedy, in whose album Robert is known to have written three of his epigrams. The names 'Elinor or Sophy' were given by Hugh Gladstone in his paper (1915), and these alternatives were followed by Wood (1922).[32] The impression was given that the names pertained to the same lady. Robert Riddell, however, had two sisters – Eleanor, who died unmarried in 1797, and Sophia, who died young. Maria Riddell named her younger daughter Sophia after the latter aunt. Miss Eleanor Riddell left a small legacy to Maria's surviving daughter Anna Maria. On balance, therefore, it seems likely that Eleanor Riddell was the recipient of this letter.

The letter began with sincere expressions of the grief which Robert felt, and he recalled 'the scenes I have past with the friend of my soul'. He assured her that these were

> sensations of no ordinary anguish.– However you, also, may be offended with some *imputed* improprieties of mine; sensibility you know I possess, and sincerity none will deny me.

One can understand Robert giving Mrs McLehose his own version of the deterioration in his relationship with Maria, placing the blame on her; but writing to one of the Riddell family who must have been acquainted with the true facts, the emphasis on the word *imputed* was either barefaced, or showed that Robert had deluded himself into thinking that, if any fault existed, it was not his. There is a hint in the next paragraph that he suspected Maria to be at the heart of the trouble:

> To oppose these prejudices which have been raised against me, is not the business of this letter. Indeed it is a warfare I know not how to wage. The powers of positive vice I can in some degree calculate, and against direct malevolence I can be on my guard; but who can estimate the fatuity of giddy caprice, or ward off the unthinking mischief of precipitate folly?

The purpose of this letter, however, was not to make excuses or cast blame on others for the rift between him and the Riddell family. Robert was anxious to retrieve the first volume of the Glenriddell Manuscripts which had been in Riddell's possession at the time of his death. He was embarrassed by this 'collection of all my trifles in verse':

> They are many of them local, some of them puerile and silly, and all of them unfit for the public eye . . . I am uneasy now for the fate of those manuscripts – Will Mrs. — have the goodness to destroy them, or return them to me? As a pledge of friendship they were bestowed; and that circumstance, indeed, was all their merit. Most unhappily for me, that merit they no longer possess.

Robert's claim to this volume was doubtful. The book itself was Robert Riddell's property from the outset, decorated with the Glenriddell coat of arms in full colour on the inside, together with the frontispiece drawing of the Nasmyth portrait and eleven lines of Helen Craik's poetry on the title page. Although Burns inscribed quite a number of his poems in the volume, the handwriting of many others shows that Glenriddell enlisted the aid of at least three amanuenses to carry out this task. Almost half the contents, in fact, were in a hand other than the poet's. Burns undoubtedly selected the material for inclusion, but equally there can be no doubt that the collection was Glenriddell's, not the poet's. Nevertheless, Eleanor Riddell apparently complied with the poet's wishes, for the volume was duly returned to Burns without demur.

Meanwhile, things were not going well for the Riddells. Four days before Glenriddell died, his brother Walter had been forced to put Woodley Park up for sale, having failed to raise the money to complete the purchase. Robert Riddell's death failed to save Walter and the will of the deceased indicates that the brothers were latterly not on the best of terms. Dr Currie, who was an intimate friend of the Riddells, said that Glenriddell had had 'little intercourse with his brother for some years past'.[33] Some indication of a coolness between Robert and Walter Riddell, or between their respective wives, is given in a letter which Burns wrote to Maria in the autumn of 1792 (CL 601). Robert was about to visit Drumlanrig with the organist Stephen Clarke:

> However, it is not likely that I shall see Glenriddel at that time; but if I should, I shall say nothing at all, & listen to nothing at all, in which you are, mediately, or immediately, concerned.– So, Vive l'amour, & vive la bagatelle! For I dare say that one, or both of these Mighty Deities are at the bottom of this most extraordinary, inexpressible, & inexplicable mystery.

What this mystery was we shall never know for certain; but it may have had some bearing on the fact that on 11 October 1792 Robert Riddell made a will, naming as his executors his brother-in-law Gilbert Kennedy and his cousin William Riddell of Camieston. Glenriddell ignored brother Walter in determining who should be responsible for carrying out his wishes. He could not exclude Walter entirely but the terms of the will made it clear that Walter's inheritance was conditional on his good behaviour. In effect the estate of Friars' Carse was to go to Walter Riddell of Woodley Park or his younger brother

> Alexander John Riddell Esqr Ensign in the forty Eight Regt of foot At the sole option of my beloved wife Mrs Elizabeth Riddell, and to either of them she shall see cause to pitch upon, by any writing she may give under her hand, at any time of her life which I here declare to be my will and Perfectly binding as if I had made the choice myself.[34]

Riddell had no illusions about Walter whom he had every good reason to regard as feckless and a spendthrift. Walter's last act before departing for the West Indies had been to execute a deed empowering his brother and John Clark to mortgage certain of his lands to pay debts due by him.[35] In fact, the earliest intimation of Walter's return to Britain was a trust disposition of Scottish lands to John Clark in repayment of various debts, signed at London on 27 May 1794.[36]

Not only did Glenriddell and his wife have a poor opinion of Walter Riddell, but they did not think much of his young wife either, and this view was shared by Elizabeth Riddell's sister. In her letter to Dr Currie of January 1798, already quoted, Rachel Kennedy asked him what he thought of Maria's extraordinary character:

> I have often been much amused with her conversation, tho' not always approving her Conduct. She uniformly professed herself *my* friend and was highly flattering in her attentions to me, but I found it quite necessary to break off all intercourse with her long before she left this Country – My opinion of Burns will be of little use to you. I am inclin'd to believe, that had his lot been cast differently, he wou'd have proved a worthy & respected Character, but his Mind was frequently [*words torn away*] circumstances which were unfavourable to *Virtue* and [*word missing*] disappointments, which his ambition had wanted, he at length became, I fear, a very dissipated and profligate fellow. His conversation appear'd to me *Eloquent* tho' not *Graceful* and his general manners as might be expected from his late introduction into polish'd Society were uncouth and awkward. He was always open to *adulation*, and bestow'd it too indiscriminately to afford any gratification to a discerning mind. Alas! poor Burns, Peace to the Manes!!!

This extraordinary passage probably tells us more about Miss Kennedy than it adds to our knowledge of either Robert or Maria. This subjective and patronising view of the poet has to be viewed through the eyes of someone who regarded herself as well bred and refined. Rachel and her sister Elizabeth were Anglo-Scots, daughters of the wealthy textile manufacturer William Kennedy from Kirkcudbrightshire who migrated to Manchester and married Ann Walter there in June 1753.[37] Significantly, even Miss Kennedy realised that her personal opinion of Burns was irrelevant to Currie's avowed intention (whatever the actual outcome) of producing a sympathetic biography. And it should not be overlooked that Rachel advised Currie not to publish the 'letter from Hell' on the grounds that the unfortunate incident was best forgotten about. One therefore has to question Currie's motive in publishing it regardless of this good advice.

Although Robert was eventually reconciled with Maria, with whom he was more than half in love, he never had any time for Glenriddell's brother or widow. In a letter to Thomson about February 1796 (CL 676), discussing subscribers to the *Select Collection*, Robert asked his publisher to regard both Elizabeth and Walter, by that time both resident in Edinburgh, as subscribers, and to call upon them for their cash:

> I mention these matters because probably you may have a delicacy on my account, as if I had presented them with their copies; a kindness neither of them deserve at my hands.

It was ironic that Robert should lump them together, for the coolness between Glenriddell's widow and his brother increased after Walter returned to Scotland in May 1794. Elizabeth Riddell took the option of selling Friars' Carse, pointedly consulting her mother-in-law and the deceased's younger brother Alexander John Riddell, but not the elder brother Walter.[38] Early in 1794, Robert made the acquaintance of John McLeod of Coldbeck in Westmorland; on 16 May he wrote to Burns expressing an interest in Friars' Carse and asking the poet to keep him informed about a possible sale. On 18 June Robert wrote to McLeod (CL 710–11):

> the fate of Carse is determined.– A majority of the trustees have fixed its *sale*.– Our friend John Clarke, whom you remember to have met with here, opposed the measure with all his might; but he was over-ruled.– He, wishing to serve Walter Riddell, the surviving brother, wanted the widow to take a given annuity, & make over to him the survivancy of the paternal estate; but luckily, the widow most cordially hates her brotherinlaw, &, to my knowledge, would rather you had the estate, though five hundred cheaper, than that Wattie should.– In the mean time, Wattie has sold his Woodleypark to Colonel Goldie, the last Proprietor.– Wattie gave 16000£ for it; laid out better than 2000£ more on it; & has sold it for 15000£.– So much for Master Wattie's sense & management which, entre nous, are about the same pitch as his worth.
>
> The Trustees have appointed a gentleman to make out an estimate of the value of the terra firma in the estate, which you know is by far the principal article in the purchase: the house & woods will be valued by some professional man.– The gentleman they have pitched on, is a Mr Wm Stewart, factor & manager for Mr Menteath of Closeburn.– Stewart is my most intimate friend; & has promised me a copy of his estimate – but please let this be a dead secret.– Stewart was the intimate & confidential friend of poor Riddell that is gone, & will be trusted & consulted in all the business; & from him I am to know every view & transaction.– I assure you it has cost me some manoeuvring to bring this to bear; but as this kind of underhand intelligence may & will be of very considerable service to you, if you are still thinking of the purchase, I have in a manner beset & waylaid my friend Stewart, untill I have prevailed on him.

Rather fancifully Robert Thornton speculated about the payment Burns expected in return for his underhand intelligence. 'Did Elizabeth Riddell discover him in the dim light of his playing Stewart? If so, she had another reason for keeping him out of her life.'[39] At any rate, Friars' Carse was sold to Dr Peter Smith, a naval surgeon, for £15,000. The proceeds went exclusively to Elizabeth Riddell, with reversion to Alexander John Riddell after her death. Walter subsequently came to an agreement with his younger brother who magnanimously undertook to divide the inheritance equally. This agreement was reached informally at first and not properly ratified until 18 May 1796,[40] but some time before that Walter had lost all or part of his promised half to Samuel and Benjamin Boddington, London merchants, by way of discharging his debts.[41] This blow followed hard on the heels of the decision of Ann Riddell of Glenriddell (widow of Walter Riddell of Newhouse) to cut her elder surviving son out of her will and leave Alexander John as her sole executor 'for the love favour and affection I have . . . and certain other causes'.[42] This explains the subsequent movements of Walter and Maria Riddell and, incidentally, provides a reason why Maria no longer felt constrained to toe the family line in ignoring Burns.

On 25 June Robert set out with John Syme on a second tour of Galloway. This was a brief trip of three days only, so it is not surprising that previous biographers either overlooked it entirely or confused it with the trip of the previous year and got the dates wrong.[43] The confusion probably arose because Syme, in his communication with Currie, omitted all mention of the second trip. Robert himself kept no journal of this tour, but several letters and poems are extant which enable us to reconstruct his itinerary.

Although very little is known concerning Robert's masonic activities after he left Ayrshire, it is on record that he joined the Dumfries St Andrew's lodge on 27 December 1791 and was elected senior warden on 30 November 1792. Robert was absent from the meeting of 6 May 1794 on which David McCulloch of Ardwall was admitted a member.[44] Whether Burns and McCulloch were acquainted prior to this or not, they certainly became close friends. Robert was probably drawn to this personable young man, ten years his junior, on account of the fact that McCulloch had until recently been living in France and had witnessed some of the turbulent events of the Revolution. At the age of nineteen he had gone to Normandy in order to learn the language and was in Paris at the fall of the Bastille. Such was his proficiency in French that he was able to move quite freely around the country for several months after the execution of King Louis and the outbreak of war between France and Britain. He returned home in the late summer of 1793 when his father was ailing and, in the absence of his two elder brothers abroad, superintended the funeral arrangements for David McCulloch Senior in January 1794. A rather high-flown testimonial to his filial piety, in the form of a letter from his mother Jane Corsane to his eldest brother Edward, was published shortly afterwards, but was somewhat negated by the minutes of Anwoth Kirk Session which recorded a charge of fornication made against him and Peggy Bailey, a serving maid at Ardwall. McCulloch never married, but in 1796 he went off to become a merchant in India and Malaya.[45]

Apart from their masonic connections, McCulloch and Burns shared an interest in Scottish song. David possessed a fine tenor voice. What Robert Aiken did for Burns's poems David McCulloch did for his songs, and the poet stated on more than one occasion that he never fully knew the beauty of his songs until he heard them sung by his young friend.

On 4 June 1794 David McCulloch rode into Dumfries to attend the county ball being held that evening in honour of the king's birthday. He was very sorry to see

> Burns walking alone on the shady side of the High Street, while the opposite was gay with successive groups of ladies and gentlemen, all drawn

together for the festivities of the night, not one of whom appeared willing to recognise him. The horseman dismounted and joined Burns, who, on his proposing to him to cross the street, said: 'Nay, nay, my young friend – that's all over now;' and quoted after a pause some verses of Lady Grizel Baillie's pathetic ballad 'His bonnet stood ance fu' fair on his brow' . . . It was little in Burns's character to let his feelings on certain subjects escape in this fashion. He, immediately after citing these verses, assumed the sprightliness of his most pleasing manner; and taking his young friend home with him, entertained him very agreeably until the hour of the ball arrived, with a bowl of his usual potation, and bonnie Jean's singing of some verses which he had recently composed.[46]

In view of the bellicose behaviour of the Loyal Natives, who spent the interval between the dinner-parties in the two largest inns and the 'grand reunion' in the Town Hall at six o'clock by strutting up and down the high street in their sashes and beribboned finery, it was merely prudent of Robert, as a notorious 'Gallican', not to court disaster by walking on the sunny side of the street. McCulloch, as a man who must have had the taint of Gallicism on him because of his recent residence in France, ought to have known better. It was probably on this occasion that McCulloch extended an invitation to Robert to visit him whenever he was in the neighbourhood of Ardwall. On 21 June Robert wrote to him (CL 712):

My long projected journey through your country is at last fixed, & on Wednesday next, if you have nothing of more importance than to take a saunter down to Gatehouse, about two or three o'clock, I shall be happy to take a draught of Mckune's best with you.

He mentioned that he would be travelling with Syme and that they would be going on to Kirroughtree, the country seat of Patrick Heron of Heron (1736–1803). Robert concluded:

Syme goes also to Kiroughtree, & let me remind you of your kind promise to accompany me there.– I will need all the friends I can muster, for I am indeed ill at ease whenever I approach your Honourables & Right Honourables.

Burns left Dumfries on the afternoon of 25 June and reached Castle Douglas that evening, intending to meet up with Syme at Gatehouse the following day. Syme appears to have gone on ahead, as he had Stamp Office business to transact in the neighbourhood. Until two years previously, Castle Douglas had been known as Carlinwark, but in 1792 it was purchased by Sir William Douglas of Gelston who got it erected into a burgh of barony, renamed in his own honour. Some years earlier Douglas had purchased lands in Wigtownshire and renamed the town on the west bank of the Cree Newton Douglas; but the name never caught on and by the end of the eighteenth century it had reverted to its original name of Newton Stewart. These antics provoked Robert's mild satire in the second Heron Election Ballad (CW 545):

> An there'll be Douglases doughty,
> New christening towns far and near.

By 1794, however, the main hostelry in the high street, where the stage-coaches between Dumfries and Stranraer changed horses, was still known as Carlinwark Inn. It was here that Robert, that evening, wrote long letters to the two ladies who came closest to sharing his most intimate confidences. Both letters showed Robert in low spirits, due to the fact that the inn was virtually deserted and, for once, he was deprived of congenial company. Both letters were dated 25 June, but the time of day was not stated; it seems likely that they were written that night.

The letter to Mrs Dunlop (CL 210) began 'Here in a solitary inn, in a solitary village, am I set by myself'. By the time he got to the letter to Mrs McLehose (CL 411-12), however, this had expanded to:

> You would laugh, were you to see me, where I am just now:- would to Heaven you were here to laugh with me, though I am afraid that crying would be our first employment.- Here am I set, a solitary hermit, in the solitary room, of a solitary inn, with a solitary bottle of wine by me –

Some explanation of his depression was conveyed to Mrs Dunlop, to whom he apologised for neglecting 'the correspondence of the most valued Friend I have on earth':

> To tell you that I have been in poor health, will not be excuse enough, though it is true.- I am afraid that I am about to suffer for the follies of my youth.- My Medical friends threaten me with a flying gout; but I trust they are mistaken.

Characteristically he perked up as he wrote, and concluded the letter with 'the first sketch of a stanza I have been framing as I passed along the road'. There followed eighteen lines of the 'Ode for General Washington's Birthday' (CW 515-16). Like 'Scots wha hae', composed in the same district almost a year earlier, this long poem was not quite what it appeared at first glance. Washington's birthday occurred on 22 February and not in June; perhaps Robert was still smarting at the recollection of the manner in which the Loyal Natives had turned the celebration of the king's birthday three weeks previously into a raucous demonstration of their patriotism. George Washington, who had recently been re-elected for a second term as president of the United States, was merely an excuse for Robert to dwell upon 'the degeneracy of kingdoms'. As in 'Scots wha hae', he waxed lyrical on the golden age of Scottish history when William Wallace (whom the recipient of this letter liked to regard as her ancestor) fought for freedom. Interestingly, he also singled out King Alfred, whose lyrical treatment by James Thomson had a profound influence on him. Robert contrasted the England which the Anglo-Saxon ruler had freed from the Danes, with the England which had now allied itself with Continental tyrants (i.e. Austria and Prussia) in an unjust war against revolutionary France.[47] Whatever gratification Mrs Dunlop might have felt at the panegyrics to William Wallace was set at naught by her 'Dear Burns' daring to condemn the present conflict. Two of Mrs Dunlop's daughters had married French royalist *émigrés* and four sons and a grandson were on active service with the British army.

The letter to Mrs McLehose was much longer and more reflective, shot through with sadness and a nostalgia for the happier times of a few years previously. It was fifteen months since Robert had last written to her, reproaching her then for omitting to let him know that she had returned from Jamaica. It does not appear that Nancy ever answered that letter, and Robert might have been tempted to let the correspondence drop; but now, in self-imposed solitary confinement, at a time when the intellectual companionship of Maria Riddell was denied him, his thoughts turned inexorably to his Edinburgh grass-widow:

> Before you ask me why I have not written you first let me be informed of you, *how* I shall write you. 'In Friendship,' you say; & I have many a time taken up my pen to try an epistle of 'Friendship' to you; but it will not do: 'tis like Jove grasping a pop-gun, after having wielded his thunder.– When I take up the pen, Recollection ruins me. Ah! my ever dearest Clarinda!– Clarinda?– What a host of Memory's tenderest offspring crowd on my fancy at that sound!– But I must not indulge that subject:– you have forbid it.

He went on to say that he had had news of her from Ainslie from whom he had recently had a letter; 'but it was so dry, so distant, so like a card to one of his Clients, that I could scarce bear to read it, & have not yet answered it'. In fact, he never did. It pained Robert to realise that the irresponsible and irrepressible companion of those carefree days, only seven years previously, had developed into such a dry old stick. It hurt him to think that Ainslie's more formal attitude had something to do with the fact that he, Burns, was no longer the celebrity he once was.

As he wrote this increasingly maudlin letter, Robert raised his glass and drank a toast to 'my dear Mrs Mack, here is your good health!' This set him to reflecting:

> You must know, my dearest Madam, that these now many years, wherever I am, in whatever company, when a married lady is called as a toast, I constantly give you; but as your name has never passed my lips, even to my most intimate friend, I give you by the name of Mrs Mack.– This is so well known among my acquaintances, that when my married lady is called for, the toast-master will say – 'O, we need not ask him who it is – here's Mrs Mac!' I have also among my convivial friends, set on foot a round of toasts, which I call, a round of Arcadian Shepherdesses; that is, a round of favourite Ladies, under female names celebrated in ancient song; & then, you are my Clarinda:– so my lovely Clarinda, I devote this glass of wine to a most ardent wish for your happiness!

This was the letter which concluded with 'Passion's Cry' (CW 501-2), followed disconcertingly with the 'Monody' on Maria Riddell.

Patrick Heron, scion of an ancient family from Newark, Nottinghamshire, had had a rather chequered career, being a partner, with William and James Douglas, in the ill-fated Ayr Bank which had crashed so spectacularly in 1773. He survived the crash and two years later married Lady Elizabeth Cochrane (1745-1811), daughter of Thomas Cochrane, eighth Earl of Dundonald. With her dowry Heron purchased the estate of Kirroughtree in Minnigaff parish about a mile north-east of Newton Stewart on the banks of the River Cree. Lady Elizabeth was a talented amateur musician and composer and in April 1794 she sent to Burns, via John Syme, the air 'Banks of Cree'. He replied on 3 April (CL 705) thanking her for the melody to which he had added the song 'Here is the Glen' (CW 513). As previously mentioned, Thomson disliked the air and published the song after Robert's death to the tune 'Flowers of Edinburgh'. Lady Elizabeth's melody was jettisoned and apparently has not survived. From the letter of April it appears that Syme was a friend of the Heron family, and it was through his connection that Robert was invited to Kirroughtree two months later.

Of the visit to Kirroughtree itself nothing is recorded. As a result of the visit, however, Robert got Patrick Heron and his brother, Major Basil Heron, to subscribe to Johnson's *Musical Museum*, as he informed the publisher on 29 June (CL 299). In the grounds of the estate there are several prehistoric cairns and the hillock known as Parliament Knowe was believed to have been a place of assembly in pre-Roman times. This may have been the inspiration of some lines 'for an Altar of Independence' (CW 557) which Robert composed and sent to Patrick Heron in July 1795.

During that bleak summer of 1794 when Robert was deprived of Maria Riddell he renewed, or rather gave a new dimension to, a friendship with Jean Lorimer (1775-1831). Robert had known her since she was a teenager when her father William had taken the lease of one of Robert Riddell's farms at Kemys Hall (or Kemmishall) two miles south-east of Ellisland. Jean's striking good looks were crowned with dazzling flaxen hair – a very unusual colour in southern Scotland in the eighteenth century. She had been born at Craigieburn near Moffat, and this inspired Robert to write verses to the old melody 'Craigieburnwood' (CW 436-7). A second version was composed in the winter of 1794 and sent to Thomson on 15 January 1795 (CL 670). The original version, however, was written in 1791 on behalf of a young Excise colleague, John Gillespie, who was smitten by Miss Lorimer – as were John Lewars, James Thomson and other Excisemen. At first Robert seems to have maintained an amused detachment as his brother officers vied with one another for the favours of the young lady. By the time Robert wrote the first version of the song, however, Gillespie had been transferred to Portpatrick whither Robert wrote teasingly to enclose the song (CL 572):

> I drank tea with the young lady at her home yesternight; & on my whispering her that I was to write to you, she begged me to inclose you

her Complnts.– In fact, the lady, to my certain knowledge, is down on her
marrow bones of repentance, respecting her usage of a certain gentleman.– I never meet with her, but you are, sooner or later, introduced on
the carpet.– Last night when she & I were a few minutes by ourselves
after tea, she says to me – 'I wonder, Mr Burns, what pet Mr Gillespie has
taken at this country, that he does not come & see his friends again . . .'
The great rivals now with Miss Jeany, are our brethren Messrs Lewars &
Thomson.– They are both deeply in love, but the Lady does not favor the
one or the other.

In fact, Jean Lorimer did not settle on any gentlemen of the Excise.
Instead, she fell in love with Andrew Whelpdale, scion of an old Penrith
family who had taken the farm of Barnhill near Moffat. He was a frequent
visitor to the Johnston family at Dumcrieff, adjacent to Craigieburn which
William Lorimer had continued to farm, and it was there that he made
young Jean's acquaintance. Whelpdale was only a year older than Jean and
still in his teens when, one night in March 1793, he eloped with her to
Gretna Green. The story goes that Whelpdale coerced Jean, threatening to
kill himself if she did not comply with his wishes. She was not quite eighteen at the time, and 'probably had no knowledge of the world'. She consented reluctantly and thereby ruined her life. The newly-weds returned to
Barnhill, but a few months later, when his debts became insurmountable,
Whelpdale abandoned his wife and his farm and fled back to Cumberland.
Twenty-three years were to elapse before she saw him again. There was
nothing left for her but to return to her parents at Kemys Hall. Before she
was nineteen, Mrs Whelpdale was in the same position as Mrs McLehose
– a married woman abandoned by her worthless husband. Perhaps because
of the irregular nature of the marriage, by the blacksmith over the anvil at
Gretna, Jean reverted to her maiden name; but legally she was still wed to
the worthless Whelpdale and for that reason was unable to remarry.

Back at Kemys Hall, keeping house for her father, Jean frequently saw
the poet and in the course of 1794 their friendship deepened into a genuine
affection. Once more Robert was in love. The biographers of Burns are
evenly divided as to the nature of this relationship. Chambers, Wallace and
other nineteenth-century scholars were quick to seize upon a passage in the
letter to Thomson dated 19 October 1794 (CL 658). Speaking of the air
'Craigieburnwood', he wrote:

> The Lady on whom it was made, is one of the finest women in Scotland;
> & in fact (entre nous) is in a manner to me what Sterne's Eliza was to him
> – a Mistress, or Friend, or what you will, in the guileless simplicity of
> Platonic love.– (Now don't put any of your squinting construction on
> this, or have any clishmaclaiver about it among your acquaintances) . . .

After a lengthy passage justifying himself, he confessed:

> I put myself in a regimen of admiring a fine woman; & in proportion to
> the adorability of her charms, in proportion you are delighted with my

verses.– The lightning of her eye is the godhead of Parnassus, & the
witchery of her smile the divinity of Helicon!

Thomson probably thought 'Methinks he doth protest too much' and,
reading between the lines, would, indeed, have looked askance at this confession. Someone, like brother Gilbert, who knew only too well Robert's
propensity for falling in love, might have recognised the old signs. Most
nineteenth-century writers, however, latched on the keywords 'Platonic
love' and resolutely turned their backs on the suggestion that there might
be anything physical about the relationship. They were also at pains to
stress, rather naïvely, that Jean Lorimer was also a close friend of Jean
Armour, citing the sole extant letter from Robert to William Lorimer,
written in August 1795 (CL 721):

> Mrs Burns desired me yesternight to beg the favor of Jeany to come and
> partake with her, and she was so obliging as to promise that she would.
> Jeany and you are all the people, besides my Edinburgh friends, whom I
> wish to see . . .

This letter, incidentally, gave the lie to the notion, current even now,[48]
that the friendship between Burns and the Lorimers declined towards the
end of his life.

The assertion that Robert had a physical love affair with Jean Lorimer
was first made by James Hogg who stated that Robert made a habit of
lodging with her at Craigieburn whenever his Excise business took him to
the Moffat area. This would certainly have been feasible in the winter of
1794-5 when Robert deputised for Alexander Findlater as District Surveyor. Hogg claimed to have had an admission from the lady herself whom
he met in Edinburgh about 1816. William Lorimer became senile before he
died in poverty and poor Jean was thrown out into the world. She became
a governess in various households in the north of England and on one occasion about 1816 visited her erstwhile husband, then imprisoned for debt at
Carlisle. After twenty-three years it is hardly surprising that she did not
recognise him; he had aged a great deal, become corpulent and partially
paralysed. There was a short-lived reconciliation and she visited him every
day for a month before returning to Scotland. She moved to Edinburgh
where she 'spent some time in a kind of vagrant life, verging on men-
dicancy, and never rising above the condition of a domestic servant'.[49]

Thomas Thorburn, a Writer to the Signet and a minor poet who contributed to Wood's *Songs of Scotland*, recorded a meeting with Jean
Lorimer about this period:

> I fell in with Chloris one evening on the Mound in Edinburgh in 1816 or
> 1817, when I was serving an apprenticeship to a WS. She made some
> amatory proposals which I declined, but I gave her a shilling, believing
> her to be an imposter. Our head clerk, however, met her some evenings
> afterwards, and adjourned to Johnnie Dowie's and discussed a bottle of

ale, and by dint of cross-questioning discovered she was the veritable Jean. I regretted afterwards I had not a jaw with her.[50]

In his chapter on 'Strictures on Scottish Songs and Ballads' James Hogg introduced a curious anecdote which sheds some more light on Jean's subsequent career. Hogg, writing in 1834, was characteristically vague regarding the date, which must have been in 1816 or 1817:

> When I lived in Edinburgh, about twenty years ago, there were three of my associates, – Mr Irvine, Mr Gibson and Mr Thomson, – found out this lady rather in bad circumstances, and attached themselves greatly to her, on account of her known connection with the star of their idolatry, Burns. She said Burns came to Craigie-burn all night every time his business called him to Moffat. I went with some of them one day to see her, and was introduced to her as the successor of Burns; but she held very light of me indeed. Her feelings were of a woman, and, though a ruined one, I loved her for them. She had a lock of his hair keeping in a box. She was then a widow apparently approaching to forty, though she might be younger. She was the ruin of a fine woman, of a fair complexion, and well-made, and I heard by her voice that she had once sung well.[51]

Jean maintained a precarious existence on the streets of Edinburgh for about a decade, but early in 1825 a gentleman discovered her and publicised her plight in the national press in the hope of raising a subscription for her relief. His wife, having sent her some newspapers containing the paragraphs which he had written, received a brief letter dated 2 March 1825:

> Burns's Chloris is infinitely obliged to Mrs — for her kind attention in sending the newspapers, and feels pleased and flattered by having so much said and done in her behalf. Ruth was kindly and generously treated by Boaz; perhaps Burns's Chloris may enjoy a similar fate in the fields of men of talent and worth.[52]

Chloris afterwards obtained a situation as housekeeper to a gentleman in Newington and lived there under the name of 'Mrs Lorimer' for several years in greater comfort than she had known since she first left her father's house. Later, however, she contracted a severe pulmonary infection, probably tuberculosis, and ultimately had to retire to a lodging in Middleton's Entry, Potterrow (close to where Burns had first met Clarinda). Here, supported by her master, she died in September 1831 at the age of fifty-six. She was laid to rest in the Preston Street cemetery where a memorial to her was erected by the Ninety Burns Club in 1901. Andrew Whelpdale, who latterly lived at Langholm, Dumfriesshire, on a small pension, survived his wife by three years.

Even before her brief, runaway marriage in March 1793, Burns was beginning to take serious notice of young Jean, who inspired 'Poortith Cauld' (CW 481–2) to the tune 'Cauld kail in Aberdeen', which Robert sent to Thomson about 7 January 1793 (CL 622). Thomson replied saying that these verses had 'too much of *uneasy* & cold reflection for this Air, which is pleasing & rather gay than otherwise'. Robert responded that 'The objections are just, but I cannot make it better.– The stuff won't bear mending; yet for *private* reasons I should like to see it in print'.

In all, Jean Lorimer inspired two dozen songs of Burns – more than any other of his heroines. Too much should not be read into this, of course; Robert was more productive than usual in the period he was working for Thomson. On 28 August 1793 Robert sent to Thomson the song 'Come let me take thee to my breast' (CW 498-9) which was also intended for 'Cauld kail in Aberdeen' but which Thomson perversely set to the Irish tune 'Ally Croker'. Thereafter references to 'Jeanie' in Robert's songs usually had Miss Lorimer in mind, rather than Jean Armour, though the long poem 'Bonie Jean' (CW 493-4) was dedicated to Jean McMurdo.

But the affair, if such it was, really gathered momentum in the summer and autumn of 1794 when Robert was deprived of the intellectual companionship of Maria Riddell. By September of that year Robert had resurrected the Arcadian conceit of a few years earlier and adopted the name Chloris for his platinum blonde young charmer. The choice of a name was first aired in a letter to Alexander Findlater that month (CL 541-2). 'I am in the clouds elsewhere,' confessed Robert to his superior officer, quoting lines from Sir Charles Sedley's Restoration comedy *The Mulberry Garden*:

> Ah, Chloris, could I now but sit
> As unconcerned as when
> Your infant beauty could beget
> Nor happiness nor pain.

He followed this quotation with the cryptic line, 'Let Yesternight – Oh yesternight!' which set him off at a tangent, recalling 'The bonie sweet Lassie I kist yestreen'. Later in this letter Robert gave the text of 'Lassie wi the lint-white locks' (CW 542), the seventeenth line of which was 'When Cynthia lights wi silver ray'. Although Jean Lorimer was clearly intended, Robert had not yet settled upon a convenient pseudonym:

> By the bye, I have not been able to please myself with verses to – 'We'll gang nae mair to yon town' – but I have pledged myself to give to the fair Arcadian, the original verses on her – 'Thine am I, my Sylvia / Celia / Cloe / Lesbia fair'.

Having toyed with these names Robert settled on Chloris for this song (CW 505). It is obvious that he borrowed the name from Sedley, apparently oblivious to the fact that this name had been besmirched by Sedley's contemporary, the notorious second Earl of Rochester, who had bestowed it on the heroine of one of his more scatalogical pieces, the shepherdess who achieved orgasm by wallowing in the filth of a pigsty. Oddly enough, the subject of Chloris also arose about the same time in a long letter

(CL 655–61) which began by asking Thomson if he knew an Irish urolagniac ditty called 'Oonagh's waterfall, or The lock that scattered Oonagh's piss', which their mutual friend Alexander Cunningham sang so delightfully. Robert regretted the want of decent verses to so charming an air, and remedied this defect by composing 'Sae flaxen were her ringlets' (CW 520). Chloris was named four times in this song alone, ending with the quatrain:

> Then, dearest Chloris, wilt thou rove
> By wimpling burn and leafy shaw,
> And hear my vows o truth and love,
> And say thou lo'es me best of a'?

Shortly afterwards there followed 'Sleep'st Thou' (CW 526). To Thomson, Robert confessed on 19 October (CL 661):

> Since the above, I have been out in the country taking a dinner with a friend, where I met with the lady whom I mentioned in the second page of this odds-&-ends of a letter.- As usual I got into song; & returning home, I composed the following – the Lovers morning salute to his Mistress.

The second stanza was a paean of praise to 'my Chloris'. This was followed in November by 'My Chloris, mark how green the groves' (CW 531) and 'Lassie wi the Lint-white Locks' (CW 528), the latter provoking Thomson to make the comment that he would 'scarce conceive a woman to be a beauty, on reading that she had lint-white locks!' In the accompanying letter (CL 662) Robert reacted to a comment in Thomson's last communication:

> I like you for entering so candidly & so kindly into the story of Ma chere Amie.- I assure you, I was never more in earnest in my life, than in the account of that affair which I sent you in my last.- Conjugal-love is a Passion which I deeply feel, & highly venerate; but somehow it does not make such a figure in Poesy as that other species of the Passion –
>
> Where Love is liberty & Nature law.[53]
>
> Musically speaking, the first is an instrument of which the gamut is scanty & confined, but the tones inexpressibly sweet; while the last, has power equal to all the intellectual Modulation of the Human Soul.- Still, I am a very Poet in my enthusiasm of the Passion.- The welfare & happiness of the beloved Object, is the *first & inviolate* sentiment that pervades my soul; & whatever pleasures I might wish for, or whatever might be the raptures they would give me, yet, if they interfere & clash with that *first* principle, it is having these pleasures at a dishonest price; & Justice forbids, & Generosity disdains the purchase!- As to the herd of the Sex, who are good for little or nothing else, I have made no such agreement with myself; but where the Parties are capable of, & the Passion is, the true Divinity of love – the man who can act otherwise than I have laid down, is a Villain!

What Thomson made of this does not appear to have been recorded. Long letters from Robert, accompanying new songs, were coming at him so thick and fast that when he wrote on 28 November he had two lengthy epistles to deal with, and confined his remarks to the songs themselves.

Almost a score of other songs dedicated to or inspired by Jean Lorimer, from 'Behold, my love, how green the groves' (CW 531) to 'O, bonie was yon rosy brier' (CW 558-9) followed in quick succession. There were also poems, ranging from the quatrain 'On Chloris requesting me to give her a sprig of blossomed thorn' (CW 534) to the inscription in six stanzas 'Tis Friendship's pledge, my young, fair Friend' (CW 557)

> written on the blank leaf of a copy of the last edition of my poems, presented to the lady whom, in so many fictitious reveries of passion, but with the most ardent sentiments of *real* friendship, I have so often sung under the name of 'Chloris'

a copy of which Robert sent to Alexander Cunningham on 3 August 1795 (CL 473). Interestingly, there is no record of any letters from Robert to Chloris, but there was the further gift of the first number of Thomson's *Select Collection* two months later.

There were no further songs, and few references, to Chloris after January 1795. Ironically, the last of the songs sent to Thomson (CL 669-70) was the second version of 'Sweet fa's the eve on Craigieburn' (CW 536), but on 2 August 1795 (CL 675) there occurred a paragraph:

> Did I mention to you, that I wish to alter the first line of the English song to Leiger m' choss, alias, The Quaker's wife – from 'Thine am I, my faithful Fair' – to 'Thine am I, my Chloris fair.' – If you neglect this alteration, I call on all the NINE, conjunctly and severally, to anathematise you!

Thomson annotated this letter, presumably when he sent it to Currie, 'N.B. The Poet afterwards disapproved of the name Chloris altogether – & restored the word here proposed to be altered'. In fairness to Burns, however, there is no evidence in his later correspondence to support Thomson's assertion, and we must therefore suppose that this was merely another example of Thomson's countermanding the dead poet's wishes.

His indiscretions of 1792 now completely forgiven, Robert began to take positive steps once again to advance his career in the Excise. On 7 January 1794, exactly a year since he had last written, Robert took up his pen to write to Graham of Fintry (CL 438-40), with a proposal for the complete reorganisation of the Dumfries Excise divisions:

> I have been myself accustommed to labour, & have no notion that a servant of the Public should eat the bread of idleness; so, what I have long digested, & am going to propose, is the reduction of one of our Dumfries Divisions.– Not only in these unlucky times, but even in the highest flush of business, my Division, though by far the heaviest, was mere trifling.– The others were likely still less.– I would plan the reduction as thus.– Let

the second Division be annihilated; & be divided among the others.- The Duties in it, are, two chandlers, a Common Brewer, & some Victuallers; these with some Tea & Spirit Stocks, are the whole Division.- The two Chandlers, I would give to the 3d, or Tobacco Division; it is the idlest of us all.- That I may seem impartial, I shall willingly take under my charge, the Common Brewer & the Victuallers.- The Tea & Spirit Stocks, divide between the Bridgend, & Dumfries 2d Itinerant Divisions: they have at present but very little, *comparatively* to do, & are quite adequate to the task.-

I assure you, Sir, that, by my plan, the Duties will be equally well charged, & thus an Officer's appointment saved to the Public.- You must remark one thing; that our Common Brewers are, every man of them in Dumfries, completely & unexceptionably, Fair Traders.- One, or two, rascally creatures are in the Bridgend Division, but besides being nearly ruined, as all Smugglers deserve, by fines & forfeitures, their business is on the most trifling scale you can fancy.-

I must beg of you, Sir, should my plan please you, that you will conceal my hand in it, & give it as your own thought.- My warm & worthy friend, Mr Corbet, may think me an impertinent inter-meddler in his department; & Mr Findlater, my Supervisor, who is not only one of the first, if not the very first of Excisemen in your Service, but is also one of the worthiest fellows in the universe; he, I know, would feel hurt at it; & as he is one of my most intimate friends, you can easily figure how it would place me, to have my plan known to be mine.-

For farther information on the Subject, permit me to refer you to a young beginner whom you lately sent among us, Mr Andrew Pearson; a gentleman that I am happy to say, from manner, abilities & attention, promises to be indeed a great acquisition to the service of your Honorable Board.

To this Robert added a postscript that, if his plan were acceptable, he would recommend 'to your humanity & justice' the present incumbent of the second division, 'a very good Officer, & is burdened with a family of small children, which, with some debts of early days, crush him much to the ground'.

The unsuspecting officer who would have lost his post had this plan gone ahead was John McQuaker. He had been in the Excise twenty-two years during which he had served in seven different towns (including Mauchline). He was indeed burdened by a large family and his problems were compounded by the loss of his wife a few years later. When he died in 1811 he was an Exciseman at Prestonpans. The Excise Character Book, however, shows that he was regarded only as 'middling good' and, in fact, he was suspended from duty for three months in May 1796 for some undisclosed offence. Significantly, his application to get a son appointed to the Excise was turned down, a clear indication that the Board thought little of the father's abilities.[54]

Robert's proposal, and the manner in which it was put forward, has been criticised. Robert was hardly being altruistic, though the greater efficiency of the Excise was the ostensible reason for writing to Graham. The latter probably saw the ploy for what it was, for there is no evidence that he either replied to Burns on the subject or put the proposal to the Board. Nothing daunted, however, Robert wrote again to Graham a month later (CL 440):

> The language of supplication is almost the only language in which I have it in my power to approach you; & I have your generous commands for coming to you with it, on every opportunity.– I hope, & know then, that you will forgive me, for mentioning to you a circumstance which has come to my knowledge, & which it is possible, though, I am afraid, by no means probable, may be of some service to me.

Somehow Robert had heard that Corbet was at the head of the Collectors' List and would shortly be promoted to one of these posts. Furthermore, Alexander Findlater seemed to be the likeliest man to take Corbet's place. This, indeed, did happen, when Corbet landed the plum job of Collector at Glasgow and Findlater then became Supervisor General at Edinburgh; but these important promotions did not take place till 1797, a year after Robert's death. Incidentally, in 1811 Findlater succeeded Corbet as Collector at Glasgow, a position he continued to hold till 1825. How such lofty moves could have benefited Burns was revealed in the letter to Graham:

> Could it be possible then, Sir, that an old Supervisor who may still be continued, as I know is sometimes the case, after they are rather too infirm for much DUTY, could not such an Officer be appointed to Dumfries, & so let the OFFICIATING JOB fall to my share?– This is a bare possibility, if it be one; so I again beg your pardon for mentioning it, & I have done with the subject.

Robert followed this rather ingenuous and unscrupulous proposal with a comment on the work he was doing for Thomson. Significantly Thomson himself was not named, but Pleyel, whom Graham doubtless knew of very well, was highlighted. Robert advanced his cause by enclosing a copy of the *Select Collection* for Graham's daughter:

> a trifling, but most fervent tribute of Gratitude, to the best Friend & truest, almost only, Patron, I have in the world: a GENTLEMAN, whose MANNER of bestowing, would give a pleasure to the feelings of unfortunate Royalty.

This letter shows only too vividly how desperate Robert had become in his pursuit of promotion, fired by growing anxieties about his deteriorating financial position. Not content to leave his obsequiousness at that, he concluded:

> Should the Chapter of Chances & Changes, which God forbid! ever place a Child of yours in the situation to need a Friend, as I have done; may they likewise find that Generous Friend, that I have found in YOU!

A letter to Findlater written about the same time (CL 541) refers to two schemes enclosed, with the enigmatic comment,

> I would not have troubled you with the collector's one, but for suspicion lest it be not right. Mr Erskine promised me to make it right, if you will have the goodness to shew him how. As I have no copy of the scheme for myself, and the alterations being very considerable from what it was formerly, I hope that I shall have access to this scheme I send you, when I come to face up to my new books.

What these schemes were, however, is not known; nor has the Mr Erskine been identified. It is tempting, however, to speculate that Graham of Fintry may have given his approval for the reorganisation of the Dumfries divisions, but unfortunately the extant Excise records are silent on the matter.

About the beginning of March 1794, Patrick Miller Junior had spoken to his friend James Perry (1756–1821), the editor and proprietor of the *Morning Chronicle*, about giving Burns a position on his literary staff. Perry, who hailed from Aberdeen, was eager to secure the regular services of the poet and offered to pay him a guinea a week, rather more than his Excise salary.[55] All that was required was a song or a poem every week, and it did not matter that these compositions were then submitted to Johnson or Thomson for their collections. The prospect of doubling his income for little additional effort must have been a very tempting one, especially as the war was continuing to affect his perquisites; but Robert, despite his anxieties about money, was mindful of the trouble he had got into with the Excise Board a year previously, and regretfully declined the offer. To Patrick Miller Junior he explained the situation (CL 699):

> Your offer is indeed truly generous, & most sincerely do I thank you for it; but in my present situation, I find that I dare not accept it.– You well know my Political sentiments; & were I an insular individual, unconnected with a wife & a family of children, with the most fervid enthusiasm I would have volunteered my services: I then could & would have despised all consequences that might have ensued.
>
> My prospect in the Excise is something, at least, it is encumbered as I am with the welfare, the very existence of near half-a-score of helpless individuals, what I dare not sport with.

He had, however, no qualms about letting Miller send Perry a copy of 'Scots wha hae', but with the proviso 'let them insert it as a thing they have met with by accident, & unknown to me'. The poem duly appeared in the *Morning Chronicle* on 8 May 1794, while 'Wilt thou be my dearie' (CW 512) appeared in the paper two days later. Robert showed an excess of prudence in this matter; although the *Chronicle* was a Whig paper it was not a subversive organ like Johnston's *Gazetteer*. Robert's caution on this occasion showed how far he had shed his old recklessness. He had not abandoned radical poetry by any means, as the Heron election ballads of

1795 were to demonstrate, but he was acutely aware of his familial responsibilities. A recurring worry, which became more acute every time his health deteriorated, was that he would die and leave his wife and little ones destitute. It was a comfort to him to know that one of the very real benefits of the Excise was the pension awarded to widows and orphans. Robert pithily summed up his motives in sticking with his Excise job in those lines (CW 306) which he is said to have penned on first being appointed to an Excise division:

> Searching auld wives' barrels,
>   Ochon, the day!
> That clarty barm should stain my laurels!
>   But, what'll ye say?
> These movin things ca'd wives an weans
> Wad move the very hearts o stanes!

With the birth of another son on 12 August 1794, named James Glencairn in honour of the late fourteenth Earl, Robert now had six children to feed. As 1794 drew to a close, however, the prospects of advancement in the Excise began to improve. Now that Britain was fully committed to the war against France there was a greater sense of solidarity at home, and as the worst excesses of the Terror abated there was less fear of revolution spreading to Britain. At any rate, Robert's political indiscretions were now forgotten. At last the importuning of January and February showed signs of paying off. He had started a long letter to Mrs Dunlop on 20 December (CL 212-14) and had got as far as giving her a copy of 'My Chloris, mark how green the groves' (CW 531) when he was interrupted by the news that Alexander Findlater had been taken ill. On or about 22 December Robert was appointed Acting Supervisor. A week later he resumed his letter:

> I assure you, what with the load of business, & what with the business being new to me, I could scarcely have commanded ten minutes to have spoken to you, had you been in town, much less to have written you an epistle.– This appointment is only temporary, & during the illness of the present incumbent; but I look forward to an early period when I shall be appointed in full form: a consummation devoutly to be wished![56] My Political sins seem to be forgiven me.

During the night of 19-20 November Robert had written the song 'Canst thou leave me thus, my Katy?' (CW 530-1) which he sent to Thomson the following morning. Although he did not say so in the accompanying letter (CL 667), it has been surmised that he intended this as a compliment to Thomson's wife, Katherine, whom he had previously promised to immortalise in song. Interestingly, in one manuscript version, the name 'Betty' was substituted, leading some editors to speculate improbably that this song was also intended as a peace-offering to Elizabeth Riddell. The song, however, with its theme of the anguish of unrequited love, was regarded by Chambers as a tentative gesture of reconciliation to Maria

Riddell: 'He conceives their estrangement as due to her inconstancy in affection'.[57] Robert appears to have sent a copy of this song to Maria soon afterwards, and to have received in response a song entitled 'Stay, my Willie, yet believe me', which Currie found among the poet's papers after his death.

After Glenriddell's death and the growing rift with his widow, Walter and Maria Riddell had left Dumfriesshire. Maria wrote a rather charming poem, 'Farewell to Nithsdale', to mark the occasion. They decided to go abroad for two years in order to economise, but by the time they reached London they found that the rapid progress of the French armies made a Continental sojourn impossible. During their brief stay in London Maria made the acquaintance of James Boswell whom she described to Smellie as 'a stranger biped, yourself always excepted'. Having aborted their plans to go abroad, Walter and Maria turned round and headed north again. This time they took a short lease of Tinwald House on the outskirts of Dumfries, 'a crazy, rambling, worm-eaten cob-web hunting chateau of the Duke of Queensberry' as she described it ruefully to Smellie. Walter Riddell was in London at the end of 1794 and Maria was alone at Tinwald House where she devoted much of her time to the education of her two daughters. She had her harp, her piano, her books and her museum of natural history, so time should never have hung heavy on her hands.

It has been assumed by most biographers that Maria was aware of the bitter lampoons Robert had composed about her and her husband, and that her subsequent forgiveness of the wayward poet demonstrated incredible magnanimity. But the Riddells were in London at the time these verses were going the rounds and if Maria ever got wind of them, she never mentioned them, either to their perpetrator or to anyone else. Indeed, when she perused Currie's 1800 edition of *The Works of Robert Burns* she did not recognise herself as the subject of the 'Monody on a Lady famed for her Caprice' (CW 511) which coincidentally came after the sonnet on the late Robert Riddell:

> The Monody that follows this little poem is very well written in its way. I had never seen it before. The two concluding lines are strongly pointed, and indeed constitute the chief, almost the whole, merit. The *idea* was a favourite one of Burns's. Before it was appropriated to the personage he calls Eliza, he had affixed it to two or three satirical squibs and epigrams, on as many successive persons who had offended him, or by whom he fancied himself slighted. This is a curious anecdote, but too scurvy a trait of the poor Bard's to be delivered over to the knowledge of his enemies. Poor Burns! Poor Human Nature![58]

What Maria would have thought, had she realised that she was the butt of these bitter lampoons, can only be imagined. Sir Hugh Gladstone alleged that 'From Esopus to Maria' (CW 539–41) was written early in 1795 *after* Robert and Maria had begun exchanging sentimental verses once more, but there is absolutely no evidence to support this view, any more than the ludicrous notion that, as Robert knew no Latin, he must have had the collaboration of Charles Sharpe of Hoddam in its composition.[59] In support of such a rash assumption Gladstone cited the venomous description of Maria by Sharpe's waspish son, Charles Kirkpatrick Sharpe (1781–1851), whose dislike of Burns was matched only by his pathological hatred of Maria. His pen-portrait, written some time after Maria died in 1808, seems to contain a garbled allusion to the Rape of the Sabine Women incident:

> There was a Lady – it is needless to outrage her ashes by recording her name – whose intimacy with B. did him essential injury – their connexion was notorious – and she made him quarrel for some time with a connexion of her own, a worthy man, to whom her deluded lover lay under many obligations. She was an affected-painted-crooked postiche – with a mouth from ear to ear – and a turned up nose – bandy legs – which however she thought fit to display – and a flat bosom, rubbed over with pearl powder, a cornelian cross hung artfully as a contrast, which was bared in the evening to her petticoat tyings, this pickled frog (for such she looked, amid her own collection of natural curiosities) Burns admired and loved – they quarrelled once, however, on account of a strolling player – and Burns wrote a copy of satirical verses on the Lady – which she afterwards kindly forgave, for a very obvious reason – amid all his bitterness he spared her in principal point, which made her shunned by her own sex, and despised by the rest of the community.[60]

Once more, we have a passage which tells us much more about the writer than his subject. The grotesque references to Maria's personal attributes do not match the beauty and charm of the sensitive portrait painted by Sir Thomas Lawrence, and 'pickled frog' can scarcely have applied to a lady who was only thirty-six when she died ten years after leaving Scotland. Sharpe could only have been a schoolboy when he saw Maria, and his description was penned twelve years later. When Maria published her *Metrical Miscellany* in 1802, young Sharpe purchased a copy and inscribed on the fly-leaf, 'This collection was published by Mrs Riddell, long the friend of Burns – her maiden name was Woodly (*sic*), she was a sister of Mr Bankes, and a worthless profligate woman'. There is no ground for supposing that Maria had an affair with the actor James Williamson, any more than that she had an affair with Burns or that she and the poet quarrelled over the actor; but clearly Maria was one of those beautiful but headstrong women (not unlike the Duchess of Gordon) resented by her own sex, who were only too ready to spread malicious gossip about her.

The date of composition of 'From Esopus to Maria' was probably much earlier than Gladstone supposed, and as the arrest and incarceration of Williamson's troupe of actors took place early in 1794 it seems fair to assume that this incident provided more immediate inspiration for the poem.

At any rate, the exchange of sentimental songs by Robert and Maria probably occurred in late November or early December 1794; perhaps the spirit of the season of goodwill to all men prevailed upon them to resolve their differences. If, as I suspect, Maria had been blithely ignorant of Robert's nasty lampoons, there was little reason for her keeping up the estrangement. Life at Tinwald House may have been busy, but it was lonely, and Maria must often have looked back on the not so distant past and missed the witty company of her poet.

This paved the way for further hesitant overtures of friendship. About the end of the year Maria sent a book to Robert. He responded with a rather stilted, third-person letter formally acknowledging her gift (CL 608):

> Mr Burns's Compliments to Mrs Riddell – is much obliged to her for her polite attention in sending him the book.– Owing to Mr B–'s being at present acting as Supervisor of Excise, a department that occupies his every hour of the day, he has not that time to spare which is necessary for any Belle Lettre pursuit; but, as he will, in a week or two, again return to his wonted leisure, he will then pay that attention to Mrs R–'s beautiful Song 'To thee, loved Nith,' which it so well deserves . . .
>
> P.S. Mr Burns will be much obliged to Mrs Riddell if she will favor him with a perusal of any of her poetical pieces which he may not have seen.

So 1794 ended on a high note, with Robert and Maria tentatively reconciled and prospects of Excise promotion looking very promising.

CHAPTER 17

The Last Years, 1795–6

O, wert thou in the cauld blast
  On yonder lea, on yonder lea,
My plaidie to the angry airt,
  I'd shelter thee, I'd shelter thee.
Or did Misfortune's bitter storms
  Around thee blaw, around thee blaw,
Thy bield should be my bosom,
  To share it a', to share it a'.

O, Wert Thou in the Cauld Blast (CW 567)

On 1 January 1795 Robert resumed his letter to Mrs Dunlop but only managed a paragraph before he was interrupted again. Pondering on the New Year and all that that meant, Robert had a sudden premonition:

What a transient business is life!– Very lately I was a boy; but t'other day I was a young man; & I already begin to feel the rigid fibre & stiffening joints of Old Age coming fast o'er my frame.

This provoked a bout of religious speculation, looking 'beyond the grave'. Again he was interrupted and the hectic business of the Excise prevented Robert from picking up his pen again until 12 January. Mrs Dunlop had lately been in London and had visited Dr Moore. Robert had just been re-reading Moore's *View of Society and Manners* and he gently reminded Mrs Dunlop that she had not returned his copy of *Zeluco*. This set him thinking of Moore's latest publication, *Journal during a Residence in France* in which Moore had used a lengthy quotation from 'Tam o Shanter':

He has paid me a pretty compliment, by quoting me, in his last Publication, though I must beg leave to say, that he has not written this last work in his usual happy manner.– Entre nous, you know my Politics; & I cannot approve of the honest Doctor's whining over the deserved fate of a certain pair of Personages.– What is there in the delivering over a per-jured Blockhead & an unprincipled Prostitute into the hands of the hangman, that it should arrest for a moment, attention, in an eventful hour, when as my friend Roscoe in Liverpool gloriously expresses it –

> When the welfare of Millions is hung in the scale
> And the balance yet trembles with fate.[1]

> But our friend is already indebted to People in power, & still looks
> forward for his Family, so I can apologise for him; for at bottom I am sure
> he is a staunch friend to liberty.– Thank God, these London trials have
> given us a little more breath, & I imagine that the time is not far distant
> when a man may freely blame Billy Pit, without being called an enemy to
> his Country.

This time Robert had gone too far. Mrs Dunlop, we must presume,
would not have been too pleased at Robert's criticism of Dr Moore, but
without doubt she was shocked and outraged at the intemperate language
in which the poet expressed his forthright opinion of Louis and Marie
Antoinette. On previous occasions she had warned him to drop the subject
of the French Revolution, but his thoughtlessness and tactlessness repelled
her. Totally oblivious to the fact that he had given such grave offence,
Robert wrote again about April (CL 214). He sent a reworking of a poem
and commented:

> Miss Keith will see that I have omitted the four lines on the ci-devant
> Commodore which gave her so much offence.– Had I known that he
> stood in no less connection than the Godfather of my lovely young
> Friend, I would have spared him for her sake.

No poem answering this description has survived, so it seems to have
received short shrift. To have unconsciously satirised Keith Dunlop's godfather would not have gone down well, but at least some allowances might
have been made; but Robert compounded the offence in closing this letter
by chiding Mrs Dunlop for her silence:

> I expected to have heard from you, how you arrived home, & how you
> found your friends; but in the hurry of momentous matters I suppose such
> a trifling circumstance had escaped your recollection.

The sarcasm in this sentence would not have escaped Mrs Dunlop and
stiffened her resolve to ignore the beastly fellow. Again, Robert does not
appear to have realised the gravity of the situation. Doubtless he had much
else to distract and preoccupy him throughout 1795, but on 31 January
1796 he wrote to Mrs Dunlop at length (CL 214–15). We can sense his
unease:

> These many months you have been two packets in my debt.– What sin of
> ignorance I have committed against so highly valued a friend I am utterly
> at a loss to guess.– Your son John, whom I had the pleasure of seeing here,
> told me that you had gotten an ugly accident of a fall, but told me also the
> comfortable news that you were gotten pretty well again.– Will you be so
> obliging, dear Madam, as to condescend on that my offence which you
> seem determined to punish with a deprivation of that friendship which

once was the source of my highest enjoyments?– Alas! Madam, ill can I afford, at this time, to be deprived of any of the small remnant of my pleasures.– I have lately drank deep of the cup of affliction.

The ensuing passage is one of the most heart-rending in any of Robert's letters. In September his daughter Elizabeth Riddell had died while on a visit to Mauchline; and the anguish at the little girl's death was exacerbated by the fact that Robert was unable to be with her at the end.

I had scarcely began to recover from that shock, when became myself the victim of a most severe Rheumatic fever, & long the die spun doubtful; until after many weeks of a sick-bed it seems to have turned up life, & I am beginning to crawl across my room, & once indeed have been before my own door in the street.

She must have been a curmudgeon indeed that could set her heart against such a *cri de coeur*; yet Mrs Dunlop ignored this pathetic communication. Robert tried one last time, writing from the Brow only days before his death (CL 215):

I have written you so often without receiving any answer, that I would not trouble you again but for the circumstances in which I am.– An illness which has long hung about me in all probability will speedily send me beyond that bourne whence no traveller returns.–[2] Your friendship with which for many years you honored me was a friendship dearest to my soul.– Your conversation & especially your correspondence were at once highly entertaining & instructive.– With what pleasure did I use to break up the seal! The remembrance yet adds one pulse more to my poor palpitating heart.

It would have been nice to think that Mrs Dunlop brought her obdurate silence to an end before it was too late but there is no evidence of a reconciliation, despite the unsubstantiated story (stoutly denied by the poet's widow) that a letter from Mrs Dunlop reached Dumfries before Robert expired. Chambers refers to a letter written to Mrs Dunlop on 23 July 1796 by John Lewars on Jean's behalf, 'in which we are told that Burns had the pleasure of receiving an explanation of Mrs Dunlop's silence', but neither this letter of Lewars nor any letter from Mrs Dunlop to Burns in July that year is extant. Of course, it is always possible that some form of verbal explanation, via a third party, was conveyed to the dying man; but Jean's emphatic denial of this must be respected. On receipt of Robert's last letter, however, Mrs Dunlop, no doubt thinking that he was exaggerating the gravity of his illness, wrote on 20 July to Gilbert Burns enquiring as to the true state of Robert's health. As Gilbert had received a letter from Robert written on 10 July (CL 358) saying 'It will be no very pleasing news to you to be told that I am dangerously ill, & not likely to get better' he knew as much as Mrs Dunlop; but Robert's assertion that he expected to remain at the seaside 'all the summer' may have lulled him into supposing that his brother was not so close to death as he made out. No letter purporting to have come from Mrs Dunlop in response to his deathbed cry has ever been produced, and we must treat this claim with suspicion, as an attempt to show Mrs Dunlop in a more charitable light. The only epistolary reaction appears to have been a letter from Mrs Dunlop to Mrs Gilbert Burns (Jean Breckenridge) at the end of July in which Mrs Dunlop acknowledged a letter giving her 'the melancholy account . . . of your worthy Brother's death'.[3] The timing of Mrs Dunlop's letters shows that, as late as 20 July, she had not forgiven Robert and was still seeking information about him in an indirect manner. Even if she *had* written to Robert on the very day she wrote to Gilbert, the poet could not possibly have received such a letter before he died.

It is clear that Robert's intemperate remarks about the King and Queen of France were merely the last straw. One can trace Mrs Dunlop's growing resentment with 'her Burns' back to the winter of 1792–3. On 23 November 1792 she expressed fear at the spread of revolutionary spirit in her neighbourhood; Robert countered this with his description of the Ça ira incident at the theatre, and the candid admission that his being a placeman gagged him from joining in the fun. A few days later Robert made his four-day visit to Dunlop House and as a result of something which happened there the correspondence significantly cooled. When Robert wrote hysterically on 5 January 1793, hurling imprecations at 'the prostituted soul of the miscreant wretch who can deliberately and diabolically plot the destruction of an honest man', Mrs Dunlop, instead of expressing sympathy and relief at Robert's lucky escape, allowed ten weeks to pass before replying. When she did get around to writing, however, she not only showed her utter disapproval of his political opinions, but revealed that she had been nursing her wrath for three months over an incident from his December visit. When she wished him to read Jenny Little's poems, Robert had retorted, 'Do I have to read them all?' Now, months later, Robert's fault recoiled upon her as if he had slapped her face: 'I never liked so little in my life as at that moment the man whom at all others I delighted to honour'. Although Mrs Dunlop eventually got over the poet's peremptory rebuff of her attempt to interest him in the rhymes of her milkmaid protégée, the memory of the incident continued to rankle. That and Robert's crass obtuseness in ignoring her repeated warnings not to offend her with his political views must have had a cumulative effect. In fairness it must be admitted that Mrs Dunlop was the last person to whom he should have unburdened himself so freely and frankly. Her very last letter to Robert (written from London on 12 January and therefore crossing in the post with his long and much-interrupted letter) had deplored the fact that Dr Moore was 'a sad Democrat' and stated candidly that in her part of Ayrshire 'we are the very pink of loyalty, and hate every word that fancy can connect with independence'. Robert completely misread the signs; but it did Mrs Dunlop no credit that such misfortunes as the death of little Elizabeth and Robert's own prolonged periods of serious illness elicited no sympathetic response. Robert's 'mother-confessor' proved to be nothing more than an unforgiving old busybody, conscious of the barriers of class and rank to the last.[4]

The undated letter which referred to Keith Dunlop's godfather, previously quoted, has not had a date assigned to it by Ferguson or Roy, but its insertion in the Oxford editions of the poet's letters implies a tentative date in August or September 1795. I would argue for an earlier date, probably in April or early May, as it was despatched with a copy of 'The Dumfries Volunteers' (CW 537–8). Although the circumstances of this poem were not mentioned in the letter, the action which Robert had taken ought, in itself, to have mollified the stern, unbending Mrs Dunlop.

During 1794 the ragged sansculottes of the French armies were everywhere triumphant and the Allies were retreating in disarray. Opinion had hardened against the Revolutionaries as news of their excesses filtered out of France. The atrocities and mass executions of the Terror were widely reported; but what united Britain against the foe more than anything else was the declaration by the Convention that no quarter would be given to prisoners. When some British cavalrymen were captured and publicly guillotined, any residual sympathy for France evaporated overnight. The year ended with the dramatic capture of the Dutch fleet, frozen in at Texel, by a squadron of French hussars. The British contingent, led by 'the grand old Duke of York', had been ignominiously chased out of Flanders. As 1795 opened, Austria, Prussia and Spain sued for peace and Britain braced itself for a French invasion. William Pitt called upon able-bodied citizens to take up arms in defence of their country. In addition to the regular army engaged in the overseas campaigns, and the fencible regiments which had been raised for home defence, Britain now had a part-time force consisting of regiments and companies of volunteers who turned out two or three times a week to drill and learn the rudiments of musketry. They were commanded by officers long past the normal retirement age, the junior officers were drawn from the county gentry, and even the NCOs and privates were usually men of some standing in the community. Henry Dundas, then Secretary of War in Pitt's Cabinet, refused a commission and was content to serve in the Edinburgh Volunteers as a private.

That the Volunteers were regarded as an élite force, very choosy about whom they admitted to their ranks, is shown by a comment by Allan Cunningham, that Robert's admission was 'not without opposition from some of the haughty Tories, who demurred about his principles'.[5] Although the Loyal Natives flocked to join the Volunteers, from the outset several of their political opponents were members. These had been named in a doggerel rhyme composed by one of the Natives:

> Ye Sons of Sedition, give ear to my song;
> Let Syme, Burns and Maxwell pervade every throng,
> With Craken, the attorney, and Mundell, the quack,
> Send Willie, the monger, to hell with a smack.

This provoked Robert to write 'Ye true Loyal Natives' (CW 515) as a contemptuous riposte. To consign William Pitt to hell was one thing; the taunt of sedition was much more serious. Hence, when the opportunity arose to affirm their loyalty to the British constitution, Burns and his friends were prompt to rally to the flag. John Syme, Robert's closest friend in Dumfries, was inevitably linked with him in the demonology of the Loyal Natives; but what of the others singled out for this poetic taunt?

William Maxwell (1760–1834) came from an old Catholic family in the Stewartry and was the second son of James Maxwell of Kirkconnell near New Abbey, across the Nith estuary from Dumfries. James was not just a Jacobite by sentiment; he was one of the few gentlemen of south-west Scotland who actually took part in the rebellion of 1745–6 and was exiled for his pains. Through the intercession of the Craiks of Arbigland, however, he was allowed to return to Scotland, and regained his estates in 1753. His son William was educated at the Jesuit college at Dinant and trained at Edinburgh as a doctor. While completing his studies in Paris, Dr Maxwell espoused the Republican cause and was a member of the National Guard present at the execution of Louis XVI. Afterwards a *canard* circulated that Maxwell had dipped his handkerchief in the blood of the decapitated king; although this story had no foundation it stuck with him till the end of his life. William was still in Paris when, on 1 February 1793, France declared war on Britain. He abandoned his uniform and made his way to one of the Channel ports whence he sailed early in March back to England. As early as 5 March he was singled out in an anti-Gallican pamphlet as 'the noted Dr Maxwell' who had been detained aboard a ship at Dover for interrogation for several hours before being permitted to land.[6] The very next day Maxwell wrote to Edmund Burke to complain about a slanderous speech which he had made in the House of Commons, accusing Maxwell of trying to purchase daggers in Birmingham to send to the French the previous year. In the tale of the 'Birmingham Daggers' we find a curious echo of the 'Rosamond Carronades' story. In fact, Maxwell's mission on behalf of the National Assembly in September 1792 to purchase arms was well documented. William was actually in London on 7 September 1792 when he advertised in the London newspapers a meeting at his house in Great Portland Street for the purpose of raising money from sympathisers in the cause of liberty. On 10 September he was in Birmingham where he placed an order for 'two to three thousand daggers at a price of a guinea a dozen'.[7] On 16 March 1794, however, the *Morning Post* reported that Dr Maxwell had had an interview with Burke who found that the good doctor was not the revolutionary firebrand he had been made out. Nevertheless, in the period between the fall of the Bastille and the outbreak of war in February 1793, Dr Maxwell had been more concerned with politics than the practice of medicine. He knew Tom Paine, Horne Tooke and other English radicals and had a hand in the formation of the radical London Corresponding Society in 1792; but he was also well connected with the most prominent Jacobins and the leaders of the Legislative Assembly in Paris. After war broke out, however, he was resigned to settling in Britain somewhere. At first he thought of obtaining a medical practice in London, but that fell through. Later he lived with relatives in Aberdeenshire before returning to Kirkconnell. In all this period he lived the life of a country gentleman, only occasionally, and in emergencies, giving medical treatment.[8]

By the end of 1793 William was domiciled at Kirkconnell but occasionally giving assistance to Dr John Gilchrist who was then the leading physician in Dumfries. In September 1794 Gilchrist was treating sixteen-year-old Jessie Staig, daughter of the Provost, and had given her no more than a few hours to live. At that point Maxwell was called in and his prescriptions wrought a dramatic improvement and eventually cured her. Robert recounted this incident to Mrs Dunlop (CL 211) adding:

> Maxwell is my most intimate friend, & one of the first [i.e. finest] characters I ever met; but on account of his Politics is rather shunned by some high Aristocrates, though his Family & Fortune entitled him to the first circles.

He enclosed an epigram composed on that occasion, 'Maxwell, if merit here you crave' (CW 519). Gilchrist introduced Maxwell to Dr James Mundell, a former naval surgeon who had retired to his ancestral home. The Mundell family hailed from Closeburn and it was in this neighbourhood that James settled for a time after leaving the Royal Navy. It was here that Mundell made the acquaintance of Burns while he was in temporary residence at the Isle in 1788. A short note (CL 485) was sent to Mundell at that time, while a second, delivered by a servant named Janet Nievison, was dated January 1790. By that time Dr Mundell was in practice in Dumfries itself. Mundell attended the Burns family there until 1794 when he was superseded by Dr Maxwell. Mundell was listed by Burns as one of the subscribers to Anderson's *Bee*, indicating that he shared the poet's radical politics.

Lumped with 'Mundell the quack' was 'Craken the attorney', in fact William McCracken (1757-1818). Professionally McCracken was embroiled with John Syme in the tangled legal affairs of James Maxwell of Kirkconnell, son of the Jacobite and elder brother of William. This, in itself, was quite sufficient for the Loyal Natives to brand McCracken as a 'Jacobin', just as people remotely connected with American radicals were branded as 'Commies' in the McCarthy era. Significantly, McCracken was one of the founder members of the Royal Dumfries Volunteers and served as secretary of its management committee.

To be sure, the membership of the Loyal Natives and the muster roll of the Volunteers were pretty well synonymous; but the Volunteers also included prominent Whigs, liberals and radicals who were eager to prove their patriotism. Indeed, some biographers have accused Robert of political opportunism, alleging that he only joined the Volunteers to deflect opprobrium. In support of this, they contended that he merely paid lip-service to the Volunteer movement and played no active part – a despicable *canard* which was destroyed when the minute-book of the Volunteers was discovered more than a century later.

At the first meeting on 31 January 1795, the founder members included Provost David Staig and his two bailies, as well as the leading professional and business men of the town. Among their names were staunch conservatives such as Wellwood Maxwell and George Duncan (cousin of the poet's biographer James Currie). But also prominent in the inaugural list were John Syme of Ryedale, Dr James Mundell and Robert Burns. Among the founder members we recognise the names of many men associated in some way with the poet: Thomas White of the Academy, Captain John Hamilton of Allershaw, the poet's landlord, William Hyslop of the Globe Inn, the banker James Gracie of 'Gracie, thou art a man of worth' (CW 420), the lawyer David Newall who had lent Robert his summer-house at the Isle, Samuel Clark and David Williamson, the tailor who supplied the Volunteers with their uniforms. Among those who enlisted at the second meeting, on 3 February, bringing the number of Volunteers to sixty-three, were John McMurdo of Drumlanrig, Alexander Findlater and John Lewars of the Excise, the lawyer William Thomson and Thomas Boyd who built Ellisland farmhouse. Another new member was the town clerk, Francis Shortt, secretary and 'poet-laureate' of the Loyal Natives who had composed the lampoon against Burns and his friends.[9] The one name conspicuous by its absence was William Maxwell.

These gentlemen signed a declaration by which they undertook to serve 'during the present war, without pay, and find our own clothing'. This interesting document, embodying the conditions of service and regulations of the corps, was anonymous, but it has been suggested that Robert had a hand in its composition. Clause 12 described the uniform: a blue coat half-lapelled with red cape and cuffs and gilt buttons with RDV engraved on them, a plain white cassimere vest with small gilt buttons, white trousers of Russia tweeling, tied at the ankle, white stockings, a black velvet stock, a round hat turned up on the left side with a gilt button, a cockade and a black feather, and black shoes tied with black ribbon. The only distinction between the officers and privates in point of dress was that the Major Commandant and the two captains wore two epaulettes, while the lieutenants wore only one and the privates none. Messrs Williamson, Rae and Johnston purchased hats at sixteen shillings each and undertook to supply uniforms to their fellow members. On 20 February 1795 the Volunteers met and declared unanimously that Colonel Arent Schuyler De Peyster should be their Major Commandant. Born in New York in 1736 of Dutch-Huguenot descent, De Peyster spent his boyhood in Holland and Britain before obtaining a commission in the 50th Foot in 1755. In an active military career spanning forty years, he served in Germany during the Seven Years War (1756–63) and in Canada (1768–85), latterly as military administrator of the Great Lakes area with the rank of colonel. From 1787 till his retirement in 1794 he served in England and Ireland. De Peyster married Rebecca Blair, daughter of Provost David Blair of Dumfries and sister of Jane Blair, John McMurdo's wife. McMurdo's daughter Arentina was named in his honour. In April 1794 De Peyster retired from the army and purchased the estate of Mavis Grove on the west bank of the Nith, three miles from Dumfries, though he also had a town house at 75 Irish Street (in more recent years the British Legion Club, but subsequently derelict).

Robert was a frequent visitor at Mavis Grove, having been introduced to De Peyster by McMurdo soon after the colonel settled there. During the winter of 1795-6 Robert was seriously ill and confined to his bed. When De Peyster wrote enquiring about his health, Robert was well enough to send a verse-epistle in January 1796 beginning 'My honor'd Colonel, deep I feel / Your interest in the Poet's weal' (CW 564-5). De Peyster was something of a poet himself, and in 1813 published a collection of verse under the title *Miscellanies by an Officer*. He had a vigorous, active life right up to the end, and died in November 1822 at the ripe old age of eighty-six.[10]

On 21 February 1795 the Volunteers elected their captains and lieutenants. John Hamilton was voted first captain and John Finnan second captain. David Newall and Wellwood Maxwell were elected first lieutenants, while Francis Shortt and Thomas White were elected second lieutenants, the commissions being gazetted by the War Office on 24 March. After the officers had been elected, the would-be Volunteers adjourned to the Assembly Rooms to ballot on who should, and who should not, be admitted to membership. This was no mere formality, as the Corps minute-book reveals. Applications had to be vetted by the Committee of Management, and it was this process which led Allan Cunningham to assert that Robert's admission to the corps was opposed by some of the Tories. In fact, although the minutes show a measure of disagreement and acrimony in regard to some candidates, no objection was raised in respect of Burns, thus refuting the statement of 'Honest Allan'.[11]

The two captains then drew the names of the men who were to serve under them, and to John Finnan of the Second Company fell the honour of drawing the name of Robert Burns. With him in this company were his great friends Dr John Harley, John Syme, James Gracie and John Lewars. On 28 March Robert mustered with fifty-seven others to take the Oath of Allegiance and sign the rules and regulations of the corps.

The Volunteers drilled several times a week in the Dock Park and also engaged in target practice. Allan Cunningham published a fanciful, if inaccurate, description of the Volunteers:

> I remember well the appearance of that respectable corps; their odd, but not ungraceful dress; white kerseymere breeches and waistcoat; short blue coat, faced with red; and round hat, surmounted by a bearskin, like the helmets of our Horse-guards; and I remember the Poet also – his very swarthy face, his ploughman-stoop, his large dark eyes, and indifferent dexterity in the handling of his arms.[12]

Cunningham added erroneously that William Maxwell joined with Syme and Burns, but this is not confirmed by the records of the Volunteers.

The diaries of William Grierson, now preserved in the Dumfries Burgh Museum, contain numerous references to the Volunteers. Grierson

(1773–1852) was not himself a member but one of his favourite recreations was to stroll down to the dock and watch the Volunteers drilling.[13] He missed the inaugural public parade on 26 March, being troubled by tooth-ache all that day. On 17 April he noted, 'Evening went to the Dock to see the Volunteers go through their Exercises. Not very proficient yet'. On 12 May he recorded, 'This day the Volunteers drum beat for the first time'. On Friday 22 May Grierson noted, 'Evening, went to the Dock and saw the Volunteers fire. Grant's Fencibles were likewise drawn up, and made a very fine appearance, there being about 700 of them'.

On 4 June, the king's birthday, a grand military parade was held at midday. The Volunteers were drawn up in the centre of Queensberry Square with the Highland Fencibles on all four sides:

> Mrs De Peyster came forward attended by about 19 ladies and presented to the Volunteers a pair of Colours which she made them a present of. Dr Burnside at the same time consecrated the colours. After that the Volunteers marched from the centre of the Fencibles till near the place where they were drawn up and fired three rounds and were answered each time by the Fencibles. Both the Volunteers and the Fencibles made a very fine appearance and fired remarkably well. The Volunteers dined together in the King's Arms and at six o' clock went with the Magistrates to the court house to drink His Majesty's health. There was none of the inhabitants invited to the Court House as was customary, which offended the people very much, it being such an old custom. After the presentation of the Colours, the Colonel addressed the Volunteers.

Grierson then appended the complete texts of Colonel De Peyster's speech and Dr Burnside's sermon.

The Duke of Portland, then Home Secretary, granted the Dumfries Volunteers £1 12s 10d for each firelock and 3s 4d for each set of accoutrements, leaving it to the men to provide themselves with uniforms. The Management Committee (who included Gracie, Syme, McCracken and Findlater as well as the officers) decided on 18 May to solicit funds from the public. Robert was the author of a petition sent to the commanding officer the very same day (CL 720) and signed by twenty-four members, including himself. Apart from the style of this letter, the theme was one close to Robert's heart:

> That our Secretary should have waited on those Gentlemen and others of that rank of life, who from the first, offered pecuniary assistance, meets our idea as highly proper but that the Royal Dumfries Volunteers should go a begging, with the burnt out Cottager and Ship-wrecked Sailor, is a measure of which we must disapprove.
>
> Please then, Sir, to call a meeting as soon as possible, and be so very good also as to put a stop to the degrading business, until the voice of the Corps be heard.

On this occasion, however, Robert was overruled, for advertisements subsequently appeared in the *Dumfries Weekly Journal* soliciting donations, and in due course lists of the donors, with the sums contributed, were also published. As a compromise, however, the Volunteers decided, on 29 May, to accept only subscriptions and donations of at least a guinea. At the first general meeting after this affair, on 22 August 1795, Robert was elected to the eight-man management committee. This is surely positive proof, if such were required, that Robert played an active part in the Volunteers and threw himself wholeheartedly into its activities. Furthermore, Robert's name features prominently in the attendance rolls, while it is conspicuously absent from the lists of fines and penalties for abstentions from parades and disciplinary offences. The discipline of the Volunteers was far more rigorous than that of the Kirk: privates and officers were fined without distinction or favour and the regulations of the corps strictly upheld. Interestingly, among the names of the defaulters we find Captain Hamilton and Lieutenant Shortt, who on 24 August were fined 2s 6d and 7s 6d respectively for being absent from parades.

The minute book of the Volunteers also exposes Dr Currie's error in stating of Burns that 'from October 1795, to the January following, an accidental complaint confined him to the house'. Robert attended a meeting of the Committee on 5 November and helped to draft a loyal address to the king after he had escaped an assassination attempt the previous month:

> Most Gracious Sovereign, – We, your Majesty's most dutiful and loyal subjects, composing the Corps of the Royal Dumfries Volunteers, penetrated by the recent and signal interposition of Divine Providence in the preservation of your most sacred person from the atrocious attempt of a set of lawless ruffians, humbly hope that your Majesty will graciously receive our unfeigned congratulations.
>
> Permitted by you, Sire, to embody ourselves for the preservation of social tranquillity, we are filled with indignation at every attempt made to shake the venerable and, we trust, lasting fabric of British Liberty.

This was Robert's last effort as a member of the committee; there is some irony in the fact that the last public act of the man who wrote those anti-Hanoverian lines at Stirling Castle should have been to help prepare this loyal address.

Few volunteer units of this period are so well documented as the Royal Dumfries Volunteers, thanks to the survival of the corps minute-book which passed from the De Peyster family to the Ewart Library in 1918. The discovery of this volume, almost a century and a quarter after the poet's death, shed valuable light on the last year of Robert's life and helped to expose the myth of 'drunkenness and dissipation', first propounded by Heron in 1797 and more recently and recklessly upheld by Henley in 1896 and Carswell in 1930. In the period up to 1918 Robert's service in the Volunteers was either ignored altogether by his biographers, or mentioned only in passing when his stirring patriotic song 'Does haughty Gaul invasion threat?' (CW 537-8) was quoted. The song that has immortalised the

Dumfries Volunteers was probably composed in the middle of April 1795. A dinner for the Volunteers was held at this time, celebrating the anniversary of Lord Rodney's naval victory over the French on 12 April 1782 which restored national pride in the closing phase of the American War. Two years earlier, at a similar commemoration in the King's Arms, Robert had composed the toast beginning 'Instead of a song, boys' (CW 484) which was published shortly afterwards in the *Dumfries Advertiser*. At the 1795 celebration Robert, as was customary, was called upon to propose a toast. On this occasion, he is said to have startled his fellow-diners with the words, 'Gentlemen, may we never see the French, nor the French see us'. Considering that the Volunteers had been raised purely for home defence, these words seem not unreasonable; nevertheless

> most of the Volunteers dropped to their seats 'like so many old wives at a field-preaching' – but not a few 'raxed their jaws' at the homely truth and humour of the poet's sentiment.[14]

Once more Robert's mouth seemed to get him into trouble. Allan Cunningham's version of the story accords with Hogg's:

> The Poet had been at a public meeting where he was less joyous than usual; as something had been expected from him, he made these verses when he went home, and sent them with his compliments to Mr Jackson, editor of the *Dumfries Journal*.[15]

Robert's organist friend Stephen Clarke set the words to music. The song first appeared in the *Edinburgh Evening Courant* of 4 May and the *Dumfries Journal* of 5 May, and was quickly copied by other newspapers and periodicals, including the *Caledonian Mercury* and the *Scots Magazine*. According to Cunningham the invasion song caught the popular imagination:

> Hills echoed with it; it was heard in every street, and did more to right the mind of the rustic part of the population than all the speeches of Pitt and Dundas, or the chosen Five-and-Forty.[16]

Indeed, it was more popular in its heyday than 'Scots wha hae' which was later adopted as Scotland's national anthem. The parallels between the song of 1795 and Claude Joseph Rouget de Lisle's song of the Army of the Rhine composed in April 1792 are startling. Of the latter, both words and music were written in a fit of patriotic excitement after a public dinner at Strasbourg where Captain Rouget de Lisle (who was the same age as Burns) was stationed. It only acquired its more familiar name of 'La Marseillaise' when it was adopted as the marching song of the volunteers from that seaport, brought into Paris to lead the assault of the extreme left on the Tuileries which took place on 20 June 1792. Incidentally, the army engineer turned composer of the French national anthem was only a moderate republican, and was later cashiered and imprisoned for his too reasonable views. Freed at the counter-revolution of 1795, he was vindi-cated when his song was adopted as the French national anthem.

At the time Robert was joining the Volunteers he was working harder than ever in the service of the Excise. Although Acting Supervisor, he con-tinued at first to draw his normal salary. The practice of the period was that the salary of the officer who was off sick for a few days continued so long as someone could be found to deputise at no additional cost. In the case of prolonged periods of illness, however, the salary was halved and a commensurate payment made to the stand-in. The unfairness of this system was mitigated on the grounds that it gave ambitious young officers an opportunity to show their mettle, with the hope that their devotion to duty would be rewarded by promotion in due course. Several of Robert's letters testify to the enormous additional burden thrust upon him as he tried to cope with Findlater's duties. Fortunately, some fragments of Robert's official diary has survived from this period, so we have a graphic record of exactly how hard he was working.

The first entry, for 23 December 1794, shows that Robert visited the Sanquhar division, the most northerly in the district. The working day began at five o'clock in the morning and went on till seven o'clock at night. During this fourteen-hour period Robert visited twelve victuallers, a tanner, a maltster, a chandler and nine tea and tobacco dealers, riding seventeen miles round the Sanquhar area. At the victuallers he took numerous gauges as well as a 'charge' – dipping the amount brewed to cal-culate the duty payable. At the tanner he counted the 'depending stock' of hides and skins which were dry and ready for sale but had not yet been stamped with the Excise seal. Sealing was not normally completed until the hides had been sold, and supervisors and officers had to 'tell over such stocks as often as possible, in order to discover whether it be decreased by goods privately taken out'.[17] The Exciseman at Sanquhar was James Graham, regarded as a 'middling' officer; but on this occasion his work and his books passed Robert's scrutiny as the latter merely noted, 'Saw nothing in the books meriting report'.

On Christmas Eve Robert was up well before dawn and riding south-wards to Thornhill at the centre of his old station, the Dumfries First Itinerary. By eight o'clock he was making his first calls there, on two victu-allers and a tanner. This day was taken up with a forty-mile tour of his old haunts, with visits to twenty victuallers and dealers in Penpont, Cairnmill, Tynron, Crossford and Dunscore, before he headed for Dumfries. At eleven o'clock that night – sixteen hours after leaving Whigham's Inn at Sanquhar – he reached his own front-door, cold and exhausted. James Hossack, the riding officer in upper Nithsdale, had only recently returned to duty after a period of suspension, so Robert paid particularly close attention to his work, but added 'nothing to report'.

In Dumfries itself John Lewars deputised for Robert, while Adam Stobie, a young expectant, stood in for Lewars. Robert now checked the town divisions, paying two visits to a common brewer, 'taking off worts – length as usual'. As these visits were taken on consecutive evenings,

Robert was relatively free during the daytime to catch up with the complicated paperwork. In the Dumfries Third Itinerary, which stretched south and east of Dumfries, Robert surveyed a papermaker at Park which entailed checking several different types of paper, each of which attracted a specific rate of duty. Ironically, the only division where Robert made adverse comment was that in which Leonard Smith officiated. He had recently been suspended from duty and since reinstatement had spent time in various Dumfries divisions covering for other officers. When checking a maltster Robert discovered that Smith had made some minor errors during his last survey and on scrutinising the books he found 'several other instances of the like nature'. The long hours on Christmas Eve were not exceptional by any means. On 17 January 1795 Robert was in the saddle from five in the morning till eight at night; on the following day he worked from seven in the morning till four in the afternoon; on 19 February from seven till six and on 23 February from five in the morning till seven in the evening. This was no eight-hour day, five-day week job. The Supervisor was on call seven days a week and at all hours of the day and night. Nor was the work of a kind that could be performed by an unintelligent man. On the contrary, it demanded considerable personal skills in dealing with both subordinate officers and often hostile traders and manufacturers. Above all, it required a high level of numeracy and a very orderly mind in keeping the elaborate set of books which were regularly examined for even the slightest irregularity, and which had to make clear every transaction.

The diary entries were subsequently initialled by Collector Mitchell who added his own report to the Excise Board:

> This diary includes 42 days, and this employed 29 surveying and transcribing diary, and so on. Mr Burns has been in every division in the district this round, and on the 5th January in two. He has very uniformly attended to charging candle and leather and taking off worts, as he has to the examination of books. Being his first effort, it would be doing him injustice not to mention that he appears, from the work of this diary, to have gone into the spirit of the duty entrusted to him.[18]

The period when Robert acted as Supervisor coincided with some of the worst winter weather ever recorded in Scotland. In Dumfries during the whole of January daytime temperatures seldom rose above freezing and the sport of curling enjoyed an unprecedented boom. The very cold weather continued the following month but on 6 February there was excessively heavy snow, followed by sleet, rain, thick fog and further snow which spread in blizzards of ferocious intensity over the ensuing four days. It was such a snowfall as no living man remembered. Most people found, on the morning of 7 February, that their houses were buried up to the windows of the upper storey. In the hollows of the Campsie Fells, near Glasgow, the snow drifted to depths of from eighty to a hundred feet. In the rural parts of Dumfriesshire the snow lay in drifts up to thirty feet deep and Robert, who had gone to Ecclefechan that day, was trapped. Snows 'of ten feet deep have impeded my progress' he told Thomson (CL 671), 'but the same obstacle has shut me up within insuperable bars'. On 12 February snow began falling early in the morning but afterwards froze hard. On Friday 13 upwards of thirty labourers were employed clearing the icebergs in the Nith that cluttered the bridges and the Whitesands. A severe storm broke on 18 February, the day of Candlemas Fair, with the result that trade was very poor. Many people were injured through falls on the icy streets. Heavy frosts, accompanied by snow, continued until the middle of March, but some roads were impassable for weeks and even in the streets of Edinburgh the snow had not entirely disappeared on the king's birthday.[19] The rigours of the work and exposure to such appalling weather must have taken their toll on Robert's constitution. No previous biographer has realised the arduousness of the work performed by Robert in this four-month period, coupled with the unparalleled ferocity of the weather at that time, and consequently its significance in the remainder of his life has never been appreciated; but it is a stark and incontrovertible fact that Robert's health deteriorated from this point onwards, and successive ailments and bouts of illness that assailed him from May 1795 onwards had a deadly cumulative effect.

At first it was expected that Findlater would soon be fully recovered and back at work in a matter of days rather than weeks; but it was not until late April that he returned to duty. This much we can glean from a letter which Robert wrote on 25 April to John Edgar, the Accountant to the Excise Board (CL 718). The latter had taken Robert to task for being late in sending in the Wine Account for the district. This was due to a combination of circumstances, one of which was that Findlater had only just returned to duty as Supervisor and Robert had assumed that he was dealing with the matter. On being informed by Mitchell that the task fell to him, Robert immediately set about it, but was delayed by James Graham having omitted to send him the Sanquhar wine books. Robert had written to Graham asking him to send the books by first post, but Graham had ignored the request:

> This, Sir, is a plain state of Facts; & if I must still be thought censurable, I hope it will be considered, that this Officiating Job being my first, I cannot be supposed to be completely master of all the etiquette of the business. If my supposed neglect is to be laid before the Honorable Board, I beg you will have the goodness to accompany the complaint with this letter.

Edgar was probably surprised at Robert's reaction; the transgression – if such it was – was so insignificant as not to merit further notice; but the tone of Robert's letter shows how anxious he was to avoid even the slightest admonition.

For four months' duty as Acting Supervisor Robert was granted the paltry sum of £12 above his normal salary. Small wonder, therefore, that he became disillusioned with the work. When Patrick Heron hinted that

he might be able to use his influence with his connections in Edinburgh
Robert replied (CL 715–16) that promotion to Supervisor was in strict
order of precedence, although the help of a friendly patron would be useful
in securing a lucrative station:

> A supervisor's income varies from about a hundred and twenty, to two
> hundred a year; but the business is incessant drudgery, and would be
> nearly a compleat bar to every species of literary pursuit.

Once he became a Supervisor, however, Robert would automatically go on
the Collectors' List. A Collector's salary ranged from £200 to almost
£1,000 and besides a handsome income Collectors had a 'life of compleat
leisure'.

> A life of literary leisure with a decent competence, is the summit of my
> wishes. It would be the prudish affectation of silly pride in me to say that
> I do not need, or would not be indebted to a political friend; at the same
> time, Sir, I by no means lay my affairs before you thus, to hook my depen-
> dant situation on your benevolence.

It is idle to speculate on what might have been, had Robert's health not
given way. In May 1795 George Thomson heard a rumour that Robert was
about to be transferred to the highly lucrative Port of Leith Division,
which suggests that Patrick Heron had been exerting himself on the poet's
behalf, but it was just a rumour. Robert replied (CL 674), 'As to what you
hint of my coming to Edinburgh, I know of no such arrangement'. A year
later, however, Graham of Fintry was apparently working on such a transfer, but Burns's untimely death prevented this from being realised.

Heron had every reason to be grateful to Robert, for he played a not
insignificant part in the election campaign of the spring of 1795. In
January that year General Stewart, long-time MP for the Stewartry of
Kirkcudbright, died. A writ for a by-election was issued the following
month to Lord Garlies, son of the Earl of Galloway, but he had used the
great storm that ravaged the south-west of Scotland in February as an
excuse to delay the election till the weather was more propitious. The
delay, however, also precipitated an outbreak of election fever without parallel since the notorious general election of 1790 when no fewer than six
men were convicted for vote-rigging in Dumfries. The Earl of Galloway
and the Tory faction threw their weight behind Thomas Gordon of
Balmaghie, nephew of James Murray of Broughton (1727–99), one of the
wealthiest landowners in the south of Scotland and MP for neighbouring
Wigtownshire. Although Murray took his title from his estate in Peeblesshire, his principal residence was Cally House near Gatehouse. Murray was
a profligate old roué who had deserted his wife, Lady Catherine Stewart,
and eloped with his niece, Grace Johnston. His immense wealth and political influence enabled him to flout convention with impunity, and his
immoral behaviour in no way affected his political association with his

wife's family, one of whose close relatives he was supporting in the election.

The Whigs backed Patrick Heron. Burns could not stand idly by in a contest marred by a Tory 'dirty tricks' campaign that sought to smear Heron by raising the spectre of the failed Ayr Bank. Robert had a genuine affection and regard for Patrick Heron whom he sincerely believed to be a man of great personal integrity; besides, his political outlook was very similar to the poet's. Robert had nothing against Gordon of Balmaghie personally, but he represented a baneful power that was immoral and corrupt and it took little encouragement for Robert to throw himself wholeheartedly into the fray. In rapid succession Robert composed three election ballads which enjoyed a wide circulation and played no small part in the defeat of the Tory candidate.

These ballads were printed locally and were eagerly perused not only by the select band of county electors but by the public at large. The first ballad (CW 543–4) was sung to the tune of 'A Man's a Man' and had the same refrain, 'For a' that and a' that' in the fifth line of each stanza. The sentiments were similar, Heron being characterised as 'The independent patriot, / The honest man, and a' that' (second stanza) and 'The independent commoner / Shall be the man for a' that' (third stanza). The fourth stanza echoed the song on which it was modelled, the line 'Wi ribban, star, and a' that' appearing twice to satirise the aristocracy.

The second ballad (CW 545–6) dealt with the election itself which was held in Kirkcudbright. In this ballad Robert concentrated on the personalities involved, the Tory supporters being mercilessly lampooned, while the Whigs were mentioned more favourably though not without the occasional sly dig. There was even an echo of the anti-clericalism of his Ayrshire days in Robert's taunts at the parish ministers of Urr and Buittle, James Muirhead (1742–1805) and George Maxwell (1762–1807). There were even more pointed references to these ministers in the third ballad, subtitled 'John Bushby's Lamentation' (CW 547–8), which Robert produced to celebrate Heron's victory:

> Whase haly priesthood nane could stain,
> For wha could dye the black?

Muirhead was something of a poet himself, and lashed out at his tormentor by rough translations of Martial's epigrams which he had printed at Edinburgh. One of these epigrams, a paraphrase of Martial's 'In Vacerram' (book XI, epigram 67) apostrophised Burns:

> For whisky; eke, most precious imp,
> Thou art a rhymester, gauger, pimp;
> Whence comes it, then, Vacerra, that
> Thou still art poor as a church-rat?

Alexander Young of Harburn, a Writer to the Signet, commented on this:

> It consists with my knowledge, that no publication in answer to the scur-
> rilities of Burns ever did him so much harm in public opinion, or made
> Burns himself feel so sore, as Dr Muirhead's translation of Martial's
> epigram. When I remonstrated with the doctor against his printing and
> circulating that translation, I asked him how he proved that Vacerras was
> a gauger as well as Burns. He answered: 'Martial calls him *fellator*, which
> means a *sucker*, or a man who drinks from the cask'.[20]

Anyone familiar with Martial's bawdry will, of course, realise that *fellator*
had the precise meaning which it enjoys to this day. Robert himself was
acquainted with Martial's epigrams through the translation by James
Elphinstone published in 1782, which he perused in Edinburgh in January
1788. Indeed, he composed an epigram of his own on Elphinstone's
translation (CW 270) which he sent to Mrs Dunlop (CL 130) and Mrs
McLehose (CL 382).

Young's comment on the election ballads as 'scurrilities' probably
reflected the perception of the upper classes regarding Robert's lampoons
and epigrams in general. The ordinary public, however, chuckled at
Robert's savage barbs. Redcastle, who drew his sword 'ne'er stained wi
gore' alluded to Walter Sloan Lawrie who had taken part in the ignomini-
ous rout at the battle of Bunker's Hill. Ever afterwards, the laird of Redcastle was habitually jeered by the mob who followed him in the streets
with cries of 'Bunker's Hill! Bunker's Hill!' Even Robert's jibes at fellow-
Whigs may not always have been accepted with good graces. The Douglas
brothers might have been mildly amused by the couplet in the second
ballad about 'Douglasses doughty, / New christening towns far and near',
but Robert surely went too far in the third ballad with the quatrain:

> But Douglasses o weight had we,
> The pair o lusty lairds,
> For building cot-houses sae fam'd,
> And christenin kail-yards.

In the second ballad Robert focused his merciless attention on 'wealthy
young Richard' Oswald, Younger of Auchencruive (1771–1841), the great-
nephew of that poor old lady whose funeral cortège had displaced him from
Whigham's inn at Sanquhar and provoked the savagely satirical 'Ode,
sacred to the memory of Mrs Oswald' (CW 342–3). In the ballad young
Oswald was dismissed with:

> But for prodigal thriftless bestowing,
> His merit had won him respect.

This is oddly at variance with Robert's praise of Oswald in the only extant
letter written by him to Syme (CL 708–9). Though undated, this letter has
been tentatively ascribed to May 1795. A letter of 23 April that year to an

unnamed correspondent (CL 717) was assigned to Richard Oswald by Chambers who first published it in 1851. This letter accompanied some unspecified verses which may have been 'Does haughty Gaul invasion threat?', for Robert went on:

> In these days of volunteering, I have come forward with my services, as poet-laureate to a highly respectable political party, of which you are a distinguished member. The enclosed are, I hope, only a beginning to the songs of triumph which you will earn in that contest.

Richard's wife Louisa 'Lucy' Johnstone of Hilton was eleven years older than him, but a celebrated beauty whom he married in 1793. The following year the Oswalds moved to Cavens, thirteen miles south-west of Dumfries, and it was then that Burns made their acquaintance. In May 1795 Robert modified 'O wat ye wha's in yon town?' (CW 541), which had originally been written for Jean Lorimer, substituting 'Lucy' for 'Jean' and sending the new version to Mrs Oswald. Lucy gave Robert her lugubrious melody entitled 'Captain Cook's Death' which he originally used for 'Thou Lingering Star' (CW 372) before settling on 'Mary's Dream' instead. Lucy Oswald went abroad for her health's sake, but died in Lisbon in 1797 of pulmonary tuberculosis.

Robert's epigrams, many of them assiduously collected by John Syme (CW 532–4), date mainly from this period and, like the election ballads, were scarcely calculated to endear the poet to influential people like Commissary Thomas Goldie, William Copland of Collieston, Captain William Roddick of Corbieton, William Graham of Mossknowe and, above all, the powerful Bushby family. John Bushby, a Dumfries lawyer and sheriff-clerk, had formerly been a partner of Douglas, Heron and Company, and manager of the Dumfries branch of the ill-fated bank. His brother William, the 'gamesome billie' of the third Heron election ballad, was alleged to have absconded with some of the bank's funds and used it to build a fortune in India. John Bushby was not unduly concerned by these lampoons, though he observed 'that he could not conceive why the poor devil [Burns] had thought proper to run a muck against all those who could best do him a service, and none of whom as far as he knew, held him at ill will'. The story goes that Burns and Bushby, at one time good friends, were estranged on account of a silly practical joke played by Bushby, while he was entertaining the poet to dinner at Tinwald Downs, his country house. Bushby pretended that the pudding was cold and Robert badly scalded his mouth when he took a hearty bite.[21]

Parliament was dissolved in May 1796 and a general election was held the following month. This prompted Robert to write his fourth Heron election ballad, subtitled 'The Trogger' (CW 549). His old adversaries, Murray of Broughton, Gordon of Balmaghie, Maxwell of Cardoness, the ministers of Buittle and Urr, the lairds of Collieston and Redcastle and, of course, John Bushby, were targeted yet again. On this occasion Heron's Tory opponent was Montgomery Stewart, younger son of the Earl of Galloway.

Oddly enough, neither the Earl (who had been savaged in previous epigrams) nor his son, the unsuccessful candidate, were mentioned in the poem. This time Robert used rhyming couplets to recite the supposed wares of a trogger or pedlar and the satire was even more bitter than before, reflecting Robert's state of health at the time. Heron was duly re-elected, but the poet did not live to see the event.

As 1795 progressed, Robert's friendship with Maria Riddell was gradually rekindled. Between March and the end of the year at least seven letters (CL 608–11) passed from Robert to Maria, enclosing a number of poems and songs. In the first of these letters Robert mentioned that he was at that moment sitting for a portrait miniature which was being painted by Alexander Reid:

> I think he has hit by far the best likeness of me ever was taken.– When you are at any time so idle, in town, as to call at Reid's painting-room, & mention to him that I spoke of such a thing to you, he will shew it you; else, he will not; for both the Miniature's existence & its destiny, are an inviolable secret, & therefore very properly trusted in part *to you*.

Some time later, however, Robert met Maria's servant, Mrs Scott, in the street and, having the miniature in his pocket, sent it by hand of this woman to Maria with a brief note. By now he had changed his mind about the portrait: 'The painter, in my opinion, has spoilt the likeness'. Perhaps his jaundiced view was coloured by his state of health: 'I am so ill as to be scarce able to hold this miserable pen to this miserable paper'.

He was in very low spirits when he wrote these words, but by the time he wrote to George Thomson in May (CL 673–4) he was in an ebullient mood. Thomson, feeling guilty about the amount of sterling material he was receiving from the poet at no cost, hit upon a charming way to show his appreciation. He had commissioned David Allan (1744–96) 'the Scottish Hogarth' to do some illustrations for the *Select Collection* and in due course despatched Allan's painting of 'The Cotter's Saturday Night' to Robert. The artist had cleverly worked Robert's portrait into the group and he was suitably flattered by the excellent likeness, derived from the Nasmyth bust-portrait:

> My phiz is *sae kenspeckle*, that the very joiner's apprentice whom Mrs Burns employed to break up the parcel (I was out of town that day) knew it at once.

And he was amused by the rascally figure of the little boy in the picture chasing the cat's tail:

> the most striking likeness of an ill-deedie, damn'd, wee, rumble-gairie hurchin of mine, whom, from that propensity to witty wickedness & manfu' mischief, which, even at twa days auld I foresaw would form the striking features of his disposition, I named Willie Nicol; after a certain Friend of mine, who is one of the Masters of a Grammar-school in a city which shall be nameless.

Robert and his friends considered Allan's likeness more striking than Nasmyth's; but he then went on to mention 'an artist of very considerable merit, just now in this town, who has hit the most remarkable likeness of what I am at this moment, that I think ever was taken of any body'. Robert's conflicting opinion of Reid's work, together with the mystery surrounding the miniature and for whom it was painted, led scholars to suppose that Reid had produced *two* miniatures. Not until DeLancey Ferguson collated the complete letter to Thomson in the late 1920s was this confusion cleared up. The subsequent history of the miniature is unknown prior to 1885 when it turned up in the collection of William F. Watson, acquired the following year by the Scottish National Portrait Gallery. There is a rumour – it is no stronger than that – that Jean Armour also sat to Reid; but no miniature identified as her portrait has ever been found.

The illness which made Burns feel so miserable at this time may have been severe rheumatism brought on by the rigours of the winter, but was probably toothache. Unfortunately, very few of Robert's letters written in 1795 actually bear a date, so that a proper chronological sequence is impossible. Two undated letters, written about mid-summer, refer to the excruciating pain Robert was then enduring. To Peter Hill he wrote enclosing no fewer than eighteen poems and epigrams (CL 324-5) – and then apologised for not writing a longer letter, because:

> at present the delightful sensations of an omnipotent TOOTH–ACH so engross all my inner man, as to put it out of my power to write Nonsense.

The enclosed epigrams were:

> mostly ill-natured, so they are in unison with my present feelings while fifty troops of infernal Spirits are riding post from ear to ear along my jaw-bones.

Even when racked with pain, Robert could still muster a wry sense of humour. Even when plagued with 'thou hell o a' diseases' Robert found some antidote in poetry, writing his 'Address to the Toothache' (CW 553) at this time. The agonies continued unabated for several weeks; to George Thomson on 3 July (CL 675) he sent 'Why, why tell thy lover' (CW 556) and 'O this is nae my ain lassie' (CW 558), concluding:

> I am at present quite occupied with the charming sensations of the TOOTH-ACH; so have not a word to spare.

Even more serious was the note sent to Maria in June or July:

> The health you wished me in your Morning's Card is I think flown from me for ever. I have not been able to leave my bed today, till about an hour ago.

But the muses had not quite forsaken him, for he sent her some lines beginning 'The trout in yonder wimpling stream' (CW 555), detached stanzas which he intended 'to interweave in some disastrous tale of a Shepherd despairing beside a clear stream'. The song was completed by 3 August. Poetry, as always, was a consolation and a powerful anodyne when mental or physical troubles assailed him.

During the summer of 1795 Robert was busy composing and revising works for both Thomson and Johnson, and most of his correspondence was taken up, directly or indirectly, with songs for their respective projects. There were also letters to old friends in Edinburgh, such as Alexander Cunningham and Robert Cleghorn, but the last dated letter of this period was written to the Birmingham gunsmith David Blair on 25 August (CL 504). Blair had presented Robert with a splendid pair of pistols in December 1788 as a token of esteem, and this began a desultory correspondence which culminated in March 1793 when Robert sent Blair a copy of the second Edinburgh Edition. In 1795 he sent Blair Lord Balmerino's dirk with a letter giving its provenance. Robert had received it from Dr Maxwell and thus it was fitting that, in the fulness of time, the case of pistols should be presented by Robert to his doctor as a dying gift. The dirk is now in the Tower at Mauchline while the pistols are in the Royal Museum of Scotland.

About August Robert wrote to Johnson (CL 301-2) 'without any apology for my laziness which indeed will admit of no apology' and got straight down to business, enclosing four new songs and comments on many others. He concluded this long letter with something completely different, a draft of a bill-head which he wished Johnson to produce for the Globe Inn:

> The Tavern-keeper, Hyslop, is a good honest fellow; & as I lie under particular obligations to him, I request that you may do it for him on the most reasonable terms . . .

Johnson designed a bill-head, with a reproduction of the globe in the centre, and sent a proof to Robert in due course for correction. Robert replied on 23 September:

> Mr Clarke will have acquainted you with the unfortunate reasons of my long silence.– When I get a little more health, you shall hear from me at large on the subject of the songs. –
> I am highly pleased with Hyslop's bills, only you have, in your usual luck, mispelt two words . . . When you have amended these two faults, which please do directly, throw off five hundred copies, & send them by the first coach or fly.

This letter is undated, being simply headed 'Weden.: Noon'; but its cover bears a poorly struck Bishop mark '–E 24', denoting *arrival* in Edinburgh on the 24 of a month, either September (1795) or February (1796). This implies posting at noon on the previous day in Dumfries, and the only month in which the 23 fell on a Wednesday was September 1795. This ties in with the reference to the printing of Hyslop's bill ordered in the previous letter. Previous editors misunderstood the significance of the postmark and dated this letter to February 1796, doubtless also misled by the reference to a 'long silence' in the first line. But this could also have alluded to a gap of several weeks in the correspondence. No letters dated September 1795 are known, so we have no inkling of the reason for Robert's silence; but it seems clear that for about a month he had been very ill, probably a recurrence of the severe depression which had dogged him since 1781, compounded by the rheumatic fever which afflicted him in June, September and December 1794. The toothache could also have been a major factor; the crudely brutal techniques of extraction then practised would have deterred all but the bravest from resorting to such an extreme, and if Robert determined to soldier on under the affliction of an alveolar abscess he risked not only loss of appetite but septicaemia. At the very least this new torment must have been extremely debilitating, particularly to someone of Robert's nervous disposition.

The Globe Inn was subsequently referred to in a letter to Thomson (CL 677) as 'my HOWFF, & where our friend Clarke & I have had many a merry squeeze'. William Hyslop, proprietor of the Globe, had been specifically named in Robert's grace beginning 'Lord, we thank, and Thee alone' (CW 408), while his son and daughter-in-law were similarly mentioned in another grace:

> O Lord, since we have feasted thus,
>   Which we so little merit,
> Let Meg now take away the flesh,
>   And Jock bring in the spirit!

William's eldest son John (1770–1835) married Margaret Geddes at South Leith on 28 October 1794.[22] Margaret was born on 20 October 1775, the daughter of David Geddes and Janet Bremner of St Cuthbert's parish. David Geddes was a native of Enzie, Banffshire, and a lapsed Catholic whose two elder brothers made names for themselves in the Catholic Church. John Geddes (1735–99), Bishop of Morocco *in partibus* and Coadjutor to Bishop Hay, the Vicar Apostolic for the Lowlands of Scotland, lived at Edinburgh and was that 'first' (i.e. best) of clergymen who befriended Burns during his sojourn in the capital. Margaret Geddes inherited her uncle's copy of the first Edinburgh Edition with the twenty-seven pages of manuscripts added by Burns. Alexander Geddes (1737–1802) also spent his life in the priesthood but is best remembered as the translator of the satires of Horace into elegant English verse. The duality of his life is best exemplified by two incidents which occurred in 1780: in May he fell foul of Bishop Hay for having attended a Presbyterian service at Banff, for which he was threatened with suspension; and shortly afterwards he received the degree of LL.D. from Aberdeen University for his services to scholarship. His ecumenism was a century and a half ahead of its time and it was said that his readiness to question idolatry and papal infallibility 'mitigated the rancour which had existed between Roman Catholics and Protestants'.[23]

Margaret Hyslop frequently visited her family in Edinburgh. Robert used her as a messenger, and it was she whom he entrusted with the business of the armorial seal which Thomson had engraved for him – yet another of those little gifts with which the publisher subtly paid his prickly contributor. John Hyslop later trained as a surgeon and he and his wife settled in London. She predeceased him and he died in 1835, but they had a daughter named Margaret who presented the Geddes Burns to Dr Henry Goadby before he emigrated to the United States in 1838. This precious volume is now preserved in the Henry E. Huntington Library at San Marino, California.[24]

Robert was just recovering from his illness late in September 1795 when he learned that his four-year-old daughter Elizabeth Riddell had died. Tantalisingly little is known about the circumstances surrounding the child's death, but she had suffered a serious illness twenty months previously and is said to have died a slow and agonising death. In the summer of 1795 she had been taken to visit her grandparents, aunts and uncles at Mauchline and it was there that she died in September.[25] This death was not unexpected, but it was a crushing blow for all that, made much worse by the fact that Robert, still convalescing, had been in no fit state to travel to Mauchline for her funeral, far less comfort her as she lay dying. This triggered off a further bout of severe depressive illness. A brief note to Maria Riddell was penned between the receipt of the bad news and the onset of the next bout of illness (CL 611):

> A severe domestic misfortune has put all literary business out of my head for some time past.– Now I begin to resume my wonted studies.– I am much correspondence in your debt; I shall pay it soon.– Clarke's Sonatas are of no use to me, & I beg you will keep them. That you, my friend, may never experience such a loss as mine, sincerely prays – RB

This undated letter was docketed '24' by Maria. There appears to be a letter missing, for the next brief note was docketed '26'. It has been tentatively dated to November 1795 (CL 611). After apologising – 'I have been a grievous sinner against all etiquette of correspondence, in not writing you long ere now' – Robert enclosed the song 'O bonie was yon rosy brier' (CW 558). There was no mention of the illness that prostrated him in the autumn of that year. Currie (1800), based on information supplied by William Maxwell, stated that, from October till the following January, Robert was confined to his house with 'an accidental complaint'. What this meant no one can now say, but it hints at an injury rather than an illness. Yet Robert himself subsequently made several tantalisingly vague references to his illness that winter, and implied that it arose out of the grief he felt at the loss of his daughter. The absence of clearly dated letters between

23 September and 17 December lends weight to a prolonged period of illness. Yet we have the curious testimony of Josiah Walker that Robert was sufficiently recovered by late November, and that he observed no unfavourable change in the poet's looks, spirits or appetite. Walker had been out of Scotland for eight years, during which his intercourse with the poet had been suspended. On returning to Scotland towards the end of 1795 he made a slight detour to Dumfries to visit his old friend, and called at his house one forenoon.

He was sitting on a window-seat reading, with the doors open, and the family arrangements going on in his presence, and altogether without that appearance of snugness which a student requires. After conversing with him for some time, he proposed a walk, and promised to conduct me through some of his favourite haunts. We accordingly quitted the town, and wandered a considerable way up the beautiful banks of the Nith. Here he gave me an account of his latest productions, and repeated some satirical ballads which he had composed, to favour one of the candidates at the last borough election . . . He repeated also his fragments of an *Ode to Liberty* with marked and peculiar energy, and showed a disposition, which, however, was easily repressed, to throw out peculiar remarks of the same nature with those for which he had been reprehended. On finishing our walk, he passed some time with me at the inn, and I left him early in the evening, to make another visit at some distance from Dumfries.

On the second morning after I returned with a friend, who was acquainted with the poet, and we found him ready to pass a part of the day with us at the inn. On this occasion, I did not think him quite so interesting as he had appeared at his outset. His conversation was too elaborate, and his expression weakened by a frequent endeavour to give it artificial strength. He had been accustomed to speak for applause in the circles which he frequented, and seemed to think it necessary, in making the most common remark, to depart a little from the ordinary simplicity of language, and to couch it in something of epigrammatic point. In his praise and censure, he was so decisive as to render a dissent from his judgment difficult to be reconciled with the laws of good-breeding. His wit was not more licentious than is unhappily too venial in higher circles, though I thought him rather unnecessarily free in the avowal of his excesses. Such were the clouds by which the pleasures of the evening were partially obscured, but frequent coruscations of genius were visible between them. When it began to grow late, he showed no disposition to retire, but called for fresh supplies of liquor, with a freedom which might be excusable as we were in an inn, and no condition had been distinctly made, though it might easily have been inferred, had the inference been welcome, that he was to consider himself as our guest; nor was it till he saw us worn out that he departed, about three in the morning . . . Upon the whole, I found this last interview not so gratifying as I had expected; although I had discovered in his conduct no errors which I had not seen in men who stand high in the favour of society, or sufficient to account for the mysterious insinuations which I had heard against his character. He on this occasion drank freely without being intoxicated, a circumstance from which I concluded, not only that his constitution was still unbroken, but that he was not addicted to solitary cordials; for if he had tasted liquor in the morning he must have easily yielded to the excess of the evening.[26]

Commentators from John Wilson (1841) to DeLancey Ferguson (1938) have rightly criticised Walker's grotesque *de haut en bas* style. Both Robert and his visitor had changed in the intervening eight years, but Walker (who as tutor to the Marquis of Tullibardine had accompanied his young charge to Eton) had been so long in the company of the high and the mighty that their patrician manner had rubbed off on him. If he were disappointed that Robert's genius only flashed intermittently, Robert was doubtless equally disappointed with Walker. Ferguson pithily concluded that, 'From the pompous superiority with which he writes of the poet, one may surmise that Burns's abrupt and decisive manner was due to irritation at being patronised by an ass'.[27]

Walker's account contrasts strongly with another alleged eye-witness account of a similar occasion which had taken place only a few months earlier. John Pattison of Kelvingrove, brother of the Paisley businessman so energetic in getting subscriptions to the first Edinburgh Edition, paid a visit to Dumfries in August 1795, on his way to stay with another brother who was a clergyman in the county. He was accompanied by his teenage son John who later wrote that when they rode up to the inn, a gentleman was seen standing on the outside stairs. Pattison hailed him as Burns:

He who had remained motionless till now rushed down the steps and caught my father by the hand, saying 'Mr Pattison, I am delighted to see you here; how do you do?' I need not say this was our immortal bard. My father continued: 'Burns, I hope you will dine with me at four o'clock.' 'Too happy, sir,' replied the poet. 'Then, may I beg of you to go with my compliments to your friend Mr Maxwell, and say I will be glad if he will do us the pleasure of joining us?' At the hour named, my father sat down at the head of the table, Dr Maxwell at the foot, and the grammar-school boy opposite Burns. Upwards of half a century has passed away; but the recollection of that day is as fresh and green in my memory as if the events recorded had occurred yesterday. It was, in fact, a new era in my existence. I had never before sat after dinner; but now I was chained to my chair till late at night, or rather early in the morning. Both Dr Maxwell and my father were highly-gifted, eloquent men. The poet was in his best vein. I can never forget the animation and glorious intelligence of his countenance, the rich, deep tones of his musical voice, and those matchless eyes, which absolutely appeared to flash fire and stream forth rays of living light. It was not conversation I heard; it was an outburst of noble sentiment, brilliant wit, and a flood of sympathy and good-will to fellow-men. Burns repeated many verses that had never seen the light, chiefly political; no impure or obscene idea was uttered, or I believe thought of; it was altogether an intellectual feast. A lofty, pure, and transcendental genius alone could have made so deep and lasting an impression on a mere boy who had read nothing, and who does not remember to have heard Burns named till that day.[28]

Between the two extremes of Walker's condescension and Pattison's gush there probably lies the truth; but sadly, perceptive and penetrating contemporary accounts of Robert's conduct and conversation at convivial gatherings with his boon companions just do not exist. The best and most objective descriptions of Burns in his last years are to be found in the correspondence of John Syme and Alexander Cunningham. Some ninety letters were written from Syme to Cunningham between 1786 and 1811 and for a hundred and twenty years they lay unread among the Cunningham family papers. They were discovered by James Ewing in 1933 and thus came too late to assist Snyder. DeLancey Ferguson[29] touched on this material briefly, while Thornton[30] made excellent use of both sides of the correspondence for the period after the poet's death when Syme in Dumfries and Cunningham in Edinburgh were the chief protagonists in the campaign to raise funds for the widow and orphans. Extracts from the correspondence pertaining to Burns were published in the *Burns Chronicle* between 1934 and 1942.[31] They form a notable addition to our knowledge of Robert's life in Dumfries and also of his posthumous history, especially the years immediately following his death.

The first two letters make no mention of Burns at all, but prove that Syme and Cunningham were well acquainted as early as 1786. The third, written from Barncailzie in January 1789, implies that it was through Cunningham that Syme got to know the poet while he was at Ellisland but coming into town every week to pick up his mail at the post office. Interestingly, they also met socially at the all too hospitable home of John Bushby: 'About a year ago he and I got almost tipsey at Tinwald Downs.' Syme regretted being unable to attend a bonspiel at the end of December 1788 when Robert played with the Dumfries curlers 'and enlivened their Beef and Kail and Tody till the small hours'. On 11 September 1790 Syme mentioned that, ten days previously, he had breakfasted at Ellisland and met 'Bonie Jean' for the first time. His first impression of the poet's wife was none too favourable: 'Methinks he has exhibited his poetical genius when he celebrated her'. Syme's comments on their mutual friend indicate vividly how much he always enjoyed his company. After Syme lost Barncailzie and was compelled to move to Dumfries as Distributor of Stamps and Collector of Stamp Duties at the end of 1791 he valued Robert more and more as an intellectual oasis in a wilderness: 'Were it not his presence, I should feel a dreary blank in the society of this town', he wrote in September 1793. By June 1792 he was writing, 'I see Burns frequently, and love him more and more'. On 8 May 1793 he wrote, 'Our friend Burns and I frequently meet – he is hitting off now and then several sweet songs on the Beauties of Dumfries and several bitter epigrams on the Boars of ditto'.

On 8 December 1793 Syme 'went to the Bard's house, and found him reading a volume like the Bible. He was in good health and spirits'. Robert had not written to Cunningham lately; the poet was annoyed because Urbani, Thomson and Cunningham had been engaging in an acrimonious correspondence in the Edinburgh newspapers and had made his name 'a subject of altercation or contradiction among you, while he was not consulted'. Robert wrote soon afterwards at length to Cunningham on the subject of Urbani's 'damned falsehood' (CL 468–9). A letter of 1 February 1794, anticipating one which Robert wrote to Cunningham on 25 February (CL 469–70), contained a descriptive paragraph:

> He comes now and then to my office and lounges half an hour in the evening, sometimes bringing a verse or two, the skin or substance of which he bids me have no mercy on. But I dare scarcely touch them. However, I have told him sometimes what seemed to me to be a feeble, harsh, or untuned note. By the bye, he mentioned a word or two in some songs he had sent Mr Thomson, which words he and you had thought fit to be supplanted by others, and these others struck me to be feebler than those supplanted. I can't recollect the particulars. He is halfway in a grand, elevated and sublime Pindaric ode to Liberty – not of the Gallic species, tho' – and in my idea he is soaring on wings which have not been used before – that is to say in plain terms, he is treating the subject in an original and superior manner.

On 15 June 1794 Syme commented on Cunningham's hope that Robert might soon make a trip to Edinburgh. But Robert was confined to Dumfries by his Excise business and 'I dare say, in part by his finances, for Robin's heart and temper are not cold and frugal'. Syme's Irish friend, a Mr Large, 'filled him and me, &c., very *fu* last Friday. A downright Irish Native and Robt. Burns in co. – I defy apathy itself to escape a doze'. While writing this letter Syme was interrupted by a visit from 'the wild Bard'. Syme had in his office the wife of a Kirkcudbright lawyer, 'a very elegant female figure of good rank':

> Her husband was out, and Robin's confounding wit began to play. He remained all day – and was, according to use and wont, charming company.

On this occasion Robert recited his reply to the Loyal Natives, a copy of which Syme enclosed for Cunningham with the warning, 'Don't let any Dumfries person see this, for one of the Savages, if he heard it, might cut Robin's pipe'. By October 1794 Syme was assiduously collecting Robert's epigrams and promised to send Cunningham his collection. Robert had now retrieved the Glenriddell Manuscript volume of his letters and promised to lend it to Cunningham. Syme himself had studied the collected letters, commenting, 'They are excellent, and of the native zest and fruit – the Bard himself'. The book containing the epigrams was sent to Cunningham on 24 November. A letter of 22 January 1795 mentioned Robert:

> He is *in statu quo*, but as he is acting *pro* Supervisor and is thereby very much occupied with that duty, which is laborious, I have not had an opportunity of eating or drinking with him these six weeks.

An undated letter written some time in the course of the year is particularly revealing:

> Burns and I are one and indivisible, but what with his occupation and mine we meet only by Starts – or at least occasionally – and we drink as many *cups* of tea as *bottles* of wine together. We are two of the best *privates* in the Dumfries Royal Volunteers. But not to flatter myself or him, I would say that hang me if I should know how to be happy were he not in the way of making me so at times.

One of the last letters written in the poet's lifetime was dated 24 February 1796. Syme was hoping to visit Edinburgh about two weeks later: 'We must have a day with Cleghorn. Mind me warmly to him'. Then he continued with an account of Robert's literary plans. It seems that Robert now intended to substitute Cunningham for Glenriddell as a would-be repository of his best literary efforts:

> Burns tells me he had (if I did not misunderstand him) a long letter very lately from you. About a month ago he mentioned a scheme he was to follow which, if he accomplishes, will prove a very agreeable treat to you. He is to sit down as the spirit moves him and write you prose and poetry on every subject which strikes him, to form a sort of Journal business of it, and when it grows thro' two or three sheets to send the foliage. This will surely be a very valuable and interesting farrago of Burnsana (is this a right term?) I have prompted him to execute the design and shall not miss giving him the spur. He and I dined tete a tete last Sunday in my Cabin – quite sober – only one bottle of port between us. I like this better than a debauch, even in an Inn. Yet when two or three are gathered together in the name of friendship and *nostri generis* – why, I would as soon have a bottle or a bottle and a half as a share of that quantity. We have a very superior young fellow here – Dr Maxwell – who, to an uncommon if not wonderful science in Physic, adds the perfect manners and mind of a gentleman. You would be much attached to him. Without him and Burns I should find this place very blank and dreary.

The spirit was willing but the flesh was weak; Robert's good intentions of supplying Cunningham with some sort of serial literary journal were never kept. Although the letters make no mention of Robert's illnesses before the very last, it is interesting to read that, in relative terms and in the context of the period, Robert, though far from abstemious, was not a heavy drinker. That Syme considered a single bottle of port between himself and Burns as the height of sobriety has to be regarded in the light of the times, when no less a figure than William Pitt habitually consumed four or five bottles of port every day and still managed to govern the country. This letter is chiefly interesting, however, for the first reference to William Maxwell who was to play a major part in the remaining months of Robert's life, as well as take a leading role in the campaign on behalf of the poet's family.

Josiah Walker's visit to Dumfries took place in November 1795 and his report on Robert's health can only be reconciled with Currie's, as well as Robert's own admission to Mrs Dunlop, if there were two separate periods of illness, the first following shortly upon the devastating news of Elizabeth Riddell's death, and the other at the end of December. Robert was absent from the meetings of the Dumfries masonic lodge on 30 November and 28 December 1795, but he was well enough to attend the meeting on 28 January 1796. These absences, of course, do not prove a thing one way or the other. But he was unwell and confined to his bed on 17 December when he sent a poetic apology to Syme declining an invitation to dine that afternoon (CW 560). On Hogmanay, the last day of the old year, he sent a verse-epistle to Collector Mitchell beginning 'Friend of the Poet tried and leal' (CW 561–2) by way of asking for a guinea advance on the next round's salary, a not uncommon practice in the Excise, and far from the desperate necessity which Snyder implied.[32] The postscript to this poetic letter alluded to the grave illness he had suffered earlier that month:

> Ye've heard this while how I've been licket,
> And by fell Death was nearly nicket:
> Grim loon! He got me by the fecket,
>   And sair me sheuk;
> But by guid luck I lap a wicket,
>   And turn'd a neuk.

The poem ended on an optimistic note, that he still had a share of health 'And by that life, I'm promised mair o't'. Sadly, time was not on his side. An undated letter to Robert Cleghorn (CL 279), tentatively assigned to Janaury 1796, also mentions the loss of his daughter and the rheumatic fever which brought Robert to the borders of the grave. 'After many weeks of a sick-bed, I am just beginning to crawl about,' he added, lending weight to the theory that the illness he had suffered since little Elizabeth's death had been continuous, but there is no doubt that this was a sweeping over-simplification. As the same phraseology occurred in the letter to Mrs Dunlop dated 31 January, however, it seems as if Robert, having been in reasonable health at the year's end, had suffered a relapse in January. He was certainly well enough again by 29 January when he wrote to Hill, sending him the customary smoked salmon (CL 325). He promised to write more fully 'in a week, or ten days', but this was, in fact, his last letter to his bookseller friend.

By February, however, he was back at work, both performing his Excise duties and plying Thomson with fresh material. Thomson had sent the latest volume of Peter Pindar to Robert, and a 'handsome, elegant present' to Jean, an expensive shawl in the latest fashion. Jean, though not the most elegant of ladies in her shape or deportment, was always well turned out; she invariably wore fine black silk stockings and boasted one of the first gingham frocks ever seen in Dumfries. An undated letter to Johnson, probably written in March (CL 302), thanked him for the copperplate on which Hyslop's bill-head had been printed, as well as printed copies of the Volunteer ballad. Robert dutifully corrected the packet of songs intended for the fifth volume of the *Museum* and sent it back with the promise, 'in a day or two, by post, expect to hear *at large*'.

Dr Currie freely acknowledged that 'the particulars respecting the illness and death of Burns were obligingly furnished by Dr Maxwell, the physician who attended him'. This statement appeared as a footnote to the passage dealing with Robert's *last* illness, in July 1796; but later biographers have assumed that Maxwell was the source of the entire seven preceding pages beginning 'Though by nature of an athletic form, Burns had in his consti-tution the peculiarities and the delicacies that belong to the temperament of genius'. Thus Currie's assertion that Robert had been confined to the house by an accidental complaint from October 1795 to January 1796 was erroneously assumed to have derived from Maxwell, and was therefore incontrovertible. The errors in this sweeping statement, demonstrable by an examination of the poet's correspondence and output in this crucial period, as well as what can be gleaned from the records of the masonic lodge and the Volunteers, could not have come from Dr Maxwell who must have known better. Consequently it would be fallacious to place any reli-ance on the ensuing passage, the source of which may have been no more than local tradition. There were plenty of malicious rumours during the poet's lifetime, and it may be that Currie's assertions were merely an amalgam of such tittle-tattle. According to Currie, 'a few days after he began to go abroad' (which would place the incident somewhere early in February 1796):

> he dined at a tavern, and returned home about three o'clock in a very cold morning, benumbed and intoxicated. This was followed by an attack of rheumatism, which confined him about a week. His appetite now began to fail; his hand shook, and his voice faultered on any exertion or emotion. His pulse became weaker and more rapid, and pain in the larger joints, and in the hands and feet, deprived him of the enjoyment of refreshing sleep. Too much dejected in his spirits, and too well aware of his real situation to entertain hopes of recovery, he was ever musing on the approaching desolation of his family, and his spirits sunk into an uniform gloom.[33]

Although the story of returning home from a late-night carousal, as given by Currie, may well be correct – we have the testimony of Walker and Lawrie regarding the lateness of the hour when such parties broke up – it was exaggerated by some later biographers, who claimed that Burns had fallen asleep in the snow, the fate which actually befell 'Holy Willie' Fisher.[34] McDowall (1870) could even point with certainty to the very spot at the head of the Globe Inn close where the poet collapsed in the snow. But this story can easily be dismissed; the weather records show that there was no snow at all in Dumfries, and only a light frost on one or two nights in January or February 1796. Instead, although temperatures were above average, this period was noted for a prolonged series of violent storms which peaked on Robert's birthday when the lead roof of the Coffee House was entirely swept off at a single stroke.[35]

The Excise records show the discharge of Robert's salary during the last five months of his life. On 3 March he received £6, which was the normal payment for an Excise round of six weeks and shows that he either performed his duties normally in the preceding period, or was on sick leave of such brief duration as not to require a substitute, with a corresponding cut in salary. The payment for the next round, however, was made on 14 April and was reduced to £3, which indicates that he was off work for much of that period. He then recovered sufficiently to resume duties (and also attended a masonic meeting on 14 April), for on 2 June he again received the full sum of £6; but the final payment on 14 July, only one week before his death, consisted of £2.[36] These cold figures chart the course of the poet's illnesses and partial recovery in this crucial period and give the lie to the story, repeated by successive biographers since 1800, that the Excise Board, 'to their honour, continued his full emoluments'. Robert Chambers even added to this by stating (1851) that a young expectant named Adam Stobie stood in for him all that time, presumably with the object of earning for Robert the reduced pay.[37]

That this was not the case was evident before Burns died, and alongside Currie's version of the payments there circulated the notion that the Excise Board had been guilty of cruelty in docking the poet's salary. Alexander Findlater, who was in the best position to know the truth of the matter, set the record straight by pointing out that when the salary of Excise officers was raised from £35 to £50 in 1788, this was done on the understanding that the £15 increase would automatically cease if the officer was off sick.[38] Robert himself complained to Alexander Cunningham on 7 July (CL 473):

> What way, in the name of thrift, shall I maintain myself & keep a horse in Country-quarters – with a wife & five children at home on 35£? I mention this, because I had intended to beg your utmost interest & all friends you can muster to move our Commissioners of Excise to grant me the full salary.– I dare say you know them all personally.

A few days later he wrote again, 'my plan is to address the Board by petition & then if any friend has thrown in his word 'tis a great deal in my favor'. The rapid deterioration in Robert's health is vividly shown in the fluctuations in his handwriting, and in particular the disintegration of his signature on the salary receipts. The last signature, made on 14 July, is so shaky as to be barely recognisable. According to Findlater, 'Commissioner Graham, regretting, I have no doubt, his inability to comply with the poet's wishes as to the full salary, sent him a private donation of £5, which, I believe, nearly or totally compensated the loss'.

Most of Robert's last letters were addressed to James Johnson or George Thomson and dealt mainly with the ongoing business of their respective song collections. Unfortunately, they are undated so they are of little help in plotting the exact course of Robert's final illness. A letter to Thomson which, from internal evidence, may be dated to April (CL 677–8) begins:

> Alas, my dear Thomson, I fear it will be sometime ere I tune my lyre again! 'By Babel streams' &c. –[39] Almost ever since I wrote you last, I have only known Existence by the pressure of the heavy hand of SICK-NESS; & have counted Time by the repercussions of PAIN! Rheumatism, Cold & Fever, have formed, to me, a terrible Trinity in Unity, which makes me close my eyes in misery, & open them without hope.

A few weeks later, however, Robert was in a more cheerful mood when he wrote to Thomson again, enclosing 'Here's a health to ane I lo'e dear' (CW 565). The heroine of this song was Jessie Lewars (1778–1855), younger daughter of John Lewars Senior, one-time Supervisor of Excise at Dumfries, and the sister of Robert's young colleague who was, in fact, the bearer of this letter – 'a young fellow of uncommon merit – indeed, by far the cleverest fellow I have met with in this part of the world'. Robert was keen to review and mend some of his previous compositions, preferring to be the author of five well-written songs than of ten otherwise. It was his dearest wish to suppress his verses to 'Cauld kail' as well as 'Laddie lie near me', as being 'neither worthy of my name, nor of your book'. Thomson, of course, ignored this and published both. Their mutual friend, Robert Cleghorn himself had been very ill about this time:

> I have great hopes that the genial influence of the approaching summer will set me to rights, but as yet I cannot boast of returning health.– I have now reason to believe that my complaint is a flying gout: – a damnable business! Do, let me know how Cleghorn is, & remember me to him.

In May 1795 Maria Riddell moved from Tinwald House to Halleaths, a mansion about two miles east of Lochmaben. Thereafter there was much less opportunity for her and Robert to meet, but their correspondence continued in a desultory way. About the beginning of June 1796 Robert wrote to Maria (CL 611–12) in reply to her invitation to join her party for the king's birthday celebrations:

> I am in such miserable health as to be utterly incapable of shewing my loyalty in any way.– Rackt as I am with rheumatisms, I meet every face with a greeting like that of Balak to Balaam – 'Come, curse me Jacob; & come, defy me Israel!'–[40] So say I, Come, curse me that East-wind; & come, defy me the North!!! Would you have me in such circumstances copy you out a Love-song? No! if I must write, let it be Sedition, or Blasphemy, or something else that begins with a B, so that I may grin with the grin of iniquity, & rejoice with the rejoicing of an apostate Angel . . . I may perhaps see you on Saturday, but I will not be at the Ball . . .

Even when racked with pain Robert could still summon up the strength to flirt with Maria, though he concluded with an apt quotation from *Hamlet* – 'Man delights not me, nor woman either!'

About the same time Robert wrote his last letter to James Johnson (CL 303). His health was now giving way, but he apologised for his silence:

> You may probably think that for some time past I have neglected you & your work; but, Alas, the hand of pain, & sorrow, & care has these many months lain heavy on me! Personal & domestic affliction have almost entirely banished that alacrity & life with which I used to woo the rural Muse of Scotia.– In the mean time, let us finish what we have so well begun . . .
>
> I am ashamed to ask another favor of you because you have been so very good already, but my wife has a very particular friend of hers, a young lady who sings well, to whom she wished to present the Scots Musical Museum, if you have a spare copy, will you be obliging as to send it by the very first Fly, as I am anxious to have it soon.

Johnson complied with this request, and on 26 June Robert presented the set to Jessie Lewars who had helped to nurse him through his recent illnesses. He inscribed verses on the fly-leaf of the first volume, beginning 'Thine be the volumes, Jessie fair' (CW 567).

Robert was increasingly depressed about his financial position. James Clarke, formerly schoolmaster at Moffat but now at Forfar, had borrowed money from him at the time of his legal problems in 1791–2 and had since repaid instalments regularly. On 26 June Robert wrote to him to press him for another guinea note (CL 596):

> Still, still the victim of affliction, were you to see the emaciated figure who now holds the pen to you, you would not know your old friend.– Whether I shall ever get about again, is only known to HIM, the Great Unknown, whose creature I am.– Alas, Clarke, I begin to fear the worst! – As to my individual Self, I am tranquil;– I would despise myself if I were not: but Burns's poor widow! & half a dozen of his dear little ones, helpless orphans, there I am weak as a woman's tear.– Enough of this! 'tis half my disease!

After thanking him for the last repayment and begging a further one by return of post Robert closed poignantly, 'Adieu dear Clarke! That I shall ever see you again, is, I am afraid, highly improbable'.

His medical friends – probably Alexander Brown as well as Maxwell – having tried physic and failed, now advised sea bathing, country air and riding. About the beginning of July Robert rode painfully out of Dumfries and headed ten miles south-east to the decayed hamlet of Brow in the parish of Ruthwell, on the shore of the Solway. Apart from the sea-bathing, the village had a small reputation as a spa, for near the shore is a chalybeate spring, on the east side of the Raffles Burn not far from the point at which it debouches into the estuary. On Maxwell's advice Robert spent the better part of three weeks at the Brow, drinking the chalybeate waters from an iron cup affixed to the side of the well. Part of the treatment recommended by Maxwell consisted of wading up to the armpits in the icy waters of the Solway – a treatment that was singularly inappropriate for a man in the last stages of emaciation and debility, and in the grip of the incurable heart disease, endocarditis.

The hamlet was used as a staging post by the cattle-drovers taking their herds south into England, and it boasted a rather rough-and-ready inn owned by James Morpeth, but run by a couple named Davidson. Robert lodged in the 'chaumer-en' (chamber-end) but no trace of this modest hostelry now exists, for it was demolished in 1863 during road-widening. Maria Riddell, who had gone to Lochmaben for her own health's sake, invited Robert to dine with her on 5 July and sent her carriage to fetch him to her lodgings. Soon afterwards she recorded her impressions of this poignant meeting:

I was struck with his appearance on entering the room. The stamp of death was imprinted on his features. He seemed already touching the brink of eternity. His first salutation was: 'Well, madam, have you any commands for the other world?' I replied, that it seemed a doubtful case which of us should be the soonest, and that I hoped he would yet live to write my epitaph. He looked in my face with an air of great kindness, and expressed his concern at seeing me look so ill, with his accustomed sensibility. At table he ate little or nothing, and he complained of having entirely lost the tone of his stomach. We had a long and serious conversation about his present situation, and the approaching termination of all his earthly prospects. He spoke of his death without any of the ostentation of philosophy, but with firmness as well as feeling, as an event likely to happen very soon, and which gave him concern chiefly from leaving his four children[41] so young and unprotected, and his wife in so interesting a situation – in hourly expectation of lying-in of a fifth. He mentioned, with seeming pride and satisfaction, the promising genius of his eldest son, and the flattering marks of approbation he had received from his teachers, and dwelt particularly on his hopes of that boy's future conduct and merit. His anxiety for his family seemed to hang heavy upon him, and the more perhaps from the reflection that he had not done them all the justice he was so well qualified to do. Passing from this subject, he shewed great concern about the care of his literary fame, and particularly the publication of his posthumous works. He said he was well aware that his death would occasion some noise, and that every scrap of writing would be revived against him to the injury of his future reputation: that letters and verses written with unguarded and improper freedom, and which he earnestly wished to have buried in oblivion, would be handed about by idle vanity or malevolence when no dread of his resentment would restrain them or prevent the censures of shrill-tongued malice or the insidious sarcasms of envy from pouring forth all their venom to blast his fame.

He lamented that he had written many epigrams on persons against whom he entertained no enmity, and whose characters he should be sorry to wound; and many indifferent poetical pieces which he feared would now, with all their imperfections on their head, be thrust upon the world. On this account, he deeply regretted having deferred to put his papers in a state of arrangement, as was now quite incapable of the exertion . . . The conversation was kept up with great evenness and animation on his side. I had seldom seen his mind greater or more collected. There was frequently a considerable degree of vivacity in his sallies, and they would probably have had a greater share, had not the concern and dejection I could not disguise damped the spirit of pleasantry he seemed not unwilling to indulge.

We parted about sunset on the evening of that day; the next day I saw him again, and we parted to meet no more![42]

On 7 July Robert wrote to Alexander Cunningham from whom he had just received a very comforting and flattering letter. Robert, heading his letter 'Brow-Sea-bathing quarters', was deeply touched, but now had no illusions about the future (CL 473):

Alas! my friend, I fear the voice of the Bard will soon be heard among you no more! For these eight or ten months I have been ailing, sometimes bedfast & sometimes not; but these last three months I have been tortured with an excruciating rheumatism, which has reduced me to nearly the last stage.– You actually would not know me if you saw me.– Pale emaciated, & so feeble as occasionally to need help from my chair – my spirits fled! fled! – but I can no more on the subject – only the Medical folks tell me that my last & only chance is bathing & country quarters & riding.

The reference to the 'Medical folks' gives the lie to Currie's insinuation that Robert, 'impatient of medical advice, as well as of every species of control', determined for himself to try the effects of bathing in the sea.[43] After bemoaning the fact that, under the regulations of the Excise, his salary was now cut, Robert referred to the song 'Lord Gregory' (CW 482) which he transcribed to accompany this letter, and then promised to send other songs after he returned to Dumfries:

Apropos to being at home, Mrs Burns threatens in a week or two, to add one more to my Paternal charge, which, if the right gender, I intend shall be introduced to the world by the respectable designation of Alexander Cunningham Burns. My last was James Glencairn, so you can have no objection to the company of Nobility.[44]

The accommodation at the Brow was rough but the Davidsons were kind to their lodger. Robert's appetite was so bad that all he could swallow was a little thin porridge laced with port. He had brought a bottle with him and when this ran out, the Davidsons having none, Robert was obliged to struggle to the nearest inn, at Clarencefield about a mile distant. The innkeeper was John Burney, Davidson's son-in-law. Robert eventually arrived at the inn, placed his empty bottle on the counter, and enquired if Burney had any port for sale, adding that 'the muckle Deil had got into his pouch' (i.e. that he had no cash). He offered his armorial seal, the recent gift of George Thomson, by way of payment, and began unfastening it from his watch fob. The landlady stamped indignantly on the floor; and her husband, taking the poet into his arms, and giving him the wine, led him gently to the door, and ended abruptly this scene of pain and shame, with tears in his eyes.[45]

One sunny afternoon Robert was well enough to pay a visit to the manse of Ruthwell where he took tea with the wife of the Revd. John Craig, and their daughter Agnes. Nine years later Agnes married the Revd. Henry Duncan, her father's assistant and successor, a man who, in 1810, founded the world's first savings bank and was joint-secretary of the Burns Mausoleum Committee. A contemporary account described this occasion:

> His altered appearance excited much silent sympathy; and the evening being beautiful, and the sun shining brightly through the casement, Miss Craig was afraid the light might be too much for him, and rose with the view of letting down the window-blinds. Burns immediately guessed what she meant; and, regarding the young lady with a look of great benignity, said: 'Thank you, my dear, for your kind attention; but oh, let him shine: he will not shine long for me!'[46]

Robert wrote several letters from the Brow. Ironically, one of them was addressed to his old adversary, his father-in-law, James Armour (CL 722). Written on 10 July and signed 'your most affectionate son', it begged that Mrs Armour (who was then visiting relatives in Fife) should come to Dumfries as quickly as possible:

> My wife thinks she can yet reckon upon a fortnight.- The Medical people order me, *as I value my existence*, to fly to seabathing & country quarters, so it is ten thousand chances to one that I shall not be within a dozen miles of her when her hour comes.- What a situation for her, poor girl, without a single friend by her on such a serious moment.-
> I have now been a week at salt water, & though I think I have got some good by it, yet I have some secret fears that this business will be dangerous if not fatal.

Once more we have Robert's statement that his 'Medical people' had advised sea-bathing; although he felt that this might have helped him, none-theless, he was not entirely convinced. This is hardly the statement of a man who would subject himself to such a desperate remedy against the wishes of his doctor as Currie implied; but, of course, Currie was probably bound by the solidarity of his profession; and at the time he wrote, Dr Maxwell was not only still alive but heavily involved with him as one of the trustees of the Burns family, so naturally no blame had to be attached to the worthy medico.

Three other letters were written that day. One was the final despairing plea for reconciliation which went to Mrs Dunlop (CL 215), the second was addressed to brother Gilbert (CL 358) giving him a bleak assessment of his health and also hinting at money worries:

I have contracted one or two serious debts, partly from my illness these many months & partly from too much thoughtlessness as to expense when I came to town that will cut in too much on the little I leave them in your hands.

This may have been a hint to Gilbert who had never made any attempt to repay the £180 which Robert had lent him in 1788. In fact, it was to be almost a quarter of a century before Gilbert cleared the capital sum, but no interest on the loan was charged because Gilbert had had the responsibility of looking after his mother, his sisters and Robert's daughter Bess. The last of the letters written that day went to Alexander Cunningham. Previous editors have misdated this letter to 12 July on account of the Edinburgh arrival date-stamp of that day, a Tuesday. It would, in fact, have been written on the Sunday and put into the Dumfries post the following day. From the tone of this letter it may be inferred that it was written *before* those to Mrs Dunlop and Gilbert. The letter, as such, was very brief, but it included a transcript of the song 'Here's a health to ane I lo'e dear' (CW 565) and ended with Robert's hopes to secure his full salary from the Excise.

On Tuesday 12 July, however, Robert wrote two longer and more urgent letters. The first was addressed to his cousin James Burness in Montrose (CL 63-4). There had been no communication between them since February 1789, but James appears to have heard of Robert's straitened circumstances and had recently written with an offer of financial assistance. Little did Robert realise that he would need to take up his cousin's generous offer so soon; but, as he explained:

> A rascal of a Haberdasher to whom I owe a considerable bill taking it into his head that I am dying, has commenced a process against me & will infallibly put my emaciated body into jail.– Will you be so good as to accommodate me, & that by return of post, with ten pounds.– O, James! did you but know the pride of my heart, you would feel doubly for me! Alas! I am not used to beg! The worst of it is, my health was coming about finely; you know & my Physician assures me that melancholy & low spirits are half my disease, guess then my horrors since this business began.– If I had it settled, I would be I think quite well in a manner.– How shall I use the language to you, O do not disappoint me! but string Necessity's curst command.–
>
> I have been thinking over & over my brother's affairs & I fear I must cut him up; but on this I will correspond at another time, particularly as I shall want your advice.–
>
> Forgive me for once more mentioning by return of Post.– Save me from the horrors of a jail!

To George Thomson he wrote in similar vein (CL 679–80), berating 'A cruel scoundrel of a Haberdasher to whom I owe an account, taking it into his head that I am dying, has commenced a process & will infallibly put me into jail'. Thomson annotated this letter before he filed it away:

This idea is exaggerated – he could not have been in any such danger at
Dumfries nor could he be in such necessity to implore aid from *Edinr*.

Nevertheless Thomson complied with Robert's wishes and sent a draft for
£5 which he actually had to borrow from George Shearer, as he was himself
overstretched at the time. James Burness likewise responded promptly with
a draft for £10. These drafts were discovered uncashed among the poet's
effects after his death.[47]

The 'cruel scoundrel of a Haberdasher' mentioned in these rather hysterical letters was David Williamson (1766–1824) who was a fellow Volunteer. It will be remembered that he was one of the three tailors appointed
to supply the Volunteers with their uniforms. Robert must have had his
uniform since the spring of 1795 but had never got around to paying his
tailor's bill. In fairness to Williamson, therefore, it should be noted that
the bill was still outstanding more than a year later. It was then that the
tailor put the matter of unpaid bills in the hands of his lawyer, Matthew
Penn, and it was the latter who had written formally to Burns, early in July
1796, demanding the settlement of the bill which stood at £7 4s. We have
seen how, on previous occasions, Robert had a very casual attitude about
settling bills, whether it be with his distinguished namesake, the
Edinburgh architect Robert Burn, or the printer of the newspaper which
advertised the roup of Ellisland. In fact, Robert had been a debtor to Williamson on previous occasions and was not at all prompt in his payments.
In March 1794, Messrs Brown & Williamson, clothiers, announced to their
customers, including Robert, that they were dissolving their partnership
and collecting the debts due to it. They enclosed an account for a balance
of £7 9s, due by him since the beginning of 1793.[48] Robert repaid this debt
in due course, but incurred a debt almost as large a few months later. The
money now owed to Williamson was quite substantial – almost two
months' Excise salary – but it might have been a hundred times as much
for all the poet's ability to pay.

Penn's was no more than the usual stock letter and contained no threat,
but Robert's mind was so unhinged with disease that the missive appeared
to him to be menacing. Had he been in good health his knowledge of business practice would have kept matters in their true perspective; as matters
stood, however, Penn's innocuous letter told on him with devastating
force. Imprisonment for debt, on the other hand, was a very real and ever-
present calamity in those times.[49] Williamson had a more felicitous connection with that other local celebrity, John Paul Jones, for his wife Jane
Young was a niece of the American admiral.

Although the threat was imaginary its consequences were real enough.
Writing to the banker James Gracie on 13 July (CL 582) Robert said that
his rheumatisms had derived great benefit from the sea-bathing, but his
loss of appetite continued. Gracie had offered a convalescent outing in his
carriage but Robert was now too weak to take him up on the offer. The following day Robert wrote one of his few known letters to his wife (CL 479).
To 'My dearest Love' he repeated the words used to Gracie the previous

day. The sea-bathing had eased his pains and he felt strengthened, but his appetite was still extremely bad:

> No flesh nor fish can I swallow; porridge and milk are the only thing I can taste. I am very happy to hear, by Miss Jess Lewars, that you are all well. My very best and kindest compliments to her, and to all the children. I will see you on Sunday.

Bathing at the Brow depended on the state of the tides and when the spring tides abated it was time to go home. This fact, mentioned in the letter to Gracie, makes a nonsense of the claim by Currie, and therefore repeated by all other biographers since 1800, that it was a renewed bout of fever which drove Robert back to Dumfries. From his correspondence it is clear that he was working to a predetermined programme. This was confirmed by the last letter written from the Brow, at noon on Saturday 16 July, to John Clark of Locharwoods (CL 706). This gentleman had been a friend of the poet for several years and was a trustee of Glenriddell's estate. By the end of that week, as the high tides abated, Robert realised that those spartan dips in the sea had not done him any lasting good:

> my hours of bathing have interfered so unluckily as to have put it out of my power to wait on you.– In the mean time, as the tides are over I anxiously wish to return to town, as I have not heard any news of Mrs Burns these two days.– Dare I be so bold as to borrow your Gig? I have a horse at command, but it threatens to rain, & getting wet is perdition.– Any time about three in the afternoon, will suit me exactly.

The reference to Miss Jess Lewars is interesting, for it illustrates the devotion of this girl, not yet eighteen years of age, to the dying poet and his family. Even during his last illness Robert, under the very eyes of his wife, beat himself into a state of poetic passion over young Jessie as she tripped around the house, ministering to the invalid and doing the domestic chores. Even as his strength was ebbing he could crack a joke with this kindly lassie. Someone, allegedly the surgeon Alexander Brown, called one day with a poster for a travelling menagerie then in Dumfries. As Brown handed the sheet to Jess, Robert seized it and wrote on it a couple of impromptu verses in red crayon, then handed it back to her saying that it was now fit to be presented to a lady. The lines were part of the group now known as 'Versicles to Jessie Lewars' (CW 566), the two stanzas known as 'The Menagerie'. Robert flirted outrageously with the girl, in verse at any rate:

> Talk not to me of savages
>   From Afric's burning sun!
> No savage e'er can rend my heart
>   As, Jessie, thou hast done.

When Jessie herself was briefly indisposed, Robert penned lines on her illness and her recovery. She was 'a seraph' whose 'purity and worth' he extolled. On another occasion she gave him a glass of watered wine, and he took up his diamond stylus to inscribe a charming toast to her on the glass. In one of his last songs 'Here's a health to ane I lo'e dear' (CW 565) he admitted the hopelessness of his love for Jessie:

> Altho thou maun never be mine,
> Altho even hope is denied,
> 'Tis sweeter for thee despairing
> Than ought in the world beside, Jessie –
> Than ought in the world beside!

The lines which Robert inscribed in Jessie's copy of the *Musical Museum* on 26 June have already been mentioned. Jessie, fittingly, inspired Robert's very last song. To the haunting air of 'Lenox love' he wrote 'O, wert thou in the cauld blast' (CW 567), surely some of the most poignant lines ever penned.

Many years later, Jessie provided Robert Chambers with her memories of Burns. The poet and his family had been next-door neighbours during most of the Mill Hole Brae period and she was able to form her judgment at close quarters. Robert was a man of simple and temperate habits 'as far as circumstances left him to his own inclinations'. Interestingly, Jessie provided a domestic angle. The poet was always anxious that his wife should have a neat and genteel appearance. Because of the fatigue of raising so many young children, poor Jean could not help sometimes being a little 'out of order'. Robert disliked this, and not only remonstrated against it in a gentle way, but did his utmost to counteract it by buying for her the best clothing he could afford. Jessie was the source of the information that Jean was one of the first ladies in Dumfries to wear a gingham gown, 'a stuff now common, but, at its first introduction, rather costly, and almost exclusively used by persons of superior conditions'. Robert would joke with Jessie about her boyfriends and speculate on which she would marry. 'There's Bob Spalding,' he would say, 'he has not as much brains as a midge could lean its elbow on; he won't do.' He claimed that poets had the second-sight and therefore he would tell her future. He said that she would marry the young lawyer James Thomson and, indeed, they were wed on 3 June 1799. After his death in 1849 Mrs Thomson lived in genteel retirement in Maxwelltown where she died in May 1855 at the age of seventy-seven.[50]

On Monday 18 July Robert returned to Dumfries in John Clark's gig. His first act – indeed, his last of which we have concrete record – was to write a despairing letter to his father-in-law (CL 722):

> Do, for heaven's sake, send Mrs Armour here immediately. My wife is hourly expecting to be put to bed. Good God! what a situation for her to be in, poor girl, without a friend! I returned from sea-bathing quarters to-day, and my medical friends would almost persuade me that I am better, but I think and feel that my strength is so gone that the disorder will prove fatal to me.

Allan Cunningham has a fanciful description of the poet's return. Cunningham was a boy of eleven and *may* have been in Dumfries at the time, but his 'eye-witness' account is probably not untypical:

> He returned on the 18th in a small spring cart; the ascent to his house was steep, and the cart stopped at the foot of the Mill-hole-brae; when he alighted he shook so much and stood with difficulty; he seemed unable to stand upright. He stooped, as if in pain, and walked tottering towards his own door: his looks were hollow and ghastly, and those who saw him then never expected to see him in life again.

The rest of Cunningham's account, however, must be taken with a pinch of salt:

> It was soon spread through Dumfries that Burns had returned from The Brow much worse than when he went away, and it was added that he was dying. The anxiety of the people, high and low, was very great. I was present and saw it. Wherever two or three were together their talk was of Burns, and of him alone. They spoke of his history, of his person, and of his works – of his witty sayings and sarcastic replies, and of his too early fate, with much enthusiasm, and sometimes with deep feeling. All that he had done, and all that they had hoped he would accomplish, were talked of: half-a-dozen of them stopped Dr Maxwell in the street, and said, 'How is Burns, sir?' He shook his head, saying, 'he cannot be worse,' and passed on to be subjected to further inquiries farther up the way. I heard one of a group inquire, with much simplicity, 'Who do you think will be our poet now?'
>
> Though Burns now knew he was dying, his good humour was unruffled, and his wit never forsook him. When he looked up and saw Dr Maxwell at his bedside, – 'Alas!' he said, 'what has brought you here? I am but a poor crow, and not worth plucking.' He pointed to his pistols, took them in his hand, and gave them to Maxwell, saying they could not be in worthier keeping, and he should never more have need of them. This relieved his proud heart from a sense of obligation. Soon afterwards he saw Gibson, one of his brother-volunteers, by the bed-side with tears in his eyes. He smiled and said, – 'John, don't let the awkward squad fire over me.'[51]

For a doctor of medicine, Currie was maddeningly vague about Robert's very last days:

> At first Burns imagined bathing in the sea had been of benefit to him: the pains in his limbs were relieved; but this was immediately followed by a new attack of fever. When brought back to his house in Dumfries, on the 18th of July, he was no longer able to stand upright. At this time a tremor pervaded his frame: his tongue was parched, and his mind sunk into delirium, when not roused by conversation. On the second and third day the fever increased, and his strength diminished. On the fourth the sufferings of this great, but ill-fated genius were terminated, and a life was closed in which virtue and passion had been at perpetual variance.

The sense of his poverty and of the approaching distress of his infant family pressed heavily on Burns as he lay on the bed of death. Yet he alluded to his indigence, at times, with something approaching to his wonted gaiety. 'What business,' said he to Dr Maxwell . . ., 'has a physician to waste his time on me? I am a poor pigeon not worth plucking. Alas! I have not feathers enough upon me to carry me to my grave.' And when his reason was lost in delirium his ideas ran in the same melancholy train; the horrors of a jail were continually present to his troubled imagination and produced the most affecting exclamations.[52]

Both paragraphs appeared in the 1800 edition, but the second paragraph was omitted from the second edition onwards. Interestingly, Currie's original draft of the second paragraph was:

And when his mind began to wander from the precincts of reason, the apprehension of want haunted his troubled imagination continually. At times he conceived himself as under confinement for debt; and under the convulsive motions which preceded his dissolution, considering himself as torn from his family to encounter the horrors of a jail, he called on his friends for assistance, exclaiming 'Maxwell! Macmurdo! Syme! will none of you relieve me?' These were the last words he uttered.[53]

In Currie's covering letter he reminded Syme:

The last exclamation etc. I minuted down from your conversation: am I right in accuracy, am I right in other respects. I have no objection to omitting this if you wish it, or to altering any thing as you may propose.

Unfortunately, although several letters of Syme to Currie are extant, the crucial letter answering this communication has not survived, and so we do not know why Syme wished Currie to omit the poet's dying words. It is extremely unlikely that Syme would have concocted the story and later thought better of it. Perhaps he thought that there was something unedifying about that last cry of despair. Certainly it did not reflect badly on Syme or his friends who, before Robert breathed his last, were already taking energetic steps to relieve Jean and her family. It is worth noting that Syme prevailed on Currie to delete a passage in his 'Reflections', particularly a sentence beginning 'With all his failings, Burns was a most affectionate parent'.

Less of the thinly-veiled moralising and a more objective clinical assessment, based on Maxwell's casenotes or recollection (after all, the event must have been relatively fresh in Maxwell's mind when he discussed it with Currie), would have been of immense value to posterity. The vacuum left by Currie's disappointingly terse account was later filled by the ever-imaginative Allan Cunningham in 1824:

Burns had laid his head quietly on the pillow awaiting dissolution, when his attendant reminded him of his medicine and held the cup to his lip.

He started suddenly up, drained the cup at a gulp, threw his hands before him like a man about to swim, and sprung from head to foot of the bed – fell with his face down, and expired with a groan.[54]

'Honest Allan' was not satisfied with this effusion, for he toned it down ten years later when preparing his first edition of the *Works*:

On the fourth day, when his attendant held a cordial to his lips, he swallowed it eagerly – rose almost wholly up – spread out his hand – sprang forward nigh the whole length of the bed – fell on his face and expired.[55]

Robert Junior, while pooh-poohing Cunningham's version, produced some details of his own in the course of 'a long and memorable conversation' which he had with Dr Robert Carruthers of Inverness many years later:

Cunningham must have been misinformed. The poet was too much crippled by disease, and too much enfeebled, for such a strange exertion. He lay a helpless wreck, his mind wandering in delirium. His last words were – 'That rascal, Matthew Penn' – an incoherent ejaculation, prompted probably by some dread of the law and a gaol – for Matthew Penn was an attorney, and the poet was a few pounds in debt.[56]

Robert Chambers, writing much later but basing his account on the eye-witness statements of those who were still alive in 1838–51 when he was gathering his material, gave a more sober description of the poet's final hours. He repeated Robert Junior's statement about his father's last words, but added a rider:

To secure quietness in the house, his four little boys were sent to John Lewars's house. Jessy tended the sick man assiduously. Findlater came occasionally to soothe the last moments of his friend. Dr Maxwell, who had watched by his bed the greater part of the night, had left, and the only persons who remained in the room were a couple of sympathetic neighbours. The children were sent for to see their father for the last time in life. They stood round the bed, while calmly and gradually he sank into his last repose. The eldest son subsequently declared that his father's last words were a muttered execration against the law agent whose letter had embittered the closing scene of his life. His mother, however, in the latest years of her life, questioned the accuracy of this statement, and it is at least possible that the son – he was only a boy of ten – may have misunderstood his father's last ejaculation.[57]

Alexander Findlater, in his lengthy letter criticising the errors and inaccuracies in Cunningham's book, added his version of events:

On the night, indeed, immediately preceding his decease, I sat by his bedside, and administered the last morsel he ever swallowed, not certainly in the form of medicine, which at that period was totally relinquished as unavailing, nor of the cordial of romance; but what was better fitted to allay his thirst, and cool his parched and burning tongue.[58]

From Jean Burns herself John McDiarmid obtained verbal 'memoranda' of the poet's last days:

> He was closely confined to bed, and was scarcely *himself* for half an hour together. By this it is meant that his mind wandered, and that his nervous system was completely unhinged. He was aware of this infirmity himself, and told his wife that she was to touch him and remind him that he was going wrong. The day before he died he called, very quickly and with a hale voice, 'Gilbert! Gilbert!' Three days before he died he got out of bed, and his wife found him sitting in a corner of the room with the bed clothes about him. Mrs Burns got assistance, and he suffered himself to be gently led back to bed. But for the fit, his strength would have been unequal to such an exertion.[59]

John Syme's letters to Alexander Cunningham in those crucial last days of the poet's life, with the accuracy of their immediacy, provide additional information, though they were silent on the actual details of Robert's death.[60] The first, written by Syme on Sunday 17 July, was in response to one from Cunningham accompanying a letter for Burns which Syme delivered personally at the Brow:

> He, poor fellow, is in a very bad state of health. I really am extremely alarmed, not only by the cadaverous aspect and shaken frame of Burns, but from the accounts which I have heard from the first Faculty here. But I entertain strong hopes that the vigor of his former stamina will conquer his present illness, and that, by care and the attention and advice he receives from Dr Maxwell, he will recover. I do not mean to alarm you, but really poor Burns is very ill. However, do not say whence you heard so.

At noon on Tuesday, however, Syme wrote again without waiting for word from Cunningham:

> I conceive it to be a task (you would not forgive me did I omit it) to mention now, that I believe it is all over with him. I am this minute come from the mournful chamber in which I have seen the expiring genius of Scotland departing with Burns. Dr Maxwell told me yesterday that he had no hopes; today the hand of Death is visibly fixed upon him. I cannot dwell on the scene. It overpowers me – yet gracious God were it thy will to recover him! He had life enough to acknowledge me, and Mrs Burns said he had been calling on you and me continually. He made a wonderful exertion when I took him by the hand – with a strong voice he said 'I am much better today – I shall be soon well again, for I command my spirits and my mind. But yesterday I resigned myself to death.' Alas, it will not do.
>
> My dear friend Cunningham, we must think on what can be done for his family. I fear they are in a pitiable condition. We will here exercise our benevolence, but that cannot be great, considering the circumscribed place &c. In the metropolis of Scotland, where men of Letters and affluence, his acquaintances and his admirers, reside, I fondly hope there will be bestowed on his family that attention and regard which ought to

flow from such a source into such a channel. It is superfluous in me to suggest such an idea to *you* . . .

The illness is – the whole system debilitated and gone, beyond the power (perhaps) of man to restore.

On Thursday 21 July Syme wrote again:

Burns departed this morning at 5 o'Clock'. I will not enlarge on the mournful subject. Indeed, I can say no more at present on this event . . .

An attempt will be made to pay that tribute on the mournful event to be mentioned in our Dumfries Newspaper, which we trust will not be a commonplace narrative. But as our paper is not published till Tewesday next, it may be late before it can appear in Edinburgh. I therefore would wish that some attention should be paid to the account which may appear in the Edinburgh papers before that time.

I have written this in a very desultory manner, being quite shaken myself by a variety of distressful emotions which the direful event has occasioned. Adieu.

John Syme was largely responsible for organising Robert's funeral. At noon on Saturday 23 July he wrote to Cunningham:

I have this minute yours of 20th, and as you wish to hear extempore occurrences I shall indulge you at present by hastily running over those circumstances which I have arranged for the dignity and splendor of the Bard's funeral obsequies. They take place on Monday at one o'Clock. His corps to be privately carried to the Town hall early in the morning. The street from thence to the Churchyard to be lined on each side by the regiment of Cinqueport Cavalry and that of the Angus shire Fencibles. A Funeral party of the Volunteers, who are to fire over his grave, march with arms reversed in front of the procession, but preceded by the bands of music of these Regiments playing the Dead March. The body of Volunteers, in full uniform, with crapes on arm, but without accoutrements, sustain the Bier. The drums of the Corps muffled &c. follow it. The Magistrates in a body next, and all the Citizens and neighbouring gentry. The Bells are to toll. This will surely be a grand and proper parade and solemnity. All ranks have testified the readiest dispositions to the above.

The Cinque Ports Cavalry, commanded by Robert Banks Jenkinson (1770–1828), made a particularly dashing spectacle. The story goes that Jenkinson refused to meet the poet – a nonsense that can easily be refuted, for the Cinque Ports Cavalry replaced the Fifeshire Cavalry at Dumfries only a few weeks before Robert died. Shortly afterwards he assumed the courtesy title of Viscount Hawkesbury, when his father became Earl of Liverpool, and later he had a brilliant political career, crowned by the premiership (1812–27). In 1797 when the Militia Act introduced selective conscription by ballot and provoked widespread riots, Hawkesbury's cavalry covered themselves in ignominy when they massacred fifteen men, women and children at Tranent, East Lothian.[61]

An account of Robert's funeral appeared in the *Dumfries Journal* on 26 July. Dr Currie's account was based on that, and fuller accounts which appeared a day or two later in the Edinburgh newspapers, but characteristically he contrived to get the date wrong, stating that 'On the evening of the 25th of July, the remains of Burns were removed to the Town-Hall, and the funeral took place on the succeeding day'. Tradition maintains that the corpse was clad in that Volunteer uniform whose payment caused its owner so much anguish at the end of his life.

A party of the volunteers, selected to perform the military duty in the church-yard, stationed themselves in the front of the procession, with their arms reversed; the main body of the corps surrounded and supported the coffin, on which were placed the hat and sword of their friend and fellow-soldier; the numerous body of attendants ranged themselves in the rear; while the Fencible regiments of infantry and cavalry lined the streets from the Town-Hall to the burial ground in the Southern church-yard, a distance of more than half a mile. The whole procession moved forward to that sublime and affecting strain of music, the *Dead March* in Saul: and three vollies fired over his grave marked the return of Burns to his parent earth! The spectacle was in a high degree grand and solemn, and accorded with the general sentiments of sympathy and sorrow which the occasion had called forth.[62]

The best account of the funeral, however, was recorded in his diary by William Grierson. Under the heading of Monday 25 July he noted:

Showery forenoon, pleasant afternoon, wet evening and night. This day at twelve o'clock went to the burial of Robert Burns, who died on the 21st aged 38 years. In respect to the memory of such a genius as Mr Burns, his funeral was uncommonly splendid. The Military here consisting of the Cinque Ports Cavalry and Angusshire Fencibles, who having handsomely tendered their services, lined the streets on both sides from the Court House to the burial ground. The Corpse was carried from the place where Mr Burns lived to the Court House last night.

Order of Procession

The firing party which consisted of twenty of the Royal Dumfries Volunteers (of which Mr Burns was a member) in full uniform with crepes on the left arm, marched in front with their Arms reversed moving in a slow and solemn time to the Dead March in Saul which was played by the military band belonging to the Cinque Ports Cavalry. Next to the firing party was the band, then the bier and corpse supported by six of the Volunteers who changed at intervals. The relations of the deceased and a number of respectable inhabitants of both town and county followed next, then the remainder of the Volunteers followed in rank and the procession closed with a guard of the Angusshire Fencibles. The great bells of the churches tolled at intervals during the time of the procession. When it arrived at the churchyard gate the funeral party formed two lines and leaned their heads on their firelocks pointed to the ground – through this space the corpse was carried and borne forward to the grave. The party then drew up alongside of it and fired three volleys over the coffin when deposited in the earth. Thus closed a ceremony which on the whole presented a solemn, grand and affecting spectacle and accorded with the general sorrow and regret for the loss of a man whose like we can scarce see again.[63]

Alone of the poet's family, Gilbert came down from Mauchline to attend the funeral. Jean herself went into labour that morning and as the cortège was making its solemn way along the crowded streets to St Michael's kirkyard she gave birth to another son. The boy was named, not after Alexander Cunningham as Burns had promised, but in honour of the doctor who delivered him. Maxwell Burns, however, turned out to be a sickly infant who followed his father to the grave only thirty-three months later.

The actual expenses of the funeral were small: 2s 6d for the grave, 3s for the mortcloth and 5s for the tolling of the town's bells. The poet's debts amounted to £14 15s, including a bill for £2 3s from Dr Brown. This indicates that Brown, rather than Maxwell, had treated Robert in the last stages of his illness. His assets amounted to drafts for £15, a library valued at £90 and the indebtedness of brother Gilbert to the tune of £183 16s 7d.[64] The notion that Burns died a pauper is therefore quite ludicrous – yet it persists to this day. People remember those anguished cries for help, written by a man who was physically at the end of his tether, and overlook the more prosaic facts revealed in the documents of the poet's executry.

CHAPTER 18

Post Mortem

Now Robin lies in his last lair,
He'll gabble rhyme, nor sing nae mair;
Cauld poverty wi hungry stare,
   Nae mair shall fear him;
Nor anxious fear, nor cankert care,
   E'er mair come near him.

To tell the truth, they seldom fash'd him,
Except the moment that they crush'd him;
For sune as chance or fate had hush'd 'em,
   Tho e'er sae short,
Then wi a rhyme or sang he lash'd 'em,
   And thought it sport.

Elegy on the Death of Robert Ruisseaux (CW 268)

Robert was hardly laid to rest when malicious slanders began to circulate. Without doubt they were in circulation while he was still alive, and he was aware of them and bitterly resented them – as his letter to Samuel Clark indicates (CL 702):

> Some of our folks about the Excise Office, Edinburgh, had & perhaps still have conceived a prejudice against me as being a drunken dissipated character.– I might be all this, you know, & yet be an honest fellow, but you know that I am an honest fellow amd am nothing of this.

This, despite actually starting the letter with the words, 'I recollect something of a drunken promise yesternight to breakfast with you this morning'. The only other letter to Clark began with the candid admission, 'I was, I know, drunk last night' and alluded to the incident with Captain Dodd which almost led to a duel. On the face of it, there is some contradiction here. How could Robert maintain that he was not 'a drunken, dissipated character' while admitting to drunkenness at the same time? The answer seems to lie in the *degree* of intoxication. Similarly Syme could boast to Cunningham that he and Burns had been quite sober when they drank only one bottle of port between them. The eighteenth century was a period notorious for hard drinking, but in the context of his times Robert could not by any stretch of the imagination be described as a hard drinker. Yet, as recently as 1963, Thornton could write: 'The fact is that Burns was a drinker, prominent in an age of hard drinkers', the implication being that Robert could hold his liquor with the best of them and better than most.[1] By way of supporting this contention, Thornton quotes from four letters – including the letter to Clark, above (but without the passage in which Robert denied his drunken, dissipated character) – as a prelude to giving the text of the celebrated 'letter from Hell' addressed to Mrs Riddell. Thornton, of course, had a particular axe to grind; he was determined to rehabilitate the reputation of Dr James Currie, and the only way to deal with the good doctor's libelling of the dead was to try to make a case that what Currie wrote was fair comment.

More recently Richard Hindle Fowler has contributed his own bizarre theories. 'There is no doubt that Burns was a habitual wine drinker in his post-Ayrshire years, and on many occasions drank to excess.'[2] This is a sweeping generalisation not supported by actual evidence; Fowler merely accepts this as fact. So, too, he adds, 'Apart from the convivial scene, he was inclined to solitary indulgence, as is made clear from many of his letters'. This is a more damning allegation than the traditional one of Burns the social drinker; but there are only two letters in which Robert mentioned drinking on his own, and in both cases the circumstances were exceptional – to Archibald Lawrie from Edinburgh on 14 August 1787 (CL 128) and to Mrs McLehose from Castle Douglas on 25 June 1794 (CL 411). There are actually thirty-six references to drink, or drinking, in about seven hundred and twenty letters, roughly a twentieth, and many of these are in jocular vein. There are times when the steadiness of Robert's hand-writing and the length, complexity and grammatical correctness of the letters give the lie to his confessions. 'I am so completely nettled with the fumes of wine, that I cannot write any thing like a letter,' he confessed to Alexander Cunningham (CL 464) – and then proceeded to give him the transcript of his latest song. That Robert could deny a charge of drunkenness in a letter beginning with an admission of a drunken promise is surely an indication that his confessions ought not to be interpreted so literally. It is singularly unfortunate that many biographers have not only taken these admissions quite literally, but have seized upon them in order to level charges of utter debauchery.

This process began before Robert was cold in his grave. Not just 'about the Excise Office' in Edinburgh, but in Dumfries itself the notion that he was less than perfect was current, although it is only fair to state that this was entertained by people who did not know him personally, but only knew of him. William Grierson, despite the appellation 'Apostle to Burns'[3] which served as the title of the edited version of his diaries published in 1981 (one suspects as a ploy to increase interest and thereby boost sales), gives no evidence in these diaries that he knew the poet at all. Grierson was born in Dumfries in 1773 and therefore was fourteen years younger than the poet. Although he was later to play a prominent part in the Mausoleum Committee, formed in December 1813, he was only twenty-three when

Burns died. The friends and acquaintances mentioned in the diaries up to 1796 were not people associated with Burns. The poet makes a solitary appearance in Grierson's journal, and that was on 25 July 1796, the day of his funeral. That account ends:

> As for his private character and behaviour, it might not have been so fair as could have been wished but whatever faults he had I believe he was always worst for himself and it becomes us to pass over his failings in silence, and with veneration and esteem look to his immortal works which will live for ever. I believe his extraordinary genius may be said to have been the cause of bringing him so soon to his end, his company being courted by all ranks of people and being of too easy and accommodating a temper which often involved him in scenes of dissipation and intoxication which by slow degrees impaired his health and at last totally ruined his constitution.[4]

William Grierson was not himself a drinker of anything more stimulating than tea (though to judge from his diary, tea-drinking loomed rather large) and one can sense his pursed-lipped disapproval of 'people being in liquor', a phrase which appears in the entries for 1 January each year with monotonous regularity. William's idea of a good time was to visit the different churches of the neighbourhood on Sundays and sample the sermons. Sermon-tasting, not wine-bibbing, was his weakness. From the frank manner in which he described his own failings it is clear that the diary was not written with a view to publication, so there is no suggestion that the comments on Burns were written for effect. They represented the sincerely held beliefs of this rather earnest young man but, as such, were probably not untypical of the perception of those who had heard of Burns without having had the privilege of knowing him personally, far less intimately.

Like William Grierson, George Thomson never met Burns, but there was less excuse for him in view of the fact that he had received fifty-seven letters from Robert over a four-year period, and ought to have known, better than most, the character of the man he was dealing with. On 22 July Alexander Cunningham informed Syme that:

> Mr Thomson has kindly undertaken to announce the Death to the Public. It will appear perhaps tomorrow or Monday, and I dare say from his pen something very elegant will be said. Another friend of mine has kindly undertaken to manage the matter at Glasgow. Were you to write J. Currie at Liverpool, something handsome may be expected.[5]

Here we have the earliest reference to Dr James Currie who, shortly thereafter, was chosen by Syme and Cunningham to edit Robert's collected works and write the biography which occupied the first of the four volumes published in 1800. Currie (1756–1805) was born at Kirkpatrick Fleming, Dumfriesshire and was a classmate of Robert Riddell at Dumfries Academy before going on to study medicine at Edinburgh. He settled at Liverpool but in 1792 purchased Dumcrieff near Moffat. John Syme acted as the factor of this estate and it may be that Currie was with Syme in Dumfries that day in 1792 when he briefly met Burns in the High Street. Some years earlier, in Liverpool, his closest friend was Graham Moore, son of Dr John Moore who presented Currie with the copy of the Kilmarnock Edition which Mrs Dunlop had sent to him in 1786. Currie was related to the McMurdo family of Dumfries and Drumlanrig as well as the Duncans of Lochrutton. Graham Moore, by then a captain in the Royal Navy, was the dedicatee of the 1800 edition of the *Life and Works*.[6]

In fact, Currie wrote to Syme first. Significantly, Robert's reputation for supposed debauchery had even penetrated as far as Liverpool. On 26 July Dr James Currie had heard of the poet's death and the same day wrote to Syme at great length about Burns:

> I assure you, I lament over his early fate. I never saw this original genius but for a few minutes, in 1792, in the streets of Dumfries. In the little conversation I had with him, which was begun rather abruptly on my part, I could easily distinguish that bold, powerful, and ardent mind, which, in different circumstances, such as the present state of the world renders familiar to the imagination, might have influenced the history of nations. What did Burns die of? What family has he left – and in what circumstances? Am I right in supposing him not a mere poet, but a man of general talents? By what I have heard, he was not very correct in his conduct; and a report goes about that he died of the effects of habitual drinking. Be so good as to tell me what you think on this point.[7]

So Currie, who had been familiar with Robert's poetry since 1787, had heard malicious rumours. It is singularly unfortunate that, in the heat of business, Syme omitted to answer this, or two subsequent letters, from Currie; and when he did get around to writing in mid-August events had moved on at such a pace that Syme probably never bothered to answer Currie's earliest questions. Thus the opportunity to scotch the rumours was lost. In light of the subsequent reputations of both biographer and biographee, the concluding paragraph of Currie's original letter is of considerable interest:

> Men of genius like Burns are sure to be envied, and even hated, by cold-blooded mediocrity and selfish prudence; and, on that account, one receives reports to their disadvantage with great distrust. As you knew this singular man, of whom much will now be said, and much enquired in future times, I wish you would give me as much of his character and of his private life as you can without inconvenience, in addition to the points I have enquired into; and I will endeavour, in one way or another, to turn it to some account.

Syme's letter of 14 August has not survived, but its contents may be inferred from Currie's answer of the following day in which he volunteered his services as biographer and editor.

George Thomson's unsigned obituary appeared in the *Glasgow Mercury* and *Edinburgh Evening Courant* of Saturday 23 July and was subsequently reprinted in other Glasgow and Edinburgh papers, as well as many of the London and provincial papers and magazines, within the next few days:

> On the 21st inst. died at Dumfries, after a lingering illness, the celebrated ROBERT BURNS. His poetical compositions, distinguished equally by the force of native humour, by the warmth and the tenderness of passion, and by the glowing touches of a descriptive pencil, will remain a lasting monument of the vigour and the versatility of a mind guided only by the lights of nature and the inspirations of genius. The public, to whose amusement he has so largely contributed, will learn with regret that his extraordinary endowments were accompanied with frailties which rendered them useless to himself and his family. The last months of his short life were spent in sickness and indigence; and his widow, with five infant children and in the hourly expectation of a sixth, is now left without any resource but what she may hope from the regard due to the memory of her husband.

Thomson is believed by some scholars to have been the author of a much longer notice which appeared in the *London Chronicle* of 28 July 1796. Many of the phrases in the shorter notice, quoted above, were repeated in the longer notice, although there were some glaring errors which incline me to question DeLancey Ferguson's attribution to Thomson.[8] The latter must surely have been aware that the 'coarse edition of his poems' was first published at Kilmarnock, and not Dumfries as stated in this article. There is, in fact, considerable ground for doubting that Thomson was the author of the *Chronicle* obituary. For similar phraseology one must turn to Henry Mackenzie's review of the Kilmarnock Edition in *The Lounger*. If Mackenzie *were* the author of this review, then the reference to Dumfries as the place of publication could have been a deliberate error to throw the reader off the scent. In view of this newspaper's wide and influential readership, the damage done by the writer's insinuations to the poet's reputation was incalculable, undeniably colouring the view of many subsequent writers. After giving a potted biography, the notice continued:

> Burns was brought to Edinburgh for a few months, everywhere invited and caressed, and at last one of his patrons procured him the situation of an Exciseman, and an income somewhat less that 50 l. per ann. We know not whether any steps were taken to better this humble income. Probably he was not qualified to fill a superior station to that which was assigned him. We know that his manners refused to partake the polish of genteel society, that his talents were often obscured and finally impaired by excess, and that his private circumstances were embittered by pecuniary distress . . . a man who possessed in an extraordinary degree the powers and failings of genius. Of the former, his works will remain a lasting monument; of the latter, we are afraid that his conduct and his fate afford but too melancholy proofs. Like his predecessor Ferguson (*sic*), though he died at an early age, his mind was previously exhausted; and the

apprehensions of a distempered imagination concurred along with the indigence and sickness to embitter the last moments of his life.

Alexander Cunningham wrote to Syme on Sunday 24 July, 'You will see in the *Courant* and *Mercury* of last night a short Panageric (*sic*) to the Memory of Poor Burns, with which I hope you will be pleased'. Clearly he saw nothing objectionable in Thomson's use of the word 'frailties' which may have been intended as a reference to the indifferent health the poet had suffered in the last year; but, of course, such a vague word was open to other interpretation. Syme, not knowing that Thomson had written the obituary, wrote to Cunningham the day after the funeral and drew attention to this feature:

> We admire the notice which was in the 'Courant' and 'Mercury', except that part which related to the *frailties &c*. We were much hurt at this and reckoned it indelicate, if not unfeelingly superfluous on that occasion. Pardon this bluntness – I mean no personal application, for I am ignorant of its author, but I cannot help saying that it was improper to wake the idea of his irregularities while the melancholy subject of his death was announced. Maxwell, McMurdo, and others were extremely wounded by it.

It is a matter for supreme regret that neither Syme, nor Maxwell, nor McMurdo, nor any of the other Dumfries gentlemen who knew Burns best, took the trouble to rebut Thomson's insinuations. Thus the innuendo of 'frailties' cancelling the poet's genius and endowments was firmly planted within days of Robert's death. Thomson's statement was repeated, with slight modifications, in the *Scots Magazine* of July 1796. The anonymous obituarist in the *Monthly Magazine* for August 1796, however, went a step further by writing that:

> Though his early days were occupied in procuring bread by the labour of his own hands, yet his nights were devoted to books and the muses, except when they were wasted in the indulgencies of the social board, to which the poet was too immoderately attached in every period of his life . . . His conduct and his fate afford but too melancholy proofs of the failings of genius.[9]

In a postscript to a letter of 6 August, Syme complained bitterly to Cunningham: 'See some damned illiberal lies in the *Morning Chronicle*. Should they be noticed? With a vengeance or how?' Cunningham, replying three days later, was smarting over the way many of the late poet's so-called friends and admirers, when approached for a donation towards the fund for the widow and family of Burns, gave him nothing but 'cold civility and humiliating advice':

> The truth is, my dear Syme, the poor Bard's *frailties* – excuse this vile word – were not only so well known here, but often I believe exaggerated,

that even the admirers of Genius cannot be prevailed on to do what we all ought – 'to forget and forgive'.

The notice which roused Syme's ire, had appeared in the *Morning Chronicle* on Monday 1 August:

> We do not wish to reflect on the liberality of the Patrons of BURNS, but they surely discovered a want of judgment in the situation which they allotted him. It was exceedingly unfortunate to make *a Poet an Exciseman*. Poor BURNS all his life time was but too apt to be led away *by the temptation of good spirits*. What then must have been the case when it became his daily occupation *to fathom the cask!*

The Revd. Dr Muirhead of Buittle could not have put it more bitchily, but we may presume that this tasteless jibe at the late poet's expense was penned by James Perry himself. As Perry had printed a number of Robert's poems and songs without ever having to pay out those guineas he once promised, this mean jibe was all the more despicable. Here again, it was most unfortunate that neither Syme nor Cunningham, by now virtually alone in their campaign to raise funds for Robert's family, were too busy to challenge this vile calumny.

The only newspaper to take a charitably independent line was the *Dumfries Journal* whose issue of 26 July contained a brief obituary written by Thomas White of the Academy. White (1758–1825) was an Englishman, a native of Hexham, Northumberland, but he taught at the Academy for forty years and eventually became rector (headmaster). He was a second-lieutenant in the Volunteers and knew Robert intimately. His obituary was fulsome, to say the least:

> His manly form and penetrating eye strikingly indicated extraordinary mental vigor.
> For originality of wit, rapidity of conception and fluency of nervous phraseology, he was unrivalled.
> Animated by the fire of Nature, he uttered sentiments which, by their pathos, melted the heart to tenderness, or expanded the mind by their sublimity: As a luminary, emerging from behind a cloud, he arose, at once, into notice; and his works and his name can never die, while divine Poesy shall agitate the chords of the human heart.[10]

White shortly afterwards composed an ode 'To the Memory of Robert Burns' which was printed as a broadside. The general tone of this panegyric was laudatory, but unfortunately the concluding lines struck an uncomfortable note:

> Upon his frailties gathering clouds descend,
> To veil all, save the POET and the FRIEND![11]

What these frailties were, was nowhere specified. That White was a close friend of the poet is undeniable. Tradition states that Robert habitually took breakfast with the White family every Saturday, and White was one of the favoured few who received a presentation copy of the 1793 Edition, as well as a copy of Voltaire's *La Pucelle* inscribed by Burns. As early as 30 August 1796 White wrote to the Royal Literary Fund in London to solicit a pension for Jean Burns: 'The improvidence of genius is proverbial; and to the list of men of genius by whom pecuniary attentions have been neglected, the name of Robert Burns must, unfortunately for his family, be added.'[12] This letter was accompanied by a letter from John Syme himself, stating that White was 'an intimate of the late Bard and has testified his regard to his memory'. Syme's letter is worth quoting at length:

> I had the pleasure of being one of Burns's principal intimates – from which situation, by his early death, I have experienced a dejection and loss that I think cannot be repaired. Few, if any, who had not the opportunities I have enjoyed can feel the regret and sorrow at being deprived of the conversation and the *mind* (if I may express myself) of this Genius who, while passion at times hurried him into indiscretions, unfolded all the loveliness of virtue & the strength of intellect.
>
> His poetical powers speak for themselves – but the powers of his language and conversation were preeminent – and can live only in the memory of his acquaintances.[13]

Here we have a clue to the 'frailties' alluded to by Thomson and White. A predisposition to alcohol, real or imaginary, was something of which Thomson could have had no knowledge; whatever he had in mind could only have been communicated to him at second- or third-hand. But Thomas White was in a good position to observe Robert's waspish wit, his irascibility, his vindictiveness over the Riddell family, his politically reckless toasts and his outbursts in convivial company. Robert's frailties arose from an ungovernable tongue rather than from the contents of any bottle. They were the indiscretions of passion.

It is untrue to suggest, as Thornton has, that by not rebutting these allegations, those who knew Robert best conceded that the charges were just. In fact Maria Riddell had them in mind when she wrote her own memoir of the poet. John Syme called on her within days of Robert's death and entreated her, as one who had the ability to write, to prepare a longer and more considered encomium for the local newspaper. At first Maria demurred, but eventually agreed so long as her identity could be concealed. Ironically, her 'Sketch' was published under the pseudonym of Candidior (which can be translated as either 'more candid' or 'too candid'). Four versions of Maria's memoir are extant, though not a single example of the *Dumfries Journal* in which it was first published appears to have survived. In reverse order, chronologically, there is the commonly accepted version, first printed by Scott Douglas in 1877–9 and reprinted by Wallace in 1896 and Maurice Lindsay in more recent years.[14] The provenance of this version has never been established, but it actually bears little resemblance to any of the 1796–1801 versions. There is the version which appeared in the second and subsequent editions of Currie from 1801 onwards, which was revised by the lady herself, angry with Currie for the version which he had printed in the edition of 1800. And then there is the proof sheet of the *Journal* article which was submitted by Maria to Syme for correction. This proof, with Syme's marginal comments, shows Maria's first thoughts written in the heat of the moment.[15] Syme referred to this proof, in a letter to Alexander Cunningham on 18 August:

> It was left with me, and I found it quite impossible. In short I wrote her a note, a free note, searing the whole with a red hot iron. I shall make no other remark but that I hope it will not gain admission into the Magazines etc. she intends sending it to. It will only cost you 4d extra, so I enclose it as you may be curious to see the thing. However, don't mention names yet, for she is still correcting and labouring at it.[16]

To what extent the article was reworked before it was eventually published will never be known, until such times as a copy of the newspaper turns up.[17] If Syme's 'red hot iron' were effective, then we may assume that the published version was considerably toned down. In the proof version such highly emotive phrases as 'irregularities of a man of Genius', 'frailties that cast their shade', 'wild effervescence of desire', 'imprudencies that sullied brighter qualifications', 'inconsistencies that sink nature', 'most rancorous malevolence', 'aversion the most acrimonious', and, most damning of all, 'a penchant for the joy-inspiring bowl', leap from the printed sheet. This was, in fact, not so much an exercise in obituary as in pure bitchery, according with the statement of Alexander Smellie, son of Maria's publisher (who visited her at Halleaths early in 1796), that although then ostensibly reconciled to Burns she was talking of the poet 'in terms of indignation and opprobrium, only perhaps too well justified by his conduct towards herself'.[18] The language was certainly moderated in 1800 and even further toned down in 1801, when Maria inserted a paragraph aiming at damage limitation:

> Conscious indeed of my own inability to do justice to such a subject, I should have continued wholly silent had misrepresentations and calumny been less industrious; but a regard to truth, no less than affection for the memory of a friend, must now justify my offering to the public a few at least of those observations which an intimate acquaintance with Burns, and the frequent opportunities I have had of observing equally his happy qualities and his failings for several years past, have enabled me to communicate.[19]

This paragraph does not appear in the Scott Douglas or subsequent versions. There is little doubt that, by the time Maria wrote these words, she was alarmed at the extent to which Robert's reputation had been besmirched. The memoir, as published in 1801, is a very fair and perceptive one, facing up to the 'inconstancy and caprice' of the poet but setting the record straight. Maria could not be certain whether 'the keenness of satire' was his forte or his foible. It remains a moot point whether, by 1801, Maria had become aware of the vicious lampoons of 1794 or not. Robert's wit, she noted,

> had always the start of his judgment, and would lead him to the indulgence of raillery uniformly acute, but often unaccompanied with the least desire to wound . . . He paid for his mischievous wit as dearly as any one could do. ''Twas no extravagant arithmetic,' to say of him, as was said of Yorick, that 'for every ten jokes he got an hundred enemies;'

Maria cited Samuel Johnson who loved 'a good hater' and she felt that Burns 'fell but little short even of the surly Doctor in this qualification, as long as the disposition to ill-will continued; but the warmth of his passions was fortunately corrected by their versatility'. Robert was 'candid and manly in the avowal of his errors, and *his avowal* was a *reparation*'.

A commonly held view in the Age of Enlightenment was that the person endowed with genius paid for this with some flaws of character. This was a comfort to ordinary mortals who could indulge their *schadenfreude* in contemplating the clay feet of their idols. Currie himself was guided by William Smellie's *Philosophy of Natural History* when he wrote that no sentient being with mental powers greatly superior to those of men, could possibly live and be happy in this world: 'If such a being really existed, his misery would be extreme'.[20] Maria echoed this in one of the more memorable passages in her memoir:

> I will not however undertake to be the apologist even of a man of genius, though I believe it is as certain that genius never was free from iregularities, as that their absolution may in great measure be justly claimed, since it is perfectly evident that the world had continued very stationary in its intellectual acquirements, had it never given birth to any but men of plain sense. Evenness of conduct, and a due regard to the decorums of the world, have been so rarely seen to move hand in hand with genius, that some have gone as far as to say, though there I cannot wholly acquiesce, that they are even incompatible; besides, the frailties that cast their shade over the splendour of superior merit, are more conspicuously glaring than where they are the attendants of mere mediocrity. It is only on the gem we are disturbed to see the dust; the pebble may be soiled, and we never regard it. The eccentric intuitions of genius too often yield the soul to the wild effervescence of desires, always unbounded, and sometimes equally dangerous to the repose of others as fatal to its own . . . The child of nature, the child of sensibility, unschooled in the rigid precepts of philosophy, too often unable to control the passions which proved a source of frequent errors and misfortunes to him, Burns made his own artless apology in language more impressive than all the argumentatory vindications in the world could do, in one of his own poems, where he delineates the gradual expansion of his mind to the lessons of the 'tutelary muse', who concludes an address to her pupil, almost unique for simplicity and beautiful poetry, with these lines:

I saw thy pulse's madd'ning play
Wild send thee pleasure's devious way;
Misled by Fancy's meteor ray,
    By passion driven;
But yet the light that led astray,
    Was *light from heaven!*[21]

In other words, whatever the waywardness of genius, it was amply redeemed by the sublimity of the poetry it produced. Maria defended a man whose conduct she had forgiven and almost forgotten, and whose true character she was in a position to understand far better than were the men whose more pretentious accounts were soon to be before the public.[22]

The first steps towards a fund for Robert's dependents were taken by Alexander Cunningham. On 20 July, the day before the poet died, Cunningham wrote to Syme and came straight to the point:

> It decidedly occurs to me, 1st. a Subscription for his Wife and Infant family – and *afterwards* the Sale of his posthumous works, Letters, Songs, &c., to a respectable London Bookseller. All that can be done shall be done by me. We must do the thing instantaneously and while the pulse of the Public will beat at the name of Burns. Pray do you know or can you inform yourself if he sold his Copy right of his Work to Creech. I suspect *not*; this would be a great fund. Creech must not be consulted or dealt with. How Burns could give him some of his late MSS. appears unaccountable upon every human principle.
>
> To you and Dr Maxwell he owes much. Indeed, I think it was a man doing himself an honour to serve Burns, and it reflects disgrace on the Eighteenth Century to have allowed him to live and die in poverty.[23]

The work of the fund-raisers was hampered by erroneous reports circulating in the press. Typical of these was the notice which appeared in the *Cumberland Paquet* of 26 July:

> On Monday, the 18th inst., at Dumfries, MR ROBERT BURNS, the Ayrshire poet, well-known, and not unworthily celebrated, for his many beautiful productions. As a testimony of respect for superior genius, a gentleman in that place requested of the widow of the deceased permission to defray the funeral expenses; this was complied with, and the obsequies of the bard were deferred till yesterday. In the meantime, we learn that numerous presents have been made by the neighbouring gentry to his relict and surviving children.

This may have been the notice which upset Syme very much when writing to Cunningham on 29 July:

> I am vexed to see accounts, false in fact and mixed with foreign matter unfriendly to his shade, published in several papers – particularly an abominable lie in the Whitehaven papers. But the Edinburgh and Dumfries papers will set matters right, and I hope correct errors &c.

Sadly, Syme had not reckoned on the ways of the press. By the time he got around to remonstrating with the several newspapers, if he ever did, Burns would have been yesterday's news. But the damage was done. The general impression may have contributed to the relative apathy of those former friends and associates, let alone the general public, who gave the fund scant support. Syme, Maxwell and McMurdo had actually called a meeting at the Dumfries Club the day before Robert's death and set the ball rolling. Originally they had high hopes that Patrick Miller of Dalswinton would take the lead in raising funds; but while Miller was quite happy to lend his name to the campaign, he was prepared to give little else, either in time or cash. Nevertheless Syme and his friends managed to raise seventy guineas for Jean and her family within a matter of days, so that the poet's debts, together with the funeral costs, could be met immediately.

While Syme laboured at Dumfries, Cunningham busied himself on Robert's behalf at Edinburgh. He turned first to Dugald Stewart and George Thomson. The latter was a dead loss from the outset, and Stewart's interest flagged within forty-eight hours, though not before he had accompanied Cunningham to call on Sir William Forbes to enlist the support of his bank in gathering subscriptions. The bank did not normally act on behalf of individuals in this manner, but Lewis Hay, a director of the bank and husband of Margaret Chalmers, helped to overcome this problem. Wild rumours in Edinburgh, that the Excise had settled on Jean a pension equivalent to Robert's full salary, and that King George himself had granted the widow a pension of £50 a year, may have helped to dampen the charity of the public. Though Cunningham laboured long and hard, by mid-April 1797 he had managed to raise only £171 19s 6d which he then remitted to the Trustees at Dumfries. Dr Currie at Liverpool raised £73 10s. By the same date, however, Syme had raised almost £500, with another £100 due and still more promised.

Cunningham's letters to Syme reveal his bitter disappointment at the miserable response his efforts elicited in Edinburgh. Robert's lines regarding the treatment of Robert Fergusson, from the 'Epistle to William Simpson' (CW 107), must have been ringing in his ears:

> My curse upon your whunstane hearts,
> Ye E'nbrugh gentry!
> The tythe o what ye waste at cartes
> Wad stow'd his pantry!

On 23 July Cunningham had called on Sir John Sinclair, for whom Robert had written an account of the Monkland Friendly Society. Cunningham hoped to enlist Sinclair's aid in writing to Henry Dundas to obtain a small annuity for the poet's widow and children. Imagine his chagrin when the baronet refused to do so, adding insult to injury by offering Cunningham a guinea for Jean. Cunningham stiffly told him that he could put himself down for that sum in any public list. 'I shall ever from my heart despise Sir John. He is a vain, poor Creature, with some ostentatious Industry and no feeling.' Cunningham had high hopes of Erskine of Mar, who had so nobly championed the poet when rumours of his dismissal were flying around, and the fact that his eldest son had married Dalswinton's daughter Janet was thought to clinch the matter; but Erskine turned out to be 'luck warm'. Cunningham confided to Syme:

> You would be surprized to know of my distress and trouble in arranging matters, and how they will go is to me very doubtful. Indeed, to tell you honestly, I despond of any Sum of consequence being obtained here.

The following day, however, Cunningham perked up. The Lord Advocate had agreed to forward his petition to Dundas regarding a pension for Jean. His confidence was shortlived because this proposal lacked the backing of prominent gentry in Dumfriesshire. The campaign was grievously hampered by the conduct of Miller of Dalswinton. Having shown his parsimony in contributing to the Dumfries fund, he refused to accept the position as guardian of the fund or to promote the plan to approach Dundas. Cunningham was pleased to report, however, that James Fergusson of Banks, Ayrshire, had offered to educate the sons of Burns free of charge at Ayr Academy where he had a number of bursaries in his own gift. This generous offer was conditional on Jean and her family moving back to Ayrshire, which Syme considered a mere formality: 'The poor woman is so passive that she would agree to any proposal coming from a friendly quarter.' When he approached Gilbert Burns about accommodating his sister-in-law and her young brood, Gilbert demurred; and Jean herself showed a surprisingly negative response, refusing point-blank to leave Dumfries.

To be sure, the picture was not entirely gloomy. Patrick Heron himself approached the Lord Advocate and, more importantly, had brought pressure to bear on Creech to surrender his claims to the copyright. He also promised to get Robert Junior a bursary to go to Glasgow University in due course. Alexander John Riddell complemented this by promising £25 per annum for four years to cover the costs of young Robert's college education.[24]

When Syme suggested to Cunningham that he should enlist the help of William Nicol, Cunningham replied that this was impossible as Nicol was 'constantly besoted and Drunk'. This was unduly harsh; Nicol was, in fact, ill at this time and was 'highly distressed by a jaundice combined with some other complaints' which turned out to be the cirrhosis of the liver that hastened him to his grave the following year. He had been informed of Robert's death by John Lewars to whom he replied on 30 August at considerable length. He apologised for his delay in answering, on account of his illness from which he was now convalescing. Nicol was distraught at the news of 'the premature death of my dearly beloved Burns' and since then 'an oppressive gloom, as deep as the darkest shades of night,' hung over him:

I can no longer view the face of Nature, with the same rapture; and social joy is blighted to me, for ever.– It gives me great pain to see, that the encomiums, passed upon him, both in the Scotch and English news-papers, are mingled with reproaches, of the most indelicate and cruel Nature. But stupidity and idiotcy rejoice, when a great and an immortal genius falls; and they pour forth their invidious reflections, without reserve, well knowing, that the dead Lion, from whose presence, they formerly scudded away, with terror, and, at whose voice they trembled through every nerve, can devour no more.[25]

On a more practical note, Nicol speculated as to what had become of the money, amounting to £700 by his estimate, which Robert had received from the first Edinburgh Edition and the sale of the copyright:

He told me he had advanced near £300 to his brother Gilbert, for the cul-tivation of his farm in Ayrshire. This affair ought to be strictly inves-tigated, a settlement made, and, in case of non-payment, an assignation to the tacks granted to Mrs Burns. I do not like the aspect of this affair. It is not improbable, such is the depravity of the human heart, that his avarice may tempt him to press his own interest to that of the large & unprovided family of his brother.

Nicol alluded to some of the wild rumours about the poet's death which he had heard in Edinburgh:

The Fanatics have now got it into their heads, that dreadful bursts of penetential sorrow issued from the breast of our friend, before he expired. But if I am not much mistaken in relation to his firmness, he would disdain to have his dying moments disturbed with the sacerdotal gloom, & the sacerdotal howls. I know he would negotiate with God alone, concerning his immortal interests.

Nicol now faded from the picture; his convalescence was shortlived and he died on 21 April 1797. Despite Cunningham's strictures, Willie Nicol's heart was in the right place, and some more sound common sense of the sort expressed in his letter would not have come amiss. Instead, Syme and Cunningham had to soldier on virtually unaided, as, one by one, the friends of Burns deserted the campaign. Increasingly they were faced with the obstructiveness, unco-operativeness and downright self-interest of people like Maria Riddell, Agnes McLehose and Robert Ainslie, Mrs Dunlop and Gilbert Burns, to say nothing of George Thomson and William Creech. The public appeal for the loan of manuscripts produced a good response – too good, in fact, for Syme and Cunningham were often bombarded with the manuscripts of poems which had long existed in printed form and thus merely confused the issue and made the work of the Trustees even harder. When it came to the letters, however, those closest to Burns proved remarkably coy, more concerned to retrieve their own letters to Robert than release Robert's letters to them. Maria Riddell, on the face of it, was among the more helpful individuals, but she used her activities on behalf of the committee to retrieve all her correspondence which was presumably consigned to the flames. To this day, not a single letter from Maria to Robert has ever come to light.

Syme and Maxwell, in the meantime, went through all the letters that were in the poet's possession at the time of his death, 'except a considerable packet of a peculiar description' which turned out to be the letters of Mrs McLehose. The protracted negotiations with this lady to retrieve her *billets doux* in exchange for a sight of Robert's letters, have already been discussed.[26] On 12 August Syme wrote to Cunningham:

> Every letter of the least imaginable merit or consequence are packed up and will be sent to you &c. for selection. We burnt the palpably useless cards &c., for I assure you they were absolutely useless for any earthly purpose and must have created a confusion &c.

Syme then discussed the packet 'of a peculiar description' at great length: 'They are letters from a female, who must have felt the genuine passion of love'. Syme and Maxwell were most impressed by this correspondence and surmised that 'the person, if alive, must have an anxious, distracted heart'. They were not to be kept long in suspense. For the time being they debated what should be done with such passionate effusions:

> Avaunt the sacrilege of destroying them or shutting them up for ever from the light. But on the other hand, can we bring them into light? If you consult on this point, let it be with one or two chosen friends – one or two of the elect – and let the seal of honour and secrecy be previously impressed.

There is no doubt that Syme and Maxwell were privileged to read letters from Clarinda which that lady subsequently destroyed. One wonders what priceless letters and documents of incalculable historical and biographical value were inadvertently consigned to the flames by these well-meaning friends, either through ignorance or misplaced good intentions. In fairness to them, theirs was an invidious task. Robert had meant to sort out his papers but never had the time nor the strength for the task; so this role devolved on his devoted friends. As early as 3 August, in fact, they had decided to purge Robert's indelicacies with the flames. A similarly drastic approach was adopted by James Currie to whom the accumulation was eventually turned over; and who knows what letters and manuscripts were destroyed in the latter part of 1796 and even later.

On 31 August Syme wrote formally to Currie inviting him to become the official biographer and editor. Currie, despite his initial enthusiasm for the task, had held back in the belief that someone who had known the poet would be better fitted for the job, and had assumed that Dugald Stewart, Maria Riddell or even Syme himself might have filled that role. Early in September he wrote to Syme expressing his reservations.[27] Syme communicated this to Cunningham on 11 September, adding that he had spent the entire forenoon writing 'a monstrous long letter' to Currie to persuade him to take on the task. Cunningham replied on 17 September endorsing Syme's view that Currie was the fittest person to become the poet's biographer. Currie himself replied to Syme on 16 September agreeing to take on the job. This was on the understanding that Cunningham would vet the poet's papers first:

> He will, of course, be very cautious whom he trusts with a sight of the naked effusions of poor Burns; for there are many that would, from mere curiosity, wish to inspect them; and several who, I fear, would be glad of an opportunity of finding in them food for their malevolence.[28]

Of the subsequent trials and tribulations of Syme, Maxwell, Cunningham and Currie in sorting, arranging, transcribing and editing the poems, songs and letters of Burns nothing need be said here. The subject has been very fully discussed and analysed by Thornton. One aspect, however, requires to be examined and that is Currie's allegations concerning the poet. An addiction to alcohol is a charge which, in one form or another, permeates Currie's biography, but the more glaring passages will suffice. Speaking of the poet's removal to Dumfries in 1791 Currie wrote:

> Hitherto Burns, though addicted to excess in social parties, had abstained from the habitual use of strong liquors, and his constitution had not suffered any permanent injury from the irregularities of his conduct. In Dumfries, temptations to *the sin that so easily beset him*, continually presented themselves; and his irregularities grew by degrees into habits. These temptations unhappily occurred during his engagements in the business of his office, as well as during his hours of relaxation; and though he clearly foresaw the consequence of yielding to them, his appetites and sensations, which could not prevent the dictates of his judgment, finally triumphed over the powers of his will.

Currie blamed Robert's celebrity for his downfall. People came from all over the country to meet him. As he could not receive them in his own home, he had perforce to take them to one or other of the taverns:

> These interviews passed at the inns of the town, and often terminated in those excesses which Burns sometimes provoked, and was seldom able to resist. And among the inhabitants of Dumfries and its vicinity, there were never wanting persons to share his social pleasures; to lead or accompany him to the tavern; to partake in the wildest sallies of his wit; to witness the strength and the degradation of his genius.[29]

Even in a discussion of Robert's politics, Currie returned to his favourite theme:

Though the vehemence of Burns's temper, increased as it often was by stimulating liquors, might lead him into many improper and unguarded expressions, there seems no reason to doubt his attachment to your mixed form of government.[30]

Not content with insinuating habitual drunkenness, Currie hinted at even greater depravity. In his more purple passages the good doctor's narrative reads like the *Rake's Progress*:

In his moments of thought he reflected with the deepest regret on his fatal progress, clearly foreseeing the goal towards which he was hastening, without the strength of mind necessary to stop, or even to slacken his course. His temper now became more irritable and gloomy; he fled from himself into society, often of the lowest kind. And in such company, that part of the convivial scene, in which wine increases sensibility and excites benevolence, was hurried over, to reach the succeeding part, over which uncontrolled passion generally presided. He who suffers the pollution of inebriation, how shall he escape other pollution? But let us refrain from the mention of errors over which delicacy and humanity draw the veil.[31]

The next paragraph held up Jean as a domestic saint by comparison:

In the midst of all his wanderings, Burns met nothing in his domestic circle but gentleness and forgiveness, except in the gnawings of his own remorse. He acknowledged his transgressions to the wife of his bosom, promised amendment, and again and again received pardon for his offences. But as the strength of his body decayed, his resolution became feebler, and habit acquired predominating strength.

This led naturally to the incident about February 1796 in which Robert was alleged to have returned home at three in the morning 'benumbed and intoxicated'. Elsewhere Currie stated that 'The fatal defect in his character lay in the comparative weakness of his volition',[32] implying that Robert was weak-willed and lacking in self-discipline. Long passages, with even longer footnotes, dilated on the temptations of other stimulants, such as tea, coffee, tobacco and opium – the 'wounds to which indolent sensibility is exposed'. Page after page in similar vein, as tedious as it is tendentious, padded out this so-called biography which was very short on substance. The plain fact is that Currie relied heavily on Syme and Gilbert for such facts of Robert's life as he could glean. Both of them travelled to Liverpool in the autumn of 1797 to confer with Currie. Gilbert had hardly seen his brother after 1788 so he was in no position to furnish details of the later years of Robert's life. Indeed, one of the reasons he did not complain about Currie's libellous statements when the book was published was that he assumed that they must be correct.

Syme himself, after years of silence, lashed out in 1819. At the inaugural meeting of the Dumfries Burns Club, which met on Robert's birthday, Vice-President Syme stated quite bluntly:

Burns has too long suffered from the combined attacks of prejudice and malignity, attacks to which some high and cruel names in the literary world have most ungenerously lent their sanction. This is not fair.[33]

Unfortunately, because Currie appears to have destroyed Syme's letters, there is no way of proving or disproving the suspicion that, somehow, Syme must have conveyed the impression of drunkenness and debauchery which coloured Currie's narrative. Yet suspicion did fall on Syme late in his life, and has unfairly lingered there ever since. In 1826 Robert Chambers visited Dumfries and interviewed the poet's friend, by that time an elderly gentleman whom he described as 'a well-bred *bon vivant*, with a rich fund of anecdote'. Syme expatiated on 'the electric flashes of the poet's eloquence at table, and the burning satiric flashes which he was accustomed to launch on those whom he disliked or who betrayed any affectation or meanness'.[34] Three years later Syme gave Chambers a description of his friend which added nothing to the record, but at this remove in time Syme conceded:

> He loved wine and would take it freely and in considerable quantities but I never saw him brutally drunk – I have seen many *gentlemen* more drunk than ever I saw Burns – I never saw Burns drink a *dram* but as any Gentleman might.[35]

Burns himself has left a candid description of his attitude to alcohol which helps to put the matter in perspective. In a volume of Sterne Robert inserted a passage:

> I love drinking now and then. It defecates the standing pool of thought. A man perpetually in the paroxysms and fevers of inebriety is like a half-drowned, stupid wretch condemned to labour unceasingly in water, but a now-and-then tribute to Bacchus is like the cold bath – bracing and invigorating.[36]

Chambers considered that Syme had 'the defects of a lively temperament' and blamed him for a curious story which had long been in circulation. This related to a conversation on some aspects of Robert's personal conduct which took place at one of their social evenings at Ryedale. According to Syme:

> I might have spoken daggers but I did not mean them: Burns shook to the inmost fibre of his frame, and drew his sword-cane, when I exclaimed: 'What! wilt thou thus, and in mine own house?' The poor fellow was so stung with remorse, that he dashed himself down on the floor.[37]

Chambers investigated this story when he interviewed Syme in 1826. The latter had only the vaguest recollection of the incident and dismissed it as a bit of histrionic horseplay, half in jest. Nevertheless Chambers felt that

Syme could not be acquitted of culpable carelessness in allowing such a story to gain serious currency.[38]

McNaught[39] asked rhetorically why did Currie not apply to Alexander Findlater, the Revd. James Gray (1770–1830) and others who knew Burns intimately in his last years. This is a good question, for it is abundantly clear to anyone reading Currie's biography that, apart from printing a version, or versions, of Maria Riddell's memoir, Currie made little or no attempt to secure eye-witness accounts of the poet. There was one other possibility overlooked by Thornton. The Revd. Thomas Duncan (1776–1858), whose eldest brother George married Currie's daughter, was, in late 1796, tutor to the Hodgson family of Ince near Liverpool and was the doctor's protégé. A letter of twenty-eight pages, believed to have been written by Duncan to Currie on 10 October 1796[40] contains a detailed critique of Burns's poems. Donald Low surmises that Currie asked his young friend for his judgment of Burns and his works. One passage is of some significance in shedding light on the prejudicial views of Burns held at the time of his death:

> I have to offer you a thousand thanks, Sir, in return for the pleasure you have been the means of procuring me. An attentive perusal of the works of our bard has convinced me of the wrong I had formerly done to his character, not only as a Poet, but also as a Man – I have now discovered what I had long suspected, that I had been accustomed to view him with the jaundiced eye of prejudice . . . How often, since the death of my countryman, have I lamented that that melancholy event should have been the first which awakened my sympathy for his sufferings – which opened my eyes to his merits!

Thomas's earlier prejudice against Burns may have been coloured by the opinions of his brother George, a fellow Volunteer but definitely among the Tory diehards of the district. Thomas Duncan's view of Burns, like that of his contemporary, William Grierson, was coloured by hearsay. But the view expressed in this letter should have tended to steer Currie away from the malicious myths of alcoholism.

By the time that Findlater and Gray, rather belatedly, came forward with their rebuttal of Currie's charges in 1814, Currie himself had been dead for almost a decade, but his work had gone through nine editions. Currie's friend, William Roscoe, admitted then that had the biographer had the testimony of these individuals in 1797, it would have modified, if not fundamentally affected, the material which he had obtained from other sources – 'an admission which surely reflects on the methods employed by Currie in collecting his materials' added McNaught.

That Currie had virtually no first-hand knowledge of his subject ought to have made him more careful in obtaining accurate testimony. It is worth noting that, when the first volume of Currie's projected four-volume work appeared in 1800, it was roundly condemned by the essayist, Charles Lamb. Writing to Samuel Taylor Coleridge, he said:

Have you seen the new edition of Burns – his posthumous works and letters? I have only been able to procure the first volume, which contains his life – very confusedly and badly written, and interspersed with dull pathological and medical discussions. It is written by a Dr Currie. Do you know the weak but well-meaning doctor? Alas! *ne sutor ultra crepitum*.[41]

There can be no doubt that Currie's impression of Robert's character was formed as a result of reading the memoir of the poet written by Robert Heron (1764–1807) which was serialised in the *Monthly Magazine* in March and June 1797.[42] It was reprinted in the *Edinburgh Magazine*, beginning in April 1797, and the *Philadelphia Magazine* the following year. It was also released late in 1797 as a separate pamphlet which enjoyed a wide circulation. In 1800 it was included in a new edition of Burns's poems published by William Magee at Belfast, and three years later in an edition by Gilbert and Hodge of Dublin. As late as 1834 Robert Chambers reproduced Heron's memoir as the only life of Burns printed in his *Biographical Dictionary of Eminent Scotsmen* where it was hailed as 'an uncommonly clear view of the life and character' of the poet. The second (1950), third (1971) and fourth (1981) editions of Hecht's biography of Burns included Heron's memoir as an appendix and it was also reproduced in full in Maurice Lindsay's *Burns Encyclopaedia*. It is astonishing that such a scurrilous piece of work should have been perpetuated in this manner. The only work of recent times where Heron's memoir has a legitimate place is in Donald Low's *Robert Burns, the Critical Heritage* (1974) which is a comprehensive collection of all the critical writings about Burns from 1786 to 1840.

Heron was born at Creehead, Galloway on 6 November 1764, the son of a weaver. He was taught at home by his mother, Jean McClimond, and did not attend the parish school till he was nine, but he was a precocious child who was employed as a pupil-teacher only two years later, and at the tender age of fourteen was appointed schoolmaster at Kelton, Kirkcudbrightshire. Here he acquired a reputation as a youthful martinet with a sadistic streak, yet his undue severity never attracted the censure meted out to James Clarke at Moffat. By 1780 he had saved sufficient money to enrol at Edinburgh University. While an undergraduate he began writing articles for newspapers and magazines. He became a licentiate of the Church of Scotland and was for a time assistant to the Revd. Dr Hugh Blair. It may have been at the home of Dr Blacklock that Heron first met Burns in the winter of 1786–7, although Heron made no mention of such a meeting in any of his writings. In the summer of 1789, however, he paid a visit to Ellisland and undertook to carry a letter from the poet to Dr Blacklock which he failed to deliver. Robert alluded to this in his verse-epistle to Blacklock (CW 370–2), despatched on 21 October 1789:

> The Ill-Thief blaw the Heron south,
> And never drink be near his drouth!
> He tauld mysel by word o mouth,
>   He'd tak my letter:
> I lippen'd to the chiel in trowth,
>   And bade nae better.

> But aiblins, honest Master Heron
> Had at the time, some dainty fair one
> To ware his theologic care on,
>   And holy study,
> And, tired o sauls to waste his lear on,
>   E'en tried the body.

Thus Robert poked gentle fun at the budding Holy Willie whose partiality to wine and women he had noted. This verse-epistle was not published till 1800, in Currie's edition, but no doubt Blacklock showed it to Heron at the time. Raymond Lamont-Brown considers that these verses triggered off a strange psychotic hatred in Robert Heron against Burns,[43] but there is no evidence in Heron's very candid and self-revealing journal to support this view. Furthermore, the acquaintance was renewed in August 1791 when Heron paid a visit to Galloway and Dumfriesshire. On 6 August, as he noted in his diary, he dined with his friends Mr (William) Bradefute (of Penpont) and James Grierson of Dalgoner in the company of the poet. On that occasion Heron recorded that Burns left the party about eleven o'clock at night.[44] By that date, however, Heron had abandoned the Church for a precarious career in journalism, although he continued as a ruling elder for New Galloway and was a delegate to the General Assembly till 1799.[45]

In 1793 he published his *Journey through the Western Counties of Scotland*. Ironically, in light of his one lasting contribution to Scottish literature, Heron's fondness for the bottle was his undoing, and in 1794 he was thrown into prison for debt. His creditors suggested that he should undertake *A History of Scotland* for Morison of Perth as a way of paying them off. The first volume, published later that year, was almost entirely written in gaol, a fact mentioned by Heron in the preface in mitigation for his 'considerable imperfections'. The excuse was naïve, for a hallmark of *all* Heron's writings was hurried composition compounded by superficiality. The *History* was published in six volumes (1794–9). In 1798 he produced a comedy at the Theatre Royal, Edinburgh, which, on its opening night, was 'hopelessly condemned before the second act' – a record without equal in the annals of the British theatre. Heron, however, attributed his lamentable failure to a conspiracy against him and promptly published his play under the title of *St Kilda in Edinburgh, or News from Camperdown, a Comic Drama in two Acts, with a Critical Preface, to which is added an Account of a famous Ass Race.* Not surprisingly, this curious production attracted absolutely no attention. Embittered and disappointed that his genius was not recognised in his native country, he moved to London in 1799. Heron had a facility for languages and it is significant that he found employment as the editor of a government newsletter aimed at the French royalist refugee community. Although he was now earning £300 a year, old habits of dissipation got the better of him and in 1806 he was committed to Newgate Prison for debt. From gaol he appealed on 2 February 1807 to the Royal Literary Fund, citing his services to literature, notably Dr Currie's avowal of his indebtedness to Heron in writing his biography of Burns. This elicited no response and Heron was left to rot in prison. By that time a chronic alcoholic, he contracted a fever and was transferred to St Pancras Hospital where he died on 13 April.[46]

His memoir of Burns, described as 'a work of some value, owing to the author's knowledge of the south-west of Scotland',[47] is a curious amalgam of the sort of vivid writing which was later to be characteristic of Allan Cunningham and a none too subtle vindictiveness, alternately praising and damning Burns. Considering that this was ostensibly an exercise in biography, this lengthy tract of almost 13,600 words is amazingly short on actual facts. Ironically it began, 'Biography is, in some instances, the most trifling and contemptible, in others, the most interesting and instructive of all the species of literary composition'. Obviously Heron thought that his work fell into the latter category when, in fact, it was a prime example of the former. In a lengthy preamble Heron set out his aims 'to trace the gradual development of the character and talents of his hero'. Heron informed his readers that 'Robert Burns was a native of Ayrshire, one of the western counties of Scotland', but the date and place of birth were not mentioned. 'His father passed through life in the condition of a hired labourer, or a small farmer', but neither the man's name nor an outline of his career was given. 'Even in that situation, it was not hard for him to send his children to the parish-school', but instead of the facts, including the endeavours of William Burnes and his neighbours to hire John Murdoch, Heron digressed at length on the parish-school system of Scotland. There was no mention of how Robert began to compose songs and poetry, or of the factors that influenced him in adolescence – other than a passing reference to the metrical psalms. Later, Heron enumerated the poets, from Ramsay to Beattie, whom Burns read, but the development of Robert's work was not traced at all.

Strangely, in view of the high moral tone adopted in the latter part of this memoir, Heron did not mention Robert's tangled love life which played a significant part in his decision to emigrate, and thus his decision to publish his poems. Instead, the notion was conveyed that his poems were passed from hand to hand and read 'with an eagerness of delight and approbation, which would not suffer him long to withhold them from the press'. Vague generalisations of this nature were the very stuff of this memoir. A subscription was proposed and eagerly taken up by those who 'sought not less to gratify their own passion for Scottish poesy, than to encourage the wonderful ploughman'. The poems were printed 'at the manufacturing village of Kilmarnock'. Heron vividly recalled the impression made by the Kilmarnock Edition (previously quoted in Chapter 10). Heron was, in fact, in Edinburgh throughout 1786, so his eye-witness account of the reception given to the poems is highly suspect. No mention was made of the fact that the edition ran to only 612 copies, nor that the great majority of these were sold in central Ayrshire. The idea that the ploughboys and maid-servants of New Galloway rushed out with their three shillings to buy the book is preposterous. The ensuing passage was probably nearer the truth:

> A copy happened to be presented from a gentleman in Ayrshire to a friend in my neighbourhood. He put it into my hands, as a work containing some effusions of the most extraordinary genius. I took it, rather that I might not disoblige the lender, than from any ardour of curiosity or expectation. 'An unlettered ploughman, a poet!' said I, with contemptuous incredulity. It was on a Saturday evening. I opened the volume, by accident, while I was undressing, to go to bed. I closed it not, till a late hour on the rising Sunday morn, after I had read over every syllable it contained.

The 'gentleman in Ayrshire' was undoubtedly the Revd. George Lawrie of Newmilns and the 'friend in my neighbourhood' was Dr Blacklock, which places this incident in Edinburgh, not Galloway, and in September 1786, not July. Indeed, Heron went on to mention 'the late amiable and ingenious Dr Thomas Blacklock' at great length. By this time, of course, Heron was Hugh Blair's assistant. What exactly were Heron's duties in this regard is not clear. He did not become a licentiate of the Church until 1789, and it is inconceivable that Heron, at twenty-two, would have been Blair's associate preacher at St Giles, a position which was filled by William Greenfield early in 1787. But Blair was also Professor of Rhetoric at the University and a leading figure among the literati, so it is probable that he employed Heron as a secretary or amanuensis in his secular duties. Suffice it to say that Heron, through his connection with Blair, moved freely in the literary circles of the capital; yet neither in his memoir nor in his journal does Heron mention his first meeting with Burns. The friendship and patronage of Blacklock were discussed at great length, but Robert's doings in Edinburgh were but sketchily outlined in the most general terms.

When it came to the genesis of the Edinburgh Edition Heron was characteristically inaccurate, stating that Burns sold his copyright to Creech for £100 (not £105) before publishing, but adding that his friends 'actively promoted a subscription for an edition to be published for the benefit of the author, ere the bookseller's right should commence'. Elsewhere, a paragraph paid tribute to Creech who 'has obligingly informed me, that the whole sum paid to the poet for the copy-right, and for the subscription copies of his book, amounted to nearly eleven hundred pounds'. The real reason for Robert hanging around Edinburgh so long was, of course, not given. Instead, Heron opined that Robert 'had consumed a much larger proportion of these gains, than prudence could approve; while he superintended the impression, paid his court to his patrons, and waited the full payment of the subscription-money'.

Approximately four hundred words were devoted to singing the praises of Henry Mackenzie

> whose writings are universally admired for an Addisonian delicacy and felicity of wit and humour, by which the CLIO of the *Spectator* is more

than rivalled; for a wildly tender pathos that excites the most exquisite vibrations of the finest chords of sympathy in the human heart; for a lofty, vehement, persuasive eloquence, by which the immortal *Junius* has been sometimes perhaps excelled, and often almost equalled!

From the fact that Heron knew how much the poet had received for his copyright, and the manner in which Creech was shown in an unusually generous light, it is not too difficult to discern the co-operation of Henry Mackenzie in the compilation of this memoir; and the effusive remarks about Mackenzie, not strictly relevant to the memoir of Burns, seem to clinch this. There was also the most illuminating point – one of the few hard facts in the entire screed – that Burns made a clear profit of 'at least, seven hundred pounds; a sum that, to a man who had hitherto lived in his indigent circumstances, would be absolutely more than the vainly expected wealth of Sir Epicure Mammon!' The memoir, however, reached its turning point with Burns in Edinburgh in 1787. From then on it was downhill all the way:

> Unfortunately, however, that happened which was natural in those unac-customed circumstances in which BURNS found himself placed . . . He was insensibly led to associate less with the learned, the austere, and the rigorously temperate, than with the young, with the votaries of intemper-ate joys, with persons to whom he was recommended chiefly by licentious wit, and with whom he could not long associate without sharing in the excesses of their debauchery . . . The enticements of pleasure too often unman our virtuous resolution, even while we wear the air of rejecting them with a stern brow. We resist, and resist, and resist; but, at last, sud-denly turn and passionately embrace the enchantress. The *bucks* of Edinburgh accomplished, in regard to BURNS, that in which the *boors* of Ayrshire had failed. After residing some months in Edinburgh, he began to estrange himself, not altogether, but in some measure, from the society of his graver friends. Too many of his hours were now spent at the tables of persons who delighted to urge conviviality to drunkenness, in the tavern, in the brothel, on the lap of the woman of pleasure. He *suffered* himself to be surrounded by a race of miserable beings who were proud to tell that they had been in the company with BURNS, and had seen BURNS as loose and as foolish as themselves.

This, coming from a boozy hack who had drunk himself into a debtor's prison only four years previously, was richly ironic. There was praise for Robert Ainslie, 'a gentleman of the purest and most correct manners, who was accustomed sometimes to soothe the toils of a laborious profession, by an occasional converse with polite literature, and with general science'. There were less complimentary remarks about William Nicol who 'in vigour of intellect, and in wild, yet generous, impetuosity of passion, remarkably resembled BURNS . . . but whose virtues and genius were clouded by habits of Bacchanalian excess'. Nicol himself had only just died when Heron wrote these words, as he noted, 'of a jaundice, with a complication of other complaints, the effects of long-continued intemperance!' As Robert Heron himself died exactly ten years later of the very ailments listed here, there is some poetic justice in this world after all.

There was a typically superficial and inaccurate account of Robert's tour of the Highlands with Nicol. A particularly unattractive aspect of Heron's memoir was his treatment of Robert's second winter in Edinburgh. This, it will be remembered, was the period when Robert was trying in vain to get Creech to settle his account, a matter which must have been common knowledge in literary circles. Yet this is how Heron describes this frustrating and unhappy period:

> He talked loudly of independence of spirit, and simplicity of manners; and boasted his resolution to return to the plough. Yet, still he lingered in Edinburgh, week after week, and month after month; perhaps expecting that one or other of his noble patrons might procure him some permanent and competent annual income, which should set him above all necessity of future exertions to earn himself the means of subsistence; perhaps unconsciously reluctant to quit the pleasures of that voluptuous town-life to which he had for some time too willingly accustomed himself.

Heron then contradicted himself by mentioning one of the real reasons: 'an accidental dislocation or fracture of an arm or a leg' – he could not even get the details right – which detained Robert longer than he had intended. A lengthy digression about those 'patrons who had called him from the plough, not merely to make him their companion in the hour of riot' who had failed to secure the poet from being 'ever over-whelmed in distress, in consequence . . . of the habits of life into which they had seduced him' probably echoed Heron's own experience and disappointments in this regard. Heron's narrative of the circumstances in which Robert eventually returned to farming bore little relation to the truth; even the poet's landlord was named as Peter Millar instead of Patrick Miller. 'BURNS, with his JANE, whom he now married, took up their residence upon his farm'. At Ellisland (not actually named), Robert's

> crosses and disappointments drove him every day more and more into dissipation; and his dissipation tended to enhance whatever was disagreeable and perplexing in the state of his affairs. He sunk, by degrees, into the boon companion of mere excisemen; and almost every drunken fellow, who was willing to spend his money lavishly in the ale-house could easily command the company of BURNS.

It seems incredible that Alexander Findlater who, in 1814 and 1834, rushed to defend the memory of his erstwhile subordinate, let Heron's outrageous libel of the Excise pass without comment. This passage paled into insignificance when Heron turned to the last years:

> In Dumfries his dissipation became still more deeply habitual. He was here exposed more than in the country, to be solicited to share the riot of

the dissolute and the idle. Foolish young men, such as writers' apprentices, young surgeons, merchants' clerks, and his brother excisemen, flocked eagerly about him, and from time to time pressed him to drink with them, that they might enjoy his wicked wit. His friend NICOL made one or two autumnal excursions to Dumfries, and when they met in Dumfries, friendship, and genius, and wanton wit, and good liquor could never fail to keep BURNS and NICOL together, till both the one and the other were as dead drunk as ever SILENUS was . . . The morals of the town were . . . deplorably corrupted; and, though a husband and a father, poor BURNS did not escape suffering by the general contamination in a manner which I forbear to describe.

It is a wonder that David Staig and the other douce burghers of Dumfries did not rise up at this slur on the town's good name. By appearing to show restraint Heron was actually leaving it to his readers' imagination to contemplate the worst excesses of debauchery, a ploy to which Currie also resorted in his biography. It was a convenient device when the author was scant of facts, but it served to heighten the effect. The other method was to throw the rotten swine's bad behaviour into stark contrast with the Christian charity of his nearest and dearest:

> In the intervals between his different fits of intemperance, he suffered still the keenest anguish of remorse and horribly afflictive foresight. His JANE still behaved with a degree of maternal and conjugal tenderness and prudence, which made him feel more bitterly the evil of his misconduct, although they could not reclaim him. At last, crippled, emaciated, having the very power of animation wasted by disease, quite broken-hearted by the sense of his errors, and of the hopeless miseries in which he saw himself and his family depressed; with his soul still tremblingly alive to the sense of shame, and to the love of virtue; yet even in the last feebleness, and amid the last agonies of expiring life, yielding readily to any temptation that offered the semblance of intemperate enjoyment; he died at Dumfries, in the summer of the year 1796, while he was yet three or four years under the age of forty.

Heron had sufficient sense to perceive that such a tale of unrelieved debauchery and depravity might strain the credulity of his readers; so it was leavened here and there by occasional praise for Robert's intellectual talents; but it is stretching a point to say, as Fowler has done, that 'No writer was ever more eulogistic on the exalted mind and poetic genius of his subject than was Heron'.[48] Fowler adds that Heron was the only writer of an extended biography on Burns who had been well acquainted with him; not only does this ignore Maria Riddell, but patently exaggerates the degree to which Heron knew Robert, as the paucity of hard facts about the poet in this memoir reveals. Burns and Heron met only twice and neither occasion was sufficiently memorable for the latter to record the fact in his otherwise frank and full diary. Burns does not feature in the Heron journal at all; but there is ample evidence that Heron regarded himself as a literary figure of genius, increasingly embittered by the failure of lesser mortals to recognise that fact; and the concomitant of this was resentment and jealousy of writers whose worth was appreciated. Prior to 1797, Heron had damned with faint praise Robert's great folkloric poem 'Hallowe'en' (CW 151–7) as well as his mock-epic 'Tam o Shanter' (CW 410–15), and implied that his fame was only transitory:

> The Poems which brought Mr. Burns into fashion, – for a winter, have all considerable merit . . . The Poem on the rustic rites and festivity of the 'Hallowe'en' is finely fanciful, and most divertingly comic; but, the subject was indeed rich in materials for the man of fancy, and humour. A later composition of Mr. Burns's, a Tale, intitled 'Alloway Kirk', in which the vulgar ideas concerning witchcraft are happily introduced, has very high merit of the same cast as 'Hallowe'en'. As a Tale, it wants indeed, the inimitable, arch simplicity of the *Tales* of Fontaine. But, it has beauties of a higher kind. I have been more entertained by it than by any of Prior's. Burns seems to have thought, with Boccacce and Prior, that some share of indelicacy was a necessary ingredient in a Tale. Pity that he should have debased so fine a piece, by any thing, having even the remotest relation to obscenity.[49]

Such a dismissive comment on two of his greatest poems would hardly have endeared Heron to Burns. As the work in which this remark was made was published in Robert's lifetime he would certainly have been made aware of it, though no mention of Heron appears in Robert's correspondence, other than the verse-epistle to Blacklock of 1789. With commendable economy, Heron recycled his literary criticism of 1793 which he repeated almost verbatim in his memoir.

Precisely what purpose this travesty was meant to serve is a mystery. Robert had been dead almost nine months when Heron's memoir was published, so it did not have the excuse of topicality. Nor could it by any stretch of the imagination be regarded as providing much-needed publicity for the widow's and orphans' fund which had closed by that time. The place of first publication is also curious. Why London and not Edinburgh? Was this long article intended to have greater impact furth of Scotland? None of these questions can be answered satisfactorily for Heron himself left no clues; but this has not deterred others from divining a sinister motive in Heron's strange performance. It has been suggested that Heron was the paid tool of Henry Mackenzie, himself the paid agent of Henry Dundas. The malevolent influence of Dundas on Robert's career has been the subject of endless (and often quite fanciful) speculation in recent years,[50] but no concrete evidence to this effect has ever been adduced. By 1797 political radicalism was dead and Britain was too fully committed in a life or death struggle with France for there to be any point in smearing Burns. Besides, the man had died a patriot; what other poet had such a funeral with full military honours? Moreover, Heron's memoir ended on an up-beat note:

It may be doubted whether he has not, by his writings, exercised a greater power over the minds of men, and by consequence, on their conduct, upon their happiness and misery, upon the general system of life, than has been exercised by any half dozen of the most eminent statesmen of the present age.

These are definitely not the words of the political mercenary, allegedly hired by Mackenzie or Dundas or Pitt himself to destroy the reputation of a dangerous radical in the same category as Tom Paine! Nevertheless, whatever the motives of Heron's memoir, as an exercise in character assassination it succeeded only too well.

Heron's memoir may have been little known in Scotland at the time it was first published; it seems to have excited little immediate reaction for I can trace no comment on it in the Scottish press at the time. But within a year it had been widely read, both in the original periodicals and as a separate pamphlet, and undoubtedly it exerted a powerful effect in forming public opinion. In 1798 Alexander Campbell alluded to it, but without countering Heron's libels:

The life of Burns is already before the public. It is written by Mr. Robert Heron, of Edinburgh. The public are anxiously looking forward to the time, when a more circumstantial account of the life and writings of our favourite poet, shall come from the pen of the Historian Medica and his friend, so well known as a physician and philosopher. It was the peculiar felicity of Burns, on his first entrance on the literary stage, to be patronized and supported, even to a degree, rarely the lot of the most consummate talents. It became, for a time, the *rage*, to use a fashionable phrase, to talk of him, to recite his pieces, and boast of having spent an evening in company with the Ayrshire bard.[51]

William Reid probably had Heron in mind when he composed his 'Monody on the Death of Robert Burns'. This was published at Glasgow in 1797 as one of the Brash & Reid chapbooks, and tried to put matters in perspective in the eighteenth stanza:

> But let us not, as chatt'ring fools,
> Proclaim his fau'ts, like envy's tools,
> Wha seek out darkness just like owls,
>   Dark, dark indeed,
> But a' his failings co'er wi' mools,   [grave-clods]
> Now since he's dead.[52]

There is no doubt, therefore, that Heron's memoir was the source of James Currie's own strictures on the poet's personal character and habits. Although his views were widely accepted at the time and for many years thereafter, for more than half a century (1896–1963) Currie was unanimously and roundly condemned by Burns enthusiasts and scholars alike. Currie was castigated as a crank and a reformed drunkard, the 'arch calumniator' and an incompetent editor. Robert Thornton's sympathetic biography has gone a long way to showing how unfair these perceptions have been, but in so doing he has insinuated that Currie must have been right to condemn the poet's drunkenness. Thornton's biography has one fatal flaw, and that is the omission of any reference to Robert Heron. Thus Currie's strictures on drunkenness and depravity, hinting at alcoholism and venereal disease, have been allowed to stand as the doctor's own opinion, though on what basis is not made clear.[53]

By late-eighteenth-century standards Currie did a reasonable job and it is all too easy for those who came after to criticise what was, in many respects, a noble, pioneering effort that served its purpose well by raising a considerable sum of money for Burns's dependents. But by 1797 Currie's mind was firmly made up; and in light of Heron's savage memoir, who can really blame him? If Syme never bothered to answer Currie's pertinent questions, he probably took this as a tacit admission that the rumours he had heard in Liverpool were only too well founded. There is no doubt, however, that Currie regarded 'the rapidly increasing use of spirituous liquors, a detestable practice, which includes in its consequences almost every evil, physical and moral'. This statement appeared in the Prefatory Remarks and applied to the Scottish peasantry in general, but inevitably it coloured his attitude towards the man who had been libelled by Heron. It also explains Currie's conviction that Robert's moral failings were so gross as to necessitate great charity on his part:

> In relating the incidents of his life, candour will prevent us from dwelling invidiously on those failings which justice forbids us to conceal; we will tread lightly over his yet warm ashes, and respect the laurels that shelter his untimely grave.[54]

The first 333 pages of the first volume of Currie's work were devoted to the poet's biography. It marked a great advance over Heron, but was inaccurate in many dates and comparatively minor details. These errors were forgivable in the circumstances, but Currie was prone to sermonising and moralising and entire pages were given over to airing his views and opinions which had little relevance to the subject of the biography. The passages referring to Burns being 'perpetually stimulated by alcohol' and those 'errors over which delicacy and humanity draw the veil' have already been discussed. These allegations, backed by endless moralising, made a considerable impression on readers of Currie's volumes over the ensuing two decades. Twenty editions appeared between 1800 and 1820 in Britain, two in the United States and one in Ireland, and in the same period rival publications incorporating the Heron memoir also enjoyed a wide circulation. In addition, there were numerous other editions which likewise carried biographical material, invariably based, to a greater or lesser extent, on the writings of Heron and Currie.[55]

Sadly those who were intimately connected with the poet, and were thus in the best position to refute the charges, kept silent for a number of years.

By the time they spoke out their rebuttal was discounted as too late. In the meantime, however, other writers were following in the footsteps of Heron and Currie and endeavouring to outdo them and each other in their exposure of the poet's failings. In 1804 David Irving published his *Lives of the Scottish Poets*. The section covering Burns began in no uncertain terms:

> Among the unfortunate sons of genius whom the present age has beheld descending into an untimely grave, we cannot hesitate in assigning a pre-eminent station to Robert Burns, a man whose native vigour of intellect elevated him far above the ordinary standard, a man whose lamentable deviations from the sober paths of life had almost degraded to a level with the outcasts of society.[56]

Dealing with the Dumfries period, Irving pulled no punches:

> His constitution was deprived of its native energies, and could only be preserved from overwhelming languor by the aid of stimulant liquors. In this deplorable state of body as well as of mind he was eager to avoid the pangs of solitary reflection, and was even incapable of relishing domestic or rational society. He rushed into the company of men whom in his purer days he would have despised and shunned; he degraded his noble faculties to so mean a level that many of his earlier friends became half ashamed of having contracted such an intimacy.

Robert Hartley Cromek published his *Reliques of Robert Burns* in 1808. In some respects this book marked progress, as Cromek made some attempt to track down people who had been connected with the late poet and obtained anecdotes from them. Unfortunately, his working methods left a great deal to be desired and created many problems for later generations of scholars. Cromek did not inject fresh evidence of depravity into this work, but in his preface he wholeheartedly endorsed the picture of Burns created by Currie:

> Whatever unhappiness the Poet was in his lifetime doomed to experience, few persons have been so fortunate in a biographer as Burns. A strong feeling of his excellencies, a perfect discrimination of his character, and a just allowance for his errors are the distinguishing features in the work of Dr Currie.[57]

Cromek's *Reliques* enjoyed immense popularity and went through several editions. Later, parts of it were cobbled together with Currie in various permutations published throughout the nineteenth century. Several of the reviews of this work themselves rank as valuable contributions to the corpus of Burns criticism.[58] Francis Jeffrey (1773–1850), writing in the *Edinburgh Review* in 1809, embellished the now generally held view of Burns's debauchery, by insinuating that he let his wife and children starve while he was 'getting fu' and unco happy':

But the leading vice in Burns's character, and the cardinal deformity indeed of all his productions, was his contempt, or affectation of contempt, for prudence, decency and regularity; and his admiration of thoughtlessness, oddity, and vehement sensibility; – his belief, in short, in *the dispensing power* of genius and social feeling, in all matters of morality and common sense . . . That profligacy is almost always selfishness, and that the excuse of impetuous feeling can hardly ever be justly pleaded for those who neglect the ordinary duties of life, must be apparent, we think, even to the least reflecting of those sons of fancy and song. It requires no habit of deep thinking, nor any thing more, indeed, than the information of an honest heart, to perceive that it is cruel and base to spend, in vain superfluities, that money which belongs of right to the pale industrious tradesman and his famishing infants; or that it is a vile prostitution of language, to talk of that man's generosity or goodness of heart, who sit raving about friendship and philanthropy in a tavern, while his wife's heart is breaking at her cheerless fireside, and his children pining in solitary poverty.[59]

Walter Scott, writing in the rival periodical, the *Quarterly Review*, added fuel to the flames. He had picked up Cromek's book with no little anxiety because the character of Burns was

such as to increase our apprehensions. The extravagance of genius with which this wonderful man was gifted, being in his later and more evil days directed to no fixed or general purpose, was, in the morbid state of his health and feelings, apt to display itself in hasty sallies of virulent and unmerited severity.[60]

It is interesting to note that both Jeffrey and Scott linked the indelicacy and vulgarity (as they saw it) of Burns's songs and poetry with his private life. Unfortunately for Burns, it was an all too common fallacy that the man who could have written so enthusiastically about 'Scotch Drink' must have been permanently soaked in whisky. Scott commented on 'the pious care with which the late excellent Dr Currie had performed the task of editing the works of Burns'. Having endorsed Currie, he continued:

We have said that Robert Burns was the child of impulse and feeling. Of the steady principle which cleaves to that which is good, he was unfortunately divested by the violence of those passions which finally wrecked him.

Scott, the patrician lawyer well on the way to his baronetcy, was on the right wing of the Tory party, and this inevitably coloured his view of Burns whom he referred to as

a plebeian, a high-souled plebeian indeed, of a citizen of Rome or Athens, but still a plebeian untinged with the slightest shade of that spirit of chivalry which since the feudal times has pervaded the higher ranks of European society.

This strange comment was provoked by reading Robert's letter to Samuel Clark in which he refused to fight a duel with Captain Dodd. Scott concluded that 'the lowness of his birth, and habits of society, prevented rules of punctilious delicacy from making any part of his education'. This and similar nonsense reflected more on the character of Scott, backward-looking, steeped in antiquarian pursuits, harking back to the romanticism of the Middle Ages and ignoring the realities of life in Dumfries in the 1790s. Scott seems to have been only too ready to give ear to gossip which was patently false. A good example of this was the tale he passed on to Lockhart:

> I heard from Mr Miller [of] Dalswinton's eldest son . . . when Burns came to stay at Dalswinton all night as he often did, he used to stipulate for a bottle of brandy in his sleeping-room and drink it well nigh out before morning.[61]

No record of an overnight stay at Dalswinton, far less a regular habit of so doing, can be found and from what we know of the poet's relations with his landlord it seems extremely unlikely. Not content with the tales of perpetual daytime intoxication we now have the spectre of solitary nocturnal drinking as well.

Next to have a go was Josiah Walker who, in 1811, provided a lengthy account of the poet's life for the two-volume edition published by the trustees of James Morison. Walker's descriptions of his two meetings with Burns, in 1787 and 1795, have already been quoted. In his introduction, however, Walker acknowledged Currie as the main source of his material, adding that the ability of his predecessor left him but little to do. Walker's patronising account, in fact, confirmed Currie's view, with such statements:

> After becoming the idol of the fashionable topers of Edinburgh and Dumfriesshire, the challenges to exhibit his Bacchanalian prowess grew so frequent that practice at last degenerated into habit.[62]

The British copyright on Currie's first edition expired at the end of 1814 and this prompted Alexander Peterkin (1780–1846), an Edinburgh lawyer who had previously edited Fergusson's poems, to produce a new edition based on Currie but prefaced by a new review of the poet's life, amounting to almost a hundred pages, with the theme:

> That the caricatures which we have been contemplating are genuine likenesses of [Burns] we distinctly deny: they have no closer resemblance to Burns than a monkey has to a man.[63]

Peterkin's robust rejection of the now universally accepted story followed a summary of the poet's career with extracts from the most offensive publications which he had encountered, roundly condemning them and arguing

the points at some length. To this Peterkin appended four letters which
had been written to himself by people who had (or claimed to have) known
Burns well, and were thus in an admirable position to substantiate his own
statements. The first was a maddeningly bland letter from Gilbert Burns,
saying little of any substance. He was hurt by the reviews of Jeffrey and
Scott:

> I am not a little surprised to see men of talents and literary taste, rake up
> the failings (real or imputed) of the dead, and lacerate the feelings of sur-
> viving friends, by presenting an overcharged picture of those failings to
> the world, and giving currency to every malicious report, founded or
> unfounded. No person can regret more than I do the tendency of *some* of
> my Brother's writings to represent irregularity of conduct as a conse-
> quence of genius, and sobriety the effect of dulness: but surely more has
> been said on that subject than the fact warrants.[64]

Gilbert shilly-shallied over his late brother's 'occasional deviations from
the paths of virtue' which he maintained were not 'the effusion of determined profligacy', but he concluded:

> Dr Currie, knowing the events of the later years of my brother's life only
> from the reports which had been propagated, and thinking it necessary,
> lest the candour of his work should be called in question to state the sub-
> stance of these reports, has given a very exaggerated view of the failings
> of my brother's life at that period, which is certainly to be regretted; but
> as the Doctor's work was not submitted to me in manuscript, nor, as far
> as I know, to any of my brother's friends at Dumfries, I had not in my
> power to set him right in that particular: and considering the excellence
> of the Doctor's work upon the whole, and how much we owed him, for
> that stupendous exertion of his benevolence, I never took any notice to
> him of my disapprobation, or of the inconsistency of this part of his work.

This was followed by a letter from James Gray (1770–1830), then master
in the High School of Edinburgh but formerly a teacher at Dumfries
Academy, with a spirited defence of the poet. This was a studied and well-
reasoned vindication of Burns:

> The fate of this great man has been singularly hard; during the greater
> part of his life, he was doomed to struggle with adverse fortune, and no
> friendly hand was stretched forth to shield him from the storm that at last
> overwhelmed him. It seemed even to have been the object of a jealous and
> illiberal policy to accelerate his ruin. His enemies have ascribed to him
> vices foreign to his nature; have exaggerated his failings, and have not
> even had the justice to relieve the deep shades of imputed depravity, by
> a single ray of virtue.[65]

Gray had a high opinion of Currie and extolled his generosity in coming
forward to rescue the widow and orphans from absolute want. He was
reluctantly compelled, however, to speak out on the principal libels in

Currie's biography. Gray drew attention to the vast amount of poetry written by Burns in his last years. 'Not many days passed . . . in which he did not compose some piece of poetry or some song designed to delight the imagination and soften the heart for ages to come.' From his own personal experience, Gray (who had become rector of the Academy in 1794) testified:

> It came under my own view professionally, that he superintended the education of his children with a degree of care that I have never seen surpassed by any parent in any rank of life whatever. In the bosom of his family, he spent many a delightful hour in directing the studies of his eldest son, a boy of uncommon talents. I have frequently found him explaining to this youth, then not more than nine years of age, the English poets, from Shakespeare to Gray, or storing his mind with examples of heroic virtue, as they live in the pages of our most celebrated English historians. I would ask any person of common candour, if employments like these are consistent with habitual drunkenness?

Not content with attacking Currie, Gray lashed out at Jeffrey, pointing out that Robert's income in his last years never rose above £75, yet by a rigid economy,

> the offspring of that spirit of independence, which regulated every action of his life – and which not even poverty could quell, – he so managed this pittance, as decently to support his family, without incurring debt, and even to have something to spare for the purpose of charity . . . It is a singular fact, that at his death, the whole amount of his debts was not twenty pounds: of this, only a few pounds were for house accounts: all the rest was for volunteer uniform. I have the authority of Mrs Burns herself for stating, that to her and her children he was uniformly kind, cheerful, and attentive; that he was an affectionate husband, and a fond father; that he never addressed her in the tone of displeasure, and that, in her presence, his brow was never clouded by a frown.

Robert Thornton, faced with such awkward and uncompromising refutation of the indictment against Burns, sought to minimise the validity of Gray's statement on the grounds that Gray was nowhere indicated in the writings of Burns as someone he even knew, and compares this negative evidence with the positive evidence of Robert's friendship with that other schoolmaster Thomas White who acknowledged (in his memorial ode) that the poet had 'frailties'.[66] But this is being very selective with the facts. Gray's position in Dumfries in the last crucial years of Robert's life is well documented, and as rector and classical master of the academy he was certainly bound to have contact with Burns whose son was then regarded as the most promising pupil in the school. Gray was, like Burns, a founder member of the Volunteers and took a prominent part in the affairs of the town library; in a small town like Dumfries their paths would have crossed in many ways. Furthermore, Gray did not deny Robert's frailties any more than Thomas White did. In fact, he faced up to them far more candidly than White, in his memorial ode, had done:

> It is not, however, denied that he sometimes mingled with society unworthy of him. He was of a social and convivial nature. He was courted by all classes of men for the fascinating power of his conversation, but over his social scene uncontrolled passion never presided. Over the social bowl, his wit flashed for hours together, penetrating whatever it struck, like the fire from heaven; but even in the hour of thoughtless gaiety and merriment, I never knew it tainted by indecency . . . In his morning hours, I never saw him like one suffering from the effects of last night's intemperance. He appeared then clear and unclouded . . . The truth is, that Burns was seldom *intoxicated*. The drunkard soon becomes besotted, and is shunned even by the convivial. Had he been so, he could not have long continued the idol of every party. It will, however, be freely confessed, that the hour of enjoyment was often prolonged beyond the limit marked by prudence; but what man will venture to affirm that, in situations where he was conscious of giving so much pleasure, he could at all times have listened to her voice.[67]

Even if Thornton could weigh such a balanced, common-sense view as this and find it wanting, he could not deny the testimony furnished to Peterkin by Alexander Findlater, who, as Robert's immediate superior in the Excise, was better qualified than anyone else to assess his character. Yet this was conveniently ignored, apart from a passing reference dismissing it as 'too late'.[68] Findlater's testimony, of course, utterly demolished Thornton's case. Findlater regretted the severity of Currie's strictures, as his *Life* had become 'a kind of text-book for succeeding commentators, who have, by the aid of their own fancies, amplified, exaggerated, and filled up the outlines he has sketched'. Findlater wryly commented:

> It is painful to trace all that has been written on this subject by Dr Currie's successors, who seem to have considered the history of the Poet as a thing like Ulysses' bow, on which each was at liberty to try his strength; and some, in order to out-do their competitors, have strained every nerve to throw all kinds of obloquy on his memory. His convivial habits, his wit and humour, his social talents, and his independent spirit, have been perverted into constant and habitual drunkenness, impiety, neglect of his professional duty, and of his family, and in short, almost every human vice: He has been branded with cowardice, accused of attempting murder and even suicide; and all this without a shadow of proof.[69]

He then proceeded systematically to demolish the allegations, insinuations and innuendoes concerning Robert's conduct as an Excise officer and his unremitting attention to duty 'which certainly was not compatible with perpetual intoxication'. This charge, Findlater averred, fell to the ground:

> I will further avow, that I never saw him, which was very frequently while he lived at Ellisland, and still more so, almost every day, after he removed

to Dumfries, but in hours of business he was quite himself, and capable of discharging the duties of his office: nor was he ever known to drink by himself, or seen to indulge in the use of liquor in a forenoon, as the statement, that he was *perpetually* under its stimulus, unequivocally implies.

Findlater concluded that 'to attempt the refutation of the various other calumnies with which his memory has been assailed, some of which are so absurd as hardly to merit any attention, does not fall in my way, though I hope they will be suitably taken notice of'. The fourth letter printed by Peterkin was written by George Thomson, but this dealt mainly with Cromek's handling of the songs of Burns and was both unimportant and irrelevant to this argument. Having done so much to vindicate Burns, however, Peterkin entirely undid his good work by reprinting Currie's biography *in toto*. As a result, Peterkin's good intentions served little purpose, amid the plethora of other editions which continued to publish Currie unchallenged.

James Gray sent a copy of Peterkin's *Review* to William Wordsworth, passing on a query from Gilbert Burns about how his brother's name could be vindicated. Wordsworth replied from Rydal Mount in January 1816 and subsequently published it in the form of a pamphlet entitled *Letter to a Friend of Robert Burns*.[70] Gilbert was motivated partly by Peterkin reviving the controversy and partly because he had now been himself approached by Cadell and Davies with a view to producing an entirely new edition of Currie's four-volume work. This, incidentally, explains why Gilbert's response to the appeal from Peterkin had been so disappointing; he did not want to say anything that might prejudice his relations with Currie's publishers. Wordsworth's pamphlet is of immense value on several counts. In the first place it contains by far the most extensive critique of Burns's work ever penned by Wordsworth, his great admirer and in some respects his successor as a Romantic poet. More importantly in this context, however, it contained Wordsworth's thoroughly trenchant attack on Currie's 'revolting account of a man of exquisite genius' and an even more savage assault on Jeffrey whose 'intellectual deformity' he now mercilessly exposed. Jeffrey's words were held up to ridicule and the hapless Edinburgh *littérateur* was subjected to withering scorn:

> It is notorious that this persevering Aristarch,[71] as often as a work of original genius comes before him, avails himself of that opportunity to re-proclaim to the world the narrow range of his own comprehension. The happy self-complacency, the unsuspecting vain-glory, and the cordial *bon-homie*, with which this part of his duty is performed, do not leave him free to complain of being hardly dealt with if any one should declare the truth, by pronouncing much of the foregoing attack upon the intellectual and moral character of Burns, to be the trespass . . . of a mind obtuse, superficial, and inept.

Unfortunately Wordsworth was so carried away with his attack on Jeffrey that he lost sight of Gray's purpose in approaching him in the first place.

Concerning the burning question whether Burns was a drunkard or not, Wordsworth had little to say. In fact, by pleading for leniency towards the dead, and by alluding to 'the black things which have been written of this great man, and the frightful ones that have been insinuated against him' without offering a rebuttal, he unwittingly left the reader with the impression that the charges were essentially correct.

Next to enter the fray was John Wilson (1785–1854), better known to posterity by his pseudonym Christopher North. He lambasted the Lake poet for attacking Jeffrey and the *Edinburgh Review*:

> With the voice and countenance of a maniac, [he] fixes his teeth in the blue cover of the *Edinburgh*. He growls over it – shakes it violently to and fro – and at last, wearied out with vain efforts of mastication, leaves it covered over with the drivelling slaver of his impotent rage.

He ended his tirade with the contemptuous line, 'We wish to have done with this lyrical ballad-monger'.[72] What was now developing into a literary quarrel, however, left the original bone of contention – Burns – out of the reckoning. William Hazlitt (1778–1830) entered the fray in a lecture 'On Burns, and the Old English Ballads' delivered at the Surrey Institution in 1818. Very properly he criticised Wordsworth for having missed the point and done little, or nothing, to repair Burns's injured reputation. Shrewdly he observed, 'It has been usual to attack Burns's moral character, and the moral tendency of his writings at the same time', but pointed out that, had he written nothing more than 'Tam o Shanter', he would have deserved immortality, and that he could never have produced this masterpiece had he not himself 'drunk full ofter of the tun than of the well'. Hazlitt, in fact, made no attempt to refute the charges (of which he had no personal knowledge one way or the other), but pleaded for a more charitable understanding:

> Poets are by nature men of stronger imagination and keener sensibilities than others; and it is a contradiction to suppose them at the same time governed only by the cool, dry, calculating dictates of reason and foresight.[73]

On 14 January 1818 George Thomson wrote to Professor Wilson, telling him that Gilbert Burns had been commissioned by Cadell and Davies to produce a new edition of his brother's works:

> This affords him a fair opportunity of correcting what has been unjustly asserted to the prejudice of the Poet's character by his different Biographers and Critics. He has accordingly written in his own mild and modest way, what he means to say; and has replied to the very strong statement which Dr Currie made as to the Poet's dissipation, and the neglect of his duties, in his latter years chiefly, by a reference to letters from Mr Findlater, now Collector of Excise at Glasgow, and Mr James Gray, of the High School, who lived in Dumfries at the time – both

having had occasion to see the Poet daily, and having been perfectly well acquainted with his habits and way of life. And surely the voluntary testimony of respectable men, speaking of what passed under their own eyes, is far better entitled to credence than any opposite statement which Dr Currie confided in, upon the information of persons unknown or from rumour.

Against the Doctor, however, Gilbert Burns does not mean to say a word; he must have been misled by his informers, and could not err otherways – for the candour and uprightness of his mind would not have permitted him to assert anything which he himself did not believe to be correct.

Unhappily, however, Dr Currie's statement has been made a text upon which the most offensive commentaries and unfounded calumnies have been raised by successive Biographers and Reviewers.[74]

Thomson asked Wilson to peruse Gilbert's paper and, if he were satisfied with this version of the fact, to write a critical review of the *Edinburgh* and *Quarterly Reviews* of Burns so that Gilbert could add it to his vindication of his injured brother. Thomson was particularly upset by Jeffrey's remarks, the overall superciliousness and condescension of the review, the strong prejudice against Burns and the burning resentment that a ploughman could have attained such an elevated rank as a poet. In particular he was angered by Jeffrey's 'illiberal and unjust account' of Burns's character and suspected that Jeffrey had only cursorily examined Burns's poetry. Interestingly, in view of the fact that Robert had addressed one of his anguished appeals for financial assistance to Thomson, the latter refuted the allegation that the poet had died in debt, saying that 'although his income from the Excise did not exceed from £40 to £70 a year, he died without being £5 in debt'. Again, he tried to put the matter of Robert's drinking into perspective:

That Burns was fond of society cannot be matter either of doubt or surprise, and it is notorious that in Scotland the society of gentlemen is seldom obtained without the circulation of the bottle. Do not gentlemen of great respectability indulge in this way without the least loss of character? And is it candid or just to reproach a man of genius, endowed with wit and the most fascinating powers of conversation, for a failing that he had in common both with his equals and his superiors?

And he reiterated Gilbert's anxiety that he would not 'on any account consent that any fault should be found with Dr Currie, because he knows it would hurt the feelings of the doctor's family'. This was asking the impossible; by this mealy-mouthed approach Gilbert made it impossible for himself to take any positive steps to repair the damage to his brother's reputation. Wilson's reply, if any, has not survived; but it is clear that he was not swayed by Thomson's arguments. A year later he wrote a lengthy article entitled 'Some Observations on the Poetry of the Agricultural and that of the Pastoral District of Scotland, illustrated by a Comparative View of the Genius of Burns and the Ettrick Shepherd'. Far from using the opportunity to rebut the charges of drunkenness and dissipation, Wilson hinted that they were true:

> There is a pathetic moral in the imperfect character of Burns, both as a poet and a man; nor ought they who delight both in him and his works, and rightly hold the anniversary of his birth to be a day sacred in the calendar of genius – to forget, that it was often the consciousness of his own frailties that made him so true a painter of human passions . . .[75]

In 1820 Gilbert produced his 'revision' for Cadell and Davies who, in expectation of a bestseller, paid an advance of £250 (equivalent to more than £30,000 in modern money), with the promise of a similar sum should the work run to a second edition. This was Gilbert's opportunity finally to set the record straight and restore his brother's reputation. The results, however, were disappointing. Gilbert's contribution to Currie's *oeuvre* consisted of a few previously unpublished letters, a trivial up-date on the poet's family, and a couple of appendices dealing with the state of the Scottish peasantry and a comment on 'my brother's habits'. The last named was pretty feeble:

> Succeeding biographers and reviewers, presuming they might go beyond Dr Currie's statements, have brought forward the most revolting calumnies and misrepresentations. To several of these I have been urged to publish answers, in order to vindicate my brother's character; but this I could never muster sufficient courage to do.[76]

This was certainly true, and Gilbert was shown up for the coward that he was. Moreover, Gilbert was a fool, given to such ridiculous statements as:

> Eager for fame, and fond of distinction . . . [Robert] endeavoured to overcome his aversion to drinking, and succeeded in being able to drink like other people.[77]

To be sure, Gilbert denied the charge of habitual or perpetual intoxication which he buttressed by quoting excerpts from Findlater and Gray, as well as printing *in extenso* another letter by Gray who now had the bit between his teeth and was losing no opportunity to vindicate his late friend. But the overall impression is that Gilbert's contribution was timid and inconsequential. It is only fair to point out, however, that Gilbert was constrained from speaking out by the explicit instructions of his publishers:

> Mr. Wordsworth has thought fit to send forth a printed letter reflecting, in terms we cannot approve, upon our late excellent friend Dr Currie's edition of your brother's writings, to which, as we must ever feel that it is not justified to any sufficient degree, we trust you will not find it necessary to pay much attention; on any minor points, respecting which your brotherly feelings may be somewhat at variance with Dr Currie's remarks,

you will doubtless be able to express yourself to your own entire satisfaction, without too severely questioning the justice which that benevolent and elegant critic may have thought due to biographical truth.[78]

Gilbert reluctantly acquiesced in this extraordinary request. In fairness to Gilbert, whose timidity and spinelessness in this matter has often been criticised, it should be noted that the Earnock MSS show that, over a period of four years, Gilbert battled, albeit ineffectually, with Cadell and Davies, not only over Currie's errors but also over 'the unlucky gleanings' of Cromek which he considered to be a 'rapacious unworthy collection'. Furthermore, Gilbert locked horns with William Roscoe in 1817–18, the latter being determined at all costs to protect the literary reputation of his late friend Currie. In the end Gilbert gave way; but by not facing up to the charges and wholeheartedly rebutting them, he was seen to be endorsing Currie; and as Currie's biography was reprinted in 1820 without a single word altered, the net result was to perpetuate the image of debauchery.

Two years later John Bumpus produced a two-volume edition with the title *Poetical Works of Robert Burns; to which are prefixed a history of the poems, by his brother, Gilbert Burns*. Bumpus cashed in on Gilbert's name, almost certainly without his knowledge or permission, by reprinting a letter from Gilbert to Currie, written in 1798 and first published in 1800. This 1822 edition, however, is noteworthy on account of the editor's remarks which showed all too clearly what had happened to the accepted opinion of Burns. His failings:

> have been detailed in this sketch of his life, from motives for which no apology is necessary: to guard ambitious and ardent minds from similar irregularities and wanderings, and to explain why such a man, after the first burst of popular applause was past, lived and died more unhappily than would probably have been the case had he never known what it was to be caressed and admired.[79]

Thus, by 1822, poor Burns was being exhibited to the public as a horrible example and a warning. Nevertheless, Burns the man continued to fascinate the public just as much as his poetry enthralled and enchanted his readers. This explains the enormous popularity of the works of John Gibson Lockhart (1828) and Allan Cunningham (1834), both of which went through many editions throughout the rest of the nineteenth century. When the latter edition appeared Findlater, then in his eightieth year, wrote at great length to rebut some of the errors in Cunningham's *Life of Robert Burns*. He was mainly concerned to set the record straight regarding the poet's verbal caution in 1792, and he corrected Cunningham's description of the deathbed scene; but on this occasion he dealt with the debauchery issue more tersely:

> The Poet . . . fell a victim to distress and premature death, from other causes than those now ascribed by his biographers. Let the noble, the

proud, the great, and the affluent, who ought to be the patrons of genius, consider this and blush![80]

Thereafter the picture of depravity in the poet's private life was gradually toned down. Even Sir Walter Scott came, in time, to revise his opinions of Burns. By mid-century, whatever failings the poet might or might not have had were beginning to recede as the light from his poetry continued undiminished. Later writers, such as Robert Chambers (1851) and Scott Douglas (1877), began the rehabilitation of Burns the man by ferreting out whatever they could from those still living who had memories of the poet. General interest in Burns was considerably stimulated by the worldwide celebrations of his centenary in 1859 and from then on the pendulum swung in the opposite direction, often veering dangerously towards uncritical bardolatry. The scholars and researchers who studied different aspects of his life and career from the 1880s onwards have helped to restore a balance and provide a fully rounded picture of Robert Burns. In the clubs and societies affiliated to the Burns Federation at one end of the spectrum, and in the groves of academe at the other, the notion of Burns the drunken debauchee has long been discredited.

Yet the early nineteenth-century view of Burns as a confirmed alcoholic lingers on in the mind of the general public. To a large extent this was due to the version of the poet's life purveyed in such sources of general knowledge as the *Encyclopaedia Britannica* where Professor Nicol's biography of Burns, deriving almost entirely from Heron and Currie, was permitted to endure until 1973 when David Daiches set the record straight. Sir Leslie Stephen's article on Burns, in the *Dictionary of National Biography*, not only repeats Currie's allegations without correction, but is a prime source of the story of the poet falling 'asleep in the open air after a carouse at the Globe Tavern'.[81] Stephen, writing in 1886, spoke of Burns 'giving way to indulgences of a discreditable kind' and added the gratuitous sneer that 'criticism of Burns is only permitted to Scotchmen of pure blood', unconsciously anticipating the furore which arose following the publication of Henley's biography of Burns a decade later.

In 1896, the centenary of the poet's death was celebrated by a rash of new editions, the foremost being the four-volume editions of Chambers (revised and extensively rewritten by Wallace) and Henley and Henderson. The latter included a biographical essay by William Ernest Henley (1849–1903), a minor English poet and critic. His criticisms, covering a wide range of authors, were often wilful and one-sided, entertaining rather than informative. His essay on Burns was an all too typical example. Thus the hoary old tales of drunkenness were revived and embellished in Henley's trenchant and picturesque prose:

> There is evidence that some time before the end he was neither a sober companion nor a self-respecting husband . . . Drink and disappointment were pretty certainly responsible between them for the mingled squalor and gloom and pathos of the end. There is nothing like liquor to make a

strong man vain of his strength and jealous of his prerogative . . .; and there is nothing like disappointment to confirm such a man in a friendship for liquor.[82]

Although Henley's intemperate language provoked a nationwide outcry at the time and a flurry of publications over the ensuing six years,[83] the Centenary Edition and its spin-offs ran to numerous reprints and variations from 1896 to 1927, helping to reinforce the traditional view. These and many other 'popular' editions, such as Archibald Fullarton's Globe and Frederick Warne's Lansdowne Poets, Albion and National editions, ensured that the notion of the poet being steeped in moral turpitude should persist. The great advances in Burns scholarship in the course of the present century, notably the Oxford editions of the Letters by DeLancey Ferguson (1931) and Ross Roy (1985) and James Kinsley's monumental three-volume edition of the Poems (1968) ought to have gone a long way to negating such misconceptions; but these scholarly works have never enjoyed the wide readership that they deserve. Similarly, the best biography of Burns, by Snyder (1932), was published in the United States and never attained its proper prominence in Britain where it was needed most, and Snyder's more ephemeral writings, admirable though they were in every respect, merely preached to the converted.[84] This objective view has been countered by the axe-grinding of Thornton (1963, 1979), Fowler (1988) and most recently by Alan Bold (1991) who is convinced that Burns was a 'bout alcoholic':

> Bout-alcoholism, with its euphoric self-indulgence dissolving into remorse as the bout shakily ends, is often associated with manic-depressive behaviour which, in turn, is often found in highly creative individuals. Poets, with their bouts of intense creativity and their bouts of despair, are understandably prone to bout-alcoholism and Burns was definitely a bout-writer producing the great poems of the Kilmarnock Edition in a short period of time (the *annus mirabilis* of 1784-5), writing songs for Johnson and Thomson in bursts. Burns's remark that 'occasional hard drinking is the devil of me' (CL 203) is a classic confession of bout-alcoholism.[85]

This argument is flawed for there is no evidence of Burns as a drinker, far less a 'bout alcoholic', in 1784-5; but as Alan Bold is a poet himself, he ought to be allowed the credit for this remarkable insight into the way poets work and behave.

A re-examination of Robert's correspondence and poetic output in light of twentieth-century scholarship coincided with several attempts to diagnose his ailments and chart the course of his physical decline. If he did not drink himself to death, what then did Burns die of? Quite independently of each other, two eminent medical men published their findings in 1926. Dr Harry B. Anderson of Toronto gave a lecture to the Toronto Burns Society in November that year and, after a detailed consideration of the poet's various illnesses as recorded in his letters, concluded that:

The case was an ordinary one of rheumatism with heart complications, shortness of breath, faintness, weakness, rapid irregular pulse (auricular fibrillation), and towards the end, fever, parched tongue and delirium, presumably due to a bacterial endocarditis which developed as a terminal infection.[86]

Earlier that year, however, following a series of articles in the *Glasgow Herald* between 4 and 9 December 1925, Sir James Crichton-Browne published his book *Burns from a New Point of View*. This enjoyed a wide circulation and ran to a second edition in 1937. More than anything else, this helped to dispel the alcoholic tradition. Sir James combined a lifelong interest in Burns with impeccable professional credentials. In studying Robert's medical history, he considered not only the memoir of Jean Armour, the account of the less reliable Gilbert and the accounts of Syme, Findlater and others who had known the poet intimately at various stages of his life, but also Robert's voluminous correspondence. With painstaking care he followed up every reference made by Robert to the malady which afflicted him almost from childhood, which at times distorted his mind and subjected him to the fits of morbidity so often mentioned in his letters and poems, and which ultimately destroyed his body before middle age had overtaken it. From the recurring references to pain, accompanied by fits of that 'melancholia which transcends all wit', Robert made abundantly clear precisely what it was that pursued him to the grave. Sir James followed the trail meticulously and built up his case, which he summed up concisely:

Burns's death was not an accidental event, but the natural consequence of a long series of events that had preceded it . . . Burns died of endocarditis, a disease of the substances and lining membrane of the heart, with the origination of which alcohol had nothing to do, though it is possible that an injudicious use of alcohol may have hastened its progress. It was rheumatism that was the undoing of Burns. It attacked him in early years, damaged his heart, embittered his life, and cut short his career . . . At Mount Oliphant, from his thirteenth to his fifteenth year, the heart trouble was well declared . . . At Mossgiel in 1784 there was an exacerbation of his disease . . . It is characteristic of the mild types of this insidious form of heart disease from which Burns suffered, that its victims, until it is far advanced, are able to go about and take an active share in affairs, as if there was nothing the matter with them. But they are visited at different intervals during its course of twenty or thirty years by feverish attacks, significant often of another milestone on the downward journey in which, with a quickened pulse, they become weak and qualmish, and are highly strung, nervous, and easily agitated.[87]

Sir James then followed in detail Burns's records of his various illnesses, and concluded with the statement, 'It will not, I think, be denied that Burns died of rheumatic endocarditis'. There the matter rested until 1982 when W. W. Buchanan and W. F. Kean of the Department of Medicine at McMaster University, Hamilton, Ontario, published a paper.[88] They advanced the theory that those predispositions to fainting fits and palpitations which Robert suffered as a teenager could have been due to attacks of paroxysmal tachycardia and nocturnal asthma. The prolonged 'nervous headache' which lasted for three weeks in 1789 suggested psychoneurosis rather than an organic disease. Other comments to Mrs Dunlop in November 1789 (CL 180) – 'a stuffed aching head and an unsound, sickly crasis' – suggested farmer's lung or one of the other hypersensitivity pneumonotides, although simple coryza (head cold) was more probable. It was conceivable that Robert's fever and 'flying gout' (migratory arthritis) could have been due to acute rheumatic fever; but there was no history of sore throats and had Robert died from acute rheumatic fever, one would have expected a terminal illness of congestive cardiac failure and not coma.

Buchanan and Keen were the first to suggest brucellosis as a possible cause of Robert's death:

> This is surprising since all the clinical features could be explained on this basis.[89] As a farmer Burns ran the well-known occupational risk of this disease. The mortality today is low with antiobiotic therapy, but death was not uncommon in the past without antibiotic therapy. The flying gout is a particularly apt description of the severe painful migratory arthritis usually affecting large joints from which Burns clearly suffered. The duration of the illness from the first mention in June 1794, to his death in July 1796, is entirely in keeping with brucellosis. *B. melitensis* is usually contracted from sheep and goats, and produces the most severe form of the illness, with a higher mortality than that caused by *B. suis* and *B. abortus*, and a bacterial endocarditis may supervene. There is no record that the poet kept goats, but he did have a pet ewe which nearly strangled herself on its tether and as a result became immortalised in two poems . . . However, these is no way of proving that Burns suffered from brucellosis unless one were to disinter his remains and demonstrate brucellar organisms! Nor, indeed, is it possible to exclude the many other conditions which could account for his death, including: polyarteritis nodosa, systemic lupus erythematosis, carcinomatosis, hepatitis, leukaemia, tuberculosis, etc.

In fact, Robert kept several sheep, not just a pet ewe, both at Lochlie and Mossgiel; and he probably kept sheep at Ellisland as well for there are references in his letters to 'ewe cheeses' which he sent as gifts to his Edinburgh friends. Buchanan and Keen added that brucellosis was first described by Marston in 1861 and the organisms identified by Sir David Bruce in 1887. Dr Maxwell has often been castigated for his poor diagnosis, but he reflected both the level of medical knowledge of the late eighteenth century and the almost total lack of diagnostic technology at the time. The stethoscope was not invented by Laennec till 1819, nor the clinical thermometer by Allnutt till 1870. Moreover, Buchanan and Keen cited a mid-nineteenth-century physician for the suspicion that Maxwell's treatment may have accelerated Robert's death. This view was propounded by Dr John Thomson in 1844, at a time when the Burns Festival on the banks of Ayr was imminent:

I proclaim that Robert Burns died the doctor's martyr; and as a very few years must sweep away all *living* testimony upon that point, I avail myself of the approaching Festival, and challenge the contradiction of all his living co-temporaries who may there congregate.

The truth stands thus: – The physician of Robert Burns believed that his liver was diseased, and placed him under a *course of mercury*. In those days a mercurial course was indeed a dreadful alternative. I know well that his mercurial course was extremely severe. In addition to this severity, his physician believed that sea-bathing was the best tonic after salivation. Thus he was sent to the Breu for sea-bathing. In the course of, I think three weeks, he returned home from sea-bathing, inflated, black with dropsy, and soon died. Among the last words I ever heard him speak, were, – Well, the doctor has made a finish of it now. Such I affirm to be the truth; – 'wha then dares battle wi' me? Come forth, thou slanderer'.[90]

In 1971 Dr J. M. A. Lenihan and colleagues of the Department of Clinical Physics and Bio-Engineering at the University of Glasgow examined a small sample of Robert's hair, provided by James F. Walker of Dundee, by neutron activation analysis. The mercury content was 8.02 parts per million, which is twice as high as the normal content, but much less than that found in dentists and laboratory workers (up to 200 parts per million). It should be noted that Robert's exposure to mercury could only have come from the medical profession, but the level found is very much below that associated with mercury poisoning. Lenihan and his colleagues were only able to examine a few hairs, none of which was very long, and had to use the whole sample to obtain sufficient sensitivity. Human hair grows at a rate of 20 cm per annum, and the hair sample could have reflected mercury treatments some time previously and not immediately prior to death. The level of mercury in hair compared with other organs remains uncertain, and perhaps only the level in the hair root will correlate with blood concentrations. On the other hand, mercury is trapped in hair to sulphydryl and disulphide groups in keratin like other heavy metals, so that normal concentrations in hair are much higher than in blood. Inorganic mercury salts, and to a lesser extent organic mercury, will lead to renal tubular damage.[91]

Buchanan and Keen concluded therefore that a large dose of an inorganic mercury salt or a moderate dose resulting in insult to already damaged kidneys could have precipitated the terminal event of uraemia and renal failure:

Were this so, and, as Dr Thomson suggested, Robert Burns died a martyr of the medical profession, it would be most ironic for one who had satirised iatrogenic disease in the poem 'Death and Doctor Hornbook':

> Whare I killed ane, a fair strae death,
> By loss o blood or want of breath,
> This night I'm free to take my aith,
>   That Hornbook's skill
> Has clad a score i' their last claith,
>   By drap an pill.

It would also be ironic if mercury were prescribed to stimulate liver function, as John Thomson implied, because such medication would tend to have the opposite effect. Thomson's statement was ignored for almost one hundred and thirty years because mercury to most people meant a treatment of venereal disease. Thomson's medical testimony was discounted as mere gossip crystallised into a notion of his own when he became possessed of medical knowledge later in life. He was only sixteen years old in 1796 and was not employed as Maxwell's assistant. Thomson, born near Lockerbie in March 1780, came to Dumfries as a small boy and attended the academy where he showed great proficiency in languages and was employed by Rector Gray as an usher or pupil-teacher from 1794 onwards. Thomson claimed that Burns habitually took an early morning walk with him in the Dock Park for the purpose of practising conversational French. He was a frequent caller at the poet's house and was therefore in a good position to observe his state of health and the treatment he was receiving. He later went to Edinburgh, where he became tutor to the family of Dr Gregory, and then studied medicine at the university where he graduated MD in June 1809. His medical expertise was thus acquired years after Burns's death, but this does not invalidate his recollections in retrospect.[92] Not until 1971, however, was Thomson's verdict vindicated by the findings of Dr Lenihan.

That Maxwell was prescribing mercury for some non-venereal ailment is clearly shown by the fact that Robert at no time exhibited or described the unmistakable symptoms of syphilis or gonorrhoea, nor was there the slightest evidence of venereal infection in Jean, who outlived him by thirty-eight years, nor signs of congenital syphilis or neonatal gonococcal blindness in any of the poet's children.

Fowler, unaware of prior publication by Buchanan and Keen, also came to the conclusion that Burns had suffered from brucellosis, a disease known, long before Marston and Bruce identified its cause, as undulant fever. Fowler considered that the poet may have contracted bovine brucellosis (*B. abortus*) which was spread in the milk of contaminated herds:

> The distressing course of brucellosis accords well with two years of suffering described by Burns, and his manner of death attracts a strong presumption of terminal pneumonia. The undulant or relapsing nature of brucellosis stems from the unusual ability of the bacillus to enter body cells, an ability shared by the malarial parasite, with re-emergence after remissions causing relapses over a long period if treatment has been ineffective or neglected. Neither brucellosis nor rheumatic carditis would have been known to Dr William Maxwell and his symptomatic treatment of either would have been ineffective.[93]

Noting Lenihan's analysis of the poet's hair, Fowler also examined the possibility that Robert had suffered heavy metal poisoning. The absence of acute mental disturbance, characteristic of sustained mercury poisoning, suggested to Fowler that mercurial administration was moderate, if, indeed, it had been administered at all. Instead, he advanced the possibility that Burns had suffered from lead poisoning, although Lenihan and his colleagues found no trace of lead in the hair sample. To my mind, the presence of mercury in the hair, taken in conjunction with John Thomson's statement in 1844, is pretty conclusive and I can see no reason for abandoning this in favour of some alternative form of heavy metal poisoning, especially when no chemical evidence is forthcoming.

What Fowler was hinting at, of course, was that Burns had absorbed lead in the form of litharge (lead oxide), a substance which was sometimes added to wine to prevent it turning into vinegar. This form of adulteration was apparently not uncommon in the inferior wines. 'He was usually hard-up in his Dumfriesshire years and he would have been on the look-out for cheaper wines,' says Fowler.[94] Lead worms could also have formed part of inexpertly built stills, and thus lead oxide could have polluted the over-rectified whisky distilled in country districts. The very symptoms in Robert's medical history as described in his correspondence, which Fowler cited to reject mercury poisoning, were highlighted to support his theory of lead poisoning. It should be noted, however, that Fowler subscribed to the view that Burns was a habitual wine drinker who, on many occasions, drank to excess; so it seems the wheel has come full circle and we are now back to the tired old *canard* of drunkenness. Doubtless this perverse view will continue to be aired periodically till the very end of time.

So where does this leave us at the moment? Bacterial endocarditis complicating rheumatic heart disease still seems, on balance, the likeliest cause of death, though brucellosis (over a period of two years) and pneumonia (as a result of the rigours of sea-bathing) cannot be ruled out.

The funds gathered in Edinburgh, Dumfries, Liverpool and London in the months following Robert's death raised about £1,200 with which government 3 per cent Reduced Stock was purchased and handed over to the provost and bailies of Ayr for the benefit of the poet's widow and family. This, together with the £1,400 raised from the proceeds of Currie's four-volume work (of which two thousand copies were sold at 31s 6d the set), provided Jean with an annuity of £60 and her family with a comfortable income. Even the illegitimate daughters, 'Dear-bought Bess' and Betty Burns, received £200 each on reaching the age of twenty-one.

Gilbert's debt to his late brother was not settled till after he received his money from Cadell and Davies in 1820. Mindful of his indebtedness and despairing of ever making a success of Mossgiel, Gilbert had offered to sell up in 1796 and discharge his debt, but Jean resolutely forbade this step. Two years later, however, Gilbert gave up his lease and moved to Dinning in Dumfriesshire, not far from Ellisland. In 1800 his cultivation of Mrs Dunlop paid off when he was appointed estate manager to Captain John Dunlop at Morham West Mains, East Lothian. John Begg, husband of Isobel Burns, took over the remainder of the Dinning lease. Four years later Gilbert became factor on the East Lothian estates of Lady Katherine Blantyre and acquired a comfortable house at Grant's Braes near Haddington. He moved there with his wife Jean and their growing brood, as well as old Agnes Brown the poet's mother, the poet's daughter Bess, and Gilbert's unmarried sisters Agnes and Annabella. Agnes married in 1804 at the rather mature age of forty-two, taking as her husband William Galt, Gilbert's farm-servant with whom she migrated to Ireland where she died, without issue, in 1834. Agnes Brown died at Grant's Braes on 14 January 1820 at the grand old age of eighty-eight. Gilbert himself died on 8 November 1827, being survived by his unmarried sister Annabella who died five years later. By Jean Breckenridge, Gilbert had eleven children one of whom, the Revd. Dr Thomas Burns, was one of the founders of Dunedin, New Zealand, in 1848 and the suburb of Mosgiel (*sic*) testifies to the Burns connection to this day. Isobel Burns, the baby of the family, married John Begg who subsequently became land steward of the Hope Vere estate at Blackwood, Lanarkshire. After her husband's accidental death in 1813 Isobel moved to East Lothian before finally settling at Bridge House, Alloway, where she died in December 1858.

Of the poet's own family, the youngest son Maxwell died on 25 April 1799 while the second son Francis Wallace died on 9 August 1803. Both were interred in the original burial plot chosen for their father in the north-east corner of St Michael's churchyard. On 19 September 1815 the coffins of the poet and his two sons were disinterred and removed to the vault beneath the mausoleum erected that year as a fitting monument. Here, in the fulness of time, Jean Armour Burns was buried on 1 April 1834. Through her long widowhood Jean continued to live in the house in the Mill Hole Brae, now renamed Burns Street. She lived in far more comfortable circumstances as a widow than she had ever done during her eight-year marriage; in 1817 William Maule of Panmure, despite having been lampooned by Burns (CW 527), settled an annuity of £50 on her, and of course she also had an Excise widow's pension. Considering the way Mrs Dunlop had treated Robert in his last years it is interesting to note that her eldest daughter, Agnes Eleanor, became Jean's closest friend. Agnes had married a French royalist, Joseph Perochon, and this couple retired to Castlebank (now Castledykes View) on the outskirts of Dumfries. Following the removal of the remains of Burns and his two sons to the Mausoleum, Jean wrote on 20 February 1816 to Mrs Perochon, giving her the original burial plot as a token of her esteem. Jean played hostess to a never-ending stream of poets, writers, literati, celebrities and devotees of her husband's poetry, answering their often impertinent questions with amazing forbearance and good humour, occasionally giving away precious books and relics which she seems not to have valued, but drawing the line at having her portrait painted by Thomas Stothard who accompanied Cromek on his tour of the Burns country in 1809 for a projected illustrated edition of Burns which never materialised.[95] In 1820 Mrs Grant of Laggan visited Jean and later described her as 'a very comely woman with plain sound sense and very good manners'.[96] Ten years later Jean, suffering from high blood pressure, had a series of strokes which left her partially paralysed and affected her speech. Thus incapacitated she lingered on until 26 March 1834.

When the Mausoleum was opened on the night before Jean's funeral the opportunity was seized to take a plastercast of the poet's skull. The pseudo-science of phrenology was then at its height and shortly afterwards George Combe compiled an elaborate report which spawned a sizeable literature on the subject. John McDiarmid was present when the vault was opened and left a vivid description of the occasion. On the lid of Robert's coffin being removed:

> There lay the remains of the great poet, to all appearances entire, retaining various traces of recent vitality, or, to speak more correctly, exhibiting the features of one who had recently sunk into the sleep of death. The forehead struck every one as beautifully arched, if not so high as might reasonably have been supposed, while the scalp was rather thickly covered with hair, and the teeth perfectly firm and white. Altogether, the scene was so imposing that the commonest workmen stood uncovered, as the late Dr Gregory did at the exhumation of the remains of King Robert Bruce, and for some moments remained inactive, as if thrilling under the effects of some undefinable emotion while gazing on all that remained of one 'whose fame is wide as the world itself'. But the scene, however imposing, was brief; for the instant the workmen inserted a shell beneath the original wooden coffin, the head separated from the trunk, and the whole body, with the exception of the bones, crumbled into dust.[97]

Archibald Blacklock, a Dumfries surgeon present at the exhumation, provided a detailed description of the poet's skull:

> The cranial bones were perfect in every respect, if we except a little erosion of their external table, and firmly held together by their sutures; even the delicate bones of the orbits, with the trifling exception of the *os unguis* in the left, were sound, and uninjured by death and the grave. The superior maxillary bones still retained the four most posterior teeth on each side, including the dentes sapientiae, and all without spot or blemish; the incisores, cuspidati, &c., had in all probability recently dropped from the jaw, for the alveoli were but little decayed. The bones of the face and palate were also sound. Some small portions of black hair, with a very few grey hairs intermixed, were observed while detaching some extraneous matter from the occiput. Indeed, nothing could exceed the high state of preservation in which we found the bones of the cranium, or offer a fairer opportunity of supplying what has so long been desiderated by phrenologists – a correct model of our immortal poet's head: and in order to accomplish this in the most accurate and satisfactory manner, every particle of sand, or other foreign body, was carefully washed off, and the plaster of Paris applied with all the tact and accuracy of an experienced artist. The cast is admirably taken, and cannot fail to prove high interesting to phrenologists and others.
>
> Having completed our intention, the skull, securely enclosed in a leaden case, was again committed to the earth, precisely where we found it.[98]

On the basis of the plastercast, George Combe produced a phrenological assessment of the poet. The skull had a circumference of twenty-two inches, larger than average. On a scale from two ('idiotcy') to twenty, Robert scored top marks for Philoprogenitiveness, Adhesiveness, Combativeness, Love of Approbation and Benevolence, a 'large' rating for Secretiveness and Self-Esteem, a 'full' rating for Order and Tune, and only an 'uncertain' rating for Language. Combe regretted the circumstances of Robert's life:

> If he had been placed from infancy in the higher ranks of life, liberally educated, and employed in pursuits corresponding to his powers, the inferior portion of his nature would have lost part of its energy, while his better qualities would have assumed a decided and permanent superiority.[99]

Phrenology, with its jargon about propensities, sentiments and perceptive faculties, sought to determine brain development from skull shape; though long since discredited with the advance of psychology, it enjoyed an immense following in the nineteenth century. One cannot help thinking that the findings of Combe and Cox benefited from hindsight and were determined by their own prejudices and preconceptions.

Robert Junior, the boy who showed such promise in his father's last years, did not live up to expectation. Through the generosity of Alexander John Riddell young Robert completed his education at Dumfries Academy, but it was a bursary known as Duchess Anne's Mortification, granted by the Duke of Hamilton, which enabled him to enrol at Glasgow University in the autumn of 1802 where he studied logic under George Jardine and won the classics medal. The following year he took James Mylne's class in moral philosophy.[100] In 1804 he moved to Edinburgh and spent one session at the university but left without graduating. At the end of that year he obtained a clerkship at the Stamp Office, through the patronage of James Shaw (a relative of Jean Breckenridge, Gilbert's wife, and then a rising alderman who subsequently became Lord Mayor of London) who brought the matter to the attention of Prime Minister Addington. Robert laboured for twenty-seven years without promotion at Somerset House. His record of service was undistinguished and latterly the complications in his domestic arrangements, together with a propensity for gambling, put him into straitened circumstances. As early as 1820 Gilbert Burns wrote confidentially to William Thomson, Jean Burns's lawyer, about his nephew:

> Mrs Burns informed me some time ago that her son Robert had been very imprudently engaged in some speculations (the nature of which I am not informed of) which had brought him into embarrassed circumstances, and that she had from time to time sent him such supplies of money as she could spare. She wrote on the 28th ult. that she had lately been informed that Robert's debts were not yet all paid, that his creditors are clamorous, and that he was in danger of being imprisoned for debt which would of course deprive him of his situation in the Stamp Office.[101]

Gilbert's payment from Cadell and Davies, in fact, went via Jean immediately back to London to settle Robert's gambling debts. Unfortunately, Robert did not learn his lesson but eventually fell back into his old ways. By July 1832 it had come to the notice of his superiors that he had fallen into debt. This embarrassing situation, coupled with what was euphemistically described as 'an ill state of health', led to his premature retirement at the early age of forty-six. On 20 July the Commissioners of Stamps applied to the Treasury for a pension. The Treasury Secretary, Thomas Spring Rice, replied on 16 August:

> I am to acquaint you that, although it does not appear that Mr Burns has any claim on account of good services to entitle him to any alteration beyond the average, yet, taking into consideration the great literary talents of his father . . . my Lords are pleased, under the circumstances of the case, to authorise you to place him on the superannuation list of your department, at the allowance of £120 per annum.[102]

The obituary notice in the *Dumfries Courier* hinted that Robert Junior 'was not well suited for the work of a public office, and, indeed, throughout his life he continued comparatively a child in matters of business'. The little boy who had been described as 'docile' matured into a man who went through life in a rather gentle, other-worldly manner. He would have been far better suited to the academic life than the civil service, and it is a wonder that he stuck to such uncongenial work so long.

On 24 March 1809, at St Marylebone parish church, Robert married Anne Sherwood. The only issue of this marriage was a daughter, Elizabeth, baptised at St Pancras Old Church on 23 August 1812.[103] Some years later Robert and Anne separated and at the age of twenty-one Eliza was taken out to India by her Uncle James where she married Assistant Surgeon Bartholomew Everitt of the East India Company medical service. They returned from India in 1839 and Dr Everitt died a year later. Their daughter Martha Burns married Matthew Thomas, a kinsman of Dr Everitt who managed the Everitt estate in Co. Wexford, Ireland, but died without issue.

While Anne Sherwood was still alive, however, Robert Junior formed a liaison with Emma Bland, daughter of the landlord of a public house in Palace Yard, Westminster. Their eldest child, Jessie, was born in 1827 while Francis William was born on 9 September 1829.[104] Jane Emma and Robert III were apparently born in 1831 and 1833 respectively, although birth entries have not been traced. On retirement from the Stamp Office, Robert Junior took his second family back to Dumfries where they resided in English Street. Here Emma Burns kept a lodging house on the upper floor of what later became Bell's Temperance Hotel while her husband augmented his substantial pension by teaching mathematics and the classics. He was a proficient musician and in his earlier years produced English verse that lacked the fire and inspiration of his father's poetry. He had a prodigious memory and great powers of application, as shown by his scholastic attainments. His enthusiasm for learning never left him, and in his latter years he devoted his time to the study of Gaelic. At the age of seventy Robert Junior died on 14 May 1857 and was the last member of the family to be interred in the Mausoleum.[105] What became of Emma Bland is not known, though it is assumed that she returned to London on the death of her common-law husband.

Francis William died young and Jessie died unmarried on 19 August 1847, but Robert III married Mary Campbell of Dumfries on 24 September 1843 [106] and they ran a private school in Loreburn Street, Dumfries, for many years until the parish school board closed it down in 1872. Robert III died in 1879 and was buried in St Mary's churchyard. He had one son, Robert Burns IV, who ran away from home and enlisted in the Scots Fusilier Guards under an assumed name. After serving at Shorncliffe, Dublin and other parts of the United Kingdom, he left the army and in 1882 obtained the position of keeper of the powder magazine at Blackhall near Edinburgh. He married Jean Palmer, daughter of a farmer in Mouswald parish, but had no family. In widowhood Jean resided in the National Burns Memorial Cottage Homes at Mauchline where she died in 1904.[107] Jane Emma married Thomas Brown, a foreman carder in a Hawick textile mill, with whom she emigrated to Guelph, Ontario. After eight years, however, they returned to Scotland and settled in Dumfries where he died in 1911. Jane Emma died on 24 September 1916 at the age of eighty-five. For a time the Browns were caretakers of Burns House, but latterly they retired to 191 High Street. They had three children, the sole survivor being Miss Jean Armour Burns Brown (1864–1937) who continued to reside in Dumfries till her death. Miss Jean bore a striking resemblance to her illustrious great-grandfather.[108]

The other surviving sons of the poet, William Nicol and James Glencairn Burns, were educated at Dumfries Academy and Christ's Hospital, London, whence they entered the service of the Honourable East India Company on cadetships procured by Sir James Shaw, the Marchioness of Hastings and Sir John Reid. The former rose to the rank of colonel and the latter to lieutenant-colonel. William married Catherine Adelaide, daughter of Richard Crone of Dublin. She died at Kulludghev, India, in June 1841, without issue, and William never remarried.

James married Sarah Robinson in 1818 and by her had three children. The eldest, Jean Isabella, died at sea on 5 June 1823 at the age of four and a half, while a son, Robert Shaw, died at Neemuch on 11 December 1821 at the age of eighteen months. Sarah herself had died at Neemuch a month previously, while giving birth to her second daughter, Sarah Eliza Maitland Tombs. The little girl was sent back to Britain and was raised by her grandmother, Jean Armour, with whom she lived till the latter's death in 1834. These were twelve happy years and till the end of her long life Sarah Burns retained the fondest memories of Dumfries and 'Bonie Jean'. One of the three authentic portraits of Jean, by Samuel McKenzie, shows her with Sarah about the age of five. Her father's second wife was Mary Beckett who died in 1844 at the age of fifty-two, leaving a daughter of fourteen. The previous year James had retired from the Indian Army and settled originally in London before moving to Cheltenham where William had already retired. In the summer of 1844 James and William, both now widowers, decided to revisit Scotland where they were reunited with their brother Robert on the banks of the Doon on 10 July, a reunion which turned into a grand public demonstration to the memory of their father.

In 1848 Sarah married Dr W. B. Hutchinson and emigrated to Australia four years later. Their first three children, Arabella Ann, Robert Burns and Arthur Vincent, died of a measles epidemic on the voyage aboard the SS *Chance*. In 1862, now widowed, Sarah returned to Cheltenham; when her father died on 18 November 1865 Sarah, with her son and three daughters, moved in with Uncle William and her step-sister Annie Burns Burns. Sarah Burns Hutchinson died at Cheltenham on 12 July 1909 in her eighty-eighth year and at her death was the nearest and oldest living descendant of the poet. Latterly she had lived with her unmarried step-sister Annie and her daughter Margaret Constance 'Daisy' Burns Hutchinson. Three of Sarah's children married, Annie Vincent Burns (Mrs Burns Scott) living in Adelaide and Mrs Violet Gowring in Eastbourne. Her son, Robert Burns Hutchinson (1855–1944), settled in Langley, Vancouver. He, in turn, had two sons and three daughters whose descendants live in various parts of Canada and the United States to this day. George Ian Burns Gowring, the only son of Mrs Gowring, carried on the line which is scattered throughout England and Wales.[109]

Robert's eldest daughter Bess married John Bishop, farm overseer to the Baillie family of Polkemmet where she died on 8 December 1816, allegedly giving birth to her seventh child. A family tree compiled by her great-grandson Alexander Freugh shows that the Bishop branch of the poet's descendants were numerous and, by 1922, scattered throughout the world.[110] Bess's younger daughter Jean married James Weir from whom was descended Lord Weir of Cathcart, the only descendant of the poet to be ennobled. The present Viscount Weir has his estate near Mauchline.

Betty Burns, daughter of the poet by Ann Park, was brought up by Jean Armour and lived at Dumfries where, on 2 June 1808, she married John Thomson, a private in the Stirlingshire Militia. The following day the regiment left Dumfries for Berwick-on-Tweed and young Mrs Thomson went there for about a year. On the regiment being posted to another part of the country in 1810 Betty went to Pollokshaws, Glasgow to live with her husband's parents. Here she raised her baby son and supported herself by doing needle-flowering for a Glasgow warehouse. Betty's fortunes took a turn for the better in 1812 when, on attaining her majority, she received £200 from the fund raised by Alderman Shaw. This enabled her to rent a house and furnish it, and it was there that her husband came when he was demobilised in 1814, to resume his trade as a hand-loom weaver. He and Betty and their large family continued to live in Pollokshaws where John died in 1869 and his wife four years later. They were buried in the Vennel cemetery and their tombstone bears two stanzas composed by their second son, Robert Burns Thomson. Betty Burns resembled her father more than any of his other children, as Hugh McDonald observed when he visited her in 1851:

> We have had the pleasure of meeting with two of the Poet's sons, on both of whom the paternal stamp was obvious; but we were more forcibly reminded of the family lineaments, as represented in the best portraits, on being introduced to Mrs Thomson than we were on that occasion.[111]

The only one of the poet's descendants who inherited his muse was the aptly named Robert Burns Thomson, born in 1818. McDonald left an interesting pen-portrait:

> He is a living *fac simile* in physical appearance of what Burns must have been in the prime of manhood. A degree more slender in person, or a shade more fair in complexion, from the nature of his employment, he possibly may be; but this we feel confident is the extent of the difference. Nor is the resemblance only physical. He has in a considerable measure the same vigorous intellect, and pithy if not rude humour, combined with a manly sense of independence, and a taste for poetry and music, in both of which arts he is indeed no mean proficient.

His song 'My Daddy's Awa at the War' attained great popularity during the Crimean War.[112] He was proud of his descent, as his sentimental poem dedicated to the memory of his famous grandfather testifies, but he made no claim to notice on account of his namesake, and resisted the temptation to issue his poems in book form. Several of his poems were published in various periodicals indicating that they were not without merit. Instead he followed in his father's footsteps as a hand-loom weaver, subsequently becoming a powerloom minder in Thornliebank and Glasgow, and later manager of Scott's textile factory. He eventually set up in business on his own account as Messrs R. B. Thomson and Company, brush manufacturers, at 38 Stockwell Street, Glasgow. He died at Shawlands on 14 April 1887 and was interred in the family lair at the Vennel. A younger brother, James Glencairn Thomson, likewise worked as a hand-loom weaver before switching to pattern-making. On his retirement in 1899 he received a public subscription of £175, and six years later a further £200. He was also granted a small pension from the government, in recognition of the eminence of his grandfather. The last survivor of the family, he died at Crossmyloof on 9 July 1911, at the age of eighty-four. The Thomson brothers were the principal guests of honour at the Burns Centenary celebrations held at the King's Arms Hall in the Trongate, Glasgow, in 1859. Margaret Thomson, youngest of Betty's daughters, was the second wife of David Wingate, the Glasgow poet. After her husband's death she resided with her brother James and died at Crossmyloof on 23 November 1898. She was interred in the family burying place, alongside the remains of Gilbert Burns Begg, the poet's nephew and son of Isabella Burns, who died at Pollokshaws on 11 January 1885 aged eighty-three.[113]

Apart from the descendants of the poet by Jenny Clow, noted in a previous chapter, there was one other liaison which allegedly resulted in an illegitimate birth. There is a strong tradition in Moffat that Helen Hyslop, 'a noted local beauty', gave birth to a daughter by Burns in 1789. The only Helen Hyslop recorded in that part of the county was born to John Hyslop and Janet Howatson at Langholm in March 1766, but no record of any child born to her appears in the parish registers of Moffat or any other district. Lawrence Burness of the Coull-Anderson Genealogical Centre, Arbroath, points out that illegitimate births were often unrecorded. The fact of Helen Hyslop Junior's existence, however, is well documented. According to a newspaper report shortly after the lady's death at the advanced age of ninety-eight, she had resided in the same little back street in which she had been born:

> Helen is said to have borne a strong resemblance to Burns in her earlier days, and indeed the likeness to the portraits of Burns was traceable to the last in the contour of the face and in the dark, bright eyes . . . Nor was the likeness confined to physical points; in her mental powers Helen showed a strain of the poetic blood. A few years ago her conversational powers and her quickness of repartee were most amusing and attractive.[114]

Jean Armour continued to live in the Millbrae Vennel until her death in 1834. Her original landlord, Captain Hamilton of Allershaw, sold the house to Dr William Maxwell and he bequeathed it to his son. About 1844 it was sold to Mrs Anna Maria Barker of Langshaw whose trustees, in turn, sold it to Colonel William Nicol Burns in 1851. It is not known who were the tenants in the eleven years after Jean Armour's death, but in 1845 the house was let to the managers of the Industrial School for the accommodation of their schoolmaster. In 1858 Colonel Burns signed a Disposition of Trust expressing the wish that the house be kept in proper repair as an interesting relic connected with his father's memory. By 1903 the Education Society was letting the house to the Town Council on a long lease at a rental only sufficient to pay the annuity of £20 to the late colonel's two nieces or their heirs. The last recipient of this annuity was Robert Burns Hutchinson, who died in the United States on 26 August 1944. Burns House was restored and formally opened by Jean Armour Burns Brown as a museum in 1935. It continues in this role to the present day, and is now under the care of the local authorities.

The poet's birthplace had a more chequered career, being for a century (1781–1881) a public house, until it was acquired by the Trustees of the Burns Monument at Alloway. Since then it has become the Mecca of Burnsians the world over, restored to more or less pristine condition, with a fine museum of Burns relics alongside. In the course of the nineteenth and early twentieth centuries, monuments and museums, statues, busts, cairns and plaques to the memory of Burns and those immortalised by their contact with him proliferated, not only all over Scotland from Aberdeen to

Portpatrick, but in various parts of England and Ireland, North America, Australia and New Zealand, wherever Scots and their descendants were scattered. At one time every Carnegie library in the United States had its obligatory bust of Burns – some 3,460 in all – but this was done away with in the 1950s. Even so, there are still upwards of 180 monuments to Burns, from Halifax, Nova Scotia, to Hokitika, New Zealand.[115] In this regard Burns far outstrips Shakespeare or any other British poet, or any other poet for that matter. Other than royalty, only Christopher Columbus and Lenin (in his heyday) have surpassed Burns in this respect.

To the poet's birthplace there came, on the fifth anniversary of his death, nine Ayrshire gentlemen who sat down to what is now regarded as the world's first Burns Supper. They dined on such homely fare as sheep's head and haggis. The 'Address to a Haggis' was recited and several toasts drunk, and a commemoration ode composed by the Revd. Hamilton Paul was delivered. The company agreed to meet again at the cottage the following January and thus the custom of celebrating the poet's birthday was initiated. Although the claim of the Greenock Burns Club to have been founded in 1801 cannot be upheld it was certainly in existence within a few years of that date. A decade later, however, the fashion for Burns Suppers was so well established that the Revd. William Peebles, whom Robert had lampooned in 'The Kirk's Alarm' (CW 359), was moved to publish his poetical treatise entitled *Burnomania; the celebrity of Robert Burns considered in a Discourse addressed to all real Christians of every Denomination*. Though Peebles vented his spleen against an 'irreligious profligate' who wrote 'vile scraps of indecent ribaldry', this did not deter the devotees of Burns from holding their celebratory dinners which, from year to year, grew in size, number and scope. Out of this developed the Burns clubs which, as a result of a meeting in London following the unveiling of the statue of Burns on the Thames Embankment in 1885, banded together to form the Burns Federation. Today, with some 400 affiliated clubs representing a membership of approximately 60,000, the Federation is a worldwide body whose annual conferences have been held in Canada, the United States and England as well as Scotland.[116]

Interest in Burns and his works is undiminished. By 1986, it was estimated that over 2,000 editions of his poems had been published, or an average of ten every year since that first blue-paper volume appeared at Kilmarnock. Biographies of Burns, critical analyses of his songs, poetry and correpondence, and books dealing with aspects of his life and work are legion; the Mitchell Library's Burns collection now runs to over 3,500 volumes. The works of Burns have been translated into almost fifty languages; Samuel Marshak's Russian editions sold over a million copies in the space of thirty years, while a Chinese edition of Burns released recently sold 100,000 copies in its initial printing. Burns continues to exert an immense appeal, as witness the press, radio and television coverage which grows steadily from year to year, not to mention the countless thousands of Burns Suppers held in every part of the globe each January. Burns has been the subject of three musicals since 1925 (a fourth is currently being put together) and there have been numerous dramatisations of various aspects of his life, including two full-length feature films.

Inevitably interest in Burns, at the time of writing, is being heightened on account of the bicentenary of his death, imminent in July 1996. As he lay dying, Robert is supposed to have turned to his wife and said, 'Jean, I'll be more thought of a hundred years after this than I am now'. By the time William Wallace completed the fourth volume of the revised Chambers edition in 1896 Robert's dying prediction had come true. Wallace concluded:

> It is safe to say that a hundred years hence he will be more thought of still. By that time the patronising Philistine, and the bourgeois critic, and the malignant detractor with his croak and leer, will have vanished into congenial obscurity. Burns will be able to speak for himself.[117]

Thanks to the scholarship of the past sixty years, we now have far more complete editions of both the prose and poetic works of Burns than Wallace could have dreamed of. As Wallace predicted, Burns can, and does, speak for himself. He is now universally recognised as one of the greatest poets of all time; no one has ever surpassed him in his ability to convey the range of moods and emotions, the joys and sorrows, humour and pathos, the hopes and yearnings, the euphoria and the heartaches experienced by all people everywhere. Not for nothing has Burns been dubbed the Bard of Humanity. The great poet is not just of his own time but for all time, and the profundities which he enunciated two hundred years ago are as valid today as ever they were. Robert Burns was born in obscurity and lived his life on the edge of poverty, a life of rough toil frequently beset by physical pain and mental anguish, time and again subjected to crushing disappointments that would have destroyed a less heroic spirit. The readiness with which the myth of dissipation was accepted after Robert's death may have been a natural reaction – few men would not have been soured by the life that was his lot – yet Robert never gave way, and refused to be crushed. We cannot but be moved and inspired by the nobility of this man who was still composing songs of matchless beauty, sung and enjoyed to this day, within days of his death. In material terms he died a poor man; but immeasurably he enriched the world.

Notes on Sources

Poems and songs of Burns are denoted by CW followed by their page number in *The Complete Works of Robert Burns* (1986) and letters are indicate by CL followed by their page number in *The Complete Letters of Robert Burns* (1987). As a rule, sources cited in the text are given in full, but for the sake of convenience frequently mentioned sources have been abbreviated.

AL	Autobiographical Letter of Burns to Dr Moore
A-Z	*Burns A-Z, the Complete Word Finder* (1990)
BC	*Burns Chronicle* followed by year of publication
BE	Maurice Lindsay, *Burns Encyclopaedia* (Hale, 1980)
Boyle	Andrew Boyle, *The Ayrshire Book of Burns-Lore* (Alloway, 1985)
Carswell	Catherine Carswell, *The Life of Robert Burns* (1930; Canongate Classics, 1990)
CH	Donald Low, *Robert Burns, the Critical Heritage* (Routledge, 1974)
Ch-Wa	Chambers and Wallace, *Life and Works of Robert Burns* 4 vols. (Chambers, 1896)
CPB	First (1) and second (2) *Commonplace Books* of Robert Burns
Cromek	Robert H. Cromek, *Reliques of Robert Burns* (Cadell and Davies, 1808)
Cunningham	Allan Cunningham, *The Works of Robert Burns with his Life*, volume I (Cochrane, 1834)
Currie	James Currie, *The Works of Robert Burns* (Cadell and Davies, 1800); later editions specifically noted
Fasti	Hew Scott, *Fasti Ecclesiae Scoticanae* (Edinburgh, 1914)
Fitzhugh (1943)	Robert Fitzhugh, *Robert Burns, his Associates and Contemporaries* (Chapel Hill, NC, 1943)
Fitzhugh (1970)	Robert Fitzhugh, *Robert Burns, the Man and the Poet* (Boston, 1970)
Fowler	Richard H. Fowler, *Robert Burns* (Routledge, 1988)
Gilfillan	Revd. George Gilfillan, *The National Burns* 4 vols. (Mackenzie, 1872)
GN	Gilbert Burns's Narrative (letter to Mrs Dunlop, 1797)
Hecht	Hans Hecht, *Robert Burns, the Man and his Work* (Alloway, 1981)
Heron	Robert Heron, *A Memoir of the Life of the Late Robert Burns* (Edinburgh, 1797)

Hilton Brown   Hilton Brown, *There Was a Lad* (Hamish Hamilton, 1949)
Kinsley   James Kinsley (ed.) *The Poems and Songs of Robert Burns* 3 vols.
               (Oxford, 1968)
Lockhart   John G. Lockhart, *Life of Robert Burns* (Minerva, 1892)
OPR   Old Parish Registers, New Register House, Edinburgh
PP   J. DeLancey Ferguson, *Pride and Passion* (OUP, 1939)
SCO   Sheriff Clerk Office
SD   W. Scott Douglas, *The Works of Robert Burns* 6 vols.(Paterson,
               1877–79)
Snyder   Franklyn B. Snyder, *The Life of Robert Burns* (Macmillan, 1932;
               Archon, 1968)
SRO   Scottish Records Office, Edinburgh
Walker   Josiah Walker, *Poems by Robert Burns* 2 vols. (Morison, 1811)

Chapter 1: Antecedents

1 Robert Chambers: *Life and Works of Robert Burns* (Edinburgh, 1851), I, 333.
2 Dr James Burnes: *Notes on his name and family* (Edinburgh, 1851), 29–30.
3 Ibid., 14–15. Alexander Carmichael (author of *Carmina Gadelica*) amplifies the story in his article 'The Land of Lorne' (*The Evergreen*, spring 1895) in which he mentions Walter Campbell of Baileandeor (near Taynuilt), outlawed for the murder of a band of travelling poets called the Strolling Satirists.
4 Chambers, op. cit., I, 335–6.
5 James Tomlinson: 'Burns's bogus armorial bearings' (BC 1980). See also Introductory Note to CW, 1st edition (1986) but emended in 2nd edition (1991).
6 W. Scott Douglas: 'The paternal ancestry of Burns', Appendix A in J. G. Lockhart: *Life of Robert Burns* (Minerva Library edn, Edinburgh, 1892).
7 Dr W. A. MacNaughton: 'Notes concerning the Burns family in Kincardineshire', *Aberdeen University Review*, V, 15–26.
8 Henry J. Rennie: 'The Burnes family in Glenbervie' (BC 1931), 28–34.
9 Revd. James C. Higgins: *The Book of Robert Burns* (Grampian Club, Edinburgh, 1891), III.
10 Rennie, op cit.
11 Rennie, op cit., in whose possession this document was in 1931.
12 Dr Charles Rogers: *Genealogical memoirs of the family of Robert Burns* (Edinburgh, 1877), 33.
13 Facsimile of the entry reproduced in *Memorial Catalogue of the Burns Exhibition* (Glasgow, 1898), facing 392.
14 Gilbert Burns to Dr James Currie, April 1798. The error was first corrected by Scott Douglas in 1882.
15 Ch-Wa I, 25.
16 Thomas McCrorie: *The Family Tree of Robert Burns* (Dumfries, 1961), but very inaccurate with regard to the poet's ancestry. He shows Robert Burnes as having five daughters, but the eldest, Margaret, was actually the daughter of William Burnes of Fordoun parish (born March 1723). The daughters of Robert Burnes were Elspit (1725), Isobel (1730), Jean (1731) and Mary (1732). Jean married her cousin John Burnes of Bogjorgan, Isobel married William Brand of Auchinblae (1770) and Mary never married (OPR Dunnottar).

17 John Ramsay of Ochtertyre: *Scotland and Scotsmen in the eighteenth century* (ed. Alex. Allardyce, Edinburgh, 1888), II, 554.
18 Kincardineshire SCO records, quoted in BC 1917, 150. Robert Burnes was also summoned on 18 December 1746 for permitting his livestock to destroy his neighbour's crops. He was assoilzied on 8 January 1747.
19 K. G. Burns: 'The poet's genealogy' (BC 1921), 120–4.
20 Snyder, 33.
21 GN.
22 Carswell, 21–7, for a highly-coloured account of William's sojourn in Edinburgh.
23 Elizabeth W. Ewing: 'Some of Burns's Ayrshire friends' (BC 1908), 35.
24 Carswell, 28–9.
25 OPR Kirkoswald. Gilbert Brown (born 1708) married Agnes Rainie on 3 June 1731. Their children were Agnes (17 March 1732), Jannet (24 February 1734), John (26 September 1736), Samuel (18 February 1739) and David (10 May 1741).
26 Revd. J. C. Muir: 'Burns in Kirkoswald' (BC 1906), 27–74. Muir says that Gilbert and Agnes had four sons and four daughters, but only two daughters and three sons are listed in OPR.
27 Ibid.
28 Allan Mitchell (ed.) *Monumental Inscriptions: Carrick* (Glasgow, 1985); OPR Kirkoswald.
29 Rogers: *Genealogical memoirs* (1877); *Book of Robert Burns* (1892), III.
30 Snyder, 38.
31 Auguste Angellier: *Robert Burns, la vie* (Paris, 1893), I; Ch-Wa I, 451n.

Chapter 2: Alloway, 1759–66

1 Carswell, 35.
2 Boyle, 25. Anciently the Curtecan. According to J. Paterson, *History of Ayrshire* (1847), I, 1999 there was no bridge over the stream till after 1791, but Boyle, 128 avers that it was bridged by the mid-17th century.
3 OPR Ayr, births.
4 Boyle, 72.
5 Elizabeth W. Ewing: 'Some of Burns's Ayrshire friends' (BC 1908), 31.
6 Letters of RB to Gavin Hamilton, 18 October 1783 (CL 65), Thomas Orr, 11 October 1784 (CL 50), John Richmond, 17 February 1786 (CL 76–7), Robert Muir, 20 March 1786 (CL 86) and Robert Aiken, 3 April 1786 (CL 91).
7 Gilbert Burns to James Currie, 24 October 1800.
8 For the subsequent history of the cottage see G. Esdaile: 'Burns's cottage and the road to it' (BC 1901), 78–90; (BC 1902), 93–99; Elizabeth Ewing (BC 1932), 31–4. A different story was given by James Grierson of Dalgoner: 'RB was born while his father resided at Doonholmgate, as gardener to Provost Fergusson of Doonholm, and did not build the cottage till several summers after Robert's birth' (letter to the *Glasgow Chronicle*, August 1817).
9 OPR Ayr, births; a reprint of the entries in the family bible appears in James Gibson *The Burns Calendar* (Kilmarnock, 1874).
10 David Watt of Doonfoot Mill, who died in October 1823, was the last person baptized in Alloway Kirk, according to an obituary notice in the *Scots Magazine*, December 1823.

11 AL (CL 249).
12 Boyle, 72.
13 RB to Captain Francis Grose, *c.* June 1790 (CL 557).
14 Carswell, 38.
15 AL (CL 249).
16 Boyle, 7.
17 John Strawhorn: *750 Years of a Scottish School: Ayr Academy, 1233–1983* (Alloway Publishing, 1983).
18 William Will: 'John Murdoch, tutor of RB' (BC 1929), 60–71.
19 Currie I, 87–8: Letter from John Murdoch to Joseph Cooper Walker, 22 February 1799.
20 Train MS, Edinburgh University Library, quoted by Fitzhugh (1943), 59.
21 AL (CL 249–50).
22 SD IV, 353.
23 Snyder, 62, n22.
24 Hugh Haliburton: *Furth in Field* (London, 1894), 225–6 contains an interesting analysis of this under the heading of 'Burns's reading books'.
25 Snyder, 44.
26 Ibid.

Chapter 3: Mount Oliphant, 1766–77

1 GN, Scott Douglas IV, 353.
2 Records of the Incorporation of Shoemakers, in Strathclyde Regional Archives, Ayr.
3 John Keats to Tom Keats, 13 July 1818. *Letters of John Keats,* ed. Hyder E. Rollins (1958), I, 331.
4 J. Cuthbert Hadden: 'Burns Topography' (BC 1893), 72–8.
5 GN.
6 Ibid. See also 'Provost Fergusson' (BC 1908), 35.
7 Burns family bible entries in *The Burns Calendar* (1874).
8 GN.
9 Ibid.
10 Carswell, 44.
11 Ibid.
12 Strawhorn, op. cit.
13 GN.
14 Ibid.
15 Carswell, 45. The thought also crossed RB's mind in January-February 1782 after the flax-dressing fiasco at Irvine.
16 Snyder, 49.
17 BC 1932, reproduced opposite 79.
18 BC 1893, 77–8. In the early 1990s it tried to cash in on the Burns connection with a restaurant 'Burns Byre' but this venture was shortlived. At the time of writing (1992) the farm is up for sale.
19 GN.
20 Ibid.
21 Ibid. The poem referred to has not survived.
22 John Murdoch to J. C. Walker, 1799, reproduced in Currie I, 90.

23 Robert's letters mention the following French books: *Angola, histoire indienne* by Rochette de la Morlière (CL 433), *Belisaire* and *Les Incas* by Jean-François Marmontel (CL 140, 232), *L'Art poetique* by Nicolas Boileau-Despreux (CL 144, 585), *Contes* of Jean de la Fontaine (CL 433, 578), and quote from the works of Racine (CL 316) and Voltaire (CL 130, 316, 687).

24 Hilton Brown, 63–4.

25 See, for example, the long letter written some time afterwards from Ellisland, 18 September 1788 (CL 237–9), containing 18 French words.

26 William Will: 'John Murdoch, Tutor of Robert Burns' (BC 1929), 60–71.

27 Ch-Wa I, 33n.

28 A reference to an exploit of one of the sons of Dr John Malcolm, in the service of the East India Company in Oudh.

29 GN.

30 Iain McDougall: 'Notes on the song' (BC 1915), 143–50.

31 Revd. Hamilton Paul: *The Poems and Songs of RB* (Ayr, 1819), v-vi.

32 *The Scotsman* (1828).

33 Chambers (1851), I.

34 Ch-Wa I, 44.

35 OPR Dalrymple, births.

36 OPR Dailly and Dreghorn.

37 1CPB.

38 GN.

Chapter 4: Kirkoswald, 1775

1 GN.

2 AL (CL 252–3).

3 *Stat. Account* (EP, 1982), VI, 406.

4 Carswell, 69.

5 *Stat. Account*, op. cit.

6 Revd. James Muir: 'Burns in Kirkoswald' (BC 1906), 27–54.

7 His tombstone in Maybole says that he died on 18 November 1844, aged 85, but the *Ayr Advertiser* of 19 December 1844 says that he died on 13 December in his 83rd year. It seems more likely that he was born in 1759 than 1761.

8 According to Rodger's tombstone he died in May 1797 aged 71, but the Kirk Session records are in his handwriting down to 3 September 1801, when it was formally minuted that he was giving up the office of Session clerk.

9 OPR Dailly. Margaret, daughter of Robert Thomson, was baptised on 5 November 1762.

10 cf letter of RB to his brother William of 5 May 1789 (CL 516).

11 CH-Wa I, 47–51.

12 Rodger must have taught him well. By dint of enterprise and extreme frugality he amassed a fortune of £100,000. His parsimony was legendary; for anecdotes see BC 1908, 140–1.

13 Carswell, 71–2.

14 Ch-Wa I, 48. A variant of the ending, quoted here, is given by Matthew Porteous (BC 1906), 42n, one of the eye–witnesses who said the debate was on the relative merits of a merchant and a sailor.

15 Revd. James Muir (BC 1906), 27–74.

16 Ch-Wa I, 50n, citing Dr Charles Rogers.

17 Muir, op. cit., 50. But the poet's correspondence belies the truth of this. RB's letter to Grose about June 1790 (CL 558) would surely have mentioned a poem if such had existed at that time; but apart from a passing reference to a Carrick farmer on an Ayr market-day there is nothing to link the narrative with the supposed composition of 1775. See also the letter to Mrs Dunlop written in November or December 1790 (CL 192). For other bibulous anecdotes of Douglas Graham see Muir, op. cit., 51ff.

18 AL (CL 253).

19 Muir, op. cit.

20 *The Letters of Robert Burns*, ed. J. DeLancey Ferguson (1931); 2nd edn. G. Ross Roy (1985), I, 3–4.

21 CL, Appendix I, 727–61.

22 The Ayr Penny Post was not established till 1828 when it covered an area as far as Dalrymple. See A. Bruce Auckland and Geoff Oxley: *Penny Posts of Scotland* (Edinburgh, 1978).

23 RB to Margaret Chalmers, 16 September 1788 (CL 238).

24 'Burns in Kirkoswald', *Macmillan's Magazine*, June 1893.

25 Ch-Wa I, 51n.

26 The influence of other poets, such as James Thomson, whom RB read at Kirkoswald, is very clearly traced by J. Logie Robertson in *Furth of Field*, and Prof. Minto in *Literature of the Georgian Era* (Edinburgh, 1894).

Chapter 5: Lochlie: the Contented Years, 1777–81.

1 'The Twa Dogs' (CW 142).

2 GN.

3 'The Lochlea Sequestration' (BC 1910), 149–52.

4 I have preferred the spelling shown in the legal documents regarding the sequestration (although in the first production in the bundle 'Lochhill' appears twice by error. RB and GB spelled it Lochlea, but it was pronounced then, as now, as 'Lochly' and the Lochlie spelling seems to be the more correct form.

5 J. Taylor Gibb (BC 1916), 128.

6 'The Lochlea Sequestration', op. cit., 151.

7 Job 3: 17.

8 SD IV, 363–4 (2) and one in Rogers, II, 153.

9 Text, including facsimile of two pages, (BC 1892), 39–42.

10 Jethro Tull: *The Horse-Hoeing Husbandry; or an essay on the Principles of Tillage and Vegetation*; Adam Dickson: *A Treatise on Agriculture*; John Taylor: *The Scriptural Doctrine of Original Sin*; James Justice: *British Gardeners' Directory*; Robert Boyle: *The Voyages and Adventures of Captain Robert Boyle*. Joseph Ritson's *Select Collection of English Songs* was not published till 1783; but RB may have meant Robert Dodsley's *Collection of Poems* which had appeared in several editions by that time. Allan Ramsay's *Tea-Table Miscellany* and *The Evergreen* both appeared in instalments between 1724 and 1727, and a complete edition of Ramsay's *Poems* was first published in 1731 and ran to many editions.

11 GN.

12 Hilton Brown, 111. Carswell, 73–4: 'The lovers' meetings were as innocent as they were sweet' and more romantic nonsense in the same vein.

13 'Now Westlin Winds' (CW 44) and 'I Dream'd I lay' (CW 45).

14 SD I, Appendix B, 329–30. Neither Stinchar nor Irvine has any relationship with the Lochlie district.
15 Revd. Hamilton Paul to Dr Robert Chambers.
16 BE.
17 Cunningham I, 29.
18 A. B. Todd: *Reminiscences of a Long Life* (Glasgow, 1906). Todd got this and other anecdotes from Hugh Merry, Annie Rankine's son. Similar versions occur in the Grierson MS, and the Scott Douglas edn. of Lockhart (1892), 27.
19 AL (CL 253). This was the last of the three songs published in the Kilmarnock Edition, 227.
20 See, for example Carswell, 65, who tells us that although RB could not sing, 'he responded quickly and unerringly to rhythm, and in spite of his rather clumsy build and cruelly rounded shoulders, he learned to dance well'.
21 Currie I, 79.
22 Quoted in *Complete Writings of Robert Burns* (Boston, 1927), VII, 23.
23 SD I, 21n. Some later biographers (notably Snyder), however, have arbitrarily moved the incident of RB's defiance to 1779, in light of the Candlish letters, op. cit.
24 *Stat. Account* VI, 645–50.
25 David Sillar to Robert Aiken, in *Poems of Robert Burns* (Edinburgh, 1811) II, 257.
26 Ibid.
27 John Taylor: *The Scriptural Doctrine of Original Sin proposed to free and candid examination* (3rd edn, 1750).
28 Matthew 18: 20, misquoted.
29 Boyle, 132.
30 H. Makinson: 'David Sillar' (BC 1915), 70–9.
31 Boyle, 134.
32 Chambers I (1851), 64n.
33 James L. Hempstead: 'Saunders Tait' (BC 1981, 72–77). See also Kay's *Portraits* (Edinburgh, 1838)II, 126. OPR Innerleithen; parents' names not given but his father's name was probably Robert Tait.
34 William Aiton: *Agricultural Report* (1811) criticized the friendly or penny societies which had lost sight of their original objectives and threw away much of their revenue 'in purchasing flags, spontoons, gorgets, crowns, coats of mail, sceptres, robes, trains, and other fooleries, and in making fool–like parades, through towns, drinking on the streets, &c'. Aiton also mentions the high-sounding titles assumed by these 'downright fools'.
35 *Poems and Songs by Alexander Tait* (Paisley, 1790), pp340, octavo, price 1s 6d. A copy of this exceedingly rare book may be seen in the Mitchell Library, Glasgow.
36 Hempstead, op. cit.
37 Currie I, 363–7.
38 GN.
39 SD I, Appendix B, 330–1.
40 John Muir: 'Burns at Galston and Ecclefechan' (1896).
41 AL. RB brings this episode in 'to crown all' after the Irvine fiasco, but from the internal evidence of the 'Begbie' correspondence scholars have placed it in the early part of 1781 and concluded that it was this rejection which led him to go to Irvine.
42 GN.

43 SD I, Appendix B, 330–1.

44 Ch-Wa I, 72.

45 This letter was first published by Scott Douglas in 1877 (vol. IV). The MS was in the Honresfield Collection examined by Ferguson in preparing his edition of 1931, but has since disappeared. In CL, I inserted the name Alison in full, solely in the interests of clarity.

46 OPR Galston.

47 J. DeLancey Ferguson: *The Letters of Robert Burns* (Oxford, 1931), Introduction. Reprinted in the second edition (1985).

48 R. H. Cromek: *Reliques* (1808), 442n.

49 William Pickering: *The Poetical Works of Robert Burns* (Aldine edn. London, 1839).

50 Davidson Cook: 'Mr A. J. Law's Collection of Burns manuscripts' (BC 1927), 23–5. For a comparison of the variant readings see Kinsley.

51 Glasgow Directories, (1787–) in the Glasgow Collection, Mitchell Library.

52 Strathclyde Regional Archives, T-BK 166/4, 1827.

53 In 1 CPB, see chapter 8, *infra*.

54 Gilfillan (1872) claimed that Montgomerie's Peggy was a Mrs Derbishire, but this is not borne out by any OPR in Great Britain.

Chapter 6: Irvine, 1781–2

1 AL (CL 253).

2 'Now Westlin Winds' (CW 44) after the Kirkoswald period.

3 Alluded to in GN.

4 For the best commentary on the sentimental influences on RB see Carol McGuirk: *Burns and the Sentimental Era* (Athens, Georgia, 1985).

5 AL (CL 253).

6 Notably Ian Grimble, in *Robert Burns* (Hamlyn, 1986).

7 GN.

8 The *Glasgow Mercury*, VI, 264 (16–23 January 1783), 25. Many writers have misunderstood the nature and purpose of the premiums.

9 Bruce P. Lenman: 'Flax and Flax-Dressing' (BC 1974), 40–3; (BC 1975), 29.

10 Henry Ranken: 'Burns in Irvine' (BC 1905), 34.

11 *Stat. Account* VI, 240–57.

12 John Strawhorn: *Irvine, Royal Burgh and New Town* (1985), 103.

13 Memorandum of Hugh Alexander of Braidmead (June 1850) who interviewed John Boyd, a cousin of the baker Montgomery Boyd. Boyd was 89 at the time so his memory may not be as reliable as could be wished. John C. Hill: *The Life and Works of Robert Burns in Irvine* (1933), based on the evidence of RB's contemporaries recollected in old age.

14 Boyle gives Peacock's name as William; Strawhorn gives it as Alexander or Samuel; 19th century accounts give the surname only. OPR Irvine show only one person of this name in this period – Samuel Peacock, whose wife was Agnes McDowgal.

15 Gilbert Brown was married three times, but contrary to popular belief, his second wife was not a Peacock. OPR Kirkoswald registers show that Gilbert married (1) Agnes Rainie (3 June 1731), (2) Margaret Blain (26 June 1744) and (3) Catharine Moat (16 April 1765). It seems more likely that Peacock (if he was related at all) was a cousin of Agnes Brown by marriage.

16 Illustrated in BC 1905, 41.

17 I am indebted to Samuel K. Gaw for information regarding the cess books.
18 Matthew 25: 11.
19 *Stat. Account.* op. cit.
20 For example, in Ian Grimble: *Robert Burns*, op. cit., 30.
21 William Hunter: *Burns as a Mason* (Edinburgh, 1858), reprinted (BC 1917), 27–62. See also R. T. Halliday: 'Burns and Freemasonry in Ayrshire' (BC 1929), 137.
22 I am indebted to John Inglis and Samuel Gaw for a transcript of the relevant entries, which have not previously been published.
23 Fowler, 224.
24 See reference to smallpox inoculation in RB's letters (CL 212, 518, 601).
25 Snyder, 75. See also James McBain: *Burns Cottage* (Glasgw, 1904).
26 Henry Ranken, op. cit., 45.
27 Ex-Provost Murchland: *A Glimpse of the Past* (Irvine, 1905), 12 – saying that RB attended lodge St Andrew's 'very often', although there is no actual record. Murchland claims that RB attended Richard Brown's admission on 27 December 1782 and stayed the night with him.
28 *Stat. Account*, op. cit.
29 Henry Ranken, op. cit., 47, quoting the unnamed introduction to *An Account of the Life and Character of Robert Burns* (not traced).
30 OPR Irvine record the baptism on 6 June. All other biographies give Brown's mother's name as Jane Whinie, based on a clerical error.
31 Currie I, 51.
32 Fowler, 180.
33 Alan Dent: *Burns in his Time* (Nelson, 1966).
34 OPR Irvine.
35 Charles L. Brodie: 'Burns's Associations with West Renfrewshire' (BC 1905), 87.
36 Revd. John C. Hill: *Burns and Irvine* (London, 1933), 36.
37 OPR Irvine. The only entry for someone of this name is 'Jean, lawful daughter of James Gardiner and Janet Caldwell his spouse, baptized 14 Sept. 1746'.
38 Henry Ranken, op. cit., 53. See also Joseph Train: *The Buchanites from First to Last* (Edinburgh, 1846). For a contemporary account of the Buchanites in Irvine see *Stat. Account*, 252–3.
39 Train, op. cit. See also R.W. MacFadzean: 'Joseph Train' (BC 1904), 84.
40 John Service (ed.): *The Memorables of Robin Cummell* (Irvine, 1913). He describes Peacock's wife as 'a terrible tairge o' a wife, and when they were haein a carousal, bringing in Newrday in the shop, she coupit owre a lichtit caun'le as she raxed for a gless, and it fell on the flure amang the tow she had been cairdin, when instantly the hoose was in a bleeze'.
41 Despite the fact that Sillar's was one of the first names on the Irvine list of subscribers to the National Burns Monument at Alloway, a 'local tradition' persists that he refused to subscribe, saying 'I cannot do so. You starved him when alive, and you cannot with good grace erect a monument to him now'. From this *canard* has grown a great deal of nonsense about a coolness between Burns and Sillar (after the latter was briefly bankrupt in 1791) which belies the recorded facts.
42 See *Robert Burns in Irvine: a Guide to Irvine Burns Club and Museum* (n.d. but c. 1985).
43 I am indebted to Sam Gaw for this information from Irvine Burns Club records.

Chapter 7: Lochlie: the Litigious Years, 1782–4

1 Fowler, 127–8, gives a detailed scientific analysis of the soil based on the *Soil Survey of Scotland*. See also B. D. Mitchell and R. A. Jarvis: *The Soils of the Country Round Kilmarnock* (HMSO, 1956), 142.

2 John Mackenzie to Josiah Walker, in Walker (1811) II, 261.

3 Revd. A. M. Paterson: 'Tarbolton and the Biographers of Burns' (BC 1957), 4.

4 See, for example, Henley and Henderson (1896).

5 David Lowe: *Burns's passionate pilgrimage, or Tait's indictment of the poet* (Glasgow, 1904).

6 'The Lochlea Sequestration' in Notes and Queries (BC 1910), 149–52.

7 John McVie: 'The Lochlie Litigation' (BC 1935), 69–87.

8 BC 1910, op. cit.

9 Fowler, 126. 100 bolls of lime was about 10 tonnes. 12 tons of limestone would yield about 7 tonnes of burnt lime (lime oxide) – a fairly thorough dressing for a moderately clayey soil.

10 The improving landowner to whom RB addressed a verse-epistle (CW 274) early in 1787.

11 New Register House, Edinburgh: Petition and Interlocutor, Court of Session, 25 August 1783.

12 Register of Acts and Decreets, Register House: Decreet of Preference, 26 November and 19 December 1783 and 27 January 1784.

13 Snyder, 81.

14 Register of Acts and Decreets, 23 November 1783.

15 John McVie, op. cit. Register of Sasines.

16 Henrietta Scott, the wealthy teenage heiress of General Scott, also bought the estates of the Earl of Glencairn and married the Marquess of Titchfield, later Duke of Portland.

17 When neebors anger at a plea
An just as wud as wud can be,
How easy can the barley-brie
      Cement the quarrel!
It's aye the cheapest lawyer's fee,
      To taste the barrel.
– 'Scotch Drink' (CW 167)
Two of the suppressed lines from 'Tam o Shanter' (A-Z, 688):
Three lawyers' tongues, turn'd inside out,
Wi lies seam'd like a beggar's clout.

18 McVie, op. cit., 86.

19 GN.

20 A facsimile of the relevant page from the minute-book appears in BC 1929, 139.

21 R. T. Halliday, op. cit., 141.

22 James L. Hempstead: 'Dr John Mackenzie, M.D.' (BC 1991), 37–43.

23 Walker II, 261–3.

24 Hilton Brown, 17.

25 Fowler, 150.

26 Somewhat above the average at the time, which was £6 per annum, plus board and lodging.

27 GN.

28 Revd. J. C. Glennie: 'Gavin Hamilton and the Kirk Session of Mauchline' (BC 1970), 20–30.
29 Hecht, 50.
30 In 'Epistle to John McMath' (CW 130).
31 Revd. Dr Andrew Edgar: *Old Church Life in Scotland* (1885–6), II, 12.
32 RB's first commonplace book, 1783–85 (1 CPB), reproduced in facsimile from the poet's MS in the possession of Sir Alfred Law of Honresfield, with transcript, introduction and notes by J.C. Ewing and Davidson Cook (Glasgow, 1938). The original, consisting of 22 stitched folio pages, has, like the rest of the Law Collection, disappeared.
33 Opinion is divided, many scholars considering that these lines were originally penned seven years earlier when the Burnes family was struggling to get free of Mount Oliphant.
34 Grierson MS, op. cit.
35 Ch-Wa I, 109–110.
36 Gilbert Burns to James Currie, April 1798.
37 Ch-Wa I, 110.
38 The last line was quoted by RB from Oliver Goldsmith's 'The Deserted Village', line 164.

Chapter 8: Mossgiel, 1784–6

1 Including, strangely, Jane Lymburn's translation of Hecht (1936) which should have taken McVie's research into account. This biography was reprinted in 1971 and 1981 without change. Even the most recent biography (by Fowler) ignored the opportunity to put the record straight.
2 See, for example, Snyder, 96, and a highly coloured account in Carswell, 108–9, who admits that her account was largely based on the poems of Saunders Tait!
3 Carswell, 117–18.
4 *Stat. Account* VI, 4445–52.
5 Ecclesiastes 7: 23.
6 Most biographies derive this from II Peter 2: 22, misquoted; but it was, in fact, verbatim from the formula used by the Church of Scotland in the ritual rebuke of fornicators. See Revd. Andrew Edgar: *Old Church Life in Scotland* 2 vols. (Paisley, 1885–6).
7 GN.
8 Fowler, 130–1.
9 Ibid., 132–3.
10 Ibid., quoting John Ramsay's account of the weather in southern Perthshire in 1783, 172.
11 Boyle, 96.
12 Angellier.
13 The Revd. Alexander McGregor of Inverness, not knowing of the older forms, derived Mossgiel from Gaelic *Màs-geal* (white or bleak ridge), but the name is almost certainly of Anglo-Saxon derivation.
14 Fowler, 134.
15 Douglas: *Scotch Peerage* II, 153–4. The title passed to his daughter Flora who married the Earl of Moira, later Marquess of Hastings.
16 Ch-Wa I, 119.

17 OPR Tarbolton.
18 Ch-Wa I, 120.
19 Grierson MS, op. cit.
20 Duncan McNaught: 'Dear-bought Bess' (BC 1909), 93.
21 Carswell, 130.
22 Snyder, 118–19.
23 Ch-Wa I, 120.
24 OPR Tarbolton.
25 *Poetical Works of William Wordsworth* (Cambridge edn), 719.
26 William Jolly: *Robert Burns at Mossgiel* (Paisley, 1881), with reminiscences of the poet by his herd-boy.
27 Grierson MS, op. cit.
28 Ibid.
29 Jolly, op. cit.
30 Robert Carruthers: *A Highland Notebook* (Inverness, 1843).
31 Ch-Wa I, 129.
32 Ibid., 129.
33 Ibid., 115.
34 Maurice Lindsay: *Robert Burns* (London, 1954), 54.
35 Fitzhugh (1970), Appendix B.
36 Sir James Crichton-Browne: *Burns from a New Point of View* (Edinburgh, 1926).
37 H. B. Anderson: 'Robert Burns, his medical friends, attendants and biographers' *Ann. Med. Hist.* (March 1928), 47–58.
38 Fowler, 214–15.
39 Ch-Wa I, 115.
40 See, for example, Revd. John C. Hill: *The Love Songs and Heroines of Robert Burns* (1961): 'He would fain have offered hand and heart to Anne Ronald but again he feared a summary dismissal'.
41 Except Ch-Wa III, 124n, which correctly identifed William Ronald of Mauchline.
42 SRO: 01:8/205, 7 October 1789.
43 Heather Ronald: 'The Ronalds of the Bennals' (BC 1988), 48–51.
44 Ch-Wa, 150n; OPR Mauchline.
45 Most biographers omit Jean's date of birth altogether. Lindsay gives 1767, Boyle 1765, Bold 27 February 1767 and Robert Burns-Begg (BC 1892) gives February 1767 but then says she died in 1834 in her 70th year.
46 Notes and Queries (BC 1907), 139 regarding the Armour Bible which had just come into the possession of Lawson Brown of Dumfries; present whereabouts unknown.
47 OPR Mauchline.
48 Boyle, 58.
49 Mauchline Kirk Session records and accounts.
50 Robert Burns-Begg: 'Bonnie Jean, a Memoir' (BC 1892), 47–71, so far the only reasonably comprehensive account of Jean Armour, but deficient in many details and vapidly hagiographical in others.
51 Duncan McNaught: 'Documents bearing on Gilbert's debt to the poet' (BC 1900), 77–90.
52 Loudoun MSS, now at Mount Stuart, Bute, and Dumfries Museum. See Alex MacMillan: 'The Letters of Jean Armour Burns' (BC 1968), 42–6 and (BC 1969), 30–4.

53 1891 Census.
54 Boyle, 88–9 gives a detailed list of the seventeen graves which have an association with RB.
55 See, for example, Ch-Wa I, 137.
56 BC 1895, 135.
57 For Jean Armour's interview with John McDiarmid in 1827 see McDiarmid: *Widow of Burns, her death, character and funeral* (Dumfries, 1834).
58 Carswell, 129–30.
59 Yvonne Stevenson: *Burns and his Bonnie Jean* (Victoria, BC, 1966).
60 John Home: *Douglas*, Act I, sc. 1 – actually quoted in this context by RB to Mrs Dunlop (CL 149).
61 Sir John Vanbrugh (1664–1726): *The Confederacy*.
62 Ecclesiastes 2: 12.
63 First quoted in Currie III, 378.
64 OPR Mauchline.
65 For the best account of the verse-epistles see Thomas Crawford: 'The Epistles' in *Critical Essays on Robert Burns* (ed. Low, London, 1975), 70–89.
66 Mauchline Kirk Session minutes, 18 November 1784.
67 Hecht (1981 edn), 51.
68 Henley and Henderson I, 379.
69 Lockhart, 60.
70 John Home: 'Black Jock Russell' (BC 1925), 77–80.
71 Allan MacLaine (BC 1955, 1–2) gives the source of the poem as 'Death and the Doctor', published in the *Scots Magazine*, January 1775.
72 Gilbert Burns to James Currie, 2 April 1798.
73 Lockhart, 60.
74 James Mackay: *Kilmarnock* (1992) recounts Goldie's varied career.
75 Gilbert Burns to James Currie, 2 April 1798, op. cit.
76 Hecht, 58.
77 Lockhart, 70n.
78 James Paterson: *The Contemporaries of Burns* (Edinburgh 1840), 26.
79 Ch-Wa I, 185n.
80 Anon: *A Letter from a Blacksmith to the Ministers and Elders of the Church of Scotland* (1759).
81 Ch-Wa I, 217n, for the opening verse of 'The Farmer's Ingle'.
82 Alan Bold: *Burns Companion* (Macmillan, 1991), 218 has a succinct summary.
83 Chambers (1851) I, 181.
84 Mauchline Kirk Session records, 1785.
85 All previous biographies give 1789, but Richmond's Edinburgh employer died in July 1787 and a business letter from Gavin Hamilton, addressed to 'Mr John Richmond, writer in Machline', dated 7 September 1787, suggests that Richmond had returned to Mauchline and set up as a lawyer on his own account by that date.
86 See, for example, Revd. Lauchlan McLean Watt: 'Burns Biography' (BC 1932), 41.
87 William Hazlitt: *Lectures on the English Poets* (1818).
88 Kinsley III, 1105.
89 Quoted in Ch-Wa I, 287–8.

Chapter 9: Two Loves

1 William Jolly: *Burns in Mossgiel*, op. cit.
2 Revd. Dr Edgar: *Lectures on Old Church Life in Scotland* (second series).
3 Ch-Wa I, 313n.
4 John Erskine: *An Institute of the Law of Scotland* (1871) I, 139.
5 Hilton Brown, 156.
6 See, for example, Robert Burns-Begg: 'Bonnie Jean' (BC 1892), 52; and Hilton Brown, 156.
7 See, for example, BE, 4.
8 Aiken's daughter later stated that many letters of RB were destroyed through the dishonesty of her father's clerk (though more likely due to carelessness).
9 John Milton: *Paradise Lost*, Book IX, lines 896–900.
10 Jeremiah 10: 21, misquoted.
11 Kirk Session records, transcribed in BC 1893, 56.
12 This phrase occurs in several letters and seems to have been a deliberate attempt by RB to imply that the event occurred much earlier than 1786. See Eric Robertson: 'Highland Mary in the writings of Burns' (BC 1893), 237.
13 Cromek: *Reliques* (1808), 237.
14 For the complete text of this letter, with a far higher proportion of deletions and second thoughts than was usual for RB's letters, see G. Ross Roy's edn of the Letters (1985), I, 39–40.
15 Edgar, op. cit., II, 402n. The last sentence is based on II Peter 2: 22. RB quoted this in his Autobiographical Letter in the context of his repeated follies in farming.
16 BC 1916, 93 which, incidentally, fixed the date of Elizabeth Burns's birth as 22 May 1785, and not November 1784 as had hitherto been believed. OPR Tarbolton gives her baptismal entry as 'Elizabeth Burns, daughter of Robert Burns in Mossgiel and Elizabeth Paton' on 24th May 1785. The omission of the customary key-words 'lawful' and 'spouse' indicated that the birth was illegitimate.
17 Matthew 8: 20, paraphrased.
18 'Second Epistle to John Lapraik', stanza 9.
19 Thomas Otway: *Venice Preserved*, Act I, sc. 1, altered.
20 Notes of Joseph Train, Laing MSS, Edinburgh University Library.
21 OPR Mauchline, 604/2, 0278.
22 Mauchline, however, did not follow the practice of some other parishes where a prominent X preceded the entries of illegitimate births.
23 Snyder, 129.
24 Cromek, 237.
25 Eric Robertson, op. cit., 35–45.
26 Snyder, 148, footnote 71.
27 William Scott Douglas: in *Proc. Soc. Ant. Scot.*, (1850).
28 Lockhart, 95n.
29 Gilfillan I, 96.
30 Ch-Wa I, 343n.
31 Snyder, 129.
32 Ch-Wa I, 432n.
33 Clark Hunter: 'How Old is Greenock Burns Club?' (BC 1991), 77–82. Greenock Burns Club were invited to rebut this before publication but their

statement (p82) did not address the facts, far less refute them, and merely reiterated the traditional beliefs of the club.

34 Cromek, 238.
35 Lockhart, 80.
36 Grierson MS, text in Fitzhugh (1970), 104–5.
37 Ch-Wa I, 431.
38 SD I, 299.
39 Ch-Wa III, 367. The original has been lost.
40 Quoted by Snyder, 132.
41 W. E. Henley and T. F. Henderson: 'The Cult of Highland Mary', *New Review* (1897).
42 Robert M. Lockhart: 'A Study in Highland Mariology', *Westminster Review* (1897).
43 George A. Aitken (ed.): *The Poetical Works of Robert Burns* (Edinburgh, 1893), I, xxxix.
44 See, for example, Ch-Wa I, Appendix VIII, 471–3.
45 Ch-Wa I, 336.
46 Duncan McNaught: 'Highland Mary, Chronology of the Episode' (BC 1915), 125–35.
47 Testimony of Andrew Smith of the Mauchline Boxworks to James Wilson of Sanquhar, *c.* 1868.
48 McNaught, op. cit.
49 Ch-Wa I, 336n.
50 Letter to *The Scotsman*, 20 October 1891.
51 John Richmond interviewed by Grierson, December 1817. Text from the Grierson MS in Laing Collection first reproduced in Fitzhugh (1943).
52 cf. the clerical rebuke to fornicators, supra.
53 Munro, op. cit., 114–18.
54 E. H. Letham: *Burns and Tarbolton* (Kilmarnock, 1900), 93.
55 Ch-Wa I, 428.
56 Greenock West parish, Register of Lairs.
57 Fowler, 185.
58 Snyder, 144.
59 Ch-Wa I, 431.
60 Archibald Macphail: 'The Beginning of an Old Song', *Greenock Telegraph*, 4 January 1921.
61 Snyder, 143.
62 For a résumé of the furore in the Scottish press see Tom Crawford's Introduction (viii-x) to Carswell, 1990 edn.
63 Revd. Lauchlan MacLean Watt, op. cit., 246.
64 Revd. Lauchlan MacLean Watt, letter to the *Times Literary Supplement*, 1932.
65 Hilton Brown, 246.
66 Fitzhugh (1970), Appendix D, 440–2.
67 Hilton Brown, 251.
68 I am indebted to Dr William Rodger for an explanation of DNA cloning and comparison techniques.

Chapter 10: Kilmarnock, 1786

1 M. Wilson: *The Ayrshire Hermit and Hurlford* (Kilmarnock, 1875).
2 Ch-Wa I, 297–8.

3 Ibid., 316.
4 Minute-book of Lodge Loudoun Newmilns Kilwinning No. 46, 1747–1795, 136. I am indebted to John Inglis for drawing this connection to my attention.
5 Ch-Wa I, Appendix VII, 468–70.
6 *Glasgow Mercury* advertisement of 6 July 1786, for the brigantine *Nancy*, Andrew Smith master, 'For freight or passage, apply to James Brown, insurance-broker, Glasgow, or to the master at Greenock'.
7 Ch-Wa I, 379n.
8 Snyder, 152.
9 Robert Heron (see Chapter 18).
10 CW 250.
11 *Glasgow Mercury*, 7 September 1786, under 'Sailings'.
12 I Samuel 16: 23.
13 Ch-Wa I, 412–13.
14 RB's own description in conversation with Josiah Walker in Edinburgh the following year. See Walker I, ciii.
15 Currie I, 136–7.
16 Ibid., 112–13.
17 *Kilmarnock Standard*, 25 June 1892; reprinted in John D. Ross: *Burnsiana* II (Paisley, 1893).
18 Currie I, 131n.
19 Ibid., 128n.
20 Ibid., 123. Currie commented, 'he complains that the lady made no reply to his effusions, and this appears to have wounded his self-love'.
21 See letter to Alexander Cunningham of 11 March 1791 (CL 461).
22 Blacklock to Lawrie, Edinburgh, 4 September 1786, Ch-Wa I, 417.

Chapter 11: Edinburgh, the First Winter, 1786–7

1 CL 92–3, previously quoted.
2 For a detailed account of this theory see *The Clarinda Conspiracy*, a novel by Alistair Campsie, (Mainstream, 1989).
3 Archibald Prentice to Professor John Wilson, 8 March 1841, subsequently published in the *Edinburgh Intelligencer*.
4 Revd. Thomas Somerville: *George Square, Glasgow* (Gardner, Paisley, n.d. [October 1891]). He was a grandson of John Prentice.
5 Train MS, Laing Coll., Edinburgh University Library; testimony of John Richmond for this and other anecdotes relating to RB's first winter in Edinburgh.
6 William Creech: *Edinburgh Fugitive Pieces* (Edinburgh, 1815).
7 Luke 11: 24.
8 Sir John Whitefoord, 4 December 1786.
9 J. Talboys Wheeler: *Madras in Olden Time*.
10 Revd. Alexander Macrae: *History of the Clan Macrae* (Dingwall, 1899), 237–41.
11 Letter to John Murdoch, 15 January 1783 (CL 55).
12 Robert Anderson to James Currie, 1799.
13 Donald Low: *Robert Burns, the Critical Heritage* (Routledge, 1974), 66.
14 Laing MSS, Edinburgh University Library.
15 Ch-Wa II, 29.
16 Ibid., 266n.

17 *The Clarinda Conspiracy*, op. cit.
18 BE, 85.
19 Lochryan MS. Full text in A–Z, 689.
20 Alexander Pope: *Essay on Man* I, 14.
21 John Logan to Henry Mackenzie (BC 1944), 25–6.
22 Dugald Stewart to James Currie, Currie I, 133–4.
23 Ch-Wa II, 79–80.
24 Sir Walter Scott to John G. Lockhart, 1827, in *Memoirs of Sir Walter Scott, Bart.* I, 166–7.
25 Ch-Wa II, 82–3.
26 Snyder, 203.
27 Blacklock to Lawrie, Ch-Wa I, 449.
28 Josiah Walker: *Poems of Robert Burns, with an account of his life*, (Edinburgh, 1811).
29 *Fasti* I, 60.
30 See I Samuel 17: 38–9.
31 PP, 252.
32 Ch-Wa II, 97–8.
33 *Glasgow Mercury*, 6 December 1786.
34 For further lurid anecdotes of Jane Maxwell, see A. Ferguson: *Henry Erskine and his Kinfolk* and *Autobiographical Sketch* (Glasgow, 1865), and J. Bulloch in *English Illustrated Magazine*, June 1897.
35 Ch-Wa II, 72.
36 *The Clarinda Conspiracy*, 23–9. The description of the love-making scene is John Cairney's.
37 At the time of her death in 1812 she was described as in her 63rd year, which would place her birth in 1749. In fact OPR St Cuthbert's shows that she was baptised on 28 February 1746.
38 Sarah Tytler and Jean Watson: *The Songstresses of Scotland* (Edinburgh, 1811).
39 Ch-Wa II, 45.
40 David Murray Lyon: 'Burns Poet Laureate of Canongate Kilwinning Lodge – a Myth' (*The Freemason*) and Hugh Peacock and Allan Mackenzie: *Robert Burns, Poet-Laureate of Lodge Canongate Kilwinning* (Edinburgh, 1894).
41 *Glasgow Mercury*, 6 December 1786.
42 Ch-Wa II, 46–7.
43 Maurice Lindsay draws attention to the fact that the opening line 'Edina, Scotia's darling seat!' inspired the well-known manufacturers of a toilet-seat to patent Edina as their brand name.
44 The full text appears in Ch-Wa II, 48–9.
45 Ibid., 58.
46 Ibid., 59.
47 Laing MSS, Edinburgh University Library.
48 The text of this alternative version appears in Ch-Wa II, 84–5.
49 'The Jolly Beggars', lines 228–33 (CW 182–91).
50 Snyder, 219.
51 Ch-Wa II, 99.
52 William Wallace (ed.): *Robert Burns and Mrs Dunlop, correspondence now published in full for the first time* (Hodder and Stoughton, London, 1898).
53 Ch-Wa II, 52–3.
54 Robert Kerr: *Memoirs of the life, writings, and correspondence of William Smellie* (Edinburgh, 2 vols., 1811).

55 Basil Skinner: *Authentic Likenesses of Robert Burns* (2nd edn. Darvel, 1990).
56 Gilbert Burns to George Thomson, 2 July 1821, Ch-Wa II, 55n.
57 James Nasmyth: *Autobiography* (John Murray, London, 1883), 34–5.
58 Ch-Wa II, 73.
59 Cromek: *Reliques*.
60 Ch-Wa II, 77.
61 *Edinburgh Evening Courant*, 19 April 1787.
62 Thomas Gray to William Palgrave, 16 September 1758.
63 *Macmillan's Magazine*, March–July 1879 (ed. William Jack), reprinted in Gilfillan IV, 317–21.
64 From the original, now preserved in the Burns Museum, Alloway.
65 See, for example, Snyder, 'By April 17, 1787 he had forgotten it entirely'.
66 Heron.
67 Moore to RB, Ch-Wa II, 94.
68 Snyder, 228.
69 James Kinsley: 'The Subscription List for the first Edinburgh Edition, 1787' (BC 1959), 26–8. The list itself, with brief annotations by Prof. J. W. Egerer, was serialized in BC to 1963 but was discontinued after the letter F.
70 Donald Low: *Two Glossaries by Robert Burns* (Stirling, 1987).
71 Mrs Dunlop to RB, 9 June 1878, quoting Dr Moore.
72 Unsigned notice in *Monthly Review* lxxvii (December 1787), 491.
73 James Maxwell: 'On the Ayr-shire Ploughman Poet or Poetaster, R. B.' in *Animadversions on Some Poets and Poetasters* (Paisley, 1788).
74 Snyder, 231, quoting an anonymous chapbook of 1787, in the British Library.
75 OPR Edinburgh. Isobella Farquhar married Lieutenant Humphrey Grahame on 20 March 1788.
76 Previously it was thought that Johnson was born about 1750. In fact he was born on 24 April 1742, son of Robert Johnson and Elizabeth Dickson, (OPR, Roxburgh).

Chapter 12: The Tours, 1787

1 Snyder, 235.
2 Ch-Wa II, 100n.
3 *Chambers Edinburgh Journal*, 28 April 1832.
4 OPR, Berwickshire. Foreman married Margaret Young at Swinton on 24 December 1788. Their daughter Margaret (born 1790) married her cousin Walter Young in 1810.
5 Hogg and Motherwell: *The Works of Robert Burns* (Glasgow, 1834–6) II.
6 Probably Alexander Horsburgh Junior (born 30 August 1761), rather than his father who was coeval with William Burnes.
7 OPR Eyemouth. Patricia Grieve married James Thomson on 29 October 1786. She was a sister of William Grieve, mentioned later.
8 Ch-Wa II, 114.
9 Ibid., 121n.
10 George Shirley: 'Burns and his Dumfries Burgess Ticket' (BC 1924), 90.
11 This interesting volume is now preserved in Dumfries and Galloway regional archives.
12 *Fasti*, III, 69.
13 Ch-Wa II, 121–2.

14 PP, 151.

15 Ch-Wa II, 121–2.

16 Even as late as 1892 Scott Douglas's enlarged edn. of Lockhart had no mention of the Cameron affair. Chambers (1851) ignores the Dumfries episode altogether.

17 Gilfillan II, xlvi.

18 Ch-Wa II, 121.

19 Most notably Fitzhugh (1970), 154.

20 Hilton Brown, 110.

21 PP.

22 International Genealogical Index, 1990. This involved the elimination of six other Margaret Camerons born in 1763–8 by following their subsequent movements, marriages and offspring. OPR Fortingall and Dull, Perthshire and Tolbooth and New Greyfriars, Edinburgh.

23 Ch-Wa II, 145–6.

24 John Milton: *Paradise Lost* I, 250–3, quoted by RB in a letter to Smith (CL 119).

25 Isobel Burns, quoted by Ch-Wa II, 125.

26 Snyder, 242–3.

27 RB to Robert Ainslie (CL 328).

28 Lodge minutes, quoted by Ch-Wa II, 139.

29 Raymond Lamont Brown (1973) and some earlier writers give Tarbert, Loch Fyne, as the furthest point of the tour, confusing it with Tarbet on the west side of Loch Lomond.

30 Ian G. Lindsay and Mary Cosh: *Inveraray and the Duke of Argyll* (EUP, 1973), 220, 272.

31 The now accepted version (CW 281) was first published by Thomas Stewart in *Poems Ascribed to Robert Burns* (Glasgow, 1801), but a shorter and substantially different version appeared in one of the Stewart and Meikle chapbooks (26 July 1799). Henley and Henderson (1896) thought that the latter was the lines actually engraved on the window, and that the longer and more polished form was elaborated by RB later.

32 Dr George Grierson: *Hints respecting Burns the Ayrshire Poet*, MS in possession of John Reid of Kingston, Glasgow, in 1867; present whereabouts unknown. The Reid Collection was apparently severely damaged or destroyed by flooding in 1831. Wallace discounted the Grierson MS because it referred to the tour in 1788, but other travellers with RB (Adair and Syme) erred in the dates of their tours, although accurate in the salient details. Wallace compounded the error by giving the date as 1878, showing how easy it is to perpetrate errors in dates.

33 From the traditional song 'We're gayly yet' in David Herd's *Ancient and Modern Scottish Songs* (Edinburgh, 1776) II, 121.

34 OPR, Ayr. George Gairdner was born at Ayr on 12 February 1758, his mother being Elizabeth McIlvain.

35 OPR, Edinburgh. *Williamson's Directory* gives 'Henry Butter of Pitlarchrie' but this was a misspelling for Pitlochrie. OPR Moulin show the marriage of Henry Butter of Faskally to Katherine Hay in 1765 and births of twin sons Henry and Patrick in October 1768. The mansion at Faskally no longer exists.

36 James L. Hempstead: 'Burns's West Highland Tour, the Grierson MS' (BC 1974), 30–7.

37 Ibid., 35–6. Fergus Roberts, former Town Clerk of Dumbarton, quoted by Hempstead; Scottish Record Society: *Roll of Dumbarton Burgesses and Guild Brethren, 1600–1846* (Edinburgh, 1937).

38 James L. Hempstead: 'The Enigma of the West Highland Tour' (BC 1983), 63; *Dumbarton and Dunbartonshire Subscribers* (typescript, 1984).

39 'A Winter Night' 4th stanza (CW 259).

40 Letter of John Taylor, Liverpool cotton-broker, to the *Liverpool Mercury*, 29 May 1847.

41 Ch-Wa II, 133.

42 Lord Cockburn: *Memorials of his Times* (ed. H. A. Cockburn, 1909).

43 Young MS, Edinburgh University Library.

44 Dr Alexander Adam (1741–1809), rector of the High School. RB had a very poor opinion of Adam on account of his quarrels with another friend Cruikshank to whom he wrote of 'that puritanic, rotten-hearted, ill-commissioned scoundrel, Adam' (CL 360).

45 Luke Fraser, Latin master at the High School.

46 Rt. Hon. Charles Hope, Lord Granton, quoted by Cockburn, op. cit. II, 205–23.

47 Facsimile edn. with an introduction and transcript by J. C. Ewing (Gowans and Gray, Glasgow, 1927).

48 Raymond Lamont Brown: *Robert Burns's Tours of the Highlands and Stirlingshire, 1787* (Ipswich, 1973) where the Lockhart-Cunningham 'emendations' are shown in square brackets. Brown believed that Lockhart and Cunningham worked from a later version of the journal, transcribed and extended by RB himself, subsequent to 1789, though no such MS has ever come to light. Snyder (244) dismissed these extensions as the work of 'Honest Allan' at his most florid.

49 George Boyack of St Andrew's communicated the four lines to the *Fifeshire Journal*, 4 November 1847.

50 'The Reproof', *Burns A-Z*, Appendix B, no. 82 (747).

51 Josiah Walker to James Currie, reproduced in Currie II, 99–103.

52 John G. Lockhart *Life of Burns* (1892), 161.

53 Ch-Wa II, 168.

54 Dr Robert Coupar to James Currie, reproduced in Currie I, 184–5.

55 Lockhart, op. cit., 163.

56 Walker I, 89.

57 Hon. George Pellew: *Life of Sidmouth* (London, 1847).

58 William B. Campbell: *A Burns Companion* (Aberdeen, 1953).

59 *Edinburgh Evening Courant*, 7 December 1786, recorded the award of the degree Ll.D. by Marischal College.

60 Ch-Wa II, 173n.

61 Archie Gordon (5th Marquess of Aberdeen): *A Wild Flight of Gordons* (Weidenfeld, 1985), 72–6.

62 J. M. Bulloch: *William Marshall, the Scots Composer* (Inverness, 1933).

63 Raymond Lamont Brown: *Robert Burns's Tour of the Highlands* (Ipswich, 1973), 46.

64 William Walker: *The Bards of Bon-Accord, 1375–1860* (Aberdeen, 1887). Brown questioned this as John Marshall began writing in 1825, but this confuses *two* poets, father and son. OPR Aberdeenshire show that John Marshall Senior, born on 23 April 1760, married Jean Beattie 7 February 1783 and their son John was born at Udny on 8 June 1790.

65 Bishop Skinner to Revd. John Skinner, in *Posthumous Works* (1809), 30–33. See also J. M. Murdoch: 'Burns and Tullochgorum' (BC 1912), 58–66.

66 OPR, Auchterhouse. Revd. David Scott had three daughters: Jean (born

12 August 1747), Elizabeth (born 9 April 1750) and Janet (born 20 February 1753).

67 Charlotte Hamilton (1763–1806). She married Dr Adair on 11 November 1789.

68 RB exaggerated slightly: there were only *five* fornicators (including Jean and himself) rebuked on that occasion (BC 1893), 56.

69 Ch-Wa II, 193n.

70 Ibid., 194.

71 RB replaced 'salvation' in 'The Holy Fair' (Kilmarnock Edn) with 'damnation' (CW 136).

72 Snyder, 253.

73 Currie I, 170.

74 A facsimile of the Geddes Burns was published by the Bibliophile Society of Boston, 1908.

75 'Hermitage, Taymouth' (CW 287–8), 'Bruar Water' (CW 290–2), 'Falls of Fyers' (CW 292) and 'Loch Turit' (CW 296–7).

76 Both versions of the 'Lines in Friars' Carse Hermitage' (CW 324–6) and 'To Robert Graham of Fintry'(CW 330–3).

77 'To the Guidwife of Wauchope House' (CW 271–2).

Chapter 13: Edinburgh, the Second Winter, 1787–8

1 John McVie: *Robert Burns and Edinburgh* (Kilmarnock, 1969), 46, 54.

2 Walker I, lxxxi.

3 Shakespeare: *Pericles*, Act V, sc. 1, misquoted.

4 Donald Low: *The Scots Musical Museum, 1787–1803*. The Introduction is of particular value.

5 Ch-Wa II, 201.

6 Clarinda to Sylvander, 31 January 1788.

7 From the use of Aberdonian words it has been deduced that David Ramsay himself (proprietor of the newspaper) wrote the poem.

8 Ch-Wa II, 211.

9 Ibid., 206.

10 Linlithgow Town Council minutes, 4 January 1859.

11 Andrew McCallum: 'Burns's Linlithgow Burgess Ticket' (BC 1944), 37.

12 *The Clarinda Conspiracy*, op. cit.

13 G. Ross Roy: *The Letters of Robert Burns* I, 180n. See also Revd. J. C. Glennie: 'Gavin Hamilton and the Kirk Session of Mauchline' (BC 1970), 20–30.

14 Ch-Wa II, 213n.

15 John Sinton: *Burns, Excise Officer and Poet* (Carlisle, 1895). OPR, Edinburgh reveals that he was born 11 April 1753, son of James Nimmo, Erskine's younger brother.

16 B. R. Leftwich: *Burns and the Excise, an account of the surviving records in official custody* (privately printed, 1936).

17 W. C. McLehose: *The Correspondence of Burns and Clarinda* (1843), Introduction. OPR, Glasgow show both the birth and baptismal dates for Agnes Craig in April 1758.

18 Agnes McLehose's account, in W. C. McLehose, op. cit.

19 Ch-Wa II, 216.

20 Ibid., 217.

21 A. Bruce Auckland and J. J. Bonar: *Penny Posts of Edinburgh and District* (Edinburgh, 1972), 7–16.

22 First advertisement in the *Caledonian Mercury*, 17 January 1774.

23 Ch-Wa II, 218–19.

24 Ibid., 220.

25 J. C. Ewing: 'The Letters of Clarinda to Sylvander' (BC 1934), 72–77. For a succinct account of the trustees' battle with Agnes McLehose, see R. D. Thornton: *James Currie, the Entire Stranger and Robert Burns* (Oliver and Boyd, 1963), 333–4.

26 W. C. McLehose, op. cit.

27 A copy of this curious work, believed to have emanated from Brydges' private press at Lee Priory, is in the Burns Collection at the Mitchell Library, Glasgow.

28 Cockburn: *Memorials of his Time*, Forbes Gray.

29 Ch-Wa II, 236; John McVie: *Robert Burns and Edinburgh*, 56.

30 Ch-Wa II, 233.

31 *The Clarinda Conspiracy*. op. cit.

32 RB's letter does, indeed, bear blots and blotches which may have been tears. The wife of the owner of this manuscript, however, suspects that his 'tears' were deliberately faked for effect.

33 Probably her cousin, William Craig.

34 Quoted in BE, 195. *Fasti*: Kemp was born on 13 January 1745, the son of the Revd. David Kemp of Gask, Perthshire, himself ordained at Trinity Gask (1770), Greyfriars (1776) and Tolbooth (1779). All three wives predeceased him.

35 Revd. George Drummond: *A Town Eclogue* (Edinburgh, 1804).

36 International Genealogical Index (Scotland) and OPR, Newburgh.

37 MS 587 (1181), National Library of Scotland.

38 Donald Low, in the Introduction (p8) to *The Scots Musical Museum, 1787–1803* (Scolar Press, Aldershot, 1991).

39 Grierson MS: last of the notes of 1814–17.

40 John McDiarmid: *Memoranda*, from Jean Armour's dictation: Affecting circumstances connected with the history of the family of Burns, *Dumfries Monthly Magazine* I, 1825.

41 Ch-Wa II, 310n.

42 *The Clarinda Conspiracy*, op. cit.

43 G. Ross Roy: *Letters of Robert Burns*, I, 251n.

44 James Stillie's advertisement (BC 1892).

45 R. D. Thornton: *Currie* op. cit., 334.

46 James Barke: 'Burns and the Ainslie Letter', *Lines Review* no. 8 (May 1955).

47 Alistair Campsie in *Glasgow Herald*, 28 January 1989.

48 Fowler, 189.

49 Ibid., Appendix C, 247–9 for a detailed discussion of the obstetrics. It should also be noted that, in a widely reported case in 1991, a woman in Northern Ireland was subjected to a brutal rape while nine months pregnant, and gave birth to a perfectly healthy baby a few days later.

50 Ibid., 189.

51 Ch-Wa II, 310.

52 OPR, Mauchline, vol. 604/2, 304.

53 G. Ross Roy: *Letters of Robert Burns* II, 233n.

54 The text of this document was first published by Snyder, Appendix C, 543–7 and reprinted in BE, 395–7.

55 Train MS.
56 In the dating of the last letters of March 1788 to Clarinda, I concur with Ferguson and Roy. Snyder, 271, following Chambers, dated some letters to the following week and put RB's departure from Edinburgh on 24 March; but as RB wrote letters form Glasgow on 20 and Mauchline on 21 March this is manifestly wrong.

Chapter 14: Ellisland, 1788–91

1 James Mackay: *Burns in Ellisland* (Dumfries, 1988), from which the salient details in this chapter are drawn.
2 Thomas Carlyle: *Reminiscences* I, 129–30.
3 *Journals of the House of Lords* (1818), LI, 542 and LV (1822), 465.
4 Patrick Miller: *General View of the Agriculture &c. of Dumfriesshire* (Edinburgh, 1812).
5 Ch-Wa II, 320n.
6 Ibid., 328n.
7 Train MS.
8 W. Gunnyon, in *Kilmarnock Standard*, 28 September 1867.
9 John Taylor Gibb (BC 1896) quoting a Miss Caldwell, who got the story from Mrs Alexander (daughter of John Richmond and Jenny Surgeoner).
10 Ch-Wa II, 335.
11 His letter of 31 May to Andrew Dunlop stated, 'I shall be in Glasgow in the middle of next week' but for what purpose is unknown.
12 Lamentations 3: 39, slightly altered.
13 Shakespeare: *Julius Caesar*, Act II, sc. 1.
14 OPR, Edinburgh reveal no specific details; she may have been one of the dozen entries for 'a poor girl, consumption', consigned to a 'town coffin' that month.
15 Parish registers of Holborn St Andrew, London.
16 Diana Van Dyk: 'From Nancy to Selinde' (BC 1985), 64.
17 M. Mathijsen: *Waarde van Lennep, brieven van de Schoolmeester* (Amsterdam, 1977).
18 *Glasgow Courier*, 23 May 1850.
19 *Illustrated London News*, 29 May 1852, 423–4: account of the punitive expedition of HMS *Cleopatra* to Borneo.
20 Snyder, 302–3.
21 Mauchline Kirk Session records, transcribed in BC 1893, 56.
22 OPR, Mauchline, 604/2 (0380).
23 Matthew 12: 33, paraphrased. The words italicised were intended as metaphors for ejaculation.
24 John Home: *Douglas*, Act I, sc. 1.
25 Jean Armour's memoir by John McDiarmid, in William McDowall: *Burns in Dumfriesshire* (Dumfries, 1870).
26 Receipt sold at Sotheby's, 24 July 1935.
27 With letters to Dunbar, 25 September (CL 284), Dugald Stewart, 20 January 1789 (CL 448–9), Lady Cunningham, 22 January 1789 (CL 496–7), Henry Erskine, 22 January 1789 (CL 224–5) and Dr Moore, 4 January 1789 (CL 257–8). The last of these gives full details of the circumstances in which the verse-epistle was composed.

28 See, for example, the letters to Ainslie, 10 October 1788 (CL 336), Bishop Geddes, 3 February 1789 (CL 507–8) and James Burness, 9 February 1789 (CL 62–3). In particular, the last states that Graham had offered RB an Excise commission.

29 For a detailed examination of the myth and the reality of this event see Elizabeth Ewing: 'Burns and the first Steamboat' (BC 1941), 40.

30 Gilbert Burns to RB, in Ch-Wa III, 17.

31 Ch-Wa II, 390–5.

32 Ibid., III, 98.

33 Cunningham, 211ff.

34 Ch-Wa III, 13n. See also letter of Revd. Richard Simpson in *Glasgow Herald*, 21 January 1896.

35 Clark's memoir to Robert Chambers (1838) in Ch-Wa III, 397–9.

36 *Stat. Account of Scotland* IV, 142n.

37 William Fullarton: *Account of Agriculture in Ayrshire* (1793), 58n. I am indebted to Sam Gaw for a sight of this very rare book.

38 Ch-Wa III, 296n.

39 Ibid., 275–6.

40 Sir Samuel Egerton Brydges, in *Metropolitan Magazine*.

41 Graham Smith: *Robert Burns the Exciseman* (Darvel, 1990), 47.

42 Charles Leadbetter: *The Royal Gauger, or Gauging Made Easy*; Jelinger Symons: *The Excise Laws Abridged and Digested*.

43 Minutes of Dumfries Quarter Sessions, in Dumfries and Galloway regional archives.

44 This statistical report is the principal proof adduced by Campsie in support of his view that the twin girls lived, and came with Jean Armour to Ellisland.

45 Robert Burnes (1719–89), elder brother of RB's father. Latterly he had been living in Stewarton where RB used to visit him on his journeys to and from Dunlop House nearby.

46 Joseph Laing Waugh: *Thornhill and its Worthies* (Dumfries, 1903), 76–80.

47 R. W. MacFadzean: 'Burns's Excise Duties and Emoluments' (BC 1898), 55–7.

48 Ch-Wa III, 210.

49 Graham Smith, op. cit.

50 Ch-Wa III, 200.

51 OPR, Dumfries.

52 Ch-Wa III, 365.

53 Cunningham.

54 Hilton Brown, 108.

55 Ch-Wa III, 365.

56 Duncan McNaught: *The Truth about Burns* (Glasgow, 1921), 174.

57 Ch-Wa III, 364.

58 Snyder, 308.

59 Fowler, 194.

60 OPR, Edinburgh.

61 CH-Wa II, 41n.

62 The volume containing this poem, among others sent to him, with RB's marginal notes was presented by Jean Armour to John Wharton (1781–1842), an Exciseman, on 29 December 1827. I am indebted to Dr Arthur Taylor, the present owner, for a sight of it.

63 *Dumfries Weekly Journal*, 28 March 1797, advertised the roup. Details of Lagganpark were supplied to Chambers by William Cairns of Torr.

64 Buchan: *Essay on the Genius, Character and Writings of James Thomson, the Poet* (London, 1792).
65 Lockhart: *Life of Burns*.
66 Snyder, 310.
67 James Thomson, quoted by William McDowall: *Burns in Dumfriesshire* (Dumfries, 1879).
68 II Samuel 12: 7.
69 William McDowall, op. cit.
70 Alexander Smith, in biographical preface to *Burns's Poetical Works* (1865).
71 Ch-Wa III, 214n.
72 Snyder, 321.
73 PP, 124.
74 Ch-Wa III, 104n.
75 Ibid., 108n.
76 Ibid., 109n.
77 Robert Thornton: 'Robert Riddell, Antiquary' (BC 1953), 44–67, based on the Gough-Paton correspondence in the National Library of Scotland, casting a great deal of light on the depth and extent of Riddell's scholarship.
78 James C. Dick: *Notes on Scottish Song by Robert Burns* (Henry Frowde, 1908).
79 The date of May 1789 has been conjectured by a postscript referring to a visit by RB and Thomas Sloan the next day.
80 For a detailed account of the subsequent history of the Glenriddell MSS see Mackay: *The Burns Federation, 1885-1985*, 185–90.
81 And even beyond 1931, for Snyder (1932) repeats Currie's interpolation, and cites Hecht (1919, English translation 1936) in dismissing RB's hand in this.
82 The copy in NLS (ex Lord Rosebery) has the date erased on the title page. The copy in the Cooper Library, Columbia, South Carolina (ex Ross Roy) has the date 1799. Both copies, however were printed on paper watermarked 1800, so publication was probably early that year – before Currie's edn was published.
83 Kinsley II and III; Gershon Legman: *The Horn Book* (New York, 1964).
84 G. Ross Roy: 'The 1827 Editions of the Merry Muses of Caledonia' (BC 1986), 32–45.
85 Ch-Wa III, 296.
86 Patrick Miller seemed to be a confirmed bachelor when, in his forties, he formed a liaison with Jean Lindsay with whom he lived at Liberton near Edinburgh. It was here that their five children were born: William (15 February 1772), Patrick (3 October 1773), Janet (25 June 1775), Thomas Hamilton (9 April 1777) and Jean (5 December 1778), all of whose births were entered in the Liberton parish register. But of an actual marriage between Patrick Miller and Jean Lindsay, the registers of the entire kingdom are silent.
87 John Corrie: *Glencairn, the Annals of an Inland Parish* (Hunter, Dumfries, 1910), 127–31.
88 MSS of John Ramsay of Ochtertyre, quoted by Alexander Allardyce: *Scotland and Scotsmen of the Eighteenth Century* (Edinburgh, 1888).
89 For a comprehensive listing of these poems see Robert Peel: 'Rags and Mags' (BC 1988), 45–8.
90 Ch-Wa III, 55.
91 Ibid., 247.
92 Fowler, 206–22.
93 James Paterson: *Contemporaries of Burns* (Edinburgh, 1840).

Chapter 15: Dumfries, the Wee Vennel, 1791–3

1 Henley and Henderson IV, 334.
2 John Nicol, in *Encyclopaedia Britannica* (1876) IV, 568. The only difference between the text of 1876 and 1973 is that the latter omits a sentence: 'To have Jacobin tendencies, to rejoice at the downfall of the Bastille, was regarded as the sign of an abandoned character, as it was twelve years ago in Scotland to embrace the cause of the Northern States in the American War'. Belatedly the entry on RB was entirely rewritten by David Daiches for the 15th edn (1974).
3 Robert Thornton: *James Currie* (1963).
4 Fowler.
5 Carswell, 324.
6 Ch-Wa III, 298.
7 Revd. Dr William Burnside: MS history of Dumfries, Ewart Library, Dumfries.
8 Ch-Wa III, 365.
9 Ibid., 371–2.
10 John McDiarmid: *Reminiscences of Mrs Burns* (Dumfries, 1827).
11 Ch-Wa III, 314. RB's account is reproduced in full.
12 Angus McNaghten: *Burns's Mrs Riddell* (Volturna, Peterhead, 1975).
13 Ibid., 30–32.
14 Robert Kerr: *Memoirs of the Life, Writings and Correspondence of William Smellie* (Edinburgh, 1811) II.
15 Graham Smith: *Burns the Exciseman*, 74.
16 Snyder, 396.
17 Henry W. Meikle: 'Burns and the capture of the Rosamond' (BC 1934), 43.
18 *Glasgow Mercury*, January 1792.
19 Lord Rosebery: *Pitt* (Macmillan, 1891), 121.
20 It appears as an untitled fragment in Alexander Smith's edn (1865), 165; but given by Gilfillan under this title. For the text see *Burns A-Z*, Appendix B, 74.
21 Carswell, 281.
22 This letter is dated by Ferguson and Roy to October 1791 but the reference to Creech publishing places it in February or March 1793.
23 *Dumfries Weekly Journal*, 3 October 1792.
24 Alexander Pope: *The Temple of Fame*, line 410.
25 Ch-Wa III, 375.
26 Ibid., 383.
27 Ibid, 384n: Charles Kirkpatrick Sharpe to Allan Cunningham, 1834.
28 Kay's *Portraits* I, 240.
29 *Dumfries Weekly Journal*, 30 October 1792.
30 BC 1896, 144–5.
31 Alexander Findlater, in *Glasgow Courier*, 13 March 1834.
32 BC 1936, facsimile, 65.
33 Minutes of the Dumfries Library, preserved in the Ewart Library.
34 Ch-Wa IV, 55.
35 Ascribed to Dorothea Benson by Allan Cunningham (1834).
36 Ch-Wa III, 401.
37 Dumfries Burgh records: criminal summons, 'The Fiscal against Jno. Lewars, 1792': deposition of Jean Murdoch.
38 Robert Thornton: *Maxwell to Burns* (1979), 164–9, including a full transcript of the documents.

Chapter 16: Dumfries: Mill Hole Brae, 1793–4.

1 From transcript by the Revd. H. Grey Graham in *The Athenaeum*, 25 July 1876.
2 Ch-Wa IV, 20–1.
3 Ibid., 19n.
4 For a full discussion of this see James Mackay: 'The Selkirk Grace, Fact and Fable' (BC 1989), 24–30.
5 Cunningham III, 311.
6 Ch-Wa IV, 317.
7 It first appeared in Fitzhugh (1943), 49.
8 Kay's *Portraits* II, 306–8 contains an account of the trial.
9 Transcript of the hearing, in *The Trial of Joseph Gerrald* (Gowans, Glasgow, 1835).
10 Fowler, 28.
11 Parliamentary proceedings of 10 March 1794.
12 G. Ross Roy, cited by Fitzhugh (1970).
13 Fitzhugh (1970), 154.
14 Alexander Pope: *Moral Essays* Epistle III, line 1.
15 See letter to Dugald Stewart, 30 July 1790 (CL 449–50).
16 Prof. John Maccunn: *Ethics of Citizenship* (McLehose, Glasgow), 66.
17 William Wycherley: *Plain Dealer* (1677): 'I weigh the man, not his title; 'tis not the King's stamp can make the metal better or heavier. Your lord is a leaden shilling which you bend every way, and which debases the stamp he bears.'
18 DeLancey Ferguson: 'Cancelled Passages in the Letters of Robert Burns and George Thomson' (BC 1929), 90–103.
19 Ibid., 101.
20 Cunningham I, 308.
21 Ch-Wa IV, 75.
22 Ibid., 76.
23 Robert Kerr: *Memoir of William Smellie* II, 360–8 reproduces Maria's letters of the period, showing that Walter Riddell was out of the country.
24 Maria Riddell to James Currie, Tunbridge Wells, July 1800.
25 Robert Thornton: 'A Letter to Dr Currie' (BC 1961), 3–5. The MS is in the Hornel Collection, Broughton House, Kirkcudbright.
26 Angus Macnaghten: *Burns's Mrs Riddell* (Volturna, Peterhead, 1975), 50–1, quoting a letter by DeLancey Ferguson, 23 December 1954. No reason for this theory was adduced.
27 'Man was made to mourn: a dirge' (CW 124), line 52.
28 Alexander Pope: *The Rape of the Lock*, Canto I, line 1, misquoted – probably a quotation from Maria's commonplace book.
29 Macnaghten, op. cit., 50.
30 *Kendal Mercury*, 10 July 1852, gives background details.
31 Hugh Gladstone: *Maria Riddell, the friend of Burns* (Dumfries, 1915), 21.
32 John M. Wood: *Robert Burns and the Riddell Family* (Dumfries, 1922).
33 Macnaghten, op. cit., 55.
34 Dumfries SCO, Commissary Records from December 1766 to December 1809, under date of registry, 28 March 1774.
35 Ibid., 28 March 1794: deed dated 28 March 1793.
36 Ibid., under date of registry, 14 June 1794.
37 Manchester Cathedral marriage registers, which show that Elizabeth Kennedy married Robert Riddell there on 23 March 1784.

38 Old Register House, Edinburgh: Register of Deeds, DUR 272, 10–20 under date of registry, 26 April 1794.

39 Robert Thornton: *James Currie*, op. cit., 303.

40 Old Register House, Register of Deeds, DAL no. 261.

41 Ibid., MACK 261, 454–8.

42 Dumfries SCO, Commissary Records, op. cit., under date of register, 16 August 1798, showing it to have been drawn and signed on 16 January 1796.

43 Snyder, 369–70, in particular thought that there had only been one tour, undertaken in 1794, and went so far as to say that Syme had got the date wrong!

44 Ch-Wa IV, 263n.

45 W. J. McCulloch: *The McCullochs of Ardwall* (Dumfries, 1968), 19–20.

46 Ch-Wa IV, 121–2, quoting Lockhart. McCulloch's youngest sister Elizabeth married Thomas Scott, Sir Walter's brother. David McCulloch was on intimate terms with the latter from whom Lockhart (Sir Walter's son-in-law) got this anecdote. Lockhart considered that RB was ostracised by polite society at this time as a result of the Friars' Carse incident.

47 William Murray: 'Poetry and Politics, Burns and Revolution' (BC 1990), 52–66.

48 BE, 222–3.

49 Ch-Wa IV, 158.

50 Thorburn to Robert Chambers, 15 February 1851.

51 Hogg and Motherwell: *Works of Robert Burns* V, 364–5.

52 Ch-Wa IV, 158.

53 Alexander Pope: *Eloisa to Abelard*, line 92.

54 Graham Smith: *Robert Burns the Exciseman*, 91.

55 At the annual rate of 52 guineas, quoted by Currie (1800), this would have been £4 12s more than RB's salary. Perry himself had received just such a start in journalism in 1777, when Urquhart of the *London General Advertiser* paid him a guinea a week for verses and light pieces.

56 Shakespeare: *Hamlet*, Act III, Sc. 1, 63.

57 Ch-Wa IV, 175.

58 'Letters of Maria Riddell to James Currie, 1796–1805: a series of 36 letters sold by Messrs Sotheby, Wilkinson and Hodge, 24 July 1918' (BC 1923), 81.

59 Gladstone, op. cit., 21.

60 Macnaghten, op. cit., 112.

Chapter 17: The Last Years, 1795–6

1 William Roscoe: 'O'er the vine-covered hills and gay regions of France'.

2 Shakespeare: *Hamlet*, Act III, Sc. 1, 78.

3 'Burns-Dunlop Correspondence' (BC 1904), 74.

4 DeLancey Ferguson: 'The Burns-Dunlop Estrangement' (BC 1930), 87–100, shows the astonishing extent to which Currie suppressed passages in RB's letters, thereby creating the mystery which long puzzled biographers. William Wallace (1898) did not have access to the crucial last letters of RB which only surfaced in 1928.

5 Cunningham, 319.

6 Arthur Young: *The Example of France: A Warning to Britain* (pamphlet, 5 March 1793).

7 French National Archives, Paris: 74394.

8 Robert Thornton: *William Maxwell to Robert Burns* (John Donald, Edinburgh, 1979).

9 William Will: *Robert Burns as a Volunteer* (Glasgow, 1919), reprinted in BC 1920, 5–30.

10 Obituary notice in *Dumfries Courier*, 21 November 1822.

11 Minute-book of the Royal Dumfries Volunteers, Ewart Library.

12 Cunningham, 319.

13 Grierson diaries, Dumfries Burgh Museum.

14 James Hogg: *Memoir of Burns* (1836), 149n.

15 Cunningham, 319.

16 Ibid., 320.

17 R. W. MacFadzean: 'Burns's Excise duties and emoluments' (BC 1898), 53–66.

18 Duncan McNaught: 'Excise MS, an important find' (BC 1912), 141–2, where it was incorrectly identified as pertaining to 1792, 'when the conduct of Burns was being enquired into by his superiors'.

19 Ch-Wa IV, 192ff.

20 Ch-Wa IV, 206n: MS of Alexander Young, a schoolfriend of Robert Riddell and James Currie and lawyer of William Nicol.

21 Ibid., 83.

22 OPR, Edinburgh parish.

23 DNB VII, 977–82: articles on Alexander and John Geddes by Thompson Cooper (1886).

24 The interesting history of this volume appears in the facsimile edn of the Geddes Burns, published by the Bibliophile Society of Boston, 1908.

25 OPR, Mauchline parish burials.

26 Josiah Walker, lxxiv-lxxv.

27 DeLancey Ferguson: *Letters of Robert Burns* II, Appendix II.

28 John Pattison, *Glasgow Courier*, January 1848.

29 DeLancey Ferguson: *The Pride and the Passion* (1939), 125–34.

30 Robert Thornton: *James Currie*, 309–50.

31 *Burns Chronicle* 1934, 53ff; 1935, 39ff; 1936, 34ff; 1938, 40ff; 1939, 77ff; 1940, 17ff and 1942, 7ff.

32 Graham Smith, op. cit., 97; Snyder, 426.

33 Currie I, 219–20.

34 Gilfillan III, xci, who says that after leaving the Globe, RB went to a brothel and there behaved so disgracefully that he was forcibly ejected, fell into the hedge opposite and fell asleep in the snow.

35 Grierson diaries, op. cit. Most of his weather notes were edited out by John Davies in the published version (1981), but the very full details in the manuscript volume show that there was absolutely no snow in Dumfries in January-February 1796.

36 SRO Excise records.

37 Robert Chambers (1851) IV, 263.

38 Alexander Findlater, in *Glasgow Courier*, 13 March 1834, p1, cols 1–2.

39 Psalms 137: 1. Currie expanded the quotation to 'By Babel streams I have sat and wept' without indicating his own interpolation by brackets.

40 Numbers 23: 7.

41 Maria had miscounted; at this time there were five children: Robert, Francis Wallace, James Glencairn, William Nicol and Betty (Ann Park's daughter).

42 Ch-Wa IV, 276–7.
43 Currie I, 220.
44 The family name of the Earl of Glencairn was Cunningham.
45 William McDowall: *Burns in Dumfriesshire* (Edinburgh, 1870), 58–60.
46 John McDiarmid: 'Affecting circumstances connected with the history of the family of Burns' *Dumfries Monthly Magazine* I (1825), based on Mrs Henry Duncan's account.
47 SRO, Commissary records, Dumfries, 6 October 1796. RB left no will and the inventory by William Wallace, a Dumfries lawyer, consisted of the £15 in the two drafts. It did not include RB's books valued at £90, nor furniture, nor the £180 owed by Gilbert.
48 Ch-Wa IV, 280n.
49 Dr Burnside's MS history of Dumfries states that in 1790, out of 70 committed to the gaol, 23 were debtors. Of these, 13 came from Dumfries and the rest from the county and the Stewartry.
50 Ch-Wa IV, 272.
51 Cunningham, 343–4.
52 Currie I, 225–31. Both paragraphs were in the 1800 edition but in subsequent editions the second paragraph was omitted.
53 Robert Thornton: *James Currie*, 189. The original text was sent by Currie to Syme on 29 December 1799.
54 Allan Cunningham: *Mirror of Literature*, 14 August 1824, 121–3.
55 Cunningham I, 345.
56 Robert Carruthers: *Highland Notebook* (Inverness, 1843), 270–2.
57 Ch-Wa IV, 284–5.
58 Findlater, op. cit.
59 Revd. P. Hately Waddell: *Life and Works of Robert Burns* (Glasgow, 1867), Appendix xxiv.
60 Syme-Cunningham correspondence II (BC 1935), 39–41.
61 Peter McNeill: *History of Tranent* (1884), 138–58.
62 Currie I, 224–5.
63 Grierson diaries.
64 Dumfries SCO, Commissary Records, 1796.

Chapter 18: Post Mortem

1 Robert Thornton: *James Currie*, 288.
2 Fowler, 241.
3 John Davies: *Apostle to Burns* (Blackwood, 1981).
4 Ibid., 63.
5 Syme-Cunningham correspondence (BC 1935), 43.
6 Thornton, op. cit.; only a portion (pp259–358) of this 460-page biography pertains to RB.
7 Currie to Syme, quoted by McNaught: 'Dr Currie and his Biography of Burns' (BC 1919), 11–12.
8 DeLancey Ferguson: 'The earliest obituary of Burns', *Modern Philology*, xxxii (November 1934), 179–84.
9 *Monthly Magazine and British Register*, August 1796, 600.
10 A photograph of White's obituary was reproduced in BC 1941, opp. 15.

11 A facsimile reproduction of this rare broadside, dated Dumfries 1796, is in the Mitchell Library Burns Collection (427588).

12 J. C. Ewing: 'The Literary Fund and Robert Burns' (BC 1934), 68–71.

13 Ibid. The Fund, only recently instituted, awarded Jean an outright payment of £25, adding another £20 in November 1801.

14 Ch-Wa IV, 520–5; BE, 305–10.

15 National Library of Scotland, 5.505. The text of Maria's proof-sheet was given in *Studies in Scottish Literature* (1968), 194–7.

16 Syme-Cunningham correspondence (BC 1936), 42.

17 The file copies of the *Dumfries Weekly Journal* were mutilated in the nineteenth century, all references to RB being cut out and pasted in a scrapbook which was at one time in the Burgh Museum but has long since disappeared. No copies of the *Journal* for 1796 are preserved in either the British Library, Colindale or the Mitchell Library, Glasgow.

18 Ch-Wa IV, 520n.

19 Currie I, 252.

20 William Smellie: *Philosophy of Natural History* I, 526.

21 'The Vision' (CW 120), lines 235–40.

22 Franklyn Snyder: 'Burns and his Biographers' (BC 1932), 57.

23 Syme-Cunningham correspondence (BC 1934), 40–1.

24 Syme to Cunningham, 2 August 1796 (BC 1935), 36.

25 Laing MSS III, 508 (59), Edinburgh University Library.

26 See Chapter 13.

27 The text of this letter was given by Duncan McNaught in BC 1919, 17–19, but it is very inaccurate. A comparison with the actual document itself reveals McNaught as guilty of those emendations of which Currie is traditionally accused. For a correct text see Thornton: *James Currie*, 347–9.

28 Duncan McNaught (BC 1919), 19–20.

29 Currie I, 203–4.

30 Ibid., 215.

31 Ibid., 218–19.

32 Ibid., 234.

33 Dumfries Burns Club, minute-book, 25 January 1819.

34 Ch-Wa IV, 217.

35 Syme to Chambers, 1829.

36 Ch-Wa IV, 428n.

37 Walter Scott, in *Quarterly Review*, I (1809), reprinted in John D. Ross, *Early Critical Reviews on Burns* (Glasgow, 1900).

38 Ch-Wa IV, 219n.

39 McNaught (BC 1919), 9.

40 Donald Low: 'An Unpublished Critique of Burns's Poetry' (BC 1970), 3–12. The letter is in the Cowie MSS, Mitchell Library.

41 E. V. Lucas (ed.) *The Letters of Charles Lamb* (1935) I, 193. The Latin tag means 'Let the cobbler stick to his rattling', a punning variation of *crepidam* (sandal or last) in Pliny *Historia Naturalis* XXXV, 85.

42 The article, merely signed 'H', appeared in two parts in the *Monthly Magazine and British Register*, iii (March 1797), 213–16 and xix (supplement to the June number), 552–62. William Nicol died on 21 April 1797, enabling the writer to work in uncomplimentary references to him also, in the second part.

43 Raymond Lamont Brown: 'Robert Burns and the Assassins' (BC 1986), 51.

44 Heron's diaries, entitled rather self-consciously *Journal of my Conduct*

(1789–98), are preserved in the Laing MSS, Edinburgh University Library. See Catherine Carswell: 'Heron, a Study in Failure' (*Scots Magazine*, October 1932).

45 Hugh Miller: *Headship of Christ* (Adam and Charles Black, Edinburgh, 1861), 145–8 gives the text of a speech by Heron to the General Assembly on the subject of Christian missions.

46 Isaac Disraeli: *Calamities of Authors* (London, 1812). See also John MacTaggart: *Scottish Gallovidian Encyclopaedia* (2nd edn, 1876) and Dr Alexander Trotter: *East Galloway Sketches* (Rae, Castle Douglas, 1901).

47 DNB IX, 702–3 (by Thomas F. Henderson). See also William McIlwraith (BC 1913), 51–65.

48 Fowler, 206.

49 Robert Heron: *Observations made in a Journey through the Western Counties of Scotland* (Edinburgh, 1793) II, 349–50.

50 Alistair Campsie: *How They Murdered Robert Burns* (play, 1987), *The Clarinda Conspiracy* (1989); Robbie Faa (Dr Robert Gilchrist): 'Historical Detection' (BC 1980), 62–3; Raymond Lamont Brown: 'Robert Burns and the Assassins' (BC 1986), 50–1.

51 Alexander Campbell: *An Introduction to the History of Poetry in Scotland* (Edinburgh, 1798), 306–8. The 'Historian Medica' was James Currie.

52 William Reid: *Poetry Original and Selected* (1797) II, 8; Hogg and Motherwell (Glasgow, 1838) V, 282.

53 Robert Thornton: *James Currie*.

54 Currie I, 24, 31.

55 Joel W. Egerer: *A Bibliography of Robert Burns* (Oliver and Boyd, 1964).

56 David Irving: 'The Life of Robert Burns' in *Lives of the Scottish Poets* (1804) II, 487–501.

57 Robert H. Cromek: *Reliques of Robert Burns* (Cadell and Davies, London, 1808).

58 Donald Low (ed.): *Robert Burns, the Critical Heritage* (1974) gives the text of several reviews, 178ff, notably those by Jeffrey and Scott.

59 *Edinburgh Review*, Janaury 1809, 249–76.

60 *Quarterly Review*, February 1809, 19–36.

61 Scott to Lockhart, 11 March 1828.

62 Walker I, xci.

63 Alexander Peterkin: *Life and Works of Robert Burns as originally edited by James Currie, MD. To which is prefixed A review of the life of Burns* (Edinburgh, 1815), 4 vols. I, xlv.

64 Gilbert Burns to Alexander Peterkin from Grant's Braes, 29 September 1814, reprinted in *Critical Heritage*, 270–2.

65 Ch-Wa IV, Appendix III, 525–30: James Gray to Alexander Peterkin, Edinburgh, 28 September 1814.

66 Thornton: *James Currie*, 315–16.

67 Ch-Wa IV, 527–8.

68 Thornton: *James Currie*, 385.

69 Ch-Wa IV, 530–2: Alexander Findlater to Alexander Peterkin, Glasgow, 10 October 1814.

70 Mitchell Library 217888. Reprinted in E. Rhys: *Literary Pamphlets* (1897) and A. B. Grosart: *Prose Works of Wordsworth* (1876) II, 4ff.

71 Aristarchus was a Greek critic who would allow no verse to pass for Homer's which he did not approve of, as Wordwsworth explains in a footnote.

72 John Wilson in *Blackwood's Magazine* I, iii (June 1817), 261–6.

73 P. P. Howe (ed.): *Complete Works of William Hazlitt* (1930) V, 127–40.

74 BC 1914, 107–10.

75 *Blackwood's Magazine* (February 1819), 521–9.

76 Gilbert Burns: *Life of Robert Burns . . . by James Currie* (Cadell and Davies, London, 1820) I, 421.

77 Ibid., 424.

78 Earnock MSS (BC 1898), 19–20: Cadell and Davies to Gilbert Burns. Gilbert replied on 8 September 1815.

79 John Bumpus: *Poetical Works of Robert Burns* (London, 1822) I, xxv.

80 Alexander Findlater, *Glasgow Courier*, 13 March 1834.

81 DNB (1886) III, 426–38, reprinted without change in 1921, 1937, 1949, 1959, 1964, 1967 and 1973.

82 Henley and Henderson IV, 337–8.

83 See, for example, James Davidson: *New Light on Burns* (1897); articles by William McIlwraith (BC 1899), Sir William R. Nicoll (BC 1903); John D. Ross: *Henley and Burns or the Critic Censured* (1901) (a collection of book reviews attacking Henley's memoir of Burns); Francis Thompson: 'Mr Henley's Burns' (*Academy*, 1897); A. H. Japp: *Robert Burns and W. E. Henley's heavyweight on him* (1899).

84 Franklyn Snyder: 'Burns and his Biographers' (BC 1932), 55–74; 'Burns's last years' (BC 1935), 53–68.

85 Alan Bold: 'Burns and Booze' in *A Burns Companion* (Macmillan, 1991), 122.

86 *Annals of Medical History* (New York, 1928) X, 58.

87 Sir James Crichton-Browne: *Burns from a New Point of View* (Hodder and Stoughton, nd [1926]).

88 W. W. Buchanan and W. F. Keen: 'Robert Burns's Illness Revisited', *Scottish Medical Journal* (1982); reprinted with revisions (BC 1991), 60–71.

89 J. A. Marston: 'Report on Fever (Malta)', *Army Medical Report* (1861) 3: 486–521; A. V. Hardy: 'Arthritis in *Brucella melitensis* infections', *Med. Clin. North America* (1937) 21, no.6, 1747–9; I. F. Huddleston: *Brucellosis in Man and Animals* (Commonwealth Fund, New York. 1939), 75–125; P. J. Kelly, W. J. Martin, A. Schriger and L. A. Weed: 'Brucellosis of the bones and joints' *Journal of the American Medical Association* (1960) 174, 347–53.

90 John Thomson: *Education, Man's Salvation from Crime, Disease and Starvation* (Edinburgh, 1844), with an appendix vindicating RB.

91 J. M. A. Lenihan, A. C. D. Leslie and H. Smith: 'Mercury in the Hair of Robert Burns', *Lancet* (1971) 2, 1030.

92 OPR, Johnstone, Dumfriesshire. John Thomson was baptised on 12 March 1780, son of John Thomson and Nelly Paterson. Additional biographical details in *Notes and Queries*, September and October 1868, and William Findlay: *Robert Burns and the Medical Profession* (Paisley, 1898).

93 Fowler, 236.

94 Ibid., 238.

95 James Gray to R. H. Cromek, 19 March 1810. Stothard did produce a sketch of Jean, which he may have drawn from memory. See *Blackwood's Magazine*, June 1836, for a memoir of Stothard by Miss Bray.

96 Cited by BE, 52.

97 John McDiarmid: 'St Michael's Church-yard, disinterment of Burns' in *Sketches from Nature* (Dumfries, 1830).

98 Archibald Blacklock: 'Description of the skull of Burns' in George Combe: *Phrenological Development of Robert Burns* (Edinburgh, 1859).

99 George Combe: 'Observations on the skull of Robert Burns', *Phrenological Journal and Miscellany*, 1 June 1834; George Combe and Robert Cox: 'An Essay on the Character and cerebral development of Robert Burns', *Phrenological Journal and Miscellany*, vol. 9, (1834–6); Lorenzo Fowler: 'Robert Burns, a Phrenological Estimate', *Phrenological Magazine* (January 1881).

100 Matriculation album of the University of Glasgow, 1802: 'Robertus Burns, filius natu maximus quondam Roberti, Poetae celeberrimi apud Mauchline in comitati de Ayr' (Robert Burns, born the eldest son of the late Robert, most celebrated poet, at Mauchline in the county of Ayr).

101 Gilbert Burns to William Thomson, 1 December 1820 (BC 1901), 88.

102 PRO, Board of Stamps and Taxes: Establishment records.

103 Birth and marriage registers of St Marylebone and St Pancras parishes, London.

104 OPR, London St Sepulchre.

105 See also Henry Kerr: 'Some personal recollections of the eldest son of the poet Burns', in John D. Ross (ed.) *Burnsiana* (1897) VI.

106 OPR, Dumfries.

107 Revd. W. McMillan: 'Robert Burns the Third' (BC 1925), 35–8.

108 'Death of a Granddaughter of Robert Burns' (BC 1917), 106–9.

109 Thomas S. McCrorie: *The Family Tree of Robert Burns* (Dumfries, 1961), with corrections from OPR.

110 BC 1922, 114.

111 Hugh McDonald: *Rambles round Glasgow* (Glasgow, 1910).

112 D. H. Edwards: *Modern British Poets* gives the text of this song.

113 Andrew McCallum: 'Descendants of Robert Burns in Pollokshaws and District' (BC 1916), 23–31.

114 *Pall Mall Gazette*, 1887.

115 James Mackay: *Burnsiana* (Darvel, 1988), 31–51.

116 James Mackay: *The Burns Federation* (Kilmarnock, 1985).

117 Ch-Wa IV, 502.

Index

743